EX LIBRIS

THE HUTCHINSON CHRONOLOGY OF WORLD HISTORY

VOLUME III

The Changing World

1776–1900

The Hutchinson Chronology of World History

Other volumes in the series:

The Ancient and Medieval World
Prehistory–AD 1491

The Expanding World
1492–1775

The Modern World
1901–1998

THE HUTCHINSON CHRONOLOGY OF WORLD HISTORY

VOLUME III

The Changing World

1776–1900

Neville Williams

Helicon

Copyright © Helicon Publishing Limited 1999
This is an extensively revised and updated edition of the
Chronology of the Modern World 1763–1992 by Neville Williams
originally published in 1966.

This edition published 1999

All rights reserved

Helicon Publishing Ltd
42 Hythe Bridge Street
Oxford OX1 2EP
England

e-mail: admin@helicon.co.uk
Web site: www.helicon.co.uk

Printed and bound by DeAgostini, Novara, Italy

ISBN 1-85986-283-7

British Library Cataloging in Publication Data

A catalog record of this book is available from the British Library.

Papers used by Helicon Publishing Ltd are natural recyclable
products made from wood grown in sustainable forests. The
manufacturing processes of both raw material and paper conform
to the environmental regulations of the country of origin.

Photo credits: Hand-coloured photographic portrait of Sitting
Bull, © Corbis-Bettmann.

Contents

Preface

The new *Hutchinson Chronology of the World History* has over 70,000 entries. *The Changing World* is the most detailed and comprehensive views of the changing world of the 18th–19th centuries available in one volume. It begins with ratification of the American Declaration of Independence, and ends with the re-election of William McKinley, the 25th President of the United States, the Boxer Rising in China and the Paris International Exhibition. During this period, the world changes more in the course of a few generations than in the previous one thousand years and sees such innovations as the automobile and airplane, the telephone and psychiatry, the camera, the radio, Coca-Cola, and the ice cream cone.

Order of Entries

The Changing World is arranged in strict chronological sequence by year, month, and day. Within each year, the entries have been carefully grouped into four main categories and 25 subcategories. Subcategories are arranged alphabetically within each main category.

Politics, Government, and Economics
   Business and Economics
   Colonization
   Human Rights
   Politics and Government
Science, Technology, and Medicine
   Agriculture
   Computing
   Ecology
   Exploration
   Health and Medicine
   Math
   Science
   Technology
   Transportation

Arts and Ideas
   Architecture
   Arts
   Film
   Literature and Language
   Music
   Theatre and Dance
   Thought and Scholarship
Society
   Education
   Everyday Life
   Media and Communication
   Religion
   Sports

Whether you are looking for a specific fact, tracing events over a period of time, or reading for pure enjoyment, the date coupled with the categories, subcategories, and indexes will help you find your way around.

Special Features

Special mini-chronologies provide at-a-glance information about important people, topics, or events of each time period. They have been designed to an overview of an event or development in a concise, easy-to-read format. For a more extensive study of the subject, the mini-chronologies provide guidelines to the dates of numerous related entries in the body of the *Chronology*. Birth and death dates of noteworthy people can be found at the end of each year in tinted boxes. Where available, birth announcements include the year of death in parentheses, e.g. (–1837), and death entries conclude with the age at death, e.g. (80).

Indexes

An extensive Main Index includes virtually every name, title, place, event, and subject appearing in the *Chronology*. The volume's vast coverage of works of art, literature, music, dance, film, theater, and scholarship can be searched using the titles index.

Special Features

Contributors and Acknowledgements

Consultant Editors

T. C. W. Blanning, *Professor of Modern European History, University of Cambridge, and Fellow of Sidney Sussex College, Cambridge, U.K.*

David Feldman, *Birkbeck College, University of London, U.K.*

Roy Porter, *Wellcome Institute for the History of Medicine, London, U.K.*

Bruce Schulman, *Professor of History, Boston University, U.S.A.*

Alison Scott, *Head, Popular Culture Library and Associate Professor of Popular Culture, Bowling Green State University, Ohio, U.S.A.*

John Sutherland, *Lord Northcliffe Professor of Modern English Literature, University College London, U.K.*

Contributing Editors
Duncan Anderson M.A., D.Phil.
Edward Barratt B.A.
Tallis Barker D.Phil., A.R.C.M.
Andrew Colquhoun B.Sc., M.A.
Sara Coombs M.A.
David Gould
Jonathan M. Hansen Ph.D.
Simon Harratt M.A., Ph.D.
John Haywood Ph.D.
Chris Holdsworth M.A., Ph.D.
Nicola Matthews B.A.
Tracy Miller
Chris Murray
Malgorzata Nawrocka-Colquhoun D.Phil.
Robert Peberdy
David Petts
Benedict Ramos
Adrian Room M.A., Dip.Ed., F.R.G.S.
Jon Rowe Ph.D.
Harold Sawdon
Christopher M. Scribner Ph.D.
Martha Y. Scribner M.A.
Harry Sidebottom M.A., D.Phil.
Giles Sparrow M.Sc.
Joe Staines B.A.
Matthew Steggle M.A., D.Phil.
Steve Williams Ph.D.

Editorial Director
Hilary McGlynn

Managing Editor
Katie Emblen

Project Manager
Susan Mendelsohn

Editors
Rachel Beckett
Chris Clark
Susan Cuthbert
Denise Dresner
Jo Linzey
Mark McGuinness
Richard Martin
Rachel Minay
Amy Myers
Kate O'Leary
Clare Ramos
Lisa Sullivan
John Wright
Karen Young

Index
Francis Coogan
Drusilla Calvert

Electronic Publishing Manager
Nick Andrews

Database Editor
Louise Richmond

Senior Technical Editor
Graham Bennett

Technical Editor
Claire Lishman

Production Director
Tony Ballsdon

Art and Design Manager
Terence Caven

Typesetting and Page Layout
Mendip Communications Ltd, Frome, Somerset

1776

POLITICS, GOVERNMENT, AND ECONOMICS

Business and Economics

MAY

2　An American mission to Paris, France, obtains a French loan of 1 million livres to support the American military effort against Britain.

Human Rights

MARCH

31　"Remember the Ladies," Abigail Adams, wife of American Continental Congressman and future president John Adams, admonishes her husband in a letter. "If particular care and attention is not paid to the Ladies we are determined to foment a Rebellion and will not hold ourselves bound by any Laws in which we have no voice, or Representation."

Politics and Government

•　At the instigation of the Marquis of Pombal, a unified administration for the Portuguese South American colonies of Maranhão and Brazil is set up in Rio de Janeiro.

•　Grigory Potemkin, favorite of Catherine II (the Great), reorganizes the Russian Black Sea fleet and begins the construction of Sevastopol harbor.

•　The Muslim Tukulor people of West Africa begin to establish a powerful state around Futa Toro on the lower Senegal.

JANUARY

6　The *corvée* (system of forced labor for the repair of roads) is abolished in France, but is restored in August the same year.

FEBRUARY

•　The British Parliament passes a Prohibitory Act, banning external trade with the American colonies in response to American military actions.

MARCH

4　American forces under George Washington seize the strategic Dorchester Heights, south of Boston,

Massachusetts, during the Continental Army's siege of the British-held city.

17　The Continental Army under George Washington forces British troops under Sir William Howe to evacuate Boston, Massachusetts.

APRIL

•　The Treaty of Copenhagen is signed between Russia and Denmark; under its terms, Catherine the Great abandons her hereditary claim through Peter III to the Danish duchy of Holstein-Gottorp.

12　The North Carolinan Convention empowers its delegates to the Colonial Convention to vote for independence from Britain.

MAY

6　American forces under Benedict Arnold are forced to abandon their siege of Quebec and are driven from Canada.

12　Chrétien de Malesherbes resigns as French minister of the interior.

12　Robert Turgot, the French comptroller general of finance, is dismissed by Louis XVI as a result of court intrigues.

15　The Virginia Convention instructs the American politician Richard Henry Lee and other delegates to Congress to propose independence. On June 7, Lee moves a resolution which declares "that these United States are and of right ought to be free and independent states."

JUNE

12　The American colony of Virginia publishes a Declaration of Rights, which serves as a model for the Bill of Rights.

JULY

4　The American Declaration of Independence, drafted by Thomas Jefferson with revisions by Benjamin Franklin and John Adams, is approved by the Continental Congress. It announces the separation of the 13 North American British colonies from Britain.

AUGUST

27　Sir William Howe's British troops defeat American forces under George Washington and Israel Putnam in the Battle of Long Island; the Americans retreat across the East River to Manhattan Island.

SEPTEMBER

9　The Continental Congress passes a resolution changing the name of the nation from the United Colonies to the United States of America.

15　British forces under Sir William Howe occupy New York, New York.

22　Nathan Hale, an American officer caught spying on the British, is hanged on Manhattan Island, New York.

American Revolution (1764–76)

1764

- The British Parliament passes a Colonial Currency Act, forbidding payments from the American colonies to Britain in "unsound" currency. The act causes a currency shortage and great resentment in the colonies.

April 5   The British Parliament passes the Sugar Act to help defray the cost of protecting Britain's expanded American empire. The act levies duties on molasses, sugar, indigo, pimento, wine, and textiles. It mandates an elaborate system of paperwork to aid enforcement. It also denies a jury trial to those accused of violating its decrees.

May   Boston lawyer James Otis repudiates the Sugar Act as "taxation without representation." He declares "absurd" the notion that a parliament sitting in England can "virtually" represent colonial interests.

August   Boston merchants begin a boycott of British luxury items in protest against the Sugar Act.

1765

May 30   The Virginia assembly adopts a set of resolutions inspired by future governor Patrick Henry. The so-called Virginia Resolves equate "British freedom" with "taxation of the people by themselves" or by "persons they annually elect to serve as members of the Assembly."

November 1   Rioters in New York protest against the Stamp Act by burning effigies of "Liberty" and the royal governor and by attacking the homes of British officials.

1766

March 18   Britain repeals the Stamp Act but simultaneously passes the Declaratory Act, which asserts Parliament's authority over the American colonies in "all cases whatsoever."

1767

June 26–July 2   The British Parliament adopts the Townshend Acts, taxing all glass, lead, paper, paints, and tea imported to the American colonies. To ensure compliance, the acts establish a Board of Customs Commissioners in Boston, a city becoming notorious for its recalcitrance.

1768

February 11   The Massachusetts Assembly's Circular Letter denounces the Townshend duties and urges other colonial legislatures to resist parliamentary taxation.

June 9–10   British customs officials seize John Hancock's sloop *Liberty* in Boston Harbor for an alleged smuggling violation. The act precipitates a riot in which the ship is reclaimed by Bostonians then recaptured the next day by the British.

July   Massachusetts governor Francis Bernard dissolves the colonial assembly for refusing to revoke the Circular Letter of February 11 urging resistance to parliamentary taxation. Deprived of a constitutional means for redressing grievances, Bostonians resort increasingly to violence.

October 1   British troops begin to arrive in Boston to quell civil disturbances there. By the end of the next year, 15,000 Bostonians share their streets with 4,000 British regulars.

1769

May 1   The British Privy Council decides to retain the duty on tea imported by the American colonies.

1770

March 5   In the "Boston Massacre," British troops fire on a raucous mob, killing five Americans and wounding six. Among the victims is Crispus Attucks, a black seaman.

OCTOBER

- The American Congress retires from Philadelphia, Pennsylvania, to Baltimore, Maryland, as British forces under Sir William Howe continue to advance across New Jersey.
- The Rockingham Whigs (a British parliamentary group led by Charles Watson-Wentworth, Marquis of Rockingham) cease to attend Parliament in protest at the continuation of the American war.
- The Swiss banker Jacques Necker is appointed finance minister in France.

11–13   American vessels commanded by Brigadier-General Benedict Arnold are defeated in two engagements by British naval forces on Lake Champlain.

NOVEMBER

20   The American-held Fort Lee, on the Hudson River, surrenders to British forces.

28   George Washington's Continental Army retreats across New Jersey into Pennsylvania as Sir William Howe's British offensive continues.

DECEMBER

25   American forces under George Washington cross the ice-strewn Delaware River in a surprise raid on Christmas night, and defeat a corps of British Hessian mercenaries at the Battle of Trenton.

SCIENCE, TECHNOLOGY, AND MEDICINE

Exploration

December 1776–79   English explorer James Cook explores the Pacific Ocean from north to south. In 1778, he passes through the Bering Strait into the Arctic Ocean, searching for the northwest passage to the Atlantic, and discovers Hawaii, where the indigenous population treats him as a god.

1772

June 10   Rhode Islanders burn the grounded British customs vessel *Gaspée*, ending a brief period of improved colonial–parliamentary relations.

1773

March 12   The Virginia House of Burgesses urges the establishment of standing committees of intercolonial correspondence. Their purpose is to enable the American colonies to respond to British parliamentary abuses with one voice.

December 16   In the Boston Tea Party, Bostonians protest against the East India Company's apparent monopoly on tea by dumping 342 chests of British tea into Boston Harbor.

1774

March 31   In the Boston Port Act, the British Parliament responds to the Boston Tea Party by closing the port of Boston. Americans regard this as the first of the so-called Intolerable Acts.

May 20   In the Massachusetts Government and Administration of Justice Acts—to Americans, the second and third Intolerable Acts—the British Parliament forbids Massachusetts citizens to meet publicly and announces that British officials accused of capital crimes in Massachusetts will be tried elsewhere.

May 26   The British Parliament dissolves the Virginia House of Burgesses for announcing its sympathy for Boston.

June 2   The British Parliament passes the Quartering Act—the last of the Intolerable Acts—which orders the people of Massachusetts to house and feed the British troops sent to pacify them.

September 5–October 27   The first Continental Congress opens in Philadelphia, Pennsylvania, and repudiates the Intolerable Acts. Before the Congress adjourns in late October, it adopts a nonimportation, nonexportation, and nonconsumption agreement. It also flirts with a new idea: that the British Parliament has no legislative or fiscal authority over the colonies whatsoever.

1775

February 27   The British Parliament accepts Lord North's conciliation plan to give the American colonies assemblies with tax-raising powers.

July 5   In a final attempt to avert the American Revolution, the Continental Congress extends the so-called Olive Branch Petition to King George III of Great Britain. The petition exhorts him to safeguard the colonists' rights by making colonial assemblies coordinate with Parliament.

July 31   The Continental Congress rejects Lord North's conciliation plan to give the American colonies assemblies with tax-raising powers.

1776

April 12   The North Carolinan Convention empowers its delegates to the Colonial Convention to vote for independence from Britain.

May 15   The Virginia Convention instructs the American politician Richard Henry Lee and other delegates to Congress to propose independence. On June 7, Lee moves a resolution which declares "that these United States are and of right ought to be free and independent states."

June 12   The American colony of Virginia publishes a Declaration of Rights, which serves as a model for the Bill of Rights.

July 4   The American Declaration of Independence, drafted by Thomas Jefferson with revisions by Benjamin Franklin and John Adams, is approved by the Continental Congress. It announces the separation of the 13 North American British colonies from Britain.

Science

- English chemist James Keir suggests that some rocks may have formed as molten material that cooled and crystallized.
- Swedish chemist Karl Wilhelm Scheele discovers uric acid in kidney stones.

Technology

- American engineer David Bushnell builds a hand-powered wooden-hulled submarine named the *Turtle*. It is used in an unsuccessful attempt to attach an explosive device to a British ship.
- English engineer John Wilkinson increases the efficiency of blast furnaces by using a steam engine to create the blast of air, in Sheffield, England.
- The first invisible ink is used by the Committee of Secret Correspondence in the American colonies.
- The machine-plane is invented.

ARTS AND IDEAS

Architecture

- Somerset House, designed by the Scottish architect William Chambers, is completed in London, England.

Arts

- The American artist Ralph Earl paints *Portrait of Roger Sherman*.
- The French artist Jean-Baptiste Pigalle completes his sculpture *Tombeau de Maurice, Maréchal de Saxe/Tomb of Maurice of Saxony* in the Church of St. Thomas in Strasbourg, France.

Literature and Language

- The Scottish-born American writer Hugh Henry Brackenridge publishes his play *The Battle of Bunkers-Hill*, a patriotic play in support of the American Revolution intended for amateur performances.

Music

- Austrian composer Wolfgang Amadeus Mozart completes his Serenade No. 7 for orchestra (K 250), the *Haffner*; his Serenade No. 5 for two orchestras (K 239), the *Serenata notturna/Nocturnal Serenade*; his Piano Concertos No. 6 (K 238), No. 7 (K 242), and No. 8 (K 246); his Piano Trio No. 1 (K 254); and his Organ Sonata in C Major (K 263).
- British aristocrat Lord Sandwich founds the Concert of Ancient Music in London, England, where no music less than 20 years old is to be played.
- English musicologist Charles Burney publishes the first volume of his *General History of Music*. The final volume appears in 1789.
- English musicologist John Hawkins publishes *The General History of the Science and Practice of Music*, an outstanding piece of scholarship that is overshadowed by Charles Burney's book of the same year.

Theater and Dance

- The anonymous play *The Blockheads*, a satire on the British, is performed in Boston, Massachusetts, shortly after the British forces have been driven out. It is a reply to the English general John Burgoyne's *The Blockade*, first performed in 1775.
- The Italian writer Vittorio Alfieri writes his tragedy *Antigone*.
- The play *Der Wirrwarr, oder Sturm und Drang/Confusion, or Storm and Stress* by the German writer Friedrich Maximilian von Klinger is performed, in Leipzig, Germany, giving its name to the *Sturm und Drang* ("Storm and Stress") romantic school of writing.
- The play *Die Soldaten/The Soldiers* by the German writer Jakob Michael Lenz is performed in Strasbourg, France, then in Germany. It is a typical example of *Sturm und Drang* romanticism.

Thought and Scholarship

- The English historian Edward Gibbon publishes the first volume of his major work *The Decline and Fall of the Roman Empire*, the most important historical work of the period. It is soon popular and controversial, with its criticisms of early Christians seen as scandalous. The eight-volume work is completed in 1788.
- The Welsh historian and moral philosopher Richard Price publishes *Observations on the Nature of Civil Liberty, the Principle of Government, and the Justice and Policy of the War with America.*

JANUARY

10 English political writer Thomas Paine publishes *Common Sense*. It denounces monarchy and proclaims that "the cause of America is in a great measure the cause of all mankind."

SOCIETY

Everyday Life

- The Continental Congress institutes a national lottery in America, to raise funds to support governmental activities.
- The first mixed drink, or cocktail, is reputedly made by Betsy Flanagan, a barmaid in Elmsford, New York. The name "cocktail" is said to possibly come from the garnish of Flanagan's creation—the tail feathers of a fowl.

Religion

- The English writer Soame Jenyns publishes his *View of the Internal Evidence of the Christian Religion*, which is soon widely translated.
- The Illuminati religious sect is formed in Ingolstadt in Bavaria by Adam Weishaupt. Closely linked to Freemasonry, the Illuminati rejected the church and sought an understanding of Divine Reason through enlightened thinking. Banished from Bavaria in the 1780s, they continued in France and elsewhere.

BIRTHS & DEATHS

JANUARY

24 E(rnst) T(heodor) A(madeus) Hoffmann, German writer, composer, and painter, born in Königsberg, Prussia (–1822).

MAY

7 Jöns Jacob Berzelius, Swedish chemist who was instrumental in establishing modern chemistry, born in Linköping, Sweden (–1848).

JUNE

11 John Constable, English landscape painter, born in East Bergholt, Suffolk, England (–1837).

AUGUST

25 David Hume, Scottish philosopher, historian, economist, and essayist, dies in Edinburgh, Scotland (65).

27 Barthold Niebuhr, German historian, born in Copenhagen, Denmark (–1831).

1777

POLITICS, GOVERNMENT, AND ECONOMICS

Human Rights

- New York adopts a constitution denying women, even those with property, the right to vote.

Politics and Government

- Spain and Portugal sign the Treaty of San Ildefonso, confirming Portugal's colonial claims to large areas in the Amazon and Paraná plains in South America.
- The Swiss Cantons form an alliance with France as a safeguard against Austrian invasion.

JANUARY

3 George Washington follows up his victory at Trenton by defeating Sir William Howe's British forces at Princeton, New Jersey.

FEBRUARY

24 Maria I becomes queen regnant of Portugal on the death of her husband, José I. She frees the Marquis of Pombal's political prisoners and banishes him.

APRIL

- French volunteers led by Marquis Marie Joseph de Lafayette and Baron Johan de Kalb begin to arrive in America to support the American struggle for independence from Britain.

JUNE

14 The Continental Congress votes to adopt a flag (designed, according to legend, by the seamstress Betsy Ross at the request of George Washington) as the national emblem of the new United States of America.

AUGUST

16 American forces under John Stark defeat a detachment from General John Burgoyne's British advance from Lake Champlain at the Battle of Bennington, Vermont.

SEPTEMBER

- Heroine Betty Zane carries gunpowder into Fort Henry, Virginia, saving it from a Native American siege during the American Revolution.
11 The British general Sir William Howe defeats American forces under Nathaniel Greene at the Battle of Brandywine, Pennsylvania.

19 American forces under Horatio Gates inflict heavy casualties on General John Burgoyne's British forces at Bemis Heights, New York.
27 British forces under Sir William Howe occupy Philadelphia, Pennsylvania.

OCTOBER

4 British troops under Sir William Howe defeat George Washington's American forces at the Battle of Germantown, Pennsylvania.
7 British forces under John Burgoyne are badly defeated by American troops under Horatio Gates in the second battle of Bemis Heights, New York.
17 The British general John Burgoyne surrenders to the Americans under Horatio Gates near Saratoga Springs, New York.

NOVEMBER

15 The American Congress adopts the Articles of Confederation of the United States of America and sends them to the states for ratification.
20 Sir William Howe's British forces capture forts Mifflin and Mercer, gaining control of the Delaware.

DECEMBER

17 The Continental Army retires to Valley Forge, outside Philadelphia, Pennsylvania, for the winter.
30 On the death of Maximilian III, the Bavarian succession passes to the elector Karl Theodor of the Palatinate, but the Holy Roman Emperor Joseph II stakes a claim to Lower Bavaria.

SCIENCE, TECHNOLOGY, AND MEDICINE

Exploration

- Scottish-born Dutch Colonel R. J. Gordon embarks on a three-year solo exploration of southern Africa, and discovers the Orange River.

Science

- French chemist Antoine-Laurent Lavoisier shows that air is made up of a mixture of gases, and that one of them (oxygen) is the substance necessary for combustion and rusting to take place. He also assigns the name "oxygen" to Joseph Priestley's dephlogisticated air.
- French scientist Charles Augustin Coulomb invents the torsion balance in which weights are measured by the amount of twist induced in a metal wire.

- Swedish chemist Karl Wilhelm Scheele describes his experiment for producing oxygen—in *Air and Fire*—and claims that air is a mixture of oxygen and nitrogen.
- Scheele discovers that silver nitrate, when exposed to light, results in a blackening effect; this is an important discovery for the development of photography.

Technology

- American engineer David Bushnell invents the torpedo.

ARTS AND IDEAS

Architecture

- French architect M. Bonnemain installs the first modern central heating system in the Château Neuf near the Pont du Pecq, St.-Germain-en-Laye, France.
- The Protestant church in Warsaw, Poland, designed by the Polish architect Simon Gottlieb Zug, is completed.

Arts

- The Spanish artist Francisco de Goya y Lucientes paints *The Sunshade*.

Literature and Language

- The American farmer and writer Robert Munford publishes his play *The Patriot*, in support of the American revolutionaries.
- The American musician and writer Francis Hopkinson (a signatory to the Declaration of Independence) publishes his satire *Letter Written by a Foreigner on the Character of the English Nation*.
- The bulk of the text of the first edition of the French *Encyclopédie/Encyclopedia*, largely the creation of the French philosopher Denis Diderot, is completed. Publication began in 1751. The entire work (with illustrations and index) is completed in 1780.

Music

- Austrian composer Wolfgang Amadeus Mozart completes his Piano Concerto No. 9 (K 271) and his Piano Sonata No. 7 (K309).
- The opera *Armide* by the German composer Christoph Gluck is first performed, in Paris, France.
- The opera *Il mondo della luna/The World on the Moon* by the Austrian composer Franz Joseph Haydn is first performed, in Eszterháza, Austria. It is based on a play by the Italian writer Carlo Goldoni.

Thought and Scholarship

- British historian and political theorist Catharine Macaulay publishes her *Address to the People of England, Scotland, and Ireland*, supporting American colonial grievances against the British government.
- The Italian writer Count Vittorio Alfieri publishes his political treatise *Della tirannide/On Tyranny*.
- The Scottish historian William Robertson publishes his *History of America*.

SOCIETY

Everyday Life

JUNE
8 Philip Lindsay, a shopkeeper in New York, New York, advertises that he has ice-cream for sale "almost any day ... for ready money."

Religion

- English clergyman, chemist, and natural philospher Joseph Priestley publishes his *Disquisition Relating to Matter and Spirit*, which affirms the importance of revelation in religion. (Though a Presbyterian minister, Priestley was accused of atheism because of his scientific work.)
June 1777–80 The German writer Gotthold Ephraim Lessing publishes *Ernst und Falk/Ernst and Falk*, dialogues in which he pleads for broad understanding in questions of religion and politics.

BIRTHS & DEATHS

MARCH
17 Roger Brooke Taney, U.S. chief justice, born in Calvert County, Maryland (–1864).

APRIL
12 Henry Clay, U.S. politician and one of the founders of the Whig Party, born in Hanover County, Virginia (–1852).

30 Karl Gauss, German mathematician, born in Brunswick, Germany (–1855).

AUGUST
c. 20 Bernardo O'Higgins, military leader who gained Chile's independence from Spain and served as first head of state 1817–23, born in Chillén, Chile (–1842).

OCTOBER
21 Samuel Foote, English actor and playwright, dies in Dover, Kent, England (57).

DECEMBER
23 Alexander I, Emperor of Russia 1801–25, born in St. Petersburg, Russia (–1825).

1778

POLITICS, GOVERNMENT, AND ECONOMICS

Colonization

- Portugal cedes Fernando Po and the Annobon Islands, in the Gulf of Guinea, West Africa, to Spain.
- The British governor-general in India, Warren Hastings, captures the French base of Chandernagore in Bengal, and an expedition under Hector Munro takes Pondicherry in the Carnatic.

Human Rights

- George Washington makes Mary Hays McCauly a sergeant in the Continental Army when she risks her life to bring water to fighting soldiers and takes her fallen husband's place on a cannon team.

Politics and Government

- American congressman Thomas Jefferson secures the passage of an act prohibiting the import of slaves into America.
- The French orientalist Abraham Hyacinthe Anquetil-Duperron publishes *Législation orientale/Oriental Law*.

JANUARY

3   Elector Karl Theodor of the Palatinate recognizes the claim of the Holy Roman Emperor Joseph II to Lower Bavaria; Austrian troops occupy the region despite the efforts of Frederick II (the Great) of Prussia to persuade Karl Theodor to resist.

FEBRUARY

6   The United States signs two treaties with France—the Treaty of Amity and Commerce and the Treaty of Alliance. The former aims to promote both countries' commercial prosperity; the latter commits France to safeguarding "the liberty, sovereignty, and independence absolute and unlimited of the United States."

17   The British prime minister Lord North presents a plan to Parliament for the conciliation of the American colonies, in response to the American treaty of alliance with France.

APRIL

5   British commissioners are appointed to negotiate with the American Continental Congress, and to offer the renunciation of Britain's right to tax the colonies.

7   The British politician William Pitt the Elder, Earl of Chatham, makes his final speech against the continuing hostilities in America.

MAY

4   The American Continental Congress ratifies the Treaty of Amity and Commerce and the Treaty of Alliance with France.

JUNE

17   The American Continental Congress rejects a British offer of peace. The American Revolution continues.

18   British general Sir Henry Clinton evacuates Philadelphia, Pennsylvania, in response to the breakdown of Anglo-American peace negotiations and the threat of a French and American blockade of the city.

28   In the Battle of Monmouth, American forces under George Washington interrupt the British retreat from Philadelphia, Pennsylvania, fighting a battle with Sir Henry Clinton's forces at Monmouth Courthouse in New Jersey.

JULY

3   A group of loyalists and Iroquois kill 360 American settlers in the Wyoming Valley of Pennsylvania.

3   Prussia, in alliance with Saxony, declares war on the Hapsburg Monarchy following the Austrian occupation of Lower Bavaria. Skirmishes between Prussia and Austria continue until May 1779.

8   A French fleet under Jean Baptiste, comte d'Estaing, arrives off the Delaware Capes.

27   A French fleet under Louis Guillouet, comte d'Orvilliers, wins a narrow victory over a British fleet under Augustus Keppel off Ushant, in the English Channel. This crucial British defeat enables units of the French Brest fleet to be sent to America and the West Indies.

AUGUST

29   American forces under John Sullivan abandon the siege of British-held Newport, Rhode Island, following the departure of the comte d'Estaing's fleet to Boston for repairs.

SEPTEMBER

- French forces seize the British island of Dominica, in the West Indies, for use as a naval base.

4   The Dutch Republic signs a treaty of amity and commerce with the American colonies.

NOVEMBER

- A British force under Admiral Sir Samuel Barrington captures the island of St. Lucia in the West Indies from the French.

11   Loyalist Walter Butler orders the slaughter of 32 American men, women, and children in the village of Cherry Valley, New York, after one of a series of raids by loyalists and Iroquois.

DECEMBER

29–January 29, 1779   British forces under Colonel Archibald Campbell occupy the largely loyalist city of Savannah, Georgia. One month later, they advance inland as far as Augusta, establishing a temporary British hold on the colony.

SCIENCE, TECHNOLOGY, AND MEDICINE

Health and Medicine

- Austrian physician Franz Mesmer first practices "mesmerism" in Paris, France; it is the forerunner of hypnotism.

Science

- In *Epoques de la nature/Epochs of Nature*, French scientist George-Louis Leclerc, comte de Buffon, reconstructs geological history as a series of stages—the first to recognize such stages. It contradicts the doctrine that the earth is only 6,000 years old.
- Italian physicist Alessandro Volta discovers and isolates methane gas.
- Swedish chemist Karl Wilhelm Scheele discovers molybdenum (atomic no. 42).
- The Société royale de médecine (Royal Society of Medicine) is established in France, to study epidemics.

Technology

- English inventor Joseph Bramah invents an improved toilet with a valve-and-siphon flushing system.

Psychology and Psychiatry (1778–1900)

1778–1844

1778
- Austrian physician Franz Mesmer first practices "mesmerism" in Paris, France; it is the forerunner of hypnotism.

1792
- French physician Philippe Pinel removes chains from mental patients in Paris, and establishes a program of modern psychiatric treatment.

1798
- Pinel publishes *Nosographie philosophique/Philosophical Nosography*, in which he describes various mental disorders and debunks the theory that mental illness is due to demonic possession.

1817
- The first insane asylum in the United States opens in Frankford, Pennsylvania.

1841
- Scottish surgeon James Braid uses hypnosis for therapeutic purposes and proposes that it is a physiological state and not due to magical fluids as commonly believed.

1844
- The American Psychiatric Association begins as the Association of Medical Superintendents of American Institutions for the Insane.

1872–1900

1872
- French physician Jean-Martin Charcot employs hypnosis to treat patients. Sigmund Freud is later one of his students.

1873
- Scottish philosopher Alexander Bain lays the foundation for physiological psychology with the publication of *Mind and Body: The Theories of Their Relation*, in which he discusses the relationship between physiology and psychology.

1880
- Austrian physician Josef Breuer relieves the symptoms of a patient being treated for hysteria by getting her to recall past experiences while under hypnosis. One of the forebears of psychoanalysis, he argues that unconscious processes produce neurotic symptoms that can be cured when the processes are made conscious. His work had a large influence on Sigmund Freud.

1882–83
- U.S. psychologist Granville Stanley Hall writes about children's lies and children's minds, pioneering child psychology.

1886
- German psychiatrist Richard Krafft–Ebling publishes *Psychopathia Sexualis*, the first study of abnormal sexual practices in humans.

1893
- British psychologist Robert Armstrong–Jones begins the modern treatment of mental diseases, at London County Council's Claybury Asylum.

1897
- The English psychologist Havelock Ellis publishes the first volume of his *Studies in the Psychology of Sex*. One of the first objective studies of human sexuality, it causes an outcry and is initially banned as obscene. The final volume is published in 1928.

1900
- Austrian psychologist Sigmund Freud publishes *Die Traumdeutung/The Interpretation of Dreams*, which interprets dreams using psychoanalytic techniques.

ARTS AND IDEAS

Arts

- The Japanese artist and poet Yosa Buson paints the hand scroll *The Narrow Path into the Back Country*.

Literature and Language

- The English writer Fanny Burney publishes anonymously *Evelina*, her first and finest novel.
- The German writer Gottfried August Bürger publishes *Gedichte/Poems*.
- The Swedish writer Johan Henrik Kellgren publishes his satirical poem "Mina löjen"/"My Laughter."

Music

- *c.* 1778 Austrian composer Franz Joseph Haydn completes his Symphony No. 69, the *Laudon*.
- Austrian composer Wolfgang Amadeus Mozart completes his Symphony No. 31 (K 297), the *Paris*; his Flute Concertos No. 1 (K 313) and No. 2 (K 314); his Piano Sonatas Nos. 8 to 13 (K 310–311 and 330–333); and his Sonatas for Piano and Violin No. 17 (K 296) and Nos. 18 to 23 (K 301–306).
- German writer Johann Gottfried Herder publishes *Stimmen der Völker in Liedern/Voices of the Peoples in Song*, the first part of his collection of German folk songs. His work encourages the study of folklore in Germany.

Theater and Dance

- The ballet *Les Petits Riens/The Little Nobodies* is first performed, in Paris, France. The music is by the Austrian composer Wolfgang Amadeus Mozart, the choreography by the French dancer Jean Noverre.
- The comedy *School for Scandal* by the Irish writer Richard Brinsley Sheridan is performed, in London, England.
- The tragedy *Fiskerne/The Fishermen* by the Danish poet Johannes Ewald is first performed, in Copenhagen, Denmark.

SOCIETY

Everyday Life

- English cabinetmaker Joseph Bramah begins manufacturing toilets, selling around 6,000 in the next 20 years. His design remains in use until around 1890.
- The French government sets up state control of brothels, with compulsory registration and medical inspection of prostitutes.

Religion

- A *Commission des Réguliers* is appointed to reform French religious houses, which leads to an edict regulating admissions and the size of monasteries.

BIRTHS & DEATHS

- Joseph Lancaster, British-born educational reformer in Britain and the United States, born in London, England (–1838).

JANUARY
10 Carolus Linnaeus, Swedish botanist and explorer who devised a system for naming plants, dies in Uppsala, Sweden (70).
26 Ugo Foscolo, Italian poet and novelist, born in Zákinthos, Greece (–1827).

FEBRUARY
25 José San Martí, Argentine revolutionary who helped lead the revolutions against Spanish rule in Argentina, Chile, and Peru, born in Yapeyú, Viceroyalty of La Plata (–1850).

APRIL
22 James Hargreaves, English inventor of the spinning jenny, dies in Nottinghamshire, England (*c.* 55).

MAY
11 William Pitt the Elder, Earl of Chatham, British statesman, dies in Hayes, Kent, England (60).
30 Voltaire (original name François-Marie Arouet), celebrated French philosopher and writer, whose major works include *Candide* (1758) and the *Dictionnaire philosophique/ Philosophical Dictionary* (1764), dies in Paris, France (83).

JULY
2 Jean-Jacques Rousseau, French philosopher whose writings provided inspiration to the leaders of the French Revolution, dies in Ermenonville, France (66).

DECEMBER
6 Joseph Louis Gay-Lussac, French chemist and physicist, a founder of meteorology, born in St.-Léonard-de-Noblat, France (–1850).
17 Humphry Davy, English chemist, inventor of the miner's safety lamp, born in Penzance, Cornwall, England (–1829).

1779

POLITICS, GOVERNMENT, AND ECONOMICS

Business and Economics

DECEMBER

- Britain ends mercantilist restrictions on Irish external trade in response to the demands of the Irish politicians Henry Flood and Henry Grattan.

Colonization

JANUARY

- French forces defeat a British attack on French colonial possessions in Senegal, West Africa, recovered from Britain in 1778.

MAY

- France abandons its colonial base at Gorée, West Africa, to Britain.

Politics and Government

- The English adventurer Sir John Acton reforms the Neapolitan army and navy, and British influence replaces that of France in Naples.

FEBRUARY

25 The American Congress authorizes a punitive expedition (May–November) against allied loyalists and Iroquois on the Pennsylvania–New York frontier. Led by General John Sullivan, the expedition succeeds in permanently weakening the Iroquois resistance.

25 Virginian military commander George Rogers Clark completes the American conquest of the Old Northwest, forcing Henry Hamilton, British lieutenant governor of Quebec, to surrender at Fort Vincennes.

MARCH

- An Irish Protestant Volunteer movement formed for the defense of Ireland from possible French invasion reaches a total of 40,000 volunteers.

MAY

13 The Treaty of Teschen ends the War of the Bavarian Succession. The Hapsburg Monarchy obtains the Inn district of Bavaria and agrees to support the reversion of the Hohenzollern principalities of Ansbach and Bayreuth to Prussia.

JUNE

16 Spain declares war on Britain, following an undertaking by France to assist in recovering Gibraltar and Florida. Spanish forces begin a siege of Gibraltar.

18 French forces capture the British island of St. Vincent in the West Indies.

JULY

6 French forces capture the British island of Grenada in the West Indies.

AUGUST

- British forces repulse an American attack on Penobscot, Maine.

SEPTEMBER

23 An American naval squadron led by John Paul Jones in the converted merchantman *Bonhomme Richard* captures the British frigate *Serapis* and armed merchantman *Countess of Scarborough* off the British coast, and takes them to the Dutch Republic.

SCIENCE, TECHNOLOGY, AND MEDICINE

Exploration

- Spanish sailor Juan Francisco de la Bodega y Quadra explores the western seaboard of North America as far North as Kayak Island off the Alaskan coast.

FEBRUARY

13 English explorer James Cook returns to Hawaii, where his crew have a disagreement with some of the indigenous population. After a hasty departure, Cook's ship, the *Resolution*, is damaged, and he is forced to land again, where he is killed in an argument over a stolen boat.

Science

- Dutch physician and plant physiologist Jan Ingenhousz discovers two respiratory cycles in plants. He concludes that sunlight is necessary for the production of oxygen by leaves.

- French scientist Charles Augustin Coulomb investigates the laws of friction.

- German astronomer Heinrich Olbers devises a method of calculating the orbits of comets.

- Swiss geologist Horace Bénédict de Saussure coins the word "geology."

American Revolutionary War (1775–83)

1775

April 19 Military action in the American Revolution begins with the skirmishes between colonials and British forces under Lieutenant Colonel Francis Smith at Lexington and Concord, Massachusetts; the British force withdraws to Boston.

June 17 British regular forces attack entrenched Massachusetts militiamen at Breed's Hill overlooking Boston. In what becomes known as the Battle of Bunker Hill, the British mount three charges and suffer terrible casualties, but hold the entrenchments at the end of the day.

1776

March 17 The Continental Army under George Washington forces British troops under Sir William Howe to evacuate Boston.

May 6 American forces under Benedict Arnold are forced to abandon their siege of Quebec and are driven from Canada.

August 27 Sir William Howe's British troops defeat American forces under George Washington and Israel Putnam in the Battle of Long Island; the Americans retreat across the East River to Manhattan Island.

September 9 The Continental Congress passes a resolution changing the name of the nation from the United Colonies to the United States of America.

September 15 British forces under Sir William Howe occupy New York, New York.

November 20 The American-held Fort Lee, on the Hudson River, surrenders to British forces.

November 28 George Washington's Continental Army retreats across New Jersey into Pennsylvania as Sir William Howe's British offensive continues.

December 25 American forces under George Washington cross the ice-strewn Delaware River in a surprise raid on Christmas night, and defeat a corps of British Hessian mercenaries at the Battle of Trenton.

1777

January 3 George Washington follows up his victory at Trenton by defeating Sir William Howe's British forces at Princeton, New Jersey.

April French volunteers led by Marquis Marie Joseph de Lafayette and Baron Johan de Kalb begin to arrive in America to support the American struggle for independence.

October 17 The British general John Burgoyne surrenders to the Americans under Horatio Gates near Saratoga Springs, New York.

December 17 The Continental Army retires to Valley Forge, outside Philadelphia, for the winter.

1778

February 6 The United States signs two treaties with France—the Treaty of Amity and Commerce and the Treaty of Alliance. The former aims to promote both countries' commercial prosperity; the latter commits France to safeguarding "the liberty, sovereignty, and independence absolute and unlimited of the United States."

July 8 A French fleet under Jean Baptiste, comte d'Estaing, arrives off the Delaware Capes.

July 27 A French fleet under Louis Guillouet, comte d'Orvilliers, wins a narrow victory over a British fleet under Augustus Keppel off Ushant, in the English Channel. This crucial British defeat enables units of the French Brest fleet to be sent to America.

September 4 The Dutch Republic signs a treaty of amity and commerce with the American colonies.

December 29 British forces under Colonel Archibald Campbell occupy the largely loyalist city of Savannah, Georgia. One month later, they advance inland as far as Augusta, establishing a temporary British hold on the colony.

1779

September 23 An American naval squadron led by John Paul Jones in the converted merchantman *Bonhomme Richard* captures the British frigate *Serapis* and armed merchantman *Countess of Scarborough* off the British coast, and takes them to the Dutch Republic.

1780

May 12 Charleston, South Carolina, surrenders to British forces under Sir Henry Clinton.

July Some 6,000 French troops under Jean-Baptiste, comte de Rochambeau, arrive at Newport, Rhode Island, to support the American military effort against Britain.

1781

March 15 The American general Nathanael Greene fights a stand-off with the British general Charles Cornwallis at the Battle of Guilford Courthouse in North Carolina. While claiming victory, Cornwallis retreats toward Wilmington.

August 1 British forces under Charles, Lord Cornwallis, occupy Yorktown, Virginia.

August 30 A French fleet of 24 ships from the West Indies under admiral François, comte de Grasse, occupies the Chesapeake Bay, Virginia, cutting the seaward communications of the British forces under Charles, Lord Cornwallis, in Yorktown.

September 5 In perhaps the decisive battle of the American Revolution, the French fleet under François, comte de Grasse, defeats off the Virginia Capes the attempt of a British fleet from New York under Admiral Thomas Graves to drive it from Chesapeake Bay. Continued French occupation of the Bay seals the fate of the British forces under Charles, Lord Cornwallis, in Yorktown.

October 19 British forces under Charles, Lord Cornwallis, surrender to the besieging American and French forces at Yorktown, after a three-week siege. The British also evacuate Charleston and Savannah.

1782

February 27 The British Parliament orders a halt to British military campaigns in North America.

November 30 The Preliminary Treaty of Paris is signed in Paris, France, between Britain and the American colonies, formally ending the American Revolution.

1783

February 14 Britain proclaims a cessation of hostilities to end the American Revolution.

February 20 America proclaims a cessation of hostilities, following the British proclamation six days earlier.

September 3 The Peace of Paris is signed between Britain on one side and France, Spain, and America on the other, ending the American Revolution. Britain recognizes the independence of the American colonies, cedes Florida to Spain, and recovers its West Indian possessions. France recovers St. Lucia, Tobago, Senegal, Gorée, and its East Indian possessions. France regains the right to fortify Dunkirk.

- The Royal Academy of Sciences is founded in Lisbon, Portugal.

Technology

- English inventor Samuel Crompton devises the spinning mule, a cross between a spinning jenny and a water-frame spinning machine; it makes possible the large-scale manufacture of thread.

Transportation

- French inventors Jean-Pierre-François Blanchard and M. Masurier construct a velocipede, a type of early bicycle, in Paris, France.

ARTS AND IDEAS

Arts

- The American artist Charles Willson Peale paints *Portrait of General George Washington Before Princeton.*

Literature and Language

- The Russian poet Gavriil Romanovich Derzhavin publishes his poem "Na smert knyazya Meshcherskogo"/"Ode on the Death of Prince Meshchersky."

February 1779–81 The English writer Samuel Johnson publishes his *Lives of the Poets.*

Music

c. 1779 Austrian composer Wolfgang Amadeus Mozart completes his Double Piano Concerto No. 10 (K 365).
- Mozart completes his Symphonies No. 32 (K 318) and No. 33 (K 319); his Mass in C (No. 16) (K 317), the *Coronation*; and his Organ Sonata in C Major (K 329).
- Italian-born English composer Muzio Clementi publishes his early keyboard sonatas (Opus 2).
- The opera *Amadis de Gaule* by the German composer Johann Christian Bach is first performed, in Paris, France.
- The opera *Iphigénia en Tauride/Iphigenia in Tauris* by the German composer Christoph Gluck is first performed, in Paris, France. The success of this opera settles the heated debate between the supporters of Gluck's French style of opera and the supporters of Nicola Puccini's Italian style in favor of Gluck.
- The opera *La vera costanza/True Constancy* by the Austrian composer Franz Joseph Haydn is first performed, in Eszterháza, Hungary.

Theater and Dance

- The comedy *The Critic* by the Irish writer Richard Brinsley Sheridan is performed, in London, England.
- The German writer Gotthold Ephraim Lessing publishes his verse play *Nathan der Weise/Nathan the Wise*, a plea for religious tolerance.
- The Imperial Ballet School opens in St. Petersburg, Russia.

Thought and Scholarship

- The English geographer James Rennel publishes his *Bengal Atlas.*

BIRTHS & DEATHS

- William Warburton, Anglican bishop of Gloucester 1759–79, and author, dies in Gloucester, England (80).

JANUARY

5 Stephen Decatur, U.S. naval hero, born in Sinepuxent, Maryland (–1820).

18 Peter Mark Roget, English physician and philologist known for his *Thesaurus of English Words and Phrases*, born in London, England (–1869).

FEBRUARY

13 James Cook, English naval captain and navigator who explored Canada's coasts and the Pacific, killed in Hawaii (50).

21 Friedrich Karl von Savigny, German jurist, born in Frankfurt am Main, Germany (–1861).

MARCH

15 William Lamb, Lord Melbourne, British prime minister 1834 and 1835–41, a Whig advisor to Queen Victoria, born in London, England (–1848).

JUNE

29 Anton Raphael Mengs, early Italian neoclassical painter, dies in Rome, Italy (51).

JULY

15 Clement Clarke Moore, U.S. scholar of Hebrew, teacher, and author of the children's Christmas ballad "A Visit From St. Nicholas" (also known as "The Night Before Christmas"), born in New York, New York (–1863).

AUGUST

1 Francis Scott Key, U.S. lawyer and author of "The Star Spangled Banner," born in Frederick, Maryland (–1843).

7 Carl Ritter, German geographer who, with Alexander von Humboldt, founded the science of modern geography, born in Quedlinburg, Prussia (–1859).

DECEMBER

6 Jean-Baptiste-Siméon Chardin, French still-life painter, dies in Paris, France (80).

SOCIETY

Everyday Life

- Due to social prejudices against breast-feeding, of a sample of 21,000 children born in Paris, France, the vast majority are sent to wet nurses and only 700 are suckled by their own mothers.
- Jean-Joseph Clausse, the chef of the French duc de Contades, makes the first *pâté de fois gras*.

Religion

- *Dialogues Concerning Natural Religion* by the Scottish philosopher David Hume are published posthumously.

Though he wrote them in the 1750s, Hume was unwilling during his lifetime to publish these attacks on the arguments for God's existence.
- Selina, Countess of Huntingdon, builds Spa Fields Chapel in London, England, but in the face of clerical opposition takes shelter under the Toleration Acts to register the chapel as a dissenting place of worship.
- The English poet William Cowper and the clergyman John Newton publish their *Olney Hymns*.
- The English scholar Robert Lowth publishes his new translation of Isaiah. Lowth was one of the first to treat the Bible as literature in its own right.

Sports

- Quarter-horse racing, in which horses race quarter-mile sprints, becomes popular in Charlottesville, Virginia.

1780

POLITICS, GOVERNMENT, AND ECONOMICS

Business and Economics

- The first hat factory in Danbury, Connecticut, is established by American entrepreneur Zadoc Benedict. Danbury subsequently becomes the center for hat manufacturing in America.

DECEMBER
13 Ireland is granted the right of free trade with Britain including direct access to British colonial markets.

Colonization

APRIL
19 Irish politician Henry Grattan demands Home Rule for Ireland in the British Parliament at Westminster.

Politics and Government

JANUARY
16 A British fleet under Sir George Rodney defeats a Spanish naval force off Cape St. Vincent, Portugal, and temporarily relieves the siege of Gibraltar.

MARCH
10 Russia creates the League of Armed Neutrality to prevent British ships from searching neutral vessels for contraband of war. The confederacy is subsequently joined by France, Spain, Austria, Prussia, Denmark, and Sweden.

APRIL
6 Lord Ashburton brings a resolution in Parliament condemning the British king, George III, for his support of Lord North's government.

MAY
12 Charleston, South Carolina, surrenders to British forces under Sir Henry Clinton during the British offensive against the southern American colonies.

JUNE
2 The Duke of Richmond proposes a bill for British parliamentary reform, including universal adult male suffrage, annual parliaments, and equal electoral areas.
2–8 The English anti-Catholic agitator Lord George Gordon heads a mob marching to Parliament with a petition to repeal the Catholic Relief Act of 1778. Riots ensue.

JULY
- Some 6,000 French troops under Jean-Baptiste, comte de Rochambeau, arrive at Newport, Rhode Island, to support the American military effort against Britain.

AUGUST
16 British forces under Charles, Lord Cornwallis, defeat an American army under Horatio Gates at Camden, South Carolina. His army then advances through North Carolina and into Virginia.

SEPTEMBER

10   Hyder Ali, sultan of Mysore, conquers most of the Carnatic (modern Karnataka) in southern India, with French support.

23   The British spy John André is captured, revealing the plot of American major general Benedict Arnold to surrender West Point to the British commander Sir Henry Clinton.

OCTOBER

•   Personal serfdom is abolished in the Hapsburg Monarchy by the Holy Roman Emperor, Joseph II.

7   American frontiersmen defeat a British force under Major Patrick Ferguson in the Battle of Kings Mountain, North Carolina.

NOVEMBER

20   Britain declares war on the United Netherlands to prevent it joining the League of Armed Neutrality created by Russia on March 10.

29   Maria-Theresa, wife and empress of Holy Roman Emperor Francis I 1745–65 and coruler of the Hapsburg Monarchy, dies in Vienna, Austria. Her son, the Holy Roman Emperor Joseph II, becomes sole ruler of the Hapsburg lands.

SCIENCE, TECHNOLOGY, AND MEDICINE

Science

c. 1780   Italian anatomist Luigi Galvani discovers the electric nature of the nervous impulse.

•   French chemist Antoine-Laurent Lavoisier demonstrates that respiration is a form of combustion.

•   Italian physiologist Lazzaro Spallanzani conducts experiments in artificial insemination, using dogs.

Technology

c. 1780   American engineer Oliver Evans develops a carding machine that combs cotton fibers in preparation for spinning.

c. 1780   Watches that can be wound without being opened are invented by the French watchmaker Abraham Louis Beréquet.

•   The circular saw is invented.

MARCH

20   Scottish engineer James Watt patents a copying machine for business letters. This style of machine remains in use until World War I.

Transportation

c. 1780   The square landau, a carriage that seats four and can be opened or closed depending on the weather, is developed in Europe. Its driver is seated on a box at the front.

c. 1780   The tumbrel cart, an unsprung, two-wheeled farm cart pulled by horses, is developed. It has the advantage that it can be tipped to release its load.

ARTS AND IDEAS

Arts

c. 1780   The Chinese artist Wang Ch'eng-p'ei paints *Two Birds on a Plum Tree.*

c. 1780   The Italian artist Francesco Guardi paints *View of the Church of Santa Maria della Salute, Venice.*

•   The Japanese artist Yosa Buson paints *Autumn Landscape* on a silk sliding door.

Literature and Language

•   Frederick the Great, king of Prussia, publishes his account of German literature *De la littérature allemande/On German Literature.* Written in French, it shows little understanding of contemporary writers such as Goethe.

•   The German writer Christoph Martin Wieland publishes his heroic poem "Oberon," one of his finest works.

Music

c. 1780   Austrian composer Franz Joseph Haydn completes his Symphonies No. 63, *La Roxolane,* and No. 53, *L'Impérial/The Imperial.*

•   Austrian composer Wolfgang Amadeus Mozart completes his Symphony No. 34 (K 338). His opera

BIRTHS & DEATHS

c. 1780   Jean Lafitte, U.S. privateer and smuggler who defended New Orleans during the War of 1812, born in France (–*c.* 1825).

APRIL

7   William Ellery Channing, U.S. Unitarian cleric, born in Newport, Rhode Island (–1842).

AUGUST

2   Etienne Bonnot de Condillac, French psychologist, philosopher, and economist, dies in Flux, France (64).

29   Jacques Louis Soufflot, French neoclassical architect who designed

the Panthéon in Paris, France, dies in Paris (67).

29   Jean-August Dominique Ingres, French neoclassical painter, born in Montauban, France (–1867).

Idomeneo is first performed in Munich, Germany, in the same year.

- French instrumentmaker Sébastien Erard makes the first piano in his workshop in Paris, France.
- The opera *La fedeltà premiata/Fidelity Rewarded* by the Austrian composer Franz Joseph Haydn is first performed, in Eszterháza, Austria.

Thought and Scholarship

MAY

4   The American Academy of Arts and Sciences is founded in Boston, Massachusetts.

SOCIETY

Education

- The Swiss educator Johann Heinrich Pestalozzi publishes *Die Abendstunde eines Linsiedlers/The*

Evening Thoughts of a Hermit, setting out his views on education, which are inspired by those of Jean-Jacques Rousseau.

Religion

- The German scholar Johann Gottfried Eichhorn publishes the first volume of his three-volume *Historische-kritische Einleitung ins Alte Testament/ Historical and Critical Introduction to the Old Testament*, one of the first systematic attempts to apply the methods of literary criticism to the Bible. The final volume appears in 1783.
- The number of Roman Catholics in England is estimated to be 70,000.

Sports

c. 1780   The fencing mask is invented by the French master, La Boessiere. It is made of metal with a horizontal eye-slit. The first wire mesh masks are introduced about 20 years later.

1781

POLITICS, GOVERNMENT, AND ECONOMICS

Business and Economics

- Jacques Necker, French finance minister, publishes *Compte rendu au Roi/Royal Accounts*; it conceals an enormous deficit, but brings discussion of public finances into the public domain for the first time in France.

DECEMBER

31   The American Congress establishes the Bank of North America in Philadelphia, Pennsylvania.

Colonization

JULY

1   Sir Eyre Coote, Irish-born British commander in chief in India, defeats Hyder Ali, Sultan of Mysore, at Porto Novo, establishing British hegemony over southern India.

NOVEMBER

13   A British force captures the Dutch settlement at Negapattam, near Madras, India.

Human Rights

- A third of the monasteries of the Austrian Empire are dissolved by Joseph II. He also makes monastic orders independent of Rome and publishes the Edict of Toleration, allowing greater freedom for Protestants and members of the Greek Orthodox Church.

Politics and Government

JANUARY

1   Veterans of the Pennsylvania division desert the Continental Army to protest against the large bounties being offered to new recruits. By the end of the month, their grievances having been redressed, most Pennsylvanians reenlist.

17   The Virginian commander Daniel Morgan wins a major victory against a British force under Sir Banastre Tarleton at the Battle of Cowpens, South Carolina.

FEBRUARY

- Catherine II (the Great) of Russia concludes a secret treaty with the Hapsburg Empire. Her aims are to drive the Ottoman Turks out of Europe, restore a Greek empire under her grandson Constantine, form a kingdom of Dacia under an Orthodox prince, and allocate Serbia and the western Balkans to Austria, and the Morea, Candia, and Cyprus to Venice.

3 A British fleet under Admiral Sir George Rodney takes the island of St. Eustatius in the West Indies from the Dutch.

MARCH

1. The Continental Congress proclaims the Articles of Confederation of the United States, after Maryland, the last state to approve, ratifies them.

15 The American general Nathanael Greene fights a stand-off with the British general Charles Cornwallis at the Battle of Guilford Courthouse in North Carolina. While claiming victory, Cornwallis retreats toward Wilmington.

MAY

• Prussia joins the League of Armed Neutrality created by Russia in 1780.

9 A Spanish force from New Orleans captures Pensacola, Florida, from the British, taking advantage of the distraction afforded by the war of the British with the colonies.

19 The French finance minister Jacques Necker is forced to resign when the queen, Marie-Antoinette, opposes his policy of raising loans to finance French participation in the American Revolution.

AUGUST

1 British forces under Charles, Lord Cornwallis, occupy Yorktown, Virginia.

30 A French fleet of 24 ships from the West Indies under Admiral François, comte de Grasse, occupies the Chesapeake Bay, Virginia, cutting the seaward communications of the British forces under Charles, Lord Cornwallis, in Yorktown, Virginia.

SEPTEMBER

5 In perhaps the decisive battle of the American Revolution, the French fleet under François, comte de Grasse, defeats off the Virginia Capes the attempt of a British fleet from New York under Admiral Thomas Graves to drive it from Chesapeake Bay. Continued French occupation of the Bay seals the fate of the British forces under Charles, Lord Cornwallis, in Yorktown.

8 A British force under Alexander Stewart defeats American troops under Nathanael Greene at the Battle of Eutaw Springs, North Carolina.

8 British troops commanded by former American commander Benedict Arnold loot and burn New London, Connecticut.

OCTOBER

13 The Holy Roman Emperor Joseph II grants a patent of religious tolerance in the Hapsburg Monarchy, together with freedom of the press.

19 British forces under Charles, Lord Cornwallis, surrender to the besieging American and French forces at Yorktown, Virginia, after a three-week siege. The British also evacuate Charleston in South Carolina and Savannah in Georgia.

SCIENCE, TECHNOLOGY, AND MEDICINE

Agriculture

• Future American president Thomas Jefferson introduces the cultivation of the tomato to the southern American colonies.

Science

• Swedish chemist Karl Wilhelm Scheele discovers the composition of the mineral calcium tungstate ("scheelite").

MARCH

13 German-born English astronomer William Herschel discovers the planet Uranus.

Technology

• Scottish engineer James Watt discovers how to convert the up-and-down motion of his steam engine into rotary motion which can then turn a shaft.

BIRTHS & DEATHS

FEBRUARY

13 Gotthold Ephraim Lessing, German dramatist and critic, dies in Braunschweig, Germany (52).

MARCH

17 Johannes Ewald, Danish lyric poet, dies in Copenhagen, Denmark (37).

18 Anne-Robert-Jacques Turgot, French economist and administrator, dies in Paris, France (53).

JUNE

9 George Stephenson, English engineer, inventor of the railroad locomotive, born in Wylam, Northumberland, England (–1848).

21 Siméon-Denis Poisson, French mathematician who applied mathematics to electromagnetic theory, born in Pithiviers, France (–1840).

JULY

6 Stamford Raffles, administrator in British East India and founder of Singapore, born at sea off Port Morant, Jamaica (–1826).

AUGUST

12 Robert Mills, U.S. neoclassical architect, born in Charleston, South Carolina (–1855).

DECEMBER

2 Zenón de Somodevilla, Marquess de la Ensenada, prime minister of Spain 1743–54, dies in Medina del Campo, Spain (79).

Transportation

- Work begins on the Siberian highway.

ARTS AND IDEAS

Arts

- The English artist Joseph Wright paints his *Portrait of Sir Brooke Boothby*.
- The French sculptor Jean Antoine Houdon carves the portrait *Seated Voltaire*, which will become one of the best-known images of the writer.
- The Swiss-born English artist Henry Fuseli paints *The Nightmare*. Capturing the Gothic mood of the period, it is one of the most vivid and macabre images of early romanticism.

Literature and Language

- The English poet George Crabbe publishes *The Library*.
- The German poet and philologist Johann Heinrich Voss publishes his translation of the *Odyssey* by the Greek poet Homer.
- The Swedish poet and critic Thomas Thorild wins a national poetry competition with *Passionerna*, a work which begins a heated literary debate on the nature of poetry. His work signals the development of romanticism in Scandinavia.

Music

- Austrian composer Franz Joseph Haydn completes his String Quartets Nos. 37–42, the *Russian* (or *Maiden*) Quartets, and his Symphony No. 73, *La Chasse*.

- Austrian composer Wolfgang Amadeus Mozart completes his Sonatas for Piano and Violin Nos. 24 to 28 (K 376–380).
- German composer Johann Adam Hiller founds the *Gewandthaus* concerts in Leipzig, Germany.

Thought and Scholarship

- The Chinese scholar and editor Ji Yun publishes *Si-ku juan-shu*, a vast anthology of Chinese texts, many of them very rare.
- The German philosopher Immanuel Kant publishes the first of his major works, the *Critique of Pure Reason*, which explores the theory of knowledge. It will become one of the central works of modern philosophy.

SOCIETY

Education

- The Swiss educational reformer Johann Heinrich Pestalozzi publishes the novel *Leonard and Gertrude*, embodying his educational theories.

Everyday Life

- The population of America is around 3.5 million. The majority live on the east coast and there is very little settlement of the rest of the country.

Media and Communication

- The Clarendon Press is founded in Oxford, England.

1782

POLITICS, GOVERNMENT, AND ECONOMICS

Colonization

JANUARY

11 The United Netherlands surrenders Trincomalee, Ceylon (modern Sri Lanka), to Britain.

Politics and Government

• The Virginia legislature adopts an emancipation law permitting citizens to liberate their slaves.

FEBRUARY

5   Spanish forces capture the British-held Spanish island of Minorca, in the western Mediterranean.

13 French forces capture the island of St. Christopher (St. Kitts) in the West Indies from Britain.

22 A motion opposing the British government's continuation of the war in America is defeated by a single vote in the House of Commons.

27 The British Parliament orders a halt to British military campaigns in North America.

MARCH

15 A motion of no-confidence in Lord North's administration is defeated in the British House of Commons by nine votes.

19 Lord North resigns as prime minister of Britain, recognizing the failure of his policy to retain British sovereignty in the American colonies.

APRIL

• The Holy Roman Emperor Joseph II repeals the third Barrier Treaty of 1715, obliging the Dutch to evacuate the garrisons in barrier towns in the Austrian Netherlands. They do so on April 18.

12 The British fleet under Admiral Sir George Rodney defeats the French fleet of the comte de Grasse in the Battle of the Saintes, ending the French threat to British possessions in the West Indies.

16 The Irish politician Henry Grattan achieves complete freedom from British legislation for Ireland.

MAY

9   British representative Thomas Grenville is sent to Paris, France, to open peace negotiations with Charles, comte de Vergennes, for France, and Benjamin Franklin for America.

17 After a British defeat at Wadgaon, India, in January 1779 and largely inconclusive warfare since, the Treaty of Salbai ends the first Anglo-Maratha war with minimal British gains.

17 British secretary of state Charles James Fox introduces a repeal of the 1720 Ireland Act, granting Ireland legislative independence (until 1800), but the parliament in Ireland is elected solely by Protestants.

30 Lord Melville carries a motion in the British Parliament recalling the British governor-general Warren Hastings from India.

JUNE

• Spain completes the conquest of Florida from Britain.

AUGUST

7   General George Washington establishes the Purple Heart, a mark of valor, as a military decoration in America.

OCTOBER

• British forces under Admiral Richard, Lord Howe, relieve Gibraltar, under siege by Spanish forces for three years.

NOVEMBER

30 The Preliminary Treaty of Paris is signed in Paris, France, between Britain and the American colonies, formally ending the American Revolution.

DECEMBER

7   Tippu Sultan succeeds his father, Hyder Ali, as sultan of Mysore, India.

SCIENCE, TECHNOLOGY, AND MEDICINE

Technology

• English pottery manufacturer Josiah Wedgwood invents the pyrometer, which he uses to measure the temperature in his pottery furnaces.

• Scottish engineer James Watt patents the double-acting steam engine, which provides power on both the upstroke and the downstroke of the piston.

• The distributing mechanism of English agriculturist Jethro Tull's seed-planting machine is improved with the addition of gears.

ARTS AND IDEAS

Arts

- The Italian artist Francesco Guardi paints *Fêtes for the Archduke Paul of Russia* and *The Concert*.

Literature and Language

- J. Hector St. John de Crevecoeur, a Frenchman who settles in New York, publishes *Letters from an American Farmer*, his book of impressions about the United States; it is especially popular abroad.
- The Dutch writers Elisabeth Wolff-Bekker and Agatha Deken publish their novel *Sara Burgerhart*.
- The English poet William Cowper publishes *Poems*, which includes his best-known work, "John Gilpin."
- The English writer Fanny Burney publishes her novel *Cecilia*.
- The first part of the *Confessions* of the French writer Jean-Jacques Rousseau (written 1765–70) are published posthumously. A very frank (and often unreliable) account of his unusual life, it is a masterpiece of autobiography. The last part appears in 1789.
- The French writer Pierre-Ambroise-François Choderlos de Laclos publishes *Les Liaisons dangereuses/Dangerous Liaisons*, a novel in the form of a series of letters, which gives a cynical account of sexual intrigue.
- The Italian scholar Girolamo Tiraboschi publishes the first volume of his 13-volume *Storia della letteratura italiana/History of Italian Literature*. The last volume appears in 1782.
- The Russian poet Gavriil Romanovich Derzhavin publishes his poem "Oda k Felitse"/"Ode to Felicia," addressed to Catherine II (the Great) of Russia.
- The Spanish writer and statesman Gaspar Melchor de Jovellanos publishes *Elogio de las bellas artes/Elegy for the Fine Arts*. Like many European writers and artists of the day, Jovellanos was beginning to find inspiration in medieval art and architecture.

December 1782–83 The German writer Johann Gottfried von Herder publishes *Vom Geist der hebräischen Poesi/The Spirit of Hebrew Poetry*.

Music

- Austrian composer Franz Joseph Haydn completes his Mass No. 6, the *Mariazellermesse*.
- Austrian composer Wolfgang Amadeus Mozart completes his Symphony No. 35 (K 385), the *Haffner*, his Piano Concerto No. 12 (K 414), and his Sonata for Piano and Violin No. 29 (K 402). He leaves Sonatas Nos. 30 and 31 unfinished.
- The opera *Il barbiere di Siviglia/The Barber of Seville* by the Italian composer Giovanni Paisiello is performed, in St. Petersburg, Russia. His masterpiece, it is based—as is Rossini's opera of the same name—on the play by the French writer Pierre-Augustin Caron de Beaumarchais.
- The opera *Orlando Paladino* by the Austrian composer Franz Joseph Haydn is first performed, in Eszterháza, Hungary.

Theater and Dance

- The English religious writer and educator Hannah More publishes *Sacred Dramas*.
- The play *Die Räuber/The Robbers*, by the German writer Friedrich Schiller, is performed, in Mannheim, Germany. Its revolutionary passion makes it an instant success.

SOCIETY

Education

- Harvard Medical School opens in Cambridge, Massachusetts.

BIRTHS & DEATHS

JANUARY

1 J(ohann) C(hristian) Bach, German composer, son of J. S. Bach, dies in London, England (47).

18 Daniel Webster, U.S. orator, politician, and lawyer, born in Salisbury, New Hampshire (–1852).

29 Daniel Auber, French composer, born in Caen, France (–1871).

MARCH

18 John C. Calhoun, U.S. politician and vice-president, and prominent defender of slavery, born in Abbeville District, South Carolina (–1850).

MAY

8 Sebastião de Carvalho, Marquis of Pombal, Portuguese reformer and virtual ruler of Portugal 1750–77, dies in Pombal, Portugal (82).

JUNE

19 Hugues-Félicité Robert de Lamennais, French priest, philosophical and political writer, born in St.-Malo, France (–1854).

JULY

1 Charles Watson-Wentworth, Marquis of Rockingham, British prime minister 1765–66 and 1782, a Whig, dies in London, England (52).

OCTOBER

9 Lewis Cass, U.S. Democrat politician and secretary of war under President Andrew Jackson, born in Exeter, New Hampshire (–1866).

NOVEMBER

1 Frederick John Ripon, Viscount Goderich, British prime minister 1827–28, a Tory, born in London, England (–1859).

DECEMBER

4 Pietro Metastasio, Italian poet who wrote for the opera, dies (81).

Everyday Life

- M. Beauvilliers opens the Grande Taverne de Londres in Paris, France, the first restaurant with individual rather than communal tables.
- New Englanders cease branding adulterers with the scarlet letter "A".

Religion

- The English clergyman, chemist, and natural historian Joseph Priestley publishes *A History of the Corruptions of Christianity*.

1783

POLITICS, GOVERNMENT, AND ECONOMICS

Colonization

JUNE

20 A British fleet under Admiral Sir Edward Hughes and a French fleet under Pierre André de Suffren fight a fierce but inconclusive battle (the last of five similar engagements) off Cuddalore, India—in parallel to the struggle on land between British and French colonial forces for dominance in southern India.

Human Rights

- Deborah Sampson, who fought in the American Revolution disguised as Robert Shurtliff, is dismissed from the army when her sex is discovered. She is awarded a veteran's pension.
- The German Jewish scholar Moses Mendelssohn publishes *Jerusalem, oder über religiöse Macht und Judentum/Jerusalem, or On Religious Power and Judaism*, a plea for freedom of conscience.

Politics and Government

- The American state of Massachusetts bans slavery.

FEBRUARY

14 Britain proclaims a cessation of hostilities to end the American Revolution.

20 America proclaims a cessation of hostilities to end the American Revolution, following the British proclamation six days earlier.

24 The Earl of Shelburne resigns as British prime minister following a resolution censuring the peace preliminaries to end the American Revolution. William Pitt the Younger and Lord North both decline to form a ministry.

APRIL

9 Tippu Sultan, the sultan of Mysore, India, forces Britain to surrender the town of Bednore.

JULY

- Britain and the Hapsburg Monarchy dissuade the Ottoman Empire from declaring war on Russia.

SEPTEMBER

3 The Peace of Paris is signed between Britain on one side and France, Spain, and America on the other, ending the American Revolution. Britain recognizes the independence of the American colonies, cedes Florida to Spain, and recovers its West Indian possessions. France recovers St. Lucia, Tobago, Senegal, Gorée, and its East Indian possessions. France regains the right to fortify Dunkirk.

OCTOBER

- Following the sack of Tiflis (Tbilisi) by Persian forces, Russia intervenes in Georgia, takes the city of Baku, and forces Irakli II of Georgia to recognize Russian sovereignty.
- The Holy Roman Emperor Joseph II delivers to the States General (parliament) of the United Netherlands a summary of the Hapsburg claims, bringing to a head the question of the navigation of the River Scheldt.

NOVEMBER

10 Charles-Alexandre de Calonne is appointed French comptroller general of finance and raises loans to solve the financial crisis following the American Revolution.

DECEMBER

24 George Washington resigns as commander of the Continental Army.

SCIENCE, TECHNOLOGY, AND MEDICINE

Agriculture

- Japan suffers its worst famine for 50 years. It continues the following year when 300,000 die of starvation.

Ecology

FEBRUARY
4–5 A massive earthquake kills over 30,000 people in nearly 200 towns in Calabria, Italy.
December 1783–84 Mt. Skaptar in Iceland erupts, killing 9,000 people, about one-fifth of the population.

Health and Medicine

- English physician Thomas Cawley correctly diagnoses diabetes mellitus by demonstrating the presence of sugar in a patient's urine.

Science

- Spanish chemists Juan José and Fausto Elhuyar discover tungsten (atomic no. 74).
- Swiss geologist Horace Bénédict de Saussure invents the hair hygrometer to measure humidity. It is based on the principle that hair lengthens when wet.

Technology

- A glass factory opens in Waterford, Ireland, establishing the world-famous Waterford crystal industry.
- English inventor Henry Cort develops a rolling mill which makes the production of iron cheaper and easier by making hammering unnecessary.
- Scottish engineer Henry Bell invents a copper cylinder for calico printing.

DECEMBER
- French aeronautical pioneer Louis-Sébastien Lenormand becomes the first person to use a parachute successfully when he jumps from Montpellier Observatory in France.

Transportation

- The French aristocrat and inventor the marquis Jouffroy d'Abbans sails the pioneering paddle-wheel steamboat *Pyroscaphe* on the River Sâone near Lyons, France.

NOVEMBER
21 Using a hot-air balloon made by Joseph and Etienne Montgolfier, Jean F. Pilâtre de Rozier and the Marquis d'Arlandes make the first human flight, in Paris, France.

DECEMBER
- French physicist Jacques-Alexandre-César Charles builds and flies the first hydrogen-filled balloon.

ARTS AND IDEAS

Architecture

- In Russia, the Tauride Palace in St. Petersburg, designed by the Russian architect Ivan Yegorovich Starov, is completed.

Arts

- The French neoclassical artist Jacques-Louis David paints *The Grief of Andromache*.
December 1783–87 The Italian neoclassical sculptor Antonio Canova creates his monument to Pope Clement XIV in the Church of SS Apostoli in Rome, Italy.

Literature and Language

- The American lexicographer Noah Webster publishes the first part of his book *A Grammatical Institute of the*

BIRTHS & DEATHS

JANUARY
23 Stendhal (pen name of Marie-Henri Beyle), French novelist, born in Grenoble, France (–1842).

FEBRUARY
6 Launcelot "Capability" Brown, English landscape designer, dies in London, England (67).

MARCH
30 William Hunter, English physician who established obstetrics as an accepted branch of medicine, dies in London, England (64).

APRIL
3 Washington Irving, U.S. writer, born in New York, New York (–1859).

28 Eyre Coote, English soldier, commander in chief of the armed forces in India 1778–83, dies in Madras, India (c. 56).

MAY
23 James Otis, American political activist just prior to the American Revolution, known for saying "Taxation without representation is tyranny," dies in Andover, Massachusetts (58).

JULY
24 Simón Bolívar, Venezuelan soldier who liberated Colombia, Peru, Ecuador, Venezuela, and Bolivia from Spanish rule, born in Caracas,

New Granada (in modern Venezuela) (–1830).

SEPTEMBER
18 Leonhard Euler, Swiss mathematician and physicist, dies in St. Petersburg, Russia (75).

OCTOBER
29 Jean d'Alembert, French mathematician, philosopher, and writer, dies in Paris, France (65).

DECEMBER
31 Thomas Macdonough, U.S. naval officer, born in The Trap, Delaware (–1825).

English Language, which becomes better known as his influential *Spelling Book*.

- The American writer David Humphreys publishes the poem "The Glory of America, or Peace Triumphant over War."
- The Bohemian (Czech) scholar Josef Dobrovský publishes *Scriptores Bohemicarum/Bohemian Texts*. Dobrovsky devoted himself to the study of Bohemian, searching in Russia and Scandinavia for books scattered during the Thirty Years' War.
- The English poet and artist William Blake publishes *Poetical Sketches*, his first book of poems.
- The English poet Thomas Crabbe publishes *The Village*, a long poem in couplets that gives a realistic view of the harshness of rural life in East Anglia, England.
- The English writer Thomas Day publishes the improving tale for children *Sandford and Merton*.
- The Serbian writer Dositej Obradović publishes his autobiography *Život i priključenija/Life and Adventures*.

Music

- Austrian composer Wolfgang Amadeus Mozart completes his Symphony No. 36 (K 425), the *Linz*, part of No. 37 (K 444), and his Piano Concertos No. 11 (K 413) and No. 13 (K 415). He leaves his Mass in C minor (No. 18) (K 427) unfinished.
- The opera *Didon/Dido* by the Italian composer Niccolò Piccinni is first performed, in Paris, France.

Thought and Scholarship

- French painters Marie-Louise-Elisabeth Vigée Le Brun and Adélaïde Labille-Guiard are admitted to the Académie Royale in France.

- The German philosopher Immanuel Kant publishes *Prolegomena zur einer jeden künftigen Metaphysik/ Prolegomena to Any Possible Metaphysic*, which tries to answer attacks on his *Critique of Pure Reason*, published in 1781.

SOCIETY

Education

- Enrollment at Yale, at 270, exceeds that of any other American college.

Everyday Life

- Churchman Junipero Serra makes the first wine in America from grape cuttings brought from Spain and replanted at the California mission San Juan Capistrano.

Media and Communication

MAY

30 The first daily newspaper in colonial America, the *Pennsylvania Evening Post*, is published.

Religion

- The English clergyman Charles Simeon starts an evangelical movement in Cambridge, England.

1784

POLITICS, GOVERNMENT, AND ECONOMICS

Business and Economics

- As the heavily indebted and inflated American economy fails, the national government proves to be incapable of raising revenue from unobliging states.

Politics and Government

- Deer hunting at night is banned in the Carolinas following several incidents in which cattle and horses are accidentally killed.
- The American states of Connecticut and Rhode Island abolish slavery.

JANUARY

6 By the terms of the Treaty of Constantinople, the Ottoman Empire acquiesces in Russia's annexation of the Crimea and the Caucasian region of Kuban.

14 The American Congress ratifies the Treaty of Paris, formally ending the American Revolution.

MARCH

8   British parliamentary opposition to the prime minister William Pitt the Younger dwindles to a majority of one.

11   Britain signs a peace treaty with Tippu Sultan of Mysore, India, ending the Second Mysore War.

APRIL

23   The American Congress adopts a land ordinance, drafted by Thomas Jefferson, facilitating the settlement of the Old Northwest.

MAY

• The Dutch defeat in the Fourth Anglo-Dutch War severely weakens the authority of Prince William V of Orange, the Stadtholder (ruler) of the United Netherlands.

20   Britain and the Dutch Republic sign a final treaty on the terms of the 1783 Peace of Paris, which ended the American Revolution.

JULY

4   The Hapsburg monarch and Holy Roman Emperor Joseph II of Austria repeals the constitution of Hungary as part of his campaign to create a unified Hapsburg empire and to break the power of the local Hungarian nobility.

AUGUST

13   William Pitt the Younger's India Act places the East India Company under a British government-appointed Board of Control and forbids interference in native affairs.

OCTOBER

• The Holy Roman Emperor and Hapsburg monarch Joseph II of Austria breaks off diplomatic relations with the Dutch Republic when two vessels from the Austrian Netherlands on the River Scheldt are fired on by the Dutch. A European crisis ensues, in which Louis XVI of France offers to mediate.

SCIENCE, TECHNOLOGY, AND MEDICINE

Agriculture

• The colony of Massachusetts contains 921,563 acres of improved land, 43,969 horses, and 237,993 horned cattle. New Jersey has 2,032,587 acres of improved land, 52,488 horses, and 102,221 horned cattle.

Exploration

• Russian fur traders establish their first permanent settlement on the North American continent, at Kodiak Island, Alaska.

• Spanish explorer Juan Pérez leaves California and travels north, exploring North America's Pacific coast as far as the Queen Charlotte Islands.

Science

• English natural philosopher Henry Cavendish discovers that water is a compound of hydrogen and oxygen.

• French mineralogist René Just Haüy establishes the science of crystallography by describing the geometric laws of crystallization.

• German-born English astronomer William Herschel discovers clouds on Mars.

• Swedish chemist Karl Wilhelm Scheele discovers citric acid.

• The first Cepheid variable star is discovered by English astronomer John Goodricke.

Technology

• American scientist and statesman Benjamin Franklin invents glasses with bifocal lenses.

• English inventor Joseph Bramah invents an improved "pick-proof" lock.

• English iron manufacturer Henry Cort discovers the "puddling process" of converting pig iron into wrought iron by stirring to burn off impurities. It revolutionizes the manufacture of iron, production of which quadruples over the next 20 years.

• Swiss inventor Aimé Argand invents an oil-burner consisting of a cylindrical wick, two concentric metal tubes to provide air, and a glass chimney to increase the draft. It gives a light ten times brighter than previous lamps and the principle is later used in gas-burners.

• U.S. engineer Oliver Evans invents an automated process for grinding grain and sifting flour; it marks the beginning of automation in America.

Transportation

• The German River Eider is linked to the Baltic by canal; it becomes the prototype canal for international ship traffic.

ARTS AND IDEAS

Architecture

• The French architect Etienne-Louis Boullé designs his *Monument for Isaac Newton*, in the form of a planetarium. It is never built.

• The theater at Besançon, France, designed by the French architect Claude-Nicolas Ledoux, is completed.

Arts

• The English artist Joshua Reynolds paints his portrait of Sarah Siddons (a well-known actress) as *The Tragic Muse*.

• The English wood engraver Thomas Bewick publishes *Select Fables*.

- The French neoclassical artist Jacques-Louis David paints one of his best-known works, *The Oath of the Horatii*.
- The Scottish artist Henry Raeburn paints *The Reverend Robert Walker Skating on Duddingston Loch*.

Literature and Language

- The Dutch writers Elisabeth Wolff-Bekker and Agatha Deken publish the first part of their novel *Willem Leevend*, one of the finest Dutch novels of the century. The final part appears in 1785.
- The French writer Bernardin de St.-Pierre publishes his *Etudes de la Nature/Studies of Nature*, a work strongly influenced by the romanticism of Jean-Jacques Rousseau. A revised third edition of 1788 contains his best-known work, the short novel *Paul et Virginie/Paul and Virginie*, an idyllic account of a young couple living in the wilderness.

Music

- Austrian composer Wolfgang Amadeus Mozart completes his Piano Concertos No. 14 (K 449), No. 15 (K 450), No. 16 (K 451), No. 17 (K 453), No. 18 (K 456), and No. 19 (K 459); his Piano Sonata No. 14 (K 457); and his Sonata for Piano and Violin No. 32 (K 454).
- Italian violinist Regina Strinsacchi finds popularity in Vienna, Austria, after years of playing in Italy. Mozart composes pieces specifically for her and even performs with her.
- The Conservatoire de Musique is founded in Paris, France. Its orginal name was Ecole Royale de Chant et de Déclamation.
- The opera *Les Danaïdes* by the Italian composer Antonio Salieri is performed in Paris, France, where he has just been appointed director of the Paris Opéra.
- The opera *Richard Cœur-de-Lion/Richard the Lion-Hearted* by the French composer André Gretry is performed, in Paris, France.

Theater and Dance

- The play *Le Mariage de Figaro/The Marriage of Figaro* by the French writer Pierre-Augustin Caron de Beaumarchais is performed, in Paris, France. An unparalleled success, it is used in 1786 as the basis of Mozart's opera.
- The tragedy *Kabale und Liebe/Cabal and Love* by the German writer Friedrich von Schiller is first performed, in Frankfurt am Main, Germany.

Thought and Scholarship

- American statesman Thomas Jefferson publishes *Notes on the State of Virginia*, in Paris, France.
- The English orientalist William Jones founds the Bengal Asiatic Society and becomes its first president.

October, 1784–91 The German writer Johann Gottfried Herder publishes his *Ideen zur Philosophie der Geschichte der Menschheit/Ideas toward a Philosophy of History*. Regarded by many as his masterpiece, this study of history anticipates the evolutionary theories of Hegel and Marx.

October, 1784–1810 The English historian William Mitford publishes his highly influential *History of Greece*.

SOCIETY

Education

- St. John's College is founded at Annapolis, Maryland.

Everyday Life

- Acadians, forced to move from Nova Scotia, Canada, to Louisiana, develop Cajun cooking, blending Canadian with native "injun" elements.

BIRTHS & DEATHS

JANUARY
28 George Hamilton-Gordon, Earl of Aberdeen, British prime minister 1852–55 of a coalition government, born in Edinburgh, Scotland (–1860).

JUNE
26 William H. Crawford, American politician who cast the deciding vote for American independence, dies in Dover, Delaware (55).

JULY
22 Friedrich Wilhelm Bessel, German astronomer whose measurements of stars allows the first interstellar distances to be determined, born in Minden, Germany (–1846).
30 Denis Diderot, French philosopher of the Enlightenment, editor of the *Encyclopédie/Encyclopedia*, dies in Paris, France (71).

AUGUST
10 Allan Ramsay, Scottish-born English portrait painter, dies in Dover, Kent, England (70).

SEPTEMBER
8 Ann Lee, English religious leader who brought the Shaker sect to America, dies in Watervliet, New York (48).

OCTOBER
20 Henry Temple, Viscount Palmerston, British statesman, prime minister 1855–58 and 1859–65, a Liberal, born in Broadlands, Hampshire, England (–1865).

27 Nicolò Paganini, Italian composer and violin virtuoso, born in Genoa, Italy (–1840).

NOVEMBER
24 Zachary Taylor, twelfth president of the United States 1849–50, a Whig, born in Montebello, Virginia (–1850).

DECEMBER
5 Phillis Wheatley, the first published black American poet, dies in Boston, Massachusetts (*c.* 31).
13 Samuel Johnson, English essayist, critic, and lexicographer, author of the *Dictionary of the English Language*, dies in London, England (74).

- Mail begins to be transported by coach in England; Bristol to London takes 17 hours.

Media and Communication

- The *Massachusetts Centinel* newspaper begins publication in Boston, Massachusetts.

Religion

FEBRUARY

28 The English evangelist John Wesley signs a deed of declaration as the charter of Wesleyan Methodism and ordains two "Presbyters" for the American Mission.

1785

POLITICS, GOVERNMENT, AND ECONOMICS

Business and Economics

JULY

6 The American Congress adopts a coinage system suggested by the Virginia delegate Thomas Jefferson. It features a gold piece worth ten dollars, a silver piece worth one dollar, and a copper piece worth one-hundredth of a dollar.

Colonization

- Russian pioneers settle on the Aleutian Islands in the north Pacific.

Politics and Government

- Spurred by delegate Thomas Jefferson, the Virginia legislature abolishes primogeniture (the automatic inheritance of all property by the eldest son).
- The state of New York abolishes slavery.

MAY

20 The American Congress adopts a second land ordinance, providing for the sale of land in the Old Northwest in tracts of 640 acres.

JULY

23 Frederick II the Great of Prussia forms the *Fürstenbund* (League of Princes) to oppose the Hapsburg monarch Joseph II's Bavarian exchange program and preserve the status quo among German states.

AUGUST

15 Louis-René-Edouard, Cardinal de Rohan, the bishop of Strasbourg and sometime French ambassador to Austria, becomes involved in the Affair of the Diamond Necklace, which increases the French monarchy's reputation for immorality and frivolity on the eve of the Revolution.

SEPTEMBER

10 Prussia signs a commercial treaty with America.

NOVEMBER

8 Under the Treaty of Fontainebleau, the Dutch Republic recognizes the Hapsburg monarch Joseph II's sovereignty over part of the River Scheldt, while Joseph abandons his claim to Maastricht, renounces the right to free navigation of the Scheldt outside his dominions, and receives 10 million guilders.

10 An alliance is pledged between France and the Dutch Republic, despite the efforts of the British envoy at The Hague.

DECEMBER

26 American Congressman James Madison's religious freedom act rescinds religious tests in the state of Virginia.

SCIENCE, TECHNOLOGY, AND MEDICINE

Agriculture

- Cultivation of potatoes begins in France.

Health and Medicine

- English physician and botanist William Withering first uses digitalis to treat heart disease.
- Porcelain teeth are introduced in America. They are introduced in France by Nicolas Dubois de Chemant in 1788.

Math

- French Enlightenment philosopher Jean-Marie-Antoine-Nicolas Caritat, marquis de Condorcet, publishes "Essai sur l'application de l'analyse à la probabilité des décisions rendues à la pluralité des voix"/"Essay on the Application of the Analysis to the Probability of Decisions Made to the Plurality of Voters," a major advance in the study of probability in the social sciences.

Science

- English chemist Henry Cavendish discovers the composition of nitric acid.
- French chemist Claude-Louis Berthollet discovers the composition of ammonia and introduces chlorine ("eau de Javel") as a bleaching agent. Previously, the only bleaching agents were sunlight and urine.
- French scientist Charles Augustin Coulomb publishes *Recherches théoriques et expérimentales sur la force de torsion et sur l'élasticité des fils de métal/Theoretical and Experimental Research on the Force of Torsion and on the Elasticity of Iron Threads*, in which he makes the first precise measurements of the electric forces of attraction and repulsion between charged bodies.
- German-born English astronomer William Herschel argues in his work *On the Construction of the Heavens* that the Milky Way galaxy is composed of individual stars and is not some luminous fluid.
- Scottish geologist James Hutton proposes the theory of uniformitarianism: that all geological features are the result of processes that are at work today, acting over long periods of time.

Technology

- English inventor Edmund Cartwright develops a steam-powered loom.

December 1785–90 English pottery manufacturer Josiah Wedgwood sets up the General Chamber of Manufacturers of Great Britain.

Transportation

JANUARY

7 French balloonist Jean Blanchard and American physicist John Jeffries cross the English Channel in a balloon.

JUNE

15 Jean-François Pilâtre de Rozier and P. A. Romain are killed while trying to cross the English Channel by balloon; they are the first casualties of modern air transport.

ARTS AND IDEAS

Architecture

- In Russia, the Palace at Pavlovsk, designed by the Scottish architect Charles Cameron, is completed.

Arts

c. 1785 The Japanese artist Maruyama Okyo paints the six-panel folding screen *Pines in Snow*.

c. 1785 The Japanese artist Torii Kiyonaga publishes his woodblock print *Cooling off by the Sumida River*.

- The English artist Alexander Cozens publishes *A New Method of Assisting the Invention in Drawing Original Compositions of Landscape*. It describes a method of landscape painting that exploits accidental dots and splashes.
- The English artist George Stubbs paints *Haymakers*.
- The English artist Joshua Reynolds paints *The Infant Hercules*.
- The English artist Thomas Gainsborough paints his *Portrait of Mrs Richard Brinsley Sheridan*.

Literature and Language

- English poet Thomas Warton becomes Britain's poet laureate, a position he holds until 1790.

BIRTHS & DEATHS

JANUARY

4 Jacob Grimm, German author (with his brother Wilhelm) of *Grimm's Fairy Tales*, born in Hanau, Germany (–1863).

MARCH

7 Alessandro Manzoni, Italian poet and novelist, born in Milan, Italy (–1873).

11 John McLean, U.S. Supreme Court justice, born in Morris County, New Jersey (–1861).

APRIL

26 John James Audubon, U.S. ornithologist, naturalist, and artist, born in Les Cayes, St.-Dominique, West Indies (now in Haiti) (–1859).

JUNE

30 James Edward Ogelthorpe, English army officer who founded Savannah, Georgia, the first British colony in Georgia, dies in Cranman Hall, Essex, England (88).

AUGUST

20 Oliver Hazard Perry, U.S. naval hero, born in South Kingston, Rhode Island (–1819).

30 Lin Tse-hsü, Chinese scholar and official whose attempt to stop the opium trade contributed to the Opium War (1839–42), born in Hou-kuan, Fukien Province, China (–1850).

NOVEMBER

21 William Beaumont, U.S. army surgeon, the first person to observe and describe digestion as it occurs in the stomach, born in Lebanon, Connecticut (–1853).

DECEMBER

6 Kitty Clive, English comedy actress, dies in Twickenham, near London, England (74).

14 Giovanni Battista Cipriani, Italian-born English neoclassical painter, dies in London, England (58).

- The Dutch poet William Bilderdijck publishes *Elius*, a work which marks the beginning of the romantic movement in Holland.
- The English poet William Cowper publishes one of his best known longer works, *The Task*.
- The German poet Friedrich Schiller writes his famous "*Freude*"/"Ode to Joy," which will be used by Beethoven in the finale of his Ninth Symphony.
- The German scholar and adventurer Rudolf Erich Raspe publishes *Baron Munchausen's Narrative of His Marvellous Travels and Campaigns in Russia*, in English.

June 1785–86 The German writer Christian Friedrich Schubart publishes *Sämtliche Gedichte/Collected Poems*.

Music

- Austrian composer Franz Joseph Haydn completes his orchestral interludes *Die sieben letzten Worte unseres Erlösers an Kreuz/The Seven Last Words of Our Savior on the Cross*. In 1796 he reworks it as a cantata. He also completes his Symphonies No. 83, *La Poule/The Hen*, and No. 85, *La Reine/The Queen*, and his String Quartets No. 43 (Opus 42) and Nos. 50 to 56 (Opus 51).
- Austrian composer Wolfgang Amadeus Mozart completes his Piano Concertos No. 20 (K 466), No. 21 (K 467), and No. 22 (K 482), and his Fantasia in C minor for solo piano (K 475).
- The Caecilian Society for the performance of sacred music is opened in London, England. It closes in 1861.

Thought and Scholarship

- A radical Dutch political manifesto published in Leiden argues that "the Sovereign is none other than the vote of the people." It reflects growing tensions between the established government of the Dutch Republic and the antiaristocratic, pro-French Patriot party.
- The English theologian and philosopher William Paley publishes *The Principles of Moral and Political Philosophy*, which sets out a form of utilitarianism.
- The German Jewish scholar Moses Mendelssohn publishes *Morgenstunden/Morning Hours*, a defense of the theology of the philosopher Leibniz.
- The German philosopher Immanuel Kant publishes his *Grundlegung zur Metaphysik der Sitten/Groundwork of the Metaphysic of Ethics*.

SOCIETY

Education

- The University of Georgia is founded at Athens, Georgia.
- The University of New Brunswick is founded at Fredericton, Canada.

Everyday Life

- H. D. Rawlings begins manufacturing soda water, in London, England.
- Men's fashion includes a coat, vest, stockings, and pumps with silver buckles. Hair is powdered and tied with a ribbon at the back.

Media and Communication

- English journalist John Walter starts publication of the *Daily Universal Register* in London, England. In 1788 the newspaper will change its name to *The Times*.

1786

POLITICS, GOVERNMENT, AND ECONOMICS

Business and Economics

- The American economy continues to deteriorate, with exports declining to a minimum.

Colonization

AUGUST

11 Penang, in the Strait of Malacca, is ceded to the British East India Company by the rajah of Kedah.

Politics and Government

- The state of New Jersey outlaws slavery.

JULY

27 The Dutch reformist Patriot party deprives William V of Orange of the command of the army of the Dutch Republic.

SEPTEMBER

- Disgruntled American Revolution veteran Daniel Shays leads an armed uprising of debtors in western Massachusetts to protest against farm foreclosures. After closing courthouses in Berkshire, Hampshire, and Worcester counties, the rebels attempt to seize the Springfield arsenal, but are beaten back by loyal militiamen.
- 11 At a meeting in Annapolis, Maryland, commissioners from New York, New Jersey, Pennsylvania, Delaware, and Virginia call for a general convention to be held at Philadelphia, Pennsylvania, in May 1787 for the purpose of making "the constitution of the Federal Government adequate to exigencies of the Union."
- 26 The British representative William Eden negotiates William Pitt the Younger's commercial treaty with France (the Eden Treaty). Many duties are reduced and France makes extensive trade concessions as a result.
- 27 The Patriot-dominated States General (parliament) of Holland separates the office of stadtholder from the role of captain general of the Netherlands armed forces; Patriot militias form in opposition to the army of the stadtholder, William V of Orange.

SCIENCE, TECHNOLOGY, AND MEDICINE

Agriculture

- Sea Island cotton is planted on the islands of this name off the coasts of South Carolina, Georgia, and Florida.

Science

- German-born English astronomer William Herschel's *Catalogue of Nebulae* is published. It is a catalog of nearly 2,500 nebulae.
- The gold-leaf electroscope is invented by English physicist Abraham Bennet. It indicates the presence of an electric charge by the mutual repulsion of two gold leaves.

Technology

- American Ezekiel Reed invents a nail-making machine.
- English gunmaker Henry Nock invents a breech-loading musket, revolutionizing weapons technology.

ARTS AND IDEAS

Arts

- The American artist John Trumbull paints *The Death of General Montgomery in the Attack on Quebec*.
- The English artist John Hoppner paints his *Portrait of a Lady*.

Literature and Language

- *An Arabian Tale, from an Unpublished Manuscript* is published anonymously. This is in fact an unauthorized translation of *Vathek*, a Gothic oriental fantasy written in French by the English writer William Beckford. Beckford republishes the original French version and then his own revised English edition.
- The American poet Philip Freneau publishes his collection *Poems*, which contains two of his best-known

poems: "The Wild Honey Suckle" and "The Beauties of Santa Cruz."

- The English orientalist William Jones discovers that Latin and Greek are related to Sanskrit; his study lays the foundation of modern comparative philology.
- The Scottish poet Robert Burns publishes *Poems Chiefly in the Scottish Dialect*, his first collection.
- The Welsh-born English writer Hester Lynch Piozzi ("Mrs. Thrale") publishes *Anecdotes of Samuel Johnson*.

Music

- Austrian composer Franz Joseph Haydn completes his Symphony No. 82, *L'Ours/The Bear*.
- Austrian composer Wolfgang Amadeus Mozart completes his Symphony No. 38 (K 504), the *Prague*; his Piano Concertos No. 23 (K 488), No. 24 (K 491), and No. 25 (K 503); his String Quartet No. 20 (K 499), the *Hoffmeister*; and his Piano Trios No. 2 (K 496) and No. 3 (K 502). His opera *Le nozze di Figaro/The Marriage of Figaro* is first performed, in Vienna, Austria. The libretto, by Lorenzo da Ponte, is based on a popular play by the French writer Pierre-Augustin Caron de Beaumarchais. He also creates soprano parts for Italian singer Maria Mandini after she defines the role of Marcellin in *The Marriage of Figaro*. Mozart's comic opera *Der Schauspieldirektor/The Impresario* is first performed in Vienna, Austria.
- The opera *Doktor und Apotheker/Doctor and Apothecary* by the Austrian composer Karl von Dittersdorf is first performed, in Vienna, Austria.

Theater and Dance

- The play *The Heiress* by the English soldier and writer John Burgoyne is performed, in London, England.

Thought and Scholarship

- The English campaigner Thomas Clarkson publishes "An Essay on the Slavery and Commerce of the Human Species," advocating abolition of the slave trade.
- The German philosopher Immanuel Kant publishes *Metaphysische Anfangsgründe der Naturwissenschaft/ Metaphysical First Principles of Science*.

SOCIETY

Religion

OCTOBER
16 Joseph II's edict establishing a single seminary at Louvain for the entire Austrian Netherlands provokes a wave of protest among the Catholic clergy.

Sports

- A rudimentary form of baseball is first played, at Princeton, New Jersey.
- French mountaineers M. G. Paccard and Jacques Balmat make the first successful ascent of Mont Blanc, the highest mountain in the Alps, southwest Europe.

BIRTHS & DEATHS

c. 1786 Sacagawea (also known as Bird Woman), a Shoshone Indian guide and interpreter who accompanies the explorers Lewis and Clark, born near modern Lemhi, Idaho (–1812).

JANUARY
4 Moses Mendelssohn, German philosopher and critic, dies in Berlin, Germany (56).
8 Nicholas Biddle, U.S. financier and editor, and president of the Second Bank of the United States, born in Philadelphia, Pennsylvania (–1844).

FEBRUARY
24 Wilhelm Grimm, German author (with his brother Jacob) of *Grimm's Fairy Tales*, born in Hanau, Germany (–1859).

MAY
21 Karl Wilhelm Scheele, Swedish chemist, dies in Köping, Sweden (44).

JUNE
13 Winfield Scott, commander of the U.S. Army, born near Petersburg, Virginia (–1866).

19 Nathanael Greene, American general during the American Revolution, dies in Mulberry Grove, Georgia (43).

AUGUST
17 David "Davy" Crockett, U.S. politician and frontiersman, born in Limestone, Tennessee (–1836).
17 Frederick II the Great, king of Prussia 1740–86, dies in Potsdam, near Berlin, Prussia (74).

NOVEMBER
18 Carl Maria von Weber, German composer, born in Eutin, Holstein, Germany (–1826).

1787

POLITICS, GOVERNMENT, AND ECONOMICS

Business and Economics

- Decimal currency is adopted in America.
- France begins trading with the Empire of Annam (modern Vietnam).
- The English philosopher Jeremy Bentham publishes his *Defence of Usury*, setting out his views on economics.

Politics and Government

- The Edict of Versailles grants a measure of religious toleration to Protestants in France.

JANUARY
- The Holy Roman Emperor Joseph II introduces a series of radical political reforms in the Austrian Netherlands, provoking riots in Louvain and Brussels.
22–May 25 A special Assembly of Notables (nobles, clergy, and magistrates) meets at Versailles, France, and rejects the proposals of the minister of finance, Charles-Alexandre de Calonne, for financial reform.

APRIL
17 The French minister of finance Charles-Alexandre de Calonne is banished to Lorraine. He is succeeded by Cardinal Etienne Loménie de Brienne, archbishop of Toulouse.

MAY
10 British politician Edmund Burke moves the impeachment before Parliament of Warren Hastings, former governor-general of India, on charges of corruption.
25–September 17 The Constitutional Convention opens in Philadelphia, Pennsylvania, with participants including George Washington (president), Benjamin Franklin, James Madison, and Edmund Randolph. The new constitution establishes a bicameral legislature whose power is counterbalanced by an executive officer, an independent judiciary, and the authority of individual states.

JUNE
28 Dutch Free Corps (citizens' militia supporting the antiaristocratic, pro-French Patriot party) units arrest Princess Wilhelmina of Orange near Gouda, in the Dutch Republic. The princess's brother, King Frederick William of Prussia, begins to prepare an invasion of the Netherlands.

JULY
6 The Parlement of Paris opposes the French minister of finance Etienne Loménie de Brienne and demands that the Estates General (parliament) be summoned.
13 Congress passes the Northwest Ordinance, providing for the political organization of the Old Northwest. It decrees that the area is to consist of no less than three and no more than five territories; when the population of a territory reaches 60,000, it is to be admitted to the union on equal terms with the existing states. Slavery is not permitted in the territories.

AUGUST
10 The Ottoman Empire declares war on Russia, in an attempt to regain the Crimea.
14 The Parlement of Paris is banished by Louis XVI to Troyes, northeast France, in an effort to curtail its growing opposition to the royal government.

SEPTEMBER
13 Prussian forces under the Duke of Brunswick invade the Netherlands, quickly overcoming desultory resistance from the Patriot Free Corps militias.
20 William V of Orange is restored as stadtholder of the Dutch Republic following the expulsion of the Patriot party by the Prussians.
24 The Parlement of Paris, banished by Louis XVI on August 14, is recalled from Troyes to Paris, France, in an effort to reconcile differences between the Parlement and the government.
28 The Constitution of the United States is submitted to the 13 American states for ratification.

OCTOBER
10 Amsterdam, the Dutch capital, surrenders to the invading Prussian forces of the Duke of Brunswick, bringing the antiaristocratic revolution in the Dutch Republic to an end.
27 The comte de Montmorin, French foreign minister, declares that France has no intention of interfering in Dutch affairs.

NOVEMBER
20 Louis XVI of France declares that the Estates General (parliament) will be summoned for July 1792.

DECEMBER
- The Hapsburg emperor Joseph II returns to Vienna, Austria, after a disappointing campaign against the Ottoman Empire.
7 Delaware becomes the first state to ratify the U.S. Constitution.
12 Pennsylvania ratifies the U.S. Constitution, becoming the second state in the Union.

18 New Jersey ratifies the U.S. Constitution, becoming the third state in the Union.

SCIENCE, TECHNOLOGY, AND MEDICINE

Science

- French chemist Antoine-Laurent Lavoisier, with collaborators, publishes *Méthode de nomenclature chimie/Method of Chemical Nomenclature*, a system for naming chemicals based on scientific principles. It is the first modern chemical textbook.
- French physicist Jacques-Alexandre Charles demonstrates that different gases expand by the same amount for the same temperature rise. It later becomes known as Charles's law.
- German physicist Ernst Chladni demonstrates sound patterns on vibrating plates (Chladni's figures).
- The German writer and polymath Johann Wolfgang von Goethe discovers the intermaxillary bone.

Transportation

AUGUST
22 American inventor John Fitch launches a steamboat on the River Delaware.

ARTS AND IDEAS

Architecture

- In Russia, the Hermitage Theater in St. Petersburg, designed by the Italian architect Giacomo Quarenghi, is completed.

Arts

c. 1787 The French artist Hubert Robert paints *Pont du Gard*.

- The English painter Joshua Reynolds paints his *Portrait of Lord Heathfield*.
- The German artist Johann Heinrich Wilhelm Tischbein paints *Goethe in the Campagna*, one of the best-known images of the German poet.

Literature and Language

- Empress Catherine II of Russia orders the compilation of an Imperial Dictionary, with 285 words translated into 200 languages.
- The German writer Johann Jakob Heinse publishes the novel *Ardinghello und die glückseligen Inseln/Ardinghell and the Blessed Islands*, based on his travels in Italy. It is widely read.
- The Italian dramatist Carlo Goldoni publishes his *Mémoires/Memoirs*.

Music

c. 1787 Austrian composer Franz Joseph Haydn completes his String Quartets Nos. 44 to 49 (Opus 50).
- Austrian composer Wolfgang Amadeus Mozart completes his Serenade No. 13 for strings (K 525), widely known as *Eine kleine Nachtmusik/A Little Night Music*; his divertimento *Ein musikalischer Spass/A Musical Joke* (K 522); his Piano Concerto No. 26 (K 537), the *Coronation*; and his String Quintets No. 3 (K 515) and No. 4 (K 516). His opera *Don Giovanni* is first performed, in Prague, Bohemia.
- Italian composer Luigi Boccherini completes his E major string quartet.

Theater and Dance

- The comedy *The Contrast* by the American dramatist Royall Taylor is first performed, in New York, New York. It is one of the first American comedies.
- The German writer and polymath Johann Wolfgang von Goethe completes the revisions of his verse play *Iphigenie auf Tauris/Iphigenia in Tauris*.
- The German writer Friedrich Schiller completes his verse play *Don Carlos*.

BIRTHS & DEATHS

FEBRUARY
13 Charles Gravier, comte de Vergennes, French foreign minister who formed an alliance with the American colonists to help them gain independence, dies in Versailles, France (67).
23 Emma Hart Willard, U.S. educator, born in Berlin, Connecticut (–1870).

MARCH
16 Georg Simon Ohm, German physicist who discovered Ohm's law, which relates electric current to voltage, born in Erlangen, Bavaria, Germany (–1854).

SEPTEMBER
10 John Crittenden, U.S. politician, born near Versailles, Kentucky (–1863).

OCTOBER
4 François-Pierre-Guillaume Guizot, French politician and historian, born in Nîmes, France (–1874).

NOVEMBER
15 Christoph Willibald von Gluck, German classical composer, dies in Vienna, Austria (73).

DECEMBER
12 Martin van Buren, eighth president of the United States 1836–40, a Democrat, born in Kinderhook, New York (–1862).

Thought and Scholarship

- American statesman and principal draftsman of the U.S. Constitution James Madison publishes *The Vices of the Political System of the United States.*

OCTOBER

October 1787–April 1788 American politician Alexander Hamilton, under the pseudonym Publius, issues the first of the "Federalist Papers" in the *New York Independent Journal*. James Madison and John Jay collaborate in the project.

SOCIETY

Education

- Franklin and Marshall College is founded in Lancaster, Pennsylvania.
- The English writer and feminist Mary Wollstonecraft publishes *Thoughts on the Education of Daughters*.
- The University of Pittsburgh is founded in Pennsylvania.

Media and Communication

- M. Lammond demonstrates a working model of the mechanical telegraph in Paris, France.

1788

POLITICS, GOVERNMENT, AND ECONOMICS

Colonization

JANUARY

18 English naval commander Arthur Phillip and his "First Fleet," consisting of 11 ships carrying 800 convicts, land at Botany Bay, in modern Australia, to found Britain's first penal settlement. Finding the area unsuitable, he moves the settlement to Port Jackson (Sydney).

26 Thomas Whittle is the first child to be born in Australia of European immigrant parents.

AUGUST

22 A British settlement is founded in Sierra Leone, West Africa, for freed slaves.

Politics and Government

- The Hapsburg monarch and Holy Roman Emperor Joseph II orders Austrian Jews to assume official naturalized German surnames.

JANUARY

2 Georgia ratifies the U.S. Constitution, becoming the fourth state in the Union.

9 Connecticut ratifies the U.S. Constitution, becoming the fifth state in the Union.

20 The Parlement of Paris presents a list of grievances against the French government to the king, Louis XVI, in effect declaring itself the defender of French liberties.

FEBRUARY

7 Massachusetts ratifies the U.S. Constitution, becoming the sixth state in the Union.

9 The Hapsburg monarch and Holy Roman Emperor Joseph II declares war on the Ottoman Empire.

13 The corruption trial of Warren Hastings, former British governor-general of India, begins in London, England.

APRIL

15 An Anglo-Dutch alliance is agreed.

28 Maryland ratifies the U.S. Constitution, becoming the seventh state in the Union.

MAY

9 The British Parliament passes a motion for the abolition of the slave trade.

23 South Carolina ratifies the U.S. Constitution, becoming the eighth state in the Union.

JUNE

- Sweden declares war on Russia, invading Russian Finland and aiming to recover the Baltic provinces lost to Czar Peter the Great at the beginning of the century.

21 New Hampshire ratifies the U.S. Constitution, becoming the ninth state in the Union and making the Constitution law.

21 The Constitution of the United States comes into force following its ratification by New Hampshire. Of the remaining four states, Virginia and New York complete ratification in 1788, North Carolina in 1789, and Rhode Island in 1790.

25 Virginia ratifies the U.S. Constitution, becoming the tenth state in the Union.

JULY

26 New York ratifies the U.S. Constitution, becoming the 11th state in the Union.

AUGUST

8 Louis XVI of France decides to summon the Estates General (parliament) for May 1789.

13 Prussia joins the Anglo-Dutch alliance to form the Triple Alliance, with the avowed aim of preserving peace in Europe.

25 The French minister of finance Etienne Loménie de Brienne resigns in the face of a major, but undeclared, crisis in French national finances.

27 Jacques Necker is recalled as French minister of finance.

SEPTEMBER

• Danish forces invade Sweden, aiming at the reconquest of former Danish territories in the south of the country while Sweden is engaged in an unsuccessful war against Russia.

13 The city of New York, New York, is proclaimed the federal capital of the United States.

NOVEMBER

• Louis XVI of France decides to summon the Assembly of Notables (nobles, clergy, and magistrates).

6 The Triple Alliance (the Dutch Republic, Britain, and Prussia) persuades Denmark and Sweden to sign the Convention of Uddevalla, providing for the evacuation of Danish troops from Sweden.

DECEMBER

17 A Russian army under Prince Grigory Potemkin takes the Black Sea port and fortress of Ochakov from the Ottoman Empire.

23 Ten square miles of land are ceded to the U.S. Congress by the state of Maryland for the site of the federal capital city, Washington, D.C.

SCIENCE, TECHNOLOGY, AND MEDICINE

Ecology

MARCH

21 A great fire in New Orleans, Louisiana, destroys nearly the entire city.

Exploration

JUNE

9 The English naturalist and explorer Joseph Banks founds the Africa Association to promote interest in exploration and trade.

Health and Medicine

• French surgeon Pierre-Joseph Desault introduces improved surgical instruments and techniques.

Math

• French mathematician Joseph Louis Lagrange publishes *Mécanique analytique/Analytical Mechanics*, an algebraic and analytical exposition of Newtonian mechanics.

Science

• French astronomer and mathematician Pierre-Simon Laplace publishes his laws of the solar system, demonstrating that planetary orbits are stable.

• Scottish geologist James Hutton's paper *Theory of the Earth* expounds his uniformitarian theory of continual change in the earth's geological features and marks a turning point in geology.

• The Linnean Society is founded in London, England.

Technology

• English inventor Thomas Mead develops a centrifugal governor for millstones. It uses a feedback mechanism to maintain a constant gap between the millstones, thus regulating the fineness of grinding.

• Scottish millwright Andrew Meikle patents a threshing machine for separating grain from straw.

• The Königsbronn Foundry in Württemberg, Germany, begins to manufacture enamel kitchenware.

ARTS AND IDEAS

Architecture

• In Germany, the Brandenburg Gate in Berlin, designed by the German architect Carl Gotthard Langhans, is completed.

Arts

• The English furniture designer George Hepplewhite publishes his *Cabinet-Maker's and Upholsterer's Guide*, containing nearly 300 designs. It will strongly influence the development of neoclassical style.

• The Japanese artist Kitagawa Utamaro publishes his series of woodblock prints *Poem of the Pillow*. Among the best-known of these erotic scenes is *Lovers on a Balcony*.

Literature and Language

• The American poet Philip Freneau publishes his collection *Miscellaneous Works*, which contains two of his best-known poems, both giving sympathetic views of Native Americans: "The Indian Burying Ground" and "The Indian Student."

• The English writer and feminist Mary Wollstonecraft publishes *Mary, a Fiction*, her first novel.

- The English-born American writer and actress Susanna Rowson publishes her novel *The Inquisitor, or Invisible Rambler*.
- The French antiquarian Jean-Jacques Barthélemy completes his *Voyage du jeune Anacharsis en Grèce/The Voyage of Young Anacharsis in Greece*, an imaginative recreation of life in Ancient Greece.

Music

c. 1788 Austrian composer Franz Joseph Haydn completes his String Quartets Nos. 57 to 59 (Opus 54), and his String Quartets Nos. 60 to 62 (Opus 55).
- American musician and writer Francis Hopkinson (a signatory to the Declaration of Independence) publishes *Seven Songs for the Harpsichord or Piano-Forte*, the first book of music published by an American. His song "My days have been so wondrous free" (1759) is arguably the first secular work in the United States.
- Austrian composer Wolfgang Amadeus Mozart completes his Symphonies No. 39 (K 543), No. 40 (K 550), and No. 41 (K 551), the *Jupiter*; his Piano Trios No. 4 (K 542), No. 5 (K 548), and No. 6 (K 564); his Piano Sonata No. 15 (K 545); and his Sonata for Piano and Violin No. 35 (K 547).

Theater and Dance

- The German writer and polymath Johann Wolfgang von Goethe completes his play *Egmont*.

Thought and Scholarship

- The American statesman Alexander Hamilton publishes *The Federalist*, a collection of 85 essays defending the U.S. Constitution. Written mainly by Hamilton, though some are by James Madison and John Jay, they appeared 1777–78 in various periodicals under the name Publius.
- The English religious writer and educator Hannah More publishes *Thoughts on the Importance of the Manners of the Great to General Society*.

- The English scholar John Lemprière publishes his *Classical Dictionary*, which will long remain the standard reference work on the classical world.
- The German historian Friedrich Johann Christoph von Schiller publishes *Geschichte des Abfalls der vereinigten Niederlande von der spanischen Regierung/History of the Revolt of the Netherlands under the Spanish Regime*.
- The German philosopher Immanuel Kant publishes the second of his major works, *Kritik der practischen Vernunft/Critique of Practical Reason*, which deals with ethics.
- The Scottish philosopher Thomas Reid publishes *Essays on the Active Powers of the Man*.

SOCIETY

Media and Communication

JANUARY
1 English journalist John Walter renames his *Universal Daily Register* newspaper *The Times*.

Religion

- The English scholar Richard Porson publishes in *Gentleman's Magazine* the first of his "Letters to Archbishop Travis" on the authenticity of parts of the New Testament.

Sports

MAY
- The English stallion Messenger arrives in America. The horse is the original sire of many of the best trotting horses in America.
30 The Marylebone Cricket Club (MCC) in London, England, codifies the laws of cricket.

BIRTHS & DEATHS

- William Strickland, U.S. architect and engineer, leading proponent of the Greek Revival style in the United States, born in Navesink, New Jersey (–1854).

JANUARY
22 George Gordon, Lord Byron, English romantic poet, born in London, England (–1824).

FEBRUARY
5 Robert Peel, British prime minister 1834–35 and 1841–46, founder of the Conservative Party, born in Bury, Lancashire, England (–1850).
22 Arthur Schopenhauer, German philosopher, born in Danzig

(modern Gdańsk), Germany (–1860).

MARCH
29 Charles Wesley, English cleric, hymn writer, and poet, cofounder of the Methodist Church with his brother John, dies in London, England (80).

APRIL
15 Georges-Louis Leclerk Buffon, French naturalist, dies in Paris, France (80).

AUGUST
2 Thomas Gainsborough, English portrait and landscape painter, dies in London, England (61).

SEPTEMBER
30 FitzRoy James Henry Somerset, Lord Raglan, British field marshal in command of the British forces during the Crimean War, born in Badminton, Gloucestershire, England (–1855).

OCTOBER
24 Sarah Josepha Buell Hale, U.S. editor and author, born in Newport, New Hampshire (–1879).

DECEMBER
14 C(arl) P(hilipp) E(manuel) Bach, German composer, second son of Johann Sebastian Bach, dies in Hamburg, Germany (74).

1789

POLITICS, GOVERNMENT, AND ECONOMICS

Business and Economics

DECEMBER

21 *Assignats* (paper money) are issued in France on the authority of the National Assembly.

Politics and Government

- Champions of the U.S. Constitution establish the Federalist Party.

MARCH

4   The U.S. Congress meets for the first time in New York, New York. Ten of the proposed twelve amendments to the Constitution are made and sent to the states for ratification.

4   The U.S. Congress meets under the Constitution for the first time. Proponents of the Constitution (federalists) outnumber opponents (antifederalists) 17–9 in the Senate and 38–26 in the House of Representatives.

APRIL

3   King Gustav III's act of unity and security in Sweden, granting him absolute powers, becomes law.

7   Selim III succeeds his uncle Abdülhamid as sultan of the Ottoman Empire.

27–28 Some 5,000 workers riot in the Faubourg St-Antoine, Paris, France, destroying the works of the printer and wallpaper manufacturer Réveillon because of his perceived threat to cut wages; about 300 civilians are killed by guards.

30 George Washington is inaugurated as the first president of the United States, with John Adams as vice-president.

MAY

5   The French Estates General (parliament) meets at Versailles.

6   French deputies of the Third Estate (the common people) refuse to meet as a separate chamber in the Estates General (parliament), demanding representation alongside the clergy and nobility.

12 The Society of Tammany, better known as Tammany Hall, meets for the first time in New York, New York. Composed of antifederalists, the society will become the foundation of the city's Democratic Party political machine during the 19th century.

JUNE

- A Spanish fleet seizes four British fishing vessels at Nootka Sound, off Vancouver Island, as colonial rivalry spreads to the northwest of the North American continent.

17 The Third Estate (representing the common people) of the Estates General (parliament) in France declares itself a National Assembly.

20 The National Assembly in France takes the "Tennis Court Oath," undertaking not to disband until a new constitution is drawn up.

23 The French revolutionary politician Honoré de Mirabeau establishes his reputation in the "royal session" of the National Assembly.

24 Most of the clergy and nobility present at the Estates General (parliament) in Paris, France, join the Third Estate's National Assembly.

JULY

4   The U.S. Congress passes its first tariff bill, levying duties on over 30 commodities.

11 The French finance minister Jacques Necker is dismissed in a royalist coup, the reactionary Louis-Auguste, baron de Breteuil, becoming principal minister. Public disturbances break out in Paris at this apparent display of high-handed royalist power.

12 The people of Paris, France, seize arms following the dismissal of the finance minister Jacques Necker, fearing a royal coup.

14 A large crowd of the common people of Paris, France, (including some 5,000 women led by Théroigne de Méricourt) storms and captures the Bastille (a medieval fortress and symbol of the *ancien régime*) in Paris. The emigration of French aristocrats begins.

15 The Commune de Paris (municipal government) is formed in Paris, France. It appoints Jean Bailly as mayor, sets up the National Guard under the Marquis de Lafayette, and is responsible for municipal administration.

27 The U.S. Congress establishes the State Department. President George Washington appoints Thomas Jefferson the first secretary of state.

31 Austrian and Russian troops under Francis, Duke of Coburg, and Count Alexander Vasilyevich Suvorov defeat an Ottoman army at Fokshany (now Focşani, Romania).

AUGUST

4   The French National Assembly in Paris removes the feudal privileges of the nobility—including seigneurial rights and hunting rights.

7   The U.S. Congress creates the War Department. Henry Knox becomes the first secretary of war.

24 Russian naval forces destroy the Swedish fleet in the Gulf of Finland.

26 The French National Assembly adopts the Declaration of the Rights of Man.

SEPTEMBER

2 The U.S. Congress establishes the Treasury Department. Alexander Hamilton becomes the first treasury secretary.

22 Austrian and Russian troops under Francis, Duke of Coburg, and Count Alexander Vasilyevich Suvorov defeat an Ottoman army at Martinesci, on the River Rymnik in Moldavia.

OCTOBER

• A revolution breaks out in the Austrian Netherlands under Henry van der Noot, following the Holy Roman Emperor Joseph II's revocation of the constitution of Brabant and Hainault.

5 French commoners, mainly women, march on the royal palace of Versailles in protest against bread prices.

6 Austrian forces under General Gideon von Laudon take Belgrade from the Ottomans.

9 The Austrian-Russian army under Francis, Duke of Coburg, and Count Alexander Vasilyevich Suvorov captures Bucharest, in Wallachia, from the Ottoman Empire.

NOVEMBER

• The Revolution Society, meeting in London, England, congratulates the French National Assembly on the storming of the Bastille.

2 Following a proposal by Charles-Maurice de Talleyrand, the bishop of Autun, church property in France is placed

"at the disposal of the nation" with the aim of selling it off to the public.

7 The French National Assembly forbids any member to accept office under Louis XVI.

12 France is divided into 80 administrative departments as the National Assembly begins a program of administrative reforms.

21 North Carolina ratifies the U.S. Constitution, becoming the 12th state in the Union.

DECEMBER

13 The Austrian Netherlands declare their independence as "the United States of Belgium."

29 Tippu Sultan, the sultan of Mysore, India, attacks the territory of the rajah of Travancore.

SCIENCE, TECHNOLOGY, AND MEDICINE

Exploration

• Scottish trader and explorer Alexander Mackenzie follows the river now named for him from Fort Chipewyan on Lake Athabasca to the Beaufort Sea section of the Arctic Ocean.

French Revolution 1789–91

1789

April 27–28 Some 5,000 workers riot in the Faubourg St-Antoine, Paris, France, destroying the works of the printer and wallpaper manufacturer Réveillon because of his perceived threat to cut wages; about 300 civilians are killed by guards.

May 6 French deputies of the Third Estate (representing the common people) refuse to meet as a separate chamber in the Estates General (parliament), demanding representation alongside the clergy and nobility.

June 17 The Third Estate of the Estates General declares itself a National Assembly.

June 20 The National Assembly takes the "Tennis Court Oath," undertaking not to disband until a new constitution is drawn up.

June 23 The revolutionary politician Honoré de Mirabeau establishes his reputation in the "royal session" of the National Assembly.

June 24 Most of the clergy and nobility present at the Estates General join the Third Estate's National Assembly.

July 11 Finance minister Jacques Necker is dismissed in a royalist coup, the reactionary Louis-Auguste, baron de Breteuil, becoming principal minister. Public disturbances break out in Paris at this apparent display of high-handed royalist power.

July 12 The people of Paris seize arms following the dismissal of finance minister Jacques Necker, fearing a royal coup.

July 14 A large crowd of the common people of Paris (including some 5,000 women led by Théroigne de

Méricourt) storms and captures the Bastille (a medieval fortress, symbol of the *ancien régime*). The emigration of French aristocrats begins.

July 15 The Commune de Paris (municipal government) is formed. It appoints Jean Bailly as mayor, sets up the National Guard under the Marquis de Lafayette, and is responsible for municipal administration.

August 4 The National Assembly removes the feudal privileges of the nobility—including seigneurial rights and hunting rights.

August 26 The National Assembly adopts the Declaration of the Rights of Man.

October 5 French commoners, mainly women, march on the royal palace of Versailles in protest against bread prices.

November 2 Following a proposal by Charles-Maurice de Talleyrand, the bishop of Autun, church property in France is placed "at the disposal of the nation" with the aim of selling it off to the public.

November 7 The National Assembly forbids any member to accept office under Louis XVI.

November 12 France is divided into 80 administrative departments as the National Assembly begins a program of administrative reforms.

1791

August 2 The declaration of Pillnitz, in which Prussia, Austria, Russia, Sweden, and Spain agree to form an alliance to restore legitimate authority in revolutionary France. France responds the following summer, declaring war on Austria and Prussia.

- Sicilian navigator Alessandro Malaspina explores the Pacific coast of South America for the Spanish, in a joint scientific and political mission.

Math

- The French mathematician Baron Augustine-Louis Cauchy completes his lifelong mathematical research, having made great advances in analysis, probability, and group theory.

Science

- French botanist Antoine-Laurent Jussieu's *Genera Plantarum/The Genera of Plants* refines Carl Linnaeus's classification of plants.
- German chemist Martin Heinrich Klaproth discovers uranium (atomic no. 92) and zirconium (atomic no. 40).
- German-born English astronomer William Herschel completes his reflecting telescope (the world's largest to date), and discovers a seventh satellite (Mimas) in the Saturnian system.

Technology

- English inventor Edmund Cartwright patents a wool-combing machine.
- English-born U.S. industrialist Samuel Slater memorizes the plans of Richard Arkwright's spinning machine and brings the technology to the United States.
- Scottish engineer James Watt develops a means of controlling the speed of his steam engine by devising a governor for it.

ARTS AND IDEAS

Architecture

- The Academy of Sciences in St. Petersburg, Russia, designed by the Italian architect Giacomo Quarenghi, is completed.
- The Virginia State Capitol in Richmond, Virginia, designed by U.S. statesman Thomas Jefferson, is completed. His "federal" style marks a return to Roman architecture, which symbolically establishes a link between U.S. and Roman republicanism.

Literature and Language

- The English clergyman and poet William Bowles publishes *Fourteen Sonnets, Elegiac and Descriptive, Written during a Tour*. Expressing a view of nature that anticipates romanticism, the sonnets are admired by the English poets Wordsworth and Coleridge.
- The English orientalist William Jones publishes his translation of the Sanskrit classic drama *Sákuntala*, by the 5th century AD writer Kálidása.
- The English poet and artist William Blake publishes his poetry collections *Songs of Innocence* and *The Book of Thel*.
- The English poet Erasmus Darwin publishes his long poem *The Loves of the Plants*.
- The French priest Joseph Amiot (or Amyot), a missionary in China, publishes his *Dictionnaire Tartare-Mantchou-Français/Tartar-Manchu-French Dictionary*, a French–Chinese dictionary. Amiot was one of the first to introduce the West to Chinese literature, history, and customs.
- The German writer Jean Paul publishes his novel *Auswahl aus des Teufels Papieren nebst einem nöthingen Aviso vom Juden Mendel/Selections from the Devil's Papers together with a Required Notice from the Jew Mendel*.
- The U.S. writer Benjamin Franklin publishes part of *The Autobiography of Benjamin Franklin*, a work he began in 1771. The first complete edition appears in 1868.
- U.S. lexicographer Noah Webster publishes *Dissertations on the English Language*, which describes an idiom of the English language peculiar to the United States.

Music

- Austrian composer Franz Joseph Haydn completes his Symphony No. 92, the *Oxford*, and also his cantata *Arianna a Naxos/Ariadne on Naxos*.
- Austrian composer Wolfgang Amadeus Mozart completes his Piano Sonatas Nos. 16 (K 570) and 17 (K 576).

Theater and Dance

- A performance of the comedy *The Recruiting Officer* by the Irish dramatist George Farquhar becomes the first

BIRTHS & DEATHS

FEBRUARY
12 Ethan Allen, American commander in the revolution, dies in Burlington, Vermont (51).

MAY
21 John Hawkins, English writer, author of *General History of the Science and Practice of Music*, the first history of music in English, dies in London, England (70).

AUGUST
6 Friedrich List, German-born U.S. economist, born in Reutlingen, Germany (–1846).

SEPTEMBER
15 James Fenimore Cooper, U.S. novelist who wrote of life on the frontier, born in Burlington, New Jersey (–1851).

15 Louis Daguerre, French painter and physicist who invented the first practical method of photography, the daguerreotype, born in Cormeilles, near Paris, France (–1851).

DECEMBER
28 Thomas Ewing, first U.S. secretary of the interior 1849–50, born in West Liberty, Virginia (–1871).

recorded performance of a play in Australia. It is acted by convicts.
- The comedy *The Father, or American Shandyism* by the U.S. dramatist William Dunlap is first performed, in New York, New York.
- The German writer and polymath Johann Wolfgang von Goethe completes his play *Torquato Tasso*.

Thought and Scholarship

- The English philosopher Jeremy Bentham publishes *Introduction to the Principles of Morals and Legislation*, which sets out his case for utilitarianism.
- The French revolutionary leader Emmanuel-Joseph Sièyes publishes his pamphlets *Qu'est-ce que le tiers-état?/What is the Third Estate?*, a defense of the right of the Third Estate (the common people, as opposed to the clergy and the aristocracy), which earns him immense popularity.
- The Welsh historian and moral philosopher Richard Price publishes *A Discourse on the Love of Our Country*, a reflection on the French Revolution.

SOCIETY

Education

- Georgetown University is founded in Washington, D.C.
- The University of North Carolina is founded at Chapel Hill.

Everyday Life

- The Japanese government bans mixed bathing and streetwalkers, and confines prostitutes to supervised brothels in the Yoshiwara section of Edo (modern Tokyo).
- There are 100 restaurants open in Paris, France.
- U.S. clergyman and inventor the Reverend Elijah Craig distills the first bourbon whiskey from corn, in Bourbon County, Kentucky.

Religion

- Pope Pius VI admits the 9th-century Decretals of Isidore, on which much papal authority was based, were forged.

1790

POLITICS, GOVERNMENT, AND ECONOMICS

Business and Economics

- English industrialist Matthew Boulton receives a patent to stamp coins using steam power.

JANUARY

14 U.S. treasury secretary Alexander Hamilton issues his Report on Public Credit, which calls for the federal government to fund the entire national debt at face value.

Human Rights

- Slaves at Mt. Vernon, George Washington's plantation in Virginia, are provided daily with a 2,800-calorie diet, mostly from corn meal, fish, and meat, a typical diet for slaves during this period.

- U.S. dramatist and critic Judith Sargent Murray writes "On the Equality of the Sexes" in the *Massachusetts* magazine.

FEBRUARY

11 The Society of Friends, better known as the Quakers, sends the U.S. Congress a petition calling for the emancipation of slaves.

Politics and Government

- In U.S. Congressional elections, Federalists attain majorities over Democratic-Republicans in the House (37–33) and Senate (16–13).

JANUARY

9 Britain, Prussia, and the Dutch Republic agree on a common policy over Belgium, but the British prime minister William Pitt the Younger refuses to recognize Belgian independence.

FEBRUARY

20 Archduke Leopold, the Grand Duke of Tuscany, becomes ruler of the Hapsburg Monarchy on the death of his brother Joseph II; in July he is elected Holy Roman Emperor as Leopold II.

MARCH

8   The National Assembly grants France's colonies self-government.

16 The "Statist" party of Henry van der Noot organizes a terrorist campaign against Francis Vonck's democratic faction in Belgium, driving them from power.

APRIL

10 The U.S. Congress establishes the Patent Office to protect and encourage new inventions.

MAY

•   The French National Assembly debates its right to declare war and make peace in the light of French treaty obligations to Spain and Anglo-Spanish friction over Nootka Sound, on the west coast of North America.

29 Rhode Island ratifies the U.S. Constitution, becoming the 13th state in the Union.

31 U.S. president George Washington signs a copyright law that will protect plays, maps, and books for a minimum of 14 years.

JULY

14 A vast rally (the Fête de la Fédération) is held in the Champ de Mars, Paris, France, on the first anniversary of the storming of the Bastille. King Louis XVI accepts the new constitution drawn up by the National Assembly.

16 The U.S. Congress provides for the construction of a new federal capital, to be located on the Potomac River near Georgetown, Maryland.

27 In the Treaty of Reichenbach, Prussia, Russia, Great Britain, and the Dutch Republic agree to allow Austria to reconquer Belgium, previously the Austrian Netherlands, in revolt since 1789.

AUGUST

•   The U.S. capital moves to Philadelphia, Pennsylvania, from New York, New York, where it remains pending construction of the new federal capital on the Potomac River near Georgetown, Maryland.

14 The Treaty of Verela ends the Swedish-Russian war, which began in June 1788, with no significant territorial changes.

31 A mutiny within the Châteauvieux regiment against its officers is suppressed with the National Constitutional Assembly's approval in Nancy, France.

SEPTEMBER

10 Jacques Necker resigns as French director general of finance (and virtual prime minister).

OCTOBER

28 Spain yields to Britain's demands for reparation over the seizure of four fishing vessels in Nootka Sound, on the west coast of North America, in June 1789, and abandons its claim to Vancouver Island.

NOVEMBER

27 Clergy in France are required to take an oath drawn up by the National Assembly to support the civil constitution.

DECEMBER

2   Austrian forces reconquer Belgium, restoring it as the Austrian Netherlands.

22 The Russian field marshal Count Alexander Vasilyevich Suvorov captures Ismail, a fortress at the mouth of the Danube, from the Ottoman Empire.

SCIENCE, TECHNOLOGY, AND MEDICINE

Exploration

•   The Scottish explorer James Bruce publishes *Travels to Discover the Source of the Nile, 1768–73*.

Health and Medicine

c. 1790 U.S. dentist John Greenwood improves the dental drill.

•   U.S. dentist Josiah Flagg builds the first dentist's chair.

Science

•   French chemist Nicolas Leblanc develops an inexpensive process for making sodium carbonate from sodium chloride (common salt). Sodium carbonate is used in making paper, soap, glass, and porcelain.

•   The English antiquarian John Frere identifies Stone Age flint tools together with the fossilized bones of extinct animals in a cave at Hoxne, southern England.

•   The German writer and polymath Johann Wolfgang von Goethe publishes his *Versuch die Metamorphose der Pflanzen zu erklären/Attempt to Explain the Metamorphosis of Plants*, a scientific study of plant forms.

NOVEMBER

13 German-born English astronomer William Herschel discovers a nebulae which he describes as a central star surrounded by a "luminous fluid." This contradicts his earlier views and he later concludes that the star was condensing out of a surrounding cloud.

Technology

•   English chemist Thomas Wedgwood makes photograms—shadowlike photographic images—by placing objects on leather sensitized with silver nitrate.

•   Industrialist Samuel Slater constructs the first U.S. cotton mill in Pawtucket, Rhode Island.

•   Scottish engineer James Watt adds a pressure-gauge to his steam engine.

Transportation

•   U.S. engineer Oliver Evans is granted the first patent for a land vehicle powered by steam.

ARTS AND IDEAS

Architecture

•   The Church of Ste. Geneviève (called the Panthéon since the French Revolution), designed by the French architect

Jacques-Germain Soufflot, is completed in Paris, France. It is one of the earliest and finest expressions of French neoclassicism.

SEPTEMBER

18 The city of Washington, D.C., is founded as the U.S. capital, when President George Washington lays the foundation stone of the Capitol building.

Arts

- The English wood engraver Thomas Bewick publishes his *History of Quadrupeds*, which establishes his career.
- The French artist Elizabeth-Louise Vigée Le Brun paints her *Self-Portrait*.
- The U.S. artist Rufus Hathaway paints *Lady With Her Pets*.

Literature and Language

- Henry James Pye becomes poet laureate in England, a position he holds until 1813.
- The English novelist Ann Radcliffe publishes her gothic novel *A Sicilian Romance*.
- The English poet and painter William Blake self-publishes his Swedenborgian poem *The Marriage of Heaven and Hell*.
- The French mystic Louis-Claude de St.-Martin publishes *L'Homme de désir/The Man of Desire*.
- The German writer Karl Philipp Moritz completes his four-volume novel *Anton Reiser*, an autobiographical work that establishes his reputation as one of the finest novelists of his day.
- The Russian writer Nikolay Mikhaylovich Karamzin publishes *Pis'ma russkogo puteshestvennika/Letters of a Russian Traveler*, recounting a tour of Europe. A popular work, it is credited with helping to create a new reading public in Russia.
- The Scottish poet Robert Burns publishes *Tam O'Shanter*, a narrative poem based on a folk legend.

- The Swedish poet Carl Michael Bellman publishes his poetry collection *Fredmans epistlar/Freeman's Epistles*, a popular song cycle.
- U.S. pioneer author Ann Eliza Bleecker publishes her accounts of American frontier conditions during the revolution.

Music

c. 1790 Austrian composer Franz Joseph Haydn completes his String Quartets Nos. 63 to 68 (Opus 64).
- Austrian composer Wolfgang Amadeus Mozart completes his Piano Concerto No. 27 (K 595); his last three String Quartets, Nos. 21 to 23, the *King of Prussia Quartets*; and his String Quintet No. 5 (K 593). His opera *Così fan tutte, ossia la scuola degli amanti/ Women Are All the Same*, or *The School for Lovers* is first performed, in Vienna, Austria.

Thought and Scholarship

- British historian and political theorist Catharine Macaulay publishes her *Observations on the Reflections of the Right Honourable Edmund Burke on the Revolution in France*, defending the French Revolution.
- The German philosopher Immanuel Kant publishes the third of his three major works, *Critique of Judgment*, which deals with aesthetics.
- The Irish-born English statesman Edmund Burke publishes *Reflections on the Revolution in France*, a condemnation of the French Revolution's violence.
- The Russian writer Alexander Nikolayevich Radishchev publishes *Puteshestvie iz Petersburga v Moskvu/Journey from Petersburg to Moscow*. A controversial book attacking serfdom and the misuse of power, it earns its author a death sentence, commuted to exile in Siberia.

BIRTHS & DEATHS

JANUARY

20 John Howard, English philanthropist and public health and prison reformer who reformed the British prison system by abolishing discharge fees, dies in Kherson, Ukraine, Russian Empire (63).

FEBRUARY

20 Joseph II, Holy Roman Emperor ruling 1765–80 with his mother, Maria Theresa, and then sole ruler 1780–90, dies in Vienna, Austria (48).

MARCH

29 John Tyler, tenth president of the United States 1841–45 on the death of William Henry Harrison, a Whig, born in Charles City County, Virginia (–1862).

APRIL

17 Benjamin Franklin, North American printer, publisher, and inventor who helped draft the Declaration of Independence and the U.S. Constitution, dies in Philadelphia, Pennsylvania (84).

MAY

21 Thomas Warton, poet laureate of England 1785–90, dies in Oxford, England (62).

JULY

14 Ernst Gideon Laudon, Austrian field marshal during the Seven Years' War 1756–63 and the Austro-Turkish War 1787–91, dies in Neutitschein, Austria (73).

17 Adam Smith, Scottish social philosopher known for *An Inquiry into the Nature and Causes of the Wealth of Nations* on *laissez-faire* economics, dies in Edinburgh, Scotland (63).

OCTOBER

21 Alphonse de Lamartine, French romantic poet and statesman, born in Mâcon, France (–1869).

DECEMBER

23 Jean-François Champollion, French linguist who translates the Rosetta Stone and founds the science of Egyptology, born in Figeac, France (–1832).

SOCIETY

Education

- Feminist commentary in *Letters on Education* by British historian and political theorist Catharine Macaulay influences writings by Mary Wollstonecraft, English educator and feminist.

Everyday Life

- French farmer Marie Harel produces the first Camembert cheese, in Orne, France. The recipe may have come from a priest from Brie, whom she sheltered during the French Revolution.
- High heels go out of fashion for women in the United States, and are replaced by sandals with bows or ribbons, rather than buckles.

- The distribution of the white population by origin in the United States is: 61% English; 10% Irish; 9% German; 8% Scottish; 3% Dutch; 2% French; 0.7% Swedish.
- The population of the city of New York, New York, reaches 30,000.
- There are 8 daily newspapers and 101 weekly newspapers in the United States.
- Women's hairstyles in France become elaborate. Some shapes are known as "a reclining dog on a hair cushion" and incorporate flowers and fruit baskets.

MARCH

1 The U.S. Congress authorizes the first national census. The document, completed in August, establishes the nation's population at 3,929,625, of which 95% live in rural areas. There are 757,208 black people in the United States, of whom 697,624 are slaves.

Fashion (1790–1889)

1790–1849

1790
- High heels go out of fashion for women in the United States, and are replaced by sandals with bows or ribbons, rather than buckles.
- Women's hairstyles in France become elaborate. Some shapes are known as "a reclining dog on a hair cushion" and incorporate flowers and fruit baskets.

1797
- Haberdasher John Hetherington creates the first top hat, in London, England.

1798
- The invention of a smallpox vaccination causes the decline of beauty patches—stars, moons, and hearts of black velvet or silk—worn by women in Europe to hide pock marks. The location of the patches had taken on meaning; i.e. worn at the corner of the mouth, the patch meant the women was willing to flirt; on the right cheek, that she was married, and so on.

c. 1800
- Schoolgirls in Europe are deprived of food, exercise, and fresh air to achieve the fashionable look of pallor and thinness.
- The first shoes in the United States designed specifically for the left and right feet are made by shoemaker William Young, in Philadelphia, Pennsylvania.

c. 1812
- The women's fashion in Britain is for dresses with very high waists, just under the bust.

c. 1815
- Men shed the pantaloons and silk stockings popular early in the century in favor of long trousers, a trend reflecting the style adopted by French revolutionaries distinguishing themselves from the nobility.
- Women's fashions adopt the stiff corset, leg-of-mutton sleeves, and full skirts, leading to the hoop skirt later in the century.

1849
- London hatters Thomas and William Bowler create the bowler hat, designed to protect the head from branches when shooting. This will become emblematic of the British middle-class professional man.

1850–89

1850
- Bavarian immigrant Levi Strauss makes the first jeans out of canvas in San Francisco, California. They are originally designed for Californian gold miners.

1853
- U.S. publisher and women's rights campaigner Amelia Jenks Bloomer adopts "bloomers," loose pants gathered at the ankles, which give women much more freedom of movement.

1856
- English tailor Thomas Burberry introduces the Burberry raincoat.

1858
- English dressmaker Charles Worth launches the first fashion house, on the rue de la Paix in Paris, France.

1865
- U.S. hatmaker John B. Stetson begins manufacturing the Stetson hat in Philadelphia, Pennsylvania.

1868
- A fashion for women's dresses with large bustles at the back is popular in the United States.

1886
October   The tuxedo gets its name when tobacco heir Griswold Lorillard wears a short black dinner jacket with satin lapels in place of the traditional tails to the Tuxedo Club in New York, New York.

1889
- The French corset-maker Hermine Cadolle creates the first bra, which frees women from the restrictions of corsets.

Religion

JULY

12 The Civil Constitution of the Clergy is established by the French National Constituent Assembly, reorganizing the church on national lines. It is to be state funded and its priests democratically elected. Jews in France are admitted to civil liberties.

Sports

c. 1790–1820 The game of bandy, a form of ice hockey still popular in parts of northern Europe, evolves in England.

1791

POLITICS, GOVERNMENT, AND ECONOMICS

Business and Economics

MARCH

3 The U.S. Congress passes the nation's first tax law. The law divides the country into 14 tax zones and levies a duty of between 20 and 30 cents a gallon on distilled spirits.

DECEMBER

12 The Bank of the United States opens in Philadelphia, Pennsylvania. It has a 20-year charter and $10 million capital, much of which comes from private investors.

Politics and Government

JANUARY

29 The revolutionary politician Honoré de Mirabeau is elected president of the French National Assembly.

MARCH

4 Vermont ratifies the U.S. Constitution, becoming the 14th state in the Union.

28 Britain increases its naval strength in an unsuccessful attempt to intimidate Russia into making peace with the Ottoman Empire.

APRIL

18 King Louis XVI of France is prevented by a riot from going to his château at St. Cloud, effectively confirming his position as a prisoner of the National Assembly and the people of Paris.

MAY

3 Poland's Four Year Sejm (parliament), in power 1788–92, introduces a new constitution, converting Poland's long-established electoral monarchy into a hereditary monarchy, giving executive power to the king and a council of state, and placing legislative power in the hands of a two-chamber Sejm. Russia opposes the changes, and promotes agitation in Poland in defense of the old constitution.

6 British North America (modern Canada) is divided into two provinces, Upper Canada (Ontario) and Lower Canada (Quebec), under the terms of the Canada Constitution Act. Each province has its own legislative assembly.

14 The British governor-general of India, Charles Cornwallis, overthrows Tippu Sultan, the sultan of Mysore, at the Battle of Seringapatam.

JUNE

21–25 King Louis XVI attempts to flee France but is caught at Varennes and brought back to Paris.

JULY

5 King Frederick William II of Prussia dismisses the long-serving Ewald, Count von Hertzberg, the foreign minister.

6 The Holy Roman Emperor Leopold II issues the "Padua Circular," a letter calling for support for King Louis XVI of France against the National Assembly.

6 The Comte d'Artois makes the city of Koblenz in Trier, Germany, the headquarters of the *émigrés* (nobles in exile from the French Revolution).

14 On the second anniversary of the fall of the Bastille, rioters in Birmingham, England, destroy the house of the dissenting clergyman, chemist, and natural historian Joseph Priestley because of his support of the French Revolution.

17 The Marquis de Lafayette's Guards open fire on a crowd demanding the abdication of King Louis XVI, in the Champ de Mars, Paris. About 50 people are killed or wounded.

AUGUST

27 By the Declaration of Pillnitz, the Hapsburg Monarchy and Prussia state that they are ready to intervene in French affairs in support of Louis XVI with the consent of other powers, but William Pitt the Younger

announces that Britain will remain neutral in the French Revolution. France sees the declaration as a threat.

SEPTEMBER

3   The new French constitution is passed by the National Assembly, making France a constitutional monarchy.
13 France annexes Avignon, a territory of the papacy since the 14th century.
30 The French National Assembly dissolves after decreeing that none of its members is eligible to serve in its designated successor, the new Legislative Assembly.

OCTOBER

October 1791–September 1792   The new Legislative Assembly convenes in Paris, France. Jacques Brissot and other members of the Girondist party urge war against the Hapsburg Monarchy.
14 The Irish Protestant nationalist Wolfe Tone founds the Society of United Irishmen as a political union of Roman Catholics and Protestants with the aim of furthering Irish parliamentary reform.

NOVEMBER

9   King Louis XVI of France vetoes a decree of the Legislative Assembly demanding the return of the *émigrés* (French nobles in exile from the Revolution) under pain of death.

DECEMBER

•   King Gustav III of Sweden offers to lead a crusade against revolutionary France.
15 After the state of Virginia ratifies the first ten amendments to the U.S. Constitution, the Bill of Rights becomes law.

SCIENCE, TECHNOLOGY, AND MEDICINE

Science

•   English mineralogist William Gregor discovers titanium (atomic no. 22).
•   Italian physiologist Luigi Galvani announces his observations on the muscular contraction of dead frogs, which he argues are caused electrically.

Technology

•   Samuel Peel patents India-rubber cloth.

ARTS AND IDEAS

Arts

•   The British artist George Morland paints *The Stable*, inspiring a vogue for scenes of everyday country life.

December 1791–94   The English furniture designer Thomas Sheraton publishes *The Cabinet-Maker and Upholsterer's Drawing Book*. His designs strongly influence the development of an elegant neoclassical style of English furniture.

Literature and Language

•   The English antiquarian Isaac D'Israeli (father of the politician and novelist Benjamin Disraeli) publishes the first part of his *Curiosities of Literature*. It is completed in 1834.
•   The English writer and actress Elizabeth Inchbald publishes her novel *A Simple Story*.
•   The English-born U.S. writer and actress Susanna Rowson publishes her novel *Charlotte Temple*, a best seller of its day in the United States and now regarded as the first U.S. novel.
•   The French writer and philosopher the Marquis de Sade publishes *Justine*, a novel whose eroticism and sadomasochism cause an outcry. The word "sadism" is derived from his name.
•   The Scottish writer James Boswell publishes his *Life of Johnson*.
•   The Swedish poet Carl Michael Bellman publishes his poetry collection *Fredmans sånger/Freeman's Songs*, a collection of drinking songs.

Music

•   Austrian composer Franz Joseph Haydn completes his Symphony No. 94, the *Surprise*; and No. 96, the *Miracle*.
•   Austrian composer Wolfgang Amadeus Mozart completes his Clarinet Concerto in A major (K 622); his *Requiem Mass* (K 626) (unfinished); his String Quintet No. 6 (K 614); and his *Variations on Schack's "Ein Weib ist das herrlichste Ding"/"A Woman is the Most Wonderful Thing"* for solo piano (K 613). His opera *Die Zauberflöte/The Magic Flute* is first performed, in Vienna, Austria, and the opera *La clemenza di Tito/The Clemency of Titus* is first performed, in Prague, Bohemia.

Theater and Dance

December 1791–1817   The German writer and polymath Johann Wolfgang von Goethe is appointed director of the Weimar theater.

Thought and Scholarship

•   The British Whig politician Edmund Burke publishes *An Appeal from the New to the Old Whigs* and *Letter to a Member of the National Assembly*, both attacking Whig support for the French Revolution.
•   The French revolutionary Louis-Antoine-Léon de St.-Just publishes *Esprit de la révolution et de la constitution de France/The Spirit of the Revolution and the Constitution of France*.
•   The French scholar Constantin Volney publishes *Les ruines, ou méditations sur les révolutions des empires/*

Ruins, or Reflections on the Revolutions of Empires, an essay on the philosophy of history that has a wide appeal in the United States and Britain as well as France.

- The Massachusetts Historical Society, the first of its kind in the United States, is founded.
- The Scottish political writer James Mackintosh publishes *Vindiciae Gallicae*, a defense of the French Revolution.

FEBRUARY

- The British-born U.S. revolutionary Thomas Paine publishes the first part of his *Rights of Man*. The second part will appear in 1792. A response to Edmund Burke's *Reflections on the French Revolution*, published in 1790, it is a vigorous defense of the French Revolution and a call for the overthrow of the British monarchy.

SOCIETY

Education

- The University of Vermont is founded at Burlington.

Everyday Life

- The English philosopher and social reformer Jeremy Bentham designs a "panopticon" prison, allowing for efficient supervision of inmates.
- The Scottish politician John Sinclair begins supervising the compilation of *The Statistical Account of Scotland*.

Religion

- The English Methodists separate from the Church of England and form the Wesleyan Methodist Church.

BIRTHS & DEATHS

JANUARY
15   Franz Grillparzer, Austrian dramatist, born in Vienna, Austria (−1872).
22   Horace Bénédict de Saussure, Swiss physicist who built the first hygrometer, dies in Geneva, Switzerland (58).

MARCH
2   John Wesley, Anglican clergyman and evangelist who, with his brother Charles Wesley, founded the Methodist movement in the Church of England, dies in London, England (87).
6   Anna Claypoole Peale, U.S. miniature painter, born in Philadelphia, Pennsylvania (−1878).

APRIL
2   Honoré-Gabriel Riquetti Mirabeau, French politician and orator, dies in Paris, France (42).
19   Richard Price, English moral philosopher and supporter of the American Revolution, dies in Hackney, London, England (68).
23   James Buchanan, fifteenth president of the United States

1856–61, a Democrat, born near Mercersburg, Pennsylvania (−1868).
27   Samuel Finley Breese Morse, U.S. painter and inventor of Morse Code, born in Charlestown, Massachusetts (−1872).

MAY
9   Francis Hopkinson, U.S. lawyer and musician, a signatory of the Declaration of Independence, dies in Philadelphia, Pennsylvania (53).

JUNE
17   Selina, Countess of Huntingdon, English Methodist evangelical revivalist, dies in London, England (83).
22   Catharine Macaulay, English historian, dies in Binfield, England (60).

SEPTEMBER
5   Giacomo Meyerbeer, German opera composer, born in Tasdorf, near Berlin, Prussia (−1864).
14   Franz Bopp, German linguist who discovered that Sanskrit is an Indo-European language and thus related to English, born in Mainz, Germany (−1867).

22   Michael Faraday, English physicist and chemist whose work contributed to a basic understanding of electromagnetism, born in Newington, Surrey, England (−1867).
26   Théodore Géricault, French painter, born in Rouen, France (−1824).

OCTOBER
16   Prince Grigory Aleksandrovich Potemkin, Russian army officer, statesman, and lover of Empress Catherine II, dies in Bessarabia, Russia (51).

DECEMBER
2   Henry Flood, Anglo-Irish statesman, leader of the group that forced England to grant political independence to Ireland, dies in Farmley, County Kilkenny, Ireland (c. 59).
5   Wolfgang Amadeus Mozart, considered one of the world's greatest composers, dies in Vienna, Austria (35).

1792

POLITICS, GOVERNMENT, AND ECONOMICS

Business and Economics

- Dollar coinage is introduced in the United States, with the opening of a mint in Philadelphia, Pennsylvania.

MAY

17 A group of brokers meeting at a coffee house in New York, New York, organize the New York Stock Exchange. The first transactions are made under a tree on Wall Street.

NOVEMBER

27 France annexes Savoy and Nice from the Kingdom of Savoy-Piedmont and opens the River Scheldt in the Austrian Netherlands to commerce.

Human Rights

- The English writer and feminist Mary Wollstonecraft publishes her *Vindication of the Rights of Woman*.

Politics and Government

- In U.S. Congressional elections, Federalists attain a majority in the Senate but cede control of the House to Democratic-Republicans (57–48).
- Manuel de Godoy, favorite and lover of Queen Maria Luisa of Spain, uses his connection with the queen to advance to the position of prime minister.
- The Republican Party forms in the United States in opposition to the perceived elitism and Anglophile sympathy of the Federalists.

JANUARY

9 Russia, deserted by the Hapsburg Monarchy and concerned over Prussian intrigues in Poland, ends the Russo-Ottoman War by the Treaty of Jassy, obtaining the Black Sea port of Ochakov and a boundary on the River Dniester, but restoring Moldavia, Bessarabia, and Wallachia to the Ottomans.

18 The states of Ansbach and Bayreuth in Germany revert to Prussia according to the terms of the Treaty of Teschen, signed on May 13, 1779.

FEBRUARY

5 Tippu Sultan, the sultan of Mysore, India, is defeated in his war with the British and Hyderabad. He cedes half of Mysore to Britain.

7 An Austro-Prussian alliance against revolutionary France is signed.

MARCH

1 Archduke Francis II succeeds his father, Leopold II, as ruler of the Hapsburg Monarchy; he is elected Holy Roman Emperor in July.

23 The republican Girondist party, under Jean Roland and Charles-François Dumouriez, forms a government in France.

29 King Gustav III of Sweden is assassinated in the course of an aristocratic coup.

APRIL

20 France declares war on the Hapsburg Monarchy following the failure of the Holy Roman Empire to renounce treaties threatening French sovereignty.

MAY

19 Russian forces invade Poland, to forestall constitutional changes designed to stabilize the Polish monarchy and thus weaken Russian influence in the country.

JUNE

1 Kentucky accepts the U.S. constitution and becomes the 15th state in the Union.

20 Crowds demonstrating against the king's refusal to pass restrictive laws against the clergy invade the Tuileries, the royal palace in Paris, France.

JULY

8 France declares war on Prussia, in response to the Austro-Prussian alliance of February 7, 1792.

25 Karl Wilhelm, Duke of Brunswick, issues a manifesto threatening the destruction of Paris by Prussian forces if the French royal family is harmed during continuing revolutionary unrest in France.

AUGUST

- Prussian and Austrian troops under Karl Wilhelm, Duke of Brunswick, invade France.

10 A huge mob storms the royal palace in the Tuileries, Paris, France, massacring the Swiss Guard. The Legislative Assembly declares the king's authority suspended. A new revolutionary Commune de Paris (municipal government) replaces the original body set up in 1789, sharing power in the French capital with a Provisional Executive Council and the Legislative Assembly.

12 The French royal family is imprisoned, on the order of the Legislative Assembly.

19–September 20 The Legislative Assembly in France dissolves the religious orders and institutes civil marriage and divorce.

SEPTEMBER

20 The Prussian invasion of France under the Duke of Brunswick is halted by French forces under generals

French Revolutionary Wars (1792–1801)

1791

AUGUST

2   The declaration of Pillnitz, in which Prussia, Austria, Russia, Sweden and Spain agree to form an alliance to restore legitimate authority in revolutionary France. France responds the following summer, declaring war on Austria and Prussia.

1792

SEPTEMBER

20   The Prussian invasion of France is halted by French forces under generals Charles-François Dumouriez and François Kellermann at the Battle of Valmy, eastern France.

NOVEMBER

6   French forces under General Charles-François Dumouriez defeat an Austrian army at Jemappes, after which they take Brussels and overrun the Austrian Netherlands (Belgium).

1793

FEBRUARY

1   France declares war on Britain and the Dutch Republic.

13   The First Coalition against France is formed by Great Britain, Austria, Prussia, the Dutch Republic, Spain, and Sardinia.

APRIL

5   The French general Charles-François Dumouriez deserts to the Austrians after his defeat at Neerwinden in the Netherlands.

JULY

23   Prussian forces under the Duke of Brunswick recapture Mainz and drive French troops from Germany.

AUGUST

28   A British force under Admiral Sir Samuel Hood occupies the key French naval base of Toulon, at the invitation of French royalists.

SEPTEMBER

6   A new French offensive under General Jean Houchard is launched in the Austrian Netherlands, where a British army under the Duke of York is defeated at Hondschoote.

OCTOBER

17   The Vendéans (French royalists) are defeated by Republican forces at Cholet, western France.

DECEMBER

19   Republican troops under Napoleon Bonaparte retake the naval base of Toulon from British and royalist forces. Many of the royalists are executed.

26   French troops under General Louis Hoche defeat an Austrian army under General Dagobert Würmser at Weissenburg, Alsace, forcing the Austrians to retreat across the Rhine.

1794

APRIL

19   Britain and Prussia sign the Treaty of The Hague, under which Britain agrees to pay subsidies for 60,000 Prussian and Dutch troops in the coalition against revolutionary France.

MAY

18   General Charles Pichegru leads French forces to victory at Tourcoing, northeast France, against an Austrian and British army commanded by Friedrich Josias, Prince of Saxe-Coburg.

JUNE

1   The British admiral Richard, Lord Howe, defeats a French fleet in the English Channel in a battle subsequently known in Britain as "The Glorious First of June."

26   A French army under General Jean-Baptiste Jourdan defeats Austrian forces at Fleurus in the Austrian Netherlands. The Austrian commander, Freidrich Josias, Prince of Saxe-Coburg, evacuates the Austrian Netherlands.

OCTOBER

•   A French army under General Jean Moreau advances as far as the River Rhine.

25   Prussia withdraws from the war against the French Republic.

1795

JANUARY

19   The French army under Charles Pichegru occupies Amsterdam, in the Dutch Republic. He captures the Dutch fleet at Texel, and his troops quickly overrun the rest of the United Netherlands.

APRIL

5   France and Prussia sign the Peace of Basel, under which France retains its conquests on the left bank of the Rhine pending the conclusion of a peace with the Holy Roman Empire, while Prussia receives territories on the right bank. Saxony, Hanover, the Bavarian Palatinate, and Hesse-Cassel also agree terms with France.

MAY

16   The Dutch Republic is reorganized under French control as the Batavian Republic, and signs an offensive and defensive alliance with France.

JUNE

27   A British naval expedition lands a force of exiled French nobles at Quiberon in Brittany, western France, to support royalist unrest in the area, but they are decisively defeated by Republican forces commanded by General Lazare Hoche.

SEPTEMBER

•   Austrian forces under the Archduke Charles reconquer the right bank of the Rhine from French forces under General Jean-Baptiste Jourdan.

6   The French republican army under General Jourdan recrosses the River Rhine, renewing its campaign against the Austrian army of the Archduke Charles.

1796

FEBRUARY

14 A British fleet under admirals John Jervis and Horatio Nelson defeat a Spanish fleet off Cape St. Vincent, Portugal.

APRIL

13 General Napoleon Bonaparte assumes command of the French campaign against the Austrians in Italy, and defeats an Austrian force at Millesimo.

22 Napoleon Bonaparte defeats the Piedmontese at Mondovi, Italy.

28 The military success of the French campaign under Napoleon Bonaparte in Italy forces the kingdom of Sardinia to abandon its Austrian alliance.

MAY

10 Napoleon Bonaparte's French army defeats the Austrians at Lodi, Italy.

15 The Italian kingdom of Sardinia signs the Peace of Cherasco with France, ceding Savoy and Nice to France.

16 The northern Italian region of Lombardy is declared a republic, under French rule.

JUNE

• The French army of General Jean-Baptiste Jourdan invades Franconia, Germany, but is driven back by Austrian forces.

23–27 General Victor Moreau's French army crosses the River Rhine at Strasbourg, aiming to link up with the army of General Jourdan in Franconia and advance on Austria.

AUGUST

15 Napoleon Bonaparte's French army defeats Austrian forces under Count Dagobert Würmser at Castiglione delle Stiviere, Italy, halting the Austrian attempt to relieve Mantua from a French siege.

19 An alliance is signed at San Ildefonso, Spain, between France and Spain against Britain. It is virtually a renewal of the 1761 Family Compact between the Bourbon rulers of the two countries.

OCTOBER

5 Spain declares war on Britain.

16 Napoleon Bonaparte creates the French-dominated Cispadane Republic in Italy by merging the Papal territories of Bologna and Ferrara and the duchy of Modena (including Reggio nell'Emilia).

1797

JANUARY

4 The French army of Napoleon Bonaparte defeats the Austrian army of General Joseph Alvintzi at Rivoli, Italy.

OCTOBER

• Napoleon Bonaparte is appointed to command French forces being assembled to invade England.

11 A British fleet under the Scottish admiral Adam Duncan defeats the fleet of the French-dominated Batavian Republic off Camperdown on the Dutch coast.

17 The Treaty of Campo Formio is signed by France and Austria after Napoleon Bonaparte's successful campaign in Italy and Tyrol. The Cisalpine and Ligurian republics are recognized, as is French possession of the Ionian Islands off the Greek coast. Austria occupies the Venetian lands east of the River Adige, including Istria, Dalmatia, and Venice, and cedes the Austrian Netherlands to France. Peace between the Holy Roman Empire and France is to be negotiated at a conference to be held at Rastatt, Germany.

1798

MAY

19 A French military expedition intending to conquer Egypt sets sail from Toulon, under the command of Napoleon Bonaparte.

JUNE

12 The French expeditionary force for Egypt occupies Malta, ruled by the Knights of St. John (whose Grand Master is Czar Paul I of Russia).

JULY

21 Napoleon Bonaparte's army in Egypt, having occupied Alexandria, defeats Mameluke forces at the Battle of the Pyramids. French domination of Egypt is established.

AUGUST

1 A British fleet under the English admiral Horatio Nelson destroys the French Toulon fleet in Aboukir Bay, Egypt, ("the Battle of the Nile") cutting the French army's communications with Europe and establishing British naval supremacy in the Mediterranean.

DECEMBER

15 French forces recapture Rome from the Austrian army of Baron Karl Mack von Lieberich, and overrun the kingdom of Naples.

24 An Anglo-Russian alliance is signed as the foundation of a Second Coalition against France.

1799

JANUARY

2 Britain joins the Russo-Ottoman alliance.

2 The French army in Egypt, commanded by Napoleon Bonaparte, advances into the Ottoman province of Syria.

MARCH

12 Austria declares war on France.

19 The French army of Egypt, under Napoleon Bonaparte, lays siege to the Syrian coastal city of Acre (Akko); it is defended by Ottoman troops aided by British forces under Sidney Smith.

25 An Austrian army under Archduke Charles defeats Jean-Baptiste Jourdan's French army at Stockach in Germany.

APRIL

5 The French army of General Barthélemy Schérer is defeated at Magnano, Italy, by an Austrian army under General Paul von Kray.

French Revolutionary Wars (1792–1801) *continued*

27 A Russo-Austrian army in Italy under the Russian field marshal Count Alexander Vasilyevich Suvorov defeats the French army of General Jean Moreau in the Battle of Cassano and occupies Turin.

MAY

20 The French army of Egypt, under Napoleon Bonaparte, abandons its siege of the Syrian coastal city of Acre.

JUNE

1 William Pitt the Younger concludes the formation of the Second Coalition of Britain, Russia, Austria, the Ottoman Empire, Portugal, and Naples against France.

4 Austrian forces under Archduke Charles defeat a French army under André Masséna at Zürich, Switzerland.

17–19 The Russo-Austrian army under the Russian field marshal Count Alexander Vasilyevich Suvorov decisively defeats the French governor of Rome, Jacques-Alexandre MacDonald, in the Battle of the Trebbia, Italy, while the French forces are advancing to relieve the army of General Victor Moreau at Genoa.

JULY

24 The French army of Egypt, under Napoleon Bonaparte, defeats an Ottoman army at Aboukir, Egypt.

AUGUST

15 Count Suvorov's Russo-Austrian army defeats French forces under Barthélemy-Catherine Joubert at Novi, Italy, and advances across the Alps toward France. Joubert is killed in the battle.

22 Napoleon Bonaparte leaves Egypt to take command of French forces in Europe.

SEPTEMBER

13 The Duke of York takes command of an Anglo-Russian army in the Netherlands, intending to reconquer the Batavian Republic and the Austrian Netherlands from France.

19 The Anglo-Russian army commanded by the Duke of York is defeated by Franco-Batavian troops at Bergen-op-Zoom in the Batavian Republic.

25–27 French forces under General André Masséna defeat a Russian army under Alexander Korsakov at Zürich, Switzerland; the main Russian force under Field Marshal Count Suvorov arrives too late, and is forced to retreat across the Alps. Austrian forces under the Archduke Charles retreat to the River Danube.

OCTOBER

18 The Anglo-Russian army commanded by the Duke of York surrenders to French and Batavian forces at Alkmaar in the Batavian Republic; Britain agrees to release all its French prisoners of war.

21 Britain declares the entire coast of the Batavian Republic to be under naval blockade.

22 Russia breaks its coalition agreement with Austria against France.

NOVEMBER

13 Austria occupies the Italian March of Ancona, on the Adriatic coast of the Papal States in central Italy.

DECEMBER

25 The Constitution of the Year VIII creates the French Consulate. It comprises three consuls, with Napoleon Bonaparte as First Consul. Britain and Austria reject French offers of peace.

Charles-François Dumouriez and François Kellermann at the Battle of Valmy, eastern France.

21 The French National Convention convenes in Paris, replacing the Legislative Assembly.

OCTOBER

19 French troops under General Adam de Custine pursue the retreating Prussian forces of the Duke of Brunswick across the Rhine, capturing the city of Mainz.

NOVEMBER

• The French radical republican party the Jacobins, under Georges Danton, wrest power from the Girondists in Paris.

6 French forces under General Charles-François Dumouriez defeat an Austrian army at Jemappes, after which they take Brussels and overrun the Austrian Netherlands (Belgium).

15 The future João VI takes power in Portugal as a result of the mental illness of his mother, Queen Maria.

19 The French National Convention offers to support all peoples wishing to overthrow their governments.

DECEMBER

5 A revolutionary coup takes place in the Swiss city of Geneva, inspired by the Revolution in France.

5 George Washington is reelected president of the United States. John Adams, the runner-up, returns to the office of vice president.

5 The trial of the French king, Louis XVI, opens before the National Convention in Paris.

15 A French decree compels all lands occupied by French troops to accept French revolutionary institutions.

SCIENCE, TECHNOLOGY, AND MEDICINE

Agriculture

• British naval captain William Bligh transplants breadfruit from the Pacific to the Caribbean where it becomes a staple food.

Exploration

• British navigator George Vancouver explores North America's Pacific coast, searching for a passage to Hudson Bay and the Atlantic, and discovers the island now named for him.

1800

JANUARY

17 The Treaty of Montluçon ends royalist disaffection in the Vendée, western France, and releases troops for a new French offensive in Europe.

MARCH

20 The French army in Egypt, commanded by General Jean Baptiste Kléber, defeats an Ottoman army at Heliopolis, and advances to Cairo, aiming to reconquer the country.

MAY

15–20 A French army commanded by Napoleon Bonaparte crosses the Great St. Bernard Pass, aiming to reconquer Italy from the Austrians.

JUNE

2 French forces under Joachim Murat occupy Milan, during Napoleon Bonaparte's renewed campaign in Italy.

14 French forces under Napoleon Bonaparte defeat the Austrians under Baron Michel Melas at the Battle of Marengo, northwest Italy, ensuring the French reconquest of Italy.

SEPTEMBER

5 A British expedition recaptures Malta from the French.

DECEMBER

3 The French general Victor Moreau defeats the Austrians under Archduke John of Austria at Hohenlinden and advances on the Austrian capital, Vienna.

16 A second Armed Neutrality of the North is agreed between Russia, Sweden, Denmark, and Prussia.

1801

DECEMBER

- The black leader Toussaint L'Ouverture achieves total control of the Franco-Spanish colony of Haiti.
- A French force under Charles Leclerc retakes the island of Haiti from the regime of Toussaint L'Ouverture, who is captured and dies in prison in France.

JANUARY

29 A convention is held between France and Spain to issue an ultimatum to Portugal to break that country's traditional allegiance with Britain.

MARCH

8 British troops under William Keith make an amphibious landing at Aboukir in French-occupied Egypt.

21 French forces stationed by Napoleon Bonaparte in Egypt are defeated near Alexandria by British troops led by General Ralph Abercromby.

JULY

12 The British admiral James Saumarez defeats a larger Franco-Spanish fleet off the coast of Morocco in the second Battle of Algeciras (having fought an inconclusive action on July 6).

SEPTEMBER

2 French forces in Egypt under General Jean Menou surrender to the British and are immediately offered free passage home, ending Napoleon Bonaparte's hopes of oriental conquest.

Health and Medicine

- A bubonic plague outbreak in Egypt kills 800,000 people.
- French physician Philippe Pinel removes chains from mental patients in Paris, France, and establishes a program of modern psychiatric treatment.

Science

- Italian physicist Alessandro Volta demonstrates the electrochemical series.

Technology

- English inventor Edmund Cartwright invents a cable-making machine.
- Scottish inventor William Murdock uses coal-gas to light his home, one of the first houses to be so lighted.

Transportation

- French physician Dominique-Jean Larrey develops the first ambulance for use on a battlefield. It is a well-sprung two-wheeled cart pulled by two horses.

- The first modern truss bridge is constructed by U.S. engineer Timothy Palmer over the Merrimack River, Maine.

ARTS AND IDEAS

Arts

- The U.S. artist John Trumbull paints *General George Washington at the Battle of Trenton*.

Literature and Language

- The Bohemian (Czech) philologist Josef Dobrovský publishes *Geschichte der böhmischen Sprache und Litteratur/History of the Bohemian Language and Literature*.
- The English poet Samuel Rogers publishes *The Pleasures of Memory*.
- The English writer Arthur Young publishes *Travels in France*, a popular account of journeys he made in the late 1780s. It becomes known for its descriptions of the French Revolution.

- The Russian writer Nikolai Mikhailovich Karamzin publishes several of his finest short stories, including the sentimental "Bednaya Liza"/"Poor Lisa."
- The U.S. writer Thomas Odione publishes his long poem *The Progress of Refinement*.

Music

- French poet and composer Claude-Joseph Rouget de Lisle writes the words and music of the revolutionary song "La Marseillaise." It was first known as "Chant de guerre de l'armée du Rhin"/"The War Song of the Army of the Rhine."
- The opera *Il matrimonio segreto/The Secret Marriage* by the Italian composer Domenico Cimarosa is first performed, in Vienna, Austria.

Theater and Dance

- The play *Henryk IV nałowach/Henry IV Hunting* by the Polish writer and director Wojciech Bogusławski is first performed, in Warsaw, Poland. Through his work as a director and theater manager, and through his many adaptations and original works, Bogusławski becomes the father of Polish theater.

Thought and Scholarship

- The English writer and feminist Mary Wollstonecraft publishes her *Vindication of the Rights of Man*, a defense of the French Revolution.

- The French revolutionary Jean-Baptiste ("Anacharsis") Cloots (or Clootz) publishes *La République du genre humain/The Republic of the Human Race*. He called himself the "spokesman of the human race."
- The German philosopher Johann Gottlieb Fichte publishes his first important work, *Versuch einer Kritik aller Offenbarung/An Attempt at a Critique of Revelation*, a work strongly influenced by Immanuel Kant.
- The Scottish philosopher Dugald Stewart publishes the first volume of his three-volume *Elements of the Philosophy of the Human Mind*. The last volume appears in 1827.
- The U.S. artist Benjamin West becomes president of the Royal Academy in London, England.
- The U.S. writer Joel Barlow publishes his political tract *Advice to the Privileged Orders*, a defense of the French Revolution.

SOCIETY

Everyday Life

- Swiss entrepreneur Jacob Schweppe sets up a company manufacturing carbonated drinks in Drury Lane, London, England. His soda water is used for health purposes, as it is said by the company to be good for indigestion, fever, and nervous illness.

BIRTHS & DEATHS

FEBRUARY

23 Joshua Reynolds, English portrait painter, dies in London, England (69).

29 Carl von Baer, German biologist, born in Piep, Estonia, Russia (–1876).

29 Gioacchino Rossini, Italian composer, born in Pesaro, Papal States (–1868).

MARCH

1 Leopold II, Holy Roman Emperor 1790–92, dies in Vienna, Austria (44).

3 Robert Adam, Scottish architect and designer, dies in London, England (64).

7 John Herschel, English astronomer known for his catalog of the stars in the southern sky, born in Slough, Buckinghamshire, England (–1871).

10 John Stuart, Earl of Bute, British prime minister 1762–63, dies in London, England (78).

MAY

13 Pope Pius IX, who reigns 1846–78, born in Senigallia, Papal States (–1878).

21 Gustave-Gaspard Coriolis, French engineer who was the first to describe the Coriolis effect (the effect of the earth's rotation on its atmosphere), born in Paris, France (–1843).

24 George Brydges Rodney, English admiral who fought naval battles against the French, Spanish, and Dutch during the American Revolution, dies in London, England (74).

JULY

18 John Paul Jones, American naval commander during the American Revolution, dies in Paris, France (45).

29 René-Nicolas de Maupeou, chancellor of France 1771–74, dies in Thuit, France (78).

AUGUST

4 Percy Bysshe Shelley, English romantic lyric poet, born in Field Place, near Horsham, Sussex, England (–1822).

4 Richard Arkwright, textile industrialist and inventor, dies in Cromford, Derbyshire (60).

5 Frederick North, British prime minister 1770–82, a Tory, dies in London, England (60).

18 John Russell, British prime minister 1846–52 and 1865–66, a Liberal, born in London, England (–1878).

29 Charles Grandison Finney, U.S. lawyer and evangelical revivalist, born in Warren, Connecticut (–1875).

OCTOBER

7 George Mason, American planter and statesman, dies in Fairfax County, Virginia (67).

NOVEMBER

26 Sarah Moore Grimké, U.S. abolitionist and feminist, born in Charleston, South Carolina (–1873).

DECEMBER

1 Nikolay Ivanovich Lobachevsky, Russian mathematician who, with János Bolyai, founded non-Euclidean geometry, born in Nizhny Novgorod, Russia (–1856).

26 Charles Babbage, British inventor who designed the first digital computer, born in Teignmouth, Devon, England (–1871).

- The first circus in the United States, run by J. B. Ricketts, performs in Philadelphia, Pennsylvania.

SEPTEMBER

22 The National Convention in Paris proclaims France a republic, and the revolutionary calendar (although not established until October 5, 1793) comes into force. It comprises 12 months of 30 days, plus 5 days (6 in a leap year); each month has 3 decades of 10 days. The extra days are added at the end of the year.

OCTOBER

12 Columbus Day is celebrated in New York, New York, for the first time.

Media and Communication

- Robert Thomas Bailey publishes the first edition of the *Farmer's Almanac*, a journal of New England agriculture and folkways.

JANUARY

4 In Belfast, Ireland, the first issue of the *Northern Star*, the newspaper of the United Irishmen (a political organization originally set up to promote a Protestant-Catholic union, but which became a separatist force), is published.

Religion

- The Baptist Missionary Society is founded in London, England.

1793

POLITICS, GOVERNMENT, AND ECONOMICS

Business and Economics

MARCH

- Britain and Russia sign a convention to ban all Baltic trade with France.
11 The British prime minister William Pitt the Younger issues Exchequer bills to raise funds for defense and for subsidies to Britain's allies in the prospective war with France.

Colonization

- British forces seize all the French settlements in India.

Human Rights

- French laws forbid women from participating in political activity, and the Revolutionary Convention declares that women, minors, the insane, and criminals cannot be citizens.

MAY

- France's first all-woman revolutionary society is founded, protesting for the right to serve in the military, to wear nontraditional clothing (especially the tricolor cockade), and to be active in politics. Leaders Claire Lacombe and Pauline Léon are both later imprisoned. The society is banned on October 10.

OCTOBER

5 The revolutionary government in France abolishes Christianity.

NOVEMBER

10 The French revolutionaries Jacques René Hébert and Pierre Chaumette organize the atheistic Feast of Reason, celebrated in St. Eustache Church, Paris, France.

Politics and Government

- Russia annexes the Khanate of the Crimea—including the Kuban region of the western Caucasus—following the steady growth of Russian influence in the Khanate after the 1774 Treaty of Kuchuk-Kainardzhi had confirmed its independence from the Ottoman Empire.
- The British governor-general of India, Charles Cornwallis, promulgates a code of justice in India on the British model. He reorganizes finances, and arranges the "permanent settlement" of Bengal.

JANUARY

23 Russia and Prussia agree on a second partition of Poland.

FEBRUARY

1 France declares war on Britain and the Dutch Republic.
12 The U.S. Congress passes a fugitive slave law barring anyone from assisting a runaway slave.

13 The First Coalition against France is formed by Great Britain, Austria, Prussia, the Dutch Republic, Spain, and Sardinia.

MARCH

4 George Washington is inaugurated president of the United States for a second term.

7 France declares war on Spain. Spanish forces invade the French-occupied territories of Roussillon and Navarre on the border between the two countries.

13 French royalists revolt in the Vendée, west France, against the revolutionary government.

15 The Traitorous Correspondence Act is passed in Britain and the Habeas Corpus Act suspended, both to curtail any possible popular support for revolutionary France.

18 French forces under General Charles-François Dumouriez are defeated at Neerwinden in the Netherlands by Austrian forces under Friedrich Josias, Prince of Saxe-Coburg, leading to the Austrian reconquest of the Austrian Netherlands.

26 The Holy Roman Empire declares war on France.

APRIL

5 The French general Charles-François Dumouriez deserts to the Austrians after his defeat at Neerwinden in the Netherlands.

6 The Committee of Public Safety is established in France as the executive organ of the revolutionary government, effectively headed by the Jacobin leader Georges Danton.

22 U.S. president George Washington proclaims U.S. neutrality in the French revolutionary wars, despite the 1778 U.S. alliance with France.

MAY

7 The Second Partition of Poland is effected, with half of Poland's remaining territory being divided between Russia and Prussia. Russia takes Lithuania and west Ukraine; Prussia takes Danzig (Gdańsk), Thorn (Toruń), Posen (Poznań), Gnesen (Gniezno), and Kalisch (Kalisz).

30 The French revolutionary Louis St-Just joins the newly formed Committee of Public Safety.

JUNE

2 The final overthrow of the Girondists by the Jacobins, and the arrest of the Girondist leader, Jacques Brissot, begins the Reign of Terror in France.

24 A revised French constitution is drawn up by a committee of the Committee of Public Safety chaired by Marie-Jean Hérault de Séchelles. It provides for a single-chamber legislature and universal manhood suffrage.

JULY

23 Prussian forces under the Duke of Brunswick recapture Mainz and drive French troops from Germany.

27 Maximilien-Françoise Robespierre, a radical Jacobin, joins the Committee of Public Safety, becoming its effective leader.

AUGUST

23 A "requisition" (levy) of all able-bodied unmarried men between 18 and 25 who are capable of military service is decreed in France.

28 A British force under Admiral Sir Samuel Hood occupies the key French naval base of Toulon, at the invitation of French royalists.

SEPTEMBER

6 A new French offensive under General Jean Houchard is launched in the Austrian Netherlands, where a British army under the Duke of York is defeated at Hondschoote.

OCTOBER

17 The Vendéans (French royalists) are defeated by Republican forces at Cholet, western France.

31 Twenty-one leading Girondists are guillotined on the authority of revolutionary tribunals in the Place de la Concorde, in Paris, France, during the Reign of Terror.

NOVEMBER

6 The French revolutionary leader "Philippe Egalité" (the Duc d'Orléans) is guillotined in Paris, France, during the Reign of Terror, accused of being an accomplice of the Girondist traitor Charles-François Dumouriez.

DECEMBER

12 The Vendéans are defeated by Republican forces at Le Mans, northwest France.

19 Republican troops under Napoleon Bonaparte retake the naval base of Toulon, southeast France, from British and royalist forces. Many of the royalists are executed.

26 French troops under General Louis Hoche defeat an Austrian army under General Dagobert Würmser at Weissenburg, Alsace, forcing the Austrians to retreat across the Rhine.

SCIENCE, TECHNOLOGY, AND MEDICINE

Ecology

• The volcano Miyi-Yama erupts in Java, Indonesia killing over 50,000 people.

APRIL

1 Nearly 53,000 people are killed by an earthquake in Unsen, Japan.

Exploration

• Scottish trader and explorer Alexander Mackenzie successfully crosses North America from Lake Athabasca off Hudson Bay to Queen Charlotte Sound on the Pacific coast.

Health and Medicine

• An epidemic of yellow fever infects almost the entire population of Philadelphia, Pennsylvania; over 4,000 people die.

Science

• French naturalist Jean-Baptiste Lamarck argues that fossils are the remains of extremely ancient, extinct species of animals and plants.

- German botanist Christian Konrad Sprengel outlines an accurate theory of plant fertilization.
- Scottish chemist Daniel Rutherford invents the first maximum–minimum thermometer.

AUGUST

1 The first metric weight system is introduced, in France.

Transportation

- French balloonist Jean-Pierre Blanchard is the first person to successfully jump from a balloon using a parachute.

ARTS AND IDEAS

Architecture

- The Brandenburg Gate (*Brandenburger Tor*) in Berlin, Prussia, designed by the German architect Karl Langhans, is completed. A ceremonial gateway, it is based on classical Greek models.
- The Łazienki Palace near Warsaw, Poland, designed by the Italian architect Dominik Merlini, is completed.

Arts

- The English artist George Stubbs paints *Soldiers of the 10th Light Dragoons*.

- The French artist Jacques-Louis David paints *The Death of Marat*, depicting the assassinated revolutionary leader Jean-Paul Marat dead in his bath.
- The German artist Gottfried Schadow sculpts the *Quadriga* (group of classical figures) for the top of the Brandenburg Gate in Berlin, Prussia.
- The Italian neoclassical sculptor Antonio Canova completes his marble carving *Cupid and Psyche*.
- The Louvre in Paris, France, becomes the national art gallery.
- The Spanish artist Francisco de Goya y Lucientes paints *Burial of the Sardine*.

Literature and Language

- The English romantic poet William Wordsworth publishes *An Evening Walk* and *Descriptive Sketches*.
- The English writer William Blake publishes his major prose work *Marriage of Heaven and Hell*. Illustrated with his own engravings, it is a satire on conventional religion and morality.

Music

- A child prodigy, the Italian virtuoso violinist Niccolò Paganini makes his debut in Genoa, Italy, at the age of 11.
- Austrian composer Franz Joseph Haydn completes his *Variations in F minor* for keyboard, and his String Quartets Nos. 69 to 71 (Opus 71) and Nos. 72 to 74 (Opus 74).

BIRTHS & DEATHS

- Elizabeth Lucas Pinckney, U.S. science educator and plantation manager, dies outside Charleston, South Carolina. She was noted for her successful cultivation of indigo.
- Francesco Guardi, Italian rococo landscape painter, dies in Venice, Italy (*c.* 81).

JANUARY

3 Lucretia Coffin Mott, U.S. Quaker, abolitionist, and women's rights advocate, born in Nantucket, Massachusetts (–1880).

21 Louis XVI, King of France 1774–92, now known as "Citizen Capet," is guillotined in Paris, France (38).

FEBRUARY

6 Carlo Goldoni, Italian dramatist who founded Italian realistic comedy, dies in Paris, France (85).

MARCH

2 Samuel Houston, politician and commander in chief in the Texas revolution, born in Rockbridge County, Virginia (–1863).

20 William Murray, Earl of Mansfield, Chief Justice of Great Britain

1756–88 who contributed to the development of commercial law, dies in London, England (88).

28 Henry Rowe Schoolcraft, U.S. ethnologist and explorer who discovered the source of the Mississippi, born in Alan County, New York (–1864).

APRIL

15 Friedrich Georg Wilhelm von Struve, German-born Russian astronomer who pioneered the study of binary stars, born in Altona, Germany (–1864).

JULY

3 John Clare, English romantic poet, born in Helpston, near Peterborough, England (–1864).

13 Jean-Paul Marat, physician and a supporter of the Jacobins, is assassinated in his bath by the Girondist Charlotte Corday (50).

15 Almira Hart Lincoln Phelps, U.S. science educator, born in Berlin, Connecticut.

OCTOBER

8 John Hancock, U.S. politician, first signatory of the U.S. Declaration of

Independence, dies in Quincy, Massachusetts (56).

16 John Hunter, English surgeon, the founder of pathological anatomy in England, dies in London, England (65).

16 Marie-Antoinette (Maria Antonia Josepha Joanna von Österreich-Lothringen), Queen Consort of King Louis XVI of France, 11th daughter of Holy Roman Emperor Francis I and Maria Theresa, is guillotined on the orders of the Committee of Public Safety in Paris, France (37).

NOVEMBER

1 Lord George Gordon, English lord who in 1780 instigated the Gordon riots against the Catholic Relief Act, dies in Newgate prison, London, England (41).

15 Jean Marie Roland, French scientist, a leader of the Girondist faction during the French Revolution, commits suicide in Bourg-Beaudoin, France (59).

Theater and Dance

- The Chestnut Street Theater in Philadelphia, Pennsylvania, opens. In 1813 it becomes the first U.S. theater to be lit by gas. It closes in 1913.

Thought and Scholarship

- Prussian political journalist Friedrich Gentz publishes his German translation of British politician Edmund Burke's *Reflections on the Revolution in France*, the first act in a sustained campaign to influence Prussian public opinion against the French Revolution.
- The English political philosopher William Godwin publishes *An Enquiry Concerning Political Justice*.
- The English scholar Richard Porson is appointed Professor of Greek at Cambridge, England, and, with Thomas Gaisford, leads a revival of classical scholarship.
- The French mathematician and philosopher Jean-Marie-Antoine-Nicolas Caritat, marquis de Condorcet, publishes *Esquisse d'un tableau historique des progrès de l'esprit humain/Sketch for an Historical Picture of the Progress of the Human Mind*. He traces the history of human development through several stages, with the French Revolution leading to the final, perfect stage.
- The French revolutionary Jean-Baptiste ("Anacharsis") Cloots (or Clootz) publishes *Base constitutionelle de la république du genre humain/A Basic Constitution of the Republic of Mankind*.
- The German philosopher Immanuel Kant publishes *Die Religion innerhalb der Grenzen des blossen Vernunft/Religion within the Boundaries of Reason*, in which he argues that although belief in God cannot be established by reason, it is acceptably based on "practical reason."

SOCIETY

Education

- Compulsory public education from the age of six is introduced in France.
- Johann Friedrich Guts Muth's *Gymnastik für die Jugend/Gymnastics for the Young*, a pioneering work on physical education, is published.
- Williams College is founded at Williamstown, Massachusetts.

Everyday Life

- Cotton thread is perfected and patented—the first patent to go to a woman—by Hannah Wilkinson Slater. Her husband, the industrial entrepreneur Samual Slater, founds the first U.S. cotton mill.

JUNE
10 The world's first public zoo opens in Paris, France.

Media and Communication

- *The American Minerva*, the first daily newspaper in New York, New York, and the second daily paper in the United States, is founded by Noah Webster.
- French inventor Claude Chappe originates semaphore and builds a long-distance signaling system in France.

Religion

- The tract *A Plea for the Poor* by the U.S. preacher John Woolman is published posthumously. It was written in 1763.
- The French revolutionary leader Jacques-René Hébert edits *Le Père Duchesne*, a journal defending the more militant form of revolution and advocating atheism.

Sports

- The government in Lexington, Kentucky, bans horse racing on the city's public streets.

1794

POLITICS, GOVERNMENT, AND ECONOMICS

Business and Economics

DECEMBER

24 A new issue of *assignats* (paper money) further depreciates the French currency.

Politics and Government

- Aga Muhammad Khan becomes ruler of Persia, founding the Qajar dynasty.
- British naval expeditions capture the French islands of the Seychelles in the Indian Ocean and Martinique, St. Lucia, and Guadeloupe in the West Indies, but Guadeloupe is later recaptured by the French.
- In U.S. Congressional elections, Federalists recover majorities in both the House (54–52) and Senate (19–13).

FEBRUARY

4 Slavery is abolished in the French colonies by the revolutionary government.

MARCH

4 The French leader of the *sans-culottes* (Paris mob), Jacques Hébert, unsuccessfully calls for a popular uprising among his followers (the Cordeliers Club, or Hébertists) as part of his political struggle against the Jacobin Georges Danton.

4 The U.S. Congress submits the Eleventh Amendment to the Constitution to the states. It denies federal courts jurisdiction in suits filed against a state by citizens of another state or another nation.

22 The U.S. Congress forbids citizens to trade slaves with foreign nations.

APRIL

3 The Polish nationalist general Tadeusz Kościuszko, leading an insurrection against Russian and Prussian domination of Poland, defeats a Russian force at Racławice.

5 The French Jacobin leaders Georges Danton and Camille Desmoulins are executed during the Reign of Terror, following a show trial organized by Maximilien Robespierre, the leader of the Committee of Public Safety.

19 Britain and Prussia sign the Treaty of The Hague, under which Britain agrees to pay subsidies for 60,000 Prussian and Dutch troops in the coalition against revolutionary France.

MAY

18 General Charles Pichegru leads French forces to victory at Tourcoing, northeast France, against an Austrian and British army commanded by Friedrich Josias, Prince of Saxe-Coburg.

JUNE

- A French army invades the Spanish frontier regions of Catalonia and Guipúzcoa.
1 The British admiral Richard, Lord Howe, defeats a French fleet in the English Channel in a battle subsequently known in Britain as "The Glorious First of June."
10 A "Law of 22 Prairial" (revolutionary calendar) increases the power of the revolutionary tribunals in France, leading to mass executions.
25 French troops under General Charles Pichegru capture Charleroi in the Austrian Netherlands from Allied forces under Friedrich Josias, Prince of Saxe-Coburg.
26 A French army under General Jean-Baptiste Jourdan defeats Austrian forces at Fleurus in the Austrian Netherlands. The Austrian commander Freidrich Josias evacuates the Austrian Netherlands.

JULY

July–November In the Whiskey Rebellion, farmers in western Pennsylvania flout the liquor tax passed by Congress in 1791. President George Washington summons the militia to quash the uprising, but by November the uprising evaporates of its own accord.

11 Following the split of the Whigs on the issue of British parliamentary reform, Lord Portland and William Wyndham enter William Pitt the Younger's cabinet, while Charles James Fox and Charles Grey lead a Whig rump of 40 politicians.

28 In France, a conspiracy by Montagnard moderates and Dantonists against the leader of the Committee of Public Safety, Maximilien Robespierre, succeeds in abolishing the Commune de Paris (municipal government). Robespierre and Louis St-Just are executed.

AUGUST

20 At the Battle of Fallen Timbers on the Ohio frontier, General Anthony Wayne shatters an army of recalcitrant Native Americans, thereby clearing the way for settlement of the Old Northwest.

26–September 6 Russian forces unsuccessfully lay siege to Warsaw, Poland, held by nationalists fighting for Polish independence.

OCTOBER

- A French army under General Jean Moreau advances as far as the River Rhine.

25 Prussia withdraws from the war against the French Republic.

NOVEMBER

9 Russian forces enter Warsaw, Poland, after six months of fighting between allied Russian and Prussian forces and nationalist Poles under Tadeusz Kościuszko.

11 The Jacobins close their club in Paris, following attacks by the antirevolutionary *"jeunesse dorée"* ("golden youth") activists.

19 The United States and Britain sign John Jay's Treaty, by which Britain agrees to relinquish its remaining authority in the Old Northwest.

DECEMBER

• Prussia and Spain open separate negotiations for peace with France.

8 The surviving Girondists are readmitted to the French National Convention.

27 A French army under General Charles Pichegru invades the Dutch Republic.

SCIENCE, TECHNOLOGY, AND MEDICINE

Ecology

• About 40,000 people are killed by an eruption of the Tunquraohua volcano in the Spanish American province of New Granada (modern Ecuador).

Math

• French mathematician Adrien Marie Legendre publishes *Eléments de géométrie*, an influential account of geometry.

Science

• English naturalist and physician Erasmus Darwin publishes *Zoonomia, or the Laws of Organic Life*, expressing his ideas on evolution (which he assumes has an environmental cause).

• Finnish chemist Johan Gadolin discovers the rare earth element yttrium (atomic no. 39)—it is used much later in color televisions.

The Industrial Revolution (1794–1873)

1794

• U.S. inventor Eli Whitney patents the cotton gin, which separates the cotton seeds from the fiber, facilitating the production of short staple cotton, which can be grown throughout the southeastern United States.

c. **1800**

• Belgian entrepreneur Lieven Bauwens smuggles the mule jenny into the Batavian Republic, spreading the Industrial Revolution in the textile industry from Britain to the rest of Europe.

1805

• French inventor Joseph-Marie Jacquard develops a loom that uses punched cards to control the weaving of cloth. Able to produce any desired pattern automatically, it stimulates the technological revolution in the textile industry and forms the basis of the automatic loom. Punched cards are also used in early computers.

1810

• Donkin & Hall establish the world's first cannery in London, England, using tin cans to package food for British naval and military forces.

1811

March 3 "Luddites" (British craftsmen and others whose livelihoods are threatened by new technology) destroy machinery in Nottingham and Yorkshire towns, England.

1812

• English inventor John Blenkinsop develops a "steam boiler on wheels;" the first practical locomotive, it employs a tooth-rack rail system and a two-cylinder engine, and hauls coal from Middleton to Leeds in Yorkshire, England.

1813

• British engineer Bryan Donkin develops a rotary printing press. This is an improvement over the flatbed press, as it allows faster printing, and spurs the development of newspapers.

• English engineer Richard Trevithick invents a rotary, steam-driven drill that improves the ability to mine hard rock.

• English inventor William Horrocks develops the power loom.

1814

• U.S. businessmen Francis Cabot Lowell and Patrick Tracey Jackson build the first textile mill to take raw cotton and convert it into finished cloth.

July 25 English engineer George Stephenson constructs the first effective steam locomotive. Called the "Bulcher," it hauls up to 30 metric tons of coal at 6.4 kph/4 mph out of mines at Killingorth Collier, Newcastle upon Tyne, England.

1833

• Philadelphia glass-producer Thomas W. Dyott introduces the paternalist concept of the factory town. Dyott's workers live in company housing and according to rules and customs governing virtually every aspect of their lives.

- German physicist Ernst Florens Friedrich Chladni suggests that meteorites have an extraterrestrial origin.

Technology

- English engineer Robert Street patents the first practical internal-combustion engine.
- English entrepreneur Josiah Spode the Elder starts to manufacture bone china in Stoke-on-Trent, Staffordshire, England.
- German inventor K. H. Klingert develops a helmeted diving suit supplied with pumped air from the surface.
- U.S. inventor Eli Whitney patents the cotton gin, which separates the cotton seeds from the fiber, facilitating the production of short staple cotton, which can be grown throughout the southeastern United States. Over the next decade, U.S. cotton production will soar.

Transportation

- The Lancaster road, the first publicly financed turnpike in the United States, opens in Pennsylvania.
- Welsh inventor Philip Vaughn invents ballbearings for use in carriage wheels.

JUNE

2 A French ordinance officer is the first to use aerial surveillance when he rises over the battlefield in a balloon, at the Battle of Maubeuge during the French Revolutionary Wars.

ARTS AND IDEAS

Literature and Language

- The English philosopher and novelist William Godwin publishes *The Adventures of Caleb Williams*, or *Things as They Are*, a novel expressing his criticisms of society.
- The English poet and artist William Blake publishes *Songs of Innocence and Experience: Shewing the Two Contrary States of the Human Soul. Songs of Innocence* had previously appeared in 1789.
- The English writer Anne Radcliffe publishes *The Mysteries of Udolpho*, a best-selling Gothic romance.
- The French poet André de Chénier writes his most famous ode, *La Jeune Captive/The Young Prisoner*, while in prison awaiting execution.
- The French writer and soldier Xavier de Maistre publishes *Voyage autour de ma chambre/A Journey around My Room*, written in prison.

Music

- Austrian composer Franz Joseph Haydn completes his Symphony No. 100, the *Military*, and No. 101, the *Clock*.
- The opera *Tammanny, or The Indian Chief*, by the English-born composer James Hewitt, is first performed,

---

1839

- British engineer James Nasmyth designs the steam hammer, an important tool for forging heavy machinery in the Industrial Revolution. He patents it on November 24, 1842.

1846

September 10 U.S. inventor Elias Howe patents a practical sewing machine; it revolutionizes garment manufacture in both the factory and home.

1851

- U.S. industrialist William Kelly develops a method of removing impurities from pig iron by injecting air into the molten mass. The oxygen in the air blast reacts with impurities to form oxides which can be separated from the slag. A key invention in the industrial revolution, it results in the production of large quantities of cheap steel.

May 1–September 18 The Great Exhibition is held in Hyde Park, London, England. Devised by Prince Albert, it is the first exhibition to display the latest technical innovations in industry, from both Britain and Europe. It features the Crystal Palace, a large iron and glass structure, designed by English architect Joseph Paxton.

1854

- French scientist Henri-Etienne St. Claire Deville develops a new process for making aluminum. Through the action of metallic sodium on aluminum chloride he produces marble-sized lumps of the metal and at the Paris Exposition in 1855 he exhibits a 7-kg/15-lb ingot. His process becomes the foundation of the aluminum industry.

- U.S. inventor Daniel Halladay develops the wind pump, an automatic windmill with a governor that keeps the milling speed constant.

1855

- U.S. chemist Benjamin Silliman publishes the *Silliman Report* in which he describes the distillation of crude oil into its various fractions (tar, naphthalene, gasoline, and solvents) and their uses in lubrication, lighting, and other purposes. His emphasis on crude oil's economic potential serves as an impetus for oil exploration and drilling.

1861

- Belgian chemist Ernest Solvay patents a method for the economic production of sodium carbonate (washing soda) from sodium chloride, ammonia, and carbon dioxide. Used to make paper, glass, and bleach, and to treat water and refine petroleum, it is a key development in the Industrial Revolution. The first production plant is established in 1863.

1868

- Chicago industrialist George M. Pullman incorporates the Pullman Palace Car Company.

1872

- Former Pennsylvania Railroad superintendent Andrew Carnegie concentrates his investment activities in steel manufacturing, laying plans for the J. Edgar Thomson Steel Works south of Pittsburgh, Pennsylvania.

1873

- The first electrically powered industrial machines begin operating in Austria; other countries quickly follow suit.

in New York, New York. This is considered the first U.S. opera.

Theater and Dance

- The English writers Samuel Taylor Coleridge and Robert Southey write the verse drama *The Fall of Robespierre*.
- The tragedy *Fatal Deception* (later known as *Leicester*) by the U.S. dramatist William Dunlap is first performed, in New York, New York.

JUNE
30 The play *Slaves of Algiers*, by the U.S. educator, dramatist, and novelist Susanna Haswell Rowson, opens in Philadelphia, Pennsylvania.

Thought and Scholarship

- The English writer and feminist Mary Wollstonecraft publishes *A Historical and Moral View of the French Revolution*.

SOCIETY

Education

- Bowdoin College is founded at Brunswick, Maine.
- Stonyhurst College, originally founded in St.-Omer, France, in 1593 as a school for English Catholics, settles in England.

- The *Ecole Polytechnique* is founded in Paris, France, to train engineers for the army and state service.
- The first *école normale* (teachers' training college) opens in France.
- The University of Tennessee is founded at Knoxville.

Everyday Life

- Powdering of men's hair goes out of fashion, after over 100 years of popularity in Europe.
- The Federal Society of Journeymen Cordwainers, one of the first U.S. labor unions, is organized in Philadelphia, Pennsylvania.
- The tricolor is adopted as the national flag of France.

Religion

- Ex-slave Richard Allen founds a black Methodist church in Philadelphia, Pennsylvania.
- The British-born U.S. revolutionary Thomas Paine publishes the first volume of his work *The Age of Reason*. An outspoken attack on traditional religious belief and practices, it is widely condemned as immoral. The last volume appears in 1796.
- The English theologian William Paley publishes *A View of the Evidences of Christianity*, a defense of Christian belief which will achieve great popularity.

JUNE
8 The revolutionary leader Maximilien Robespierre presides over the Feast of the Supreme Being in Paris, France.

BIRTHS & DEATHS

JANUARY
6 Rebecca Pennock Lukens, U.S. industrial executive, born in Coatesville, Pennsylvania (–1854).
16 Edward Gibbon, English historian, author of *The Decline and Fall of the Roman Empire*, dies in London, England (57).

MARCH
24 Jacques René Hébert ("Père Duchesne"), French political journalist and leader of the Parisian workers during the French Revolution, is guillotined in Paris, France (36).

APRIL
5 Camille Desmoulins, influential French journalist and pamphleteer during the French Revolution, dies in Paris, France (34).
5 Georges-Jacques Danton, leader in the French Revolution instrumental in overthrowing the monarchy and establishing France's First Republic, is guillotined in Paris, France (35).

8 Jean-Marie-Antoine-Nicolas Caritat, marquis de Condorcet, philosopher of the Enlightenment, dies in Bourg-la-Reine, France (50).
10 Matthew Perry, U.S. naval officer, born in South Kingston, Rhode Island (–1858).

MAY
8 Antoine-Laurent Lavoisier, French scientist, the founder of modern chemistry, is guillotined by the revolutionary authorities in Paris, France (50).
24 William Whewell, English philosopher of science, born in Lancaster, England (–1866).
27 Cornelius Vanderbilt, U.S. shipping and railroad magnate, born in Port Richmond, Staten Island, New York (–1877).
30 Zilpah P. Grant Banister, U.S. educator, born in Norfolk, Connecticut.

JUNE
19 Richard Henry Lee, U.S. statesman and orator, and signatory of the Declaration of Independence, dies in Chantilly, Virginia (62).
27 Wenzel Anton von Kaunitz, chancellor of Austria 1753–92, dies in Vienna, Austria (83).

JULY
28 Maximilien François Robespierre, French Jacobin leader during the French Revolution, is guillotined in Paris, France (36).

AUGUST
30 Stephen Watts Kearny, U.S. Army officer who seized New Mexico for the United States and helped retake California during the Mexican War (1846–48), born in Newark, New Jersey (–1848).

NOVEMBER
28 Baron Friedrich von Steuben, Prussian major general in the American Revolution, dies in Remsen, New York (64).

1795

POLITICS, GOVERNMENT, AND ECONOMICS

Colonization

FEBRUARY

• The Dutch Republic surrenders Ceylon (modern Sri Lanka) to Britain following the French conquest of the Republic itself.

SEPTEMBER

• A British force under Major General James Craig captures the Dutch colony of the Cape of Good Hope, southern Africa, for Prince William V of Orange, a refugee in England following the French invasion of the United Netherlands.

Human Rights

FEBRUARY

21   The National Convention formally separates church and state in France, allowing public worship in private homes.

Politics and Government

• The Speenhamland Act is passed to provide economic relief for the poor in Britain.

JANUARY

3   Russia and Austria sign a secret treaty for a third partition of the remaining Polish territory.

19   The French army under Charles Pichegru occupies Amsterdam, in the Dutch Republic. He captures the Dutch fleet at Texel, and his troops quickly overrun the rest of the United Netherlands.

29   In the Naturalization Act, the U.S. Congress makes five years' residency and the disavowal of foreign allegiances and hereditary titles requisites of citizenship.

FEBRUARY

9   The Italian Grand Duchy of Tuscany makes peace with France.

15   The Vendéans (French royalist rebels) sign the Peace of La Jaunaie, accepting the authority of the French republican government.

APRIL

1   On "Germinal 12" of the revolutionary calendar, a mob invades the National Convention in Paris, France,

demanding bread. Reactionary agitation against the Convention spreads throughout France.

5   France and Prussia sign the Peace of Basel, under which France retains its conquests on the left bank of the Rhine pending the conclusion of a peace with the Holy Roman Empire, while Prussia receives territories on the right bank. Saxony, Hanover, the Bavarian Palatinate, and Hesse-Cassel also agree terms with France.

MAY

16   The Dutch Republic is reorganized under French control as the Batavian Republic, and signs an offensive and defensive alliance with France.

20   On "Prairial 1" of the revolutionary calendar, popular unrest again threatens the National Convention in Paris, France, leading to the "White Terror" purge of extreme revolutionaries and the end of Montagnard influence in the Convention.

JUNE

• French naval forces recapture the island of St. Lucia, in the West Indies, from Britain.

25   The Imperial duchy of Luxembourg capitulates to France.

27   A British naval expedition lands a force of exiled French nobles at Quiberon in Brittany, western France, to support royalist unrest in the area, but they are decisively defeated by Republican forces commanded by General Lazare Hoche.

JULY

27   Spain signs a peace treaty with France, ceding the western part of the Caribbean island of San Domingo (now Haiti) to France.

AUGUST

22   A third French constitution is approved by the National Convention, vesting executive power in five directors (the Directory).

23   Prussia joins the secret Austro-Russian agreement of March 1, 1795 to partition the remaining Polish territory.

SEPTEMBER

• Austrian forces under the Archduke Charles reconquer the right bank of the Rhine from French forces under General Jean-Baptiste Jourdan.

6   The French republican army under General Jourdan recrosses the River Rhine, renewing its campaign against the Austrian army of the Archduke Charles.

20   A French army under General Charles Pichegru occupies Mannheim, Germany.

OCTOBER

1   The Austrian Netherlands is formally annexed by France.

5   French republican general Napoleon Bonaparte disperses royalist rebels marching against the National

Convention in Paris with a "whiff of grapeshot," making him a national figure.

24 Prussia, Austria, and Russia occupy the remaining Polish territory in the so-called "Third Partition;" Prussia takes Warsaw and lands between the Bug and the Niemen rivers, Austria takes Kraków and Galicia, and Russia the area between Galicia and the River Dvina.

27 Thomas Pinckney, the U.S. minister to Britain, negotiates the Treaty of San Lorenzo between the United States and Spain. It settles the southern U.S. boundary with Florida and grants the United States the right to navigate the Mississippi River through Spanish territory.

NOVEMBER

• Following an attack on King George III, the British prime minister William Pitt the Younger introduces the Treasonable Practices and Seditious Meetings bills, forbidding meetings of more than 50 persons without advance notice to a magistrate.

4 The Directory (a ruling executive of five directors) is formally established in France.

24 The French general Barthélemy Schérer defeats an Austrian army at Loano, Piedmont, in northern Italy.

25 Stanislas II Poniatowski abdicates as king of Poland following the Third Partition of his country between Prussia, Russia, and Austria.

SCIENCE, TECHNOLOGY, AND MEDICINE

Exploration

JUNE

21 The Scottish explorer Mungo Park begins to trace the course of the River Niger, west Africa.

Health and Medicine

• Scurvy is greatly reduced among British sailors by supplying them with lemons.

Technology

• English inventor Joseph Bramah invents a hydraulic press capable of exerting a force of several thousand metric tons.

• French chemist Nicolas Conté devises a new method of making pencil leads; ground graphite is mixed with clay into thin rods which are then fired.

ARTS AND IDEAS

Arts

c. 1795 The Japanese artist Kitagawa Utamaro publishes his series of woodblock prints *The Twelve Hours of the Green Houses*, which includes *The Courtesan Kisegawa of the Pine Needle House*.

• The Japanese artist Toshusai Sharaku publishes his woodblock print *The Actor Nakamura Konozo as Boatman Kanagawaya no Gon*. Toshusai Sharaku is the leading figure in the depiction of actors in the Kabuki theater, a popular genre of Japanese print.

• The U.S. artist Charles Willson Peale paints *Staircase Group*.

Literature and Language

• The English poet Walter Savage Landor publishes his *Poems*.

• The German scholar Friedrich August Wolf publishes *Prolegomena to Homer*, in which he argues that the *Iliad* and *Odyssey* were not written by Homer but were put together gradually from a range of traditional ballads.

• The German writer and polymath Johann Wolfgang von Goethe publishes his poetry collection *Römische Elegien/Roman Elegies*.

• The German writer Friedrich von Schlegel publishes his essay "Über das Studium der griechischen Poesie"/"On the Study of Greek Poetry."

• The German writer Jean Paul publishes his novel *Hesperus*.

• The German writer Johann Heinrich Voss publishes one of his finest poetic works, the idyll "Luise."

June 1795–96 The German writer and polymath Johann Wolfgang von Goethe publishes *Wilhelm Meister's Lehrjahre/Wilhelm Meister's Apprenticeship*, a novel charting a young man's journey to emotional and intellectual maturity.

Music

• Austrian composer Franz Joseph Haydn completes his Symphonies No. 103, the *Paukenwirbel/Drum Roll*, and No. 104, the *London*.

• German composer Ludwig van Beethoven completes his Piano Concerto No. 2 in B (Opus 19) and publishes his Piano Sonatas Nos. 1, 2, and 3 (Opus 2).

JULY

14 In France, "La Marseillaise," originally written as a royalist rallying song, is adopted as the national anthem.

Theater and Dance

• The English dramatist and actor Charles Dibdin publishes his *History of the English Stage*.

Thought and Scholarship

• The French scholar Charles-François Dupuis publishes *Origine de tous les cultes/The Origins of Religion*, which arouses an interest in Upper Egypt.

• The German philosopher Immanuel Kant publishes *Zum ewigen Frieden/On Perpetual Peace*.

SOCIETY

Education

- Educator Joseph Lakanal sets out his plans for *écoles centrales* (secondary schools) in France.
- The German writer Friedrich Johann Christoph von Schiller publishes his *Über die ästhetische Erziehung des Menschen in einer Reihe von Briefen/Letters Concerning the Aesthetic Education of Mankind*.
- The Institut de France is founded in Paris to replace the abolished royal academies. It is grouped in three "classes": mathematical and physical sciences, moral and political sciences, and literature and fine art.
- Union College is founded in Schenectady, New York.

Everyday Life

- European women's fashion allows for more freedom and greater comfort in attempts to emulate a Roman style.
- French chef Nicolas Appert begins experiments on preserving food in hermetically sealed containers.

Religion

- Maynooth College, a Roman Catholic seminary, is founded by an act of the Irish parliament to prevent priests from traveling for instruction to the European mainland, where they might come under the influence of revolutionary ideas.

BIRTHS & DEATHS

c. 1795   Dred Scott, subject of the celebrated U.S. Supreme Court slavery case *Scott v. Sandford* (which took place in 1857 and ruled that persons born as slaves remained in servitude even on free soil), born a slave in Southampton County, Virginia (–1858).

c. 1795   Wiremu Kingi (also known as William King or Te Rangitake), Maori chief who led the resistance to European colonization of New Zealand's North Island, born in Manukorihi, New Zealand (–1882).

JANUARY
3   Josiah Wedgwood, English pottery designer and manufacturer, dies in Etruria, Staffordshire, England (65).

FEBRUARY
27   Francis Marion, American military leader, dies in Berkeley County, South Carolina (63).

MAY
10   Augustin Thierry, French historian, born in Blois, France (–1856).
19   James Boswell, Scottish diarist, friend and biographer of Samuel Johnson, dies in London, England (56).

OCTOBER
1   Margaretta Angelica Peale, U.S. still-life painter, born in Philadelphia, Pennsylvania.

31   John Keats, English romantic lyric poet, born in London, England (–1821).

NOVEMBER
2   James K. Polk, eleventh president of the United States 1845–49, a Democrat, born in Mecklenburg County, North Carolina (–1849).

DECEMBER
4   Thomas Carlyle, Scottish historian and essayist, born in Ecclefechan, Dumfrieshire, Scotland (–1881).
20   Leopold von Ranke, German historian, born in Wiehe, Saxony, Germany (–1886).

1796

POLITICS, GOVERNMENT, AND ECONOMICS

Politics and Government

- Aga Muhammad, the shah of Persia, seizes the rebel region of Khorasan, in Khuzistan, finally ending the influence of the descendents of Nadir Shah in Persian politics.
- British forces capture the Dutch, Spanish, and French possessions of Demerara, Essequibo, Berbice, St. Lucia, and Grenada in the West Indies, but abandon Corsica to the French.
- In U.S. Congressional elections, Federalists retain majorities in the House (58–48) and Senate (20–12).

FEBRUARY
14 A British fleet under admirals John Jervis and Horatio Nelson defeat a Spanish fleet off Cape St. Vincent, Portugal.

MARCH
- The British prime minister William Pitt the Younger begins negotiations for peace with France.
5 Royalist uprisings in the Vendée and Brittany, western France, are finally put down by Republican forces.
9 The French general Napoleon Bonaparte marries Joséphine de Beauharnais, widow of the Vicomte de Beauharnais.

APRIL
13 General Napoleon Bonaparte assumes command of the French campaign against the Austrians in Italy, and defeats an Austrian force at Millesimo.
22 Napoleon Bonaparte defeats the Piedmontese at Mondovi, Italy.
28 The military success of the French campaign under Napoleon Bonaparte in Italy forces the kingdom of Sardinia to abandon its Austrian alliance.

MAY
10 Napoleon Bonaparte's French army defeats the Austrians at Lodi, Italy.
10 The radical French pamphleteer François-Noël Babeuf, organizer of the insurrectionist "Committee of Equals," fails in his move to restore the French constitution of 1793.
15 The French army commanded by Napoleon Bonaparte enters Milan, Italy.
15 The Italian kingdom of Sardinia signs the Peace of Cherasco with France, ceding Savoy and Nice to France.

16 The northern Italian region of Lombardy is declared a republic, under French rule.

JUNE
- The French army of General Jean-Baptiste Jourdan invades Franconia, Germany, but is driven back by Austrian forces.
1 Tennessee ratifies the U.S. constitution and becomes the 16th state in the Union.
23–27 General Victor Moreau's French army crosses the River Rhine at Strasbourg, aiming to link up with the army of General Jourdan in Franconia and advance on Austria.

JULY
- Britain captures the Italian island of Elba.

AUGUST
15 Napoleon Bonaparte's French army defeats Austrian forces under Count Dagobert Würmser at Castiglione delle Stiviere, Italy, halting the Austrian attempt to relieve Mantua from a French siege.
19 An alliance is signed at San Ildefonso, Spain, between France and Spain against Britain. It is virtually a renewal of the 1761 Family Compact between the Bourbon rulers of the two countries.
29 General Jourdan's French army in Germany is defeated by an Austrian army under the Archduke Charles at Amberg.

SEPTEMBER
3 Archduke Charles's Austrian army defeats General Jourdan's French forces at Würzburg, Germany. Jourdan resigns his command.
19 The U.S. president George Washington, having refused to accept nomination for a third term in office, delivers his farewell address.

OCTOBER
5 Spain declares war on Britain.
16 Napoleon Bonaparte creates the French-dominated Cispadane Republic in Italy by merging the Papal territories of Bologna and Ferrara and the duchy of Modena (including Reggio nell'Emilia).

NOVEMBER
- Britain's Royal Navy withdraws from the Mediterranean following Spain's declaration of war.
15 The French army of Napoleon Bonaparte defeats an Austrian army under General Joseph Alvintzi at Arcole, Italy.
17 Paul I becomes emperor of Russia on the death of his mother, Catherine II the Great.

DECEMBER
- A French military expedition under Lazare Hoche to Bantry Bay, Ireland, fails because of adverse weather conditions.
7 John Adams defeats Thomas Jefferson in the U.S. presidential election by three electoral votes to become

the second president of the United States. Jefferson is elected vice president.
19 The French Directory (five-man ruling executive) refuses further negotiations with Britain.

SCIENCE, TECHNOLOGY, AND MEDICINE

Exploration

- Scottish explorer Mungo Park explores 450 km/280 mi of the Niger River. He publishes his account, *Travels in the Interior of Africa*, in 1799.

Health and Medicine

- English physician Edward Jenner performs the first vaccination against smallpox.

Science

- French anatomist Georges Cuvier identifies bones found near the River Meuse as belonging to a giant prehistoric animal, the mosasaur.
- French astronomer Pierre-Simon Laplace, in *Exposition du système du monde/Account of the System of the World*, enunciates the "nebular hypothesis," that the solar system formed from a cloud of gas; it forms the basis of modern theory.
- German chemist Johann Tobias distills pure ethyl alcohol.

Technology

- French balloonist Joseph Montgolfier invents the hydraulic ram to raise water using the power of waterfalls.
- Philadelphia, Pennsylvania, begins to experiment with gas illumination.
- Spanish inventor Francisco Salva links Madrid to Arunjez, Spain (50 km/44 mi), with an electric telegraph. Signals are generated by electrostatic machines and detected by people holding the ends of the wires.

ARTS AND IDEAS

Architecture

- The Harrison Gray Otis House in Boston, Massachusetts, designed by the U.S. architect Charles Bulfinch—the United States's first native-born professional architect—is completed.

Arts

- The U.S. artist Gilbert Stuart paints *George Washington (The Lansdowne Portrait)*.

Literature and Language

- The English writer Fanny Burney publishes her novel *Camilla: or, A Picture of Youth*.

BIRTHS & DEATHS

c. 1796   James "Jim" Bowie, U.S. frontiersman and folk hero, colonel in the Texan forces during the Mexican War, born in Logan County, Kentucky (–1836).

FEBRUARY
17 James Macpherson, Scottish poet, dies in Belville, Inverness, Scotland (59).
22 Adolphe Quetelet, Belgian mathematician who was one of the first to apply statistics to social phenomena, born in Ghent, Belgium (–1874).

MARCH
11 Francis Wayland, U.S. Baptist cleric, educator, and moral philosopher, born in New York, New York (–1865).

MAY
4 William Hickling Prescott, U.S. historian, born in Salem, Massachusetts (–1859).

8 François Mignet, French historian and archivist, born in Aix-en-Provence, France (–1884).

JUNE
1 Sadi Carnot, French scientist who provided the theoretical basis of steam engines known as the Carnot cycle, born in Paris, France (–1832).
25 Czar Nicholas I, Russian emperor 1825–55, born in Tsarskoye Selo, near St. Petersburg, Russia (–1855).

JULY
26 George Catlin, U.S. artist whose paintings depict scenes of Native Americans, born in Wilkes-Barre, Pennsylvania (–1872).
26 Jean Baptiste Camille Corot, French landscape painter, born in Paris, France (–1875).
31 Robert Burns, national poet of Scotland, dies in Dumfries, Scotland (37).

AUGUST
27 Sophia Smith, U.S. philanthropist and founder of Smith College, born in Hatfield, Massachusetts (–1870).

OCTOBER
7 Thomas Reid, Scottish philosopher who advocated a "philosophy of common sense," dies in Glasgow, Scotland (86).

NOVEMBER
17 Catherine II the Great, German-born empress of Russia 1762–96 who brought Russia into the political and cultural life of Europe, dies in Tsarskoye Selo, near St. Petersburg, Russia (67).

- The English writer Matthew "Monk" Lewis publishes his Gothic horror novel *The Monk*.
- The German writer Jean Paul publishes his novel *Leben des Quintus Fixlein/The Life of Quintus Fixlein*.
- The U.S. writer Joel Barlow publishes his best-known poem, "Hasty Pudding," a mock epic.

Music

- Austrian composer Franz Joseph Haydn completes his Mass No. 7, the *Paukenmesse/Kettle Drum Mass*, and Mass No. 8 in B flat, the *Missa Sancti Bernardi*, or *Heiligmesse/Holy Mass*.
- German composer Ludwig van Beethoven completes his Cello Sonatas 1, 2, and 3 (Opus 5).

Thought and Scholarship

- The British statesman Edmund Burke publishes his *Letters on a Regicide Peace*, in which he argues that free speech may have to be limited. He also publishes "A Letter to a Noble Lord," attacking the Duke of Bedford, who had criticized him for accepting a pension.
- The French royalist diplomat Joseph de Maistre publishes *Considérations sur la France/Thoughts on France*. A fervent opponent of the French Revolution, de Maistre is the most eloquent critic of 18th-century rationalism.
- The German philosopher Johann Gottlieb Fichte publishes *Grundlage des Naturrechts nach Principien der Wissenschafts/The Science of Rights*.

December 1796–1811   The German publisher Friedrich Arnold Brockhaus publishes *Konversations-Lexicon/Conversational Vocabulary*, the first German encyclopedia. The first edition is edited by R. G. Löbel, subsequent editions by Brockhaus.

SOCIETY

Everyday Life

- *American Cookery* by Amelia Simmons is one of the earliest cookbooks to focus on U.S. ingredients and foods, such as flapjacks and johnnycakes.
- A method of extracting the sediment from champagne, which leads to the first clear sparkling wines, champagnes, and pink champagnes, is developed by French winemaker Nicole-Barbe Clicquot (now famous as Veuve Clicquot).
- Billiards becomes a popular pastime in the United States, especially in the South.
- In Baltimore, Maryland, 8% of households are headed by women, most of whom are widows.

Religion

- The English theologian Richard Watson publishes *An Apology for Christianity*, a reply to the skeptical arguments of Thomas Paine's *The Age of Reason*, published in 1794.

Sports

- The leading Spanish matador José Delgado Pepe Hillo publishes his influential treatise on bullfighting, *La Tauromaquia/Bullfighting*.

1797

POLITICS, GOVERNMENT, AND ECONOMICS

Business and Economics

FEBRUARY
- The Bank of England suspends cash payments because of a run on bullion caused by the expense of the war against France.

MAY
- A British naval force under the Scottish admiral Adam Duncan blockades the Texel, the major route for European maritime trade via the Netherlands.

Colonization

JULY
9   The Cisalpine Republic is created as a French satellite state, from the Cispadine Republic and parts of Lombardy and Venetia.

Politics and Government

- The Russian emperor Paul I issues legislation limiting peasants' work for their landlords to three days a week and decrees succession to property by strict seniority.

JANUARY

4 The French army of Napoleon Bonaparte defeats the Austrian army of General Joseph Alvintzi at Rivoli, Italy.

26 A final treaty formalizing the Third Partition of Poland is signed by representatives of Russia, Prussia, and Austria.

FEBRUARY

• A British expedition under the Scottish general Ralph Abercromby captures the French island of Trinidad, in the West Indies.

2 The duchy of Mantua, Italy, surrenders to the French army of Napoleon Bonaparte.

19 Pope Pius VI cedes Romagna, Bologna, and Ferrara to France under the Treaty of Tolentino. Napoleon Bonaparte's French army begins advances through Tyrol toward Vienna, Austria.

MARCH

• The British general Gerard, Lord Lake, quells a rebellion of United Irishmen and Irish nationalists in Ulster, Ireland, attempting to take advantage of Britain's war with France.

4 John Adams is inaugurated as second president of the United States.

APRIL

15 A mutiny erupts on board Royal Navy ships anchored at Spithead, off Portsmouth, England. The government meets the sailors' grievances.

18 A preliminary peace between Austria and France is signed at Leoben, Austria.

MAY

2 A naval mutiny breaks out at the Nore anchorage in the Thames estuary, London, England.

16 The Venetian Republic signs an alliance with France and makes changes to its constitution in the hope of avoiding incorporation into a French-dominated republic.

JUNE

6 Napoleon Bonaparte establishes the French-dominated Ligurian Republic in Genoa, Italy.

28 France occupies the Ionian Islands, off the west coast of Greece.

30 The naval mutiny at the Nore anchorage in the Thames estuary, London, England, is suppressed. The sailors' leader, Richard Parker, is hanged from the yardarm.

JULY

• Charles-Maurice de Talleyrand, the worldly bishop of Autun, becomes French foreign minister.

SEPTEMBER

4 In the coup of 18 Fructidor (revolutionary calendar) in France, Paul Barras purges the Directory (of which he is a member) of Royalists.

OCTOBER

• Napoleon Bonaparte is appointed to command French forces being assembled to invade England.

October–December France and Britain hold unsuccessful peace talks in Lille, northern France.

11 A British fleet under the Scottish admiral Adam Duncan defeats the fleet of the French-dominated Batavian Republic off Camperdown on the Dutch coast.

17 The Treaty of Campo Formio is signed by France and Austria after Napoleon Bonaparte's successful campaign in Italy and Tyrol. The Cisalpine and Ligurian republics are recognized, as is French possession of the Ionian Islands off the Greek coast. Austria occupies the Venetian lands east of the River Adige, including Istria, Dalmatia, and Venice, and cedes the Austrian Netherlands to France. Peace between the Holy Roman Empire and France is to be negotiated at a conference to be held at Rastatt, Germany.

18 In what becomes known as the "XYZ affair," U.S.–French relations deteriorate after a U.S. delegation to France is humiliated by three emissaries of the French foreign minister Charles-Maurice de Talleyrand.

NOVEMBER

7 Richard Colley, the Marquess of Wellesley, is appointed British governor-general of India.

16 Frederick William III succeeds his father, Frederick William II, as king of Prussia and continues his father's policy of neutrality in the war against revolutionary France.

DECEMBER

16 A conference opens at Rastatt, Germany, to arrange a peace between France and the Holy Roman Empire.

29 France occupies Mainz, Germany, in accordance with the terms of the Treaty of Campo Formio.

SCIENCE, TECHNOLOGY, AND MEDICINE

Ecology

• An earthquake destroys the city of Quito in the Spanish American province of New Granada (modern Ecuador), killing 41,000 people.

Math

• The French mathematician Joseph-Louis Lagrange publishes *Théorie des fonctions analytiques/Theory of Analytical Functions*, which introduces the modern notation for derivatives.

Science

• English chemist Smithson Tennant proves that diamonds consist of carbon.

• French anatomist Georges Cuvier establishes the science of comparative anatomy with the publication of *Tableau élémentaire de l'histoire naturelle des animaux/An Elementary Natural History of Animals*.

• French chemist Louis-Nicolas Vauquelin discovers chromium (atomic no. 24).

• French eyeglasses-maker P. L. Guinand invents a new way to make optical glass.

December 1797–98 English natural philosopher Henry

Cavendish first calculates the gravitational constant in Newton's theory.

Technology

- English bone china is developed by English pottery manufacturer Josiah Spode when he adds bone ash to hard-paste porcelain.
- English engineer Henry Maudslay invents the carriage lathe, which permits the operator to use the lathe without holding the metal-cutting tool.
- English inventor Edmund Cartwright invents an engine that runs on alcohol.

Transportation

- English engineer Richard Trevithick builds high-pressure working models of stationary and moving steam locomotives.
- Horses are used to draw wagons on iron rails laid on some roads in Shropshire, England.

ARTS AND IDEAS

Architecture

- The U.S. builder Asher Benjamin publishes *The Country Builder's Assistant*. One of the first U.S. architectural design books, it has an important impact on the development of U.S. building.

Arts

- The English artist J. M. W. Turner paints *Moonlight: A Study at Millbank*.
- The English wood engraver Thomas Bewick publishes *Land Birds*, one of his finest set of engravings. It is the first part of his work *A History of British Birds*. The second part appears in 1804.
- The German artist Wilhelm von Schadow sculpts *Princesses Luise and Frederika*.
- The Spanish artist Francisco de Goya y Lucientes paints his *Portrait of the Duchess of Alba*.
- The U.S. artist John Trumbull completes his painting *The Declaration of Independence*, one of the best-known images of the period.

Literature and Language

- The English novelist Anne Radcliffe publishes her best-selling Gothic romance *The Italian*, in response to Matthew "Monk" Lewis's *The Monk*, published in 1796.
- The English poet and essayist Robert Southey publishes *Letters Written During a Short Residence in Spain and Portugal*.
- The English poet Samuel Taylor Coleridge writes one of his best-known poems, "Kubla Khan." It is published in 1816.
- The Italian writer Ugo Foscolo publishes his ode *A Bonaparte liberatore/To Bonaparte the Liberator*.
- The Scottish scholar Alexander Fraser Tytler publishes his influential "Essay on the Principles of Translation."

December 1797–99 The German poet Friedrich Hölderlin publishes his elegiac novel *Hyperion*.

Music

c. 1797 Austrian composer Franz Joseph Haydn completes his String Quartets Nos. 75 to 80 (Opus 76).
- The opera *Médée/Medea* by the Italian composer Luigi Cherubini is performed, in Paris, France.

Theater and Dance

- The German writer Ludwig Tieck publishes *Volksmärchen/Folk Tales*, a collection of folk tales,

BIRTHS & DEATHS

- Sojourner Truth, freed slave turned orator, born in Ulster County, New York (–1883).

JANUARY
31 Franz Schubert, Austrian composer, born in Vienna, Austria (–1828).

MARCH
2 Horace Walpole, English author of Gothic romances and letter writer, dies in London, England (80).
26 James Hutton, Scottish geologist who formulated the theory of uniformitarianism, dies in Edinburgh, Scotland (70).
27 Alfred de Vigny, French romantic poet, novelist, and dramatist, born in Loches, France (–1863).

APRIL
16 Louis Adolphe Thiers, French statesman, journalist, and historian, first president of the Third Republic 1871–73, born in Marseille, France (–1877).

JULY
8 Edmund Burke, Irish-born British statesman, political thinker, and writer, dies in Beaconsfield, Buckingham, England (68).

AUGUST
30 Mary Wollstonecraft Shelley, English writer, author of *Frankenstein*, born in London, England (–1851).

NOVEMBER
14 Charles Lyell, Scottish geologist, who developed uniformitarian geology which laid the foundation for evolutionary biology, born in Kinnordy, Forfarshire, Scotland (–1875).
29 Gaetano Donizetti, Italian opera composer, born in Bergamo, Cisalpine Republic (–1848).

DECEMBER
13 Heinrich Heine, German poet, born in Düsseldorf, Germany (–1856).

under the name Peter Lebrecht. He also completes a play set in the Middle Ages, *Karl von Berneck*.
- The play *Tieste/Thyestes* by the Italian writer Ugo Foscolo is performed, in Venice, Italy, making its young author famous.

Thought and Scholarship

- The French writer François-René de Chateaubriand publishes his "Essai sur les révolutions"/"Essay on Revolutions," a comparative survey of revolutions ancient and modern.
- The German philosopher Immanuel Kant publishes *Die Metaphysik der Sitten/The Metaphysics of Morals*.
- The German philosopher Friedrich von Schelling publishes *Ideen zu einer Philosophie der Natur/Ideas for a Philosophy of Nature*.
- U.S. churchman and geographer Jedidiah Morse publishes *The American Gazetteer*, the nation's first gazetteer.

SOCIETY

Education

- The British educationist Andrew Bell publishes *An Experiment in Education*, advocating teaching by a

"monitorial" system, with better pupils instructing the slower ones.
- The Swiss educator Johann Heinrich Pestalozzi publishes *Meine Nachforschungen über den Gang der Natur in der Entwicklung des Menschengeschlechts/My Inquiry into the Course of Nature in the Development of Mankind*.

Everyday Life

- Haberdasher John Hetherington creates the first top hat, in London, England.

Media and Communication

SEPTEMBER
5   Freedom of the press is restrained in France, with the new ruling Directorate retaining the right to prohibit publication. Some newspapers are suppressed for periods of up to two years.

Religion

- English moral and religious campaigner William Wilberforce publishes *A Practical View of the Prevailing Religious System of Professed Christians*.
- The religious edict introduced in Prussia in 1788, imposing censorship in education and penalties for heresy, is repealed.

1798

POLITICS, GOVERNMENT, AND ECONOMICS

Colonization

- British military forces take the region of modern Honduras in central America from the Spanish colonial authorities.

Politics and Government

- In U.S. Congressional elections, Federalists retain majorities in the House (64–42) and Senate (19–13).

JANUARY
8   The Eleventh Amendment to the U.S. Constitution becomes law.
22   A French-style Directory (ruling executive) is established in the Batavian Republic.
24   The French-dominated Lemanic Republic is proclaimed in Geneva, Switzerland.

FEBRUARY
11   French forces occupy Rome, Italy.
15   The French-dominated Roman Republic is proclaimed in central Italy. Pope Pius VI refuses to surrender his temporal power and leaves Rome for Valence, France.

MARCH
- The influential Spanish prime minister and mastermind of the Franco-Spanish Treaty of San Ildefonso against Britain, Manuel de Godoy, is forced to resign, following the Spanish naval defeat by Britain off Cape St. Vincent.
29   Swiss revolutionaries proclaim the pro-French Helvetian Republic.

APRIL

- The United States prepares for war with France following publication of the dispatches of the U.S. ministers who negotiated with the French Directory in the "XYZ affair" in October 1797.
- 26 The Swiss city of Geneva is annexed by France.

MAY

- 19 A French military expedition intending to conquer Egypt sets sail from Toulon, southeast France, under the command of Napoleon Bonaparte.
- 23 A rebellion of United Irishmen and Catholic Irish nationalists against British rule breaks out in Ireland.

JUNE

- 12 The French expeditionary force for Egypt occupies Malta, ruled by the Knights of St. John (whose Grand Master is Czar Paul I of Russia).
- 18–July 6 In three Alien Acts passed in as many weeks, the U.S. Congress extends the naturalization period from 5 to 14 years and empowers the president to deport dangerous aliens.
- 21 British forces commanded by Gerard, Lord Lake, defeat the Catholic Irish rebels at Vinegar Hill, County Wexford, Ireland, so ending the Irish Rebellion.

JULY

- 14 The U.S. Congress passes the Sedition Act, designed to stifle internal political dissent by suppressing press criticism of the U.S. president and his administration. The act's blatant partisanship invites scorn from Thomas Jefferson and James Madison, among others, and ultimately discredits the Federalist Party.
- 21 A Navy Department is created in the United States to equip squadrons for attack on French shipping and possessions in the West Indies.
- 21 Napoleon Bonaparte's French army in Egypt, having occupied Alexandria, defeats Mameluke forces at the Battle of the Pyramids. French domination of Egypt is established.

AUGUST

- 1 A British fleet under the English admiral Horatio Nelson destroys the French fleet in Aboukir Bay, Egypt ("the Battle of the Nile") cutting the French army's communications with Europe and establishing British naval supremacy in the Mediterranean.
- 19 France signs a formal alliance with the Helvetian Republic.
- 22 A French force of 1,200 men commanded by General Jean Humbert lands at Killala Bay in Ireland, with the aim of supporting Irish rebels against British rule.

SEPTEMBER

- The Ottoman Empire declares war on France.
- 1 Britain signs a treaty of alliance with the nizam (ruler) of Hyderabad, India. The treaty is the first step in reducing Hyderabad to the status of a subsidiary ally of Britain.
- 5 A law enforcing mass conscription is passed by the Directory (ruling executive) in France, at the instigation of General Jean-Baptiste Jourdan.

OCTOBER

- 27 The French expedition to Ireland under General Jean Humbert surrenders to British forces at Balinasloe, County Galway, having arrived too late to prevent the defeat of the Catholic Irish rebels at Vinegar Hill, County Wexford.

NOVEMBER

- A British expedition recaptures the island of Minorca from Spain (it was occupied by Spain in 1782).
- A French army commanded by General Barthélemy-Catherine Joubert occupies the Italian kingdom of Piedmont.
- 16–December 24 Following the passage of the Alien and Sedition Acts, the Virginia and Kentucky legislatures pass resolutions to nullify any act of Congress in any state which considers it to be unconstitutional.
- 29 King Ferdinand IV of the Italian kingdom of Naples declares war against France and occupies Rome.

DECEMBER

- 4 France declares war on the Italian kingdom of Naples.
- 9 French forces under General Joubert force King Charles Emmanuel of Sardinia to abdicate.
- 15 French forces recapture Rome from the Austrian army of Baron Karl Mack von Lieberich, and overrun the kingdom of Naples.
- 24 An Anglo-Russian alliance is signed as the foundation of a Second Coalition against France.

SCIENCE, TECHNOLOGY, AND MEDICINE

Agriculture

- John "Johnny Appleseed" Chapman, Swedish-born U.S. missionary and nurseryman, plants his first apple orchard, in Pennsylvania.

Ecology

NOVEMBER

- 17–21 New England is hit by a snowstorm that buries houses in huge drifts; hundreds of people die.

Exploration

- The English explorer and naval surgeon George Bass proves that Tasmania, off south Australia, is an island.

Health and Medicine

- English physician Edward Jenner announces the discovery of a vaccination against smallpox in *Inquiry into the Causes and Effects of Variolae Vaccinae*.
- The French physician Philippe Pinel publishes *Nosographie philosophique/Philosophical Nosography*, in which he describes various mental disorders and debunks the theory that mental illness is due to demonic possession.
- English economist and clergyman Thomas Malthus publishes *Essay on the Principles of Population* in which he argues that population increases geometrically while food production increases only arithmetically, resulting in competition; this insight is later a key idea for the English naturalist Charles Darwin.

Math

- Norwegian mathematician Caspar Wessel introduces the vector representation of complex numbers.

Science

- British manufacturer Charles Tennant improves the manufacture of chloride of lime.
- English natural philosopher Henry Cavendish determines the mean density of the earth; it is 5.5 times as dense as water.
- French astronomer Pierre-Simon Laplace predicts the existence of black holes.
- U.S.-born British physicist and inventor Benjamin Thompson, Count Rumford, demonstrates experimentally the theory that heat is the increased motion of particles.

Technology

- Frenchman Nicholas-Louis Robert invents a paper-making machine.
- German printer Alois Senefelder invents lithography.

Transportation

- The first lock in North America is built on the Sault Ste. Marie Canal joining Lake Superior with Lake Huron.

ARTS AND IDEAS

Architecture

- The English neoclassical architect John Soane publishes his *Sketches in Architecture*.
- The Massachusetts State House in Boston, designed by the U.S. architect Charles Bulfinch, is completed.

Arts

- The Scottish artist Henry Raeburn paints *Isabella McLeod, Mrs James Gregory*.

Literature and Language

- The English poet Samuel Taylor Coleridge publishes the poems "Fear in Solitude," "Frost at Midnight," and "France: an Ode."
- The English poets William Wordsworth and Samuel Taylor Coleridge publish *Lyrical Ballads*. A collaboration that marks the true beginning of English romantic poetry, it includes Coleridge's "The Rime of the Ancient Mariner."
- The English writer William Godwin publishes *Memoirs of the Author of the Vindication of the Rights of Woman*, a biography of the English writer and feminist Mary Wollstonecraft.
- The German writer and critic Friedrich Schlegel publishes *Geschichte der Poesie der Griechen und Römer/A History of Greek and Roman Poetry*.
- The German writer and philosopher Christoph Friedrich Nicolai publishes his satirical novel *Leben und Meinungen Sempronius Gundiberts eines deutschen Philosophen/The Life and Thoughts of Sempronius Gundibert, German Philosopher*, attacking the pretensions of German philosophy.
- The German writer Novalis publishes the *Blütenstaub/Pollen*, a collection of poetic fragments.
- The U.S. writer Charles Brockden Brown publishes *Wieland*, a gothic romance, and *Alcuin*. Written in support of women's rights (it was inspired by the writings of the English writer and feminist Mary Wollstonecraft), *Alcuin* is considered one of the first U.S. feminist books.

Music

- Austrian composer Franz Joseph Haydn completes his Mass No. 9 in D minor, the *Nelson*, and his oratorio *Die Schöpfung/The Creation*.
- German composer Ludwig van Beethoven completes his Piano Concerto No. 1 in C (Opus 15). This is in fact his second piano concerto. He also completes his Violin Sonatas Nos. 1, 2, and 3 (Opus 12).

Theater and Dance

- The English writer and actress Elizabeth Inchbald publishes her translation (from August von Kotzebue's

BIRTHS & DEATHS

JANUARY
19 Auguste Comte, French philosopher, founder of sociology and positivism, born in Montpellier, France (−1857).

APRIL
26 Ferdinand Delacroix, French painter, born in Charenton-St.-Maurice, France (−1863).

JUNE
29 Giacomo Leopardi, Italian poet, scholar, and philosopher, born in Recanati, Papal States (−1837).

JULY
2 John Fitch, U.S. entrepreneur who pioneered the construction of steamboats in the United States, dies in Bardstown, Kentucky (55).

AUGUST
21 James Wilson, U.S. lawyer and theorist, signatory of the Declaration of Independence, dies in Edenton, North Carolina (55).

21 Jules Michelet, French nationalist historian, born in Paris, France (−1874).

DECEMBER
4 Luigi Galvani, Italian physician who investigated electrical conduction in living tissues, dies in Bologna, Italy (61).

German original) of the play *Lover's Vows*, which features in the narrative of Jane Austen's *Mansfield Park*.

- The German actor and dramatist August Wilhelm Iffland becomes director of the Berlin Royal Theater in Germany.
- The play *Victor, ou l'enfant du forêt/Victor, Child of the Forest* by the French dramatist René-Charles Guilbert de Pixérécourt is first performed, in Paris, France. Pixérécourt—who wrote about 120 plays—is the leading figure in the development of melodrama.
- The tragedy *André* by the U.S. dramatist William Dunlap is first performed, in New York, New York.

Thought and Scholarship

- The German philosopher Johann Gottlieb Fichte publishes *Das System der Sittenlehre nach den Prinzipen der Wissenschaftslehre/A System of Ethics on Scientific Principles*.

SOCIETY

Education

- The University of Louisville is founded at Louisville, Kentucky.

Everyday Life

- The invention of a smallpox vaccination causes the decline of beauty patches—stars, moons, and hearts of black velvet or silk—worn by women in Europe to hide pock marks. The location of the patches had taken on meaning; i.e., worn at the corner of the mouth, the patch meant the women was willing to flirt; on the right cheek, that she was married, and so on.

Media and Communication

- German journalist Johann Cotta founds the newspaper *Allgemeine Zeitung* in Leipzig, Saxony.

Religion

- Omiki-san Nakayama founds Tenri Kyo, a major Shinto sect. She teaches that the root of suffering and illness comes from the mind.

Sports

- *c.* 1798 The game of "baseball" is referred to in Jane Austen's *Northanger Abbey*.
- Diomed, the first winner of the Epsom Derby, is sold for 50 guineas to John Hoomes of Virginia. The horse is brought to the United States where Colonel Miles Selden buys him for £1,000. Diomed sires the dominant line of 19th-century U.S. racehorses.

◆

1799

POLITICS, GOVERNMENT, AND ECONOMICS

Business and Economics

- In Philadelphia, Pennsylvania, the first strike by a labor organization, the Federal Society of Cordwainers (shoemakers), succeeds after nine days.

JULY
19 The Russian government grants the Russian-American Company the monopoly of trade in Alaska.

Colonization

- The Carnatic (modern Karnataka) and Mysore, India, are placed under British administration.

JANUARY
23–June 19 The French-dominated Parthenopean Republic is established in Naples.

Politics and Government

JANUARY
2 Britain joins the Russo-Ottoman alliance.
2 The French army in Egypt, commanded by Napoleon Bonaparte, advances into the Ottoman province of Syria.

FEBRUARY
8 Cardinal Fabrizio Ruffo, the newly appointed papal vicar-general of the kingdom of Naples begins a

counterrevolutionary campaign against the French occupation of the kingdom; by June his advancing forces recapture the city of Naples itself.

MARCH

1 Ottoman and Russian forces complete the conquest of the French-occupied Ionian Islands, off western Greece, which are organized as a republic under Ottoman protection.

12 Austria declares war on France.

19 The French army of Egypt, under Napoleon Bonaparte, lays siege to the Syrian coastal city of Acre (Akko); it is defended by Ottoman troops aided by British forces under Sidney Smith.

25 An Austrian army under Archduke Charles defeats Jean-Baptiste Jourdan's French army at Stockach in Germany.

25 French troops occupy the Grand Duchy of Tuscany.

APRIL

5 The French army of General Barthélemy Schérer is defeated at Magnano, Italy, by an Austrian army under General Paul von Kray.

8 The peace conference between France and the Holy Roman Empire at Rastatt, Germany, opened on December 16, 1797, is dissolved without agreement.

27 A Russo-Austrian army in Italy under the Russian field marshal Count Alexander Vasilyevich Suvorov defeats the French army of General Jean Victor Moreau in the Battle of Cassano and occupies Turin.

MAY

4 Tippu Sultan, the sultan of Mysore, India, is killed at Seringapatam, after it is captured by the British. His kingdom is divided between Britain and the nizam (ruler) of Hyderabad.

20 The French army of Egypt, under Napoleon Bonaparte, abandons its siege of the Syrian coastal city of Acre (Akko).

JUNE

1 The British prime minister William Pitt the Younger concludes the formation of the Second Coalition of Britain, Russia, Austria, the Ottoman Empire, Portugal, and Naples against France.

4 Austrian forces under Archduke Charles defeat a French army under André Masséna at Zürich, Switzerland.

17–19 The Russo-Austrian army under the Russian field marshal Count Suvorov decisively defeats the French governor of Rome, Jacques-Alexandre MacDonald, in the Battle of the Trebbia, Italy, while the French forces are advancing to relieve the army of General Moreau at Genoa.

JULY

12 Political associations are banned in Britain.

20 Charles-Maurice de Talleyrand resigns as French foreign minister.

24 The French army of Egypt, under Napoleon Bonaparte, defeats an Ottoman army at Aboukir, Egypt.

AUGUST

15 Count Suvorov's Russo-Austrian army defeats French forces under Barthélemy-Catherine Joubert at Novi, Italy, and advances across the Alps toward France. Joubert is killed in the battle.

22 Napoleon Bonaparte leaves Egypt to take command of French forces in Europe.

SEPTEMBER

13 The Duke of York takes command of an Anglo-Russian army in the Netherlands, intending to reconquer the Batavian Republic and the Austrian Netherlands from France.

19 The Anglo-Russian army commanded by the Duke of York is defeated by Franco-Batavian troops at Bergen-op-Zoom in the Batavian Republic.

25–27 French forces under General Masséna defeat a Russian army under Alexander Korsakov at Zürich, Switzerland; the main Russian force under Field Marshal Count Suvorov arrives too late, and is forced to retreat across the Alps. Austrian forces under the Archduke Charles retreat to the River Danube.

OCTOBER

9 Napoleon Bonaparte lands at Fréjus, southern France, on his return from Egypt.

18 The Anglo-Russian army commanded by the Duke of York surrenders to French and Batavian forces at Alkmaar in the Batavian Republic; Britain agrees to release all its French prisoners of war.

21 Britain declares the entire coast of the Batavian Republic to be under naval blockade.

22 Russia breaks its coalition agreement with Austria against France.

NOVEMBER

9 Napoleon Bonaparte overthrows the ruling Directory (ruling executive) in France in the coup of 18 Brumaire (revolutionary calendar).

13 Austria occupies the Italian March of Ancona, on the Adriatic coast of the Papal States in central Italy.

DECEMBER

25 The Constitution of the Year VIII creates the French Consulate. It comprises three consuls, with Napoleon Bonaparte as First Consul. Britain and Austria reject French offers of peace.

SCIENCE, TECHNOLOGY, AND MEDICINE

Agriculture

• Beets gain importance as a vegetable in Europe.

Exploration

• German explorer Alexander von Humboldt arrives in the Spanish viceroyalty of New Granada (in the area of modern Venezuela), at the start of his five years of exploration in South America.

• The Scottish traveler Mungo Park publishes his *Travels in the Interior of Africa*, in 1795–97.

Health and Medicine

• A bubonic plague in North Africa kills 300,000 people.

Math

- The German mathematician Karl Friedrich Gauss proves the fundamental theorem of algebra: that every algebraic equation has as many solutions as the exponent of the highest term.

December 1799–1825 French mathematician and physicist Pierre-Simon Laplace publishes the five-volume *Traité de mécanique céleste/Celestial Mechanics*, which extends and corrects Isaac Newton's theories of the solar system.

Science

- French chemist Joseph-Louis Proust discovers that the elements in a compound are combined in definite proportions.
- The U.S.-born British inventor and physicist Benjamin Thompson, Count Rumford, procures a charter for the Royal Institution (a scientific society) in Britain, with the naturalist and explorer Joseph Banks as first president.

Technology

- French inventor Philippe Lebon is granted a patent for a system of heating and lighting from coal gas.

ARTS AND IDEAS

Arts

- The French artist Anne-Louis Girodet de Roucy paints *Mademoiselle Lange as Danäe*.
- The French artist Jacques-Louis David paints *Les Sabines/The Rape of the Sabine Women*.
- The Spanish artist Francesco de Goya publishes *Los Caprichos*, a set of etchings that bitterly satirize Spanish society and the church. They are seized by the Inquisition.

Literature and Language

- The English poet Thomas Campbell publishes *The Pleasures of Hope*, a poem in couplets.
- The German writer Friedrich von Schlegel publishes his autobiographical novel *Lucine*.
- The German writer Novalis publishes *Geistliche Leider/Devotional Songs*.
- The U.S. writer Charles Brockden Brown publishes two novels: *Arthur Mervyn* and *Edgar Huntly*.

Music

c. 1799 Austrian composer Franz Joseph Haydn completes his String Quartets Nos. 81 to 82 (Opus 77) and his Mass No. 10, the *Theresienmesse/Theresa Mass*.

The Elements (1799–1898)

1799
- French chemist Joseph-Louis Proust discovers that the elements in a compound are combined in definite proportions.

1803
- English chemist and physicist John Dalton formulates his atomic theory of matter: that all elements are made of minute indestructible particles, called atoms, that are all identical.

1804
- English chemist and physicist William Hyde Wollaston discovers the element rhodium (atomic no. 45) and develops a powder-metallurgy method of purifying platinum—valuable in chemical research.

1807
October English chemist Humphry Davy isolates the elements potassium (element no. 19) and sodium (element no. 11) by passing an electric current through their chemical compounds.

1808
- Humphry Davy isolates the alkaline-earth metals magnesium (element no. 12), calcium (element no. 20), strontium (element no. 38), and barium (element no. 56).

1811
- French chemist Bernard Courtois accidentally discovers the element iodine (atomic no. 53), when he adds too much sulfuric acid to kelp ash and obtains a violet vapor that condenses to a black crystalline substance. He calls it "substance X." Humphry Davy names it iodine in 1813.

1815
- English chemist William Prout hypothesizes that the atomic weight of any element is a whole number ratio of the atomic weight of hydrogen. It proves valuable in the classification of elements.

1823
- Swedish chemist Jöns Jakob Berzelius isolates silicon (element no. 14).

1825
- Danish scientist Hans Christian Oersted isolates aluminum (element no. 13) in powdered form, and Jöns Jakob Berzelius isolates titanium (element no. 22).

1831
- Jöns Jakob Berzelius discovers isomerism—the relation of two or more compounds of the same element with the same number of atoms but which differ in structural arrangement and properties.

- German composer Ludwig van Beethoven completes his Piano Sonata No. 8 (Opus 13), the *Pathétique*.

Theater and Dance

- The German writer Friedrich Schiller completes *Wallenstein*, a trilogy of plays that is the greatest historical drama in German literature.
- The play *The Italian Father* by the U.S. dramatist William Dunlap is first performed, in New York, New York.

Thought and Scholarship

- The German writer Johann Gottfried Herder publishes *Metakritik/Metacriticism*, an attack of the philosophies of Immanuel Kant and Johann Gottlieb Fichte, and the first of his *Briefen zur Beförderung der Humanität/ Letters on the Progress of Mankind*. The last appears in 1797.
- The Scottish political writer James Mackintosh publishes his *Introduction to the Law of Nature and Nations*.

December 1799–1805 The English historian Sharon Turner publishes his *History of England from the Earliest Period to the Norman Conquest*. His work encourages a serious study of Britain's ancient past.

SOCIETY

Media and Communication

NOVEMBER
- After the Brumaire coup (November 9) in France more than 50 Paris newspapers are suppressed. By 1811 only four remain, the same number as before the French Revolution.

Religion

- The Church Missionary Society and the Religious Tract Society are founded in London, England.
- The German theologian Friedrich Schleiermacher publishes his *Über die Religion: Reden an die Bebildeten unter ihren Verächtern/Religion: Speeches to its Cultured Despisers*. Seeking to locate a belief in God in intuition and feeling rather than dogma, Schleiermacher's works will be one of the profoundest influences on modern Protestant theology.

1841
- French chemist Eugène-Melchior Péligot isolates uranium (element no. 92).
- Jöns Jakob Berzelius observes chemical allotropy (two different forms of the same element) in carbon.

1852
- English chemist Edward Frankland develops the idea of chemical valence: that atoms of an element combine only with a given number of atoms of another element. It forms the foundation of modern structural chemistry.

1858
- Italian chemist Stanislao Cannizzaro differentiates the atomic and molecular weight of an element.

1859
- German chemists Robert Wilhelm von Bunsen and Gustav Kirchhoff discover that each element emits a characteristic wavelength of light. It initiates spectrum analysis, a valuable tool for both chemist and astronomer.

1860
- Robert Wilhelm von Bunsen and Gustav Kirchhoff discover the element cesium (element no. 55).

1868
- English astronomer Norman Lockyer and, independently, French astronomer Pierre-Jules Janssen, discover helium (element no. 2) through spectroscopic observations of the sun.

1869
- Based on the fact that the elements exhibit recurring patterns of properties when placed in order of increasing atomic weight, Russian chemist Dmitry Ivanovich Mendeleyev develops the periodic classification of the elements. He leaves gaps for elements yet to be discovered.

1886
- French chemist Henri Moissan isolates the highly reactive halogen element fluorine (element no. 9).

1894
- British physicist John William Strutt (3rd Baron Rayleigh) and Scottish chemist William Ramsay isolate the inert gas argon (element no. 18).

1898
- British chemists William Ramsay and Morris William Travers discover the noble gases neon (element no. 10), krypton (element no. 36), and xenon (element no. 54).
- French chemists Pierre and Marie Curie discover the radioactive elements radium (element no. 88) and polonium (element no. 84). Radium is discovered in pitchblende and is the first element to be discovered radiochemically.

BIRTHS & DEATHS

- Lazaro Spallanzani, Italian physiologist who contributed to the study of animal reproduction, dies in Pavia, Cisalpine Republic (70).

FEBRUARY

24 Georg Christoph Lichtenberg, German physicist and satirist who discovered the principle of xerography, dies in Ober-Ramstadt, near Darmstadt, Hesse, Germany (56).

28 Ignaz von Döllinger, German historical scholar and Roman Catholic theologian, born in Bamberg, Germany (–1890).

MARCH

29 Edward Stanley, Earl of Derby, British prime minister 1852, 1858, and 1866, a Conservative, born in Knowsley Park, Lancashire, England (–1869).

MAY

4 Tippu Sultan, Sultan of Mysore 1782–99, dies in battle in Seringapatam, India (c. 49).

18 Pierre-Augustin Caron de Beaumarchais, French comic dramatist, dies in Paris, France (67).

20 Honoré de Balzac, French novelist whose writings helped establish the modern form of the novel, born in Tours, France (–1850).

JUNE

6 Patrick Henry, American antifederalist and orator who declared "Give me liberty or give me death" at the start of the American Revolution, dies in Red Hill, Virginia (63).

7 Alexander Pushkin, Russian poet, novelist, and dramatist, born in Moscow, Russia (–1837).

AUGUST

5 Richard Howe, English admiral during the French Revolution, dies (73).

8 Nathaniel B. Palmer, U.S. sea captain and Antarctic explorer, born in Stonington, Connecticut (–1877).

29 Pope Pius VI, who was pope 1775–99, dies in Valence, France (81).

OCTOBER

18 Christian Friedrich Schönbein, German chemist, born in Metzingen, Germany (–1868).

20 James Iredell, U.S. associate justice, dies in Edenton, North Carolina (48).

DECEMBER

6 Joseph Black, British chemist and physicist, dies in Edinburgh, Scotland (71).

14 George Washington, commander in chief during the American Revolution, and first president of the United States 1789–97, dies and is buried in Mt. Vernon, Virginia (67).

◆

1800

POLITICS, GOVERNMENT, AND ECONOMICS

Business and Economics

c. 1800 The Belgian entrepreneur Lieven Bauwens smuggles the mule jenny into the Batavian Republic, spreading the Industrial Revolution in the textile industry from Britain to the rest of Europe.

- The British socialist Robert Owen opens a model factory at New Lanark, Scotland.
- U.S. sailors in New York, New York, strike over wages, causing riots.

JANUARY

18 The decree establishing the Bank of France is promulgated. The bank's close relationship with the government forms the basis of French public finance.

NOVEMBER

7 The Russian emperor Paul I imposes an embargo on British vessels in Russian ports until Britain restores Malta to the Knights of St. John.

Human Rights

c. 1800 Schoolgirls in Europe are deprived of food, exercise, and fresh air to achieve the fashionable look of pallor and thinness.

SEPTEMBER

30 The British prime minister William Pitt the Younger advocates Catholic emancipation in Britain.

Politics and Government

- In U.S. Congressional elections, Democratic-Republicans attain majorities in the House (69–36) and Senate (18–13).
- The 2nd Combination Acts modify earlier legislation but retain the ban on labor unionism in Britain.

JANUARY

17 The Treaty of Montluçon ends royalist disaffection in the Vendée, western France, and releases troops for a new French offensive in Europe.

FEBRUARY

19 Napoleon Bonaparte, as First Consul of France, establishes himself in the royal palace in the Tuileries, Paris.

MARCH

20 The French army in Egypt, commanded by General Jean Baptiste Kléber, defeats an Ottoman army at Heliopolis, and advances to Cairo, aiming to reconquer the country.

28 The Act of Union with Britain is passed by the Irish Parliament.

APRIL

• Paul von Kray succeeds Archduke Charles as commander in chief of the Austrian army.

MAY

• The former secretary of state Manuel de Godoy returns to power, as Prince of the Peace, in Spain.

9 A French army under General Victor Moreau defeats the Austrian army of General Paul von Kray at Biberach in Württemberg, Germany.

15–20 A French army commanded by Napoleon Bonaparte crosses the Great St. Bernard Pass, aiming to reconquer Italy from the Austrians.

JUNE

• The U.S. departments of state are moved from Philadelphia, Pennsylvania, to Washington, D.C., the new seat of government.

2 French forces under Joachim Murat occupy Milan, during Napoleon Bonaparte's renewed campaign in Italy.

14 French forces under Napoleon Bonaparte defeat the Austrians under Baron Michel Melas at the Battle of Marengo, northwest Italy, ensuring the French reconquest of Italy.

14 The French commander in Egypt, Jean Baptiste Kléber, is assassinated by a fanatic in Cairo just as he is beginning to govern the country.

SEPTEMBER

5 A British expedition recaptures Malta from the French.

OCTOBER

• Napoleon Bonaparte, First Consul of France, promises the Grand Duchy of Tuscany, with the title of king, to the Duke of Parma, son-in-law of Charles IV of Spain.

NOVEMBER

• In the U.S. presidential election, the Republicans Thomas Jefferson and Aaron Burr each receive 73 electoral votes. Federalists John Adams and Charles Pinckney secure 65 and 64 votes respectively. As stipulated by the U.S. Constitution, the election goes to the House of Representatives, where Jefferson is elected president.

DECEMBER

3 The French general Victor Moreau defeats the Austrians under Archduke John of Austria at Hohenlinden and advances on the Austrian capital, Vienna.

16 A second Armed Neutrality of the North is agreed between Russia, Sweden, Denmark, and Prussia.

24 The discovery of a plot to assassinate the First Consul Napoleon Bonaparte, in Paris, France, enables him to deport democratic republicans to French Guiana, South America.

SCIENCE, TECHNOLOGY, AND MEDICINE

Exploration

c. 1800 Seal fur traders operating on the island of South Georgia in the South Atlantic discover the outlying regions of the Antarctic Peninsula.

Health and Medicine

• The Company of Surgeons, in London, England, becomes The Royal College of Surgeons.

Science

• English physicist Thomas Young publishes *Outlines and Experiments respecting Sound and Light* which proposes a wave theory of light.

• German-born English astronomer William Herschel discovers the existence of infrared solar rays.

• Italian physicist Alessandro Volta invents the voltaic pile made of discs of silver and zinc—the first battery.

• Scottish chemist William Cruickshank purifies water by adding chlorine.

APRIL

9 English chemist Humphry Davy publishes *Researches, Chemical and Philosophical, Chiefly Concerning Nitrous Oxide* detailing the effects of nitrous oxide, later used as the first anesthetic.

Technology

c. 1800 A pasta-making machine is invented in Naples, Italy.

• English army officer Henry Shrapnel invents shrapnel for the British army.

• English engineer Henry Maudslay improves his screw-cutting lathe so that it can cut screws of varying pitches.

• U.S. inventor Eli Whitney makes muskets with interchangeable parts.

Transportation

• U.S. inventor Robert Fulton builds a copper-covered submarine, the *Nautilus*, and conducts trials in France on the River Seine.

April 1800–06 French engineers build a road over the Simplon Pass; it becomes a major link between southern and central Europe.

ARTS AND IDEAS

Architecture

- The Bank of Pennsylvania, in Philadelphia, designed by the English-born U.S. architect Benjamin Latrobe, is completed. His design marks a rejection of the prevailing Roman style in favor of classical Greek architecture.
- U.S. engineer James Finley builds the first suspension bridge in the United States.

Arts

- The English artist George Stubbs paints *Hambletonian, Rubbing Down.*
- The French artist Jacques-Louis David paints his *Portrait of Mme Récamier* and *Napoleon Crossing the Alps.*
- The French artist Marie-Guillemine Benoits paints his *Portrait of a Black Woman.*
- The Spanish artist Francisco de Goya y Lucientes paints *Charles IV and his Family.*

Literature and Language

- *c.* 1800   The U.S. churchman and writer Mason Locke Weems publishes his biography *The Life and Memorable Actions of George Washington.* This colorful account—which includes in its 1806 edition the first telling of the story of the young Washington's inability to lie about cutting down a cherry tree—does much to create the popular image of Washington.
- *The Farmer's Boy* by the English poet Robert Bloomfield, with woodcuts by the artist Thomas Bewick, becomes the first best seller of English verse.
- The Chinese scholar and editor Ji Yun publishes *Yunwei caotang biji,* a collection of popular Chinese folk tales and fables.
- The English poets William Wordsworth and Samuel Taylor Coleridge publish the second edition of their *Lyrical Ballads* (first published in 1798). This contains Wordsworth's celebrated and controversial preface, in which he defends the use of everyday words in poetry. It becomes one of the central texts of English romanticism.
- The Franco-Swiss writer Madame de Staël publishes *De la littérature considérée dans ses rapports avec les institutions sociales/On Literature Considered in Relation to Social Institutions.*
- The German writer Friedrich von Schlegel publishes his essay "Brief über den Roman"/"Letter on the Novel."
- The German writer Novalis publishes the prose lyrics "Hymnen an die Nacht"/"Hymns to the Night."
- The Irish writer Maria Edgeworth publishes her novel *Castle Rackrent.*

Music

- German composer Ludwig van Beethoven completes his Symphony No. 1 in C major (Opus 21), his String Quartets Nos. 1 to 6 (Opus 18), and his Violin Sonata in A minor (Opus 23).

- The opera *Le Calife de Bagdad/The Caliph of Baghdad* by the French composer François Adrien Boïeldieu is first performed, in Paris, France.

Theater and Dance

- The French statesman Joseph Fouché establishes theater censorship in France.
- The German writer Friedrich Johann Christoph von Schiller completes his historical play *Maria Stuart,* one of his greatest works.
- The play *Coelina, ou l'enfant du mystère/Coelina, Child of Mystery* by the French dramatist René-Charles-Guilbert de Pixérécourt is first performed, in Paris, France.

Thought and Scholarship

- The German philosopher Johann Gottlieb Fichte publishes *Die Bestimmung des Menschen/The Vocation of Man.*
- The German theologian Friedrich Schleiermacher publishes *Monologen/Monologues,* a study of ethics.

APRIL
24 The U.S. Congress authorizes the establishment of the Library of Congress in Washington, D.C.

SOCIETY

Education

- Downing College is founded at Cambridge University, England.

NOVEMBER
1 Middlebury College is founded in Middlebury, Vermont.

Everyday Life

- Boston Female Asylum in Massachusetts, the first charitable institution for women in the United States, is established by U.S. businesswoman Elizabeth Peck Perkins.
- Four-tined forks begin to be used in the United States, rather than the two- and three-tined forks formerly used.
- A postal service is introduced in the city of Berlin, Prussia.
- The birth rate in the United States is over seven per woman, which is the highest in the world.
- The first shoes in the United States designed specifically for the left and right feet are made by shoemaker William Young, in Philadelphia, Pennsylvania.
- The population of the world is estimated at 870 million, with over 20% of people living in Europe.
- U.S. census data show a 35.1% increase in the population, which has climbed to 5.3 million since 1790.

November 1800–50   A revolution in retail and wholesale trade occurs: specialization transforms the urban retail market, replacing the general store with individual stores for hardware, groceries, dry goods, furnishing, books, tobacco, etc. Cash-only sales policies are instituted around 1806.

DECEMBER
25   King George III's wife, Queen Charlotte, introduces the Christmas tree to the British court.

Media and Communication

- There are 24 daily newspapers and 241 weekly newspapers in the United States.
- U.S. editor and publisher Margaret Bayard Smith establishes a newspaper called the *National Intelligencer* in Washington, D.C., with her husband, Samuel Harrison Smith.

Religion

MARCH
14   The Italian cardinal Luigi Chiaramonti, backed by the influential French cardinal Jean Maury, is elected as Pope Pius VII.

Sports

c. 1800   Horse racing is well established in Virginia, with Broad Rock, Fairfield, Newmarket, and Tree Hill the leading venues.
- Gouging, a rough form of wrestling in which the object is to gouge out the opponent's eyeball, gains popularity in the backwoods region of the Ohio River valley in the United States.

BIRTHS & DEATHS

JANUARY
1   Louis Jean Marie Daubenton, French naturalist and paleontologist, dies in Paris, France (83).

7   Millard Fillmore, thirteenth president of the United States 1850–53, a Whig, born in Locke Township, New York (–1874).

23   Edward Rutledge, U.S. politician, a signatory of the Declaration of Independence and governor of South Carolina, dies in Charleston, South Carolina (50).

FEBRUARY
11   William Henry Fox Talbot, English chemist, archeologist, and pioneer of photography, born in Melbury Abbas, Dorset, England (–1877).

APRIL
15   James Clark Ross, British naval officer who explored the Arctic and Antarctic, born in London, England (–1862).

16   George Charles Bingham, Lord Lucan, British cavalry commander who mistakenly orders the Charge of the Light Brigade (October 25, 1854) during the Crimean War, born in London, England (–1888).

25   William Cowper, English poet, dies in East Dereham, Norfolk, England (68).

MAY
7   Niccolò Piccinni, Italian operatic composer, dies in Passy, France (72).

9   John Brown, U.S. abolitionist whose antislavery campaign contributes to the initiation of the American Civil War, born in Torrington, Connecticut (–1859).

19   Sarah Miriam Peale, U.S. portrait painter, born in Philadelphia, Pennsylvania (–1885).

JUNE
14   Jean-Baptiste Kléber, French general during the French Revolution, dies in Cairo, Egypt (47).

21   John Rutledge, U.S. chief justice who helped write the U.S. Constitution, dies in Charleston, South Carolina (60).

JULY
31   Friedrich Wöhler, German chemist, born in Escherheim, near Frankfurt am Main, Germany (–1882).

SEPTEMBER
6   Catharine Esther Beecher, U.S. educational reformer and writer, born in East Hampton, Long Island, New York (–1878).

OCTOBER
2   Nat Turner, U.S. slave who led a briefly successful slave revolt, born in Southampton County, Virginia (–1831).

25   Thomas Babington Macaulay, English historian, poet, and Whig politician, born in Rothley Temple, Leicestershire, England (–1859).

26   Helmuth von Moltke, chief of the German general staff whose victories lead to German unification, born in Parchim, Germany (–1891).

DECEMBER
24   Ferdinand Keller, Swiss archeologist who excavated prehistoric Alpine lake dwellings on Lake Zürich, born in Marthalem, Switzerland (–1881).

29   Charles Goodyear, U.S. inventor who discovered how to vulcanize rubber, born in New Haven, Connecticut (–1860).

1801

POLITICS, GOVERNMENT, AND ECONOMICS

Business and Economics

- The Philadelphia bookseller Mathew Carey helps establish the American Company of Booksellers in New York, New York.

Colonization

SEPTEMBER

9   France obtains part of Guiana in South America.

Politics and Government

- The black leader Toussaint L'Ouverture achieves total control of the Franco-Spanish colony of Haiti.
- A French force under Charles Leclerc retakes the island of Haiti from the regime of Toussaint L'Ouverture, who is captured and dies in prison in France.

JANUARY

- The U.S. president John Adams appoints former secretary of state John Marshall as chief justice of the U.S. Supreme Court.
1   The Act of Union creates the United Kingdom of Great Britain and Ireland, bringing Ireland under direct control of the Parliament in Westminster.
14 Britain places an embargo on vessels of the Armed Neutrality of the North, the confederation of Russia and Sweden—joined later by Denmark (February 27) and Prussia (March 3)—formed to defend their trading rights in defiance of Britain's attempt to blockade Napoleonic France.
29 A convention is held between France and Spain to issue an ultimatum to Portugal to break that country's traditional allegiance with Britain.

FEBRUARY

- The U.S. Congress passes the Judiciary Act of 1801, creating 16 circuit courts. In one of his last acts as U.S. president, John Adams fills the offices of the new courts with Federalist judges, thereby ensuring Federalist influence well into the Democratic-Republican Thomas Jefferson's presidential term.

9   The Treaty of Lunéville, following the French defeat of Austria in Napoleon Bonaparte's campaign of 1800–01, marks the virtual destruction of the Holy Roman Empire. France gains all territory west of the Rhine, including Belgium and Luxembourg. The Grand Duchy of Tuscany is ceded to the Duchy of Parma to form the new kingdom of Etruria, and recognition is given to the Batavian, Cisalpine, Helvetian, and Ligurian republics.

MARCH

3   Britain seizes Danish and Swedish islands in the West Indies, principally St. Thomas and St. Croix (because Denmark and Sweden are allied with France in the Revolutionary Wars).
3   Prussia decides to join the Armed Neutrality of the North (the confederation of Russia, Sweden, and Denmark formed to defend their rights to export goods to Napoleonic France in defiance of Britain's attempt to blockade that country).
4   Thomas Jefferson, the third U.S. president, is the first to be inaugurated in Washington, D.C. He admonishes the young nation against becoming involved in "entangling alliances."
8   British troops under William Keith make an amphibious landing at Aboukir in French-occupied Egypt.
21 French forces stationed by Napoleon Bonaparte in Egypt are defeated near Alexandria by British troops led by General Ralph Abercromby.
21 The Treaty of Aranjuez is signed between France and Spain, formalizing their ultimatum to Portugal to break its traditional allegiance to Britain. Spain also agrees to cede the North American territory of Louisiana to France.
23 Czar Paul I of Russia is assassinated by military officers concerned by his dangerous mental instability. He is succeeded by his son, Alexander I.
28 The Peace of Florence is signed between Napoleonic France and the Italian kingdom of Naples, by which British vessels are to be excluded from Neapolitan ports.
29 An embargo is placed on British vessels in Danish ports; Danish forces, allied to Napoleonic France, enter the free city of Hamburg in Germany in order to close the River Elbe.

APRIL

2   British vice admiral Horatio Nelson is victorious against the Danish fleet in the Battle of Copenhagen, fought in retaliation for Danish actions against Britain in closing the River Elbe.
3   The electorate of Hanover (ruled by the British monarch, George III) is overrun by Prussian troops.
9   Following their defeat by the British under Nelson at the Battle of Copenhagen, the Danes are forced to consent to a truce by which they abstain from the Armed Neutrality of the North (formed by Russia, Sweden,

Denmark, and Prussia to defend their right to export goods to Napoleonic France).

14　The English Habeas Corpus Act is suspended to allow the detention of political suspects without trial.

MAY

- The Tripolitan War begins between the United States and the Barbary state of Tripoli (modern Libya) in North Africa after Tripoli insults the U.S. flag. The larger cause of the war is U.S. unwillingness to pay tribute to Tripoli's Barbary pirates.

JUNE

6　The Treaty of Badajoz formally ends the war between Spain and Portugal over Portugal's traditional allegiance to Britain. Portugal cedes the province of Olivenza and agrees to close its ports to British ships.

17　The Armed Neutrality of the North (the confederation of Russia, Sweden, Denmark, and Prussia, formed to defend their right to export goods to Napoleonic France) breaks up with the signing of the Treaty of St. Petersburg between Britain, Russia, and Prussia, which recognizes British right of search of merchant vessels.

19　A maritime convention is signed between Russia and Britain as further formal reconciliation, following the signing of the Treaty of St. Petersburg on June 17.

27　The French-held city of Cairo, Egypt, is taken by British troops.

JULY

12　The British admiral James Saumarez defeats a larger Franco-Spanish fleet off the coast of Morocco in the second Battle of Algeciras (having fought an inconclusive action on July 6).

15　A concordat with the papacy drawn up by Napoleon Bonaparte effectively places the church in France under state control. The pope is allowed to keep the Papal States, with the exception of Ferrara, Bologna, and Romagna, which are annexed by France.

SEPTEMBER

2　French forces in Egypt under General Jean Menou surrender to the British and are immediately offered free passage home, ending Napoleon Bonaparte's hopes of oriental conquest.

12　Czar Alexander I of Russia announces the annexation of the kingdom of Georgia and George XIII, Regent of Georgia, recognizes the Russian decision instead of accepting the traditional suzerainty of Persia.

29　The Treaty of Madrid between France and Portugal confirms the Treaty of Badajoz, ending the war between Portugal and Spain.

OCTOBER

1　Preliminaries of peace are signed between Britain and France; Britain is to restore all maritime conquests, except Trinidad and Ceylon (Sri Lanka), to France, Spain, and the Netherlands; France agrees to evacuate Naples and the Papal States; the integrity of Portugal is recognized; the independence of the Ionian Islands is agreed upon; both French and British armies are to evacuate Egypt, which is to be restored to the Ottoman Empire, and Malta is to be restored to the Knights of St. John by Britain.

23　Denmark signs the Treaty of St. Petersburg, joining Britain, Russia, and Prussia in recognizing British right of search of merchant vessels.

SCIENCE, TECHNOLOGY, AND MEDICINE

Agriculture

- U.S. nurseryman John Chapman—"Johnny Appleseed"—enters the Ohio valley with appleseeds collected from Philadelphia cider presses and distributes them to pioneers.

Exploration

October 1801–03　English navigator Matthew Williams, aboard HMS *Investigator*, surveys the coast of New South Wales, and completes the first circumnavigation of Australia.

Health and Medicine

- English physician and physicist Thomas Young announces that the cause of astigmatism is a lack of symmetry in the curvature of the cornea.

Math

- German mathematician Karl Friedrich Gauss publishes *Disquisitiones Arithmeticae/Discourses on Arithmetic*, which deals with relationships and properties of integers and leads to the modern theory of algebraic equations.

Science

- Dutch botanist Christiaan Hendrik Persoon publishes *Synopsis fungorum/An Overview of Fungi*, a description of various fungi. It is the founding text of modern mycology.
- English chemist and physicist John Dalton formulates the law of partial pressure in gases—Dalton's Law—that states that each component of a gas mixture produces the same pressure as if it occupied the container alone.
- English chemist Charles Hatchett discovers the metallic element niobium (atomic no. 41), which he calls columbium.
- English physician and physicist Thomas Young discovers the interference of light when he observes that light passing through two closely spaced pinholes produces alternating bands of light and dark in the area of overlap. He thereby establishes the wave theory of light.
- French anatomist Marie-François-Xavier Bichat publishes *Anatomie générale/General Anatomy*, which investigates the various bodily tissues and organs and is one of the first books in histology.
- French biologist Jean-Baptiste de Lamarck establishes the classification of invertebrates in *Système des animaux sans vertèbres, ou table générale des classes/ System of Invertebrate Animals, or General Table of Classes*.

- French mineralogist René-Just Häuy publishes *Traité de minéralogie/Treatise on Mineralogy*, a theory of the crystal structure of minerals that establishes him as one of the founders of crystallography.
- German astronomer Johann Elert Bode, the first cartographer to draw boundaries between adjacent constellations, publishes *Uranographia*, a catalog of 17,240 stars, which also contains 20 star maps.
- German mathematician Karl Friedrich Gauss calculates the orbit of Ceres, discovered earlier in the year. His technique allows other astronomers to locate it.
- German physicist Johann Wilhelm Ritter discovers ultraviolet rays when he notes that silver chloride decomposes faster in invisible than visible light. He also discovers electroplating.
- Spanish mineralogist Andrés Manuel del Rio discovers vanadium (atomic no. 23).

JANUARY
1   The Italian astronomer Giuseppe Piazzi discovers the first asteroid, Ceres.

MAY
- German astronomer Heinrich Olbers discovers the second asteroid, Pallas. He is convinced that asteroids are the remains of a disintegrated planet lying between Mars and Jupiter.

Technology

- English navigator Edward Massey invents a mechanical "log" which uses a rotor, gears, and a dial to determine the speed of a ship.
- French engineer Philippe Lebon lights the Hotel Seignelay in Paris, France, with "thermolampes." It is the first public building to be lit with gas.

JANUARY
- U.S. engineer Eli Whitney demonstrates the effectiveness of interchangeable parts when he asks president-elect Thomas Jefferson to choose parts from piles of disassembled muskets and reassemble them.

Transportation

DECEMBER
24   English engineer Richard Trevithick builds a steam-powered carriage that he successfully drives up a hill in Camborne, Cornwall, England.

ARTS AND IDEAS

Architecture

- The city hall building, designed by Joseph Manigault, is built in Charleston, South Carolina; it is one of the premier examples of postcolonial studied architecture.

OCTOBER
- The first water flows through the new Philadelphia aqueduct, providing the burgeoning city of Philadelphia, Pennsylvania, with a much needed resource.

Arts

- The Elgin marbles (ancient Greek sculptures collected by the Earl of Elgin, mostly from the Acropolis in Athens, Greece) are brought to London, England. They are placed in the British Museum in 1816.
- The English artist J. M. W. Turner paints *Calais Pier*.
- The French artist Jean-Auguste-Dominique Ingres paints *The Ambassadors of Agamemnon*.
- The Spanish artist Francisco José de Goya y Lucientes paints his *Portrait of Don Manuel de Godoy*.
- The U.S. artist Rembrandt Peale paints *Rubens Peale with a Geranium*.

Literature and Language

- *Vespro/Evening* and *Notte/Night*—the last two parts of the long poem in four parts *Il giorno/The Day* by the Italian poet Giuseppe Parini—are published posthumously.
- The English poet Robert Southey publishes his verse epic *Thalaba the Destroyer*.
- The French writer François-Auguste-René, vicomte de Chateaubriand, publishes his novel *Atala*, a romantic epic about Native Americans.
- The U.S. writer Charles Brockden Brown publishes his novel *Clara Howard*.

Music

- Austrian composer Franz Josef Haydn completes his Mass No. 11 in B flat, the *Schöpfungsmesse/The Creation Mass*, and his secular oratorio *Die Jahreszeiten/The Seasons*.
- German composer Ludwig van Beethoven completes his Piano Sonata No. 15 (Opus 28), the *Pastorale*; his Piano Concerto No. 3 in C minor (Opus 37); and his Violin Sonata in F (Opus 24), the *Spring Sonata*.

Theater and Dance

- The ballet *Die Geschöpfe des Prometheus/The Creatures of Prometheus*, with music (Opus 43) by the German composer Ludwig van Beethoven, is first performed, in Vienna, Austria. The choreography is by the Italian dancer Salvatore Viganò.
- The tragedy *Die Jungfrau von Orleans/The Maid of Orleans* by the German writer Friedrich Johann Christoph von Schiller is first performed, in Leipzig, Germany.

SOCIETY

Education

- The University of South Carolina is founded in Columbia, South Carolina.

Everyday Life

- Frontier culture evolves in the western United States. Forms of entertainment—logrolling, barbecuing, whiskey drinking, gambling on horses or card playing, hunting, shooting, and dancing country reels and jigs— reflect the character of the frontier.
- Josiah Bent of Massachusetts constructs a Dutch oven in his home and creates the first cold water crackers; they gain immediate popularity in New England (partially because they are believed to aid digestion), and eventually, around the world.
- The Act of Union, formally uniting Britain and Ireland, is marked with the incorporation of the cross of St. Patrick into the design of the British flag.
- The first accurate censuses, taken in 1800 and 1801, provide population statistics for: Italy, 17.2 million; Spain, 10.5 million; Great Britain, 10.4 million; Ireland, 5.2 million; the United States, 5.3 million; also for London, England, 864,000; Paris, France, 547,756; Vienna, Austria, 231,050; Berlin, Germany, 183,294, and New York, New York, 60,515.

October 1801–1900 Popular social dances include the waltz and the polka (introduced from Europe c. 1830), and folk dances such as the cakewalk, the Washington Post, and the barn dance.

Media and Communication

October 1801–09 Joseph Dennie edits the *Port Folio* in which he expresses his strong Federalist opinions; he attacks Thomas Jefferson so avidly that he is tried (but acquitted) for seditious libel.

NOVEMBER

16 The *New York Evening Post* begins publication in the United States under the direction of the politicians John Jat and Alexander Hamilton.

Religion

- A religious revival, called the Second Great Awakening, stretches westward with its hellfire sermons; it defines frontier evangelical Protestantism in the first quarter of the century.
- Congregationalists and Presbyterians combine their overtaxed resources in the Plan of Union to carry religion to frontier settlements; it is one of the most successful cooperative endeavors in U.S. church history, allowing ministers to serve in either church.

Sports

- The English antiquary Joseph Strutt's *Sports and Pastimes of the People of England* is published.

BIRTHS & DEATHS

JANUARY

11 Domenico Cimarosa, Italian composer of comic opera, dies in Venice, Italy (51).

FEBRUARY

21 John Henry Newman, English clergyman who led the Oxford Movement in the Church of England and later became a Roman Catholic cardinal, born in London, England (–1890).

MAY

16 William Seward, U.S. secretary of state 1861–69 who purchased Alaska from Russia in 1867 for $7.2 million, born in Florida, New York (–1872).

JUNE

1 Brigham Young, U.S. religious leader of The Church of Jesus Christ of Latter-day Saints who led converts to colonize the U.S. West and established a base at Salt Lake City, born in Whitingham, Vermont (–1877).

14 Benedict Arnold, American general and traitor during the American Revolution, dies in London, England (60).

JULY

14 Johannes Peter Müller, German physiologist and philosopher, born in Koblenz, Germany (–1858).

NOVEMBER

3 Vincenzo Bellini, Italian operatic composer, born in Catania, Sicily (–1835).

1802

POLITICS, GOVERNMENT, AND ECONOMICS

Business and Economics

- Income tax (introduced in 1799) is abolished in Britain after much public protest following the (temporary) end of the war with France that it was introduced to pay for.

Colonization

AUGUST

26 France annexes the island of Elba, off the coast of Tuscany (Italy), abandoned by Britain in 1797.

SEPTEMBER

21 Napoleon Bonaparte incorporates the Italian duchy of Piedmont into the French republic.

Human Rights

APRIL

26 An amnesty for French émigrés is announced to try to conciliate dissident elements under Napoleon Bonaparte's regime.

Politics and Government

- In the U.S. congressional elections, the Democratic-Republicans retain majorities in the House of Representatives (102–39) and Senate (25–9).

JANUARY

26 Napoleon Bonaparte becomes president of the Italian Republic (the former Cisalpine Republic), further strengthening French control in Italy.

FEBRUARY

- The U.S. Congress authorizes President Thomas Jefferson to arm U.S. merchant ships in the face of continuing Barbary pirate attacks off North Africa.

MARCH

27 The Treaty of Amiens is signed between Britain and France, based on the preliminaries agreed on October 1, 1801; it achieves (briefly) the complete pacification of Europe.

30 Sweden signs the 1801 Treaty of St. Petersburg, joining Britain, Russia, Prussia, and Denmark in recognizing British right of search of merchant vessels.

APRIL

- U.S. president Thomas Jefferson signs the Enabling Act, establishing guidelines by which U.S. territories can become states.

MAY

19 The *Légion d'Honneur* (order of merit) is created by Napoleon Bonaparte, membership in which is to be awarded to individuals for service to the state.

JUNE

29 A new Genoese constitution makes the city subordinate to France, which is extending its influence through Italy.

AUGUST

2 Napoleon Bonaparte becomes First Consul for life in France, with the right to appoint his successor, underlining his dictatorial control of the country.

16 The Fifth Constitution, or Constitution of the Year XII, is introduced in France, strengthening Napoleon Bonaparte's position as First Consul. The Senate, which is controlled by him, is enlarged, while the Tribunate and the legislative bodies lose influence.

OCTOBER

15 Napoleon Bonaparte intervenes in the civil war in Switzerland between the towns and the forest cantons. Using his newly won authority in the region, he styles himself "Mediator of the Helvetic League" and imposes a settlement.

23 At Poona in India, the maharaja (prince) Jaswant Rao Holkar of Indore defeats both Baji Rao, the peshwa of Poona, head of the Maratha confederacy and sympathetic to the British, and Madhoji Rao Sindhia of Gwalior, the most powerful figure in central India.

DECEMBER

31 By the Treaty of Bassein, the peshwa of Poona, India, effectively surrenders his independence to the British East India Company, agreeing not to make treaties without consulting the British and to accept the protection of a large British force.

SCIENCE, TECHNOLOGY, AND MEDICINE

Ecology

- German scientist C. W. Boeckmann invents the hygrometer for measuring humidity; it uses two thermometers, one exposed to the air and one wrapped in cotton.

- Prussian naturalist and explorer Alexander von Humboldt discovers huge deposits of guano in Peru that he investigates as a potential source of nitrates. Export of large quantities to Europe, where it is used for fertilizer and explosives, begins in 1809.

Exploration

- English explorers John Truter and William Somerville explore Bechuanaland (modern Botswana) in southern Africa, penetrating almost to Lake Ngami.
- Prussian explorer and naturalist Alexander von Humboldt explores the area of modern Ecuador in South America, and attempts to climb the 6,000-m/20,000-ft Mt. Chimborazo. He reaches 5,800 m/19,300 ft before being forced to turn back.

Health and Medicine

- English physician and physicist Thomas Young postulates that the eye requires only three receptors to see the full spectrum, instead of receptors for each color as is generally believed. In the same year, he applies his wave theory of light to calculate the approximate wavelengths of the seven colors in the spectrum.
- French physician Pierre Henri Nysten experiments with electrical cardiac stimulation on guillotined corpses.

Science

- English astronomer William Herschel discovers that some stars revolve around others, forming binary pairs. He catalogs 848 of them.
- English chemist Humphry Davy discovers that passing an electric current through metal strips heats them to incandescence.
- English scientist William Hyde Wollaston discovers dark (Fraunhofer) lines in the solar spectrum. They are caused by the absorption of specific wavelengths of the sun's radiation by gaseous elements in the atmosphere.
- French biologist Jean-Baptiste de Lamarck is the first to use the term "biology."
- French chemist and physicist Joseph-Louis Gay-Lussac demonstrates that all gases expand by the same fraction of their volume when subjected to the same temperature increase; it permits the establishment of a new temperature scale.
- German physicist Johann Wilhelm Ritter invents the dry voltaic cell.
- Italian jurist Gian Domenico Romagnosi observes that an electric current deflects a magnetic needle. The observation is announced in an obscure newspaper and is later rediscovered by Danish physicist Hans Christian Oersted.
- Scottish physicist John Leslie accurately explains capillary action.
- Swedish chemist Anders Gustaf Ekeberg discovers tantalum (atomic no. 73).

December 1802–05 French zoologist Pierre-André Latreille publishes his 14-volume work *Histoire naturele générale et particulière des crustacés et insectes/Comprehensive Natural History of Crustaceans and Insects.*

Technology

- English inventor George Bodley develops the cast-iron enclosed kitchen stove. Consisting of heated hot plates, side oven, hot water tank, and a central fire grate which burns coal, coke, peat or wood, it replaces open fires for cooking purposes.
- English physicist Thomas Wedgwood announces to the British Royal Institution that by using a camera obscura he can create images projected on paper saturated with silver nitrate. He is unable to fix the images and they quickly fade.
- The U.S. chemicals manufacturer E. I. Du Pont de Nemours and Co. begins operations in Delaware.

December 1802–08 English engineer Henry Maudslay and French-born British engineer Marc Isambard Brunel develop a mass-production line for making pulley blocks for sailing ships. Ten workers can make as many pulley blocks per year as 110 workers achieved previously.

OCTOBER

11 French aeronaut André-Jacques Garnerin patents the parachute. In September 1802 he parachutes 2,440 m/8,000 ft into Grosvenor Square, London, England.

Transportation

- Scottish engineer William Symington launches the world's first paddlewheel steamer, the *Charlotte Dundas*, which acts as a tugboat on the Forth and Clyde Canal. The 17-m/56-ft long steam-driven vessel runs at 13 kph/8 mph and uses a piston rod connected directly to the crankshaft.

MARCH

- English engineer Richard Trevithick takes out a patent for a high-pressure steam engine for "driving carriages." By allowing the steam to expand within the cylinder, higher pressures are achieved and the engine can be made smaller and lighter without loss of power. It is an essential invention in the development of steam locomotives.

ARTS AND IDEAS

Architecture

- The Four Courts, in Dublin, Ireland, designed by the Irish architect James Gandon, are completed.
- The mock-Gothic castle of Löwenburg at Schloss Wilhelmshöhe, near Kassel, Germany, designed by the German architect Heinrich Christoph Jussow, is completed.

Arts

- The English artist John Constable paints *The Stour Valley*, one of his earliest works.
- The English artist Thomas Girtin completes *The Eidometropolis*, a vast panorama of London, England, (which is later lost).

- The French artist Anne-Louis Girodet de Roucy paints *Ossian Receiving the Generals of the Republic*.
- The French artist François-Pascal, baron Gérard, paints *Mme Récamier* and *Napoleon Crossing the Alps*.
- The Italian artist Antonio Canova sculpts *Napoleon Bonaparte*.

Literature and Language

- The Franco-Swiss writer Madame de Staël publishes her novel *Delphine*.
- The Italian writer Ugo Foscolo publishes his novel *Ultime lettere di Jacopo Ortis/The Last Letters of Jacopo Ortis*, an attack on Napoleon's decision to cede Venice to Austria. Many consider it the first modern Italian novel.

March 1802–03 The Scottish poet and novelist Walter Scott publishes his three-volume collection of ballads *Minstrelsy of the Scottish Border*.

Music

- Austrian composer Franz Josef Haydn completes his Mass No. 12, the *Harmoniemesse*.
- German composer Ludwig van Beethoven completes his *Moonlight* Piano Sonata (Opus 27, no. 2), his Symphony No. 2 in D (Opus 36), and his piano work *7 Bagatelles* (Opus 33).
- The opera *Une folie/An Act of Folly* by the French composer Etienne-Nicolas Méhul is first performed, in Paris, France.

Thought and Scholarship

- The American Academy of Arts is incorporated in New York, New York.
- The English philosopher Jeremy Bentham publishes *Civil and Penal Legislation*.
- The English theologian William Paley publishes *Natural Theology*, which contains a celebrated version of the argument from design (to prove God's existence).
- The French social thinker Claude-Henri de Rouvroy, comte de St.-Simon, publishes *Lettres d'un habitant*

de Genève à ses contemporains/Letters of a Genevan to His Contemporaries.

- U.S. mathematician and astronomer Nathaniel Bowditch publishes *The New American Practical Navigator*. Based on corrected tables from J. H. Moore's *The Practical Navigator*, Bowditch's book goes through 60 editions and sets the standards for maritime navigation.

APRIL

- The U.S. Library of Congress publishes its *Catalogue of Books, Maps, and Charts, Belonging to the Library of the Two Houses of Congress*, the nation's first library catalog.

SOCIETY

Education

- St. Mary's University is founded in Halifax, Nova Scotia, Canada.
- The German philosopher and educator Johann Friedrich Herbart publishes *Pestalozzis Idee eines ABC der Anschauung/Pestalozzi's Idea for an ABC of Sense Perception*.

MAY

1 Napoleon Bonaparte reforms the French system of education, introducing *lycées* (state run secondary schools) which are run with military discipline.

JULY

- The U.S. Military Academy opens at West Point, New York.

Everyday Life

- Based on the work of German chemist Franz Karl Archard, King Frederick Wilhelm III of Prussia, builds the world's first sugar beet factory at Cunern, Silesia. Sugar beet becomes the second most import source of sugar after sugar cane.
- The banjo clock, designed by U.S. clockmaker Simon Willard to hang on a bracket on a wall, appears in U.S. homes for the first time.

BIRTHS & DEATHS

FEBRUARY

26 Esek Hopkins, first commodore of the U.S. navy 1775–83, dies in Providence, Rhode Island (84).

26 Victor Hugo, French romantic novelist, born in Besançon, France (–1885).

JULY

22 Marie-François-Xavier Bichat, French physiologist who founded the science of histology, dies in Lyon, France (31).

24 Alexandre Dumas (*père*), French novelist best known for *The Count*

of Monte Cristo and *The Three Musketeers* (both 1844), born in Villers-Cotterêts, France (–1870).

SEPTEMBER

19 Lajos Kossuth, Hungarian political reformer who led Hungary's fight to gain independence from Austria, born in Monok, Hungary (–1894).

OCTOBER

2 Samuel Adams, U.S. politician and signatory of the Declaration of Independence, dies in Boston, Massachusetts (80).

31 Benoît Fourneyron, French engineer who invented the water turbine, born in St-Etienne, France (–1867).

NOVEMBER

15 George Romney, English portrait painter, dies in Kendal, Westmorland, England (68).

DECEMBER

6 Paul-Emile Botta, French archeologist whose discovery of the palace of the Assyrian king Sargon I in 1843 sparked other excavations in Mesopotamia, born in Turin, Italy (–1870).

- The Health and Morals of Apprentices Act in Britain restricts their working hours to 12 a day, bans night working, and prevents the recruitment of orphans aged under 9.
- U.S. entrepreneur Gideon Putnam builds the first hotel in the United States in Saratoga Springs, New York; it differs from other establishments because of its emphasis on service and lodging rather than food and drink.

Religion

- The French writer François-Auguste-René, vicomte de Chateaubriand, publishes his defense of religion *Le Génie du Christianisme/The Genius of Christianity*.

Sports

- The state of New York prohibits horse races, except those held by jockey clubs. The law is not relaxed until 1821, when public horse racing is allowed in Queens County.

1803

POLITICS, GOVERNMENT, AND ECONOMICS

Business and Economics

- Income tax is reintroduced in Britain.

APRIL
14 A reorganization of the Bank of France gives it a monopoly of note issue, stabilizing French finance.

Colonization

JANUARY
- The U.S. president Thomas Jefferson dispatches the minister plenipotentiary James Madison to France and Spain to purchase New Orleans and East and West Florida. France surprises Jefferson by offering the entire Louisiana territory to the United States.

Politics and Government

- The U.S. Supreme Court, in the case *Marbury v. Madison*, rules unconstitutional the Judiciary Act of 1801, thereby initiating the process of judicial review.
19 Napoleon Bonaparte, First Consul of France (later Napoleon I, Emperor of France), has the Act of Mediation passed in Switzerland, whereby the federal structure of government is weakened and the cantons (political divisions) regain their independence.
19 The U.S. Congress extends federal laws to Ohio.

25 The Enactment of Delegates of the Empire (*Reichdeputationshauptschluss*) at the Diet (legislative assembly) of Regensburg, Oberpfalz, reconstructs the German states. Most of the ecclesiastical estates, free imperial cities, and smaller princes lose their independence, while Bavaria and Prussia greatly improve their positions in a reorganization that proves to be a step toward eventual German unification. Under the Treaty of Lunéville (February 1801) those states and rulers who lost territory on the west bank of the Rhine were to be compensated with indemnities and territory east of the Rhine. In practice this means that the highly complex medieval arrangements are more practically reconfigured to the satisfaction of the leading rulers.

APRIL
30 The United States purchases Louisiana and New Orleans from the French, in contravention of the terms of the Treaty of San Ildefonso of October 1, 1800. Including in effect the entire western half of the drainage basin of the River Mississippi, the purchase, for a total sum (including interest) of $27,267,622, increases the nation's territory by 140%.

MAY
16–18 Britain and France go to war again (the start of the Napoleonic Wars) because of Napoleon Bonaparte's interference in Italian and Swiss affairs, and because of Britain's refusal to part with Malta immediately despite its agreement to do so in the 1802 Treaty of Amiens.
17 Britain places its first embargo on all French and Dutch ships in British ports.

JUNE
1–10 French forces invade the British-ruled electorate of Hanover.
6 British forces occupy the French Caribbean possessions of St. Lucia and Tobago.
24 Abortion becomes a statutory crime in Britain (it was previously only an ecclesiastical crime).

Napoleonic Wars (1803–15)

1803

AUGUST

23 Camps are established at St.-Omer, France, and Bruges in French-occupied Belgium, for the army with which Napoleon Bonaparte, First Consul of France (later Napoleon I, Emperor of France), intends to invade Britain. Work begins on assembling an invasion flotilla.

1805

AUGUST

25–September 3 The French emperor Napoleon I's "Army of England" leaves Boulogne, France, to march south against Austria.

OCTOBER

20 The Austrian army under Baron Karl Mack von Leiberich, encamped at Ulm on the River Danube, is outflanked by Napoleon's army. Mack surrenders with 30,000 men.

21 A Royal Navy fleet commanded by the English admiral Horatio Nelson defeats the combined Franco-Spanish fleet under Vice Admiral Pierre Villeneuve in the Battle of Trafalgar. Nelson is mortally wounded in the action, but the battle confirms Britain's naval superiority and removes any possibility of a French invasion of Britain.

DECEMBER

2 Napoleon entices the much larger Russo-Austrian forces ranged against him to overextend themselves before effecting a crushing defeat upon them in the Battle of Austerlitz, in Moravia.

1806

OCTOBER

9 Prussia's ultimatum to France concerning Prussian retention of Hanover expires and it declares war.

14 Napoleon decisively defeats the Prussians under Prince Hohenlohe at Jena in Saxony; Marshal Louis Davout simultaneously defeats the Saxons under the Duke of Brunswick at Auerstadt, also in Saxony.

27 Napoleon occupies the Prussian capital, Berlin.

NOVEMBER

21 Napoleon introduces the "Continental System" through the Berlin Decrees, closing continental (European) ports to British vessels and declaring all British ports to be in a state of blockade, in an attempt to counter Britain's control of the sea.

1807

JANUARY

7 Britain declares a blockade of the coasts of France and of Napoleon's allies, and that all ships trading in ports where Britain is excluded are liable to capture, in retaliation for the Continental System introduced by Napoleon in November 1806.

FEBRUARY

8 Napoleon's army catches up with the retreating Russian and Prussian forces at Eylau in eastern Prussia; an indecisive battle causes heavy losses to both sides.

APRIL

26 By the Convention of Bartenstein, Russia and Prussia form an alliance to drive France out of the German states.

JUNE

14 The French army under Marshal Jean Lannes roundly defeats a combined Russo-Prussian force under Count Levin August Bennigsen at the Battle of Friedland in eastern Prussia.

JULY

7 The Treaty of Tilsit (Prussia) ends the war between France and Russia. Napoleon, having defeated Austria and now Russia and Prussia, is the master of continental Europe. Russia agrees to the establishment of a Grand Duchy of Warsaw (as a French satellite in eastern Europe), recognizes the Confederation of the Rhine (association of German states under French protection), agrees to close all ports to British ships, and, by a secret agreement, Czar Alexander I agrees to coerce Denmark, Sweden, and Portugal into joining the alliance against Britain. In return he is given a free hand against Sweden in Finland and the Ottoman Empire in the Danubian provinces (Moldavia and Wallachia).

SEPTEMBER

2–5 A British fleet bombards the port of Copenhagen, Denmark, in the knowledge that Napoleon plans to use the powerful Danish fleet against Britain.

NOVEMBER

19 France invades Portugal for refusing to enter the Continental System and close its ports to Britain, marking the beginning of the Peninsular War.

29 The Portuguese royal family, the Braganzas, flee to Brazil under the protection of the British admiral Sidney Smith, taking with them the fleet that Napoleon intended to use against Britain.

1808

MARCH

3 French forces under Marshal Joachim Murat occupy the Spanish capital, Madrid.

MAY

2 A Spanish rising against the French (the *Dos Mayo*) begins in the occupied capital, Madrid. This is the start of the extensive guerrilla warfare that continues throughout the Peninsular War.

AUGUST

1 A British expedition under Arthur Wellesley (later Duke of Wellington) lands in Portugal to oppose Napoleon.

1 Napoleon's brother Joseph, the new king of Spain, flees from Madrid in fear of Spanish rebels.

21 A British army under Wellesley defeats the French at Vimiero, near Lisbon, Portugal.

30 The Convention of Cintra is agreed between the British commander, Hew Dalrymple, and the French commander, General Andoche Junot, allowing the latter to withdraw his troops from Portugal.

DECEMBER

13 The Spanish capital, Madrid, surrenders to Napoleon, who has taken personal command of French forces in the Iberian Peninsula.

1809

JANUARY

1 The Spanish Supreme Junta and Britain agree not to make a separate peace with Napoleon.

6 General John Moore, commanding the British army in Spain, is killed at the Battle of Coruña, having drawn the French emperor Napoleon away from Lisbon and Madrid.

FEBRUARY

8 Francis I of Austria, fearing Napoleon will overrun and dismember Austria, decides to launch a preemptive war against France.

APRIL

10 The Tyrolese revolt against Bavarian oppression as the Austrian army marches through Bavaria against the French, beginning a period of rebellion and civil war.

19–20 Napoleon defeats the Austrian army under Archduke Charles at Abensberg, Bavaria.

22 Arthur Wellesley lands at Lisbon to take command of British forces in Portugal.

22 Napoleon defeats the Austrian army under Archduke Charles at Eckmühl in Bavaria.

MAY

12 British forces under Arthur Wellesley defeat the French under Marshal Nicolas-Jean Soult at Oporto and force them to retreat from Portugal.

13 The French army takes the Austrian capital, Vienna.

21–22 After the Battle of Aspern-Essling against the Austrians, Napoleon is forced to retreat across the River Danube. France calls on Russian support against Austria, which is given halfheartedly.

JULY

5–6 Napoleon defeats the Austrian army under Archduke Charles in the Battle of Wagram, near Vienna, although the Austrian army retreats in good order.

12 Austria sues for peace with France and the Armistice of Znaim (Moravia) is signed.

28 A British expedition to Walcheren (the Netherlands) to help the Austrians by diverting Napoleon's attention from the Danube fails due to bad planning and the ravages of disease. The force is withdrawn.

28 The British under Arthur Wellesley are victorious at the Battle of Talavera in Spain over the French who afterwards fall back to Madrid. Wellesley is subsequently created Viscount Wellington.

1810

APRIL

19 Under the influence of the South American nationalist Simón Bolívar, the Junta in Venezuela breaks away from Napoleonic Spain, refusing to recognize Joseph Bonaparte and proclaiming allegiance to Ferdinand VII, the hereditary king of Spain.

MAY

22 A revolt breaks out in the Spanish viceroyalty of New Granada against Joseph Bonaparte's regime. Three days later another revolt breaks out in Rio de la Plata.

JULY

1 Louis Bonaparte, King of the French-dominated Kingdom of Holland, abdicates under pressure from his brother, Napoleon. Napoleon annexes the Netherlands, making it part of the Empire of the French.

OCTOBER

• British and Portuguese forces commanded by Arthur Wellesley, Viscount Wellington, hold the lines of Torres Vedras, the name given to the defensive emplacements his forces have created around the Portuguese city of the same name, throughout the month. The besieging French force runs short of supplies, and is forced to withdraw.

1811

MAY

• The U.S. warship *President* sinks the British gunboat *Little Belt* in retaliation for Britain's forcible enlistment of a U.S. soldier two weeks previously. Nine British sailors are killed and 12 are injured.

6 Wellington defeats the French at Fuentes d'Onoro, near Ciudad Rodrigo, in Portugal. Napoleon subsequently replaces the unsuccessful Marshal André Masséna with Marshal Auguste Marmont.

16 A British force under General William Beresford checks the French advancing on Portugal, under Marshal Nicolas-Jean Soult, at Albuhera, near Badajoz, Spain.

AUGUST

8 British forces occupy Dutch-held Java in the East Indies (the Netherlands having been incorporated into the Empire of the French).

1812

JANUARY

19 British forces under Wellington take Ciudad Rodrigo, Spain, one of the main passages between Spain and Portugal. French forces reoccupy Swedish Pomerania and the island of Rügen to put pressure on Sweden to end clandestine trade with Britain and to dissuade it from entering an anti-French alliance with Russia.

MARCH

29 The secretary of the council of state, Count Mikhail Speransky, the architect of Russia's pro-French policies, is replaced by the conservative vice admiral Shishkov as Czar Alexander I turns decisively against Napoleon.

APRIL

6 British forces capture the strategically important city of Badajoz on the border of Portugal and Spain.

Napoleonic Wars (1803–15) *continued*

MAY

28 The Treaty of Bucharest ends the war between Russia and the Ottoman Empire. Russia obtains Bessarabia (an area of southeast Europe bordered by the rivers Dniester and Prut) and withdraws its demand for the provinces of Moldavia and Wallachia. The peace enables Czar Alexander I to act against Napoleon.

JUNE

24 Napoleon crosses the River Niemen and begins his invasion of Russia. Rivalry with Russia has been brewing for some years, and Napoleon has assembled a huge army of 500,000 infantry and 100,000 cavalry (the *Grande Armée*).

28 The *Grande Armée* under Napoleon crosses the River Vilna in pursuit of the retreating Russian army, and occupies the city of Vilna (modern Vilnius), capital of Russian Poland.

JULY

18 By the Treaty of Örebro, Britain joins Russia and Sweden in a formal alliance against France.

22 British forces, under Viscount Wellington, decisively defeat the French, under Marshal Auguste Marmont, on the Spanish–Portuguese border at Salamanca, and subsequently advance into Spain.

AUGUST

12 British forces under Wellington enter the Spanish capital, Madrid, following the retreat of the French forces and its evacuation by King Joseph Bonaparte.

17–18 Russian forces commanded by Marshal Michel Andreas Barclay de Tolly are defeated by the French *Grande Armée* at Smolensk, which is then occupied by the French.

SEPTEMBER

7 The Russian army, now under the command of Marshal Mikhail Ilarionovich Kutuzov, is defeated by the French *Grande Armée* at the Battle of Borodino, and obliged to retreat and abandon the Russian capital, Moscow. Napoleon makes a significant mistake in failing to mobilize his reserves and destroy the retreating army.

14–18 The French *Grande Armée* enters and occupies the Russian capital, Moscow, burning much of the city. Following the defeat of the main Russian forces, the French are now subjected to constant wearying harassment by mounted troops.

19 British forces are forced by the French army under Marshal Auguste Marmont to withdraw from the city of Burgos in northern Spain.

OCTOBER

18 A detachment commanded by Marshal Joachim Murat from the French *Grande Armée* in Russia is defeated by Russian forces at Vinkaro.

19 Having failed to deliver a knockout blow against the Russians, Napoleon's *Grande Armée* begins to retreat from Moscow as winter sets in.

NOVEMBER

26–28 As the retreating *Grande Armée* crosses the River Beresina in Russia, it is attacked by Russian forces under Marshal Mikhail Ilarionovich Kutuzov and Count Ludwig Adolf Wittgenstein and sustains very heavy losses.

DECEMBER

5 Hearing news of the coup against him, Napoleon leaves his troops under the command of Marshal Joachim Murat in Russia and sets out for Paris (where he arrives on December 18). The remnants of his *Grande Armée* struggle back to France, a bare 10,000 effective troops remaining from the 500,000 who set out for Moscow.

30 By the Convention of Tauroggen with Russia, without the knowledge of King Frederick Wilhelm III, the Prussian field marshal Johann, Count Yorck von Wartenburg, commander of the Prussian contingent in Napoleon's *Grande Armée*, breaks away from the French alliance and becomes temporarily neutral.

1813

FEBRUARY

28 Prussia agrees, by the Alliance of Kalisz with Russia, to conduct a joint campaign in Saxony and Silesia against Napoleon and the Confederation of the Rhine (association of German states under French protection). Prussia is to regain all territory lost since 1806. An invitation to join the war is extended to Britain and Austria, and the agreement becomes the genesis of the Fourth Coalition against France.

MARCH

17 King Frederick Wilhelm III of Prussia declares war against France.

18 After a patriotic outbreak in Hamburg against the French, the city is taken from its French garrison by advancing Russian forces.

MAY

2 Napoleon defeats a Prussian and Russian army at Lützen (Gross-Gorschen) near Leipzig, Saxony, but is unable to destroy his opponents.

20–21 The indecisive Battle of Bautzen, near Dresden, Saxony, between the French and Russo-Prussian armies results in heavy losses on both sides.

JUNE

4–August 10 The armistice of Poischwitz, Austria, between the allies (Prussia and Austria) and France is arranged after allied requests through the mediation of the Austrian foreign minister Klemens Metternich. Napoleon uses the time to train his cavalry.

14–15 Having only a small army of its own, Britain undertakes to pay subsidies to support Russia and Prussia in the war with France.

21 British forces under Viscount Wellington completely rout the French army of Marshal Jean-Baptiste Jourdain at Vittoria in northern Spain, forcing Joseph Bonaparte to flee back to France.

27 By the Treaty of Reichenbach with Prussia and Russia, Austria agrees to declare war on France on July 20 if the French refuse the conditions of peace.

JULY

26–August 1 A French force, under Marshal Nicolas-Jean Soult, tries to reenter Spain and is definitively repulsed by British forces at the Battle of Sorrauren.

AUGUST

12 Austria declares war against Napoleon. The allies (Austria, Prussia, and Russia) can now put 500,000 men in the field, with armies in Silesia, Bohemia, and northern Germany.

23 French forces under General Nicolas-Charles Oudinot are defeated by the Prussian general Friedrich von Bülow at Grossbeeren, preventing them from marching on the Prussian capital, Berlin.

26 The French, under General Jacques MacDonald, are defeated at Katzbach, Prussia, by the Prussian general Gebhard von Blücher.

26–27 In the Battle of Dresden, in Saxony, Napoleon defeats the allied army from Bohemia, having arrived unexpectedly after the Austrian general Karl Philipp, Prince zu Schwarzenberg, had attacked the French under Marshal Gouvion St.-Cyr.

SEPTEMBER

6 The French marshal Michel Ney is defeated by Prince Jean-Baptiste Bernadotte of Sweden's Northern Army at Dennewitz as he attempts to take Berlin.

9 The French-held city of San Sebastián in northern Spain capitulates to the British army after a siege lasting since August 31.

9 The Treaty of Teplitz confirms the Reichenbach agreement of June 27 uniting Russia, Prussia, and Austria against France.

OCTOBER

8 Bavaria joins the allies against France by the Treaty of Ried with Austria, and leaves the Confederation of the Rhine (the association of German states under French protection).

14 Bavaria makes a formal declaration of war against France.

16–19 Opposed by the Prussian army in the northwest and Austro-Russian forces in the south, the French army under Napoleon is heavily defeated in the "Battle of the Nations" at Leipzig in Saxony, and retreats. Allied victory leads to the dissolution of the Confederation of the Rhine (the association of German states under French protection) and of the kingdom of Westphalia.

NOVEMBER

8 The allies offer peace proposals to Napoleon in Frankfurt by which France would be left with the boundaries of the Alps and the Pyrenees, keeping Belgium, Nice, and Savoy.

DECEMBER

1 By the Declaration of Frankfurt, the allies resolve to invade France because of Napoleon's vague reply to their peace proposals.

10 British troops besiege the southern French port of Bayonne.

21 The Austrian forces of Field Marshal Karl Philipp, Prince zu Schwarzenberg, enter France through Switzerland.

31 The Prussian army under General Gebhard von Blücher crosses the River Rhine into France near Mannheim.

1814

JANUARY

11 Joachim Murat, King of Naples, deserts Napoleon and joins the allies, Prussia and Austria, in a bid to preserve his throne.

30 In the Battle of La Rothière in France, Napoleon attempts to stop General Gebhard von Blücher's Prussians joining up with the Austrian army of Field Marshal Karl Philipp, Prince zu Schwarzenberg. Blücher attacks the French first and the Austro-Russian army completes the victory.

FEBRUARY

5–March 19 Peace negotiations between the allies and Napoleon at Châtillon-sur-Seine, France, are futile as Napoleon refuses to accept the 1791 frontier of France.

8 Napoleon pushes Karl Philipp's Austro-Russian army back 65 km/40 mi at the Battle of Montereau, France, despite being heavily outnumbered.

MARCH

7 Napoleon I inflicts a heavy defeat on General Gebhard von Blücher's Prussian forces at Craonne, 40 km/25 mi from Paris. Blücher subsequently links up with Bernadotte's Swedish army approaching from the northeast and faces Napoleon's force of 30,000 with a combined army of 100,000 men.

9 The allies sign the Treaty of Chaumont, by which they agree not to negotiate a separate peace with Napoleon and to insist on his acceptance of the 1791 frontiers of France.

9–10 At the Battle of Laon, in northern France, the combined allied army compels Napoleon to withdraw further into France.

12 British forces, advancing from the south of France, capture the port of Bordeaux.

30 The French marshals Auguste Marmont and Edouard Mortier attempt unsuccessfully to resist the superior forces of Karl Philipp, Blücher, and Bernadotte drawn up outside Paris, France. Following his defeat by Karl Philipp, Napoleon is left stranded far to the east.

31 Auguste Marmont surrenders the French capital, Paris, to the allies. Napoleon who has been rushing to rejoin the battle, halts at Fontainebleau, southeast of Paris. The Senate declares the throne forfeited following the flight of the empress Marie-Louise.

APRIL

1 The Senate appoints a provisional French government in Paris, following the triumphant entry of the allies into the capital.

10 Arthur Wellesley, Viscount Wellington, defeats the French marshal Nicolas-Jean Soult and drives his army out of Toulouse. He is subsequently created Duke of Wellington.

11 By the Treaty of Fontainebleau, Napoleon abdicates unconditionally and is banished to the principality of Elba, an island off the west coast of Italy, on an annuity of 2,000,000 francs. Queen Marie-Louise is given the duchies of Gustalla, Parma, and Piacenza.

Napoleonic Wars (1803–15) *continued*

MAY

3 King Louis XVIII of France enters Paris, following the abdication of Napoleon.

NOVEMBER

1 The Congress of Vienna, convened to decide the final settlement of the Napoleonic Wars, formally opens in Austria.

1815

MARCH

1 Napoleon, having escaped from the island of Elba, lands in the south of France at Cannes and marches on the capital, Paris, with growing support.

19 King Louis XVIII of France flees from Paris, before the advance of Napoleon.

20 Napoleon enters Paris, and the "Hundred Days" (Napoleon's second period of rule) begin. Over the next

two days he forms a government composed primarily of his former ministers.

25 Austria, Britain, Prussia, and Russia form the Fifth Coalition against Napoleon to maintain the established order in Europe. Each agrees to send 150,000 men into the field.

MAY

3 Neapolitan forces commanded by Joachim Murat, King of Naples, are defeated at Tolentino, near Ancona, by the Austrian army.

JUNE

16 The French army under Napoleon defeats a Prussian force under General von Blücher at Ligny, Belgium, in an attempt to split the Prussian army from the Anglo-Dutch army under Arthur Wellesley, Duke of Wellington. The Prussians manage to retreat in good order and, instead of moving west, retire to the north, in order to be able to link up with Wellington.

JULY

15 A camp is established at Boulogne, France, for the "Army of England" with which Napoleon Bonaparte intends to invade once his fleet can operate safely.

23 The radical Robert Emmet, leader of the United Irishmen, attempts to stage a rising against British rule in Ireland.

AUGUST

3 The second Anglo-Maratha War begins in India when British troops take the offensive against the Sindhia dynasty of Gwalior.

23 Camps are established at St.-Omer, France, and Bruges in French-occupied Belgium, for the army with which Napoleon Bonaparte intends to invade Britain. Work begins on assembling an invasion flotilla.

SEPTEMBER

23 The British soldier and statesman Arthur Wellesley (later Duke of Wellington) defeats the Daulat Rao Sindhia of Gwalior at the Battle of Assaye in India, but is subsequently recalled by superiors alarmed at his forthright actions.

OCTOBER

19 By a convention with France, Spain is declared neutral in the Napoleonic Wars and is to enforce Portugal's neutrality.

DECEMBER

30 Daulat Rao Sindhia of Gwalior, India, finally submits to British forces.

SCIENCE, TECHNOLOGY, AND MEDICINE

Agriculture

December 1803–04 Thousands die in India from starvation during a famine caused by drought and the destruction of crops by locusts.

Ecology

- English meteorologist Luke Howard gives names to the cloud types (cirrus, cumulus, stratus, and nimbus), and recognizes that their shapes reflect their causes.

APRIL

- John James Audubon becomes the first person in the United States to band birds for scientific purposes, when he tags some phoebes.

Science

- English botanist and entomologist Adrian Harvey Haworth publishes *Lepidoptera Britannica/Butterflies of Britain*, the first complete description of several hundred British moths and butterflies.
- English chemist and physicist John Dalton formulates his atomic theory of matter: that all elements are made of minute indestructible particles, called atoms, that are all identical. He also devises a system of chemical symbols and arranges the relative weights of atoms in a table.
- English scientist William Hyde Wollaston discovers the element palladium (atomic no. 78).
- French chemist Claude-Louis Berthollet publishes *Essai de statique chimique/Essay on Chemical Statistics*, in

18 Napoleon engages it in the decisive Battle of Waterloo, near the Belgian village of that name, south of Brussels. Wellington manages to hold back the French attack until the Prussian army under Blücher, having avoided pursuit by a French detachment under Marshal Emmanuel de Grouchy, begins to arrive in the late afternoon. As the Prussians begin to attack the French right flank, Wellington orders a counterattack, forcing the French into a retreat which soon turns into a rout.

22 Napoleon abdicates for a second time, having being given the choice of resignation or deposition by the French Chambers.

JULY

7–8 The allies, mainly Austrian and Prussian forces, reenter Paris, enabling King Louis XVIII to return (July 8) to the royal palace of the Tuileries.

AUGUST

2 By agreement between Prussia, Austria, Britain, and Russia, Napoleon is banished to St. Helena, a desolate island in the Atlantic Ocean.

1818

SEPTEMBER

27–November 21 A conference is held in Aachen between Austria, Prussia, Russia, Britain, and France to discuss the indemnity imposed on France after its defeat in the Napoleonic Wars.

OCTOBER

9 The allies (Britain, Prussia, Austrian Empire, and Russia) agree to evacuate the army of occupation from France by November 30, as the French war indemnity is being paid.

which he notes that the completeness of chemical reactions depends partly on the masses of the reacting substances. He thus begins the study of physical chemistry.

- Swedish chemist Jöns Jakob Berzelius discovers cerium (atomic no. 58).

Technology

- English inventor Robert Ransome develops a cast-iron, self-sharpening plow.
- Henry Shrapnel's shell (invented 1784) is adopted by the British army.
- Scottish engineer William Murdock invents a steam gun.
- U.S. farmer Thomas Moore patents a refrigerator with an icebox.

Transportation

- English engineer Richard Trevithick builds a second steam carriage, the *New Castle*, which he runs through the streets of London, England, at a speed of 10 kph/6 mph.
- The Surrey Iron Railroad between Croydon and Wandsworth, England, is built; the first freight railway, it uses horse-drawn carriages.
- U.S. inventor Robert Fulton demonstrates a steamboat on the River Seine in Paris, France; it attracts little interest.

April 1803–22 Scottish engineer Thomas Telford constructs the 100-km/60-mi Caledonian Canal, linking Scotland's east and west coasts.

MAY

- Less than four years before the U.S. engineer and inventor Robert Fulton launches his first steamboat, the U.S. surveyor Benjamin Henry Latrobe denigrates the feasibility of steam locomotion in a report to the American Philosophical Society.

ARTS AND IDEAS

Architecture

- Benjamin Henry Latrobe is appointed surveyor of public buildings by President Thomas Jefferson. He designs the south wing of the U.S. Capitol and alterations to the White House.
- The Rotunda in the Bank of England, in London, designed by the English architect John Soane, is completed. It is later destroyed.

Arts

- The Danish artist Bertel Thorvaldsen sculpts *Jason and the Golden Fleece*.
- The Scottish artist Henry Raeburn paints *The Macnab*.
- The U.S. artist Benjamin West paints *Christ Healing the Sick*.

Music

- Austrian composer Franz Josef Haydn completes his String Quartet No. 83 (Opus 103).
- German composer Ludwig van Beethoven completes his Symphony No. 3 (Opus 55), the *Eroica*, and his Violin Sonata in A major (Opus 47), the *Kreutzer Sonata*.

Theater and Dance

- The play *Die Braut von Messina/The Bride of Messina* by the German writer Friedrich Johann Christoph von Schiller is first performed.

Thought and Scholarship

- The English economist Thomas Robert Malthus publishes *An Essay on the Principle of Population; or, a View of its Past and Present Effects on Human Happiness*. This is a much expanded version of his 1798 tract.
- The French economist Jean-Baptiste Say publishes *Traité d'économique politique/Treatise on Political Economy*.
- The U.S. historian Samuel Miller publishes *A Brief Retrospect of the Eighteenth Century*.
- The U.S. novelist William Wirt publishes *Letter of the British Spy*, a seminal work in the cultural study of the American South.
- Salisbury, Connecticut, becomes the first town in the United States to boast a publicly supported library. The library has been established by a gift from Boston publisher Caleb Bingham.

SOCIETY

Education

- Joseph Lancaster, an English Quaker schoolmaster, publishes *Improvements in Education as it Respects the Industrious Classes*, describing the "monitor system" by which older children take responsibility for teaching younger ones.

Religion

- Massachusetts Universalists adopt the Winchester Profession, asserting the oneness of God and the freedom of the will.

SEPTEMBER
- Catholics in Boston, Massachusetts, dedicate the city's first Catholic church.

BIRTHS & DEATHS

FEBRUARY
2   Albert Sydney Johnston, Confederate general and the designated second in command of all Confederate forces at the beginning of the Civil War, born in Washington, Kentucky (–1862).

MARCH
14   Fredrich Gottlieb Klopstock, German poet, dies in Hamburg, Germany (78).

MAY
12   Justus von Liebig, German chemist who was active in the fields of organic chemistry, biochemistry, and agricultural chemistry, born in Darmstadt, Hesse-Darmstadt (–1873).
25   Ralph Waldo Emerson, U.S. writer and leading proponent of New England Transcendentalism, born in Boston, Massachusetts (–1882).

JULY
31   John Ericcson, Swedish-born U.S. naval engineer who invented the screw propeller, born in Långbanshyttan, Sweden (–1889).

SEPTEMBER
28   Prosper Mérimée, French dramatist, historian, and archeologist, born in Paris, France (–1870).

OCTOBER
8   Vittorio Alfieri, Italian poet, dies in Florence, Italy (54).

NOVEMBER
5   Pierre Choderlos de Laclos, French author who pioneered the psychological novel, dies in Taranto, Parthenopean Republic (62).

29   Christian Doppler, Austrian physicist who described the change in frequency of light and sound waves emitted by a moving object relative to an observer, born in Salzburg, Austria (–1853).

DECEMBER
11   Hector Berlioz, French composer, born in Côte-St.-André, France (–1869).
18   Johann Gottfried von Herder, German poet, critic, and philosopher, dies in Weimar, Saxe-Weimar (now Germany) (59).

1804

POLITICS, GOVERNMENT, AND ECONOMICS

Business and Economics

FEBRUARY

- In a letter to the French economist Jean-Baptiste Say, the U.S. president Thomas Jefferson depicts the United States as a nation whose physical and natural abundance "enables every one who will labor to marry young, and to raise a family of any size. Our food, then, may increase geometrically with our laborers, and our births, however multiplied, become effective."

Colonization

OCTOBER

9 The settlement of Hobart, Tasmania, is founded under the British lieutenant governor David Collins.

Politics and Government

- Boys as young as five or six are being used to clean chimneys in Britain. Legislation is passed preventing the apprenticing of boys under nine and limiting the working day to a maximum of eight hours; these laws are often broken.
- In the U.S. congressional elections, the Democratic-Republicans retain majorities in the House of Representatives (116–25) and Senate (27–7).
- The U.S. president Thomas Jefferson appoints the South Carolina jurist William Johnson to the U.S. Supreme Court.

JANUARY

25 A Royalist plot against Napoleon Bonaparte, First Consul of France (later Napoleon I, Emperor of France), is discovered by the police in Paris, France.

FEBRUARY

- The U.S. naval lieutenant Stephen Decatur burns the U.S. warship *Philadelphia*, captured by Barbary pirates the previous year, in Tripoli (modern Libya) harbor, North Africa.

MARCH

- The U.S. Congress passes the Louisiana Territory Act, dividing the new land in half to create the Territory of

Orleans in the south and the District of Louisiana in the north.

20–21 The Duc d'Enghien, believed on flimsy evidence to be the Royalists' candidate to replace Napoleon Bonaparte, is kidnapped from Baden in Germany by French troops and executed after a summary trial.

21 The Civil Code (renamed the Code Napoleon in 1807) is promulgated in France, providing a uniform civil law (previously French law was split between Roman law in the south and custom law in the north).

APRIL

16 War begins between the British East India Company and the Maratha maharaja Jaswant Rao Holkar of Indore in India.

MAY

16 Napoleon Bonaparte is proclaimed emperor of France by the Senate and Tribunate.

JULY

- The U.S. vice president Aaron Burr mortally wounds the former U.S. treasury secretary Alexander Hamilton in a duel. Burr challenged Hamilton to a duel after Hamilton had implicated Burr in an alleged plot to withdraw New York and New England from the Union.

AUGUST

11 Francis II of Austria assumes the title of hereditary emperor of Austrian possessions (though he still retains the title of Holy Roman Emperor).

SEPTEMBER

- The 12th amendment to the U.S. Constitution becomes law. It stipulates that electors will vote separately for the president and vice president. Formerly, the runner-up in the presidential election automatically became vice president.

OCTOBER

27 The liberal reformer Baron Heinrich vom Stein is appointed Prussian minister of trade.

NOVEMBER

6 Francis II, Emperor of Austria, makes a secret treaty with Russia to resist further French aggression in Italy.

11 Austria and Russia make a declaration to maintain the unstable Ottoman Empire against French expansion in the Balkans and the Near East.

13–17 British troops defeat the forces of the Maratha maharaja Jaswant Rao Holkar of Indore.

DECEMBER

- Americans reelect Thomas Jefferson as U.S. president and elect former New York governor George Clinton as vice president.

2 Napoleon Bonaparte crowns himself emperor as Napoleon I in Paris, France. Pope Pius VII officiates at the coronation.

12 Spain reluctantly declares war on Britain at the instigation of France.

SCIENCE, TECHNOLOGY, AND MEDICINE

Agriculture

- The soybean is first grown in the United States.
- Washington, D.C., plays host to the first agricultural fair in the United States, where farmers and entrepreneurs market ideas as well as agricultural goods.

Ecology

December 1804–07 German naturalist and explorer Alexander von Humboldt draws maps with isotherms (lines joining locations with the same mean temperature) and isobars (lines joining locations with the same mean barometric pressure).

Exploration

- The North American bison population is estimated to be about 60 million at this time, based on the sighting of huge herds by the U.S. explorers Meriwether Lewis (private secretary to President Thomas Jefferson) and William Clark (a U.S. army officer); they departed St. Louis, Missouri (in May) for the Dakota territory on the first leg of their epic journey to find a land route to the Pacific Ocean.

Science

- English chemist and physicist William Hyde Wollaston discovers the element rhodium (atomic no. 45) and develops a powder-metallurgy method of purifying platinum—valuable in chemical research.
- English chemist and physicist John Dalton proposes the law of multiple proportions which states that when two elements combine to form more than one compound the weights of one element combine with a fixed weight of the other in a ratio of small whole numbers. The law provides strong support for his atomic theory.
- English chemist Smithson Tennant discovers and isolates osmium (atomic no. 76) and iridium (atomic no. 77).
- German astronomer Karl Harding discovers Juno, the third asteroid to be discovered.
- Scottish physicist John Leslie publishes *An Experimental Inquiry into the Nature and Properties of Heat*.
- Swiss plant physiologist Nicolas-Théodore de Saussure publishes *Recherches chimiques sur la végétation/ Chemical Research on Vegetation*, in which he demonstrates that plants require nitrogen from the soil, and increase in weight through the absorption of water and carbon dioxide.

August

24 French physicists Jean Biot and Joseph-Louis Gay-Lussac ascend to a height of 4,000 m/13,000 ft in a hydrogen balloon to study the effects of altitude on fluctuations in the earth's magnetic field.

September

16 Gay-Lussac ascends to a height of 7,016 m/23,018 ft in a hydrogen balloon; a record unbeaten for 50 years. He takes measurements of the earth's magnetism, temperature, air pressure, and chemical composition, and determines that at that altitude the air contains the same percentage of oxygen (21.49%) as on the ground.

Technology

- French confectioner Nicolas Appert opens the world's first factory to vacuum-pack goods, in Massey, near Paris, France.
- German inventor Friedrich Albrecht Winzer develops an oven to manufacture coal gas.
- September 1804–05 Cornish mining engineer Arthur Woolf patents a high-pressure compound steam engine that uses the steam twice at descending pressures and doubles the thermal efficiency of James Watt's engine.

Transportation

- U.S. engineer John Stevens builds a steamship, *Little Juliana*, using two Archimedes screws to propel it. He also uses a multitube, high-pressure steam engine connected directly to the boiler.
- U.S. inventor Oliver Evans builds a five-horsepower steam engine, which he drives 2.4 km/1.5 mi through Philadelphia, Pennsylvania. Its original purpose is to propel a scow, a water vehicle for dredging and cleaning docks.

February

21 English engineer Richard Trevithick builds the first steam railroad locomotive, and on a wager runs it on a 16 km/10 mi track at the Pen-y-darren Ironworks in South Wales carrying 10 tons of iron and 70 passengers.

December

1 English aviation pioneer George Cayley develops an instrument to measure wind resistance. About this time he also begins to construct models of gliders with fixed wings, fuselage, lifts and a rudder—the basic configuration of the modern airplane.

ARTS AND IDEAS

Architecture

- The Coonskin Library opens in Marietta, Ohio, as settlers exchange coonskins for books.

Arts

- The French artist Antoine-Jean Gros paints *The Plague at Jaffa*.
- The U.S. artist John Vanderlyn paints *The Death of Jane McCrea*.
- The English wood engraver Thomas Bewick publishes *Water Birds*, the second part of his classic *A History of British Birds*. The first part appeared in 1797.

Literature and Language

- The autobiography of the Danish poet Johannes Ewald, *Levnet og meninger/Life and Opinions*, an early classic of Danish literature, is published posthumously.
- The English poet and artist William Blake publishes his epic poem *Jerusalem*, his most richly illustrated book.

Music

- German composer Ludwig van Beethoven completes his Piano Sonata No. 21 (Opus 53), the *Waldstein*, and his 3 Violin Sonatas (Opus 30).
- The opera *Milton* by the Italian composer Gaspare Spontini is first performed, in Paris, France.

Theater and Dance

- The play *Wilhelm Tell* by the German writer Friedrich Johann Christoph von Schiller is first performed, in Weimar, Germany.

Thought and Scholarship

- The New York investor John Pintard oversees the establishment of the New York Historical Society.
- The Scottish philosopher Thomas Brown publishes *Inquiry into the Relation of Cause and Effect*.
- The Society of Painters in Water-Colours (later called the Water Colour Society) is founded, in England.

SOCIETY

Education

- Ohio University is founded in Athens, Ohio.

Everyday Life

- The first recorded shipment of bananas to the United States arrives from Cuba aboard the merchant ship *Reynard*. An organized fruit trade does not begin until 1885.
- The first restaurant guide, *Almanach des Gourmands/ Gourmands' Almanac*, written by Alexandre-Balthazar-Laurent Grimod de la Reynière, lists 500 restaurants in Paris, France.
- Two patents for galluses, better-known as garter belts, are granted in the United States.

BIRTHS & DEATHS

FEBRUARY

12   Immanuel Kant, German philosopher whose work had a major influence on subsequent philosophy, dies in Königsberg, Prussia (80).

16   Charles Pichegru, French general, is found strangled with his cravat in Temple prison, Paris, France (43).

APRIL

- Jacques Necker, Swiss banker and director of finance of France 1771–81, 1788–89, and 1789–90, dies in Coppet, Switzerland (71).

5   Matthias Schleiden, German botanist who, with Theodor Schwann, established cell theory, born in Germany (–1881).

MAY

13   Alexey Stepanovich Khomyakov, Russian poet who led the Slavophile movement which lauded the Russian way of life, born in Moscow, Russia (–1860).

JUNE

1   Michael Ivanovich Glinka, Russian composer, born in Novospasskoye, Russia (–1857).

JULY

1   George Sand (pseudonym of Lucie Dudevant), French romantic novelist, born in Paris, France (–1876).

4   Nathaniel Hawthorne, U.S. author best known for *The Scarlet Letter* (1850) and *The House of Seven Gables* (1851), born in Salem, Massachusetts (–1864).

12   Alexander Hamilton, U.S. Federalist Party politician who influenced the adoption of a strong central government and was the First Secretary of the Treasury 1789–95, dies in New York, New York, after a duel (c. 48).

28   Ludwig Feuerbach, German philosopher who argued that God is nothing but the outward projection of human nature, born in Landshut, Bavaria (now in Germany) (–1872).

NOVEMBER

23   Franklin Pierce, fourteenth president of the United States 1853–57, a Democrat, born in Hillsboro, New Hampshire (–1869).

DECEMBER

2   Philippe Lebon, French engineer who invented illuminating gas, is murdered by prowlers in Paris, France (37).

10   Karl Gustav Jacob Jacobi, German mathematician who developed the theory of elliptic function, born in Potsdam, Prussia (now Germany) (–1851).

21   Benjamin Disraeli, Earl of Beaconsfield, British prime minister 1868 and 1874–80, a Conservative, born in London, England (–1881).

23   Charles-Augustin Ste.-Beuve, French historian and literary critic, born in Boulogne, France (–1869).

1805

POLITICS, GOVERNMENT, AND ECONOMICS

Business and Economics

- French inventor Joseph-Marie Jacquard develops a loom that uses punched cards to control the weaving of cloth. Able to produce any desired pattern automatically, it stimulates the technological revolution in the textile industry and forms the basis of the automatic loom. Punched cards are also used in early computers.
- Philadelphia cordwainers (shoemakers and leather workers) are convicted of criminal conspiracy in the first labor dispute to be adjudicated in a U.S. court.
- Internal customs duties in Prussia are abolished under the minister of trade, Baron Heinrich vom Stein, while the rest of central Europe preserves anticompetitive legislation.

MAY

5   Great Britain begins to clamp down on U.S. trade with the West Indies, which results in the loss of its friendship with the United States and leads to war in 1812.

Colonization

JUNE

4   The Ligurian Republic (Italy) is annexed by France, which thus gains the port of Genoa.

SEPTEMBER

23   The duchies of Parma, Piacenza, and Gustalla in Italy are annexed by France.

Politics and Government

MARCH

- Thomas Jefferson is inaugurated as U.S. president for a second term.

APRIL

- The Tripolitan War begins to turn in the United States's favor when a force led by the U.S. naval commander William Eaton seizes the port of Derna (Darnah, in modern Libya), North Africa.
- 4–July 7   The British vice admiral Horatio Nelson pursues a Franco-Spanish fleet under Vice Admiral Pierre Villeneuve to the West Indies and back without success.

11   By the Treaty of St. Petersburg, Britain and Russia agree to form a European league for the liberation of the northern German states and Italy, and to protect the Netherlands, Switzerland, and the Italian kingdom of Naples from French domination. Britain is to finance Russia and other potential members of the Third Coalition against France.

MAY

26   Emperor Napoleon I of France crowns himself king of Italy in Milan Cathedral.

JUNE

- The U.S. naval officer John Rodgers secures a peace treaty with the Barbary state of Tripoli (modern Libya), North Africa, by which Tripoli pledges to quit its harassment of U.S. merchant ships and release the crew of the captured U.S. warship *Philadelphia* in exchange for $60,000.

JULY

22   British admiral Robert Calder's naval squadron clashes with the Franco-Spanish fleet of Vice Admiral Pierre Villeneuve off Cape Finisterre, northwest Spain; two French ships are captured, but Villeneuve escapes to the southern Spanish port of Cadiz.

AUGUST

9   Austria joins Britain, Russia, and Sweden as the signatories of the Treaty of St. Petersburg in alliance against France.

25–September 3   Napoleon I's "Army of England" leaves Boulogne, France, to march south against Austria.

SEPTEMBER

8   The Austrian army of Baron Karl Mack von Leiberich opens hostilities against France by invading Bavaria and takes up positions near Ulm, on the River Danube.

OCTOBER

20   The Austrian army under Baron Karl Mack von Leiberich, encamped at Ulm on the River Danube, is outflanked by Napoleon's army. Mack surrenders with 30,000 men.

21   A Royal Navy fleet commanded by the English admiral Horatio Nelson defeats the combined Franco-Spanish fleet under Vice Admiral Villeneuve in the Battle of Trafalgar. Nelson is mortally wounded in the action, but the battle confirms Britain's naval superiority and removes any possibility of a French invasion of Britain.

NOVEMBER

23   A peace treaty is signed between the British East India Company and the Maratha prince Daulat Rao Sindhia of Gwalior, India, ending the war between them on terms favorable to British trade.

DECEMBER

2　The French emperor Napoleon I entices the much larger Russo-Austrian forces ranged against him to overextend themselves before effecting a crushing defeat upon them in the Battle of Austerlitz, in Moravia.

15　By the Treaty of Schönbrunn with France, Prussia cedes Cleves, Neuchâtel, and Ansbach, and accepts French territorial gains in Germany and Italy. In return Prussia is allowed to occupy Hanover in order to prevent it joining the coalition against Napoleon.

26　By the peace of the Treaty of Pressburg between Austria and France, the Austrians recognize French gains in Italy and give up the Tyrol and all possessions in Italy and southern Germany so that Bavaria and Württemberg become kingdoms. Baden becomes a grand duchy.

SCIENCE, TECHNOLOGY, AND MEDICINE

Ecology

- British navy commander Francis Beaufort devises the Beaufort wind force scale.

Exploration

- A Shoshone scout, Sacajawea, joins the U.S. explorers Meriwether Lewis and William Clark, sharing her valuable knowledge of edible plants and interpreting for the explorers.
- Scottish explorer Mungo Park leads an expedition to the River Niger in West Africa, but is drowned after being ambushed at Bussa.

JULY

- Lewis and Clark reach the headwaters of the Missouri River, dashing their hope of finding an easy passage to the Pacific Ocean.

AUGUST

- The U.S. army lieutenant Zebulon Montgomery Pike embarks on an attempt to locate the headwaters of the Mississippi River.

NOVEMBER

- Lewis and Clark reach the Pacific Ocean via the Columbia River.

Science

- French physicist Joseph-Louis Gay-Lussac determines the relative proportions of hydrogen and oxygen in water by measuring the proportions of the gases that combine.

Technology

- British artillery officer William Congreve invents the Congreve rocket. Consisting of a rocket 103 cm/40.5 in

long, and a stabilizing stick 4.9 m/16 ft long, it has a range of 1.8 km/1.1 mi, and is used during the Napoleonic Wars and the War of 1812. It is immortalized in the song "The Star-Spangled Banner."

- English engineer Richard Trevithick uses his high-pressure steam engine to operate an iron-rolling mill and to propel a barge with the aid of paddlewheels.
- U.S. engineer Oliver Evans builds a prototype of a compressed-ether refrigeration machine.

Transportation

- The Philadelphia entrepreneur Stephen Girard begins production of merchant ships destined for the China–West Indies trade.
- U.S. inventor Oliver Evans runs an amphibious dredger called *Orukter Amphibolos* through the streets of Philadelphia; 9 m/30 ft long, with a continuous chain of buckets as well as wheels, it runs on land and water and is the first powered vehicle to operate on roads in the United States.

ARTS AND IDEAS

Arts

- The Brazilian artist Aleijadhino completes his sculptures *The Twelve Prophets*, the finest baroque sculptures in South America.
- The English artist J. M. W. Turner paints *Shipwreck*.
- The English artist John Sell Cotman paints *Greta Bridge*.
- The German artist Philipp Runge paints *The Morning*.
- The Spanish artist Francisco José de Goya y Lucientes paints his *Portrait of Doña Isabel Cobos de Porcal*, *The Clothed Maja*, and *The Nude Maja*. He is summoned by the Inquisition and asked to explain why he has painted a nude (a rare subject in Spanish art).

Literature and Language

- The Boston satirist Mercy Otis Warren publishes her *History of the Rise, Progress, and Termination of the American Revolution*.
- The English poet Robert Southey publishes his epic poem *Madoc*.
- The English poet William Wordsworth finishes the first version of his autobiographical work *The Prelude*. It is published in a heavily changed format in 1850. The 1805 version is not published until 1926.
- The French writer François-Auguste-René, vicomte de Chateaubriand, publishes his novel *René, ou les effets de la passion/René, or the Effects of Passion*.
- The Scottish poet and novelist Walter Scott publishes his long narrative poem *The Lay of the Last Minstrel*.

Music

- German composer Ludwig van Beethoven completes his Piano Sonata No. 23 (Opus 57), the *Appassionata*, and his overture *Leonora No 1* (Opus 138).
- German writers Achim von Arnim and Clemens Brentano publish *Des Knaben Wunderhorn/The Boy's Magic Horn*, an important collection of German folk songs. The composer Gustav Mahler sets many of them to music.
- Italian musician Niccolò Paganini begins to tour Europe as a virtuoso violinist.
- Beethoven's opera *Fidelio, oder der Triumph der ehelichen Liebe/Fidelio, or the Triumph of Married Love* is first performed, in Vienna, Austria.

Thought and Scholarship

- The U.S. painter Charles Willson Peale establishes the Pennsylvania Academy of Fine Arts, the oldest existing art institute in the United States.

SOCIETY

Everyday Life

- Frederick Tudor, a businessman from Boston, Massachusetts, makes the first significant shipment of ice from New England to Martinique. Over a 15-year period, changes in cutting, storing, and shipping technology allow profitable shipments to Havana, New Orleans, and India.

Religion

- The German immigrant George Rapp establishes the Rappites, a religious utopian community, in the new town of Harmony, Pennsylvania.
- The Universalist Boston clergyman Hosea Ballou publishes his *Treatise on Atonement*.

Sports

JULY
8 The U.S. boxer Bill Richmond defeats Jack Holmes of Britain at Cricklewood Green, near London, England, to become the first black American to win a prize fight.

BIRTHS & DEATHS

FEBRUARY
1 Auguste Blanqui, French socialist revolutionary, born in Puget-Théniers, France (–1881).

MARCH
21 Jean Baptiste Greuze, French portrait painter, dies in Paris, France (79).

APRIL
2 Hans Christian Andersen, Danish storyteller, born in Odense, Denmark (–1875).

MAY
7 William Petty-Fitzmaurice, Earl of Lansdowne, prime minister of England 1782–83, dies in London, England (67).
9 Johann Christoph Friedrich von Schiller, German dramatist and poet, dies in Weimar, Saxe-Weimar (45).
25 William Paley, English Anglican priest, theologian, and utilitarian philosopher, dies in Lincoln, Lincolnshire, England (61).
28 Luigi Boccherini, Italian composer who was instrumental in developing the string quartet, dies in Madrid, Spain (62).

JUNE
22 Giuseppe Mazzini, Italian revolutionary and founder of Young Italy, a secret revolutionary society which strove for Italian unity, born in Genoa, Italy (–1872).

JULY
29 Alexis Charles-Henri-Clérel de Tocqueville, French political scientist, historian, and politician, born in Paris, France (–1859).

OCTOBER
21 Horatio Nelson, British naval commander who won decisive battles against France in the Revolutionary and Napoleonic Wars, is killed at sea off Cape Trafalgar, Spain (46).

NOVEMBER
19 Ferdinand de Lesseps, French diplomat who built the Suez Canal, born in Versailles, France (–1894).

DECEMBER
6 Jean-Eugène Robert-Houdin, French magician who founded modern magic, born in Blois, France (–1871).
12 William Lloyd Garrison, U.S. newspaper editor and leader of the abolitionist (antislavery) movement, born in Newburyport, Massachusetts (–1879).
23 Joseph Smith, U.S. prophet whose writings along with the Bible form the theological basis of The Church of Jesus Christ of Latter-day Saints, born in Sharon, Vermont (–1844).

1806

POLITICS, GOVERNMENT, AND ECONOMICS

Business and Economics

- Two hundred New York shoemakers launch the nation's first industrial strike in an attempt to secure higher wages and fair working conditions. The strike leaders are indicted for criminal conspiracy.
- U.S. businessman William Colgate opens a candle and soap factory in New York, New York. This will grow into the Colgate–Palmolive–Peet commercial empire.

APRIL
- The U.S. Congress prohibits the import of many British goods in response to Britain's seizure of U.S. ships and impressment of U.S. sailors.

Politics and Government

- In the U.S. congressional elections, the Democratic-Republicans retain majorities in the House of Representatives (118–24) and Senate (28–6).
- The former U.S. vice president Aaron Burr becomes involved in an alleged conspiracy to create an independent nation in the southwest United States.
- The U.S. president Thomas Jefferson appoints the New York jurist Henry B. Livingston to the U.S. Supreme Court.
- The Virginia legislature passes a law requiring free blacks to leave the state.

JANUARY
8   Britain occupies the Dutch colony of the Cape of Good Hope (southern Africa).

FEBRUARY
15   A Franco-Prussian treaty against Britain is concluded, under which Prussia agrees to close its ports to British ships as part of the French emperor Napoleon I's attempt to stifle British trade.
15   French troops enter Naples, Italy. Napoleon's brother, Joseph Bonaparte, immediately begins administrative reform in the Italian kingdom.

MARCH
30   Joseph Bonaparte becomes king of Naples.

APRIL
1   Britain declares war on Prussia, following the seizure of the electorate of Hanover.

4   Britain begins blockading the French coast.

MAY
- The future U.S. president Andrew Jackson mortally wounds the U.S. lawyer Charles Dickinson in a duel, after Dickinson allegedly insults Jackson's wife.

JUNE
4   The British general John Stuart defeats a small French force at Maida in Calabria, southern Italy, but subsequently withdraws to his base on the island of Sicily.
5   Louis Bonaparte, brother of Emperor Napoleon I of France, becomes king of the French-dominated Kingdom of Holland (the Netherlands).
27   The city of Buenos Aires in the Spanish American viceroyalty of Rio de La Plata surrenders to a small British force.

JULY
12   The Confederation of the Rhine is established under the protection of France, uniting Bavaria, Württemberg, Mainz, Baden, and eight lesser German principalities. These come under a French constitution, are subject to the Napoleonic legal system, and agree to provide troops for Napoleon's armies.
18   The French marshal André Masséna captures Gaeta in southern Italy.

AUGUST
6   The Holy Roman Empire comes to an end; Francis II formally resigns as Holy Roman Emperor and becomes Francis I, Emperor of Austria.
8   The Argentine city of Buenos Aires is retaken from the British by the Spanish.
25   The Nuremberg publisher Johann Philipp Palm is executed by the French authorities for allegedly producing the pamphlet "Germany in her Deep Distress," calling for patriotic opposition to French occupation.

OCTOBER
1   Prussia issues an ultimatum to France concerning Prussian retention of Hanover, which it believes the emperor Napoleon I intends to restore to Britain as part of a peace settlement.
7   Napoleon begins to march north with his *Grande Armée* from Bavaria to Prussia.
9   Prussia's ultimatum to France concerning Prussian retention of Hanover expires and it declares war.
14   Napoleon decisively defeats the Prussians under Prince Hohenlohe at Jena in Saxony; Marshal Louis Davout simultaneously defeats the Saxons under the Duke of Brunswick at Auerstadt, also in Saxony.
16   War breaks out between the Ottoman Empire and Russia. The French emissary in Istanbul persuades

Sultan Selim III to tighten his grip on the disputed Danubian provinces (Moldavia and Wallachia), which leads Russia to invade them.

27 The French emperor Napoleon I occupies the Prussian capital, Berlin.

NOVEMBER

7 The Baltic port city of Lübeck, held by the Prussian army under General Gebhard von Blücher, surrenders to French forces.

11 All the major Prussian fortresses, including Spandau, Stettin (modern Szczecin), Küstrin (modern Kostrzyń), and Magdeburg, are now in French hands.

21 The French emperor Napoleon I introduces the "Continental System" through the Berlin Decrees, closing continental (European) ports to British vessels and declaring all British ports to be in a state of blockade, in an attempt to counter Britain's control of the sea.

28 Marshal Joachim Murat leads a French force into Warsaw, Poland, in pursuit of the retreating Prussian and Russian armies.

DECEMBER

10 Saxony joins the Confederation of the Rhine (an association of German states under French protection) by the Treaty of Posen (Poznań) with France, and the elector, Frederick Augustus, becomes king.

15 The French emperor Napoleon I, marching east in pursuit of the retreating Russian and Prussian army, enters Warsaw, Poland.

26 French forces under Marshal Jean Lannes engage a Russian army under Count Levin August Bennigsen at Pułtusk in Russia. The French are unable to prevent their opponents from retreating further and both sides retire to their winter quarters.

27 A Russian army sacks the city of Bucharest, in the Ottoman Danubian province of Wallachia.

SCIENCE, TECHNOLOGY, AND MEDICINE

Exploration

JULY

- The U.S. explorer Zebulon Montgomery Pike embarks on an expedition through the American Southwest.

SEPTEMBER

- The U.S. explorers Meriwether Lewis and William Clark arrive in St. Louis, Missouri, after 28 months of travel. They return with a wealth of information about the geography and natural history of the American West.

NOVEMBER

- Zebulon Montgomery Pike arrives at the site of what will become known as Pike's Peak, in Colorado.

Science

- German chemist Friedrich Wilhelm Saturner isolates morphine—the first painkiller—from opium.

Technology

- English engineer Joseph Bramah invents a printing machine that prints serial numbers on bank notes.
- English physicist Benjamin Thompson, Count von Rumford, invents the coffee percolator, in an attempt to persuade workmen in Munich, Germany, to consume less alcohol.
- Scottish merchant Patrick Clark develops a cotton thread strong enough to replace the silk and linen thread currently in use.
- The U.S. entrepreneur David Melville erects the first gas street lights on Pelham Street in Newport, Rhode Island.

OCTOBER

7 English printer Ralph Wedgewood patents carbon paper (paper impregnated with ink so as to produce a copy on an underlying sheet when written on) in London, England.

Transportation

- A steam dredger is used to clear docks in London, England. It is powered by one of Richard Trevithick's high-pressure steam engines.
- The U.S. Congress approves construction of the 725-km/450-mi Natchez Trace Parkway between Natchez, Mississippi, and Nashville, Tennessee. Following an old Native trail, it is the most important highway in the Southwest.

ARTS AND IDEAS

Architecture

- U.S. millwright Timothy Palmer builds the first long covered bridge in the United States. Spanning the Schuylkill River, Philadelphia, Pennsylvania, its center span is 55 m/180 ft long; the cover keeps off the snow.

Arts

- The Brera art gallery opens in Milan, Italy.
- The French artist Antoine-Jean Gros paints *The Battle of Aboukir*.
- The Scottish artist David Wilkie paints *Village Politicians*.

Literature and Language

- The U.S. lexicographer Noah Webster publishes his *Compendious Dictionary of the English Language*, the first of his dictionaries. His larger dictionary appears in 1828.

Music

- German composer Ludwig van Beethoven completes his Symphony No. 4 in B flat (Opus 60); his Violin Concerto in D (Opus 61); his Piano Concerto No. 4 in G (Opus 58); his String Quartets Nos. 7, 8, and 9 (Opus 59), the *Rasoumovsky Quartets*; and his overture *Leonora No 3* (Opus 72a).

Thought and Scholarship

- The German grammarian Johann Christoph Adelung publishes *Mithridates*, a history of languages and dialects.
- The German philosopher Johann Gottlieb Fichte publishes *Die Grundzüge des gegenwärtigen Zeitalters/ The Characteristics of the Present Age.*
- The German poet and historian Ernst Moritz Arndt publishes the first volume of his four-volume *Geist der Zeit/Spirit of the Age.* The last volume appears in 1818. His passionately patriotic works do much to inspire the German national revival.

SOCIETY

Education

- A school in New York, New York, adopts the educational system of the English educator Joseph Lancaster. In the so-called Lancaster system, senior pupils serve as teachers for their more junior peers, making learning more affordable.

- The German philosopher and educator Johann Friedrich Herbart publishes *Allgemeine Pädagogik/A Universal Pedagogy.*
- The world's first agricultural high school (gymnasium) opens in Möglin, near Berlin, Prussia (now Germany).

Everyday Life

- British naval captain Thomas Cochrane drops the first aerial propaganda, using kites from his ship to drop leaflets in France from his position in the Bay of Biscay.

JANUARY
1　Emperor Napoleon I abolishes the French Republican calendar.

Media and Communication

NOVEMBER
15　The first issue of the *Yale University Literary Cabinet*, the first college magazine in the United States, is published.

Religion

- The French emperor Napoleon I convokes a Sanhedrin (Jewish council) and establishes a consistory, a body to oversee Jewish affairs.
- The German biblical scholar Wilhelm De Wette publishes *Introduction to the Old Testament.*

Sports

JUNE
10　The first recorded harness race in the United States (a trotting race) takes place in Harlem, New York.

BIRTHS & DEATHS

JANUARY
14　Matthew Fontaine Maury, U.S. naval officer and one of the founders of oceanography, born in Spotsylvania County, Virginia (–1873).
16　Nicolas Leblanc, French chemist who discovered a process of making sodium bicarbonate from salt, dies in St.-Denis, France (*c.* 64).
23　William Pitt the Younger, prime minister of Britain 1783–1801 and 1804–06, a Tory, dies in London, England (46).

MARCH
6　Elizabeth Barrett Browning, English poet and wife of the English poet Robert Browning, born in Durham, England (–1861).

APRIL
9　Isambard Kingdom Brunel, British marine engineer who built the first

transatlantic steamer the *Great Western* (1838), and the *Great Eastern* (1858), the largest ship in the world for 40 years, born in Portsmouth, England (–1859).

MAY
20　John Stuart Mill, English utilitarian philosopher and economist, born in London, England (–1873).

JUNE
12　John Augustus Roebling, German-born U.S. architect who pioneered the construction of suspension bridges and designed the Brooklyn Bridge, born in Mülhausen, Prussia (–1869).

JULY
10　George Stubbs, English painter, dies in London, England (81).

AUGUST
22　Jean-Honoré Fragonard, French rococo painter, dies in Paris, France (73).

23　Charles-Augustin de Coulomb, French physicist who formulated Coulomb's law which relates the forces of electrical charges to the distance between them, dies in Paris, France (69).

OCTOBER
22　Thomas Sheraton, English cabinetmaker who gave his name to a type of Georgian furniture, dies in Soho, London, England (55).
25　Henry Knox, American general during the American Revolution, dies in Thomastown, Maine (56).
28　Charlotte Smith, English novelist and poet, dies in Tilford, near Farnham, Surrey, England (57).

1807

POLITICS, GOVERNMENT, AND ECONOMICS

Business and Economics

- The French emperor Napoleon I introduces a Commercial Law Code in France. It is published hastily in response to the collapse of the Récamier firm, which has been trading illegally.

JANUARY

7   Britain declares a blockade of the coasts of France and of Napoleon's allies, and that all ships trading in ports where Britain is excluded are liable to capture, in retaliation for the Continental System (closure of European ports to Britain) introduced by Napoleon in November 1806.

NOVEMBER

11 Britain declares a blockade of continental (European) ports. It makes trade in goods produced by blockading countries illegal and requires all neutrals to call at a British port before proceeding to other European countries.

DECEMBER

17 Napoleon issues the Milan Decrees against British trade, extending the Berlin Decrees of November 21, 1806, which introduced the Continental System.

Politics and Government

- U.S. president Thomas Jefferson appoints the Kentucky jurist Thomas Todd to the U.S. Supreme Court.
- War begins in Finland between its current ruler, Sweden, and the expansionist Czar Alexander I of Russia, who has been given a free hand in Sweden by the Treaty of Tilsit.

JANUARY

- The U.S. satirists Washington and William Irving and James Kirke Paulding introduce *Salmagundi*, a series of satirical pamphlets depicting the excesses of Jeffersonian democracy.
- 4   Baron Heinrich vom Stein, the Prussian trade minister, is replaced because of his abrasive manner and demand for complete control of policy.

FEBRUARY

8   The French emperor Napoleon I's army catches up with the retreating Russian and Prussian forces at Eylau in eastern Prussia; an indecisive battle causes heavy losses to both sides.

19 A British fleet under Admiral John Duckworth forces its way through the Dardanelles to support Russia in its war against the Ottoman Empire.

MARCH

- The U.S. Congress prohibits the African slave trade, with effect from January 1, 1808.
- 2   The British fleet under Admiral John Duckworth, having arrived in Ottoman waters in February to support Russia in its war against the Ottoman Empire, is forced to withdraw, losing two ships.
- 5   The British foreign secretary, Earl Grey, introduces a Roman Catholic Army and Navy Service Bill to enable Catholics to hold commissions, in a bid to conciliate Irish activists. The bill is successfully opposed by King George III and Lord Sidmouth, Lord President of the Council.
- 15–April 27   French forces capture the Prussian port of Danzig (modern Gdańsk) and hold it against Russian and Prussian efforts to retake it.

APRIL

26 By the Convention of Bartenstein, Russia and Prussia form an alliance to drive France out of the German states.

MAY

29 The Ottoman sultan Selim III is deposed by janissaries (members of his bodyguard) opposed to his reforms and is replaced by Mustafa IV.

JUNE

14 The French army under Marshal Jean Lannes roundly defeats a combined Russo-Prussian force under Count Levin August Bennigsen at the Battle of Friedland in eastern Prussia.

27 Britain joins the Convention of Bartenstein, formed by Russia and Prussia in April to drive France out of the German states.

JULY

7   The Treaty of Tilsit (Prussia) ends the war between France and Russia. The French emperor Napoleon I, having defeated Austria and now Russia and Prussia, is the master of continental Europe. Russia agrees to the establishment of a Grand Duchy of Warsaw (as a French satellite in eastern Europe), recognizes the Confederation of the Rhine (association of German states under French protection), agrees to close all ports to British ships, and, by a secret agreement, Czar Alexander I agrees to coerce Denmark, Sweden, and Portugal into joining the alliance against Britain. In return he is given a free hand against Sweden in Finland and the Ottoman Empire in the Danubian provinces (Moldavia and Wallachia).

9   By a separate Treaty of Tilsit with France, Prussia loses half its territory, including all its possessions west of the River Elbe to France and all Polish territories, which are to form the Grand Duchy of Warsaw under the king of Saxony, and, by a secret agreement, promises to join the Continental System and exclude British ships from Prussian ports.

19   The Grand Duchy of Warsaw is established from Prussian territory in accordance with the Treaty of Tilsit. France's ally Frederick Augustus, King of Saxony, becomes its ruler, establishing a strong Napoleonic presence in eastern Europe.

20   France and Russia sign a peace treaty ending hostilities.

August

8   Jérôme Bonaparte, brother of the French emperor Napoleon I, is created king of Westphalia (made up of former Prussian possessions west of the River Elbe), and the city of Erfurt (formerly Prussian) is incorporated into France.

24   Czar Alexander I of Russia fails to ratify the Franco-Russian peace treaty of July 20.

September

•   A circuit court in Richmond, Virginia, acquits the former U.S. vice president Aaron Burr of treason in an alleged move to create an independent nation in the American Southwest.

2–5   A British fleet bombards the port of Copenhagen, Denmark, in the knowledge that the French emperor Napoleon I plans to use the powerful Danish fleet against Britain.

7   Napoleon suppresses the French Tribunate, thus consolidating his dictatorship.

7   The Danish fleet surrenders following the British attack on Copenhagen, and is confiscated by Britain.

7   Under the threat of advancing French forces recently freed from the war against Prussia, King Gustavus IV Adolphus cedes the German province of Swedish Pomerania to France.

October

4   Baron Heinrich vom Stein becomes Prussia's principal minister. He will superintend the initial period of Prussian reform following its total defeat in the war with France.

14   In an attempt to modernize Prussian agriculture, the medieval feudal system of tenure, in which peasants are tied to their landlords and the land they work, is ended by an Act of Emancipation.

27   By the Treaty of Fontainebleau, Spain and France agree to conquer Portugal to enable the French emperor Napoleon I to deny Britain access to its ports.

29   Denmark allies itself with France against Britain.

November

7   Russia breaks off relations with Britain, amounting to a declaration of war (as a result of the Treaty of Tilsit with France).

19   France invades Portugal for refusing to enter the Continental System and close its ports to Britain, marking the beginning of the Peninsular War.

29   The Portuguese royal family, the Braganzas, flee to Brazil under the protection of the British admiral Sidney Smith, taking with them the fleet that the French emperor Napoleon I intended to use against Britain.

December

•   The U.S. president Thomas Jefferson signs the Embargo Act, prohibiting exports to France and Britain. The act is designed to compel France and England to lift restrictions on U.S. trade imposed during the war between the two European powers.

SCIENCE, TECHNOLOGY, AND MEDICINE

Ecology

•   British inventor William Cubitt develops "patent sails." Used on windmills, they automatically adjust the sails to the speed and direction of the wind.

•   German geographer Alexander von Humboldt, and French botanist Aimé Bonpland, in *Voyage aux régions équinoxiales du Nouveau Continent, 1799–1804/ Voyage to the Equitorial Regions of the New Continent, 1799–1804*, describe the climate, vegetation, and physical geography of South America.

Science

•   English physician and physicist Thomas Young enunciates "Young's modulus," a measurement of the elasticity of a material defined as the stress divided by the strain.

•   German astronomer Heinrich Olbers discovers the fourth asteroid, Vesta.

•   U.S. president Thomas Jefferson establishes the U.S. Coast Survey.

October

•   English chemist Humphry Davy isolates the elements potassium (atomic no. 19) and sodium (atomic no. 11) by passing an electric current through their chemical compounds.

Technology

•   German promoter Frederick Albert Winsor's National Light and Heat Company lights one side of Pall Mall, London, England, with gas lamps.

•   A line-throwing device is invented for use in lifeboats and lifesaving.

•   British engineer Matthew Murray builds a "portable" steam engine for use in ships; it becomes the prototype for subsequent engines.

•   English chemist Humphry Davy invents the first arc lamp; a 2,000-cell battery creates an electric arc across a gap of 100 mm/4 in between two charcoal conductors.

•   English inventors Henry and Sealy Fourdrinier receive a patent for an improved version of Nicolas-Louis Robert's papermaking machine. Their new "Fourdrinier machine" allows production of paper in continuous sheets.

- English scientist William Hyde Wollaston develops the camera lucida. It projects an image, using a four-sided prism, onto a flat surface, so that it can be traced.
- French inventor Joseph-Nicéphore Niepce makes two heliotrope (sundrawing) prints of an engraved portrait—the first photomechanical reproduction process.
- An internal combustion engine is invented in France. Called the "Pyréolophore," it works on a piston and cylinder system.
- Scottish clergyman Alexander Forsyth invents the percussion ignition for guns; he uses an explosive chemical charge which detonates when struck by a hammer. It allows operation in wet weather and leads to the development of breech loaders.

Transportation

- French inventor Isaac de Rivas patents a gas-powered vehicle. It uses hydrogen as fuel and the valves and ignition are hand-operated.

AUGUST

17–18 U.S. engineer Robert Fulton's paddleboat *Steamboat* makes a 240-km/150-mi trial run on the Hudson River from Albany to New York, New York. Completed in 32 hours (sailing ships take 4 days), averaging 7.6 kph/ 4.7 mph, it is equipped with side paddles and a Boulton and Watt engine. The following year it is refurbished and renamed the *Clermont* and begins to ply the Hudson River.

ARTS AND IDEAS

Arts

c. 1807 The English artist J. M. W. Turner paints *The Thames near Walton Bridge* and *Sun Rising in a Mist*.
- The French artist Jacques-Louis David completes his painting *Coronation of Napoleon*.
- The U.S. artist Gilbert Stuart paints his *Portrait of Thomas Jefferson*.

Literature and Language

- The Boston Athenaeum, Boston, Massachusetts, opens as a meeting place and research institute for the city's literati.
- The English poet George Gordon, Lord Byron, publishes *Hours of Idleness*, a collection of early verse.
- The English poet William Wordsworth publishes *Ode: Intimations of Immortality* and *Poems, in Two Volumes*.
- The English writers Charles and Mary Lamb publish *Tales from Shakespeare*.
- The Franco-Swiss writer Madame de Staël publishes her novel *Corinne*.
- The Italian writer Ugo Foscolo publishes *Dei sepolcri/Of the Graveyards*, a long patriotic poem attacking Napoleon.
- The U.S. writer Joel Barlow publishes his national epic *The Columbiad*. An earlier version, *The Vision of Columbus*, appeared in 1787.

Music

- German composer Ludwig van Beethoven completes his overture *Coriolan* (Opus 62) and his Mass in C major (Opus 86).
- The opera *Joseph* by the French composer Etienne-Nicolas Méhul is first performed, in Paris, France.
- The opera *La vestale/The Vestal Virgin* by the Italian composer Gaspare Spontini is first performed, in Paris, France.

Thought and Scholarship

- The German classical scholar Friedrich August Wolf publishes *Darstellung der Altertumswissenschaft/Science of Antiquity*.
- The German jurist and economist Gottlieb Hufeland publishes his book *New Foundations of Political Economy*, advocating liberal economic reform.

BIRTHS & DEATHS

JANUARY
19 Robert E. Lee, Confederate general who commanded the Southern armies during the American Civil War, born in Stratford, Westmoreland County, Virginia (−1870).

FEBRUARY
3 Joseph E. Johnston, U.S. Confederate general, born near Farmville, Virginia (−1891).
27 Henry Wadsworth Longfellow, U.S. poet, born in Portland, Maine (−1882).

APRIL
9 John Opie, English historical and portrait painter, dies in London, England (45).

MAY
28 Jean Louis Rodolphe Agassiz, U.S. naturalist, born in Motier, Switzerland (−1873).

JULY
4 Giuseppe Garibaldi, Italian soldier whose conquest of Sicily and Naples helped unify Italy, born in Nice, France (−1882).

NOVEMBER
5 Angelica Kauffmann, Swiss neoclassical painter, dies in Rome, Italy (66).
24 Joseph Brant, Mohawk chief who led four of the six Iroquois tribes against the Americans during the American Revolution, dies near Brantford, Ontario, Canada (65).

- The German philosopher Georg Wilhelm Friedrich Hegel publishes *Phänomenologie des Geistes/ Phenomenology of Spirit*. His first major work, it gives a sketch of his elaborate metaphysical system.
- The Swiss economist and historian Jean-Charles-Léonard Sismonde de Sismondi publishes the first volume of his 16-volume *Histoire des républiques italiennes du moyen âge/History of the Italian Republics in the Middle Ages*. The last volume appears in 1818. The work has a major impact on the development of Italian nationalism.

JULY

7   The liberal German general Gerhard von Scharnhorst publishes his *Manifesto* detailing plans for Prussian military reform, which are soon implemented. He recommends a small core of professional soldiers supported by a large militia.

SOCIETY

Education

- The German writer Jean Paul publishes *Levana*, a treatise on education.

Religion

- Connecticut missionaries form the Connecticut Tract Society to distribute Christian literature.
- The "New Methodists," founded by U.S. religious leader Jacob Albright, hold the first Convention of the U.S. Evangelical Association.

Sports

- The Ascot Gold Cup horse race is established at Ascot, Berkshire, England.

1808

POLITICS, GOVERNMENT, AND ECONOMICS

Business and Economics

JANUARY

- The U.S. Congress passes a second Embargo Act, designed to compel France and Britain to open their ports to U.S. shipping despite the war between the two European states.

FEBRUARY

28   Austria joins the French emperor Napoleon I's Continental System and supports the closure of European ports to Britain.

MARCH

- Frustrated at its inability to alter French and British mercantile policy, the U.S. Congress passes a third Embargo Act, no more effective than its predecessors.

APRIL

6   The U.S. merchant John Jacob Astor establishes the American Fur Company in New York State.

Colonization

JANUARY

1   Sierra Leone becomes a British crown colony.

MARCH

16   Czar Alexander I of Russia proclaims Finland to be a Russian province (it has been captured from Sweden as a result of the war begun in 1807 after Russia's signing of the Treaty of Tilsit).

MAY

30   The French emperor Napoleon I annexes Tuscany (previously created the kingdom of Etruria in 1801), allowing it seats in the French Senate and legislature.

Human Rights

- The English churchman and writer Sydney Smith publishes *Letters of Peter Plymley*, arguing in favor of Catholic emancipation in Britain.
- The French emperor Napoleon I abolishes the Inquisition in Spain and Italy.

Politics and Government

- In the U.S. congressional elections, the Democratic-Republicans retain majorities in the House of Representatives (94–48) and Senate (28–6).

- The French marshal Joachim Murat becomes king of Naples, succeeding Joseph of Naples who is now king of Spain.
- The Tennessee congressman George W. Campbell, a Democratic-Republican, wounds his colleague Barent Gardenier, a Federalist from New York, New York, in a duel.

JANUARY

1 The United States prohibits the import of slaves from Africa.

FEBRUARY

2 A French force under General Sextius Miollis occupies Rome after Pope Pius VII refuses to recognize the Kingdom of Naples, grant a concordat with the Confederation of the Rhine (association of German states under French protection) on the same lines as that agreed with France, or join in the alliance against Britain.

16 French troops in Spain for the war with Portugal become openly hostile toward Spain.

29 French forces take the city of Barcelona, Spain, aiming to conquer the country as part of Emperor Napoleon I's consolidation of French control of southern Europe.

MARCH

3 French forces under Marshal Joachim Murat occupy the Spanish capital, Madrid.

17 A French decree places Jews under more direct state control. A synagogue is to be provided in every *département* with more than 2,000 Jews, with a controlling consistory to aid in conscription to the army. Strict rules are placed on the freedom of Jews to trade and lend money.

18 Manuel de Godoy, the Spanish chief minister, is driven from office by popular protest at his pro-French policy which is seen as having encouraged Emperor Napoleon I's ambitions in Iberia and left Spain open to French attack.

19 Charles IV of Spain abdicates in favor of his son, Ferdinand, being too closely associated with the francophile policy of his ousted chief minister, Manuel de Godoy.

APRIL

- Defying the U.S. Congress in the course of the Napoleonic Wars, the French emperor Napoleon I issues the Bayonne Decree, ordering the seizure of all U.S. ships entering French and Italian ports. From the emperor's perspective, U.S. ships are the veritable property of Britain.

MAY

2 A Spanish rising against the French (the *Dos Mayo*) begins in the occupied capital, Madrid. This is the start of the extensive guerrilla warfare that continues throughout the Peninsular War.

6 The French emperor Napoleon I compels King Charles IV and Crown Prince Ferdinand to renounce the Spanish throne.

JUNE

6 The *Tugendbund* (Society of Virtue), a German nationalist movement, is founded in Königsberg, East Prussia.

9 The Austrian *Landwehr*, a militia of all men aged 19–25 who are not in the regular army, is created on the

initiative of Johann Philipp, Count von Stadion, the foreign minister.

15 Joseph of Naples, brother of the French emperor Napoleon I, becomes king of Spain.

15–August 15 In the first siege of Saragossa, northeastern Spain, the Spanish garrison and local population resist French attempts to reopen the main line of communications with central Spain and Portugal.

17 Czar Alexander I of Russia, suspecting French intentions against Russia, promises to restore privileges in Finland (captured by Russia from Sweden) to try to secure its allegiance.

JULY

7 Mahmud II succeeds Mustafa IV as sultan of the Ottoman Empire; the latter is dethroned. Mahmud II is a cousin of the deposed Selim III, and his determination and ability enable him to carry on Selim's administrative and military reforms.

19 French forces under General Pierre Dupont are surrounded and forced to surrender by the Spanish in the Battle of Baylen in Spain.

AUGUST

1 A British expedition under Arthur Wellesley (later Duke of Wellington) lands in Portugal to oppose the French emperor Napoleon I.

1 Napoleon's brother Joseph, the new king of Spain, flees from Madrid in fear of Spanish rebels.

21 A British army under Wellesley defeats the French at Vimiero near Lisbon, Portugal.

30 Following the British defeat of French forces in Portugal, the Convention of Cintra is agreed between the British commander, Hew Dalrymple, and the French commander, General Andoche Junot, allowing the latter to withdraw his troops from Portugal.

SEPTEMBER

8 The French emperor Napoleon I forces Prussia to limit its army to 42,000 men.

OCTOBER

12 The French emperor Napoleon I and Czar Alexander I of Russia meet in Erfurt (a former Prussian city, now under French rule). Napoleon reaffirms Russian rights in the Danubian provinces of the Ottoman Empire (Moldavia and Wallachia) and Finland in return for Russia's agreement to support France against Austria if the latter takes advantage of French reverses in Portugal and Spain and declares war.

NOVEMBER

19 Municipal councils are introduced in Prussia; because of the limits imposed by the French emperor Napoleon I on Prussia's army, these become the focus for Prussian military revival.

24 Prussian ministries are transformed into modern administrative organs responsible for specific functions rather than simply for geographical areas.

DECEMBER

- Americans elect James Madison of the Democratic-Republican Party as U.S. president and George Clinton as vice president.

13 The Spanish capital, Madrid, surrenders to Emperor Napoleon I, who has taken personal command of French forces in the Iberian Peninsula.

16 Following Prussian principal minister Baron Heinrich vom Stein's reforms and obvious desire to throw off French domination, Napoleon declares him an "Enemy of France" by imperial decree and he flees into hiding.
16 The French marshal Gouvion St.-Cyr defeats Spanish forces commanded by the Swiss general Aloys Reding at Cardadeu, Spain.
20–February 20, 1809   In the second siege of Saragossa, northeastern Spain, Spanish forces attempt, unsuccessfully, to disrupt French lines of communication between central Spain and Portugal.
21 The French marshal Gouvion St.-Cyr defeats the Spanish under General Aloys Reding, at Molins de Rey, near Barcelona, Spain.

SCIENCE, TECHNOLOGY, AND MEDICINE

Ecology

December 1808–14   Scottish-born U.S. ornithologist Alexander Wilson publishes the nine-volume *American Ornithology* that establishes ornithology in the United States.

Science

- English chemist Humphry Davy isolates the alkaline-earth metals magnesium (atomic no. 12), calcium (atomic no. 20), strontium (atomic no. 38), and barium (atomic no. 56).
- French physicist Etienne Malus discovers the polarization of light by reflection.
- French physicists Joseph-Louis Gay-Lussac and Louis-Jacques Thénard discover the element boron (atomic no. 5).

AUGUST

- English chemist and physicist John Dalton publishes *New System of Chemical Philosophy* that examines his chemical research and atomic theory, and establishes the quantitative system of chemistry.

DECEMBER

31 French chemist Joseph-Louis Gay-Lussac, in *The Combination of Gases*, announces that gases combine chemically in simple proportions of volumes, and that the contraction in volume observed when they combine is a simple relation to the original volume of the gases—Gay-Lussac's Law.

Technology

- German artist Ferdinand Piloty produces the first color lithographs.

Transportation

- English engineer Richard Trevithick sets up in London, England, giving novelty rides on the engine *Catch-me-who-can*. He soon abandons the construction of steam locomotives because the weight of his engines fracture the cast-iron rails.
- The steamboat *New Orleans* becomes the first steamboat to ply the Mississippi and Ohio rivers. It travels at 13 kph/8 mph downstream and 5 kph/3 mph upstream.

ARTS AND IDEAS

Arts

- The English artist J. M. W. Turner paints *The Battle of Trafalgar*. The painting causes controversy because of its factual inaccuracy.
- The French artist Anne-Louis Girodet de Roucy paints *The Entombment of Atala*.
- The French artist Jean-Auguste-Dominique Ingres paints *The Valpinçon Bather* and *Oedipus and the Sphinx*.
- The French artist Pierre-Paul Prud'hon paints *The Rape of Psyche*.
- The German artist Caspar David Friedrich paints *The Cross on the Mountains* and becomes one of the leading exponents of German romanticism.
- The Italian artist Antonio Canova sculpts *Pauline Bonaparte Borghese as Venus*.
- The Spanish artist Francisco José de Goya y Lucientes paints his *Portrait of King Ferdinand VII of Spain on Horseback*.

BIRTHS & DEATHS

FEBRUARY

14 John Dickinson, U.S. statesman who was the principle author of the Declaration of Independence and helped prepare the Articles of Confederation, dies (75).

APRIL

20 Honoré Daumier, French caricaturist and painter known for his satirization of French politicians and society, born in Marseille, France (–1879).
20 Louis-Napoléon Bonaparte (Napoleon III), Emperor of France 1852–71, born in Paris, France (–1873).

JUNE

3 Jefferson Davis, president of the Confederate States of America 1861–65, born in Christian County, Kentucky (–1889).

DECEMBER

29 Andrew Johnson, seventeenth president of the United States 1865–69, a Democrat, born in Raleigh, North Carolina (–1875).

Literature and Language

- The autobiography *Vita di Vittorio Alfieri/The Life of Vittorio Alfieri* by the Italian writer Count Vittorio Alfieri is published posthumously.
- The German writer Friedrich von Schlegel publishes his *Geschichte der alten und neuen Literatur/The History of Literature Ancient and Modern.*
- The Scottish poet and novelist Walter Scott publishes the long narrative poem *Marmion: A Tale of Flodden Field.*
- The Danish churchman and poet Nikolai Frederik Severin Grundtvig publishes *Nordens mythologi/ Northern Mythology*, a landmark in the study of Icelandic sagas and Norse mythology.

Music

- German composer Ludwig van Beethoven completes his Symphonies No. 5 in C minor (Opus 67) and No. 6 in F, the *Pastoral* (Opus 68), and his Cello Sonata in A major (Opus 69).

Theater and Dance

- The comedy *Der zerbrochene Krug/The Broken Jug* by the German dramatist Heinrich Wilhelm von Kleist is first performed, produced by Johann Wolfgang von Goethe, in Weimar, Germany.
- The German poet Johann Wolfgang von Goethe publishes part one of his verse drama *Faust*. The second part appears in 1832.

- The play *The Indian Princess, or La Belle Sauvage* by the U.S. dramatist James Nelson Barker is first performed, in Philadelphia, Pennsylvania. It gives a romanticized account of the life of Pocahontas, and becomes the first U.S. play to be performed in London, England.

Thought and Scholarship

- The German philosopher Johann Gottlieb Fichte publishes *Reden an die deutsche Nation/Addresses to the German Nation*. This work plays an important role in the development of German nationalism.
- The New York Academy of Fine Arts is founded in New York, New York.

SOCIETY

Media and Communication

- *The Times* sends Henry Crabb Robinson as special correspondent to the Peninsular Campaign in Spain during the Napoleonic conflict, making him in effect the first war correspondent.
- The University of Maryland law professor John Elihu Hall establishes the *American Law Journal*, the first of its kind.

Religion

DECEMBER
- The Philadelphia pastor William White establishes the nation's first Bible Society.

1809

POLITICS, GOVERNMENT, AND ECONOMICS

Business and Economics

- The Boston Crown Glass Company is incorporated in Boston, Massachusetts.

MARCH
- Having repealed the Embargo Act of 1807, the U.S. Senate passes the Non-Intercourse Act, authorizing trade

with all nations except Britain and France, who are to be denied access to U.S. ports. Trade with Britain and France will be reestablished once they recognize the rights of U.S. ships.
- The U.S. senator Timothy Pickering of Massachusetts wins repeal of the Embargo Act of December 1807, which has devastated New England shipping without affecting Britain or France.

AUGUST
- The U.S. president James Madison reapplies the Non-Intercourse Act to Britain after the latter reneges on a promise to end its restrictions on U.S. trade.

Colonization

- Britain captures the Caribbean islands of Martinique and Cayenne from the French.

SEPTEMBER

17 Russia obtains Finland by the Peace of Frederikshavn with Sweden. The two countries have been at war, largely because of conflict about ownership of Finland, since 1807.

Human Rights

FEBRUARY

- In a letter to the French Catholic priest Henri Grégoire, the former U.S. president Thomas Jefferson qualifies statements he made in *Notes on Virginia about African Americans* that alleged physical and intellectual inferiority. Those statements, Jefferson admits, were at best tentative.

Politics and Government

JANUARY

1 The Spanish Supreme Junta and Britain agree not to make a separate peace with the French emperor Napoleon I.
5 Britain, now in opposition to Russia, concludes the Treaty of the Dardanelles with Russia's enemy, the Ottoman Empire.
6 General John Moore, commanding the British army in Spain, is killed at the Battle of Coruña, having drawn the French emperor Napoleon I away from Lisbon, Portugal, and Madrid, Spain.

FEBRUARY

8 Francis I of Austria, fearing the French emperor Napoleon I will overrun and dismember Austria, decides to launch a preemptive war against France.
25 The French marshal Gouvion St.-Cyr defeats a Spanish force under the Swiss general Aloys Reding at the Battle of Valls in Spain.

MARCH

- The former U.S. president Thomas Jefferson retires to Monticello, Virginia, after 44 years of public service.
1 The Prussian General Staff is created under General Gerhard von Scharnhorst.
4 James Madison is inaugurated as the fourth president of the United States.
29 King Gustavus IV Adolphus of Sweden is forced to abdicate after military defeats in war with Denmark.

APRIL

- The U.S. president James Madison proclaims the U.S. boycott of British trade to be over, after Britain promises to end restrictions against U.S. shipping, with effect from June 10.
4 Britain agrees to provide Austria with a monthly subsidy of £150,000 for the war with France and to invade the Scheldt region of the French-dominated Kingdom of Holland.
10 The Tyrolese revolt against Bavarian oppression as the Austrian army marches through Bavaria against the French, beginning a period of rebellion and civil war.

19–20 The French emperor Napoleon I defeats the Austrian army under Archduke Charles at Abensberg, Bavaria.
22 Austrian forces under Archduke Ferdinand occupy Warsaw, capital of the French satellite Grand Duchy of Warsaw (Poland).
22 The British soldier and statesman Arthur Wellesley (later Duke of Wellington) lands at Lisbon to take command of British forces in Portugal.
22 Napoleon defeats the Austrian army under Archduke Charles at Eckmühl in Bavaria.
25 The British in India conclude a treaty of friendship with the Sikhs at Amritsar, fixing the boundary of British influence in the northwest at the River Sutlej.
26 Britain restricts the limits of its naval blockade to the Netherlands, France, and the Italian states.

MAY

5 Russian action against the Turks in southeastern Europe is renewed.
12 British forces under Arthur Wellesley defeat the French under Marshal Nicolas-Jean Soult at Oporto and force them to retreat from Portugal.
13 The French army takes the Austrian capital, Vienna.
17 The French emperor Napoleon I issues an imperial decree annexing the Papal States, following their occupation by France in February 1808.
21–22 After the Battle of Aspern-Essling against the Austrians, Napoleon is forced to retreat across the River Danube. France calls on Russian support against Austria, which is given halfheartedly.

JUNE

3 Austrian forces occupying Warsaw, capital of the Grand Duchy of Warsaw, are compelled to withdraw by advancing Russian and Polish forces, and the city again comes under French control.
5 Charles XIII becomes king of Sweden.

JULY

- The Shawnee chief Tecumseh inaugurates a crusade to rally Native American groups along the U.S. frontier in defense of their land.
5–6 The French emperor Napoleon I defeats the Austrian army under Archduke Charles in the Battle of Wagram, near Vienna, although the Austrian army retreats in good order.
6 Pope Pius VII, having excommunicated Napoleon after the annexation of the Papal States, is taken prisoner by the French.
12 Austria sues for peace with France and the Armistice of Znaim (Moravia) is signed.
16 A revolt breaks out in Upper Peru against Spanish authority.
28 A British expedition to Walcheren (the Netherlands) to help the Austrians by diverting Napoleon's attention from the Danube fails due to bad planning and the ravages of disease. The force is withdrawn.
28 The British soldier and statesman Arthur Wellesley is victorious at the Battle of Talavera in Spain over the French who afterwards fall back to Madrid. Wellesley is subsequently created Viscount Wellington.

SEPTEMBER

4 The British prime minister, the Duke of Portland, resigns because of ill health.

21 The British secretary of state for war and the colonies, Lord Castlereagh, and the foreign secretary, George Canning, fight a duel over the latter's attempts to have Castlereagh removed from the War Office due to alleged incompetence. Canning is wounded in the thigh.

26 The Ottoman Empire is defeated by the Russians at Brailoff and subsequently at Silestria (both fortresses in the Danubian provinces of Moldavia and Wallachia).

OCTOBER

4 The Tory politician Spencer Perceval becomes prime minister of Britain.

8 Klemens Metternich becomes foreign minister of Austria. He will be at the center of European affairs for the next 40 years.

14 By the peace of Schönbrunn concluding the war of 1809, Austria cedes the Illyrian provinces (Carniola, Trieste, Carinthia, Croatia, and Dalmatia) to France, Galicia to the Grand Duchy of Warsaw and Russia, and Salzburg and the Inn District to Bavaria. It also joins the Continental System (supporting the closure of European ports to Britain), recognizes French authority in Portugal, Spain, and Italy, and pays an indemnity.

NOVEMBER

19 The Spanish are defeated at Ocana and the French overrun all of Andalusia, with the exception of Cadiz, which remains the capital of free Spain.

DECEMBER

16 The French emperor Napoleon I is divorced from Joséphine de Beauharnais by an act of the Senate because of her failure to provide him with an heir.

SCIENCE, TECHNOLOGY, AND MEDICINE

Agriculture

- The French surgeon Odette Phillippe introduces the grapefruit into the United States.

Health and Medicine

- U.S. physician Ephraim McDowell removes a 9-kg/20-lb ovarian tumor from Jane Todd Crawford, who lives another 30 years. It is the first such operation that is successful and it demonstrates the feasibility of abdominal surgery.

Math

- German mathematician Karl Friedrich Gauss describes the least-squares method for minimizing errors in calculations in *Theoria Motus Corporum Coelestium/ Theory of the Movement of Heavenly Bodies*.

Science

- French biologist Jean-Baptiste de Lamarck publishes *Philosophie zoologique/Zoological Philosophy* in which he theorizes that organs improve with use and degenerate with disuse and that these environmentally adapted traits are inheritable.
- French mineralogist René-Just Häuy publishes *Tableau comparatif/Comparative Tables*, one of the first classifications of minerals.
- U.S. geologist William Maclure publishes *Observations on the Geology of the United States*, the first geological survey of the eastern United States.

Technology

- British inventor John Heathcoat develops a lace-making machine. It simulates the movements of bobbins as used by lace-workers.
- Joseph Bramah, inventor of the water closet, patents the compound fountain pen in Britain. It uses a nib consisting of a goose quill cut into sections, and a holder. Previously, the entire quill had been used.
- U.S. inventor Joseph Hawkins receives a patent for producing imitation mineral water—carbonated water.

ARTS AND IDEAS

Architecture

- The country house Monticello, designed by the U.S. statesman Thomas Jefferson as his home, is completed on his estate in Virginia. It is an outstanding example of the Palladian style in the United States.

Arts

- A group of artists form the Brotherhood of St. Luke (later known as the Nazarenes) in Vienna, Austria, to regenerate German religious art by returning to the styles of the early Italian Renaissance. The leading figure is the German artist Friedrich Johann Overbeck.
- The German artist Caspar David Friedrich paints *Abbey in the Oak Wood*.
- The German artist Philipp Otto Runge completes his allegorical cycle of paintings *The Four Phases of Day*.
- The Scottish artist Henry Raeburn paints *Portrait of Mrs Spiers*.

Literature and Language

- The English poet George Gordon, Lord Byron, publishes *English Bards and Scots Reviewers*, a satire attacking British writers and reviewers including Walter Scott, Samuel Taylor Coleridge, and William Wordsworth.
- The English writer Hannah More publishes her novel *Coelebs in Search of a Wife*.

Surgery (1809–96)

1809
- U.S. physician Ephraim McDowell removes a 9-kg/20-lb ovarian tumor from Jane Todd Crawford, who lives another 30 years. It is the first such operation that is successful and it demonstrates the feasibility of abdominal surgery.

1817
- English surgeon James Parkinson describes the central nervous system disorder now known as Parkinson's disease.

1819
- British surgeon James Blundell makes the first human-to-human blood transfusion. The patient survives for 56 hours.

1822
June 6   U.S. army surgeon William Beaumont begins the study of digestion when he treats a French-Canadian trapper wounded in the stomach by a shotgun blast. The wound has failed to heal and the remaining fistula allows examination of digestive processes.

1826
- French physician Pierre Salomon Ségalas, using a candlelit speculum (mirror), performs the first endoscopy when he examines a patient's bladder.

1846
September 30   U.S. dentist William Thomas Morton gives the first successful demonstration of ether as an anesthetic during a dental operation to extract a tooth.

1853
- British surgeon John Snow administers chloroform to Queen Victoria during the birth of Prince Leopold. It subsequently becomes a generally accepted anesthetic.

1858
- British physician Henry Gray publishes *Anatomy of the Human Body, Descriptive and Surgical* (*Gray's Anatomy*). It remains the standard text in anatomy for over 100 years.

1867
June 15   U.S. physician John Stough Bobbs performs the first successful gallstone operation.

1873
- Austrian surgeon Theodor Billroth performs the first operation to remove the larynx.

1876
- Swiss surgeon Emil Kocher is the first to remove the thyroid gland to treat goiter.

1877
October 26   English surgeon Joseph Lister performs the first operation to repair a fractured kneecap. Conducted under antiseptic conditions, its success convinces other surgeons of the value of antisepsis.

1881
- Austrian surgeon Theodor Christian Albert Billroth initiates modern abdominal surgery by removing the cancerous lower part of a patient's stomach.
- U.S. surgeon William Stewart Halsted discovers that blood can be returned to a patient's body after it has been aerated.

1884
- Austrian surgeon Carl Koller is the first to use cocaine as a local anesthetic, which he uses during eye operations to block nerve impulses. He uses it on a suggestion from Sigmund Freud. U.S. surgeon William Stewart Halsted experiments with it on himself the following year and becomes addicted.

November 25   German-born British surgeon Rickman John Godlee performs the first operation to remove a brain tumor.

1885
- U.S. surgeon William West Grant performs the first successful appendectomy.

1886
- German surgeon Ernst Gustav Benjamin von Bergmann introduces steam sterilization of surgical instruments and dressings.
- U.S. pharmaceutical company Johnson and Johnson produces the first individually wrapped ready-to-use sterile surgical dressings.

1893
July 10   U.S. surgeon Daniel Hale Williams performs the first open-heart surgery, on a patient who has been wounded by a knife. The patient lives for another 20 years.

1896
- Polish surgeon Johannes von Mikulicz–Radecki introduces the gauze mask worn by surgeons during surgery.

- The French writer François-Auguste-René, vicomte de Chateaubriand, publishes his prose epic *Les Martyrs, ou le triomphe de la religion chrétienne/The Martyrs, or the Triumph of the Christian Religion.*
- The German writer Jean Paul publishes his novels *Dr Katzenbergers Badereise/Dr. Katzenberger's Journey to the Spa* and *Des Feldpredigers Schmelzle Reise/Army Chaplain Schmelzle's Journey.*
- The German writer Johann Wolfgang von Goethe publishes his novel *Wahlverwandtschaften/The Elective Affinities.*
- The Russian writer Ivan Andreyevich Krylov publishes his first book of popular verse fables, *Basni.*

Music

- German composer Ludwig van Beethoven completes his Piano Concerto No. 5 in E flat (Opus 73), the *Emperor*, and his String Quartet No. 10 (Opus 74), the Harp Quartet.
- The opera *Ferdinand Cortez* by the Italian composer Gaspare Spontini is first performed, in Paris, France.

Thought and Scholarship

- The English economist David Ricardo publishes *The High Price of Bullion or Proof of the Depreciation of Bank Notes.*

- The New York satirist Washington Irving publishes his comic *A History of New York from the Beginning of the World to the End of the Dutch Dynasty, by Diedrich Knickerbocker*, a Federalist burlesque of Jeffersonian democracy.

SOCIETY

Education

- Miami University is founded in Oxford, Ohio.

Everyday Life

- Quack medicines are popular in the United States. One of the most popular concoctions is "Hamilton's Essence and Extract of Mustard: for Rheumatism, Gout, Palsy, Swelling, Numbness, etc."

Sports

- The 2,000 Guineas horse race is established at Newmarket, England.

BIRTHS & DEATHS

JANUARY

4   Louis Braille, French educator and inventor of a writing system for the blind, born in Coupvray, France (–1852).

15   Pierre-Joseph Proudhon, French socialist and journalist, born in Besançon, France (–1865).

19   Edgar Allan Poe, U.S. poet, critic and short-story writer, born in Boston, Massachusetts (–1849).

FEBRUARY

3   Felix Mendelssohn (-Bartholdy), German composer, born in Hamburg, Germany (–1847).

12   Abraham Lincoln, seventeenth president of the United States 1861–65, a Republican, born in Hodgenville, Kentucky (–1865).

12   Charles Robert Darwin, English naturalist who developed the theory of evolution through natural selection, born in Shrewsbury, Shropshire, England (–1882).

15   Cyrus Hall McCormick, U.S. industrialist who invented the first practical reaper, born in Rockbridge County, Virginia (–1884).

MARCH

7   Jean-Pierre-François Blanchard, French balloonist who was the first person to cross the English Channel by air, dies in Paris, France (55).

31   Nicolay Gogol, Russian novelist, born near Poltava, Ukraine (–1852).

MAY

31   Franz Josef Haydn, Austrian classical composer, dies in Vienna, Austria (77).

JUNE

8   Thomas Paine, British-born American political pamphleteer whose writings influenced the American Revolution, dies in Boston, Massachusetts (72).

14   English naval commander Henry Keppel born (–1904).

JULY

15   Friedrich Henle, German pathologist who pioneered histology, born in Fürth, Bavaria (now in Germany) (–1885).

AUGUST

6   Alfred Lord Tennyson, English poet, born in Somersby, Lincolnshire, England (–1892).

29   Oliver Wendell Holmes, U.S. physician and poet, born in Cambridge, Massachusetts (–1894).

OCTOBER

11   Meriwether Lewis, U.S. explorer who, with William Clark, led the first expedition across North America to the Pacific Northwest 1804–06, dies near Nashville, Tennessee (35).

30   William Henry Cavendish Bentinck, Duke of Portland, prime minister of England 1783 and 1807–09, dies in Bulstrode, Buckinghamshire, England (71).

DECEMBER

24   Kit Carson, U.S. frontiersman, born in Madison County, Kentucky (–1868).

29   William Ewart Gladstone, prime minister of Britain 1868–74, 1880–85, 1886, and 1892–94, a Liberal, born in Liverpool, England (–1898).

1810

POLITICS, GOVERNMENT, AND ECONOMICS

Business and Economics

- Donkin & Hall establish the world's first cannery in London, England, using tin cans to package food for British naval and miltary forces.
- Ireland is in economic crisis as its population increases to around 6 million, and poverty increasingly results from archaic inheritance laws that encourage the subdivision of ever-smaller family agricultural plots.

MAY

- The U.S. Congress passes Macon's Bill Number Two, restoring trade with Britain and France, notwithstanding their continuing mercantile hostility resulting from the war between them. The bill promises to reward the first country—whether Britain or France—to reinstate normal trade relations by boycotting the other.

JULY

- Leaders of the local Journeymen Cordwainers (shoemakers and leather workers) are convicted of conspiracy in New York, New York, for authorizing a labor strike. They are fined $1 each and made to pay trial costs.

AUGUST

- The French emperor Napoleon I promises the United States that France will normalize trade relations if the U.S. president James Madison boycotts trade with Great Britain.
- 5   The Trianon Tariff is introduced, whereby Emperor Napoleon I places a 50% tax on all colonial imports into France, in an effort to raise revenue.

OCTOBER

- As part of his ongoing battle with British trade, by the Decrees of Fontainebleau (issued October 18 and 25) the French emperor Napoleon I orders the confiscation and burning of British goods found within Napoleonic states and establishes tribunals to try persons accused of importing illicit wares.

NOVEMBER

- 1   The French emperor Napoleon I revokes the Berlin and Milan decrees with regard to U.S. trade to try to foment animosity between Britain and the United States.
- 2   The Prussian chancellor of state, Karl August, Prince von Hardenberg, introduces a modern taxation system

which excludes no one and abolishes the rules limiting employment in certain trades to guild members, thus increasing economic competition.

DECEMBER

- 31   In retaliation for French strangulation of European trade, Czar Alexander I of Russia introduces new tariffs aimed at French goods.

Colonization

- Guadeloupe, the last French colony in the West Indies, is taken by British forces.

JULY

- 9   Emperor Napoleon I annexes the Netherlands, making it part of the Empire of the French.
- 10   The French marshal Michel Ney takes the frontier town of Ciudad Rodrigo in Spain which has held back French forces from reinvading Portugal. A British force takes the French possessions of Bourbon and Mauritius in the Indian Ocean.

Politics and Government

- In the U.S. congressional elections, the Democratic-Republicans retain majorities in the House of Representatives (108–36) and Senate (30–6).
- Obstinate fighting between Ottoman and Russian forces continues all year in the Ottoman Danubian provinces of Moldavia and Wallachia.
- The U.S. Supreme Court, in the case *Fletcher v. Peck*, rules unconstitutional a Georgia law, thereby applying the principle of judicial review to the states.

JANUARY

- 1–October 10   Cadiz, the capital of free Spain, is besieged by French forces.
- 6   By the Treaty of Paris, Sweden agrees to join the Continental System, closing European ports to Britain, and recovers Pomerania from France in return.

FEBRUARY

- 11   The French emperor Napoleon I marries the archduchess Marie-Louise of Austria.
- 17   The French Senate issues a decree stating that spiritual authority cannot be exercised by a foreign power within the empire, which Pope Pius VII, in captivity at Savona in Italy, unconditionally rejects.
- 21   The Tyrolese patriot leader Andreas Hofer is shot after the failure of the Tyrolese revolt against Bavaria.

MARCH

- 23   By the Rambouillet Decrees (kept secret until May), the French emperor Napoleon I orders the sale of all U.S. ships that have been seized for violation of French decrees.

APRIL

9   A riot occurs in London, England, in support of the member of Parliament Sir Francis Burdett, who has been imprisoned by the government for his radical views. Burdett advocated liberal measures such as parliamentary reform, Catholic emancipation, prison reform, and freedom of speech; his imprisonment resulted from a letter he published in William Cobbet's *Political Register*, in which he declared the conduct of the House of Commons illegal in imprisoning a radical orator.

19   Under the influence of the South American nationalist Simón Bolívar, the Junta in Venezuela breaks away from Napoleonic Spain, refusing to recognize Joseph Bonaparte and proclaiming allegiance to Ferdinand VII, the hereditary king of Spain.

MAY

22   A revolt breaks out in the Spanish viceroyalty of New Granada against Spanish authority.

25   A revolt breaks out in the Spanish viceroyalty of Rio de la Plata, South America, against Joseph Bonaparte's regime.

JUNE

6   Karl August, Prince von Hardenberg, another reforming liberal, succeeds Baron Heinrich vom Stein in Prussia as chief minister.

JULY

1   Louis Bonaparte, King of the French-dominated Kingdom of Holland, abdicates under pressure from his brother, the French emperor Napoleon I.

19   Queen Louise of Prussia dies. Despite the attempts of Napoleon to sully her reputation, she was much loved and was very important for Prussian self-esteem at a time of military disaster.

AUGUST

18   Charles XIII of Sweden adopts the French general Jean-Baptiste Bernadotte as his heir, following the death of the crown prince Christian.

SEPTEMBER

•   U.S. settlers in Spanish West Florida rebel against their Spanish rulers. They seize the Spanish garrison at Baton Rouge and proclaim a republic.

16   A revolt breaks out in Mexico in favor of independence from Spain.

18   The Junta in Chile revolts against Joseph Bonaparte's rule in Spain and assumes authority.

OCTOBER

•   British and Portuguese forces commanded by Arthur Wellesley, Viscount Wellington, hold the lines of Torres Vedras, the name given to the defensive emplacements his forces have created around the Portuguese city of the same name, throughout the month. The besieging French force runs short of supplies, and is forced to withdraw.

•   The U.S. president James Madison annexes West Florida, which will become part of the Orleans territory.

25   King George III celebrates his 50th anniversay as monarch of Great Britain.

DECEMBER

10   The French emperor Napoleon I annexes the German ports of Hanover, Bremen, Hamburg, Lauenburg, and Lübeck to try to prevent the smuggling of British goods into Europe.

SCIENCE, TECHNOLOGY, AND MEDICINE

Agriculture

December 1810–59   U.S. cotton production, the vast majority of which is grown in the southern states, rises from 171,000 bales in 1810 to just under 5.4 million in 1859.

Ecology

•   Scottish-born U.S. ornithologist Alexander Wilson observes a flock of passenger pigeons 400 km/250 mi long which he estimates contains 2 billion birds. The passenger pigeon becomes extinct in 1914.

Exploration

OCTOBER

28–July 14, 1811   David Thompson, an English explorer working for the North Western Company, successfully crosses the Rocky Mountains and navigates down the Columbia River to the Pacific Ocean.

Health and Medicine

•   German physician Samuel Hahnemann lays the foundations of homoeopathy with the publication of *Organon der rationellen Heilkunst/Organ of Rational Medicine*.

•   Nearly 25,000 people die from yellow fever in Barcelona and Cadiz, Spain.

Math

•   French mathematician Jean-Baptiste-Joseph Fourier publishes his method of representing functions by a series of trigonometric functions.

Science

•   French chemist Louis-Nicolas Vauquelin identifies nicotine as the active ingredient in tobacco.

•   German physicist Thomas Johann Seebeck discovers that silver chloride takes on the color of the incident light it is exposed to.

•   Scottish physicist John Leslie is the first to create artificial ice—he freezes water using an air pump.

Technology

•   English inventor Peter Durand patents the first tin-plated steel container.

- French chef Nicolas Appert publishes the results of his food preservation experiments in *L'Art de conserver, pendant plusieurs années, toutes les substances animales et végétales/The Art of Preserving All Kinds of Animal and Vegetable Substances for Many Years*, making the techniques available to others.
- French-born English engineer Marc Isambard Brunel applies his mass-production methods to manufacturing footwear for the British army.
- German inventor Rudolph Ackerman develops a differential gear that allows carriages to turn sharp corners; it is later used on "horseless carriages."
- The first hay-mowing machine is introduced in the United States.
- U.S. inventor Oliver Evans builds a mechanized flour mill in Pittsburgh, Pennsylvania—the first to be powered by steam.

Transportation

- The 100-km/60-mi-long St. Quentin Canal opens. Linking Paris and Le Havre to the North Sea and the English Channel, it has a 5.6-km/3.5-mi-long tunnel.

ARTS AND IDEAS

Architecture

- The most famous U.S. suspension bridge in the 19th century, the Newburyport Bridge designed by John Templeman, is completed; it has a span of 81.6 m/ 224 ft.

Arts

c. 1810 The German artist Caspar David Friedrich draws his *Self-Portrait* and (1810) paints *Monk by the Sea*.
- The German artist Philipp Otto Runge paints *The Artist's Parents and His Children*.
- The Spanish artist Francisco José de Goya y Lucientes begins his series of engravings *Los desastres de la guerra/The Disasters of War*, which he completes in about 1815. They are not published until 1863.

Literature and Language

- Friedrich Christoph Perthes edits the literary magazine *Das vaterlandische Museum* in Hamburg, Germany.
- The Dutch writer Willem Bilderdijk publishes his unfinished verse epic *De ondergang der eerste wareld/ The Destruction of the First World*.
- The English poet George Crabbe publishes *The Borough*, a long poem describing life in a country town.
- The German dramatist Heinrich Wilhelm von Kleist publishes *Erzählungen/Tales*. Among the best-known of these tales are "Die Marquise von O"/"The Marquise of

O" and "Das Erdbeben in Chili"/"The Earthquake in Chile."
- The German scholar Georg Friedrich Creuser publishes the first volume of his four-volume *Symbolik und Mythologie der alten Völker, besonders der Griechen/ The Symbolism and Mythology of the Ancients*. The last volume appears in 1812.
- The German writer Friedrich von Schlegel publishes *Über die Sprache und Weisheit der Indien/Concerning the Language and Wisdom of India*.
- The Scottish poet and novelist Walter Scott publishes his narrative poem *The Lady of the Lake*.
- The U.S. lawyer and writer Charles Jared Ingersoll publishes *Inchiquin, the Jesuit's Letters*.

Music

- German composer Ludwig van Beethoven completes his incidental music for *Egmont* (Opus 84), a drama by the German writer Goethe; his Piano Sonata No. 26 (Opus 81a), the *Lebewohl*, also known as *Les Adieux*; and his String Quartet No. 11 (Opus 95).
- The opera *La cambiale di matrimonio/The Bill of Marriage*, by the Italian composer Gioachino Antonio Rossini, is first performed, in Venice, Italy.

Theater and Dance

- The play *Das Käthchen von Heilbronn/Katherine of Heilbronn* by the German dramatist Heinrich Wilhelm von Kleist is first performed, in Vienna, Austria.

Thought and Scholarship

- French anatomist Franz Gall and Austrian anatomist Johann Spurzheim publish *Anatomie et physiologie du système nerveux/Anatomy and Physiology of the Nervous System*, which establishes the "science" of phrenology; the idea that intelligence and personality traits can be determined from skull shape.
- The English writer and critic William Hazlitt publishes *On the Rise and Progress of Modern Philosophy*.
- The Franco-Swiss writer Madame de Staël publishes *De l'Allemagne/Germany*. A study of German culture and society, it is seen as anti-French and banned on the orders of Napoleon.
- The Presbyterian clergyman and scholar Samuel Stanhope Smith publishes *An Essay on the Causes of the Variety of Complexion and Figure of the Human Species*, an early account of evolution.

SOCIETY

Education

- Berlin University is founded by German scholar, diplomat, and educator Wilhelm von Humboldt, who believes education is necessary to produce patriotic citizens. The German nationalist philosopher Johann Gottlieb Fichte is installed as rector.

Everyday Life

- The U.S. census lists the population at 7,239,881, an increase from the 1800 figure of approximately 5,297,000.

OCTOBER

1 The Berkshire Cattle Show, forerunner of the county fair and one of the most popular institutions in U.S. culture, is held in Pittsfield, Massachusetts.

Media and Communication

- The U.S. printer and editor Isaiah Thomas publishes *History of Printing in America*.

JULY

- The U.S. periodical *Agricultural Museum* is first published in the Georgetown section of Washington, D.C.

Religion

- The Congregationalist Church establishes the American Board of Commissioners for Foreign Missions, the nation's first missionary society.
- The Connecticut minister Lyman Beecher joins in establishing the Connecticut Moral Society.
- The U.S. Presbyterian dissenters Thomas and Alexander Campbell establish the Brush Run Church in Pennsylvania.

BIRTHS & DEATHS

JANUARY

23 John Hoppner, English portrait painter, dies in London, England (57).

MARCH

1 Frédéric Chopin, French composer known for his works for piano, born in Zelazowa, Poland (–1849).

2 Pope Leo XIII, Italian pope 1878–1903, born in Carpineto, Romano, Papal States (–1903).

7 Cuthbert Collingwood, English naval commander who was second in command to Horatio Nelson at the Battle of Trafalgar, dies at sea en route to England (61).

15 Charles-Forbes-René, comte de Montalembert, French orator, politician, and historian, born in London, England (–1870).

MAY

21 Charles Geneviève d'Eon de Beaumont ("Le Chevalier d'Eon"), French secret agent who disguised himself as a woman, dies in London, England (81).

23 Margaret Fuller, U.S. transcendentalist author, born in Cambridgeport, Massachusetts (–1850).

28 Crown Prince Christian of Sweden dies during a fit of apoplexy.

JUNE

8 Robert Schumann, German romantic composer, born in Zwickau, Saxony (–1856).

26 Joseph-Michel Montgolfier, French aeronaut who, with his brother Jacques-Etienne, developed the hot-air balloon, dies in Balaruc-les-bains, France (69).

JULY

5 P(hineas) T(aylor) Barnum, U.S. showman and promoter who popularized the three-ring circus, born in Bethel, Connecticut (–1891).

AUGUST

10 Count Camillo Benso di Cavour, Italian politician who was instrumental in bringing about the unification of Italy, born in Turin, Italy (–1861).

SEPTEMBER

29 Elizabeth Cleghorn Stevenson, English novelist and biographer (under the name "Mrs. Gaskell") of the novelist Charlotte Brontë, born in Chelsea, London, England (–1865).

NOVEMBER

18 Asa Gray, U.S. botanist who classified much of the flora of the United States, born in Sauquoit, New York (–1888).

DECEMBER

7 Theodor Schwann, German histologist who founded modern cell theory, born in Neuss, Prussia (–1882).

11 Alfred de Musset, French romantic poet and playwright, born in Paris, France (–1857).

1811

POLITICS, GOVERNMENT, AND ECONOMICS

Business and Economics

- The U.S. fur merchant John Jacob Astor extends his monopoly over the industry by acquiring two-thirds of control over the new South West Company.

FEBRUARY

- The U.S. president James Madison restores the boycott on British trade in response to the French emperor Napoleon I's promise, of the previous August, to normalize trade relations with the United States.
- 20 Austria declares itself bankrupt as a result of the massive military mobilizations it has made and the sharp decline in its revenues following the 1809 Treaty of Schönbrunn.

MARCH

- 3 "Luddites" (British craftsmen and others whose livelihoods are threatened by new technology) destroy machinery in Nottingham and Yorkshire towns, England.

NOVEMBER

- 5 The U.S. president James Madison recommends that Congress prepare for hostilities against Britain, in view of the British orders in council on trade and violation of the 48-km/30-mile limit (off the U.S. coast).

Colonization

APRIL

- A group of U.S. colonists sponsored by the U.S. fur merchant John Jacob Astor arrive at the mouth of the Columbia River, in the present-day state of Washington.

JULY

- 5 Venezuela declares its independence from Spain and adopts a constitution under the influence of the South American nationalist Simón Bolívar and Francisco de Miranda, having disavowed allegiance to Ferdinand VII of Spain.

AUGUST

- 14 Paraguay achieves independence from Spain.

Human Rights

- A slave insurrection outside New Orleans, Louisiana, claims the lives of one planter and an estimated 75 slaves.

Politics and Government

- In a sensational plagiarism case, the U.S. editor Isaac Mitchell from Poughkeepsie, New York, and the teacher Daniel Jackson from Plattsburg, New York, both claim authorship of the same novel. Though Jackson has distributed the novel by a slightly different name, authorship of *The Asylum; or, Alonzo and Melissa* is granted posthumously to Mitchell.
- New York State enacts a general incorporation law, providing private charters to corporate investors.
- U.S. president James Madison appoints the Massachusetts jurist Joseph Story and Maryland jurist Gabriel Duvall to the U.S. Supreme Court.

JANUARY

- The U.S. Congress passes a secret resolution authorizing the United States to annex Spanish East Florida upon the assent of local officials or in the event of foreign occupation.
- 22 By annexing Oldenburg, near Hanover, to increase his hold on Baltic trade, the French emperor Napoleon I further alienates Czar Alexander I of Russia whose brother-in-law is the heir apparent to the grand duchy.

FEBRUARY

- 10 The Russians take Belgrade, Serbia, and capture the Ottoman army in their war with the Ottoman Empire in the Danubian provinces (Moldavia and Wallachia).

MARCH

- 1 Mehmet Ali, the Ottoman viceroy in Egypt, deals with internal opposition to his rule by massacring its Mameluke leaders at a banquet held for them in Cairo.

MAY

- The U.S. warship *President* sinks the British gunboat *Little Belt* in retaliation for Britain's forcible enlistment of a U.S. soldier two weeks previously. Nine British sailors are killed and twelve are injured.
- U.S.–British relations deteriorate after the British warship *Guerrière* stops the U.S. vessel *Spitfire* and forcibly enlist a U.S. sailor, off Sandy Hook, New York.
- 6 Britain's Viscount Wellington (Arthur Wellesley) defeats the French at Fuentes d'Onoro, near Ciudad Rodrigo, in Portugal. Emperor Napoleon I subsequently replaces the unsuccessful Marshal André Masséna with Marshal Auguste Marmont.
- 16 A British force, under General William Beresford, checks the French advancing on Portugal, under Marshal

Nicolas-Jean Soult, at Albuhera (Albuera), near Badajoz, Spain.

JUNE

1   The new Civil Code is promulgated throughout the Austrian Empire, excepting Hungary, to standardize its laws.

17–July 6   A National Council of the French clergy meets in Paris to settle the disputes between Emperor Napoleon I and Pope Pius VII over the role and influence of the papacy. It is dissolved when it refuses to support Napoleon's orders unless the Pope does.

AUGUST

8   British forces occupy Dutch-held Java in the East Indies (the Netherlands having been incorporated into the Empire of the French).

SEPTEMBER

14   An edict issued in Prussia by the chief minister Karl August, Prince von Hardenberg, ends restrictions on land sale and ownership, providing for peasant proprietorship and more productive agriculture.

OCTOBER

29   The French emperor Napoleon I threatens to occupy the Prussian capital, Berlin, unless Prussia cancels its military plans for rapprochement with Russia.

NOVEMBER

•   The Shawnee chief Tecumseh leads a failed attack against 800 U.S. soldiers commanded by William Henry Harrison, the governor of the territory of Indiana, near the Tippecanoe River in northern Indiana. Harrison is credited with destroying Tecumseh's uprising, and nicknamed the "Hero of Tippecanoe."

SCIENCE, TECHNOLOGY, AND MEDICINE

Ecology

DECEMBER

16   The first, and largest, earthquake recorded in the United States destroys the city of New Madrid, Missouri. Two other earthquakes hit the town on January 23 and February 7, 1812.

Exploration

•   English scholar and eccentric Thomas Manning, disguised as a Chinese doctor, explores Tibet and becomes the first Englishman to reach the capital, Lhasa, a city closed to Europeans, before being expelled.

Health and Medicine

•   An anonymous writer publishes what is believed to be the first U.S. book on child care, *The Maternal*

Physician; A Treatise on the Nurture and Management of Infants, from the Birth until Two Years Old, Being the Result of Sixteen Years' Experience in the Nursery.

Math

•   French mathematician Siméon-Denis Poisson publishes *Traité de mécanique/Treatise on Mechanics*, which discusses the application of mathematics to magnetism, electricity, physics, and mechanics.

Science

•   French chemist Bernard Courtois accidentally discovers the element iodine (atomic no. 53), when he adds too much sulfuric acid to kelp ash and obtains a violet vapor that condenses to a black crystalline substance. He calls it "substance X." Humphry Davy names it iodine in 1813.

•   German astronomer Wilhelm Olbers theorizes that pressure from solar radiation always forces the tail of a comet to point away from the sun.

•   Italian physicist Amedeo Avogadro proposes Avogadro's law which states that equal volumes of different gases under the same temperature and pressure conditions will contain the same number of molecules.

•   Scottish physicist David Brewster discovers the law now named for him that describes the behavior of polarized light.

•   Swedish chemist Jöns Jakob Berzelius introduces the modern system of chemical symbols.

Technology

•   Frieberg, Saxony, is the first city to be illuminated by coal gas lights.

•   German printer Friedrich Koenig, working in London, England, develops a mechanical press. Gears are used to control the raising and lowering of the platen, the movement of the bed, and the inking of the rollers. With German printer Andreas Bauer, he also designs a press with a cylindrical platen, which holds the sheet of paper.

•   U.S. inventor John Hall patents a breech-loading rifle.

Transportation

•   The U.S. entrepreneur John Stevens opens a steamboat ferry between New York, New York, and Hoboken, New Jersey. He is forced to shut down operations when the U.S. engineer and inventor Robert Fulton, who possesses a monopoly on steamboat enterprises in New York State, threatens a lawsuit.

•   Steam power is used in Leeds, England, for conveying coal on a railroad.

December 1811–37   The Cumberland Road, or National Road, is constructed. It is the first federal highway in the United States, running from Cumberland, Maryland, to the Ohio River.

ARTS AND IDEAS

- The German writer Johann Wolfgang von Goethe publishes the first part of his autobiography *Dichtung und Wahrheit/Poetry and Truth*.

Arts

- The American Museum opens in New York, New York, featuring the latest scientific and artistic developments.
- The Danish artist Bertel Thorvaldsen sculpts *Procession of Alexander the Great*.
- The English artist John Constable paints *Dedham Vale, Morning*.
- The English artist Thomas Lawrence paints *Portrait of Benjamin West*.
- The English sculptor Francis Leggatt Chantrey sculpts the portrait bust *The Reverend J Horne-Tooke*.
- The German critic and literary historian August Wilhelm Schlegel publishes *Vorlesungen über dramatische Kunst und Literatur/Lectures on Dramatic Art and Literature*, in which he draws a distinction between classical and romantic art.

Literature and Language

- The English writer Jane Austen publishes her novel *Sense and Sensibility*. She began work on it in 1797.
- The German writer Friedrich Heinrich Karl de La Motte, Baron Fouqué, publishes *Undine*, a fairy tale.

Music

- German composer Ludwig van Beethoven completes his Piano Trio in B flat (Opus 97), the *Archduke*, and his overture and incidental music for August von Kotzebue's play *König Stephan/King Stephen*, written for the opening night of the German Theater in Budapest in 1812.
- The opera *Abu Hassan* by the German composer Carl Maria von Weber is first performed, in Munich, Germany.

Theater and Dance

- The tragedy *Aiace/Ajax*, by the Italian writer Ugo Foscolo, is first performed, in Milan, Italy.

Thought and Scholarship

- Scottish anatomist Charles Bell publishes *New Idea of the Anatomy of the Brain*, in which he distinguishes between sensory and motor nerves.
- The German historian Berthold Georg Niebuhr publishes the first volume of his influential *Römische*

BIRTHS & DEATHS

JANUARY
8   Christoph Friedrich Nicolai, German writer and bookseller, a leader of the German Enlightenment, dies in Berlin, Germany (74).

FEBRUARY
9   Nevil Maskelyne, English astronomer who developed a method of determining longitude by observing the moon, and published *The British Mariner's Guide* (1763) and the *Nautical Almanac* (1766), dies in Greenwich, London, England (78).

MARCH
20   François-Charles-Joseph, heir to the throne of the French emperor Napoleon I, is born. He is given the title of king of Rome.
31   Robert Wilhelm von Bunsen, German chemist who discovered that each element emits light of a characteristic wavelength and who invented the Bunsen burner, born in Göttingen, Germany (–1899).

APRIL
5   Robert Raikes, English journalist and philanthropist who founded the Sunday school movement which taught children reading and the

catechism on Sundays, dies in Gloucester, England (74).

JUNE
14   Harriet Beecher Stowe, U.S. writer, author of *Uncle Tom's Cabin*, born in Litchfield, Connecticut (–1896).

JULY
18   William Makepeace Thackeray, English novelist who wrote *Vanity Fair*, born in Calcutta, India (–1863).

AUGUST
3   Elisha Graves Otis, U.S. inventor who built the first safety elevator, born in Halifax, Vermont (–1861).
21   William Kelly, U.S. steelmaker who invented the pneumatic method of making steel, born in Pittsburgh, Pennsylvania (–1888).
31   Louis-Antoine de Bougainville, French navigator who explored the South Pacific, dies in Paris, France (81).
31   Théophile Gautier, French novelist, poet, and journalist, born in Tarbes, France (–1872).

SEPTEMBER
8   Peter Simon Pallas, German geologist whose theory of the formation of mountain ranges recognized that rocks display a

temporal sequence, dies in Berlin, Germany (69).
30   Thomas Percy, English antiquarian and author of *Reliques of Ancient English Poetry* (1765), dies in Dromore, County Down, Ireland (82).

OCTOBER
22   Franz (Ferencz) Liszt, Hungarian pianist and composer, born in Raiding, Hungary (–1886).
25   Evariste Galois, French mathematician who developed group theory algebra, born in Bourg-la-Reine, France (–1832).
27   Isaac Merrit Singer, U.S. inventor who developed the sewing machine and brought it into popular use, born in Pittstown, New York (–1875).
29   (Jean-Joseph-Charles-) Louis Blanc, French socialist who developed the idea of worker-controlled "social workshops," born in Madrid, Spain (–1882).

NOVEMBER
26   Zeng Guofan, Chinese administrator and military leader who suppressed the Taipeng Rebellion, born in Xiangxiang, Hunan Province, China (–1872).

Geschichte/History of Rome. The last volume appears in 1832.

SOCIETY

Everyday Life

- The population of Great Britain is 12.5 million, an increase of 2.1 million during the previous decade. The population of London, England, exceeds 1 million.

Religion

- Large numbers of Welsh Protestants leave the Anglican Church in the "Great Schism."

Sports

- Swiss mountaineers Rudolf and Hieronymus Meyer climb the Jungfrau in the Swiss Alps.
- The Prussian educator Friedrich Ludwig Jahn, a founding father of modern gymnastics, establishes the Turnverein gymnastic society in Berlin, the Prussian capital.
- The Reverend J. Ramsey of Gladsmuir, Scotland, publishes *An Account of the Game of Curling* in Edinburgh, Scotland. It is the earliest known book on the sport.
- Thousands of spectators in New York, New York, watch the first noteworthy rowing race in the United States, between the *Knickerbocker* of New York and the *Invincible* of New Jersey.

SEPTEMBER

28 An estimated crowd of 40,000 at Wymondham, England, watch the English prizefighter Tom Cribb defeat Tom Molineaux, a freed slave from Virginia.

1812

POLITICS, GOVERNMENT, AND ECONOMICS

Business and Economics

- French chef Nicolas Appert opens the first commercial canning factory, outside Paris, France.
- When the British navy's blockade of the European coast prevents silk reaching Britain, James and Patrick Clark in Paisley, Scotland, begin to manufacture cotton sewing thread as an alternative.

JANUARY

19 British forces under Arthur Wellesley, Viscount Wellington, take Ciudad Rodrigo, Spain, one of the main passages between Spain and Portugal. French forces reoccupy Swedish Pomerania and the island of Rügen to put pressure on Sweden to end clandestine trade with Britain and to dissuade it from entering an anti-French alliance with Russia.

FEBRUARY

24 Prussia agrees to allow free passage for French troops across its territory, to provide troops in the event of war with Russia, and to adhere to the Continental System of closing European ports to Britain, after pressure from the French emperor Napoleon I.

APRIL

11 Two Luddites (British craftsmen whose livelihoods are threatened by new technology) are shot dead as they break into Rawford's Mill in Yorkshire, England, to smash newly delivered looms.

Colonization

JUNE

26 The Polish diet (parliament) declares Poland independent from Russia, Prussia, and Austria, denouncing its partition between these powers.

JULY

31 The Venezuelan Republic falls to Spanish forces and Francisco de Miranda, Venezuelan revolutionary and leader in the revolution against Spanish rule in Venezuela, is arrested.

Human Rights

MARCH

11 A Prussian edict states that Jews are simply another religious community like any other, and removes citizenship restrictions on them. Seventy thousand take the opportunity to become Prussian citizens.

APRIL

19 Lucy Brewer of the United States disguises herself and, under the name Nicolas Baker, serves as a member of the all-male crew of the *Constitution* for three years.

Politics and Government

- In the U.S. congressional elections, the Democratic-Republicans retain reduced majorities in the House of Representatives (112–68) and Senate (27–9).

JANUARY

1 After 50 years of preparation, the new Civil Code comes into effect throughout the Austrian Empire, except Hungary, standardizing its laws.

MARCH

- In preparation for war with Britain, the U.S. Congress authorizes $11 million in war bonds, the first of their kind.
- The U.S. Congress passes the nation's first foreign aid act to help relieve the victims of an earthquake in Venezuela.

4 Richard Colley, Marquess Wellesley, resigns as British foreign secretary because of lack of support for the Peninsular campaign and is replaced by Lord Castlereagh.

16 Worried by the expansion of Russian influence in the Danubian provinces (Moldavia and Wallachia) of the Ottoman Empire, Austria agrees to provide an army for the French emperor Napoleon I, who in return guarantees the integrity of the Ottoman Empire and promises to restore the Illyrian provinces (Carniola, Trieste, Carinthia, Croatia, and Dalmatia) to Austria.

19 The Spanish cortes (national assembly) promulgates a liberal constitution, whose provisions include universal suffrage, under the rule of a hereditary monarch.

29 The secretary of the council of state, Count Mikhail Speransky, the architect of Russia's pro-French policies, is replaced by the conservative vice admiral Shishkov as Czar Alexander I turns decisively against Emperor Napoleon I.

APRIL

6 British forces capture the strategically important city of Badajoz on the border of Portugal and Spain.

9 Under the secret Treaty of Åbo, Sweden agrees to aid Russia by creating a diversion against the French in northern Germany, while in return Czar Alexander I suggests Swedish annexation of Danish Norway as compensation for the loss of Finland to Russia under the 1809 Peace of Frederikshavn.

14 Louisiana becomes the 18th state in the Union.

27 William Horsfall, a Yorkshire mill owner, is murdered by Luddites (British craftsmen whose livelihoods are threatened by new technology).

MAY

28 The Treaty of Bucharest ends the war between Russia and the Ottoman Empire. Russia obtains Bessarabia, (an area of southeast Europe bordered by the rivers Dniester

---

Anglo–American War of 1812 (1812–15)

1812

June 19 The U.S. Congress passes resolutions of war against Britain, beginning the War of 1812, after suffering years of perceived mercantile humiliation as a result of Britain's war with France.

August 15 Native Americans allied with Britain in the War of 1812 attack and kill U.S. traders and their families fleeing Fort Dearborn, the site of present-day Chicago, Illinois.

August 16 U.S. brigadier general William Hull surrenders Detroit to a British force without firing a shot, an act that will earn him a court martial two years later. The loss of the fortress forces the postponement of U.S. plans for an invasion of Canada.

August 19 In a naval engagement off Nova Scotia, the U.S. warship *Constitution* defeats its British counterpart *Guerrière*.

October In a naval battle on Lake Erie, U.S. forces commanded by Lieutenant Jesse Duncan Elliott capture two British warships, HMS *Detroit* and HMS *Caledonia*.

October 13 British troops under Isaac Brock defeat a U.S. force at Queenstoun Heights in Lower Canada, preventing further U.S. attempts to invade Canada.

December 29 The U.S. warship *Constitution* sinks the British warship *Java* off the coast of Brazil.

1813

February 24 The U.S. warship *Hornet* captures the British ship *Peacock*.

April 24 U.S. forces led by army lieutenant Zebulon Montgomery Pike capture York (present-day Toronto), Canada, from the British. Pike perishes in the battle.

June 1 The British warship *Shannon* captures its U.S. counterpart *Chesapeake* off the Massachusetts coast.

August 14 The British warship *Pelican* defeats its U.S. opponent *Argus* off the coast of England.

September 3 The U.S. warship *Enterprise* defeats the British ship *Boxer* off the Maine coast.

September 10 The U.S. wins the Battle of Lake Erie, consolidating its hold on the Great Lakes.

October 5 U.S. troops defeat a British force at the Battle of the Thames River in Upper Canada (modern Ontario). The Shawnee chief Tecumseh, allied with the British, perishes in the battle, causing his four-year-old Indian Confederacy to disintegrate.

1814

August 24 At the Battle of Bladensburg, a British landing force defeats American militia, opening the way to Washington, D.C.. British forces then burn the White House and other public buildings in Washington, in apparent retaliation for the U.S. destruction of York.

September 11 U.S. naval forces defeat their British counterparts at the Battle of Lake Champlain.

1815

January 8 At the Battle of New Orleans, the British suffer 2,600 casualties; the Americans suffer only 13, while making frontal assaults on strongly entrenched positions.

February The U.S. Senate ratifies the Treaty of Ghent (signed on December 24, 1814), formally ending the war.

and Prut) and withdraws its demand for the provinces of Moldavia and Wallachia. The peace enables Czar Alexander I to act against the French emperor Napoleon I.

JUNE

- The U.S. Congress authorizes the Treasury to issue $5 million of new notes.
18 The U.S. Congress passes resolutions of war against Britain (beginning the War of 1812) after suffering years of perceived mercantile humiliation as a result of Britain's war with France.
19 The United States formally declares war against Britain after Britain's failure to revoke trade restrictions aimed at damaging French trade but also causing severe hardship in the United States.
24 The French emperor Napoleon crosses the River Niemen and begins his invasion of Russia. Rivalry with Russia has been brewing for some years, and Napoleon has assembled a huge army of 500,000 infantry and 100,000 cavalry (the *Grande Armée*).
28 The French *Grande Armée* under Napoleon crosses the River Vilna in pursuit of the retreating Russian army, and occupies the city of Vilna (modern Vilnius), capital of Russian Poland.

JULY

- In a sermon about the War of 1812, the pacifist Boston Congregational minister William Ellery Channing asserts the compatibility of patriotism and dissent.
- The U.S. Congress doubles import tariffs to help defray the cost of war with Britain.
7 Britain makes peace with Russia and Sweden.
14 The French emperor Napoleon I, unwilling to offend Prussia or Austria whose interests would be threatened by the reconstitution of a Polish state, refuses to acknowledge the Polish declaration of independence of June 26, and forfeits valuable Polish support in the French war with Russia.
18 By the Treaty of Örebro, Britain joins Russia and Sweden in a formal alliance against France.
22 British forces under Arthur Wellesley, Viscount Wellington, decisively defeat the French, under Marshal Auguste Marmont, on the Spanish–Portuguese border at Salamanca, and subsequently advance into Spain.

AUGUST

12 British forces under Arthur Wellesley, Viscount Wellington, enter the Spanish capital, Madrid, following the retreat of the French forces and its evacuation by King Joseph Bonaparte.
15 Native American peoples allied with Britain in the War of 1812 attack and kill U.S. traders and their families fleeing Fort Dearborn, the site of present-day Chicago, Illinois.
16 The U.S. brigadier general William Hull surrenders Detroit to a British force without firing a shot, an act that will earn him a court martial two years later. The loss of the fortress forces the postponement of U.S. plans for an invasion of Canada.
17–18 Russian forces commanded by Marshal Michel Andreas Barclay de Tolly are defeated by the French *Grande Armée* at Smolensk, which is then occupied by the French.
19 In a naval engagement off Nova Scotia, the U.S. warship *Constitution* defeats its British counterpart *Guerrière*.

SEPTEMBER

7 The Russian army, now under the command of Marshal Mikhail Ilarionovich Kutuzov, is defeated by the French *Grande Armée* at the Battle of Borodino, and obliged to retreat and abandon the Russian capital, Moscow. Emperor Napoleon I makes a significant mistake in failing to mobilize his reserves and destroy the retreating army.
14–18 The French *Grande Armée* enters and occupies the Russian capital, Moscow, burning much of the city. Following the defeat of the main Russian forces, the French are now subjected to constant wearying harassment by mounted troops.
19 British forces are forced by the French army under Marshal Auguste Marmont to withdraw from the city of Burgos in northern Spain.

OCTOBER

- In a naval battle on Lake Erie, U.S. forces commanded by Lieutenant Jesse Duncan Elliott capture two British warships, HMS *Detroit* and HMS *Caledonia*.
13 British troops under Isaac Brock defeat a U.S. force at Queenstoun Heights in Lower Canada, preventing further U.S. attempts to invade Canada.
18 A detachment commanded by Marshal Joachim Murat from the French *Grande Armée* in Russia is defeated by Russian forces at Vinkaro.
19 Having failed to deliver a knockout blow against the Russians, Emperor Napoleon I's *Grande Armée* begins to retreat from Moscow as winter sets in.
23 Reacting against Napoleon's impoverishment of France and apparently insatiable ambition, General Claude-François de Malet conspires to dethrone Napoleon, install King Louis XVIII, and end the Napoleonic Wars.
24 At the Battle of Maloyaroslavets, the Russian army under Marshal Mikhail Kutuzov blocks the French *Grande Armée*'s favored line of retreat from Moscow, forcing it to take a more circuitous one through barren countryside.
29 General Claude-François de Malet is executed for conspiring against Napoleon.

NOVEMBER

26–28 As the retreating French *Grande Armée* crosses the River Beresina in Russia, it is attacked by Russian forces under Marshal Mikhail Ilarionovich Kutuzov and Count Ludwig Adolf Wittgenstein and sustains very heavy losses.

DECEMBER

- James Madison is reelected U.S. president. The Massachusetts politician Elbridge Gerry replaces George Clinton as vice president.
5 Hearing news of the coup against him, the French emperor Napoleon I leaves his troops under the command of Marshal Joachim Murat in Russia and sets out for Paris (where he arrives on December 18). The remnants of his *Grande Armée* struggle back to France, a bare 10,000 effective troops remaining from the 500,000 who set out for Moscow.
29 The U.S. warship *Constitution* sinks the British warship *Java* off the coast of Brazil.
30 By the Convention of Tauroggen with Russia, without the knowledge of King Frederick Wilhelm III, the

Prussian field marshal Johann, Count Yorck von Wartenburg, commander of the Prussian contingent in Napoleon's *Grande Armée*, breaks away from the French alliance and becomes temporarily neutral.

SCIENCE, TECHNOLOGY, AND MEDICINE

Agriculture

- Two strains of corn are crossbred in the United States to produce the first hybrid corn.

Exploration

FEBRUARY

- The U.S. fur trader and explorer William Hunt arrives in Astoria, Oregon, from St. Louis, Missouri, having charted some of what will become known as the Oregon Trail.

AUGUST

22 Swiss explorer Johann Ludwig Burckhardt discovers the ancient city of Petra (Jordan), capital of an Arab kingdom *c.* 312 BC–AD 650.

Health and Medicine

- The Philadelphia physician Benjamin Rush publishes *Medical Inquiries and Observations upon the Diseases of the Mind*.
- Cholesterol is discovered.

Science

- English chemist Humphry Davy publishes *Elements of Chemical Philosophy*, in which he discusses his work on electrochemistry.
- French mathematician and astronomer Pierre-Simon Laplace publishes *Théorie analytique des probabilités/ Analytical Theory of Probabilities*. It describes the mathematical tools he has invented for predicting the probabilities of occurrence of natural events and is the first complete theoretical account of probability.
- French zoologist Georges Cuvier, publishes *Recherches sur les ossements fossiles de quadrupèdes/Research on the Fossil Bones of Quadrupeds*, and establishes comparative vertebrate paleontology. He theorizes that the extinction of species has been caused by great catastrophes such as sudden land upheavals and floods.
- The Academy of Natural Sciences is founded in Philadelphia, Pennsylvania.

Technology

- The world's first steam threshing machine is powered by one of Richard Trevithick's high-pressure steam engines.

Transportation

- *c.* 1812 The Baltimore clipper ship is introduced by U.S. shipbuilders; its revolutionary design—it has a great expanse of sail and hull that offers little water resistance—makes it one of the fastest ships afloat.
- English inventor John Blenkinsop develops a "steam boiler on wheels;" the first practical locomotive, it employs a tooth-rack rail system and a two-cylinder engine, and hauls coal from Middleton to Leeds in Yorkshire, England.
- Scottish engineer Henry Bell's steamship *Comet* plies the Clyde River. The first commercially successful steamship in Europe, it heralds the era of steam navigation in Europe.

ARTS AND IDEAS

Architecture

- The City Hall in New York, New York, designed by the French-born architect Joseph-François Manqin and the U.S. architect John McComb, is completed.

Arts

- *c.* 1812 The English artist J. M. W. Turner paints *Snowstorm: Hannibal Crossing the Alps*.
- The French artist Théodore Géricault paints *An Officer of the Chasseurs*.
- The Spanish artist Francisco José de Goya y Lucientes paints *The Duke of Wellington* and *The Colossus*.

Literature and Language

- The English poet George Gordon, Lord Byron, publishes the first two cantos of *Childe Harold's Pilgrimage*. Further cantos appear in 1816 and 1818. Based on the wanderings of a typical "Byronic hero," it becomes an immediate success.
- The German biblical scholar Heinrich Friedrich Wilhelm Gesenius publishes his *Hebräisches und Chaldäisches Handwörterbuch/Hebrew and Chaldaic Dictionary*.
- The German folklorists and philologists Jakob Ludwig Carl Grimm and his brother Wilhelm Carl Grimm publish the first volume of their *Kinder and Hausmärchen/Fairy Tales*. A second volume appears in 1815 and a third in 1822.
- The Scottish-born U.S. mapmaker John Melish publishes *Travels in the United States*.
- The U.S. writer James Kirke Paulding publishes *The Diverting History of John Bull and Brother Jonathan*, a comic history of the United States.

Music

- Austrian composer Franz Schubert completes his *Salve Regina* for voice and orchestra (D 27); his *Kyrie* in D minor (D 31); and his String Quartets No. 1 (D 18) and No. 2 (D 32).

- German composer Ludwig van Beethoven completes his Symphonies No. 7 in A (Opus 92) and No. 8 in F (Opus 93), and his Violin Sonata in G major (Opus 96), which is revised in 1815.
- The opera *La pietra del paragone/The Touchstone*, by the Italian composer Gioachino Antonio Rossini, is first performed, in Milan, Italy.

Thought and Scholarship

- The Danish churchman and poet Nikolai Frederik Severin Grundtvig publishes his world history *Verdens krønike/World Chronicle*.
- The German philosopher Georg Wilhelm Friedrich Hegel publishes the first part of his *Wissenschaft der Logic/The Science of Logic*. In this work he sets out his famous three-part "dialectic" of thesis, antithesis, and synthesis. The second part appears in 1816.
- The Massachusetts publisher Isaiah Thomas endows the American Antiquarian Society in Worcester, Massachusetts.

SOCIETY

Education

- Hamilton College is founded in Clinton, New York.
- Lycoming College is founded in Williamsport, Pennsylvania.

Everyday Life

c. 1812   The women's fashion in Britain is for dresses with very high waists, just under the bust.

Media and Communication

c. 1812   During the War of 1812, the term "Uncle Sam" is first used to refer to the U.S. federal government. First printed in the Troy, New York, *Post* on September 3, 1813, the term may have originated from Samuel Wilson, a U.S. Army supply inspector known as Uncle Sam.

- The *New England Journal of Medicine* begins publication in Boston, Massachusetts.

Religion

- The U.S. Congregationalist missionary Adoniram Judson departs for India at the forefront of a wave of U.S. missionary activity.

Sports

August 1812–29   The English sports writer Pierce Egan publishes *Boxiana: or, Sketches of Ancient and Modern Pugilism*.

BIRTHS & DEATHS

- Edmund Malone, Irish-born English Shakespearean scholar, dies in London, England (70).

FEBRUARY
7   Charles Dickens, English novelist of the Victorian era, born in Portsmouth, England (–1870).

MARCH
18   John Horne Tooke, English political agitator for parliamentary reform, dies in Wimbledon, Surrey, England (75).
20   Jan Ladislav Dussek, Bohemian composer and pianist, dies in St. Germain-en-Laye, France (52).

APRIL
6   Alexander Ivanovich Herzen, Russian journalist and political activist who argued that Russian

socialism would be achieved through a peasant revolt, born in Moscow, Russia (–1870).
20   George Clinton, soldier, governor of New York 1777–95 and 1801–04, and vice president of the United States 1804–12, dies in Washington, D.C. (72).
22   James Andrew Dalhousie, British governor-general of India 1847–56 who conquered and annexed most of the independent states on the subcontinent, born in Dalhousie Castle, Scotland (–1860).
26   Alfred Krupp, German industrialist who manufactured armaments, born in Essen, Grand Duchy of Berg (–1887).

MAY
7   Robert Browning, English poet, born in London, England (–1889).
12   Edward Lear, English landscape painter and writer of nonsense verse, born in Highgate, London, England (–1888).

SEPTEMBER
19   Mayer Amschel Rothschild, German financier who began the Rothschild banking dynasty, dies in Frankfurt, Germany (78).

NOVEMBER
16   John Walter, English editor, the founder of *The Times* newspaper in 1788, dies in Teddington, Middlesex, England (73).

1813

POLITICS, GOVERNMENT, AND ECONOMICS

Business and Economics

- The Boston textile mogul Francis Cabot Lowell incorporates the Boston Manufacturing Company, the first integrated factory in the United States.
- The British East India Company's monopoly of trade with India is abolished, but its monopoly in China continues.

JANUARY

10 Fourteen Luddites (British craftsmen rebelling against new technology) are executed in York, England, for frame-breaking (smashing looms and other machinery).

Colonization

JULY

7 Venezuela becomes independent from Spain for the second time with the South American nationalist Simón Bolívar as virtual dictator.

NOVEMBER

6 Mexico declares itself independent of Spain.

Politics and Government

FEBRUARY

24 The U.S. warship *Hornet* captures the British ship *Peacock*, in a naval engagement.

28 Prussia agrees, by the Alliance of Kalisz with Russia, to conduct a joint campaign in Saxony and Silesia against the French emperor Napoleon I and the Confederation of the Rhine (association of German states under French protection). Prussia is to regain all territory lost since 1806. An invitation to join the war is extended to Britain and Austria, and the agreement becomes the genesis of the Fourth Coalition against France.

MARCH

- James Madison is inaugurated as U.S. president for a second term.

3 Britain concludes the Treaty of Stockholm with Sweden. The latter agrees to supply an army of 30,000 men to fight the French in return for British subsidies and a promise not to oppose Swedish union with Norway (currently under Danish rule).

17 King Frederick Wilhelm III of Prussia declares war against France.

18 After a patriotic outbreak against the French in Hamburg, capital of the province of Hamburg, the city is taken from its French garrison by advancing Russian forces.

27 A combined Russo-Prussian force occupies Dresden, the capital of Saxony, forcing the pro-French king Frederick Augustus to flee.

APRIL

24 U.S. forces led by army lieutenant Zebulon Montgomery Pike capture York (present-day Toronto), Canada, from the British. Pike perishes in the battle.

MAY

2 The French emperor Napoleon I defeats a Prussian and Russian army at Lützen (Gross-Gorschen) near Leipzig, Saxony, but is unable to destroy his opponents.

20–21 The indecisive Battle of Bautzen, near Dresden, Saxony, between the French and Russo-Prussian armies results in heavy losses on both sides.

JUNE

1 The British warship *Shannon* captures its U.S. counterpart *Chesapeake* off the Massachusetts coast.

4–August 10 The armistice of Poischwitz, Austria, between the allies (Prussia and Austria) and France is arranged after allied requests through the mediation of the Austrian foreign minister Klemens Metternich. The French emperor Napoleon I uses the time to train his cavalry.

14–15 Having only a small army of its own, Britain undertakes to pay subsidies to support Russia and Prussia in the war with France.

21 British forces under Viscount Wellington completely rout the French army of Marshal Jean-Baptiste Jourdain at Vittoria in northern Spain, forcing Joseph Bonaparte to flee back to France.

27 By the Treaty of Reichenbach with Prussia and Russia, Austria agrees to declare war on France on July 20 if the French refuse the conditions of peace.

JULY

26–August 1 A French force, under Marshal Nicolas-Jean Soult, tries to reenter Spain and is definitively repulsed by British forces, under Viscount Wellington, at the Battle of Sorrauren.

28–August 10 The Congress of Prague between France, Prussia, and Austria begins to discuss a peace settlement but is dissolved.

AUGUST

- The Creek War begins when Creek warriors commanded by William Weatherford (Red Eagle) kill

500 U.S. settlers at Fort Mims, near present-day Mobile, Alabama.

12   Austria declares war against the French emperor Napoleon I. The allies (Austria, Prussia, and Russia) can now put 500,000 men in the field, with armies in Silesia, Bohemia, and northern Germany.

14   The British warship *Pelican* defeats its U.S. opponent *Argus* off the coast of England.

23   French forces under General Nicolas-Charles Oudinot are defeated by the Prussian general Friedrich von Bülow at Grossbeeren, preventing them from marching on the Prussian capital, Berlin.

26   The French, under General Jacques MacDonald, are defeated at Katzbach, Prussia, by the Prussian general Gebhard von Blücher.

26–27   In the Battle of Dresden, in Saxony, the French emperor Napoleon I defeats the allied army from Bohemia, having arrived unexpectedly after the Austrian general Karl Philipp, Prince zu Schwarzenberg, had attacked the French under Marshal Gouvion St.-Cyr.

September

3   The U.S. warship *Enterprise* defeats the British ship *Boxer* off the Maine coast.

6   The French marshal Michel Ney is defeated by Prince Jean-Baptiste Bernadotte of Sweden's Northern Army at Dennewitz as he attempts to take the Prussian capital, Berlin.

9   The French-held city of San Sebastián in northern Spain capitulates to the British army under Viscount Wellington, after a siege lasting since August 31.

9   The Treaty of Teplitz confirms the Reichenbach agreement of June 27 uniting Russia, Prussia, and Austria against France.

10   The U.S. wins the Battle of Lake Erie against the British in the War of 1812, consolidating its hold on the Great Lakes of North America.

October

5   U.S. troops defeat a British force at the Battle of the Thames River in Upper Canada (modern Ontario). The Shawnee chief Tecumseh, allied with the British, perishes in the battle, causing his four-year-old Indian Confederacy to disintegrate.

8   Bavaria joins the allies against France by the Treaty of Ried with Austria, and leaves the Confederation of the Rhine (the association of German states under French protection).

8   British forces, under Viscount Wellington, cross the River Bidassoa and enter France from Spain.

12   By the peace of the Treaty of Gulistan, Persia cedes the Caucasus region to Russia, continuing the extension of Russian influence southward.

14   Bavaria, having joined the allies on October 8, makes a formal declaration of war against France.

16–19   Opposed by the Prussian army in the northwest and Austro-Russian forces in the south, the French army under Napoleon is heavily defeated in the "Battle of the Nations" at Leipzig in Saxony, and retreats. Allied victory leads to the dissolution of the Confederation of the Rhine (the association of German states under French protection) and of the kingdom of Westphalia.

26   After a rising in the Italian states, the Austrians defeat Napoleon's son-in-law, Eugène de

Beauharnais, at Valsarno, thus regaining a foothold in Italy.

31   The city of Pamplona in Spain finally surrenders to a British force.

November

•   The U.S. army general John Coffee leads a raid on the Creek village of Talladega, in present-day Alabama. Coffee's men kill about 500 Creeks in retaliation for the Creek attack on Fort Mims the previous August.

8   The allies offer peace proposals to Emperor Napoleon I in Frankfurt by which France would be left with the boundaries of the Alps and the Pyrenees, keeping Belgium, Nice, and Savoy.

10   The British army under Viscount Wellington defeats French forces, under Marshal Nicolas-Jean Soult, at Toulouse, France.

15–17   French forces are expelled from the Netherlands after uprisings by the Dutch.

16   The French emperor Napoleon I replies evasively to the peace proposals offered by the allies on November 8.

30   William of Orange (later King William I) returns to the Netherlands.

December

1   By the Declaration of Frankfurt, the allies resolve to invade France because of Emperor Napoleon I's vague reply to their peace proposals.

10   British troops under Viscount Wellington besiege the southern French port of Bayonne.

11   By the Treaty of Valençay, Napoleon agrees to restore Ferdinand VII as king of Spain, in a bid to win an ally.

21   The Austrian forces of Field Marshal Karl Philipp, Prince zu Schwarzenberg, enter France through Switzerland.

29   The Swiss diet (parliament) votes for a restoration of the old constitution and revokes Napoleon's 1802 Act of Mediation.

31   The Prussian army under General Gebhard von Blücher crosses the River Rhine into France near Mannheim.

SCIENCE, TECHNOLOGY, AND MEDICINE

Agriculture

•   English chemist Humphry Davy publishes *Elements of Agricultural Chemistry* in which he summarizes the state of agricultural knowledge with regard to fertilizers.

Exploration

•   English settler-farmer Gregory Blaxland becomes the first European to cross the Blue Mountains of Australia, inland from the settlement at Sydney, opening up the interior to exploration. William Lawson and William Charles Wentworth accompany him on the expedition.

•   Swiss explorer Johann Ludwig Burckhardt discovers the ancient temples of Abu Simbel, Egypt.

Science

- French chemist and physicist Pierre-Louis Dulong discovers the explosive nitrogen trichloride.
- Scottish physicist John Leslie publishes *Experiments and Instruments Depending on the Relations of Air to Heat and Moisture*.
- Swiss botanist Augustin Pyrame de Candolle publishes *Théorie élémentaire de la botanique/Elementary Theory of Botany* in which he coins the word "taxonomy," introduces the idea of homology in plants, and argues that the basis of plant classification should be anatomy and not physiology.

Technology

- British engineer Bryan Donkin develops a rotary printing press. This is an improvement over the flatbed press, as it allows faster printing, and spurs the development of newspapers.
- English engineer George Clymer invents the "Columbia" printing-press, which eliminates the screw process.
- English engineer Richard Trevithick invents a rotary, steam-driven drill that improves the ability to mine hard rock.
- English inventor Charles Plinth invents the soda siphon.
- English inventor William Horrocks develops the power loom.

Transportation

MARCH

13 English inventor William Hedley patents a steam locomotive that depends on friction between the wheels and rail rather than a rack-and-tooth system. Known as "Puffing Billy," it hauls coal trucks 8 km/5 mi from the Wylam colliery in Northumberland, England, to Lemington-on-Tyne.

ARTS AND IDEAS

Arts

- The English artist David Cox publishes the first part of his *Treatise on Landscape Painting and Effect in Water Colours*. The second part appears in 1814.
- The English artist J. M. W. Turner paints *Frosty Morning*.
- The U.S. artist Washington Allston paints *The Dead Man Restored to Life by the Bones of the Prophet Elisha*.

Literature and Language

- The English poet George Gordon, Lord Byron, publishes the poem "Bride of Abydos."

BIRTHS & DEATHS

JANUARY

18 Joseph Farwell Glidden, U.S. inventor who developed the first commercially successful barbed wire, born in Charlestown, New Hampshire (–1906).

20 Christoph Martin Wieland, German poet, dies in Weimar (now in Germany) (79).

21 John C(harles) Frémont, U.S. explorer who opened up California for development, born in Savannah, Georgia (–1890).

FEBRUARY

12 James Dana, U.S. geologist who developed geology in the United States, born in Utica, New York (–1895).

MARCH

19 David Livingstone, Scottish missionary and explorer who explored much of East Africa in search of the source of the Nile, born in Blantyre, Lancashire, Scotland (–1873).

APRIL

10 Joseph Lagrange, Italian-French mathematician who established the fields of analytical and celestial mechanics, dies in Paris, France (77).

19 Benjamin Rush, U.S. physician and political leader who was one of the signatories of the Declaration of Independence, dies in Philadelphia, Pennsylvania (67).

MAY

5 Søren Kierkegaard, Danish philosopher who founded existentialist philosophy, born in Copenhagen, Denmark (–1855).

22 (Wilhelm) Richard Wagner, German dramatic composer and theorist who wrote the operatic sequence *Der Ring des Nibelungen/The Ring of the Nibelung*, born in Leipzig, Germany (–1883).

JUNE

8 David Dixon Porter, Union naval officer during the Civil War, born in Chester, Pennsylvania (–1891).

28 Gerhard Johann von Scharnhorst, Prussian general who introduced the general staff system, dies in Prague, Bohemia (57).

JULY

12 Claude Bernard, French physiologist who discovered the role of the pancreas and liver in digestion, and the regulation of blood supply by vasomotor nerves, born in St-Julien, France (–1878).

SEPTEMBER

30 John Rae, Scottish physician and explorer of the Canadian Arctic, born near Stromness, Orkney Islands, Scotland (–1893).

OCTOBER

5 Tecumseh, Shawnee chief, orator, and military leader who fought with the British during the War of 1812, dies in battle near the Thames River, Upper Canada, modern Ontario (c. 55).

10 Giuseppe Fortunino Francesco Verdi, Italian operatic composer, born in Le Roncole, near Busseto, Duchy of Parma (–1901).

23 Ludwig Leichhardt, Prussian explorer who covered extensive areas of Australia, born in Trebatsch, Prussia (–1848).

- The English poet Percy Bysshe Shelley publishes his first major poem, *Queen Mab, a Philosophical Poem*. After surveying political and social evils, it sets out a utopian ideal for society.
- The English writer Jane Austen publishes her novel *Pride and Prejudice*. She completed it in 1797 under the title *First Impressions*.
- The English writer Robert Southey publishes his biography *The Life of Nelson*.
- The German poet and historian Ernst Moritz Arndt publishes the poem "Was ist das deutsche Vaterland?"/ "What is the German Fatherland?" This and his other patriotic poems and songs reflect the growing tide of nationalism in Germany.
- The German writer Adelbert von Chamisso publishes his tale *Peter Schlemihls wundersame Geschichte/Peter Schlemihl's Remarkable Story*.

Music

- Austrian composer Franz Schubert completes his Symphony No. 1 in D (D 82) and his String Quartets No. 3 (D 36), No. 4 (D 46), No. 5 (D 68), and No. 6 (D 74).
- German composer Ludwig van Beethoven completes his *Wellingtons Sieg* (Opus 91), known as *Wellington's Victory* or *The Battle Symphony*.
- The opera *Tancredi*, by the Italian composer Gioachino Antonio Rossini, is first performed in Venice, Italy.

Thought and Scholarship

- The Franco-Swiss writer Benjamin Constant publishes *De l'Esprit de conquête et de l'usurpation/On the Spirit of Conquest and Usurpation*.
- The Welsh social reformer Robert Owen publishes *A New View of Society*.

SOCIETY

Education

- Colby College is founded in Waterville, Maine.

Media and Communication

- The *Boston Daily Advertiser*, begins publication under the editorship of Nathan Hale. Strongly biased toward the Whig Party, the successful newspaper later combines with the *Boston Record* when it is purchased by William Randolph Hearst in 1917.
- The Boston Congregationalist minister William Ellery Channing joins liberal colleagues in establishing the religious periodical *Christian Disciple*.

SEPTEMBER
- The Philadelphia publisher John W. Scott establishes the nation's first religious weekly, *Religious Remembrancer*.

1814

POLITICS, GOVERNMENT, AND ECONOMICS

Business and Economics

- The Boston textile mogul Francis Cabot Lowell's Boston Manufacturing Company begins operations in Waltham, Massachusetts. The Waltham mill is the first mechanized factory in the United States to integrate the manufacturing process from the raw material to the finished product.

Colonization

AUGUST
13 The Cape Colony in southern Africa becomes a British colony while other former Dutch colonies are restored, apart from Demerara, Essequibo, and Berbice in South America, which become British Guiana.

Politics and Government

- British troops set fire to the U.S. Library of Congress, destroying all but a few of the most valuable books.
- In the U.S. congressional elections, the Democratic-Republicans retain majorities in the House of Representatives (117–65) and Senate (25–11).
- The French government introduces legislation which makes abortion illegal, unless the mother's life is at risk.

JANUARY

- In the ongoing Creek War, Creek warriors repel three attacks by U.S. militiamen in present-day Alabama.
- The administration of U.S. president James Madison receives a British proposal to begin peace negotiations to end the War of 1812.
- 11 Joachim Murat, King of Naples, deserts the French emperor Napoleon I and joins the allies, Prussia and Austria, in a bid to preserve his throne.
- 14 By the Treaty of Kiel with Sweden, Denmark cedes Norway in return for Pomerania and the island of Rügen in Germany. Norwegians are guaranteed their rights and property.
- 14 In a separate treaty with Britain, Denmark, which has been allied with France through the Continental System of closing European ports to Britain, regains all lost territories with the exception of the island of Heligoland in the North Sea which, just off the German coast, is strategically useful to Britain.
- 30 In the Battle of La Rothière in France, French emperor Napoleon I attempts to stop General Gebhard von Blücher's Prussians joining up with the Austrian army of Field Marshal Karl Philipp, Prince zu Schwarzenberg. Blücher attacks the French first and the Austro-Russian army completes the victory.

FEBRUARY

5–March 19   Peace negotiations between the allies and the French emperor Napoleon I at Châtillon-sur-Seine, France, are futile as Napoleon refuses to accept the 1791 frontier of France.
- 8 Napoleon pushes the Austrian field marshal Karl Phillip's Austro-Russian army back 65 km/40 mi at the Battle of Montereau, France, despite being heavily outnumbered.
- 27 Karl Philipp defeats French forces at Bar-sur-Aube, France.

MARCH

- U.S. army troops under Andrew Jackson defeat a force of Creeks at the Battle of Horseshoe Bend, Alabama, ending the Creek War.
- 7 The French emperor Napoleon I inflicts a heavy defeat on General Gebhard von Blücher's Prussian forces at Craonne, 40 km/25 mi from Paris, France. Blücher subsequently links up with Prince Jean-Baptiste Bernadotte's Swedish army approaching from the northeast and faces Napoleon's force of 30,000 with a combined army of 100,000 men.
- 9 The allies sign the Treaty of Chaumont, by which they agree not to negotiate a separate peace with Napoleon and to insist on his acceptance of the 1791 frontiers of France.
- 9–10   At the Battle of Laon, in northern France, the combined allied army compels Napoleon to withdraw further into France.
- 12 British forces under Viscount Wellington, advancing from the south of France, capture the port of Bordeaux.
- 19 Pope Pius VII is freed from his captivity under the French in Savona, Italy.
- 20 Having diverted his army south to try to cut the approaching Karl Philipp's supply lines, Napoleon is defeated by him at Arcis-sur-Aube, France.
- 30 The French marshals Auguste Marmont and Edouard Mortier attempt unsuccessfully to resist the superior forces of Karl Philipp, Blücher, and Bernadotte drawn up outside Paris, France. Following his defeat by Schwarzenberg, Napoleon is left stranded far to the east.
- 31 Marmont surrenders the French capital, Paris, to the allies. Napoleon, who has been rushing to rejoin the battle, halts at Fontainebleau, southeast of Paris. The Senate declares the throne forfeited following the flight of the empress Marie-Louise.

APRIL

- 1 The Senate appoints a provisional French government in Paris, following the triumphant entry of the allies into the capital.
- 8 The national assembly in Norway meets to discuss a constitution, as Norway has declared itself independent in defiance of the Treaty of Kiel. It decides on a limited monarchy.
- 10 Britain's Viscount Wellington defeats the French marshal Nicolas-Jean Soult and drives his army out of Toulouse, in southern France. He is subsequently created Duke of Wellington.
- 11 By the Treaty of Fontainebleau, the French emperor Napoleon I abdicates unconditionally and is banished to the principality of Elba, an island off the west coast of Italy, on an annuity of 2,000,000 francs. Queen Marie-Louise is given the duchies of Gustalla, Parma, and Piacenza.

MAY

- 3 King Louis XVIII of France enters Paris, following the abdication of French emperor Napoleon I.
- 4 King Ferdinand VII of Spain annuls the liberal constitution of the cortes (national assembly), one of the first of a wave of antidemocratic acts performed by royalty returning to office after Napoleon's defeat.
- 30 By the First Treaty of Paris, the French recognize the frontier of 1792, agree to recognize the independence of the Netherlands, and the Italian and the German states, and promise to end the slave trade. The Netherlands and Belgium are united as an independent state under William I. Under a secret treaty, Austria is to receive Venetia and the kingdom of Sardinia, Genoa.

JUNE

- 4 King Louis XVIII of France issues a constitutional charter, making clear however that he is taking up the throne on his hereditary right, not by a contract with the people, and that the constitution is granted as a gift from the king.

AUGUST

- British forces sack and burn Washington, D.C., in apparent retaliation for the U.S. destruction of York (present-day Toronto), Canada.
- 14 By the Convention of Moss in Norway, Sweden recognizes the Norwegian constitution, with the provision that King Frederick VI must renounce his throne and Norway come under Swedish rule.

SEPTEMBER

- U.S. naval forces defeat their British counterparts at the Battle of Lake Champlain.

OCTOBER

- 10 The British governor-general of India, Francis Rawdon-Hastings, Earl of Moira, declares war on the Gurkhas of Nepal, a fierce mountain people living in the northeast of India.

26 The electorate of Hanover is proclaimed a kingdom by the British prince regent, acting in the name of his father, King George III.

NOVEMBER

1 The Congress of Vienna, convened to decide the final settlement of the Napoleonic Wars, formally opens in Austria.

4 The Norwegian constitution is established. Christian VII of Denmark is elected king of Norway.

11 King Charles XIII of Sweden is elected to the Norwegian throne.

13 Russia hands over Saxony to Prussia, an action opposed by Austria, the German states, and France, as Czar Alexander I wishes to obtain Poland in exchange. This would make Russia and Prussia the dominant powers in central Europe, rather than creating a stable balance of power.

DECEMBER

• The United States and Britain sign the Treaty of Ghent, ending the War of 1812. The most contested issues—Britain's impressment of U.S. sailors, U.S. commercial rights, and the Northwest boundary dispute—remain unresolved.

December 1814–January 1815 Federalist delegates from five New England states opposed to the War of 1812 attend a secret convention in Hartford, Connecticut, where they contemplate secession and float diverse proposals designed to safeguard sectional interests. The Treaty of Ghent to end the war, signed midway through the convention, takes the air out of these renegades' sails, effectively destroying the Federalist party.

SCIENCE, TECHNOLOGY, AND MEDICINE

Exploration

• A Christian mission station is established in the Bay of Islands on New Zealand's North Island; it acts as a base for the earliest European exploration of the island's interior.

December 1814–15 Swiss explorer Johann Ludwig Burckhardt, working for the British Royal Geographical Society, visits and describes the Muslim holy cities of Mecca and Medina in Arabia.

Science

• French physician Matthieu Orfila publishes *Traité de toxicologie/Treatise on Toxicology*, which examines inorganic poisons and animal venoms and establishes the science of experimental toxicology.

• Swedish chemist Jöns Jakob Berzelius publishes *Theory of Chemical Proportions and the Chemical Action of Electricity*, establishing himself as one of the founders of modern chemistry. He also publishes *An Attempt to Establish a Pure Scientific System of Mineralogy through the Use of the Electrochemical Theory of Chemical Proportions*, an extensive chemical classification of

minerals in which he classifies over 2,000 chemical compounds.

JULY

25 German physicist Joseph von Fraunhofer plots more than 500 absorption lines (Fraunhofer lines) and discovers that the relative positions of the lines is constant for each element. His work forms the basis of modern spectroscopy.

Technology

• *The Times* of London, England, is produced on the first steam-driven stop-cylinder press, which prints 1,000 sheets per hour.

• British merchant J. Thomson patents a flintlock pistol with a nine-chamber revolving magazine.

• U.S. businessmen Francis Cabot Lowell and Patrick Tracey Jackson build the first textile mill to take raw cotton and convert it into finished cloth.

• U.S. clockmaker Eli Terry patents a "perfected wooden clock" with interchangeable parts. It is the first mass-produced clock.

Transportation

JULY

25 English engineer George Stephenson constructs the first effective steam locomotive. Called the "Bulcher" it hauls up to 30 metric tons of coal at 6.4 kph/4 mph, out of mines at Killingorth Collier, Newcastle upon Tyne, England.

OCTOBER

• U.S. engineer Robert Fulton launches the world's first steam warship, *Demologos* (dubbed the *Fulton*). Heavily gunned and armored, it is unique in that its paddlewheel is located between two parallel hulls. It is never used in battle.

ARTS AND IDEAS

Arts

c. 1814 The English artist John Constable paints *The Mill Stream*.

• The French artist Jean-Auguste-Dominique Ingres paints *La Grande Odalisque*.

• The Spanish artist Francisco José de Goya y Lucientes paints *The 2nd of May, 1808* and *The 3rd of May, 1808*. Both pictures depict atrocities carried out by the French during their invasion of Spain. He also paints his *Portrait of King Ferdinand VII of Spain in the Uniform of a General*

• The U.S. artist John Vanderlyn paints *Ariadne Asleep on the Island of Naxos*.

Literature and Language

• The English poet George Gordon, Lord Byron, publishes his narrative poem *The Corsair*.

- The English poet William Wordsworth publishes his long philosophical poem *The Excursion*.
- The English writer Jane Austen publishes her novel *Mansfield Park*.
- The German poet Friedrich Rückert publishes *Deutsche Gedichte/German Poems*.
- The German writer Ernst Theodor Amadeus Hoffmann publishes the first volume of his stories *Phantasiestücke in Callots Manier/Fantasy Pieces in the Manner of Callot*. The last volume appears in 1815. His stories of the macabre and the supernatural become very popular.
- The Scottish poet and novelist Walter Scott anonymously publishes his first novel, *Waverley*. Its popularity encourages him to turn from narrative verse to novels.

Music

- Austrian composer Franz Schubert writes the song "Gretchen am Spinnrade"/"Gretchen at the Spinning Wheel" (D 118). The text is from Goethe's *Faust*, published in 1808. He also completes his Mass in F major (D 105) and his String Quartets No. 7 (D 94) and No. 8 (D 112).

OCTOBER
19 The *Baltimore Patriot* publishes "The Defense of Fort McHenry" by Francis Scott Key. The poem captures many imaginations; it is renamed "The Star-Spangled Banner" and is designated the U.S. national anthem by an act of Congress.

Thought and Scholarship

- The French social thinker Claude-Henri de Rouvroy, comte de St.-Simon, publishes *De la Réorganisation de la société européenne/On the Reorganization of European Society*.
- The U.S. editors Nicholas Biddle and Paul Allen of Philadelphia, Pennsylvania, publish a *History of the Expedition under the Command of Captains Lewis and Clark*, based on the papers of the U.S. explorers Meriwether Lewis and William Clark.
- The U.S. political philosopher John Taylor of Virginia publishes *An Inquiry into the Principles and Policy of the Government of the United States*, a critique of Federalist politics and ideology.

SOCIETY

Education

- The U.S. educator Emma Willard establishes the Middlebury Female Academy, a school for young women, in Middlebury, Vermont.
- The city of Pittsburgh, Pennsylvania, establishes the first major library west of the Allegheny Mountains.

Religion

- The Connecticut Tract Society joins with similar missionary groups to form the American Tract Society.

MAY
5 Pope Pius VII restores the Inquisition and revives the *Index Librorum Prohibitorum* (a list of banned books) and the Jesuit Order.

BIRTHS & DEATHS

- Joseph-Ignace Guillotin, French physician who invented the guillotine, dies (*c.* 76).

JANUARY
27 Johann Gottlieb Fichte, German philosopher, dies in Berlin, Prussia (52).

MARCH
29 Claude Michel ("Clodion"), French rococo sculptor, dies in Paris, France (75).

MAY
29 Joséphine de Beauharnais, Empress of France 1804–10 and consort of Napoleon I, dies in Malmaison, France (50).
30 Mikhail Alexandrovich Bakunin, Russian revolutionary, born in Premukhine, Russia (–1876).

JULY
25 Charles Dibdin, popular English composer, actor, and theatrical manager, dies in London, England (69).

29 Samuel Colt, U.S. firearms manufacturer who invented the Colt revolver, born in Hartford, Connecticut (–1862).

AUGUST
10 John Clifford Pemberton, Confederate general in the Civil War who unsuccessfully defended Vicksburg, born in Philadelphia, Pennsylvania (–1881).
13 Anders Jonas Ångström, Swedish physicist who founded spectroscopy, born in Lögdö, Sweden (–1874).
21 Benjamin Thompson, later Count Rumford, English physicist who established the theory that heat is a form of motion, and founded the Royal Institution of Great Britain, dies in Auteuil, France (61).

OCTOBER
4 Jean-François Millet, French painter, born in Gruchy, near Gréville, France (–1875).

15 Mikhail Yuryevich Lermontov, Russian romantic poet and novelist, born in Moscow, Russia (–1841).

NOVEMBER
13 Joseph Hooker, Union general in the American Civil War, born in Hadley, Massachusetts (–1879).
23 Elbridge Gerry, Vice President of the United States 1813–14 and a signatory of the U.S. Declaration of Independence, dies in Washington, D.C. (70).

DECEMBER
2 The Marquis de Sade, French writer whose erotic novels and stories led to the term "sadism," dies in Charenton, near Paris, France (74).

1815

POLITICS, GOVERNMENT, AND ECONOMICS

Colonization

MARCH

2   The kingdom of Kandy, Ceylon (Sri Lanka), is incorporated into the British Empire.

MAY

25   Czar Alexander I of Russia proclaims Poland to be part of Russia.

JUNE

4   Denmark cedes Pomerania and the island of Rügen to Prussia in return for part of the duchy of Lauenburg.

OCTOBER

10   A British force occupies Ascension Island in the south Atlantic Ocean.

Human Rights

- The U.S. abolitionist Paul Cuffe transports 38 black Americans to Africa, inaugurating the U.S. colonization movement.

Politics and Government

- Jean Lafitte, a notorious pirate who preyed on Spanish ships, helps the United States in the Battle of New Orleans in return for a U.S. pardon. After the battle, he resumes his piracy, but his actions during the battle of New Orleans make him a folk hero in the United States.

JANUARY

- Ironically, the United States wins its most decisive victory in the War of 1812 two weeks after the signing of the Treaty of Ghent bringing the war to an end. The victory occurs in New Orleans, Louisiana, where an outnumbered U.S. force under the command of Andrew Jackson repels a British force led by Edward Pakenham, taking 2,036 British prisoners.

3   By a secret treaty, Austria, Britain, and France form a defensive alliance against Prusso-Russian plans to solve the Saxon and Polish problems.

10   Britain declares war against the king of Kandy, a mountain kingdom in the interior of Ceylon (Sri Lanka)

and the only part of the island not controlled by Britain, following friction between his followers and British subjects.

FEBRUARY

- New York, New York, receives news of the Treaty of Ghent ending the War of 1812, signed in December 1814.
- The U.S. Senate ratifies the Treaty of Ghent, formally ending the War of 1812.

MARCH

- Flushed by the U.S. victory over Britain in the Battle of New Orleans, the U.S. Congress declares war on Algiers, a haven for pirates attacking U.S. ships in the Mediterranean.

1   French emperor Napoleon I, having escaped from the island of Elba, lands in the south of France at Cannes and marches on the capital, Paris, with growing support.

19   King Louis XVIII of France flees from Paris, before the advance of Napoleon.

20   Napoleon enters Paris, France, and the "Hundred Days" (Napoleon's second period of rule) begin. Over the next two days he forms a government composed primarily of his former ministers.

25   Austria, Britain, Prussia, and Russia form the Fifth Coalition against Napoleon to maintain the established order in Europe. Each agrees to send 150,000 men into the field.

APRIL

5   Britain's Duke of Wellington arrives in Brussels, in French-occupied Belgium, to lead the British and Dutch forces against the French emperor Napoleon I.

10   Austria sends a diplomatic note to Joachim Murat, King of Naples, declaring war against him for occupying the Italian cities of Rome, Florence, and Bologna.

MAY

3   Neapolitan forces commanded by Joachim Murat, King of Naples, are defeated at Tolentino, near Ancona, by the Austrian army.

18   A peace treaty is concluded between Prussia, Russia, and Austria and the king of Saxony, Frederick Augustus, previously allied with the French emperor Napoleon I.

25   Recognizing the popular nationalistic spirit in Prussia that has contributed much to the defeat of Napoleon, King Frederick Wilhelm III promises a constitution in Prussia.

JUNE

- In the U.S. war against Algerian pirates in the Mediterranean, the U.S. commodore Stephen Decatur captures the Algerian warships *Estido* and *Mashouda*, killing the *Mashouda*'s commander Hammida.
- A peace treaty ends the U.S.–Algerian war in the Mediterranean.

2 Posing as the savior of the liberties of the French republic from the restored Bourbon monarchy in France, Napoleon I issues the liberal constitution of "Le Champ de Mai."

9 The Congress of Vienna closes after its Final Act is passed. The Netherlands, Belgium, and Luxembourg are united to form the United Netherlands (by an act of May 31), Switzerland is to be neutral, East Poland is ceded to Russia and the Western Provinces of Poland to Prussia, Kraków becomes an independent republic, Lombardy and Venetia are restored to Austria, Prussia gains the Rhineland and the northern region of Saxony, Hanover obtains East Friesland and Hildesheim, the German Confederation is established under the presidency of Austria (by an act of June 8), the Bourbon monarch Ferdinand VII is restored in Spain, the Braganza dynasty returns to the Portuguese throne, Ferdinand IV is recognized as king of the Two Sicilies, the pope and the minor Italian princes are restored, and Britain retains the majority of its overseas conquests, including Malta and Heligoland.

16 The French army under French emperor Napoleon I defeats a Prussian force under General Gebhard von Blücher at Ligny, Belgium, in an attempt to split the Prussian army from the Anglo-Dutch army under Arthur Wellesley, Duke of Wellington. The Prussians manage to retreat in good order and, instead of moving west, retire to the north, in order to be able to link up with Wellington.

18 Napoleon, having pursued Wellington's Anglo-Dutch army, engages it in the decisive Battle of Waterloo, near the Belgian village of that name, south of Brussels. Wellington manages to hold back the French attack until the Prussian army under General Gebhard von Blücher, having avoided pursuit by a French detachment under Marshal Emmanuel de Grouchy, begins to arrive in the late afternoon. As the Prussians begin to attack the French right flank, Wellington orders a counterattack, forcing the French into a retreat which soon turns into a rout.

22 Napoleon abdicates for a second time, having being given the choice of resignation or deposition by the French Chambers.

July

• The United States and the Barbary state of Tunis, North Africa, sign a treaty by which Tunis agrees not to molest U.S. ships on the Mediterranean Sea.

7 The "White Terror" begins in southern France, as fanatical royalists attack revolutionary elements, Bonapartists, and Protestants.

7–8 The allies, mainly Austrian and Prussian forces, reenter the French capital, Paris, enabling King Louis XVIII to return (July 8) to the royal palace of the Tuileries.

August

2 By agreement between Prussia, Austria, Britain, and Russia, the former French emperor Napoleon I is banished to St. Helena, a desolate island in the Atlantic Ocean.

September

26 The anti-Liberal Holy Alliance is formed by Austria, Russia, and Prussia, to maintain the settlement of the Congress of Vienna.

October

6 The British prince regent supports the principles of the Holy Alliance formed by Austria, Russia, and Prussia, but avoids any commitments involving Britain.

13 The former king of Naples, Joachim Murat, is court-martialed and shot after a farcical attempt to regain his Italian kingdom.

November

5 Through a treaty with Russia, Austria, and Prussia, Britain establishes a protectorate over the Ionian Islands off the coast of Greece.

20 By the Second Treaty of Paris, France's borders are reduced to those of 1789. It yields territory to Savoy and to Switzerland, and agrees to restore captured art treasures and pay an indemnity, while the Quadruple Alliance between Austria, Prussia, Russia, and Britain is renewed.

27 Czar Alexander I of Russia issues a Polish constitution in an attempt to appease the Poles (having proclaimed Poland to be part of Russia on May 25).

December

• U.S. president James Madison urges Congress to adopt legislation authorizing a major nationalization campaign. Among other improvements, Madison calls for expansion of the U.S. navy, reorganization of the militia, enlargement of the Military Academy, a stable monetary system, a federal tariff to protect U.S. industry, and a reliable communications infrastructure.

2 A peace treaty between Britain and the rajah of Nepal is signed, extending the frontiers of British power, but war is soon resumed.

7 Marshal Michel Ney, counted among the greatest of the French emperor Napoleon I's generals, is shot to appease extreme royalists, following his trial for treason. Having had four horses shot from under him at Waterloo in an attempt to die an honorable death in battle, Ney commands the firing squad himself.

16 The Portuguese colony of Brazil is made an empire under João, the prince regent of Portugal.

SCIENCE, TECHNOLOGY, AND MEDICINE

Ecology

April

5 Tambora volcano, on Sumbawa island in the Netherlands East Indies, erupts violently, killing 50,000 people. Its height diminishes by 1,220 m/4,000 ft, while dust clouds affect the world's climate.

Math

• English physician and philologist Peter Roget invents the "log-log" slide rule.

Science

- English chemist Humphry Davy recognizes that hydrogen is the key element in acids.
- English chemist William Prout hypothesizes that the atomic weight of any element is a whole number ratio of the atomic weight of hydrogen. It proves valuable in the classification of elements.
- French physicist Augustin-Jean Fresnel shows that light has transverse waves—he thus explains the diffraction of light.

April 1815–22 French biologist Jean-Baptiste de Lamarck publishes *Histoire naturelle des animaux sans vertèbres/ Natural History of Invertebrate Animals*, in which he maintains that museum collections should form the basis for revising biological classifications.

Technology

- British artillery officer William Congreve improves the accuracy of his rocket by mounting the guide stick in the center of five equally spaced jets.
- English chemist Humphry Davy invents the miner's safety lamp. It does not ignite marsh gas in the mines which causes explosions.
- U.S. inventor Joshua Shaw develops the percussion cap—a metal cone containing explosives and used for firing bullets.

Transportation

- Scottish inventor John Loudon McAdam begins building roads around Bristol, Avon, England. Comprised of two grades of large crushed stone for good drainage and to support the load, and covered by a surface of compacted smaller stones to form a pavement to withstand wear and tear and to shed water to the drainage ditches, they are the most advanced roads built to date.

ARTS AND IDEAS

Architecture

- U.S. engineer Theodore Burr builds the world's largest timber-truss bridge over the Susquehanna River at Lancaster, Pennsylvania. It is 110 m/360 ft long and uses arches to strengthen the trusses. It serves as the model for future timber-truss bridges.

JULY
- The city of Baltimore, Maryland, begins construction of the nation's first monument to George Washington, the first president of the United States.

Arts

c. 1815 The English artist J. M. W. Turner paints *Crossing the Brook*.

c. 1815 The U.S. artist Ammi Phillips paints *Portrait of Harriet Leavens*.
- Pope Pius VII sends the Italian artist Antonio Canova to Paris, France, to secure the return to Rome of works of art looted by the former French emperor Napoleon I.
- The English artist John Constable paints *Golding Constable's Flower Garden*.
- The Italian sculptor Antonio Canova sculpts *Three Graces*.
- The Spanish artist Francisco José de Goya y Lucientes paints *Self-Portrait at the Age of 69*.

Literature and Language

- The English poet William Wordsworth publishes the long poem *The White Doe of Rylstone*.
- The German brothers Christian and Friedrich Leopold, Counts of Stolberg-Stolberg, publish *Vaterländische Gedichte/Poems of the Fatherland*.
- The German folklorists Jakob Ludwig Carl Grimm and his brother Wilhelm Carl Grimm publish the second volume of their famous *Kinder and Hausmärchen/Fairy Tales*. The first volume appeared in 1812, and a third volume will appear in 1822.
- The German writer Ernst Theodor Amadeus Hoffmann publishes the first volume of his novel *Die Elixiere des Teufels/The Devil's Elixir*. The second volume appears in 1816.
- The Italian writer Alessandro Manzoni publishes his religious poems *Inni sacri/Sacred Hymns*.
- The Scottish writer Walter Scott publishes his novel *Guy Mannering*.
- The U.S. writer William Cullen Bryant publishes the poem "To a Waterfowl," one of his best-known works.

Music

- Austrian composer Franz Schubert completes his Symphony No. 2 in B flat (D 125); his Mass in G major (D 167); his Piano Sonatas No. 1 (D 157), left incomplete, and No. 2 (D 279); his Symphony No. 3 in D (D 200); and his song *Erlkönig/The Erl King* (D 328), using a poem by the German poet Goethe.
- French writer Pierre-Jean Béranger publishes *Chansons morales/Moral Songs*, a collection of songs and poems. Critical of Napoleon and the Bourbon Restoration, Béranger's songs become very popular.
- German composer Ludwig van Beethoven completes his Cello Sonatas in C major and D major (Opus 102), and his overture *Nemensfeier* (Opus 115), written for the names-day festival of Emperor Francis II of Austria in 1815.

Theater and Dance

- The comedy *Yankee in England*, by the U.S. writer David Humphreys, is published.

Thought and Scholarship

- The English economist Thomas Robert Malthus publishes *An Inquiry into the Nature and Progress of Rent*.

- The English economist David Ricardo publishes *The Influence of a Low Price of Corn on the Profits of Stock*, an attack on the British Corn Laws.
- The Franco-Swiss writer Benjamin Constant publishes *Principes de politiques/The Principles of Politics*.
- The German jurist Friedrich Karl von Savigny publishes the first volume of his *Geschichte des römischen Rechts im Mittelalter/History of Roman Law in the Middle Ages*. The final volume appears in 1831.
- The Scottish philosopher Dugald Stewart publishes *Progress of Metaphysical, Ethical, and Political Philosophy*.
- The U.S. Library of Congress acquires much of the former U.S. president Thomas Jefferson's private library, which includes many rare books.

SOCIETY

Education

- The Boston Society for the Moral and Religious Instruction of the Poor begins Sunday school education.

Everyday Life

c. 1815 Men shed the pantaloons and silk stockings popular early in the century in favor of long trousers, a trend reflecting the style adopted by French revolutionaries distinguishing themselves from the nobility.

c. 1815 Women's fashions adopt the stiff corset, leg-of-mutton sleeves, and full skirts, leading to the hoop skirt later in the century.

Media and Communication

- The critical quarterly *North American Review* begins publication in Boston, Massachusetts.

Sports

- In rowing, eights are raced at Oxford University, England, for the first time.
- The Royal Yacht Squadron, the oldest sailing club still in existence, is established in London, England, as the Yacht Club. It is renamed the Royal Yacht Club in 1820 before adopting its current name in 1830.

BIRTHS & DEATHS

JANUARY
11 John A. Macdonald, prime minister of Canada 1867–73 and 1878–91, a Liberal-Conservative, born in Glasgow, Scotland (–1891).
16 Henry W. Halleck, U.S. general in chief of the Union forces during the American Civil War, born in Westernville, New York (–1872).

FEBRUARY
24 Robert Fulton, U.S. engineer who built the first practical steamships and submarines, dies in New York, New York (49).

MARCH
5 Franz Mesmer, Austrian physician who used mesmerism (now known as hypnotism) to treat patients, dies in Meersburg, Austria (80).

APRIL
1 Otto von Bismarck, founder and first chancellor of the German Empire 1871–90, born in Schönhausen, Brandenburg (–1898).

24 Anthony Trollope, English novelist, born in London, England (–1882).

JUNE
1 James Gillray, English caricaturist known for his political cartoons of King George III, dies in London, England (58).

SEPTEMBER
9 John Singleton Copley, U.S. painter noted for his portraits and historical studies, dies in London, England (77).
28 Nicolas Desmarest, French geologist who discovered that basalt is volcanic in origin and thus disproved the theory that all rocks are formed by sedimentation, dies in Paris, France (90).

OCTOBER
12 William J. Hardee, Confederate general during the American Civil War, born near Savannah, Georgia (–1873).

NOVEMBER
2 George Boole, English mathematician who developed Boolean algebra which is central to computer operations, born in Lincoln, England (–1864).
29 Ii Naosuke, Japanese feudal lord who was responsible in 1854 for Japan signing the Perry Convention ending its isolationist policy, born in Hikone, Japan (–1860).

DECEMBER
7 Michel Ney, French marshal during the Napoleonic Wars, is executed for treason in Paris, France (46).
8 Adolf Menzel, German painter, born in Breslau, Prussia (now Wrocław, Poland) (–1905).
31 George G(ordon) Meade, U.S. army officer who defeated the Confederate Army at Gettysburg in 1863 during the American Civil War, born in Cadiz, Spain (–1872).

1816

POLITICS, GOVERNMENT, AND ECONOMICS

Business and Economics

JANUARY
- U.S. public debt exceeds $100 million for the first time, reaching $127,335,000.

MARCH
- The U.S. Congress drafts the nation's first protective tariff, in response to an inundation of British manufactures following the War of 1812.

APRIL
- The U.S. Congress charters the Second Bank of the United States. Intended to last 20 years, the bank is capitalized at $35 million, four-fifths of which will be owned by private investors.

DECEMBER
- The Provident Institution for Savings, the first U.S. savings bank, opens in Boston, Massachusetts.

Colonization

DECEMBER
12 Britain restores Java to the United Netherlands, having confiscated it in 1811 when the Kingdom of Holland was allied to France.

Politics and Government

- At a dinner honoring his naval victories over the Barbary pirates the previous year, the U.S. commodore, Stephen Decatur, utters the immortal toast, "Our Country! In her intercourse with foreign governments may she always be in the right; but our country, right or wrong."
- In the U.S. congressional elections, the Democratic-Republicans retain majorities in the House of Representatives (141–42) and Senate (34–10).

FEBRUARY
7 The South American revolutionary leader Simón Bolívar is entrusted by the independent Congress of New Granada with political and military control in the invasion of the Spanish colony of Venezuela from Haiti.

MARCH
- The Democratic-Republicans nominate the U.S. secretary of state James Monroe of Virginia for president and the New York politician Daniel D. Tompkins for vice president.
- The U.S. Supreme Court, in the case *Martin v. Hunter's Lessee*, asserts its right to hear appeals of state court rulings.
3 Income tax is abolished in Britain after the government is defeated in the House of Commons.
20 Maria I, the insane queen of Portugal, dies. She is succeeded by her son, John VI.

MAY
5 Grand Duke Karl August of Saxe-Weimar grants the first German constitution, formally establishing limited political rights for his subjects.

JUNE
- Citizens of the Indiana territory draft a state constitution in preparation for Indiana's admission to the Union.
21 The United Netherlands join the Holy Alliance formed between Austria, Russia, and Prussia in 1815.

JULY
- U.S. army troops massacre the Seminole garrison at Fort Apalachicola in East Florida.
9 At the Congress of Tucuman, the United Provinces of La Plata (Argentina) declare independence from Spain.

AUGUST
8 Bavaria joins the Holy Alliance formed between Austria, Russia, and Prussia in 1815.

SEPTEMBER
5 King Louis XVIII of France dissolves the ultra-conservative Chambre Introuvable (Chamber of Deputies convened in 1815) and changes the voting system so that moderate deputies obtain a majority in the ensuing election.

NOVEMBER
5 The diet (national assembly) of the German Confederation (the newly created association of German states set up to replace the Holy Roman Empire) opens at Frankfurt am Main, Hesse province, under Klemens, Prince Metternich, the Austrian chief minister.

DECEMBER
- Americans elect the U.S. secretary of state James Monroe as president and the New York politician Daniel D. Tompkins as vice president.
2 The Spa Fields Riots take place in England when a crowd of around 200 people, assembled to hear demands for political reform, marches on London and is dispersed by troops.
11 Indiana becomes the 19th state in the Union.

SCIENCE, TECHNOLOGY, AND MEDICINE

Agriculture

- There is a serious famine in Ireland with the failure of the potato crop.

Technology

- Baltimore, Maryland, becomes the first U.S. city to be illuminated with gas lighting.
- British army captain George Manby devises the modern compressed-air fire extinguisher.
- Dutch musician Dietrich Nikolaus Winkel invents the metronome (not German musician Johann Nepomuk Maelzel to whom its invention is often attributed).
- French inventors J. J. Cochot and A. Brunet patent a circular saw with tempered steel teeth.
- French physician René Laënnec invents the stethoscope to detect cardiovascular diseases.
- French-born British engineer Marc Isambard Brunel patents a knitting machine that can knit fabric in tubes.
- Scottish clergyman Robert Stirling patents the Stirling hot-air engine. It is powered by the expansion and displacement of air inside an externally heated cylinder. It is forgotten until the Dutch company Philips becomes interested in it in the 1970s.

APRIL

- French inventor Joseph-Nicéphore Niepce records a view from his workroom window on paper sensitized with silver chloride, but he is only partially able to fix the image.

JUNE

- The Gas Light Company of Baltimore, Maryland, becomes the first municipal gas company in the United States.

Transportation

- The "celeripede" is invented in France. A two-wheeled ancestor of the bicycle, it is propelled by pushing the feet against the ground, but cannot be steered.

FEBRUARY

- The state of New Jersey grants what is believed to be the nation's first railroad charter to retired U.S. army colonel John Stevens for a never completed railroad intended to link the Delaware and Raritan rivers.

OCTOBER

7   U.S. riverboat captain Henry Miller Shreve launches his steamboat *Washington* on the Mississippi. With a tall second deck, and a high pressure steam engine mounted above the water line on a shallow hull, it can navigate the shallowest waters of the river. The innovations become the prototype design for the Mississippi steamboats that dominate the economy and agriculture of the middle U.S. states until 1870.

ARTS AND IDEAS

Architecture

- The Exchange (Bourse) in St. Petersburg, Russia, designed by the Swiss architect Thomas de Thomon, is completed.

Arts

- The English artist John Constable paints *Wivenhoe Park*.
- The Spanish artist Francisco José de Goya y Lucientes completes his set of engravings *Tauromaquia/ Bullfighting*.

Literature and Language

- The English poet and critic Leigh Hunt publishes his book of verse *The Story of Rimini*.
- The English poet George Gordon, Lord Byron, publishes his narrative poem "The Siege of Corinth."
- The English poet Percy Bysshe Shelley publishes the poem "Alastor, or the Spirit of Solitude."
- The English poet Samuel Taylor Coleridge publishes his poetry collection *Christabel and Other Poems*. Its best-known poem is the fragment "Kubla Khan, or A Vision in a Dream," written in 1797.
- The English writer Jane Austen publishes her novel *Emma*.
- The English writer Thomas Love Peacock publishes his comic novel *Headlong Hall*, a satire on contemporary intellectual debate.
- The Franco-Swiss writer Benjamin Constant publishes his autobiographical novel *Adolphe*, a thinly disguised account of his relationship with the writer Madame de Staël.
- The German philologist Franz Bopp publishes *Über das Conjugationssystem der Sanskritsprache in Vergleichung mit jenem der griechischen, lateinischen, persischen und germanischen Sprachede/On the System of Conjugation in Sanskrit Compared with Those in Greek, Latin, Persian and German*. A major work in comparative linguistics, it shows that these languages derive from a common ancestor.
- The Italian poet Giacomo Leopardi writes the poem "Apressamento della morte"/"The Approach of Death."
- The Scottish poet and novelist Walter Scott publishes his novels *The Antiquary* and *Old Mortality*.
- The U.S. etymologist John Pickering publishes *A Vocabulary of Words and Phrases Peculiar to the United States*.
- The U.S. writer George Tucker publishes *Letters from Virginia*, a collection of satirical essays.
- The U.S. writer Samuel Woodworth publishes his novel *Champions of Freedom*.

Music

- Austrian composer Franz Schubert completes his Symphonies No. 4 in C minor (D 417), the *Tragic*, and

No. 5 in B flat (D 485); his Mass in C major (D 452); his String Quartet No. 11 (D 353); and his Piano Sonatas No. 3 (D 459) and No. 4 (D 537).

- The opera *Il barbiere di Siviglia/The Barber of Seville*, by the Italian composer Gioachino Antonio Rossini, is first performed in Rome, Italy. It is first performed in Britain in 1818 (in London, England), and in the United States in 1819 (in New York, New York).

Thought and Scholarship

- The German philosopher Georg Wilhelm Friedrich Hegel publishes the second part of his *Wissenschaft der Logic/The Science of Logic*. The first part appeared in 1812.
- The Russian writer Nikolay Mikhaylovich Karamzin publishes the first volume of his 12-volume *Istoriya gosudarstva rossiyskogo/History of the Russian State*. The last volume appears in 1829. A classic work, it is influential in the development of the study of both Russian history and Russian literature.
- The Welsh social reformer Robert Owen publishes *An Address to the Inhabitants of New Lanark*.

SOCIETY

Education

- Harvard College establishes its Divinity School as a distinct, Christian institution.

Everyday Life

- New York State opens a prison in the town of Auburn. Combining individual sleeping cells with group meals

and activities, the facility serves as a model for U.S. prison development.
- English stationer John Letts publishes the first desk calendar, in London, England. His company will grow to become one of the largest producers of calendars.

JUNE
- The New York Federalist De Witt Clinton helps create the Grand Encampment of Knights Templar, an esoteric politico-religious club.

Media and Communication

OCTOBER
- The English politician and journalist William Cobbett publishes the first edition of his radical newspaper the *Political Register* in Britain.

Religion

- The American Bible Society is created in New York, New York, to distribute Bibles to the poor.
- The U.S. Methodist clergyman and former slave Richard Allen establishes the African Methodist Episcopal Church in Philadelphia, Pennsylvania.
- The Boston Congregationalist minister, William Ellery Channing, joins in establishing the Peace Society of Massachusetts.

APRIL
- The new African Methodist Episcopal Church of Philadelphia, Pennsylvania, elects the founder Richard Allen as its first bishop.

Sports

- In what is regarded as the first prize fight in the United States, U.S. boxer Jacob Hyer defeats his fellow countryman Tom Beasley under London Prize Ring rules.

BIRTHS & DEATHS

JANUARY
27 Samuel Hood, British admiral during the Seven Years' War, the American War of Independence, and the French Revolution, dies (91).

MARCH
31 Jean François Ducis, French dramatist who introduced Shakespeare to the French stage, dies in Versailles, France (82).

APRIL
21 Charlotte Brontë, English novelist who wrote *Jane Eyre* (1847), born in Thornton, Yorkshire, England (–1855).

JUNE
5 Giovanni Paisiello, Italian operatic composer, dies in Naples, Italy (75).

JULY
21 Paul Julius, Baron von Reuter, German-born British reporter who established Reuter's news agency, born in Kassel, Hesse (–1899).
31 George Henry Thomas, Union general during the Civil War, born in Southampton County, Virginia (–1870).

AUGUST
4 Russell Sage, U.S. financier and philanthropist who financed much of the U.S. railroad system, born in Shenandoah, New York (–1906).

NOVEMBER
3 Jubal A. Early, Confederate general whose defeats in 1864 and 1865 led to the end of the American Civil

War, born in Franklin County, Virginia (–1894).
6 Gouverneur Morris, U.S. statesman and financial expert who established the U.S. decimal coinage system 1781–85, dies in Morrisania, New York (64).

DECEMBER
13 Werner von Siemens, German electrical engineer who developed the telegraph industry, born in Lenthe, Prussia (–1892).

1817

POLITICS, GOVERNMENT, AND ECONOMICS

Business and Economics

JANUARY

- The Second Bank of the United States opens in Philadelphia, Pennsylvania.

Human Rights

- The black American Reverend Richard Allen and the abolitionist James Forten lead 3,000 black Philadelphians in a protest against the colonization movement to transport free black Americans back to Africa.
- Robert Finley, Bushrod Washington, Henry Clay, and John Randolph found the American Colonization Society to transport free black Americans back to Africa.

Politics and Government

JANUARY

28 George, the British prince regent, is fired at as he returns by coach from the state opening of Parliament in London, England.

FEBRUARY

5 A new electoral law limiting the franchise is introduced in France, calculated to give the middle class more power and thus stabilize the regime.
10 Britain, Prussia, Austria, and Russia agree to decrease the size of the army of occupation in France.

MARCH

- In one of his final acts in office, the U.S. president James Madison vetoes a Bonus Bill providing a permanent fund for internal improvements. The president believes such action requires a constitutional amendment.
- The U.S. Congress divides the Mississippi territory in two, creating the Alabama territory and the prospective state of Mississippi.
3 The Prussian chancellor Karl August, Prince von Hardenberg, establishes councils of state with advisory powers to supervise Prussia's separate provinces.
4 James Monroe is inaugurated as fifth president of the United States.

11 The "March of the Blanketeers" from Manchester to London, England, to protest at the suspension of the Habeas Corpus Act (allowing imprisonment without trial) is broken up at Stockport by the local yeomanry.

APRIL

- The United States and Britain sign the Rush–Bagot Convention, reducing U.S. and British naval tonnage on the Great Lakes.

MAY

5 Sweden joins the Holy Alliance formed between Austria, Russia, and Prussia in 1815.

SEPTEMBER

9 The ultra-royalists (extreme conservatives dedicated to absolutist monarchist rule) lose seats in the French election.
23 By a treaty with Britain, Spain agrees to end the slave trade.

OCTOBER

18 At the Wartburg festival in Jena, German students gather to celebrate the anniversaries of the death of the German Protestant reformer Martin Luther and the "Battle of the Nations" at Leipzig (the defeat of Napoleon I), demonstrating the growing popularity of nationalism in Germany.
30 The South American revolutionary leader Simón Bolívar organizes an independent government of Venezuela, but not on liberal lines.

NOVEMBER

- The First Seminole War erupts between the Seminole people of Florida and southern Georgia settlers over disputed land.
5 The third Anglo-Maratha War against the British in India begins with attacks at Poona, Nagpur, and Indore. The Maratha confederacy is an alliance of the most powerful Indian leaders led by Baji Rao, the peshwa of Poona.

DECEMBER

- General Andrew Jackson assumes command of the U.S. army forces sent to pursue the Seminoles in East Florida.
10 Mississippi becomes the 20th state in the Union.
21 British forces under the English general Thomas Hyslop decisively defeat the army of Holkar II of Indore, leader of one of the major Maratha clans, at Mahidput, west-central India, during the third Anglo-Maratha War.

SCIENCE, TECHNOLOGY, AND MEDICINE

Agriculture

- Irish farmer James Murray invents superphosphate, a fertilizer made from bones and sulfuric acid.
- U.S. statesman Henry Clay imports Hereford cattle into the United States from Britain. They soon become the dominant breed in the country.

Health and Medicine

- English surgeon James Parkinson describes the central nervous system disorder now known as Parkinson's disease.
- The first asylum for the mentally ill in the United States opens in Frankford, Pennsylvania.

Science

- English physician and physicist Thomas Young explains the polarization of light—the alignment of light waves so that they vibrate in the same plane (light waves normally vibrate at right angles to the direction of travel).
- French chemists Joseph Pelletier and Joseph-Bienaimé Caventou isolate chlorophyll.
- German astronomer Friedrich Wilhelm Bessel develops the "Bessel function," a mathematical function that explains the movement of three stellar objects whose gravitational effects influence each other.
- German chemist Friedrich Stromeyer discovers the metallic element cadmium (atomic no. 48).
- Swedish chemist Jöns Jakob Berzelius discovers selenium (atomic no. 34).
- Swedish chemist Johan August Arfwedson discovers lithium (atomic no. 3).
- The French zoologist Georges Cuvier publishes *Le Règne animal distribué d'après son organisation/The Animal Kingdom, Distributed According to its Organization*, in which he breaks away from the view that animals can be arranged in a linear sequence leading to humans and argues instead that they should be classified according to their anatomical organization.

AUGUST
- The Boston Linnaean Society is summoned to Gloucester, Massachusetts, to investigate reports of an enormous sea serpent said to measure 30 m/100 ft long and 1 m/3 ft in diameter.

Technology

- The U.S. entrepreneur Thomas Gilpin provides the first custom-designed machine-made paper produced in the United States.
- Welsh inventor Richard Roberts invents a screw-cutting lathe, metal planer, gearcuttng machine, and gas meter.

Transportation

- The Staten Island ferry between Staten Island and Manhattan, New York, begins operating.

JULY
- Construction begins on New York's Erie Canal, designed to connect the Great Lakes to the Atlantic Ocean via the Hudson River. The canal is 584 km/ 363 mi in length, and runs from Buffalo to New York, New York. When completed it has 83 locks.

ARTS AND IDEAS

Arts

- The English artist John Constable paints *Flatford Mill*.
- The English sculptor Francis Leggatt Chantrey sculpts *The Sleeping Children*.
- The U.S. artist Benjamin West paints *Death on a Pale Horse, or The Opening of the First Five Seals*.

Literature and Language

- The English poet George Gordon, Lord Byron, publishes his dramatic poem *Manfred*.
- The English poet Samuel Taylor Coleridge publishes his poetry collection *Sybilline Leaves*.
- The English writer and critic William Hazlitt publishes his critical study *Characters of Shakespeare*.
- The English writers Percy Bysshe Shelley and Mary Shelley publish *History of a Six Weeks' Tour*, describing their travels in Europe.
- The Massachusetts poet William Cullen Bryant publishes "Thanatopsis," a metaphysical investigation into life and death.
- The Swedish poet Erik Johan Stagnelius publishes his epic poem *Waldimir den Store/Vladimir the Great*.
- The U.S. writer James Kirke Paulding publishes *Letters from the South*.

Music

- Austrian composer Franz Schubert completes his Piano Sonatas No. 5 (D 557), No. 6 (D 566), No. 7 (D 567), and No. 8 (D 575); and the song *Der Tot und das Mädchen/Death and the Maiden* (D 531).
- Italian-born English composer Muzio Clementi publishes *Gradus ad Parnassum/Steps to Parnassus*, a popular collection of piano exercises.
- The opera *La gazza ladra/The Thieving Magpie*, by the Italian composer Gioachino Antonio Rossini, is first performed, in Milan, Italy.

Theater and Dance

- The Drury Lane Theatre in London, England, becomes the first theater in the world to be lit entirely by gas.

- The play *Die Ahnfrau/The Actress* by the Austrian dramatist Franz Grillparzer is first performed, in Vienna, Austria.
- The San Carlo Opera House in Naples, Italy, which burned down in 1816, reopens.

Thought and Scholarship

- The English economist David Ricardo publishes his most important work, *Principles of Political Economy and Taxation.*
- The German scholar Philipp Böckh publishes *Die Staatshaushaltung der Athener/The Public Economy of Athens.*
- The German philosopher Georg Wilhelm Friedrich Hegel publishes the first part of his *Enzyklopädie der Philosophischen Wissenschaften im Grundrisse/Encyclopedia of Philosophical Science in Outline.* The second part appears in 1827.
- The Spanish priest and historian Juan Antonio Llorente, once the secretary of the Inquisition, publishes the first part of his *Histoire critique de l'inquisition d'Espagne/Critical History of the Inquisition in Spain*, in Paris, France. The second part appears in 1818.

July 1817–59 German geographer Carl Ritter publishes *Earth Science in its Relation to Nature and the History of Man.* The first of 19 volumes surveying world geography, it establishes him as cofounder, along with Alexander von Humboldt, of modern geography.

- The University of Michigan is founded in Ann Arbor, Michigan.
- U.S. educator Thomas Hopkins Gallaudet establishes the first U.S. public school for hearing disabled students, in Hartford, Connecticut.

Everyday Life

- Cup plates, chinaware with a center indention, are developed to hold a tea cup while the drinker sips from the saucer. They go out of fashion before the American Civil War when saucer-drinking is considered poor manners.
- Thomas Adams produces the first chewing gum from chicle, the coagulated juice of the sapodilla, a tropical American fruit tree.

Media and Communication

- The Ohio abolitionist Charles Osborn begins publication of *Philanthropist*, an antislavery newspaper.

Religion

- The French writer on religion Félicité Lamennais publishes *Essai sur l'indifférence en matière de religion/Essay on Indifference to Religion.*

SOCIETY

Education

- The English journalist William Cobbett credits the average U.S. farmer with a higher degree of literacy than his European counterpart.

BIRTHS & DEATHS

JANUARY

1 Martin Heinrich Klaproth, German chemist who discovered uranium, zirconium, and cerium, dies in Berlin, Germany (73).

APRIL

4 André Masséna, French general during the French Revolution and the Napoleonic Wars, dies in Paris, France (58).

JUNE

30 Abraham Gottlob Werner, German geologist who founded the Neptunian school of geology which held the belief that all rocks were sedimentary in origin, dies in Freiberg, Germany (66).

JULY

12 Henry David Thoreau, U.S. essayist, poet, and philosopher, born in Concord, Massachusetts (–1862).

14 Madame de Staël (Anne-Louise-Germaine Necker, Baroness de Staël-Holstein), French novelist and writer, dies in Paris, France (51).

18 Jane Austen, English novelist, dies in Winchester, England (41).

AUGUST

6 Pierre Samuel Du Pont de Nemours, French economist and statesman, dies in Eleutherian Mills, near Wilmington, Delaware (77).

OCTOBER

15 Tadeusz Kościuszko, Polish army officer who led a Polish uprising against the Russian Empire, dies in Solothurn, Switzerland (71).

23 Pierre-Athanase Larousse, French encyclopedist, born in Toucy, France (–1875).

NOVEMBER

7 Jean-André Deluc, Swiss-born English geologist, dies in Windsor, Berkshire, England (90).

28 Hisamitsu Shimazu, Japanese feudal lord who was one of the leaders in the rebellion against the Tokugawa shogunate, born in Kagoshima, Japan (–1887).

30 Theodor Mommsen, German historian, born in Garding, Schleswig (–1903).

1818

POLITICS, GOVERNMENT, AND ECONOMICS

Business and Economics

- The American Fur Company agent Solomon Laurent Juneau establishes a trading post on Lake Michigan at the future site of Milwaukee, Wisconsin.
- The branch of the Second Bank of the United States in Baltimore, Maryland, collapses, precipitating a financial panic.
- The New England Glass Company opens in Cambridge, Massachusetts.

MAY

28 The Prussian Tariff Reform Act makes taxes and tariffs standard throughout Prussia.

Colonization

FEBRUARY

12 The Spanish colony of Chile proclaims itself independent.

APRIL

5 Chilean forces under the Argentine soldier and statesman José de San Martín defeat a Spanish army at Maipú, Chile, thereby safeguarding the independence of their new state.

JUNE

2 The leader of the Maratha confederacy in India, Baji Rao, the peshwa of Poona, surrenders to the British forces of Francis Rawdon-Hastings, Marquess of Hastings and governor-general of Bengal. Britain annexes the peshwa's lands, effectively destroying the Maratha Confederacy, the last significant rival to British domination of the subcontinent.

NOVEMBER

20 The South American revolutionary leader Simón Bolívar formally declares Venezuela independent of Spain.

Politics and Government

- In the U.S. congressional elections, the Democratic-Republicans retain majorities in the House of Representatives (156–27) and Senate (35–7).

- The U.S. attorney general's office becomes formalized, despite the fact that Congress will not establish the Department of Justice until 1870.
- The U.S. state of Connecticut abolishes property qualifications for voting.
- U.S. forces under the command of General Andrew Jackson rout the Seminole people in Spanish-controlled Florida, thus clearing the way for Spain's cession of Florida to the United States in 1819.

JANUARY

- Having been burned by the British during the War of 1812, the U.S. presidential residence in Washington, D.C., reopens with a new coat of white paint. The residence will be known hereafter as the White House.

6 Under the Treaty of Mundoseer, the dominions of the Maratha Holkar dynasty of Indore are combined administratively with the Rajput states of northwest India, and come under British protection.

FEBRUARY

5 On the death of King Charles XIII of Sweden, Prince Jean-Baptiste Bernadotte (the Napoleonic marshal adopted as heir in 1810) succeeds to the throne as King Charles XIV, founding a new dynasty.

APRIL

- The U.S. Congress adopts a flag with 13 stripes and stars, equal to the number of U.S. states.
- The U.S. Senate ratifies the Rush–Bagot Convention, reducing U.S. and British naval tonnage on the Great Lakes.

MAY

- U.S. forces under General Andrew Jackson seize the Spanish settlement at Pensacola, East Florida, under the pretense that it harbors Seminole fugitives.

26 A Bavarian constitution is proclaimed, providing for a diet (assembly) of two chambers, limited freedom of speech, and legal equality.

JUNE

3 The Indian territory of Baji Rao, Peshwa of Poona, comes under British control via the Bombay presidency following his defeat in the third Maratha War.

30 The suspension of the Habeas Corpus Act in Britain (allowing imprisonment without trial) is extended until March 1, 1819.

JULY

1–25 A British election is held and the Whig opposition increases its number of seats in Parliament.

AUGUST

22 A liberal constitution is introduced into the German state of Baden, providing for a diet (assembly) of two chambers, legal equality, and fiscal reforms.

SEPTEMBER

27–November 21   A conference is held in Aachen between Austria, Prussia, Russia, Britain, and France to discuss the indemnity imposed on France after its defeat in the Napoleonic Wars.

OCTOBER

9   The allies (Britain, Prussia, Austrian Empire, and Russia, the victorious powers in the Napoleonic Wars) agree to evacuate the army of occupation from France by November 30, as the French war indemnity is being paid.

20   By a convention between the United States and Britain, the border between Canada and the United States is defined as the 49th Parallel, and a ten-year joint occupation of the territory of Oregon is agreed. The United States and Britain reach an accord that grants U.S. fishermen access to waters off Newfoundland and Labrador in exchange for U.S. renunciation of claims to the waters off other British territories.

NOVEMBER

15   France is invited to join the Concert of Europe and meet with the other major European states to discuss international problems when they arise.

15   The Quadruple Alliance between Russia, Austrian Empire, Prussia, and Britain is renewed to watch over France and protect it against revolution, although Britain refuses to make a formal alliance with France or its allies.

DECEMBER

3   Illinois becomes the 21st state in the Union.

21   Armand du Plessis, duc de Richelieu, resigns as prime minister in France and is succeeded by Elie, duc de Decazes, after the October elections show increasing support for the left.

SCIENCE, TECHNOLOGY, AND MEDICINE

Ecology

- French scientist François de Larderel exploits the energy of geothermal emissions of steam at Larderello, Italy.

Exploration

APRIL

April–August   Scottish explorer John Ross leads a British naval expedition in search of a Northwest Passage to the Pacific. He reaches Lancaster Sound, to the north of Baffin Island in modern Canada, but is deceived by a mirage into thinking his path is blocked.

Health and Medicine

- French chemist Jean-Baptiste-André Dumas uses iodine to treat goiters.

Science

- German astronomer Friedrich Wilhelm Bessel, in *Fundamenta Astronomiae/Fundamental Principles of Astronomy*, records the positions of 50,000 stars on the basis of James Bradley's observations; it is the most accurate star catalog to date.
- Hydrogen peroxide is discovered and used as a bleach.

Technology

- British locksmith Jeremiah Chubb invents a tumbler lock that is pick-proof.
- French-born British engineer Marc Isambard Brunel develops the tunneling shield that permits tunneling in water-bearing rocks.
- German inventor Alois Senefelder publishes *Vollständiges Lehrbuch der Steindruckerey/A Complete Course of Lithography*, which reveals the secrets of lithographic printing. He also begins to apply the process to color printing.
- German printers Friedrich Koenig and Andreas Bauer design a printing press that uses two cylinders to print both sides of a sheet of paper.
- U.S. engineer Eli Whitney invents a milling machine to manufacture parts for firearms. It will also be used to make parts for other manufactured items.
- U.S. inventor E. Collier develops a turning cylinder revolver consisting of five cylinders that have to be turned manually.

SEPTEMBER

- The U.S. inventor Seth Boyden begins manufacturing patent leather in Newark, New Jersey.

Transportation

- New York merchants establish the Black Ball Line, the first successful Atlantic packet service to sail on published schedules.
- The first all-iron ship is built; iron plates riveted to each other replace wooden planks.

APRIL

6   German inventor Karl von Drais de Sauerbrun exhibits his *draisienne*, a two-wheeled bicycle propelled by pushing the feet along the ground, with a padded seat and a swiveling steering mechanism. It becomes popular in Britain the following year and is known as the "hobby horse."

ARTS AND IDEAS

Arts

c. 1818   The English artist John Crome paints *The Poringland Oak*.

c. 1818   The German artist Caspar David Friedrich paints *Wanderer above the Sea of Fog*.

- The English artist Edwin Henry Landseer paints *Fighting Dogs getting Wind*.
- The French artist Jacques-Philippe de Loutherbourg paints *Coalbrookdale by Night*, one of the earliest works to feature industrial subjects, in this case iron furnaces.
- The Spanish artist Francisco José de Goya y Lucientes completes his set of engravings *Los Proverbios/Proverbs*.
- The U.S. artist Washington Allston paints *Elijah in the Desert*.

Literature and Language

- The Danish philologist Rasmus Christian Rask publishes *Undersøgelse om det gamle Nordiske eller Islandske Sprogs Oprindelse/Essay on the Origin of the Old Norse or Icelandic Tongue*, a landmark in the development of comparative linguistics.
- The English poet John Keats publishes *Endymion: A Poetic Romance*.
- The English reformer and writer William Cobbett publishes *A Grammar of the English Language*.
- The English writer and critic William Hazlitt publishes *Lectures on the English Poets*.
- The English writer Mary Wollstonecraft Shelley publishes the Gothic novel *Frankenstein, or the Modern Prometheus*. The novel is published anonymously, although the authorship becomes known in 1823.

- The English writer Thomas Love Peacock publishes his comic novel *Nightmare Abbey*, a satire on contemporary literary figures such as Coleridge, Byron, and Shelley.
- The Scottish poet and novelist Walter Scott publishes two novels: *Heart of Midlothian* and *Rob Roy*.
- Two novels by the English writer Jane Austen are published posthumously: *Northanger Abbey* (an early Austen novel that makes fun of the taste for Gothic novels) and *Persuasion*.

Music

- Austrian composer Franz Schubert completes his Symphony No. 6 in C major (D 589) and writes his Piano Sonatas No. 9 (D 613), left incomplete, and No. 10 (D 625).
- German composer Ludwig van Beethoven completes his Piano Sonata No. 29 (Opus 106), the *Hammerklavier*.
- The opera *Mosè in Egitto/Moses in Egypt* by the Italian composer Gioachino Antonio Rossini is first performed, in Naples, Italy.

Theater and Dance

- The tragedy *Brutus, or the Fall of Tarquin* by the U.S. dramatist John Howard Payne is first performed, in New York, New York.

BIRTHS & DEATHS

APRIL

29 Alexander II, Czar of Russia 1855–81 who was responsible for emancipating the Russian serfs, born in Moscow, Russia (–1881).

MAY

5 Karl Marx, Prussian political theorist, economist, and sociologist whose ideas formed the basis of communism, born in Trier, Prussia (–1883).

10 Paul Revere, American silversmith and folk hero of the American Revolution who, on April 18, 1775, warned Boston that the British were coming, dies in Boston, Massachusetts (83).

25 Jacob Burckhardt, Swiss cultural historian, born in Basel, Switzerland (–1897).

28 Pierre Gustave Toutant Beauregard, Confederate general during the American Civil War, born near New Orleans, Louisiana (–1893).

JUNE

3 Louis Faidherbe, French colonial administrator who was instrumental in establishing France's colonial empire in Africa, born in Lille, France (–1889).

17 Charles-François Gounod, French operatic composer known best for *Faust* (1859), born in Paris, France (–1893).

JULY

1 Ignaz Philipp Semmelweis, Hungarian physician who discovered the cause of puerperal fever and introduced antiseptic practices into medicine, born in Buda, Hungary, Austrian Empire (–1865).

14 Joseph-Arthur Gobineau, French ethnologist whose theories of race influenced European racial policies, born in Ville-d'Avray, France (–1882).

28 Gaspard Monge, French mathematician who pioneered analytical geometry, dies in Paris, France (72).

30 Emily Brontë, English novelist known for *Wuthering Heights* (1847), born in Thornton, Yorkshire (now West Yorkshire), England (–1848).

SEPTEMBER

12 Richard Jordon Gatling, inventor of the Gatling machine gun, born in Maney's Neck, North Carolina (–1903).

OCTOBER

8 Abigail Adams, wife of the second president of the United States John Adams, whose correspondence provided insights into U.S. life in the early years of the country's existence, dies in Quincy, Massachusetts (73).

NOVEMBER

2 Samuel Romilly, English lawyer noted for his reforms of English criminal law, commits suicide in London, England (61).

9 Ivan Sergeyevich Turgenev, Russian novelist, poet, and playwright, born in Oryol, Russia (–1883).

21 Lewis Henry Morgan, U.S. anthropologist whose study of kinship among the Iroquois helped establish anthropology in the United States, born near Aurora, New York (–1881).

- The tragedy *Sappho* by the Austrian dramatist Franz Grillparzer is first performed, in Vienna, Austria.

Thought and Scholarship

- *Considérations sur la révolution/Reflections on the Revolution* by the Franco-Swiss writer Madame de Staël is published posthumously.
- The English historian Henry Hallam publishes *The View of the State of Europe in the Middle Ages*.

SOCIETY

Education

- Dalhousie University is founded in Halifax, Nova Scotia, Canada.
- St. Louis University is founded in St. Louis, Missouri.

- Yale Medical School is founded in New Haven, Connecticut.

Everyday Life

- Pork producers in Cincinnati, Ohio, begin marketing the salt pork that will make the city famous.
- The U.S. retailer Henry Sands Brooks opens an apparel store in New York, New York, that serves as the foundation for Brooks Brothers.

Media and Communication

- U.S. chemist Benjamin Silliman begins the *American Journal of Science*.

Religion

- The U.S. educator–moralist Timothy Dwight publishes *Theology, Explained and Defended*.

1819

POLITICS, GOVERNMENT, AND ECONOMICS

Business and Economics

- A financial panic grips the U.S. economy caused by, among other things, an over-extension of credit, real estate speculation, and declining European demand for U.S. agricultural products.
- In the face of economic depression, U.S. manufacturers lobby Congress for higher protective tariffs.

Politics and Government

- The U.S. Congress separates the territory of Maine from Massachusetts in anticipation of Maine becoming an independent state.
- The U.S. Supreme Court, in the case *Dartmouth College v. Woodward*, rules that corporate charters are protected by the constitution's contract clause.
- The U.S. Supreme Court, in the case *McCulloch v. Maryland*, endorses Congress's charter of the Second Bank of the United States. Though the Constitution does

not specifically grant Congress the authority to charter a bank, such authority is implied from the Constitution's "necessary and proper" clause.

FEBRUARY

- The United States and Spain sign the Transcontinental Treaty, by which Spain cedes East Florida to the United States in exchange for U.S. recognition that West Texas was not part of the Louisiana Purchase. The treaty also extends U.S. territorial claims to the Pacific.
- The New York representative James Tallmadge introduces an amendment to a Missouri statehood bill that thrusts the vexing problem of slavery squarely before the U.S. Congress. The so-called Tallmadge Amendment proposes that Missouri slaves shall become free at the age of 25 and prohibits the future importation of slaves into the state. Bound to upset the balance between free and slave states, the Tallmadge Amendment is eventually dropped.
- 22 The U.S. Congress ratifies the Adams–Onis Treaty to obtain Florida from Spain.

MARCH

- The U.S. Congress passes the nation's first immigration law, designed to systemize immigration accounting.
- 23 August von Kotzebue, a German dramatist and alleged Russian agent, is assassinated by a nationalistic German student in Mannheim, Grand Duchy of Baden.

APRIL

- 24 After lengthy negotiations with Britain, the Ottoman Empire obtains Parga from the Ionian Islands.

MAY

1 Freedom of the press is introduced in France.

AUGUST

16 The "Peterloo Massacre" takes place in England when a crowd of 60,000 people gathered in St. Peter's Fields, Manchester, to listen to speeches on parliamentary reform and repeal of the Corn Laws, is charged on by the yeomanry. Eleven people are killed and 400 injured.

SEPTEMBER

20 The Frankfurt diet (assembly) of the German Confederation sanctions the Carlsbad Decrees by which freedom of the press is abolished, universities are placed under state supervision, and all political agitation is to be suppressed in an attempt to check revolutionary and liberal movements in Germany.

25 The German state of Württemberg is given a constitution similar to those recently established in Baden and Bavaria, providing for limited parliamentary representation.

OCTOBER

10 Prussia concludes a tariff treaty with the German state of Schwarzburg–Sonderhausen, the beginning of the creation of a German customs union or *Zollverein*.

NOVEMBER

11 The Austrian chief minister Klemens, Prince Metternich, uses his influence to convene a conference in Vienna, Austria, to discuss a modification of the Federal Act of the German States that would make it impossible for them to pursue liberal policies.

DECEMBER

14 Alabama becomes the 22nd state in the Union.

17 After a successful military campaign in New Granada against the Spanish colonial forces, the South American revolutionary leader Simón Bolívar becomes president of the newly formed Republic of Great Colombia, nominally consisting of the Spanish colonies of New Granada, Quito, and Venezuela.

SCIENCE, TECHNOLOGY, AND MEDICINE

Exploration

- British soldier Captain George Sadlier becomes the first European for three hundred years to cross Arabia.

December 1819–20 English admiral Edward Parry leads a British Royal Naval expedition to find the Northwest Passage. He passes the limit reached by John Ross's expedition of 1818 and enters Viscount Melville Sound in the Canadian Arctic, but is stopped by ice north of Banks Island.

December 1819–21 Russian navigator Fabian Gottlieb von Bellingshausen completes a circumnavigation of the Southern Ocean, and, in early 1820, sights the ice shelf of continental Antarctica.

Health and Medicine

- British surgeon James Blundell makes the first human-to-human blood transfusion. The patient survives for 56 hours.
- French physician Jean-Louis-Marie Poiseuille is the first to use a mercury manometer to measure blood pressure.
- Sumatra is struck by a cholera epidemic.

Science

- English astronomer and chemist John Herschel discovers that hyposulfate of soda acts as a solvent for (the otherwise insolvent) salts of silver that are used as a fixative in photography.
- French physicists Pierre-Louis Dulong and Alexis-Thérèse Petit formulate the Dulong–Petit law that states that the specific heat of an element, times its atomic weight, is a constant. It proves useful in establishing atomic weights.
- From observations of the crystallization of phosphates and arsenates, German chemist Eilhardt Mitscherlich propounds the theory of isomorphism. It explains the similarity in crystalline structure between different chemical compounds.
- German astronomer Johann Encke discovers the short-period comet (Encke's comet), which returns every 3.29 years.

JUNE

- Danish physicist Hans Christian Oersted discovers electromagnetism when he observes that a magnetized compass needle is deflected by an electric current.

Technology

- A cultivator for removing weeds is invented in the United States.
- French engineer Charles Cagniard de La Tour invents the siren.
- German inventor Augustus Siebe develops a diving suit consisting of a metal helmet fitted to a leather suit. Air supplied by a pressure pump keeps the water-level below the diver's chin.
- U.S. farmer Jethro Wood invents a cast-iron plow with an improved moldboard; built in standard pieces for easy replacement of parts, it becomes the standard plow of the period.

Transportation

- The world's first omnibus service begins in Paris, France; within a decade the idea spreads to other major cities.

MAY

22–June 30 The U.S. ship *Savannah* crosses the Atlantic from Georgia Port, Georgia, to Liverpool, England. It is the first steamship to make the crossing, although steam propulsion is used for only a fraction of the journey.

ARTS AND IDEAS

Architecture

- City planners lay the groundwork for the city of Memphis, Tennessee, on the banks of the Mississippi River.
- U.S. army engineers construct Fort Snelling on the future site of Minneapolis, Minnesota.

May 1819–26   Scottish engineer Thomas Telford constructs the 177-m/580-ft Menai suspension bridge over the Menai Straits between Bangor, Wales, and the island of Anglesey. The first modern suspension bridge, it uses chains of wrought-iron links suspended from masonry towers at either end. Lacking stiffening girders it is vulnerable to high winds.

Arts

- The English artist John Constable paints *The White Horse*.
- The French artist Jean-Auguste-Dominique Ingres paints *Roger and Angelica*.
- The German artist Caspar David Friedrich paints *Two Men Contemplating the Moon* and *Chalk Cliffs at Rügen*.
- The German artist Wilhelm von Schadow sculpts *Marshal Blücher*.
- The Prado in Madrid, Spain, opens as the national museum of fine art.
- The Spanish artist Francisco José de Goya y Lucientes paints his *Portrait of Doña Antonia Zárate*.
- The U.S. artist Washington Allston paints *Moonlit Landscape*.

Literature and Language

- The English Orientalist Horace Hatman Wilson publishes his *Sanskrit-English Dictionary*.
- The English poet George Crabbe publishes *Tales of the Hall*.
- The English poet George Gordon, Lord Byron, publishes the first part of his "epic satire" *Don Juan*, one of his most important works. Other parts appear in 1821, 1823, and 1824. He also publishes his narrative poem *Mazeppa*.
- The English publisher and writer William Hone publishes his political satire *The Political House that Jack Built*.
- The German folklorist and philologist Jakob Ludwig Carl Grimm publishes *Deutsche Grammatik/German Grammar*, one of the major works of 19th-century linguistics.
- The German writer Johann Wolfgang von Goethe publishes his poetry collection *West-östlicher Divan/ Divan of East and West*.
- U.S. essayist and short-story writer Washington Irving publishes *The Sketch Book of Geoffrey Crayon, Gent.*, which includes popular tales such as *Rip Van Winkle* and *The Legend of Sleepy Hollow*. The book is a great success in both the United States and Britain.

MARCH

March–July   The *Croaker Papers*, a series of satirical poems published anonymously, are printed in the *Evening Post* and the *National Advertiser* in New York, New York. The authors are U.S. poet Fitz-Greene Halleck and writer and druggist Joseph Rodman Drake.

Music

- Austrian composer Franz Schubert completes his Piano Quintet in A major (D 667), *Die Forelle/The Trout*, and his Piano Sonata No. 11 (D 664).
- The opera *Semiramide riconosciuta/Semiramide Rewarded* by the German composer Giacomo Meyerbeer is first performed, in Turin, Italy.

Theater and Dance

- The play *She Would Be A Soldier* by the U.S. writer Mordecai Manuel Noah is first performed, in New York, New York.

Thought and Scholarship

- The German philosopher Arthur Schopenhauer publishes *Die Welt als Wille und Vorstellung/The World as Will and Idea*. His major work, it has a profound influence on German culture.
- The Swiss economist and historian Jean-Charles-Léonard Sismonde de Sismondi publishes *Nouveaux Principes d'économie politique/New Principles of Political Economy*.

SOCIETY

Education

- Colgate University is founded in Hamilton, New York.
- Norwich University, a private military and technical institute, opens in Northfield, Vermont.
- The University of Cincinnati is founded in Cincinnati, Ohio.
- The University of Virginia is founded in Charlottesville, Virginia. Its chief architect is the U.S. statesman and polymath Thomas Jefferson.
- The U.S. educator Emma Willard moves her school for young women to Waterford, New York.

Everyday Life

- François-Louis Cailler sets up a chocolate factory in Vevey, Switzerland. It is the first to produce chocolate in bars.
- The U.S. fishmongers Ezra Daggett and Thomas Kensett establish what is believed to be the first U.S. food canning enterprise in New York, New York.

APRIL

- The English immigrant Thomas Wildey establishes a U.S. branch of the English fraternal organization the Independent Order of Odd Fellows, in Baltimore, Maryland.

Media and Communication

- The U.S. abolitionist Charles Osborn moves from Ohio to Jonesboro, Tennessee, where he publishes the weekly antislavery periodical *Manumission Intelligencer*.

APRIL

- John Stuart Skinner, a farmer from Baltimore, Maryland, publishes the periodical *American Farmer*.

Religion

- U.S. Methodists dispatch their first missionary, Bishop George, to convert Francophone settlers in Louisiana.
- The Boston minister William Ellery Channing delivers an address entitled "Unitarian Christianity," a seminal work in the Unitarian religion.
- The French royalist diplomat Joseph de Maistre publishes *Du Pape/The Pope*, a defense of papal infallibility.
- The German theologian Georg Hermes publishes *Philosophische Einleitung in die Christkatholische Theologie/Philosophical Introduction to Christian Theology*, an attempt to combine Catholic theology and German philosophy.

BIRTHS & DEATHS

JANUARY

14 John Wolcot ("Peter Pindar"), English satirist, dies in London, England (80).

FEBRUARY

8 John Ruskin, English writer and artist who led the Gothic Revival movement, born in London, England (–1900).

14 Christopher Latham Sholes, U.S. inventor of the typewriter, born near Mooresburg, Pennsylvania (–1890).

22 James Russell Lowell, U.S. poet, critic, and diplomat, born in Cambridge, Massachusetts (–1891).

MARCH

23 August von Kotzebue, German dramatist and novelist, dies in Mannheim, Grand Duchy of Baden (57).

APRIL

15 Oliver Evans, U.S. inventor who developed the high-pressure steam engine and built the first automated production line in the United States, dies in New York, New York (73).

MAY

8 Kamehameha I, the king of Hawaii who united the Hawaiian islands, dies in Kailua, Hawaii (c. 61).

24 Victoria, Queen of the United Kingdom of Great Britain and Ireland 1837–1901, Empress of India 1876–1901, born in London, England (–1901).

31 Walt Whitman, U.S. journalist, essayist, and poet, born in West Hills, New York (–1892).

JUNE

10 Gustave Courbet, French realist painter of everyday events, born in Orléans, France (–1877).

20 Jacques Offenbach, French composer who creates the *opérette*, or comic opera, born in Cologne, Germany (–1880).

JULY

9 Elias Howe, U.S. inventor who developed the first practical sewing machine, born in Spencer, Massachusetts (–1867).

19 Gottfried Keller, Swiss writer, born in Zürich, Switzerland (–1890).

AUGUST

1 Herman Melville, U.S. novelist, short-story writer, and poet who wrote *Moby Dick*, born in New York, New York (–1891).

23 Oliver Hazard Perry, U.S. naval hero who defeated the British in the

Battle of Lake Erie during the War of 1812, dies at sea en route to the United States from South America (34).

26 Albert, Prince Consort, advisor, and husband to Queen Victoria of the United Kingdom of Great Britain and Ireland, born in Schloss Rosenau, Germany (–1861).

SEPTEMBER

6 William Rosecrans, Union general during the Civil War, born in Kingston Township, Ohio (–1898).

18 (Jean-Bernard-)Léon Foucault, French physicist who invented Foucault's pendulum to demonstrate that the earth rotates, born in Paris, France (–1868).

OCTOBER

20 The Bab (adopted name of Mirza Ali Muhammad), founder of the Baha'i faith, born in Shīrāz, Persia (–1850).

NOVEMBER

22 George Eliot (pseudonym of Mary Anne Evans), English novelist, born in Chilvers Coton, Warwickshire, England (–1880).

1820

POLITICS, GOVERNMENT, AND ECONOMICS

Colonization

NOVEMBER

25 A temporary truce is concluded between Spain and Colombia as King Ferdinand VII of Spain is faced with revolution at home, but he still refuses to uphold Colombian independence under Simón Bolívar, and war is soon resumed.

Human Rights

FEBRUARY

• Eighty-six free black Americans depart the United States for Sierra Leone, the British-founded colony for freed slaves in west Africa.

Politics and Government

• In the U.S. congressional elections, the Democratic-Republicans retain majorities in the House of Representatives (158–25) and Senate (44–4).
• The U.S. state of Massachusetts abolishes property qualifications for voting.

JANUARY

1 A revolution begins in Spain due to King Ferdinand VII's failure to adhere to the constitution of 1812 and his sending of troops to South America to put down risings in the Spanish colonies that have attracted much popular support in Spain itself.

FEBRUARY

13 Charles-Ferdinand d'Artois, duc de Berry, sole heir to the French throne, is assassinated by a radical determined to end the Bourbon line.
20 Elie, duc de Decazes, is dismissed as prime minister of France after the assassination of Charles-Ferdinand d'Artois, duc de Berry, and is succeeded by his predecessor, the more right-wing Armand du Plessis, duc de Richelieu.

MARCH

• The U.S. Congress passes legislation known as the Missouri Compromise, which admits Maine and Missouri to the Union as free and slave states

respectively. The legislation also prohibits slavery above the latitude 36° 30', the southern boundary of Missouri.
• The U.S. Congress passes the Missouri Enabling Act, authorizing citizens of Missouri to draw up a state constitution.
3 Maine becomes the 23rd state in the Union.
6 The "Missouri Compromise" is decided by the U.S. Congress, allowing Missouri to enter the Union as a slave state and Maine as a nonslave state, and banning slavery in all Louisiana Purchase territories north of Missouri's southern border.
6–April 14 The general election in Britain returns the existing Tory government.
7 King Ferdinand VII of Spain is forced by popular pressure to restore the constitution of 1812 and to abolish the Inquisition, the body responsible for upholding Catholicism in Spain.
26 The Law of General Security is passed in France, allowing for the arrest of anyone suspected of plotting against the king.
30 French prime minister Armand du Plessis, duc de Richelieu, reestablishes censorship of the press.

APRIL

• The U.S. Congress passes legislation that enables settlers to purchase 80-acre land tracts for $100, $1.25 per acre.

MAY

• Arthur Thistlewood and James Watson, leaders of the Cato Street Conspiracy to murder British cabinet ministers, are executed for treason.
15 The final act of the Conference of Vienna is passed, authorizing the German Confederation to intervene in the affairs of member states unable to maintain public order and the principles of conservative government.

JUNE

6 A new electoral law in France regulates the electoral colleges and introduces a system of "double-voting," resulting in increased influence for the right.
8 The Frankfurt diet (assembly) of the German Confederation approves the act passed at the Conference of Vienna on May 15 allowing for the interference of the Confederation in the affairs of member states threatened by revolutionary action.

JULY

2–7 A revolt breaks out in the Italian kingdom of Naples, due to the misrule of King Ferdinand IV, at the instigation of the Carbonari and secret societies dedicated to obtaining political reform and national unification. It results in the promise of a constitution similar to that in Spain.

AUGUST

24 A revolution breaks out in Oporto, Portugal, caused by discontent at King John VI living in Brazil and English

influence in the government. Its leaders demand a constitution.

SEPTEMBER

29 Henri, comte de Chambord, is born. The son of the assassinated Duc de Berry, he is heir to the French throne.

OCTOBER

23 A conference at Troppau, Germany, meets to discuss possible action against revolutionary movements in Europe. It is attended by Austria, Russia, and Prussia, and by plenipotentiaries from France and Britain.

NOVEMBER

19 A Preliminary Protocol is issued at Troppau, Germany, by Austria, Russia, and Prussia, expelling those nations undergoing revolutions from the Concert of Europe and allowing other states to intervene to crush revolts by force if necessary.

DECEMBER

• James Monroe and Daniel D. Tompkins are reelected as U.S. president and vice president respectively.

16 Britain repudiates the Preliminary Protocol on controlling future revolutions within Europe issued by Austria, Russia, and Prussia on November 19.

17 The conference between Austria, Russia, Prussia, France, and Britain at Troppau, Germany, is adjourned until January 1821, when the powers are to meet in Laibach.

SCIENCE, TECHNOLOGY, AND MEDICINE

Exploration

• The U.S. ethnologist Henry Rowe Schoolcraft travels to the Midwest to study Native American customs.

• The U.S. explorer and engineer Stephen Long transverses the territory of the Platte and Arkansas rivers, returning with descriptions of many varieties of unknown flora and fauna.

JANUARY

14 English naval officer Edward Bransfield lands on Deception Island in Antarctica, and plants the Union Jack and buries a bottle containing coins there. He sights high, snow-covered mountains to the south on January 20—the first sighting of mainland Antarctica.

Health and Medicine

• Thousands of people die in cholera epidemics in China and the Philippines.

Math

c. 1820 German mathematician Karl Friedrich Gauss introduces the normal distribution curve ("Gausian distribution")—a basic statistical tool.

• French mathematician Charles-Thomas de Colmar develops the first mass-produced calculator—the "arithmometer."

Science

c. 1820 French physicist André Ampère develops an instrument that uses a needle to measure the flow of electricity. It is the first measurement of electricity.

• French chemists Joseph Pelletier and Joseph-Bienaimé Caventou isolate the antimalarial drug quinine, as well as the other alkaloids brucine, cinchonine, colchicine, strychnine, and veratrine.

• French physicist André Ampère formulates Ampère's law, which states the relationship between a magnetic field and the electric current that produces it.

• German inventor Johann Schweigger develops the first galvanometer for measuring the intensity and direction of an electric current.

Technology

c. 1820 German mathematician Karl Friedrich Gauss invents the heliotrope, an instrument that increases the accuracy of surveying by using sunlight.

• French physicist Augustin-Jean Fresnel develops the Fresnel lens, a compound lens that narrows a light beam. It is used in lighthouses.

ARTS AND IDEAS

Architecture

• The city of Indianapolis is established on Indiana's White River.

Arts

c. 1820 The Spanish artist Francisco José de Goya y Lucientes paints *Fantastic Vision*.

• The ancient Greek sculpture the *Venus de Milo* (created in about 150 BC) is discovered on the Greek island of Melos.

• The English artist John Constable paints *Harwich Lighthouse*.

• The English artist John Martin paints *Belshazzar's Feast*.

• The English poet and artist William Blake begins work on his illustrations to the *Book of Job*.

• The French artist Théodore Géricault completes his painting *The Raft of the Medusa*, a grim depiction of a recent shipwreck. It becomes one of the major works of romanticism.

• The Spanish artist Francisco José de Goya y Lucientes paints *Saturn Devouring One of His Children*. This is one of the "Black Pictures" he paints on the walls of his own house, private works that are dark, savage, and violent.

- The U.S. entrepreneur Lambert Hitchcock begins production of his Hitchcock chair in Hitchcockville, Connecticut.

Literature and Language

- The English poet John Keats publishes the first version of his epic poem *Hyperion*. A second version appears posthumously in 1856. He also publishes the poems *The Eve of St. Agnes* and *Ode to a Nightingale*.
- The English poet Percy Bysshe Shelley publishes the poems *Prometheus Unbound* and *Ode to the West Wind*.
- The French poet Alphonse Marie Louis de Lamartine publishes *Méditations poétiques/Poetic Meditations*.
- The Russian poet Alexander Pushkin publishes his romantic epic *Ruslan i Lyudmila/Ruslan and Ludmila*. It is the basis of the opera *Ruslan and Ludmila*, which is written in 1842 by the Russian composer Mikhail Ivanovich Glinka.
- The Scottish poet and novelist Walter Scott publishes his novel *Ivanhoe*.

JANUARY

- U.S. literary pretensions suffer a blow when the English clergyman and essayist Sydney Smith muses, "In the four corners of the globe, who in the world reads an American book? or goes to an American play? or looks at an American picture or statue?"

Music

- Austrian composer Franz Schubert completes his *Lazarus* oratorio (D 689) and writes his *Quartettsatz*, a movement intended for *String Quartet No 12* (D 703), which was never completed.

- The opera *Margherita d'Anjou* by the German composer Giacomo Meyerbeer is first performed, in Milan, Italy.
- The operetta *Die Zwillingsbrüder/Twin Brothers* (D 647) by the Austrian composer Franz Schubert is first performed, in Vienna, Austria.

Thought and Scholarship

- *c.* 1820   English physician and physicist Thomas Young makes substantial advances in the decipherment of the Rosetta Stone—the key to understanding Egyptian hieroglyphics.
- The English economist Thomas Robert Malthus publishes *Principles of Political Economy*.
- The German writer Johann Joseph von Görres publishes *Teutschland und die Revolution/Germany and the Revolution*.

SOCIETY

Education

- Indiana University is founded in Bloomington, Indiana.
- The U.S. states of New York and New Hampshire establish the nation's first state-supported libraries.
- Two new libraries are founded in New York, New York for middle-class readers: the Mercantile Library Association and the Apprentices Library Association.

Everyday Life

- The U.S. census lists the population at 9,638,453, up from roughly 7,240,000 in 1810.

BIRTHS & DEATHS

JANUARY
29   George III, King of Great Britain and Ireland 1760–1820, dies in Windsor Castle, Berkshire, England (81).

FEBRUARY
8   William Tecumseh Sherman, Union general during the American Civil War, born in Lancaster, Ohio (–1891).

15   Susan B(rownell) Anthony, U.S. suffragist whose work eventually led to women's suffrage in the United States (1920), born in Adams, Massachusetts (–1906).

MARCH
11   Benjamin West, U.S.-born English historical painter, dies in London, England (81).

22   Stephen Decatur, U.S. naval hero, dies in a duel in Bladensburg, Maryland (41).

30   Anna Sewell, British author who wrote *Black Beauty*, born in Yarmouth, Norfolk, England (–1878).

APRIL
20   Arthur Young, English writer on agriculture, economics, and politics, dies in London, England (78).

MAY
12   Florence Nightingale, "Lady of the Lamp," English nurse who was in charge of nursing the British troops during the Crimean War and who established nursing as a profession for women, born in Florence, Italy (–1910).

23   James Buchanan Eads, U.S. engineer who in 1874 built the first major bridge over the Mississippi River at St. Louis, Missouri, born in Lawrenceburg, Indiana (–1887).

JUNE
6   Henry Grattan, Anglo-Irish politician, leader of the movement that compelled Britain to free the Irish legislature from British control, dies in London, England (83).

SEPTEMBER
3   Benjamin Henry Latrobe, British-born U.S. architect who worked on the Capitol Building in Washington, D.C., dies in New Orleans, Louisiana (55).

26   Daniel Boone, U.S. frontiersman, dies in St. Charles, Missouri (85).

NOVEMBER
28   Friedrich Engels, German socialist philosopher who, with Karl Marx, wrote *The Communist Manifesto* (1848) which laid the foundations of modern communism, born in Barmen, Prussia (now Germany) (–1895).

Media and Communication

- The Tennessee abolitionist Elihu Embree publishes the antislavery journal *Emancipator*.
- William Swaim, an abolitionist from Greensboro, North Carolina, publishes the antislavery paper *Patriot*.
- By 1820, only 4 of the 1,634 newspapers founded in Colonial North America and the United States since 1704 have lasted more than 50 years.

Sports

c. 1820 Squash rackets, a version of rackets with a softer ball, is invented and developed at Harrow School, London, England.

- The first football games are played in U.S. colleges. The game is a form of hazing by sophomores inflicted on freshmen by kicking the freshmen instead of the ball. The game is banned in the 1830s because of the high number of injuries.

JULY

15 The U.S. climber Edwin James makes the first successful ascent of the 4,298-m/14,100-ft Pike's Peak in the Rampart of the Rocky Mountains, Colorado.

1821

POLITICS, GOVERNMENT, AND ECONOMICS

Business and Economics

MAY

7 The British Africa Company, a private enterprise created to exploit African economic resources, is dissolved because of heavy expenses incurred, and Sierra Leone, Gambia, and the Gold Coast are taken over by the British government to form British West Africa.

Colonization

- The American Colonization Society purchases the colony of Liberia on Africa's west coast, to which it will begin sending black Americans in 1822.

JULY

28 Peru proclaims itself formally independent of Spain.

SEPTEMBER

15 Guatemala declares itself independent of Spain and aligns itself with Mexico.

29 The Portuguese cortes (national assembly) annuls King John IV's introduction of a liberal constitution in Brazil and recalls his son, the regent, from there in an attempt to reintroduce the old colonial system.

NOVEMBER

28 Panama declares itself independent of Spain and joins the Republic of Colombia.

DECEMBER

- The U.S. slaveholder and real estate speculator Stephen Austin establishes the first U.S. settlement in Texas, San Felipe de Austin.

1 The West Indian colony of San Domingo establishes itself as a republic independent of Spain.

Politics and Government

- New York State abolishes property qualifications for voting.

JANUARY

12–May 12 Britain, Russia, Prussia, Austria, and France meet in Laibach to continue their discussions on how to control any future revolts and revolutions in Europe.

26 The Portuguese cortes (national assembly) meets to discuss a constitution.

FEBRUARY

- A revolt occurs in the Ottoman province of Wallachia against the oppressive rule of the Turks.

13 At the Congress of Laibach, Austria agrees to King Ferdinand IV's request to send an army into his Italian kingdom of Naples to suppress the revolt there.

24 King John VI of Portugal promises to introduce the progressive clauses of the Portuguese constitution into Brazil.

MARCH

- The U.S. Supreme Court, in the case *Cohens v. Virginia*, asserts the supremacy of federal law over state law in cases of civil rights.

- U.S. president James Monroe is inaugurated for a second term.

6 A revolt occurs in the Ottoman province of Moldavia against Turkish rule. The rebels appeal to Czar

Alexander I of Russia for help, and the prospect of a successful Russian-supported revolt while the Ottoman authorities are preoccupied with defeating regional warlords prompts a first (unsuccessful) rebellion in Greece.

7   The rebels opposing King Ferdinand IV in the Italian kingdom of Naples are crushed at Rieti by the Austrian army.

10   A revolution, influenced by the Carbonari, begins in the Italian kingdom of Piedmont to put the heir apparent, Prince Charles Albert Carignan, on the throne because he is believed to be a liberal.

13   King Victor Emmanuel I of the Italian kingdom of Piedmont abdicates and proclaims his brother Prince Charles Felix, not Prince Charles Albert (the heir apparent), to be his successor.

16   Prince Charles Felix issues a decree forcing the heir apparent, Charles Albert, to renounce his claim to the throne of the Italian kingdom of Piedmont.

23   The Austrian army enters the Italian kingdom of Naples and restores King Ferdinand IV to the throne.

APRIL

8   The Austrian army intervenes in the dispute over the succession to the throne of the Italian kingdom of Piedmont and defeats the supporters of Prince Charles Albert at Novara.

22   After several revolutionary outbreaks in the Ottoman province of Morea in which the Greeks massacre Turks, the Greek patriarch of Constantinople, the head of the Greek Orthodox Church, is murdered by the Turks as a reprisal and a reign of terror begins.

22   King John VI of Portugal issues a decree in Brazil (confirming an earlier decree of March 27), establishing a regency there under his son Dom Pedro.

MAY

9   A constitution is decreed in Portugal under which feudalism and the Inquisition are abolished and a single elective chamber is established in which the king is to have only a suspensory vote.

JUNE

19   The Ottoman army defeats the Greek rebels at Dragashan,

War of Greek Independence (1821–27)

1821

March 6   A revolt occurs in the Ottoman province of Moldavia against Turkish rule. The rebels appeal to Czar Alexander I of Russia for help, and the prospect of a successful Russian-supported revolt while the Ottoman authorities are preoccupied with defeating regional warlords prompts a first (unsuccessful) rebellion in Greece.

April 22   After several revolutionary outbreaks in the Ottoman province of Morea in which the Greeks massacre Turks, the Greek patriarch of Constantinople, the head of the Greek Orthodox Church, is murdered by the Turks as a reprisal and a reign of terror begins.

June 19   The Ottoman army defeats the Greek rebels at Dragashan.

October 5   Greek rebels take the town of Tripolitza in the Ottoman province of Morea in their ongoing struggle against the Ottoman Empire, massacring the Ottoman population there.

1822

January 13   Greek independence from the Ottoman Empire is formally proclaimed by the assembly at Epidaurus.

February 5   The assassination of Ali of Janina, the Ottoman ruler in the Greek province of Morea who revolted against Ottoman rule, enables the Ottoman Empire to concentrate its forces against the Greeks.

April 22   The Ottoman fleet captures the Greek island of Chios, which has rebelled against the Ottoman Empire, and massacres its Christian inhabitants or sells them as slaves.

June 18   A Greek flotilla under Admiral Konstantin Kanaris routs the Ottoman fleet in the Strait of Chios in reprisal for the atrocities carried out by the Turks on the island of Chios.

July 7   Ottoman troops begin their invasion of Greece. The Turks overrun the peninsula north of the Gulf of Corinth.

1824

April 4   The Greek island of Crete is captured by the Egyptians, who are assisting the Ottoman Empire in its war with the Greeks.

July 7   The Ottoman Empire captures the Greek island of Ipsara.

October 10   The Greek army inflicts a very heavy defeat on the Turks at Mitilini, on the Greek island of Lesbos.

1825

February 24   Egyptian forces land in the Ottoman province of Morea to support the Turks and begin to subdue the rebelling Greeks.

July 24   The Greek provisional government passes proposals to place the country under British protection (subsequently rejected by the British government).

1826

April 4   The St. Petersburg Protocol is signed between Britain and Russia, agreeing that the Greek problem should be solved by establishing the complete autonomy of Greece under Ottoman suzerainty.

1827

October 20   The Battle of Novorian is fought, in which a combined British, French, and Russian fleet destroys a Turkish–Egyptian fleet lying at anchor.

1828

August 9   Over the next year, Egyptian and Turkish forces evacuate Greece supervised by a European expeditionary force.

24 The South American revolutionary leader Simón Bolívar ensures the independence of Venezuela from Spain by defeating the Spanish army of General Miguel de la Torre at Carabobo, near Caracas. A subsequent congress of the republic of Great Colombia (to which Venezuela is now added) at Cúcuta, Colombia, reorganizes the administration of the new republic, constitutionally limiting Bolívar's powers as president.

JULY

19 The coronation of King George IV of Britain takes place at Westminister Abbey, London, England. Queen Caroline is not admitted to the ceremony.

26 Relations are severed between the Ottoman Empire and Russia, after the Ottoman Empire's refusal to protect its Christian subjects in the Balkans.

AUGUST

• Missouri becomes the 24th state in the Union.

SEPTEMBER

• The United States and the Seminole nation conclude a treaty relegating the Seminoles to a barren tract of land on the Florida peninsula, from which they are to depart westward within 20 years.

• Czar Alexander I claims the Pacific coast of North America north of the 51st parallel for Russia, sparking controversy with the United States and Britain, which have jointly claimed the territory.

OCTOBER

5 Greek rebels take the town of Tripolitza in the Ottoman province of Morea in their ongoing struggle against the Ottoman Empire, massacring the Ottoman population there.

DECEMBER

12 Armand du Plessis, duc de Richelieu, is succeeded as French prime minister by Jean Villèle, ending the rule of the right center and leading to a period of reaction under the ultra-conservatives.

SCIENCE, TECHNOLOGY, AND MEDICINE

Exploration

SEPTEMBER

• The U.S. merchant Stephen Becknell departs Independence, Missouri, for Santa Fé, New Mexico, on what will become known as the Santa Fé Trail.

Math

• French mathematician Baron Augustine-Louis Cauchy publishes *Cours d'analyse/A Course in Analysis*, which sets mathematical analysis on a formal footing for the first time.

Science

• English physicist Michael Faraday builds an apparatus that transforms electrical energy into mechanical energy—the principle of the electric motor.

• German physicist Thomas Seebeck discovers thermoelectricity—the conversion of heat into electricity—when he generates a current by heating one end of a metal strip comprising two metals joined together.

SEPTEMBER

• U.S. meteorologist William Redfield discovers that during a hurricane trees are toppled toward the northwest in Connecticut, and toward the southeast 80 km/50 mi further west, demonstrating that tropical storms are cyclones.

Transportation

• The world's first iron-hulled steamship, the *Aaron Manby*, steams from Birmingham, England, to Paris, France, where it enters service on the River Seine.

ARTS AND IDEAS

Architecture

• St. Mary's Roman Catholic Cathedral in Baltimore, Maryland, designed by the English-born U.S. architect Benjamin Henry Latrobe, is completed, the first large-scale cathedral to be built in North America.

• Brighton Pavilion in Brighton, England, designed by the English architect John Nash, is completed. Combining Indian and Chinese elements, it epitomizes the Picturesque style.

• The Schauspielhaus theater in Berlin, Germany, designed by the German architect Karl Friedrich Schinkel, is completed.

Arts

c. 1821 The German artist Caspar David Friedrich paints *Moonrise Over the Sea*.

• The Danish artist Bertel Thorvaldsen designs the sculpture *The Lion of Lucerne*.

• The English artist John Constable paints *The Haywain*, one of his best-known works, and *Salisbury Cathedral from the Bishop's Grounds*.

• The German artist Christian Daniel Rauch sculpts the portrait bust *Johann Wolfgang von Goethe*.

Literature and Language

• Cherokee warrior Sequoyah develops a syllabary of 86 symbols in which to write the Cherokee language. The Cherokees soon begin writing books, and publish a newspaper, the *Cherokee Phoenix* in 1828, in their own language, making them the first Native American nation to adopt European-style literacy.

• The English diplomat John Bowring publishes *Specimens of the Russian Poets*, which introduces Russian literature to an English readership.

• The English poet Percy Bysshe Shelley publishes *Adonais: An Elegy on the Death of John Keats*.

• The English writer and critic William Hazlitt publishes his collection of essays *Table Talk*.

- The English writer Thomas De Quincey publishes his autobiographical *Confessions of an English Opium Eater* in the *The London Magazine*.
- The German writer Ernst Theodor Amadeus Hoffmann publishes his collection of stories *Die Serapionbrüder/ The Serapion Brothers*.
- The German writer Johann Wolfgang von Goethe publishes his novel *Wilhelm Meisters Wanderjahre/ Wilhelm Meister's Wandering Years*. The final version appears in 1829.
- The memoirs *Dix Années d'exil/Ten Years of Exile* by the Franco-Swiss writer Madame de Staël is published posthumously.
- The Russian poet Alexander Pushkin publishes his narrative poem *Kavkazsky plennik/Prisoner of the Caucasus*.
- The Scottish poet and novelist Walter Scott publishes his novel *Kenilworth*.
- The Scottish writer John Galt publishes his novel *Annals of the Parish*.
- The U.S. writer James Fénimore Cooper publishes his adventure novel *The Spy*.

Music

- German piano tuner Friedrich Buschmann invents the harmonica.
- The opera *Der Freischütz/The Freeshooter* by the German composer Carl Maria von Weber is first performed, in Berlin, Germany.

Theater and Dance

- The play *Prinz Friedrich von Homburg/The Prince of Homberg* by the German dramatist Heinrich Wilhelm von Kleist is published posthumously.

Thought and Scholarship

- The French social thinker Claude-Henri de Rouvroy, comte de Saint-Simon, publishes *Du Système industriel/ The Industrial System*.
- The Scottish philosopher James Mill publishes *Elements of Political Economy*.
- The German philosopher Georg Wilhelm Friedrich Hegel publishes *Grundlinien der Philosophie des Rechts/ Philosophy of Right*.
- The Swiss economist and historian Jean-Charles-Léonard Sismonde de Sismondi publishes the first volume of his 31-volume *Histoire des Français/History of the French*. The last volume appears in 1844.
- The U.S. scholar and moralist Timothy Dwight publishes *Travels in New England and New York*, a seminal work in U.S. cultural and environmental studies.
- The Scottish writer Frances Wright publishes *Views of Society and Manners in America*.

September 1821–22 French Egyptologist Jean-François Champollion deciphers the Egyptian hieroglyphics on the Rosetta Stone.

SOCIETY

Education

- Amherst College is founded in Amherst, Massachusetts.
- Boston English High School opens in Boston, Massachusetts. It is the first free public school in the United States.
- The U.S. educator Emma Willard founds the Troy Female Seminary in Troy, New York, to provide higher

BIRTHS & DEATHS

FEBRUARY

3 Elizabeth Blackwell, the first woman to receive a medical degree in the United States, born in Counterslip, Gloucestershire, England (–1910).

23 John Keats, English romantic lyric poet, dies in Rome, Italy (26).

26 Joseph de Maistre, French author, moralist, and diplomat, dies in Turin, Kingdom of Sardinia (67).

APRIL

9 Charles Pierre Baudelaire, French poet, born in Paris, France (–1867).

MAY

2 Hester Lynch Piozzi, English author and friend of Samuel Johnson, dies in Clifton, Bristol, England (81).

5 Napoleon I (Napoleon Bonaparte), French general, First Consul 1799–1804, and emperor of France 1804–15, dies in exile on the island of St. Helena in the South Atlantic (52).

8 William Henry Vanderbilt, U.S. railroad magnate and philanthropist, born in New Brunswick, New Jersey (–1885).

JULY

13 Nathan Bedford Forrest, outstanding Confederate cavalry general during the American Civil War and later founder of the Ku Klux Klan, born near Chapel Hill, Tennessee (–1877).

16 Mary Baker Eddy, founder of the Christian Science movement, born in Bow, near Concord, New Hampshire (–1910).

AUGUST

31 Hermann Ludwig von Helmholtz, German philosopher best known for articulating the law of conservation of energy, born in Potsdam, Prussia (now in Germany) (–1894).

OCTOBER

11 Fyodor Mikhailovich Dostoyevsky, Russian novelist best known for

Crime and Punishment (1866) and *The Brothers Karamazov* (1879–80), born in Moscow, Russia (–1881).

13 Rudolf Virchow, German pathologist who pioneered the use of cell theory to explain disease, born in Schivelbein, Pomerania, Russia (–1902).

17 Alexander Gardner, U.S. photographer of the American Civil War and of Native Americans, born in Paisley, Scotland (–1882).

DECEMBER

12 Gustave Flaubert, French realist novelist best known for *Madame Bovary* (1857), born in Rouen, France (–1880).

25 Clara Barton, U.S. schoolteacher who founded the U.S. Red Cross, born in Oxford, Massachusetts (–1912).

education for women. Her teaching methods serve as a model for European and U.S. educational institutions for women.

- George Washington University is founded in Washington, D.C.
- McGill University is founded in Montreal, Canada.

Everyday Life

c. 1821 Coffee is used generally throughout the United States, although it is criticized by temperance advocates and some who believe it to be an aphrodisiac.
- France has a population of 30.4 million; Britain, 20.8 million (of which Ireland comprises 6.8 million); the Italian states, 18 million; the Austrian Empire, 12 million; the United States, 9.6 million; and the combined populations of Prussia, Bavaria, Saxony, and the duchies, principalities and free cities of Germany, 26.1 million.
- The Fulton Fish Market opens on the East River, New York, New York.
- The world's first natural gas well is sunk at Fredonia, New York. Lead pipes distribute the gas to consumers for lighting and cooking.

September 1821–30 Emigration to the United States from Britain is 27,489 and from Ireland 54,338.

Media and Communication

- The itinerant U.S. abolitionist Benjamin Lundy edits the monthly magazine *Genius of Universal Emancipation*, which propounds a program for slave emancipation and colonization.
- The Philadelphia, Pennsylvania entrepreneurs Samuel C. Atkinson and Charles Alexander establish the weekly periodical *Saturday Evening Post*.

Sports

- The New York state assembly rescinds a 19-year ban on horse racing.
- The first organized horse race over hurdles takes place at Bristol, England.
- U.S. inventor Thomas Roys invents the rocket harpoon for hunting whales.

1822

POLITICS, GOVERNMENT, AND ECONOMICS

Business and Economics

- The Philadelphia publisher Matthew Carey publishes *Essays on Political Economy*, in which he advances the benefit of a high protective tariff to encourage manufacturers.

JUNE
24 A partial repeal of the British Navigation Acts (which protect British shipping interests) allows foreign ships to bring goods from European ports and also opens up West Indian trade with the United States.

Colonization

JANUARY
13 Greek independence from the Ottoman Empire is formally proclaimed by the assembly at Epidaurus.

OCTOBER
12 Brazil becomes formally independent of Portugal and Dom Pedro is proclaimed Emperor Pedro I.

DECEMBER
2 The government of the former Spanish colony of San Salvador, in the Bahamas, not wishing to be united with Mexico, asks to be incorporated in the United States.

Politics and Government

- At the urging of private traders, the U.S. Congress abolishes the so-called "Indian factory system," a network of federally operated trading posts designed to secure the allegiance of Native American ethnic groups to the United States.
- In the U.S. congressional elections, the Democratic-Republicans retain majorities in the House of Representatives (187–26) and Senate (44–4).

JANUARY
13 A revolutionary Greek assembly adopts a liberal republican constitution.

FEBRUARY
5 The assassination of Ali of Janina, the Ottoman ruler in the Greek province of Morea who revolted against

Ottoman rule, enables the Ottoman Empire to concentrate its forces against the Greeks.

MARCH

- The U.S. president James Monroe urges Congress to extend diplomatic recognition to La Plata, Brazil, Chile, Peru, Colombia, Mexico, and the Federation of Central American States. Congress obliges on May 4.

APRIL

22 The Ottoman fleet captures the Greek island of Chios, which has rebelled against the Ottoman Empire, and massacres its Christian inhabitants or sells them as slaves.

MAY

- U.S. president James Monroe vetoes legislation erecting a toll on the Cumberland (or National) Road, connecting Cumberland, Maryland, and Wheeling, West Virginia. The president maintains that the federal government has no authority to operate a public road.
19 General Agustín de Itúrbide, having temporarily suppressed the movement for independence in Mexico, is elected emperor by the Constitutional Congress.

JUNE

- The authorities in Charleston, South Carolina, foil a slave rebellion orchestrated by local freeman Denmark Vesey. Scores of slaves and free blacks are arrested. Vesey and 34 others are hanged.
18 A Greek flotilla under Admiral Konstantin Kanaris routs the Ottoman fleet in the Strait of Chios in reprisal for the atrocities carried out by the Turks on the island of Chios.

JULY

7 The Ottoman invasion of Greece to suppress its revolt against the Ottoman Empire begins. The Turks overrun the peninsula north of the Gulf of Corinth.

SEPTEMBER

23 A Portuguese constitution is decreed, providing for liberty, legal equality, a single chamber which the king may not dissolve until its period of four years has expired, and a constitutional monarchy.

OCTOBER

20 The Congress of Verona opens, attended by representatives of Austria, Prussia, France, Russia, and Britain, to discuss European problems, notably the revolutions in Spain and Greece.

NOVEMBER

19 A French plan for intervention in Spain is tentatively accepted by the other powers at the Congress of Verona after opposition from Austria, Prussia, and Britain to an outright invasion. France is allowed to intervene in Spain if it is attacked or if the Spanish rebels depose King Ferdinand VII.

DECEMBER

14 The Congress of Verona on European problems comes to an end, having failed to discuss the Greek War of Independence.

SCIENCE, TECHNOLOGY, AND MEDICINE

Ecology

- A cyclone in Bengal kills 50,000 people.
- Canton in China is destroyed by fire.

OCTOBER

- Galungung volcano on Java erupts killing over 4,000 people.

Exploration

October 1822–24 Scottish fur trader James Weddell, surveying the South Atlantic, reaches a latitude of nearly 75° S and longitude of 35° W in the Southern Ocean, sailing into the Weddell Sea (named for him).

Health and Medicine

- New York, New York, is struck by yellow fever; thousands flee the city.
- The first U.S. patent is awarded to C. M. Graham, for artificial teeth.

JUNE

6 U.S. army surgeon William Beaumont begins the study of digestion when he treats a French-Canadian trapper wounded in the stomach by a shotgun blast. The wound has failed to heal and the remaining fistula allows examination of digestive processes.

Math

- French mathematician Jean-Victor Poncelet systematically develops the principles of projective geometry in *Traité des propriétés projectives des figures/ Treatise on the Projective Properties of Figures*.
- French mathematician Augustin-Louis Cauchy formulates the basic mathematical theory of elasticity; he defines stress as the load per unit area of the cross-section of a material.
- French mathematician Jean-Baptiste-Joseph Fourier publishes *Théorie analytique de la chaleur/Analytical theory of heat*, introducing a technique now known as Fourier analysis, which has widespread applications in mathematics, physics, and engineering.

Science

- German scientist Friedrich Mohs introduces a scale for specifying the hardness of minerals.
- Mary Anning discovers the first fossil to be recognized as that of a dinosaur—an *Iguanodon*—in Devon, England.
- The world's largest deposit of platinum is discovered in the Urals.

Technology

- U.S. inventor William Church patents the world's first typesetting machine in Britain. It consists of a keyboard and a magazine, in which the letters of type are stored. Pressing a key releases the corresponding letter in the magazine. Since the letters are delivered in a continuous row, words must be divided, and the line justified, by hand. •

ARTS AND IDEAS

Architecture

- St. Pancras Church in London, England, designed by the English architects Henry William Inwood and his father William Inwood, is completed, one of the finest examples of the Gothic Revival style.
- The Senate in Helsinki, Finland, designed by the German architect Carl Ludwig Engel, is completed.

Arts

c. 1822 The U.S. artist Raphaelle Peale paints *Venus Rising from the Sea – a Deception (After the Bath)*.
- The English artist John Martin paints *Destruction of Herculaneum*.

- The English artist John Constable paints *Yarmouth Harbour*.
- The French artist Eugène Delacroix paints *Dante and Virgil Crossing the Styx*.
- The German artist Caspar David Friedrich paints *Woman at the Window*.
- The Scottish artist David Wilkie paints *Chelsea Pensioners Reading the Gazette of the Battle of Waterloo*.
- The U.S. artist and inventor Samuel Finley Breese Morse paints *The Old House of Representatives*.
- The U.S. artist Charles Willson Peale paints *The Artist in His Museum*.

Literature and Language

- The French writer Alfred Victor, comte de Vigny, publishes *Poèmes/Poems*.
- The French writer Victor Hugo publishes *Odes et poésies diverses/Diverse Odes and Poems*.
- The German folklorists Jakob Ludwig Carl Grimm and his brother Wilhelm Carl Grimm publish the third volume of their famous *Kinder- und Hausmärchen/Fairy Tales*. Earlier volumes appeared in 1812 and 1815.
- The Italian writer Ugo Foscolo publishes his long poem *Le grazie/The Graces*. Fragments appeared in 1803 and 1818.
- The Russian poet Alexander Pushkin publishes his narrative poem *Bratya razboyniki/The Robber Brothers*.

BIRTHS & DEATHS

JANUARY
2 Rudolf Clausius, German physicist who formulated the second law of thermodynamics, born in Kölin, Prussia (now Koszalin, Poland) (–1888).
6 Heinrich Schliemann, German archeologist who excavated Troy, Mycenae, and Tiryns, born in Neubukow, Mecklenburg-Schwerin, Germany (–1890).
12 (Jean-Joseph-) Etienne Lenoir, Belgian inventor who built the first commercially successful internal combustion engine and the first automobile to be equipped with one, born in Mussy-la-Ville, Belgium (–1900).

FEBRUARY
25 William Pinkney, U.S. attorney general under President James Madison, dies in Washington, D.C. (57).

MARCH
16 John Pope, Union general during the Civil War, born in Louisville, Kentucky (–1892).
25 Albrecht Ritschl, German Lutheran theologian, born in Berlin, Germany (–1889).

APRIL
26 Frederick Law Olmsted, U.S. landscape architect who designed Central Park in New York, New York, born in Hartford, Connecticut (–1903).
27 Ulysses S. Grant, U.S. general who commanded the Union army during the last two years of the American Civil War and president 1863–77, born in Point Pleasant, Ohio (–1885).

MAY
26 Edmond de Goncourt, French writer, born in Nancy, France (–1896).

JUNE
25 E(rnst) T(heodor) A(madeus) Hoffmann, German writer, composer, and painter, dies in Berlin, Germany (46).

JULY
8 Percy Bysshe Shelley, English romantic lyric poet, dies at sea off Livorno, Tuscany, Italy (29).
22 Gregor Mendel, Austrian monk and botanist who laid the mathematical foundations of genetics, born in Heinzendorf, Austria (–1884).

AUGUST
19 Jean-Baptiste Joseph Delambre, French astronomer, dies in Paris, France (72).

SEPTEMBER
28 Louis Pasteur, French microbiologist who proved that microorganisms cause disease and fermentation and developed the process of pasteurization, born in Dole, France (–1895).

OCTOBER
13 Antonio Canova, Italian neoclassical sculptor, dies in Venice, Italy (64).

NOVEMBER
26 Karl August, Prince von Hardenberg, Prussian statesman who maintained the integrity of Prussia during the Napoleonic Wars, dies in Genoa, Italy (77).

DECEMBER
10 César (-Auguste) Franck, Belgian-born French composer, born in Liège, the United Netherlands (now in Belgium) (–1890).
24 Matthew Arnold, English poet and social critic, born in Laleham, Middlesex, England (–1888).

- The Swedish churchman and poet Esaias Tegnér publishes his popular narrative poem *Axel*.
- The U.S. writer John Neal publishes his novel *Logan, A Family History*.
- The U.S. writer Washington Irving publishes *Bracebridge Hall, or the Humourist*, a collection of sketches.

Music

- Austrian composer Franz Schubert stops work on his Symphony No. 8 in B minor (D 759), the *Unfinished*, but completes his Mass in A flat (D 678). He also completes his opera *Alfonso und Estrella* (D 732). It is first performed in 1854, in Weimar, Germany. In this year, he also writes his *Wanderer Fantasy* (D 760).
- German composer Ludwig van Beethoven completes his Mass in D major (Opus 123), the *Missa Solemnis*. He also completes his last piano sonata, No. 32 (Opus 111).
- The Royal Academy of Music is founded in London, England.

Theater and Dance

- The drama *Adelchi* by the Italian writer Alessandro Manzoni is first performed.

Thought and Scholarship

- The French writer Stendhal publishes his study *De l'Amour/On Love*.
- The German Association for Science is founded in Leipzig.

SOCIETY

Education

- Hobart College is founded as Geneva College in Geneva, New York.

JUNE

6   The president of the council of French universities is placed in charge of all education and of all teachers, thus ensuring clerical influence in education.

Everyday Life

- The English social reformer Francis Place publishes *Illustrations ... of the Principles of Population*, which advocates birth control.
- The streets of Boston, Massachusetts, are lit by gas for the first time.

Media and Communication

MARCH

17   A new press law in France prohibits the sale of newspapers unless they are approved by the government. Offenders are to be tried in royal courts, where magistrates take orders from government officials.

DECEMBER

20   *The Sunday Times* is founded in London, England, by its parent organization *The Times*, but with an independent editorial policy.

1823

POLITICS, GOVERNMENT, AND ECONOMICS

Politics and Government

- In eight separate acts of Parliament, the British home secretary Robert Peel abolishes the death penalty for over 100 crimes in Britain.
- U.S. army troops shatter an alliance of Sac, Fox, Winnebago, Pottawatomie, and Kickapoo peoples forged by the Sac chief Black Hawk to thwart U.S. expansion into Illinois.

- U.S. president James Monroe appoints New York jurist Smith Thompson to the U.S. Supreme Court.

JANUARY

31   Russia, Austria, France, and Prussia demand the abolition of the liberal Spanish constitution of 1812, but the cortes (national assembly) refuses. The ambassadors of those countries leave the Spanish capital, Madrid.

MARCH

19   Emperor Agustín de Itúrbide of Mexico is forced to abdicate by insurgents.

25   The British government formally recognizes the Greeks as belligerents in their war with the Ottoman Empire.

APRIL

6   The French army crosses the River Bidassoa and enters Spain to begin its attempt to reimpose conservative monarchical government there.

JUNE

5 Provincial diets, assemblies consisting of representatives of the nobility, middle class, and peasants, are established in Prussia.

11 King Ferdinand VII of Spain refuses to leave the capital, Madrid, in the face of the French invasion and is declared to be temporarily incapacitated. A provisional regency of the cortes (national assembly) is established to govern in the meantime.

18 King John VI annuls the Portuguese constitution of 1822 after risings against his rule and against the loss of Brazil.

JULY

• The U.S. secretary of state John Quincy Adams informs Russia that the United States will not recognize Russia's claim of September 4, 1821 to the Pacific coast of North America north of the 51st parallel.

1 The former Spanish colonies of Guatemala, San Salvador, Nicaragua, Honduras, and Costa Rica form the Confederation of the United Provinces of Central America.

AUGUST

31 The French army intervening against the Spanish liberal rebels led by Major Rafael de Riego storms the Trocadero in southern Spain and enters the rebel-held port of Cadiz.

SEPTEMBER

10 The South American revolutionary leader Simón Bolívar, having landed in Peru, is recognized as dictator and prepares to fight Spanish royalist forces.

OCTOBER

1 King Ferdinand VII of Spain, having been restored by the French who have crushed the Spanish rebellion, issues a decree for the execution of his enemies, and a reign of tyranny begins.

NOVEMBER

13 Emperor Pedro I dissolves the Brazilian assembly after several conspiracies against him, and a council of state is subsequently established to draw up a constitution for Brazil.

DECEMBER

2 The "Monroe Doctrine" is announced by the U.S. president James Monroe. It excludes European powers from interfering in the politics of any of the American republics and closes the entire American continent to colonial settlements by them.

SCIENCE, TECHNOLOGY, AND MEDICINE

Exploration

• Lake Chad, Central Africa, is discovered by British explorer Walter Oudney.

Health and Medicine

• Cholera strikes the Russian city of Astrakhan on the Caspian Sea, gateway to the rest of Europe.
• German physician Friedrich Adolphe Wilde invents the diaphragm contraceptive device.

Math

• English mathematician Charles Babbage begins construction of the "difference engine," a machine for calculating logarithms and trigonometric functions.

Science

• Bohemian physiologist Jan Purkinje classifies the various types of fingerprints, recognizing that they can be used as means of identification.
• English chemist Michael Faraday liquefies chlorine (for use in bleaches and water purification). He also discovers that certain gases condense until they cool when placed under constant pressure, a principle later used in refrigeration.
• English engineer William Sturgeon demonstrates the world's first electromagnet by wrapping a current-carrying wire around an iron bar. The 200-g/7-oz magnet can support 4 kg/9 lb and is an essential invention in the development of electric motors and the electric telegraph.
• French chemist Eugène-Michel Chevreul discovers the chemical processes involved in making soap, thus permitting industrial production.
• Italian botanist Giovanni Battista Amici proves the existence of sexual processes in flowering plants, by observing pollen approaching the plant ovary.
• Swedish chemist Jöns Jakob Berzelius isolates silicon (atomic no. 14).

Technology

• British inventor Francis Ronalds sets up a telegraph system on his estate at Hammersmith using wires attached to a battery at the transmitter end and to electrodes marked with a letter at the receiving end. He offers it to the British Admiralty which rejects the offer.
• U.S. inventor Jacob Perkins develops a steam engine capable of 1,400 psi (pounds per square inch).

Transportation

• English engineer Samuel Brown develops an internal combustion engine that uses hydrogen as a fuel and has separate combustion and working cylinders. He uses it to drive a vehicle up Shooter's Hill in London, England.
• The British government adopts John Loudon McAdam's method of road building—"Macadamization"—greatly facilitating transport and communication. It is quickly adopted in the United States.

ARTS AND IDEAS

Architecture

- The New Admiralty in St. Petersburg, Russia, designed by the Russian architect Adrian Dmitryevitch Zakharov, is completed.

Arts

- The Hudson River school, a group of U.S. painters rebelling against traditional design and preferring the European, more romantic portrayal of nature, begins to attract critical acclaim. The forerunners of the group include Thomas Cole, Ashe B. Durand, and Thomas Dought.
- The Norwegian artist Johan Christian Clausen Dahl paints *View from a Window over Pillnitz*.

Literature and Language

- The French poet Alphonse Marie Louis de Lamartine publishes *Nouvelles Méditations poétiques/New Poetic Meditations*.
- The French writer Stendhal publishes his critical study *Racine et Shakespeare/Racine and Shakespeare*, one of the first manifestos of romantic literature in France.
- The German writer Johann Wolfgang von Goethe publishes his lyric poem *Die Marienbader Elegie/The Marienbad Elegy*.
- The U.S. writer James Fenimore Cooper publishes *The Pioneers*, the first of the "Leatherstocking" novels.
- The U.S. writer James Kirke Paulding publishes the novel *Konigsmarke, the Long Finne*, a satire on the adventure stories of contemporary writers such as Walter Scott and James Fenimore Cooper.

Music

- Austrian composer Franz Schubert completes his opera *Fierrabras* (D 796). It is first performed in 1835, in Vienna, Austrian Empire. He also completes his incidental music (D 797) for the play *Rosamunde, Fürstin von Cypern/Rosamund, Princess of Cyprus* by Helmina von Chézy; his Piano Sonata No. 12 (D 784); and his song cycle *Die schöne Müllerin/The Fair Maid of the Mill* (D 795).
- German composer Ludwig van Beethoven completes his Symphony No. 9 in D minor, the *Choral* (Opus 125), and his variations on a waltz theme suggested by the Austrian music publisher Anton Diabelli (Opus 120).
- The opera *Euryanthe* by the German composer Carl Maria von Weber is first performed, in Vienna, Austria.
- The opera *Jessonda* by the German composer Ludwig Spohr is first performed, in Kassel, Germany.
- The opera *Leicester* by the French composer Daniel-François-Esprit Auber is first performed, in Paris, France. It is based on a story by Walter Scott.

Theater and Dance

- The play *Clari, or The Maid of Milan* by the U.S. dramatist John Howard Payne is first performed, in London, England. It is best remembered for the song "Home, Sweet Home."

Thought and Scholarship

- The French statesman and historian Adolph Thiers publishes the first volume of his ten-volume *Histoire de la Révolution française/History of the French Revolution*. The last volume appears in 1827.
- The Philadelphia author Charles Jared Ingersoll publishes *The Influence of America on the Mind*, a defense of U.S. politics and culture.
- The U.S. statesman John Taylor publishes *New Views of the Constitution*.

BIRTHS & DEATHS

- Mathew Brady, U.S. photographer known for his photographs of the American Civil War, born near Lake George, New York (–1896).

FEBRUARY

15 Li Hongzhang, leading 19th-century Chinese statesman who attempted to modernize China, born in Hefei, Anhwei province, China (–1901).

26 John Philip Kemble, English actor and theater manager, dies in Lausanne, Switzerland (66).

28 (Joseph-) Ernest Renan, French philosopher, historian, and religious scholar, born in Tréguier, France (–1892).

MARCH

14 Charles François Dumouriez, French general during the French Revolution who later defected to the Austrians, dies in Turville Park, Buckinghamshire, England (84).

APRIL

23 Joseph Nollekens, English neoclassical sculptor, dies in London, England (85).

JULY

8 Henry Raeburn, Scottish portrait painter, dies in Edinburgh, Scotland (66).

AUGUST

2 Lazare Carnot, French general who was instrumental in organizing the revolutionary forces during the French Revolution, dies in Magdeburg, Prussian Saxony (now Germany) (70).

20 Pope Pius VII, Italian pope 1800–23, dies in Rome (81).

SEPTEMBER

16 Francis Parkman, U.S. historian who wrote *England and France in North America*, born in Boston, Massachusetts (–1893).

DECEMBER

6 Max Müller, German Orientalist and philologist, born in Dessau, Germany (–1900).

SOCIETY

Education

- Trinity College is founded in Hartford, New York.

Religion

MAY

12 The Catholic Association is established in Ireland by the nationalist Daniel O'Connell to agitate for Catholic Emancipation (the removal of legal restrictions on Catholics) and independence.

SEPTEMBER

28 After the death of Pope Pius VII on August 20, the Italian clergyman Annibale Sermattei Della Genga is elected Pope Leo XII. He is pope until 1829.

Sports

- The first school gymnastics program in the United States is established at Round Hill School, Massachusetts, by Charles Beck, a disciple of the Prussian gymnastics pioneer Friedrich Ludwig Jahn.

MAY

27 A crowd of 60,000 at the Union race course, New York, New York, watch American Eclipse representing the North defeat Sir Henry, representing the South, in a best two-of-three contest. Such contests become a feature of U.S. horse racing in the 19th century.

NOVEMBER

- During a game of football (soccer) at Rugby School, England, William Webb Ellis, a pupil, picks up the ball and runs with it. This is traditionally regarded as the origin of the game of rugby, but it is several years before the game at the school becomes predominantly a handling as opposed to a kicking game.

1824

POLITICS, GOVERNMENT, AND ECONOMICS

Business and Economics

- English Quaker John Cadbury opens a tea and coffee shop in Birmingham, England, the beginnings of the Cadbury confectionery company.
- Textile weavers in Pawtucket, Rhode Island, strike for better wages and shorter hours in what is believed to be the first work stoppage involving women in the United States.
- The first recorded strike by women workers (weavers) takes place in Pawtucket, Rhode Island.
- Paolo Agnese sets up the first commercial pasta factory, in Imperia, Italy.

Colonization

DECEMBER

9 The Spanish army is defeated at the Battle of Ayacucho, Peru, by South American liberation forces under José de Sucre, and Peru achieves its independence.

12 Spanish royalist forces agree to leave South America.

31 The British foreign secretary George Canning recognizes the independence of Buenos Aires, Mexico, and Colombia, violating the Monroe Doctrine of 1823, which claims sole influence for the United States in the Americas.

Human Rights

- The radical Scots immigrant Frances Wright tours the United States, promoting abolition, temperance, women's rights, birth control, and public education.

Politics and Government

- New York State holds the nation's first nominating convention in which citizens select the electors of nominees for governor and lieutenant governor.
- The U.S. congressional elections mark a new course in U.S. political history: the faltering Federalist Party disintegrates and the Democratic-Republican Party splits into two camps, one a proadministration faction led by the secretary of state John Quincy Adams, the other an antiadministration faction led by the war hero Andrew Jackson. The proadministration faction attains slim majorities in both the House of Representatives (105–97) and Senate (26–20).

FEBRUARY

10 The South American revolutionary leader Simón Bolívar is proclaimed emperor of Peru.

24 The British governor-general of India, Lord Amherst, declares war against the Burmese as the latter have violated the territory of the British East India Company by capturing the island of Shahpuri.

MARCH

2 The U.S. Supreme Court, in the case *Gibbons v. Ogden*, removes the monopolies granted to steamboat operators on rivers, thus opening navigation of U.S. waterways to all steamboats and upholding federal jurisdiction in the regulation of interstate commerce.
27 A decree is issued in Brazil for the election of deputies to a legislative assembly, as part of Emperor Pedro I's constitutional reforms.

APRIL

• The United States and Russia settle the controversy over the northernmost coast of North America. Russia is granted the territory north of latitude 54° 40', in exchange for Russia's lifting of a fishing ban off its North American territorial waters.
4 The Greek island of Crete is captured by the Egyptians, who are assisting the Ottoman Empire in its war with the Greeks.
30 The garrison of Lisbon, Portugal, revolts against King John VI and recognizes his younger son, Dom Miguel, as ruler. The latter has placed himself at the head of a movement for restoring the absolutist rights of his father.
30 The U.S. Congress passes the Road Survey Act authorizing the Army Corps of Engineers to survey possible road and canal routes.

MAY

11 British forces take Rangoon, the Burmese capital, in their war with the Burmese.

JULY

7 The Ottoman Empire captures the Greek island of Ipsara.

AUGUST

• The Marquis de Lafayette, French hero of the American Revolution, arrives in the United States for a year-long visit commemorating his and France's contribution to that war.
• The U.S. state of Illinois abolishes slavery.
24 Simón Bolívar, Emperor of Peru, defeats Spanish forces at Junín in Peru.

SEPTEMBER

16 King Louis XVIII of France dies and is succeeded by his brother, Charles X.

OCTOBER

• The former Spanish colony of Mexico becomes a republic.
10 The Greek army inflicts a very heavy defeat on the Turks at Mitilini, on the Greek island of Lesbos.

DECEMBER

• In the U.S. presidential election, none of the four candidates gains a majority, leaving the House of Representatives to decide between John Quincy Adams and Andrew Jackson (recipients of the two highest totals of electoral votes) the following February.

SCIENCE, TECHNOLOGY, AND MEDICINE

Ecology

• Over 10,000 people die in St. Petersburg, Russia, when an ice jam causes the Neva River to flood.

Exploration

• The Geographical Society of Paris, France, offers a reward of 10,000 francs to any explorer who can reach and safely return from the sub-Saharan city of Timbuktu in Mali.
• The U.S. fur merchant Jedediah Strong Smith identifies a route through the Rocky Mountains that becomes known as the South Pass, affording access to the Green River of the future state of Utah.

Math

• German mathematician and astronomer Friedrich Wilhelm Bessel discovers a class of functions, now called Bessel functions, that arise in many areas of physics.
• Niels Henrik Abel of Norway proves that equations involving powers of x greater than four cannot be solved using a standard formula like that used for quadratic equations.
• Swiss mathematician Jakob Steiner develops inversive geometry.

Science

• English biochemist William Prout discovers that hydrochloric acid is the primary agent of digestion.
• French chemists Jean-Baptiste-André Dumas and C. Prevost show that sperm is essential to fertilization.
• Swedish chemist Jöns Jakob Berzelius isolates zirconium (atomic no. 40).
• Swiss botanist Augustin Pyrame de Candolle begins his 17-volume classification of plants *Prodromus systematis naturalis regni vegetabilis/Treatise on the Classification of the Plant Kingdom*. Completed in 1873 by his son Alphonse, it replaces Lamarck's classification system and serves as the model for future systems.
• French scientist Sadi Carnot publishes *Réflexions sur la puissance motrice du feu et sur les machines propres à développer cette puissance/Thoughts on the Motive Power of Fire, and on Machines Suitable for Developing that Power*, a pioneering study of thermodynamics in which he explains that a steam engine's power results from the decrease in temperature from the boiler to the condenser. He also describes the "Carnot cycle" whereby heat is converted into mechanical motion and mechanical motion converted into heat—the basis of the second law of thermodynamics.

Technology

- English mason Joseph Aspdin patents Portland cement. More water-resistant than other cements, it quickly becomes widely used.
- U.S. inventor William Church improves the printing press by adding a device to the cylinder to pick up, hold, and then release the sheets of paper.

Transportation

- French engineer Marc Séguin builds the world's first wire-cable suspension bridge over the Rhône River at Touron, France.

ARTS AND IDEAS

Architecture

- The Chapelle Expiatoire in Paris, France, designed by the French architect Pierre Fontaine, is completed.
- The Second Bank of the United States, in Philadelphia, Pennsylvania, designed by the U.S. architect William Strickland, is completed. It is among the finest U.S. examples of the Greek Revival style, its façade modeled on a Greek temple.

Arts

- The British government buys the paintings of financier John Julius Angerstein, a collection which will form the basis of the National Gallery in London, England.
- The English artist John Flaxman sculpts *Pastoral Apollo*.
- The French artist Eugène Delacroix paints *The Massacre at Chios*, a depiction of a contemporary event from the War of Greek Independence.

- The French artist Jean-Auguste-Dominique Ingres paints *The Vow of Louis XIII*.
- The German artist Caspar David Friedrich paints *Arctic Shipwreck*.
- The German artist Friedrich Johann Overbeck paints *Entry of Christ into Jerusalem*.
- The Spanish artist Francisco José de Goya y Lucientes paints *Bullfight* and *The Milkmaid of Bordeaux*.

Literature and Language

- The English poet George Gordon, Lord Byron, completes the publication of his "epic satire" *Don Juan*. Other parts appeared in 1819, 1821, and 1823.
- The English writer Mary Mitford publishes the first volume of her account of village life *Our Village: Sketches of Rural Life, Character and Scenery*. The final volume appears in 1832. The sketches began to appear in *Lady Magazine* in 1819.
- The English writer Walter Savage Landor publishes the first of his *Imaginary Conversations*, dialogues between famous historical figures.
- The Italian poet Giacomo Leopardi publishes his poetry collection *Canzoni e versi/Songs and Verses*.
- The Massachusetts abolitionist Lydia Maria Child publishes *Hobomok*, a sentimental novel celebrating the Native American.
- The Scottish historian Thomas Carlyle publishes his translation of Goethe's *Wilhelm Meisters Wanderjahre/ Wilhelm Meister's Wandering Years*, published in 1821. Carlyle is to play a major role in introducing English readers to German literature.
- The Scottish poet and novelist Walter Scott publishes his novel *Redgauntlet*.
- The U.S. writer George Tucker publishes his novel *The Valley of the Shenandoah*.
- The U.S. writer Washington Irving publishes *Tales of a Traveler*.

BIRTHS & DEATHS

- David Bushnell, U.S. inventor who built the *Turtle*, the first effective submarine, dies in Warrenton, Georgia (82).

JANUARY
21 Thomas "Stonewall" Jackson, one of the ablest Confederate generals in the American Civil War, born in Clarksburg, Virginia (–1863).
26 Théodore Géricault, French painter, dies in Paris, France (32).

FEBRUARY
14 Winfield Scott Hancock, Union general during the American Civil War and Democratic presidential candidate in 1880, born in Montgomery County, Pennsylvania (–1886).

MARCH
3 Giovanni Battista Viotti, Italian violinist and composer, dies in London, England (68).
8 Jean-Jacques-Régis de Cambacérès, French statesman who drafted the Code Napoleon, or Code Civil, dies in Paris, France (70).
12 Gustav Robert Kirchoff, German physicist who, with Robert Wilhelm von Bunsen, helped establish spectrum analysis, born in Königsberg, Prussia (–1887).

APRIL
19 George Gordon, Lord Byron, English romantic poet, dies in Missolonghi, Greece (36).

MAY
16 Edmund Kirby-Smith, commander of all Confederate forces west of the Mississippi for two years during the Civil War, born in St. Augustine, Florida (–1893).

AUGUST
8 Friedrich August Wolf, German classical scholar, the founder of modern philology, dies in Marseille, France (65).

SEPTEMBER
4 Josef Anton Bruckner, Austrian composer, born in Ansfelden, Austria (–1896).
16 Louis XVIII, King of France by title (he declared himself king) 1795–1814, and in fact 1814–24, dies in Paris, France (68).

Music

- Austrian composer Franz Schubert completes his String Quartets No. 13 (D 804) and No. 14 (D 810), *Der Tot und das Mädchen/Death and the Maiden.*
- German composer Felix Mendelssohn completes his Symphony No. 1 (Opus 11).

Thought and Scholarship

- The German historian Leopold von Ranke publishes *Geschichten der romanischen und germanischen Völker, 1494–1535/History of the Roman and Teutonic People, 1494–1535.*
- The German philosopher and educator Johann Friedrich Herbart publishes *Wissenschaft neu gegrundet auf Erfahrung, Metaphysik, und Mathematik/Psychology as Knowledge Newly Founded on Experience, Metaphysics, and Mathematics.*
- The Italian historian Carlo Botta publishes *Storia d'Italia dal 1789 al 1814/The History of Italy from 1789 to 1814.*

SOCIETY

Education

- At the age of 15 French educator Louis Braille develops a system of raised dots for the blind to read. The Braille system is published in 1829.
- Rensselaer Polytechnic Institute is founded in Troy, New York.

Everyday Life

- British member of Parliament Colonel Richard Martin founds the Society for the Prevention of Cruelty to Animals.

Media and Communication

- *Sunday School Magazine* is published in the United States.
- *Le Globe* newspaper is issued in Paris, France, edited by liberal journalist Paul Dubois.
- The *Christian Disciple* becomes the *Christian Examiner,* beginning a trajectory that will make it the leading religious periodical of the mid-19th century.

SEPTEMBER

29 The 1820 law censoring the French press is suspended, but the policy of the new king of France, Charles X, is generally illiberal.

Religion

- The ecumenical American Sunday School Union is established in the United States, as Sunday schools proliferate.

DECEMBER

4 The Catholic Association, founded by the Irish politician Daniel O'Connell, votes for the institution of a "Catholic Rent" to fund its activities, which quickly generates a huge income.

JANUARY

- Kenyon College is founded in Gambier, Ohio, as the Theological Seminary of the Protestant Episcopal Church.

1825

POLITICS, GOVERNMENT, AND ECONOMICS

Business and Economics

- Six hundred carpenters strike in Boston, Massachusetts, for a ten-hour day.
- The Suffolk Bank in Boston, Massachusetts, introduces the Suffolk, or pyramid, system by which rural banks agree to maintain deposits in the Suffolk Bank in

exchange for the Suffolk Bank redeeming rural bank notes.

Colonization

MARCH

- The new Mexican state of Texas-Coahuila authorizes U.S. colonization, begun by the U.S. slaveholder and real estate speculator Stephen Austin under Spanish rule in 1823.

AUGUST

6 Bolivia (Upper Peru) proclaims itself independent of Peru at a congress at Chuquisaca, Upper Peru.

25 Uruguay declares itself independent of Brazil.

29   Portugal recognizes Brazilian independence under Emperor Pedro I.

Human Rights

MAY

17   A Roman Catholic Relief Bill to give Catholics in Britain full parliamentary rights, moved by the radical member of Parliament Francis Burdett, is rejected by the House of Lords on its second reading.

Politics and Government

JANUARY

4   King Ferdinand I of Naples dies and is succeeded by his son, Francis I.

FEBRUARY

- After the failure of any presidential candidate to receive a majority the previous December, the U.S. House of Representatives selects John Quincy Adams as president over Andrew Jackson.
- The U.S. and Creek leaders sign a treaty by which the Creeks surrender their land in Georgia and agree to depart for the West by September 1826. The treaty is repudiated by the majority of the Creeks.

24   Egyptian forces land in the Ottoman province of Morea to support the Turks and begin to subdue the rebelling Greeks.

28   An Anglo-Russian treaty is signed over the latter's territory on the northwest coast of America and over the two countries' respective rights in the Pacific Ocean.

MARCH

4   John Quincy Adams is inaugurated as sixth president of the United States.

APRIL

15   A French law makes sacrilege a capital offense, part of King Charles X's attempts to uphold the position of the church in France.

27   A French law of indemnity compensates nobles for losses they incurred in the French Revolution.

JUNE

6   The Greeks, in revolt against the Ottoman Empire, put forward proposals to place themselves under British protection.

JULY

24   The Greek provisional government, hard-pressed in its revolt against the Ottoman Empire by simultaneous invasions of Greece by Ottoman and Egyptian armies, passes proposals to place the country under British protection (subsequently rejected by the British government).

SEPTEMBER

19   The Hungarian diet (national assembly) is reconvened after 13 years, and because of Hungarian discontent the Austrian emperor, Francis I, agrees to triennial meetings.

DECEMBER

1   Alexander I, Emperor of Russia 1801–25 who was instrumental in defeating the French emperor Napoleon I, dies in Taganrog, Russia, and is succeded by Nicholas I, his younger brother.

10   Brazil declares war against Argentina following Argentine support for a secessionist movement in the Brazilian Banda Oriental provinces (modern Uruguay).

SCIENCE, TECHNOLOGY, AND MEDICINE

Ecology

- A forest fire in New Brunswick, Canada, destroys over 1.62 million ha/4 million acres and several towns.

Exploration

FEBRUARY

25   British vet, explorer, and East India Company agent William Moorcroft, having journeyed for five years and crossed the Himalayas into Tibet, reaches Bukhara.

Science

- French physicist André Ampère publishes *Electrodynamics*, in which he formulates the mathematical laws governing electric currents and magnetic fields. It lays the foundation for electromagnetic theory.
- Danish scientist Hans Christian Oersted isolates aluminum (atomic no. 13) in powdered form.
- English astronomer John Herschel invents the actinometer for measuring the sun's light energy.
- English scientist Michael Faraday isolates benzene by distilling whale oil.
- German physicists Wilhelm Eduard Weber and Ernst Heinrich Weber publish *Treatise on Magnetic Waves*, which investigates the earth's magnetism and explains how a substance may be unmagnetized.
- Scottish botanist David Douglas discovers the Douglas Fir on the northwest coast of America.
- Swedish chemist Jöns Jakob Berzelius isolates titanium (atomic no. 22).

Technology

- English engineer Samuel Brown develops a water-cooling system to cool engines.
- French engineer Jacques de Montgolfier designs the uniflow engine, a steam engine that exhausts steam in the center of the cylinder.
- The British company Sharp, Roberts, and Company develops an automatic spinning mule.

- The U.S. glassmaker Deming Jarves opens his glassworks in Sandwich, Massachusetts, employing one of the first mechanical glass pressers.
- U.S. inventor Thomas Kensett receives a patent for a tin-plated can.
- John Ayrton develops the traumatrope, a device that gives the illusion of motion.

Transportation

- English engineer George Cayley invents caterpillar treads.
- U.S. engineer John Stevens constructs the first steam locomotive to run on rails in the United States. It runs on a short circular track at his home in Hoboken, New Jersey.

SEPTEMBER

27 The Stockton to Darlington railroad in England opens. Built by George Stephenson, it is the world's first public railroad to carry steam trains. Stephenson's locomotive *Active* carries 450 passengers at 24 kph/15 mph over the 43-km/27-mi track.

OCTOBER

25 The canal boat *Seneca Chief* opens the Erie Canal. Linking the Great Lakes with the Hudson River, it opens the Midwest to settlement.

October 1825–43 English engineer Isambard Kingdom Brunel's Thames Tunnel, the first under a river, is constructed. Its success on opening to pedestrian traffic prompts British solicitor Charles Pearson to propose the construction of a subway system for London, England.

ARTS AND IDEAS

Architecture

- The Kasino at Schloss Glienicke, near Potsdam, Germany, designed by the German architect Karl Friedrich Schinkel, is completed.
- The rebuilding of the town of Karlsruhe, Germany, planned by the German architect Friedrich Weinbrenner, is completed.

Arts

- The English artist John Constable paints *Leaping Horse*.
- The English artist Samuel Palmer paints *Early Morning*.
- The English artist William Etty paints *The Combat: Woman Pleading for the Defeated*.
- The German artist Peter von Cornelius paints the fresco *The Last Judgment* in the Ludwigskirche in Munich, Germany.
- The U.S. artist Sarah Miriam Peale paints *A Slice of Water Melon*.

Literature and Language

- The Ecuadorian poet José Joaquín Olmeda publishes his heroic poem "La victoria de Junín: canto a Bolívar"/ "The Victory at Junín: Song to Bolívar."
- The English historian Thomas Babington, Lord Macaulay, publishes his "Essay on Milton" in the literary journal the *Edinburgh Review*.
- The English writer and critic William Hazlitt publishes *The Spirit of the Age; or Contemporary Portraits*, one of his finest collections of essays.
- The Italian writer Alessandro Manzoni publishes *I promessi sposi/The Betrothed*, one of the great novels of Italian literature.
- The Swedish churchman and poet Esaias Tegnér publishes his epic cycle *Frithjofs Saga/The Saga of Frithjof*, based on Scandinavian myths.

Music

- Austrian composer Franz Schubert completes his Symphony No. 9 in C major (D 944), the *Great*; his Piano Sonatas No. 13 (D 840), No. 14 (D 845), and No. 15 (D 850); and writes the song *Nacht und Träume/ Night and Dreams* (D 827).
- German composer Ludwig van Beethoven completes his String Quartets No. 12 (Opus 127) and No. 15 (Opus 132).

Theater and Dance

- The comedy *The Forest Rose* by the U.S. writer Samuel Woodworth is first performed, in New York, New York.
- The tragedy *König Ottokars Glück und Ende/King Ottocar's Rise and Fall* by the Austrian dramatist Franz Grillparzer is first performed, in Vienna, Austria.

Thought and Scholarship

- The French historian Augustin Thierry publishes *Histoire de la conquête d'Angleterre par les Normands/ History of the Norman Conquest of England*, widely considered his most important book.
- The U.S. writer James Kirke Paulding publishes *John Bull in America, or the New Munchausen*.

SOCIETY

Everyday Life

- New York State opens a reformatory for juvenile boys, the first to operate under the so-called "cottage system."

JANUARY

- The British social reformer Robert Owen establishes the secular utopian community New Harmony, Indiana, on the grounds of the German-born U.S. visionary George Rapp's old settlement, Harmony.

Media and Communication

- The periodical *American Traveler* is published in Boston, Massachusetts, as travel becomes increasingly fashionable.
- The Presbyterian religious periodical *Biblical Repertory* begins publication.

Sports

MAY

16   The New York Trotting Club opens the first purpose-built trotting course in the United States, the Union Course, Long Island, New York.

BIRTHS & DEATHS

c. 1825   Jean Lafitte, U.S. privateer and smuggler who defended New Orleans during the War of 1812, dies (*c.* 45).

JANUARY

25   George Edward Pickett, Confederate general during the Civil War, born in Richmond, Virginia (–1875).

APRIL

11   Ferdinand Lassalle, German socialist who was instrumental in founding the German Labor movement, born in Breslau, Prussia (now Wrocław, Poland) (–1864).

16   Henry Fuseli, Swiss-born English painter, dies in Putney, London, England (84).

MAY

7   Antonio Salieri, Austrian composer, dies in Vienna, Austria (74).

19   Claude-Henri de Rouvroy, comte de Saint-Simon, French social reformer, one of the founders of Christian Socialism, dies in Paris, France (65).

20   Antoinette Brown Blackwell, U.S. Congregationalist and Unitarian minister, and the first woman minister in the United States, born in Henrietta, New York (–1921).

JUNE

1   John Hunt Morgan, U.S. Confederate guerrilla, leader of "Morgan's Raiders," born in Huntsville, Alabama (–1864).

11   Daniel P. Tompkins, U.S. vice president under James Monroe, dies in Staten Island, New York (50).

OCTOBER

10   Paul Kruger, Boer statesman who founded the Afrikaaner nation and was instrumental in initiating the Second Anglo-Boer War, born in Cradock district, Cape Colony, southern Africa (–1904).

25   Johann Strauss, Austrian composer of Viennese waltzes and operettas, born in Vienna, Austria (–1899).

NOVEMBER

9   A(mbrose) P(owell) Hill, Confederate general in the American Civil War, born in Culpeper, Virginia (–1865).

10   Thomas Macdonough, U.S. naval officer who defeated the British at the Battle of Plattsburg in the War of 1812, dies at sea en route from the Mediterranean to New York, New York (41).

14   Johann Paul Friedrich Richter ("Jean Paul"), German novelist, dies in Bayreuth, Bavaria (62).

29   Jean-Martin Charcot, French physician and one of the founders of modern neurology, born in Paris, France (–1893).

DECEMBER

8   Eli Whitney, inventor of the cotton gin, dies in New Haven, Connecticut (59).

29   Jacques-Louis David, French neoclassical painter known for his paintings of historical events, dies in Brussels, in the Kingdom of the United Netherlands (now in Belgium) (77).

1826

POLITICS, GOVERNMENT, AND ECONOMICS

Business and Economics

- U.S. economist Langdon Byllesby publishes *Observations on the Sources and Effects of Unequal Wealth*.

Politics and Government

- In the U.S. congressional elections, the Jacksonian or antiadministration faction of the Democratic-Republicans attains majorities in the House of Representatives (119–94) and Senate (28–20).
- The U.S. state of Pennsylvania makes kidnapping a felony, thus nullifying the federal fugitive slave law of 1793.
- U.S. president John Quincy Adams appoints the Kentucky jurist Robert Trimble to the U.S. Supreme Court.

JANUARY

- Representatives of the U.S. government and Creek leaders sign the Treaty of Washington, revising the treaty of the previous February. The new treaty requires the Creeks to cede less territory and grants them an additional year before departing the ceded land.

FEBRUARY

24 By the Treaty of Yandabu, ending the Burmese War, the British gain Assam, Arakan, and Terasserim, while the Burmese pay an indemnity and come under British influence.

MARCH

10 King John VI of Portugal dies and is succeeded by his son, Emperor Pedro I of Brazil, as King Pedro IV.
25 The Brazilian constitution is promulgated, establishing a hereditary monarchy and a general assembly of two chambers.

APRIL

- The U.S. secretary of state Henry Clay fights a duel with the Virginia representative John Randolph in which neither party is hurt. Randolph had allegedly insulted Clay and the administration of President John Quincy Adams.
4 The St. Petersburg Protocol is signed between Britain and Russia, agreeing that the Greek problem should be

solved by establishing the complete autonomy of Greece under Ottoman suzerainty.
5 Russia gives an ultimatum to the Ottoman Empire over Serbia and the Danubian provinces (Moldavia and Wallachia), stating that they must be evacuated by Ottoman troops and be the subject of a final settlement.
22 Ibrahim, son of the governor of Egypt Mehmet Ali, acting on behalf of the Ottoman Empire, takes the Greek town of Missolonghi.
29 A liberal constitution is promulgated in Portugal, providing for a hereditary monarchy with legislative power in the hands of a cortes (national assembly) of two chambers.

MAY

2 King Pedro IV waives his right of accession to the Portuguese throne in order to remain emperor in Brazil; his daughter, Maria da Gloria, is to become queen, provided that Dom Miguel, Pedro IV's brother, marries her.

JUNE

- Ailing former U.S. president and founding father John Quincy Adams utters the words "Independence now and Independence forever!"—to be read on the 50th anniversary of the Declaration of Independence.
19 Mahmud II, Sultan of the Ottoman Empire, decrees that his politically powerful bodyguard, the janissaries, should be disbanded. They revolt and are subsequently massacred.
20 A treaty of commerce is agreed between Siam (modern Thailand) and Britain, under which Perak and Selangor are declared independent, Kedah becomes Siamese territory, and Britain obtains the Isle of Pangkor and the Sembilan Islands.

JULY

15 The Pan-American Congress ends without agreement on uniting the South American republics.

AUGUST

- In a stirring eulogy to the former U.S. president and founding father John Adams, who died on July 4, the U.S. politician and orator Daniel Webster quotes Adams as having declared boldly in 1776, "Sink or swim, live or die, survive or perish, I give my hand and heart to this vote" (in favor of the U.S. Declaration of Independence).

SEPTEMBER

28 Russia declares war against Persia over its encroachment into the Transcaucasian region.

OCTOBER

7 The Akkerman Convention settles the problem of the Danubian provinces (Moldavia and Wallachia) and

Serbia, with the Turks evacuating key fortresses and allowing Russia full access to the Dardanelles.

30   The new Portuguese cortes (national assembly), vested with legislative rights by the constitution of April 29, meets for the first time.

DECEMBER

12   The British foreign secretary George Canning agrees to send troops to Portugal to counteract the threat of a Spanish invasion in support of Dom Miguel, who is trying to obtain the throne from the rightful heir, Maria da Gloria.

19   A treaty of commerce between Prussia and Mecklenburg–Schwerin advances the idea of a *Zollverein* (customs union) between the German states.

SCIENCE, TECHNOLOGY, AND MEDICINE

Exploration

AUGUST

- The U.S. merchant and explorer Jedediah Strong Smith departs the Great Salt Lake, Utah, for San Gabriel Mission, California, where he arrives on November 27. Smith's expeditions help chart the American West.

Science

- English administrator Stamford Raffles founds the Royal Zoological Society in London, England.
- English astronomer John Herschel begins to measure the parallax of stars—the apparent shift in a star's position relative to a neighbor caused by the earth's revolution around the sun. He thus conclusively proves that the earth revolves around the sun.
- English chemist H. Hennel and French chemist G. S. Sérullas independently synthesize alcohol.
- French chemist Antoine-Jérôrome Balard discovers bromine (atomic no. 35).
- French physician Pierre Salomon Ségalas, using a candlelit speculum (mirror), performs the first endoscopy when he examines a patient's bladder.
- German astronomer Heinrich Olbers formulates the paradox named for him: why is the night sky dark if there are an infinite number of stars?
- Italian physicist Leopoldo Nobili invents the astatic galvanometer that measures small electric currents without interference from the earth's magnetism.

Technology

- *c.* 1826   Axes, shovels, spades, and other implements begin to be produced by machines rather than by hand in the United States.
- English inventor James Sharp develops the first practical gas cooker, which he installs in his home.

- Scottish inventor Patrick Bell develops a mechanical reaper. Its success is limited, however, because it has to be pushed.
- Using a camera obscura and an eight-hour exposure, French inventor Joseph-Nicéphore Niepce takes a crude photograph of his barnyard from a window on his estate. It is the world's first photograph. He uses light-sensitive bitumen of Judea (a type of asphalt) to fix the image on a pewter plate. He also makes two prints of an engraved portrait using light to reproduce the image on chemically sensitized paper; it is the first example of a photochemical reproduction process.

Transportation

- The Dutch steamship *Curaçao* crosses the Atlantic; most of the journey is done under sail rather than by using the paddlewheels.
- The Granite Railway, a 4.8-km/3-mi track for hauling granite, is built in Massachusetts—the first railroad in the United States.
- The world's first railroad tunnel is built on the Liverpool–Manchester railroad in England.

ARTS AND IDEAS

Architecture

- The University of Virginia in Charlottesville, Virginia, designed by the U.S. statesman Thomas Jefferson, is completed. Among its outstanding buildings is the Rotunda, a library based on the Pantheon in Rome, Italy.
- French-born British engineer Marc Isambard Brunel builds the world's first floating landing piers, at Liverpool, England.
- The U.S. architect Alexander Parris lays the foundations of Quincy Market, Boston, Massachusetts, which will become a hub of commerce.

Arts

- The English artist John Constable paints *The Cornfield*.
- U.S. artist and inventor Samuel Finley Breese Morse paints his *Portrait of the Marquis de Lafayette*.

Literature and Language

- The English poet Elizabeth Barrett Browning publishes her poetry collection *Essay on Mind, with Other Poems*.
- The English statesman and writer Benjamin Disraeli, Earl of Beaconsfield, publishes his novel *Vivian Grey*.
- The French writer Alfred Victor, comte de Vigny, publishes his historical novel *Cinq mars/The Fifth of March*.
- The German poet Heinrich Heine publishes the first of his four volumes of travel reflections *Reisebilder/Travel Pictures*.

- The German writer Joseph, Baron von Eichendorff, publishes his novel *Aus dem Leben eines Taugenichts/ Memoirs of a Good-for-Nothing*.
- The Scottish poet and novelist Walter Scott publishes his novel *Woodstock*.
- The U.S. missionary and novelist Timothy Flint publishes *Recollections of the Last Ten Years*, an account of life in the Mississippi Valley.
- The U.S. writer James Fenimore Cooper publishes his novel *The Last of the Mohicans*.

Music

- Austrian composer Franz Schubert completes his String Quartet No. 15 (D 887) and his Piano Sonata No. 16 (D 894), and writes the song *An Sylvia* (D 891), using a text translated from Shakespeare.
- German composer Felix Mendelssohn completes his orchestral work *A Midsummer Night's Dream*.
- German composer Ludwig van Beethoven completes his String Quartets No. 13 (Opus 130), No. 14 (Opus 131), and No. 16 (Opus 135).
- The opera *Elvida* by the Italian composer Gaetano Donizetti is first performed, in Naples, Italy.
- The opera *Oberon* by the German composer Carl Maria von Weber is first performed, in London, England.

Theater and Dance

- The tragedy *Superstition* by the U.S. dramatist James Nelson Barker is published.

Thought and Scholarship

- The foremost U.S. legal scholar James Kent publishes the first of his four-volume *Commentaries on American Law*.

SOCIETY

Education

- Case Western Reserve University is founded in Cleveland, Ohio.
- Furman University is founded in Greenville, South Carolina.
- Lafayette College is founded in Easton, Pennsylvania.
- The German literature instructor Charles Follen introduces gymnastics into the Harvard College curriculum. Gymnastics is already common in German universities.

Everyday Life

- Streets in Berlin, Germany, begin to be lit with gas lamps.
- The radical thinker Richard Carlile writes *Every Woman's Book*, a birth control manual.

FEBRUARY

- A group of U.S. reformers found the American Temperance Society, to seek the regulation and (ultimately) prohibition of alcohol throughout the nation.

Media and Communication

- The U.S. minister and temperance crusader William Collier establishes the temperance movement journal *National Philanthropist*.

BIRTHS & DEATHS

FEBRUARY

9   John A. Logan, U.S. congressman and Union general during the Civil War, born in Jackson County, Illinois (–1886).

22   Charles Willson Peale, U.S. painter noted for his paintings of leaders of the American Revolution, born in Queen Annes County, Maryland (85).

MARCH

29   Wilhelm Liebnecht, German Socialist who cofounded the German Social Democratic Party, born in Giessen, Hesse (–1900).

APRIL

6   Gustave Moreau, French Symbolist painter, born in Paris, France (–1898).

JUNE

5   Carl Maria von Weber, German composer, dies in London, England (39).

JULY

4   John Adams, second president of the United States 1797–1801, a Federalist, dies in Braintree, Massachusetts (90).

4   Thomas Jefferson, third president of the United States 1801–09, a Democratic-Republican, dies in Monticello, Virginia (83).

SEPTEMBER

17   Georg Friedrich Berhard Riemann, German mathematician whose work in geometry influenced relativity theory, born in Breselenz in the kingdom of Hanover (–1866).

DECEMBER

1   William Mahone, Confederate general during the Civil War, railroad magnate and politician, born in Southampton County, Virginia (–1895).

7   John Flaxman, English neoclassical sculptor and designer, dies in London, England (71).

Religion

- The U.S. Congregationalist Church creates the American Home Missionary Society to propagate the Bible in the American South.

1827

POLITICS, GOVERNMENT, AND ECONOMICS

Business and Economics

- The German-born U.S. economist Friedrich List publishes *Outlines of American Political Economy*, which makes the case for protective tariffs to promote U.S. manufacturing.
- The U.S. merchant banker Phillip E. Thomas and associates incorporate the Baltimore and Ohio Railroad, designed to compete for business with the Erie Canal.

Politics and Government

JANUARY
1 British forces arrive in Lisbon to defend Queen Maria of Portugal against possible attack by Spain in support of Dom Miguel.
26 Peru secedes from Colombia in protest at dictator Simón Bolívar's alleged tyranny.

FEBRUARY
- Sectional animosity stirs in the U.S. Senate as the vice president John C. Calhoun, a southerner, casts the deciding vote in defeating a proposed tariff on raw and finished wool, designed to protect northern manufacturing.
- The U.S. Supreme Court, in the case *Martin v. Mott*, upholds the president's authority to call out the militia in cases of emergency.
20 Brazilian forces are defeated at the Battle of Ituziango by the combined armies of Uruguay and Argentina.

MARCH
- In acknowledgment of the growing importance of the U.S. postal service, Congress raises the salary of the postmaster general to the same level as that of other cabinet officers.

APRIL
4 A diplomatic note is sent from Russia, France, and Britain to Sultan Mahmud II of the Ottoman Empire urging a truce in his war with Greece.
10 The Tory foreign secretary George Canning becomes prime minister of Britain, forming a government of liberal Tories and moderate Whigs.
29 Count Capo d'Istria is elected president of Greece.
30 King Charles X of France dissolves the French National Guard (a militia) by decree after a period of civil unrest. The decree is unpopular among the middle classes who dominate it.

JUNE
5 The Ottoman army captures the Acropolis and enters Athens in its war with the Greek rebels.
9 An Ottoman manifesto rejects the allied note of April 4 recommending a truce with Greece.
18 A concordat between the United Netherlands and Pope Leo XII is signed, allowing the Dutch greater influence in their church affairs.
21 The British home secretary Robert Peel reforms the criminal law by further reducing the number of capital offenses, abolishing the immunity of clergy from arrest in cases of felony, and recodifying offenses against property in a simplified form.
24 The French prime minister Jean Villèle uses a royal ordinance to censor the press.

JULY
- Delegates from 13 northern, industrialized U.S. states attend a convention in Harrisburg, Pennsylvania, to call for a protective tariff.
- The Protocol of St. Petersburg between Britain and Russia agreeing that Greece should be independent is extended into a treaty to include France.
3 King Pedro IV of Portugal (Emperor Pedro I, of Brazil) appoints Dom Miguel lieutenant general of Portugal to rule in his place.
6 The Treaty of London is signed by which Russia, Britain, and France agree to recognize the autonomy of Greece and so force Sultan Mahmud II of the Ottoman Empire to make peace with the Greeks.

AUGUST

- The United States and Britain sign a treaty extending their joint occupation of the Oregon country, between the California border and the Russian-occupied part of North America (modern Alaska).
- 16 Sultan Mahmud II of the Ottoman Empire rejects the attempt of Russia, France, and Britain to force him to make peace with the Greeks.

OCTOBER

- 1 Russia defeats Persian forces in its war with Transcaucasia and takes Erivan in Armenia.
- 20 The Ottoman and Egyptian fleets are destroyed by allied (British, French, and Russian) squadrons in the Battle of Navarino, in the Greek War of Independence.

NOVEMBER

- The Creek nation cedes its remaining land in the southeastern United States to the federal government and departs for the Midwest.
- 17–24 In the French elections the ultra-conservatives are defeated by the liberal opposition.

DECEMBER

- 26 Sultan Mahmud II of the Ottoman Empire rejects the right of the allies to mediate in the war between the Ottoman Empire and Greece.

SCIENCE, TECHNOLOGY, AND MEDICINE

Ecology

- French engineer Benoît Fourneyron builds the world's first water turbine. It generates 6 horsepower.

Exploration

December 1827–30 Indian-born English explorer Charles Sturt and his guide Hamilton Hume explore the Australian interior, discovering and following the Darling and Murray rivers. Their expedition disproves the popular theory among settlers and Europeans of a great inland sea at the heart of the continent, and encourages settler interest in South Australia.

Health and Medicine

- British physician Richard Bright describes the inflammation of the structures in the kidney that produce urine, in *Reports of Medical Cases*. It is now called Bright's disease.

Math

- German mathematician Karl Friedrich Gauss introduces the subject of differential geometry that describes features of surfaces by analyzing curves that lie on it—the intrinsic-surface theory.

Science

- English chemist John Walker invents the friction match ("Lucifer"); made with antimony sulfide and potassium chloride, it is ignited by drawing it through sandpaper.
- Estonian embryologist Karl von Baer reports the discovery of eggs in mammals and humans in *Epistola de ovo mammalium et hominis generis/On the Mammalian Egg and the Origin of Man*. It dispels the idea of the preformation of the embryo.
- German chemist Friedrich Wöhler produces aluminum in bar form.
- German physicist Georg Ohm formulates Ohm's Law, which states that the current flowing through an electric circuit is directly proportional to the voltage, and indirectly proportional to the resistance.

December 1827–38 U.S. ornithologist John James Audubon publishes the first volume of his multivolume work *Birds of America*.

Technology

- U.S. inventor Jacob Perkins develops an improved uniflow engine.
- William Nicol develops a polarizing microscope and a method of grinding sections of rock to transparent thinness.

Transportation

- Hammersmith Bridge opens in London, England. It is the world's first suspension bridge made of stone and metal.
- The first railroads in continental Europe are built: a horse-drawn tramway between Budweis, Bohemia, and Linz, Austria, and the St.-Etienne to Andrézieux railroad in France. The latter uses horses and carries only freight.

FEBRUARY

- 28 The Baltimore and Ohio Railroad becomes the first railroad in the United States to be chartered to carry freight and passengers. The railroad is built to compete with the Erie Canal, which is taking business away from Baltimore, Maryland.

NOVEMBER

- French inventor Onésiphore Pecqueur invents the differential gear for use on steam-driven vehicles. It transmits the power from the engine to the wheels while allowing them to turn at different speeds when the vehicle goes around corners.

ARTS AND IDEAS

Architecture

- Regent Street in London, England, designed by the English architect John Nash, is completed.
- The County Records Office in Charleston, South Carolina, designed by the U.S. architect Robert Mills, is completed.

- The U.S. army colonel Henry H. Leavenworth constructs Fort Leavenworth on the Missouri River in the future state of Kansas. The fort serves as a embarkation point for settlers heading west along the Santa Fé Trail.

Arts

- The English artist John Constable paints *The Chain Pier, Brighton*.
- The French artist Camille Corot paints *The Bridge at Narni*.
- The French artist Eugène Delacroix paints *The Death of Sardanapalus*.
- The French artist Jean-Auguste-Dominique Ingres paints *The Apotheosis of Homer*.

Literature and Language

- The Boston writer Sarah Josepha Hale publishes *Northwood*, an antislavery novel.
- The critical literary journal *Western Monthly Review* begins publication in the United States.
- The English churchman and poet John Keble publishes his collection of religious poems *The Christian Year*.
- The English poet John Clare publishes his cycle of poems *The Shepherd's Calendar*.
- The English writers Alfred Tennyson, Charles Tennyson Turner, and Frederick Tennyson publish the (misnamed) *Poems by Two Brothers*.
- The French writer Stendhal publishes *Armance*, his first novel.
- The French writer Victor Hugo publishes his *Preface* to his unstaged drama *Cromwell*. The *Preface* becomes one of the most important manifestos of the French romantic movement.
- The German poet Heinrich Heine publishes his poetry collection *Buch der Lieder/Book of Songs*.
- The U.S. novelist James Fenimore Cooper publishes his novel *The Prairie*.
- The U.S. writer Edgar Allan Poe publishes *Tamerlane and Other Poems* anonymously.

- The U.S. writer George Tucker publishes his satirical novel *A Voyage to the Moon*, under the pseudonym Joseph Atterley.

Music

- Austrian composer Franz Schubert completes his *Deutsche Messe/German Mass* (D 872); his Piano Trios No. 1 (D 898) and No. 2 (D 929); and his song cycle *Winterreise/Winter Journey* (D 911).
- The opera *Il pirata/The Pirate* by the Italian composer Vicenzo Bellini is first performed, in Milan, Italy.

Thought and Scholarship

- The German philosopher Georg Wilhelm Friedrich Hegel publishes the second part of his *Enzyklopädie der philosophischen Wissenschaften im Grundrisse/ Encyclopedia of Philosophical Science in Outline*. The first part appeared in 1817.
- The Italian poet Giacomo Leopardi publishes *Operette morali/Minor Moral Works*, a collection of philosophical dialogues.

SOCIETY

Education

- The U.S. state of Massachusetts adopts the nation's first compulsory education law, mandating tax-supported schools in every Massachusetts community with 500 families or more. The law also makes the study of U.S. history obligatory.
- The University of Toronto is founded in Ontario, Canada.

Everyday Life

- English clergyman Thomas Malthus's sixth edition of his 1798 pamphlet *An Essay on the Principle of Population* expresses the view that the poor laws only

---

BIRTHS & DEATHS

FEBRUARY

17 Johann Heinrich Pestalozzi, Swiss educator who advocated educating the poor, dies in Brugg, Switzerland (81).

MARCH

5 Alessandro Volta, Italian physicist who invented the electric battery, dies in Como, Lombardy, Italy (82).

5 Pierre-Simon de Laplace, French mathematician and astronomer who demonstrated the stability of the solar system, dies in Paris, France (77).

26 Ludwig van Beethoven, German classical romantic composer, dies in Vienna, Austria (56).

APRIL

10 Lewis Wallace, Union general during the Civil War and author of *Ben-Hur*, born in Brookville, Indiana (–1905).

22 Thomas Rowlandson, English painter and caricaturist, dies in London, England (70).

OCTOBER

10 Ugo Foscolo, Italian poet and novelist, dies in Turnham Green, near London, England (49).

11 Christian Ditley, Count Reventlow, Danish politician whose agricultural reforms abolished serfdom in Denmark, dies in Lolland, Denmark (79).

DECEMBER

7 Saigo Takamori, Japanese leader who led the rebellion that overthrew the Tokugawa shogunate and then later rebelled against the new Imperial government, born in Kagoshima, Japan (–1877).

encourage large families; he encourages people to marry late and to exercise "moral restrain" as a means of economic control.

- The first Mardi Gras celebrations take place in New Orleans, Louisiana, introduced by French students.

November 1827–38 A period of Irish and German migration to the United States begins due to a severe winter in 1829, increased legislation against German Jews, economic stress in Ireland, and Irish factionalism.

MAY

- The Ohio inventor and anarchist Josiah Warren opens his self-styled "equity" store in Cincinnati, Ohio, where he charges customers little above cost with the aim of demonstrating the principle of "labor for labor."

Media and Communication

- The *American Quarterly Review*, a literary, legal, and political journal, is published in Philadelphia, Pennsylvania.
- The U.S. entrepreneur and reformer Arthur Tappan establishes the *Journal of Commerce* in New York, New York, to promote both commerce and morality.

Sports

JUNE

4–5 The inaugural cricket match between Oxford University and Cambridge University takes place at the Lord's ground, London, England. The game ends in a tie.

JULY

- The first U.S. swimming academy opens, in Boston, Massachusetts.

1828

POLITICS, GOVERNMENT, AND ECONOMICS

Business and Economics

- Prussia forms a customs union with Hesse-Darmstadt, extending its free trade area.
- The Boston businessman Willard Phillips publishes *A Manual of Political Economy*, in which he defends the protective tariff as good for both New England and the United States as a whole.
- U.S. workers staging what is believed to be the nation's first factory strike in Patterson, New Jersey, are greeted by the state militia, summoned for the first time to quash industrial unrest.

MAY

- The U.S. president John Quincy Adams signs the so-called "Tariff of Abominations," raising import duties on various foreign manufactures. The tariff alienates southerners who purchase European agricultural implements and who fear that reciprocal tariffs will injure their cotton economy.

DECEMBER

- The South Carolina legislature repudiates the "Tariff of Abominations," passed in May. The vice president John C. Calhoun, a South Carolina native, articulates his

state's rights position in the controversial pamphlet "South Carolina Exposition and Protest."

Colonization

AUGUST

27 Uruguay is formally proclaimed independent at the preliminary peace ending the war between Brazil and Argentina.

Politics and Government

- In the U.S. congressional elections, the Democrats attain majorities over the National Republicans in the House of Representatives (139–74) and Senate (26–22).
- The Democratic Party emerges under the leadership of the Tennessee senator Andrew Jackson and New York political operator Martin Van Buren. The Democrats endorse the old Democratic-Republican principles of agrarianism, personal liberty, and suspicion of special interests. They garner support from northern and southern farmers and hard-pressed northern urban denizens.
- The National Republican Party emerges under the leadership of the U.S. president John Quincy Adams. The National Republicans promote the secretary of state Henry Clay's strong nationalist platform of a protective tariff, a national bank, federally funded internal improvements, and cautious distribution of land grants.

JANUARY

3   Jean Villèle resigns as prime minister of France after election defeats in November 1827.

5   Jean-Baptiste, vicomte de Martignac, becomes prime minister of a moderate administration in France.

18 A commercial treaty between the German states of Bavaria and Württemberg abolishes customs duties on their common frontier.

25 Arthur Wellesley, Duke of Wellington, becomes prime minister of a Tory administration in Britain.

FEBRUARY

22 The Peace of Turkmanchai ends the Russo-Persian War. Persia cedes part of Armenia, including Erivan, to Russia.

26 Dom Miguel takes the oath to his brother, King Pedro IV (resident in Brazil), as regent of Portugal.

MARCH

3   Pedro IV abdicates as king of Portugal.

APRIL

4   British troops are recalled from Portugal by the British prime minister, the Duke of Wellington.

14 A new press law in France reduces censorship, but press trials are still to be held by government-influenced tribunals and not conducted by juries.

26 Russia declares war on the Ottoman Empire in support of Greek independence.

JUNE

16 The French prime minister Jean-Baptiste, vicomte de Martignac, attacks the Jesuits, prohibiting religious orders from teaching unless sanctioned by the state.

23 Dom Miguel is proclaimed king of Portugal, following a peaceful coup d'état.

JULY

7   The Belgian Clerical and Liberal parties unite after King William I has estranged the Clericals by concluding the concordat of 1827.

19 The London Protocol is issued by Britain, Russia, and France, allowing France to intervene in the Ottoman province of Morea to evacuate hostile troops in order to secure Greek independence.

AUGUST

6   The Egyptian leader Mehmet Ali agrees to Britain's demand to withdraw his forces from Greece.

OCTOBER

11 The Russians occupy the Black Sea port of Varna in the war against the Ottoman Empire.

NOVEMBER

16 A London Protocol, issued by France, Britain, and Russia, guarantees the independence of the province of Morea and the Cyclades islands, Greece.

SCIENCE, TECHNOLOGY, AND MEDICINE

Ecology

- Prussian meteorologist Heinrich Wilhelm Dove discovers that winds in tropical storms circulate counterclockwise in the northern hemisphere and clockwise in the southern hemisphere.

DECEMBER

28 An earthquake at Echigo, Japan, kills 30,000 people.

Exploration

APRIL

20 French explorer René Caillié successfully reaches the city of Timbuktu in Mali, traveling from the West African coast disguised as an Arab, and returning across the Sahara Desert to Morocco.

Health and Medicine

- Amalgam, an alloy of mercury and silver, is used to fill teeth for the first time.

Math

- English mathematician George Green introduces a theorem that enables volume integrals to be calculated in terms of surface integrals. He also publishes *Essay on the Application of Mathematical Analysis to the Theory of Electricity and Magnets*, in which he applies mathematics to the properties of electric and magnetic fields.

- Norwegian mathematician Niels Abel begins the study of elliptic functions.

Science

- Estonian embryologist Karl von Baer describes the notochord, the development of the neural folds into the nervous system, and the main brain vesicles in *Über die Entwicklungsgeschichte der Thiere/On the Development of Animals*. In doing so he establishes the science of comparative embryology.

- French physiologist Henri Dutrochet discovers osmosis—the passage of a solvent through a semipermeable membrane.

- German chemist Friedrich Wöhler synthesizes urea from ammonium cyanate. It is the first synthesis of an organic substance from an inorganic compound and signals the beginning of organic chemistry. He also isolates the alkaline-earth metal element beryllium (atomic no. 4).

- Nicotine is first isolated.

- Scottish botanist Robert Brown observes the continuous motion of tiny particles in a liquid solution, now known as Brownian motion.
- Swedish chemist Jöns Jakob Berzelius discovers the element thorium (atomic no. 90).

Technology

- English inventor John Mitchell introduces the machine-made steel pen point.
- English inventor Samuel Jones patents the "promethean match," a glass bead containing acid, and coated with flammable chemicals. Breaking the glass with a small pair of pliers, or the teeth, ignites the paper the bead is wrapped in.
- U.S. inventor John Thorpe develops a ring spinning machine which controls the thread during spinning, allowing continuous spinning. It is simpler and more productive than Crompton's spinning mule, which it soon replaces.

Transportation

- French engineer Marc Séguin develops a multiple fire-tube boiler, replacing the water-tube boiler of earlier steam engines. Robert Stephenson installs one in his locomotive the *Rocket* the following year.

April 1828–50   The 300-km/185-mi-long Chesapeake and Ohio (C & O) Canal is constructed. It runs from Washington, D.C., to Cumberland, Maryland, and crosses the Alleghenies.

JULY

- A ground-breaking ceremony on the Baltimore and Ohio Railroad in the United States marks the ascendancy of the "iron horse" (railroad).

ARTS AND IDEAS

Architecture

- The German architect Heinrich Hübsch publishes *In welchem Style sollen wir bauen?/In Which Style Should We Build?*

Arts

- The English artist John Constable paints *Dedham Vale*.
- The U.S. artist John Quidor paints *Ichabod Crane Pursued by the Headless Horseman*.

Literature and Language

- The English poet and critic Leigh Hunt publishes his reminiscences *Lord Byron and Some of His Contemporaries*. A later edition is published as *Autobiography* in 1850.
- The Russian writer Yevgeny Abramovich Baratynsky publishes his narrative poem *Bal/The Ball*.
- The U.S. lexicographer Noah Webster publishes his two-volume *An American Dictionary of the English Language*, which becomes the classic dictionary of U.S. English. He published a shorter dictionary in 1806.
- The U.S. missionary and writer Timothy Flint publishes his novel *The Life and Adventures of Arthur Clenning*.
- The U.S. writer John Neal publishes his novel *Rachel Dyer*, based on the Salem witch trials.
- The U.S. writer Nathaniel Hawthorne publishes his first novel, *Fanshawe*, anonymously.

Music

- Austrian composer Franz Schubert completes his Mass in E flat (D 950); his String Quintet in C major (D 956);

BIRTHS & DEATHS

FEBRUARY
1   Meyer Guggenheim, Swiss-born U.S. industrialist who built up the largest mining corporation in the United States, born in Langnau, Switzerland (–1905).
8   Jules Verne, French author who pioneered modern science fiction writing, born in Nantes, France (–1905).
11   De Witt Clinton, U.S. statesman, instigator of the Erie Canal, dies in Albany, New York (58).

MARCH
20   Henrik Johan Ibsen, Norwegian poet and playwright whose works include *Peer Gynt* (1867) and *A Doll's House* (1879), born in Skien, Norway (–1906).

APRIL
6   Gustave Moreau, French Symbolist painter, born in Paris, France (–1898).
16   Francisco José de Goya y Lucientes, Spanish painter and engraver known for his depiction of contemporary events, dies in Bordeaux, France (81).
21   Hippolyte-Adolphe Taine, French critic and Positivist historian, born in Vouziers, France (–1893).

MAY
12   Dante Gabriel Rossetti, English Pre-Raphaelite painter and poet, born in London, England (–1882).

JULY
15   Jean-Antoine Houdon, French rococo sculptor, dies in Paris, France (88).

AUGUST
12   William Blake, English poet and engraver, dies in London, England (70).
22   Franz Josef Gall, German anatomist who founded the "science" of phrenology, dies in Paris, France (70).

SEPTEMBER
9   Lev Nikolayevich ("Leo") Tolstoy, Russian author best known for *War and Peace* and *Anna Karenina*, born in Yasnaya Polyana, Russia (–1910).

NOVEMBER
14   James B. McPherson, Union general during the Civil War, born in Sandusky County, Ohio (–1864).
19   Franz Schubert, Austrian composer, dies in Vienna, Austria (31).

his Piano Sonatas No. 17 (D 958), No. 18 (D 959), and No. 19 (D 960); and his *Impromptus* for piano.
- The character and song "Jim Crow" is introduced in Louisville, Kentucky, by Thomas Dartmouth "Daddy" Rice, a black-faced number that becomes a staple of traveling minstrel shows in the United States. Later the phrase "Jim Crow" comes to mean "segregated."
- The opera *Le Comte Ory/Count Ory* by the Italian composer Gioachino Antonio Rossini is first performed, in Paris, France.

Thought and Scholarship

- The English historian William Francis Patrick Napier publishes the first volume of his *History of the Peninsular War*. The last volume appears in 1840.
- The German folklorist and philologist Jakob Ludwig Carl Grimm publishes *Deutsche Rechtsaltertümer/ German Legal Antiquities*.
- The Scottish philosopher Dugald Stewart publishes *Philosophy of the Active and Moral Powers of Man*.
- The U.S. writer Washington Irving publishes *History of the Life and Voyages of Christopher Columbus*.

SOCIETY

Education

- The Presbyterian minister John Finley Crowe establishes Hanover College in Hanover, Indiana. The school's mandate is to train Presbyterian ministers.

Media and Communication

- The *Southern Review*, an expression of the culture of the American South, begins publication in Charleston, South Carolina.
- The U.S. writer and journalist Sarah Josepha Hale publishes the periodical *Ladies' Magazine* in Boston, Massachusetts.

FEBRUARY
- The Cherokee people publish the first Native American newspaper, the *Cherokee Phoenix*, in Echota, Georgia.

1829

POLITICS, GOVERNMENT, AND ECONOMICS

Business and Economics

MAY
27 Prussia obtains support for its progressive commercial policy from the German states of Bavaria and Württemberg.

OCTOBER
- The luxurious Tremont Hotel in Boston, Massachusetts, opens with a magnificent banquet. It sets the standard for opulence in what will become the hotel's heyday.

Human Rights

- The black American abolitionist David Walker publishes his *Appeal to the Colored Citizens of the World*, a ringing denunciation of slavery and a call to arms.

- The British governor-general of India, Lord George Bentinck, secures the abolition of "suttee" (the burning of a widow on her husband's funeral pyre) in Bengal.

Politics and Government

- The British home secretary Robert Peel founds the Metropolitan Police force to patrol London, England.
- The U.S. president Andrew Jackson offers to buy Texas from Mexico. Mexico declines.
- The U.S. Workingmen's Party emerges in several cities of the industrialized northeast, attracting a loose coalition of newspaper editors and labor organizations committed to universal suffrage, abolition of debtors prisons, ready access to credit, and compulsory tax-supported public schooling.
- U.S. president Andrew Jackson appoints the Ohio jurist and former U.S. postmaster general John McLean to the U.S. Supreme Court.

MARCH
4 Andrew Jackson is inaugurated as seventh president of the United States.
5 The Roman Catholic Relief Bill is passed by the British House of Commons.
22 A London Protocol on Greece modifies the Protocol of November 1828, extending the guarantee of

independence by Britain, Russia, and France to include continental Greece and the island of Euboea.

APRIL

13 The Roman Catholic Relief Bill passes the Lords, in Britain, allowing Catholics to sit and vote in Parliament, giving them the right to vote, and making them eligible for all military, civil, and corporate offices except those of Regent, Lord Chancellor of England, and Lord Lieutenant of Ireland. They are to take an oath denying the pope has the power to interfere in domestic affairs and recognizing the legitimacy of Britain's protestant monarchs.

AUGUST

6 The French prime minister Jean-Baptiste, vicomte de Martignac, is dismissed after alienating both liberals and conservatives with his proposals to change the electoral law.

8 King Charles X of France appoints Auguste, Prince de Polignac, as prime minister, an ultra-conservative who does not possess the confidence of the Chamber, in a move away from responsible government.

SEPTEMBER

14 The Treaty of Adrianople ends the Russo-Ottoman War and the Greek War of Independence. Sultan Mahmud II of the Ottoman Empire recognizes the London Protocol of March 1829 which guarantees the territory of Greece and the independence of the Danubian provinces (Moldavia and Wallachia) and of Serbia. Russia obtains land south of the Caucasus.

SCIENCE, TECHNOLOGY, AND MEDICINE

Health and Medicine

- Irish physician Robert Collins reduces hospital mortality by disinfecting hospital rooms with chlorine.
- Scottish physician James Simpson installs the world's first water purification system, in London, England. Using sand filtration, it purifies water from the River Thames.

Math

- French mathematician Evariste Galois introduces the theory of groups—collections whose members obey simple rules of addition and multiplication but which are necessary for solving higher algebraic equations. Group theory is now fundamental to modern algebra and has applications in quantum theory.
- Russian mathematician Nikolay Ivanovich Lobachevsky develops hyperbolic geometry, in which a plane is regarded as part of a hyperbolic surface shaped like a saddle. It is the beginning of non-Euclidean geometry.

Science

- French mathematician Gustave Gaspard Coriolis writes *Du calcul de l'effet des machines/On the Calculation of Mechanical Action* in which he is the first to use the term "kinetic energy."
- Scottish chemist Thomas Graham formulates the law named for him on the diffusion rates of gases. He also devises a dialysis method of separating colloids from crystalloids and thereby establishes the science of colloidal chemistry.
- U.S. scientist Joseph Henry develops a more powerful electromagnet by insulating the wire instead of the iron bar.

Technology

- Scottish inventor James Beaumont Neilson introduces a process for preheating the blast air in blast furnaces. By producing very high temperatures it triples the amount of iron produced per tonne of coal, thus allowing lower-grade iron and coal ores to be used, and larger smelters to be constructed.
- The first electromagnetic clock is invented.
- The first mechanical elevator is installed, in the Coliseum in Regent's Park, London, England.
- U.S. inventor William Austin Burt patents the Typographer, the first patented typewriter. A handle is used to select the letter which is then inked on a pad and pressed on the paper.

Transportation

- The Welland Canal, Canada, opens, connecting lakes Erie and Ontario and bypassing Niagara Falls.

JULY

4 English entrepreneur George Shillibeer begins a horse-drawn omnibus service in London, England; buses seat 22 and are pulled by 3 horses.

OCTOBER

- The Chesapeake and Delaware Canal, linking the Delaware River to Chesapeake Bay, opens to boat traffic.

10–14 George and Robert Stephenson's *Rocket* wins the Liverpool and Manchester Railway competition with an average speed of 58 kph/36 mph without a load, and 26 kph/16 mph with a 40 tonne load. Using a multiple fire-tube boiler, rather than the single flue boiler other contestants use, its design sets the pattern for future railroad locomotives.

ARTS AND IDEAS

Architecture

- The General Post Office in London, England, designed by the English architect Robert Smirke, is completed (later demolished).

- The White House in Washington, D.C., is completed. Work began on the "President's House" in the 1790s to a design by the Irish-born architect James Hoban, the style a refined neoclassicism. The building was burned down by the British in 1814 and work began again. Alterations to Hoban's designs were made by President Thomas Jefferson and the architect Benjamin Henry Latrobe.

Arts

c. 1829 The English artist J. M. W. Turner paints *Ulysses Deriding Polyphemus*.
- The English artist John Constable paints *Hadleigh Castle*.
- The first lithographed cartoon appears in the United States; the process is faster than wood cuttings or engravings.

Literature and Language

- Karl Baedeker publishes the first of his travel guidebooks, in German, a guide to Koblenz, Prussia. He will go on to produce versions of his books in German, English, and French, describing other locations in Europe, North America, and the Orient.
- The French writer Alfred de Musset publishes *Contes d'Espagne et d'Italie/Stories of Italy and Spain*.
- The French writer Honoré de Balzac publishes his novel *Les Chouans*, the first volume of his series *La Comédie humaine/The Human Comedy*.
- The French writer Stendhal publishes his travel book *Promenades dans Rome/Walks in Rome*.
- The U.S. writer James Fenimore Cooper publishes his novel *The Wept of Wish-ton-Wish*.

Music

- English inventor Charles Wheatstone patents the concertina, which uses a bellows and two reeds to produce a note on a draw or press of the bellows.

- French composer Hector Berlioz completes his piece for voice and orchestra (part of a cantata never completed) *La Mort de Cléopâtre/The Death of Cleopatra*.
- The Armenian Cyrill Demian (living in Vienna) patents the accordion.
- The opera *Guillaume Tell/William Tell* by the Italian composer Gioachino Antonio Rossini is first performed, in Paris, France. It is based on a play by the German writer Friedrich Johann Christoph von Schiller, published in 1804. It is first performed in Britain in 1830 (in London, England), and in the United States in 1831 (in New York, New York).

Thought and Scholarship

- The English poet and historian Henry Hart Milman publishes *History of the Jews*.
- The French historian François Guizot publishes *Histoire de la civilisation en France/The History of French Civilization*.
- The German historian Leopold von Ranke publishes *Die serbische Revolution/The Serbian Revolution*.
- The German-born U.S. political scientist Francis Lieber publishes the first volumes of his 13-volume *Encyclopedia Americana*.
- The Scottish philosopher James Mill publishes *Analysis of the Human Mind*.
- The U.S. writer Thomas Skidmore publishes *The Rights of Man to Property*.

SOCIETY

Education

- The French educator Louis Braille's *Procédé pour écrire les paroles/A System for Writing Words* is the first book in braille to be published.
- The U.S. educator James H. Coffin establishes the nation's first vocational training school, the Fellenberg Manual Labor Institution, in Fellenberg, Massachusetts.

BIRTHS & DEATHS

JANUARY
6 Josef Dobrovský, Czech language scholar who founded comparative Slavic linguistics, dies in Brno, Moravia, Austrian Empire (75).

FEBRUARY
10 Pope Leo XII, Italian pope 1823–29, dies in Rome (68).

APRIL
26 Theodor Billroth, Austrian surgeon who founded modern abdominal surgery, born in Bergen, Prussia (–1894).

MAY
17 John Jay, U.S. lawyer and first chief justice of the U.S. Supreme Court

1789–95, dies in Bedford, New York (83).

JUNE
- Geronimo, Apache Native American chief who fought the U.S. military during the 1870s and early 1880s, born in No-Doyohn Canyon, Mexico (–1908).
8 John Everett Millais, English painter who was a founding member of the Pre-Raphaelite Brotherhood, born in Southampton, Hampshire, England (–1896).
26 Johann Heinrich Tischbein, German painter, dies in Eutin, Oldenburg (now Germany) (78).

SEPTEMBER
7 Friedrich August Kekulé von Stradonitz, German chemist who laid the theoretical foundations of organic chemistry, born in Darmstadt, Hesse (–1896).

DECEMBER
18 Jean-Baptiste Pierre Antoine de Monet, Chevalier de Lamarck, French biologist who believed that acquired traits are inheritable, dies in Paris, France (85).

MARCH

- The U.S. physician John Dix Fisher establishes the New England School for the Blind in Boston, Massachusetts. It is the nation's first school for visually impaired students.

Everyday Life

- The U.S. fur merchant Hall J. Kelley establishes the American Society for Encouraging the Settlement of the Oregon Country, in Boston, Massachusetts.

Media and Communication

- The *Revue des Deux Mondes* is first issued in France, edited by François Buloz. It is relaunched in 1831.

Religion

MARCH

31 After the death of Pope Leo XII on February 10, the Italian clergyman Francesco Saverio Castiglioni is elected Pope Pius VIII. He is pope until 1830.

Sports

SEPTEMBER

- The *American Turf Register and Sporting Magazine*, the first journal in the United States devoted to sports, is published by John Stuart Skinner in Baltimore, Maryland.

1830

POLITICS, GOVERNMENT, AND ECONOMICS

Colonization

MAY

13 Ecuador secedes from Colombia to escape the dictatorial rule of Simón Bolívar.

SEPTEMBER

11 Ecuador is recognized as an independent republic and granted a constitution by Colombia, under which it is to be part of the Confederation of Colombia.
22 Venezuela secedes from Colombia and becomes an independent sovereign state.

Human Rights

- By this year, the American Colonization Society has transported 1,420 black Americans back to Africa.
- Black American abolitionists meet in Philadelphia, Pennsylvania, "to devise ways and means for the bettering of our condition."
- "Suttee" (the burning of a widow on her husband's funeral pyre) is abolished in Bombay and Madras, India, under the British governor-general of India, Lord George Bentinck.

Politics and Government

- In the U.S. congressional elections, the Democrats retain majorities in the House of Representatives (141–58) and Senate (25–21).
- The French writer and priest Abbé Hughes Félicité Robert de Lamennais advocates a combination of Catholicism and liberalism.
- The Russian statesman Count Mikhail Speransky codifies Russian law chronologically in the *Svod Zakonoff Rossiyskoy Imperiy/Digest of the Laws of the Russian Empire* (45 volumes with commentaries).
- U.S. president Andrew Jackson appoints the Pennsylvania jurist Henry Baldwin to the U.S. Supreme Court.

JANUARY

- In what will become known as the Webster–Hayne debate, the U.S. senators Daniel Webster of Massachusetts and Robert Y. Hayne of South Carolina engage in a gripping oratorical duel about the respective merits of federal sovereignty and states' rights in the U.S. Congress, with Webster arguing for the Union and Hayne for the states.

FEBRUARY

3 Greece is declared independent of the Ottoman Empire at the London Conference and granted the protection of France, Russia, and Britain.

MARCH

18 King Charles X of France's appointment of the right-wing Auguste, Prince de Polignac, as prime minister is denounced by the French Chambers.
29 King Ferdinand VII of Spain, at the instigation of the liberal queen Christina, publishes the law of 1789, canceling earlier legislation giving precedence to male heirs to the throne.

APRIL

- Mexico calls a moratorium on further U.S. settlement of Texas. The Mexican constitution forbids slavery, but the majority of U.S. settlers in Texas retain slaves.
- 27 Simón Bolívar resigns as president of Colombia following the breakaway of Ecuador from Colombia.

MAY

- U.S. president Andrew Jackson vetoes legislation authorizing construction of the Maysville Road in Kentucky. The president maintains that Congress has no authority to undertake internal improvements within individual states. He approves legislation, however, funding improvements to the Cumberland Road, an interstate highway connecting Cumberland, Maryland, and Wheeling, West Virginia.
- 16 King Charles X of France dissolves the Chambers, which oppose him, and calls an election.
- 28 The U.S. Congress passes the Indian Removal Act, requiring Native Americans living east of the Mississippi River to move into the Oklahoma territory.

JUNE

- 4 Antonio José de Sucre, former president of Bolivia and the South American revolutionary leader Simón Bolívar's most able general, is assassinated in Colombia.
- 26 King George IV of Britain dies and is succeeded by his brother William IV, Duke of Clarence.

JULY

- The U.S. government forces the Auk and Fox leaders to sign a treaty ceding land in southern Wisconsin and northern Illinois and requiring their peoples to migrate west into Iowa territory.
- 5 France lands a force in Algeria, in an attempt to conquer territory, and takes Algiers.
- 19 The Liberal opposition obtains a majority in the French elections.
- 25 King Charles X of France issues the three ordinances of St.-Cloud for controlling the press, dissolving the Chamber of Deputies, and having antigovernment voters removed from the electoral lists following the victory of the Liberal opposition in the elections.
- 27–29 Revolutionary action known as the "Three Glorious Days" flares up in Paris and other areas of France following the publication of the ordinances of St.-Cloud by King Charles X.
- 29 A group of moderate constitutional monarchists form a "City Committee" and place themselves at the head of the crowd rebelling in Paris, France, to prevent leadership of the movement falling to republicans.
- 30 The "City Committee" representing the demonstrators in Paris, France, issues a proclamation demanding the accession of Louis Philippe, duc d'Orléans, the liberal head of the younger branch of the Bourbon family.

AUGUST

- 1 King Charles X of France appoints Louis Philippe, duc d'Orléans, as Lieutenant Général (ruler) of France.
- 2 Charles X abdicates as king of France following continued opposition to his rule.
- 9 Louis Philippe, duc d'Orléans, accepts the offer of the Chambers to become king of France, founding the Orléanist monarchy. The Orléanists are the younger branch of the French royal family of Bourbon.

- 11 The first ministry of King Louis Phillipe's reign in France is formed, comprising a range of moderate and progressive liberals led by Jacques Lafitte, Casimir Périer, and François Guizot.
- 14 A new constitutional charter is published in France, establishing a constitutional monarchy, allowing for the initiation of legislation in Chambers, ensuring the permanent suppression of press censorship, and ending the status of Catholicism as the state religion.
- 25 A revolution is staged in Belgium against union with the Dutch (with whom the Belgians were amalgamated as the United Netherlands after the Napoleonic Wars).

SEPTEMBER

- The Anti-Masonic Party, headed by U.S. politician William Wirt, becomes the first major third party in U.S. history.
- 9 Revolts occur in Saxony, Hesse, and Brunswick following the arrival of news of the revolution in France and the abdication of Charles X.

NOVEMBER

- 2 A progressive ministry is formed in France under Jacques Lafitte.
- 8 King Francis I of Naples dies and is succeeded by his liberal son King Ferdinand II.
- 15 Four ministers of Charles X, the deposed king of France, are tried for treason.
- 18 The Belgian National Congress declares the country independent of the United Netherlands.
- 21 The trial of the ministers of the deposed Charles X of France ends in rioting when they are sentenced to life imprisonment and not death as the crowds want.
- 22 Charles, Earl Grey, becomes prime minister of a Whig government in Britain, with Viscount Palmerston as foreign secretary, following the resignation of the Tory Arthur Wellesley, Duke of Wellington.
- 22 The Belgian National Congress votes for a monarchy (but excludes the Dutch royal family, the House of Orange, on November 24).
- 29 An insurrection in Poland against Russian domination is brought to a head by the intention of Czar Nicholas II of Russia to use Polish forces against the rebellions in Belgium and France, with whom the nationalist, liberal Polish revolutionaries are in sympathy.

DECEMBER

- After a year of political wrangling about the constitutionality of federally sponsored internal improvements, the U.S. president Andrew Jackson argues in his annual message that internal improvements have to be national in extent to pass constitutional muster.
- 20 At the London Conference, Britain, France, the Austrian Empire, Prussia, and Russia support Belgium's decision to separate from the Netherlands.

SCIENCE, TECHNOLOGY, AND MEDICINE

Exploration

MARCH

22 British explorers Richard and John Lander begin to explore the lower course of the River Niger in West Africa. During the year they successfully sail down to its delta, establishing the river's course for the first time in European cartography.

Health and Medicine

- An outbreak of cholera in Astrakhan on the Caspian Sea the previous year spreads to the interior of Russia, then across Europe, killing millions of people.

Math

c. 1830 English mathematician Charles Babbage creates the first accurate actuarial tables.

- French mathematician Siméon-Denis Poisson introduces "Poisson's ratio," which deals with stresses and strains on materials.

Science

- English microscopist Joseph Lister establishes the theoretical principles behind the construction of lenses free from chromatic and spherical distortion.
- French chemist Jean-Baptiste-André Dumas discovers a method of burning organic compounds to determine their nitrogen content.
- Swedish chemist Nils Sefström rediscovers the element vanadium (atomic no. 23), originally discovered in 1801 by the Spanish mineralogist Manuel del Rio.

JULY

July–April 1833 Scottish geologist Charles Lyell publishes his three-volume work *Principles of Geology* in which he argues that geological formations are the result of presently observable processes acting over millions of years. It creates a new time frame for other sciences such as biology and paleontology.

Technology

- English inventor James Perry makes a more flexible pen by cutting slits down the sides of the nib and a small hole at the top of a central slit running down to the point.
- French inventor Barthélemy Thimonnier patents the first sewing machine. Eighty are constructed to make French army uniforms but are destroyed the following year by a mob of tailors fearing unemployment.
- U.S. inventor Jacob Perkins develops a hot-water radiator for central heating.

- U.S. inventor Thaddeus Fairbanks develops the platform scale. Objects placed on a platform are weighed through a series of levers and an extension with slotted weights and a small sliding weight.
- U.S. inventors Edwin Budding and John Ferrabee invent the lawn mower in Britain. It will become a success with the growing popularity of lawn tennis.

Transportation

c. 1830 The sporting gig, a two-wheeled one-horse carriage, appears.

- A surface condenser is invented that provides fresh water for steam boilers; it makes oceangoing steamships possible.
- English inventor Thomas Cochrane invents an air lock; it is used for harbor, bridge, and tunnel construction.
- The U.S. engineer Robert L. Stevens invents the T-rail and the railroad spike, innovations that will spur the development of the railroad, and uses wooden ties on a bed of crushed stone.
- U.S. inventor Peter Cooper constructs the *Tom Thumb*, the first steam locomotive built in the United States.

JANUARY

7 The first section of the 611-km/380-mi Baltimore and Ohio Railroad, between Baltimore and Ellicott's Mills, opens. It is the first public railroad in the United States.

SEPTEMBER

15 The Liverpool and Manchester Railway opens. The first railroad to carry both passengers and freight, its success sparks widespread railroad building in Britain and the United States.

DECEMBER

25 The South Carolina Canal and Rail Road Company begins the United States's first scheduled passenger service using the steam locomotive the *Best Friend of Charleston*, which pulls four loaded passenger cars on the 9.6-km/6-mi track from Charleston to Hamburg, South Carolina.

ARTS AND IDEAS

Architecture

- The Altes Museum in Berlin, Germany, designed by the German architect Karl Friedrich Schinkel, is completed.
- The Eastern State Penitentiary at Cherry Hill, Philadelphia, Pennsylvania, designed by the U.S. architect John Haviland, is completed.
- The remodeling of Buckingham Palace in London, England, to designs by the English architect John Nash, is completed.
- The U.S. surveyor and engineer James Thompson lays plans for the city of Chicago, Illinois.

Arts

c. 1830 The English artist J. M. W. Turner paints *Music at Petworth*.

c. 1830 The Russian artist Alexey Venetsianov paints *Summer*.
- The English artist Samuel Palmer paints *Coming from Evening Church*.
- The French artist and caricaturist Honoré Daumier is briefly imprisoned for depicting the French king Louis Philippe as the character Gargantua created by the French writer Rabelais in 1532.
- The French artist Eugène Delacroix paints *Liberty Leading the People* and *Portrait of Baron Schwitters*.
- The U.S. artist William Sidney Mt. paints *Rustic Dance After a Sleighride*.

Literature and Language

- The English poet Alfred, Lord Tennyson publishes *Poems Chiefly Lyrical*. Among its best-known poems is "Mariana."
- The French writer Honoré de Balzac publishes *Scènes de la vie privée/Scenes from Private Life*, a collection of stories.
- The French writer Stendhal publishes his novel *Le Rouge et le noir/The Scarlet and the Black*.
- The U.S. preacher William Ellery Channing publishes *Remarks on American Literature*.
- The U.S. writer James Fenimore Cooper publishes his novel *The Water-Witch*.

Music

- German composer Robert Schumann completes his *Abegg Variations* for piano (Opus 1).
- The opera *Der Alchymist/The Alchemist* by the German composer Ludwig Spohr is first performed, in Kassel, Germany.
- The opera *Fra Diavolo* by the French composer Daniel-François-Esprit Auber is first performed, in Paris, France.

Theater and Dance

- The comedy *The Lion of the West*, a satire on backwoodsmen such as Davy Crockett by the U.S. writer James Kirke Paulding, is first performed, in New York, New York.
- The play *The Triumph at Plattsburg* by the U.S. dramatist Richard Penn Smith is first performed, in Philadelphia, Pennsylvania.
- The Russian poet Alexander Pushkin publishes *Malenkiye tragedi/Little Tragedies*, a collection of four short dramas. Among the best known is *Motsart i Salyeri/Mozart and Salieri*.
- The tragedy *Hernani* by the French writer Victor Hugo is first performed, in Paris, France. The play causes a riot, with clashes between defenders of established, classical theater and the play's supporters, who hail it a masterpiece of new (romantic) theater.

Thought and Scholarship

- The French sociologist Auguste Comte publishes the first part of his *Cours de philosophie positive/Course of Positive Philosophy*. The final part appears in 1842.
- Italian writer and political activist Giuseppe Mazzini publishes *La filosophia della musica/The Philosophy of Music*.
- The Museum of Science is founded in Boston, Massachusetts.

SOCIETY

Education

- The American Institute for Instruction opens in Boston, Massachusetts, to promote educational development.
- The University of Richmond is founded in Richmond, Virginia.
- The Yale educators Jeremiah Day and James L. Kingsley publish *Reports on the Course of Instruction in Yale College*.

BIRTHS & DEATHS

MAY
16 Jean-Baptiste-Joseph Fourier, French mathematician who provided a mathematical theory of heat, dies in Paris, France (62).

JUNE
26 George IV, King of Great Britain and Ireland 1820–30, previously regent 1811–20, dies in Windsor, Berkshire, England (67).

JULY
10 Camille Pissaro, French impressionist painter, born in St. Thomas, Danish West Indies (–1903).

AUGUST
18 Franz Josef, Emperor of Austria 1848–1916 and King of Hungary 1867–1916 who created the Austro-Hungarian Empire, born in Schloss Schönbrunn near Vienna, Austria (–1916).

SEPTEMBER
8 Frédéric Mistral, French poet, born in Maillane, France (–1914).

OCTOBER
5 Chester A. Arthur, twenty-first president of the United States 1881–84, a Republican, born in Fairfield, Virginia (–1886).
24 Beva Ann Lockwood, U.S. lawyer, presidential candidate in 1884, and the first woman to practice law before the U.S. Supreme Court, born in Royalton, New York (–1917).

NOVEMBER
8 Oliver O. Howard, Union general in the American Civil War, born in Leeds, Maine (–1909).
30 Pope Pius VIII, Italian pope 1829–30, dies in Rome, Italy (69).

DECEMBER
8 Benjamin Constant de Rebecque, Franco-Swiss novelist best known for his book *Adolphe* (1816), dies in Lausanne, Switzerland (63).
10 Emily Dickinson, U.S. poet, born in Amherst, Massachusetts (–1886).
17 Simón Bolívar, Venezuelan soldier who liberated Colombia, Peru, Ecuador, Venezuela, and Bolivia from Spanish rule, dies in Santa Marta, Colombia (47).

Everyday Life

- Angostura bitters are marketed; created by Dr. J. G. B. Siegert in Angostura (now Ciudad Bolívar), Venezuela, they are originally intended as a tonic for poor appetite.
- The Scottish-born U.S. social reformer Robert Dale Owen publishes *Moral Physiology*, the first U.S. book about birth control.
- The U.S. census lists the nation's population at 12,866,020, up from roughly 9,638,000 in 1820.
- The U.S. minister and health reformer Sylvester Graham introduces the Graham cracker, made from coarse whole-wheat flour.
- The world population is around 1 billion.

Media and Communication

- The Philadelphia moralist Louis Antoine Godey begins publication of the monthly miscellany *Godey's Lady's Book*.

Religion

- The U.S. Christian fundamentalist Alexander Campbell establishes the Disciples of Christ church, which subsequently becomes one of the principal evangelical Protestant denominations in the United States.

APRIL

- The U.S. visionary Joseph Smith founds The Church of Jesus Christ of Latter-day Saints in Fayette, New York.

Sports

- "Town ball," a rudimentary form of baseball which later becomes known as the Massachusetts Game, is played widely in New England.

1831

POLITICS, GOVERNMENT, AND ECONOMICS

Business and Economics

NOVEMBER

11 Silk weavers in Lyons, France, riot in protest at low wages.

Human Rights

- Boston abolitionist William Lloyd Garrison founds the New England Anti-Slavery Society which begins publication of the *Liberator* in January.
- The Georgia Senate offers a $5,000 reward for the apprehension and conviction of Boston abolitionist William Lloyd Garrison, who targets southerners as well as northerners with abolitionist literature.

AUGUST

21 U.S. slave-preacher Nat Turner launches a massive slave uprising in Southampton County, Virginia. Within a day, local militia and federal troops restore order, but not before some 70 whites and 100 blacks are killed in the melee. Turner himself is not apprehended.

OCTOBER

30 Some six weeks after leading the bloodiest slave uprising in U.S. history, escaped slave Nat Turner is apprehended in Southampton County, Virginia.

NOVEMBER

- Virginian lawyer Thomas Gray transcribes "The Confessions of Nat Turner," an autobiographical account by Turner of the Virginia slave revolt he led, and publishes it at a profit shortly after Turner is hanged on November 11, 1831.

Politics and Government

- The British East India Company annexes the Indian state of Mysore, using a peasant revolt as evidence of alleged local misgovernment.

JANUARY

5 A constitution is granted in Hesse-Cassel, following the revolt of September 1830.
25 The Polish diet (national assembly) declares Poland independent of Russia and the rule of the Russian tsars.

FEBRUARY

2 Pope Gregory XVI is elected. He is believed by many to have liberal sympathics.
3 Revolutionary outbreaks occur in the Italian provinces of Modena and Parma and the Papal States, influenced by the 1830 revolution in France.
3 The Belgians elect Louis, duc de Nemours, the son of King Louis Philippe of France, as their king. However,

Abolition of U.S. Slavery (1783–1866)

1783–1819

1783–86
- Massachusetts, Connecticut, Rhode Island, New York, and New Jersey ban slavery.

1793
February 12   The U.S. Congress passes a fugitive slave law barring anyone from assisting a runaway slave.

1807
March   The U.S. Congress prohibits the African slave trade, with effect from January 1, 1808.

1815
- U.S. abolitionist Paul Cuffe transports 38 black Americans to Africa, inaugurating the U.S. colonization movement.

1817
- The black American Reverend Richard Allen and the abolitionist James Forten lead 3,000 black Philadelphians in a protest against the colonization movement.

1819
February   New York representative James Tallmadge introduces an amendment to a Missouri statehood bill that thrusts the vexing problem of slavery squarely before the U.S. Congress. The so-called Tallmadge Amendment proposes that Missouri slaves shall become free at the age of 25 and prohibits the future importation of slaves into the state. Bound to upset the balance between free and slave states, the Tallmadge Amendment is eventually dropped.

1820–44

1820
March 6   The "Missouri Compromise" is decided by the U.S. Congress, allowing Missouri to enter the Union as a slave state and Maine as a nonslave state, and banning slavery in all Louisiana Purchase territories north of Missouri's southern border.

1824
August   Illinois abolishes slavery.

1831
August 21   Slave-preacher Nat Turner launches a massive slave uprising in Southampton County, Virginia. Within a day, local militia and federal troops restore order, but not before some 70 whites and 100 blacks are killed in the melee. Turner is hanged for leading the August uprising.

1834
October   A proslavery mob destroys the homes of some 40 black Americans, as an antiabolitionist riot rips through Philadelphia, Pennsylvania.

1837
February 6   The U.S. House of Representatives adopts a resolution denying slaves the right of petition enjoyed by white citizens.

November 7   A proslavery mob in Alton, Illinois, lynches abolitionist publisher Elijah P. Lovejoy and destroys his printing press.

1838
February 14   Plymouth representative John Quincy Adams inundates the U.S. House of Representatives with 350 petitions protesting slavery and the annexation of Texas.

December 3   Ohio congressman Joshua R. Giddings becomes the first avowed abolitionist to sit in the U.S. House of Representatives.

1839
- Massachusetts abolitionist Theodore Dwight Weld publishes "American Slavery As It Is," which Harriet Beecher Stowe credited with inspiring *Uncle Tom's Cabin*.

1841
October 27   Slaves aboard the American vessel *Creole* spark an international incident when they mutiny off the coast of Virginia and sail for the Bahamas. The British government of the Bahamas arrests the leaders of the mutiny but frees the remaining slaves, against U.S. protests.

Louis Philippe prevents his son becoming king of the Belgians, as it would give France a measure of influence in Belgium unacceptable to Britain.

7   The Belgian constitution is proclaimed, assigning executive power to a hereditary king who governs through ministers responsible to a legislative body, establishing an independent judiciary, and providing for freedom of worship, education, and the press.

MARCH
- The Italian revolutionary Giuseppe Mazzini, in exile in Marseille, France, founds the "Young Italy" movement which aims to unite Italy and introduce democracy.

3   Austrian troops occupy the revolutionary Italian provinces of Parma and Modena.

4   John Quincy Adams becomes the first former president to return to Congress, where he represents Plymouth, Massachusetts, in the U.S. House of Representatives.

8   A constitution is proclaimed in the German kingdom of Hanover following persistent unrest there since the 1830 revolution in France.

13   Casimir Périer becomes prime minister of a strict liberal government in France.

APRIL
7   Emperor Pedro I of Brazil abdicates in favor of his son in order to return to Portugal to aid his daughter, Queen Maria II, who is being challenged by his brother, Dom Miguel, for the throne.

MAY
21   The powers of Europe send a memorandum to Pope Gregory XVI, advising him to reform the political and administrative system of the Papal States to avert further revolutionary action.

1842

- The U.S. Supreme Court, in *Priss v. Pennsylvania*, declares unconstitutional a Pennsylvania law of 1826 forbidding the capture and return of fugitive slaves.

1844

- Abolitionist William Lloyd Garrison publishes "Address to the Friends of Freedom and Emancipation in the United States," an antislavery call-to-arms.

1850–66

1850

September 9 California becomes the 31st state in the Union. Its constitution prohibits slavery.

September 18 As part of the Compromise of 1850, the U.S. Congress passes the Fugitive Slave Law, requiring northerners to return escaped slaves to their masters.

September 20 As part of the Compromise of 1850, the U.S. Congress abolishes the slave trade in the District of Columbia.

1852

April 20 Harriet Beecher Stowe publishes *Uncle Tom's Cabin* in book form. The book, previously serialized in the antislavery broadsheet *National Era*, is instantly controversial and popular, selling 1.2 million copies by mid-1853.

July 5 Abolitionist Frederick Douglass delivers his address "What to the Slave is the Fourth of July?" in Rochester, New York. Douglass criticizes Americans for their hypocritical celebration of liberty in the face of human bondage.

1857

March In the case *Dred Scott v. Sandford*, the U.S. Supreme Court rules that black Americans cannot be citizens of the United States. The Court also denies Congress the right to prohibit slavery anywhere without due process of law, thereby invalidating the Missouri Compromise of 1820.

1858

August Illinois congressman Abraham Lincoln and Illinois senator Stephen A. Douglas, candidates for Douglas' Illinois senate seat, engage in a series of extraordinary political debates about the future of slavery in the United States. Published in newspapers around the country, the debates make Lincoln a household name.

1861

March The Confederate Congress adopts the Confederate constitution. It maintains state sovereignty and protects slavery.

1862

July Union major general David Hunter marshals fugitive slaves into Union ranks. They become the first black American troops to participate in the Civil War.

September 22 U.S. president Abraham Lincoln announces that he will emancipate the slaves as a war measure, to take effect from January 1, 1863.

1863

January 1 The Emancipation Proclamation goes into effect, but it "frees" slaves only in territory held by the Confederacy.

1865

March Confederate president Jefferson Davis signs legislation providing for the conscription and arming of slaves.

August Mississippi and North Carolina repeal their secession ordinances and abolish slavery.

December The 13th Amendment to the U.S. Constitution, prohibiting slavery, becomes law.

1866

April The U.S. Congress passes the Civil Rights Act over President Andrew Johnson's veto. The legislation grants citizenship and equal civil rights to black Americans.

26 Polish forces are defeated by the Russian army at Ostrołęnke, following Poland's declaration of independence.

JUNE

4 The Belgian Congress proclaims Leopold of Saxe-Coburg king of Belgium, a candidate acceptable to both Britain and France.

26 The London Conference of Britain, France, Prussia, Russia, and Austria issues Eighteen Articles for peace preliminaries between Belgium and the Netherlands as a substitute for the January Protocols. These are more favorable to the Belgians but are rejected by the Dutch.

27 The U.S. government and Black Hawk, chief of the Sauk, sign a treaty by which the Sauk agree to leave their land in Illinois and move to Iowa.

JULY

5 A reform edict drawn up by the papal secretary of state Cardinal Tomasso Bernetti does not substantially alter the political system in the Papal States.

AUGUST

2 Dutch troops invade Belgium to try to impose a settlement over the secession of Belgium from the United Netherlands, as the Dutch are unhappy over the peace preliminaries agreed by the great powers in London, England, on June 26.

SEPTEMBER

4 The German state of Saxony is granted a constitution, following the revolt of September 1830.

8 Russia takes the Polish capital, Warsaw, after a two-day battle and the Polish revolt for independence collapses.

9 The president of the Council of the Provisional Government of Greece, Count Capo d'Istria, is assassinated after hostility to his bureaucratic methods.

14 The London Conference of Britain, France, Russia, Prussia, and Austria issues Twenty-four Articles, intended to constitute a preliminary peace settlement between Belgium and the Netherlands.

NOVEMBER

15 A treaty incorporating the Twenty-four Articles of October 14 for the separation of the Netherlands and Belgium is accepted by Austria, France, Britain, Prussia, Russia, and Belgium.

17 Venezuela, Ecuador, and New Granada (now Colombia) dissolve the Union of Colombia (of 1819) and New Granada becomes an independent state.

DECEMBER

• Further risings take place in the Papal States against Pope Gregory XVI's upholding of the conservative political system.

12 At the first national nominating convention, the National Republican Party nominates Henry Clay for president.

29 A law abolishing hereditary peerages and replacing them with life peerages gives King Louis Phillipe of France more power over the upper chamber and undermines the attempts of ultra-conservatives to restore absolutism.

SCIENCE, TECHNOLOGY, AND MEDICINE

Agriculture

• U.S. industrialist Cyrus Hall McCormick invents the mechanical reaper (patented in 1834) permitting one person to do the work of five.

Exploration

• English navigator John Biscoe, sailing for the London whaling company Enderby Brothers, discovers the Indian Ocean coast of Antarctica, naming it Enderby Land.

JUNE

1 John Ross, Scottish Arctic explorer, with his nephew James Clark Ross, becomes the first European to reach the magnetic north pole, on the Boothia Peninsula in northern Canada—over 20° from the geographical North Pole at this time.

Health and Medicine

• Cholera and famine lead to 900,000 deaths in Europe.
• English physiologist Marshall Hall writes *Experimental Essay on the Circulation of the Blood*, in which he denounces bloodletting and is the first to show that the capillaries bring the blood into contact with the body's tissues.

Science

• German chemist Justus von Liebig and, independently, U.S. chemist Samuel Guthrie, discover chloroform.
• Italian physcisist Macedonio Melloni makes discoveries in radiant heat through the thermomultiplier.
• Peregrine Phillips develops the contact process for producing sulfuric acid.
• Scottish botanist Robert Brown discovers the nucleus in plant cells.
• Swedish chemist Jöns Jakob Berzelius discovers isomerism—the relation of two or more compounds of the same element with the same number of atoms but which differ in structural arrangement and properties.

AUGUST

29 English chemist Michael Faraday discovers electromagnetic induction—the production of an electric current by change in magnetic intensity (and also the principle of the electric generator). U.S. scientist Joseph Henry makes the same discovery independently of Faraday, and shortly before him, but does not publish his work.

OCTOBER

• English physicist Michael Faraday makes the first transformer.

DECEMBER

27–October 2, 1836 The English naturalist Charles Darwin undertakes a five-year voyage, to South America and the Pacific, as naturalist on the *Beagle*. The voyage convinces him that species have evolved gradually but he waits over 20 years to publish his findings.

Technology

• English leather merchant William Bickford invents the safety fuse for use with explosives.
• French inventor Charles Sauria makes friction matches using yellow phosphorous, sulfur, and potassium chlorate, which are not liable to spontaneous combustion and which light when struck.
• German mining engineer Wilhelm Albert makes the first stranded wire-rope. It is used to haul loads in his mine in Saxony.
• U.S. inventor Seth Boyden patents a method for making malleable cast iron.
• U.S. scientist Joseph Henry constructs an electric telegraph that operates over a distance of 1.6 km/1 mi. By turning an electromagnet on and off, which attracts and releases a piece of iron, he develops a pattern of clicks.

Transportation

• U.S. engineer Matthias William Baldwin develops a steam-tight boiler that doubles the pressure of previous steam engines and allows locomotives to reach speeds of 96 kph/60 mph.

- U.S. entrepreneur Abraham Bower begins a horse-drawn 12-seater omnibus service in New York, New York—the city's first public transit operation.

December 1831–40 Railroad construction proceeds at a rapid pace in Britain and the eastern United States. The railroads provide an all-weather, fast, and inexpensive means of transporting large volumes of goods and people, revolutionizing agriculture, manufacturing, and travel, and having a catastrophic effect on canals and stagecoaches.

ARTS AND IDEAS

Architecture

- London Bridge, designed by the British architects George and John Rennie, is completed in London, England.
- The Caffè Pedrocchi in Padua, Italy, designed by the Italian architects Antonio Gradenigo and Giuseppe Japelli, is completed.

Arts

- The "Barbizon School" of artists, including Jean-François Millet and Pierre Rousseau, first exhibit in the Salon in Paris, France.
- The English artist John Constable paints *Salisbury Cathedral from the Meadows*.
- The French artist Camille Corot paints *The Forest of Fontainebleau*.
- The French artist Paul Delaroche paints *The Princes in the Tower*.
- The U.S. artist William Sidney Mt. paints *Dancing on the Barn Floor*.

Literature and Language

- The English ironmonger and poet Ebenezer Elliott publishes *Corn Law Rhymes*, verses attacking the Corn Laws.
- The English writer Thomas Love Peacock publishes his comic novel *Crotchet Castle*.
- The French writer Honoré de Balzac publishes the novels *Peau de Chagrin/The Ass's Skin* and *Le Chef-d'oeuvre inconnu/The Forgotten Masterpiece*.
- The French writer Victor Hugo publishes his poetry collection *Les Feuilles d'automne/Autumn Leaves* and his novel *Notre-Dame de Paris/The Hunchback of Notre Dame*.
- The Italian poet Giacomo Leopardi publishes his poetry collection *Canti/Songs*.
- The Swedish writer and feminist Fredrika Bremer publishes her novel *Familjen H/The H. Family*. Bremer introduces the domestic novel into Swedish literature.
- The U.S. writer James Kirke Paulding publishes the novel *The Dutchman's Fireside*.
- The U.S. writer James Fenimore Cooper publishes his novel *The Bravo*.

- The U.S. writer John Greenleaf Whittier publishes *Legends of New England in Prose and Verse*.

Music

- French composer Hector Berlioz completes his *Symphonie fantastique/Fantastic Symphony*.
- German composer Felix Mendelssohn completes his choral work *Die erste Walspurgisnacht/The First Halloween Night* (Opus 60).
- German composer Robert Schumann completes his *Papillons/Butterflies*, 12 short pieces for solo piano (Opus 2).
- The opera *Robert le Diable/Robert the Devil* by the German composer Giacomo Meyerbeer is first performed, in Paris, France. It is first performed in Britain in 1832 (in London, England), and in the United States in 1834 (in New York, New York).
- The opera *Zampa* by the French composer Louis Joseph Ferdinand Hérold is first performed, in Paris, France.
- The operas *La sonnambula/The Sleepwalking Girl* and *Norma*, both by the Italian composer Vicenzo Bellini, are first performed, in Milan, Italy.

JULY

4 "America the Beautiful" is sung publicly for the first time, at the Park Street Church in Boston, Massachusetts. The words are the work of Baptist minister Samuel Francis Smith; the tune is borrowed from the British anthem "God Save the King."

Theater and Dance

- The play *The Gladiator* by the U.S. writer Robert Montgomery Bird is first performed, in Philadelphia, Pennsylvania.
- The Russian poet Alexander Pushkin publishes his verse drama *Boris Godunov*, which he completed in 1825.
- The tragedy *Des Meeres und der Liebe Wellen/The Waves of Sea and Love* by the Austrian dramatist Franz Grillparzer is first performed, in Vienna, Austria.

SOCIETY

Education

- La Grange College is founded in La Grange, Georgia.
- New York University is founded in New York, New York.
- Wesleyan University is founded in Middletown, Connecticut.

DECEMBER

26 Philadelphia merchant-millionaire Stephen Girard dies, leaving his fortune for the creation of the Girard College, Philadelphia. It is a secondary school for orphaned white boys, founded with the provision that no minister of any creed, denomination, or sect be allowed to visit, or to sit on its board.

Everyday Life

- The population of Britain is 12.2 million, Ireland, 7.7 million, and the United States, 12.8 million.

December 1831–40 Emigration to the United States is 75,810 from Britain and 207,381 from Ireland.

AUGUST

10 William Driver, a ship's captain from Salem, Massachusetts, coins the term "Old Glory" in reference to the U.S. flag.

Religion

- The U.S. founder of The Church of Jesus Christ of Latter-day Saints, Joseph Smith, relocates its headquarters from Fayette, New York, to Kirtland, Ohio.
- The U.S. preacher and moralist Lyman Beecher publishes "The Necessity of Revivals to the Perpetuity of Our Civil and Religious Institutions."

AUGUST

- U.S. religious leader William Miller founds the second Adventists in the United States.

BIRTHS & DEATHS

c. 1831   Sitting Bull, Sioux chief who was responsible for the massacre of George Custer and all the men under his command at the Battle of the Little Bighorn, born near Grand River, Dakota Territory (–1890).

JANUARY

14 Henry MacKenzie, Scottish novelist, poet, and playwright, dies in Edinburgh, Scotland (85).

31 Barthold Georg Niebuhr, German historian, dies in Bonn, Prussia (54).

MARCH

6 Philip H. Sheridan, Union general in the Civil War, born in Albany, New York (–1888).

JUNE

29 (Heinrich Friedrich) Karl, Reichsfreiherr vom und zum Stein, chief minister of Prussia 1807–08 who formed the final European coalition against Napoleon, dies in Schloss Cappenberg, Westphalia (73).

JULY

4 James Monroe, fifth president of the United States 1817–25, a Democratic Republican, dies in New York, New York and is buried in Richmond, Virginia (73).

AUGUST

5 Sébastien Erard, French piano- and harp-maker who pioneered the construction of the modern form of the piano, dies near Passy, France (79).

OCTOBER

6 (Julius Wilhelm) Richard Dedekind, German mathematician who gave an arithmetical definition to irrational numbers, born in Braunschweig, Brunswick (–1916).

NOVEMBER

11 Nat Turner, U.S. slave who led a briefly successful slave revolt, is hanged in Jerusalem, Virginia (31).

14 Georg Wilhelm Friedrich Hegel, German philosopher of the idealist school, dies in Berlin, Germany (61).

19 James A. Garfield, twentieth president of the United States 1881, a Republican, born near Orange, Ohio (–1881).

1832

POLITICS, GOVERNMENT, AND ECONOMICS

Business and Economics

- U.S. president Andrew Jackson vetoes legislation chartering the Second Bank of the United States.

JULY

10   U.S. president Andrew Jackson vetoes legislation renewing the charter of the Bank of the United States. Jackson maintains that the bank is a monopoly controlled by foreigners.

NOVEMBER

24   South Carolina sparks the so-called Nullification controversy by calling a state convention to nullify the federal tariffs of 1828 and early 1832. The convention also threatens to withdraw South Carolina from the Union.

DECEMBER

10   U.S. president Andrew Jackson responds to South Carolina's nullification ordinance by equating secession with treason and threatening to use force if necessary to uphold federal law.

Colonization

- Massachusetts abolitionist William Lloyd Garrison publishes *Thoughts on African Colonization*, explaining why he withdrew his support for the colonization movement.

Human Rights

- Virginian Thomas R. Dew publishes "Review of the Debate in the Virginia Legislature of 1831 and 1832," recounting one of the South's last frank discussions about the institution of slavery.

MAY

9   The U.S. government and the Seminoles sign the Treaty of Payne's Landing, by which the Seminoles agree to leave Florida for land belonging to the Creek people, west of the Mississippi River.

Politics and Government

- In U.S. Congressional elections, the Democrats and National Republicans each retain 20 seats in the Senate,

with 8 seats going to other parties. In the House, Democrats retain a 147–43 majority over the National Republicans.

JANUARY

19   An Austrian army arrives in Bologna to put down the revolt against conservative government in the Papal States.

19   Austrian troops, under Count Josef Radetzky, occupy Ancona after fresh risings in the Papal States (at the end of 1831) and remain until 1838.

21   New York senator William Learned Marcy coins the term "spoils," in a speech defending political patronage within the Democratic Party.

FEBRUARY

23   A French fleet docks at Ancona to dispute Austria's intervention in Italian affairs by sending troops to deal with the revolt against conservative government in the Papal States.

26   The Polish constitution is abolished following the crushing of the Polish rebellion for independence by Russia. A new organic statute is imposed by Czar Nicholas I of Russia allowing for partial autonomy, but its provisions are never implemented as Poland is Russified under its new viceroy, Marshal Ivan Paskevich.

29   New Granada's (now Colombia) constitution is proclaimed, providing for a republican system of government with a Congress of two chambers.

MARCH

23   The Third Reform Bill for revision of the British political system is passed by the House of Commons.

APRIL

6   The Sacs return to Illinois from Iowa, upsetting white settlers and inaugurating the Black Hawk War (named for the Sac chief Black Hawk).

10   A French law excludes the families of Charles X and Napoleon I from France.

10   The Ottoman Empire declares war on Mehmet Ali, its representative in Egypt, who is in effect independent. He is demanding the Ottoman province of Syria as his reward for aiding the Ottoman Empire in the War of Greek Independence.

30   Caroline de Bourbon, a leading legitimist conspirator, lands at the southern French port of Marseille in an unsuccessful attempt to start a rising to put Charles X back on the French throne.

MAY

5   Ibrahim, son of Mehmet Ali of Egypt, takes the Ottoman port of Acre in Egypt's war with the Ottoman Empire.

21   The Democratic Party formally adopts its name at the national convention in Baltimore, Maryland.

27   The Hambach Festival of South German Democrats, a gathering of the supporters of political reform and unification, advocates armed revolt.

JUNE

5   Riots break out in Paris, France, after the funeral of the leading republican General Maximilien Lamarque.

16   The French prime minister Casimir Périer is one of many Parisians to die of cholera.

28   Klemens, Prince Metternich, of Austria has his Six Articles passed by the diet (assembly) of the German Confederation, giving the diet the right to prevent member states implementing liberal reforms.

JULY

9   Dom Pedro, the father of Maria da Gloria, Queen of Portugal, takes the city of Oporto with the aid of Britain and France and the forces of Maria's rival, Dom Miguel, are defeated.

AUGUST

2   In the Black Hawk War, Illinois militia general Henry Atkinson commands a massacre of Sac women, children, and old men at the mouth of Wisconsin's Bad Axe River.

8   The British East India Company, under Governor-General William Bentinck, annexes Cathar after its residents ask for British protection.

8   The Greek National Assembly elects the liberal prince Otto of Bavaria king as Otto I.

SEPTEMBER

21   The United States and the Sac and Fox people sign a treaty ending the Black Hawk War. The Native Americans agree to remain west of the Mississippi River.

OCTOBER

6   Queen Maria Cristina, wife of the sick king Ferdinand VII of Spain, is appointed regent, leading to a partial liberalization of policy.

11   The former Napoleonic marshal Nicholas-Jean Soult, duc de Dalmie, becomes prime minister of France in an administration containing François Guizot, Adolphe Thiers, and Achille, duc de Broglie, which stabilizes French politics.

15   Maria Cristina, the queen–regent of Spain, extends an amnesty to many political exiles.

NOVEMBER

7   Caroline de Bourbon, a leading legitimist conspirator (supporting the royal house of Bourbon), is arrested following her unsuccessful attempt to stage a rising in France.

DECEMBER

21   Egyptian forces rout the Ottoman army at the Battle of Konieh in the war between the two countries.

23   The French take the city of Antwerp, forcing the Netherlands to recognize the independence of Belgium.

SCIENCE, TECHNOLOGY, AND MEDICINE

Agriculture

- U.S. agriculturalist Edmund Ruffian writes *An Essay on Calcareous Manures*, in which he shows that soil acidity can be reduced by the application of calcareous earths.

Health and Medicine

- A cholera epidemic arrives in the United States from Canada, killing thousands of people in this year alone.
- English physician Thomas Hodgkin first describes the lymphatic cancer, Hodgkin's disease.
- Reclining dentists' chairs are first introduced, in England, designed by English surgeon James Snell.

Math

- Swiss mathematician Jakob Steiner founds synthetic geometry with the publication of *Systematic Development of the Dependency of Geometrical Forms on One Another*.

Science

- English physicist William Sturgeon constructs an electric motor.
- French chemist Pierre-Jean Robiquet isolates the analgesic codeine from opium.
- French inventor Hippolyte Pixii builds the first magneto or magneto-electric generator. A magnet rotates in front of two coils to produce an alternating current, making it the first induction electric generator and the first machine to convert mechanical energy into electrical energy.
- G.-E. Merkel of Paris, France, and J. Siegal of Austria develop friction matches without phosphorous.
- German astronomer Wilhelm Olbers predicts the earth will pass through the tail of Biela's comet, causing panic in Europe.
- German chemist Justus von Liebig investigates the constitution of ether-alcohol and founds *Annalen der Pharmacie*, which later becomes the major chemical journal *Annalen der Chemie*.
- German chemists Justus von Liebig and Friedrich Wöhler discover radicals—chemical groups that remain unchanged through a variety of reactions. Their investigations into the structure of oil of bitter almonds (benzaldehyde) represent the first attempts to understand the structure of organic compounds.

JULY

- U.S. scientist Joseph Henry discovers the phenomenon of self-induction—the production of electric current when a conductor is disconnected from a battery.

Technology

- Belgian inventor Joseph Plateau develops the phenakistoscope, a device which creates the illusion of motion. It consists of a disc, with images in reverse, located around the center, and which is rotated in front of a mirror. The illusion of motion is created by observing the images in the mirror through slits on the disc.
- English inventor Charles Wheatstone invents the stereoscope, a device for viewing pictures in three dimensions.
- French engineer Benoît Fourneyron develops a water turbine capable of 50 horsepower.
- John Matthews creates the soda fountain, a machine for carbonating water, which he then sells at his store in New York, New York.
- The U.S. artist and inventor Samuel Finley Breese Morse begins development of an electric telegraph machine.
- U.S. engineer William Avery builds the first practical steam turbine; it is used to power sawmills.

July, 1832–1834 U.S. inventor Walter Hunt improves on Barthélemy Thimonnier's sewing machine by developing one that uses two threads.

Transportation

- The *Ann McKim*, the first of a new class of clipper ship, is launched in the United States.
- The 580-km/360-mi Göta Canal from Göteborg to Stockholm is completed in Sweden, connecting the North Sea to the Baltic.

NOVEMBER

14 The New York and Harlem Railroad begins operation in New York, New York. It consists of two horse-drawn cars that travel on tracks in the pavement. The cars have a capacity of 40 and travel at about 19 kph/12 mph.

ARTS AND IDEAS

Architecture

- The University of Helsinki, Finland, designed by the German architect Carl Ludwig Engel, is completed.

Arts

c. 1832 The German artist Caspar David Friedrich paints *Large Enclosure.*
- The French artist Jean-Auguste-Dominique Ingres paints his *Portrait of Louis-François Bertin.*
- The U.S. artist George Catlin paints *Keokuk, The Watchful Fox, Chief of the Tribe.* Beginning in 1832, and traveling from Montana to Florida, Catlin paints over 500 images of Native Americans. They form one of the most important records of the indigenous cultures of North America.

Literature and Language

- The Austrian writer Nikolaus Lenau publishes *Gedichte/Poems.*
- The English poet Alfred, Lord Tennyson publishes *Poems.* Among its best-known poems are "The Lotus-Eaters" and "The Lady of Shalott."
- The French writer George Sand publishes her novel *Indiana.*
- The French writer Honoré de Balzac publishes *Contes drôlatiques/Droll Stories.*
- The German writer Eduard Friedrich Mörike publishes his novel *Maler Nolten/Painter Nolten.*
- The Italian writer Silvio Pellico publishes *Le mie prigioni/My Imprisonment.*
- The Russian lexicographer and folklorist Vladimir Ivanovich Dahl publishes *Russkie skazki/Russian Fairy Tales.*
- The Swedish writer Carl Jonas Love Almqvist publishes the first volume of his *Törnrosens bok/The Thornrose Book.* He publishes many volumes in the series, which includes selections of his prose and verse.

Music

- German composer Felix Mendelssohn completes his Symphony No. 5 (Opus 107), the *Reformation.*
- Massachusetts educator Lowell Mason establishes the Boston Academy of Music.
- The opera *L'elisir d'amore/The Love Potion* by the Italian composer Gaetano Donizetti is first performed, in Milan, Italy.

Theater and Dance

- The German poet Johann Wolfgang von Goethe publishes part two of his verse drama *Faust.* The first part appeared in 1808.
- The tragedy *Le Roi s'amuse/The King Amuses Himself* by the French writer Victor Hugo is first performed, in Paris, France. It later provides the basis for the opera *Rigoletto,* which is written in 1851 by the Italian composer Giuseppe Fortunino Francesco Verdi.

Thought and Scholarship

- The Swedish historian Erik Gustaf Geijer publishes the first volume of his three-volume *Svenska folkets historia/History of the Swedes.* The last volume appears in 1836.

SOCIETY

Education

- The Presbyterian Church founds Wabash College in Crawfordsville, Indiana.

- Zürich University is founded in Switzerland.

APRIL

7   Pennsylvania College, later known as Gettysburg College, is founded in Gettysburg, Pennsylvania.

Media and Communication

SEPTEMBER

1   The *New York Sun* begins publication under the direction of Benjamin Day.

Religion

- Pope Gregory XVI issues an encyclical condemning freedom of conscience and of the press.
- The English teacher and historian Thomas Arnold publishes *Essay on Church Reform.*

BIRTHS & DEATHS

JANUARY

23   Edouard Manet, French realist painter and important 19th-century artist, born (−1883).

27   Lewis Carroll (pen name of Charles Lutwidge Dodgson), English novelist who wrote *Alice's Adventures in Wonderland* (1865), born in Daresbury, Cheshire, England (−1898).

MARCH

4   Jean-François Champollion, French linguist, who translated the Rosetta Stone and founded Egyptology, dies in Paris, France (41).

10   Muzio Clementi, Italian-born English pianist and composer, often called the "father of the piano," dies in Evesham, Worcestershire, England (79).

22   Johann Wolfgang von Goethe, German poet, novelist, dramatist, and philosopher, dies in Weimar, Saxe-Weimar (now Germany) (82).

MAY

13   Georges Cuvier, French zoologist who established the sciences of comparative zoology and paleontology, dies in Paris, France (62).

31   Evariste Galois, French mathematician who developed group theory algebra, dies in a duel in Paris, France (20).

JUNE

6   Jeremy Bentham, English philosopher and chief proponent of utilitarianism, dies in London, England (84).

9   Friedrich Gentz, German politician and writer known for his criticisms of the French Revolution, dies in Vienna, Austria (67).

10   Nikolaus August Otto, German engineer who developed the four-stroke ("Otto cycle") internal combustion engine, born in Holzhausen, in Nassau, Germany (−1891).

AUGUST

16   Wilhelm Wundt, German psychologist, the founder of experimental psychology, born in Neckarau, near Mannheim, Baden, Germany (−1920).

24   Sadi Carnot, French scientist who provided the theoretical basis of steam engines known as the Carnot cycle, dies in Paris, France (36).

SEPTEMBER

21   Walter Scott, Scottish novelist, poet, historian, and biographer who developed the historical novel, dies in Abbotsford, Roxburgh, Scotland (61).

25   William Le Baron Jenny, U.S. civil engineer and architect who built the first skyscraper, in Chicago, Illinois, born in Fairhaven, Massachusetts (−1907).

30   Frederick Sleigh Roberts (Lord Roberts), British field marshal during the Anglo-Afghan War 1878–80, and the Second Anglo-Boer War 1899–1902, born in Cawnpore, India (−1914).

NOVEMBER

29   Louisa May Alcott, U.S. author of children's books, best known for *Little Women* (1869), born in Germantown, Pennsylvania (−1888).

DECEMBER

28   Gustav Eiffel, French civil engineer who built the Eiffel Tower for the Paris Exhibition in 1867, born in Dijon, France (−1923).

1833

POLITICS, GOVERNMENT, AND ECONOMICS

Business and Economics

- Philadelphia glass-producer Thomas W. Dyott introduces the paternalist concept of the factory town. Dyott's workers live in company housing and according to rules and customs governing virtually every aspect of their lives.
- The British East India Company's trading rights with China are transferred to individual merchants.

MARCH

2   To head off the showdown between South Carolina and the federal government over the tariff issue, U.S. president Andrew Jackson signs legislation reducing the tariff over the next ten years. But the tariff legislation is accompanied by the inflammatory Force Act which affirms the president's right to use force to ensure state compliance with federal law.

23   Prussia establishes a *Zollverein* (customs union) in Germany, incorporating Bavaria, Hesse-Darmstadt, and Württemberg, from which Austria is excluded.

SEPTEMBER

23   U.S. president Andrew Jackson replaces Secretary of the Treasury William J. Duane with Roger B. Taney, after Duane refuses to comply with Jackson's order to remove government deposits from the Bank of the United States, an institution against which the president was conducting a long-running campaign.

OCTOBER

1   The administration of U.S. president Andrew Jackson withdraws federal deposits from the Bank of the United States and puts them in state banks.

DECEMBER

26   Kentucky senator Henry Clay introduces two resolutions censuring U.S. president Andrew Jackson for his removal of federal deposits from the Bank of the United States.

Human Rights

- Massachusetts abolitionist Lydia Maria Child publishes *An Appeal in Favor of That Class of Americans Called Africans,* a book that converts many Northerners to abolitionism.

- The New York abolitionist Arthur Tappan joins representatives of local antislavery societies to form the American Anti-Slavery Society in Philadelphia, Pennsylvania. Though moderate in origin, the organization quickly falls under the influence of the radical William Lloyd Garrison.

Politics and Government

- Massachusetts becomes the last state in the Union to maintain the legal separation of church and state.
- The U.S. Congress establishes the Congressional Temperance Society in Washington, D.C.
- The U.S. Supreme Court, in *Barron v. Baltimore*, rules that state governments are not beholden to respect the federal Bill of Rights.

JANUARY

1   Britain proclaims sovereignty over the Falkland Islands (claimed by Argentina in 1820).

FEBRUARY

2   An attempt by the "Young Italy" movement (the followers of Giuseppe Mazzini) to seize Savoy fails.

20   Russian ships enter the Bosporus on the way to Constantinople to assist the Ottoman Empire in its war with Egypt.

MARCH

4   U.S. president Andrew Jackson is inaugurated for a second term.

4   Colonel Henry Dodge forms the first independent U.S. cavalry unit, the First Regiment of Dragoons, at Fort Jefferson, Missouri.

15   In the final salvo of the controversy over the tariff laws, South Carolina repeals its nullification ordinance of the previous November, but nullifies the recent Force Act as a face-saving gesture.

20   The United States and Siam (modern Thailand) sign a commercial treaty in Bangkok.

APRIL

- A Coercion Act for Ireland gives the Lord Lieutenant, Lord Edward Stanley, the power to suppress meetings, try suspects by court martial, and impose an all-night curfew.

3   An attempt by German revolutionaries to take over the diet (assembly) of the German Confederation in Frankfurt in protest against the repressive articles of June 1832 is easily crushed.

MAY

3   The Ottoman Empire recognizes the independence of Egypt (ostensibly a part of the Ottoman Empire but in fact already autonomous) and cedes the provinces of Syria and Aden to its ruler Mehmet Ali.

21   The Dutch conclude an armistice of indefinite length, suspending their war with Belgium over Belgian independence from the United Netherlands.

22   A constitution in Chile ends internal unrest and creates an oligarchic, conservative regime, giving greater power to the president and establishing Roman Catholicism as the state religion.

JUNE

●   The diet (assembly) of the German Confederation in Frankfurt appoints a central commission to ensure radical elements are suppressed in its member states.

28   François Guizot's Primary Education Law in France provides for "moralizing" religious education under the secular control of local mayors and prefects. Guizot has been the minister of public instruction since 1832.

JULY

8   By the Treaty of Unkiar-Skelessi, a defensive alliance between the Ottoman Empire and Russia, Sultan Mahmud II of the Ottoman Empire agrees to close the Dardanelles to all but Russian ships.

24   The Portuguese capital, Lisbon, is evacuated by the forces of the challenger to the throne, Dom Miguel, and occupied by the supporters of Dom Pedro and Maria II (known as Maria da Gloria).

AUGUST

14   The Church Temporalities Act is passed by the British Parliament reducing the number of bishoprics in Ireland, where only one in ten of the population are Protestant.

SEPTEMBER

10–20   A conference is held at Münchengrätz, attended by Russia, Prussia, and Austria to discuss European problems, particularly the weakness of the Ottoman Empire.

21   The U.S. and Muscat (Oman) sign a commercial treaty.

22   Maria da Gloria, Queen of Portugal, returns to the capital, Lisbon, after it has been evacuated by the rival claimant Dom Miguel's forces and reoccupied by her supporters.

26   A new liberal constitution is granted in the German kingdom of Hanover by King William IV of Britain.

29   King Ferdinand VII of Spain dies and is succeeded by his infant daughter Queen Isabella II.

OCTOBER

15   Prussia, Russia, and Austria agree to support the integrity of the Ottoman Empire and to further the Holy Alliance by assisting one another in time of war.

SCIENCE, TECHNOLOGY, AND MEDICINE

Agriculture

●   U.S. agriculturalist Edmund Ruffian begins the periodical *Farmer's Journal*, in which he warns that current farming practices will exhaust the soil. He advocates crop rotation, contour plowing, and the use of fertilizers.

●   U.S. inventor Obed Hussey develops a mechanical reaper rivaling that of Cyrus Hall McCormack patented in 1834.

October 1833–37   Japan is hit by famine.

Computing

●   Charles Babbage creates his "analytical engine" in England; it is a prototype of the modern computer, using levers, rods, and gears to perform calculations.

Health and Medicine

c. 1833   German physician Gustav Henle describes in detail the structures of the eye and brain.

●   Bohemian physiologist Jan Purkinje discovers the sweat glands in the skin.

●   U.S. army surgeon William Beaumont publishes *Experiments and Observations on the Gastric Juice and the Physiology of Digestion*—the first detailed book on human digestion.

Science

●   English physicist Michael Faraday announces the basic laws of electrolysis: that the amount of a substance deposited on an electrode is proportional to the amount of electric current passed through the cell, and that the amounts of different elements are proportional to their atomic weights.

●   French chemist Anselme Payen discovers and isolates diastase from barley; it is the first enzyme to be isolated.

●   Moravian baron Karl von Reichenbach discovers creosote.

October 1833–37   Swiss-born U.S. paleontologist Jean-Louis Agassiz publishes *Recherches sur les poissons fossiles/Research on Fossil Fish*, in which he classifies nearly 1,700 fossil fishes.

Technology

●   Balloon-framing, a wood-frame technique, is developed by U.S. carpenter Augustus Deodat Taylor; it revolutionizes house construction in the United States.

●   English optician Peter Barlow develops an achromatic (noncolor-distorting) lens for microscopes.

●   German mathematician Karl Friedrich Gauss, and German physicist Wilhelm Eduard Weber, construct an electromagnetic telegraph. It uses two copper wires and a compasslike mechanism for detecting the electric current, and carries messages 2.3 km/1.4 mi over housetops in Göttingen.

●   Swedish engineer John Ericsson exhibits a caloric, or heat engine, which uses superheated air to produce 5 horsepower.

●   U.S. inventor Samuel Colt introduces his six-shooter revolver.

●   Xavier Progin develops the first typewriter with a manual keyboard. Letters are placed on separate hammers.

Transportation

- The Ohio and Erie Canal, connecting the Great Lakes to the Mississippi River, opens to commercial traffic.

ARTS AND IDEAS

Arts

- The Scottish gardener and designer John Claudius Loudon publishes *Encyclopedia of Cottage, Farm, and Villa Architecture and Furniture*.
- The U.S. artist Thomas Cole paints *The Titan's Goblet*.

Literature and Language

- The English poet Robert Browning publishes *Pauline: A Fragment of a Confession* anonymously.
- The French writer George Sand publishes her novel *Lélia*.
- The French writer Honoré de Balzac publishes the novel *Eugénie Grandet*.
- The literary journal *Knickerbocker Magazine* begins publication in New York, New York, under the editorship of Willis G. and Lewis G. Clark.
- The Russian poet Alexander Pushkin publishes his novel in verse *Yevgeny Onegin/Eugene Onegin*, his major work. He began writing it in 1823. It quickly becomes one of the best-known works of Russian literature and is used as the basis for the 1879 opera by the Russian composer Peter Illich Tchaikovsky.
- The Scottish historian Thomas Carlyle publishes *Sartor Resartus, the Life and Opinions of Herr Teufelsdröckh*, a philosophical satire, in *Fraser's Magazine*. It appears as a book in 1836.
- The U.S. writer John Neal publishes his novel *The Down-Easters*.

Music

- German composer Felix Mendelssohn completes his Symphony No. 4 (Opus 90), the *Italian*.
- German composer Robert Schumann completes his piano piece *Impromptus on a Theme by Clara Wieck* (Opus 5).

Thought and Scholarship

- The French historian Jules Michelet publishes the first volume of his 24-volume *Histoire de France/History of France*. The last volume appears in 1867.
- The German poet Heinrich Heine publishes *Französische Zustände/French Affairs*, a collection of his newspaper articles on France.
- The institutional center of French liberal thought, the Académie des Sciences Morales et Politiques, is revived in France.

SOCIETY

Education

- Haverford College is founded in Haverford, Pennsylvania.
- Oberlin College is founded in Oberlin, Ohio. It is the first coeducational college in the country.
- The University of Delaware is founded in Newark, Delaware.
- Congregationalist minister Abiel Abbot helps establish the nation's oldest local, tax-supported public library in Peterborough, New Hampshire.

Media and Communication

March 1833–37 The rise of the "penny press," or low-cost papers, includes the *New York Sun* founded in

---

BIRTHS & DEATHS

MAY
7 Johannes Brahms, German composer, born in Hamburg, Germany (–1897).

JULY
5 Joseph-Nicéphore Niepce, French inventor who took the first permanent photograph, dies in Chalon-sur-Saône, France (68).

AUGUST
20 Benjamin Harrison, twenty-third president of the United States 1889–93, a Republican, born in North Bend, Ohio (–1901).
28 Edward Burne-Jones, English artist and designer, born in Birmingham, England (–1898).

SEPTEMBER
7 Hannah More, English religious author and educator of the poor, dies in Bristol, England (88).
27 Rammohan Ray, Indian religious leader and political activist who founded the Hindu–Protestant movement Brahmo Samaj, dies in Bristol, England (61).

OCTOBER
21 Alfred Nobel, Swedish chemist who invented dynamite and founded the Nobel prizes, born in Stockholm, Sweden (–1896).

NOVEMBER
12 Alexander Porfiryevich Borodin, Russian composer, born in St. Petersburg, Russia (–1887).

13 Edwin Booth, U.S. actor of Shakespearean tragedy, born in Bel Air, Maryland (–1893).
19 Wilhelm Dilthey, German philosopher who developed a philosophy of the humanities and social sciences, born in Biebrich, near Wiesbaden, now in Germany (–1911).
23 Jean-Baptiste Jourdan, French general and marshal of France, dies in Paris, France (71).

DECEMBER
6 John Singleton Mosby, U.S. Confederate guerrilla during the Civil War, born in Edgemont, Virginia (–1916).

1833 by Benjamin H. Day, and the *New York Morning Herald*, founded in 1835 by James Gordon Bennett.

Religion

- The English churchman John Henry Newman publishes the first of his *Tracts for the Times*, pamphlets on

religious subjects that become an important expression of the Oxford Movement (a reform movement within the Anglican Church). They appear until 1841, written also by John Keble, Isaac Williams, and Edward Bouverie Pusey.

◆

1834

POLITICS, GOVERNMENT, AND ECONOMICS

Business and Economics

FEBRUARY

14 Workers in Lyons, France, strike in protest at a bill to repress republican societies and labor unions.

APRIL

9 A revolt by silk weavers in Lyons, France, lasts four days before being crushed by the army, after the French government attempts to suppress labor union activities.

JUNE

24 The U.S. Senate rejects U.S. president Andrew Jackson's nomination of Roger B. Taney for the post of treasury secretary in protest of Jackson's heavy-handed banking policy.

28 The U.S. Congress passes the Second Coinage Act, which raises the silver–gold ratio from 15:1 to 16:1.

Human Rights

- U.S. abolitionist minister James G. Birney publishes "Letter to the Ministers and Elders," exhorting clergymen to adopt the cause of abolition.

JULY

- During an antiabolitionist riot in New York, New York, a proslavery mob breaks into the house of abolitionist Lewis Tappan and destroys his furnishings.

AUGUST

1 Slavery is abolished throughout the British Empire, thanks largely to the efforts of the English philanthropist and politician William Wilberforce.

OCTOBER

- A proslavery mob destroys the homes of some 40 black Americans, as a antiabolitionist riot rips through Philadelphia, Pennsylvania.

28 The U.S. government orders the Seminoles to evacute Florida, as stipulated by a treaty of May 1832.

Politics and Government

- Diverse anti-Jacksonian politicians and businessmen coalesce under the leadership of Daniel Webster of Massachusetts, Henry Clay of Kentucky, and John C. Calhoun of South Carolina to form the American Whig Party.

- In U.S. Congressional elections, Democrats retain majorities in the House (145–98) and Senate (27–25).

FEBRUARY

17 The United States and Spain sign the Van Ness Convention in Madrid, settling an old territorial dispute.

MARCH

28 U.S. president Andrew Jackson protests against the Senate's adoption of a censure resolution against him for removing federal government deposits from the Bank of the United States. The Senate strikes the censure resolution from the Congressional Record the next year.

APRIL

12 A republican rising in Paris, France, is crushed by troops commanded by the liberal deputy Adolphe Thiers, and 150 republicans are arrested.

22 Britain, France, Spain, and Portugal form the Quadruple Alliance to uphold liberal constitutions in Portugal and Spain. This is in response to the claim asserted by Don Carlos, brother of the late King Ferdinand VII, who threatens to seize the Spanish throne from his infant niece Isabella II.

JUNE

30 The U.S. Congress creates the Department of Indian Affairs, to oversee federal policy.

JULY

7   A civil war begins in Spain as Don Carlos, brother of the late King Ferdinand VII of Spain, claims the throne occupied by the infant queen Isabella II. The Carlists are supported by the Catholic Church, the Basques, and other conservative elements, and are opposed by Britain and France.

AUGUST

13   An official government of French possessions in north Africa is constituted.

15   The South Australia Act is passed by the British Parliament, allowing for the establishment of a colony there.

SEPTEMBER

24   Dom Pedro of Portugal dies, leaving his daughter, Maria da Gloria, to rule alone.

OCTOBER

16   The Houses of Parliament in London, England, are destroyed by fire.

SCIENCE, TECHNOLOGY, AND MEDICINE

Agriculture

- Cyrus Hall McCormack patents his reaper, which, while not the first of its kind, is the most effective—he sells 4,000 in 1856 and 23,000 the next year—and revolutionizes U.S. agriculture.
- The British Raj oversees the systematic growing of tea in India; this will result in a decline in the market for Chinese tea.

Exploration

JUNE

15   U.S. explorer-merchant Nathaniel Jarvis Wyeth establishes Fort Hall as a military and trading post on the Oregon Trail in southeast Idaho.

Science

- English inventor Charles Wheatstone uses a revolving mirror to measure the speed of electricity in a conductor.
- Estonian physicist Heinrich Lenz formulates the electromagnetic law that an induced current is in a direction that opposes the charge that produces it.
- French chemist Jean-Baptiste-André Dumas formulates the law of substitution by showing that halogens can replace hydrogen in organic compounds.
- French chemist Jean-Baptiste Boussingault discovers that plants absorb nitrogen through the soil and carbon from carbon dioxide in the air.
- French chemists Jean-Baptiste-André Dumas and Eugène-Melchior Péligot isolate methyl alcohol.
- French physicist Benoît-Pierre Clapeyron develops the second law of thermodynamics: entropy always increases in a closed system.

- French physicist Jean-Charles Peltier discovers the Peltier effect: the emission or absorption of heat by an electric current depending on the direction of current. In the 1960s the effect is used for refrigeration.
- German chemist Friedlieb Ferdinand Runge is the first to obtain the simple phenol carbolic acid.
- German chemist Justus von Liebig develops melamine—the basis for synthetic resins such as "Formica" and "Melmac."
- German physiologist Ernst Heinrich Weber writes *De Tactu/Concerning Touch*, in which he introduces the ideas of the smallest perceivable difference between stimuli, and sensory thresholds.
- The English microscopist Joseph Lister discovers the true shape of red blood cells.

June 1834–38   English astronomer John Herschel, at the Cape of Good Hope, catalogs the locations of 68,948 stars in the southern hemisphere.

Technology

- English manufacturer James Sharp produces the first commercial gas stove.
- English mathematician William George Horner develops the zoetrope, a motion picture device that is an improvement over the phenakistoscope. It consists of two discs with images on one side observed through slits on the other.
- U.S. inventor Jacob Perkins develops, in Britain, a compression machine that, by alternate compression and expansion of gases freezes water—the beginning of gas refrigeration.

Transportation

- English architect Joseph Aloysius Hansom patents the hansom cab, an enclosed two-wheeled carriage with a raised driver's seat at the rear. With room for two passengers it becomes the most popular cab in London, England.
- The journal *Lloyd's Register of Shipping* is launched in London, England, containing records of all large merchant ships.
- U.S. blacksmith Thomas Davenport constructs the first battery-powered electric motor. He uses it to operate a small car on a short section of track—the first streetcar.

ARTS AND IDEAS

Architecture

- The Merchants' Exchange in Philadelphia, Pennsylvania, designed by the U.S. architect William Strickland, is completed.

Arts

c. 1834   The U.S. artist Edward Hicks paints *The Peaceable Kingdom*, one of the best-known images of U.S. naive art. He paints this scene several times.

- The French artist and caricaturist Honoré Daumier publishes his lithograph *Rue Transnonain, 14 April 1834.*

- The French artist Eugène Delacroix paints *Women of Algiers*.
- The French artist Théodore Chassériau paints *Two Sisters*.
- The Glyptothek (Sculpture Museum) in Munich, Germany, designed by the German architect Leo von Klenze, is completed.
- The Swiss wax modeler Marie Tussaud opens her waxwork exhibition in London, England.
- The U.S. artist and writer William Dunlap publishes the *Rise and Progress of the Arts of Design in the United States*.
- The U.S. artist Asher Brown Durand paints *The Capture of Major André*.
- The U.S. artist Henry Inman paints his *Self-Portrait*.

Literature and Language

- The English writer Edward Bulwer Lytton publishes his novel *Last Days of Pompeii*.
- The French literary critic Charles-Augustin Ste.-Beuve publishes the autobiographical novel *Volupté/ Voluptuousness* anonymously.
- The Russian critic Vissarion Grigoryevich Belinsky publishes his influential collection of critical essays *Literaturnye mechtaniya/Literary Musings*.

- The Russian poet Alexander Pushkin publishes the short story "Pikovaya dama"/"Queen of Spades."
- The U.S. writer William Gilmore Simms publishes his novel *Guy Rivers*.
- Virginian Thomas W. White establishes the literary-critical journal *Southern Literary Messenger* at Richmond, Virginia.

Music

- French composer Hector Berlioz completes his orchestral work *Harold en Italie/Harold in Italy*, inspired by Lord Byron's poem *Childe Harold's Pilgrimage* published in 1812.

Theater and Dance

- The play *The Broker of Bogatá* by the U.S. writer Robert Montgomery Bird is first performed, in Philadelphia, Pennsylvania.
- The tragedy *Der Traum ein Leben/The Dream a Life* by the Austrian dramatist Franz Grillparzer is first performed, in Vienna, Austria.

BIRTHS & DEATHS

- Dimitry Ivanovich Mendeleyev, Russian chemist who developed the periodic table of the elements, born in Tobolsk, Siberia, Russia (–1907).

JANUARY

12 William Wyndham Grenville, English politician who abolished the British slave trade, dies in Dropmore, Buckinghamshire, England (74).

13 Horatio Alger, U.S. writer and biographer, born in Revere, Massachusetts (–1899).

17 August Weismann, German biologist, one of the founders of genetics who developed a "germ plasm" theory of inheritance, born in Frankfurt am Main, now in Germany (–1914).

FEBRUARY

6 Edwin Klebs, German physician who, with Friedrich Löffler, discovered the diphtheria bacillus, born in Königsberg, Prussia (–1913).

12 Friedrich Schleiermacher, German theologian who founded modern Protestant theology, dies in Berlin, Germany (65).

16 Ernst Haeckel, German zoologist and evolutionist, born in Potsdam, Prussia (now in Germany) (–1919).

26 Aloys Senefelder, German printer who invented lithography, dies in Munich, Germany (62).

MARCH

17 Gottlieb Daimler, German mechanical engineer who built one of the first successful cars powered by an internal combustion engine, born in Schorndorf, Württemberg (now Germany) (–1900).

MAY

20 Marie-Joseph-Paul-Yves-Roch-Gilbert de Motier, marquis de Lafayette, French aristocrat and political leader who fought against the British during the American Revolution, dies in Paris, France (76).

JUNE

19 Charles Maddon Spurgeon, English Baptist preacher and founder of churches and of Spurgeon's Bible College, born in Kelvedon, Essex, England (–1892)

JULY

14 James Whistler, U.S.-born British artist, born in Lowell, Massachusetts (–1903).

19 Edgar Degas, French artist known for his paintings, drawings, and bronzes of the human figure in motion, born in Paris, France (–1917).

25 Samuel Taylor Coleridge, English romantic poet, literary critic, and philosopher, dies in Highgate, London, England (61).

AUGUST

7 Joseph-Marie Jacquard, French inventor of the Jacquard loom which used punched cards to control the pattern and which revolutionized the textile industry, dies in Ouillins, France (82).

18 Marshall Field, U.S. entrepreneur who began Field's department stores, born near Conway, Massachusetts (–1906).

22 Samuel Pierpont Langley, U.S. aeronautics pioneer who built the first heavier-than-air flying machine, born in Roxbury, Massachusetts (–1906).

SEPTEMBER

2 Thomas Telford, Scottish civil engineer who built the Menai Bridge in Wales, dies in London, England (77).

DECEMBER

23 Thomas Malthus, English economist and demographer who theorized that population growth, unless checked, would always outstrip the food supply, dies in St. Catherine, near Bath, England (68).

Thought and Scholarship

- *Deontology; or the Science of Morality* by the English philosopher Jeremy Bentham is published posthumously.
- Massachusetts statesman-scholar George Bancroft publishes his magisterial *History of the United States*.
- The French socialist Victor Considérant publishes the first part of his *Destinée sociale/Social Destiny*. The final part appears in 1838.
- The German historian Leopold von Ranke publishes the first part of his *Die römischen Päpste, ihre Kirche, und ihre Staat/The Roman Popes, their Church and State.* The final volume appears in 1836.
- The U.S. writer James Fenimore Cooper publishes his political tract *A Letter to His Countrymen.*

SOCIETY

Education

- The University of the Ozarks is founded in Clarksville, Arkansas.
- Tulane University is founded in New Orleans, Louisiana.
- Wake Forest University is founded in Winston-Salem, North Carolina.
- Wheaton College is founded in Norton, Massachusetts.

Everyday Life

- The Philadelphia Club is founded in Philadelphia, Pennsylvania. It is the first gentleman's club in the country.
- Tomatoes begin to be eaten as food in the United States (despite their 300-year presence), but will not become popular until 1900 since they are commonly believed to be poisonous.
- U.S. author Jonathan Harrington Green publishes *Gambling Unmasked; or, The Personal Experience of the Reformed Gambler, J H Green*. It contains the first published reference to the game of poker.

Religion

- The French writer on religion Félicité Lamennais publishes *Paroles d'un croyant/Words of a Believer.*

Sports

SEPTEMBER

- The first game of lacrosse on a marked-out pitch is played in Montreal, Lower Canada, between Algonquin and Iroquois teams.

1835

POLITICS, GOVERNMENT, AND ECONOMICS

Business and Economics

- Inventor John Ireland Howe establishes the Howe Manufacturing Company in Salem, New York. The enterprise makes pins in a single operation devised by Howe in 1832.

MAY

12 The German state of Baden joins the *Zollverein* (customs union) established by Prussia in 1833.

Human Rights

- Massachusetts Unitarian pastor William Ellery Channing publishes his antislavery pamphlet "Slavery."
- The U.S. reformer Lydia Maria Child publishes *History of the Conditions of Women in Various Ages and Nations.*

OCTOBER

21 Proslavery Bostonians rough-up abolitionist William Lloyd Garrison, compelling city policemen to escort Garrison to jail for his own protection.

Politics and Government

- Prince Miloš Obrenović of Serbia grants a constitution in the Ottoman province of Serbia, but soon withdraws it at Sultan Mahmud II of the Ottoman Empire's demand.
- The governor of Buenos Aires Juan Manuel de Rosas becomes dictator of Argentina.

- U.S. president Andrew Jackson names Georgia congressman James M. Wayne to the U.S. Supreme Court.

JANUARY

- Anti-Jacksonian Democrats in Tennessee and Alabama nominate Tennessee senator Hugh L. White for president in next year's election. White will capture only these two states. Massachusetts Whigs nominate Daniel Webster, who will face opposition within his own party, and will win only his own state.
- The U.S. Senate rejects President Andrew Jackson's nomination of Maryland jurist and former U.S. attorney general Roger B. Taney to the U.S. Supreme Court.
- 25 A French force under Marshal Bertrand Clauzel dislodges the Algerian leader Abd al-Kader from Tafna, Algeria.
- 30 U.S. president Andrew Jackson becomes the first U.S. president targeted by an assassin's bullet as malcontent Richard Lawrence takes aim at the chief executive while he attends the funeral of South Carolina representative Warren Ransom Davis. Fortunately, Lawrence misfires.

MARCH

2 Emperor Francis I of Austria dies and is succeeded by his son Ferdinand I.

MAY

20 Democrats nominate Vice President Martin Van Buren for president and Kentucky's Richard M. Johnson for vice president.

JUNE

26 The Algerian nationalist leader Abd al-Kader heavily defeats the French army under General Camille Trézel at Macta, Algeria.

JULY

28 An assassination attempt is made on the French king, Louis Philippe, by a lone republican, Giuseppe Fieschi.

SEPTEMBER

9 The "September Laws" in France severely censor the press and suppress the radical movement in response to renewed fears of republican violence.

NOVEMBER

- The Second Seminole War breaks out when the Seminole chief Osceola refuses to lead his people out of Florida and into Oklahoma Territory.
- 24 The U.S.-backed Texas provincial government marshals the Texas Rangers, a mounted police force.

DECEMBER

- The U.S. and Cherokees sign the Treaty of New Echota, by which the Cherokees agree to surrender their land in Georgia in exchange for $5,600,000.

SCIENCE, TECHNOLOGY, AND MEDICINE

Ecology

- U.S. meteorologist James Pollard Espy studies the energy sources of storms and explains frontal systems with attendant condensation and precipitation.

Exploration

- British army officer James Wellsted explores the Hadramaut region of southern Arabia, and discovers the remains of the 2,000-year-old Hadrami civilization.
- French naturalist Godfrey Thomas Vigne explores the Karakoram Mountains north of Kashmir in Central Asia, and is the first European to report the huge glacier systems there.

Health and Medicine

- English physician James Paget discovers the parasitic worm *Trichina spiralis* which causes trichinosis.
- French physician Charles Gabriel Pravaz invents the hypodermic syringe.

Math

- Belgian statistician Adolphe Quetelet publishes *Sur l'Homme et le développement de ses facultés/A treatise on Man and the Development of his Faculties*, in which he presents the idea of the "average man" in whom measurements of various traits are normally distributed around a central value.
- French mathematician Siméon-Denis Poisson publishes *Théorie mathématique de la chaleur/Mathematical Theory of Heat*.
- French mathematician Gustave Coriolis describes the inertial forces acting on a rotating body that act at right angles to the direction of rotation. The Coriolis force causes wind and current systems to rotate to the right in the northern hemisphere and to the left in the southern.

Science

- c. 1835 French chemist Anselme Payen discovers cellulose, the basic component of plant cells.
- German chemist Justus von Liebig discovers the process of silvering—making mirrors by coating glass with silver.
- Swedish chemist Jöns Jakob Berzelius first uses the word "catalysis"—the increased rate of a chemical reaction induced by the addition of another material that remains unchanged after the reaction.

Technology

- English scientist William Henry Fox Talbot publishes a paper describing the paper negative. He exposes paper infused with silver chloride to light, which then separates into fine silver and dark tones from which he can take positive prints.
- U.S. manufacturer Samuel Colt patents a six-shot revolver with a rotating cartridge cylinder. Each time the trigger is pulled a new bullet moves in front of the barrel. Its effective range is 23 m/75 ft.

NOVEMBER

23 Scottish-U.S. inventor Henry Burden patents a machine to mass-produce horseshoes in Troy, New York. Burden can produce 60 horseshoes a minute.

Transportation

MAY

5 The Brussels–Mechelen railroad line opens in Belgium, the first passenger railroad in Europe.

DECEMBER

7 The Nuremberg–Fürth railroad, the first railroad in Germany, opens.

ARTS AND IDEAS

Architecture

- The Arc de Triomphe, designed by the French architect Jean-François-Thérèse Chalgrin, is completed in Paris, France.

Arts

- c. 1835 The German artist Caspar David Friedrich paints *The Stages of Life*.
- The English pioneer of photography William Henry Fox Talbot creates *Picture of a Latticed Window*, the oldest existing photographic negative.
- The French artist Théodore Rousseau paints *The Descent of the Cattle from Pasture*.
- The U.S. artist Henry Inman paints *Newsboy*.
- The U.S. artist Hiram Powers sculpts *Portrait of Andrew Jackson*.
- The U.S. artist Thomas Doughty paints *In Nature's Wonderland*.
- The U.S. artist William Sidney Mt. paints *Bargaining for a Horse*.

Literature and Language

- The Danish writer Hans Andersen publishes *Eventyr, fortalte for børn/Tales, Told for Children*, his first collection of fairy tales.
- The English historian and poet Henry Hart Milman publishes *Nala and Damayanti and Other Poems*, translations from Sanskrit literature.
- The English poet Robert Browning publishes his dramatic poem *Paracelsus*.
- The English writer Edward Bulwer Lytton publishes his novel *Rienzi*.
- The English writer Mary Mitford publishes *Belford Regis: Sketches of a Country Town*.
- The French writer Alfred Victor, comte de Vigny, publishes the collection of stories *Servitude et grandeur militaires/Military Servitude and Grandeur*, one of his most important works.
- The French writer Honoré de Balzac publishes the novel *Le Père Goriot/Father Goriot*.
- The French writer Théophile Gautier publishes his novel *Mademoiselle de Maupin*.
- The Italian poet Giacomo Leopardi publishes a further collection of his poems, *Canti/Songs*.
- The Russian writer Nikolay (Vasilyevich) Gogol publishes his novel *Myortvye dushi/Dead Souls*, and his short story "Shinel"/"The Overcoat" both major works of Russian literature.
- The U.S. writer William Gilmore Simms publishes his novel *The Partisan*.

Music

- German composer Ludwig Spohr completes his Symphony No. 4, *Die Weihe der Töne/The Power of Sound*.
- German composer Richard Wagner completes his *Christopher Columbus* overture.
- German composer Robert Schumann completes his Piano Sonatas No. 1 (Opus 11) and No. 3 (Opus 14), and his piano piece *Carnival: Scènes mignonnes sur quatre notes/Little Scenes on Four Notes* (Opus 9).
- Hungarian composer Franz Liszt completes his piano work *Album d'un voyageur/A Traveler's Album*.
- The opera *Lucia di Lammermoor* by the Italian composer Gaetano Donizetti is first performed, in Naples, Italy. It is based on a story by Scottish writer Walter Scott.

Theater and Dance

- The drama *Chatterton* by the French writer Alfred Victor, comte de Vigny, is first performed, in Paris, France. His most important work, it is based on the brief life of the English poet Thomas Chatterton.
- The German writer Georg Büchner writes his play *Dantons Tod/Danton's Death*. It is published in 1850 and first performed in 1902.

Thought and Scholarship

- The U.S. historian Jared Sparks publishes *The Life of Washington*.
- The English historian Connop Thirlwall publishes the first volume of his *History of Greece*. The last volume appears in 1844.
- The English politician Richard Cobden publishes the pamphlet *England, Ireland and America*, a defense of free trade.

- The French historian Alexis Charles-Henri-Clérel de Tocqueville publishes the first part of his *De la Démocratie en Amérique/Democracy in America*. The last part appears in 1840.

SOCIETY

Education

- Ohio's Oberlin College, founded in 1833, admits students regardless of color.
- The Congregationalist Church establishes Marietta College, in Marietta, Ohio.

DECEMBER
21 The Presbyterian Church establishes Oglethorpe University in Milledgeville, Georgia.

Everyday Life

- The Society for the Prevention of Pauperism is established in Boston, Massachusetts.
- Boston minister Joseph Tuckerman founds the Association of Delegates from the Benevolent Societies of Boston.

JULY
8 The Liberty Bell cracks in Philadelphia, Pennsylvania, while tolling the death of chief justice John Marshall, who died on July 6.

DECEMBER
16 Extensive fire in New York, New York, destroys 674 buildings and causes over $15 million in damage.

Media and Communication

MAY
- The *New York Herald* is founded by Scottish-born U.S. publisher James Gordon Bennet. It costs one cent.

Religion

- The German theologian David Friedrich Strauss publishes *Das Leben Jesu kritisch bearbeitet/The Life of Jesus Critically Examined*. Asserting that many elements of the life of Jesus are to be understood as "myth" rather than literal fact, the book is highly controversial.
- Unitarian pastors William Henry Channing of Cincinnati and James Freeman Clarke of Louisville establish the *Unitarian-Transcendentalist Monthly Western Messenger*.
- The German folklorist and philologist Jakob Ludwig Carl Grimm publishes *Deutsche Mythologie/German Mythology*.

Sports

- A crowd of around 30,000 people at the Union horse-racing course, Long Island, watch Henry Stannard from Connecticut win a $1,000 prize for completing a 16-km/10-mi foot race in less than an hour.

BIRTHS & DEATHS

MARCH
12 Simon Newcomb, Canadian-born U.S. astronomer and mathematician who constructed tables giving the daily positions of celestial bodies, born in Wallace, Nova Scotia, Canada (–1909).

APRIL
21 Samuel Slater, British-born founder of the U.S. cotton textile industry, dies in Webster, Massachusetts (66).

JUNE
2 Pope Pius X, Italian pope 1903–14, born in Riese, Venetia, Austrian Empire (–1914).
6 John Marshall, U.S. chief justice who founded the system of constitutional law in the United States, dies in Philadelphia, Pennsylvania (79).

SEPTEMBER
23 Vincenzo Bellini, Italian operatic composer, dies in Puteaux, France (33).

OCTOBER
9 (Charles-) Camille Saint-Saëns, French composer whose work includes *Samson et Dalila*, and *Carnaval des animaux/Carnival of the Animals*, born in Paris, France (–1921).
31 Adolph von Baeyer, German chemist who discovered the structure of indigo for which he received the Nobel Prize for Chemistry in 1905, born in Berlin, Germany (–1917).

NOVEMBER
25 Andrew Carnegie, U.S. steel magnate and philanthropist, born in Dunfermline, Fife, Scotland (–1919).
30 Mark Twain (pseudonym of Samuel Langhorne Clemens), U.S. author who creates the characters Tom Sawyer and Huckleberry Finn, born in Florida, Missouri (–1910).

DECEMBER
1 Nicholas Baptiste (adopted name of Anselme Baptiste), French actor, dies in Les Batignolles, France (74).

1836

POLITICS, GOVERNMENT, AND ECONOMICS

Business and Economics

MARCH

23 The U.S. Mint turns out the first coins produced by a steam-powered press.

JULY

11 The U.S. treasury department issues a circular announcing that only gold and silver pieces will be deemed acceptable payment for public lands.

Colonization

- Adelaide becomes the capital of the newly formed British colony of South Australia.

SEPTEMBER

1 U.S. missionaries Marcus Whitman and H. H. Spalding inaugurate the settlement of the Oregon Territory near the present-day site of Walla Walla, Washington.

Human Rights

- A proslavery mob destroys the press of abolitionist publisher James Birney, who narrowly escapes with his life.
- Reformer Ernestine L. Rose presents the New York State legislature with a petition demanding the right of women to hold property in their own names.
- The U.S. writer Richard Hildreth publishes *The Slave, or Memoirs of Archy Moore*, one of the first U.S. antislavery novels.

Politics and Government

- In the U.S. Congressional elections, Democrats retain majorities in the House (108–107).
- The Communist League is founded in Paris, France, by emigré German intellectuals. Originally called the League of the Just, it becomes the Communist League after Karl Marx and Friedrich Engels join in 1847.
- U.S. president Andrew Jackson appoints Virginia jurist Philip P. Barbour to the U.S. Supreme Court.

FEBRUARY

22 The first ministry of the moderate liberal Adolphe Thiers is formed in France, temporarily stabilizing French politics.

MARCH

- The U.S. Senate confirms President Andrew Jackson's nomination of former U.S. attorney general Roger B. Taney to the U.S. Supreme Court.

2 Texas declares its independence from Mexico, but the United States does not recognize the Republic of Texas.

6 Two hundred Texans are killed at the isolated fortress of Alamo in San Antonio, Texas, when 3,000 Mexicans commanded by general Antonio Lopes de Santa Anna overrun the Republic of Texas garrison.

APRIL

21 Republic of Texas general Sam Houston defeats his Mexican counterpart General Antonio Lopes de Santa Anna at the Battle of San Jacinto, thereby securing the independence of Texas and ending the Texas–Mexican War.

MAY

25 The U.S. House of Representatives adopts a gag rule, effectively tabling antislavery petitions.

JUNE

15 Arkansas becomes the 25th state in the Union.

JULY

2 The U.S. Congress passes legislation ordering postmasters to deliver all newspapers and pamphlets, regardless of content, under penalty of imprisonment. The act follows reports that some southern postmasters were refusing to deliver abolitionist literature.

AUGUST

13 The Tithes Commutation Act is passed in Britain, solving the problem of the Irish paying tithes to the Irish church by commuting this payment to a state land tax.

17 The Federation of Peru and Bolivia is proclaimed by the Bolivian dictator Andrés de Santa Cruz, creating a more powerful political unit under his control.

SEPTEMBER

6 Adolphe Thiers is forced to resign as French prime minister after proposing an invasion of Spain in support of the liberal regent Queen Maria Cristina.

6 Louis-Mathieu, comte Molé, forms a conservative government in France.

OCTOBER

22 Sam Houston is inaugurated first president of the Republic of Texas.

30 Louis-Napoléon Bonaparte, the nephew of Napoleon I, fails to spark a revolt against King Louis Phillipe of France among the garrison at Strasbourg as a first step

to seizing power and is subsequently exiled to the United States.

NOVEMBER

11 Chile, threatened by the increase in power of its neighbors by confederation, declares war on the Peru–Bolivia Federation.

DECEMBER

7 Americans elect Martin Van Buren president. No vice presidential candidate wins a majority, compelling the Senate to select the vice president for the first time in U.S. history. The Senate chooses Kentucky politician Richard M. Johnson.

SCIENCE, TECHNOLOGY, AND MEDICINE

Ecology

- Mt. Hekla erupts in Iceland causing widespread damage.

Exploration

December 1836–38 Boer farmers from Cape Colony, southern Africa, wishing to escape British rule, begin the Great Trek to the Northeast, exploring and founding settlements in the modern Transvaal and Orange Free State.

Math

- French mathematician Jean-Victor Poncelet publishes *Cours de mécanique appliquée aux machines/A Course in Mechanics Applied to Machines*; it introduces the use of mathematics to machine design.

Science

- Albert Gallatin publishes "A Synopsis of the Indian Tribes" and later publishes other essays on Native Americans, laying the foundation for U.S. ethnology.
- English chemist Edward Davy makes the inflammable welding gas acetylene.
- French chemist Jean-Baptiste-André Dumas establishes the alcohol series.
- French physicist Edmund Becquerel discovers the photovoltaic effect when he observes the creation of a voltage between two electrodes, one of which is exposed to light.
- German physiologist Theodor Schwann discovers pepsin, the first known animal enzyme to be isolated.
- The Danish archeologist Christian Jürgensen Thomsen orders archeological artifacts according to their material: stone, bronze, and iron. The idea later becomes formalized as the Stone Age, Bronze Age, and Iron Age.
- The process of galvanization (coating with zinc) is developed in France.
- U.S. botanist Asa Gray writes *Elements of Botany*, the first textbook on botany.

Technology

- English chemist Edward Davy designs an electromagnetic repeater for amplifying and relaying telegraphic signals.
- English chemist John Frederic Daniell invents the Daniell cell, a battery that generates a steady current during continuous operation—an improvement over the voltaic cell which loses power over time.
- English engineer William Sturgeon establishes the monthly journal *Annals of Electricity*.
- English inventor William Fothergill Cooke develops a telegraph system consisting of three needles and six wires.
- French inventor Ignace Dubus-Bonnel produces woven-glass fabrics—the first fiberglass.
- German gunsmith Nikolaus von Dreyse invents the needle-gun, which uses a long needle-like firing pin to detonate the bullet's charge.
- Swedish engineer John Ericsson patents a screw propeller. Other screw propellers are patented about this time by British engineer Francis Pettit Smith (1836), Austrian engineer Joseph Ressel (1832), Scottish engineer Robert Wilson (1832), and U.S. engineer John Stevens (1826).
- U.S. inventor Samuel Lane develops a combined harvesting and threshing machine. Combines do not come into general use until the 1930s.

Transportation

- The first public horse-drawn railroad in Russia begins service.
- The first steamship to sail the Pacific Ocean, the *Beaver*, is assembled in Vancouver, Washington.

APRIL

18 The Long Island Railroad, New York, begins operating.

JULY

21 The Champlain and St. Lawrence Railroad, between Laprarie and St. John, Quebec, opens—the first railroad in Canada.

ARTS AND IDEAS

Architecture

- Construction begins of the Washington Monument on the mall in Washington, D.C.
- The Church of Notre Dame-de-Lorette in Paris, France, designed by the French architect Louis Lebas, is completed.
- The country house Andalusia, near Philadelphia, Pennsylvania, designed by the U.S. architect Thomas Ustick Walter, is completed.
- The English architect and designer Augustus Welby Northmore Pugin publishes his book *Contrasts*. Arguing in favor of medieval architecture, he plays a leading role in the Gothic revival.

- The Halls of Justice (The Tombs) in New York, New York, designed by the U.S. architect John Haviland, is completed. It is the best-known example of the short-lived revival of Ancient Egyptian styles.
July 1836–42 The Croton dam in New York state is constructed. It is the first large masonry dam in the United States.

Arts

- The English artist Phiz creates his first illustrations for Charles Dickens's novels (the first being *The Pickwick Papers*).
- The U.S. artist Thomas Cole paints *The Oxbow (The Connecticut River near Northampton)* and *The Course of Empire*.
- The French artist François Rude sculpts *La Marseillaise*, a relief on the Arc de Triomphe in Paris, France.

Literature and Language

- The English writer Catherine Grace Gore publishes her novel *Mrs Armytage, or Female Domination*.
- The English writer Charles Dickens publishes his first book, *Sketches by Boz*, a collection of essays and stories that appeared in periodicals. A second volume of sketches is published in 1837.
- The English writer Frederick Marryat publishes his adventure novel *Mr Midshipman Easy*.
- The French writer Alfred de Musset publishes his memoirs *La Confession d'un enfant du siècle/ Confessions of a Child of the Century*.
- The German writer Karl Leberecht Immermann publishes his novel *Die Epigonen/The Late-Comers*.
- The Italian politician and writer Francesco Domenico Guerazzi publishes his novel *L'assedio di Firenze/The Siege of Florence*.

Music

- The opera *Das Liebesverbot/Forbidden Love* by the German composer Richard Wagner is first performed, in Magdeburg, Germany. It is based on William Shakespeare's play *Measure for Measure*.
- The opera *Les Huguenots/The Huguenots* by the German composer Giacomo Meyerbeer is first performed, in Paris, France.
- The opera *Zhizn za tsarya/A Life for the Czar* by the Russian composer Mikhail Ivanovich Glinka is first performed, in St. Petersburg, Russia.

Theater and Dance

- The Austrian writer Nikolaus Lenau publishes his verse drama *Faust*.
- The play *El trovador/The Troubadour* by the Spanish dramatist Antonio García Gutiérrez is first performed.
- The satire *Revizor/The Government Inspector* by the Russian writer Nikolay Gogol is first performed, in Moscow, Russia.

Thought and Scholarship

- The German philosopher Arthur Schopenhauer publishes *Über den Willen in der Natur/On the Will in Nature*.
- The Swiss economist and historian Jean-Charles-Léonard Sismonde de Sismondi publishes *Etudes sur les constitutions des peuples libres/Study of the Constitutions of Free Peoples*.
- The U.S. poet and essayist Ralph Waldo Emerson publishes the essay *Nature*, one of the central works of the U.S. literary and philosophical movement Transcendentalism.

BIRTHS & DEATHS

JANUARY
30 Betsy Ross, U.S. seamstress who designed the first U.S. flag, dies in Philadelphia, Pennsylvania (84).

FEBRUARY
18 Ramakrishna, Hindu religious leader, born in Hooghly, Bengal state, India (–1886).
24 Winslow Homer, U.S. artist noted for his seascapes, born in Boston, Massachusetts (–1910).

MARCH
6 Davy Crockett, U.S. frontiersman and politician, is killed at the Alamo, San Antonio, Texas (49).

APRIL
7 William Godwin, English social philosopher and political journalist who wrote about atheism, anarchy, and individual freedom, born in Wisbech, Cambridgeshire, England (79).

MAY
17 Joseph Norman Lockyear, English astronomer who discovered helium, born in Rugby, Warwickshire, England (–1920).
18 Wilhelm Steinitz, Austrian chess master, world champion 1866–94, born in Prague, Austria-Hungary (–1900).
24 Joseph Rowntree, industrial reformer and philanthropist, born in York, England (–1925).

JUNE
10 André Marie Ampère, French physicist who founded the science of electromagnetism, dies in Marseille, France (61).
20 Emmanuel Joseph Sieyès, French clergyman and constitutional theorist who played a major role in bringing Napoleon I to power, dies in Paris, France (88).

23 James Mill, Scottish Utilitarian philosopher, historian, and economist, dies in London, England (63).
26 Claude Joseph Rouget de Lisle, French soldier, composer of "La Marseillaise," the French national anthem, dies in Choisy-le-Roi, France (76).
28 James Madison, fourth president of the United States 1809–17, a Democratic-Republican, dies in Montpelier, Virginia (85).

SEPTEMBER
7 Henry Campbell-Bannerman, British prime minister 1905–08, a Liberal, born in Glasgow, Scotland (–1908).

NOVEMBER
18 William Schwenk Gilbert, English playwright known for his works produced with Arthur Seymour Sullivan, born in London, England (–1911).

SOCIETY

Education

- Emory University is founded in Atlanta, Georgia.
- German immigrant Constantine Hering opens the North American Academy of Homeopathic Healing Art in Allentown, Pennsylvania.
- U.S. educator William Holmes McGuffey issues his first and second *Eclectic Readers*, moral and literary lesson books.

July 1836–57 William H. McGuffey publishes his "eclectic readers," the most popular how-to-read texts in U.S. public schools. McGuffey also stresses a self-help ethos.

Everyday Life

July

4 Missionaries Narcissa Prentiss Whitman and Eliza Hart Spalding become the first white women to pass into Oregon Territory, where they settle in the company of their husbands.

Media and Communication

- The launch of *La Presse* and *Le Siècle* means newspapers in France become more affordable.

Religion

- The English theologian Edward Bouverie Pusey publishes *On the Holy Eucharist* in the *Tracts for The Times* series, begun in 1833.

Sports

- The inaugural Prix du Jockey Club horse race, the French Derby, is run at Chantilly, northeast of Paris, France.
- The Waterloo Cup coursing (hunting with greyhounds) competition, which comes to be regarded as the "Blue Riband of the Leash," is held for the first time, in England.

1837

POLITICS, GOVERNMENT, AND ECONOMICS

Business and Economics

- William Procter and his brother-in-law James Gamble set up a soap and candle business in Cincinnati, Ohio, which will be the foundation of the successful Procter and Gamble company.

May

10 Inflation and speculation spark panic in U.S. financial circles, precipitating the closing of over 600 banks and spawning a six-year depression.

Colonization

June

6 The Republic of Natal is formally established by Dutch settlers in southern Africa and a constitution is proclaimed.

Human Rights

- U.S. abolitionist preacher Theodore Weld publishes *The Bible Against Slavery*, castigating the hypocrisy of proslavery Christians.

November

7 A proslavery mob in Alton, Illinois, lynches abolitionist publisher Elijah P. Lovejoy and destroys his printing press.

Politics and Government

- In the Second Seminole War, the U.S. Army seizes Seminole chief Osceola, who approaches U.S. commanders under a flag of truce for the purpose of negotiating.

- The U.S. Supreme Court, in *Charles River Bridge v. Warren Bridge Co*, asserts the right of states to encourage economic competition at the cost of existing charter-holders.
- U.S. president Martin Van Buren appoints Tennessee jurist John McKinley and Alabama congressman John Catron to the U.S. Supreme Court.

JANUARY

1   The U.S. Congress passes the Distribution Bill, by which the federal government plans to disperse its budget surplus. The financial panic of the following May thwarts the bill's implementation.

26   Michigan becomes the 26th state in the Union.

FEBRUARY

- The U.S. Supreme Court, in *New York v. Miln*, upholds a New York state law requiring ship captains to file reports on immigrant cargo.

6   The U.S. House of Representatives adopts a resolution denying slaves the right of petition enjoyed by white citizens.

MARCH

3   In one of his last acts in office, U.S. president Andrew Jackson recognizes the Republic of Texas.

3   The U.S. Congress increases the number of Supreme Court justices from seven to nine.

4   Democrat Martin Van Buren is inaugurated eighth president of the United States.

MAY

30   The Treaty of Tafna grants the Algerian leader Abd al-Kader the interior of Algeria while France gains the coastline.

JUNE

18   A progressive constitution is proclaimed in Spain providing for national sovereignty, a representative house of two chambers, the absolute veto of the crown over legislation, and restricted suffrage.

20   On the death of King William IV of Britain his niece, Queen Victoria, succeeds to the throne.

20   The German kingdom of Hanover is automatically separated from Britain when Queen Victoria comes to the British throne because Salic Law forbids female monarchs, and the conservative Ernest Augustus, Duke of Cumberland, the eldest surviving son of George III of Britain, becomes king.

JULY

7   King Ernest Augustus of the German kingdom of Hanover suppresses the Hanoverian constitution.

NOVEMBER

11   Louis Joseph Papineau, the speaker in the Legislative Assembly, leads a rebellion in French-speaking Lower Canada. This is the result of conflicts between the British governor and the legislative councils on the one hand and the popularly elected assemblies on the other, and of friction between French and British settlers.

22   The Lower Canadian rebels against British rule defeat government forces at St. Denis, Lower Canada.

24   The rebels in Lower Canada are decisively defeated at St. Charles, Lower Canada.

DECEMBER

5   British-born Canadian journalist and reformer William Lyon Mackenzie leads a revolt against British rule in Upper Canada.

12   King Ernest Augustus of Hanover dismisses seven professors of Göttingen University, including the German nationalist ethnologists Jacob and Wilhelm Grimm, who oppose his revocation of the constitution.

13   William Lyon Mackenzie, leader of the revolt against British rule in Upper Canada, sets up a provisional government for Upper Canada from headquarters on Navy Island in the Niagara River, and prepares for an invasion of Canada.

29   U.S.–Canadian relations become strained after Canada burns the U.S. ship *Caroline*, killing a U.S. seaman. The ship had been supplying Canadian revolutionaries with contraband on the Niagara River near Buffalo, New York.

SCIENCE, TECHNOLOGY, AND MEDICINE

Health and Medicine

- Smallpox kills 15,000 Native Americans along the Missouri River.
- Bohemian physiologist Jan Purkinje discovers large nerve cells in the cerebellum with branching extensions; they are now called Purkinje cells.
- English physiologist Marshall Hall describes the reflex action of nerves in his paper "On the Functions of the Medulla Oblongata and Medulla Spinalis, and on the Excito-motor System of Nerves." The British medical profession denounces the idea as absurd.

Math

- French mathematician Siméon-Denis Poisson publishes *Recherches sur la probabilité des jugements/Researches on the Probabilities of Opinions*, in which he establishes the rules of probability and describes the Poisson distribution.

Science

- French chemist Henri-Victor Regnault devises a classification system for coal based on its chemical composition.
- French physiologist Henri Dutrochet establishes chlorophyll's essential role in photosynthesis.
- German astronomer Friedrich Struve publishes *Micrometric Measurement of Double Stars*, a catalog of over 3,000 binary stars.
- German chemist Karl Friedrich Mohr enunciates the theory of conservation of energy.
- U.S. geologist James Dana publishes *System of Mineralogy*, which is still the standard text on mineralogy.

Technology

- English architect Joseph Paxton develops the ridge-and-furrow construction technique to produce stronger roofs. He later uses the technique to construct the Crystal Palace, London, England.
- English scientists Charles Wheatstone and William Cooke patent a telegraph system for use on railroads.
- French engineer Benoît Fourneyron builds a water turbine which rotates at 2,300 revolutions per minute and generates 60 horsepower. Weighing only 18 kg/40 lb, and with a wheel only 0.3 m/1.0 ft in diameter, it is far more productive than the waterwheel and is used to power factories, especially the textile industry, in Europe and the United States.
- German scientist Moritz Hermann von Jacobi, in Russia, develops electroplating; first with silver and then with nickel and chrome.
- U.S. blacksmith John Deere introduces his first steel bladed plow at Grand Detour, Illinois.
- U.S. inventors John and Hiram Pitts patent a threshing machine that separates the chaff from the grain.

December 1837–48 The Croton Aqueduct is constructed. Extending 73 km/45.5 mi from the reservoir created by the Croton dam, it supplies New York, New York, with water.

ARTS AND IDEAS

Arts

- The English artist Edwin Landseer paints *The Old Shepherd's Chief Mourner*.
- The French pioneer of photography Louis-Jacques-Mandé Daguerre takes *Still Life in Studio*, one of the earliest daguerreotypes, a photographic technique he invented.

Literature and Language

- English journalist Harriet Martineau publishes *Society in America*, a largely favorable account of her travels through the young republic.
- English teacher Isaac Pitman devises the first practical system of shorthand, which is based on phonetic principles. He publishes details in his book *Stenographic Sound Hand*.
- German teacher Georg Friedrich Grotefend publishes *New Contributions to a Commentary on the Persepolitan Cuneiform Writing* in which he deciphers Persian cuneiform script.
- The English churchman and writer Richard Harris Barham begins publishing *Ingoldsby Legends*, mock-medieval ballads, in journals.
- The English writer Charles Dickens publishes his first novel, *The Pickwick Papers*, and begins to publish his novel *Oliver Twist* in the magazine *Bentley's Miscellany*. It is published as a book in 1838.

- The English writer William Makepeace Thackeray begins to publish his comic sketches *The Yellowplush Correspondence* in *Fraser's Magazine*. They are published in his *Comic Tales and Sketches* in 1841.
- The Flemish writer Hendrik Conscience publishes his novel *In't wonderjaar/In The Year of Miracles*.
- The Russian poet Alexander Pushkin publishes his long poem *Medny vsadnik/The Bronze Horseman*. One of the first works to focus on the "little man," it is of major importance in the development of Russian literature.
- The Russian writer Mikhail Yuryevich Lermontov writes *Smert' poeta/Death of Pushkin*, an elegy on the death of Pushkin. Though unpublished (it is an attack on the corruption of court circles), it is widely read in manuscript.
- The Swedish writer and feminist Fredrika Bremer publishes her novel *Grannarna/Neighbors*.
- The U.S. writer George Tucker publishes his *Life of Thomas Jefferson*.
- The U.S. writer Nathaniel Hawthorne publishes his story collection *Twice-Told Tales*, which includes "The Maypole of Merrymount" and "The Minister's Black Veil." The stories originally appeared in the periodical *The Token*. An enlarged edition appears in 1842.
- The U.S. writer Robert Montgomery Bird publishes his novel *Nick of the Woods, or The Jibbenainosay*.
- The U.S. writer Washington Irving publishes the biography *The Adventures of Captain Bonneville*, based on Bonneville's papers.

Music

- French composer Hector Berlioz completes his *Requiem* (Opus 5), the *Grande Messe des morts/High Mass for the Dead*.
- German composer Robert Schumann completes his *Davidsbündlertänze/Dances for the League of David* for piano (Opus 6) and his piano pieces *Etudes symphoniques/Symphonic Studies* (Opus 13).

Theater and Dance

- The German writer Georg Büchner completes his play *Woyzeck*. It is published in 1879 and first performed in 1913. It is the basis of the opera *Wozzeck*, which is written in 1925 by Alban Berg.
- The play *Svend Dyrings hieus/Sven Dyring's House* by the Danish writer Henrik Hertz is first performed, in Copenhagen, Denmark.

Thought and Scholarship

- *A Brief Historical Relation of State Affairs from September 1678 to April 1714* by the English historian and diarist Narcissus Luttrell is published posthumously.
- Philadelphia economist Henry C. Carey publishes volume one of his three-volume work *Principles of Political Economy*, in which he delineates a moderate *laissez-faire* position that includes a protective tariff.

- The Scottish historian Thomas Carlyle publishes *French Revolution*, a colorful history that establishes his reputation.

AUGUST

31 Massachusetts essayist Ralph Waldo Emerson delivers his address "The American Scholar" to the Phi Beta Kappa Society of Harvard College in Cambridge, Massachusetts. He calls on U.S. thinkers to promote an indigenous intellectual tradition, informed by the old, but inspired by unmediated experience with the new.

SOCIETY

Education

- French educator Louis Braille perfects his communication code for the blind.
- The German educationist Friedrich Wilhelm Froebel opens the first kindergarten near Blankenburg.

APRIL

20 The Massachusetts Senate creates the first state board of education in the United States. State senator and educator Horace Mann assumes the board's presidency.

NOVEMBER

8 Mt. Holyoke Seminary opens in Holyoke, Massachusetts. It is the first college in the U.S. established specifically for women.

Everyday Life

- *A Manual of Politeness for Both Sexes* states that it is vulgar for a lady to cross her knees over one another and join the hands around them when sitting.
- Charles Lewis Tiffany opens a store selling stationery and fancy goods in New York, New York: this will grow into the world-famous jewelry store, Tiffany's.
- The American Moral Reform Society convenes for the first time in Philadelphia, Pennsylvania, dedicating itself to promote education, temperance, thrift, and personal responsibility.
- Popular in U.S. magazines are temperance stories, in which the evils of drinking are exemplified by zealously imbibing husbands who come to unfortunate ends. U.S. book stores carry other popular temperance items, such as annuals and gift books.

Media and Communication

- The *Baltimore Sun* begins publication in Baltimore, Maryland.
- The French government sets up a national news agency, *Agence Havas*. It will be known as *Agence France-Presse* from 1945.
- The literary and political monthly *United States Magazine and Democratic Review* begins publication in Washington, D.C.
- U.S. financier Alfred Lewis Vail devises "Morse Code" for use with the telegraph system designed by U.S. artist and inventor Samuel Finley Breese Morse, using dots and dashes to represent letters and numbers.

BIRTHS & DEATHS

- Ducos du Hauron, French physicist who invented the first practical method of color photography, born in Langon, France (–1920).

JANUARY

2 Mily Alexseyevich Balakirev, Russian composer, born in Nizhny Novogorod, Russia (–1910).

19 William Williams Keen, the first brain surgeon in the United States, born in Philadelphia, Pennsylvania (–1932).

20 Sir John Soane, English architect, dies in London, England (83).

FEBRUARY

10 Alexander Pushkin, Russian poet, novelist, and dramatist, dies in St. Petersburg, Russia (37).

MARCH

1 William Dean Howells, U.S. novelist, born in Martins Ferry, Ohio (–1920).

18 Stephen Grover Cleveland, twenty-second (1885–89) and twenty-fourth (1893–97) president of the United States, a Democrat, born in Caldwell, New Jersey (–1908).

31 John Constable, English landscape painter, dies in London, England (59).

APRIL

5 Algernon Charles Swinburne, English poet and critic, born in London, England (–1909).

17 J(ohn) P(ierpont) Morgan, U.S. financier, born in Hartford, Connecticut (–1913).

MAY

27 "Wild Bill" (James Butler) Hickok, U.S. marksman, army scout, and gambler, born in Troy Grove, Illinois (–1876).

JUNE

14 Giacomo Leopardi, Italian poet, scholar, and philosopher, dies in Naples, Italy (38).

20 William IV, King of Great Britain and Ireland 1830–37, dies in Windsor Castle, England (71).

JULY

8 William C. Quantrill, Confederate guerrilla, whose troops raided towns with union sympathies during the Civil War, born in Canal Dover, Ohio (–1865).

SEPTEMBER

2 Zhang Zhidong, Chinese reformer who tried to modernize China, born in Xingyi, China (–1909).

DECEMBER

26 George Dewey, U.S. naval commander who defeated the Spanish in Manila harbor during the Spanish–American War, permitting the United States to acquire the Philippines, born in Montpelier, Vermont (–1917).

1838

POLITICS, GOVERNMENT, AND ECONOMICS

Business and Economics

- When the economic panic of 1837 leaves them without money or stock for their paper business, John and Lyman Hollingsworth from Massachusetts create the first manila paper using hemp rope, sails, and canvas.

Colonization

DECEMBER

16 The Boers (Dutch settlers) decisively defeat a Zulu army at Blood River, in retaliation for the attack on Pieter Retief's force on February 6, and secure their position in Natal, southern Africa.

Human Rights

- Philadelphia abolitionist Sarah Moore Grimke publishes "Letters on the Equality of the Sexes, and the Condition of Women," a vindication of women's rights.

FEBRUARY

14 Plymouth, Massachusetts, representative John Quincy Adams inundates the U.S. House of Representatives with 350 petitions protesting slavery and the annexation of Texas.

OCTOBER

- The Cherokees begin to depart Georgia for Oklahoma Territory on what is known as the Trail of Tears. Some 10% of the Cherokees are thought to have perished from sickness and maltreatment at the hands of the U.S. military under the command of General Winfield Scott.

DECEMBER

3 Ohio congressman Joshua R. Giddings becomes the first avowed abolitionist to sit in the U.S. House of Representatives.

Politics and Government

- In U.S. Congressional elections, Democrats retain majorities in the House (124–118) and Senate (28–22).

JANUARY

5 President Martin Van Buren proclaims U.S. neutrality in the Canadian rebellion.

13 The United States apprehends a group of Canadian revolutionaries who had been launching strikes against the Canadian government from U.S. territory on Navy Island in the Niagara River.

26 Tennessee becomes the first U.S. state to adopt legislation prohibiting the sale of alcohol.

30 Seminole chief Osceolo dies in a U.S. Army prison, as the guerrilla tactics of his Seminole warriors continue to frustrate the U.S. Army.

FEBRUARY

6 A Boer (Dutch settler) expeditionary force under Pieter Retief in Natal, southern Africa, is attacked by Zulus.

10 The British government temporarily suspends the Legislative Assembly of Lower Canada following the revolt against British rule.

MAY

29 John Lambton, Earl Durham, arrives in Quebec as the British governor in chief of all Canada.

JUNE

12 The U.S. Congress divides the Wisconsin Territory, creating the new Iowa Territory, which includes present-day Iowa, North and South Dakota, and part of Minnesota.

JULY

31 An Irish Poor Law is enacted, based on the British Poor Law Amendment Act of August 1834.

OCTOBER

1 Britain begins the First Anglo-Afghan War to consolidate its influence over the Afghans and to prevent Russia increasing its power in the region, which constitutes a threat to British interests in India.

9 John Lambton, Earl Durham, resigns his position as British governor in chief of Canada after criticism of him for leniency toward the rebels against British rule.

10 Austrian troops evacuate the Italian Papal States, except for Ferrara (which they have occupied since January 1832), having secured the position of the conservative cardinal Tomasso Bernetti, Papal Secretary of State.

12 The Republic of Texas retracts its request to become part of the United States.

NOVEMBER

27 A French force occupies the Mexican port of Veracruz in support of the claims for compensation of French victims of civil unrest in Mexico.

30 Mexico declares war on France after the French occupation of the port of Veracruz.

DECEMBER

24 The sultan of the Ottoman Empire, Mahmud II, supported by Russia, limits the authority of Prince Milosh Obrenović in Serbia.

SCIENCE, TECHNOLOGY, AND MEDICINE

Exploration

December 1838–42 U.S. navigator John Wilkes leads an expedition to survey large areas of the Antarctic coastline; many of the charts he produces later prove inaccurate.

MAY
18 The U.S. Congress authorizes commander Charles Wickes to explore the South Pacific Ocean and survey the northwest coast of the United States.

Science

- Dutch chemist Gerard Johann Mulder coins the word "protein."
- French chemist Charles Frédéric Kuhlmann synthezises nitric acid.
- French chemist Théophile-Jules Pelouze discovers that cotton can explode if dipped in concentrated nitric acid.
- French physician Charles Cagniard de la Tour demonstrates that fermentation is caused by yeast cells.
- German botanist Matthias Jakob Schleiden publishes the article "Contributions to Phytogenesis," in which he recognizes that cells are the fundamental units of all plant life. He is thus the first to formulate cell theory.
- German chemist Justus von Liebig demonstrates that animal heat is due to respiration. He also provides the first adequate definition of an acid—"a compound containing hydrogen in a form in which it can be replaced by a metal."
- German embryologist Robert Remak discovers nonmedullated nerve fibers.
- German mathematician Karl Friedrich Gauss publishes *Allgemeine Theorie des Erdmagnetismus/Unified Theory of the Earth's Magnetism*, in which he demonstrates that 95% of the earth's magnetic field originates in the interior of the earth.
- German physicist Karl August Steinheil discovers that the earth acts as a conductor and can replace the return wire in telegraph systems.
- Italian chemist R. Piria synthesizes salicylic acid, the basic ingredient in aspirin, from willow bark.

OCTOBER
11 Using the method of parallax, German astronomer Friedrich Bessel calculates the star 61 Cygni to be 10.3 light-years away from earth. It is the first determination of the distance of a star other than the sun.

Technology

- German scientist Augustus Siebe invents an airtight diving suit with ventilation valves.
- U.S. inventor David Bruce invents a type-casting machine that melts metal to make characters for typesetting.

- U.S. inventor Samuel Howd patents an inward flow water turbine.

JANUARY
6 The U.S. artist and inventor Samuel Finley Breese Morse and financier Alfred Louis Vail make the first successful public demonstration of an electric telegraph.

Transportation

APRIL
8 English engineer Isambard Kingdom Brunel's ship *Great Western* is launched. It is the largest ship in the world (65 m/212 ft long) and the first steamship built specifically for oceanic service.
23 The *Great Western* and *Sirius*, both built by Isambard Brunel, are the first steamships to cross the Atlantic entirely under steam, arriving in New York, New York, only hours apart. They make the crossing in half the time (15 days) sailing ships take. The *Sirius*, which arrives first, uses a condenser to recover fresh water from the boiler, and the *Great Western* is a wooden paddle steamer driven by two engines.

ARTS AND IDEAS

Architecture

- The Arco della Pace in Milan, Italy, a ceremonial arch designed by the Italian architect Marchese Luigi Cagnola, is completed.
- The National Gallery in London, England, designed by the English architect William Wilkins, is completed.

Arts

c. 1838 The English artist J. M. W. Turner paints *The Fighting Téméraire*.
- The French artist and caricaturist Honoré Daumier completes his series of lithographs *Robert Macaire*.
- The U.S. artist John Quidor paints *A Battle Scene from Knickerbocker's History*.
- The U.S. artist William Page paints his *Portrait of John Quincy Adams*.

Literature and Language

- The English writer Charles Dickens begins publishing *The Life and Adventures of Nicholas Nickleby* in serial form. It appears as a book in 1839.
- The English writer Robert Surtees publishes *Jorrocks's Jaunts and Jollities*, a collection of comic stories.
- The Flemish writer Hendrik Conscience publishes his historical novel *De leeuw van Vlaanderen/The Lion of Flanders*, which becomes one of the most popular books in Flemish literature.
- The German poet Eduard Friedrich Mörike publishes *Gedichte/Poems*.
- The German writer Karl Leberecht Immermann publishes his novel *Münchhausen*.

- The U.S. poet Henry Wadsworth Longfellow publishes his poem "A Psalm of Life" in the *Knickerbocker Magazine*.
- The U.S. writer Edgar Allan Poe publishes his novel *The Narrative of Arthur Gordon Pym*.
- The U.S. writer James Fenimore Cooper publishes the novels *Homeward Bound* and *Home as Found*.
- The U.S. writer Joseph Clay Neal publishes *Charcoal Sketches, or Scenes in a Metropolis*, a satirical look at Philadelphia, Pennsylvania.
- The U.S. writer William Gilmore Simms publishes his novel *Richard Hurdis*.

Music

- German composer Robert Schumann completes his Piano Sonata No. 2 (Opus 22), which he began in 1833. He also completes his piano pieces *Kinderscenen/Scenes from Childhood* (Opus 15).
- Hungarian composer Franz Liszt completes his piano work *Etudes d'exécution transcendante d'après Paganini/Transcendental Studies after Paganini*. They are revised in 1851.
- Swedish singer Jenny Lind makes her debut in Stockholm. She sings in the opera *Der Freischütz/The Freeshooter*, written in 1821 by Carl Maria von Weber.
- The opera *Benvenuto Cellini* by the French composer Hector Berlioz is first performed, in Paris, France.

Theater and Dance

- Actress Elisa Rachel's début as Camille in Corneille's *Horace* at the Théatre Français in Paris, France, begins the revival of French classical drama.

- The play *Ruy Blas* by the French writer Victor Hugo is first performed, in Paris, France. It is widely considered his finest play.

Thought and Scholarship

- French historian Alexis Charles-Henri-Clérel de Tocqueville's *De la Democratie en Amerique* appears in the United States under the English title *Democracy in America*.
- The English teacher and historian Thomas Arnold publishes the first volume of his *History of Rome*. The project is left unfinished.
- The U.S. historian William Hickling Prescott publishes *History of the Reign of Ferdinand and Isabella*.

SOCIETY

Education

- Acadia University is founded in Wolfville, Nova Scotia, Canada.
- Duke University is founded in Durham, North Carolina.
- Massachusetts music teacher Lowell Mason convinces the Boston School Committee to include music instruction as part of the public school curriculum.

Everyday Life

- German physician Friedrich Wilde develops the contraceptive rubber cap. This is the first use of rubber for medical purposes.

BIRTHS & DEATHS

JANUARY
13 John Scott, later Earl of Eldon, chancellor of England 1801–27, dies in London, England (86).

FEBRUARY
16 Henry Adams, U.S. historian and author who is known for his autobiography *The Education of Henry Adams*, born in Boston, Massachusetts (–1918).
18 Ernst Mach, Austrian physicist and philosopher who established the principles of supersonics, born in Chirlitz-Turas, Moravia, Austrian Empire (–1916).

APRIL
2 Léon Gambetta, French politician who organized the defense of France during the Franco–German War 1870–71, born in Cahors, France (–1882).

MAY
10 John Wilkes Booth, U.S. actor who assassinated the U.S. president Abraham Lincoln, born near Bel Air, Maryland (–1865).

17 Charles de Talleyrand-Périgord, French statesman and diplomat, dies in Paris, France (84).

JULY
8 Ferdinand (Adolf August Heinrich) Graf von Zeppelin, German builder of rigid dirigible airships, born in Konstanz, Baden, Germany (–1917).

AUGUST
3 Yamagata Aritomo, Japanese soldier and statesman, first prime minister of Japan 1889–91 and 1898–1900, responsible for turning Japan into a military power, born in Hagi, Japan (–1922).

SEPTEMBER
2 Liloukalani, first Hawaiian queen and last reigning sovereign of Hawaii 1891–95, born in Honolulu, Hawaii (–1917).
29 Henry Hobson Richardson, U.S. architect who revived the Romanesque style in the United States, born in Priestly Plantation, Louisiana (–1886).

OCTOBER
3 Black Hawk, Native North American leader whose refusal to leave his ancestral lands resulted in the Black Hawk War in 1832, dies in Des Moines River, Iowa (71).
8 John Hay, U.S. secretary of state 1898–1905 who was responsible for the "Open Door Policy" with regard to China, born in Salem, Indiana (–1905).
24 Joseph Lancaster, British-born educational reformer in Britain and the United States, dies in New York, New York (60).
25 Georges (Alexandre-César-Léopold) Bizet, French composer, born in Paris, France (–1875).

DECEMBER
24 John Morley, English author, critic, and statesman, born in Blackburn, Lancashire, England (–1923).

- Hoop rolling becomes a popular past-time with ladies in New York, New York.

Media and Communication

- The *Bombay Times and Journal of Commerce* begins publication in Bombay, India, to serve the British residents of western India. The name will be changed to the *Times of India* in 1861.

Religion

JANUARY

12 The Church of Jesus Christ of Latter-day Saints departs from Kirtland, Ohio, for Independence, Missouri, as the economic depression tightens its grip on the eastern United States.

Sports

- The Narragansett Boat Club of Providence, Rhode Island, is founded. It is the oldest boat club still in existence in the United States.

1839

POLITICS, GOVERNMENT, AND ECONOMICS

Human Rights

- Massachusetts abolitionist Theodore Dwight Weld publishes "American Slavery As It Is," which Harriet Beecher Stowe credited with inspiring *Uncle Tom's Cabin*.
- The American Anti-Slavery Society splits into radical and moderate wings over the question of women's leadership within the organization. Moderates, led by New Yorker Lewis Tappan, establish the American and Foreign Anti-Slavery Society, who also subsequently found the Liberty Party to combat constitutional and legal impediments to emancipation.
- The United States becomes embroiled in an international controversy after the U.S. Navy apprehends a Spanish vessel of mutinous slaves. Secretary of State John Forsyth aims to turn the cargo of slaves over to Spain, but Massachusetts abolitionist John Quincy Adams files suit, ultimately securing the captives' liberation.

Politics and Government

- Mississippi grants women full property rights.
- Mississippi prohibits the sale of alcohol in amounts less than one gallon.

- The Chinese government bans the use of opium, putting an end to the lucrative opium trade, in which Britain was a major player.
- The U.S. Supreme Court, in *Bank of Augusta v. Earle*, invokes the interstate commerce clause, upholding the right of a corporation chartered in one state to pursue business in other states.

1839–1846 The so-called Antirent War erupts in Albany County, New York, when descendants of Dutch patroon Stephen Van Rensselaer attempt to collect back rent from farmers living on the old Rensselaer estate. It will take seven years to settle the land dispute.

JANUARY

20 The Battle of Yungay, resulting in a victory for Chile against the Peru–Bolivia Federation, leads to the dissolution of the Federation.

FEBRUARY

11 The Durham Report on the state of affairs in Canada, produced by the former British governor in chief of Canada, John Lambton, Earl Durham, is presented to the House of Lords in London, England. It recommends that Upper and Lower Canada should be merged and, while remaining under British control, genuine power should be given to the local inhabitants.

12 The so-called Aroostock War begins between the United States and Canada, after U.S. land agent Rufus McIntire is seized by Canadian lumberjacks in a disputed territory between New Brunswick, Canada, and Maine. Both the United States and Canada marshal forces as if ready to fight, but U.S. general Winfield Scott convinces the two sides to negotiate their differences.

19 Spanish general Rafael Maroto, leader of the moderate Carlists, executes several more extreme generals and courtiers plotting against him, paving the way for an end to the civil war in Spain.

20 The U.S. Congress prohibits duelling in the District of Columbia.

24 Uruguay declares war against Argentina, following Argentine attempts to subvert the government of Uruguay.

MARCH

9 French forces withdraw from Mexico, whose government agrees to compensate French victims of civil riots in Mexico.

APRIL

11 The United States and Mexico sign a treaty granting U.S. citizens the right to arbitrate property claims against the Mexican government.

19 The Treaty of London is signed, agreeing the territorial arrangements for the separation of Belgium and the Netherlands. Luxembourg, disputed between the two, becomes an independent grand duchy, and the River Scheldt is opened to the ships of both the Netherlands and Belgium.

21 The Ottoman army invades Syria because of continuing friction between the Ottoman Empire and Mehmet Ali, the viceroy of Egypt.

JUNE

13 Prince Milosh Obrenović of Serbia abdicates because of lack of support in the country and is succeeded by his son, Milan.

24 Ibrahim, the son of Viceroy Mehmet Ali of Egypt, routs the Ottoman forces attempting to recover Syria from Egyptian control at Nezib, Syria.

JULY

1 Following the defeat of the Ottoman army at Nezib, Syria, the Ottoman fleet sails to Alexandria, Egypt, and voluntarily surrenders to Mehmet Ali, the viceroy of Egypt.

1 Sultan Mahmud II of the Ottoman Empire dies and is succeeded by his 16-year-old son, Abdul Mejid.

7 The First Opium War between China and Britain begins after the Chinese authorities seize and burn cargoes of opium due to be exported from China by British merchants, in an attempt to combat smuggling of the drug.

9 Prince Milan Obrenović of Serbia dies and is succeeded by his brother, Michael.

27 Britain, Russia, Austria, Prussia, and France inform Abdul Mejid, the new young sultan of the Ottoman Empire, that they will support him against Mehmet Ali, the viceroy of Egypt.

AUGUST

7 The Afghan capital, Kabul, is captured by British troops.

12 The "Sacred Month" begins, as some workers in Lancashire and the northeast of England strike in support of the People's Charter.

23 The Chinese port of Hong Kong is taken by the British in the First Opium War with China.

31 General Rafael Maroto and General Baldomero Espartero, leaders of the two sides in the Spanish civil war, agree a peace formula at Vergara, Spain, conceding some of the demands of the insurgent Carlists.

SEPTEMBER

25 The Republic of Texas gains diplomatic recognition from France.

NOVEMBER

3 A Reform Decree in the Ottoman Empire guarantees the life, liberty, and property of all subjects, a liberal measure designed to cement Western support for the Ottoman Empire.

3 The First Opium War between Britain and China gains momentum when a British frigate sinks a Chinese fleet of junks.

13 The new Liberty Party holds its first national convention in Warsaw, New York. The Party nominates moderate New York abolitionist James G. Birney for president and Francis J. Lemoyne for vice president.

DECEMBER

3 King Frederick VI of Denmark dies and is succeeded by his nephew, Christian VIII.

7 Whigs nominate William Henry Harrison, victorious general of the Battle of Tippecanoe in 1811, for president and Virginian John Tyler for vice president. The duo inspires the campaign slogan, "Tippecanoe and Tyler too."

SCIENCE, TECHNOLOGY, AND MEDICINE

Exploration

- The Ottoman viceroy of Egypt, Muhammad Ali, allows a series of trade missions by European traders south along the White Nile into East Africa. Travelers on these missions soon discover the limit of the river's navigable reaches, at Juba in the Sudan.

December 1839–43 English naval officer James Clark Ross leads a Royal Naval expedition in search of the magnetic south pole. He discovers the Ross Sea (1841), Ross Ice Shelf, Ross Island, Victoria Land, and active Antarctic volcanoes, although he does not reach the pole, which lies inland.

Health and Medicine

- The world's first dental school is founded in Boston, Massachusetts.

Science

- English physicist Michael Faraday discovers that each element has a specific electrical inductive capacity.
- German physiologist Theodor Schwann publishes *Microscopic Investigations on the Accordance in the Structure and Growth of Plants and Animals*, in which he argues that all animals and plants are composed of cells. Along with Matthias Schleiden, he thus founds modern cell theory.
- Scottish geologist Robert Murchison publishes *The Silurian System*, a geological treatise which establishes the geological sequence of the Early Paleozoic rocks (395–500 million years old).
- Swedish chemist Carl Mosander discovers the metallic element lanthanum (atomic no. 57).
- U.S. inventor Isaac Babbitt develops a white metal, an alloy of tin, antimony, and copper, called Babbitt metal, which has antifriction properties and is used for bearings.

December 1839–55 English physicist Michael Faraday publishes *Researches in Electricity*, summarizing his discoveries.

Technology

- British engineer James Nasmyth designs the steam hammer; an important tool for forging heavy machinery in the Industrial Revolution. He patents it on November 24, 1842.
- British physicist William Robert Grove makes the first fuel cell, a device that produces electricity from the conversion of the chemical energy of the fuel.
- English astronomer and chemist John Herschel, independently of English photography pioneer William Henry Fox Talbot, invents the process of photography on sensitized paper. He is the first to apply the terms "positive" and "negative" to photographic images and uses sodium hyposulfite instead of sodium chloride.
- U.S. inventor Charles Goodyear vulcanizes rubber by adding sulfur and then heating it.

JANUARY

9   French physicist Louis-Jacques-Mandé Daguerre announces to the French Academy of Arts and Science that he can produce permanent positive images on a copper plate coated with silver iodide that is exposed to bright sunlight for 20–30 minutes. The image is developed with mercury vapor, and fixed in a salt solution. His "daguerreotype" proves to be a dead end, overtaken by Fox Talbot's production of a photographic negative a few weeks later.

Transportation

- Steam engines begin operating on the New York and Harlem Railroad.
- The Brougham one-horse carriage for town use appears.
- The first railroad in Italy, Naples–Portici, opens.

JULY

- English inventors Charles Wheatstone and William Cooke demonstrate an electric telegraph on the Paddington–West Drayton railroad line.

ARTS AND IDEAS

Arts

- The U.S. artist and inventor Samuel Finley Breese Morse takes the first daguerreotype photographs in the United States, only weeks after the process has been revealed in Paris, France.
- The U.S. artist Erastus Salisbury Field paints his *Portrait of Joseph B Moore and His Family*.
- The U.S. artist Henry Inman paints *Georgianna Buckham and Her Mother*.

Literature and Language

- The French writer Stendhal publishes his novel *La Chartreuse de Parme/The Charterhouse of Parma*.
- The U.S. novelist Daniel Pierce Thompson publishes his popular adventure tale *The Green Mountain Boys*.
- The U.S. writer Edgar Allan Poe publishes *Tales of the Grotesque and Arabesque* and the short story "The Fall of the House of Usher" in *Burton's Gentleman's Magazine*.
- The U.S. writer Henry Wadsworth Longfellow publishes his poetry collection *Voices of the Night* and the novel *Hyperion*.

MARCH

23   The acronym "OK," standing for the phonetic "Oll Korrect," appears in the *Morning Post* in Boston, Massachusetts.

Music

- French composer Hector Berlioz completes his dramatic symphony *Roméo et Juliette/Romeo and Juliet*.
- German composer Robert Schumann completes his piano pieces *Faschingsschwank aus Wein/Vienna*

BIRTHS & DEATHS

JANUARY

19   Paul Cézanne, French postimpressionist painter whose work led to the development of cubism, born in Aix-en-Provence, France (–1906).

FEBRUARY

11   Josiah Willard Gibbs, U.S. theoretical physicist, born in New Haven, Connecticut (–1903).

MARCH

21   Modest Petrovich Mussorgsky, Russian composer, born in Karevo, Russia (–1881).

JUNE

17   William Bentinck, British governor-general of India 1828–35 whose reforms eventually led to India's independence over 100 years later, dies in Paris, France (64).

JULY

8   John D(avison) Rockefeller, U.S. industrialist who founded Standard Oil, and philanthropist who founded the Rockefeller Foundation, born in Richford, New York (–1937).

AUGUST

28   William Smith, English geologist who developed the science of stratigraphy, dies in Northampton, Northamptonshire, England (70).

SEPTEMBER

10   Charles Sanders Peirce, U.S. logician and philosopher who advocated Pragmatism, born in Cambridge, Massachusetts (–1914).

19   George Cadbury, English businessman who developed the Cadbury Brothers chocolate-manufacturing firm, born in Birmingham, Warwickshire, England (–1922).

NOVEMBER

15   William Murdock, Scottish inventor who pioneered the use of coal gas for lighting, dies in Birmingham, Warwickshire, England (85).

DECEMBER

5   George A(rmstrong) Custer, U.S. cavalry officer and Civil War general, born in New Rumley, Ohio (–1876).

Carnival Pranks (Opus 26) and *Drei Romanzen/Three Romances* (Opus 28).
- Hungarian composer Franz Liszt completes his piano transcription of Johann Sebastian Bach's *Fantasia and Fugue* in G minor.

Thought and Scholarship

- John Lowell, Jr., founds the Lowell Institute in Boston, Massachusetts, to provide free public lectures by eminent scholars.
- The German historian Leopold von Ranke publishes the first part of his *Deutsche Geschichte im Zeitalter der Reformation/German History in the Reformation Era*. The final part appears in 1843.

SOCIETY

Education

- Boston University is founded in Boston, Massachusetts.
- The Institute of Physiology is founded at Breslau, Silesia (now Wrocław, Poland).
- The Massachusetts board of education sponsors the first state-supported institute to train school teachers.

- The University of Missouri is founded at Columbia, Missouri.

Everyday Life

- The French statesman and historian Louis Blanc publishes *L'Organisation du travail/The Organization of Work*, which proposes a system of national workshops.

Religion

- Massachusetts biblical scholar Andrews Norton publishes "A Discourse on the Latest Form of Infidelity," a response to Ralph Waldo Emerson's "Divinity School Address."
- Massachusetts Unitarian pastor George Ripley publishes "The Latest Form of Infidelity Examined," refuting Andrews Norton's renunciation of Emerson's "Divinity School Address."
- The American Sunday School Union publishes *The Tree and Its Fruits*, a book that purports the idea that the good die easily but the evil die with difficulty.

Sports

- The Detroit Boat Club is founded in Michigan.

1840

POLITICS, GOVERNMENT, AND ECONOMICS

Business and Economics

- Cotton textiles become the leading U.S. industry, with 1,778,000 spindles and 75,000 workers.

Colonization

- The first colony set up by Britain's New Zealand Company is established at Port Nicholson (modern Wellington harbor) on the southern tip of the North Island of New Zealand.

Human Rights

- U.S. abolitionist Lucretia Mott is turned away from the World's Anti-Slavery Society convention in London, England, which refuses to admit women.

Politics and Government

- In U.S. Congressional elections, Whigs attain majorities in the House (133–102) and Senate (28–22).
- The United States, Great Britain, the Netherlands, and Belgium join France in recognizing the Republic of Texas.

JANUARY
- Abortive risings in suppport of the People's Charter take place in Dewsbury and Sheffield, England.
8   The U.S. House of Representatives adopts a gag rule that effectively turns away antislavery petitions.

FEBRUARY
5   By the Treaty of Waitangi, New Zealand Maori chiefs surrender their sovereignty to the British government.

10 Queen Victoria of Great Britain marries her cousin Prince Albert of the German duchy of Saxe-Coburg-Gotha.

MARCH

31 U.S. president Martin Van Buren issues an executive order establishing a ten-hour workday for federal employees.

MAY

5 Democrats nominate President Martin Van Buren for a second term.

JUNE

6 The Carlist wars of succession in Spain end when the Carlist forces under Ramón Cabrera retreat into France.
7 King Frederick Wilhelm III of Prussia dies and is succeeded by his son Frederick Wilhelm IV.

JULY

15 Russia, Britain, Prussia, and Austria form the Quadruple Alliance in support of the Ottoman Empire and by the Treaty of London offer Egypt to its ruler and Ottoman opponent, Mehmet Ali, as a hereditary possession and also southern Syria for life, provided he gives up Crete and northern Syria. He refuses, in the hope of French aid.
23 The British Parliament passes an act for the union of Upper and Lower Canada with equal representation for both of the former provinces.

AUGUST

6 King Ernest Augustus of the German kingdom of Hanover imposes a new constitution, giving himself increased power.
6 Louis-Napoléon Bonaparte, the nephew of Napoleon I, fails in his attempt to stage a rising against the French king, Louis Philippe, at Boulogne, France.

SEPTEMBER

11 The Egyptian-held Ottoman city of Beirut is bombarded by British forces supporting the Ottoman Empire to compel Viceroy Mehmet Ali of Egypt to submit and accept the terms for peace offered in July by the Treaty of London.

OCTOBER

7 King William I of the Netherlands, unwilling to grant constitutional reform, abdicates in favor of his son, William II.
12 Queen Maria Cristina, regent for the young Isabella II of Spain, abdicates after calls for more progressive policies.
28 The French prime minister Adolphe Thiers is forced to resign after attempting to obtain French aid for the viceroy of Egypt, Mehmet Ali, in his war with the Ottoman Empire.

NOVEMBER

3 The bombardment and capture of the Egyptian-held Syrian city of Acre by British forces supporting the Ottoman Empire compels the Egyptian commander Ibrahim to evacuate all Syria.
5 By the Convention of Alexandria the Egyptian viceroy Mehmet Ali agrees to the terms of the Treaty of London of July 15, ending the Ottoman–Egyptian war.
5 The First Anglo-Afghan War ends when Afghan forces surrender to the British in Afghanistan.

DECEMBER

2 Americans elect William Henry Harrison president and John Tyler vice president.
15 Napoleon I's remains are brought for burial at the war veterans' hospital of Les Invalides in Paris, France.

SCIENCE, TECHNOLOGY, AND MEDICINE

Agriculture

c. 1840 The vine powdery mildew *Inciluna necator* is controlled in Europe, by spraying with lime sulfur and by sulfur dusting; it is the first control of an insect pest by chemical means.
• German chemist Justus von Liebig demonstrates that treating bones (which are used for fertilizer) with acid increases the availability of their nutrients to plants.
December 1840–50 Wheat becomes an increasingly important cash crop in the United States; production in 1839 is nearly 85 million bushels and climbs to over 100 million bushels in 10 years.

Exploration

• English settler and explorer Edward Eyre explores the desert northwest of Adelaide in southern Australia, and discovers Lake Torrens and Lake Eyre.

JANUARY

19 U.S. explorer Charles Wilkes claims part of Antarctica for the United States.

Health and Medicine

• Dr. Horace A. Hayden helps establish the American Society of Dental Surgeons in New York, New York.
• German physician Gustav Jacob Henle suggests that infectious diseases are caused by living microscopic organisms.
• U.S. physician Willard Parker establishes a clinic at the College of Physicians and Surgeons in New York, New York.
January 1840–60 A cholera pandemic kills millions of people worldwide.

Science

• Bohemian physiologist Jan Purkinje first uses the term "protoplasm," applying it to embryonic tissues.
• British physicist William Robert Grove lights an auditorium with platinum coils in inverted glasses sealed with water, which are heated to incandescence.
• English biochemist William Prout classifies food components into water, fats, carbohydrates, and proteins.

- English microscopist John Dancer takes the first photographs of microscopic objects; they are magnified up to 20 times.
- English philosopher William Whewell publishes *The Philosophy of Inductive Sciences, Founded upon Their History*, in which he describes how the sciences use induction to arrive at general propositions.
- English physicist James Joule publishes *Production of Heat by Voltaic Electricity*, in which he states his law that the amount of heat produced per second in any conductor by an electric current is proportional to the product of the square of the current and the resistance of the conductor.
- German astronomer Friedrich Bessel explains the irregularities in the orbit of Uranus as due to the gravitational effects of an unknown planet (later identified as Neptune).
- German chemist Christian Schönbein discovers ozone.
- German chemist Justus von Liebig publishes *Die organische Chemie in ihrer Anwendung auf Agrikulturchemie und Physiologie/Organic Chemistry in its Application to Agriculture and Physiology*, which establishes agricultural chemistry as an applied science. He argues that the chemical analysis of plants should determine the substances present in fertilizers.
- Harvard College professor William Cranch Bond erects the first astronomical observatory in the United States.
- Italian optician Giovanni Battista Amici introduces the oil-immersion technique for observing specimens under the microscope. By immersing the objective lens in a drop of oil placed on top of the specimen light aberrations are minimized and magnifications up to 6,000 times achieved.
- Swiss chemist Charles Choss demonstrates that calcium is needed for proper bone development.
- Swiss embryologist Rudolf Albert von Kölliker identifies spermatozoa as cells.
- Swiss-born U.S. naturalist Jean-Louis Agassiz describes the motion and behavior of glaciers in *Etudes sur les glaciers/Studies of Glaciers*. He argues that Europe was covered by great sheets of ice in the geologically recent past.
- U.S. astronomer John William Draper takes the first photograph of the moon.

Technology

- English scientist William Henry Fox Talbot improves his earlier photographic process and produces the calotype, a negative-positive photographic system.
- Hungarian mathematician József Petzval develops an improved camera lens.
- Scottish inventor Alexander Bain devises the first electric clock.
- Swiss scientist Gottfried Keller prepares paper from ground wood. Until now the principal fiber for paper has been provided by rags.

January 1840–90 Currier and Ives in the United States produce over 7,000 different lithograph prints that sell more than 10 million copies.

Transportation

- There are 4,530 km/2,816 miles of railroad in the United States, 2,142 km/1,331 mi in Great Britain, and 483 km/300 mi in France.

ARTS AND IDEAS

Architecture

- Helsinki Cathedral in Finland, designed by the German architect Carl Ludwig Engel, is completed.
- The Ludwigskirche church in Munich, Bavaria, designed by the German architect Friedrich von Gärtner, is completed.
- The remodeling of the Place de la Concorde and the Champs Elysées in Paris, France, to designs by the German-born architect Jakob Ignaz Hittorf, is completed.

Arts

c. 1840 The English artist J. M. W. Turner paints *The Slave Ship*.
- The U.S. artist Asher Brown Durand paints *The Evening of Life*.
- The U.S. artist Horatio Greenough sculpts *George Washington*.
- The U.S. artist Thomas Cole completes his cycle of paintings *The Voyage of Life*.

Literature and Language

- The English writer Charles Dickens begins publishing his novel *The Old Curiosity Shop* in serial form. It appears as a book in 1841.
- The French writer Prosper Mérimée publishes his novel *Colomba*.
- The Irish writer Charles James Lever publishes his novel *Charles O'Malley*.
- The Russian writer Mikhail Yuryevich Lermontov publishes his novel *Geroy nashego vremeni/A Hero of Our Time*.
- The U.S. lawyer and writer Richard Henry Dana, Jr., publishes *Two Years Before the Mast*, a classic account of life at sea (he sailed on a brig from Boston, Massachusetts, to California).
- The U.S. literary journal *The Dial*, the quarterly of the transcendental movement, is first published. It closes in 1844, having produced 16 issues. Its editors are Margaret Fuller, Ralph Waldo Emerson, and Henry David Thoreau.
- The U.S. poet Henry Wadsworth Longfellow publishes his poem "The Wreck of the Hesperus" in the journal *New World*.
- The U.S. writer James Fenimore Cooper publishes his novel *The Pathfinder* and *The Deerslayer*, which is the last of his *Leatherstocking* novels. The first appeared in 1823.

Music

c. 1840 Belgian instrumentmaker Adolphe Sax invents the saxophone. He registers his invention in 1846.

- French composer Hector Berlioz completes his orchestral work *Grande Symphonie funèbre et triomphale/Great Funereal and Triumphal Symphony*.
- German composer Felix Mendelssohn completes his choral symphony, the *Lobgesang/Hymn of Praise* (Opus 52).
- German composer Richard Wagner completes his *Faust* overture.
- German composer Robert Schumann completes his *Liederkreis/Song Cycle* (Opus 39), settings of poems by the German poet Joseph, Baron von Eichendorff, and *Frauenliebe und Leben/Woman's Love and Life* (Opus 42). He also completes his *Liederkreis/Song Cycle* (Opus 24) and *Dichterliebe/Poet's Love* (Opus 48), both settings of poems by the German poet Heinrich Heine.
- Hungarian composer Franz Liszt completes his piano transcription of Hector Berlioz's *Symphonie fantastique/ Fantastic Symphony*.
- The opera *La Fille du régiment/Daughter of the Regiment* by the Italian composer Gaetano Donizetti is first performed, in Paris, France.

Theater and Dance

- The play *Judith* by the German dramatist Christian Friedrich Hebbel is first performed, in Berlin, Germany.

Thought and Scholarship

- New England clergyman-writer Orestes Brownson publishes *The Laboring Classes*, a sympathetic account of workers' grievances.

- The French historian Augustin Thierry publishes *Récits des temps mérovingiens/Narratives of Merovigian Times*.
- The French literary critic Charles-Augustin Ste.-Beuve publishes the first volume of his three-volume *Histoire de Port-Royal/History of Port Royal*. The last volume appears in 1860.
- The French political writer Etienne Cabet publishes *Voyage en Icarie*, a "philosophical and social romance" describing a communist utopia.
- The French socialist Pierre-Joseph Proudhon publishes *Qu'est-ce-que la Propriété?/What is Property?* It contains the famous proposition: "Property is theft."
- The French writer on religion Félicité Lamennais publishes the first part of his *Esquisse d'une philosophie/ Sketch for a Philosophy*. The last part appears in 1846.
- U.S. philosopher Albert Brisbane publishes *Social Destiny of Man*, a Fourierist defense of utopian social communities.

SOCIETY

Everyday Life

- By adding quinine to its soda water, the Schweppes company creates tonic water.
- James Pimm, of Pimm's Oyster Bar in London, England, develops Pimms No.1, a mixture of gin, liqueurs, herbs, and spices made to an undisclosed recipe. From 1859 it is available in bottled form.
- The U.S. Census lists the nation's population at 17,069,453, up from roughly 12,901,000 in 1830.

BIRTHS & DEATHS

c. 1840 Chief Joseph, Nez Percé chief who led his people on a 1,600-km/1,000-mi journey to escape the U.S. army, born in Wallowa Valley, Oregon Territory (–1904).

JANUARY
22 Johann Friedrich Blumenbach, German physiologist who was one of the first to make a scientific classification of races, dies in Göttingen, Germany (87).

FEBRUARY
22 August Bebel, German socialist who founded the German Social Democratic Party, born in Deutz near Cologne, Germany (–1913).

MARCH
2 Wilhelm Olbers, German astronomer and physician who discovered several asteroids and comets, dies in Bremen, Germany (81).

30 Charles Booth, English sociologist who was one of the first to apply statistics to social problems, born in Liverpool, England (–1916).

APRIL
2 Emile Zola, French novelist and critic who founded the Naturalist movement, born in Paris, France (–1902).
25 Siméon-Denis Poisson, French mathematician who applied mathematics to electromagnetic theory, dies in Sceaux, France (58).
27 Edward Whymper, English mountaineer who was the first to climb the Matterhorn, born in London, England (–1911).

MAY
7 Peter Illich Tchaikovsky, leading 19th-century Russian composer who, among a great variety of works, composed the music for the

ballets *Swan Lake*, *The Nutcracker*, and *Sleeping Beauty*, born in Votkinsk, Russia (–1893).
13 Alphonse Daudet, French novelist, born in Nîmes, France (–1897).

JUNE
2 Thomas Hardy, English novelist and poet, born in Bockhampton, Dorset, England (–1928).

OCTOBER
27 Niccolò Paganini, Italian composer and violin virtuoso, dies in Nice, France (57).

NOVEMBER
12 Auguste Rodin, French sculptor reknowned for his realistic treatment of the human figure, born in Paris, France (–1917).
14 Claude Monet, French impressionist painter, born in Paris, France (–1926).

MAY

1 The world's first postage stamp, the Penny Black, is issued in Britain, the first adhesive stamp to be used commercially.

Media and Communication

• The New England Transcendentalist Club publishes *The Dial*, a quarterly literary, philosophical, and religious magazine edited by Margaret Fuller.

Religion

• The periodical *Beacon* appears in New York, New York, repudiating religion as an opiate of the laboring masses.

Sports

c. 1840 Horse racing thrives in the United States, particularly in Kentucky where there are nearly 20 racecourses in operation.

• Ski jumping is invented in Norway by Sondre Nordheim.

JANUARY

1 The first recorded bowling tournament in the United States is held at Knickerbocker Alleys, New York.

1841

POLITICS, GOVERNMENT, AND ECONOMICS

Business and Economics

AUGUST

• U.S. president John Tyler vetoes a bill creating a Fiscal Bank of the United States. The president opposes the legislation because it gives the states no role in approving the establishment of branch banks.

19 The U.S. Congress passes a federal bankruptcy law, designed to ease the burden of the continuing depression.

SEPTEMBER

11 All but one member of U.S. president John Tyler's cabinet resigns in protest over his recent veto of legislation creating the Fiscal Bank of the United States.

Colonization

JANUARY

20 British sovereignty is proclaimed over the Chinese port of Hong Kong.

MAY

3 New Zealand is formally proclaimed a British colony.

Human Rights

OCTOBER

27 Slaves aboard the American vessel *Creole* spark an international incident when they mutiny off the coast of Virginia and sail for the Bahamas. The British government of the Bahamas arrests the leaders of the mutiny but frees the remaining slaves, against U.S. protests.

Politics and Government

• The Pre-Emption Distribution Act in the United States gives rights to squatters who take up locations on surveyed public lands.

• U.S. president John Tyler appoints Virginia jurist Peter V. Daniel to the U.S. Supreme Court.

FEBRUARY

13 Sultan Abdul Mejid of the Ottoman Empire accepts the Treaty of London, which awards Egypt to Mehmet Ali, the viceroy of Egypt, as a hereditary possession.

MARCH

4 William Henry Harrison is inaugurated ninth president of the United States.

APRIL

4 After one month in office, U.S. president William Henry Harrison dies of pneumonia. He is succeeded by Vice President John Tyler.

MAY

8 General Baldomero Espartero is appointed regent of Spain (replacing Queen Maria Cristina) as Isabella II is still under age.

JULY

13 By the Convention of the Straits, the European powers guarantee Ottoman independence and the Dardanelles and Bosporus are closed to warships of all nations in peacetime (thus overthrowing the 1833 Treaty of Unkiar-Skelessi).

13 France joins Russia, Britain, Prussia, and Austria in the Quadruple Alliance of July 1840 and promises to uphold the integrity of the Ottoman Empire (having previously considered extending French influence in the Near East by backing the reforming ruler of Egypt, Mehmet Ali).

NOVEMBER

2   The Second Anglo-Afghan War begins when the Afghans rise and massacre British army officers.

SCIENCE, TECHNOLOGY, AND MEDICINE

Exploration

- English settler and explorer Edward Eyre leads an expedition along the Great Australian Bight—Australia's southern coast. His journey from the Spencer Gulf to King George Sound proves that it is not a suitable route for normal travel. He becomes the first European to cross the continent from east to west.

Health and Medicine

- Massachusetts reformer Dorothea Dix launches a two-year investigation into the mistreatment of the insane in Massachusetts.

Math

- German mathematician Carl Gauss publishes a treatise on geometrical optics in which he develops formulae for calculating the position and size of the image formed by a lens of given focal length.

Science

- French chemist Auguste Laurent obtains pure carbolic acid through the distillation of pit coal.
- French chemist Eugène-Melchior Péligot isolates uranium (atomic no. 92).
- French geologists Jean-Baptiste Elie de Beaumont and Ours Dufrénoy produce a geological map of France.
- German astronomer Friedrich Bessel deduces the elliptical distortion of the earth—the amount it departs from a perfect sphere—to be $\frac{1}{299}$.
- German physician Gustav Jacob Henle discovers that "ductless glands" secrete their products directly into the bloodstream.
- Scottish geologist Roderick Murchison proposes naming the Permian geologic period 225–280 million years ago after the Perm region in Russia.

- Swedish chemist Jöns Jakob Berzelius observes chemical allotropy (two different forms of the same element) in carbon.

Technology

- British inventor Joseph Stevenson develops the pile driver for use in sinking bridge foundations.
- English chemist Alexander Parkes discovers a cold vulcanization process of waterproofing fabrics.
- English mechanical engineer Joseph Whitworth standardizes the size of threads on screws, which becomes internationally accepted.
- English physicist Frederik de Moleyns receives the first patent for an incandescent lamp. It consists of an evacuated glass sphere containing powdered charcoal between two platinum filaments. The passage of an electric current heats the charcoal to incandescence producing light.
- German chemist Robert Wilhelm von Bunsen invents the carbon–zinc battery.
- Steam-operated fire pumps begin to replace bucket brigades and hand-operated pumps in New York, New York.
- The U.S. artist and inventor Samuel Finley Breese Morse patents his electromagnetic telegraph.
- U.S. engineer Henri Rossiter Worthington develops a direct-action steam pump, which has a steam piston connected to a water piston. Activating the steam piston also activates the water piston which pumps water to the boiler.

November 1841–45 U.S. inventor Thomas Jackson Rodman develops a method of making canons stronger by cooling them from the inside around a hollow core, and allowing other layers to cool and shrink on the outside. He also invents perforated-cake gunpowder which burns evenly, preventing gun barrels from exploding.

Transportation

- There are 2,410 km/1,500 mi of railroad in Great Britain.

SEPTEMBER

19 The Strasbourg to Basel railroad opens. It is the first international railroad line.

ARTS AND IDEAS

Architecture

- The Dresden Opera House, designed by the German architect Gottfried Semper, is completed in Germany.
- The English architect Augustus Pugin publishes *The True Principles of Pointed Architecture*.

Arts

- The French artist Eugène Delacroix paints *The Entry of the Crusaders into Jerusalem*.

- The U.S. artist George Catlin publishes *The Manners, Customs, and Conditions of the North American Indians*. His book—and his hundreds of paintings—arouse great interest in Native American cultures.
- The U.S. artist William Sidney Mt. paints *Cider Making*.

Literature and Language

- The English writer Catherine Grace Gore publishes her novel *Cecil, or the Adventures of a Coxcomb*.
- The French writer Honoré de Balzac publishes his novel *Une Ténébreuse Affaire/A Shady Affair*.
- The U.S. poet and essayist Ralph Waldo Emerson publishes his first volume of *Essays*. Among the essays are "The Over-Soul," "Self-Reliance," and "Friendship."
- The U.S. writer Edgar Allan Poe publishes the short stories "The Murders in the Rue Morgue" and "Descent into the Maelström" in *Graham's Magazine*.

Music

- French composer Hector Berlioz completes his set of songs *Les Nuits d'été/Summer Nights* (Opus 7), settings of poems by Théophile Gautier.
- German composer Robert Schumann completes his Symphony No. 1 (Opus 38), the *Frühling/Spring*.
- The opera *Les Diamants de la couronne/The Crown Diamonds* by the French composer Daniel-François-Esprit Auber is first performed, in Paris, France.

Theater and Dance

- The ballet *Giselle*, by the Italian choreographer Jean Coralli and the French choreographer Jules Joseph Perrot, is first performed, in Paris, France.

Thought and Scholarship

- Massachusetts transcendentalists establish the Utopian community of Brook Farm outside Boston, Massachusetts, designed to strike an ideal balance between physical and intellectual labor.
- Scottish surgeon James Braid uses hypnosis for therapeutic purposes and proposes that it is a physiological state and not due to magical fluids as commonly believed.
- The French statesman and historian Louis Blanc publishes *Histoire de dix ans/The History of Ten Years*, an attack on the July Monarchy.
- The German philosopher Rudolf Hermann Lotze publishes *Metaphysics*.
- The German philosopher Arthur Schopenhauer publishes *Die Beiden Grundprobleme der Ethik/The Two Fundamental Problems of Ethics*.
- The German-born U.S. economist Friedrich List publishes *National System of Political Economy*.
- The Scottish historian Thomas Carlyle publishes *On Heroes, Hero-Worship, and the Heroic in History*.
- The U.S. reformer Catherine E. Beecher publishes "A Treatise on Domestic Economy," emphasizing the civic importance of women's domestic role.

SOCIETY

Education

- Fordham University is founded in New York, New York.
- Queen's University is founded at Kingston, Ontario, Canada.

BIRTHS & DEATHS

JANUARY
28 Henry Morton Stanley, Welsh-born U.S. newspaper correspondent and explorer who rescued David Livingstone in the Congo, born in Denbigh, Wales (–1904).

FEBRUARY
25 Pierre-Auguste Renoir, French impressionist painter, born in Limoges, France (–1919).
26 Evelyn Baring, Lord Cromer, who, as British ambassador to Egypt 1883–1907, had a significant influence on Egypt's development, born in Cromer Hall, Norfolk, England (–1917).

MARCH
8 Oliver Wendell Holmes, legal historian, philosopher, and justice of the U.S. Supreme Court, born in Boston, Massachusetts (–1935).

APRIL
4 William Henry Harrison, ninth president of the United States in 1841, a Whig, dies in Washington, D.C., one month after his inauguration (68).

JUNE
1 David Wilkie, Scottish genre and portrait painter, and printmaker, dies at sea near Gibraltar (55).

JULY
27 Mikhail Yuryevich Lermontov, Russian romantic poet and novelist, killed in a duel in Pyatigorsk, Russia (26).

SEPTEMBER
8 Antonín Dvořák, Bohemian composer who is known for the influence of folk music in his works, born in Nelahozeves, near Prague, Bohemia (–1904).

28 Georges Clemenceau, French journalist and prime minister 1917–20 who helped draft the Treaty of Versailles in 1919, born in Mouilleron-en-Pareds, France (–1929).

OCTOBER
14 Ito Hirobumi, Prime Minister of Japan 1885–88, 1892–96, 1898, and 1900–01, who helped modernize Japan, born in Suo province, Japan (–1909).

NOVEMBER
9 Edward VII, King of Great Britain and Ireland 1901–10, born in London, England (–1910).
20 Wilfrid Laurier, Prime Minister of Canada 1896–1916, a Liberal, born in St.-Lin, Quebec, Lower Canada (–1919).

Everyday Life

- An anonymous cobbler in Boston, Massachussets, inspires the concept of probation, posting bail for a drunkard whom he then shepherds to solvency.
- Arc lamps light streets in Paris, France.
- Populations: Great Britain, 18,534,000; Ireland, 8,175,000; United States, 17,063,353. Principal cities: London, England, 2,235,344; Paris, France, 935,261; Vienna, Austria, 356,870; Berlin, Germany, 300,000; New York, New York, 312,710.
September 1841–50   Emigration to the United States is 267,044 from Britain and 780,719 from Ireland.

Media and Communication

- The *New York Tribune* is founded by U.S. journalist Horace Greeley.

Religion

- Boston Transcendentalist Elizabeth Palmer Peabody publishes *A Glimpse of Christ's Idea of Society*.
- Massachusetts Unitarian clergyman Theodore Parker publishes "A Discourse of the Transient and Permanent in Christianity," a defense of religion as systematized intuitive belief.

OCTOBER

29   Roman Catholic bishop John Joseph Hughes sparks a nativist outcry in New York, New York, when he urges state legislators to appropriate funds for Catholic schools.

Sports

- U.S. boxer Tom Hyer, son of self-proclaimed boxing champion Jacob Hyer, claims the title for himself, beating his first challenger, John McCluster. He holds the title until 1849.

1842

POLITICS, GOVERNMENT, AND ECONOMICS

Business and Economics

- U.S. entrepreneur Morris Robinson founds Mutual Life of New York, the nation's first mutual life insurance company.

Human Rights

- The U.S. Supreme Court, in *Priss v. Pennsylvania*, declares unconstitutional a Pennsylvania law of 1826 forbidding the capture and return of fugitive slaves.

Politics and Government

- A new constitution is granted to the U.S. state of Rhode Island.
- In a move designed to thwart British and French encroachment in Hawaii, the U.S. formally declares Hawaii's independence.

- In U.S. Congressional elections, Whigs retain a slim majority in the U.S. Senate (28–25) but surrender control of the House to the Democrats (142–79).
- Rhode Island dissident Thomas W. Dorr launches Dorr's Rebellion, which seeks to modernize Rhode Island's outdated and restrictive government charter.
- The Massachusetts Supreme Judicial Court, in *Commonwealth v. Hunt*, asserts the legality of labor unions and maintains labor's right to strike.
1842–43   War breaks out between the independent Boer (Dutch) settlers and British forces in Natal, southern Africa.

JANUARY

1   British forces under General William Elphinstone capitulate at Kabul, the capital of Afghanistan, in the Second Anglo-Afghan War.
1   British forces under Charles James Napier, British general and colonial administrator, begin the conquest of the Indian province of Sind (in modern-day Pakistan).
13   Most of General William Elphinstone's British forces are massacred by Afghan troops at Gandalak, Afghanistan, in the Second Anglo-Afghan War.

MARCH

3   Massachusetts governor John Davis signs legislation limiting the workday of child factory workers to ten hours.

APRIL

18   In Dorr's Rebellion, the followers of Rhode Island dissident Thomas W. Dorr install him as governor of

Rhode Island, prompting the traditionally elected governor Samuel W. King to impose martial law.

MAY

18 The self-proclaimed governor of Rhode Island, Samuel Dorr, and his followers try unsuccessfully to seize the state armory.

AUGUST

29 By the Treaty of Nanking ending the First Opium War between Britain and China, Canton, Shanghai, and other Chinese ports are opened to Britain, which is permitted to establish consular facilities and obtains a large indemnity.

30 The U.S. Congress passes legislation raising tariffs to their 1832 level.

OCTOBER

10 A rising is staged in Barcelona, Spain, against the Spanish regent General Baldomero Espartero by republicans and merchants suffering from his repression of contraband.

10 The First Anglo-Afghan War, begun by a British invasion in 1839 to counter perceived Russian and Persian expansionism in the region, ends in British defeat. After the massacre of over 3,000 British and Indian troops retreating from a popular revolt in Kabul in January, a punitive expedition reoccupying the country is withdrawn by the British government.

DECEMBER

1 U.S. Navy captain Alexander S. MacKenzie tries and hangs midshipman Philip Spencer, son of the secretary of war John C. Spencer, for conspiring to mutiny aboard the Navy vessel *Somers*.

4 The Spanish regent General Baldomero Espartero bombards the city of Barcelona and the revolt against him there is soon crushed.

SCIENCE, TECHNOLOGY, AND MEDICINE

Agriculture

- English agronomist John Bennet Lawes patents superphosphate—the first artificial fertilizer—by treating phosphate rock with sulfuric acid. The following year he opens a superphosphate factory.

Exploration

- The U.S. Congress authorizes explorer John C. Frémont to identify a northern route to Oregon through the Wyoming Territory's South Pass.

Health and Medicine

- English physician Edwin Chadwick publishes *Report on an Enquiry into the Sanitary Condition of the Labouring Population of Great Britain*. It indicates that the working classes have far higher disease rates than middle and upper classes because of poor sanitary conditions. It leads to public health legislation.

- U.S. surgeon Crawford Williamson Long is the first to use ether as an anesthetic in an operation. He does not publish his findings until 1849.

Science

- Austrian physicist Christian Doppler publishes *Über das farbige Licht der Doppelsterne*/*On the Colored Light of Double Stars*, in which he describes how the frequency of sound and light waves changes with the motion of their source relative to the observer—the "Doppler effect." He also theorizes that the wavelength of light from a star will vary according to the star's velocity relative to earth.

- British paleontologist Richard Owen coins the term "dinosaur" to describe the great reptiles that inhabited the earth until 65 million years ago.

- English naturalist Charles Darwin writes a 35-page summary of his theory of evolution. He shows it only to close friends.

- German astronomer Friedrich Bessel accurately explains that the wavy course of Sirius is due to the existence of a companion star—the first binary star to be discovered.

- German chemist Robert Wilhelm von Bunsen synthesizes cacodyl, the first organometallic compound.

- German physicist Julius Robert von Mayer publishes *Law of Conservation of Energy*, in which he recognizes that heat and mechanical energy are aspects of the same phenomenon—the first law of thermodynamics.

- Polish embryologist Robert Remak discovers that the early embryo consists of three layers: ectoderm, mesoderm, and endoderm.

May 1842–45 Irish astronomer William Parsons Rosse builds the 180-cm/72-in reflecting telescope Leviathan. Used to observe nebulae, its size is not exceeded until the 250-cm/100-in Mt. Wilson Observatory telescope is built in 1917.

Technology

- German electrical engineer Ernst Werner von Siemens patents an electroplating process.

- The first underwater telegraph cable is laid by U.S. artist and inventor Samuel Finley Breese Morse. It is made of copper but is short-lived.

- U.S. engineer James Buchanan Eads invents a diving bell that allows him to walk along the Mississippi river bottom to salvage losses from riverboat accidents.

- U.S. inventors M. A. Cravath and I. M. Cravath develop the disc plow. It uses a round concave disc of hardened steel to reduce friction.

Transportation

- The first wire suspension bridge in the United States is built by U.S. engineer Charles Ellet over the Schuylkill River, Philadelphia. It employs five wire cables on each side and has a span of 109 m/358 ft.

- There are 558 km/336 mi of railroad in France.

MAY

8   The Paris–Versailles train jumps the track and catches fire, trapping passengers inside the wooden carriages; 100 people die. It is the world's first serious train accident.

ARTS AND IDEAS

Architecture

- The Church of the Madeleine in Paris, France, designed by the French architect Pierre-Alexandre Vignon, is completed, replacing an earlier Madeleine by Pierre Contant d'Ivry (built in 1764). On Napoleon's orders, this new building is not a church, but a "temple to glory."
- The Customs House (later the Federal Hall National Memorial) in New York, New York, designed by the U.S. architects Ithiel Town and Alexander Jackson Davis, is completed.
- The United States Treasury Building in Washington, D.C., designed by the U.S. architect Robert Mills, is completed.

Arts

- P. T. Barnum, best known as a circus impressario, opens Barnum's American Museum in New York, New York.
- The French artist Jean-Auguste-Dominique Ingres paints his *Portrait of Baron James de Rothschild*.
- The French artist Théodore Rousseau paints *Marshy Landscape*.

- The French pioneer of photography Hippolyte Bayard takes *The Cutting of the Rue Tholoze*.

Literature and Language

- Due to low postal rates for newspapers and improvements in the printing process, inexpensive publishing begins in the United States, allowing novels to be sold in a newspaper format for as little as 6¼ cents. The trend forces publishers to print affordable paperback novels.
- The English historian Thomas Babington, Lord Macaulay, publishes *Lays of Ancient Rome*, a sequence of poems on Roman history.
- The English writer Alfred, Lord Tennyson, publishes *Poems*, which contains revised versions of "The Lotus-Eaters" and "The Lady of Shalott," and new works such as "Morte d'Arthur," "Locksley Hall," and "Ulysses."
- The English writer Charles Dickens publishes his account of his travels in the United States, *American Notes for General Circulation*.
- The German writer Annette von Droste-Hülshoff publishes her novel *Die Judenbuche/The Jew's Beech Tree*.
- The U.S. writer Edgar Allan Poe publishes the short story "Masque of the Red Death" in *Graham's Magazine*.
- The U.S. writer Henry Wadsworth Longfellow publishes *Ballads and Other Poems*.

Music

- German composer Felix Mendelssohn completes his Symphony No. 3 (Opus 56), the *Scotch*. He began work on it in 1830.

BIRTHS & DEATHS

- Crazy Horse (Ta-Sunko-Whitko), Oglala Sioux Native American chief who, with Chief Sitting Bull, killed the U.S. general George Custer and massacred his troops at the Battle of the Little Bighorn in 1876, born near Rapid City, South Dakota (–1877).

JANUARY

11   William James, U.S. pragmatist philosopher and functionalist psychologist, born in New York, New York (–1910).

FEBRUARY

4   Georg Brandes, Danish literary critic, born in Copenhagen, Denmark (–1927).

MARCH

18   Stéphane Mallarmé, French Symbolist poet, born in Paris, France (–1898).

23   Stendhal (pen name of Marie Henri Beyle), French novelist, dies in Paris, France (59).

MAY

12   Jules Massenet, French operatic composer, born in Montaud, near St.-Etienne, France (–1912).

13   Arthur Seymour Sullivan, British composer of operettas with William Schwenk Gilbert, born in London, England (–1900).

JUNE

11   Carl von Linde, German engineer who developed a process of liquefying gases and laid the foundation of the science of refrigeration, born in Berndorf, Bavaria (–1934).

JULY

25   Jean-Charles-Léonard Simonde de Sismondi, Swiss economist and historian, dies in Chêne, near Geneva, Switzerland (69).

OCTOBER

- Bernardo O'Higgins, military leader who gained Chile's independence from Spain and served as first head of state 1817–23, dies in exile in Peru (*c.* 65).

2   William Ellery Channing, U.S. Unitarian cleric, dies in Bennington, Vermont (62).

NOVEMBER

12   John William Strutt, Baron Rayleigh, English physicist who experimented in optics and microscopy, and (with William Ramsay) discovered and isolated argon, born in Maldon, Essex, England (–1919).

DECEMBER

21   Peter Alexeyevich Kropotkin, Russian revolutionary, born in Moscow, Russia (–1921).

- German composer Robert Schumann completes his three String Quartets (Opus 41).
- Italian composer Gioachino Antonio Rossini completes his oratorio *Stabat Mater*.
- The opera *Nabucodonosor* (later known as *Nabucco*) by the Italian composer Giuseppe Fortunino Francesco Verdi is first performed, in Milan, Italy. It is first performed in Great Britain in 1846 (in London, England), and in the United States in 1848 (in New York, New York).
- The opera *Rienzi* by the German composer Richard Wagner is first performed, in Dresden, Germany. It is based on a novel by the English writer Edward Bulwer Lytton. It is first performed in the United States in 1878 (in New York, New York, New York), and in Britain in 1879 (in London, England).
- The opera *Ruslan i Lyudmila/Ruslan and Ludmila* by the Russian composer Mikhail Ivanovich Glinka is first performed, in St. Petersburg, Russia. It is based on a work by the poet Alexander Pushkin, written in 1820.
- The Philharmonic Society of New York is founded under the U.S. musician Ureli Corelli Hill. It is reorganized in 1909 and is now known as the New York Philharmonia Orchestra.

SOCIETY

Education

- Notre Dame University is founded in Notre Dame, Indiana.

- Villanova University is founded in Philadelphia, Pennsylvania.

Everyday Life

- The Sons of Temperance, a society to promote abstinence from alcohol, is founded in New York, New York.
- Tom Thumb is exhibited by U.S. showman P. T. Barnum in the United States. No taller than 64 cm/25 in through his teens, Tom Thumb is only 102 cm/40 in tall at full maturity.

MAY

5–7 Fire destroys 4,219 buildings in Hamburg (25% of the city). Over 100 people are killed.

Media and Communication

- D. K. Whitaker founds the *Southern Quarterly Review*, a proslavery journal, in Charleston, South Carolina.
- The first photograph to be printed in a newspaper appears in the English newspaper *The Times*.

Religion

- The German writer Johann Joseph von Görres publishes *Christliche Mystik/Christian Mysticism*.

1843

POLITICS, GOVERNMENT, AND ECONOMICS

Colonization

APRIL

11 A British act of Parliament separates Gambia from Sierra Leone, west Africa, as a crown colony.

MAY

4 Natal in southern Africa is proclaimed a British colony.

AUGUST

8 Britain formally annexes the Indian province of Sind (in modern-day Pakistan), having militarily subdued its inhabitants.

DECEMBER

13 Basutoland in southern Africa becomes a native state under British protection.

Politics and Government

- Rhode Island authorities arrest local revolutionary Thomas W. Dorr and sentence him to life in prison.
- The United States and Hawaii sign a treaty guaranteeing Hawaii's independence.

MAY

2   U.S. settlers in the Oregon Territory establish a local government at Champoeg and draw up a territorial constitution.

10   French troops under Marshal Thomas Bugeaud defeat the Algerian ruler Abd al-Kader's army in the decisive battle of the war between the two countries over territory.

JUNE

•   Protestant zealots within the Native American Association found the American Republican Party in New York, New York.

17   The Maoris revolt against British rule in New Zealand, resentful at the encroachment of British settlers on their land.

JULY

15   General Ramón Narváez, representing the moderate faction in Spanish politics, deposes the progressive regent General Baldomero Espartero.

AUGUST

23   Mexican president Antonio Lopes de Santa Anna warns the U.S. Tyler administration not to attempt the annexation of the Republic of Texas.

31   The Liberty Party nominates Kentucky abolitionist James G. Birney for president and Ohio senator Thomas Morris for vice president.

SEPTEMBER

15   King Otto I of Greece convokes a national assembly in deference to a popular rising against his misrule.

OCTOBER

8   Anglo-Chinese commercial treaties confirm the provisions of the 1842 Treaty of Nanking.

NOVEMBER

28   Britain and France recognize the independence of Hawaii.

SCIENCE, TECHNOLOGY, AND MEDICINE

Agriculture

•   English agronomist John Bennet Lawes and English chemist Joseph Henry Gilbert establish the Rothamsted Experimental Station, Hertfordshire, England, the world's first agricultural research station. They also discover that nitrogen, potassium, and phosphorus are necessary for plant growth.

Computing

•   English mathematician Ada Byron, Countess Lovelace, writes a program for Charles Babbage's analytical engine—the first computer program.

Exploration

MAY

22   A wagon train transporting some 1,000 U.S. settlers departs Independence, Missouri, for the Oregon Territory. It reaches Oregon in October.

29   U.S. explorer John C. Frémont departs Kansas City, Missouri, for Oregon. On this trip, Frémont will chart a secure course to Oregon, returning with reliable information about western flora and fauna.

Health and Medicine

•   Over 13,000 people die from yellow fever along the Mississippi river valley.

•   U.S. physician and author Oliver Wendell Holmes maintains that puerperal fever (a disease common to women at childbirth) is contagious and recommends that attending doctors wash their hands and wear clean clothes.

•   U.S. reformer Dorothea Dix publishes *Memorial to the Legislature of Massachusetts*. Her report inspires reform in the treatment of the mentally ill.

Math

•   English mathematician Arthur Cayley is the first person to investigate spaces with more than three dimensions.

•   Irish mathematician William Rowan Hamilton invents quaternions, which make possible the application of arithmetic to three-dimensional objects.

Science

•   English physicist James Joule determines the value for the mechanical equivalent of heat (now known as the joule), that is the amount of work required to produce a unit of heat.

•   English physicist Michael Faraday develops electroplating by coating metals with nickel.

•   German astronomer Samuel Heinrich Schwabe discovers that sunspots and the effects of solar disturbances have a cycle of about 11 years.

•   German biologist Emil du Bois-Reymond demonstrates that the human nervous system uses electricity to communicate between different parts of the body.

•   German physicist Georg Ohm postulates that the ear analyzes complex sounds into a combination of simple tones that can be expressed mathematically.

•   Swedish chemist Carl Mosander discovers the rare-earth metals erbium (atomic no. 68) and terbium (atomic no. 65).

Technology

c. 1843   Mechanical piston drills begin to be used in mining.

•   English inventor Charles Wheatstone patents the Wheatstone bridge, a device that measures electrical resistance.

- Scottish inventor Alexander Bain patents a device for the transmission and reproduction of graphic matter—the principle of facsimile machines.
- The U.S. Congress appropriates $30,000 to construct a telegraph demonstration line between Washington, D.C., and Baltimore, Maryland.
- U.S. arms manufacturer Samuel Colt develops a mine that is exploded by an electric charge—the first device to be exploded by remote control.
- U.S. inventor Charles Thurber designs the "chirographer," a typewriter consisting of a cylinder with letters mounted on it that are actuated by pressing on them. However, the first practical typewriter is not constructed until 1867 by Christopher L. Sholes.

Transportation

- The U.S. steamship *Princeton* is launched. It is the world's first propeller-driven battleship and has 10 large guns. Warships switch to propellers about this time since paddlewheels are vulnerable.

JULY

19 English engineer Isambard Kingdom Brunel's ship *Great Britain* is launched. It is the world's largest ship (98 m/322 ft long; weighing 3,332 metric tons/3,270 tons), with six masts and a screw propeller, and becomes the first propeller-driven iron ship to cross the Atlantic.

ARTS AND IDEAS

Architecture

MARCH

- The Zola arched dam is built near Aix-en-Provence, France.

Arts

- English illustrator John Calcott Horsley designs the first Christmas card.
- The English artist J. M. W. Turner paints *The Sun of Venice Going to Sea*.
- The English writer and art critic John Ruskin publishes the first volume of his five-volume *Modern Painters*, a broad-ranging discussion of art which defends the works of J. M. W. Turner. The last volume appears in 1860.
- The French artist Jean-François Millet paints his *Portrait of Pauline Ono*.
- The French pioneer of photography Hippolyte Bayard takes *Garden Tools and a Straw Hat*.
- The Scottish pioneers of photography David Octavius Hill and Robert Adamson take *Sandy Linton and His Boat and Bairns*.
- The U.S. artist Hiram Powers sculpts *The Greek Slave*.
- The U.S. artist William Page paints *Cupid and Psyche*.

Literature and Language

- The English poet William Wordsworth becomes poet laureate, a position he holds until 1850.

- The English writer Charles Dickens publishes *A Christmas Carol*. Its central character is the miser Scrooge.
- The English writer Edward Bulwer Lytton publishes his novel *Last of the Barons*.
- The English writer George Borrow publishes *The Bible in Spain*, an account of his travels in Spain and Portugal.
- The U.S. writer James Russell Lowell publishes *Poems*.

Music

- French composer Hector Berlioz publishes *Traité de l'instrumentation/Treatise on Instrumentation*.
- German composer Richard Wagner completes his choral work *Das Liebesmahl der Apostel/The Love Feast of the Apostles*.
- German composer Robert Schumann completes his cantata *Das Paradies und die Peri/Paradise and the Peri* (Opus 50).
- The opera *Die fliegende Holländer/The Flying Dutchman* by the German composer Richard Wagner is first performed, in Dresden, Germany. It is first performed in Britain in 1870 (in London, England), and in the United States in 1876 (in Philadelphia, Pennsylvania).
- The opera *Don Pasquale* by the Italian composer Gaetano Donizetti is first performed, in Paris, France.
- The opera *The Bohemian Girl* by the Irish composer Michael William Balfe is first performed, in London, England. It is first performed in the United States in 1844 (in New York, New York).

Theater and Dance

- The play *Kong Renés datter/King René's Daughter* by the Danish writer Henrik Hertz is first performed, in Copenhagen, Denmark.

Thought and Scholarship

- Massachusetts historian William Hickling Prescott publishes *History of the Conquest of Mexico*, an epic tale of Montezuma's encounter with Cortez.
- The Danish philosopher Søren Aabye Kierkegaard publishes *Enten–Eller/Either/Or*, his first major philosophical work, and *Frygt og baeven/Fear and Trembling*. His analysis of choice makes this work one of the early classics of Existentialism.
- The English philosopher John Stuart Mill publishes *The System of Logic*.
- The Scottish historian Thomas Carlyle publishes *Past and Present*, in which he compares life in the Middle Ages to life in Victorian England.
- U.S. reformer Albert Brisbane establishes the Utopian community North American Phalanx at Redbank, New Jersey. Based on the teachings of French social philosopher Charles Fourier, the North American Phalanx remains viable for over a decade.

SOCIETY

Education

- Holy Cross College is founded in Worcester, Massachusetts.

Everyday Life

- Babbitt's Best Soap, the first powdered laundry detergent, is sold in New York, New York, by U.S. inventor and manufacturer Isaac Babbitt.
- The Association for Improving the Condition of the Poor is founded in New York, New York.
- The Manufacture Française des Tabacs, in France, is the first company to produce cigarettes commercially.

Media and Communication

SEPTEMBER

- *The Economist* magazine is launched, with James Wilson as editor, in London, England.

Religion

JULY

12 The Church of Jesus Christ of Latter-day Saints founder Joseph Smith announces that God has sanctioned polygamy among the Latter-day Saint community.

Sports

- William Weeks, a student, introduces rowing to Harvard University, in Cambridge, Massachusetts.
- Rowing and sailing become popular sports for the upper classes in the United States.

OCTOBER

10 The first U.S. futurity horse race, the Peyton Stakes, is held at Nashville, Tennessee.

BIRTHS & DEATHS

JANUARY
20 Paul Cambon, French ambassador to Britain 1898–1920 who was responsible for the 1904 "Entente Cordiale" between Britain and France, born in Paris, France (–1924).

FEBRUARY
19 Adelina Patti, Italian soprano, born in Madrid, Spain (–1919).

APRIL
15 Henry James, U.S.-born British novelist and playwright, born in New York, New York (–1916).

MAY
10 Benito Pérez Galdós, Spanish novelist, born in Las Palmas, Canary Islands, Spain (–1920).
28 Noah Webster, U.S. lexicographer known for his *American Dictionary of the English language*, dies in New Haven, Connecticut (84).

JUNE
15 Edvard Grieg, Norwegian nationalist composer, born in Bergen, Norway (–1907).

JULY
2 Samuel Christian Friedrich Hahnemann, German physician who founded homeopathy as a system of alternative medicine, dies in Paris, France (88).
25 Charles Macintosh, Scottish chemist, inventor of waterproof material, dies near Glasgow, Scotland (76).

SEPTEMBER
19 Gustave-Gaspard Coriolis, French engineer who was the first to describe the Coriolis force, dies in Paris, France (50).

NOVEMBER
10 John Trumbull, U.S. painter and author noted for his paintings of the American Revolution, dies in New York, New York (87).

DECEMBER
11 Robert Koch, German physician who discovered the bacilli responsible for tuberculosis and cholera, and founded the science of bacteriology, born in the German free city of Clausthal (–1910).
18 Smith Thompson, U.S. politician and jurist, dies in Poughkeepsie, New York (75).

1844

POLITICS, GOVERNMENT, AND ECONOMICS

Business and Economics

- Silesian loom weavers revolt in protest at the economic depression and the decline of their trade caused by competition from modern technology, and are brutally repressed.

DECEMBER

12 The Rochdale Society of Equitable Pioneers, the first modern cooperative society, is founded in England.

Colonization

MAY

5 The British colony of Natal in southern Africa is combined with Cape Colony for administrative purposes.

Human Rights

- Abolitionist William Lloyd Garrison publishes "Address to the Friends of Freedom and Emancipation in the United States," an antislavery call-to-arms.

Politics and Government

- Along with the fate of Texas, the question of the United States's northern boundary with Canada dominates the U.S. presidential election. Most U.S. partisans believe that U.S. territory should extend to latitude 54° 40′. Democratic presidential candidate James K. Polk adopts the slogan "Fifty-four Forty or Fight."
- In U.S. Congressional elections, Democrats attain majorities in both the House (143–77) and Senate (31–25).
- Maine grants women full property rights.
- The governor of Rhode Island pardons local revolutionary Thomas W. Dorr, whose democratic insurrection prompts reform of the state's outdated governing system.

MARCH

8 King Oscar I of Sweden accedes to the throne on the death of his father, Charles XIV (the former Napoleonic marshal Jean-Baptiste Bernadotte).

16 A constitution is granted by King Otto I of Greece, establishing a representative system of two chambers, the Senate and the Chamber of Deputies.

APRIL

12 The United States and the Republic of Texas sign the Texas Annexation Treaty, making Texas a U.S. territory.

27 U.S. presidential candidates Democrat Martin Van Buren and Whig Henry Clay announce their opposition to the annexation of Texas. Both maintain that such a move undertaken without Mexico's consent will precipitate war with Mexico.

MAY

1 Whigs nominate Kentucky senator Henry Clay for president and New Jersey politician Theodore Frelinghuysen for vice president.

29 Democrats nominate Tennessee congressman James K. Polk for president and Pennsylvania politician George M. Dallas for vice president.

JUNE

6 Czar Nicholas I of Russia visits London, England, and suggests partition of the Ottoman Empire should it become any weaker.

8 The treaty for the annexation of Texas by the United States is defeated in the U.S. Senate.

JULY

3 The United States and China sign a commercial treaty providing U.S. merchant access to five Chinese ports.

AUGUST

6 A French force under François, prince de Joinville, begins hostilities against the Arabs of Morocco to gain territory for France.

20 President John Tyler withdraws from the presidential race, becoming the first sitting president not to run for a second term.

SEPTEMBER

10 The French war against the Arabs in Morocco ends with the Treaty of Tangier which resolves territorial matters.

DECEMBER

4 Americans elect Democrats James K. Polk president and George M. Dallas vice president.

4 The U.S. House of Representatives lifts the gag rule, which had effectively stifled antislavery petitions.

SCIENCE, TECHNOLOGY, AND MEDICINE

Ecology

- The last great auk *Pinguinus impennis* is killed. The penguin-like flightless auk lived in the North Atlantic before being hunted to extinction.
- French zoologist Henri Milne-Edwards, off the coast of Sicily, is the first to study underwater marine life.

Exploration

December 1844–46 Indian-born English explorer Charles Sturt attempts to cross the Australian continent from south to north, heading north from Adelaide through the Stony Desert, but is forced to turn back by the intense heat of the Simpson Desert.

Health and Medicine

- Polish embryologist Robert Remak discovers the nerve cells in the heart now known as Remak's ganglia.
- The American Psychiatric Association begins as the Association of Medical Superintendents of American Institutions for the Insane.

Math

- French mathematician Joseph Liouville finds the first transcendental numbers—numbers that cannot be expressed as the roots of an algebraic equation with rational coefficients.

Science

- German chemist Heinrich Rose rediscovers and names the element niobium (atomic no. 41), first discovered by British chemist Charles Hatchett in 1801.
- Russian chemist Karl Klaus discovers the platinum element ruthenium (atomic no. 44).

Technology

- English calico printer John Mercer discovers that caustic soda increases the luster and strength of cotton and its affinity for dyes. The process becomes known as mercerization.
- French scientist Lucien Vidie invents the aneroid barometer. It detects changes in air pressure through the deformation of an evacuated metal tube.
- German electrical engineer Ernst Werner von Siemens invents a technique for reproducing print. The print to be copied is raised into relief on zinc plates.
- German engineer Gottlob Keller develops an effective process for making paper from wood pulp, which

reduces the cost of newspaper production and helps the growth of mass media.
- Scottish engineer William Fairbairn introduces the Lancashire boiler, an improved cylindrical steam engine boiler with two flues.
- The world's first telegraph line, connecting Washington, D.C., and Baltimore, Maryland, becomes operational.
- U.S. physician John Gorrie develops a refrigeration machine that uses the compression and expansion of air to provide ice for his hospital.

ARTS AND IDEAS

Arts

- The English artist J. M. W. Turner paints *Rain, Steam, and Speed*, the first major art work to feature a train.
- The U.S. artist Asher Brown Durand paints *View of the Catskills*.
- The U.S. artist Francis William Edmonds paints *The Image Peddler*.

December 1844–46 The English pioneer of photography William Henry Fox Talbot publishes *The Pencil of Nature*, an album of his photographs. Among its best-known images is *The Open Door*.

Literature and Language

- The English historian and writer Alexander Kinglake publishes *Eothen*, an account of his travels in the Near East.
- The English poet and critic Leigh Hunt publishes his critical study *Imagination and Fancy*.
- The English statesman and writer Benjamin Disraeli, Earl of Beaconsfield, publishes his novel *Coningsby, or the New Generation*.
- The French writer Alexandre Dumas *père* publishes his adventure novels *Les Trois Mousquetaires/The Three Musketeers* and *Le Comte de Monte-Cristo/The Count of Monte Cristo*.
- The French writer Marie-Joseph ("Eugène") Sue begins publishing his novel *Le Juif errant/The Wandering Jew* in serial form. It is published as a book in 1845.
- The German poet Heinrich Heine publishes his verse satire *Deutschland: ein Wintermärchen/Germany: A Winter's Tale* and *Neue Gedichte/New Poems*.
- The German poet Friedrich Rückert publishes *Liebesfrühling/The Dawn of Love*.
- The German writer Hermann Ferdinand Freiligrath publishes his poetry collection *Glaubensbekenntnis/Statement of Conscience*. Because of his commitment to revolutionary politics, his works are banned and he has to leave Germany.
- The Hungarian poet Sándor Petőfi publishes *Versek/Poems*. His poems are quickly accepted as the most important and inspiring expressions of Hungarian nationalism.
- The U.S. essayist Ralph Waldo Emerson publishes his second volume of *Essays*. Among them are "The Poet" and "Nature."

Music

- German composer Felix Mendelssohn completes his Andante and Variations in D for organ, and his choral work *Hör mein Bitten/Hear My Prayer*. Its best-known section is "O for the wings of a dove."
- The opera *Ernani* by the Italian composer Giuseppe Fortunino Francesco Verdi is first performed, in Venice, Italy. It is taken from a story by French writer Victor Hugo. It is first performed in Britain in 1844 (in London, England), and in the United States in 1847 (in New York, New York).

Theater and Dance

- The play *Don Juan Tenorio* by the Spanish writer José Zorrilla y Moral is first performed, in Madrid, Spain. A retelling of the Don Juan story, it becomes the most popular Spanish play of the 19th century.
- The play *Maria Magdalena* by the German dramatist Christian Friedrich Hebbel is first performed.

Thought and Scholarship

- New Jersey journalist-reformer Parke Godwin publishes *Democracy, Constructive and Pacific*, an early account of social democracy.
- Scottish writer Robert Chambers publishes *The Vestiges of the Natural History of Creation*, which dispels the idea of divine creation and anticipates some of Charles Darwin's conclusions.
- The Danish philosopher Søren Aabye Kierkegaard publishes *Begrebet Angst/The Concept of Dread* and *Philosophishe Smuler/Philosophical Fragments*.
- The English philosopher John Stuart Mill publishes *Unsettled Questions of Political Economy*.
- The Swiss economist and historian Jean-Charles-Léonard Sismonde de Sismondi publishes the last volume of his 31-volume *Histoire des Français/History of the French*. The first volume appeared in 1821.
- U.S. reformer Albert Brisbane launches the Utopian community Alphadelphia Phalanx in Kalamazoo County, Michigan. Alphadelphia is modeled on Brisbane's thriving establishment in Redbank, New Jersey, but the new one will not last three years.

JULY

- In a series of editorials published over the course of the month, Whig presidential candidate Henry Clay endorses the principle of U.S. annexation of Texas as long as it can be accomplished "without dishonor, without war."

BIRTHS & DEATHS

JANUARY

7 St. Bernadette of Lourdes, French peasant girl whose visions of the Virgin Mary lead to the establishment of the shrine at Lourdes, born in Lourdes, France (–1879).

FEBRUARY

15 Henry Addington Sidmouth, British prime minister 1801–04, a Tory, dies in Richmond, Surrey, England (86).

17 Montgomery Ward, U.S. merchant who introduced the mail-order method of selling, born in Chatham, New Jersey (–1913).

20 Ludwig Eduard Boltzmann, Austrian physicist who developed the science of statistical mechanics, born in Vienna, Austria (–1906).

27 Nicholas Biddle, U.S. financier, editor, and president of the Second Bank of the United States, dies in Philadelphia, Pennsylvania (58).

MARCH

18 Nicolay Andreyevich Rimsky-Korsakov, Russian composer, born in Tikhvin, near Novgorod, Russia (–1908).

24 Bertel Thorvaldsen, Danish sculptor, dies (73).

30 Paul Verlaine, French lyric poet, leader of the Symbolists, born in Metz, France (–1896).

31 Andrew Lang, Scottish writer known for his collections of fairy tales, born in Selkirk, Scotland (–1912).

APRIL

4 Charles Bulfinch, U.S. architect who transformed the city of Boston, dies in Boston, Massachusetts (80).

16 Anatole France, French writer and winner of the Nobel Prize for Literature in 1921, born in Paris, France (–1924).

MAY

21 Henri Rousseau, French painter, born in Laval, France (–1910).

JUNE

27 Joseph Smith, U.S. prophet whose writings, along with the Bible, form the theological basis of The Church of Jesus Christ of Latter-day Saints, dies in Carthage, Illinois (38).

JULY

25 Thomas Eakins, U.S. realist painter, born in Philadelphia, Pennsylvania (–1916).

27 John Dalton, English chemist who developed an atomic theory of matter, dies in Manchester, England (77).

AUGUST

17 Menelik II, King of the Ethiopian kingdom of Shewa 1865–69 and Emperor of Ethiopia 1889–1913, born in Ankober, Shewa (–1913).

30 Friedrich Ratzel, German geographer and ethnologist, born in Karlsruhe, Baden (now Germany) (–1904).

OCTOBER

15 Friedrich Wilhelm Nietzsche, German philosopher and critic, especially of Christianity, born in Röcken, Saxony, Prussia (–1900).

23 Louis Riel, Canadian Métis leader who led an uprising against the Canadian government, born in Assiniboia, Saskatchewan, Canada (–1885).

NOVEMBER

25 Carl Friedrich Benz, German engineer who built the first practical car, born in Karlsruhe, Germany (–1929).

DECEMBER

13 John Henry Patterson, U.S. manufacturer who developed the cash register and founded the National Cash Register Company (NCR), born near Dayton, Ohio (–1922).

SOCIETY

Education

- The State University of New York is founded at Albany, New York.
- The University of Mississippi is founded in Oxford, Mississippi.

Everyday Life

- The New York Prison Association is established to address the deplorable state of released convicts.

JUNE

6   English dry goods clerk George Williams founds the Young Men's Christian Association (YMCA), in London, England.

26   U.S. President John Tyler marries Julia Gardiner in New York, New York.

Media and Communication

- U.S. labor advocate George Henry Evans reestablishes his moribund newspaper *Workingman's Advocate*.

MAY

24   The first public telegraph line is strung 60 km/37 mi between Washington, D.C., and Baltimore, Maryland. The first message is transmitted by U.S. artist and inventor Samuel Finley Breese Morse who asks "What hath God wrought?"

Religion

- Twenty-four people die and two churches are burned during Protestant–Catholic riots in Philadelphia, Pennsylvania.
- Having converted from Unitarianism to Catholicism, writer Orestes Brownson founds *Brownson's Quarterly Review*.
- The French theologian Jacques-Paul Migne publishes the first volume of his 171-volume *Encyclopédie théologique/Theological Encyclopedia*. The final volume appears in 1866.

JUNE

27   A mob murders The Church of Jesus Christ of Latter-day Saints Church founder Joseph Smith and his brother Hyrum in Carthage, Illinois.

Sports

- The first steeplechase horse race in the United States is run at Hoboken, New Jersey.

JULY

- The New York Yacht Club is founded.

OCTOBER

16   An estimated crowd of over 25,000 at the Beacon Race Course, near New York, New York, watch "pedestrians" (professional runners) from the United States and Britain compete over 16 km/10 mi for a prize of $1,000.

1845

POLITICS, GOVERNMENT, AND ECONOMICS

Business and Economics

- New York labor organizers create the Industrial Congress of the United States.

APRIL

4   The British prime minister Robert Peel's second "Free-Trade" Budget repeals export duties entirely, and duties on many imports are limited or abolished.

JUNE

6   An Anglo-French expedition is sent to Madagascar to quell opposition to European traders.

Human Rights

- Escaped slave Frederick Douglass publishes *Narrative of the Life of Frederick Douglass*, an influential abolitionist tract.
- Massachusetts transcendentalist Margaret Fuller publishes "Woman in the Nineteenth Century," a seminal text in U.S. feminism.

Politics and Government

- U.S. president James K. Polk names jurists Levi Woodbury of New Hampshire and Samuel Nelson of New York to the U.S. Supreme Court.

JANUARY

23 The U.S. Congress decrees the first Tuesday after the first Monday of November to be the universal election day for presidential elections.

FEBRUARY

28 The U.S. Congress approves the annexation of the Republic of Texas.

MARCH

3 Florida becomes the 27th state in the Union.

4 Democrat James K. Polk is inaugurated 11th president of the United States.

6 Mexico formally protests the U.S. annexation of Texas.

11 Further Maori risings take place against British rule in New Zealand, following revolts in 1843 and 1844.

28 Mexico severs diplomatic relations with the United States.

MAY

23 A new moderate constitution is granted in Spain, by which the monarch recovers the right to nominate the Senate and press and judicial rights are limited.

JUNE

15 The Polk administration assures Texas that the U.S. government will protect the territory from any attack by Mexico.

23 The Congress of the Republic of Texas approves annexation by the United States.

JULY

- John L. Lewis, editor of *United States Magazine and Democratic Review*, coins the term "manifest destiny" in reference to the U.S. annexation of Texas.

NOVEMBER

10 President James K. Polk dispatches Louisiana representative John Slidell to Mexico to repair U.S.–Mexican relations and to offer the Mexican government $5 million for the purchase of New Mexico and $35 million for California.

DECEMBER

- Texas becomes the 28th state in the Union.

11 The First Anglo-Sikh War breaks out in northwest India when the powerful Sikh army crosses the Sutlej River to attack British territories in central Hindustan, after a period of growing tension following the death of the Sikh maharaja Ranjit Singh.

12 The *Sonderbund*, an armed league of the seven Catholic cantons in Switzerland, is formally established to protect Catholic interests.

20 John Slidell, U.S. minister plenipotentiary (diplomat of ambassadorial or cabinet rank with full powers to negotiate substantive agreements on behalf of the state), sent to Mexico by President James K. Polk to repair U.S.–Mexican relations, is turned away by the Mexican government.

21 British forces under Major General Sir Hugh Gough, British commander in chief in India, defeat the Sikhs at Firozshah (modern Firozpur), northwest India, in the First Anglo-Sikh War.

SCIENCE, TECHNOLOGY, AND MEDICINE

Agriculture

c. 1845 The clearing of forests in New Zealand by the increasing number of European settlers begins, to make room for sheep farms.

- The potato blight fungus *Phytophthora infestans* causes potato crops to fail throughout Europe. In Ireland, where the potato is a staple, over half the crop is lost causing devastating famine. Over 1 million die and 1.5 million emigrate over the next 2 years.

Exploration

MAY

18 English explorer John Franklin leads a new expedition in search of the last link in the long-sought Northwest Passage through the Canadian Arctic, but the project ends in disaster, with all the crew perishing in 1847–48 to the west of King William Island.

Health and Medicine

- German pathologist Rudolf Virchow describes the first case of leukemia.

- U.S. dentist Horace Wells uses nitrous oxide as an anesthetic to perform painless dental operations. In January 1845 he gives a demonstration in which the patient proves unresponsive.

Math

- English mathematician Arthur Cayley publishes *Theory of Linear Transformations*, which lays the foundation of the school of pure mathematics.

- French mathematician Baron Augustine-Louis Cauchy proves the fundamental theorem of group theory, subsequently known as Cauchy's theorem.

Science

- Austrian chemist Anton von Schrötter discovers red phosphorous, which enables the production of safety matches as it does not spontaneously combust.

- English physicist Michael Faraday discovers diamagnetism. He also discovers that a magnetic field rotates the plane of polarization of a light beam—the Faraday effect.

- German chemist August Wilhelm von Hofmann develops a method of preparing aniline dye from benzene.

- German chemist Hermann Kolbe synthesizes acetic acid from carbon disulfide—the first organic compound to be synthesized from inorganic materials.

- German physicist Friedrich Wöhler determines the specific gravity, ductility, color, and other properties of aluminum, and isolates metallic aluminum in pinhead-sized amounts.

- German zoologist Carl von Siebold describes the unicellular nature of protozoa and describes the function of the cilia.

May 1845–51   English archeologist Austen Henry Layard excavates the Mesopotamian city of Nimrud.

May 1845–58   German naturalist and explorer Alexander von Humboldt lays the basis of modern geography with the publication of *Kosmos/Cosmos*, in which he arranges geographic knowledge in a systematic fashion.

Technology

- English engineer William Armstrong invents a hydraulic crane.
- English inventor Thomas Wright obtains the first patent for an arc lamp.
- French gunsmith Nicolas Flobert invents rim priming for cartridges.
- French inventor Josué Heilmann develops a machine for combing cotton and wool.
- German chemist Christian Schönbein discovers the explosive compound nitrocellulose, or guncotton.
- Scottish engineer William McNaught develops a compound steam engine where the high and low pressure cylinders are at opposite ends of the beam.
- Scottish engineer William Fairbairn develops a riveting machine that is used to manufacture steam boilers.
- U.S. artist and inventor Samuel Finley Breese Morse establishes his telegraph system in France and extends his telegraph line to New York and Boston.

May 1845–51   U.S. industrialist Erastus Brigham Bigelow develops the power loom, which allows carpets and tapestries to be made faster and in asymmetrical patterns.

Transportation

- Scottish inventor Robert Thomson patents the pneumatic tire. Although used for 1,931 km/1,200 mi on a horsedrawn Brougham carriage, pneumatic tires are not used again until the end of the century.
- The first asphalt road laid is London Road, Nottingham, England.
- The screw-propelled ship *Rattler* has a tug of war with the paddlewheeler *Alecto*. The *Rattler* pulls the *Alecto* away at 2.5 knots, demonstrating the superiority of the screw propeller.
- U.S. naval architect John Willis Griffiths launches the first extreme clipper ship, the *Rainbow*. Extreme clippers become the fastest ships afloat.

ARTS AND IDEAS

Architecture

- The restoration of Notre-Dame Cathedral in Paris, France, revives interest in the Gothic style.

- The Royal Botanic Gardens and Herbarium are founded in Melbourne, Australia.
- Work begins on Marseille Cathedral in France, designed by the French architect Léon Vaudoyer. It is completed in 1893.

Arts

c. 1845   The U.S. artist George Caleb Bingham paints *Fur Traders Descending the Missouri*.

- The German artist Adolph von Menzel paints *Room with an Open Window*.
- The U.S. artist Thomas Cole paints *View Across Frenchman's Bay*.
- The U.S. artist William Sidney Mt. paints *Eel Spearing at Setauket*.

Literature and Language

- The Argentine statesman and writer Domingo Faustino Sarmiento publishes *Civilización y barbarie: vida de Juan Facundo Quiroga/Civilization and Barbarity: A Life of Facundo Quiroga*. The single most important South American book published in the 19th century, it is a biography that focuses on the question of Latin American identity.
- The Danish writer Meïr Aron Goldschmidt publishes his novel *En Jøde/The Jew*.
- The English statesman and writer Benjamin Disraeli, Earl of Beaconsfield, publishes his novel *Sybil, or the Two Nations*, which gives a vivid picture of poverty in 19th-century Britain.
- The French writer Prosper Mérimée publishes his novella *Carmen*. It provides the story for the opera *Carmen*, which is written in 1875 by Georges Bizet.
- The German writer Heinrich Hoffmann publishes *Der Struwwelpeter/Slovenly Peter*, a collection of cautionary tales that becomes a classic of children's literature.
- The U.S. writer Edgar Allan Poe publishes *The Raven and Other Poems* and the short stories "The Pit and the Pendulum," "The Tell-Tale Heart," and "The Purloined Letter" in the *Broadway Journal*.

Music

- German composer Robert Schumann completes his piano pieces *Albumblätter/Leaves from an Album* (Opus 124).
- Hungarian composer Franz Liszt completes his work for piano (later orchestrated by Busoni) *Rapsodie espagnole/Spanish Rhapsody*.
- The opera *Leonora* by the U.S. composer and critic William Henry Fry is first performed, in Philadelphia, Pennsylvania, and then New York, New York. It is widely seen as the first important U.S. opera.
- The opera *Tannhäuser und der Sängerkrieg auf Wartburg/Tannhäuser and the Singing Contest of Wartburg* by the German composer Richard Wagner is first performed, in Dresden, Germany. It is first performed in the United States in 1859 (in New York, New York), and in Britain in 1876 (in London, England). A revised version appears in 1861.

Thought and Scholarship

- The English social economist William Thomas Thornton publishes *Over-Population and Its Remedy*.
- The French historian Adolphe Thiers publishes the first volume of his 20-volume *L'Histoire du consulat et de l'empire/History of the Consulate and Empire*. The last volume appears in 1865.
- The German political philosophers Karl Marx and Frederich Engels publish *Die heilige Familie/The Holy Family*, an attack on Hegel's philosophy.
- The Scottish writer Thomas Carlyle publishes his edition of *Cromwell's Letters and Speeches*.

SOCIETY

Education

- Massachusetts educator Horace Mann publishes "Lectures on Education."

OCTOBER
10 The U.S. Naval Academy opens at Annapolis, Maryland.

Everyday Life

- Over 1,000 buildings in New York, New York, are destroyed by fire.

- Henry Jones of Bristol, England, creates self-raising flour.
- The fraternal organization Temple of Honor is founded in New York, New York.
- The total British state expenditure reaches £54.8 million annually.
- U.S. labor advocate George Henry Evans establishes the National Reform Association.
- U.S. physicians William Shecut and Horace Harvel Day patent the first adhesive bandage, Allcock's Porous Plaster.

MARCH
17 English rubber-manufacturer Stephen Perry patents rubber bands for stationery use.

Media and Communication

- Henry Clay's political machine establishes the *American Whig Review*, a literary and political magazine published to promote the congressman's presidential aspirations.

AUGUST
28 U.S. inventor Rufus Porter founds the scientific magazine *Scientific American*.

Sports

SEPTEMBER
13 The Knickerbocker Club, New York, New York, codifies the rules of baseball.

BIRTHS & DEATHS

MARCH
3 Georg Cantor, Russian mathematician who established set theory, born in St. Petersburg, Russia (–1918).
10 Alexander III, Emperor of Russia 1881–94 who instituted a policy of Russification, born in St. Petersburg, Russia (–1894).
27 Wilhelm Konrad Röntgen, German physicist who discovered X-rays, born in Lennep, Prussia (–1923).

MAY
12 August Schlegel, German scholar and critic, dies in Bonn, Germany (77).

15 Elie Metchnikoff, Russian zoologist who discovered the process of phagocytosis, born near Kharkov, Ukraine, Russia (–1916).

JUNE
8 Andrew Jackson, seventh president of the United States 1829–37, a Democrat, dies at the Hermitage, near Nashville, Tennessee (78).
18 (Charles-Louis-) Alphonse Laveran, French physician who discovered the malaria parasite, born in Paris, France (–1922).

JULY
17 Charles Grey, Earl Grey, British Whig prime minister 1830–34, dies in Howick, Northumberland, England (81).

AUGUST
16 Gabriel Lippmann, French physicist who produced the first color photographic plate, born in Hollerich, Luxembourg (–1921).

OCTOBER
23 Sarah Bernhardt, French actress, born in Paris, France (–1923).

DECEMBER
31 Nikola Pašić, Prime Minister of Serbia 1891–92, 1904–05, 1906–08, 1909–11, and 1912–18, and Prime Minister of the Kingdom of the Serbs, Croats, and Slovenes (later Yugoslavia) 1918, 1921–24, and 1924–26, born in Zaječar, Serbia (–1926).

1846

POLITICS, GOVERNMENT, AND ECONOMICS

Business and Economics

- Alexander Turney Stewart opens the Marble Dry Goods Palace on Broadway in New York, New York. It is the first department store and the largest store in the world.
- An agricultural and industrial depression in France causes widespread distress.
- The French socialist Pierre-Joseph Proudhon publishes the economic tract *Système des contradictions économiques, ou philosophie de la misère/The System of Economic Contradictions, or the Philosophy of Misery.*

Human Rights

- James D. B. De Bow establishes *De Bow's Review*, a political monthly supportive of slavery, nullification, and John C. Calhoun.
- The beginnings of native segregation are seen in the British colony of Natal, southern Africa, where the first location commission sets up preserves for immigrant Zulus.

AUGUST

- In the controversial Wilmot Proviso, Pennsylvania congressman David Wilmot proposes banning slavery from any territory acquired from Mexico in the Mexican–American War. Several attempts to pass the legislation fail in the U.S. Senate.

Politics and Government

- In U.S. Congressional elections, Democrats retain a majority in the Senate (36–21), while surrendering to Whig control of the House (115–108).
- New York state outlaws perpetual leases on the estates of the original Dutch patroons, thus ending the seven-year land dispute known as the Antirent War.
- President James K. Polk appoints Pennsylvania jurist Robert C. Grier to the U.S. Supreme Court.
- The Walker Tariff replaces the tariff passed by the Whig administration of John Tyler in 1842 in the United States.

JANUARY

- President James K. Polk sends U.S. troops into the disputed territory between Nueces and Rio Grande rivers on the Texas–Mexico border.

28 The British East India Company's forces under General Harry Smith defeat the Sikhs at Aliwal, northwest India, in the course of the First Anglo-Sikh War.

FEBRUARY

10 British forces under Major General Sir Hugh Gough defeat the Sikhs at Sobrahan (modern Sobraon), northwest India, in the First Anglo-Sikh War.

14 A rising against Russian rule in the city of Kraków, the center of Polish nationalism, begins and swiftly spreads throughout Poland.

MARCH

9 By the Treaty of Lahore ending the First Anglo-Sikh War in India, Britain gains territory beyond the Sutlej River, the previous boundary of British India. Punjab becomes a British protectorate.

12 A liberal revolt begins in the Sicilian capital, Palermo, against the ruler of Sicily, Ferdinand II of Naples.

12 Austrian and Russian troops occupy the city of Kraków, suppressing the Polish rebellion against Austrian rule. The city and its environs had been established as an independent republic, although in fact remaining under Austrian rule, at the Congress of Vienna in 1815.

APRIL

25 General Zachary Taylor, commander of U.S. troops on the Texas–Mexico border, dispatches news to President James K. Polk that Mexico has attacked U.S. forces on U.S. territory.

27 The U.S. Congress authorizes President James K. Polk to abrogate the treaty of 1818 providing for joint U.S.– British occupation of the Oregon territory.

30 U.S. forces in southern Texas come under attack from the Mexican army, which crosses the Rio Grande onto U.S. soil.

MAY

3 U.S. troops at Fort Texas come under siege from Mexican forces.

4 Michigan becomes the first state in the Union to abolish the death penalty.

5 Nationalist German professors meet in Frankfurt ("The Intellectual Diet of the German People") to discuss German unification.

8 In the first pitched battle of the Mexican–American War, U.S. forces defeat the Mexicans at the Battle of Palo Alto.

9 U.S. troops under the command of Zachary Taylor push the Mexicans back across the Rio Grande into Mexico at the Battle of Resaca de la Palma.

9 President James K. Polk and Congress receive news that Mexican forces attacked U.S. troops in Texas on April 24.

13 The U.S. Congress passes a declaration of war with Mexico and authorizes President James K. Polk to marshal 50,000 volunteers.

16   The supporters of the Portuguese claimant to the throne, Dom Miguel, force Costa Cabral, Count of Thomar, the effective ruler of Portugal while Maria da Gloria is still under age, into exile.

18   General Zachary Taylor leads U.S. troops across the Rio Grande River into Mexico in the Mexican–American War.

25   Louis-Napoléon Bonaparte, the nephew of Napoleon I, escapes from Ham in France (where he has been imprisoned since his unsuccessful attempt to seize power in France in 1840) and travels to London, England.

JUNE

12   A mammoth meeting of Liberals in Brussels demands political reform in Belgium.

14   In the so-called Bear Flag Revolt, a group of U.S. settlers declares California's independence from Mexico.

15   The United States and Britain sign the Oregon Treaty, establishing the U.S.–Canadian border at the 49th parallel.

JULY

8   King Christian VIII of Denmark declares the Danish state indivisible in a direct response to the movement for independence in the predominantly German duchies of Schleswig and Holstein.

AUGUST

17   The U.S. naval commander Robert F. Stockton proclaims U.S. annexation of California, which had been declared an independent republic on June 14.

28   The British Possessions Act grants Canada the right to fix its own tariffs, giving it a greater measure of financial independence.

SEPTEMBER

17   The German Confederation asserts its right to exert influence in the Danish-governed duchies of Schleswig and Holstein (ethnically Schleswig is half Danish and half German, Holstein mostly German).

25   U.S. forces under Zachary Taylor seize Monterrey, Mexico.

OCTOBER

10   Queen Isabella II of Spain is married to the Duke of Cadiz, Don Francisco de Asis, while her sister Princess Maria Louisa Fernanda marries the Duc de Montpensier, the youngest son of the French king, Louis Philippe, giving France undue influence in Spain. Fears of British opposition to the marriages weaken the Orléanist monarchy in France.

DECEMBER

28   Iowa becomes the 29th state in the Union.

SCIENCE, TECHNOLOGY, AND MEDICINE

Agriculture

- The Irish potato crop fails again, as in 1845, and famine increases despite organized relief.

Exploration

December 1846–48   British New Zealand Company surveyor Thomas Brunner, accompanied by his Maori guide Ekehu, explores South Island's mountainous west coast.

Health and Medicine

December 1846–53   German physician Gustav Jacob Henle publishes *Handbook of Rational Pathology*. One of the first books in modern pathology, it describes diseased organs according to their normal physiological functions.

SEPTEMBER

30   U.S. dentist William Thomas Morton gives the first successful demonstration of ether as an anesthetic during a dental operation to extract a tooth. He uses it in Boston, Massachusetts, on October 16, to anesthetize a patient while removing a tumor from his neck.

Math

- French mathematician Evariste Galois's research on the resolubility of algebraic equations is published posthumously.

Science

- British physicist William Grove, in his book *On the Correlation of Physical Forces*, enunciates the conservation of energy principle (a year before German physicist Hermann Ludwig von Helmholtz).
- English paleontologist Richard Owen publishes *Lectures on Comparative Anatomy and Physiology of the Vertebrate Animals*, one of the first textbooks on comparative vertebrate anatomy.
- French physiologist Claude Bernard discovers that pancreatic secretions break down fat molecules into fatty acids and glycerin.
- German botanist Hugo von Mohl uses the word protoplasm to describe the main living substance in a cell. It leads to the development of cell physiology.
- German industrialist Carl Zeiss opens a factory at Jena to produce microscopes and other optical instruments.
- German zoologist Carl von Siebold publishes *Lehrbuch der vergleichenden Anatomie/Textbook of Comparative Anatomy*, one of the first textbooks in comparative anatomy that is based on actual observation rather than philosophical discussion.
- Italian botanist Giovanni Battista Amici establishes the circulation of sap in plants.
- Italian chemist Ascanio Sobrero first prepares the powerful explosive nitroglycerin.

SEPTEMBER

23   German astronomer Johann Gotfried Galle discovers the planet Neptune on the basis of French astronomer Urbain Le Verrier's calculations of its position.

OCTOBER

- British astronomer William Lasell discovers Triton, one of Neptune's two moons—only a month after the planet itself is discovered.

Technology

- U.S. blacksmith John Deere invents a one-piece steel plow and moldboard, making it possible to plow effectively the black soils of the U.S. midwest.
- U.S. industrialist Erastus Brigham Bigelow erects the nation's first gingham factory at Clinton, Massachusetts.
- U.S. inventor Royal E. House develops a printing telegraph that uses a 28-key keyboard, typewriter ribbon and a simple tape printer.

FEBRUARY

2 French inventor Jean-Aimé Balan patents the first breeze blocks used in construction.

SEPTEMBER

10 U.S. inventor Elias Howe patents a practical sewing machine; it revolutionizes garment manufacture in both the factory and home.

Transportation

- English inventor Daniel Gooch develops eight-wheeled locomotives that can attain speeds of over 100 kph/60 mph. They set a pattern for subsequent locomotives.
- Spurred by the competition of the Baltimore and Ohio Railroad and Erie Canal, a group of Philadelphia investors incorporate the Pennsylvania railroad to connect Philadelphia and Pittsburgh.

ARTS AND IDEAS

Architecture

- The Royal College of Physicians, designed by the Scottish architect Thomas Hamilton, is completed, in Scotland.
- The Trinity Church in New York, New York, designed by the U.S. architect Richard Upjohn, is completed. It is one of the leading examples of American Gothic Revival.

Arts

- The English artist George Frederick Watts paints *Paolo and Francesca*.
- The French artist Jean-François Millet paints *Oedipus Unbound*.
- The German writer Friedrich Theodor Vischer publishes the first volume of his *Ästhetik oder Wissenschaft des Schönen/Aesthetics, the Science of the Beautiful*. The final volume appears in 1857.

Literature and Language

- The English artist and poet Edward Lear publishes his collection of verse *Book of Nonsense*.
- The English sisters Charlotte, Emily, and Anne Brontë publish *Poems by Currer, Ellis and Acton Bell*.
- The French literary critic Charles-Augustin Ste.-Beuve publishes *Portraits contemporains/Contemporary Portraits*, a collection of essays.
- The French writer George Sand publishes her novel *La Mare au diable/The Devil's Pond*.
- The French writer Honoré de Balzac publishes his novel *La Cousine Bette/Cousin Bette*.
- The German writer Hermann Ferdinand Freiligrath publishes his poetic cycle *Ça Ira/That Will Do*.
- The Russian writer Fyodor Mikhaylovich Dostoyevsky publishes his novels *Bednyye lyudi/Poor Folk* and *Dvoynik/The Double*.
- The U.S. poet Henry Wadsworth Longfellow publishes *The Belfry of Bruges and Other Poems*.
- The U.S. writer Edgar Allan Poe publishes his essay "The Philosophy of Composition" in *Graham's Magazine* and the short story "The Cask of Amontillado" in *Godey's Lady's Magazine*.
- The U.S. writer John Greenleaf Whittier publishes *Voices of Freedom*, a collection of his antislavery poems, the best-known of which is "Massachusetts to Virginia."
- The U.S. writer Nathaniel Hawthorne publishes his story collection *Mosses From an Old Manse*, which includes "Young Goodman Brown" and "Rappaccini's Daughter."
- The U.S. writer Thomas Bangs Thorpe publishes his collection of humorous tales *The Mysteries of the Backwoods*.
- The U.S. writer Herman Melville publishes *Typee, a Peep at Polynesian Life*.

Music

- French composer Hector Berlioz completes his dramatic cantata *La Damnation de Faust/The Damnation of Faust* (Opus 24), based on Goethe's play *Faust*, written in 1808. Berlioz began work on this piece in 1828.
- German composer Felix Mendelssohn completes his oratorio *Elias/Elijah* (Opus 70). It is first performed in Birmingham, England, in 1846.
- German composer Robert Schumann completes his Symphony No. 2 (Opus 61).
- The opera *Attila* by the Italian composer Giuseppe Fortunino Francesco Verdi is first performed, in Venice, Italy.

Thought and Scholarship

- Charles Grandison Finney publishes "Lectures on Systematic Theology."
- English diplomat Henry Creswicke Rawlinson publishes *Persian Cuneiform Inscription at Belhistun*, his translation and analysis of the cuneiform inscription of Darius I Hystapis at Behistun, Persia, which opens up Assyrian history.

- The English historian George Grote publishes the first volume of his *History of Greece*. The final volume appears in 1856.
- The German philosopher and anthropologist Theodor Waitz publishes *Foundations of Psychology*.
- The German political philosophers Karl Marx and Frederick Engels complete their book *Die deutsche Ideologie/German Ideology*, setting out their concept of history. The text is not published until 1932.
- The U.S. Congress establishes the Smithsonian Institution in Washington, D.C., "for the increase and diffusion of knowledge," with money left by British scientist and millionaire James Smithson.

SOCIETY

Education

- Bucknell University is founded in Lewisburg, Pennsylvania.

Everyday Life

- French chemist Joseph Dubonnet invents the alcoholic drink Dubonnet.

Media and Communication

September 1846–47 U.S. inventor Richard M. Hoe pioneers the first rotary printing press. Installed in Philadelphia, Pennsylvania, the next year, the press turns out 9,000 newspapers per hour.

Religion

JUNE
15 Cardinal Mastai-Ferretti, at this time regarded as a liberal, is elected Pope Pius IX.

Sports

JUNE
19 In what is regarded as the first real baseball game (played under the rules modified in 1845 by the Knickerbocker Club), the Knickerbocker Club plays the New York Club at the Elysian Fields, Hoboken, New Jersey.

BIRTHS & DEATHS

FEBRUARY
26 William F. Cody ("Buffalo Bill"), U.S. buffalo hunter and Wild West showman, born in Scott County, Iowa (–1917).

MARCH
17 Friedrich Wilhelm Bessel, German astronomer whose measurements of stars allowed the first interstellar distances to be determined, dies in Königsberg, Prussia (now Kaliningrad, Russia) (61).

MAY
18 Peter Carl Fabergé, Russian goldsmith and jewelry designer, born in St. Petersburg, Russia (–1920).

JUNE
1 Pope Gregory XVI, who was pope 1831–46, dies in Rome, Italy (80).
11 John Franklin, English admiral and explorer, dies near King William Island, British Arctic Islands, while trying to find the Northwest Passage (61).
27 Charles Stewart Parnell, Irish nationalist who led the movement for Irish home rule, born in Avondale, County Wicklow, Ireland (–1891).

SEPTEMBER
25 Wladimir Köppen, Russian-born German meteorologist who maps the climatic zones of the earth, born in St. Petersburg, Russia (–1940).

OCTOBER
6 George Westinghouse, U.S. industrialist who was responsible for the use of alternating current, rather than direct current, in the United States, born in Central Bridge, New York (–1914).

NOVEMBER
25 Carry Nation, U.S. temperance militant who attacked bars with a hatchet, born in Garrard County, Kentucky (–1911).
30 Friedrich List, German-born U.S. economist, dies in Kufstein, Austria (57).

1847

POLITICS, GOVERNMENT, AND ECONOMICS

Business and Economics

- The German political philosopher Karl Marx publishes (in French) *La Misère de la philosophie/The Misery of Philosophy*, an attack on Pierre-Joseph Proudhon's *Système des contradictions économiques, ou philosophie de la misère/The System of Economic Contradictions, or the Philosophy of Misery*, published in 1846.

Colonization

AUGUST

26 Liberia, the colony established in west Africa for freed U.S. slaves, is proclaimed an independent republic under the presidency of Joseph Roberts.

Human Rights

- U.S. abolitionists, black and white, meet in Troy, New York, to resist oppression and promote black American education and civil rights.

Politics and Government

- Vermont passes legislation granting wives dominion over property held at the time of their marriage or acquired thereafter.

FEBRUARY

3 A United Diet is summoned by the Prussian king, Frederick Wilhelm IV, in a development of the constitutional process. While not democratically elected, this new national assembly is given the right of veto of state finances.

22–23 In the Mexican–American War, U.S. general Zachary Taylor defeats his Mexican counterpart Santa Anna at the Battle of Buena Vista.

MARCH

3 The Liberals obtain a majority in the Table of Deputies, the lowest representative assembly in Austrian-governed Hungary, and issue the "March laws," a ten-point program demanding responsible government.

9 In the Mexican–American War, a U.S. amphibious expedition under the command of General Winfield Scott lands near the Mexican fortress city of Veracruz.

22–29 U.S. forces lay siege to the Mexican fortress at Veracruz, capturing the fortress within a week. They then advance on Mexico City.

APRIL

18 U.S. forces under General Winfield Scott defeat the Mexican army at Cerro Gordo, en route to Mexico City.

JUNE

6 The United States and Mexico begin peace negotiations to end the Mexican–American War.

JULY

4 The moderate liberal French politician and former prime minister Adolphe Thiers holds the first reform banquet in Paris, France, to publicize the case for a limited extension of the franchise.

17 Austrian troops occupy Ferrara, after disappointment at the failure of Pope Pius IX to institute political reforms in the Papal States leads to unrest.

AUGUST

20 U.S. forces defeat the Mexican army at Churubusco, en route to Mexico City.

SEPTEMBER

8 U.S. forces defeat the Mexican army at the Battle of Molino del Rey, outside Mexico City.

9 The moderate liberal François Guizot becomes French prime minister at a time when the country is subjected to severe political and economic unrest.

13 U.S. forces seize Chapultepec, gaining access to Mexico City.

14 U.S. general Winfield Scott leads a column of triumphant U.S. troops down the main boulevard of Mexico City.

OCTOBER

21 Civil war begins in Switzerland, following the Catholic cantons' refusal on July 20 to dissolve their armed league, the *Sonderbund*, in the face of a liberal, anticlerical majority in the diet.

SCIENCE, TECHNOLOGY, AND MEDICINE

Ecology

- Nearly 34,000 people die in an earthquake in Zenkojil, Japan.

ARTS AND IDEAS

SEPTEMBER

9   Gold is discovered in California and leads to the first "gold rush."

Exploration

- Lost and starving in the Sierra Nevada mountains, a group of U.S. settlers known as the Donner party resorts to cannibalism.

Health and Medicine

- German physiologist Carl Ludwig invents the kymograph, a device used to record muscular motion and changes in blood pressure. It is still used today.
- Scottish physician James Simpson, in *Account of a New Anaesthetic Agent 1847*, first describes the use of chloroform as an anesthetic. He uses it to assist women during childbirth.

September 1847–48   Over 15,000 people die from an influenza epidemic in London, England.

MAY

7   The American Medical Association is founded by U.S. physician Nathan Smith Davis, in Philadelphia, Pennsylvania.

Math

- English mathematician Augustus de Morgan proposes two laws of logic that are now known as de Morgan's laws.
- The English mathematician George Boole publishes *The Mathematical Analysis of Logic*, in which he shows that the rules of logic can be treated mathematically. Boole's work lays the foundation of computer logic.

Science

- English physicist James Joule discovers the law of conservation of energy—the first law of thermodynamics.
- German physicist Franz Neumann states the mathematical laws of electrical induction—the process of converting mechanical energy into electrical.
- German physicist Hermann Ludwig von Helmholtz presents his paper "On the Conservation of Energy" to the Physical Society of Berlin. In it he demonstrates the law of conservation of energy by showing that perpetual motion machines are impossible.

Technology

- French clockmaker Antoine Redier invents the first modern alarm clock.
- French gunsmith B. Houiller patents the first cartridge. It consists of a powder charge in a case with a percussion cap and projectile.
- German electrical engineer Ernst Werner von Siemens suggests that gutta-percha (a type of rubber) be used to insulate telegraph wires, which allows them to be used for submarine cables.
- Scottish inventor David Brewster improves the stereoscope by using lenses that produce the three-dimensional effect by combining two dissimilar binocular pictures.
- U.S. inventor Alfred Ely Beach patents a typewriter which uses an inked ribbon.
- U.S. inventor Richard Hoe eliminates the to-and-fro movement of flatbed printing presses by patenting a revolving or rotary press. Because the type is mounted on a large cylinder, printing is continuous and rapid. Known as the "lightning press," it can print over 8,000 sheets per hour and greatly contributes to the spread of newspapers.

Transportation

May 1847–49   U.S. engineer Charles Ellet spans the Ohio River at Wheeling, Virginia, with the world's first long-span wire-cable suspension bridge. Built for the Baltimore & Ohio Railroad, its central span of 308 m/1,010 ft makes it the longest suspension bridge built to date.

ARTS AND IDEAS

Architecture

- The British Museum in London, England, designed by the English architect Robert Smirke, is completed, a leading example of the Greek revival style.
- The Customs House in Boston, Massachusetts, designed by the U.S. architect Ammi Burnham Young, is completed.

Arts

- The French artist Eugène Delacroix completes his frescoes in the library of the Palais de Luxembourg, in Paris, France.

Literature and Language

- The Brazilian poet Dias Gonçalves publishes *Primeiros cantos/First Poems*.
- The English historian James Anthony Froude publishes "Shadows in the Clouds," an autobiographical essay dealing with his religious doubts.
- The English statesman and writer Benjamin Disraeli, Earl of Beaconsfield, publishes his novel *Tancred, or The New Crusade*.
- The English writer Anne Brontë publishes her first novel, *Agnes Grey*, under the name Acton Bell.
- The English writer Frederick Marryat publishes his historical novel *The Children of the New Forest*, which becomes a classic of children's literature.

- The English writer William Makepeace Thackeray begins publishing his novel *Vanity Fair* in serial form. It appears as a book in 1848.
- The U.S. essayist Ralph Waldo Emerson publishes *Poems*.
- The U.S. poet Henry Wadsworth Longfellow publishes his long epic poem *Evangeline, a Tale of Acadie*.
- The U.S. writer Herman Melville publishes *Omoo, a Narrative of Adventures in the South Seas*.

OCTOBER

- The English writer Charlotte Brontë publishes her second novel, *Jane Eyre*, under the name Currer Bell. (Her first novel, *The Professor*, does not appear until 1857.)

DECEMBER

- The English writer Emily Brontë publishes her only novel, *Wuthering Heights*, under the name Ellis Bell.

Music

- German composer Robert Schumann completes his Piano Trios No. 1 (Opus 63) and No. 2 (Opus 80).
- The opera *Macbeth* by the Italian composer Giuseppe Fortunino Francesco Verdi (and based on the tragedy by William Shakespeare) is first performed, in Florence, Italy. It is first performed in the United States in 1858 (in New York, New York), and in Britain in 1860 (in Manchester).
- The opera *Martha* by the German composer Friedrich von Flotow is first performed, in Vienna, Austria.
- U.S. songwriter Stephen Foster writes "Camptown Races" and "Oh Susanna."

SEPTEMBER

11   "Oh Susanna" is performed for the first time at a concert in Pittsburgh, Pennsylvania; it is the first of Foster's many popular folk tunes to gain widespread success.

Thought and Scholarship

- The French historian Jules Michelet publishes the first volume of his *Histoire de la Révolution française/ History of the French Revolution*. The last volume appears in 1853.
- The French statesman and historian Louis Blanc publishes the first volume of his *Histoire de la Révolution française/History of the French Revolution*. The final volume appears in 1862.
- The German historian Leopold von Ranke publishes the first part of his *Neun Bücher preussischer Geschichte/ Memoirs of the House of Brandenburg and History of Prussia, during the Seventeenth and Eighteenth Centuries*. The concluding part appears in 1848.
- The U.S. historian William Hickling Prescott publishes *The Conquest of Peru*.

SOCIETY

Education

- The University of Iowa is founded in Iowa City.

Everyday Life

- Harrison W. Crosby produces canned tomatoes in Easton, Pennsylvania.
- U.S. baker's apprentice Hanson Gregory invents the ring doughnut, in Camde, Maine.
- In *The Evil Tendencies of Corporal Punishment as a Means of Moral Discipline in Families and Schools*, U.S. educator Lyman Cobb repudiates corporal punishment.

JULY

1   The U.S. Post Office Department issues the first official U.S. postage stamps, in five and ten cent denominations.

BIRTHS & DEATHS

FEBRUARY
11   Thomas Alva Edison, prolific U.S. inventor who invented the light bulb, phonograph, and motion picture projector, born in Milan, Ohio (–1931).

MARCH
3   Alexander Graham Bell, Scottish-born U.S. scientist who invented the telephone, born in Edinburgh, Scotland (–1922).

APRIL
10   Joseph Pulitzer, U.S. newspaper editor and publisher who established the Pulitzer prizes, born in Makó, Hungary (–1911).

MAY
7   Archibald Philip Primrose, fifth Earl of Rosebery, British prime minister 1894–95, a Liberal, born in London, England (–1929).
15   Daniel O'Connell, Irish nationalist leader who, as a member of the British House of Commons, fought for the rights of Irish Catholics, dies in Genoa, Sardinia (71).

JULY
4   James Anthony Bailey, one of the originators of the Barnum and Bailey Circus, born in Detroit, Michigan (–1906).

SEPTEMBER
5   Jesse James, U.S. bank and train robber, born near Centerville, Missouri (–1882).

OCTOBER
2   Paul von Hindenburg, German field marshal, president of the Weimar Republic 1925–34, born in Posen, Prussia (now Poznań, Poland) (–1934).

NOVEMBER
4   Felix Mendelssohn(-Bartholdy), German composer, dies in Leipzig, Germany (38).

Religion

JULY

24 The Church of Latter-day Saints leader Brigham Young leads a group of Latter-day Saints to what is now Salt Lake City, Utah, where they establish their headquarters.

- Connecticut Congregationalist minister Horace Bushnell publishes "Views of Christian Nurture," a critique of Calvinist dogmatism.
- The U.S. Congregationalist preacher Henry Ward Beecher begins his ministry at Plymouth Congregational Church in Brooklyn, New York. He makes its pulpit a national platform for the temperance and antislavery movements.

1848

POLITICS, GOVERNMENT, AND ECONOMICS

Business and Economics

- Midwestern grain merchants establish the Chicago Board of Trade to regulate the exchange of warehouse receipts, which circulate as currency throughout the region.
- U.S. industrialist Cyrus Hall McCormick moves McCormick Harvester from Virginia to Chicago, where it will become a major U.S. enterprise.

Colonization

FEBRUARY

3 The British general Harry Smith annexes territory in southern Africa between the Orange and the Vaal rivers.

AUGUST

29 The Boers (Dutch settlers) in southern Africa are defeated at Boomplaats in the Orange Free State by British forces, and retire across the Vaal River, ensuring British sovereignty over the Orange River.

Human Rights

- Black American civil rights proponents found the Citizens Union of Pennsylvania to attain full citizenship rights for black Americans.

JULY

19 U.S. women's rights advocates Lucretia Mott and Elizabeth Cady Stanton convoke the Seneca Falls Convention where, along with a host of others, they issue the "Declaration of Sentiments," demanding full citizenship rights.

Politics and Government

- In U.S. Congressional elections, Democrats attain majorities in both the House (112–109) and Senate (35–25).
- New York State grants women full property rights.

JANUARY

20 King Christian VIII of Denmark dies and is succeeded by his liberal son Frederick VII, who is nevertheless committed to retaining the duchies of Schleswig and Holstein despite their claims for independence.

FEBRUARY

2 The United States and Mexico sign the Treaty of Guadeloupe Hidalgo, ending the Mexican–American War. In exchange for some $18 million, Mexico recognizes Texas as part of the United States and cedes 500,000 square miles of territory encompassing all of the future states of California, Nevada, and Utah, and part of the future states of New Mexico, Arizona, Colorado, and Wyoming.

10 King Ferdinand II of Naples proclaims a liberal constitution, after failing to secure Austrian help in defeating the rebellion in Sicily.

17 Grand Duke Leopold of the Italian state of Tuscany is forced by the proclamation of a constitution for the kingdom of Naples to grant one in Tuscany in order to forestall a revolution.

22 Crowds assemble in Paris, France, to demand parliamentary reform but are dispersed by the National Guard.

24 King Louis Phillipe of France abdicates in favor of his grandson, Louis-Philippe-Albert, comte de Paris, but a Republican provisional government containing the socialist Louis Blanc is established under Alphonse de Lamartine.

MARCH

3 A revolution breaks out in Budapest and on March 15 the Hungarian diet (national assembly) is subsequently granted the reforms it advocated in March 1847, making it effectively independent under Austrian rule.

5 A constitution is granted for the dual Italian kingdom of Sardinia–Piedmont by its king, Charles Albert.

12–15 A revolution in Vienna, the Austrian capital, begins with demonstrations by liberal students, inspired by the revolutions in Paris, France, and Budapest, Hungary.

13 The Austrian chief minister, Klemens, Prince Metternich, resigns following protests against his conservative rule and an assembly of the States–General, the Austrian representative body, is promised.

14 A constitution for the Papal States is promulgated reluctantly by Pope Pius IX, in response to the revolutions in the rest of Italy.

17 A revolution begins in Austrian-occupied Venetia after news arrives of the success of the Italian, French, and Viennese revolts. An independent Venetian Republic is proclaimed, with the revolutionary leader Daniele Manin as president of a provisional government.

17 Demonstrations in the Prussian capital, Berlin, begin a revolution in Prussia for political reform and the creation of a united Germany.

17 King William II of the Netherlands appoints a committee to revise the constitution in order to forestall unrest following news of the revolutions in Italy and Austria.

18 The duchies of Schleswig and Holstein declare independence of Denmark at Rendsburg, Holstein.

18–22 A five-day revolution (the *Cinque Giornate*) begins in the Italian city of Milan against Austrian rule of Lombardy.

20 A revolt takes place in the Italian duchy of Parma, demanding a constitution.

20 The Second Anglo-Sikh War begins in India, arising out of the Sikh aristocracy's discontent at British administration and the subsequent murder of two British officers.

21 King Frederick VII of Denmark announces his decision to incorporate the duchy of Schleswig (half Danish, half German) fully into Denmark.

22 King Charles Albert of Sardinia–Piedmont declares war on Austria in an attempt to check Austrian influence and unify Italy under his leadership.

22 Spanish prime minister Ramón Narváez suspends the cortes (national assembly) to try to prevent the spread of revolution in Europe to Spain.

24 The German elements in the duchies of Schleswig and Holstein form a government and Prussia recognizes the autonomy of the duchies.

26 Demonstrations for reform in Madrid, the Spanish capital, are easily crushed.

31 A German Ante-Parliament (*Vorparlament*) of liberal deputies meets at Frankfurt to decide the format of a formal German national parliament.

APRIL

8 Emperor Ferdinand I of Austria promises to grant Bohemia a constitution.

8 The Austrian army of Count Joseph Radetzky, attempting to contain the rebellion in Lombardy, northern Italy, is defeated by Piedmontese troops at Goito, Lombardy.

13 Sicily, having revolted against the rule of the Bourbon King Ferdinand II of the Two Sicilies, declares itself independent of Naples.

25 Emperor Ferdinand I of Austria grants a constitution in response to the Viennese revolt against his rule, allowing limited representative government.

25 Papal forces under General Giacomo Durando join Sardinia–Piedmont in its war against Austria.

29 Pope Pius IX dissociates himself from the movement for Italian unification.

MAY

2 A Prussian force invades Denmark in support of the independent German government of the combined duchies of Schleswig and Holstein.

4 A French National Assembly meets, after elections based on universal male suffrage, in which the moderate Republicans have a majority.

15 A left-wing rising takes place in Paris, France, following news of the suppression of the Polish revolt for independence. Workers overturn the government and set up a provisional administration, but this is immediately suppressed.

15 The revolt in the Italian kingdom of Naples against King Ferdinand II is suppressed and the government chambers are dissolved.

15 There is a second rising in Vienna, Austria, against the new constitution, demanding greater concessions. In response, the constitution is repealed.

17 Emperor Ferdinand I of Austria flees from widespread radical disturbances in the capital, Vienna, to Innsbruck in Tyrol.

18 A National Assembly composed of liberal delegates elected from all over Germany meets in Frankfurt and suspends the German Confederation prior to discussing a more unified organization of the German states.

22 A Prussian National Assembly meets in the capital, Berlin.

26 An ill-planned rising in County Tipperary, Ireland, is easily put down by British troops.

26 Democrats nominate Michigan senator Lewis Cass for president and Kentucky politician William O. Butler for vice president.

29 Austrian troops defeat a Tuscan force at Curtatone in their assault on the Italian revolutionary states.

29 Wisconsin becomes the 30th state in the Union.

30 Piedmontese troops defeat the Austrians at the second Battle of Goito, Lombardy.

JUNE

2 A Pan-Slav Congress (in fact largely made up of Bohemian representatives) meets in Prague, Bohemia, under the presidency of Francis Palacky.

3 The U.S. Senate approves the Treaty of New Granada, providing the U.S. right of way across the Isthmus of Panama.

9 Whigs nominate Mexican–American War hero Zachary Taylor for president and New Yorker Millard Fillmore for vice president.

10 The Austrian army of Count Joseph Radetzky, fighting against the revolutions in Italy and against the Italian kingdom of Sardinia–Piedmont, defeats the Piedmontese at Vicenza, in the Austrian-ruled Veneto.

10 The Austrian authorities dismiss the governor of Croatia, Count Josip Jellačić, as he is becoming dangerously associated with movements for Croatian national unity.

17 Austrian troops under Prince Alfred von Windischgrätz crush a Bohemian revolt against Austrian rule in Prague, Bohemia.

23 The "June Days" begin in France with the construction of barricades by workers determined to protect the national workshops erected in March from government attempts to close them.

29 The Frankfurt parliament of German liberals elects Archduke John of Austria to be regent of the Reich with which they plan to replace the German Confederation.

JULY

7 Russia, concerned at the spread of revolution through Europe, invades the Danubian principalities of the Ottoman Empire at the request of the Ottoman government to put down revolts there.

22 An Austrian Reichstag (constituent assembly) is convened in Vienna. It draws up a new, democratic constitution.

25 An Austrian army under Count Josef Radetzky defeats the Piedmontese at Custozza, reestablishing Austrian control of Lombardy.

25 The Habeas Corpus Act is suspended in Ireland, allowing imprisonment without trial, because of fears of an insurrection following the revolutions in Europe and the repeated failure of the potato crop.

27 Despite the success of Austria in putting down liberalism in the Italian republics, Venice, Sardinia–Piedmont, and Lombardy formally unite as a symbolic beginning to Italian unification.

AUGUST

9 Following the decisive Piedmontese defeat at Custozza in the Veneto, an armistice is concluded between Austria and Sardinia–Piedmont at Vigevano, Lombardy, by which Sardinia–Piedmont gives up Lombardy and accepts the status quo as it existed in Italy before the revolutions.

9 The Free Soil Party nominates former president Martin Van Buren for president and Massachusetts congressman Charles Francis Adams for vice president.

11 Sardinian troops are expelled from the Italian republic of Venice when the terms of the Vigevano armistice of August 9 between Sardinia–Piedmont and Austria become known, and the revolutionary Daniele Manin is restored as dictator.

12 Emperor Ferdinand I of Austria returns to the capital, Vienna, the revolutionary situation having stabilized with the end of the Austro-Italian war in Italy.

26 The Truce of Malmö is made between Denmark and Prussia ending the war over the duchies of Schleswig and Holstein. The truce establishes an armistice that lasts for 17 months, during which Schleswig–Holstein is jointly administered by Austria and Prussia.

SEPTEMBER

7 The feudal practice of serfdom, by which peasants are tied to the land and controlled by their landlords to whom they owe dues of service, is abolished in Austria.

11 King Ferdinand II of the Italian kingdom of Naples signs an armistice with the rebellious island of Sicily, but the insurgents continue to resist.

12 Following the defeat of the *Sonderbund* (the armed league of the seven Catholic cantons), Switzerland adopts a new constitution by which the states become a federal union with strong central government.

17 Count Josip Jellačić leads a Croat invasion of Hungary, disputing Magyar domination of the Hapsburg monarchy's Slav peoples.

24 The leading Hungarian nationalist Lajos Kossuth is proclaimed president of a committee for national defense, following Croatia's mobilization against Hungary.

OCTOBER

6 A third revolution takes place in the Austrian capital, Vienna, at the news that the government is to crush the revolt in Hungary.

13 The Qajar shah Muhammad of Persia dies, leaving his son Nasir Ud-Din to deal with his legacy of bad government.

31 Government forces under Prince Alfred von Windischgrätz take the Austrian capital, Vienna, from the insurgents after the third Viennese revolution of October 6.

NOVEMBER

3 The Prussian general Friedrich von Wrangel restores royal control of Berlin.

4 The constitution of the Second Republic is promulgated in France with a single chamber, a strong president, and direct universal suffrage.

7 Mexican–American War hero Zachary Taylor is elected as U.S. president and Millard Fillmore as vice president.

10 Ibrahim, acting as viceroy of Egypt because of the senility of his father, Mehmet Ali, dies and is succeeded by Abbas I.

15 Pellegrino Rossi, the papal premier, is assassinated by a fanatical democrat and Pope Pius IX is forced to constitute a liberal ministry in the Papal States under Carlo Muzzarelli.

16 A popular insurrection flares up in Rome, Italy, demanding liberal political reforms in the Papal States.

24 Pope Pius IX flees to Gaeta following the popular insurrection in Rome.

27 The Austrian prime minister Felix, Prince zu Schwarzenberg, issues the "Kremsier program", which proclaims the indivisibility of the Hapsburg Empire and so in effect rules out any possibility of a Greater Germany.

30 The Austrian field marshal Prince Alfred von Windischgrätz defeats the Hungarian insurgents, in support of Lajos Kossuth, under Arthur von Görgei at Mór, Hungary.

DECEMBER

2 The mentally unstable emperor Ferdinand I of Austria abdicates in favor of his nephew Franz Josef I.

5 The Prussian National Assembly is dissolved and a constitution is imposed that includes universal male suffrage, but the ultimate authority of King Frederick Wilhelm IV is maintained.

10 Louis-Napoléon Bonaparte, the nephew of Napoleon I, is elected president of France by a massive majority. He subsequently appoints his first government, made up mostly of moderate ministers from the Orléanist regime.

27 The German National Assembly in Frankfurt proclaims the fundamental rights of political and national freedom.

SCIENCE, TECHNOLOGY, AND MEDICINE

Ecology

JANUARY

24 U.S. prospector James Marshall discovers gold in the millrace at Sutter's Mill on the American River near Sacramento, California.

Exploration

December 1848–49 German explorers Johann Ludwig Krapf and Johannes Rebmann travel into the interior of Africa from its eastern coast, exploring the region of Kenya, and becoming the first Europeans to sight Mounts Kilimanjaro (Rebmann, May 1848) and Kenya (Krapf, December 1849).

December 1848–60 Nine separate expeditions search for the lost Franklin expedition to the Arctic north of Canada. The British admiral Robert McClure and the crew of his search ship HMS *Investigator*, traveling eastward from the Beaufort Sea, confirm (September 9, 1850) that the McClure Strait north of Banks Island completes the Northwest Passage.

Health and Medicine

- Cholera reaches London, England, and Paris, France, from India.
- Hungarian obstetrician Ignaz Philipp Semmelweis discovers that puerperal infection ("childbed fever"), which causes maternal mortality rates as high as 30% in some European hospitals, is caused by infection. He advises all attending physicians, midwives, and students to wash their hands in chlorinated water before each examination. Although this dramatically reduces infection in the Vienna hospital where he works, few other hospitals follow his procedures.
- December 1848–49 During another cholera epidemic in Britain, British physician John Snow traces the source to dirty water and bad sanitation.

Science

- English paleontologist Richard Owen publishes *On the Archetypes and Homologies of the Vertebrate Skeleton* in which he defines homology and analogy in relation to the structural similarities of organs or structures.
- French physicist Armand Fizeau shows how the shift in wavelength of the light from stars can be used to measure their relative velocities.
- Scottish physicist William Thomson (later Lord Kelvin), devises the absolute temperature scale. He defines absolute zero as –273°C/–459.67°F, where the molecular energy of molecules is zero. He also defines the quantities currently used to describe magnetic forces:

magnitude of magnetic flux, beta, and H the magnetizing force.

- The first wind and current charts for the North Atlantic are compiled by U.S. naval officer Matthew Fontaine Maury.
- The Société des Ingénieurs Civils de France is founded.

MAY

22 French chemist Louis Pasteur establishes the field of stereochemistry when he discovers two mirror-image forms of tartaric acid that polarize light in opposite directions.

SEPTEMBER

20 The American Association for the Advancement of Science (AAAS) is founded in Boston, Massachusetts.

Technology

- French scientists Alexandre Becquerel and Abel Niépce de Saint-Victor produce the first color photographs using coatings of silver chloride. They are unable to fix the images.
- New York and Chicago are linked by a telegraph line.
- U.S. locksmith Linus Yale patents a pin tumbler lock.

Transportation

- The Illinois–Michigan Canal is completed. It connects the Great Lakes and the Mississippi River and results in the explosive growth of Chicago.

ARTS AND IDEAS

Architecture

- The Bogardus Factory, in New York, New York, designed by its owner, the U.S. architect James Bogardus, is completed. It is the first building to have a cast-iron façade.

Arts

- The English artist George Frederick Watts paints *Roland Pursuing Morgan Le Fay*.
- The English artist John Everett Millais paints *Lorenzo and Isabella*.
- The English artists William Holman Hunt, John Everett Millais, and Dante Gabriel Rossetti found the Pre-Raphaelite Brotherhood. Rejecting the materialism and industrialization of Victorian England, they seek an art which has the moral and religious integrity of the medieval world.
- The French artist and caricaturist Honoré Daumier completes his series of lithographs *Les Gens de justice/ Lawyers*.
- The French artist Jean-François Millet paints *The Winnower*.
- The U.S. artist William Caton Woodville paints *Politics in an Oyster House*.

Literature and Language

- The English historian James Anthony Froude publishes "Nemesis of Faith," an autobiographical essay.
- The English writer Anne Brontë publishes her novel *The Tenant of Wildfell Hall*, under the name Acton Bell.
- The English writer Elizabeth Cleghorn Gaskell publishes her novel *Mary Barton*.
- The English writer William Makepeace Thackeray begins to publish his novel *The History of Pendennis* in serial form. It is published as a book in 1850.
- The French writer Alexandre Dumas *fils* publishes his novel *La Dame aux camélias/The Lady of the Camelias*. It is performed as a successful play in 1852, which is the basis of Verdi's 1853 opera *La traviata/The Fallen Woman*.
- The French writer François-Auguste-René, vicomte de Chateaubriand, publishes the first part of his autobiographical *Mémoires d'outre-tombe/Memoirs from Beyond the Grave*.
- The French writer George Sand publishes her novel *François le Champi/The Country Waif*.
- The French writer Henry Murger begins to publish his novel *Scènes de la vie de Bohème/Scenes from Bohmian Life* in serial form. It appears as a book in 1851 and is the basis of Giacomo Puccini's 1896 opera *La Bohème*.

- The French writer Léonard-Sylvain-Julien Sandeau publishes his novel *Mademoiselle de la Seiglière*.
- The German folklorist and philologist Jakob Ludwig Carl Grimm publishes *Geschichte der deutschen Sprache/History of the German Language*.
- The U.S. poet John Greenleaf Whittier publishes the semifictional romance *Leaves from Margaret Smith's Journal*.
- The U.S. abolitionist writer and poet James Russell Lowell publishes the verse satire *A Fable for Critics*, which contains portraits of a wide range of U.S. writers including Ralph Waldo Emerson, Henry Wadsworth Longfellow, Edgar Allan Poe, and Nathaniel Hawthorne.

Music

- German composer Robert Schumann completes his set of songs *Liederalbum für die Jugend/Song Album for the Young* (Opus 79).
- Hungarian composer Franz Liszt completes his Symphonic Poem *Les Préludes/The Preludes*.
- Russian composer Mikhail Ivanovich Glinka completes his orchestral fantasy *Kamarinskaya/Wedding Song*.

BIRTHS & DEATHS

- Wyatt Earp, U.S. law officer and gunslinger, born in Monmouth, Illinois (–1929).

FEBRUARY
5 Joris Karl Huysmans (born Charles-Marie-Georges Huysmans), French novelist, born in Paris, France (–1907).
23 John Quincy Adams, sixth president of the United States 1825–29, a Republican, dies in Washington, D.C. (80).
27 Ellen Terry, English actress popular in both Britain and the United States, born in Coventry, Warwickshire, England (–1928).

MARCH
1 Augustus Saint-Gaudens, U.S. sculptor, born in Dublin, Ireland (–1907).
29 John Jacob Astor, U.S. fur magnate and investor in New York property, dies in New York, New York (84).

APRIL
4 Ludwig Leichhardt, Prussian explorer, writes his last letter and dies sometime after this date while trying to cross Australia (c. 35).
8 Gaetano Donizetti, Italian opera composer, dies in Bergamo, Lombardy (now Italy) (50).

MAY
23 Otto Lilienthal, German aeronautical pioneer who made more than 2,000 glider flights, born in Anklam, Prussia (–1896).

JUNE
7 Paul Gauguin, French postimpressionist painter, born in Paris, France (–1903).

JULY
4 François de Chateaubriand, French romantic author known for his memoirs and his accounts of Native Americans, dies in Paris, France (79).
25 Arthur James Balfour, British prime minister 1902–05, a Conservative, born in Whittinghame, East Lothian, Scotland (–1930).

AUGUST
7 Jöns Jacob Berzelius, Swedish chemist who was instrumental in establishing modern chemistry, dies in Stockholm, Sweden (68).
12 George Stephenson, English engineer, inventor of the railroad locomotive, dies in Chesterfield, Derbyshire, England (67).

OCTOBER
31 Stephen Watts Kearny, U.S. Army officer who seized New Mexico for the United States and helped retake California during the Mexican–American War 1846–48, dies in St. Louis, Missouri (54).

NOVEMBER
8 Gottlob Frege, German mathematician who founded mathematical logic, born in Wismar, Mecklenburg-Schwerin (now Germany) (–1925).
24 William Lamb, Viscount Melbourne, British prime minister 1834 and 1835–41, a Whig advisor to Queen Victoria, dies in London, England (69).

DECEMBER
9 Joel Chandler Harris, U.S. author, creator of "Uncle Remus," born in Eatonton, Georgia (–1908).
19 Emily Brontë, English novelist known for *Wuthering Heights* (1847), dies in Haworth, Yorkshire (now West Yorkshire), England (30).

Thought and Scholarship

- US abolitionist writer and poet James Russell Lowell publishes the satirical "Biglow Papers" (first series), opposing the Mexican–American war.
- The English historian Thomas Babington, Lord Macaulay, publishes the first volume of his *History of England from the Accession of James II*. The final volume appears in 1861.
- The English philosopher John Stuart Mill publishes *The Principles of Political Economy*.
- The German political philosophers Karl Marx and Friedrich Engels publish *Manifest der Kommunistischen Partei/Manifesto of the Communist Party*, one of the central works of Marxism. It contains the famous lines: "Workers of the world unite. You have nothing to lose but your chains."

SOCIETY

Education

- Rhodes College is founded in Memphis, Tennessee.
- The University of Ottawa is founded in Ottawa, Ontario, Canada.
- The University of Wisconsin is founded at Madison, Wisconsin.

NOVEMBER

1 U.S. educator Samuel Gregory establishes the Boston Female Medical School, the first medical school for women.

Everyday Life

- John Curtis of Bangor, Maine, produces the first commerical chewing gum, "State of Maine Pure Spruce Gum."
- U.S. visionary John Humphrey Noyes establishes the Oneida Community, an industrial utopia in Oneida, New York.

MARCH

6 National workshops are erected in France by the socialist Louis Blanc, who claims for the unemployed the "right to work."

DECEMBER

5 In his annual message to Congress, President James K. Polk inspires the California gold rush, waxing lyrical about the fortunes to be won in the foothills of the Sierra Nevada.

Media and Communication

- A group of New York journalists form the Associated Press to establish more efficient and faster news lines.

1849

POLITICS, GOVERNMENT, AND ECONOMICS

Business and Economics

- The watchmaking American Horologe Company is established in Waltham, Massachusetts.

JUNE

26 The Navigation Acts protecting British shipping are finally repealed to develop free trade.

OCTOBER

10 The "October Manifesto" is published in Canada to generate support for union with the United States after Britain's repeal of the Navigation Acts in June increases the economic depression.

Colonization

- Russia continues to extend its territory at the expense of Persia.

MARCH

29 Britain annexes the Indian province of Punjab.

NOVEMBER

22 Britain's Cape Colony in southern Africa forbids the landing of convicts and forces the ship carrying them from Britain to sail on to Tasmania.

Human Rights

- The U.S. campaigner for women's rights Amelia Bloomer begins to reform women's dress in the United States, making it more practical.

Politics and Government

JANUARY

13 A Sikh army is narrowly defeated at Chillianwalla, India, by British troops under Major General Sir Hugh Gough during the Second Anglo-Sikh War, brought about by the revolt of the Sikh governor of Multan against British control.

23 A circular note is sent by the Prussians to the other German states informing them that Prussia is ready to assume the leading role in the creation of a closer German union which is to exclude Austria.

FEBRUARY

7 Grand Duke Leopold II of the Italian state of Tuscany flees to Siena to escape republican agitation in Florence.

9 The Papal States in Italy are proclaimed a republic (the Roman Republic) under the Italian patriot Giuseppe Mazzini.

21 British forces under Major General Sir Hugh Gough defeat the Sikhs at Gujarat, India, in the decisive battle of the Second Anglo-Sikh War.

MARCH

3 The U.S. Congress creates the Department of Interior, combining under one cabinet office the old General Land Office, Patent Office, Pension Office, Bureau of Indian Affairs, and the Bureau of the Census.

3 The U.S. Congress establishes the Minnesota Territory, in which slavery is prohibited.

4 The Kremsier Constitution is promulgated in Austria, giving all national groups considerable autonomy, but is immediately replaced by a constitution in which the territories are deemed indivisible.

5 Zachary Taylor is inaugurated 12th president of the United States.

12 The Italian kingdom of Sardinia–Piedmont ends the truce it made with Austria in August 1848, making another attempt to end Austrian influence and unite Italy.

12 The Sikhs surrender to the British at Rawalpindi, India, ending the Second Anglo-Sikh War.

13 The Neapolitan parliament is dissolved by King Ferdinand II of Naples, worried by the revolutions in Tuscany and Rome.

23 The Austrian army of Count Joseph Radetzky decisively defeats the Piedmontese army of King Charles Albert of Sardinia–Piedmont at Novara, Piedmont, ending the war between them. Charles Albert, who had renewed the war only because of radical pressure, abdicates in favor of his son Victor Emmanuel II.

24 A radical Italian nationalist uprising begins in Brescia, in the Austrian-ruled Veneto, Italy, against rule from Vienna.

27 The German National Assembly announces its constitution for a federal German state.

28 The German National Assembly in Frankfurt elects King Frederick Wilhelm IV of Prussia "Emperor of the Germans," head of their proposed union of German states.

29 Britain annexes the Indian province of Punjab by a treaty with the maharajah of Lahore, following the surrender of the Sikh army on March 12.

APRIL

3 King Frederick Wilhelm IV of Prussia is unwilling to take the crown of a new united Germany from the people and wishes instead to receive it from the German princes. His vague reply is taken by the German National Assembly as a refusal.

3 The radical Italian nationalist revolt in Brescia, in the Veneto, Italy, is put down by Austrian troops.

4 A rebellion breaks out in Montreal, Canada, against British rule.

12 Grand Duke Leopold II of Tuscany returns to power following an Austrian invasion to quell the radical revolution that had caused him to flee. His reliance on Austria costs the formerly liberal duke a great deal of popular support.

14 The Hungarian diet (national assembly) proclaims the country independent from Austria, with Lajos Kossuth as governor–president.

25 A French expedition under General Nicolas-Charles Oudinot lands in the Papal States to restore the Pope while encouraging him to make liberal reforms and to counter Austrian influence in Italy.

MAY

1 The Convention of Balta Liman is signed by which the joint Russo-Ottoman occupation of the formerly Ottoman Danubian principalities of Moldavia and Wallachia is established for seven years.

3–8 Republican revolts take place in Dresden, Saxony, but are suppressed by Prussian troops.

4 In a futile gesture the German National Assembly in Frankfurt calls on the German states to unite according to the provisions of the Frankfurt constitution of March 27, and is ignored.

14 Austria withdraws its deputies from the German National Assembly in Frankfurt.

15 The capital of Sicily, Palermo, is entered by Neapolitan forces to end the revolt in Sicily, which is forced to resubmit to monarchical rule from the Italian kingdom of Naples.

21 The core of the deputies to the German National Assembly in Frankfurt withdraw, having been unable to organize a peaceful parliamentary union of the German states.

26 The "Three Kings' League" of Prussia, Saxony, and Hanover is formed to promote closer German unity under Prussian leadership.

JUNE

5 A liberal constitution is granted in Denmark, establishing a limited monarchy and guaranteeing civil liberties.

6 The rump of the German National Assembly moves to Stuttgart following its expulsion from Frankfurt.

13 Left-wing riots in Paris, France, are easily defeated, providing an opportunity for President Louis-Napoléon Bonaparte to crack down on his rivals. Republican riots in Paris and Lyons, in protest at French military support of the pope, are also put down.

JULY

3 French troops enter Rome despite resistance by the Italian patriot Giuseppe Garibaldi, and restore Pope Pius IX, ending the radical Roman Republic.

10   Peace preliminaries are concluded between Denmark and Prussia to end the war over the duchies of Schleswig and Holstein.

23   The Republican revolt in the German state of Baden is put down by Prussian troops.

AUGUST

2   Mohammad Ali, the ruler of Egypt, dies and power devolves to his grandson Abbas I.

6   The Peace of Milan ends the war between Sardinia–Piedmont and Austria, reestablishing Austrian influence in Italy.

13   The army of Lajos Kossuth's Hungarian Republic capitulates at Vilagos, Hungary, after determined but hopeless resistance, to Russian troops under General Ivan Paskievich, sent to aid Austria in putting down the Hungarian revolt.

28   The Italian republic of Venice submits to Austrian troops after a five-week siege.

SEPTEMBER

1   California holds a constitutional convention independent of Congressional legislation. California voters ratify the state constitution, which prohibits slavery.

SCIENCE, TECHNOLOGY, AND MEDICINE

Agriculture

- Agricultural cooperative land banks are founded in Germany.

Ecology

- British meteorologist William Reid demonstrates that hurricanes in the northern hemisphere rotate and curve along paths opposite in direction to those in the southern hemisphere.

Exploration

- Scottish missionary David Livingstone becomes the first European to cross the Kalahari Desert in southwest Africa, discovering Lake Ngami (since dried out) on its northern side on August 1.

September, 1849–1855   The British government sponsors an expedition to the western Sudan (central West Africa), led by the antislavery campaigner James Richardson. In 1850 the German geographer and explorer Heinrich Barth joins the expedition, becoming its leader on the death of Richardson in 1851 at Lake Chad. Under Barth, the expedition successfully crosses the Sahara to the Niger River, visits Timbuktu, and maps large areas of West Africa.

Health and Medicine

- British-born U.S. physician Elizabeth Blackwell receives her medical degree from the Geneva Medical School of Geneva College (now Hobart and William Smith colleges) in New York. She is the first woman to receive such a degree.
- Nearly 10,000 California gold miners die from scurvy.

Science

- British geologist Henry Clifton Sorby demonstrates that minerals can be identified by their optical properties.
- English archeologist Austen Henry Layard discovers the Mesopotamian city of Nineveh where he unearths the palace of Sennacherib and thousands of cuneiform tablets.
- English chemist Edward Frankland isolates amyl alcohol (pentanol).
- French physicist Armand Fizeau measures the velocity of light to within 5% of the value accepted today.

September 1849–84   English paleontologist Richard Owen publishes *A History of British Fossil Reptiles*.

Technology

- British-born U.S. engineer James Bicheno Francis develops the highly efficient Francis turbine in which the inward flow of water follows a radius to emerge near the shaft. It is the principal turbine used today.
- French army officer Claude-Etienne Minié invents the Minié ball, a cylindrical bullet which increases the range of rifles from 200 m/650 ft to 1,000 m/3,300 ft, and which is subsequently used by all European armies and in the American Civil War.
- French inventor Eugène Bourdon invents the Bourdon tube, the most commonly used industrial pressure gauge for measuring the pressures of liquids and gases.
- U.S. inventor George Henry Corliss patents the Corliss-valve engine which has separate intake and exhaust valves at each end of the cylinder allowing the admission and exhaust of steam to be controlled, and thus saving heat.

Transportation

- The Transisthmian Railroad is constructed across the Isthmus of Panama. It is built initially to transport goldseekers to California.

September 1849–50   English engineer Robert Stephenson builds the Britannia Bridge, a tubular railroad bridge, over the Menai Strait, Wales.

ARTS AND IDEAS

Architecture

- English architect Joseph Paxton builds the Victoria regia Lily House, a greenhouse to house the *Victoria regia* lily.

It is the first building to use ridge and furrow construction and to have a curtain wall hung from the girders. The design serves as the model for the Crystal Palace, London, England.
- The English writer and art critic John Ruskin publishes his influential treatise on architecture *The Seven Lamps of Architecture*.
- The Laing Store, in New York, New York, designed by the U.S. architect James Bogardus, is completed. It is one of the first public buildings to have a cast-iron façade, a feature which allows the use of prefabricated parts.

- The French literary critic Charles-Augustin Ste.-Beuve begins publishing informal essays in several newspapers in Paris, France, a practice he continues until 1869. These become known as his "Causeries du lundi"/ "Monday Chats."
- The U.S. essayist Henry David Thoreau publishes *A Week on the Concord and Merrimack Rivers*.
- The U.S. writer Herman Melville publishes his novels *Mardi/Tuesday* and *Redburn: His First Voyage*.
- The U.S. writer James Kirke Paulding publishes the novel *The Puritan and His Daughter*.

Arts

- The French artist Gustave Courbet paints *After Dinner at Ornans* and *Funeral at Ornans*. The unadorned realism of the latter causes a scandal when it is exhibited at the official Salon in Paris. Courbet becomes the leading figure in the development of realism.
- The German artist Alfred Rethel completes his set of wood-engravings *The Dance of Death*.
- The German-born Canadian artist Cornelius David Krieghoff paints *Winter Landscape*.
- The U.S. artist Asher Brown Durand paints *Kindred Spirits*.

Literature and Language

- The English poet and critic Matthew Arnold publishes *The Strayed Reveller and Other Poems*.
- The English writer and churchman Charles Kingsley publishes his novel *Alton Locke: Tailor and Poet*.
- The English writer Charles Dickens begins to publish his novel *David Copperfield* in serial form. It is published as a book in 1850. Its full title is: *The Personal History, Experience and Observations of David Copperfield the Younger, of Blunderstone Rookery, Which He Never Meant to be Published on Any Account*.
- The English writer Charlotte Brontë publishes her novel *Shirley*, under the name Currer Bell.

Music

- Austrian composer Josef Anton Bruckner completes his *Requiem*.
- German composer Robert Schumann completes his *Manfred* overture (Opus 115), based on a verse drama by the English poet George Gordon, Lord Byron; his piano pieces *Waldscenen/Woodland Scenes* (Opus 82); and his orchestral work *Introduction and Allegro appassionato* (Opus 92).
- Hungarian composer Franz Liszt completes his work for piano and orchestra *Totentanz/Dance of Death*, his piano transcription of Richard Wagner's overture *Tannhäuser*, and his piano work *Sonetti del Petrarca/ Petrarch Sonnets*, which includes the *Dante Sonata*.
- The opera *Die lustigen Weiber von Windsor/The Merry Wives of Windsor* by the German composer Otto Nicolai (and based on the play by English dramatist William Shakespeare) is first performed, in Berlin, Germany. It is first performed in the United States in 1863 (in Philadelphia, Pennsylvania), and in Britain in 1864 (in London, England).
- The opera *Le Prophète/The Prophet* by the German composer Giacomo Meyerbeer is first performed, in Paris, France. It is first performed in Britain in 1849 (in London, England), and in the United States in 1850 (in New Orleans, Louisiana).
- The song "Oh Bury Me Not on the Lone Prairie" is written by U.S. composer George N. Allen; the lyrics are from the poem "The Ocean Burial" by E. H. Chapin.

BIRTHS & DEATHS

JANUARY
22   August Strindberg, Swedish playwright and novelist who developed expressionist drama, born in Stockholm, Sweden (–1912).

MARCH
19   Alfred von Tirpitz, German admiral who built up the German navy prior to World War I, born in Küstrin (modern Kostrztń), Prussia (–1930).

MAY
10   Hokusai, Japanese painter and printmaker, dies in Edo (now Tokyo), Japan (88).

JUNE
15   James K. Polk, eleventh president of the United States 1845–49, a

Democrat, dies in Nashville, Tennessee (53).

JULY
12   William Osler, Canadian physician who transformed medical training in North America by emphasizing clinical experience, born in Bond Head, Canada West (now Ontario), Canada (–1919).

AUGUST
12   Albert Gallatin, U.S. statesman, diplomatist, financier, and ethnologist, who served as secretary of the Treasury, dies in Astoria, New York (88).

SEPTEMBER
26   Ivan Petrovich Pavlov, Russian physiologist who developed the idea

of conditioned reflex through his work on salivating dogs, born in Ryazan, Russia (–1936).

OCTOBER
7   Edgar Allan Poe, U.S. poet, critic, and short-story writer, dies in Baltimore, Maryland (40).
17   Frédéric Chopin, French composer known for his works for piano, dies in Paris, France (39).

DECEMBER
12   Marc Isambard Brunel, British engineer who perfected a method of tunneling under water, dies in London, England (80).

Theater and Dance

MAY

10 Twenty-two people perish and fifty-six are wounded when the militia is called in to quell a riot outside the Astor Place Opera House in New York, New York. The riot is sparked by followers of the U.S. actor Edwin Forest who have taken umbrage at critical remarks made by Forest's rival, the British actor William Charles Macready.

Thought and Scholarship

- Massachusetts essayist Henry David Thoreau publishes "Resistance to Civil Government," in which he justifies withholding a poll tax to a government supportive of the Mexican–American War.
- The English historian John Mitchell Kemble publishes *History of the Saxons in England.*
- The German composer Richard Wagner publishes his essay *Die Kunst und die Revolution/Art and Revolution.*
- The U.S. historian Francis Parkman publishes *The Oregon Trail.*

SOCIETY

Everyday Life

- Some 80,000 prospectors arrive in California in the first year of the gold rush.

- English tea wholesaler Henry Charles Harrod buys a grocery store in London, England, which will grow to become one of the world's most famous department stores.
- French tailor M. Jolly-Bellin invents dry-cleaning.
- In London, England, the hatters Thomas and William Bowler create the bowler hat, designed to protect the head from branches when shooting. This will become emblematic of the British middle-class professional man.
- The U.S. mail is carried by stagecoach across the United States on the Santa Fé trail.
- Walter Hunt invents the safety pin.

Religion

- Connecticut Congregationalist minister Horace Bushnell publishes *God in Christ*, repudiating the concept of the Trinity in favor of the oneness of God.
- Pope Pius IX issues a papal encyclical condemning socialism and communism.

Sports

DECEMBER

21 The first skating club in the United States, the Skater's Club of the City and County of Philadelphia, is formed in Pennsylvania.

1850

POLITICS, GOVERNMENT, AND ECONOMICS

Business and Economics

- A single coinage is introduced into Switzerland, following the closer constitutional union of the cantons (political regions).

Colonization

AUGUST

17 Britain buys forts on the west African Gold Coast from Denmark.

Human Rights

- A convention of free black Americans, at Columbus, Ohio, resolves to fight oppression and promote education and economic opportunity for blacks.

JANUARY

29 Kentucky senator Henry Clay introduces eight resolutions designed to quell the political storm over the fate of slavery in the territories acquired from Mexico.

OCTOBER

23 Two years after the Seneca Falls Convention, women's rights advocates convoke a national women's rights convention in Worcester, Massachusetts.

25 Proslavery partisans establish the Southern Rights Convention to combat antislavery propaganda.

Politics and Government

- A group of Protestant zealots creates the fraternal organization the Supreme Order of the Star-Spangled Banner, the precursor to the American (Know-Nothing) Party.
- In U.S. Congressional elections, Democrats retain majorities in the House (140–88) and Senate (35–24).

JANUARY

2   The U.S. Senate ratifies a commercial treaty between the United States and El Salvador.

15   The British fleet blockades the Greek port of Piraeus, Athens, to force Greece to compensate Don Pacifico, a Moorish Jew who is a British subject, for damages sustained when a mob sacked his house in Athens.

31   A liberal constitution is granted in Prussia establishing limited parliamentary representation.

FEBRUARY

23   Hanover leaves the Three Kings' League (Prussia, Saxony, and Hanover) aimed at furthering German unity under Prussian influence.

27   Austria and the German states of Bavaria, Saxony, and Württemberg agree proposals for a German union under Austrian influence.

APRIL

19   The United States and Britain sign the Clayton–Bulwer Treaty, providing for joint custody of a canal to be built across the central American isthmus.

27   The Greek government submits to British demands for compensation over the Don Pacifico affair (concerning the British subject whose house in Athens was sacked), following the British fleet's blockade of the capital.

29   The Erfurt Parliament summoned by King Frederick Wilhelm IV of Prussia is prorogued, having approved his plans for a Prussian-led unification of Germany. However, the important south German states have not attended, favoring Austria over Prussia.

MAY

10   Austria revives the pre-1848 diet (assembly) of the German Confederation in Frankfurt under Felix, Prince zu Schwarzenberg, to counter Prussian attempts at German unification.

25   New Mexico forms its own government without Congressional consent. The New Mexico constitution prohibits slavery.

31   President Louis-Napoléon Bonaparte of France replaces universal suffrage with a limited franchise following left-wing electoral successes.

JUNE

6   The British foreign secretary Lord Palmerston survives a parliamentary attack on his conduct of foreign affairs, notably the Don Pacifico affair in Greece, with his *Civis Romanus sum/I am a Roman Citizen* speech in which he argues for the defense of the rights of British subjects everywhere.

6   The Irish Tenant League is founded in Ireland by the Irish nationalists Charles Gavan Duffy and Frederick Lucas to agitate for fair treatment of Irish tenant farmers by their (predominantly English) landlords.

JULY

2   The Peace of Berlin is agreed between Prussia and Denmark, formally ending the war over the duchies of Schleswig and Holstein without substantially changing the status of the duchies.

9   U.S. president Zachary Taylor dies of cholera. He is succeeded by Vice President Millard Fillmore, who is sworn in the next day as 13th president of the United States.

AUGUST

2   The Treaty of London between Britain, France, Russia, Denmark, and Sweden confirms the provisions of the Peace of Berlin on the status of the duchies of Schleswig and Holstein.

5   The British Parliament passes the Australia Government Act, granting representative government to South Australia, Tasmania, and Victoria (which is separated from New South Wales).

8   The ex-king of France, Louis Philippe, dies and the Orléanist claim to the French throne is now upheld by his grandson Louis-Philippe-Albert, comte de Paris.

SEPTEMBER

9   California becomes the 31st state in the Union. Its constitution prohibits slavery.

9   The U.S. Congress passes the Texas and New Mexico Act, establishing the boundaries of Texas and New Mexico, and the Utah Act, establishing the boundary of Utah. As part of the so-called Compromise of 1850, the fate of slavery in the prospective states of New Mexico and Utah will be decided by the principal of popular sovereignty.

18   As part of the Compromise of 1850, the U.S. Congress passes the Fugitive Slave Law, requiring northerners to return escaped slaves to their masters.

20   As part of the Compromise of 1850, the U.S. Congress abolishes the slave trade in the District of Columbia.

26   French president Louis-Napoléon Bonaparte clamps down further on opposition to his rule, restricting the freedom of the press.

28   The U.S. Congress prohibits flogging in the Navy and Merchant Marine.

28   U.S. president Millard Fillmore names Church of Latter-day Saints leader Brigham Young governor of Utah Territory.

OCTOBER

10   The Taiping Rebellion breaks out in China under Hong Xiuquan, who takes the cities of Nanjing and Shanghai, proclaims himself emperor, and attacks Beijing.

11   The national liberal Count Camillo Benso di Cavour becomes a minister in the Italian kingdom of Sardinia–Piedmont, where he begins economic reforms.

NOVEMBER

28   As a result of Russian mediation, Felix, Prince zu Schwarzenberg, of Austria and Otto von Manteuffel of Prussia sign the Punctation of Olmütz, by which Prussia subordinates itself to Austria and recognizes the Frankfurt diet (assembly) of the German Confederation.

SCIENCE, TECHNOLOGY, AND MEDICINE

Agriculture

c. 1850 Cable plowing, in which a stationary engine draws a plow attached to a cable through a field, is introduced by English farmer Thomas Aveling.

• Jersey cows are first imported into the United States from England.

Ecology

c. 1850 U.S. physicist Joseph Henry arranges for telegraph offices to have meteorological equipment installed in exchange for weather information telegraphed to the Smithsonian Institution. By 1860 there are over 500 stations involved, and the information allows the production of the first daily weather maps.

• The last salmon for 120 years are taken from the Thames River in England, which is now heavily polluted.

JULY

25 Prospectors discover gold on the Rouge River in Oregon.

Exploration

• English explorer Francis Galton explores Damaraland in Africa.

• German geographer Heinrich Barth explores Central Africa.

Health and Medicine

c. 1850 German physician Carl Reinhold Wunderlich begins the practice of taking a patient's temperature with a thermometer as a regular diagnostic procedure.

• The Massachusetts Sanitary Commission publishes the Shastuck Report. Commissioned because of the recurrent epidemics of yellow fever, cholera, smallpox, typhoid, and typhus, it reviews living conditions in Boston and recommends the provision of a public-health organization consisting of a state health department with local health boards in each town.

Math

• Russian mathematician Pafnuty Lvovich Chebyshev publishes *On Primary Numbers*, in which he further develops the theory of prime numbers.

Science

c. 1850 British physicist William Grove demonstrates that steam in contact with a hot platinum wire decomposes into hydrogen and oxygen, thus proving the thermal dissociation of atoms within a molecule.

c. 1850 French naturalist Antonio Snider-Pellegrini suggests that the similarities among European and North American plant fossils could be explained if the two continents were once in contact.

• British chemist Alexander Parkes discovers a method of extracting silver from lead—by melting and combining the lead with zinc.

• French physician Casimir-Joseph Davaine transmits anthrax to healthy sheep by inoculating them with the blood of animals dying of the disease. He then discovers microscopic rod-shaped bodies in their blood, becoming one of the first to observe the organisms responsible for the disease.

• French physicist Jean Foucault establishes that light travels slower in water than in air. He also measures the velocity of light to within 1% of its true speed.

• German mathematical physicist Rudolf Clausius formulates the second law of thermodynamics in *Über die Bewegende Kraft der Wärme/On the Driving Power of Heat*.

• German physicist Hermann Ludwig von Helmholtz establishes the speed of nervous impulses (27 m/90 ft per second).

• In his paper entitled "On the Power of Soils to Absorb Manure," British chemist John Way describes how potassium in the soil is replaced by equal amounts of magnesium and chloride—the first description of the phenomena of ion exchange.

• Italian physicist Macedonia Melloni invents a radiometer for measuring radiant energy.

Technology

c. 1850 An improved steam hammer, using a steam-driven piston that actuates the hammer directly, permitting rapid operation with precise control, comes into general use in England. It becomes important for making rails.

c. 1850 French photographer Louis-Désiré Blanquart-Evrard develops albumen photographic paper, a light-sensitive paper coated with albumen (egg-white).

• British inventor Francis Bakewell invents a "copying telegraph" that can transmit images or print painted with varnish on one conducting roller to another. It is an early version of the facsimile machine and a forerunner of television.

• English engineer Jacob Brett lays the first long-distance submarine telegraph cable, between Dover, England, and Calais, France.

• English engineer William Armstrong invents a hydraulic accumulator that can supply pipes with water at 42 ksi/600 psi.

• French inventor Ferdinand Carré devises a refrigeration machine in which the expansion of liquid ammonia produces temperatures as low as −30°C/−122°F.

• Gutta-percha (rubber) hoses begin to replace watering cans.

• The first modern children's baby carriages in Britain appear (designed to be pushed rather than pulled), with manufacturers John Allen and A. Babin both putting products on the market.

- U.S. inventor John Fairbank patents a typewriter that is fed with a continuous roll of paper. In the same year, U.S. inventor Oliver Eddy patents a typewriter with a ribbon and a piano keyboard for inputting letters.

Transportation

- German inventor Sebastian Bauer builds *Le Plongeur-Marin*, one of the first submarines.
- Railroad mileage in operation: United States, 14,400 km/9,072; Great Britain, 9,791 km/6,119; France 3,627 km/2,267 mi (1851).
- English engineer George Stephenson's cast-iron railroad bridge at Newcastle upon Tyne, England, opens.

ARTS AND IDEAS

Architecture

- The Library of Ste. Geneviève in Paris, France, designed by the French architect Pierre-François-Henri Labrouste, is completed.

Arts

- The English artist John Everett Millais paints *Christ in the House of his Parents*.
- The French artist Eugène Delacroix completes his fresco on the ceiling of the Salon d'Apollon in the Louvre, in Paris, France.
- The French artist Théodore Chassériau paints *Arab Horsemen Carrying Away Their Dead*.
- The set of engravings *Proverbios/Proverbs* by the Spanish artist Francisco José de Goya y Lucientes is published posthumously.
- Théodore Rousseau, French landscape artist and founder of the Barbizon School, paints *On The Outskirts of the Forest of Fontainebleau*.

Literature and Language

- *Harper's Monthly Magazine*, a literary journal, begins publication in New York, New York.
- The English artist and poet Dante Gabriel Rossetti publishes his poem "The Blessed Damozel" in the Pre-Raphaelite journal *The Germ*.
- The English poet Alfred, Lord Tennyson, publishes *In Memoriam*, a long elegy on the death of his friend Arthur Hallam, anonymously. He becomes poet laureate, a position he holds until 1892.
- The English poet and critic Leigh Hunt publishes *Autobiography*, a reworking of his earlier *Lord Byron and Some of His Contemporaries*, originally published in 1828.
- The English writer Elizabeth Barrett Browning publishes her poetry collection *Poems*, which contains the sonnet sequence *Sonnets from the Portuguese*.

- The lecture "The Poetic Principle" by the U.S. writer Edgar Allan Poe is published posthumously in *The Union Magazine*.
- The U.S. novelist Nathaniel Hawthorne publishes *The Scarlet Letter*, a tale of the tragic consequences of concealed guilt.
- The U.S. photographer Mathew Brady publishes *The Gallery of Illustrious Americans*, portraits of leading figures in U.S. life during the 1840s.
- The U.S. poet John Greenleaf Whittier publishes the sequel of *Legends of New England in Prose and Verse*, *Song of Labor*.
- The U.S. writer Herman Melville publishes his novel *White-Jacket, or The World in a Man-of-War*.

Music

c. 1850 Hungarian composer Franz Liszt completes his piano work *Liebesträume/Love Dreams*, three nocturnes, and (1850) his Symphonic Poem *Prometheus* and his piano work *Consolations*.

- French composer Hector Berlioz completes his *Te Deum* (Opus 22).
- German composer Richard Wagner publishes *Das Judentum in der Musik/Judaism in Music*, in which he attacks what he sees as the corrupting influence of Jews in music, and in particular the works of Giacomo Meyerbeer. In the same year, his opera *Lohengrin* is first performed, in Weimar, Germany. The wedding march from the opera becomes widely used at marriage services.
- German composer Robert Schumann completes his Symphony No. 3 (Opus 97), the *Rhenish*. In the same year, his opera *Genoveva* is first performed, in Leipzig, Germany.
- Italian songwriter Teodoro Cottrau composes the popular song "Santa Lucia."
- The opera *Stiffelio* by the Italian composer Giuseppe Verdi is first performed, in Trieste, Italy.

Theater and Dance

- The play *Catilina/Catiline*, the first play by the Norwegian dramatist Henrik Johan Ibsen, is first performed, in Christiania (Oslo), Norway.
- The play *Die Erbförster/The Hereditary Forester* by the German writer Otto Ludwig is first performed.
- The Russian writer Alexander Nikolayevich Ostrovsky publishes his comedy *Bankrot/The Bankrupt*. An exposure of financial misdealings, it is banned and Ostrovsky is dismissed from the Russian government service.

Thought and Scholarship

- The German-American philosopher Francis Lieber coins the term "penology" to refer to the study of penal systems.
- The Russian political thinker Alexander Ivanovich Herzen publishes *S togo berega/From Another Shore*, which sets out his view that the course of history is not determined, but subject to chance and human intervention.

- The Scottish social historian Thomas Carlyle publishes his *Latter-Day Pamphlets*.
- The U.S. essayist Ralph Waldo Emerson publishes his collection of essays *Representative Men*, a catalog of six stalwarts (Plato, Swedenborg, Montaigne, Shakespeare, Napolean, and Goethe) whose greatness enables mankind to recognize the divine essence in itself.

SOCIETY

Education

- Oregon State University is founded at Corvallis, Oregon.
- The University of Rochester is founded in Rochester, New York.
- The University of Utah is founded at Salt Lake City, Utah.

OCTOBER

12 The Woman's Medical College of Pennsylvania opens in Philadelphia, Pennsylvania.

Everyday Life

- A state old-age pension program is instituted in France.
- Bavarian immigrant Levi Strauss makes the first jeans out of canvas in San Francisco, California. They are originally designed for Californian gold miners.
- Black American workers in New York, New York, establish the American League of Colored Laborers to promote industrial and business opportunities for black youth.
- Some 370,000 immigrants arrive in the United States, many of them from Ireland.
- The Pinkerton Detective Agency is founded in the United States by Scottish-U.S. detective Allan Pinkerton; the agency's motto is "We Never Sleep."
- The U.S. Census lists the nation's population at 23,191,876, up from roughly 17,120,000 in 1840.

JULY

1 The U.S. Post Office Department introduces postal service west of the Missouri River. The new link connects Independence, Missouri, and Salt Lake City, Utah.

Media Communication

- There are 254 daily newspapers published in the United States.

BIRTHS & DEATHS

FEBRUARY

12 William Morris Davis, U.S. geographer, geologist, and meteorologist who pioneered the science of geomorphology, born in Philadelphia, Pennsylvania (–1934).

MARCH

7 Thomas Masaryk, founder and first president of Czechoslovakia 1918–35, born near Göding, Moravia, Austrian Empire (–1937).

31 John C. Calhoun, U.S. vice president 1825–32, who was proslavery and advocated individual states' rights, dies in Washington, D.C. (68).

APRIL

16 Marie Tussaud, French artist and founder of Madame Tussaud's wax museum in London, England, dies in London (88).

23 William Wordsworth, English romantic poet, and poet laureate 1843–50, dies in Grasmere, Westmorland, England (80).

MAY

9 Joseph-Louis Gay-Lussac, French chemist and physicist who investigated the properties of gases and was a founder of meteorology, dies in Paris, France (71).

12 Henry Cabot Lodge, U.S. Republican senator 1893–1924, born in Boston, Massachusetts (–1924).

JUNE

24 Horatio Herbert Kitchener, British field marshal who conquered the Sudan, was commander in chief during the Boer War, and who, as secretary of state for war, organized the British armed forces at the start of World War I, born near Listowel, County Kerry, Ireland (–1916).

JULY

2 Robert Peel, British prime minister 1834–35 and 1841–46, founder of the Conservative Party, dies in London, England (62).

9 Margaret Fuller, U.S. transcendentalist author, dies at sea (40).

9 The Bab (adopted name of Mirza Ali Muhammad), founder of the Baha'i faith, is executed in Tabriz, Persia (30).

9 Zachary Taylor, twelfth president of the United States 1849–50, a Whig, dies in Washington, D.C. (65).

AUGUST

5 Guy de Maupassant, French short-story writer in the Naturalist school, born near Dieppe, France (–1893).

17 José San Martí, Argentine revolutionary who helped lead the revolutions against Spanish rule in Argentina, Chile, and Peru, dies in Boulogne-sur-Mer, France (71).

18 Honoré de Balzac, French novelist whose writings helped establish the modern form of the novel, dies in Paris, France (51).

26 Louis Philippe, King of the French 1830–48, dies in Claremont, Surrey, England (76).

SEPTEMBER

2 A. G. Spalding, U.S. baseball player and sporting goods manufacturer, born in Byron, Illinois (–1915).

2 Eugene Field, U.S. journalist and poet, born in St. Louis, Missouri (–1895).

NOVEMBER

13 Robert Louis Stevenson, Scottish novelist who wrote *Kidnapped*, *Treasure Island*, and *The Strange Case of Dr Jekyll and Mr Hyde*, born in Edinburgh, Scotland (–1894).

22 Lin Tse-hsü, Chinese scholar and official whose attempt to stop the opium trade contributed to the Opium War 1839–42, dies in Chaozhou, Kwangtung Province, China (65).

- The *Christian Almanac*, a religious almanac in the United States, has a circulation of 300,000.

c. 1850 John Jacques, the British sports goods manufacturer, makes the first croquet sets.

1851

POLITICS, GOVERNMENT, AND ECONOMICS

Business and Economics

- At the Great Exhibition in England, German industrialist Alfred Krupp exhibits a steel ingot weighing 1,952 kg/4,300 lb—the largest cast to date.

MARCH

3 The U.S. Congress authorizes production of three-cent coins.

Colonization

- The French government begins the transportation of convicts to its colonies.

JULY

1 Victoria, Australia, is proclaimed an independent British colony.

Human Rights

FEBRUARY

- A Boston mob rescues a fugitive slave named Shadrach from his captors, provoking tension between North and South.

Politics and Government

- The German diet (assembly) in Frankfurt appoints a Reaction Committee to control its small states and prevent the passing of liberal reforms.
- The Massachusetts legislature passes a law allowing towns to tax their residents in order to support free libraries.
- U.S. president Millard Fillmore appoints Massachusetts jurist Benjamin R. Curtis to the U.S. Supreme Court.

FEBRUARY

22 The Whig prime minister of Britain, Lord John Russell, resigns after having been defeated in a Reform Bill debate on February 20, but as Lord Stanley is unable to form a Conservative administration, he returns as prime minister on the same day.

MARCH

16 Spain agrees a concordat with the papacy by which Catholicism becomes the sole faith in Spain and the church gains control of education and the press.

MAY

16 Censorship of the Prussian press is revived to suppress the diffusion of radical ideas.

16 Prussia again recognizes the reestablishment of the German Confederation under Austrian leadership at the Dresden Conference (as it did at the Punctation of Olmütz in 1850).

JUNE

2 The legislature in the U.S. state of Maine passes legislation prohibiting the manufacture and distribution of alcohol.

AUGUST

24 Cuban ex-patriot Narciso Lopez leads an unauthorized and disastrous mission to wrest Cuba from Spanish control. Undertaken against the will of the Fillmore administration, Lopez had secured private backing from U.S. speculators.

NOVEMBER

18 King Ernest Augustus of the German kingdom of Hanover dies and is succeeded by his son, George V.

DECEMBER

2 The French president Louis-Napoléon Bonaparte carries out a coup d'état to extend his presidency and give him more power.

9 Conservative Spanish prime minister Bravo Murillo dismisses the cortes (national assembly), arrests radicals, and closes newspapers.

21 A plebiscite in France approves Louis-Napoléon Bonaparte's coup and extension of presidential powers.

31 The Austrian constitution of 1849 is abolished, consolidating the return to conservative rule in the Hapsburg Empire.

SCIENCE, TECHNOLOGY, AND MEDICINE

Ecology

- Australian sheep station manager Edward Hammond Hargreaves sparks a gold rush when he discovers gold in new South Wales, Australia.

Health and Medicine

December 1851–54 Over 250,000 people (approximately 2% of the population) die from tuberculosis in Britain.

Science

- British astronomer William Lasell discovers Ariel and Umbriel, two satellites of Uranus.
- French scientist Jean-Bernard-Léon Foucault proves that the earth rotates by using a pendulum 67 m/220 ft long (Foucault's pendulum), in Paris, France. The pendulum always swings in the same plane and the earth rotates underneath it.
- German botanist Hugo von Mohl discovers that the secondary walls of plant cells are of a fibrous structure.
- German botanist Wilhelm Friedrich Hofmeister publishes *On the Germination, Development, and Fructification of the Higher Cryptogamia and on the Fructification of the Coniferae*, in which he discovers the alternation of generations in ferns and mosses, and establishes the relationships between the conifers (gymnosperms) and flowering plants (angiosperms).
- Scottish physicist William Thomson publishes his essay "On the Dynamical Theory of Heat," which states that energy in a closed system tends to become unusable waste heat—the second law of thermodynamics.

Technology

- English astronomer Warren de la Rue takes the first photograph of a solar eclipse.
- English scientist William Henry Fox Talbot takes the first high-speed flash photograph. He uses a spark produced from the discharge of a Leyden jar battery for the flash.
- English sculptor F. Scott Archer develops the wet-collodion photographic process. Collodion-coated (nitrocellulose) glass plates are exposed in the camera while still wet and then developed and fixed immediately. It permits instantaneous exposures but requires photographers in the field to take portable darkrooms.
- French inventor Aimé Laussedat invents photogrammetry, the art of using photographs from different angles to measure buildings and make maps.
- German inventor Heinrich Ruhmkorff invents the Ruhmkorff coil, an induction coil capable of producing sparks across a gap of 30 cm/1 ft, which later develops into an alternating-current transformer.

- German physicist Hermann Ludwig von Helmholtz invents the ophthalmoscope, which is used to examine the blood vessels of the retina. He also invents the ophthalmometer, which is used to measure the eye for eyeglasses.
- The first electric fire alarm in the United States is installed by William Channing and Moses Farmer, in Boston, Massachusetts.
- U.S. clergyman Lorenzo Lorraine Langstroth invents the moveable-frame beehive which provides a base for the bees and allows honeycombs to be built and removed without destroying the nest. It revolutionizes the beekeeping industry and soon spreads throughout the world.
- U.S. industrialist William Kelly develops a method of removing impurities from pig iron by injecting air into the molten mass. The oxygen in the air blast reacts with impurities to form oxides which can be separated from the slag. A key invention in the industrial revolution, it results in the production of large quantities of cheap steel.

December 1851–60 Photographic exposure times become short enough to capture movement.

May

1–September 18 The Great Exhibition is held in Hyde Park, London, England. Devised by Prince Albert, it is the first exhibition to display the latest technical innovations in industry, from both Britain and Europe. It features the Crystal Palace, a large iron and glass structure designed by English architect Joseph Paxton.

August

12 U.S. inventor Isaac Merrit Singer patents the first practical domestic sewing machine for general use, in Boston, Massachusetts. His design, which enables continuous and curved stitching, and allows any part of the material to be worked on, sets the pattern for all subsequent sewing machines.

Transportation

- Construction of the Pacific Railroad (later the Missouri Pacific Railroad), the first railroad west of the Mississippi, begins.
- The bridge over the Medway at Rochester, Kent, England, is built. It is the first in which workers use a compressed air chamber, or pneumatic caisson, to dig bridge foundations underwater.
- The iron mill at Dowlais, Wales, produces iron railroad rails 37 m/120 ft long, and H-shaped beams 15 m/50 ft long.
- U.S. engineer George Washington Whistler completes the 650-km/404-mi Moscow to St. Petersburg railroad.

ARTS AND IDEAS

Architecture

- The Crystal Palace, in London, England, designed by the English architect and engineer Joseph Paxton, is completed. Designed to house the Great Exhibition of 1851, it is of a revolutionary design employing only prefabricated units of glass and iron and is the largest building in the world, 564 m/1,851 ft long, 139 m/456 ft wide, and 20 m/66 ft tall. It is destroyed by fire in 1936.

- The English writer and art critic John Ruskin publishes the first part of his three-part study of architecture and society *The Stones of Venice*. The second and third parts appear in 1853.
- The equestrian monument to Frederick the Great, in Berlin, Germany, designed by the German artist Christian Daniel Rauch and the German architect Karl Friedrich Schinkel, is completed.

JULY

- Renovation of the U.S. Capitol begins in Washington, D.C.

Arts

- The English illustrator John Tenniel begins drawing cartoons for *Punch* magazine. He works for *Punch* until 1901.
- The French artist Camille Corot paints *Dance of the Nymphs*.
- The French artist Jean-Auguste-Dominique Ingres paints *Portrait of Mme Moitessier*.
- The German-born U.S. artist Emanuel Leutze paints *Washington Crossing the Delaware*.
- The U.S. artist Frederic Edwin Church paints *New England Scenery*.
- The U.S. artist Seth Eastman paints *Lacrosse Playing Among the Sioux Indians*.

Literature and Language

- The Brazilian poet Dias Gonçalves publishes *Ultimos cantos/Last Poems*.
- The English writer George Borrow publishes *Lavengro: The Scholar – The Gypsy – The Priest*, a fictionalized autobiography.
- The French writer Gérard de Nerval publishes *Voyage en Orient/Journey to the Orient*.
- The German poet Heinrich Heine publishes his third and last poetry collection, *Romanzero*.
- The Russian writer Ivan Sergeyevich Turgenev publishes his short story "Dnevnik lishnego cheloveka"/"Diary of a Superfluous Man." The "superfluous man" becomes a key character type in 19th-century Russian literature.
- The Scottish historian Thomas Carlyle publishes his biography *The Life of John Sterling*.
- The U.S. writer Herman Melville publishes *Moby Dick, or the Whale*, his major work and one of the great U.S. novels of the 19th century.
- The U.S. writer Nathaniel Hawthorne publishes his novel *The House of Seven Gables*.

Music

- German composer Richard Wagner publishes *Oper und Drama/Opera and Drama*, in which he sets out his highly influential ideas on the nature of opera and operatic performance.
- German composer Robert Schumann completes his Symphony No. 4 (Opus 120). It is in fact second in order of composition (written in the early 1840s), but it is later revised. He also completes his overture for Shakespeare's *Julius Caesar* (Opus 128), his two Violin Sonatas (Opus 105 and Opus 121), and his Piano Trio No. 3 (Opus 110).
- Hungarian composer Franz Liszt completes his Symphonic Poem *Mazeppa* and revision of his piano work *Etudes d'exécution transcendante/Transcendental Studies*.
- The opera *Rigoletto* by the Italian composer Giuseppe Verdi is first performed, in Venice, Italy. It is based on the play *Le Roi s'amuse/The King Amuses Himself*, published in 1832 by Victor Hugo. The opera is first performed in Britain in 1853 (in London, England), and in the United States in 1855 (in New York, New York).
- U.S. songwriter Stephen Foster writes "Old Folks at Home," also known as "Swanee River."

Thought and Scholarship

- South Carolina senator John C. Calhoun's "A Disquisition on Government" appears posthumously.
- The English social scientist Herbert Spencer publishes *Social Statistics, or the Conditions Essential to Human Happiness Specified*.
- The English writer Charles Dickens publishes *A Child's History of England*.
- The Italian philosopher Vincenzo Gioberti publishes *Il rinnovamento civile d'Italia/On the Civic Renewal of Italy*.
- The U.S. anthropologist Lewis Henry Morgan publishes *League of the Ho-dé-no-sau-nee, or Iroquois*, one of the earliest scientific studies of Native Americans.
- The U.S. historian Francis Parkman publishes *History of the Conspiracy of Pontiac*.
- U.S. reformer Stephen Pearl Andrews publishes *The Science of Society*, advocating an individualist social system known as Pantarchy.

DECEMBER

24 Two-thirds of the Library of Congress in Washington, D.C., is destroyed by fire.

SOCIETY

Education

- Northwestern University is founded in Evanston, Illinois.
- The University of Minnesota is founded in Minneapolis–St. Paul, Minnesota.

MARCH

15 An act drawn up by the French minister of education, Frederick, vicomte de Falloux, is passed, reintroducing clerical control of education in France.

Everyday Life

- As the United States becomes increasingly wealthy, women's fashions grow more expensive, with much use of silk and velvet.
- Bax and Co. produce a waterproof coat in London, England, using a new method, chemically treating wool. They call the result Aquascutum, and it is worn by soldiers fighting in the Crimea.
- British umbrella manufacturer Samuel Fox is the first to use a steel rib structure for the umbrella, thereby introducing a lighter and more practical product.
- John Henry Anderson, a magician from Scotland, tours the United States, charging 50 cents for his magic performances.
- Populations (in millions) are China, 430; German States and free cities, 34; France, 33; Britain, 20.8; Ireland, 6.5; Italy, 24; United States, 23; Austrian Empire, 16.
- The Asylum for Friendless Boys is established in New York, New York.
- The Young Men's Christian Association (YMCA), an English organization founded in 1844, establishes branches in Boston, Massachusetts, and Montreal, Canada.
- U.S. dairyman Jacob Fussell establishes the first wholesale ice-cream business in the United States, in Baltimore, Maryland.
- Almost three-quarters of San Francisco, California, is destroyed by fire.

March 1851–60   Emigration to the United States from Britain is 423,964 and from Ireland 914,119, the latter a record number, in the wake of the 1845 potato crop failure.

Media and Communication

- German businessman Paul Julius, Baron von Reuter, founds the Reuters News Agency, in London, England.
- The editor of the *Terre Haute Express* in Indiana urges young readers: "Go West, young man, go West," a quote incorrectly attributed to *New York Tribune* editor Horace Greeley.

SEPTEMBER

18   *The New York Times* newspaper is launched in the United States, edited by Henry J. Raymond.

Sports

MAY

27   Adolf Anderssen of Germany wins the first-ever international chess tournament, held in London, England, and is subsequently regarded as the world champion.

BIRTHS & DEATHS

JANUARY

27   John James Audubon, U.S. naturalist and artist known for his paintings of birds, dies in New York, New York (65).

FEBRUARY

1   Mary Wollstonecraft Shelley, English writer, author of *Frankenstein*, dies in London, England (53).

18   Karl Gustav Jacob Jacobi, German mathematician who developed the theory of elliptic function, dies in Munich, Bavaria (now Germany) (46).

MARCH

15   Emil Behring, German bacteriologist who founded the science of immunology and received the first Nobel Prize for Physiology or Medicine in 1901, born in Hansdorf, Prussia (–1917).

MAY

7   Adolf von Harnack, German theologian and church historian, born in Dorpat (now Tartu), Estonia (–1930).

21   Léon Bourgeois, French prime minister 1895–96 who received the Nobel Peace Prize in 1920, born in Paris, France (–1925).

JULY

8   Arthur Evans, English archeologist, excavator of the Minoan city of Knossos in Crete, born in Nash Mills, Hertfordshire, England (–1941).

10   Louis Daguerre, French painter and physicist who invented the first practical method of photography, the daguerreotype, dies in Bry-sur-Marne, France (62).

SEPTEMBER

13   Walter Reed, U.S. Army surgeon who proved that yellow fever is transmitted by mosquitos, born in Belroi, Virginia (–1902).

14   James Fenimore Cooper, U.S. novelist who wrote of life on the frontier, dies in Cooperstown, New York (61).

OCTOBER

2   Ferdinand Foch, French commander of the Allied forces at the end of World War I, born in Tarbes, France (–1929).

NOVEMBER

6   Charles Henry Dow, U.S. financial journalist who established the Dow–Jones average, born in Sterling, Connecticut (–1902).

26   Nicolas-Jean Soult, French military leader and politician, dies in St.-Amans-Soult, France (82).

DECEMBER

10   Melvil Dewey, U.S. librarian who introduced the Dewey decimal system of cataloging books, born in Adams Center, New York (–1931).

19   J(oseph) M(allord) W(illiam) Turner, English romantic landscape painter, dies in London, England (76).

1852

POLITICS, GOVERNMENT, AND ECONOMICS

Business and Economics

- The U.S. beer brewing partnership of Adolphus Busch and Eberhard Anheuser begins in St. Louis, Missouri.

Human Rights

JULY

5   Abolitionist Frederick Douglass delivers his address "What to the Slave is the Fourth of July?" in Rochester, New York. Douglass criticizes Americans for their hypocritical celebration of liberty in the face of human bondage.

Politics and Government

- In U.S. Congressional elections, Democrats retain control of the U.S. House (159–71) and Senate (38–22).

JANUARY

14   A new French constitution gives the president dictatorial power.

17   The Sand River Convention is made between the Boers (Dutch settlers) and the British government, allowing the Boers to establish the South African Republic (Transvaal).

22   The royal family of Orléans is banished from France by presidential decree.

FEBRUARY

3   Juan Manuel de Rosas is overthrown as dictator of Argentina at the Battle of Caseros by the insurgent Justo de Urquiza, supported by Brazilian and Uruguayan forces.

17   President Louis-Napoléon Bonaparte introduces further repressive measures in France, including censorship of the press.

APRIL

1   The Second Anglo-Burmese War breaks out after the expiry of a British ultimatum to the king of Burma to pay compensation to British merchants following disputes between the traders and local inhabitants.

MAY

8   The Treaty of London between Britain, France, Russia, Prussia, Austria, and Sweden guarantees the integrity of Denmark, following the conflict between Prussia and Denmark over the duchies of Schleswig and Holstein.

JUNE

6   Democrats nominate former New Hampshire senator Franklin D. Pierce for president and Alabama politician William R. King for vice president.

21   The U.S. Whig Party nominates Mexican–American War veteran Winfield Scott for president and North Carolina congressman William A. Graham for vice president.

30   A British act of Parliament grants a new constitution providing for representative government for the colony of New Zealand.

AUGUST

11   Free-Soilers (opponents of the extension of slavery into frontier territories) nominate New Hampshire abolitionist senator John P. Hale for president and Indiana congressman George W. Julian for vice president.

NOVEMBER

4   The Italian patriot Count Camillo Benso di Cavour becomes prime minister of the Italian kingdom of Sardinia–Piedmont.

21   A plebiscite is held in France which supports the revival of a French empire.

DECEMBER

2   The Second French Empire is proclaimed. President Louis-Napoléon Bonaparte becomes Emperor Napoleon III.

10   The Spanish prime minister Bravo Murillo announces plans to abolish parliamentary government in Spain.

12   British forces under General Henry Godwin annex Pegu (Lower Burma) in the Second Anglo-Burmese War.

14   The Spanish prime minister Bravo Murillo is made to resign by Queen Isabella II because of the destabilizing effect of his plans for a return to absolutist government.

SCIENCE, TECHNOLOGY, AND MEDICINE

Ecology

- Eight pairs of English sparrows (*Passer domesticus*) are imported into Brooklyn, New York. Within 100 years their range extends across North America.

Exploration

- German geographer Heinrich Barth explores Lake Chad in central Africa.

Health and Medicine

- German physician Karl von Vierordt develops a method of counting red blood cells that becomes important in diagnosing anemia.
- Swiss embryologist and histologist Rudolf Albert von Kölliker publishes *Handbuch der Gewebelehre des Menschen/Handbook of Human Histology*, the first textbook in histology, and the first to discuss tissues in terms of cell theory.

JANUARY

15 New York philanthropist Sampson Simson creates Mt. Sinai Hospital, originally called Jews' Hospital.

OCTOBER

6 A group of U.S. pharmacists establishes the American Pharmaceutical Association.

Math

- British mathematician James Joseph Sylvester establishes the theory of algebraic invariants—algebraic-equation coefficients which remain unchanged when the coordinate axes are altered or rotated.

Science

- English chemist Edward Frankland develops the idea of chemical valence: that atoms of an element combine only with a given number of atoms of another element. It forms the foundation of modern structural chemistry.
- English physicist James Joule and Scottish physicist William Thomson, discover that an expanding gas cools (the Joule–Thomson effect). The phenomenon is used in the refrigeration industry.
- French chemist Charles Gerhardt classifies organic compounds into four types: hydrogen, hydrogen chloride, ammonia, and water.
- German physician Robert Remak discovers that the growth of tissues, including diseased tissues, involves both the multiplication and division of cells.
- Irish astronomer Edward Sabine demonstrates a link between sunspot activity and disturbances in the earth's magnetic field.

Technology

- English scientist William Henry Fox Talbot patents a photolythic engraving method which involves photographing images through a fine mesh and developing them on sensitized steel plates. It leads to the development of photogravure.
- French inventor François Beltzung patents a screwtop for bottles.
- U.S. inventor and machine-shop owner Elisha Otis installs, in a factory in Albany, New York, a freight elevator equipped with an automatic safety device that prevents it from falling if the lifting chain or rope breaks. This leads to the passenger elevator, making the building of skyscrapers more practical. The first permanent Otis and Son elevator is installed in E. V. Haughwort and Co., a department store in New York, New York, in 1857.

Transportation

- German industrialist Alfred Krupp manufactures the first seamless steel railroad tire.
- The United States Mail Steamship Company's *Pacific* sets a world speed record, crossing the Atlantic in less than ten days (from New York, New York, to Liverpool, England).

JULY

30 The British ship *John Bowes*, enters service. It is the first tramp steamer (a merchant ship that does not make regularly scheduled runs).

SEPTEMBER

24 French engineer Henri Giffard flies the first steam-powered airship a distance of 28 km/17 mi, at an average speed of 10 kph/6 mph. Cigar-shaped and filled with hydrogen, it is 44 m/144 ft long, and uses a 160-kg/350-lb steam engine to turn a three-blade propeller 3.3 m/11 ft in diameter at 119 rpm. It is the first application of a propeller to flight.

ARTS AND IDEAS

Architecture

- King's Cross Station, in London, England, designed by the English architect Lewis Cubitt, is completed. It is one of the finest railroad stations of the 19th century.
- The Houses of Parliament, in London, England, designed by the English architect Charles Barry, are completed, one of the most prominent examples of the Gothic Revival style. The interiors are by Augustus Pugin.

Arts

- The Dutch artist Johan Barthold Jongkind paints *The Quai d'Orsay*.
- The English artist Ford Madox Brown paints *The Last of England*.
- The French photographer Blanquart Evrard publishes *Album photographique de l'artiste et de l'amateur/A Photographic Album by Artists and Amateurs*, one of the most important collections of early French photographs.
- The U.S. artist George Caleb Bingham paints *The County Election*.
- The U.S. artist William Caton Woodville paints *Sailor's Wedding*.

Literature and Language

- The English writer Charles Dickens publishes his novel *Bleak House* in serial form. It is published as a book in 1853.
- The English writer Matthew Arnold publishes *Empedocles on Etna, and Other Poems*.

- The English writer Mary Mitford publishes *Recollections of a Literary Life*.
- The English writer William Makepeace Thackeray publishes his novel *The History of Henry Esmond*.
- The French writer Théophile Gautier publishes his poetry collection *Emaux et camées/Enamels and Cameos*.
- The Russian writer Ivan Sergeyevich Turgenev publishes his collection of short stories *Zapisky okhotnika/A Sportsman's Sketches*.
- The U.S. writer Herman Melville publishes his novel *Pierre, or The Ambiguities*.
- The U.S. writer Nathaniel Hawthorne publishes his novel *The Blithedale Romance* and his story collection *The Snow-Image and Other Twice-Told Tales*, which includes "Ethan Brand."

APRIL

20 Harriet Beecher Stowe publishes *Uncle Tom's Cabin* in book form. The book, previously serialized in the antislavery broadsheet *National Era*, is instantly controversial and popular, selling 1.2 million copies by mid-1853.

Music

- German composer Johannes Brahms completes his Piano Sonata No. 2 (Opus 2) and the first of his *Ungarische Tänze/Hungarian Dances* for piano.
- German composer Robert Schumann completes his Mass (Opus 147) and Requiem (Opus 148).

Thought and Scholarship

- African-American writer Martin R. Delany publishes *The Condition, Elevation, Emigration, and Destiny of the Colored People of the United States*, calling on blacks to emigrate to a state of their own creation.
- English philosopher Herbert Spencer coins the term "evolution" in *The Development Hypothesis*.
- South Carolina antisuffragist Louisa S. McCord publishes "Enfranchisement of Women" and "Woman and Her Needs," both of which maintain the moral superiority of women's traditional domestic role.
- The English diplomat and historian Henry Creswicke Rawlinson publishes his *History of Assyria*.
- The English teacher and reformer Mary Carpenter publishes *Juvenile Delinquents: Their Condition and Treatment*.
- The French scholar Léopold-Victor Delisle joins the Bibliothèque Nationale in Paris, France, where he makes a major contribution to the development of paleography (the study of handwritten historical material).

BIRTHS & DEATHS

JANUARY

4 Joseph Joffre, French general who was commander in chief 1914–16 of the French armies on the Western Front during World War I, born in Rivesaltes, France (–1931).

6 Louis Braille, French educator and inventor of a writing system for the blind, dies in Paris, France (43).

FEBRUARY

24 George Augustus Moore, Irish novelist, born in Ballyglass, County Mayo, Ireland (–1933).

25 Thomas Moore, Irish poet, satirist, composer, and musician, dies in Wiltshire, England (72).

MARCH

1 Théophile Delcassé, French foreign minister 1898–1905 and 1914–15, who was responsible for arranging European alliances prior to World War I, born in Pamiers, France (–1923).

4 Nikolay (Vasilyevich) Gogol, Russian novelist, dies in Moscow, Russia (41).

21 Doc (John Henry) Holliday, U.S. gambler, dentist, and gunslinger, baptized in Griffin, Georgia (–1887).

MAY

• Calamity Jane (Martha Jane Burke), U.S. frontierswoman, born near Princeton, Missouri (–1903).

1 Santiago Ramón y Cajal, Spanish histologist who, with Camillo Golgi, established that the neuron is the basic unit of the nervous system, born in Petilla de Aragón, Spain (–1934).

JUNE

25 Antonio Gaudí, Spanish architect known for his free-flowing forms and rich colors, born in Reus, Spain (–1926).

29 Henry Clay, two-time U.S. presidential candidate and a leading senator and congressman during the 1810s and 1820s, dies in Washington, D.C. (75).

SEPTEMBER

12 Herbert Henry Asquith, British prime minister 1908–16, a Liberal, born in Morley, Yorkshire (now West Yorkshire), England (–1928).

14 Arthur Wellesley, Duke of Wellington, British army commander and Tory prime minister 1828–30, dies in Walmer Castle, Kent, England (83).

23 William Stewart Halsted, U.S. surgeon who established the first surgical school in the United States at Johns Hopkins University, Baltimore, Maryland, born in New York, New York (–1922).

28 Henri Moissan, French chemist who developed the electric arc furnace for preparing new substances, born in Paris, France (–1907).

OCTOBER

2 William Ramsay, Scottish chemist who discovered the noble gases neon, krypton, and xenon, born in Glasgow, Scotland (–1916).

9 Emil Fischer, German chemist who investigated purines and sugars, born in Euskirchen, Prussia (now Germany) (–1919).

24 Daniel Webster, U.S. orator, politician, and lawyer, dies in Marshfield, Massachusetts (70).

DECEMBER

15 Henri Becquerel, French physicist who discovered radioactivity, born in Paris, France (–1908).

19 Albert Abraham Michelson, German-born U.S. physicist who, with Edward Morley, established that the speed of light is a constant, born in Strelno, Prussia (–1931).

- The German historian Leopold von Ranke publishes the first part of his *Französische Geschichte, vornehmlich im sechzehnten und siebzehnten Jahrhundert/History of France, Principally in the Sixteenth and Seventeenth Centuries*. The final volume appears in 1861.

SOCIETY

Education

- Six thousand out of eight thousand public school teachers are women, in Boston, Massachusetts.
- Antioch College is founded in Yellow Springs, Ohio.
- Laval University is founded in Quebec City, Canada.
- Massachusetts passes legislation requiring children between the ages of 8 and 14 to attend school for a minimum of 12 weeks per year.
- Tufts University is founded in Medford, Massachusetts.

Everyday Life

- The Butchers' Guild of Frankfurt introduces frankfurters in Germany.

NOVEMBER

5   The American Society of Civil Engineers is launched in New York, New York, as the American Society of Engineers and Architects.

Media and Communication

- British publisher Samuel Orchart Beeton launches the first mass-market women's magazine, the *Englishwoman's Domestic Magazine*. Its popularity is partly due to the contributions of his wife, Isabella Beeton, on domestic management.

Religion

- Polygamy becomes a tenet of The Church of Latter-day Saints' faith in the United States.

MAY

9   The U.S. Roman Catholic Church Council meets for the first time in Baltimore, Maryland.

OCTOBER

- U.S. minister Thomas Gallaudet establishes St. Ann's Church for deaf mutes in New York, New York.

Sports

AUGUST

3   The first Yale against Harvard eights rowing race takes place at Lake Winnipesaukee, New Hampshire. Harvard wins the 3.2-km/2-mi race by four lengths.

1853

POLITICS, GOVERNMENT, AND ECONOMICS

Business and Economics

- The German-born instrument maker Heinrich Engelhard Steinway founds the company of Steinway and Sons in New York, New York, making pianos.

FEBRUARY

- The U.S. Congress passes the Coinage Act, reducing the silver content of U.S. coins.

Colonization

SEPTEMBER

24   France annexes the territory of New Caledonia in the south Pacific Ocean.

DECEMBER

11   Britain annexes Nagpur, one of the leading Maratha states in India.

Human Rights

- A convention of black Americans, meeting at Rochester, New York, establishes the National Council of Colored People.
- German-American political philosopher Francis Lieber publishes *On Civil Liberty and Self-Government*.

FEBRUARY

1 Paulina Wright Davis and Caroline H. Dall publish *Una*, the first women's suffrage magazine, in Washington, D.C.

Politics and Government

- A group of U.S. anti-Catholic, anti-immigrant Protestants forms the Native American Party (popularly known as the Know-Nothings) to safeguard the rights of so-called Native Americans against immigrants from Europe. The party's popular name derives from its members' refusal to divulge their beliefs.
- U.S. president Franklin D. Pierce appoints Alabama jurist John A. Campbell to the U.S. Supreme Court.

JANUARY

29 Emperor Napoleon III of France marries the Spanish Countess Eugénie de Montijo at the royal palace of the Tuileries in Paris.

MARCH

- Franklin D. Pierce is inaugurated as 14th president of the United States.
- The U.S. Congress separates the Oregon Territory (now attaining the population level deemed necessary for full statehood) from its northern, largely unsettled half, reorganized as the Washington country.

APRIL

19 Prince Alexander Menshikov, the Russian emissary to the Ottoman Empire, demands for Russia the right to protect the Christian subjects of the Ottoman Empire.

MAY

1 A new constitution in Argentina is not acceptable to Buenos Aires, which claims a special status because of its importance as the region's main port.
21 The Ottoman Turks reject Russia's ultimatum of April 19, extending Russian influence in the Ottoman Empire, and Prince Alexander Menshikov leaves the Ottoman capital, Constantinople.
31 Czar Nicholas I of Russia orders the occupation of the Danubian principalities of Wallachia and Moldavia following his dispute with the Ottoman Empire over Russian influence in the Ottoman Empire.

JUNE

20 Peace is made between Britain and Burma, but the Burmese king refuses to sign a treaty giving Britain Pegu (Lower Burma) and a state of war continues.

JULY

- U.S. commodore Matthew Calbraith Perry sails into Tokyo Bay, having been dispatched by President Millard Fillmore to establish diplomatic relations with Japan.
1 Cape Colony in southern Africa obtains a constitution from Britain establishing an elected legislative council.
2 The Russian army crosses the River Pruth and invades Moldavia as part of Russia's attempt to increase its influence in Ottoman territory.
28 The "Vienna Note," a preliminary to a conference to discuss the problems caused by the weakness of the Ottoman Empire in southeast Europe, is submitted to Russia by Austria.

OCTOBER

4 The Ottoman Empire issues an ultimatum to Russia to evacuate the Danubian principalities of Moldavia and Wallachia within 15 days, stating that Russian failure to do so will amount to war.

NOVEMBER

15 Queen Maria II of Portugal (known as Maria da Gloria) dies and is succeeded by her young son Pedro V, who initially rules under a regency.
30 The Ottoman fleet is destroyed by the Russians off Sinope, on the Black Sea, ending hopes of peacefully resolving the tension over Russian involvement in Ottoman affairs.

DECEMBER

- The United States and Mexico agree to the Gadsden Purchase, named for U.S. minister to Mexico James Gadsden. The United States acquires 77,700 sq km/29,644 sq mi of territory along the southern borders of Arizona and New Mexico in exchange for $10 million.

SCIENCE, TECHNOLOGY, AND MEDICINE

Ecology

- The Forest of Fontainebleau in France becomes the first designated nature reserve.
- The giant redwood *Wellingtonia gigantea*, the largest tree in the world, which can grow to over 100 m/330 ft high, is discovered in California.

Exploration

- British explorer and translator Richard Burton, disguised as an Afghan pilgrim, reaches Mecca during the Muslim month of pilgrimage, but is thwarted in his attempts to cross Arabia by fighting in the interior.

NOVEMBER

11–September 11, 1855 Scottish missionary and explorer David Livingstone undertakes a great expedition from Linyanti on the River Zambezi to Luanda in Portuguese Angola, to attempt to establish an alternative trade to slavery. Reaching Luanda on May 31, 1854, he begins the return journey on September 20.

Health and Medicine

- British surgeon John Snow administers chloroform to Queen Victoria during the birth of Prince Leopold. It subsequently becomes a generally accepted anesthetic.
- Fighting in the Crimean War, many British soldiers pick up the habit of smoking from their Ottoman comrades.

Science

- French physicist Jean Foucault invents the gyroscope.
- French physiologist Claude Bernard demonstrates the glycogenic function of the liver.
- French physiologist Claude Bernard discovers that the vasomotor nerves function to regulate the supply of blood to the organs by widening or narrowing the blood vessels.

Technology

- Don Luis Susini establishes the world's first mass-production system for making cigarettes, in Havana, Cuba.
- German miners begin to use a compressed-air drill.
- There are 3 million daguerreotypes, an early form of photograph, produced in the United States.
- U.S. inventor Alfred Ely Beach patents a typewriter that produces embossed letters for the blind.
- U.S. inventor Richard Hoe improves his rotary press, developing the web press which can print 18,000 sheets per hour on both sides.

SEPTEMBER

2   French inventor Pierre Carpentier patents corrugated iron sheeting.

Transportation

- Albany industrialist Erastus Corning incorporates the New York Central Railroad, a combination of small railroad lines in upstate New York.
- British engineer James Berkley completes India's first railroad, the 32-km/20-mi Bombay–Thana line.
- Canadian-born U.S. naval architect David Oman McKay builds the *Great Republic*, the world's largest sailing ship (99 m/325 ft long and weighing 4,627 metric tons/4,555 tons).
- English baron George Cayley constructs a glider that carries his driver 500 m/1,640 ft—the first crewed glider flight.
- The steamship *Monumental City* sails from San Francisco, California, to Melbourne, Australia—the first steamship to cross the Pacific.
- There are 48,000 km/30,000 mi of railroad track in the United States, up from 14,400 km/9,000 mi in 1850.

MARCH

- The U.S. Congress authorizes the War Department to identify a suitable route for a transcontinental railroad.

ARTS AND IDEAS

Architecture

- The French architect Georges-Eugène, baron Haussmann, becomes Prefect of the Seine Department and begins reconstruction of Paris, France, using long wide avenues that converge on focal points. He begins with the Bois de Boulogne.

- The Hippodrome, a theater that seats 4,600 people, opens in New York, New York.

Arts

- The English artist William Holman Hunt paints *The Light of the World* and *The Awakening Conscience*.
- The French artist Gustave Courbet paints his *Portrait of Pierre-Joseph Proudhon*.
- The U.S. artist Frederick Edwin Church paints *Niagara*.
- The U.S. artist Sanford Robinson Gifford paints *Summer Afternoon*.

Literature and Language

- Fanny Fern's *Fern Leaves from Fanny's Portfolio*, a book of sentimental poems, sells more than 70,000 copies.
- The Austrian writer Adalbert Stifter publishes his story collection *Bunte Steine/Colored Stones*.
- The English churchman and writer Charles Kingsley publishes his historical novel *Hypatia*.
- The English writer Charlotte Mary Yonge publishes her novel *The Heir of Redclyffe*, which quickly becomes a best seller.
- The English writer Charlotte Brontë publishes her novel *Villette*, under the name Currer Bell.
- The English writer Elizabeth Cleghorn Gaskell publishes her novel *Cranford*.
- The English writer Matthew Arnold publishes *Poems: A New Edition*. It contains "The Scholar Gipsy" and "Sohrab and Rustum."
- The French historian and critic Hippolyte-Adolphe Taine publishes *Essai sur les fables de La Fontaine/An Essay on the Fables of La Fontaine*.
- The French writer Charles-Marie-René Leconte de Lisle publishes *Poèmes antiques/Antique Poems*.
- The French writer Victor Hugo publishes his poetry collection *Les Châtiments/Punishments*.
- The U.S. writer Harriet Beecher Stowe publishes *A Key to Uncle Tom's Cabin*, a defense against hostile criticism of her antislavery novel *Uncle Tom's Cabin*, published in 1852.
- The U.S. writer Nathaniel Hawthorne publishes *Tanglewood Tales*, a collection of tales for children based on Greek myths.

Music

- German composer Johannes Brahms completes his Piano Sonatas No. 1 (Opus 1) and No. 3 (Opus 5).
- Hungarian composer Franz Liszt completes his Piano Sonata in B minor.
- The opera *Il trovatore/The Troubadour* by the Italian composer Giuseppe Verdi is first performed, in Rome, Italy. It is first performed in both Britain and the United States in 1855 (in London, England, and New York, New York). His opera *La traviata/The Fallen Woman* is also first performed, in Venice, Italy. It is based on the novel *The Lady of the Camelias*, published in 1848 by Alexandre Dumas *fils*. It is first performed in both Britain and the United States in 1856 (in London, England, and New York, New York).

- U.S. songwriter Stephen Foster writes "My Old Kentucky Home."

Theater and Dance

- The comedy *Die Journalisten/The Journalists* by the German writer Gustav Freytag is first performed.

Thought and Scholarship

- Massachusetts polymath Richard Hildreth publishes *Theory of Politics*, an economic interpretation of history based on the social philosophy of Robert Owen.
- The English theologian Frederick Denison Maurice publishes *Theological Essays*. Because of his controversial questioning of the doctrine of eternal punishment, he is expelled from his professorship at King's College, London, England, in the same year.
- The German historian Heinrich von Sybel publishes the first volume of his *Geschichte der Revolutionszeit, 1789–95/A History of the French Revolution*. The final volume appears in 1858.
- The Swiss art historian Jakob Christoph Burckhardt publishes *Die Zeit des Konstantins des Grossen/The Age of Constantine the Great*.

SOCIETY

Education

- The University of Florida opens at Gainesville, Florida.
- Washington University opens at St. Louis, Missouri.

Everyday Life

- Anne Pamela Cunningham establishes the Mt. Vernon Ladies' Association to transform George Washington's plantation into a national shrine.
- The British confectionery company Fry's produces the chocolate bar Fry's Chocolate Stick, later renamed Fry's Chocolate Cream.
- The U.S. chef George Crum creates potato chips in Saratoga Springs, New York. The product is so popular that general commercial production begins almost immediately.
- Tighter licensing laws in Scotland make pubs close at 11 p.m. and all day on Sunday. Illicit stills proliferate as a result.
- U.S. publisher and women's rights campaigner Amelia Jenks Bloomer adopts "bloomers," loose trousers gathered at the ankles, which give women much more freedom of movement.

JULY

14 The first World's Fair, modeled on the Great Exhibition of London, England, in 1851, opens in New York, New York.

Religion

- The German theologian Johann Jakob Herzog publishes the first volume of his 22-volume *Realencyklopädie für protestantische Theologie und Kirche/Encyclopedia of Protestant Theology and the Protestant Church*. The last volume appears in 1868.

BIRTHS & DEATHS

FEBRUARY

3 Hudson Maxim, U.S. inventor and manufacturer of explosives, born in Orneville, Maine (–1927).

9 Leander Starr Jameson, British statesman who, with Cecil Rhodes, tried to unite southern Africa under British rule, born in Edinburgh, Scotland (–1917).

MARCH

17 Christian Doppler, Austrian physicist who described the change in frequency of light and sound waves emitted by a moving object relative to an observer (the Doppler effect), dies in Vienna, Austria (49).

19 K'ang Youwei, Chinese social reformer, born in Kwangtung Province, China (–1927).

30 Vincent van Gogh, Dutch painter whose work inspired the expressionists, born in Zundert, the Netherlands (–1890).

APRIL

25 William Beaumont, U.S. army surgeon and the first person to observe and describe digestion as it occurs in the stomach, dies in St. Louis, Missouri (67).

JUNE

3 William Flinders Petrie, British archeologist and Egyptologist who developed a method of dating cultures by comparing pottery fragments, born in Charlton, London, England (–1942).

JULY

5 Cecil Rhodes, English financier, prime minister of Cape Colony 1890–96, and philanthropist who established the Rhodes scholarships at Oxford University, England, born in Bishop's Stortford, Hertfordshire, England (–1902).

SEPTEMBER

20 Chulalongkorn, King of Siam (modern Thailand) 1868–1910 whose modernizing reforms prevented Thailand from becoming a European colony, born in Bangkok, Siam (–1910).

21 Heike Kamerlingh Onnes, Dutch physicist who discovered superconductivity, born in Groningen, the Netherlands (–1926).

NOVEMBER

5 Marcus Samuel, businessman, philanthropist, cofounder of Shell Transport and Trading Company, later Shell Oil, born in London, England (–1927).

27 Bat Masterson (nickname of Batholemew Masterson), Canadian-born U.S. lawman, gambler, and saloon keeper, born in Henryville, Canada East (now Quebec) (–1921).

Sports

- West Australian becomes the first horse to win the English Triple Crown (2,000 Guineas, Derby, and St. Leger).

1854

POLITICS, GOVERNMENT, AND ECONOMICS

Business and Economics

DECEMBER

- New York lawyers and entrepreneurs George H. Bissell and "Stonewall" J. Eveleth establish the Pennsylvania Rock Oil Company, the nation's first petroleum corporation.

Colonization

OCTOBER

- In the so-called Ostend Manifesto, the U.S. ministers to Spain, France, and Britain draft a memorandum to secretary of state William L. Marcy justifying the purchase or, if necessary, forcible seizure of Cuba from Spain. Widespread opposition to the move prompts Marcy to reject the idea.

Human Rights

- Virginia lawyer and writer George Fitzhugh publishes *Sociology for the South*, an apology for slavery and indictment of industrial capitalism.

APRIL

26 Boston abolitionist Eli Thayer organizes the Massachusetts Emigrant Aid Society (renamed the New England Emigrant Aid Society in 1855); its purpose is to promote the settlement of antislavery groups in the territory of Kansas.

JUNE

- The fugitive slave Anthony Burns becomes a celebrity in Boston when he is seized by federal deputies and returned to the South despite city-wide opposition.

Politics and Government

- Connecticut and Rhode Island pass personal liberty laws, designed to thwart the capture and return of fugitive slaves.
- In U.S. Congressional elections, Democrats attain a majority over the new Republican Party in the Senate (40–15), but cede control to Republicans in the House (108–83).

FEBRUARY

- A group of 50 disgruntled members of the U.S. Whig Party, Free-Soilers (opponents of the extension of slavery into frontier territories), and antislavery Democrats meet in Ripon, Wisconsin, to discuss forming a new political party. This meeting sows the seeds for the formation of the Republican Party.
23 The Convention of Bloemfontein is signed by which the British agree to evacuate southern African territory north of the Orange River, allowing for the establishment of an independent Orange Free State by Dutch settlers.

MARCH

- The United States and Japan sign the Treaty of Kanagawa, establishing a U.S. consulate in Japan and providing U.S. ships limited access to several Japanese ports.
12 Britain and France conclude an alliance with the Ottoman Empire against Russia.
26 Charles III, the Duke of Parma, ruler of the Italian duchy of Parma, is murdered.
27–28 France (March 27) and Britain (March 28) issue an ultimatum to Russia to withdraw from the Danubian principalities of Moldavia and Wallachia.

APRIL

12 Buenos Aires adopts a separate constitution from Argentina, proclaiming the port's right to levy tariffs on traffic passing through it independently.
20 Austria and Prussia conclude a defensive alliance against Russian expansion in response to the tension in southeast Europe.

MAY

- U.S. president Franklin D. Pierce signs the controversial Kansas–Nebraska Act, creating the territories of Kansas and Nebraska. The act virtually repeals the Missouri

Crimean War (1854–56)

1854

SEPTEMBER

14 Britain and France land unopposed in the Crimea to begin the Crimean War with Russia over its attempt to increase its power in southeast Europe at the expense of the Ottoman Empire.

20 British and French troops are victorious over Russian forces at the Battle of the Alma.

OCTOBER

17 British and French forces begin the siege of the Russian-held city of Sevastopol in the Crimea.

17 In the Battle of Balaclava the British defeat a strong Russian push towards the harbor.

NOVEMBER

• English nurse Florence Nightingale arrives in Scutari, Ottoman Empire, and introduces sanitary measures in an effort to reduce deaths from cholera, dysentery, and typhus.

5 British and French forces defeat the Russians at the Battle of Inkerman.

14 A torrential storm bursts over the Crimean city of Sevastopol while it is under siege by the British and French, wrecking allied supply ships and causing chaos and considerable loss of life.

DECEMBER

9 English poet Alfred, Lord Tennyson, publishes "The Charge of the Light Brigade," a poetic description of the disastrous attack on October 25, 1854 by the Light Brigade at the Battle of Balaclava.

1855

JANUARY

26 The Italian kingdom of Sardinia–Piedmont joins Britain, France, Austria, and Prussia in the Crimean War against Russia.

APRIL

4 An electric telegraph line is established between London, England, and Balaclava on the Black Sea, allowing immediate reporting on the Crimean War.

JUNE

7–18 Two Allied assaults on Sevastopol are repelled with heavy casualties.

SEPTEMBER

8 In a renewed assault, the French take the Malakoff, a key Russian defensive position, which makes the continued defence of Sevastopol untenable.

11 British and French forces enter the Crimean city of Sevastopol after the besieged Russians withdraw.

NOVEMBER

21 Sweden joins an alliance with Britain, France, and the Ottoman Empire against Russia.

28 The Ottoman fort of Kars in Transcaucasia is taken by Russian forces.

DECEMBER

29 An Austrian ultimatum to Russia threatens war unless Russia accepts the "Vienna Points" of August 1854, with the additional neutrality of the Black Sea and cession of Bessarabia.

1856

FEBRUARY

25 A peace conference to end the war in the Crimea opens in Paris, France, attended by representatives of Britain, France, Austria, the Ottoman Empire, Sardinia–Piedmont and Russia.

MARCH

30 The integrity of the Ottoman Empire is recognized by the signatories to the Treaty of Paris ending the Crimean War, which guarantees the Danubian principalities. Russia cedes Bessarabia, the Black Sea is to be neutral, and the River Danube is to be free to ships of all nations.

APRIL

15 Britain, France, and Austria guarantee the integrity and independence of the Ottoman Empire in a further treaty after signing the Treaty of Paris.

Compromise of 1820 by stipulating that the fate of slavery in Kansas and Nebraska (both north of the 36th parallel) will be determined by popular sovereignty.

5 Britain declares that the Monroe Doctrine (stating that the interference of non-American states in affairs of any part of North or South America will be treated as an act of aggression by the United States) should not be regarded as binding on European countries.

26 France and Britain occupy the Greek port of Piraeus, Athens, after declaring a blockade of Greece for attempting to attack the Ottoman Empire, and Greece subsequently promises neutrality.

JUNE

• The United States and Canada sign the Reciprocity Treaty, opening U.S. markets to Canadian products in return for U.S. fishing rights in Canadian waters.

3 An Austrian ultimatum to Russia against carrying its war with the Ottoman Empire across the Balkans forces Russia to retreat from the Danubian principalities of Moldavia and Wallachia.

14 The Ottoman Empire agrees that Austria should occupy and defend the Danubian principalities of Moldavia and Wallachia until the end of the Ottoman war with Russia.

JULY

• The Republican Party is launched in Jackson, Michigan. The party outlines a Free-Soil platform, opposing the extension of slavery into frontier territories and sharply at odds with the Kansas–Nebraska Act.

AUGUST

3 The progressive general Baldomero Espartero becomes prime minister of Spain with General Enrique O'Donnell as minister of war.

8　The "Four Points" issued by Britain, Austria, and France from the Austrian capital, Vienna, state their conditions of peace with Russia to be Russia's abandonment of its claim to a protectorate over the Ottoman sultan's Christian subjects, revision of the Straits settlement in the interests of European powers, free passage of the mouth of the River Danube, and a guarantee of the integrity of the Danubian principalities of Moldavia and Wallachia, and of Serbia.

22　Austria occupies the Danubian principalities of Moldavia and Wallachia following the withdrawal of the Russian army.

SEPTEMBER

14　Britain and France land unopposed in the Crimea to begin the Crimean War with Russia over its attempt to increase its power in southeast Europe at the expense of the Ottoman Empire.

20　British and French troops are victorious over Russian forces at the Battle of the Alma in the Crimean War.

OCTOBER

10　The Prussian Upper House is reconstituted to give increased influence to large landowners, making the legislative process more conservative.

17　English and French forces begin the siege of the Russian-held city of Sevastopol in the Crimea.

25　British and French forces win a narrow victory over Russia at great cost at Balaclava in the Crimea, following cavalry charges of the British Light and Heavy Brigades.

NOVEMBER

5　British and French forces defeat the Russians at the Battle of Inkerman.

DECEMBER

2　Austria concludes an alliance with Britain and France under which its Italian possessions are guaranteed during the Crimean War in return for Austria's defense of the Danubian principalities of Moldavia and Wallachia against possible Russian attack.

SCIENCE, TECHNOLOGY, AND MEDICINE

Ecology

- English naturalist Philip Henry Gosse builds the first institutional aquarium in England for the protection of marine animals.

OCTOBER

5　A tsunami levels 5,000 buildings in Yamato, Iga, and Isehits, Japan; 2,400 people are killed.

NOVEMBER

14　A torrential storm bursts over the Crimean city of Sevastopol while it is under siege by the British and French, wrecking allied supply ships and causing chaos and considerable loss of life.

Exploration

November 1854–55　British explorers Richard Burton and John Hanning Speke travel to the interior of Somaliland, in East Africa.

November 1854–62　Welsh naturalist Alfred Russel Wallace explores the East Indies between Singapore and New Guinea, and identifies the precise boundary between Asia and Australasia from their different fauna.

Health and Medicine

- A typhus epidemic spreads from the Russian to the British and French troops in the Crimea. More men die of disease during the Crimean War than are killed by enemy action.
- English physician John Snow traces a local epidemic of cholera and typhoid to a communal pump in Broad Street, London, England. He discovers that the well's water supply is being contaminated by a leakage from a neighboring sewage tank.

NOVEMBER

- English nurse Florence Nightingale arrives in Scutari, Ottoman Empire, and introduces sanitary measures in an effort to reduce deaths from cholera, dysentery, and typhus during the Crimean War.

Math

- English mathematician George Boole publishes *The Laws of Thought*, in which he outlines his system of symbolic logic now known as Boolean algebra.
- English mathematician Arthur Cayley makes important advances in group theory.
- German mathematician Georg Friedrich Bernhard Riemann formulates his concept of non-Euclidean geometry in *On the Hypotheses forming the Foundation of Geometry*. He also gives a lecture entitled "Über die Hypothesen welche der Geometrie zu Grunde liegen"/"On the Hypotheses that Lie at the Foundation of Geometry," in which he shows the connection between geometry and our assumptions about the universe.

Science

- English astronomer George Biddell Airy calculates the mass of the earth by swinging a pendulum at the top and bottom of a deep coal mine and measuring the different gravitational effects on it.
- French scientist Henri-Etienne St. Claire Deville develops a new process for making aluminum. Through the action of metallic sodium on aluminum chloride he produces marble-sized lumps of the metal and at the Paris Exposition in 1855 he exhibits a 7-kg/15-lb ingot. His process becomes the foundation of the aluminum industry.
- German biologist Christian Ehrenberg publishes *Microgeology* and establishes micropaleontology, the study of fossil microorganisms.
- U.S. naval officer Matthew Fontaine Maury maps the depth of the North Atlantic to 4,000 fathoms (7,300 m/ 23,950 ft).

Technology

- At Varna, Bulgaria, allied army commanders use the telegraph to communicate with their troops during the Crimean War—the first military use of the telegraph.
- Italian inventor Guiseppe Devincenzi patents an early form of the electric typewriter, in London, England.
- U.S. inventor Daniel Halladay develops the wind pump, an automatic windmill with a governor that keeps the milling speed constant.
- U.S. inventor Peter Cooper manufactures the first structural-iron beams that are used for constructing buildings.
- U.S. inventor Walter Hunt, who had earlier patented the safety pin, invents the paper collar.
- U.S. inventor Elisha Graves Otis demonstrates his safety elevator at the Crystal Palace Exposition in New York by riding in it and ordering the rope to be cut.

NOVEMBER

- The destruction of the Ottoman wooden frigates by Russian shells in the naval action at Sinope, in the Ottoman Empire, emphasizes the need for armor plating on warships.

Transportation

- The era of the great U.S. clipper ships reaches it zenith when the vessel *Flying Cloud* sails from New York, New York, to San Francisco, California, via Cape Horn, in 89 days and 8 hours.
- The Vienna–Trieste railroad (between Italy and Austria) is completed. Employing a 1.6-km/1-mi-long tunnel through the Semmering Pass, it is the world's first mountain railroad.

FEBRUARY

- The Chicago Rock Island Line railroad reaches the Mississippi, linking the Great Lakes to the river via Chicago.

ARTS AND IDEAS

Architecture

- Paddington Railway Station, in London, England, designed by the English engineer Isambard Kingdom Brunel and the English architect Thomas Henry Wyatt, is completed.
- The Dresden Art Gallery, in Germany, designed by the German architect Gottfried Semper, is completed.

Arts

- The Austrian artist Moritz von Schwind paints frescoes at Wartburg Castle at Eisenach, Thuringia, Germany, which depict the life of St. Elisabeth of Hungary.
- The English artist John Everett Millais paints *Ophelia*.
- The French artist Gustave Courbet paints *The Meeting*.

- The French artist Jean-Auguste-Dominique Ingres paints *Joan of Arc at the Coronation of Charles VII* and *Portrait of La Comtesse d'Haussonville*.
- The French graphic artist Charles Meryon completes his series of etchings *Eaux-fortes sur Paris/Etchings of Paris*.

Literature and Language

- The U.S. poet and essayist Henry David Thoreau publishes *Walden, or Life in the Woods*. His best-known work, it records his life in a cabin on the shore of Walden Pond in eastern Massachusetts between 1845 and 1847.
- The English writer Coventry Patmore publishes *The Betrothal*, the first part of his novel in verse *Angel in the House*. Subsequent parts appear in 1856, 1860, and 1862.
- The English writer Charles Dickens publishes his novel *Hard Times*.
- The French historian Ernest Renan publishes *Histoire général des langues sémitiques/A General History of the Semitic Languages*.
- The French writer Gérard de Nerval publishes *Les Filles du feu/The Girls of Fire*, which contains one of his best-known stories, "Sylvie," and his poetry collection *Chimères/Chimeras*.
- The French writer George Sand publishes her autobiography *Histoire de ma vie/The Story of My Life*.
- The German folklorist and philologist Jakob Ludwig Carl Grimm publishes the first volume of his *Deutsches Wörterbuch/German Dictionary*. The project is not completed until 1954.
- The Hungarian writer Mór Jókai publishes his novel *Egy magyar nábob/A Hungarian Nabob*.
- The Swiss writer Gottfried Keller publishes the first part of his autobiographical novel *Der grüne Heinrich/Green Henry*, his best-known work. The final part appears in 1855.
- The U.S. writer Timothy Shay Arthur publishes his novel *Ten Nights in a Barroom and What I Saw There*.
- U.S. fur merchant John Jacob Astor endows the Astor Library in New York, New York, with a bequest of $400,000.

DECEMBER

9   The English poet Alfred, Lord Tennyson publishes his poem "The Charge of the Light Brigade," a poetic description of the disastrous attack on October 25, 1854 by the Light Brigade at the Battle of Balaclava, during the Crimean War.

Music

- Austrian composer Josef Anton Bruckner completes his *Missa solemnis/Solemn Mass*.
- French composer Hector Berlioz completes his oratorio *L'Enfance du Christ/The Childhood of Christ* (Opus 25). Berlioz began work on this piece in 1828.
- German composer Johannes Brahms completes his Piano Trio No. 1 (Opus 8). It is revised in 1889.
- Hungarian composer Franz Liszt completes his Symphonic Poem *Orpheus* and the first of his three

volumes of piano works, *Année de pèlerinage: Suisse/ Years of Pilgrimage: Switzerland.*

- U.S. songwriter Stephen Foster writes "Jeanie with the Light Brown Hair."

Theater and Dance

- The play *Bednost ne porok/Poverty is No Crime* by the Russian dramatist Alexander Nikolayevich Ostrovsky is first performed, in Moscow, Russia.
- The play *Le Gendre de Monsieur Poirier/The Son-in- Law of Monsieur Poirier* by the French writers Emile Augier and Léonard-Sylvain-Julien Sandeau is first performed, in Paris, France.

Thought and Scholarship

- The German historian Theodor Mommsen publishes the first volume of his *Römische Geschichte/History of Rome.* The last volume appears in 1856.
- The Provençal writer Frédéric Mistral founds the Félibrige Society for the revival of Provençal culture.

SOCIETY

Everyday Life

- The first baby show takes place, in Springfield, Ohio.
- The Boston Public Library opens in Boston, Massachusetts.

Media and Communication

- The newspaper *Le Figaro* is launched in Paris, France.

Sports

- Flora Temple becomes the first trotting horse to complete 1.6 km/1 mi in under 2 minutes 20 seconds, at Kalamazoo, Michigan.
- The British climber Alfred Wills climbs the Wetterhorn from Grindelwald in the Alps, an event which is regarded as the start of mountaineering as a sport. Within the next 11 years all the Alpine peaks are reached except La Meije.

BIRTHS & DEATHS

JANUARY

1　James George Frazer, Scottish anthropologist, folklorist, and classical scholar best known for his multivolume work *The Golden Bough* (1890), born in Glasgow, Scotland (–1941).

FEBRUARY

9　Baron Edward Henry Carson, Irish politician who led the revolt against British Home Rule for all of Ireland, born in Dublin, Ireland (–1935).

27　(Hugues-) Félicité (-Robert de) Lamennais, French priest, philosophical and political writer, dies in Paris, France (71).

MARCH

14　Paul Ehrlich, German medical researcher who discovered the first effective treatment for syphilis, born in Strehlen, Silesia, Prussia (now Strzelin, Poland) (–1915).

23　Alfred Milner, British colonial administrator whose reforms and attitudes are instrumental in beginning the Boer War 1899–1902, born in Giessen, Hesse-Darmstadt (–1925).

APRIL

6　William Strickland, U.S. architect and engineer, leading proponent of

the Greek Revival style in the United States, dies in Nashville, Tennessee (*c.* 66).

29　Jules-Henri Poincaré, French mathematician, theoretical astronomer, and philosopher of science, born in Nancy, France (–1912).

JULY

3　Leoš Janáček, Bohemian operatic composer whose music is intimately connected with the inflections of his native tongue, born in Hukvaldy, Moravia, Austrian Empire (–1928).

7　Georg Simon Ohm, German physicist who discovered Ohm's law, which relates electric current to voltage, dies in Munich, Germany (67).

12　George Eastman, U.S. inventor, manufacturer, and philanthropist who introduced the Kodak camera, born in Waterville, New York (–1932).

AUGUST

20　Friedrich Schelling, German Idealist philosopher, dies in Bad Ragaz, Switzerland (79).

SEPTEMBER

1　Engelbert Humperdinck, German operatic composer known best for

Hansel and Gretel (1893), born in Siegburg, Hanover (now Germany) (–1921).

OCTOBER

20　(Jean-Nicolas-) Arthur Rimbaud, French Symbolist poet, born in Charleville, France (–1891).

NOVEMBER

3　Jokischi Takamine, Japanese biochemist who isolated adrenaline (epinephrine), the first hormone to be isolated from natural sources, born in Takaoka, Japan (–1922).

6　John Philip Sousa, U.S. bandmaster and composer of military marches, born in Washington, D.C. (–1932).

21　Benedict XV, who was pope 1914–22, born in Pegli, Sardinia (–1922).

DECEMBER

10　Henry Rowe Schoolcraft, U.S. ethnologist and explorer who discovered the source of the Mississippi, dies in Washington, D.C. (71).

1855

POLITICS, GOVERNMENT, AND ECONOMICS

Politics and Government

- The government of the British colony of Victoria in Australia restricts Chinese immigration.

JANUARY

26 The Italian kingdom of Sardinia–Piedmont joins Britain, France, Austria, and Prussia in the Crimean War against Russia.

FEBRUARY

- The U.S. Congress passes legislation making children born abroad to U.S. parents citizens of the United States.
- U.S. president Franklin Pierce signs legislation creating the U.S. Court of Claims, where citizens can take their grievances against the federal government.
2 Panama is given federal status by a constitutional amendment.
6 The former foreign secretary Lord Palmerston becomes prime minister of a Liberal administration in Britain.

MARCH

- Violence and fraud mar Kansas' territorial election, as proslavery partisans from Missouri cross into Kansas to swell the ranks of proslavery legislators. Despite evidence of fraud, the Pierce administration endorses the election results.
2 The reactionary czar Nicholas I of Russia dies and is succeeded by the more moderate Alexander II.
30 By the Treaty of Peshawar, Britain and Afghanistan form an alliance against Persia.

MAY

- In a sign of deteriorating relations between North and South, South Carolina congressman Preston S. Brooks severely beats Massachusetts congressman Charles Sumner on the floor of the U.S. House of Representatives. Sumner had insulted Brooks' uncle, South Carolina senator Andrew P. Butler.
5 King George V of the German kingdom of Hanover abolishes its liberal institutions at the demand of the conservative diet (assembly) of the German Confederation.

JUNE

1 A bill to enable the sale of church lands to peasant proprietors is passed in Spain, provoking riots protesting at the infringement of the status of the Catholic Church.

JULY

- New York State prohibits the production and distribution of alcohol.
16 The British Parliament establishes responsible government throughout the Australian states, except for Western Australia.

AUGUST

18 An Austrian concordat with the Pope gives the clergy control of education, censorship, and matrimonial law.

SEPTEMBER

- Antislavery partisans in Kansas hold their own territorial election in the town of Big Springs. They marshal an army to combat their proslavery rivals, as Kansas divides into two armed camps.
11 British and French forces enter the Crimean city of Sevastopol after the besieged Russians within capitulate.

OCTOBER

- Antislavery partisans in Kansas write the Topeka Constitution, outlawing slavery and providing for a governor and state legislature.

NOVEMBER

21 Sweden joins an alliance with Britain, France, and the Ottoman Empire against Russia.
28 The Ottoman fort of Kars in Transcaucasia is taken by Russian forces.

DECEMBER

29 An Austrian ultimatum to Russia threatens war unless Russia accepts the "Vienna Points" of August 1854, with the additional neutrality of the Black Sea and cession of Bessarabia.

SCIENCE, TECHNOLOGY, AND MEDICINE

Exploration

NOVEMBER

3–May 20, 1856 Scottish missionary and explorer David Livingstone completes his crossing of the African continent by traveling eastward from Linyanti on the River Zambezi to Quelimane in Portuguese East Africa, visiting and naming the Victoria Falls (November 17, 1855) on the way.

Health and Medicine

- English physiologist Marshall Hall further develops artificial respiration to aid victims of drowning.

Science

- English astronomer John Russell Hind discovers the first dwarf nova, U Geminorum. The star brightens by a factor of nearly 40 in a matter of a days before returning to its normal brightness.
- French physiologist Claude Bernard discovers that ductless glands produce hormones, which he calls "internal secretions."
- German biologist Rudolf Virchow discovers that "every cell is derived from a cell"—the principle of cell division.
- Irish astronomer William Parsons observes the spiral structure of some galaxies including the Crab Nebulae, and the Great Nebula in Orion.
- Swedish inventor J. E. Lundström patents the safety match. The combustible chemicals are separated so that it lights only when struck on a chemically-impregnated surface.
- U.S. chemist Benjamin Silliman publishes the *Silliman Report* in which he describes the distillation of crude oil into its various fractions (tar, naphthalene, gasoline, and solvents) and their uses in lubrication, lighting, and other purposes. His emphasis on crude oil's economic potential serves as an impetus for oil exploration and drilling.
- U.S. navy officer Matthew Fontaine Maury publishes *Physical Geography of the Sea*, the first textbook on oceanography.
- U.S. physician Abraham Gesner extracts kerosene from raw petroleum, which he uses for medicinal purposes. Previously it had been extracted from coal tar and shale oil. Others also extract kerosene which they promote as a fuel.

November 1855–56 English naturalist Philip Henry Gosse publishes *Manual of Marine Zoology*, the first thorough book on the subject.

Technology

c. 1855 German glass-blower Heinrich Geissler invents the Geissler tube. The forerunner of the neon tube, it consists of an evacuated glass tube with an electrode at each end and is filled with a rarefied gas. The tube lights up when an electric current is passed through it.
- British chemist Alexander Parkes invents "Parkesine," the first plastic.
- Austrian engineer Franz Köller adds tungsten to steel to make tungsten steel. It is used as a high-speed cutting steel as it retains its hardness at high temperatures.
- British-born U.S. inventor David Hughes patents a printing telegraph, which quickly becomes the standard in Europe.
- French inventor Alphonse Poitevain invents the collotype printing process, which accurately reproduces photographs.
- The English firm of Smith and Phillips introduce the first gas oven.

- U.S. inventor Richard Smith Lawrence develops the turret lathe which allows a variety of cutting, drilling, reaming, and boring tools to be attached.
- U.S. manufacturer Samuel Colt opens an armory at Hartford, Connecticut. Using 1,400 machine tools, he develops the use of interchangeable parts to a high degree and revolutionizes the manufacture of small arms.

Transportation

- German inventor Sebastian Bauer builds *Le Diable-Marin/The Marine Devil*, an iron submarine 15.8 m/52 ft long, with a crew of 11, 4 of whom work a treadmill to turn a screw propeller. Bauer takes the first underwater photographs through the submarine's windows.
- The Sault Ste. Marie Canal, between lakes Superior and Huron, is completed. It bypasses the St. Mary's River rapids and makes the Great Lakes a navigable waterway.
- The Wabash Canal is completed linking the Ohio River with Lake Erie.

MARCH
- German-born U.S. engineer Augustus Roebling completes the 250-m/821-ft-long Niagara Falls Suspension Bridge across the Niagara Gorge between Ontario, Canada, and New York state. It is the first suspension bridge strong enough to withstand high winds and heavy railroad locomotives.

APRIL
21 The first bridge across the Mississippi, between Rock Island, Illinois, and Davenport, Iowa, opens to rail traffic.

AUGUST
29 The worst U.S. train accident to date occurs on the Camden and Amboy Railroad near Burlington, New Jersey; 21 people are killed and 75 injured.

August 1855–59 The Royal Albert Bridge over the Tamar River at Saltash, Cornwall, England, is built by English engineer Isambard Kingdom Brunel. To build it he uses a pneumatic caissment, an 11-m/35-ft diameter iron cylinder, which is sunk through 21 m/70 ft of water and 5 m/16 ft of mud to allow the bridge's foundations to be built on the rock bottom.

ARTS AND IDEAS

Architecture

- The Church of St. Eugène in Paris, France, designed by the French architect Louis-Auguste Boileau, is completed.
- The Smithsonian Institution, in Washington, D.C., designed by the U.S. architect James Renwick, is completed.

Arts

- The Canadian artist Robert Scott Duncanson paints *Pompeii*.
- The English photographer Roger Fenton takes *Captain Turner, Coldstream Guards*. This is one of the many pictures of the Crimean War taken by Fenton.
- The French artist Gustave Courbet paints *The Artist's Studio*. When it is rejected by the official committee selecting works for the Paris Exposition Universelle (World Fair), he sets up his own exhibition, the *Pavillion du Réalisme* (Realist Pavilion), at the Exposition.

Literature and Language

- Cambridge, Massachusetts, bookstore owner John Bartlett compiles and publishes the first edition of his now famous *Familiar Quotations*.
- The English churchman and writer Charles Kingsley publishes his historical novel *Westward Ho!*
- The English poet Alfred, Lord Tennyson, publishes *Maud and Other Poems*.
- The English poet Robert Browning publishes his collection of poetry *Men and Women*.
- The English writer Anthony Trollope publishes his novel *The Warden*.
- The English writer Charles Dickens publishes his novel *Little Dorrit* in serial form. It is published as a book in 1857.
- The English writer Elizabeth Cleghorn Gaskell publishes her "social problem" novel *North and South*.
- The English writer George Meredith publishes his prose fantasy *The Shaving of Shagpat: An Arabian Entertainment*.

- The English writer William Makepeace Thackeray publishes his comic fairy tale *The Rose and the Ring* under the name Michael Angelo Titmarsh.
- The French writer Gérard de Nerval publishes his tale *Aurélia*. His work has an important influence on the development of the Symbolist movement.
- The German writer Gustav Freytag publishes his novel *Soll und Haben/Should and Have*.
- The Russian writer Leo Tolstoy publishes the first part of his collection of stories *Sevastopolskiye rasskazy/Sevastopol Sketches*. The second part appears in 1856.
- The U.S. editor Evert Augustus Duyckinck publishes *The Cyclopedia of American Literature*.
- The U.S. humorist Mortimer Neal Thomson publishes *Doesticks, What He Says*, sketches of New York life.
- The U.S. poet Walt Whitman publishes his poetry collection *Leaves of Grass*, his most important work and one of the major works of 19th-century U.S. literature.
- The U.S. writer Henry Wadsworth Longfellow publishes his long narrative poem *The Song of Hiawatha*, one of his best-known works.
- The U.S. writer Herman Melville publishes his novel *Israel Potter: His Fifty Years of Exile*.
- The U.S. writer Thomas Bulfinch publishes *The Age of Fable*, a collection of ancient myths.

Music

- Hungarian composer Franz Liszt completes his *Missa Solemnis/Solemn Mass*.
- The opera *Les Vêpres siciliennes/Sicilian Vespers*, by the Italian composer Giuseppe Verdi, is first performed, in Paris, France. It is first performed in Britain in 1859 (in London, England), and in the United States in 1859 (in New York, New York).

BIRTHS & DEATHS

FEBRUARY
23 Karl Friedrich Gauss, German mathematician, dies in Göttingen, Germany (77).

MARCH
2 Czar Nicholas I, Emperor of Russia 1825–55, dies in St. Petersburg, Russia (58).
3 Robert Mills, U.S. neoclassical architect, dies in Washington, D.C. (73).
24 Andrew W. Mellon, U.S. secretary of the Treasury 1921–32 and philanthropist, born in Philadelphia, Pennsylvania (–1937).
31 Charlotte Brontë, English novelist who wrote *Jane Eyre* (1847), dies in Haworth, Yorkshire (now West Yorkshire), England (38).

JUNE
14 Robert M. La Follette, U.S. senator 1906–25 and leader of the Progressive Movement, born in Primrose, Wisconsin (–1925).
28 FitzRoy James Henry Somerset, Lord Raglan, British field marshal in command of the British forces during the Crimean War, dies near Sevastopol, Crimea, Russia (66).

AUGUST
7 Stanley J. Weyman, British writer of historical romance, born in Ludlow, Shropshire, England (–1928).

SEPTEMBER
10 Robert Koldewey, German architect and archeologist who excavated Babylon, born in Blankenburg am Harz, Duchy of Brunswick (–1925).

NOVEMBER
5 Eugene Debs, U.S. labor leader and five-time presidential candidate for the Socialist Party, born in Terre Haute, Indiana (–1926).
11 Søren Kierkegaard, Danish philosopher who founded Existentialist philosophy, dies in Copenhagen, Denmark (42).

Theater and Dance

- The play *Zwischen Himmel und Erde/Between Heaven and Earth* by the German writer Otto Ludwig is first performed.
- The Russian writer Ivan Sergeyevich Turgenev publishes his comedy *Mesyats v derevne/A Month in the Country*. One of the masterpieces of 19th-century Russian theater, it is first performed professionally in 1872, in Moscow, Russia.

Thought and Scholarship

- The English poet and historian Henry Hart Milman publishes *The History of Latin Christianity*.
- The English scholar William Whewell publishes *Elements of Morality*.
- The English social scientist Herbert Spencer publishes *Principles of Psychology*, in which, several years before Charles Darwin's *The Origin of Species*, he sets out a theory of evolution.
- The French social reformer Pierre-Guillaume-Frédéric Le Play publishes *Les Ouvriers européens/The Workers of Europe*, the first comparative study of working-class incomes.
- The Scottish philosopher Alexander Bain publishes *Sense and the Intellect*.
- The U.S. historian William Hickling Prescott publishes *Philip II*.
- The U.S. writer Washington Irving publishes the first volume of his five-volume *Life of Washington*. The last volume appears in 1859.

SOCIETY

Education

- Michigan State University is founded in East Lansing, Michigan.
- New York educator Henry Barnard publishes the *American Journal of Education*.
- Pennsylvania State University is founded in State College, Pennsylvania.
- Trenton State College, a teacher education institution, is founded in Ewing, New Jersey.

Everyday Life

- The Paris International Exposition is held in France.
- The Young Women's Christian Association (YWCA), a counterpart to the Young Men's Christian Association (YMCA), is founded in London, England.

Media and Communication

- A telegraph cable is laid across the Mediterranean by English engineer Charles Tilston Bright.

APRIL
4   An electric telegraph line is established between London, England, and Balaclava on the Black Sea, allowing immediate reporting on the Crimean War.

1856

POLITICS, GOVERNMENT, AND ECONOMICS

Business and Economics

- The system of hire purchase is introduced in the United States, by the Singer sewing machine manufacturing company.
- Western Union begins its meteoric rise to the top of the U.S. telegraph industry.

Colonization

FEBRUARY
13 Britain annexes the northern Indian province of Oudh, which increases hostility to British rule in India.

JULY
12 Natal, formerly part of the British Cape Colony in southern Africa, is established as a separate British crown colony with an elected assembly.

Politics and Government

- A British act of Parliament grants self-government to the Australian state of Tasmania.
- Civil war begins in Zululand (in modern Natal, South Africa) on the death of Mpande between his sons Cetewayo and Mbulazi.

- During the civil war between the two rival claimants to power in Zululand, Cetewayo kills his brother Mbulazi at the Battle of Tugela River.
- In U.S. Congressional elections, Democrats attain majorities in both the House (118–92) and Senate (36–20).

FEBRUARY

- The American Party, popularly known as the Know-Nothings, nominates former president Millard Fillmore for president and Tennessee politician Andrew J. Donelson for vice president.
- The new Republican Party holds its first national assembly in Pittsburgh, Pennsylvania.
18 A Reform Edict guarantees the life, honor, and property of all subjects throughout the Ottoman Empire, abolishes the civil power of the heads of the Christian churches, ends torture, provides for large-scale reform of prisons, and establishes religious freedom.
25 A peace conference to end the war in the Crimea opens in Paris, France, attended by representatives of Britain, France, Austria, the Ottoman Empire, Sardinia–Piedmont, and Russia.

MARCH

16 The birth of the Prince Imperial, Eugène Louis Jean Joseph, the son of Emperor Napoleon III, ensures there is a line of Bonapartist succession to the French throne.
30 The integrity of the Ottoman Empire is recognized by the signatories to the Treaty of Paris ending the Crimean War, which guarantees the Danubian principalities. Russia cedes Bessarabia, the Black Sea is to be neutral, and the River Danube is to be free to ships of all nations.

APRIL

15 Britain, France, and Austria guarantee the integrity and independence of the Ottoman Empire in a further treaty after signing the Treaty of Paris ending the Crimean War.
16 The Declaration of Paris abolishes privateering, defines the nature of contraband and blockade, and recognizes the principle of "free ships, free goods," moves designed to facilitate free trade even in times of war.

MAY

24 The U.S. slavery abolitionist John Brown orders the Massacre of Pottawatomie Creek in the "War for Bleeding Kansas" in the United States, in which five slavery supporters are murdered by free-staters.
27 In a liberal move, Czar Alexander II of Russia grants an amnesty (from 1848) for Polish insurgents (against Russian rule).

JUNE

- Democrats nominate former U.S. minister to Britain James Buchanan for president and Kentucky senator John C. Breckinridge for vice president.

JULY

- The U.S. adventurer William Walker becomes president of Nicaragua.
12 Austria grants an amnesty for the Hungarian insurgents of 1848–49.
14 The Spanish Liberal prime minister Baldomero Espartero is sacked by Queen Isabella II.

AUGUST

- The U.S. Congress passes copyright legislation protecting the rights of playwrights.

SEPTEMBER

- The rump of the U.S. Whig Party (most of the former Whigs having joined the new Republican Party) nominates former president Millard Fillmore and Tennessee politician Andrew J. Donelson for president and vice president, respectively.
3 An unsuccessful rising of Prussian royalists takes place in Neuchâtel canton, Switzerland (a possession of the king of Prussia that proclaimed itself a republic in 1848).
15 The Spanish prime minister Enrique O'Donnell reestablishes the liberal Spanish constitution of 1845, with the additional provision for an annual assembly of the cortes (national assembly).

OCTOBER

8 The *Arrow* Incident, when a ship flying the British flag is boarded by Chinese who arrest members of its crew, provokes the outbreak of the Second Opium War.
14 The Spanish constitution reintroduced by Prime Minister Enrique O'Donnell is annulled after his dismissal.

NOVEMBER

- Americans elect Democrat candidate James Buchanan of Pennsylvania as president of the United States.
1 War breaks out between Britain and Persia after the latter occupies the city of Herat in Afghanistan (known as "the key of India").
3–4 The British fleet bombards the Chinese port of Canton (Guangzhou) during the Second Opium War.

DECEMBER

2 The frontier between France and Spain is defined.
6 The South African Republic (Transvaal) is organized under the political leadership of Marthinius Wessel Pretorius, from the four republics of Lydenburg, Potchefstroom, Zontpansberg, and Utrecht.
12 Ramón Narváez is made prime minister in Spain following Queen Isabella II's dismissal of Enrique O'Donnell. Narváez had lost power temporarily in 1851 and was briefly exiled as special ambassador to France.

SCIENCE, TECHNOLOGY, AND MEDICINE

Ecology

- The first national storm warning system is established in France.

Science

- Austrian monk and botanist Gregor Mendel begins experiments breeding peas that will lead him to the laws of heredity.

- English chemist William Henry Perkin synthesizes the first artificial aniline dye ("mauve"). His commercial production of it the following year leads to the development of other dyes and lays the foundation of the synthetic organic chemical industry.
- French chemist and microbiologist Louis Pasteur establishes that microorganisms are responsible for fermentation, thus establishing the discipline of microbiology.
- French hydraulic engineer Henri Darcy develops a law to estimate the flow of groundwater.
- German botanist Nathaniel Pringsheim is the first to notice fertilization when he observes sperm entering the ovum in plants.
- German naturalist Johann Fuhrott discovers the first fossil remains of a Neanderthal in Quaternary bed in Feldhofen Cave near Hochdal cave above the Neander Valley, Germany. They cause immediate debate about whether they are the remains of ancient humans or the deformed bones of a modern human.
- German scientist Theodore Bilharz discovers the parasitic worm that causes schistosomiasis (bilharzia).

Technology

- English inventor Henry Bessemer obtains a patent for the Bessemer converter which converts cast iron into steel by injecting air into molten iron to remove carbon and increase the temperature of the molten mass. It allows iron to be poured and thus shaped and brings down prices.
- English mechanical engineer Joseph Whitworth designs a machine that can measure to an accuracy of 0.000001 inch.
- German-born British engineer William Siemens invents a regenerative smelting furnace which preheats the air supplied to a furnace resulting in high-temperature flames. Patented in 1858, it permits the production of ductile steel for boiler plating.
- The world's first oil refinery opens at Ploieşti, Romania.
- U.S. artist and inventor Samuel Finley Breese Morse's receiver is changed from an inker, which printed the Morse code onto a recording wheel, to a sounder, which makes an audible click which the operator translates, making the reception of messages far quicker.

Transportation

- California's first railroad connects Sacramento to Folsom.

ARTS AND IDEAS

Architecture

- The U.S. architect James Bogardus publishes *Cast-Iron Buildings: Their Construction and Advantages.*

Arts

- The English artist John Everett Millais paints *Autumn Leaves.*
- The French artist Gustave Courbet paints *Two Women on the Banks of the Seine.*
- The French artist Jean-Auguste-Dominique Ingres paints *La Source/The Spring.*
- The U.S. artist William Sidney Mt. paints *The Banjo Player.*

Literature and Language

- Christian von Bunsen's book *Signs of the Times* revives the Liberal movement in Prussia.
- The English explorer and translator Richard Burton publishes his travel book *First Footsteps in Africa.*
- The English poet Elizabeth Barrett Browning publishes her novel in verse *Aurora Leigh* (the first printing is incorrectly dated 1857).
- The English writer Coventry Patmore publishes *The Espousals,* the second part of his novel in verse *Angel in the House.* The first part appeared in 1854, and subsequent parts appear in 1860 and 1862.
- The English writer Charles Reade publishes his novel *It Is Never Too Late to Mend,* an attack on English prisons.
- The French writer Gustave Flaubert publishes his novel *Madame Bovary* in serial form. Appearing as a book in 1857, it is one of the major French novels of the 19th century.
- The German writer Eduard Friedrich Mörike publishes his tale *Mozart auf der Reise nach Prag/Mozart on His Journey to Prague.*
- The Russian writer Ivan Sergeyevich Turgenev publishes his novel *Rudin.*
- The U.S. humorist Mortimer Neal Thomson publishes *Plu-ri-bus-tah, A Song That's By No Author,* a parody of Longfellow's *Hiawatha.*
- The U.S. poet John Greenleaf Whittier publishes his collection of poems *The Panorama and Other Poems,* which contains "The Barefoot Boy."
- The U.S. writer Harriet Beecher Stowe publishes *Dred, A Tale of the Great Dismal Swamp*; although popular, its sales do not rival those of her first novel that attacked slavery, *Uncle Tom's Cabin.*
- The U.S. writer Herman Melville publishes his story collection *Piazza Tales,* which includes "Bartleby the Scrivener."

Music

- German composer Johannes Brahms completes his Prelude and Fugue in A minor for organ.
- Hungarian composer Franz Liszt completes his *Dante Symphonie/Dante Symphony.*
- The opera *Rusalka,* by the Russian composer Alexander Dargomyzhsky, is first performed in St. Petersburg, Russia. It is based on a work by the Russian poet Alexander Pushkin.
- U.S. college student Benjamin Russell Hanby writes the song "Darling Nelly Gray."

Thought and Scholarship

- The English historian James Anthony Froude publishes the first volume of his *History of England from the Fall of Wolsey to the Death of Elizabeth*. The final volume appears in 1870.
- The French historian Alexis Charles-Henri-Clérel de Tocqueville publishes the first part of *L'Ancien Régime et la révolution/The Ancient Regime and the Revolution*.
- The French historian Ernest Renan publishes *Etudes d'histoire religieuse/Studies in Religious History*.
- The German philosopher Rudolf Hermann Lotze publishes the first volume of his *Mikrokosmus/Microcosm*, which sets out his religious philosophy. The last part appears in 1864.
- The U.S. historian John Lothrop Motley publishes *Rise of the Dutch Republic*.

SOCIETY

Education

- Auburn University is founded in Auburn, Alabama.
- Charles Toussaint and Gustav Langenscheidt found the first-ever correspondence school, teaching languages, in Germany.

- German-American educator Mrs. Carl Schurz opens the first kindergarten in the United States at Watertown, Wisconsin.
- The University of Maryland is founded at College Park, Maryland.

Everyday Life

- English tailor Thomas Burberry introduces the Burberry raincoat.
- U.S. businessman and inventor Gail Borden patents condensed or evaporated milk, which contains sugar to inhibit bacterial growth.
- U.S. inventor Alexander Twinning produces ice on a commercial scale using a vapor compression machine.

Media and Communication

- The magazine *Harper's Weekly* is launched, in New York, New York, by the publishers Harper & Brothers.
- The German newspaper *Frankfurter Zeitung* is launched in Frankfurt am Main.

Religion

- Massachusetts minister Charles H. Leonard presides at the first celebration of Children's Day at the Universalist Church of the Redeemer in Chelsea, Massachusetts.

BIRTHS & DEATHS

JANUARY
12 John Singer Sargent, Italian-born U.S. painter, born in Florence, Italy (–1925).

FEBRUARY
17 (Christian Johann) Heinrich Heine (born Harry Heine), German poet, dies in Paris, France (58).
24 Nikolay Ivanovich Lobachevsky, Russian mathematician who, with János Bolyai, founded non-Euclidean geometry, dies in Kazan, Russia (63).

APRIL
5 Booker T. Washington, U.S. educator and black American spokesman between 1895 and 1915, born in Franklin County, Virginia (–1915).
24 Henri-Philippe Pétain, French general during World War I, born in Cauchy-à-la-Tour, France (–1951).

MAY
6 Robert Edwin Peary, U.S. explorer who was the first to reach the North Pole, born in Cresson, Pennsylvania (–1920).
6 Sigmund Freud, Austrian neurologist, founder of

psychoanalysis, born in Freiberg, Moravia (now Příbor, Czech Republic) (–1939).
22 Augustin Thierry, French historian, dies (61).

JUNE
22 (Henry) Rider Haggard, English novelist and creator of the character Tarzan, born in Bradenham Hall, Norfolk, England (–1925).

JULY
10 Nikola Tesla, Croatian-born U.S. electrical engineer who discovered the rotating magnetic field and invented a polyphase system of alternating current, born in Smiljan, Croatia (–1943).
23 Bal Gangadhar Tilak, Indian mathematician, philosopher, and militant nationalist, a leader of the Indian independence movement, born in Ratnagiri, India (–1920).
26 George Bernard Shaw, Irish dramatist, literary critic, and socialist propagandist, born in Dublin, Ireland (–1950).
29 Robert Schumann, German romantic composer, dies in

Endenich, near Bonn, Germany (46).

SEPTEMBER
3 Louis Sullivan, U.S. architect who designed some of the first skyscrapers, born in Boston, Massachusetts (–1924).

OCTOBER
16 Oscar Wilde, Irish poet and dramatist, born in Dublin, Ireland (–1900).

DECEMBER
11 Georgy Velentinovich Plekhanov, founder of the Marxist movement in Russia, born in Gualovka, Russia (–1918).
18 J(oseph) J(ohn) Thomson, English physicist, discoverer of the electron, born in Cheetham Hill, near Manchester, England (–1940).
22 Frank B(illings) Kellogg, U.S. secretary of state 1925–29, born in Potsdam, New York (–1937).
28 (Thomas) Woodrow Wilson, twenty-eighth president of the United States 1913–21, a Democrat, born in Staunton, Virginia (–1924).

- The English theologian Arthur Penrhyn Stanley publishes *Sinai and Palestine*.
- The English theologian Edward Bouverie Pusey publishes *The Doctrine of the Real Presence*.

Sports

- The sporting newspaper *The Spirit of the Times* refers to baseball as the "national pastime."

1857

POLITICS, GOVERNMENT, AND ECONOMICS

Business and Economics

FEBRUARY
- The U.S. Congress bans foreign coins as legal tender.

MARCH
- The U.S. Congress passes the Tariff Act, lowering import duties approximately 20%.

AUGUST
24 The New York branch of the Ohio Life Insurance and Trust Co. fails, precipitating a financial panic that slows the U.S. economy.

Human Rights

- North Carolina writer Hinton R. Helper publishes *The Impending Crisis of the South*, repudiating slavery and endorsing free labor.
- Richmond editor George Fitzhugh publishes *Cannibals All! or, Slaves Without Masters*, in defense of slavery.

JANUARY
- There should be "No union with slaveholders," cries Massachusetts abolitionist William Lloyd Garrison at the State Disunion Convention in Worcester, Massachusetts.

NOVEMBER
20 Czar Alexander II of Russia appoints a committee to study the problem of the emancipation of Russia's millions of serfs.

Politics and Government

- Michigan and Maine pass personal liberty laws designed to thwart the capture and return of fugitive slaves.

MARCH
- James Buchanan is inaugurated as the 15th president of the United States.
4 The Peace of Paris ends the Anglo-Persian war provoked by the Persian occupation of the city of Herat in Afghanistan in 1856, with the shah of Persia, Nasir Ud-Din, recognizing the independence of Afghanistan.

MAY
- The Massachusetts legislature imposes a literacy test as a requisite for voting in the commonwealth.
10 A revolt of Sepoys (Indian soldiers employed by the British East India Company) at Meerut, north India, begins the Indian Mutiny against the British, caused by ethnic discontent at British rule.
26 Under pressure from Britain and France, Prussia renounces its sovereignty over the Swiss canton of Neuchâtel.

JUNE
1 Britain's Royal Navy destroys the Chinese fleet during the Second Opium War.
6 Rebellious Indians begin their siege of the British-held north Indian city of Cawnpore (now Kanpur).
14 A commercial treaty is signed between France and Russia. France is developing freer trade and Russia is more receptive to western ideas under Czar Alexander II.
27 British soldiers and male residents of the northern Indian city of Cawnpore are executed after surrendering to their Indian besiegers, despite having been given a promise of safe-conduct.

JULY
15 British women and children, taken by Indian rebels after the surrender of the city of Cawnpore, are executed.

AUGUST
15 The Italian National Association is formed by the Italian soldier and patriot Giuseppe Garibaldi to work for Italian unification under the leadership of Sardinia–Piedmont.

SEPTEMBER
- Incited by a member of The Church of Jesus Christ of Latter-day Saints extremist, Native Americans kill 120 settlers bound for California at the Mountain Meadows Massacre in Utah.

20 The rebel-held Indian city of Delhi is captured by British forces after a siege which began in June.
25 A British force, led by Major General Henry Havelock and Sir James Outram, temporarily relieves the northern Indian city of Lucknow but cannot lift its siege by Indian insurgents.

OCTOBER

• The voters of Kansas elect an antislavery legislature in a carefully supervised territorial election.
October–December Proslavery partisans draft the Lecompton Constitution, which permits slavery, in a rigged constitutional convention held in Lecompton, Kansas. The Lecompton Constitution is approved on December 31, when antislavery Kansans refuse to partake in the referendum.
10 King Frederick Wilhelm IV of Prussia suffers a stroke.
10 The Irish Republican Brotherhood (whose members are known as Fenians) is founded in New York, New York, to fight for Irish independence from Britain.

NOVEMBER

16 British troops, under the Scottish general Sir Colin Campbell, commander of the forces in India, future field marshal and Baron Clyde, relieve the north Indian city of Lucknow, besieged by Indian rebels.

DECEMBER

6 British forces recapture the rebel-held city of Cawnpore (now Kanpur) from Indian rebel forces.
29 A combined British and French force takes the Chinese port of Canton (Guangzhou) during the Second Opium War (the French having joined the British to secure trading rights in China).

SCIENCE, TECHNOLOGY, AND MEDICINE

Agriculture

• There is widespread cattle disease in Europe.

Ecology

MARCH

21 A severe earthquake hits Tokyo, Japan, and over 107,000 people die in the ensuing fire.

JUNE

27 *Scientific American* warns that whale oil, used for lighting, may soon run out due to overhunting.

Exploration

June 1857–59 British explorers John Hanning Speke and Richard Burton explore inland east Africa, becoming the first Europeans to reach Lake Tanganyika (February 1858). Speke continues northward, and on July 30, 1858 he visits and names Lake Victoria, which he guesses to be the source of the River Nile.

Health and Medicine

• British-born U.S. physician Elizabeth Blackwell establishes the New York Infirmary for Women and Children in New York, New York, a hospital staffed entirely by women.
• English nurse Florence Nightingale, in a confidential report to the Royal Commission on the Health of the Army, gives evidence of the appalling health conditions of the British army; it leads to the establishment of the Army Medical School.

Math

June 1857–1936 English mathematician Karl Pearson introduces a number of fundamental concepts to the study of statistics.

Science

• Austrian geologist Eduard Suess declares that mountains and continents are formed by the movement of portions of the earth's crust and not simply by vertical uplift.
• French chemist and microbiologist Louis Pasteur demonstrates that lactic fermentation that spoils milk is due to a living organism.
• German mathematical physicist Rudolf Clausius develops the mathematics of the kinetic theory of heat and demonstrates that evaporation occurs when more molecules leave the surface of a liquid than return to it, and that the higher the temperature, the greater the number of molecules that will leave.

Technology

• French inventor Léon Scott de Martinville constructs the "phonoautograph." A precursor to the phonograph, it consists of a diaphragm that vibrates in response to sound and which traces a line on a rotating cylinder.
• French physicist Alexandre Becquerel develops a process of coating electric discharge tubes with luminescent materials; it eventually leads to the fluorescent lamp.
• Scottish-born Australian inventor James Harrison develops a vapor-compression machine using ether as the refrigerant. It is the first to be used in the brewing industry and for freezing meat for shipment.
• The first permanent electric street lighting is installed in the rue Impériale in Lyons, France.

MARCH

23 Elisha Graves Otis constructs a passenger lift for E. V. Haughwort and Co. in New York, New York, the first one to be installed in a department store.

Transportation

SEPTEMBER

• The U.S. steamship *Central America* sinks during a hurricane off Charleston, South Carolina, killing 470 people. Three metric tons of gold are also lost.

September 1857–71 French engineer Germain Sommeiller builds the 12-km/7-mi-long Mont Cenis Tunnel in the Alps, between France and Switzerland. He pioneers the use of compressed-air drills and, in the later stages, dynamite, in the construction of long-distance rock tunneling. A rail tunnel, it is also the first long-distance tunnel to be driven from both ends.

ARTS AND IDEAS

Architecture

- U.S. landscape architect Frederick Law Olmsted lays plans for the the 340-ha/840-acre Central Park, on the outskirts of New York. It first opens in 1858 in an uncompleted state and is officially opened in 1876.

Arts

- The French artist Jean-François Millet paints *The Gleaners*.
- The Swiss artist Arnold Böcklin paints *Pan in the Reeds*.
- The U.S. artist George Caleb Bingham paints *The Jolly Flatboatmen*.
- The U.S. artist John Frederick Kensett paints *Beacon Rock, Newport Harbor*.

Literature and Language

- British army officer Henry Creswicke Rawlinson deciphers the Mesopotamian cuneiform.
- The Austrian writer Adalbert Stifter publishes his novel *Der Nachsommer/Indian Summer*.
- The English writer Anthony Trollope publishes his novel *Barchester Towers*.
- The English writer Dinah Maria Muloch publishes her novel *John Halifax, Gentleman*.
- The English writer Elizabeth Cleghorn Gaskell publishes her *Life of Charlotte Brontë*.
- The English writer George Borrow publishes his autobiographical *The Romany Rye*.
- The English writer George Eliot publishes the stories "Scenes from Clerical Life" in *Blackwood's Magazine*. They are published as a book in 1858.
- The English writer Thomas Hughes publishes *Tom Brown's Schooldays*, which becomes a classic of English "public school" literature.
- The English writer William Makepeace Thackeray begins to publish his novel *The Virginians* (which he also illustrates) in serial form. It appears as a book in 1859.
- The French literary critic Charles-Augustin Ste.-Beuve publishes *Etude sur Virgile/A Study of Virgil*.
- The French writer Charles Baudelaire publishes his poetry collection *Les Fleurs du mal/Flowers of Evil*, one of the major works of 19th-century European poetry. It is banned for obscenity and the author, publishers, and printers are fined. An enlarged edition appears in 1861.

- The Norwegian writer Bjørnstjerne Martinius Bjørnson publishes his tale *Synnøve solbakken/Trust and Trial*.
- The U.S. essayist Ralph Waldo Emerson publishes his poem *Brahma*.
- The U.S. writer Delia Bacon publishes *The Philosophy of the Plays of Shakespeare Unfolded*, which inaugurates the "Baconian heresy"—the theory that the Elizabethan writer and statesman Francis Bacon wrote Shakespeare's plays.
- U.S. author Herman Melville publishes *The Confidence-Man*, a bleak satire on the era's egotism and commercialism.

Music

- German composer Johannes Brahms completes his Organ Prelude and Fugue in G minor.
- Hungarian composer Franz Liszt completes his *Faust Symphonie/Faust Symphony*. It is based on Goethe's verse drama *Faust*, published in 1808. He also completes his Symphonic Poem *Hunnenschlacht/Battle of the Huns*.
- The hymn "We Three Kings of Orient" is written by English-U.S. clergyman John Henry Hopkins.
- U.S. composer James Pierpont publishes the song "Jingle Bells," originally written in 1850 with the title "One-Horse Open Sleigh."

Thought and Scholarship

- Boston lecturer Henry James, Sr., publishes *Christianity the Logic of Creation*, reiterating his faith in the "the immanence of God in the unity of mankind."
- The English historian Henry Thomas Buckle publishes the first part of his *History of Civilization*. The second part appears in 1861.
- The French historian and critic Hippolyte-Adolphe Taine publishes *Les Philosophes français du dix-neuvieme siècle/French Philosophers of the 19th Century*.

SOCIETY

Education

- Illinois State University is founded in Normal, Illinois.
- Michigan State College of Agriculture opens. It is the first agricultural college in the United States.
- The Indian universities of Calcutta, Bombay, and Madras are founded.
- The University of the South is founded in Sewanee, Tennessee.

Everyday Life

- The first toilet paper, Gayetty's Medicated Paper, is launched in the United States.

- The German cartoonist and poet Wilhelm Busch begins working for the German newspaper *Fliegende Blätter*. His work over the next 12 years plays an important role in the development of cartoons, in particular the captionless comic strip.

Media and Communication

- *The Atlantic Monthly*, a journal of literature, art, and politics, is first published in Boston, Massachusetts. Its editor is the poet J. R. Lowell.

Sports

- Horse racing begins at Longchamp near Paris, France.
- The Alpine Club, a British mountaineering society, is founded. Within the next 17 years similar clubs are founded in Austria, Switzerland, Italy, Germany, and France.

BIRTHS & DEATHS

FEBRUARY

12 Eugène Atget, French photographer known for his photographs of everyday life in Paris, born in Libourne, near Bordeaux, France (–1927).

15 Mikhail Ivanovich Glinka, Russian composer, dies in Berlin, Germany (53).

18 Max Klinger, German painter and sculptor, born in Leipzig, Germany (–1920).

22 Heinrich Hertz, German physicist who studied electromagnetic waves, born in Hamburg, Germany (–1894).

22 Robert Stephenson Smyth Baden-Powell, founder of the Boy Scouts and Girl Guides, born in London, England (–1941).

26 Emile Coué, French pharmacist who introduced the phrase "Every day and in every way, I am becoming better and better" into psychotherapy, born in Troyes, France (–1926).

MARCH

11 Manuel Quintana, Spanish patriot and neoclassical poet, dies in Madrid, Spain (84).

18 Rudolf Diesel, German engineer who invented the diesel engine, born in Paris, France (–1913).

APRIL

18 Clarence Darrow, U.S. criminal lawyer who defended Tennessee schoolteacher John T. Scopes for preaching Darwinism, born near Kinsman, Ohio (–1938).

MAY

2 Alfred de Musset, French romantic poet and playwright, dies in Paris, France (46).

2 Frederick Scott Archer, English inventor who developed the wet collodion process, the first photographic process that allowed multiple copies of pictures to be made, dies in London, England (*c.* 44).

13 Ronald Ross, British bacteriologist who discovered that malaria is transmitted by mosquitos, born in Almora, India (–1932).

31 Pius XI, who was pope 1922–39, born in Desio, Lombardy, Austrian Empire (–1939).

JUNE

2 Edward Elgar, English composer, born in Broadheath, Worcestershire, England (–1934).

JULY

- Saad Zaghlul, Egyptian statesman, leader of the nationalist movement that gained Egypt's independence, born in Ibyanah, Egypt (–1927).

30 Thorstein Veblen, U.S. economist and social scientist, born in Manitowoc County, Wisconsin (–1929).

SEPTEMBER

5 Auguste Comte, French philosopher and the founder of positivism in the social sciences, dies in Paris, France (59).

13 Milton Snavely Hershey, U.S. manufacturer who founded the Hershey Chocolate Corporation, born near Hockersville, Pennsylvania (–1945).

15 William Howard Taft, twenty-seventh president of the United States 1909–13, a Republican, born in Cincinnati, Ohio (–1930).

17 Konstantin Eduardovich Tsiolkovsky, Russian aeronautics and astronautics scientist who pioneered rocket and space travel research, born in Izhevskoye, Russia (–1935).

NOVEMBER

26 Ferdinand de Saussure, Swiss linguist whose ideas about the structure of language laid the foundation of modern linguistics, born in Geneva, Switzerland (–1913).

27 Charles Scott Sherrington, English physiologist who laid the foundation for understanding the functioning of the nervous system, born in London, England (–1952).

DECEMBER

3 Joseph Conrad (pen name of Józef Teodor Konrad Korzeniowski), Polish-born British novelist whose works include *Heart of Darkness*, *Nostromo*, and *Chance*, born in Berdichev, Poland (–1924).

15 George Cayley, English engineer who founded the science of aerodynamics, dies in Scarborough, Yorkshire (now North Yorkshire), England (83).

1858

POLITICS, GOVERNMENT, AND ECONOMICS

Colonization

AUGUST

2   British Columbia in Canada is organized as a British colony following the discovery of gold there.

NOVEMBER

8   The formal independence of Montenegro is accepted by the sultan of the Ottoman Empire, together with the borders of the former Ottoman possession as fixed by France, Britain, Prussia, Russia, and the Ottoman Empire, following friction between Montenegro and the Ottomans.

Human Rights

- Alexander II begins emancipation of Russian serfs.

JULY

23 The Jews Relief Act abolishes the legal bar to Jews becoming members of the British Parliament.

AUGUST

- Illinois congressman Abraham Lincoln and Illinois senator Stephen A. Douglas, candidates for Douglas's Illinois senate seat, engage in a series of extraordinary political debates about the future of slavery in the United States. Published in newspapers around the country, the debates make Lincoln a household name.
- The U.S. Congress submits the proslavery Lecompton Constitution to the citizens of Kansas Territory for a final vote. Voters reject the document and Kansas becomes a free territory.

OCTOBER

- New York senator William Henry Seward, in a speech in Rochester, New York, labels the sectional controversy over slavery an "irrepressible conflict."

Politics and Government

- In U.S. Congressional elections, Democrats retain their majority in the Senate (38–26), but cede control of the House to Republicans (113–101).
- Kansas and Wisconsin pass personal liberty laws, designed to thwart the capture and return of fugitive slaves.

- Ottawa is designated as the capital of Canada.
- The Tokugawa shogun (military ruler) of Japan, Iesada, dies and is succeeded by Iemochi.
- U.S. president James Buchanan appoints Maine jurist Nathan A. Clifford to the U.S. Supreme Court.

JANUARY

- In an extra-legal referendum, antislavery partisans in Kansas defeat the proslavery Lecompton Constitution. The referendum has no legal influence on the U.S. federal government's deliberations on the Kansas constitution.

14 The Italian patriot Felice Orsini, who calls Napoleon III a "traitor to Italy," fails in his attempt to assassinate the French emperor.

FEBRUARY

18 The British government's Conspiracy to Murder Bill, designed to deal with foreign revolutionaries who use London, England, as a base in the aftermath of the Orsini affair (attempted assassination of Emperor Napoleon III of France by the Italian patriot Felice Orsini), is defeated.

APRIL

1   The Granadian Confederation is formed in South America from provinces in the former Colombian Federation.

MAY

- Minnesota becomes the 32nd state in the Union.

JUNE

19 Hugh Rose defeats the Indian insurgent commander Tanti Topi at Gwalior, India, during the Indian Mutiny.

26 The Treaty of Tianjin between China and Britain ends the Second Opium War, by which China opens more ports to British commerce and legalizes the opium trade. A similar treaty is signed between the Chinese and the French on June 27.

JULY

7   General Enrique O'Donnell returns to power in Spain, stabilizing politics by forming a broad-based administration containing clericals and progressives.

8   The British declare the Indian Mutiny officially at an end.

20 Emperor Napoleon III of France and Count Camillo Benso di Cavour, Prime Minister of the Italian kingdom of Sardinia–Piedmont, begin their meetings at Plombières, France, to plan the extension of French and Sardinian–Piedmontese power in Italy.

AUGUST

2   The powers of the British East India Company are transferred to the British crown. India is Britain's greatest imperial asset, and the Company is deemed inadequate to administer it after the mutiny of 1857.

19   Austria, Prussia, France, Britain, Russia, the Ottoman Empire, and Sardinia–Piedmont agree that the Ottoman possessions of Moldavia and Wallachia should be granted considerable autonomy.

26   An Anglo-Japanese commercial treaty provides for a relaxation of Japanese trade restrictions and the establishment of permanent British diplomatic representation in Japan.

OCTOBER

7   King Frederick Wilhelm IV of Prussia is declared incapable of government after suffering two strokes, and his brother Wilhelm is made regent.

DECEMBER

7   France and Spain blockade Cochin-China (now part of Vietnam) following attacks on European missionaries and traders.

23   The Serbian diet (national assembly) deposes Alexander Karageorgevič, the son of the murdered nationalist leader Kara George, and declares Milosh Obrenovič (who abdicated in June 1839) king again.

SCIENCE, TECHNOLOGY, AND MEDICINE

Exploration

MARCH

12–July 23 1864   Scottish missionary and explorer David Livingstone leads an unsuccessful mission to Africa to navigate the Zambezi River from its estuary to the Victoria Falls. Nevertheless, he successfully explores the area around Lake Nyasa, and reports optimistically on its prospects for colonization.

Health and Medicine

- British physician Henry Gray publishes *Anatomy of the Human Body, Descriptive and Surgical* (*Gray's Anatomy*). It remains the standard text in anatomy for over 100 years.
- Dutch ophthalmologist Frans Donders reports that far sightedness is due to a shortened eyeball, which results in light rays converging behind the retina. It permits the scientific manufacture of corrective lenses.
- The first powered dental drill is constructed. Invented by U.S. inventor James Beall Morrison, it is driven by a foot pedal.

Math

- English mathematician Arthur Cayley invents matrices (rectangular arrays of numbers) and studies their properties in *A Memoir on the Theory of Matrices*.

Science

- English chemists W. H. Perkin and B. F. Duppa synthesize glycine, the first amino acid to be manufactured.
- German biologist Rudolf Virchow publishes *Die Cellularpathologie in ihrer Begründung auf physiologische und pathologische Gewebenlehre/Cellular Pathology as Based upon Physiological and Pathological Histology*. In it he expands his ideas on the cell as the basis of life and disease, establishing cellular pathology as essential in understanding disease.
- German chemist August Wilhelm von Hofmann manufactures the artificial dye magenta.
- German chemist Friedrich Kekulé publishes *Uber die Konstitution und die Metamorphosen der chemischen Verbindungen und Über die chemische Natur des Kohlenstoffs/On the Constitution and Changes of Chemical Compounds and on the Chemical Nature of Carbon*, in which he shows that carbon atoms can link together to form long chains—the basis of organic molecules.
- German chemist Johann Griess, while working in an English brewery laboratory, develops the first azo dyes, a synthetic organic dye with nitrogen forming a key group (the azo group) in the dye's chemical structure.
- German physicist Hermann Ludwig von Helmholtz propounds a theory of vortex motion.
- Italian chemist Stanislao Cannizzaro differentiates the atomic and molecular weight of an element.
- Stone tools in situ with Pleistocene animals are discovered by English school-master William Pengelly at Windmill Hill Cave at Brixham, Dorset, England. They demonstrate that human beings are as old as now extinct animals, thus founding the science of prehistory.
- The U.S. social scientist Henry Charles Carey publishes the first volume of his *Principles of Social Science*. The final volume appears in 1859.

JULY

1   English naturalists Charles Darwin and Alfred Russel Wallace contribute a joint paper on the variation of species to the Linnaean Society of London, England, stating their conclusions about natural selection and evolution.

Technology

- French engineer Germain Sommeiller develops the compressed-air ram or drill.
- French inventor Louis Ducos du Hauron patents a method of making color photographs. He uses color filters and prints on zinc plates.
- Scottish physicist William Thomson invents the mirror galvanometer (patented in 1867), which is used as a telegraph receiver for underwater cables.
- South Foreland lighthouse in Kent, England, is equipped with electric arc lamps; it is the first lighthouse to be powered by electricity.
- Swedish scientist Goran Göransson redesigns English engineer Henry Bessemer's converter for making steel, increasing reliability.

- The French photographer Nadar flies his balloon *The Giant* over France taking the world's first aerial photographs.
- The Prussian army is entirely equipped with breech-loading "needle-guns," more effective than the traditional muzzle-loading rifle.
- U.S. engineer Lyman Blake invents a machine that can sew the soles of shoes to the upper part, in Abingdon, Massachusetts.

AUGUST

16 Queen Victoria of Britain and U.S. president James Buchanan are the first to exchange messages on the first successful Atlantic telegraph cable laid between Valentia, Ireland, and Newfoundland, Canada. The cable lasts for only 27 days.

Transportation

- The first asphalt street surface is laid, in Paris, France.

JANUARY

31 English engineer Isambard Kingdom Brunel's steamship *Great Eastern* is launched. With a displacement of 19,222 metric tons/18,918 tons, and 211 m/692 ft long, it is the largest ship in the world. It has two sets of engines that drive two screw propellers and two paddlewheels, and is the first steamship with a double iron hull. Its design serves as the prototype for modern ocean liners.

ARTS AND IDEAS

Architecture

- St. Patrick's Cathedral in New York, New York, designed by the U.S. architect James Renwick, is completed. It is one of the best-known examples of American Gothic Revival.
- The Cathedral of St. Isaac of Dalmatia, in St. Petersburg, Russia, designed by the French architect August Ricard Montferrand, is completed.
- U.S. inventor James Bogardus publishes *Cast Iron Buildings: Their Construction and Advantages*, which popularizes his method of constructing buildings by supporting their weight by columns rather than by walls. It is an important step in the development of skyscrapers.

Arts

- The English artist Edwin Landseer sculpts the lions for the base of Nelson's Column in Trafalgar Square, London, England.
- The U.S. artist Charles Loring Elliott paints his *Portrait of Mrs Thomas Goulding*.
- The U.S. artist James Abbot McNeill Whistler completes his set of engravings *Twelve Etchings from Nature (The French Set)*.

- The U.S. artist Martin Johnson Heade paints *Rhode Island Landscape*.

Literature and Language

- The English writer, designer, and social reformer William Morris publishes his poetry collection *The Defence of Guenevere and Other Poems*.
- The French writer Octave Feuillet publishes *Roman d'un jeune homme pauvre/Novel of a Poor Young Man*.
- The Russian writer Aleksey Feofilaktovich Pisemsky publishes his novel *Tysyacha dush/A Thousand Souls*.
- The U.S. poet Henry Wadsworth Longfellow publishes his long poem *The Courtship of Miles Standish*.

Music

- French composer César Franck completes his *Messe solennelle/Solemn Mass*.
- French composer Hector Berlioz completes his opera *Les Troyens/The Trojans*. Because of its length (five acts) it is not staged until 1863.
- German composer Johannes Brahms completes his Piano Concerto No. 1 (Opus 15).
- German composer Richard Wagner completes his *Fünf Gedichte von Mathilde Wesendonck/Five Wesendonck Songs*, settings of poems by the poet Mathilde Wesendonck.
- Hungarian composer Franz Liszt completes his Symphonic Poem *Hamlet*.
- The comic opera *Orphée aux enfers/Orpheus in the Underworld* by the German-born French composer Jacques Offenbach is first performed, in Paris, France. It is an immediate success and popularizes the French dance the cancan.
- The opera *Der Barbier von Bagdad/The Barber of Baghdad* by the German composer Peter von Cornelius is first performed, in Weimar, Germany.
- The song "The Yellow Rose of Texas" is written by a composer known only as "J. K."
- U.S. songwriter J. Warner writes the song "The Old Grey Mare (Get Out of the Wilderness)."

Thought and Scholarship

- The U.S. writer Oliver Wendell Holmes publishes *The Autocrat of the Breakfast Table*, a collection of essays that appeared in *The Atlantic Monthly* between 1857 and 1858.
- The Scottish historian Thomas Carlyle publishes the first volume of his biography *Frederick the Great*. The final volume appears in 1865.

SOCIETY

Education

- Iowa State University is founded at Ames, Iowa.
- The Cooper Union college opens in New York, New York, offering a variety of educational programs for the

working classes, funded by a donation from U.S. industrialist Peter Cooper.

Everyday Life

- About 100,000 Americans move west in reaction to the discovery of gold at two sites in the Colorado territory.
- Collectors form the Numismatic and Antiquarian Society in Philadelphia, Pennsylvania, to organize various coin collecting activities.
- English chemist Erasmus Boyd patents tonic water (sweetened soda water with quinine) in London, England.
- The English dressmaker Charles Worth launches the first fashion house, on the rue de la Paix in Paris, France.
- The U.S. branch of the Young Women's Christian Association is founded in New York, New York.
- U.S. merchant Rowland H. Macy opens the dry goods business in New York, New York, that will blossom into Macy's department store.
- U.S. metalworker John L. Mason patents a system for airtight jars in the United States, which makes the preservation of food in the home easier.

Religion

- Connecticut Congregationalist minister Horace Bushnell publishes *Nature and the Supernatural*, a repudiation of Transcendental philosophy.
- The Swiss-born U.S. biblical scholar Philip Schaff publishes the first volume of *A History of the Christian Church*. The final volume appears in 1890.

Sports

- Australian cricketer Thomas Wills and his cousin Henry Colden Harrison devise Australian Rules football, and help to form the first club, Melbourne Football Club.
- The Schuylkill Navy, which becomes the most important rowing organization in the United States, is formed in Philadelphia, Pennsylvania.

MARCH

10 Twenty-five clubs from the New York area form the National Association of Baseball Players.

JULY

20 The first known baseball admittance charges are made at a series of three games at the Fashion Race Course, Long Island, between a New York All-Star and a Brooklyn All-Star team. A crowd of around 1,500 people pay 50 cents each to watch each of the games.

BIRTHS & DEATHS

MARCH

4 Matthew Perry, U.S. naval officer who ended Japan's isolation, dies in New York, New York (63).

APRIL

- Emile Durkheim, French sociologist and founder of sociology, born in Epinal, France (–1917).
23 Max Planck, German theoretical physicist who was the originator of quantum theory, born in Kiel, in the duchy of Schleswig (–1947).
28 Johannes Peter Müller, German physiologist and philosopher, dies in Germany (56).

JUNE

10 Robert Brown, Scottish botanist who discovered Brownian motion, dies in London, England (84).

29 George Washington Goethals, U.S. army engineer who supervised the construction of the Panama Canal 1907–14, born in Brooklyn, New York, New York (–1928).

JULY

9 Franz Boas, U.S. anthropologist, the founder of relativist anthropology in the United States, born in Minden, Prussia (–1942).
14 Emmeline Pankhurst, militant English suffragist, born in Manchester, England (–1928).
26 Edward Mandell House, advisor to U.S. president Woodrow Wilson, born in Houston, Texas (–1938).

SEPTEMBER

16 Andrew Bonar Law, Canadian-born British Conservative politician, prime minister 1922–23, born in Kingston, New Brunswick, Canada (–1923).

NOVEMBER

17 Robert Owen, Welsh reformer, manufacturer, and utopian socialist, dies in Newtown, Wales (87).
20 Selma Lagerlöf, Swedish novelist, born in Mårbacka, Sweden (–1940).

DECEMBER

23 Giacomo Puccini, Italian operatic composer, born in Lucca, Tuscany, Italy (–1924).

1859

POLITICS, GOVERNMENT, AND ECONOMICS

Colonization

- Queensland secedes from New South Wales and becomes a separate British colony in Australia, with its capital at Brisbane.

Human Rights

- Harriet E. Wilson completes *Our Nig: Sketches from the Life of a Free Black, in a Two-Story White House, North, Showing That Slavery's Shadows Fall Even There*, the first novel published in the United States by a black American author.

MAY

9–19 The Southern Commercial Convention, meeting in Vicksburg, Mississippi, calls for an end to the ban on the importation of slaves, which has been in place since 1808.

OCTOBER

- Abolitionist fanatic John Brown leads 21 followers on an unsuccessful raid of the U.S. arsenal at Harper's Ferry, Virginia. Brown aims to foment an antislavery uprising among northern abolitionists, free-blacks, and fugitive slaves.

DECEMBER

- John Brown is executed for leading a raid on the U.S. arsenal at Harper's Ferry, Virginia, in October.

Politics and Government

JANUARY

19 A formal treaty of alliance is made between France and the Italian kingdom of Sardinia–Piedmont, prior to the attempt to unify much of Italy under Sardinian–Piedmontese rule.

FEBRUARY

- Oregon becomes the 33rd state in the Union.

MARCH

- The U.S. Supreme Court, in *Abelman v. Booth*, upholds the Fugitive Slave Law of 1850 in a case overturning a Wisconsin personal liberty law.

APRIL

- Elections in Britain see Liberal gains but the government of Prime Minister Edward Stanley, Lord Derby, is still in a minority.
17 A French decree offers an amnesty for political offenders and an extension of political rights. Emperor Napoleon III wants to increase Republican activity in France as a counterweight to clerical disapproval of the incorporation of the Papal States in a unified Italy.
19 Austria issues an ultimatum to the Italian kingdom of Sardinia–Piedmont to disarm unconditionally within three days.
27 A peaceful revolution occurs in the Italian state of Tuscany and Grand Duke Leopold II flees. Similar peaceful risings follow in Modena and Parma.
29 Austrian forces cross the frontier of the Italian kingdom of Piedmont to dispute Sardinian–Piedmontese plans for Italian unification.

MAY

3 France declares war on Austria in response to the Austrian invasion of the Italian kingdom of Piedmont to dispute plans for Italian unification.
22 King Ferdinand II of Naples dies, and is succeeded by Francis II.

JUNE

4 Austrian forces attempting to stop Italian unification are defeated at Magenta in Lombardy, Italy, by French troops.
12 Henry Temple, Lord Palmerston, forms a Liberal administration in Britain, following the failure of Edward Stanley, Lord Derby's, Conservative government to gain a majority in elections to the House of Commons.
14 Prussia begins to mobilize against France in support of Austria, opposing the unification of Italy.
24 Austrian forces, opposing the unification of Italy, are defeated in a decisive battle at Solferino, near Verona, Italy, by French and Piedmontese forces.

JULY

- Kansans ratify an antislavery constitution in preparation for statehood.
8 King Oscar I of Sweden dies and is succeeded by Charles XV.
11 The preliminary Peace of Villafranca temporarily ends the conflict between France and Austria. Austria is to cede the Italian states of Parma and Lombardy to France, for subsequent cession to Sardinia–Piedmont; Tuscany and Modena are to be restored to their prerevolutionary rulers, and Venice is to remain Austrian. The treaty causes the Sardinian–Piedmontese prime minister Count Camillo Benso di Cavour to resign in disgust.

OCTOBER

22 Spain declares war against the Moors in Morocco. The prime minister Enrique O'Donnell believes territorial aggrandisement at the expense of Spain's traditional enemies will prove popular.

NOVEMBER

11 The Treaty of Zürich confirms the preliminary Peace of Villafranca of July 11, formally ending the war between France and Austria.

SCIENCE, TECHNOLOGY, AND MEDICINE

Ecology

- Prospectors in western Nevada discover the so-called Comstock Lode, the nation's richest silver deposit to date.

AUGUST

28 U.S. engineer Edwin Drake drills the world's first oil well, at Titusville, Pennsylvania. Drilled to a depth of 21 m/69 ft, it produces 1,818 l/400 gal per day. His success, coinciding with a growing demand for oil products, especially kerosene, leads to further drilling.

Health and Medicine

- British physician Alfred Baring Garrod publishes *Treatise on Gout and Rheumatic Gout* in which he demonstrates that gout is caused not by overindulgence, but by an excess of uric acid in the blood which can be controlled through avoiding foods containing purine.

Math

- German mathematician Georg Friedrich Bernhard Riemann makes a conjecture about a function called the zeta function. Riemann's hypothesis is still unproved, but is an important key to understanding prime numbers.

Science

- German chemist Albert Niemann first isolates cocaine from the leaves of the coca plant *Erythroxylum coca*.
- German chemists Robert Wilhelm von Bunsen and Gustav Kirchhoff discover that each element emits a characteristic wavelength of light. It initiates spectrum analysis, a valuable tool for both chemists and astronomers.

August 1859–62 German astronomer Friedrich Argelander publishes *Bonner Durchmusterung/Bonn Survey*, a star catalog listing over 324,000 stars and their magnitudes in the northern hemisphere.

NOVEMBER

24 Charles Darwin publishes *On the Origin of Species by Natural Selection*, which expounds his theory of evolution by natural selection, and by implication denies the truth of biblical creation and God's hand in nature. It sells out immediately and revolutionizes biology.

Technology

- Belgian inventor Etienne Lenoir builds the first internal combustion engine in Paris, France. Operating on coal gas, it has only a 4% efficiency.
- French artillery officer Amédée Mannheim invents the first modern slide rule that has a cursor or indicator.
- French physicist Gaston Planté invents the electric accumulator or rechargeable storage battery. The first electric storage battery, it is now widely used in vehicles.
- U.S. businessman George Bissell distills kerosene from crude oil and markets it as lamp fuel.

Transportation

- French naval architect Stanislas-Henri-Laurent Dupuy de Lôme builds the *Gloire*, the first ironclad battleship. Its iron plates are 11 cm/4.5 in thick.

APRIL

25 Construction of the Suez Canal begins in Egypt.

ARTS AND IDEAS

Architecture

- The Church of All Saints in Margaret Street, London, England, designed by the English architect William Butterfield, is completed.
- The Red House, Bexleyheath, England, designed for the writer and artist William Morris by the English architect Philip Speakman Webb, is completed. It marks a return to vernacular traditions in building.

Arts

c. 1859 The French artist Jean-Léon Gérôme paints *The Gladiators*.

- The French artist Camille Corot paints *Macbeth*.
- The French artist Edouard Manet paints *The Absinthe Drinker*.
- The French artist Edgar Degas paints *The Belleli Family*.
- The French artist Jean-Auguste-Dominique Ingres paints *The Turkish Bath*.
- The French artist Jean-François Millet paints *The Angelus*. Through reproductions, this becomes one of the best-known images in late 19th-century France.
- The French photographer Nadar takes his *Portrait of Sarah Bernhardt*.
- The U.S. artist Eastman Johnson paints *Old Kentucky Home: Life in the South*.
- The U.S. artist Frederic Edwin Church paints *The Heart of the Andes*.
- The U.S. artist George Innes paints *Hakensack Meadows, Sunset*.

Literature and Language

- The English poet Alfred, Lord Tennyson, begins publishing his sequence of poems *Idylls of the King*, based on the legend of King Arthur. The last poem is published in 1872.
- The English writer Charles Dickens publishes his novel *A Tale of Two Cities*.
- The English writer Edward Fitzgerald publishes *The Rubaiyat of Omar Khayyam of Naishapur* anonymously. A translation of the poetry of the 12th-century Persian poet and astronomer 'Umar Khayyām, it becomes very popular.
- The English writer George Eliot publishes her novel *Adam Bede*.
- The English writer George Meredith publishes his novel *The Ordeal of Richard Feverel*.
- The French novelist Victor Hugo publishes *La Légende des siècles/The Legend of the Centuries*, short epics based on classical myths.
- The French Provençal writer Frédéric Mistral publishes his epic poem *Mirèio*.
- The Russian writer Ivan Alexandrovich Goncharov publishes his comic novel *Oblomov*.
- The Russian writer Ivan Sergeyevich Turgenev publishes his novel *Dvoryanskoye gnezdo/Home of the Gentry*.
- The U.S. writer Harriet Beecher Stowe publishes her novel *The Minister's Wooing*.

Music

- The opera *Faust* by the French composer Charles-François Gounod is first performed, in Paris, France. It is based on Goethe's verse drama *Faust*, published in 1808.
- The opera *Un ballo in maschera/A Masked Ball* by the Italian composer Giuseppe Verdi is first performed, in Rome, Italy.
- U.S. entertainer and member of the Virginia Minstrels Dan Emmett writes the song "Dixie (I Wish I Was in Dixie's Land)."

Theater and Dance

- The play *Groza/The Thunderstorm* by the Russian dramatist Alexander Nikolayevich Ostrovsky is first performed, in Moscow, Russia.
- The play *The Octoroon* by the Irish dramatist Dion Boucicault is first performed, in New York, New York. It is the first U.S. play in which a black person is portrayed seriously.

Thought and Scholarship

- The English philosopher John Stuart Mill publishes *On Liberty*. His most important work, it is an attempt to safeguard the rights of individuals in a democratic society.
- The German historian Leopold von Ranke publishes the first part of his *Englische, vornehmlich im sechzehnten und siebzehnten Jahrhundert/History of England Principally in the Sixteenth and Seventeenth Centuries*. The final part appears in 1868.
- The German political philosopher Karl Marx publishes *Zur Kritik der politischen Ökonomie/Criticism of Political Economy*.
- The Scottish philosopher Alexander Bain publishes *The Emotions and the Will*.
- The Spanish writer Pedro Antonio de Alarcón y Ariza publishes *Diario de un testigo de la guerra de Africa/Diary of a Witness of the War in Africa*, an account of a war in Morocco.

SOCIETY

Everyday Life

- The Mt. Vernon Ladies' Association dedicates George Washington's estate in Mt. Vernon, Virginia, a national shrine.
- The world's first children's playgrounds are created in Queen's and Phillips Parks in Manchester, England, when horizontal bars and swings are installed.

Sports

- The Cachar Club, the first polo club of the modern era, is founded in Assam, India.
- The Australian landowner Thomas Austin imports two dozen English rabbits so that he can shoot them for sport: the rabbits multiply rapidly, causing a major agricultural problem in Australia.

JUNE

30 The French tightrope walker Charles Blondin crosses Niagara Falls, between Canada and the United States, on a tightrope. About 25,000 people witness the crossing, which takes five minutes.

JULY

1 Amherst defeats Williams 66–32 at Pittsfield, Massachusetts, in the first ever intercollegiate baseball game.

NOVEMBER

12 Jules Leotard performs the first flying trapeze act, at the Cirque Napoléon in Paris, France. He also gives his name to the tight-fitting costume he wears.

BIRTHS & DEATHS

JANUARY

6 Samuel Alexander, Australian philosopher, born in Sydney, Australia (–1938).

9 Carrie Chapman Catt, U.S. feminist leader whose activities led to women's suffrage in the United States in 1920, born in Ripon, Wisconsin (–1947).

27 Kaiser Wilhelm II, German emperor and king of Prussia 1888–1918, born in Potsdam, near Berlin, Prussia (–1941).

28 Frederick John Ripon, Viscount Goderich, British prime minister 1827–28, a Tory, dies in Putney, Surrey, England (76).

28 William Hickling Prescott, U.S. historian, dies in Boston, Massachusetts (62).

FEBRUARY

19 Svante Arrhenius, Swedish chemist who received the Nobel Prize for Chemistry in 1903 for his discovery that certain substances dissociate in water into ions, born in Vik, Sweden (–1927).

MARCH

8 Kenneth Grahame, Scottish author of *The Wind in the Willows* (1908), born in Edinburgh, Scotland (–1932).

16 Alexander Stepanovich Popov, Russian physicist and electrical engineer who invented the radio independently of the Italian inventor Guglielmo Marconi, born in Turinskye Rudniki, Russia (–1906).

APRIL

3 Washington Irving, U.S. writer, dies in Tarrytown, New York (76).

8 Edmund Husserl, German philosopher, founder of phenomenology, born in Prossnitz, Moravia, Austrian Empire (–1938).

16 Alexis Charles-Henri-Clérel de Tocqueville, French political scientist, historian, and politician, dies in Cannes, France (53).

MAY

2 Jerome K. Jerome, English comic writer best known for *Three Men in a Boat*, born in Walsall, Staffordshire, England (–1927).

6 Alexander von Humboldt, German naturalist and explorer, dies in Berlin, Germany (89).

15 Pierre Curie, French physicist who, with his wife Marie Curie, discovered radium and polonium, born in Paris, France (–1906).

22 Arthur Conan Doyle, Scottish novelist who created the detective Sherlock Holmes, born in Edinburgh, Scotland (–1930).

JUNE

11 Klemens, Prince Metternich, Austrian statesman, dies in Vienna, Austria (86).

AUGUST

11 Christiaan Eijkman, Dutch physiologist whose discovery that beriberi is caused by a nutritional deficiency led to the discovery of vitamins, born in Nijkerk, the Netherlands (–1930).

SEPTEMBER

3 Jean Léon Jaurès, French socialist leader who united various socialist groups into one Socialist Party, born in Castres, France (–1914).

15 Isambard Kingdom Brunel, British marine engineer who built the first transatlantic steamer, the *Great Western* (1838), and the *Great Eastern* (1858), the largest ship in the world for 40 years, dies in Westminster, London, England (53).

28 Carl Ritter, German geographer who, with Alexander von Humboldt, founded the science of modern geography, dies in Berlin, Germany (80).

OCTOBER

12 Robert Stephenson, English Victorian civil engineer noted for his bridges, especially the Britannia Bridge over the Menai Strait, Wales, dies in London, England (55).

18 Henri Bergson, French philosopher who was the first to elaborate process philosophy, born in Paris, France (–1941).

20 John Dewey, U.S. philosopher and one of the main founders of pragmatism, born in Burlington, Vermont (–1952).

27 Theodore ("Teddy") Roosevelt, twenty-sixth president of the United States 1901–09, a Republican, born in New York, New York (–1919).

DECEMBER

2 John Brown, U.S. abolitionist whose antislavery campaign contributed to the initiation of the American Civil War, dies in Charleston, Virginia (59).

5 English literary critic and scholar Sidney Lee born in London, England (–1926).

5 John Jellicoe, British admiral of the fleet during World War I, born in Southampton, England (–1935).

16 Wilhelm Grimm, German author (with his brother Jacob) of *Grimm's Fairy Tales* (1812), dies in Berlin, Germany (73).

1860

POLITICS, GOVERNMENT, AND ECONOMICS

Business and Economics

- Europe buys 80% of U.S. exports.
- The leading U.S. export is baled cotton, with a value of $192 million.
- Pig-iron production stands at 3.9 million tons in Britain, 0.9 million tons in France, and 0.8 million tons in the United States.

FEBRUARY

- Shoemakers in Lynn, Massachusetts, strike for higher wages and the right to organize a union. On April 10 management accedes to the first demand, raising wages by 10%.

Colonization

APRIL

26 A peace is agreed between Spain and Morocco, ending Spain's war of attempted colonization.

JULY

7 Russia founds the port of Vladivostok in the vicinity of the Korean border as it continues to expand into Asia.

Human Rights

- U.S. writer E. N. Elliott edits *Cotton Is King* and *Pro-Slavery Arguments*.

Politics and Government

- In U.S. Congressional elections, Republicans attain majorities over Democrats in the House (105–43) and Senate (31–10).

JANUARY

20 Italian nationalist politician Count Camillo Benso di Cavour is recalled as Sardinian–Piedmontese prime minister, giving renewed hope to Italian patriots.
23 The Cobden–Chevalier Treaty (negotiated between the British Liberal politician and economist Richard Cobden and the French economist Michel Chevalier) establishes a substantial degree of free trade between Britain and France.

FEBRUARY

26 Spanish forces defeat the Moroccans at the Battle of Wadi Ras in a bid to gain territory in Morocco.

MARCH

5 The size of the Austrian Imperial Council (Reichsrat) is increased by the "March Patent," centralizing imperial control in opposition to Hungarian demands for autonomy.
11–15 Plebiscites in the Italian states of Tuscany, Emilia, Parma, Modena, and Romagna declare their populations in favor of union with Sardinia–Piedmont (a major step toward Italian unification).
17 The Second Maori War breaks out in New Zealand, arising out of grievances against British settlers encroaching on aboriginal territory.
24 Sardinia–Piedmont cedes Nice and Savoy to France by the Treaty of Turin, the price agreed at the pact of Plombières for French support of Sardinian–Piedmontese extension of power in Italy.

MAY

- Republicans nominate former Illinois congressman Abraham Lincoln for president and Maine senator Hannibal Hamlin for vice president in the United States.
- The U.S. Congress passes the Morrill Tariff Bill, which protects U.S. manufacturers from foreign competition.
5 The Italian soldier and patriot Giuseppe Garibaldi and his Redshirts ("The Thousand") sail from Genoa, northwest Italy, to attempt to complete the unification of Italy.
27 Garibaldi and his followers take the city of Palermo in Sicily in their attempt to incorporate it into the kingdom of Italy.

JUNE

- Northern Democrats meeting in Baltimore, Maryland, nominate Illinois senator Stephen A. Douglas for president and Georgia politician Herschel V. Johnson for vice president in the United States. Their choice of Johnson represents an (unsuccessful) attempt to end the schism between Northern and Southern wings of the party.
- Southern Democrats meeting in Baltimore, Maryland, nominate Kentucky senator John C. Breckinridge for president and Oregon settler Joseph Lane for vice president in the United States.
- The U.S. Congress creates the Government Printing Office.

AUGUST

12 The reforming King Danilo I of Montenegro is assassinated.
22 The Italian soldier and patriot Giuseppe Garibaldi lands on the Italian mainland to make war on the kingdom of Naples.

SEPTEMBER

5 Britain, Austria, France, Prussia, Russia, and the Ottoman Empire sign a treaty agreeing to restore order in the Ottoman province of Syria after a massacre of Christians by an Islamic sect, the Druses.

7 The Italian soldier and patriot Giuseppe Garibaldi and his followers enter Naples as part of their attempt to unify Italy, forcing King Francis II of Naples to flee.

8 A rising in favor of union with Italy begins in the Papal States.

11 King Victor Emmanuel II of Sardinia–Piedmont invades the Papal States (which he intends to annex as part of a unified Italy under his sovereignty).

18 Piedmontese forces invading the Papal States under Prime Minister Count Camillo Benso di Cavour defeat papal troops at Castelfidardo.

21 Anglo-French troops defeat Chinese forces at Ba Lizhao in the war over European trading rights in China.

OCTOBER

12 British and French forces occupy Beijing, China, in reprisal for the seizure of the British representative Harry Parkes during the war over European trading rights.

20 The October Diploma amends the Austrian constitution, restoring the federal institutions as they existed before 1848. The Hapsburg territories are granted considerable autonomy in the hope of conciliating the subject nationalities.

21–22 Plebiscites in the Italian kingdoms of Naples and Sicily support motions for union with the kingdom of Sardinia–Piedmont.

24 By the Treaty of Beijing, the Chinese ratify the Treaty of Tianjin with Britain (of June 26, 1858) and recognize the treaty of June 27, 1858 with France.

26 The revolutionary Italian patriot Giuseppe Garibaldi meets King Victor Emmanuel II of Sardinia–Piedmont near Naples and salutes him as king of Italy.

NOVEMBER

• Abraham Lincoln is elected as president of the United States, though these "States" will not remain "United" for long.

24 Emperor Napoleon III of France concedes the right of a yearly debate on government policy to the French legislature.

• South Carolina responds to the election of Abraham Lincoln as president of the United States by seceding from the Union.

DECEMBER

• Militia of the self-styled independent republic of South Carolina seize the federal arsenal and occupy Fort Moultrie and Castle Pinckney in Charleston harbor.

• To stave off imminent civil war, Kentucky senator John J. Crittenden proposes to extend the Missouri Compromise line of 36° 30′ across the nation. President-elect Abraham Lincoln, among others, helps kill the so-called Crittenden Compromise.

SCIENCE, TECHNOLOGY, AND MEDICINE

Agriculture

• U.S. scientist John Curtis publishes *Farm Insects*, the first book to deal with insect pests, and their economic impact.

Ecology

• Oil production stands at 500,000 barrels in the United States, and 8,542 barrels in Romania.

• Potassium deposits at Stassfurt, near Magdeburg, Germany, are exploited. They are the world's most important source of potash before World War I.

Exploration

December 1860–63 British adventurer John Hanning Speke returns to Lake Victoria in Africa, sponsored by the Royal Geographical Society. He and James Augustus Grant explore the lake's western shores, visit the kingdom of Buganda, and identify the Nile's exit from the lake at Ripon Falls on July 28, 1862.

AUGUST

August–June 1861 Irish settler Robert Burke and English surveyor William Wills lead an expedition out of Victoria to cross Australia from south to north. The four-man advance party turns back only a few miles from the coast of the Gulf of Carpentaria and misses the support party in the desert of Cooper Creek; only one member of the expedition, John King, survives.

Health and Medicine

c. 1860 French chemist Louis Pasteur develops the process of pasteurization: sterilizing milk and other beverages by heating to a high temperature for a few minutes to kill microorganisms.

• English nurse Florence Nightingale establishes the Nightingale School for Nurses. The first nursing school in England, it establishes nursing as a profession for women.

• French physician Etienne Lancereaux suggests that diabetes is due to a disorder of the pancreas.

• German chemists H. A. Kolbe and E. Lautemann synthesize salicylic acid, the active ingredient in aspirin, from inorganic chemicals.

• German pathologist Friedrich von Zenker describes the clinical symptoms of the disease trichinosis, caused by nematode worm larvae.

Science

c. 1860 By observing sunspots, English astronomer Richard Carrington discovers that the sun rotates faster at the equator than at the poles.

- German chemist Robert Wilhelm von Bunsen and German physicist Gustav Kirchhoff discover the element cesium (atomic no. 55).
- German physicist Gustav Fechner publishes *Elemente der Psychophysik/Elements of Psychophysics*, in which he develops experimental techniques for measuring sensations in relation to the magnitude of the stimulus.
- The chemical congress at Karlsruhe, Germany, settles the problem of atomic weights.

Technology

- English inventor Edward Alfred Cowper develops the hot-blast stove for smelting iron; it is eight times more efficient than blast-furnaces using cold air.
- English inventor R. Catchpole applies air brakes to the "patent" sails of windmills, allowing them to work in lighter winds.
- U.S. gunsmith B. Tyler Henry patents the lever-action repeating rifle. It is used widely during the American Civil War.

Transportation

- c. 1860   The open four-wheeled phaeton carriage appears, in Britain. It is driven by the rider without the need of a special driver.
- c. 1860   The Victorian two-passenger carriage appears, in Britain.
- British engineer John Russel builds the *Warrior*, the world's first iron-hulled battleship.
- The first Japanese-built steamship, the *Kanrinmaru*, is launched.
- There are 49,292 km/30,808 mi of railroad track in operation in the United States, 14,595 km/9,122 mi in Britain, 9,469 km/5,918 mi in France, and 3,200 km/2,000 mi in Canada.

ARTS AND IDEAS

Arts

- c. 1860   The U.S. artist William Page paints his *Portrait of Mrs William Page*.
- The English artist William Holman Hunt paints *The Discovery of Our Saviour in the Temple*.
- The French artist Edouard Manet paints *The Guitarist*.
- The French artist Edgar Degas paints *Young Spartans Exercising*.
- The German-born U.S. artist Emanuel Leutze completes his fresco *Westward the Course of Empire Takes its Way* in the U.S. Capitol building in Washington, D.C.
- The Swiss art historian Jakob Christoph Burckhardt publishes *Die Kultur der Renaissance in Italien/The Culture of the Renaissance in Italy*. His most important work, it has a profound effect on the study of art history.
- The U.S. artist Frederic Edwin Church paints *Twilight in the Wilderness*.

- The U.S. artist John Quincy Adams Ward sculpts *Indian Hunter*.

Literature and Language

- Dime novels, or inexpensive, mass-marketed paperback books, first appear in the United States, published by Erastus Beadle. The first such novel is *Malaeska: The Indian Wife of the White Hunter* by the U.S. writer Ann Sophia Stephens. Popular dime-novel characters include Deadwood Dick, Calamity Jane, and Kit Carson.
- The English writer Charles Dickens begins to publish his novel *Great Expectations* in serial form. It is published as a book in 1861.
- The English writer Coventry Patmore publishes *Faithful for Ever*, the third part of his novel in verse *Angel in the House*. The first and second parts appeared in 1854 and 1856, and the final part appears in 1862.
- The English writer George Eliot publishes her novel *The Mill on the Floss*.
- The English writer William Wilkie Collins publishes his novel *The Woman in White*.
- The Russian writer Ivan Sergeyevich Turgenev publishes his novel *Nakanune/On the Eve*.
- The U.S. writer Nathaniel Hawthorne publishes his novel *The Marble Faun*.
- The U.S. writer Oliver Wendell Holmes begins to publish his novel *The Professor* serially in *The Atlantic Monthly*. It is published as a book in 1861 under the title *Elsie Venner: A Romance of Destiny*.

Music

- U.S. songwriter Stephen Foster writes "Old Black Joe."

Theater and Dance

- The comedy *Le Voyage de Monsieur Perrichon/The Voyage of Monsieur Perrichon* by the French dramatist Eugène-Marin Labiche is first performed, in Paris, France. Labiche is the leading figure in the development of French farce.
- The comedy *Les Pattes de mouche/A Scrap of Paper* by the French dramatist Victorien Sardou is first performed, in Paris, France.
- The melodrama *The Colleen Bawn* by the Irish dramatist Dion Boucicault is first performed, in New York, New York.

Thought and Scholarship

- The English philosopher John Stuart publishes *A Treatise on Representative Government*.
- The French writer Charles-Forbes-René, comte de Montalembert, publishes the first volume of *Les Moines d'Occident/The Monks of the West*. The last volume appears in 1877.
- The U.S. essayist Ralph Waldo Emerson publishes his collection of lectures *The Conduct of Life*.
- The U.S. historian John Lothrop Motley publishes the first volume of his *History of the United Netherlands*. The last volume appears in 1867.

JUNE

30 At the Oxford meeting of the British Association, Bishop Samuel Wilberforce and biologist Thomas Henry Huxley debate creationism versus evolutionism.˙

SOCIETY

Education

- Louisiana State University and Agricultural and Mechanical College is founded in Baton Rouge, Louisiana.

- Olympia Brown enrolls in the theological seminary at St. Lawrence University, becoming the first American woman to study theology alongside men.
- U.S. educator Elizabeth Palmer Peabody opens the first English-speaking kindergarten in Boston, Massachusetts.

Everyday Life

- British publisher Jeremiah Smith invents the self-adhesive envelope.
- John Newnham invents the snap fastener in England.

BIRTHS & DEATHS

- George Washington Carver, U.S. agricultural chemist who transformed agriculture in the U.S. Southwest by developing over 300 products from peanuts, born near Diamond Grove, Missouri (–1943).

JANUARY

10 Charles Roberts, Canadian nationalist poet, editor, and novelist, born in Douglas, New Brunswick, Canada (–1943).

17 Anton Chekhov, Russian writer and dramatist known for his mastery of the short story, born in Taganrog, Russia (–1904).

25 Charles Curtis, U.S. Republican politician, vice president under Herbert Hoover 1929–33, born in Kansas Territory (now Kansas) (–1936).

MARCH

13 Hugo Wolf, Austrian composer, born in Windischgraz, Austria (–1903).

19 William Jennings Bryan, U.S. lawyer, three-time Democratic presidential candidate, and prosecuting attorney in the Scopes trial against Tennessee schoolteacher John T. Scopes for teaching Darwinism, born in Salem, Illinois (–1925).

24 Ii Naosuke, Japanese feudal lord who was responsible for Japan signing the Perry Convention of 1854 ending Japan's isolationist policy, is ambushed and killed in Edo, Japan (44).

APRIL

7 W(ill) K(eith) Kellogg, U.S. industrialist who founded the W. K. Kellogg company to manufacture breakfast cereals, born in Battle Creek, Michigan (–1951).

MAY

2 Theodor Herzl, Hungarian-born Austrian Zionist who promoted an international effort to establish a Jewish homeland, born in Budapest, Hungary (–1904).

9 J(ames) M(atthew) Barrie, Scottish dramatist and novelist, author of *Peter Pan*, born in Kirriemuir, Scotland (–1937).

21 Willem Einthoven, Dutch physiologist who developed the electrocardiograph, born in Semarang, Java, Netherlands East Indies (–1927).

31 Walter Sickert, German-born English painter, most important of the English impressionists, born in Munich, Germany (–1942).

JUNE

23 Baldwin Spencer, English anthropologist who worked with the Australian Aborigines, born in Stretford, Lancashire, England (–1929).

JULY

1 Charles Goodyear, U.S. inventor who discovered how to vulcanize rubber, dies in New York, New York (59).

7 Gustave Mahler, Austrian composer, born in Kalište, Bohemia, Austrian Empire (–1911).

20 British educator and reformer Margaret McMillan born in New York, New York (–1931).

AUGUST

20 Raymond Poincaré, French statesman, prime minister in 1912, and president of the Third Republic during World War I, born in Barle-le-Duc, France (–1934).

SEPTEMBER

6 Jane Addams, U.S. social reformer and Nobel Peace Prize winner in 1931, born in Cedarville, Illinois (–1935).

13 John J. Pershing, U.S. Army general, commander of the U.S. Expeditionary Force in Europe during World War I, born in Laclede, Missouri (–1948).

13 Ralph Connor (Charles William Gordon), Canadian author and Presbyterian minister, born in Glengarry County, Ontario, Canada (–1937).

21 Arthur Schopenhauer, German philosopher, dies in Frankfurt am Main, Germany (72).

OCTOBER

5 Alexey Stepanovich Khomyakov, Russian poet who led the Slavophile movement which lauded the Russian way of life, dies in Ryazan, near Moscow, Russia (56).

12 Elmer Ambrose Sperry, U.S. inventor who developed the gyroscopic compass and stabilizers now used in most guidance and stabilizing systems, born in Cortland, New York (–1930).

NOVEMBER

18 Ignacy Paderewski, Polish pianist, composer, and statesman, prime minister of Poland in 1919, born in Kuryłówka, Russian Poland (–1941).

DECEMBER

14 George Hamilton-Gordon, Earl of Aberdeen, British prime minister 1852–56, dies in London, England (76).

19 James Andrew Dalhousie, British governor-general of India 1847–56 who conquered and annexed most of the independent states on the subcontinent, dies in Dalhousie Castle, Scotland (48).

- The British Adulteration of Food Law is passed after medical testimony that some food coloring is fatally poisonous.
- The U.S. Census lists the nation's population at 31,443,321, up from approximately 23,261,000 in 1850.

APRIL

3 The Pony Express begins mail service between St. Louis, Missouri, and Sacramento, California. Riders change horses at 157 stations along the 2,897-km/1,800-mi route and mail takes ten days. Within a few months it is made obsolete by the establishment of the transcontinental telegraph system.

Religion

- The *Catholic Times* newspaper is launched in Britain.
- The Russian Orthodox Church establishes a monastery and a hospice in Jerusalem, Israel.

Sports

- The game of croquet is introduced into the United States from England.
- The Olympic Country Club, one of the world's first athletic clubs, is founded in San Francisco, California.

APRIL

4 A vast crowd assembles at a field in Farnborough, England, to watch a prize fight between Tom Sayers of England and John C. Heenan of the United States. The bout lasts 42 rounds and ends as a draw.

OCTOBER

17 A 3-round 36-hole strokeplay competition for professional golfers at Prestwick, Scotland, regarded as the first British Open golf championship, is won by Scottish golfer Willie Park, Sr.

♦

1861

POLITICS, GOVERNMENT, AND ECONOMICS

Business and Economics

- Michaux et Cie, the first bicycle manufacturing company, opens in Paris, France.
- U.S. banker Jay Cooke founds the investment banking house Jay Cooke & Co. in Philadelphia, Pennsylvania, which will help finance the Union war effort.
- Coal production stands at 83.6 million tons in Britain, 6.8 million tons in France, and 0.3 million tons in Russia.
- Iron production stands at 3.7 million tons in Britain, 2.8 million tons in the United States, and 0.2 million tons in Germany.

1861–65 The United States, or the North, has a booming economy during the Civil War as production and profits soar. There is inflation, too; prices rise 117% and wages rise just 43%.

AUGUST

- The U.S. Congress passes an income tax levy to help defray the cost of the Civil War, the first national income tax in the United States.

Colonization

FEBRUARY

25 French forces defeat the Vietnamese at Jiloa, enabling France to expand into Cochin-China (part of modern Vietnam).

MARCH

18 Spain reannexes its former West Indian colony of San Domingo at the island's request.

Human Rights

MARCH

3 An edict emancipating serfs on private Russian estates is proclaimed, ending the medieval practice which ties them to their landlords.

OCTOBER

23 Serfs on royal estates in Russia are partially liberated following the emancipation of serfs on private land earlier in the year.

Politics and Government

October 1861–65 800,000 people emigrate to the United States during the Civil War.

JANUARY

- Alabama, Florida, Georgia, Louisiana, and Mississippi secede from the Union.
- Kansas becomes the 34th state in the Union, notwithstanding the rash of southern state secessions.

American Civil War (1861–65)

1861

APRIL

- The Union Navy begins a largely effective blockade of the Confederate coastline, which will last throughout the war.
- 12–14 Confederate forces fire on the federal garrison at Fort Sumter, Charleston, South Carolina, at 4:30 am, thus inaugurating the American Civil War.
- 19 U.S. president Abraham Lincoln responds to what he calls the southern "insurrection" by calling for 75,000 volunteers for a three-month term. In response, Virginia secedes from the Union.

JULY

- 21 Union and Confederate forces clash at Bull Run (Manassas, in Confederate parlance), Virginia, in the first real engagement of the American Civil War. At first, Union troops appear to gain the advantage, but Confederate reinforcements turn the Union army on its heels.

NOVEMBER

- 1 Lincoln names George B. McClellan to succeed Winfield Scott as commander of the U.S. Army. Scott retired the previous day.

1862

FEBRUARY

- 6 Union general Ulysses S. Grant captures Fort Henry on the Tennessee River from the Confederates in the American Civil War.

MARCH

- 8–9 The Confederate warship *Merrimack* and the ironclad warship *Virginia* sink the Union *Cumberland* and *Congress* at Hampton Roads, Virginia, but are forced to withdraw by the ironclad Union vessel *Monitor*, in the first battle between two ironclad warships.

APRIL

- 6 Union and Confederate soldiers clash at Shiloh, Tennessee, with the Union forces getting the better of the battle by the end of the second day. Each side suffers roughly 10,000 casualties.

MAY

- 1 Union naval forces under the command of Captain David Farragut seize the strategic port of New Orleans, Louisiana, near the mouth of the Mississippi River.

JUNE

- 1 Confederate president Jefferson Davis appoints Robert E. Lee commander of the Confederate Army of Northern Virginia.
- 25–July 1 In a series of engagements known as the Seven Days Battles, Union general George B. McClellan encounters Robert E. Lee just outside Richmond, Virginia. Despite gaining the advantage six out of seven days, McClellan's forces never proceed to Richmond, the Confederate capital.

JULY

- Union major general David Hunter marshals fugitive slaves into Union ranks. They become the first black American troops to participate in the Civil War.
- 12 The U.S. Congress creates the Medal of Honor to reward noncommissioned officers and privates for heroism.

- 22 Lincoln informs his cabinet that he will issue a proclamation emancipating slaves in territories in rebellion against the United States as an exigency of war.

AUGUST

- 29–30 In the Second Battle of Bull Run (known to Confederates as Second Manassas), Confederate forces effectively block a Union advance on the Confederate capitol, Richmond, Virginia.

SEPTEMBER

- 17 In the Battle of Antietam, Maryland, (Sharpsburg, in Confederate parlance), the Union army foils a Confederate advance on Washington, D.C. Some 23,000 soldiers fall on this, the war's costliest day of fighting. President Lincoln uses the Union "victory" as a pretext for issuing the Emancipation Proclamation five days later.
- 22 Lincoln announces that he will emancipate the slaves as a war measure, to take effect from January 1, 1863. The proclamation applies only to slaves in Confederate-held territory—in other words, slaves over whom Lincoln has no practical jurisdiction whatsoever.

NOVEMBER

- 5 Frustrated by the leadership of General George B. McClellan, Lincoln relieves McClellan as commander of the Army of the Potomac, replacing him with Ambrose E. Burnside.

DECEMBER

- 13 At the Battle of Fredericksburg, Virginia, out-manned Confederate forces repel another Union advance on the Confederate capitol at Richmond. In one of its worst defeats, the Union suffers nearly 13,000 casualties.

1863

JANUARY

- 1 The Emancipation Proclamation goes into effect, but it "frees" slaves only in territory held by the Confederacy.

MARCH

- 3 The U.S. Congress passes a conscription act, requiring male citizens and would-be citizens between the ages of 20 and 45 to register for the draft. The legislation allows conscripts to buy a substitute for a fee of $300.

MAY

- 2–4 In one of the most humiliating Union defeats of the war, 60,000 Confederate troops defeat a Union force over twice that size at the Battle of Chancellorsville. The Confederacy suffers the most grievous loss, however, as the outstanding Confederate general Thomas "Stonewall" Jackson is mortally wounded by one of his own men and dies on May 10.
- 22–July 4 Union forces under Ulysses S. Grant begin a siege of the last major Confederate stronghold on the Mississippi River, the fortress at Vicksburg, Mississippi.

JULY

- 1–December 19 The Union Army raises 997,127 soldiers in four different conscription efforts.
- 4 Union forces under Grant capture the Confederate stronghold of Vicksburg, Mississippi, establishing Union control of the entire Mississippi River.

13–16 Antidraft riots erupt in New York, New York, mainly over the Conscription Act's provision for wealthy conscripts to buy their way out of military service. Some 1,000 people are killed or wounded, many of them black Americans.

SEPTEMBER

19–20 Confederate forces under Braxton Bragg win a clear but strategically indecisive victory over a Union army commanded by William Rosecrans at the Battle of Chickamauga, Tennessee. The Confederacy loses 18,000 men, the Union 16,000.

NOVEMBER

19 Lincoln delivers the Gettysburg Address at the dedication of the Civil War cemetery at Gettysburg, Pennsylvania. He reiterates the principles of freedom, equality, and democracy embodied in the U.S. constitution.

23–25 Union forces attain command of a crucial railroad junction at the Battle of Chattanooga, Tennessee, thus strengthening the Union's grip on Confederate supply lines.

DECEMBER

8 Lincoln offers amnesty to southerners willing to take an oath of loyalty to the United States.

1864

DECEMBER

- The mansion and grounds of Confederate general Robert E. Lee and his wife Mary, in northern Virginia, are confiscated by the Union government, and portions are used for a cemetery for Union soldiers. After the end of the Civil War, the site becomes Arlington National Cemetery.

FEBRUARY

17 The Confederate submarine *Hunley* sinks the Union warship *Housatonic* in the first successful submarine assault in history.

MARCH

10 Lincoln appoints Ulysses S. Grant general in chief of the U.S. Army.

APRIL

12 Confederate troops under the command of Nathan Bedford Forrest massacre black American Union soldiers captured in the Confederate seizure of Fort Pillow, Tennessee.

20 Reports of atrocities at Confederate prison camps prompt the Union War Department to reduce rations in Union prison camps.

MAY

5–6 At the Battle of the Wilderness, near Spotsylvania, Virginia, Union and Confederate forces fight a costly draw, dashing the hopes of a decisive victory on both the Northern and Southern home-fronts.

JUNE

- At the Battle of Cold Harbor, Virginia, a Confederate army repels a Union army nearly twice its size. In the aftermath, Union general Grant begins a prolonged siege of Petersburg, Virginia, that will last to the end of the war.

SEPTEMBER

- Union forces under William Tecumseh Sherman occupy Atlanta, Georgia.

OCTOBER

- In a daring raid designed to damage Union morale and thereby influence the presidential election, Confederate lieutenant Bennett H. Young robs three banks in the town of St. Albans, Vermont. After failing to set light to the town, Young and his mavericks retreat to Canada, where they are arrested.

NOVEMBER

- American voters in the Union states reelect Abraham Lincoln as president.

- Confederate arsonists attempt unsuccessfully to set fire to New York, New York.

- Union general William Tecumseh Sherman begins his notorious march through Georgia, starting from Atlanta and marching toward Savannah.

DECEMBER

- Sherman's forces occupy Savannah, Georgia, minutes after the Confederate defenders depart.

1865

FEBRUARY

- Columbia, South Carolina, is burned, though debate rages whether the fires were set by advancing Union soldiers or the retreating Confederate army.

- The Confederate Congress transfers complete control of the Confederate military from President Jefferson Davis to the commander of the Army of Northern Virginia, Robert E. Lee.

18 The Confederate port of Charleston, South Carolina, besieged by the U.S. Navy since 1861, surrenders.

MARCH

- Confederate commander Robert E. Lee requests an audience with his Union counterpart Ulysses S. Grant to discuss peace terms. President Lincoln refuses the request.

- Confederate president Jefferson Davis signs legislation providing for the conscription and arming of slaves.

3 At the Battle of Five Forks, Confederate general Robert E. Lee attempts unsuccessfully to break the Union siege of Petersburg, Virginia. Lee's effort having failed, the Confederates retreat to Richmond.

APRIL

- In the face of a Union onslaught, Lee orders the evacuation of the Confederate capital, Richmond, Virginia.

- Union forces capture Richmond, Virginia after four years of trying.

9 The Confederate Army of Northern Virginia under Robert E. Lee surrenders to Union general Ulysses S. Grant at Appomattox Courthouse, Virginia.

26 Confederate forces under Joseph E. Johnston surrender to the Union forces at Durham, North Carolina.

MAY

26 The surrender of the last Confederate army at Shreveport, near New Orleans, Louisiana, ends the American Civil War.

2 King Frederick Wilhelm IV of Prussia dies and is succeeded by his brother Wilhelm I.

- South Carolina, Mississippi, Florida, Alabama, Georgia, and Louisiana form the Confederate States of America in a constitutional convention at Montgomery, Alabama.

- Texas secedes from the Union.

- The Confederate Provisional Congress selects Mississippi senator Jefferson Davis as president and Georgia congressman Alexander Stephens as vice president.

8 The British chancellor of the Exchequer, William Ewart Gladstone, introduces the Post Office Savings Bill to enable small savings to be invested through the Post Office.

8 Union forces seize Roanoke Island, North Carolina.

13 King Francis II of Naples surrenders at the fortress of Gaeta in Naples to the revolutionary Italian patriot Giuseppe Garibaldi's forces, which are attempting to unify Italy by force.

18 The Italian parliament proclaims Victor Emmanuel II of Sardinia–Piedmont king.

26 The Austrian political system is centralized by the "February Patent" which gives greater power to the central parliament, Emperor Franz Josef having decided to bring Hungary under closer control.

27 The "Warsaw Massacre" takes place when a Polish crowd demonstrating against Russian rule is fired on in Warsaw by Russian troops.

MARCH

- Abraham Lincoln is inaugurated as 16th president of the United States.

- In one of his last acts in office, U.S. president James Buchanan signs legislation creating the Nevada Territory.

- The Confederate Congress adopts the Confederate constitution, which maintains state sovereignty and protects slavery. It also adopts the so-called "Stars and Bars," the Confederate Flag.

17 The kingdom of Italy is formally proclaimed by the first Italian parliament, with Victor Emmanuel II of Sardinia–Piedmont as king.

APRIL

12–14 Confederate forces fire on the federal garrison at Fort Sumter, Charleston, South Carolina, at 4:30 am, thus inaugurating the American Civil War.

19 The Union Navy begins a largely effective blockade of the Confederate coastline, which will last throughout the war.

- U.S. president Abraham Lincoln responds to what he calls the southern "insurrection" by calling for 75,000 volunteers for a three-month term. In response, Virginia secedes from the Union.

10 Finland obtains a constitution from Russia.

MAY

- Arkansas and North Carolina secede from the Union.

- Richmond, Virginia, becomes the capital of the Confederate States of America.

JUNE

- Tennessee secedes from the Union.

25 Sultan Abdul Mejid of the Ottoman Empire dies and is succeeded by his brother Abdul Aziz.

JULY

- Union and Confederate forces clash at Bull Run (Manassas, in Confederate parlance), Virginia, in the first real engagement of the American Civil War. At first, Union troops appear to gain the advantage, but Confederate reinforcements turn the Union army on its heels.

AUGUST

21 The Hungarian diet (national assembly) is dissolved after opposition to the "February Patent" introduced by the Austrian parliament to limit its power, government subsequently being carried out by an Imperial Commission.

SEPTEMBER

- The Union Navy wins the first naval battle of the Civil War, which occurs at Pensacola, Florida.

2 Prussia concludes a commercial treaty with China at the Chinese port of Tianjin.

OCTOBER

31 A London Convention is agreed between Britain, Spain, and France to protect their interests in Mexico, following its suspension of payments of foreign debts.

NOVEMBER

- Union forces seize Port Royal Island, off the southern coast of South Carolina.

1 U.S. president Abraham Lincoln names George B. McClellan to succeed Winfield Scott as commander of the U.S. Army. Scott retired the previous day.

11 Emperor Napoleon III of France grants a limited extension of the financial powers of the French legislature.

11 King Pedro V of Portugal dies and is succeeded by Louis I.

DECEMBER

23 Sultan Abdul Aziz of the Ottoman Empire agrees to the unification of the Ottoman provinces of Moldavia and Wallachia as Romania.

SCIENCE, TECHNOLOGY, AND MEDICINE

Agriculture

- Hungarian-born U.S. viticulturist Agoston Haraszthy de Mokcsa introduces over 300 different varieties of grape vines into California, initiating the state's wine industry.

Ecology

- There is severe flooding in Warsaw, Poland, due to excessive rainfall.

Exploration

December, 1861–62 Scottish settler and explorer John McDouall Stuart successfully crosses the Australian continent from south to north, from Adelaide to Arnhem Land near modern Port Darwin, after five preparatory expeditions since 1858.

Health and Medicine

- French microbiologist Louis Pasteur develops the germ theory of disease.
- French surgeon Paul Broca discovers that articulate speech is controlled in the front temporal regions of the brain. Discovered while operating on a speech-impaired man with a brain tumor, it is the first time the localization of brain function has been demonstrated. The area is now known as the convolution of Broca.

Science

- Belgian chemist Ernest Solvay patents a method for the economic production of sodium carbonate (washing soda) from sodium chloride, ammonia, and carbon dioxide. Used to make paper, glass, and bleach, and to treat water and refine petroleum, it is a key development in the Industrial Revolution. The first production plant is established in 1863.
- English chemist William Crookes discovers the element thallium (atomic no. 81).
- English entomologist H. W. Bates publishes his paper "Contributions to the Insect Fauna of the Amazon Valley," in which he describes many of the over 14,000 insects (8,000 of which had previously been unknown) that he has collected.
- German chemists Robert Wilhelm von Bunsen and Gustav Kirchhoff discover the alkali metal rubidium (atomic no. 37) by means of spectrum analysis.
- German physicist Gustav Kirchhoff determines the composition of the sun's atmosphere by analyzing its spectrum.
- German zoologist Max Schultze defines the cell as consisting of protoplasm and a nucleus, a structure he recognizes as fundamental in both plants and animals.
- Irish telegrapher Joseph May observes that the electrical resistance of instruments made from selenium is affected by sunlight; a phenomenon subsequently used in the construction of televisions.
- Scottish chemist Thomas Graham develops a process for separating gases by atmolysis which is based on the principle that different molecules diffuse through a semipermeable membrane at different rates.
- The fossil remains of *Archaeopteryx* are found at Solnhofen, Germany. The earliest known bird, it has many reptilian features and is 55–190 million years old.

Technology

- Australian inventor T. S. Mort builds the first machine-chilled cold store at Sydney, Australia.
- English inventor Thomas Walker refines the patent log for measuring the distance and speed of ships.

- German engineer Nikolaus August Otto constructs an internal combustion engine that runs on gasoline.
- German physicist Johann Reis transmits musical tones over 100 m/300 ft using a device he calls a telephone.
- Scottish physicist James Clerk Maxwell demonstrates that color photographs can be produced by photographing through three primary-color filters and then combining the images.

December 1861–70 Kerosene lamps come into widespread use as kerosene becomes plentiful and whale oil scarce. They are safer, cleaner, more efficient, and easier to operate than earlier oil lamps.

JANUARY

15 U.S. inventor Elisha Graves Otis invents a steam elevator.

Transportation

- French inventor Pierre Michaux and his son Ernst construct the first successful bicycle with pedals. The pedals are attached to the front wheel, and because it has steel tires and no springs it is called the "bone-shaker."

January 1861–65 Railroads play a major role in a war for the first time, during the American Civil War.

OCTOBER

- The U.S. Navy begins construction of the *Monitor*, one of the world's first steel-hulled warships.

ARTS AND IDEAS

Architecture

- The State Capitol in Columbus, Ohio, designed by the U.S. architect Thomas Ustick Walter, is completed.

Arts

- The U.S. artist George Innes paints *Delaware Water Gap*.
- The U.S. artist John Quidor paints *Embarkation from Communipaw*.
- The U.S. photographer Mathew Brady, working with teams of photographers, takes over 3,500 photographs of the American Civil War. These vivid images of the horrors of the conflict have a profound effect on the image of war in the public mind.

Literature and Language

- Former slave Harriet A. Jacobs publishes her memoir *Incidents in the Life of a Slave Girl*.
- The English writer Charles Reade publishes his novel *The Cloister and the Hearth: A Tale of the Middle Ages*.
- The English writer George Eliot publishes her novel *Silas Marner*.

- The English writer Mrs. Henry Wood publishes her novel *East Lynne*, which becomes an international best seller.
- The French writer Charles Baudelaire publishes the second, enlarged, edition of his poetry collection *Les Fleurs du Mal/Flowers of Evil*.
- The Russian lexicographer and folklorist Vladimir Ivanovich Dahl publishes *Tolkovyi slovar' zhivogo veliko-russkogo yazyka/Dictionary of the Living Russian Tongue*, the first major Russian dictionary.
- The Russian writer Fyodor Mikhaylovich Dostoyevsky publishes his novel *Unizhennyye i oskorblyonnyye/The Insulted and Injured*.

Music

- A revised version of the opera *Tannhäuser und der Sängerkrieg auf Wartburg/Tannhäuser and the Singing Contest of Wartburg* by the German composer Richard Wagner is first performed, in Paris, France. The original version appeared in 1845, in Dresden, Germany.
- English composer and church organist William Monk writes the hymn "Abide With Me," using words by Scottish clergyman Henry Lyte.
- French composer Georges Bizet completes his orchestral work *Scherzo et marche funèbre/Scherzo and Funeral March*.
- The Royal Academy of Music is founded in London, England.

Thought and Scholarship

- The English jurist Henry James Sumner Maine publishes *Ancient Law*.
- The German political philosopher Ferdinand Lassalle publishes *System der erworbenen Rechte/System of Assigned Rights*.
- The Italian historian Pasquale Villari publishes his *Storia di Gerolamo Savonarola/The Life of Savonarola*.

SOCIETY

Education

- The English social scientist Herbert Spencer publishes *Education, Moral, Intellectual, Physical*.
- The Massachusetts Institute of Technology opens in Cambridge, Massachusetts.
- The University of Washington is founded in Seattle, Washington.
- Vassar College is founded in Poughkeepsie, New York.
- Yale University in New Haven, Connecticut, confers the nation's first Ph.D.

BIRTHS & DEATHS

JANUARY
14 Mehmed VI, last sultan of the Ottoman Empire 1918–22, born (–1926).

FEBRUARY
15 Alfred North Whitehead, English mathematician and philosopher, born in Ramsgate, Kent, England (–1947).

APRIL
4 John McLean, U.S. Supreme Court justice, dies in Cincinnati, Ohio (76).
8 Elisha Graves Otis, U.S. inventor who built the first safety elevator, dies in Yonkers, New York (49).

MAY
6 Rabindranath Tagore, Bengali poet and mystic, born in Calcutta, India (–1941).
19 Nellie Melba, Australian soprano, born in Richmond, near Melbourne, Australia (–1931).

JUNE
6 Count Camillo Benso di Cavour, Italian politician who was instrumental in bringing about the unification of Italy, dies in Turin, Italy (50).

19 Douglas Haig, Earl Haig, British field marshal who commanded the British forces in France during most of World War I, born in Edinburgh, Scotland (–1928).
20 Frederick Gowland Hopkins, English biochemist who discovered vitamins, born in Eastbourne, East Sussex, England (–1947).
30 Elizabeth Barrett Browning, English poet and wife of the English poet Robert Browning, dies in Florence, Italy (55).

AUGUST
8 William Bateson, English biologist who founded the science of genetics, born in Whitby, Yorkshire (now North Yorkshire), England (–1926).

OCTOBER
10 Fridtjof Nansen, Norwegian explorer, oceanographer, and statesman, born in Store-Frøen, near Christiania (now Oslo), Norway (–1930).
25 Friedrick Karl Savigny, German jurist, dies in Berlin, Germany (81).

NOVEMBER
2 Georgy Yevgenyevich Lvov, Russian social reformer and head of the first Russian provisional government after the Russian Revolution in 1917, born in Popovka, near Tula, Russia (–1925).
6 James A. Naismith, Canadian-born U.S. physical education director who invented the game of basketball, born in Almonte, Ontario, Canada (–1939).

DECEMBER
4 Lillian Russell, U.S. actress and singer, born in Clinton, Iowa (–1922).
8 William Crapo Durant, U.S. industrialist who founded General Motors, born in Boston, Massachusetts (–1947).
14 Albert, Prince Consort, advisor, and husband of Queen Victoria of the United Kingdom of Great Britain and Ireland, dies in Windsor, Berkshire, England (42).

Everyday Life

- Isabella Beeton writes her *Book of Household Management*, a comprehensive domestic manual for housewives and mothers in Britain based on her articles in the *Englishwoman's Domestic Magazine*.
- The population of Russia is 76 million, 32 million in the United States, 25 million in Italy, 23.1 million in Britain, and 5.7 million in Ireland.

October 1861–70   Emigration to the United States from Britain totals 606,896; from Ireland it is 435,779.

Media and Communication

- A telegraph wire is strung across the United States between New York, New York, and San Francisco, California; it follows the route of the pony express which it now makes redundant.
- Jessie White Mario becomes the first female foreign correspondent for a newspaper when she writes on post-unification Italy for the *Morning Star* in London, England.

AUGUST

- The *New York Post* newspaper loses its postal privileges for 18 months because of its open hostility to the Union's war effort.

Religion

- The German Catholic theologian Johann Joseph Ignaz von Döllinger publishes *Über Kirche und Kirchen: Papsthum und Kirchenstaat/The Church and the Churches: Papacy and the Church State*, which attacks papal claims to temporal power.

Sports

- Deerfoot, a Seneca Native American foot racer, tours Britain and wins all his races.

NOVEMBER

- The Melbourne Cup horse race, the premier race in Australian flat racing, is run for the first time.

◆

1862

POLITICS, GOVERNMENT, AND ECONOMICS

Politics and Government

- In U.S. Congressional elections, Republicans retain majorities in the U.S. House (103–80) and Senate (39–12).
- The U.S. Congress establishes the Agriculture Department.
- U.S. president Abraham Lincoln appoints jurists David Davis of Illinois, Noah H. Swayne of Ohio, and Samuel F. Miller of Iowa to the U.S. Supreme Court.

JANUARY

14   The Prussian parliament refuses to vote for increases in the army budget, beginning a standoff between King Wilhelm I and parliament.

FEBRUARY

2   France purchases the towns of Menton and Roquebrune from Monaco, extending its influence in southern Europe.

6   The Union general Ulysses S. Grant captures Fort Henry on the Tennessee River from the Confederates in the American Civil War.

MARCH

8–9   The Confederate warship *Merrimack* and the ironclad warship *Virginia* sink the Union *Cumberland* and *Congress* at Hampton Roads, Virginia, but are forced to withdraw by the ironclad Union vessel *Monitor*, in the first battle between two ironclad warships.

10   Britain and France recognize the independence of Zanzibar, the commercial center of east and central Africa.

APRIL

6   Union and Confederate soldiers clash at Shiloh, Tennessee, with the Union forces getting the better of the battle by the end of the second day. Each side suffers roughly 10,000 casualties.

MAY

1   Union naval forces under the command of captain David Farragut seize the strategic port of New Orleans, Louisiana, near the mouth of the Mississippi River.

5   Mexican troops heavily defeat a French force attempting to enforce the payment of Mexico's debts at the Battle of Puebla.

11   The Confederate ironclad warship *Virginia* is scuttled in Norfolk, Virginia by retreating Confederate troops, after

being defeated in the first battle between ironclad warships on March 8 by the Union *Monitor*.

20 U.S. president Abraham Lincoln signs the Homestead Act, providing settlers with 160 acres of land at a nominal fee in order to spur development of the West.

JUNE

1 Confederate president Jefferson Davis appoints Robert E. Lee commander of the Confederate Army of Northern Virginia.

5 The Treaty of Saigon is signed between France and Annam (part of modern Vietnam) by which France annexes half of Cochin-China (also part of modern Vietnam), which has been under blockade since 1858.

15 Ottoman troops bombard Belgrade, Serbia, after a Serb rising against Ottoman rule.

25–July 1 In a series of engagements known as the Seven Days Battles, Union general George B. McClellan encounters Confederate general Robert E. Lee just outside Richmond, Virginia. Despite gaining the advantage on six out of seven days, McClellan's forces never proceed to Richmond, the Confederate capital.

JULY

• Union major general David Hunter marshals fugitive slaves into Union ranks. They become the first black American troops to participate in the Civil War.

2 U.S. president Abraham Lincoln signs the Morrill Act, providing states with 30,000 acres of land per senator and congressman on which to erect agricultural and industrial colleges.

11 U.S. president Abraham Lincoln appoints Henry W. Halleck general in chief of the Union army.

12 The U.S. Congress creates the Medal of Honor to reward noncommissioned officers and privates for heroism.

22 The U.S. president Abraham Lincoln informs his cabinet that he will issue a proclamation emancipating slaves in territories in rebellion against the United States as an exigency of war.

AUGUST

2 A commercial treaty is signed between France and Prussia, continuing the development of free trade in Europe.

20 Imperial Chinese forces led by the U.S. adventurer Frederick Ward defeat the Taiping rebels at the Battle of Tzeki, near Shanghai.

29 The Italian soldier and patriot Giuseppe Garibaldi attempts to conquer Rome and make it part of Italy, but is captured at Aspromonte by Italian troops sent to protect the papacy and forestall foreign intervention.

29–30 In the Second Battle of Bull Run (known to Confederates as Second Manassas), Confederate forces effectively block a Union advance on the Confederate capitol, Richmond, Virginia.

SEPTEMBER

15 Confederate general Thomas "Stonewall" Jackson seizes the Union arsenal at Harper's Ferry, Virginia.

17 In the Battle of Antietam, Maryland (Sharpsburg, in Confederate parlance), the Union army foils a Confederate advance on Washington, D.C. Some 23,000 soldiers fall on this, the war's costliest day of fighting. President Abraham Lincoln uses the Union "victory" as

a pretext for issuing the Emancipation Proclamation five days later.

22 The conservative German politician Otto von Bismarck is appointed chancellor of Prussia by King Wilhelm I to deal with the impasse created between the king and parliament on increases in military spending.

22 The U.S. president Abraham Lincoln announces that he will emancipate the slaves as a war measure, to take effect from January 1, 1863. The proclamation applies only to slaves in Confederate-held territory—in other words, slaves over whom Lincoln has no practical jurisdiction whatsoever.

29 The Prussian chancellor Otto von Bismarck makes a speech in the Prussian parliament in which he declares that Germany will be united by "Blood and Iron" (rather than liberal good intentions).

OCTOBER

7 The Prussian diet (state assembly) again rejects an increase in the military budget and is adjourned, so that Chancellor Otto von Bismarck rules without a budget for four years.

22 The garrison in Athens, Greece, revolts against the incompetent government of King Otto I.

NOVEMBER

5 Frustrated by the leadership of General George B. McClellan, President Abraham Lincoln relieves McClellan as commander of the Army of the Potomac, replacing him with Ambrose E. Burnside.

DECEMBER

4 Britain, France, and Russia agree not to fill the vacant Greek throne with a member of their royal families.

13 At the Battle of Fredericksburg, Virginia, out-manned Confederate forces repel another Union advance on the Confederate capitol at Richmond. In one of its worst defeats, the Union suffers nearly 13,000 casualties.

31–January 2, 1863 At the Battle of Murfreesboro, Tennessee, Union and Confederate forces fight to a bloody draw, with each side sustaining some 9,000 casualties.

SCIENCE, TECHNOLOGY, AND MEDICINE

Agriculture

MAY

20 The U.S. Congress passes the Homestead Act, reducing the price of western lands and contributing to a westward agricultural expansion.

Health and Medicine

• Dutch ophthalmologist Frans Cornelius Donders discovers that astigmatism is caused by the distorted shape of the cornea which diffuses light rays instead of focusing them.

- U.S. doctor Dio Lewis publishes *The New Gymnastics for Men, Women, and Children* in the United States, a popular book that stresses the link between physical activity and good health.

Science

c. 1862 English astronomer Warren de la Rue takes stereoscopic photographs of the sun and moon.
- French archeologist Ferdinand Fouqué begins the excavation of Santorini, Greece, which was destroyed by the eruption of Thera about 2000 BC. He discovers houses and pottery decorated with frescoes indicating the existence of an ancient Aegean culture previously unknown.
- French microbiologist Louis Pasteur demonstrates that ammonia is produced by the fermentation of urea by the microscopic organism *Micrococcus ureae*.
- German chemist Friedrich Wöhler discovers that water decomposes calcium carbonate into lime and acetylene.
- German biochemist Ernst Felix Hoppe-Seyler prepares hemoglobin in crystalline form.
- German botanist Julius von Sachs proves that starch is produced by photosynthesis.
- Scottish physicist William Thomson, using the earth's temperature, estimates the earth to be between 20 and 400 million years old.
- Scottish-born German astronomer Johann von Lamont discovers the electrical current within the earth's crust.
- Swedish physicist Anders Ångström discovers that the sun's atmosphere contains hydrogen.
- U.S. astronomer Alvan Clark observes the companion star of Sirius—the first white dwarf to be discovered.

Technology

- French engineer Alphonse Beau de Rochas patents a four-stroke internal combustion engine, although it is never built.
- English engineer John Allen demonstrates a high-speed horizontal steam engine at the London International Exhibition; its speed is double that of other engines and it serves as a model for subsequent high-speed engines.
- French inventor Pierre Michaux patents the ball bearing, which is first used in bicycles.
- Joseph Brown constructs a universal milling machine.
- U.S. engineer Charles Ellet builds a steam-powered ram. Union forces use it to gain control of the Mississippi River during the American Civil War.

NOVEMBER
- U.S. inventor Richard Gatling patents a ten-barrel, crank-operated machine gun; it can fire 320 rounds per minute.

Transportation

- Belgian-born French inventor Etienne Lenoir constructs the first automobile with an internal combustion engine and makes a 10-km/6-mi trip.
- The U.S. Congress passes the Pacific Railroad Act, authorizing construction of the first transcontinental railroad.

JANUARY
30 Swedish-born U.S. engineer John Ericsson's ironclad warship *Monitor* is launched. Steam-powered and propeller-driven, and with an armored revolving gun turret, its design sets the pattern for future warships.

MAY
9 The first steel rails are laid down at the Camden Goods Station in London, England, manufactured by Henry Bessemer and Company.

ARTS AND IDEAS

Architecture

- The Town Hall in Halifax, Yorkshire (now West Yorkshire), England, designed by the English architect Charles Barry, is completed.

Arts

c. 1862 The French artist Honoré Daumier paints *Third Class Carriage*.
- The English artist Augustus Egg paints *Travelling Companions*.
- The English artist William Powell Frith paints *The Railway Station*.
- The French artist Edouard Manet paints *Lola de Valence* and *Olympia*, a painting of a naked prostitute. Refused by the official Academy, it is exhibited in 1863 at the "Salon des Refusés," where it causes a public outcry.
- The U.S. artist James Abbot McNeill Whistler paints *Symphony in White No 1: The Girl in White*.
- The U.S. artist Sanford Robinson Gifford paints *Kauterskill Clove*.

Literature and Language

- The English writer Coventry Patmore publishes *The Victories of Love*, the final part of his novel in verse *Angel in the House*. Earlier parts appeared in 1854, 1856, and 1860.
- The English writer Christina Georgina Rossetti publishes her poetry collection *Goblin Market and Other Poems*.
- The English writer George Meredith publishes his sonnet sequence *Modern Love*.
- The French writer Gustave Flaubert publishes his historical novel *Salammbô*.
- The French writer Victor Hugo publishes his novel *Les Misérables*.
- The Russian writer Fyodor Mikhaylovich Dostoyevsky publishes his novel *Zapiski iz myortvogo domo/Notes from the House of the Dead*.
- The Russian writer Ivan Sergeyevich Turgenev publishes his novel *Ottsy i deti/Fathers and Sons*. Depicting the conflict between conservatives and radicals, the book is attacked by both.

The Automobile (1862–1900)

1862

- Belgian-born French inventor Etienne Lenoir constructs the first automobile with an internal combustion engine and makes a 10-km/6-mi trip.

1875

- Austrian engineer Siegfried Marcus builds one of the first automobiles powered by gasoline. It is the oldest existing automobile.

1876

- German engineer Nikolaus Otto patents the four-stroke internal combustion engine, the prototype of modern engines. Its development marks the beginning of the end of the age of steam. More than 30,000 are built in the following decade.

1882

- German engineer Gottlieb Daimler builds a gasoline engine.

1885

- Belgian-born French inventor Etienne Lenoir develops the electrical spark plug.

January 26 German mechanical engineer Karl Friedrich Benz patents a three-wheeled vehicle powered by a two-cycle, single-cylinder internal combustion engine, pioneering the development of the automobile. His vehicle achieves a speed of 14.4 kph/9 mph.

1887

March 4 Gottlieb Daimler fits his engine to a four-wheeled carriage to produce a four-wheeled automobile.

1891

- French inventors René Panhard and Emile Levassar create a vehicle to a design which becomes the basis for modern automobiles, by putting the engine at the front (which improves traction for the front wheels) and by replacing the typical leather drive-belt with a transmission, gear shift, and clutch. It is the first vehicle to be designed as an automobile rather than a modified "horseless" carriage.

1894

- U.S. inventor Elmer Ambrose Sperry begins to make the first electric automobiles built in the United States.

1895

- French bicycle tire manufacturer Edouard Michelin introduces his pneumatic automobile tires.

1896

June 4 U.S. industrialist Henry Ford tests his "Quadricycle" automobile, in Detroit, Michigan. It consists of a buggy frame mounted on four bicycle wheels and is powered by a four horsepower internal combustion engine.

1897

- German engineer Rudolf Diesel produces a 25-horsepower compression engine. Its high efficiency and simple design make it an immediate success.

1898

- The French firm of Renault Frères produces the first automobile to have the transmission connected directly to the engine. It has three forward and one reverse gears, which are selected with a gear shift.

1900

November 10 The first U.S. National Automobile Show opens at Madison Square Gardens, New York, New York, with 31 exhibitors.

Music

- Hungarian composer Franz Liszt completes his orchestral work *Mephistowaltzer/Mephisto Waltz* No. 1 and oratorio *Die Legende von der heilige Elisabeth/The Legend of St. Elizabeth*.
- The opera *Béatrice et Bénédict* by the French composer Hector Berlioz is first performed, in Paris, France. It is based on Shakespeare's *Much Ado about Nothing*.
- The opera *La forza del destino/The Force of Destiny* by the Italian composer Giuseppe Verdi is first performed, in St. Petersburg, Russia.
- U.S. abolitionist and poet Julia Ward Howe writes the lyrics for "The Battle Hymn of the Republic," which are set to the tune of the hymn "Glory, Glory, Hallelujah," attributed to William Steffe.

Theater and Dance

- The French actress Sarah Bernhardt makes her début at La Comédie Française in Paris, France.

Thought and Scholarship

- Black American Episcopal minister Alexander Crummell publishes *The Future of Africa*.
- Designer and conservationist Frederick Law Olmsted publishes *The Cotton Kingdom, a Traveler's Account of Life in the American South*.
- Swiss humanitarian Henri Dunant, in his book *Un Souvenir de Solferino/A Memory of Solferino*, proposes the establishment of international relief societies. It leads to the founding of the first Red Cross societies in 1864.
- The English diplomat and historian Henry Creswicke Rawlinson publishes the first volume of *The Five Great Monarchies of the Ancient Eastern World*. The final volume appears in 1867.
- The English philosopher John Stuart Mill publishes *Utilitarianism*, an influential work on moral philosophy.
- The English social scientist Herbert Spencer publishes *The First Principles*.
- The English writer and art critic John Ruskin publishes *Unto this Last*, essays on political economy.
- The German socialist Ferdinand Lassalle's *The Working-Man's Programme* advocates a system of state socialism.

SOCIETY

Education

- The University of South Dakota is founded in Vermillion, South Dakota.

Everyday Life

- The first casino opens in Monte Carlo, Monaco.
- The International Exhibition, a world trade fair, takes place in London, England.

- U.S. bartender Jerry Thomas creates the Dry Martini cocktail in San Francisco, California.
- The Peabody Trust is set up by U.S. philanthropist George Peabody to promote housing for the poor.

Sports

- The first ever hockey club, Blackheath Hockey Club, is formed at Blackheath, London, England.

DECEMBER

25 A baseball game between Union army teams at Hilton Head, South Carolina, is watched by an estimated crowd of 40,000 people.

BIRTHS & DEATHS

JANUARY

10 Samuel Colt, U.S. firearms manufacturer who invented the Colt revolver, dies in Hartford, Connecticut (47).

18 John Tyler, tenth president of the United States 1841–45, a Whig, dies in Richmond, Virginia (71).

23 David Hilbert, German mathematician, born in Königsberg, Prussia (now Kaliningrad, Russia) (–1943).

24 Edith Wharton, U.S. author, born in New York, New York (–1937).

29 Frederick Delius, English composer, born in Bradford, Yorkshire (now West Yorkshire), England (–1934).

MARCH

28 Aristide Briand, 11 times prime minister of France and winner of the Nobel Peace Prize in 1926, born in Nantes, France (–1932).

31 Arthur Griffith, Irish journalist and nationalist, founder of Sinn Féin (1905) and president of the Irish Republic (1922), born in Dublin, Ireland (–1922).

APRIL

3 James Clark Ross, British naval officer who explored the Arctic and Antarctic, dies in Aylesbury, Buckinghamshire, England (61).

6 Albert Sydney Johnston, Confederate general and the designated second in command of all Confederate forces at the beginning of the Civil War, is killed in battle at Shiloh, Tennessee (59).

MAY

6 Henry David Thoreau, U.S. essayist, poet, and philosopher, dies in Concord, Massachusetts (44).

JULY

2 William Bragg, English physicist who shared with his son, (William) Lawrence Bragg, the 1915 Nobel Prize for Physics for work in X-ray crystallography, born in Wigton, Cumberland, England (–1942).

14 Gustav Klimt, Austrian painter, born in Vienna, Austria (–1918).

24 Martin Van Buren, eighth president of the United States 1837–41, a Democrat, dies in Kinderhook, New York (79).

AUGUST

5 Joseph Merrick, the "Elephant Man," severely deformed professional "freak," born in Leicester, England (–1890).

19 (Auguste) Maurice Barrès, influential French writer and

politician, born in Charmes-sur-Moselle, France (–1923).

22 Claude Debussy, French composer, born in St.-Germain-en-Laye, France (–1918).

29 Maurice Maeterlinck, Belgian Symbolist poet and playwright, born in Ghent, Belgium (–1949).

SEPTEMBER

11 O. Henry (pen name of William Sydney Porter), U.S. short-story writer and novelist, born in Greensboro, North Carolina (–1910).

27 Louis Botha, first prime minister of South Africa 1910–19, born in Greytown, Natal (–1919).

OCTOBER

19 Auguste Lumière, French inventor who, with his brother Louis, developed the Cinématographe, the first practical film camera and projector, born in Besançon, France (–1954).

NOVEMBER

15 Gerhart Hauptmann, German poet, playwright, and novelist, born in Bad Salbrunn, Silesia, Prussia (–1946).

DECEMBER

23 Henri Pirenne, Belgian educator and scholar, born in Verviers, Belgium (–1935).

1863

POLITICS, GOVERNMENT, AND ECONOMICS

Business and Economics

FEBRUARY

25 The U.S. Congress passes the National Banking Act, creating a system of federally chartered banks.

Colonization

AUGUST

11 A French protectorate is formally established over Cambodia, extending French influence in southeast Asia.

Politics and Government

- The pro-European king of Madagascar, Radama II, is overthrown and killed.
- U.S. president Abraham Lincoln appoints California jurist Stephen J. Field to the U.S. Supreme Court.

JANUARY

- U.S. president Abraham Lincoln orders his officers to respect the right to religious worship in Union-occupied Confederate territory.
1 The Emancipation Proclamation goes into effect, but it "frees" slaves only in territory held by the Confederacy.
22 A Polish insurrection against Russian rule begins when the Polish National Committee, a conspiratorial body, publishes a manifesto demanding the reconstitution of an independent Polish state.
22 On the death of Muhammad Said, Ismail (son of the former khedive Ibrahim) becomes khedive of Egypt.

FEBRUARY

3 Greece elects Prince Alfred, second son of Queen Victoria of Britain, as its king in succession to the deposed King Otto, but the British government rejects this decision because of its agreement with France and Russia of December 4, 1862 proscribing undue influence in Greece.
8 Prussia allies with Russia to suppress the Polish revolt through a convention drawn up by Gustav, Count von Alvensleben, chief advisor to the Prussian king Wilhelm I (the "Alvensleben Convention").

24 The U.S. Congress establishes the Arizona Territory from part of the New Mexico Territory.
27 Enrique O'Donnell resigns as Spanish prime minister, ending a period of liberalism in Spanish politics.

MARCH

3 Russian-ruled Poland is divided into provinces in an attempt to break up nationalist feeling.
3 The U.S. Congress creates the Idaho Territory.
3 The U.S. Congress passes a conscription act, requiring male citizens and would-be citizens between the ages of 20 and 45 to register for the draft. The legislation allows conscripts to buy a substitute for a fee of $300.
30 Prince William of Denmark is recognized as king of Greece and takes the title of George I.

MAY

- The Finnish diet (national assembly) is reconstructed by Czar Alexander II of Russia in return for Finnish opposition to the Polish rebellion against Russian rule.
2–4 In one of the most humiliating Union defeats of the war, 60,000 Confederate troops defeat a Union force over twice that size at the Battle of Chancellorsville. The Confederacy suffers the most grievous loss, however, as the outstanding Confederate general Thomas "Stonewall" Jackson is mortally wounded by one of his own men and dies on May 10.
4 Maori risings begin again in New Zealand in protest at the actions of British settlers.
22–July 4 Union forces under Ulysses S. Grant begin a siege of the last major Confederate stronghold on the Mississippi River, the fortress at Vicksburg, Mississippi.

JUNE

- The anti-Western Japanese Choshu clan fire on French, U.S., and Dutch ships in Japanese waters.
1 The Liberal opposition gains many seats in the French election in protest at Emperor Napoleon III's foreign policies.
1 U.S. president Abraham Lincoln defends the right of the *Chicago Times* to publish a speech unflattering to him and supportive of the Confederacy.
6 Civil war breaks out in Afghanistan on the death of its ruler, Dost Muhammad, between his son Sher Ali and his grandson (Sher Ali's nephew) Abd ʾar-Rahman.
7 French forces take Mexico City in their bid to bring Mexico under French control.
20 West Virginia, separated from Virginia during the Civil War, becomes the 35th state in the Union.

JULY

1–December 19, 1864 The Union Army raises 997,127 soldiers in four different conscription efforts.
4 Union forces under Ulysses S. Grant capture the Confederate stronghold of Vicksburg, Mississippi,

establishing Union control of the entire Mississippi River.

13–16 Antidraft riots erupt in New York, New York, mainly over the Conscription Act's provision for wealthy conscripts to buy their way out of military service. Some 1,000 people are killed or wounded, many of them black Americans.

AUGUST

15 British naval forces bombard Kagoshima, the capital of the Japanese Satsuma clan, after Britain fails to obtain satisfaction for the Satsuma murder of a British subject.

16 The German princes meet in Frankfurt to reform the German Confederation on lines favorable to Austria and its allies, but nothing is agreed as Austria opposes liberal demands (championed by Prussia) for a popular franchise.

SEPTEMBER

19–20 Confederate forces under Braxton Bragg win a clear but strategically indecisive victory over a Union army commanded by William Rosecrans at the Battle of Chickamauga, Tennessee. The Confederacy loses 18,000 men, the Union 16,000.

NOVEMBER

11 The French politician Adolphe Thiers forms the Third Party in France to oppose Napoleon III's imperial rule.

14 A conference opens between Britain, France, Austria, Russia, and Prussia to decide on the status of the British-held Ionian Islands.

15 King Frederick VII of Denmark dies and is succeeded by his liberal son Christian IX, who is determined to pursue his father's policies with regard to the duchy of Schleswig.

18 King Christian IX of Denmark signs the new Danish constitution incorporating the duchy of Schleswig into Denmark.

19 U.S. president Abraham Lincoln delivers the Gettysburg Address at the dedication of the Civil War cemetery at Gettysburg, Pennsylvania. He reiterates the principles of freedom, equality, and democracy embodied in the U.S. constitution.

23–25 Union forces attain command of a crucial railroad junction at the Battle of Chattanooga, Tennessee, thus strengthening the Union's grip on Confederate supply lines.

DECEMBER

8 U.S. president Abraham Lincoln offers amnesty to southerners willing to take an oath of loyalty to the United States.

SCIENCE, TECHNOLOGY, AND MEDICINE

Ecology

- The first modern weather maps are published by the Paris Observatory.

AUGUST

13–15 Three days of earthquakes in Peru and Colombia cause 70,000 deaths.

Exploration

- Dutch explorer Alexandrine-Pieternella-Françoise Tinné explores the Bahr al-Ghazal, a network of swamps in southern Sudan that feed the White Nile.

Health and Medicine

- French parasitologist Casimir-Joseph Davaine shows that anthrax is due to the presence of rodlike microorganisms in the blood. It is the first disease of animals and humans to be shown to be caused by a specific microorganism.
- French physiologist Etienne-Jules Marey invents the sphygmomanometer to record blood pressure graphically. It is still used today.
- Over 30,000 people die in Britain from an epidemic of scarlet fever.

Science

- English astronomer William Huggins uses the spectra of stars to show that they are composed of the same elements that exist on the earth and the sun.
- English biologist Thomas Henry Huxley publishes *Evidence as to Man's Place in Nature*, in which he demonstrates that gorillas and chimpanzees are anatomically closer to humans than monkeys.
- English geologist Charles Lyell publishes *The Geological Evidence for the Antiquity of Man*, in which he provides evidence for human evolution.
- German chemist Adolf von Baeyer synthesizes barbituric acid, the first barbiturate drug.
- German chemist J. Willbrand discovers the chemical explosive trinitrotoluene (TNT). It is not used as an explosive until 1904.
- German physicist Hermann Ludwig von Helmholtz publishes *On the Sensation of Tone As a Physiological Basis or a Theory of Music*, in which he traces sensations through the sense organs and nerves to the brain.

MARCH

3 The National Academy of Sciences is established in the United States. It acts as an adviser to the U.S. government in scientific and technological matters.

Technology

- English geologist Henry Clifton Sorby examines the microstructure of steel, leading to the development of metallurgy as a science.
- Italian physicist Giovanni Caselli patents the "pantelegraph": a device consisting of two separated, but synchronized, pendulums with metallic pointers, one of which traces a message on a metal plate and the other of which makes a copy of it—the first facsimile machine. The Paris–Lyon telegraph line in France is used to provide a public telefacsimile service, using this device.

- U.S. businessman Samuel Van Syckel constructs the world's first oil pipeline. About 5 cm/2 in in diameter, it connects his refinery to the railroad station in Pitthole, Pennsylvania, 11 km/7 mi away.
- U.S. crude petroleum production reaches 2,611,000 barrels per year.

Transportation

- French engineer Jean-Jacques Farcot develops an automatic hydraulic-linkage device for controlling a ship's rudder from the bridge—the first servomechanism.
- New Zealand's first railroad opens, between Christchurch and Ferrymead.
- U.S. railroad engineers establish the Brotherhood of Locomotive Engineers, the nation's first railroad union.

JANUARY

10 The Metropolitan Railway opens between Faringdon Street and Bishops' Road, Paddington, in London, England. The world's first subway system, it is 6 km/3.75 mi long, uses steam locomotives, and carries 9.5 million passengers during the first year.

OCTOBER

10 French aeronaut Félix Nadar ascends above Paris in his giant balloon *Le Géant*, which is equipped with a complete photographic laboratory.

ARTS AND IDEAS

Architecture

- The Befreiungshall (Hall of Liberation)—a Greek-style temple commemorating German liberation from the empire of Napoleon I, near Kelheim, Germany— designed by the German neoclassical architect Leo von Klenze, is completed.
- The Heinrichshof building, designed by the Danish architect Theophil von Hansen, is completed in Vienna, Austria.
- The Propyläea in Munich, Germany, a monumental gateway designed by the German architect Franz Karl Leo von Klenze, is completed.

Arts

- c. 1863 The French artist Edgar Degas paints his *Portrait of Thérèse Degas, Duchess Morbilli*.
- French emperor Napoleon III orders a special exhibition in Paris of works of art refused by the Academy—the "Salon des Refusés."
- The Dutch artist Johan Barthold Jongkind paints *Le Havre*.

- The English artist and poet Dante Gabriel Rossetti paints *Beata Beatrix/Blessed Beatrix*.
- The French artist Edouard Manet paints *Déjeuner sur l'herbe/Luncheon on the Grass*. It causes an outcry when it is exhibited in the Salon in 1865, where it is condemned as badly painted and obscene because of its composition of nude female figures and male figures in everyday dress. He also paints *Spanish Dancers*.
- The German artist Hans von Marées paints *Diana Bathing*.
- The U.S. artist Albert Bierstadt paints *The Rocky Mountains, Lander's Peak*.
- The U.S. artist David Gilmour Blythe paints *Libby Prison*.
- The U.S. artist Elihu Vedder paints *The Questioner of the Sphinx*.
- The U.S. artist John Frederick Kensett paints *View Near West Point on the Hudson River*.
- The U.S. artist Thomas Crawford completes *The Progress of Civilization*, sculptures for the pediment of the United States Capitol in Washington, D.C.

Literature and Language

- The English writer Charles Kingsley publishes his children's classic *The Water Babies*.
- The French historian and critic Hippolyte-Adolphe Taine publishes *Histoire de la littérature anglaise/ History of English Literature*.
- The French philosopher and lexicographer Maximilien-Paul-Emile Littré publishes the first part of his *Dictionnaire de la langue française/Dictionary of the French Language*. The final part appears in 1872.
- The French writer Charles Baudelaire publishes his essay "*Le Peintre de la vie moderne*"/"The Painter of Modern Life." A study of the French artist Constantin Guy, it is an important work in the development of modernism.
- The Hungarian writer Mór Jókai publishes his novel *Az új földesúr/The New Landlord*.
- The Russian writer Leo Tolstoy publishes his novel *Kazaki/Cossacks*.
- The U.S. writer Nathaniel Hawthorne publishes his essay collection *Our Old Home: A Series of English Sketches*.

Music

- German composer Johannes Brahms completes his piano work *Variations on a Theme by Paganini* (Opus 35).
- The opera *Les Pêcheurs de perles/The Pearl Fishers* by the French composer Georges Bizet is first performed, in Paris, France. It is first performed in Britain in 1887 (in London, England), and in the United States in 1893 (in Philadelphia, Pennsylvania).
- The opera *Les Troyens/The Trojans* by the French composer Hector Berlioz is first performed, in Paris, France. Because of its length it is staged as two operas: *La Prise de Troie/The Sack of Troy* and *Les Troyens à Carthage/The Trojans at Carthage*.
- U.S. composer Patrick Sarsfield Gilmore writes the song "When Johnny Comes Marching Home."

Thought and Scholarship

- The English historian Samuel Rawson Gardiner publishes the first volume of his *History of England from the Accession of James I*. The final volume appears in 1901.
- The English historian Alexander William Kinglake publishes the first volume of his eight-volume *History of the War in the Crimea*. The final volume appears in 1887.
- The French historian Ernest Renan publishes his *Vie de Jésus/Life of Jesus*. The book is controversial because it treats Jesus as a purely historical figure and denies any supernatural aspects to his life. He also publishes the first volume of his *Histoire des origines du christianisme/History of the Origins of Christianity*. The final volume appears in 1904.

SOCIETY

Education

- Boston College is founded as a Jesuit university in Chestnut Hill, Massachusetts.

Everyday Life

- A roller-skating craze takes off in the United States and Europe, lasting until the 1870s.
- English inventor Frederick Walton patents linoleum in London, England.
- German inventor Johann Faber develops the propelling pencil.
- The French company Source Perrier launches its naturally carbonated Perrier mineral water.

BIRTHS & DEATHS

JANUARY

1   Pierre, Baron de Coubertin, French administrator responsible for the revival of the Olympic Games and who serves as the first president of the International Olympic Committee 1896–1925, born in Paris, France (–1937).

17 David Lloyd George, Welsh Liberal politician, British prime minister 1916–22, born in Manchester, England (–1945).

17 Konstantin Stanislavsky, Russian actor, director, and producer who founded the Moscow Arts Theater, born in Moscow, Russia (–1938).

19 Werner Sombart, German historical economist, born in Ermsleben, Saxony, Prussia (–1941).

FEBRUARY

9   Anthony Hope (pen name of Anthony Hope Hawkins), English novelist best known for *The Prisoner of Zenda* (1894), born in London, England (–1933).

20 French painter, printer, and designer Lucien Pissarro, son of Camille Pissarro (1830–1903), born (–1944).

27 George Herbert Mead, U.S. Pragmatist philosopher, born in South Hadley, Massachusetts (–1931).

MARCH

12 Gabriele D'Annunzio, Italian writer and politician, born in Pescara, Italy (–1938).

27 Frederick Henry Royce, English industrialist, joint founder of the Rolls-Royce company, born in Huntingdonshire, England (–1933).

APRIL

29 William Randolph Hearst, U.S. newspaper publisher, born in San Francisco, California (–1951).

MAY

10 Thomas "Stonewall" Jackson, one of the ablest Confederate generals in the American Civil War, dies from pneumonia in Guiney's Station, Virginia, eight days after being accidentally shot by one of his own men (39).

JULY

10 Clement Clarke Moore, U.S. scholar of Hebrew, teacher, and author of the children's Christmas ballad "A Visit From St. Nicholas" (also known as "The Night Before Christmas"), dies in Newport, Rhode Island (83).

26 John Crittenden, U.S. politician, dies in Frankfort, Kentucky (75).

26 Sam Houston, U.S. politician, president of the Republic of Texas 1836–38 and 1841–44, dies in Huntsville, Texas (70).

30 Henry Ford, U.S. industrialist who developed the mass-production of cheap Ford cars, born in Wayne County, Michigan (–1947).

AUGUST

13 (Ferdinand-Victor-) Eugène Delacroix, French romantic painter of historical and contemporary events, known for his use of color, dies in Paris, France (65).

SEPTEMBER

17 Alfred de Vigny, French romantic poet, novelist, and dramatist, dies in Paris, France (66).

20 Jacob Grimm, German author (with his brother Wilhelm) of *Grimm's Fairy Tales* (1812), dies in Berlin, Germany (78).

23 Arthur Henderson, British Labour politician who was one of the main organizers of the Labour Party, born in Glasgow, Scotland (–1935).

NOVEMBER

14 Leo Hendrik Baekeland, Belgian-born U.S. inventor of Bakelite, born in Ghent, Belgium (–1944).

21 Arthur Quiller-Couch ("Q"), English poet and anthologist who compiled *The Oxford Book of English Verse* 1900, born in Bodmin, Cornwall, England (–1944).

DECEMBER

7   R. W. Sears, U.S. mail-order merchant who developed the large retail company Sears, Roebuck, and Co., born in Stewartville, Minnesota (–1914).

12 Edvard Munch, Norwegian painter of psychological subjects such as *The Scream*, born in Löten, Norway (–1944).

16 George Santayana, Spanish-born U.S. philosopher and poet, born in Madrid, Spain (–1952).

18 Franz Ferdinand, Austrian archduke whose assassination sparked World War I, born in Graz, Austria (–1914).

24 William Makepeace Thackeray, English novelist who wrote *Vanity Fair*, dies in London, England (52).

- The U.S. Cutting Company produces the first canned peaches.
- U.S. president Abraham Lincoln establishes the annual national Thanksgiving holiday on the last Thursday in November.

FEBRUARY

17 The International Red Cross is founded in Geneva, Switzerland.

DECEMBER

8 The Church of La Compañia, in Santiago, Chile, burns down, killing 2,500 people.

Media and Communication

- *Le Petit Journal*, the first cheap newspaper in France, is launched.

Sports

- The Grand Prix de Paris horse race is first run at Longchamp, Paris, France. It is the first time that the

term "Grand Prix" is used in the title of a sporting event.
- U.S. inventor James L. Plimpton of New York, New York, patents the four-wheeled roller skate.

MAY

5 Joe Coburn wins the U.S. heavyweight boxing championship, knocking out Mike McCoole in the 63rd round in their fight in Charleston, South Carolina.

JUNE

- The first independent athletics club of the modern world, the Mincing Lane Athletics Club, is founded in London, England.

OCTOBER

26 The Football Association is founded in London, England, by the representatives of 11 soccer clubs. Their purpose is to establish "a definite code of rules for the regulation of the game." All clubs are from the London area.

1864

POLITICS, GOVERNMENT, AND ECONOMICS

Business and Economics

- "In God We Trust" appears for the first time on the new U.S. two-cent piece.

JUNE

- The U.S. Congress passes the Internal Revenue Act, raising income taxes.

Colonization

MARCH

29 Following the conference of the European powers on their status, the Ionian Islands are ceded by Britain to Greece.

OCTOBER

30 The Peace of Vienna concludes the German–Danish war, by which Denmark cedes the duchies of Schleswig, Holstein, and Lauenberg to Austria and Prussia.

Politics and Government

- In U.S. Congressional elections, the Republican Party retains its majorities in the House (149–42) and Senate (42–10).
- The mansion and grounds of Confederate general Robert E. Lee and his wife Mary, in northern Virginia, are confiscated by the Union government, and portions are used for a cemetery for Union soldiers. After the end of the Civil War, the site becomes Arlington National Cemetery.

JANUARY

13 As a limited liberal measure, the Zemstvo Law in Russia establishes provincial councils with limited responsibilities for public services but with none for the police.

16 Austria and Prussia send an ultimatum to Denmark for the repeal of its new constitution incorporating the duchy of Schleswig, and form an alliance in case of its rejection.

FEBRUARY

1 Austro-Prussian troops enter Schleswig in opposition to Denmark's incorporation of the disputed territory.

17 The Confederate submarine *Hunley* sinks the Union warship *Housatonic* in the first successful submarine assault in history.

20 At the Battle of Olustee, Florida, Confederate forces under the command of General Joseph Finegan repel a Union attempt to seize control of Florida.

MARCH

10 U.S. president Abraham Lincoln appoints Ulysses S. Grant general in chief of the U.S. Army.

APRIL

10 Archduke Maximilian of Austria accepts the title offered by Napoleon III of emperor of Mexico, following French military victories there in an attempt to enforce the payment of European debts. France wishes to establish a liberal, Catholic empire in Mexico.

12 Confederate troops under the command of Nathan Bedford Forrest massacre black American Union soldiers captured in the Confederate seizure of Fort Pillow, Tennessee.

18 Danish forces are defeated at Düppel, Denmark, and German troops invade Denmark in the war over the duchies of Schleswig and Holstein.

20 Reports of atrocities at Confederate prison camps prompt the Union War Department to reduce rations in Union prison camps.

25 The British foreign secretary Lord John Russell calls a London Conference of Britain, Russia, France, Austria, and Prussia to solve the disputes over the duchies of Schleswig and Holstein.

MAY

1 Brazil, Argentina, and Uruguay form a military alliance against the Paraguayan dictator Francisco Solano López.

5–6 At the Battle of the Wilderness, near Spotsylvania, Virginia, Union and Confederate forces fight a costly draw, dashing the hopes of a decisive victory on both the Northern and Southern home-fronts.

26 The U.S. Congress creates the Montana Territory from part of Idaho Territory.

JUNE

• At the Battle of Cold Harbor, Virginia, a Confederate army repels a Union army nearly twice its size. In the aftermath, Union general Grant begins a prolonged siege of Petersburg, Virginia, that will last to the end of the war.

• Republicans renominate Abraham Lincoln for president and Tennessee governor Andrew Johnson for vice president.

25 At the London Conference on the disputes over the duchies of Schleswig and Holstein, the Prussian chancellor Otto von Bismarck makes demands he knows Denmark will not concede to prevent a settlement being negotiated before Prussia can achieve a military victory.

29 Prussia captures Alsen, Denmark, and the bulk of the Danish army in the war over the duchies of Schleswig and Holstein.

JULY

19–21 British forces under General Charles Gordon assist imperial troops under Zeng Guofan in taking the city of Nanjing, ending the Taiping Rebellion in China.

AUGUST

• Democrats nominate general George B. McClellan for president and Ohio politician George H. Pendleton for vice president.

SEPTEMBER

• Union forces under William Tecumseh Sherman occupy Atlanta, Georgia.

5–8 British, French, and Dutch fleets attack the Japanese in the Shimonoseki Straits in reprisal for the closure of ports and expulsion of foreigners by the Japanese Choshu clan.

9 The reactionary Ramón Narváez becomes prime minister of Spain.

15 A Franco-Italian convention is signed under which the Kingdom of Italy renounces its claim to Rome, and Florence becomes the Italian capital in place of Turin.

OCTOBER

• In a daring raid designed to damage Union morale and thereby influence the presidential election, Confederate lieutenant Bennett H. Young robs three banks in the town of St. Albans, Vermont. After failing to set light to the town, Young and his mavericks retreat to Canada, where they are arrested.

• Nevada becomes the 36th state in the Union.

22 Japan agrees to pay an indemnity to Britain, France, and the Netherlands following the Shimoneseki incidents of September 5–8.

NOVEMBER

• American voters in the Union states reelect Abraham Lincoln as president.

• Confederate arsonists attempt unsuccessfully to set fire to New York, New York.

• Union general William Tecumseh Sherman begins his notorious march through Georgia, starting from Atlanta and marching toward Savannah.

28 An advanced new democratic constitution in Greece does away with the upper Chamber of Deputies.

29 A village of Cheyenne and Arapaho people are massacred at Sand Creek, Colorado, by the U.S. colonel John M. Chivington's Third Colorado Cavalry. The attack is a punishment against the two groups for murdering isolated settlers and raiding stage routes, which they did to protest against being ordered off their land.

DECEMBER

• Union forces under William Tecumseh Sherman occupy Savannah, Georgia, minutes after the Confederate defenders depart.

• U.S. president Abraham Lincoln appoints former Ohio senator Samuel P. Chase to the U.S. Supreme Court.

1 The Russian judiciary is reformed, introducing Western ideas such as the separation of judicial and administrative power and equality for everybody before the law.

SCIENCE, TECHNOLOGY, AND MEDICINE

Ecology

• A 12-m/39-ft tidal wave near Coringa, India, kills 50,000 people and 100,000 cattle; disease following the storm kills another 30,000.

• Norwegian engineer Sven Foyn invents the gun-launched harpoon with an explosive head. It permits hunting the faster and more plentiful fin, sei, and blue whales and ushers in the era of modern whaling.

OCTOBER

1 A cyclone in Calcutta, India, kills nearly 70,000 people and destroys most of the city.

5 About 45,000 people die in India when the Ganges River overflows.

• Yosemite National Park, California, is established. It is the first state park and becomes a national park in 1894.

Exploration

• Colonel T. G. Montgomerie of the British Survey Team in India begins the training of native agents, or "Pundits," to explore and survey Tibet.

SEPTEMBER

15 English explorer John Hanning Speke's claim to have established the source of the River Nile is disputed in Britain by his rival Richard Burton. Speke is killed in a shooting accident on the day of a debate between the two men organized by the British Association for the Advancement of Science.

OCTOBER

October 1864–65 English explorer Samuel Baker and his Hungarian wife Florence von Sass, friends of John Hanning Speke, investigate the upper reaches of the Nile in Africa, and discover that it flows out of Lake Victoria into another lake, Lake Albert. They do not establish the full course of the river, however.

Health and Medicine

• The Geneva Convention prescribes immunity in war zones for the Red Cross League, founded by the Swiss doctor and philanthropist Henri Dunant to care for those wounded in war.

Math

• French mathematician Joseph Bertrand publishes *Treatise on Differential and Integral Calculus*.

Science

• By examining their spectra, English astronomer William Huggins demonstrates that the Orion Nebula (and hence all nebulae) consists of gases, while the Andromeda Nebula is composed of stars and is therefore a galaxy.

• English philosopher Herbert Spencer coins the term "survival of the fittest" in *Principles of Biology*.

• Scottish physicist James Clerk Maxwell introduces mathematical equations that describe the electromagnetic field and predict the existence of radio waves.

Technology

• British scientists B. J. Sayce and W. B. Bolton introduce silver bromide emulsions to photography.

• English engineer Robert Whitehead invents the modern torpedo in Austria. Powered by a compressed-air engine, and a single propeller, it is 4 m/14 ft long, 36 cm/14 in in diameter, weighs 136 kg/300 lb, achieves a speed of six knots, and has a range of about 640 m/2,100 ft.

• English inventor James Slater patents a precision-made drive-chain; it is used for industrial machines and bicycles.

• French engineers Pierre and Emile Martin, and British engineer William Siemens, simultaneously develop the open-hearth process for making steel using a regenerative gas-fired furnace. By using hot waste gases to heat the furnace, high quality steel is produced in bulk, and scrap steel can be melted and reused.

• The first commercial production of Bessemer steel begins at Wyandotte, Michigan.

• Two French naval officers develop the 44.5-m/146-ft long *Plongeur*, the first submarine powered by an air-driven engine.

Transportation

• Austrian engineer Siegfried Marcus builds a pioneering automobile powered by a single-cylinder internal combustion engine. He dismantles it after the first test run because the rear wheels have to be lifted off the ground to start the engine since the engine lacks a clutch.

• Chicago industrialist George M. Pullman builds *Pioneer*, the first especially constructed sleeping car for railroads.

JULY

15 Two trains collide at Shohla, Pennsylvania, killing 148 people in the worst U.S. train crash to date.

ARTS AND IDEAS

Architecture

• The English housing reformer Octavia Hill begins reform of workers' tenement dwellings in St. Marylebone, London, England.

Arts

• The French artist Camille Corot paints *Homage to Delacroix*, a group portrait that includes the poet Baudelaire, the artists Whistler and Manet, and Corot himself.

• The U.S. artist Elihu Vedder paints *The Lair of the Sea Serpent*.

• The U.S. artist James Abbot McNeill Whistler paints *Caprice in Blue and Gold No 2*.

• The U.S. artist Sanford Robinson Gifford paints *Twilight in the Adirondacks*.

• The U.S. artist William Rimmer sculpts *Alexander Hamilton*.

Film

MARCH

1 French physicist Arthur-Louis Ducos du Hauron patents a device for taking and projecting moving pictures, although he does not build the device.

Literature and Language

- *Les Destinées, Le Journal d'un poète/Destinies: The Journal of a Poet* by the French writer Alfred Victor, comte de Vigny, is published posthumously.
- *The Maine Woods*, a collection of magazine articles by the U.S. poet and essayist Henry David Thoreau, is published posthumously.
- The English churchman and writer John Henry Newman publishes *Apologia Pro Vita Sua*, his spiritual autobiography. A revised version appears in 1865.
- The English writer Anthony Trollope begins to publish his novel *The Small House at Allington* in serial form. It is published as a book in 1865.
- The English writer Charles Dickens begins to publish his novel *Our Mutual Friend* in serial form. It is published as a book in 1865.
- The French writer Jules Verne publishes his adventure novel *Le Voyage au centre de la Terre/Voyage to the Center of the Earth*.
- The French writers Jules and Edmond de Goncourt (brothers) publish their novels *Renée Mauperin* and *Germinie Lacerteux*.
- The German writer Wilhelm Raabe publishes his novel *Der Hunger pastor/The Hunger-Pastor*.

- The Russian writer Fyodor Mikhaylovich Dostoyevsky publishes his novel *Zapiski iz podpolya/Notes from the Underground*.
- The Russian writer Leo Tolstoy publishes the first part of his epic novel *Voyna i mir/War and Peace*. The second part appears in 1869.
- The U.S. poet John Greenleaf Whittier publishes his collection of poems *In War Time and Other Poems*, which contains his most famous poem, "Barbara Frietchie."

Music

- Austrian composer Josef Anton Bruckner completes his Mass No. 1 in D minor. He revises it in 1876 and 1882.
- The opera *Mireille*, by the French composer Charles-François Gounod, is first performed, in Paris, France.
- The operetta *La Belle Hélène/Beautiful Helen*, by the German-born French composer Jacques Offenbach, is first performed in Paris, France.
- U.S. songwriter Stephen Foster writes "Beautiful Dreamer."

BIRTHS & DEATHS

JANUARY
1 Alfred Stieglitz, U.S. photographer who advocated photography as an art form, born in Hoboken, New Jersey (–1946).

MARCH
14 Casey Jones, U.S. railroad engineer and folk hero, born in Missouri (–1900).
17 Roger Brooke Taney, U.S. chief justice who in the Dred Scott decision ruled that blacks were not citizens and could thus not sue in a federal court, dies in Washington, D.C. (86).

APRIL
21 Max Weber, German sociologist and political economist who developed the idea of the "Protestant Ethic," which relates Protestantism to capitalism, born in Erfurt, Prussia (–1920).

MAY
2 Giacomo Meyerbeer, German opera composer, dies in Paris, France (73).
19 Nathaniel Hawthorne, U.S. author best known for *The Scarlet Letter* (1850) and *The House of Seven Gables* (1851), dies in Plymouth, New Hampshire (59).
20 John Clare, English romantic poet known for his poems of English peasantry, dies in St. Andrew's Asylum, Northampton, England (71).

JUNE
4 Nassau William Senior, English economist, dies in London, England (73).
11 Richard Strauss, German composer, born in Munich, Germany (–1949).
21 Heinrich Wölfflin, Swiss historian and writer on aesthetics, born in Basel, Switzerland (–1945).
25 Walther Hermann Nernst, German scientist who formulated the third law of thermodynamics, born in Briesen, Prussia (–1941).

JULY
22 James B. McPherson, Union general during the Civil War, is killed near Atlanta, Georgia (35).
24 Frank Wedekind, German actor and dramatist, born in Hanover, Germany (–1918).

AUGUST
23 Eleutherios Venizelos, Greek politician, prime minister of Greece 1910–15, 1917, 1924, and 1928–30, born in Mourniés, Crete (–1936).
31 Ferdinand Lassalle, German socialist who was instrumental in founding the German Labor movement, dies near Geneva, Switzerland, from wounds inflicted during a duel three days earlier (39).

SEPTEMBER
4 John Hunt Morgan, Confederate guerrilla, leader of "Morgan's Raiders," is killed in Greenville, Tennessee (38).
15 John Hanning Speke, British explorer who discovered Lake Victoria, the source of the Nile, is killed in a hunting accident near Corsham, Wiltshire, England (37).

NOVEMBER
9 Dmitry Iosifovich Ivanofsky, Russian microbiologist who discovered viruses, born in Nizy, Russia (–1920).
23 Friedrich Georg Wilhelm von Struve, German-born Russian astronomer who pioneered the study of binary stars, dies in St. Petersburg, Russia (71).
24 Henri de Toulouse-Lautrec, French artist who depicted the personalities of Parisian night life, born in Albi, France (–1901).

DECEMBER
8 George Boole, English mathematician who developed Boolean algebra, which is central to computer operations, dies in Ballintemple, Ireland (49).

Theater and Dance

- The play *Kongsemnerne/The Pretenders* by the Norwegian writer Henrik Johan Ibsen is first performed, in Christiania (now Oslo), Norway.

Thought and Scholarship

- The English teacher and social reformer Mary Carpenter publishes *Our Convicts*.
- The French historian Numa Denis Fustel de Coulanges publishes *La Cité antique/The City in Antiquity*.
- The French political economist Pierre-Guillaume-Frédéric Le Play publishes *La Réforme sociale en France/Social Reform in France*.
- The Scottish jurist and historian James Bryce publishes *The Holy Roman Empire*.

SOCIETY

Education

- Marquette University is founded in Milwaukee, Wisconsin.
- The Quaker-affiliated Swarthmore College is founded in Swarthmore, Pennsylvania.
- The universities of Belgrade in Serbia and Bucharest in Romania are founded.
- The University of Denver is founded in Denver, Colorado.

Everyday Life

- Dutch brewer Gerard Heineken launches Heineken beer.
- The (First) International Working Men's Association is founded in London, England, by the German philosopher, economist, and social theorist Karl Marx to coordinate the activities of workers' associations worldwide.

Media and Communication

- The newspaper *Neue Freie Presse* is launched in Vienna, Austria.

Religion

DECEMBER

8 A papal *Syllabus Errorum/Syllabus of Errors* condemns the errors of the 19th century—nationalism, naturalism, socialism, communism, and freemasonry.

Sports

- The Saratoga horse-racing course opens in Saratoga Springs, New York.

MARCH

3 England's Cambridge and Oxford universities compete in the first-ever interuniversity athletics meeting.

APRIL

15 The first known horse show is held by the Royal Dublin Society, in Dublin, Ireland.

1865

POLITICS, GOVERNMENT, AND ECONOMICS

Business and Economics

APRIL

- U.S. president Andrew Johnson lifts restrictions on trade with all ex-Confederate states except Texas.

Colonization

JANUARY

27 A treaty between Spain and Peru recognizes the independence of the former Spanish colony, following ongoing friction since the latter's cession.

MARCH

27 The independent British colony of Kaffraria is incorporated with Cape Colony in southern Africa.

MAY

5 A revolt of the inhabitants of the Caribbean island of San Domingo forces Spain to renounce its sovereignty over the colony, reacquired in March 1861.

Human Rights

DECEMBER

24 Former Confederate cavalry commander Nathan Bedford Forrest founds the Ku Klux Klan, allegedly as a social club for Confederate veterans and their families.

Politics and Government

- The authorities in Britain's Australian colonies refuse to accept further shipments of transported British criminals. As a result, longer, harsher sentences are introduced in Britain.
- The capital of New Zealand is moved from Auckland to Wellington following outbreaks of fighting between the native Maori peoples and European settlers near the former capital.
- The French minister of education Victor Duruy's law making secondary education more liberal and relevant to pupils' needs is passed.
- The U.S. Post Office Department introduces free mail delivery in cities with populations over 50,000.
- The U.S. War Department names nurse Clara Barton to head a committee to identify soldiers missing in the Civil War.

FEBRUARY

- Columbia, South Carolina, is burned, though debate rages whether the fires were set by advancing Union soldiers or the retreating Confederate army.
- The Confederate Congress transfers complete control of the Confederate military from President Jefferson Davis to the commander of the Army of Northern Virginia, Robert E. Lee.
- U.S. president Abraham Lincoln meets with Confederate peace commissioners aboard the vessel *River Queen* at Hampton Roads, Virginia. The meeting produces no progress toward peace.
18 The Confederate port of Charleston, South Carolina, besieged by the U.S. Navy since 1861, surrenders.

MARCH

- Confederate commander Robert E. Lee requests an audience with his Union counterpart Ulysses S. Grant to discuss peace terms. U.S. president Abraham Lincoln refuses the request.
- Confederate president Jefferson Davis signs legislation providing for the conscription and arming of slaves.
- The U.S. Congress creates the Freedman's Bureau to provide ex-slaves with economic and educational assistance.
- U.S. president Abraham Lincoln is inaugurated for a second term. In his Second Inaugural Address, he exhorts Americans to pursue "with malice toward none... a just and lasting peace among ourselves and with all nations."
3 At the Battle of Five Forks, Confederate general Robert E. Lee attempts unsuccessfully to break the Union siege of Petersburg, Virginia. Lee's effort having failed, the Confederates retreat to Richmond.
18 The dictator of Paraguay, President Francisco Solano López, seizes Argentine territory, provoking a war against Argentina, Brazil, and Uruguay.

APRIL

- In the face of a Union onslaught, Confederate general Robert E. Lee orders the evacuation of the Confederate capital, Richmond, Virginia. Union forces capture Richmond, after four years of trying.
9 The Confederate Army of Northern Virginia under Robert E. Lee surrenders to Union general Ulysses S. Grant at Appomattox Courthouse, Virginia.
14 Confederate malcontent John Wilkes Booth shoots President Abraham Lincoln at Ford's Theater in Washington, D.C.; Lincoln dies early the next morning. Booth is killed by a posse of federal soldiers on April 26. Vice President Andrew Johnson is sworn in as the 17th president of the United States.
26 Confederate forces under Joseph E. Johnston surrender to the Union forces at Durham, North Carolina.

MAY

- Ex-Confederate president Jefferson Davis is apprehended by U.S. soldiers at Irwinville, Georgia.
- U.S. president Andrew Johnson issues a far-reaching amnesty proclamation for former Confederate soldiers.
26 The surrender of the last Confederate army at Shreveport, near New Orleans, Louisiana, ends the American Civil War.
30 A commercial treaty is signed establishing greater freedom of trade between Britain and the German *Zollverein* (customs union).

JUNE

29 The reactionary leader Ramón Narváez, having taken his conservative policies too far, is dismissed as Spanish prime minister and replaced by the progressive general Enrique O'Donnell.

AUGUST

- A Mississippi state convention repeals its secession ordinance and abolishes slavery.
14 The Convention of Gastein temporarily resolves the question of the administration of the duchies of Schleswig and Holstein (ceded to Austria and Prussia by Denmark). Austria receives Holstein and Prussia obtains Schleswig and the port city of Kiel, while purchasing the duchy of Lauenburg.

SEPTEMBER

2 The war in New Zealand between colonial settlers and several Maori tribes ends when the British governor issues a proclamation of peace.
20 The 1861 February Patent, which centralized the Austrian political system, is temporarily suspended following Hungarian demands for autonomy.
26 A Native Rights Act in New Zealand recognizes the Maori people as natural-born subjects of Queen Victoria of Great Britain, and institutes a land court to hear their grievances against colonial settlers who have dispossessed them of their lands.

OCTOBER

4 The Prussian chancellor Otto von Bismarck and the French emperor Napoleon III meet at Biarritz, France, where Napoleon recognizes Prussian supremacy in Germany and a united Italy.
10 The United States demands the recall of French troops stationed in Mexico in support of the French-appointed emperor, Maximilian I.

29 The Liberal politician Lord John Russell becomes prime minister of Great Britain.

NOVEMBER

- North Carolina repeals its secession ordinance and prohibits slavery.

DECEMBER

- Radical Republicans in the U.S. Congress create a Joint Committee on Reconstruction, resolving to punish former Confederate states if they do not demonstrate remorse for seceding, and to guarantee the full emancipation of black American slaves.
- The 13th Amendment to the U.S. Constitution, prohibiting slavery, becomes law.
- 10 King Leopold I of Belgium dies and is succeeded by his son, Leopold II.
- 12 A new constitution in Sweden abolishes the traditional four estates and replaces them with two chambers, following long-standing demands for political reform.
- 12 The Koloszvár (modern Cluj) diet (assembly) in Transylvania, dominated by Hungarians, passes a decree for the reincorporation of Transylvania in Hungary.

SCIENCE, TECHNOLOGY, AND MEDICINE

Exploration

December 1865–66   German explorer Gerhard Rohlfs makes the first European crossing of the central Sahara, traveling from Tripoli on the Mediterranean coast via the River Niger to Lagos in west Africa.

Health and Medicine

- French physiologist Claude Bernard publishes *Introduction à la médecine expérimentale/An Introduction to the Study of Experimental Medicine*, in which he stresses the need for experimentation and hypothesis in medicine. It challenges earlier views of vitalism and indeterminism.
- Paris, France, is struck by a cholera epidemic in which nearly 200 people die per day.

AUGUST

12 English surgeon Joseph Lister first uses phenol (carbolic acid) as an antiseptic during surgery, to kill germs.

Math

- German mathematician and physicist Julius Plücker invents line geometry.
- German mathematician August Möbius describes a strip of paper that has only one side and one edge. Now known as the Möbius strip, it also remains in one piece when cut down the middle.

Science

- Austrian monk and botanist Gregor Mendel publishes a paper in the *Proceedings* of the Natural Science Society of Brünn that outlines the fundamental laws of heredity.
- English geologist Henry Clifton Sorby develops a spectrum microscope for analyzing the light from organic pigments.
- French microbiologist Louis Pasteur reports his discovery that heating wine kills the microorganisms that cause it to turn to vinegar. The process becomes known as pasteurization.
- French physiologist Claude Bernard develops the concept of homeostasis when he notes that "all the vital mechanisms, varied as they are, have only one object: that of preserving constant the conditions of life."
- German botanist Julius von Sachs, in *Handbuch der Experimental Physiologie der Pflanzen/A Handbook on the Experimental Physiology of Plants*, discusses the transport of water in the roots of plants.
- German botanist Julius von Sachs demonstrates that chlorophyll is contained within chloroplasts, and not diffused throughout the cell.
- German chemist Friedrich Kekulé suggests that the benzene molecule has a six-carbon ring structure. His theory refines current knowledge of organic chemistry.
- Maria Mitchell of Massachusetts becomes the first woman professor of astronomy when she receives an appointment to Vassar College in Poughkeepsie, New York.
- Russian physiologist Ivan M. Sechenov publishes *Reflexes of the Brain*, in which he argues that psychic processes have a physiological basis.

Technology

- An air-filled container mounted on the back of a diver and with an automatic valve—the forerunner of the modern aqualung—is developed in France.
- French chemist George Leclanché invents the zinc-carbon battery—the first dry cell battery.
- German chemist Hermann Johann Philipp Sprengel constructs a pump that creates a vacuum high enough to meet the needs of electric light bulbs. The inability to create a good vacuum has hindered their development.
- German inventor Ernst Busch develops a biconvex photographic lens that eliminates much of the distortion of camera lenses.
- Paul Schutzenberger invents "celanese" acetate rayon; it is not commercially produced until 1904.
- Swedish inventor Alfred Nobel invents the blasting cap. Used to detonate nitroglycerin safely and dependably, it expands the use of explosives in industry.
- The first mechanical dishwasher is invented.
- U.S. industrialist John Davidson Rockefeller founds the first large oil refinery, near Cleveland, Ohio.
- U.S. inventor Linus Yale patents the Yale lock.
- U.S. inventor Thaddeus Lowe develops an ice-making machine.
- U.S. inventor William Bullock develops a rotary press that prints on a roll of paper instead of single sheets, and includes a device for cutting the paper once it is printed. It is capable of producing 12,000 newspapers an hour.

Transportation

APRIL

- Around 1,700 Americans, 1,450 of them returning Union soldiers, die in an explosion aboard the steamship *Sultana* on the Mississippi River near Memphis, Tennessee.

ARTS AND IDEAS

Architecture

- The City Hall in Boston, Massachusetts, designed by the U.S. architects Arthur Gilman and Gridley Bryan, is completed.
- The wings and dome of the United States Capitol in Washington, D.C., designed by the U.S. architect Thomas Ustick Walker, are completed.

Arts

- The French artist Claude Monet paints *The Snow-Covered Road at Honfleur*.
- The French artist Edgar Degas paints *Lady with Chrysanthemums*.
- The French artist Eugène Boudin paints *The Jetty at Deauville*.
- The U.S. artist Winslow Homer paints *Prisoners from the Front*.

Literature and Language

- The English churchman and writer John Henry Newman publishes his dramatic monologue *The Dream of Gerontius*. It is set to music by Edward Elgar in 1900.
- The English poet Algernon Charles Swinburne publishes his verse drama *Atalanta in Calydon*.
- The English writer and mathematician Lewis Carroll publishes *Alice's Adventures Under Ground*, later known as *Alice's Adventures in Wonderland*.
- The English writer Matthew Arnold publishes *Essays in Criticism*.
- The German cartoonist and poet Wilhelm Busch publishes *Max und Moritz/Max and Moritz*, a collection of his satirical verse with his own illustrations.
- The U.S. humorist Henry Shaw publishes the fiction book *Josh Billings, His Sayings*.
- The U.S. poet Walt Whitman publishes his poetry collection *Drum Taps*. It contains his well-known "When Lilacs Last in The Dooryard Bloom'd," an elegy on the death of President Abraham Lincoln.
- The U.S. writer Mark Twain publishes his story "The Celebrated Jumping Frog of Calaveras County" in the New York *Saturday Press*.

Music

- Bohemian composer Antonín Leopold Dvořák completes his Symphony No. 1, *Zlonické zvony/Bells of Zlonice*, the score of which is lost and is not rediscovered until 1923. He also completes his Symphony No. 2.
- German composer Johannes Brahms completes his Cello Sonata No. 1 (Opus 38).
- Henry Clay Work writes the popular song "Marching Through Georgia" to commemorate the successes of General William Tecumseh Sherman's army.
- Hungarian composer Franz Liszt completes his orchestral work *Rákóczymarsch/Rákóczy March*.
- Russian composer Nikolay Andreyevich Rimsky-Korsakov completes his Symphony No. 1.
- The opera *Tristan und Isolde/Tristan and Isolde* by the German composer Richard Wagner is first performed, in Munich, Germany. It includes the *Liebestod* sung by Isolde.

Thought and Scholarship

- The English historian William Edward Hartpole Lecky publishes *A History of the Rise and Influence of Rationalism in Europe*.
- The English philosopher John Stuart Mill publishes *Auguste Comte and Positivism*.
- The U.S. historian Francis Parkman publishes *Pioneers of France in the New World*.
- The English historian John Robert Seeley publishes *Ecce Homo/Behold the Man*, a life of Christ.

SOCIETY

Education

- Cornell University is founded in Ithaca, New York.
- Lehigh University is founded in Bethlehem, Pennsylvania.
- The University of Kentucky is founded at Lexington, Kentucky.
- The University of Maine is founded in Orono, Maine.
- Yale University in New Haven, Connecticut, establishes the nation's first department of fine arts.

Everyday Life

- British stamp dealer J. W. Scott sets up a business in New York, New York, and stimulates the growing hobby of stamp collecting and trading in the United States.
- The first Le Printemps ("Spring") department store is opened in Paris, France.
- The North British Rubber Co. begins manufacturing rubber wellington boots, in Scotland.
- U.S. hatmaker John B. Stetson begins manufacturing the Stetson hat in Philadelphia, Pennsylvania.

Media and Communication

- *Harper's Weekly*, an illustrated weekly news magazine in the United States that reported extensively on the Civil War, has a press run of 250,000 copies.
- Construction of the New York–Paris overland telegraph route connecting the United States and France begins. Built northwestward from British Columbia in Canada and eastward from St. Petersburg in Russia, its surveyed route takes it across the Bering Strait. Construction halts the following year with the laying of transatlantic cables.
- The *San Francisco Examiner* daily newspaper begins circulation.
- The *San Francisco Chronicle* daily newspaper begins circulation as the *Daily Dramatic Chronicle*.
- The political weekly magazine the *Nation* is founded in New York, New York, edited by E. L. Godkin.
- U.S. financier Cyrus West Field and Scottish physicist William Thomson, Lord Kelvin, use Isambard Kingdom Brunel's steamship the *Great Eastern* to lay the first successful transatlantic telegraph cable.

Religion

JULY

2   William and Catherine Booth launch their Christian Mission in Britain, which they will later name the Salvation Army.

Sports

- Horse-racing commences at Saratoga Springs, New York, the oldest racecourse still in existence.

JULY

13   Edward Whymper, an English artist and pioneering mountaineer, becomes the first person to climb the Matterhorn, in the Alps, southern central Europe. On the descent, four of his companions fall to their deaths.

AUGUST

19   A professional race in Manchester, England, to determine "the champion miler of England" between professional runners William "Crowcatcher" Lang and William Richards results in the first recorded mile below 4 minutes 20 seconds, with both runners crossing the line in 4 minutes 17.25 seconds.

BIRTHS & DEATHS

JANUARY

19   Pierre-Joseph Proudhon, French socialist and journalist, dies in Paris, France (56).

FEBRUARY

17   Ernst Troeltsch, German theologian and philosopher, born in Haunstetten, near Augsburg, Bavaria (–1923).

APRIL

2   A(mbrose) P(owell) Hill, Confederate general in the American Civil War, is killed in battle at Petersburg, Virginia (39).

9   Charles Proteus Steinmetz, German-born U.S. electrical engineer and politician who developed the mathematics of alternating circuits, born in Breslau, Prussia (now Wrocław, Poland) (–1923).

9   Erich Ludendorff, German field marshal in World War I, born in Kruszewnia, near Poznań, Prussian Poland (–1937).

15   Abraham Lincoln, sixteenth president of the United States 1861–65, a Republican, is assassinated in Washington, D.C. (56).

26   John Wilkes Booth, U.S. actor who assassinated the U.S. president Abraham Lincoln, is killed by soldiers near Port Royal, Virginia (26).

JUNE

3   George V, King of Great Britain and Ireland 1910–36, born in London, England (–1936).

6   William C. Quantrill, Confederate guerrilla, whose troops raided towns with union sympathies during the Civil War, dies in Louisville, Kentucky (27).

8   Joseph Paxton, English landscape gardener who designed the Crystal Palace for the Great Exhibition of 1851, dies in Sydenham, near London, England (63).

13   W(illiam) B(utler) Yeats, Irish poet, dramatist, and nationalist, born in Sandymount, Dublin, Ireland (–1939).

AUGUST

13   Ignaz Philipp Semmelweis, Hungarian physician who discovered the cause of puerperal fever and introduced antiseptic practices into medicine, dies in Vienna, Austria (47).

27   Charles Dawes, U.S. vice president 1925–29 who developed the Dawes Plan for organizing Germany's war reparations after World War I, born in Marietta, Ohio (–1951).

SEPTEMBER

2   William Rowan Hamilton, Irish astronomer and mathematician who developed the theory of quaternions, dies in Dublin, Ireland (60).

OCTOBER

1   Paul Dukas, French composer who is best known for *The Sorcerer's Apprentice* (1897), born in Paris, France (–1935).

18   Henry Temple, Viscount Palmerston, British statesman, prime minister 1855–58 and 1859–65, a Liberal, dies in Brocket Hall, Hertfordshire, England (80).

NOVEMBER

2   Warren G. Harding, twenty-ninth president of the United States 1921–23, a Republican, born in Corsica, Ohio (–1923).

8   Tom Sayers, British boxer who participated in the first international heavyweight boxing match in 1860, dies in London, England (38).

12   Elizabeth Cleghorn Stevenson, English novelist (under the name "Mrs. Gaskell") and biographer of the novelist Charlotte Brontë, dies near Alton, Hampshire, England (55).

DECEMBER

8   Jean Sibelius, Finnish composer, born in Hämeenlinna, Finland (–1957).

30   Rudyard Kipling, English novelist, short story writer, and poet, born in Bombay, India (–1936).

1866

POLITICS, GOVERNMENT, AND ECONOMICS

Business and Economics

- The first strip mines in the United States open near Danville, Illinois. Horsedrawn plows and scrapers remove overburden, which is hauled away in carts and wheelbarrows.
- Three-fourths of U.S. imports are manufactured goods, while three-fourths of U.S. exports are crude materials or crude foodstuffs.

MAY

- The U.S. Congress creates a five-cent piece consisting of roughly 25% nickel and 75% copper. The coin will become known as the nickel.
- 11 "Black Friday" in London, England, sees scenes of commercial panic following the collapse of the merchant bank Overend and Gurney.

JUNE

- 25 Japan concludes a tariff convention with Britain, France, the Netherlands, and the United States, as it continues to open itself to the West.

Politics and Government

- The Göteborg system of state control of sales of spirits is introduced in Sweden.
- The Republican Party retains control of the House (143–39) and Senate (42–11) in U.S. Congressional elections.
- The U.S. Supreme Court, in *Ex Parte Milligan*, rules that military commissions may only try civilians in the immediate vicinity of a theater of war.

JANUARY

- 14 Peru declares war on Spain in resentment over clauses in the treaty of January 27, 1865 by which Peru's independence was recognized.

FEBRUARY

- 12 Federal officials in Washington, D.C., commemorate Abraham Lincoln's birthday for the first time.
- 17 The Habeas Corpus Act is suspended in Ireland after Irish nationalist unrest, allowing the imprisonment of suspects without trial.
- 23 Prince Alexander Cuss of Romania is dethroned following his attempt to redistribute church lands to the peasantry.

APRIL

- President Andrew Johnson declares insurrection over in Virginia, Tennessee, North Carolina, South Carolina, Georgia, Alabama, Florida, Mississippi, Louisiana, and Arkansas.
- The U.S. Congress passes the Civil Rights Act over President Andrew Johnson's veto. The legislation grants citizenship and equal civil rights to black Americans.
- 8 An offensive and defensive alliance is signed between Prussia and Italy.

JUNE

- 7 Prussian troops march into the Austrian-ruled duchy of Holstein. The Prussian chancellor, Otto von Bismarck, wants to provoke war with Austria and end its influence in Germany.
- 8 Prussian troops annex the duchy of Holstein in the war with Denmark over Schleswig and Holstein.
- 12 A secret treaty is agreed between Austria and France, by which the French emperor Napoleon III promises French neutrality in Austria's coming war with Prussia provided that Austria cedes Venice, which France will in turn hand over to Italy.
- 14 The German Federal Diet (legislative assembly) votes for mobilization against Prussian intervention in the Austrian-ruled duchy of Holstein, at which Prussian delegates declare the German Confederation at an end.
- 15–16 Prussia invades the German states of Saxony, Hanover, and Hesse, which, as Austria's allies, have opposed Prussia's entry into the Austrian-ruled duchy of Holstein.
- 20 Italy declares war on Austria in accordance with its treaty with Prussia of April 8.
- 24 Austrian forces under Archduke Albert defeat the Italians at Custozza, in Venice, following an Italian declaration of war in support of Prussia.
- 29 Prussian troops defeat the Hanoverian army at Langensalza in the Seven Weeks' War between Prussia and Austria and its allies.

JULY

- The U.S. Congress overrides President Andrew Johnson's veto of the New Freedmen's Bureau Bill. The legislation establishes military tribunals for individuals who deprive black Americans of their civil rights.
- 3 The Prussians defeat the Austrians at Sadowa (Königgrätz), Bohemia, in the decisive battle of the Seven Weeks War.
- 4 Emperor Napoleon III of France announces the cession of the Italian state of Venice by Austria following the Austrian defeat in the Seven Weeks War with Prussia, as agreed in the treaty between Prussia and Austria of June 12.
- 20 The Italian fleet is destroyed by the Austrian navy under Admiral Wilhelm von Tegetthoff off Lissa in Dalmatia

Seven Weeks War (1866)

JUNE

7   Prussian troops march into the Austrian-ruled duchy of Holstein. The Prussian chancellor Otto von Bismarck wants to provoke war with Austria and end its influence in Germany.

14   The German Federal Diet (legislative assembly) votes for mobilization against Prussian intervention in the Austrian-ruled duchy of Holstein, at which Prussian delegates declare the German Confederation at an end.

15–16   Prussia invades the German states of Saxony, Hanover, and Hesse, which as Austria's allies have opposed Prussia's entry into Holstein.

20   Italy declares war on Austria in accordance with its treaty with Prussia of April 8.

24   Austrian forces under Archduke Albert defeat the Italians at Custozza, in Venice.

29   Prussian troops defeat the Hanoverian army at Langensalza.

JULY

3   The Prussians defeat the Austrians at Sadowa (Königgrätz), Bohemia, in the decisive battle of the Seven Weeks War.

20   The Italian fleet is destroyed by the Austrian navy under Admiral Wilhelm von Tegetthoff off Lissa in Dalmatia.

AUGUST

23   The Peace of Prague is agreed between Prussia and Austria whereby Austria is to be excluded from Germany, while the German states of Hanover, Hesse, Nassau, and Frankfurt are to be incorporated with Prussia. The south German states are to be independent, but the states north of the River Main are to form a confederation under Prussia, which also obtains Austrian Silesia and territory from Saxony and from the south German states.

---

during the war arising from Italy's support of Prussia in the Seven Weeks War between Austria and Prussia.

26   A preliminary peace treaty ending the Seven Weeks War between Prussia and Austria is agreed at Nikolsburg, Bohemia.

28   The Danish constitution is altered in favor of the king and Upper House as, following the loss of the dissentient territories of Schleswig and Holstein, conservative elements exploit the lack of need of a progressive constitution.

AUGUST

•   President Andrew Johnson declares insurrection over in Texas and civil government restored throughout the United States.

•   The Japanese shogun (military ruler) Iemochi dies and is succeeded by Yoshinobu.

7   Prussia makes a treaty with the pro-Austrian German state of Baden ending the war between them, including a secret military alliance against France.

10   A treaty is agreed between Bolivia and Chile whereby territory between the Andes Mountains and the Pacific Ocean is to be ceded to Chile.

12   An Austro-Italian armistice ends the conflict between the two which has accompanied the Seven Weeks War between Prussia and Austria.

13   Prussia concludes a treaty of peace with the south German state of Württemberg, Austria's ally in the Seven Weeks War, which includes a secret military alliance against France.

22   Prussia signs a treaty with the pro-Austrian German state of Bavaria ending the war between them, and containing a secret military alliance against France.

23   The Peace of Prague between Prussia and Austria confirms the preliminary Peace of Nikolsburg (July 26) whereby Austria is to be excluded from Germany, while the German states of Hanover, Hesse, Nassau, and Frankfurt are to be incorporated with Prussia, the south German states are to be independent, but the states north of the River Main are to form a confederation under Prussia, which also obtains Austrian Silesia and

territory from Saxony and from the south German states.

SEPTEMBER

2   After a long period of unrest under Ottoman authority, the island of Crete revolts and decrees union with Greece.

3   Having defeated Austria and established Prussia as the leading power in Germany, the Prussian chancellor Otto von Bismarck obtains an indemnity from a grateful Prussian diet (state assembly) for having ruled without parliamentary approval of government budgets, ending the constitutional conflict that began in 1862.

20   Prussia annexes the German states of Hanover, Hesse, Nassau, and Frankfurt, as agreed by the Peace of Prague of August 23.

OCTOBER

3   The war between Austria and Italy, arising from Italy's support of Prussia against Austria in the Seven Weeks War, is formally ended by the Treaty of Vienna, with Italy receiving Venice from Austria.

21   Peace is agreed between Prussia and the German state of Saxony, Austria's ally.

21–22   Plebiscites in Venice result in support for a union with the kingdom of Italy.

24   The German Confederation is formally ended following Prussia's defeat of Austria for control of Germany.

DECEMBER

24   Schleswig and Holstein are incorporated in Prussia, in accordance with the terms of the Peace of Prague of August 23.

SCIENCE, TECHNOLOGY, AND MEDICINE

Agriculture

- Cattle from San Antonio, Texas, are first driven north on the Chisholm trail (named for the scout Jesse Chisholm) to the cattle-shipping depot of the Kansas Pacific Railroad at Abilene, Kansas. Between 1867 and 1871, 1.5 million head of cattle are driven along the trail and then shipped by train to markets in the east.
- Famine, caused by drought, kills nearly 1.5 million people in India.

Exploration

JANUARY

28 Scottish explorer David Livingstone embarks on his final expedition in Africa, sponsored by the Royal Geographical Society, to establish the true source of the Nile. All outside contact with him is lost after he reaches Lake Tanganyika, and reports of his death circulate.

JUNE

June–June 1868 French naval officers Ernest-Marc-Louis Doudart de Lagrée and Marie-Joseph-François Garnier explore the Mekong River, recording huge regions of unmapped territory in Southeast Asia and becoming the first Europeans to enter China's Yunnan province from the south, but failing to achieve their aim of opening the area to commercial development.

Health and Medicine

- A cholera epidemic in Europe kills 300,000 people; a related epidemic in the United States kills 50,000.
- English physician Thomas Clifford Allbut develops the clinical thermometer. Previous thermometers were over 30 cm/1 ft long and required 20 minutes to register a temperature.
- The British Sanitary Act is passed. It is the first public health law based on scientific principles.
- The first public health administration is established with the creation of a municipal board of health in New York, New York.

Math

- *Elements of Quaternions* by Irish mathematician William Rowan Hamilton is published posthumously. Quaternions make possible the application of arithmetic to three-dimensional objects.

Science

- German embryologist Ernst Haeckel proposes a third category of living beings intermediate between plants and animals. Called Protista, it consists mostly of microscopic organisms such as protozoans, algae, and fungi.

- German embryologist Ernst Haeckel postulates the biogenetic law that ontogeny recapitulates phylogeny—that the evolutionary development of the species is reproduced in the development of the animal embryo.

Technology

- British engineer J. H. Greathead develops a tunneling shield; it permits tunnels to be dug under the foundations of buildings, thus avoiding the disruption caused by the cut-and-cover method. It is used to build the City and South London Railway's "tube" subway tunnels in London, England.
- British manufacturer John Dallmeyer develops a photographic objective lens with two symmetrical elements placed either side of a diaphragm. The lens reduces distortion and eliminates the problem of haloes.
- Charles Brown and Heinrich Sulzer improve the efficiency of the steam engine by using superheated steam that does not condense on the cylinder walls.
- English inventor C. M. Spencer develops the automatic lathe.
- French physician François Carlier invents the chemical fire extinguisher. Containing a mixture of sodium bicarbonate and sulfuric acid, it is the first fire extinguisher to use a product other than water, and extinguishes fires on materials such as gasoline by creating a film that cuts the supply of air to the fire.
- German electrical engineer Werner von Siemens invents the self-excited generator that can be started by the residual magnetism in its electromagnet. Use of an electromagnet rather than a steel magnet allows electricity to be produced in great quantity.
- The French army is equipped with the Chassepot 11-mm Fusil d'Infantrie Modèle 1866 rifle, developed by French gunsmith Antoine-Alphonse Chassepot; it has a faster firing rate and greater range than other contemporary rifles. It is first used effectively in the Franco-Prussian War.
- U.S. inventor J. Ousterhoudt patents a tin can with a key opener.
- U.S. manufacturer Oliver Fisher Winchester develops the Winchester repeating rifle.

Transportation

- U.S. inventor James Caroll takes out the first U.S. patent for a pedal bicycle.

ARTS AND IDEAS

Architecture

- The Gare du Nord railroad station in Paris, France, designed by the German-born French architect Jakob Ignaz Hittorf, is completed.

Arts

- The French artist Claude Monet paints *Terrace at Ste.-Adresse*.
- The Italian artist Giovanni Fattori paints *La Rotonda dei Palmieri*.
- The National Archeological Museum is established in Athens, Greece, to house the world's finest collection of Greek antiquities.
- The U.S. artist Albert Bierstadt paints *Storm in the Rocky Mountains*.

Literature and Language

- The English poet Algernon Charles Swinburne publishes *Poems and Ballads*.
- The English writer Christina Georgina Rossetti publishes her poetry collection *The Prince's Progress and Other Poems*.
- The French writer Alphonse Daudet publishes his collection of stories *Lettres de mon moulin/Letters from My Windmill*.
- The French writer Victor Hugo publishes his novel *Les Travailleurs de la mer/Toilers of the Sea*.
- The Russian writer Fyodor Mikhaylovich Dostoyevsky publishes his novel *Prestupleniye i nakazaniye/Crime and Punishment*, the first of his major novels.
- The U.S. poet John Greenleaf Whittier publishes his collection of poems *Snow-Bound*.
- The U.S. writer Herman Melville publishes his poetry collection *Battle Pieces and Aspects of the War*.

Music

- Austrian composer Josef Anton Bruckner completes his Symphony No. 1. He revises it in 1868, 1877, and 1884. He also completes his Mass No. 2. The final version appears in 1882.
- Hungarian composer Franz Liszt completes his piano work *Deux Légendes/Two Legends*.
- Russian composer Peter Illyich Tchaikovsky completes his Symphony No. 1, *Winter Dreams*.
- The opera *Mignon* by the French composer Charles-Louis-Ambroise Thomas is first performed, in Paris, France. It is first performed in Britain in 1870 (in London, England), and in the United States in 1871 (in New Orleans, Louisiana).
- The opera *Prodaná Nevěstá/The Bartered Bride* by the Bohemian composer Bedřich Smetana is first performed, in Prague, Bohemia.
- The operetta *La Vie parisienne/Parisian Life* by the German-born French composer Jacques Offenbach is first performed, in Paris, France.
- U.S. composer J. A. Butterfield and U.S.-Canadian journalist George Washington Johnson write the song "When You and I Were Young, Maggie."

Thought and Scholarship

- The French lexicographer Pierre-Athanase Larousse publishes the first volume of his 17-volume *Grand Dictionnaire universel du XIX siècle/Universal Dictionary of the 19th Century*. The last volume appears in 1876.

SOCIETY

Education

- Carleton College is founded at Northfield, Minnesota.
- Drew University is founded at Madison, New Jersey.
- The University of Kansas is founded at Lawrence, Kansas.
- The University of New Hampshire is founded at Durham, New Hampshire.

JUNE
22 A measure introduced by the French Liberal minister of education Victor Duruy establishes a legal requirement for communities of over 500 to provide education for girls.

Everyday Life

- British tour organizer Thomas Cook offers the first organized tours to the United States.
- Swiss company Nestlé launches its first product, formula milk for babies.
- The Young Women's Christian Association (YWCA), founded in England, opens its first U.S. branch in Boston, Massachusetts.
- Nearly 2,500 buildings are destroyed by fire in Quebec City, Canada.

APRIL
- U.S. philanthropist Henry Bergh establishes the American Society for the Prevention of Cruelty to Animals (ASPCA), modeled after its English predecessor.

JULY
- Fire devastates the city of Portland, Maine, wreaking an estimated $10 million damage.

AUGUST
- The first National Labor Congress convenes in Baltimore, Maryland.

DECEMBER
- The Cadbury brothers of Birmingham, England, produce Cadbury's Cocoa Essence. It is the first successful drinking chocolate.

Media and Communication

- U.S. scientist Mahlon Loomis transmits the first telegraph message over radio waves. It is sent between two mountains in West Virginia using kites to support the aerials.

JULY
- Work is completed on the Atlantic telegraph cable connecting the United States and Britain.

Sports

- Baseball grows rapidly in the post-Civil War period as returning soldiers bring the game to their hometowns. Membership in the National Association of Baseball Players increases to 237, an increase of 146 on the previous year.
- James L. Plimpton, three years after inventing the modern four-wheeled roller skate, opens the first roller skating rink in the United States, the Atlantic House Rink, Newport, Rhode Island.

July 1866–67   A new set of boxing rules is drafted in Britain under the auspices of John Sholto Douglas, Marquess of Queensberry. With their insistence on the wearing of padded gloves, three-minute rounds, and a count of ten for knockouts, they herald the beginning of modern boxing.

MARCH
23   The first ever national athletics championships are staged by the Amateur Athletic Club at Beaufort House, Welham Green, London, England.

BIRTHS & DEATHS

- John Ringling, U.S. impresario who managed the Ringling Brothers circus, born in McGregor, Iowa (–1936).

JANUARY
23   Thomas Love Peacock, English author, dies in Weymouth, Dorset, England (80).
29   Romain Rolland, French novelist and dramatist, born in Clamecy, France (–1944).

FEBRUARY
25   Benedetto Croce, Italian historian and philosopher who championed the idea of unrestricted freedom, born in Pescasseroli, Italy (–1952).
26   Herbert Henry Dow, U.S. chemist who established the Dow Chemical Company in 1887, born in Belleville, Canada (–1930).

MARCH
6   William Whewell, English philosopher of science, dies in Cambridge, England (71).

APRIL
3   James Barry Munnik Hertzog, Prime Minister of South Africa 1924–39, born near Wellington, Cape Colony (now Cape Province, South Africa) (–1942).

MAY
17   Erik Satie, French composer, born in Honfleur, France (–1926).

JUNE
17   Lewis Cass, U.S. politician and secretary of war 1831–36 under

President Andrew Jackson, a Democrat, dies in Detroit, Michigan (83).

JULY
20   Berhard Riemann, German mathematician whose work in geometry influenced relativity theory, dies in Selasca, Italy (39).
28   Beatrix Potter, English writer of children's books, who created Peter Rabbit, Mrs. Tiggy-Winkle, and other characters, born in South Kensington, London, England (–1943).

AUGUST
13   Giovanni Agnelli, Italian industrialist who founded the Fiat car company and supplied the Italian military with its war machines during both world wars, born in Villar Perosa, Italy (–1945).

SEPTEMBER
1   James Corbett, "Gentleman Jim," U.S. world heavyweight boxing champion who was the first to box scientifically, born in San Francisco, California (–1933).
4   Simon Lake, U.S. engineer who built the *Argonaut*, the first submarine to operate in the open ocean, born in Pleasantville, New Jersey (–1945).
21   H(erbert) G(eorge) Wells, English novelist, sociologist, and historian, who wrote *The Time Machine, The War of the Worlds*, and *The Invisible

Man*, born in Bromley, Kent, England (–1946).
25   Thomas Hunt Morgan, U.S. zoologist and geneticist who established the chromosomal theory of inheritance through his work on the fruit fly, born in Lexington, Kentucky (–1945).

OCTOBER
6   Reginald Aubrey Fessenden, Canadian-U.S. pioneer of long-distance radio broadcasts, born in Milton, Quebec, Canada (–1932).
12   Ramsay MacDonald, British politician, first Labour Party prime minister of Britain in 1924, prime minister again in 1929, and in a coalition government 1931–35, born in Lossiemouth, Moray, Scotland (–1937).

NOVEMBER
8   Herbert, Lord Austin, English automobile manufacturer, born in Little Missenden, Buckinghamshire, England (–1941).

DECEMBER
14   Roger Fry, English art critic, artist, and supporter of the postimpressionist movement, born in London, England (–1934).
16   Wassily Kandinsky, Russian-born artist, founder of the Abstract art movement, born in Moscow, Russia (–1944).

1867

POLITICS, GOVERNMENT, AND ECONOMICS

Business and Economics

- U.S. author Horatio Alger publishes *Ragged Dick*, the first of some 130 didactic novels that broadcast the ideal of the self-made man.

Politics and Government

- New York, New York, passes legislation designed to ameliorate tenement housing conditions.
- The states of New York, Illinois, and Missouri enact legislation instituting an eight-hour working day.

JANUARY

- The U.S. Congress overrides President Andrew Johnson's veto to pass legislation granting suffrage to black American men in the District of Columbia.

FEBRUARY

- The U.S. Congress authorizes a survey for a canal across the isthmus of Panama.
- 12 A Fenian rising seeking Irish independence from Britain begins in County Kerry, Ireland.
- 17 The Hungarian diet (national assembly) is opened and the constitution of 1848 restored. Government by *Ausgleich* ("compromise") begins, allowing for a dual monarchy under which the Magyars gain autonomy in Hungary while Austria continues to govern the rest of the Hapsburg territories, with unitary foreign and war policies.

MARCH

- Nebraska becomes the 37th state in the Union.
- The U.S. Congress overrides President Andrew Johnson's veto to pass the Reconstruction Act. It divides the South into five military districts, each under the command of a military governor. Civil government will be restored on an individual basis as states rejoin the Union.
- The U.S. Congress overrides President Andrew Johnson's veto to pass the second Reconstruction Act. It requires ex-Confederate states to register all eligible voters in pursuance of state constitutional conventions.
- The U.S. Congress passes the Tenure of Office Act, requiring the president to attain senate consent before dismissing federal officials appointed with senate

consent. The legislation aims to thwart President Johnson's attempt to replace cabinet members appointed by Lincoln with individuals of his own choosing.
- The U.S. Congress submits the 14th Amendment, guaranteeing national and state citizenship to black Americans, to the states.
- 5 Abortive Fenian risings, seeking Irish independence from Britain, occur in Dublin and Munster, Ireland.
- 9 The United States purchases the 1,524,640-sq km/586,400-sq mi Alaska Territory from Russia for $7,200,000.
- 12 Emperor Napoleon III of France withdraws French support for Emperor Maximilian I of Mexico, who is faced with a powerful revolt of the local population.
- 29 The British North America Act establishes the Dominion of Canada comprising Quebec, Ontario, Nova Scotia, and New Brunswick, confederated provinces with a central parliamentary government under a British governor-general.

APRIL

- 16 The constitution of the new Prussian-dominated North German Confederation is proclaimed.

JUNE

- 8 Emperor Francis Joseph I of Austria is crowned king of Hungary in the capital, Buda (now Budapest), as part of the separation of Hungary as an autonomous national unit under the *Ausgleich*.
- 19 Emperor Maximilian I of Mexico is executed by rebels led by President Benito Juárez.

JULY

- The U.S. Congress passes the third Reconstruction Act over President Johnson's veto. The legislation requires ex-Confederate states to adopt the 15th Amendment, guaranteeing black American voting rights, as a precondition of readmission to the Union.
- 1 The constitution of the new North German Confederation with Prussia at its head comes into effect.
- 13 The Spanish cortes (national assembly), elected under conservative pressure, votes away its rights.
- 23 Russia forms a governor-generalship over Turkestan, continuing the expansion of its influence in central Asia.
- 31 The British politician William Torrens secures the passage of the Artisans' and Labourers' Dwellings Act in Britain, empowering local authorities to clear slums.

AUGUST

- 8 Ferdinand Bebel becomes the first socialist to be elected to the North German Reichstag (legislative assembly).
- 15 The Second Reform Act extends the franchise in Britain and redistributes parliamentary seats to reflect increasing urbanization. The electorate is roughly doubled from 1 to 2 million.

21 A British act of Parliament regulates the hours and conditions of work for children, young persons, and women in workshops.

SEPTEMBER

18 Fenians (Irish terrorists seeking Ireland's independence from Britain) attack a prison van in Manchester, England, in an attempt to free imprisoned colleagues, and a policeman is killed.

OCTOBER

• Alaska becomes a U.S. territory.

27 The Italian soldier and patriot Giuseppe Garibaldi begins his march on Rome, in a second attempt to incorporate it into the kingdom of Italy.

28 A French force lands at Civitavecchia, northwest of Rome, to defend the Pope against the advance of Garibaldi.

NOVEMBER

3   The Italian soldier and patriot Giuseppe Garibaldi, defeated by French and papal troops at Mentana, north of Rome, is sent as a captive to the island of Caprera, off Sardinia, Italy.

5   The progressive former Spanish prime minister Enrique O'Donnell dies, which represents a blow to Spanish political stability.

9   Matsuhito becomes Japanese emperor at the head of a movement to restore the rights of the emperor over those of the shogun (military ruler).

DECEMBER

• Emperor Maximilian I refuses to leave Mexico at Emperor Napoleon III of France's request.

13 A Fenian (Irish terrorist) attempt to blow open the prison at Clerkenwell in London, England, kills 12 people.

21 The new Austrian constitution incorporating the system of dual control, with Hungary semi-independent, is promulgated.

SCIENCE, TECHNOLOGY, AND MEDICINE

Agriculture

DECEMBER

4   Minnesota farmer Oliver H. Kelley establishes the National Grange of the Patrons of Husbandry in Washington, D.C., a fraternal and educational association for farmers popularly called the Grangers.

Ecology

• Diamonds are discovered in southern Africa along the Orange and Vaal rivers.

Exploration

• Pundit Nain Singh explores Tibet for the British Survey of India, searching for the source of the River Indus and reaching the Tibetan gold fields.

Health and Medicine

• Scottish physician Thomas Lauder Brunton publishes *A Textbook of Pharmacology, Therapeutics and Materia Medica*; the first extensive British treatise on pharmacology.

• Scottish physician Thomas Lauder Brunton finds amyl nitrate relieves the pain of angina pectoris.

JUNE

15 U.S. physician John Stough Bobbs performs, in Indianapolis, Indiana, the first successful gallstone operation.

Science

• French chemist and microbiologist Louis Pasteur disproves the theory of spontaneous generation when he demonstrates that microorganisms present in the air cause food to decompose.

• German chemist August Wilhelm von Hofmann discovers formaldehyde.

• German scientist Hermann Ludwig von Helmholtz publishes *Handbook of Physiological Optics* that develops the idea, contrary to Immanuel Kant, that concepts of time and space are due to experience.

• Swedish chemist Alfred Nobel patents dynamite. It consists of 75% nitroglycerin and 25% of an absorbent material known as ghur which makes the explosive safe and easy to handle.

• Swedish physicist Anders Ångström is the first to examine the Aurora Borealis spectroscopically.

• U.S. chemist Benjamin Chew Tilgham uses sulfurous acid to produce wood pulp for making paper.

Technology

• A stock ticker teletype machine to print records of stock transactions is developed at the Stock Exchange in New York, New York.

• French engineer Léon Edoux develops the hydraulic column elevator. Water is injected under pressure into a vertical shaft to raise the elevator, which acts like a piston on a column of water. Draining the water lowers the elevator.

• French gardener Joseph Monier patents reinforced concrete by adding steel rods, bars, or mesh to the concrete. It dramatically increases the tensile strength of the concrete, making it capable of sustaining heavy stresses.

• U.S. inventors Lucien Smith and Alphonso Dabb file patents for barbed wire, although no machine yet exists to produce it in quantity.

• U.S. printer Christopher Latham Sholes constructs the first practical typewriter.

Transportation

- The Cincinnati bridge is constructed in Cincinnati, Ohio. At 332 m/1,089 ft, it is the longest suspension bridge built to date.
- The first elevated railroad is built in Manhattan, New York, along Ninth Avenue. Initially operated as a cable car, it converts to steam engines in 1871.
- The first transpacific steamship service is inaugurated by the Pacific Mail Steamship Company, which begins regular service between San Francisco, California, and Hong Kong (China) and Yokohama.
- The railroad between Innsbruck, Austria, and Bolzano, Italy, is completed through the 1,370-m/4,500-ft-high Brenner Pass, one of the major passes through the Alps.
- U.S. steamship operator Cornelius Vanderbilt takes over the New York Central Railroad.

ARTS AND IDEAS

Architecture

- The Church of St. Augustin in Paris, France, designed by the French architect Victor Baltard, is completed.
- The Dominion Parliament House in Ottawa, Canada, designed by the Canadian architect Thomas Fuller, is completed. It is destroyed by fire in 1916.
- The Galleria Vittorio Emanuele, a covered arcade in Milan, Italy, is completed.

Arts

- The English furnituremaker Bruce Talbert publishes *Gothic Forms Applied to Furniture*.
- The English photographer Julia Margaret Cameron takes her *Portrait of Sir John Herschel*. One of the outstanding Victorian photographers, Cameron photographed many eminent figures of the period.
- The French artist Frédéric Bazille paints *The Artist's Family*.
- The French artist Henri Fantin-Latour paints his *Portrait of Edouard Manet*.
- The Paris Exposition Universelle (World Fair) in France introduces Japanese art to the West. Its influence can be seen in the works of artists as varied as French-born Edward Degas, U.S.-born James Whistler, and Dutch-born Vincent van Gogh.
- The U.S. artist Albert Bierstadt paints *Emigrants Crossing the Plains*.
- The U.S. artist Edmonia Lewis sculpts *Forever Free*.

Literature and Language

- The Australian writer Adam Lindsey Gordon publishes his collection of poems *Sea Spray and Smoke Drift*.
- The Belgian writer Charles de Coster publishes *La Légende et les aventures héroïques, joyeuses, et glorieuses d'Ulenspiegel/The Glorious Adventures of Till Eulenspiegel*.
- The English writer Anthony Trollope publishes his novel *Last Chronicle of Barset*.
- The English writer Ouida publishes her novel *Under Two Flags*.
- The French writer Emile Zola publishes his novel *Thérèse Raquin*.
- The Russian writer Ivan Sergeyevich Turgenev publishes his novel *Dym/Smoke*.
- The U.S. essayist Ralph Waldo Emerson publishes his poetry collection *May-Day and Other Poems*.
- The U.S. writer Oliver Wendell Holmes publishes his novel *The Guardian Angel*.

Music

- Austrian composer Johann Strauss completes his *Blauen Donau/Blue Danube* waltz.
- Hungarian composer Franz Liszt completes his oratorio *Christus*.
- Russian composer Alexander Porfiryevich Borodin completes his Symphony No. 1.
- Russian composer Modest Petrovich Mussorgsky completes his orchestral work *Night on the Bare Mountain*.
- The opera *Don Carlos* by the Italian composer Giuseppe Verdi is first performed, in Paris, France. It is first performed in Britain in 1867, and in the United States in 1877 (in New York, New York).
- The opera *La Jolie Fille de Perth/The Fair Maid of Perth* by the French composer Georges Bizet is first performed, in Paris, France. It is based on a story by the Scottish writer Walter Scott.
- The opera *Roméo et Juliette* by the French composer Charles-François Gounod is first performed, in Paris, France. It is based on William Shakespeare's tragedy *Romeo and Juliet*.
- U.S. composer R. E. Eastburn writes the song "Little Brown Jug."

Theater and Dance

- The Norwegian dramatist Henrik Johan Ibsen publishes his verse play *Peer Gynt*. It is first performed in 1876.

Thought and Scholarship

- The German political philosopher Karl Marx publishes the first volume of *Das Kapital/Capital*, his major work and the central text of communism.
- The U.S. historian Francis Parkman publishes *The Jesuits in North America in the Seventeenth Century*.

SOCIETY

Education

- Classes begin at the University of Illinois at Urbana-Champaign.

- Howard University is founded at Washington, D.C.
- New England philanthropist George Peabody bequeaths $3.5 million to promote school construction and teacher training in the United States.
- West Virginia University is founded at Morgantown, West Virginia.

- Canada adopts lacrosse as its national game and establishes the National Lacrosse Association. In the same year, it is introduced to Britain by a party of the Caughnawages people, touring with the Canadian promoter W. B. Johnson.

JUNE

19 Ruthless, ridden by J. Gilpatrick, wins the inaugural Belmont Stakes horse race at Jerome Park, New York.

Everyday Life

- Liebig's Soluble Food for Babies, developed in Germany by Baron Justus von Liebig, is the first commercial baby food.

Sports

c. 1867 The game of badminton, based on the old English game of battledore and shuttlecock (itself based on an ancient Chinese game), is devised at Badminton Hall, Gloucestershire, England, by the family and friends of the Duke of Beaufort.

BIRTHS & DEATHS

JANUARY

17 Jean-August-Dominique Ingres, French neoclassical painter, dies in Paris, France (87).

FEBRUARY

3 The Japanese emperor Komei dies.
7 Laura Ingalls Wilder, U.S. author known for her book *Little House on the Prairie*, born in Lake Pepin, Wisconsin (–1957).

MARCH

25 Arturo Toscanini, Italian conductor, born in Parma, Italy (–1957).
29 Cy Young, U.S. professional baseball player, born in Gilmore, Ohio (–1955).

APRIL

10 George William Russell (pseudonym "AE"), Irish poet and mystic, born in Lurga, County Armagh, Ireland (–1935).
16 Wilbur Wright, U.S. pioneer of aviation who, with his brother Orville, was the first to achieve sustained powered flight, born near Millville, Indiana (–1912).
18 Robert Smirke, English architect, dies in Cheltenham, Gloucestershire, England (86).

MAY

14 Kurt Eisner, German socialist leader who organized the revolution that overthrew the Bavarian monarchy in 1918, born in Berlin, Germany (–1919).

JUNE

4 Carl Mannerheim, Finnish military leader who defended Finland from the Soviet Union during World War

II and who was Finland's first president 1944–46, born in Villnäs, Finland (–1955).

8 Frank Lloyd Wright, U.S. architect and author who developed a "Prairie style" of architecture, born in Richland Center, Wisconsin (–1959).
17 John Robert Gregg, Irish-born U.S. inventor who developed the shorthand system named for him, born in Rockcorry, County Monaghan, Ireland (–1948).
28 Luigi Pirandello, Italian playwright, novelist, and short-story writer, born in Agrigento, Sicily, Italy (–1936).

JULY

8 Käthe Kollwitz, German graphic artist and sculptor, born in Königsberg, Prussia (–1945).
31 Benoît Fourneyron, French engineer who invented the water turbine, dies in Paris, France (64).
31 S(ebastian) S(pering) Kresge, U.S. businessman who established over 1,000 discount stores throughout the United States, born in Bald Mount, Pennsylvania (–1966).

AUGUST

3 Stanley Baldwin, British prime minister 1923–24, 1924–29, and 1935–37, a Conservative, born in Bewdley, Worcestershire, England (–1947).
14 John Galsworthy, English novelist and playwright, born in Kingston Hill, Surrey, England (–1933).
25 Michael Faraday, English physicist and chemist whose work contributed to a basic understanding

of electromagnetism, dies in Hampton Court, Surrey, England (76).

31 Charles Baudelaire, French poet, dies in Paris, France (46).

OCTOBER

3 Elias Howe, U.S. inventor who developed the first practical sewing machine, dies in Brooklyn, New York, New York (48).
23 Franz Bopp, German linguist who discovered that Sanskrit is an Indo-European language and thus related to English, dies in Berlin, Germany (76).

NOVEMBER

7 Marie Curie (born Skłodowska), Polish-born French physicist who, with her husband Pierre Curie, discovered polonium and radium, and who won the Nobel Prize for Physics in 1903 and for Chemistry in 1911, born in Warsaw, Poland (–1934).
12 Sun Zhong Shan (Sun Yat-sen), leader of the Chinese Nationalist Party (Guomindang) which overthrew the Manchu dynasty, first president of the Republic of China 1911–12, and de facto ruler 1923–25, born in Xiangshan, Guangdong Province, China (–1925).

DECEMBER

5 Józef Piłsudski, Polish revolutionary and statesman, first president 1918–22 of the newly independent Poland, born in Zulów, Poland (–1935).

1868

POLITICS, GOVERNMENT, AND ECONOMICS

Business and Economics

- Chicago industrialist George M. Pullman incorporates the Pullman Palace Car Company.
- William Rand and Andrew McNally start a printing company in the United States, which will later grow to become the world's leading map publisher.

Colonization

MARCH

12   The south African chief Moshoeshoe I is granted British protection from the Boers (Dutch settlers), making Basutoland (modern Lesotho) a British protectorate.

Human Rights

- U.S. suffragist Susan B. Anthony introduces the suffrage newspaper *The Revolution*.
- Women's rights advocates Julia Ward Howe and Carolina Severance establish the New England Woman's Club to promote the civil rights of women.

Politics and Government

- In U.S. Congressional elections, Republicans retain majorities in the House (149–63) and Senate (56–11).

JANUARY

3   The Tokugawa shogunate (military government) is abolished in Japan, having ruled since 1603, and the Meiji dynasty is restored under Emperor Matsuhito.

FEBRUARY

- U.S. president Andrew Johnson dismisses Secretary of War Edwin M. Stanton without Senate consent, thereby violating the Tenure of Office Act of March 1867. As a result, the U.S. House of Representatives votes to impeach the president.

MARCH

- The U.S. Congress passes the fourth Reconstruction Act. Designed to thwart the South's disenfranchisement of black American voters, the legislation stipulates that state constitutions will be ratified or rejected based on majorities tallied against the number of votes cast rather than against the number of eligible voters.

- The U.S. Senate begins the impeachment trial of President Andrew Johnson.

APRIL

6   The Japanese emperor Matsushito formally agrees to rule with a popularly elected assembly.

25   The conservative Spanish prime minister Ramón Narváez dies, weakening the position of Queen Isabella II.

MAY

- Republicans nominate General Ulysses S. Grant for president and Indiana congressman Schuyler Colfax for vice president.
- The Grand Army of the Republic, a civil war veterans' association, designates the last Monday in May (traditionally May 30) Decoration Day—the day on which civil-war graves are to be festooned.
- The U.S. Senate twice votes 35–19 to impeach President Andrew Johnson. Both times the vote falls short of the necessary two-thirds majority.

11   Freedom of the press is granted in France in response to calls for political liberalization.

12   The city of Samarkand is occupied by the Russians as they press further into central Asia.

JUNE

- The U.S. Congress overrides President Andrew Johnson's veto to pass legislation granting Congressional representation to North Carolina, South Carolina, Georgia, Alabama, Florida, and Louisiana.
- The U.S. Congress passes legislation instituting an eight-hour working day for federal employees.

10   King Michael III of Serbia is murdered by followers of the Karageorgević dynasty and succeeded by his cousin Milan IV.

11   A limited right of public meeting is allowed in France, continuing Emperor Napoleon III's limited liberalization.

JULY

- Democrats nominate New York governor Horatio Seymour for president and Missouri senator Francis P. Blair, Jr., for vice president.
- The 14th Amendment to the U.S. Constitution, guaranteeing black American citizenship, becomes law.

7   The Third Maori War breaks out in New Zealand between the aboriginal inhabitants and British settlers encroaching on their land.

AUGUST

8   France concludes a commercial treaty with Madagascar, which also recognizes Hova power (the dominant people on the island).

SEPTEMBER

17   A Liberal revolution begins against Queen Isabella II of Spain under Marshal Juan Prim.

18 The Spanish admiral Juan Topete issues a Liberal manifesto in Cadiz, Spain, in support of the revolt against Queen Isabella II, calling for an end to absolutist rule.

28 Royalist forces are defeated by rebels opposing Queen Isabella II of Spain at Alcolea.

29 The major political factions in Madrid, Spain, dissatisfied with Queen Isabella's extremism, unite to depose her.

30 Queen Isabella II of Spain flees to France and is declared deposed, following the Liberal revolt against her rule.

NOVEMBER

- Americans elect Ulysses S. Grant to become the 18th president of the United States.

DECEMBER

- Jefferson Davis, President of the ex-Confederacy, goes on trial for treason at Richmond, Virginia.

- U.S. president Andrew Johnson proclaims a general amnesty for all who participated in what he calls the "insurrection or rebellion" against the United States.

3   The English statesman William Ewart Gladstone forms a Liberal ministry in Britain after victory over the Conservatives in the general election.

31 Coalition forces (Brazil, Argentina, and Uruguay) at war with Paraguay enter Asunción, Paraguay.

SCIENCE, TECHNOLOGY, AND MEDICINE

Agriculture

- Cattle dealer J. G. McCoy establishes Abilene, Kansas, as a major cattle depot.

- French chemist and microbiologist Louis Pasteur isolates two different strains of the bacilli which are killing the silkworm larvae of France's silk industry. He recommends destroying infected colonies to prevent contagion.

- European vines are attacked by the aphid *phylloxera*, brought in on imported U.S. vines.

Ecology

- A tsunami over 21 m/66 ft high kills over 25,000 people in Hawaii and Chile.

- San Francisco, California, is hit by an earthquake measuring 7.0 on the Richter scale. A large number of buildings are destroyed causing $300,000 worth of damage. Only five people are killed.

- English meteorologist Alexander Buchan begins the use of weather maps for forecasting, with the publication of a map showing the movement of a cyclonic depression across North America and Europe. It marks the start of modern meteorology.

AUGUST

13 An earthquake in Peru kills 25,000 people and causes $300 million damages.

Science

- English astronomer Norman Lockyer and French astronomer Pierre-Jules Janssen announce, independently, a method of spectroscopically observing solar prominences without waiting for an eclipse to block out the sun's glare.

- English astronomer Norman Lockyer and, independently, French astronomer Pierre-Jules Janssen, discover helium (atomic no. 2) through spectroscopic observations of the sun. Lockyer discovers that solar prominences are due to an upheaval in the outer layer of the sun called the chromosphere.

- English chemist Henry Deacon invents a process for the production of chlorine by the catalytic oxidation of hydrogen chloride.

- English chemist William Perkin synthesizes the natural red dye alizarin, which is used to dye cotton, silk, and wool, and coumarin, the first artificial perfume.

- English naturalist Charles Darwin publishes an elaboration of *Origin of Species* entitled *The Variation of Animals and Plants under Domestication*, in which he tries—unsuccessfully—to account for the inheritance of characteristics.

- English naturalist Thomas Henry Huxley makes the first classification of the dinosaurs, creating the order Ornithoscelida and two suborders.

- French geologist Louis Lartet is the first to discover the skeletal remains of anatomically modern humans, in a cave near Cro-Magnon, France. They are 35,000 years old.

- German botanists Nathaniel Pringsheim and Julius von Sachs discover the specialized organelles in plant cytoplasm called plastids.

- German embryologist Ernst Haeckel publishes *The History of Creation* in which he expresses his views on evolution.

- Swedish physicist Anders Ångström expresses the wavelengths of Fraunhofer lines in units of 10^{-10} m, a unit now known as the angstrom.

- The metric system of weights and measures is adopted in Japan.

NOVEMBER

23 French physicist Louis Ducos du Hauron patents a technique for taking color photographs. Photographs are taken through green, orange, and violet filters and then printed on sheets of gelatin containing red, blue, and yellow pigments—the complementary colors of the negatives. A color photograph is produced by superimposing the three positive transparencies.

Technology

- A revolving wheelcutter is introduced in Britain. It permits undercutting coal seam.

- German chemist Robert Wilhelm von Bunsen invents the filter pump.

- The British decorator Benjamin Maughan invents the domestic gas water heater.

- U.S. entrepreneur Philip Danforth Armour opens a meatpacking factory in Chicago, Illinois.

- U.S. inventor Charles Henry Gould invents the stapler. Used mainly by bookbinders, it dispenses with the need to sew many books.
- U.S. inventor William Remington patents a nickel electroplating process.
- U.S. machine-toolmaker William Sellars standardizes the system of screw threads in the United States.
- U.S. printer Christopher Latham Sholes develops a typewriter with a "QWERTY" keyboard that permits documents to be typed faster than they can be written out. The position of the keys reduces the chance of them jamming.

Transportation

- English engineer John Stringfellow builds a model triplane. Its design is adopted by future airplane developers.
- Former Confederate army officer Eli Hamilton Janney patents the automatic railroad "knuckle" coupler, which is safer than the link and pin linkage that it replaces.
- Models of helicopters are displayed at the London Aeronautical Exhibition, in England.
- The first regularly scheduled railroad dining car goes into operation in the United States; made by George M. Pullman, it is named "Delmonico," after the famous restaurant in New York, New York.
- The world's first traffic lights are installed in front of the House of Commons, London, England, to help pedestrians cross the street. They consist of red and green gas lamps which are alternately raised and lowered.
- U.S. inventor George Westinghouse introduces the air brake on U.S. railroads, significantly improving railroad safety.
- U.S. inventor William Davis patents a refrigerated metal railcar. Filled with ice, it is used to transport fish, meat, and fruit.

ARTS AND IDEAS

Arts

- The English artist George Frederick Watts paints his *Portrait of Thomas Carlyle*.
- The French artist Edouard Manet paints his *Portrait of Emile Zola* and *The Execution of Emperor Maximilian*.
- The French artist Paul Cézanne paints *Rape*.
- The French artist Pierre-Auguste Renoir paints *Alfred Sisley and His Wife*.
- The U.S. artist Martin Johnson Heade paints *Thunder Storm on Narragansett Bay*.
- The U.S. photographer Carlton Watkins publishes *The Yosemite Book*, an album of nature photographs.

Literature and Language

- *Passages from the American Notebooks* by the U.S. writer Nathaniel Hawthorne is published posthumously.
- The English poet Robert Browning publishes the first part of his long poem *The Ring and the Book*. The final part appears in 1869.

- The English writer Wilkie Collins publishes his novel *The Moonstone*.
- The English writer, designer, and social reformer William Morris publishes the first part of his long poem *The Early Paradise*. The final part appears in 1870.
- The German philosopher Friedrich Nietzsche publishes *Gözendammerung/Twilight of the Idols*.
- The Russian writer Fyodor Mikhaylovich Dostoyevsky publishes the first part of his novel *Idiot*. The second part appears in 1869.
- The U.S. writer Francis Bret(t) Harte publishes his stories "The Luck of Roaring Camp" in the journal *Overland Monthly*.
- The U.S. writer Louisa May Alcott publishes her novel *Little Women*. The second part appears in 1869.

Music

- Austrian composer Josef Anton Bruckner completes his Mass No. 3. The final version appears in 1893.
- French composer Georges Bizet completes his orchestral work *Marche funèbre/Funeral March* in B minor.
- German composer Johannes Brahms completes his choral work *Ein deutsche Requiem/A German Requiem*, his cantata *Rinaldo*, and his song cycle *Die schöne Magelone/The Fair Magelone* (Opus 33).
- German composer Max Bruch completes his Violin Concerto No. 1.
- Hungarian composer Franz Liszt completes his *Requiem*.
- Norwegian composer Edvard Grieg completes his Piano Concerto (Opus 16).
- Russian composer Nikolay Andreyevich Rimsky-Korsakov completes his Symphony No. 2, the *Antra*.
- Russian composer Peter Illyich Tchaikovsky completes his *Valse Caprice* for piano (Opus 4).
- The opera *Die Meistersinger von Nürnberg/The Mastersingers of Nuremberg* by the German composer Richard Wagner is first performed, in Munich, Germany.
- U.S. church organist Lewis H. Redner and U.S. pastor Philips Brooks write the hymn "O Little Town of Bethlehem."
- U.S. composer Horatio Richmond Palmer writes the hymn "Yield Not to Temptation."

Thought and Scholarship

- The Scottish philosopher Alexander Bain publishes *Mental and Moral Science*.

SOCIETY

Education

- The University of California is founded at Berkeley.
- Wayne State University is founded in Detroit, Michigan.
- Chicago millionaire Walter Loomis Miller bequeaths $2 million to establish a public library in Chicago, Illinois.

Everyday Life

- A fashion for women's dresses with large bustles at the back is popular in the United States.
- A pneumatic mail system, consisting of 400 km/250 mi of tubes laid out in a circle, is installed in Paris, France. It operates for over 100 years.
- The fraternal organization Benevolent Protective Order of Elks is established in New York, New York.
- The U.S. banker Edmund McIlhenny creates Tabasco sauce.
- British travel operator Thomas Cook offers the first organized tours to the Middle East.

MARCH
- Senior U.S. shoemakers establish the Order of the Knights of St. Crispin to protect themselves from upstart competitors.

Media and Communication

- Georgia publisher W. A. Hemphill establishes the newspaper *Atlanta Constitution*.
- The *World Almanac* is published for the first time, by the U.S. newspaper the *New York World*.
- The *Overland Monthly* newspaper is founded in San Francisco, California, with Francis Bret(t) Harte as editor.

Sports

c. 1868   Bicycling, or "velocipeding," is introduced to the United States from Europe.

MAY
31   The earliest known bicycle race, a 2-km/1.25-mi event for velocipedes at Parc de St.-Cloud, Paris, France, is won by the British rider James Moore.

SEPTEMBER
- The Scottish golfer Tom Morris, Jr., wins the first of four consecutive British Open victories. At the 166 yard eighth hole he hits the first recorded hole-in-one in competitive play. At 17 years 249 days, he remains the youngest player ever to win the event.

NOVEMBER
11   The first U.S. amateur track and field meeting is held at the Empire City Skating Rink, New York, New York, by the recently formed New York Athletic Club.

BIRTHS & DEATHS

FEBRUARY
11   Jean-Bernard-Léon Foucault, French physicist who invented Foucault's pendulum to demonstrate that the earth rotates, dies in Paris, France (48).
23   W. E. B. Du Bois, U.S. sociologist and black leader, born in Great Barrington, Massachusetts (−1963).

MARCH
22   Robert Andrews Millikan, U.S. physicist who developed a method of determining the electric charge on a single electron, born in Morrison, Illinois (−1953).
28   Maxim Gorky, Russian novelist and short-story writer, born in Nizhny Novogorod, Russia (−1936).

APRIL
1   Edmond Rostand, French dramatist who wrote *Cyrano de Bergerac*, born in Marseille, France (−1918).

MAY
7   Lord Henry Brougham, British Whig politician who was lord chancellor of England 1830–34 and who founded the University of London, dies in Cannes, France (89).
18   Nicholas II, Czar of Russia 1895–1917, born in Tsarskoye Selo, near St. Petersburg, Russia (−1918).

23   Kit Carson, U.S. frontiersman and Native American agent, dies in Fort Lyon, Colorado (58).

JUNE
1   James Buchanan, fifteenth president of the United States 1857–61, a Democrat, dies near Lancaster, Pennsylvania (77).
6   Robert Falcon Scott, British naval officer and explorer who tried to reach the South Pole, born in Devonport, Devon, England (−1912).
14   Karl Landsteiner, Austrian-born U.S. immunologist who discovered the ABO and MN blood groups and Rhesus factor, born in Vienna, Austria (−1943).
18   Miklós Horthy, Hungarian general and head of state 1920–44, born in Kenderes, Hungary (−1957).
29   George Ellery Hale, U.S. astronomer who developed the Hale telescope at Mt. Palomar, California, born in Chicago, Illinois (−1938).

JULY
12   Stefan George, German lyric poet, born in Büdesheim, near Bingen, Germany (−1933).
14   Gertrude Bell, English writer and administrator who helped establish the Hashimite dynasty in Baghdad,

born in Washington Hall, Durham, England (−1926).

AUGUST
29   Christian Friedrich Schönbein, German chemist who discovered ozone, dies in Sauersberg near Baden-Baden, Germany (68).

OCTOBER
23   Frederick William Lanchester, English automobile manufacturer who built the first British automobile powered by an internal combustion engine, born in London, England (−1946).

NOVEMBER
13   Gioacchino Rossini, Italian composer, dies in Passy, near Paris, France (76).
24   Scott Joplin, U.S. composer and pianist known as the "King of Ragtime," born in Bowie County, Texas (−1917).

DECEMBER
9   Fritz Haber, German chemist who discovered a method of producing ammonia cheaply, born in Breslau, Silesia, Prussia (now Wrocław, Poland) (−1934).
24   Emanuel Lasker, German chess master, world champion 1894–1920, born in Berlinchen, Prussia (−1941).

1869

POLITICS, GOVERNMENT, AND ECONOMICS

Business and Economics

- Baptist Sunday school superintendent Francis Wayland Ayer founds the United States's first modern advertising agency.
- Foreigners invest $1.5 billion in the United States; U.S. interests invest $100 million overseas.
- Henry John Heinz goes into partnership with L. C. Noble and launches his first food product, horseradish in jars, in the United States.

SEPTEMBER
- In what becomes known as Black Friday, the crooked machinations of investors Jay Gould and James Fisk inspire panic on the U.S. gold market.

Human Rights

- Arabella Mansfield becomes the first woman to be admitted to the bar in the United States, in Iowa.
- The English philosopher John Stuart Mill publishes "The Subjection of Women," an essay arguing for sexual equality.
- The U.S. state of Wyoming enfranchises women and gives them the right to hold office.

MAY
- Elizabeth Cady Stanton and Susan B. Anthony establish the National Woman Suffrage Association.

Politics and Government

- The Russian anarchist Mikhail Alexandrovich Bakunin founds the Social Democratic Alliance to agitate for spontaneous revolution.
- The song "Come Home Father ," written by Henry Clay Work for a dramatization of the play *Ten Nights in a Barroom* by Timothy Shay Arthur in 1864, is adopted as the anthem of the U.S. Prohibition Party.
- Tunisia accepts control by Britain, Italy, and France because of its bankruptcy.

FEBRUARY
- Treason charges against ex-Confederate president Jefferson Davis are dropped in the wake of President Andrew Johnson's general amnesty of the previous December.

MARCH
- Ulysses S. Grant is inaugurated 18th president of the United States.

APRIL
- After ratifying the 15th Amendment, guaranteeing black American male suffrage, Virginia, Georgia, Mississippi, and Texas are readmitted to the Union.

JUNE
1   A new Spanish constitution is promulgated following the deposition of Queen Isabella II in 1868, providing for the continuation of monarchical government.

JULY
12   Genuine legislative power is granted to the French National Assembly by Emperor Napoleon III following agitation for political reform, while he preserves imperial control.

SEPTEMBER
9   The National Prohibition Party is formed in Chicago, Illinois, to agitate for temperance (prohibition of alcohol).

OCTOBER
11   The Red River Rebellion begins in Canada when mixed-blooded rebels, led by the half-Irish, half-Native American rebel Louis Riel, stop a survey team near Winnipeg, Manitoba, fearing the government wants to seize their land.

NOVEMBER
19   The Canadian government purchases territories in the northwest belonging to the Hudson Bay Company.

DECEMBER
- The Wyoming Territory becomes the first U.S. state or territory to grant suffrage to women.

SCIENCE, TECHNOLOGY, AND MEDICINE

Agriculture

- French naturalist Leopold Trouvelot imports gypsy moths (*Porthetria dispar*) into Massachusetts, United States, to start a silk industry, but they escape to become a major pest of forest and fruit trees.
- Coffee plantations in Ceylon (Sri Lanka) and Java are destroyed by coffee rust *Hamileia vastatrix*. Over the next 20 years it spreads throughout southeast Asia leading to a widespread conversion to tea cultivation.

Ecology

- English meteorologist Alexander Buchan produces the first weather maps showing the average monthly and annual air pressure for the world. They provide information about the atmosphere's circulation.
- U.S. astronomer Abbe Cleveland begins issuing daily weather bulletins.
- German embryologist Ernst Haeckel coins the word "ecology."

Exploration

- Civil War veteran John Wesley Powell becomes the first U.S. citizen to navigate the Colorado River through the Grand Canyon, a feat he accomplished with one arm.
- German explorer Gustave Nachtigal begins a six-year expedition to the Sahara and the Sudan.

Health and Medicine

- Massachusetts establishes the first state board of health.
- Norwegian physician Gerhard Henrik Armauer Hansen discovers the leprosy bacillus *Mycobacterium leprae*.
- German physician Paul Langerhans discovers irregularly-shaped sections of endocrine tissue in the pancreas that secrete glucagon and insulin, which are essential for normal human metabolism. The sections are now known as the islets of Langerhans.

Science

- Based on the fact that the elements exhibit recurring patterns of properties when placed in order of increasing atomic weight, Russian chemist Dmitry Ivanovich Mendeleyev develops the periodic classification of the elements. He leaves gaps for elements yet to be discovered.
- English anthropologist and eugenicist Francis Galton publishes *Hereditary Genius, its Laws and Consequences*, founding the science of eugenics. He argues that the physical and mental characteristics of humans can be improved through selective marriages.
- English naturalist Thomas Henry Huxley, in *Protoplasm, the Physical Basis of Life* argues that life could develop from inorganic chemicals.
- Swiss biochemist Johann Miescher discovers a nitrogen and phosphorous material in cell nuclei that he calls nuclein but which is now known as the genetic material DNA.

Technology

- U.S. scientist John Wesley Hyatt, in an effort to find a substitute for the ivory in billiard balls, invents (independently of Alexander Parkes) celluloid. The first artificial plastic, it can be produced cheaply in a variety of colors, is resistant to water, oil, and weak acids, and quickly finds use in making such things as combs, toys, and false teeth.
- "Cup and cone" ball-bearings are invented.
- Belgian electrical engineer Zénobe-Théophile Gramme invents the first commercially practical generator of direct current (DC). It produces a continuous current at high voltages. It is a primary stimulus to the further development of electric power.
- French physicist Louis Ducos du Hauron publishes *Les Couleurs en photographie: Solution du problème/Colors in Photography: Solution of the Problem*, in which he identifies the additive and subtractive system of color photography.
- The first electric washing-machine is built.
- U.S. inventor Thomas Alva Edison develops the first electric voting machine; the first one is authorized for use in 1892.

JANUARY

- U.S. inventor Thomas Edison develops a duplex telegraph which can transmit two messages simultaneously on the same wire.

Transportation

- The British clipper ship *Cutty Sark* is launched. It is one of the largest sailing ships at 65 m/212 ft long.
- The first chain-driven bicycle is built by the firm of A. Guilmet and Meyer.
- The French manufacturer G. Anthoni manufactures the first bicycle with four gears.
- U.S. Baptist minister Jonathan Scobie invents the rickshaw to transport his invalid wife around Yokohama, Japan. It comes into widespread use throughout the area.
- U.S. inventor George Westinghouse patents the air brake for railroads. They are made compulsory in the United States in 1893.

MAY

10 The first U.S. transcontinental railroad is completed when the Union Pacific Railroad, building west, and the Central Pacific Railroad, building east, meet at Promontory Point, Utah. It is 2,832 km/1,770 mi long.

JULY

- The Hannibal Bridge in Kansas City, Missouri, opens. Built by U.S. engineer Frederick Joy, it is the first permanent bridge to span the Missouri River.

NOVEMBER

17 French diplomat and engineer Ferdinand de Lesseps completes the 168-km/105-mi-long Suez Canal in Egypt that links the Mediterranean and the Red Sea, and which reduces the route from Europe to Asia by 8,000 km/5,000 mi.

ARTS AND IDEAS

Architecture

- The Pont de Chatelleraut, the first notable reinforced concrete bridge, is built, in Paris, France.

Arts

- The French artist Edgar Degas paints *The Orchestra of the Opéra*.

- The French artist Edouard Manet paints *Lunch in the Studio*.
- The French artist Jean-Baptiste Carpeaux sculpts *The Dance*.
- The French artist Paul Cézanne paints *The Magdelene*.
- The French artist Pierre-Auguste Renoir paints *Le Grenouillère*.
- The U.S. artist John Frederick Kensett paints *Lake George*.
- The U.S. artist Thomas Moran paints *Spirit of the Indian*.
- The U.S. artist Winslow Homer paints *Long Beach, New Jersey*.

Literature and Language

- The English writer R. D. Blackmore publishes his novel *Lorna Doone*.
- The French novelist Gustave Flaubert publishes his novel *L'Education sentimentale/A Sentimental Education*.
- The French writer Victor Hugo publishes his novel *L'Homme qui rit/Laughing Man*.
- The Perkins Institute in Boston, Massachusetts, produces the first novel in raised type for blind people, Charles Dickens' *The Old Curiosity Shop*.
- The Russian writer Ivan Alexandrovich Goncharov publishes his novel *Obryv/The Precipice*.
- The U.S. writer Francis Bret(t) Harte publishes his stories "The Outcasts of Poker Flat" in the journal *Overland Monthly*.
- The U.S. writer Harriet Beecher Stowe publishes her novel *Oldtown Folks*.
- The U.S. writer Mark Twain publishes *The Innocents Abroad, or The New Pilgrims' Progress*, a book of humorous travel stories that originated from sketches published in newspapers.

Music

- German composer Johannes Brahms completes the last of his *Ungarische Tänze/Hungarian Dances* for piano and his *Liebesliederwalzer/Love Song Waltzes* for piano and voices (Opus 52).
- The opera *Das Rheingold* by the German composer Richard Wagner is first performed, in Munich, Germany. It is the first part of his *Der Ring des Nibelungen/The Ring of the Nibelung* cycle of operas.
- The opera *Voyevoda/Dream on the Volga* by the Russian composer Peter Illyich Tchaikovsky is first performed, in Moscow, Russia. In the same year, he completes the first version of his overture *Romeo and Juliet*; the final version appears in 1880.
- U.S. composer Frank Campbell and U.S. lyricist Billy Reeves write the song "Shoo Fly, Don't Bother Me."

Theater and Dance

- The comedy *Froufrou* by the French writer Ludovic Halévy is first performed, in Paris, France.

Thought and Scholarship

- The English historian William Edward Hartpole Lecky publishes *A History of European Morals from Augustus to Charlemagne*.
- The English philosopher James Knowles founds the Philosophical Society in London, England.
- The English social economist William Thomas Thornton publishes *On Labour*.
- The English social scientist and literary critic Walter Bagehot publishes *Physics and Politics*.
- The English writer Matthew Arnold publishes *Culture and Anarchy*. His major work, it is a study of the moral, intellectual, and religious perplexities of Victorian society.
- The Russian political thinker Alexander Ivanovich Herzen publishes his open letter "K staromu tovarishchy"/"To An Old Comrade." Addressed to the anarchist Bakunin, it rejects the legitimacy of violent revolution.
- The U.S. historian Francis Parkman publishes *The Discovery of the Great West*.

SOCIETY

Education

- Harvard University dean Nathaniel S. Shaler offers the first informal summer school course in the United States.
- Purdue University is founded in West Lafayette, Indiana.
- Southern Illinois University is founded at Carbondale, Illinois.
- The University of Nebraska is founded at Lincoln, Nebraska.

Everyday Life

- French chemist Hippolyte Mège-Mouriés patents margarine.

December
- Black American delegates to the Colored National Labor Convention meet in Washington, D.C., to promote the interests of black workers.

Media and Communication

November
4 English astronomer Norman Lockyer begins publication of the weekly science journal *Nature*.

Sports

- Henry Chadwick, a New York journalist and baseball administrator, publishes the first annual baseball handbook, the precursor of *Spalding's Official Baseball Guide*.

- The All England Croquet Club is founded in Wimbledon, London. Eleven years later it is retitled the All England Lawn Tennis and Croquet Club.
- The Cincinnati Red Stockings, the first U.S. professional baseball club, are founded by Harry Wright.
- Water polo, originally called "football in the water," is invented in England.

NOVEMBER

6   Rutgers defeats Princeton 6–4 at New Brunswick, New Jersey, in the first intercollegiate football match. The game is played under modified English Football Association (soccer) rules, however over the next few years most of the major schools in the eastern United States take up rugby.

Religion

- Roman Catholics in Britain number 950,000, of whom 750,000 are Irish immigrants.

November 1869–70   At the First Vatican Council, a council of the Roman Catholic Church convened by Pope Pius IX, liberalism is condemned. On July 18, 1870, the council issues the "Declaration of Papal Infallibility," declaring that papal pronouncements on spiritual questions are not questionable.

BIRTHS & DEATHS

FEBRUARY

14   Charles Thomson Rees Wilson, Scottish physicist who invented the cloud chamber to study radioactivity, cosmic rays, and X-rays, born in Glencorse, Midlothian, Scotland (–1959).

28   Alphonse de Lamartine, French romantic poet and statesman, dies in Paris, France (79).

MARCH

8   Hector Berlioz, French composer, dies in Paris, France (65).

18   (Arthur) Neville Bowes Chamberlain, British prime minister 1937–40, a Conservative, born in Birmingham, Warwickshire, England (–1940).

21   Florenz Ziegfeld, U.S. theatrical producer known for his Ziegfeld Follies, a revue show based on the Folies Bergères, which ran annually 1907–31, born in Chicago, Illinois (–1932).

29   Aleš Hrdlička, U.S. anthropologist who theorized that Native North Americans migrated from Asia, born in Humpolec, Bohemia (–1943).

29   Edwin Landseer Lutyens, English architect who planned the city of New Delhi, India, born in London, England (–1944).

JULY

22   John Augustus Roebling, German-born U.S. architect who pioneered the construction of suspension bridges and designed the Brooklyn Bridge, dies in Brooklyn Heights, New York (63).

AUGUST

8   Roger Fenton, English photographer who covered the Crimean War, dies in London, England (c. 50).

SEPTEMBER

12   Peter Mark Roget, English physician and philologist known for his *Thesaurus of English Words and Phrases*, dies in Malvern, Worcestershire, England (90).

25   Rudolf Otto, German theologian, philosopher, and historian, born in Peine, Prussia (–1937).

OCTOBER

2   Mahatma Gandhi (honorific name of Mohandas Karamchand Gandhi), leader of the nationalist movement to free India from British rule, born in Porbandar, India (–1948).

8   Frank Duryea, U.S. inventor who, with his brother Charles Duryea, built the first practical automobile powered by an internal combustion engine in the United States, born in Washburn, Illinois (–1967).

8   Franklin Pierce, fourteenth president of the United States 1853–57, a Democrat, dies in Concord, New Hampshire (64).

13   Charles-Augustin Ste.-Beuve, French historian and literary critic, dies in Paris, France (64).

23   Edward Stanley, Earl of Derby, British prime minister in 1852, 1858–59, and 1866–68, a Conservative, dies in London, England (70).

23   John Heisman, U.S. football coach who introduced a number of innovations to the game, born in Cleveland, Ohio (–1936).

NOVEMBER

22   André Gide, French writer and humanist, born in Paris, France (–1951).

DECEMBER

30   Stephen Leacock, Canadian humorist and author, born in Swanmore, Hampshire, England (–1944).

31   Henri Matisse, French painter, sculptor, illustrator, and designer, born in Le Cateau, France (–1954).

1870

POLITICS, GOVERNMENT, AND ECONOMICS

Business and Economics

- The Atlantic Refining Company incorporates in New Jersey.
- The U.S. oil company now known as the Exxon Corporation is incorporated as the Standard Oil Company in Ohio. Its directors include John D. Rockefeller.
- The world production of steel is 560,000 tons (half by Great Britain).
- Coal production (in millions of tons) in selected countries: Great Britain, 110.4; United States 35; Germany, 294; Austria-Hungary, 13; France, 12.
- Iron production (in millions of tons) in selected countries: Great Britain, 5.9; United States, 1.6; Germany, 1.3; France, 1.2; Russia, 0.4.

JANUARY

10 U.S. industrialist John D. Rockefeller founds the Standard Oil Company in Ohio; it quickly comes to dominate the U.S. oil industry.

Politics and Government

- In U.S. Congressional elections, Republicans retain majorities in the House (134–104) and Senate (52–17).
- The Home Rule Association is founded by the Irish politician Isaac Butt to agitate for Irish independence.
- The Massachusetts assembly establishes the nation's first state bureau of labor.
- U.S. president Ulysses S. Grant appoints Pennsylvania congressman William Strong and New Jersey jurist Joseph P. Bradley to the U.S. Supreme Court.

JANUARY

- The Grant administration presents the Senate with a treaty providing for U.S. annexation of the Dominican Republic, which had achieved independence from Spain in 1865.
- The U.S. Congress authorizes the Virginia legislature to send representatives to Congress providing that its members swear never to amend their constitution in such a way as to deny black American civil or political rights.

- U.S. cartoonist Thomas Nast introduces the donkey as the symbol of the Democratic Party in an edition of *Harper's Weekly*.
1 The traditionally pro-Austrian German state of Baden decides to seek entry to the Prussian-dominated North German Confederation.
2 The moderate politician Emile Ollivier becomes French prime minister, but is forced to admit more progressive members to his ministry.

FEBRUARY

- Congress creates the U.S. Weather Bureau.
- The U.S. Congress authorizes the Mississippi legislature to send representatives to Congress providing that its members swear never to amend their constitution in such a way as to deny black American civil or political rights.

MARCH

- The 15th Amendment to the U.S. Constitution, guaranteeing black American voting rights, becomes law.
- The U.S. Congress authorizes the Texas legislature to send representatives to Congress providing that its members swear never to amend their constitution in such a way as to deny black American civil or political rights. Mississippi senator Hiram R. Revels becomes the first black American to sit in the U.S. Congress.
1 Paraguayan president Francisco Solano López is killed in the war against the combined forces of Brazil, Argentina, and Uruguay.

APRIL

20 The Senate in France is made an Upper House, sharing legislative powers with the National Assembly, further liberalizing the political system of the Second Empire.

MAY

12 A Fenian (Irish terrorist) attack from Vermont on Quebec, Canada, fails.
12 Manitoba is made a Canadian province, which helps to end the Red River Rebellion by mixed-blood rebels over territory.

JUNE

- The U.S. Congress creates the Department of Justice.
- The U.S. Senate rejects a treaty providing for U.S. annexation of the Dominican Republic.
25 Queen Isabella II of Spain abdicates in Paris, France, in favor of her son Alfonso (XII), having been driven from power by Liberal rebels.
28 A decree issued in Russia by the reforming czar Alexander II liberalizes the structure of municipal government.

JULY

- The U.S. Congress authorizes the Georgia legislature to send representatives to Congress.

Franco-Prussian War (1870–71)

1870

JULY

13 A French ultimatum to Prussia not to renew its attempts to put a Hohenzollern ruler on the Spanish throne results in the "Ems Telegram," a conciliatory message from King Wilhelm I of Prussia provocatively rewritten by the Prussian chancellor Otto von Bismarck to incite war.

19 France declares war on Prussia following its receipt of the "Ems Telegram."

AUGUST

4 The French army, led by Marshal Marie-Edmé-Patrice-Maurice MacMahon, duc de Magenta, is defeated at Weissenberg, Bavaria, by Prussian forces under Crown Prince Frederick.

6 French forces are defeated by the Prussians at Wörth and Spicheren in Alsace.

16 Prussian forces defeat the French at Vionville and Mars-la-Tour, France.

18 The French are again defeated by the Prussians at Gravelotte and St. Privat, France.

19 The siege of French troops in the fortress of Metz, northeast France, by advancing Prussians begins.

SEPTEMBER

1 The French army is defeated by the Prussians at Sedan, France, in the decisive battle of the Franco-Prussian War.

2 Emperor Napoleon III of France capitulates to the Prussians at Sedan, France, conceding defeat in the Franco-Prussian War.

4 The French defeat leads to a revolt in Paris against the government of Napoleon III. A provisional government of national defense is set up to continue the war against Prussia and a republic is proclaimed.

4 The regime of Napoleon III is overthrown in Paris after his capture by Prussian forces.

19 Prussian forces begin the siege of Paris, whose inhabitants are in revolt against Napoleon III and continue the war against Prussia.

OCTOBER

27 French troops besieged by the Prussians in Metz surrender.

28 French forces surrender to Prussian forces in Strasbourg, France.

1871

JANUARY

19 French forces still contesting Prussian victory are defeated at St. Quentin, France.

28 Paris, besieged by Prussian forces since September 1870, capitulates and an armistice with Germany is signed.

MARCH

18 A left-wing rising begins in Paris, when soldiers sent to requisition cannons stationed in the city side with the populace, who wish to establish their own radical government and continue the war with Prussia.

MAY

10 The Peace of Frankfurt formally ends the Franco-Prussian War. France is to cede Alsace-Lorraine to Germany, pay an indemnity of 5 milliards of francs, and be subject to military occupation until payment is completed.

---

2 News reaches France of the acceptance of the vacant Spanish throne by Prince Leopold of Hohenzollern, unacceptably extending Prussian influence over Spain.

12 Prince Leopold of Hohenzollern's acceptance of the Spanish throne is withdrawn by his father, King Wilhelm I of Prussia, because of the threat of war with France over the matter.

13 A French ultimatum to Prussia not to renew its attempts to put a Hohenzollern ruler on the Spanish throne results in the "Ems Telegram," a conciliatory message from King Wilhelm I of Prussia provocatively rewritten by the Prussian chancellor Otto von Bismarck to incite war.

19 France declares war on Prussia following its receipt of the "Ems Telegram" of July 13.

30 Austria revokes its 1855 concordat with the papacy following the promulgation of the decree of papal infallibility.

AUGUST

1 An Irish Land Act passed by the British government provides for loans to peasants to buy land, and grants compensation for eviction and for improvements made to premises they have rented.

4 The French army, led by Marshal Marie-Edmé-Patrice-Maurice MacMahon, duc de Magenta, is defeated at Weissenberg, Bavaria, by Prussian forces under Crown Prince Frederick during the Franco-Prussian War provoked by the "Ems Telegram" of July 13.

6 French forces are defeated by the Prussians at Wörth and Spicheren in Alsace.

8 By a British act of Parliament, Western Australia is granted representative government.

9 Prussia guarantees Belgian neutrality in the Franco-Prussian War.

11 Britain and France guarantee the integrity of Belgium in the conflict between France and Prussia.

16 Prussian forces defeat the French at Vionville and Mars-la-Tour, France.

18 The French are again defeated by the Prussians at Gravelotte and St. Privat, France.

19 The siege of French troops in the fortress of Metz, northeast France, by advancing Prussians begins.

SEPTEMBER

1 The French army is defeated by the Prussians at Sedan, France, in the decisive battle of the Franco-Prussian War.

2 Emperor Napoleon III of France capitulates to the Prussians at Sedan, France, conceding defeat in the Franco-Prussian War.

4 The French defeat in the Franco-Prussian War leads to a revolt in Paris, France, against the government of Emperor Napoleon III. A provisional government of

national defense is set up to continue the war against Prussia and a republic is proclaimed.

4 The regime of Emperor Napoleon III is overthrown in Paris, France, after his capture by Prussian forces.

19 Prussian forces begin the siege of Paris, France, whose inhabitants are in revolt against Emperor Napoleon III and continue the war against Prussia.

20 Italian troops led by King Victor Emmanuel II enter Rome and take over the city following the withdrawal of French troops on the fall of Emperor Napoleon III of France.

OCTOBER

9 Rome is made the capital of Italy by decree, with King Victor Emmanuel II of Italy formally incorporating Rome and the Roman provinces into Italy.

27 French troops besieged by the Prussians in Metz, northeast France, surrender.

28 French forces continuing the Franco-Prussian War surrender to Prussian forces in Strasbourg, France.

NOVEMBER

16 Armadeo, Duke of Aosta and son of King Victor Emmanuel II of Italy, is elected king of Spain by the cortes (national assembly).

23 A treaty of alliance between the Prussian-led North German Confederation and the former Austrian ally Bavaria is signed, following the Prussian victory in the Franco-Prussian War which establishes it as the strongest power in central and western Europe.

DECEMBER

• The North Carolina legislature impeaches governor William Woods Holden, replacing him with Tod R. Caldwell.

12 The (Catholic) German Center Party is established to defend the Catholic interests of the south German states which have recently joined the Prussian (and Protestant) dominated German Empire.

SCIENCE, TECHNOLOGY, AND MEDICINE

Agriculture

• Canadian fruit-grower Alan MacIntosh propagates the MacIntosh apple.

December 1870–1910 The sorghum plant is introduced in the United States. It is used for forage and for making syrup.

Ecology

• Diamond fields are discovered in the Orange Free State, southern Africa.

• The National Botanical Garden of Belgium is established in Brussels.

Exploration

• Swedish explorer Adolf Erik Nordenskjöld makes the first known expedition to the interior of Greenland.

June 1870–80 Russian explorer and naturalist Nikolay Mikhailovich Przhevalsky crosses the Gobi Desert from Lake Baikal to Kalgan, 160 km/100 mi from Beijing in China. He subsequently explores the northern side of the Tibetan plateau from Mongolia, but is not permitted to enter Lhasa, the Tibetan capital.

Science

• British philosopher William Kingdon Clifford foreshadows Albert Einstein's theory of general relativity with his publication of "On the Space-Theory of Matter," in which he suggests that matter and energy are different forms of curved space.

• German archeologist Heinrich Schliemann begins archeological excavations at Hissarlik, in Anatolia (modern Turkey), the site of the ancient city of Troy.

• German archeologist Alexander Conze arranges pottery styles in chronological order which permits the comparative dating of stratified sites.

• German chemist Robert Wilhelm von Bunsen invents the ice calorimeter, which uses ice to measure the heat given off during a chemical reaction.

• The Science Museum of Victoria is established at Melbourne, Australia.

Technology

• U.S. inventor Richard Hoe improves his rotary printing press by printing on both sides of the paper.

• U.S. inventor William Bullock invents a device for automatically folding newspapers; he incorporates it into his rotary press.

Transportation

• English engineer William Froude builds a model-testing tank in Torquay, Devon, to test the physical laws affecting ships on scale models, influencing subsequent ship design.

• English inventor James Starley makes the first "pennyfarthing" bicycle, so named because the difference in size between the wheels resembles the difference between the largest and smallest British coins.

• English inventors James Starley and William Hillman patent the Ariel Cycle, the first lightweight metal bicycle.

• The Suez Canal in Egypt is used by 436,000 tons of shipping; 71% of the traffic is British shipping.

ARTS AND IDEAS

Architecture

• Keble College, Oxford University, Oxford, England, designed by the English architect William Butterfield, is completed.

- St. Pancras railroad station opens in London, England. Built by British architect William Barlow, it uses wrought-iron trussed arches with a span of 74 m/243 ft, and a height of 30 m/100 ft to create one of the world's largest enclosed spaces.

JANUARY
- Construction begins on the Brooklyn Bridge, New York, New York, which will connect Brooklyn to Manhattan.

Arts

- The English artist John Everett Millais paints *The Boyhood of Raleigh*.
- The French artist Berthe Morisot paints *The Artist's Sister and Their Mother*.
- The U.S. Congress incorporates the Corcoran Art Gallery in Washington, D.C.

Film

- English scientist William Henry Fox Talbot reduces photographic exposure time to one-hundredth of a second, making moving pictures feasible.

Literature and Language

- *Passages from the English Notebooks* by the U.S. writer Nathaniel Hawthorne is published posthumously.
- Charles Scribner founds *Scribner's Monthly*, a literary journal.
- The English artist and poet Dante Gabriel Rossetti publishes *Poems*.
- The English statesman and writer Benjamin Disraeli, Earl of Beaconsfield, publishes his novel *Lothair*.
- The English writer Charles Dickens leaves his last novel, *The Mystery of Edwin Drood*, unfinished.
- The French writer Jules Verne publishes his novel *Vingt Mille Lieues sous les mers/Twenty Thousand Leagues Under the Sea*.
- The Hungarian writer Mór Jókai publishes his novel *Fekete gyémántok/Black Diamonds*.
- The U.S. writer Francis Bret(t) Harte publishes *The Luck of Roaring Camp and Other Stories*, which includes, along with the title story, "The Outcasts of Poker Flats" and "Tennessee's Partner." The stories first appeared in the magazine *Overland Monthly*.

Music

- German composer Richard Wagner completes his orchestral work *Siegfried Idyll*, written to celebrate his wife's birthday. In the same year, his opera *Die Walküre/The Valkyrie* is first performed, in Munich, Germany. It is the second part of his *Der Ring des Nibelungen/The Ring of the Nibelung* cycle of operas.

Theater and Dance

- The ballet *Coppélia, ou La Fille aux yeux d'émail/ Coppelia, or the Girl with Enamel Eyes* by the French composer Léo Delibes is first performed, in Paris, France. The choreography is by the French choreographer Arthur St.-Léon.

Thought and Scholarship

- The French historian and critic Hippolyte-Adolphe Taine publishes *De l'Intelligence/On Intelligence*.
- The U.S. essayist Ralph Waldo Emerson publishes his collection of lectures *Society and Solitude*.

SOCIETY

Education

- A University Extension Lectures Board is established in Cambridge, England, to provide lecturers for British mechanics institutes and other bodies for the education of workers.
- Colorado State University is founded at Fort Collins, Colorado.
- Harvard and Yale universities launch extensive graduate studies programs.
- Ohio State University is founded at Columbus, Ohio.
- St. John's University is founded in New York, New York.
- Syracuse University is founded in Syracuse, New York.

Everyday Life

c. 1870   The British drinks company Schweppess produces ginger ale.
- The Irish doctor Thomas Barnardo opens the East End Juvenile Mission in London, England, as a refuge for impoverished young boys.
- The Jürgens Mekaniske Establissement in Copenhagen, Denmark, begins manufacturing the *Skrivekugle*, the first commercial typewriter.
- The U.S. Census lists the nation's population at 39,818,449, up from roughly 31,515,000 in 1860.
- U.S. inventor William W. Lyman patents his design for a gripping can opener with a cutting wheel.

JUNE
5   A fire in Constantinople, in the Ottoman Empire, kills 900 people.

OCTOBER
1   The British Post Office issues the world's first postcards.

Media and Communication

- A telegraph link between Britain and India opens.
- The British newspaper the *Daily Telegraph* has the largest circulation in the world, with sales in excess of 250,000 copies.

Religion

- Black bishop Robert Paine founds the Colored Methodist Episcopal Church in the town of Jackson, Tennessee.
- The English churchman John Newman publishes *The Grammar of Assent*, a defense of religious belief.

Sports

- The National Association for the Promotion of the Interests of the Trotting Turf, later renamed the National Trotting Association, is founded in the United States.

AUGUST

8 The U.S. yacht *Magic* defeats the British challenger *Cambria* in the inaugural America's Cup race.

BIRTHS & DEATHS

c. 1870 "Typhoid Mary" (nickname of Mary Mallon), U.S. cook and a carrier of typhoid who caused several outbreaks of the disease in the New York City area during the early 1900s, born (–1938).

c. 1870 Edwin S. Porter, U.S. pioneer filmmaker who introduced creative dramatic editing, born in Scotland (–1941).

c. 1870 Sundance Kid (nickname of Harry Longarbaugh), U.S. train and bank robber, born in Phoenixville, Pennsylvania (–*c.* 1909).

JANUARY

8 Primo de Rivera, Spanish general, dictator of Spain 1923–30, born in Cadiz, Spain (–1930).

21 Alexander Ivanovich Herzen, Russian journalist and political activist who argued that Russian socialism would be achieved through a peasant revolt, dies in Paris, France (57).

FEBRUARY

7 Alfred Adler, Austrian psychiatrist who introduced the idea of the inferiority complex, born in Penzing, Austria (–1937).

12 English music hall artist "Marie Lloyd" (pseudonym of Matilda Wood) born in London, England (–1922).

MARCH

4 English poet, wood-engraver, and critic Thomas Sturge Moore, brother of philosopher George Moore (1873–1958), born in Hastings, Surrey, England (–1944).

13 Charles Forbes-René, comte de Montalembert, French orator, politician, and historian, dies in Paris, France (59).

29 George Henry Thomas, Union general during the American Civil War, dies in San Francisco, California (53).

29 Paul-Emile Botta, French archeologist whose discovery of the palace of the Assyrian king Sargon I in 1843 sparked other excavations in Mesopotamia, dies in Achères, France (68).

APRIL

22 Vladimir Ilyich Lenin, founder of the Russian Communist Party, leader of the Russian Revolution, and head of the Soviet Union 1917–24, born in Simbirsk, Russia (–1924).

MAY

6 James Young Simpson, British physician, the first to use chloroform as an anesthetic in obstetrics and the first to use ether in Britain, dies in London, England (58).

24 Benjamin Cardozo, justice of the U.S. Supreme Court, born in New York, New York (–1938).

24 Jan Christian Smuts, Boer soldier and statesman, prime minister of South Africa 1919–24 and 1939–48, born in Bovenplaats, near Riebeeck, Cape Colony (–1950).

JUNE

9 Charles Dickens, English novelist of the Victorian era, dies in Gad's Hill, Chatham, Kent, England (58).

13 Jules Bordet, Belgian bacteriologist who received the Nobel Prize for Physiology or Medicine in 1919 for his discovery of immune factors in the blood, born in Soignies, Belgium (–1961).

17 Kitaro Nishida, Japanese philosopher who attempted to integrate Western philosophy with Japanese spiritual traditions, born near Kanazawa, Japan (–1945).

JULY

29 George Dixon, Canadian-born U.S. bantamweight boxer and the first black person to win a boxing championship, born in Halifax, Canada (–1909).

AUGUST

19 Bernard Baruch, U.S. presidential advisor who helped draft the United Nations policy with regard to controlling atomic energy, born in Camden, South Carolina (–1965).

31 Maria Montessori, Italian educator, born in Chiaravalle, near Ancona, Italy (–1952).

SEPTEMBER

23 Prosper Mérimée, French dramatist, historian, and archeologist, dies in Cannes, France (66).

OCTOBER

12 Robert E. Lee, Confederate general who commanded the Southern armies during the American Civil War, dies in Lexington, Virginia (63).

DECEMBER

5 Alexandre Dumas (*père*), French novelist best known for *The Count of Monte Cristo* and *The Three Musketeers* (both 1844), dies in Puys, France (68).

6 William S. Hart, U.S. silent-film actor known for his Westerns, born in Newburgh, New York (–1946).

18 "Saki" (pseudonym of Hector Hugh Munro), Scottish writer, born in Akyab, Burma (–1916).

1871

POLITICS, GOVERNMENT, AND ECONOMICS

Business and Economics

- The investment house Drexel, Morgan & Company opens at 23 Wall Street, in lower Manhattan, New York, New York.
- B. F. Goodrich Co. is founded in Akron, Ohio, by the U.S. chemist Benjamin Franklin Goodrich. The company's first product is rubber fire hose, to replace leather hoses that crack in the cold.
- Coal production (in millions of tons) for selected countries: Great Britain, 117.4; United States, 35; Germany, 29.4; France, 13.3; Austria-Hungary, 12.5.
- Iron production (in millions of tons) for selected countries: Great Britain, 6.6; France, 2.5; Germany, 1.4.

DECEMBER

4   Germany adopts the gold standard, tying the value of its currency to the price of gold.

Colonization

JULY

20 The British colony of British Columbia joins the Dominion of Canada.

AUGUST

8   The British protectorate of Basutoland (modern Lesotho) is united with Cape Colony in southern Africa.

Politics and Government

- Arsonists destroy the French royal residence, the Tuileries Palace, as well as parts of the Louvre, in Paris, France.
- The new U.S. Department of Justice establishes the federal prison system.

JANUARY

18 Following the defeat of Emperor Napoleon III of France in the Franco-Prussian War, King Wilhelm I of Prussia is proclaimed German emperor at Versailles in France, the North German Confederation having been enlarged to include all the German states except Austria-Hungary.

19 French forces still contesting Prussian victory in the Franco-Prussian War are defeated at St. Quentin, France.

28 The French capital, Paris, besieged by Prussian forces since September 1870, capitulates and an armistice with Germany is signed.

FEBRUARY

12 The French National Assembly convened after the fall of Emperor Napoleon III in the Franco-Prussian War meets at Bordeaux, France.

17 The veteran French Liberal statesman Adolphe Thiers becomes head of the executive of the French National Assembly, committed to a program of peace with Germany.

21 The U.S. Congress grants the District of Columbia a territorial government.

26 A preliminary peace between France and Germany is signed at Versailles, France.

28 In the face of southern disenfranchisement of black American men, the U.S. Congress adopts legislation providing for federal supervision of elections in cities with populations above 20,000.

MARCH

3   The U.S. Congress passes the Indian Appropriation Act, making all Native Americans wards of the federal government and annulling all treaties with indigenous North American tribes.

4   U.S. president Ulysses S. Grant establishes a civil service commission in the United States.

13 The London Conference between the great powers of Europe revokes the Black Sea clauses of the Treaty of Paris of 1856 and gives Russia the freedom to deploy its forces in the Black Sea (following Russia's independent repudiation of these clauses in October 1870).

18 A left-wing rising begins in Paris, France, when soldiers sent to requisition cannons stationed in the city side with the populace, who wish to establish their own radical government and continue the war with Prussia.

22 A commune is set up in Lyons, France, along the lines of the Paris Commune (provisional national government). The following day a similar commune is set up in Marseille.

26 The extreme left-wing Paris Commune is formally established in the French capital by popular elections.

APRIL

16 The newly established German Empire receives a constitution remodeled from that of the North German Confederation (of which it is a development).

MAY

1   One year after the Legal Tender Act of 1862 had been declared unconstitutional on the grounds that it represented an abuse of federal power, a newly constituted U.S. Supreme Court upholds the act in the *Knox v. Lee* case, exposing President Ulysses S. Grant to charges of court-packing.

8 The United States and Britain sign the Treaty of Washington, by which they agree to arbitrate U.S. claims for damages incurred by Confederate ships built or outfitted by Britain.

10 The Peace of Frankfurt formally ends the Franco-Prussian War. France is to cede Alsace-Lorraine to Germany, pay an indemnity of 5 milliards of francs, and be subject to military occupation until payment is completed.

13 The Law of Guarantees in Italy declares the pope's person inviolable and allows him possession of the Vatican (following the incorporation of the papal lands into the kingdom of Italy).

21–28 In "Bloody Week" in Paris, France, fighting between government troops and demonstrators ends in the defeat of the extreme left-wing Paris Commune (provisional national government) at a cost of 20,000–30,000 lives.

JULY

12 Irish Catholics and Protestants riot in New York, New York, leaving 52 people dead.

31 The discovery of the U.S. politician William Marcy "Boss" Tweed's "Ring" in New York, New York, reveals his organization of a systematic defrauding of the city treasury.

AUGUST

14 Local government boards are created in England to control the administration of the Poor Law and other municipal functions.

17 The British Liberal politician Edward Cardwell's army reforms reorganize the British army, abolishing the purchase of commissions and establishing trained reserve forces.

29 Feudal fiefdoms are abolished in Japan and replaced with a series of prefectures.

31 The French Liberal statesman Adolphe Thiers is elected the first president of the Third Republic in France.

SEPTEMBER

4 Public outcry at the influence-peddling of the Democratic political machine in New York, New York, based at Tammany Hall, results in the formation of a citizens' committee to investigate the influence and activities of its chief organizer William Marcy "Boss" Tweed.

SCIENCE, TECHNOLOGY, AND MEDICINE

Agriculture

- The U.S. Congress establishes the U.S. Commission on Fish and Fisheries under the directorship of U.S. naturalist Spencer Fullerton Baird. The Commission undertakes research into fish behavior, introduces foreign species into the United States, and increases the commercial availability of fish through operating hatcheries.

Ecology

- A wooden pipeline 25 km/40 mi long is completed at Rochester, New York, to transport natural gas. It is the world's first long-distance fuel pipeline.

JULY

July 1871–September 1880 Prairie farms in the United States and Canada are destroyed by swarms of the Rocky Mountain locust *Melanoplus spretus* and the migratory locust *Melanoplus sanguinipes*.

OCTOBER

8–14 Over 500,000 ha/1.2 million acres of Wisconsin forest are destroyed by fire. The town of Peshtigo is burned to the ground, with 1,152 deaths in the worst fire in U.S. history.

Exploration

OCTOBER

23–March 14, 1872 Welsh-born U.S. journalist Henry Stanley reaches Lake Tanganyika in Africa in search of the lost Scottish explorer David Livingstone, who he finds at the trading settlement of Ujiji. Together they explore the lake's northern reaches, and establish that it is not the source of the Nile. Livingstone refuses to leave Africa with Stanley.

Health and Medicine

- German surgeon F. Steiner is the first to use electrical cardiac stimulation to successfully restart a patient's heart.
- The swivel dentist's chair is invented in the United States.

Math

- German mathematician Karl Theodor Wilhelm Weierstrass discovers a curve that, while continuous, has no definable gradient at any point.

Science

- Austrian physicist Ludwig Boltzmann describes the general statistical distribution of energies among the molecules in a gas.
- Belgian mathematician Adolphe Quetelet initiates the science of anthropometry with the publication of *L'Anthropométrie/Anthropometrie*, in which he is the first to apply statistical methods to the measurement of the human body.
- English anthropologist Edward Burnett Tylor provides the first scientific definition of culture in his book *Primitive Culture: Researches into the Development of Mythology, Philosophy, Religion, Language, Art, and Custom*. It allows the comparative study of social institutions.
- English naturalist Charles Darwin publishes *The Descent of Man, and Selection in Relation to Sex*, in which he applies his evolutionary theory to humans and also elaborates the theory of sexual selection.

- English physicist John William Strutt, Baron Rayleigh, explains that the sky is blue because of the scattering of light by small particles in the atmosphere.
- German chemist Adolf von Baeyer synthesizes fluorescein, a red fluorescent marker used as a visible tracer in dilutions of one part per 40 million.
- Italian astronomer Giovanni Schiaparelli observes a network of lines on Mars which he calls *canali* ("channels"). The word is mistakenly translated as "canals" and leads to widespread speculation that they were constructed by intelligent beings.
- The French social reformer Pierre-Guillaume-Frédéric Le Play publishes *L'Organisation de la famille/The Organization of the Family*.
- The German archeologist Heinrich Schliemann discovers a cache of valuables and jewelry at Hissarlik, Anatolia (modern Turkey), hidden at the time of the destruction of Troy II in 2050 BC. It is greeted erroneously as "the Treasure of Priam."
- U.S. paleontologist Charles Marsh discovers the first *Pterodactyl* skeleton, an extinct flying lizard.

Technology

- English doctor Richard Leach Maddox and English chemist Joseph Wilson Swan replace the collodion wet-emulsion photographic plate with a dry, silver-bromide sensitized, gelatin-emulsion plate. The gelatin emulsions go on sale in 1873 and the plates in 1876. They revolutionize photography.
- German chemist Hermann Sprengel develops a new type of explosive in Britain in which one of the ingredients, combined just prior to use, is a liquid.

Transportation

- Grand Central Station opens in New York, New York.
- October 1871–80   Steamships begin to replace sailing ships for transporting cargo, and steel-hulls begin to replace iron-hulls. More efficient engines reduce fuel requirements by nearly 50%.
- October 1871–80   Railroads replace steamboats as the main mode of transport in the United States.

ARTS AND IDEAS

Architecture

- The great fire of Chicago, Illinois, destroys much of the city. This, combined with a rapid growth of the city's prosperity, means that architects are given the opportunity to develop radically new ideas during the 1880s and 1890s. One of the most important results will be the Chicago School, a group of architects—including Jenny, Burnham & Root, and Sullivan—who will play a major role in the development of the skyscraper.
- October 1871–72   French engineer Jules Saulnier builds the Meunier Chocolate factory in Noisiel, France. It is

the first building to have a proper iron skeleton; previous ones had been constructed of metal cages or cells joined together.

Arts

c. 1871   The U.S. artist William Rimmer sculpts *Dying Centaur*.
- The French artist Paul Cézanne paints *The Black Marble Clock*.
- The Russian artist Vasily Vasilyevich Vereshchagin paints *The Apotheosis of War*.
- The U.S. artist Eastman Johnson paints *The Old Stagecoach*.
- The U.S. artist Thomas Eakins paints *Max Schmitt in a Single Scull*.

Literature and Language

- Self-taught U.S. ethnologist Lewis Henry Morgan publishes *Systems of Consanguinity and Affinity*, which posits the existence of a kinship system common among all Native Americans.
- The English writer and mathematician Lewis Carroll writes the children's classic *Through the Looking-Glass*.
- The English writer George Eliot publishes the first part of her novel *Middlemarch: A Study of Provincial Life*. The last part appears in 1872.
- The English writer Thomas Hardy publishes *Desperate Remedies*, his first published novel.
- The French writer Emile Zola publishes his novel *La Fortune des Rougon/The Rougon Family*, the first novel in his *Les Rougon–Macquart* series. His intention is to create a comprehensive and scientific picture of French society.
- The U.S. writer Walt Whitman publishes his poem "Passage to India."

Music

- English composer Arthur Seymour Sullivan and English clergyman Sabine Baring-Gould write the hymn "Onward Christian Soldiers."
- English composer Arthur de Lulli writes the tune "Chopsticks."
- French composer Camille St.-Saëns completes his symphonic poem *Le Rouet D'Omphale/Omphale's Spinning Wheel*.
- French composer Georges Bizet completes his piano work *Jeux d'enfants/Children's Games*.
- German composer Johannes Brahms completes his *Schicksalslied/Song of Destiny*, a setting of a poem by the German poet Hölderlin for chorus and orchestra (Opus 54). He also completes his *Triumphlied/Song of Triumph*, a setting of the biblical Book of Revelation for chorus and orchestra (Opus 55).
- German composer Richard Wagner completes his *Kaisermarsch/Emperor's March*, written to celebrate the German victory in the Franco-Prussian War.
- Russian composer Peter Illyich Tchaikovsky completes his *Nocturne and Humoreske* for piano (Opus 10) and his String Quartet No. 1 (Opus 11).

- The opera *Aïda* by the Italian composer Giuseppe Verdi is first performed, in Cairo, Egypt (to celebrate the opening of the Suez Canal).

- The first college daily newspaper, *The Daily Illinois*, is published at the University of Illinois.
- The University of Arkansas is founded at Fayetteville.

Thought and Scholarship

- The English economist William Stanley Jevons publishes *Theory of Political Economy*.
- The English writer and art critic John Ruskin begins to publish *Fors Clavigera*, a monthly publication of lectures on art and social issues, delivered to working men.
- The German economist Adolph Wagner publishes *The Social Question*.
- The German historian Theodor Mommsen publishes the first volume of his *Römische Staatsrecht/Roman Constitutional Law*. The last volume appears in 1888.
- The U.S. poet Walt Whitman publishes his political tract *Democratic Vistas*, arguing that democracy and individualism are compatible.

Everyday Life

- Populations of selected countries (in millions): Germany, 41; United States, 39; France, 36.1; Japan, 33; Italy, 26.8; Great Britain, 26; Ireland, 5.4.
- Spanish acrobats performing in London, England, introduce the safety net for circus performers.
- U.S. showman P. T. Barnum opens his circus in Brooklyn, New York, advertising it as the "Greatest Show on Earth."

OCTOBER

8–10   Over 250 people are killed and 90,000 made homeless when fire destroys nearly 10.4 sq km/4 sq mi of Chicago and causes $200 million in property damage. Steam-powered fire engines are used to help extinguish the blaze.

SOCIETY

Education

- Keble College is founded at Oxford University, Oxford, England.
- Smith College is founded in Northampton, Massachusetts.

Religion

- The German Catholic theologian Johann Joseph Ignaz von Döllinger is excommunicated by the archbishop of Munich for refusing to accept Vatican decrees.

JULY

7   The German government begins its *Kulturkampf* (cultural struggle) with the Catholic Church, when Chancellor Otto von Bismarck suppresses the Roman Catholic department for spiritual affairs.

BIRTHS & DEATHS

FEBRUARY
4   Friedrich Ebert, German Social Democrat who was president of the Weimar Republic 1919–25, born in Heidelberg, Germany (–1925).

MARCH
27   Heinrich Mann, German novelist and essayist, born in Lübeck, Germany (–1950).

MAY
11   John Herschel, English astronomer known for his catalog of the stars in the southern sky, dies in Collingwood, Kent, England (79).
12   Daniel-François-Esprit Auber, French composer, dies in Paris, France (89).

JUNE
13   Jean-Eugène Robert-Houdin, French magician who founded modern magic, dies in St. Gervais, France (65).
17   James Weldon Johnson, poet, diplomat, and anthologist of black culture, born in Jacksonville, Florida (–1938).
22   William McDougall, British-born U.S. psychologist who laid the foundation of social psychology, born in

Chadderton, Lancashire, England (–1938).

JULY
10   Marcel Proust, French novelist who wrote *A la Recherche du temps perdu/Remembrance of Things Past* (1913–27), born in Auteuil, France (–1922).
23   Cordell Hull, U.S. secretary of state 1933–44 who lowered tariffs to stimulate international trade and received the Nobel Peace Prize in 1944, born in Overton County, Texas (–1955).

AUGUST
13   Karl Liebknecht, German Social Democrat who cofounded the Spartacus League, which evolved into the German Communist Party, born in Leipzig, Germany (–1919).
19   Orville Wright, U.S. pioneer of aviation who, with his brother Wilbur, was the first to achieve sustained powered flight, born in Dayton, Ohio (–1948).
27   Theodore Dreiser, U.S. naturalist and novelist, born in Terre Haute, Indiana (–1945).

30   Ernest Rutherford, New Zealand physicist and investigator of radioactivity, born in Spring Grove, New Zealand (–1937).

SEPTEMBER
6   English banker Montagu Norman, governor of the Bank of England 1920–44, born (–1950).
28   Pietro Badoglio, Italian general who arranged Italy's armistice with the allies during World War II, born in Grazzano Monferrato, Italy (–1956).

OCTOBER
18   Charles Babbage, English inventor who designed the first digital computer, dies in London, England (78).
26   Thomas Ewing, first U.S. secretary of the interior 1849–50, dies in West Liberty, Virginia (81).
30   Paul Valéry, French poet, essayist, and critic, born in Sète, France (–1945).

NOVEMBER
1   Stephen Crane, U.S. novelist known for his book *The Red Badge of Courage* (1895), born in Newark, New Jersey (–1900).

Sports

- The American National Rifle Association is founded by National Guard officers. Target rifle shooting becomes one of the most popular sporting activities of the decade in the United States.

JANUARY

26 The Rugby Football Union is founded in London, England.

MARCH

17 Baseball's first fully professional league, the National Association of Professional Baseball Players, is formed in New York, New York.
27 Scotland defeats England in the first ever rugby international, played at Raeburn Place, Edinburgh, Scotland, in front of 4,000 spectators.

1872

POLITICS, GOVERNMENT, AND ECONOMICS

Business and Economics

- Former Pennsylvania Railroad superintendent Andrew Carnegie concentrates his investment activities in steel manufacturing, laying plans for the J. Edgar Thomson Steel Works south of Pittsburgh, Pennsylvania.

FEBRUARY

2 The Netherlands sell their trading posts on the Gold Coast of Africa to Britain in return for a free hand in Sumatra.

Colonization

NOVEMBER

2 The Boston town meeting creates a Committee of Correspondence, charging it with safeguarding colonial rights in concert with committees established throughout the colony. Several weeks later, Boston politician Samuel Adams issues a scathing first report.

Politics and Government

- Cetewayo succeeds his father, Mpande, as ruler in Zululand (part of modern Natal, South Africa).
- Compulsory military service is introduced in Japan.
- In the U.S. Congressional elections, the Republicans retain majorities in the House (194–92) and Senate (49–19).

- The Licensing Act restricts the sale of alcohol in Britain.
- The Russian anarchist Mikhail Alexandrovich Bakunin is expelled from the (First) International Working Men's Association at The Hague Conference in the Netherlands as his anarchism contradicts orthodox Marxism.
- U.S. president Ulysses S. Grant appoints New York jurist Ward Hunt to the U.S. Supreme Court.

JANUARY

12 Yohannes IV becomes emperor of Abyssinia (now Ethiopia).
25 Henri, comte de Chambord, the Legitimist (elder branch of the Bourbons) pretender to the French throne, issues his Antwerp Declaration, countering suggestions of "a Revolution Monarchy" being established following the deposition of Emperor Napoleon III in 1870.

FEBRUARY

8 The British viceroy of India, Richard Southwell Bourke, Earl of Mayo, is murdered by a Pathan protesting at British rule in India while on a visit to the Andaman Islands.
22 The new Prohibition Party nominates Pennsylvania politician James Black for president and Michigan politician John Russell for vice president.

MARCH

19 The British politician Charles Dilke, declaring himself a Republican, calls for an inquiry into Queen Victoria's expenditure.

APRIL

26 The proclamation of Don Carlos, Duke of Madrid, as Charles VII of Spain leads to the Second Carlist War as his followers dispute the authority of the ruling king Amadeo I.

MAY

4 Carlist forces are defeated by the government in the Second Carlist War in Spain and the pretender to the throne, Don Carlos, escapes to France.

JUNE

6 The Republicans nominate Ulysses S. Grant for president and Massachusetts senator Henry Wilson for vice president.

25 The Jesuits are expelled from Germany in the ongoing *Kulturkampf* (cultural struggle) between the state and the Catholics.

JULY

1 The Cape Colony theologian and Dutch Reformed Church minister Thomas François Burgers is elected president of the Transvaal Republic, in southern Africa.

9 The Democrats nominate *New York Tribune* editor Horace Greeley for president and Missouri governor Benjamin Gratz for vice president.

28 France adopts conscription and the establishment of a large standing army in response to its defeat by Prussia in 1870.

SEPTEMBER

7 A meeting of the three emperors Wilhelm, Alexander, and Franz Josef in Berlin, Germany, leads to a tacit entente between Germany, Russia, and Austria-Hungary to uphold authoritarian rule in Europe.

14 The Geneva court of arbitration finds Britain legally responsible for the depredations caused by the *Alabama* and other cruisers supplied by Britain to the Confederacy during the American Civil War, awarding the United States $15,500,000 damages.

OCTOBER

21 The German emperor Wilhelm I, called on to adjudicate between Britain and the United States over the disputed ownership of the island of St. Juan off Vancouver, Canada, decides in favor of the United States.

NOVEMBER

5 Ulysses S. Grant is reelected president of the United States.

5 U.S. women's rights advocate Susan B. Anthony and several others are arrested for casting ballots in the presidential election.

22 Louis Philippe, comte de Paris, the Orléanist heir to the French throne, accepts compensation for the confiscation of his estates, thereby undercutting moves to make him king.

DECEMBER

2 In the so-called Credit Mobilier scandal, the U.S. House of Representatives votes to appoint a commission to investigate reports of "kickbacks" made to U.S. congressmen by directors of the Union Pacific railroad.

9 The German chancellor Otto von Bismarck's County Organization Bill, for remodeling local government in Prussia at the expense of nobles' powers, passes the Upper House after the special creation of 25 extra peers.

SCIENCE, TECHNOLOGY, AND MEDICINE

Agriculture

- U.S. plant breeder Luther Burbank develops the Burbank potato. During the next 50 years he develops over 800 new varieties of plants.

Ecology

- The first oil well is sunk in the Baku oil field in Russia: the world's largest until the 1940s.
- U.S. entrepreneur William Tell Coleman discovers huge deposits of borax in Nevada. The major source of the mineral until the 1930s, it becomes known as colemanite and is used to manufacture ceramics, metals, and soap.

Exploration

- After the departure from Africa of his friend Henry Stanley, Scottish explorer David Livingstone continues his search for the source of the Nile, traveling far south of its true source, and eventually dying in May 1873 at Chitambo in modern Zambia.
- British explorer Ney Elias, accompanied by a Chinese attendant, begins a 4,000-km/2,500-mi journey from China, across the Gobi Desert and Siberia, and into Russia.

Health and Medicine

- Austrian surgeon Theodor Billroth is the first to remove a part of the esophagus and rejoin the remaining sections.
- French physician Jean-Martin Charcot employs hypnosis to treat patients. Sigmund Freud is later one of his students.
- U.S. dentist Alexander Morrison invents the pneumatic dentist's chair which can be tilted back.
- U.S. inventor Thomas Edison discovers diagnostic radiology (fluoroscopy), when he observes that his assistant's hair has fallen out and his scalp ulcerated while developing a fluorescent roentgen-ray lamp.

Math

- German mathematician Richard Dedekind demonstrates how irrational numbers (those that cannot be written as a fraction) may be defined formally.

Science

- German botanist Ferdinand Julius Cohn publishes *Untersuchungen über Bakterien/Researches on Bacteria*.

The first major work on bacteriology, it classifies bacteria on the basis of their morphology and physiology.

- U.S. astronomer Henry Draper develops astronomical spectral photography and takes the first photograph of the spectrum of a star—that of Vega.

DECEMBER

7–May 26, 1876 The British ship *Challenger* undertakes the world's first major oceanographic survey. Under the command of the Scottish naturalist Wyville Thomson, it discovers hundreds of new marine animals, and finds that at 2,000 fathoms the temperature of the ocean is a constant 2.5°C/36.5°F.

Technology

- Edmund Barbour invents the adding machine with printed totals and subtotals.
- Scottish physicist William Thomson (later Lord Kelvin) develops a sounding-machine (the "Kelvin") for determining depth at sea.
- U.S. engineer George Baily Brayton invents a continuous combustion engine that involves preliminary compression of the fuel mixture; it serves as the basis for subsequent turbine engines.
- U.S. inventor Thomas Edison patents the electric typewriter.

MAY

- Russian physicist Alexandre de Lodyguine installs 200 graphite-filament electric lights at the Admiralty dock in St. Petersburg, Russia. The glass globes filled with nitrogen are expensive to maintain and unreliable.

NOVEMBER

23 Adelaide and Port Darwin in Australia are connected by telegraph wire; soon afterwards the line is extended to Asia and Europe.

Transportation

- French engineer Amédée Bollé achieves a record speed of 40 kph/25 mph in a steam-driven vehicle.
- German engineer Paul Haenlein builds the first airship that uses an internal combustion engine as a power source; its fuel is taken from the gas in the balloon.
- Irish-born U.S. engineer William Robinson patents an automatic electric signaling system for railroads.
- Italian businessman Giovanni Pirelli opens a store in Milan, the start of his world-famous business making tires and other rubber products.
- The world's first oil tanker is built.

November 1872–80 The 14.5-km/9-mi-long St. Gotthard Tunnel between Lucerne, Switzerland and Milan, Italy is constructed.

OCTOBER

14 The 29 km-/18-mi-long Tokyo–Yokohama railroad opens; built by English engineers, it is the first railroad in Japan.

DECEMBER

- The U.S. ship the *Marie Celeste* is found adrift without crew in the Atlantic Ocean, undamaged and with its cargo intact.

ARTS AND IDEAS

Architecture

- The Albert Memorial in London, England (built in memory of Prince Albert), designed by the English architect George Gilbert Scott, is completed.

Arts

- Illustrations of the slums of London, England, by the French artist Paul Doré appear in the book *London: A Pilgrimage*.
- The French artist Berthe Morisot paints *Paris Seen From the Trocadéro*.
- The French artist Camille Corot paints *Corner of the Table*, a group portrait that includes the French poets Rimbaud and Verlaine.
- The French artist Claude Monet paints *Impression: Sunrise*. It is this painting which gives impressionism its name.
- The French artist Edgar Degas paints *Dancing Class at the Ballet School*.
- The French artist Pierre-Auguste Renoir paints *Pont Neuf*.
- The Russian artist Ilya Yefimovich Repin paints *Boat Pullers on the Volga*.
- The Russian artist Ivan Nikolayevich Kramskoy paints *The Temptation of Christ*.
- The Swiss artist Arnold Böcklin paints *Battle of the Centaurs*.
- The U.S. artist James Abbot McNeill Whistler paints *Arrangement in Grey and Black No 1: The Artist's Mother*.
- The U.S. artist Martin Johnson Heade paints *Jungle Orchids and Hummingbirds*.
- The U.S. artist William Rimmer paints *Flight and Pursuit*.
- The U.S. artist Winslow Homer paints *Snap the Whip*.

Literature and Language

- *Kindertotenlieder/Children's Death Songs* by the German poet Friedrich Rückert (Friedrich Raimar) are published posthumously. He wrote them in 1824 when his two children died. They are set to music by the Austrian composer Gustav Mahler in 1904.
- The Danish literary critic Georg Brandes Morris Cohen publishes the first part of his *Hovedstrømninger i det 19de aarhundredes litteratur/Main Currents in 19th-Century Literature*. The final part appears in 1890.
- The English writer Charles Stuart Calverley publishes *Fly Leaves*, a selection of his parodies of famous poets.
- The English writer Samuel Butler publishes his satirical novel *Erewhon*.
- The English writer Thomas Hardy publishes his novel *Under the Greenwood Tree*.
- The French writer Alphonse Daudet publishes his collection of stories *Aventures prodigieuses de Tartarin de Tarascon/The Marvelous Adventures of Tartarin de Tarascon*.

- The French writer Jules Verne publishes his novel *La Tour du monde en quatre-vingt jours/Around the World in Eighty Days* in serial form. It is published as a book in 1873.
- The U.S. poet Henry Wadsworth Longfellow publishes his long poem *Christus: A Mystery*.
- The U.S. writer Mark Twain publishes *Roughing It*.
- The U.S. writer William Dean Howells publishes his first novel, *Their Wedding Journey*.

Music

- Austrian composer Josef Anton Bruckner completes his Symphony No. 2. He revises it in 1875–76, with J. Herbeck in 1877 and 1891–92.
- French composer Georges Bizet completes *L'Arlésienne/ The Maid of Arles*, incidental music for a play of that name by the French writer Alphonse Daudet.

- Russian composer Peter Illyich Tchaikovsky completes his Symphony No. 2, the *Ukrainian*.
- The opera *Boris Godunov* by the Russian composer Modest Petrovich Mussorgsky is completed in its revised form, the original having been finished in 1869.
- The opera *The Stone Guest* by the Russian composer Alexander Dargomyzhsky is first performed, in St. Petersburg, Russia. It is based on a work by the poet Alexander Pushkin.
- The operetta *La Fille de Madame Angot/Madame Angot's Daughter* by the French composer Alexandre Charles Lecocq is first performed, in Paris, France.

Theater and Dance

- The play *Mesyats v derevne/A Month in the Country*, by the Russian writer Ivan Sergeyevich Turgenev, is first performed, in Moscow, Russia. It was published in 1855.

BIRTHS & DEATHS

c. 1872 Grigory Yefimovich Rasputin, Siberian peasant and mystic who influenced the Russian czar Nicholas II and tsarina Alexandra, born in Pokrovskoye, Siberia, Russia (–1916).

JANUARY

6 Alexander Scriabin, Russian composer, born in Moscow, Russia (–1915).

9 Henry W. Halleck, U.S. general in chief of the Union forces during the American Civil War, dies in Louisville, Kentucky (56).

21 Franz Grillparzer, Austrian dramatist, dies in Vienna, Austria-Hungary (81).

31 Zane Grey, prolific U.S. author of Westerns, born in Zanesville, Ohio (–1939).

MARCH

3 Wee Willie Keeler, U.S. baseball player, born in Brooklyn, New York (–1923).

7 Piet Mondrian, Dutch abstract painter, born in Amersfoort, the Netherlands (–1944).

10 Giuseppe Mazzini, Italian revolutionary and founder of Young Italy, a secret revolutionary society that strove for Italian unity, dies in Pisa, Italy (66).

12 Zeng Guofan, Chinese administrator and military leader who suppressed the Taipeng Rebellion, preserving China's Imperial regime, dies in Nanjing, China (60).

19 Sergei Pavlovich Diaghilev, Russian arts promoter who did much to revive ballet in Europe, born in Novgorod province, Russia (–1929).

APRIL

2 Samuel Finley Breese Morse, U.S. painter and inventor of Morse Code, dies in New York, New York (80).

9 Léon Blum, French prime minister 1936–37, a Socialist, and the first Jewish premier of France, born in Paris, France (–1950).

MAY

10 Marcel Mauss, French anthropologist who examined the relationship between social structure and forms of exchange, born in Epinal, France (–1950).

18 Bertrand Russell, British philosopher, born in Trelleck, Monmouthshire, Wales (–1970).

JUNE

6 Alexandra (Alexandra Fyodorovna), consort of the Russian emperor Nicholas II, whose misrule while he was at war led to the Russian Revolution, born in Darmstadt, Germany (–1918).

JULY

1 Louis Blériot, French aviator who in 1909 was the first person to fly across the English Channel, born in Cambrai, France (–1936).

4 Calvin Coolidge, thirtieth president of the United States 1923–29, a Republican, born in Plymouth, Vermont (–1933).

5 Edouard Herriot, French politician, leader of the Radical Party and prime minister of France 1924–25, 1926, and 1932, born in Troyes, France (–1957).

16 Roald Amundsen, Norwegian explorer, the first person to reach the South Pole, born in Christiania (now Oslo), Norway (–1928).

SEPTEMBER

13 Ludwig Feuerbach, German philosopher who argued that God is nothing but the outward projection of human nature, dies in Rechenberg, Germany (68).

OCTOBER

4 Roger Keyes, British admiral whose attack on Zeebrugge, Belgium, April 22–23, 1918, closed the Strait of Dover to German submarines, born in Tundiani Fort, India (–1945).

10 William Seward, U.S. secretary of state 1861–69 who purchased Alaska from Russia in 1867 for $7.2 million, dies in Auburn, New York (71).

23 Théophile Gautier, French novelist, poet, and journalist, dies in Neuilly-sur-Seine, France (61).

27 Emily Post, U.S. expert on social graces, who wrote *Etiquette: The Blue Book of Social Usage*, born in Baltimore, Maryland (–1960).

NOVEMBER

6 George G(ordon) Meade, U.S. army officer who defeated the Confederate army at Gettysburg in 1863 during the American Civil War, dies in Philadelphia, Pennsylvania (56).

DECEMBER

7 Johan Huizinga, Dutch historian, born in Groningen, the Netherlands (–1945).

23 George Catlin, U.S. artist whose paintings depict scenes of Native North Americans, dies in Jersey City, New Jersey (76).

Thought and Scholarship

- The German philosopher Friedrich Nietzsche publishes *Die Geburt der Tragödie aus dem Geiste der Musik/The Birth of Tragedy from the Spirit of Music*.

SOCIETY

Everyday Life

- Chicago merchant Aaron Montgomery Ward establishes the nation's first mail-order house, providing merchandise for a largely agricultural market.
- Lyman Bloomingdale and his brothers Gustave and Joseph, the family behind the great U.S. department store Bloomingdale's, open their Great East Side Store in New York, New York.
- Yellowstone National Park is created in Wyoming and Montana. The world's first national park, it is also the United States's largest at 898,000 ha/2.2 million ac.

APRIL

10 U.S. secretary of agriculture Julius Sterling Morton institutes Arbor Day, a public holiday during which U.S. citizens are encouraged to plant trees. Over one million are planted the first Arbor Day. All states eventually accept it as public holiday.

JULY

1 A telegraph line is established between Britain and Australia.

NOVEMBER

9 An explosion in a four-story Boston warehouse results in a fire that destroys almost 800 buildings in a 65-acre section of the city and causes $75 million in property damage.

Religion

- The U.S. religious leader Charles Taze Russell founds the religious movement the Jehovah's Witnesses, their main belief being that the end of the world is imminent. Their zeal in finding converts helps them to grow quickly.
- The German theologian David Friedrich Strauss publishes *Der alte und der neue Glaube/The Old Faith and the New*. Arguing that Christianity is dead, and that a new faith must be created combining art and science, the book is highly controversial.
- U.S. Presbyterian divine Charles Hodge publishes *Systematic Theology*, defending biblical authority and comparing theological exegesis to natural science.

Sports

MARCH

16 A crowd of 2,000 at the Oval cricket ground in London, England, watch Wanderers, a team of ex-public school players, defeat the Royal Engineers 1–0 to win the inaugural Football Association (FA) Cup (soccer) final.

NOVEMBER

30 At the West of Scotland cricket ground at Patrick, near Glasgow, England and Scotland tie 0–0 in the first ever official international association football (soccer) match.

1873

POLITICS, GOVERNMENT, AND ECONOMICS

Business and Economics

- Germany adopts the mark as its national coinage.

FEBRUARY

12 The U.S. Congress passes the Coinage Act discontinuing the minting of silver. The act inaugurates prolonged controversy between partisans of bimetallism and staunch supporters of the gold standard.

MAY

10 The British Parliament passes the Tea Act. By eliminating English export duties on tea while maintaining the import duty in the colonies, the act enables merchants of the struggling East India Company to under-price U.S. competitors.

24 A financial crisis begins in Vienna, Austria, following a stock-market crash, and spreads to other European capitals.

SEPTEMBER

18 The failure of the investment house Jay Cooke & Co. in Philadelphia, Pennsylvania, precipitates a financial panic and a prolonged economic depression.

Colonization

- Andrew Clarke, British governor of the Straits Settlements (comprising Singapore, Malacca, Penang, Cocos Islands, Christmas Island, and Labuan), places British residents in several of the Malay states, increasing British influence in the Malay Peninsula.

JULY

1 Prince Edward Island, formerly a separate province, joins the Dominion of Canada.

AUGUST

12 Russia assumes suzerainty of the Khanates of Khiva and Bukhara, pushing further into central Asia.

Human Rights

JUNE

5 Slave markets and the export of slaves are abolished by the sultan of Zanzibar, under pressure from the British representative John Kirk.

Politics and Government

- The Flemish language is admitted in the courts of Flanders as a concession by the Belgian government to Flemings.
- The office of Statholder (or king of Sweden's lieutenant) in Norway is abolished as Norway demands greater independence.
- The U.S. Congress censures Massachusetts representatives Oakes Ames and James Brooks for their part in the Credit Mobilier–Union Pacific railroad scandal, exposed toward the end of the previous year.

JANUARY

9 The former French emperor Napoleon III dies, and the youth of his only son, Eugène, aged 17, delays hopes of a Bonapartist restoration in France.

FEBRUARY

11 King Amadeo I of Spain abdicates because of the disorder caused by conflict between the Republicans and Carlists.

16 A republic is proclaimed in Spain following the abdication of King Amadeo I.

MARCH

3 The U.S. Congress passes the Salary Act, raising the salaries of president, congressmen, Supreme Court justices, and Cabinet officers.

3 The U.S. Congress passes the Comstock Law, named for moral crusader Anthony Comstock, prohibiting the distribution of pornographic literature through the U.S. mail.

4 Ulysses S. Grant is inaugurated U.S. president for a second term.

APRIL

4 The Dutch begin a war against the sultan of Achin in northwest Sumatra.

4 War breaks out between Britain and the Ashanti in west Africa (modern Ghana) as a result of British attempts to stop King Kofi Kari-Kari's slave trade.

23 Massive monarchist demonstrations take place in Madrid, Spain.

MAY

6 A military convention is signed between Germany and Russia strengthening the unofficial entente to uphold authoritarian rule in Europe that was agreed in Berlin, Germany, in September 1872.

11–14 Adalbert Falk, the Prussian minister of public worship, introduces the "May Laws," subjecting the clergy to state control as part of the German government's campaign against the Catholic Church.

24 French president Adolphe Thiers is deposed by the monarchist Assembly, and the antidemocratic candidate

Marie-Edmé-Patrice-Maurice MacMahon, duc de Magenta, is elected in his place.

AUGUST

5   Henri, comte de Chambord, the Legitimist (Bourbon) pretender to the French throne, and Louis Philippe, comte de Paris, the Orléanist candidate, come to an understanding that Henri should rule and be succeeded by Louis Philippe in the event of a restoration of the monarchy.

SEPTEMBER

8   Because of the recent Carlist risings, the Spanish republican statesman Emilio Castelar is made ruler of Spain by the cortes (national assembly) to restore order under a centralized republic.

9   Italian statesman Marco Minghetti forms a ministry in Italy following the breakup of Giovanni Lanza's government.

15 The German army occupying France to ensure payment of the indemnity agreed at the end of the Franco-Prussian War leaves the country.

OCTOBER

17 Henri, comte de Chambord, the Legitimist (Bourbon) claimant to the French throne, replies to demands made by the Orléanists as a requirement for supporting him in a letter from Frohsdorf, in which he states his uncompromising Legitimism.

20 Ecuador becomes a theocracy as President Gabrial García Moreno introduces an unprecedented amount of papal control.

22 An alliance of the emperors of Germany, Russia, and Austria-Hungary (the *Dreikaiserbund*) formalizes the agreement between them of 1872 to uphold autocratic government in Europe.

27 The Legitimist (Bourbon) heir to the French throne, Henri, comte de Chambord, ends hopes of a restoration of the French monarchy by refusing to accept the tricolor as the national flag.

31 Spanish officials intercept the U.S. vessel *Virginus* bound for Cuba with munitions destined for the Cuban revolutionaries. The Spanish execute the eight U.S. citizens among the *Virginus*'s crew.

NOVEMBER

7   The Canadian prime minister John Macdonald resigns over corruption charges.

11 The Croats are granted a considerable measure of internal self-government by Austria-Hungary.

11 The rival cities of Buda and Pest are statutorily united to form the capital of Hungary.

19 The notorious political operator William Marcy "Boss" Tweed is convicted of fraud and sentenced to 12 years' imprisonment.

20 The monarchist majority in the French chamber confers presidential powers for seven years upon the autocratic Marie-Edmé-Patrice-Maurice MacMahon, duc de Magenta.

DECEMBER

12 The papal nuncio (diplomatic representative) is expelled from Switzerland in response to increased tension between the Vatican and the Swiss government.

SCIENCE, TECHNOLOGY, AND MEDICINE

Agriculture

- A widespread famine occurs in Bengal, India, following crop failure.
- U.S. farmer George Grant imports Aberdeen Angus bulls from Scotland into the United States.
- In the first example of biological pest control, British-born U.S. entomologist Charles Riley exports the acarid *Rhizoglyphus phylloxerae* to France to destroy aphids.
- U.S. inventor Fred Hatch constructs the first modern cylindrical grain silo.

Health and Medicine

- Austrian surgeon Theodor Billroth performs the first operation to remove the larynx.
- English physician William Budd publishes *Typhoid Fever, Its Nature, Mode of Spreading, and Prevention*, in which he establishes the infectious nature of the disease.
- French neurologist Jean-Martin Charcot founds modern neurology with the publication of his multivolume *Leçons sur les maladies du système nerveux/Lectures on the Diseases of the Nervous System*.
- Austrian physician Josef Breuer discovers that the semicircular canals in the inner ear function to maintain balance.
- German Egyptologist George Maurice Ebers discovers a papyrus text at Thebes. Known as the Ebers papyrus, it is dated to 1500 BC and is the oldest medical work known, containing over 700 folk remedies for various afflictions.

Science

- Dutch physicist Johannes Van der Waals introduces the idea of weak attractive forces between molecules.
- German physicist Ernst Abbe discovers that to distinguish two separate objects under the microscope the distance between them must be more than half the wavelength of the light that illuminates them. The discovery becomes important in the later development of electron and X-ray microscopes.
- Scottish philosopher Alexander Bain lays the foundation for physiological psychology with the publication of *Mind and Body: The Theories of Their Relation*, in which he discusses the relationship between physiology and psychology.
- Scottish physicist James Clerk Maxwell publishes *A Treatise on Electricity and Magnetism*, in which he provides a mathematical model of electromagnetic waves and identifies light as being one such wave.
- Scottish physicist William Thomson reforms the mariner's compass by mounting thin cylindrical bars on silk thread.

- The German archeologist Heinrich Schliemann announces he has discovered the ancient city of Troy at the site of Hissarlik in Anatolia (modern Turkey).
- Willoughby Smith confirms that the electrical conductivity of selenium increases with the amount of illumination; it proves to be an important discovery in the development of television.

MAY

- British Assyriologist George Smith discovers and deciphers cuneiform tablets at Nineveh containing the *Epic of Gilgamesh*, which describes a great flood similar to that in the Bible.

Technology

- At the Vienna Exhibition, Belgian electrical engineer Zénobe-Théophile Gramme discovers that his dynamo can be operated as an electric motor.
- German chemist Hermann Vogel discovers that the addition of green aniline dye to photographic emulsions increases their sensitivity to green light. The subsequent addition of other dyes makes color photography possible.
- Russian scientist A. A. Tavrisov develops a method for the continuous distillation of petroleum.
- The first electrically powered industrial machines begin operating in Austria; other countries quickly follow suit.
- U.S. manufacturer Samuel Colt produces the single-action "Peacemaker" revolver, the most popular firearm in the West.

Transportation

- U.S. coach builder F. Forder introduces the hansom cab into New York, New York, and Boston, Massachusetts.

APRIL

1 The steamship *Atlantic* runs aground at Halifax, Nova Scotia, Canada; over 500 people die.

AUGUST

1 U.S. engineer Andrew Smith Hallidie introduces the cable-car in San Francisco, California. Drawn on an endless cable in a slot between the rails, the cars are pulled up hills horse-drawn carriages are unable to climb. Other cable-cars are subsequently introduced in Seattle and other coastal cities.

ARTS AND IDEAS

Architecture

- The British naval commander Fairfax Moresby founds Port Moresby on the south coast of New Guinea in the west Pacific Ocean.

Arts

c. 1873 The French artist Camille Corot paints *Algerian Girl Reclining*.

- The French artist Berthe Morisot paints *The Cradle*.
- The French artist Edgar Degas paints *The Cotton Office*.
- The French artist Paul Cézanne paints *The House of the Hanged Man* and *A Modern Olympia*.
- The French artist Pierre Puvis de Chavannes paints *L'Eté/Summer*.
- The Russian artist Ilya Yefimovich Repin paints *Muzhiki na Volge/The Volga Boatmen*.
- The U.S. artist George Innes paints *The Monk*.
- The U.S. artist Thomas Moran paints *The Chasm of the Colorado*.
- The U.S. artist Winslow Homer paints *Breezing Up*.

Literature and Language

- The English philosopher John Stuart Mill publishes his *Autobiography*, one of the classic 19th-century autobiographies.
- The French writer Arthur Rimbaud publishes his prose poems *Une Saison en enfer/A Season in Hell*.
- The German writer Paul Johann Ludwig von Heyse publishes his novel *Kinder der Welt/Children of the World*.
- U.S. writers Mark Twain and C. D. Warner publish *The Gilded Age*, a tale of egotism and corruption in the aftermath of the Civil War.

Music

- Austrian composer Josef Anton Bruckner completes his Symphony No. 3. He revises it in 1874 and 1877.
- Bohemian composer Antonín Leopold Dvořák completes his Symphony No. 3 and his String Quartet in A minor (Opus 16).
- French composer Camille St.-Saëns completes his symphonic poem *Phaëton*.
- French composer Georges Bizet completes his orchestral work *Jeux d'enfants/Children's Games* (setting of earlier piano pieces).
- German composer Johannes Brahms completes his *Ungarische Tänze/Hungarian Dances*, orchestrations of several of his *Hungarian Dances* for piano.
- Russian composer Peter Illyich Tchaikovsky completes his symphonic fantasy *Groza Butia/The Tempest*.
- The opera *The Maid of Pskov* by the Russian composer Nikolay Andreyevich Rimsky-Korsakov is first performed, in St. Petersburg, Russia. It is later renamed *Ivan the Terrible* by the impresario Sergey Pavlovich Diaghilev.

Theater and Dance

- The play *Snegurochka/The Snow Maiden* by the Russian dramatist Alexander Nikolayevich Ostrovsky is first performed.

Thought and Scholarship

- *New York Tribune* editor Whitelaw Reid publishes "The Scholar in Politics," which weighs the costs and benefits of marrying two apparently distinct fields.

- Massachusetts Unitarian minister Octavius B. Frothingham publishes *Religion of Humanity*.
- The English social scientist Herbert Spencer publishes *The Study of Sociology*.
- The English writer and critic Walter Horatio Pater publishes *Studies in the History of the Renaissance*.

SOCIETY

Education

- Vanderbilt University is founded in Nashville, Tennessee.

Everyday Life

- The first meat refrigeration plant in Australia is built by Australian wool merchant T. S. Mort and French engineer E. Nicolle.
- The National Aquarium is established at Woods Hole, Massachusetts, and is the first public aquarium in the country. It is moved to Washington, D.C., in 1888.

MAY
- New York State inaugurates Memorial Day, commemorating soldiers who gave their lives in the American Civil War.

Religion

- A group of midwestern Jewish congregations in the United States establishes the Union of American Hebrew Congregations.

JULY
1 Monasteries are dissolved in Italy following the absorption of the papal lands.

Sports

- The British major Walter Clopton Wingfield invents the game of "Sphairistiké," a direct precursor of lawn tennis, largely based on real tennis, squash, and badminton. The game becomes known as lawn tennis or tennis-on-the-lawn, and his rules for the game, as revised by the Marylebone Cricket Club, form the basis of the code drafted in 1877 by the All England Croquet and Lawn Tennis Club for the first Wimbledon tournament.
- The first British Open golf championship to be played in St. Andrews, Scotland, is won by Scottish golfer Tom Kidd.

MAY
27 The inaugural Preakness Stakes horse race is won by Survivor ridden by U.S. jockey G. Barbee at the Pimlico Race Track, Baltimore, Maryland.

AUGUST
18 The first successful ascent of the 4,418-m/14,494-ft Mt. Whitney, California, is made by Charles Begole, A. H. Johnson, and John Lucas.

BIRTHS & DEATHS

JANUARY
2 St. Theresa, French Carmelite nun, canonized in 1925, born in Alençon, France (−1897).
9 Hayyim Nahman Bialik, leading Hebrew poet, born in Rädi, Russia (−1934).
9 Louis-Napoléon Bonaparte (Napoleon III), Emperor of France 1852–71, dies in Chislehurst, Kent, England (64).

FEBRUARY
1 Matthew Fontaine Maury, U.S. naval officer and one of the founders of oceanography, dies in Lexington, Virginia (67).
10 Justus von Liebig, German chemist who was active in the fields of organic chemistry, biochemistry, and agricultural chemistry, dies in Munich, Germany (69).
27 Enrico Caruso, Italian operatic tenor and the first leading musician to record his voice, born in Naples, Italy (−1921).

APRIL
1 Sergey Vasilevich Rachmaninov, Russian composer and piano virtuoso, born in Oneg, near Semenovo, Russia (−1943).

25 Félix d'Hérelle, French-Canadian microbiologist who discovered the bacteriophage, a virus that infects bacteria, born in Montreal, Canada (−1949).

MAY
1 David Livingstone, Scottish missionary and explorer who explored much of East Africa in search of the source of the Nile, dies in Chitambo, Barotseland (Zambia) (59).
8 John Stuart Mill, English utilitarian philosopher and economist, dies in Avignon, France (67).
22 Alessandro Manzoni, Italian poet and novelist, dies in Milan, Italy (88).
23 Leo Baeck, Jewish rabbi and theologian who was the spiritual leader for German Jews under Nazi Germany, born in Lissa, Germany (−1956).

AUGUST
26 Lee De Forest, U.S. physicist and inventor who invented the audion vacuum tube, a major component of early radios, telephones, televisions, and computers, born in Council Bluffs, Iowa (−1961).

SEPTEMBER
9 Max Reinhardt, Austrian-born U.S. theatrical director who helped found the Salzburg Festival, born in Baden, near Vienna, Austria (−1943).

OCTOBER
23 William D. Coolidge, U.S. physical chemist and inventor of the X-ray tube, born in Hudson, Massachusetts (−1975).
30 Francisco Madero, Mexican revolutionary and president of Mexico 1911–13 who overthrew the dictator Porfirio Díaz, born in Parras, Mexico (−1913).

NOVEMBER
4 G(eorge) E(dward) Moore, British realist philosopher, born in London, England (−1958).
6 William J. Hardee, Confederate general during the American Civil War, dies in Wytheville, Virginia (58).

DECEMBER
7 Willa Cather, U.S. novelist, born in Winchester, Virginia (−1947).
14 Jean-Louis Agassiz, U.S. naturalist, dies in Cambridge, Massachusetts (66).

1874

POLITICS, GOVERNMENT, AND ECONOMICS

Business and Economics

- British travel operator Thomas Cook introduces the world's first traveler's checks.
- The Ottoman Empire's finances collapse because of heavy borrowing abroad.

Colonization

MARCH

15 France assumes a protectorate over Annam (part of modern Vietnam), which breaks off its vassalage to China.

OCTOBER

25 Britain annexes the Fiji islands in the southwest Pacific Ocean.

Human Rights

DECEMBER

7 Approximately 70 black Americans are killed during a riot in Vicksburg, Mississippi, sparked by the dismissal of a sheriff sympathetic to black American rights.

Politics and Government

- Canada adopts voting by ballot on a single day.
- Civil marriage is made compulsory in Germany as part of the *Kulturkampf* (cultural struggle) with the Catholic Church.
- In the U.S. Congressional elections, the Republicans retain a majority in the Senate (45–29) while ceding control of the House to the Democrats (169–109).
- U.S. president Ulysses S. Grant appoints Ohio jurist Morrison R. Waite chief justice of the U.S. Supreme Court.

JANUARY

2 Emilio Castelar retires as Spanish prime minister.
3 Spanish marshal Francisco Serrano becomes dictator of Spain as the head of an interim military government.

FEBRUARY

4 King Kofi Kari-Kari of the Ashanti, west Africa (modern Ghana), signs a treaty promising to end human sacrifices and open the country to British trade. The British general Garnet Wolseley burns the capital, Kumasi, ending the war between the Ashanti and Britain.

MAY

5 At the Gotha Conference in Germany, German Marxists and Lassalleans unite to form the Socialist Working Men's Party.
5 Further May Laws are issued in Germany requiring the Catholic clergy to work through the state, following attempts at passive resistance to the *Kulturkampf* (cultural struggle).
5 The Swiss constitution is revised to centralize authority, and the federal court receives more power.

JUNE

20 The U.S. Congress revokes the District of Columbia's territorial government, installing a governing commission in its place.

JULY

7 Denmark grants Iceland self-government with a representative Althing (parliament).

AUGUST

8 The Bolivia–Chile boundary is fixed by convention as the parallel 24°S, lessening ongoing tension between the two countries.
21 In a sensational civil-court case, the U.S. preacher Henry Ward Beecher goes on trial in Brooklyn, New York, for allegedly committing adultery with Elisabeth Tilton, wife of the writer Theodore Tilton.

SEPTEMBER

15 The Prince of Wales visits France, the first British royal visit to France since the revolution of 1789, conferring Britain's approval on the French Republic.

OCTOBER

4 Harry von Arnim, the former German ambassador in Paris, France, is arrested in Germany on a charge of embezzling state papers, but in reality because he has been undermining the French Republic, which the German chancellor, Otto von Bismarck, supports.

NOVEMBER

24 The exiled Alfonso (XII), the son of Isabella II who abdicated in his favor, comes of age and declares a constitutional monarchy in Spain.
25 A group of southern and western farmers in the United States forms the Greenback Party, committed to inflating the U.S. currency in order to relieve farmers' debt burden.

DECEMBER

19 Harry von Arnim, the former German ambassador to Paris, France, is found not guilty of handling state papers but guilty of an offense against public order and sentenced to three months in prison.

29–31   Spanish generals rally to Alfonso, the exiled son of Queen Isabella II, who is proclaimed king of Spain as Alfonso XII.

SCIENCE, TECHNOLOGY, AND MEDICINE

Computing

- English economist William Stanley Jevons constructs a logical machine that he refers to as an "abecedarium."

Ecology

- Austrian meteorologist Julius von Hann discovers that 90% of atmospheric water vapor is found below 5,500 m/18,000 ft, thus demonstrating that mountain ranges act as barriers to the transport of water vapor.

Exploration

- English naval officer Verney Lovett Cameron leads a Royal Geographical Society expedition to East Africa in search of the Scottish explorer David Livingstone. When he learns of the great explorer's death, he diverts his course and conducts a thorough survey of the southern part of Lake Tanganyika, then follows the Congo–Zambezi watershed westward to reach Angola on the west coast of Africa.

NOVEMBER
12–August 12, 1877   Welsh-born U.S. journalist and explorer Henry Stanley explores the shores of Lake Victoria and circumnavigates Lake Tanganyika before traveling down the Congo River (now the Zaïre) to Africa's west coast, establishing beyond argument that Lake Victoria is the principal source of the Nile.

Health and Medicine

- Austrian surgeon Theodor Billroth develops the study of the bacterial causes of fever associated with wounds with the publication of *Untersuchungen über die Vegetationsformen von Coccobacteria septica/ Investigations of the Vegetal Forms of Coccobacteria septica*.
- English physician James Paget describes the cancerous condition of the breast, now known as Paget's disease.
- Fluorides are discovered to prevent tooth decay.
- U.S. physician Andrew Taylor Still founds the health-care profession of osteopathy with his conviction that disease can be cured through correctly manipulating the joints.

Math

- German mathematician Georg Cantor is the first person rigorously to describe the notion of infinity.

Science

- Austrian physicist Ludwig Boltzmann develops the basic principles of statistical mechanics when he demonstrates how the laws of mechanics and the theory of probability, when applied to the motions of atoms, can explain the second law of thermodynamics.
- Dutch chemist Jacobus Henricus van't Hoff and French chemist Joseph-Achile Le Bel, independently and simultaneously, develop stereochemistry by proposing a three-dimensional structure for organic molecules including a tetrahedron-shaped molecule for carbon.
- German chemist Othman Zeidler reports the synthesis of dichlorodiphenyl-trichloroethane (DDT). He has no idea of its insecticidal properties.
- Irish physicist George Johnstone Stoney names the electron and estimates the value of its charge.
- The German psychologist Wilhelm Wundt publishes *Grundzüge der physiologischen Psychologie/Principles of Physiological Psychology*.
- U.S. astronomer Henry Draper photographs the transit of Venus.

Technology

- English chemist William Blanchard Bolton develops a process of washing nitrates out of photographic emulsions in the development of photographic plates.
- French engineer Jean-Maurice-Emile Baudot patents a binary telegraph code in which each letter is represented by a combination of five current-on or current-off signals; it soon replaces Morse Code as the main telegraphic alphabet.
- U.S. inventor Elisha Gray constructs a telephone receiver but does not have a transmitter.
- U.S. inventor Joseph Glidden designs a machine for making barbed wire. Inexpensive and easy to put up, it transforms the open range of the western United States into fenced pastureland.
- U.S. inventor Thomas Alva Edison invents the quadruplex telegraph which simultaneously sends two messages in opposite directions on the same telegraph line.

Transportation

- English inventor H. J. Lawson develops the "safety bicycle." Because it has two equal-sized wheels, rubber tires, and is powered by an endless chain between the pedals and the rear wheel, it has greater stability and is easier to brake than other bicycles.
- Passenger liners cross the Atlantic in 7 days averaging about 16 knots.
- The first New York, electric streetcars begin operating.

JULY
4   The St. Louis Bridge over the Mississippi River at St. Louis, Missouri, is officially opened. Built by U.S. engineer James Buchanan Eads, it consists of three hollow-steel arch trusses each over 150 m/500 ft long, making it the longest bridge in the world. A landmark in engineering, the arches are cantilevered so they can be raised, the foundations are planted to record depths of 30 m/100 ft, and it pioneers the use of structural steel.

ARTS AND IDEAS

Architecture

- The Sherman House, designed by the U.S. architects Daniel Hudson Burnham and John Wellborn Root, is completed in Chicago, Illinois.

Arts

c. 1874 The U.S. artist James Abbot McNeill Whistler paints *Nocturne in Black and Gold: Falling Rocket*. This picture is attacked by the English art critic John Ruskin as "a pot of paint... flung in the public's face." Whistler sues for libel, and though he wins his case, he is awarded only a farthing (quarter of a penny) in damages.
- The first impressionist exhibition is held in Paris, France, with works by (among others) Cézanne, Degas, Pissarro, and Sisley.
- The French artist Berthe Morisot paints *The Butterfly Chase*.
- The French artist Edouard Manet paints *Argenteuil*.
- The French artist Pierre-Auguste Renoir paints *La Loge/ At the Theater*.
- The French-born English artist James Tissot paints *Ball on Shipboard*.
- The U.S. artist Thomas Ball sculpts *The Emancipation Group*.

Literature and Language

- The English writer Thomas Hardy publishes his novel *Far from the Madding Crowd*.
- The French writer Alphonse Daudet publishes his novel *Fromont jeune et Risler aîné/Fromont the Younger and Risler the Elder*.
- The French writer Gustave Flaubert publishes his novel *La Tentation de St. Antoine/The Temptation of St. Anthony* (a work he began in 1839).
- The French writer Paul Verlaine publishes his poetry collection *Romances sans paroles/Songs without Words*.
- The French writer Victor Hugo publishes *L'Année terrible/The Terrible Year*, poems on the Franco-Prussian War of 1870.
- The Spanish writer Pedro Antonio de Alarcón y Ariza publishes his novel *El sombrero de tres picos/The Three-Cornered Hat*. It is used as the basis of the ballet *The Three-Cornered Hat*, which is written in 1919 by the Spanish composer Manuel de Falla.

Music

- Bohemian composer Antonín Leopold Dvořák completes his Symphony No. 4.
- French composer Camille St.-Saëns completes his symphonic poem *Danse macabre/Macabre Dance*.
- Italian composer Giuseppe Verdi completes his *Requiem*.

- Russian composer Modest Petrovich Mussorgsky completes his piano work *Pictures at an Exhibition*. This is orchestrated by several composers, notably by the French composer Maurice Ravel in 1922.
- Russian composer Peter Illyich Tchaikovsky completes his String Quartet No. 2 (Opus 22). In the same year, his opera *The Life of a Guardsman* is first performed, in St. Petersburg, Russia.
- The opera *Dvě vdovy/The Two Widows* by the Bohemian composer Bedřich Smetana is first performed, in Prague, Bohemia.
- The operetta *Giroflé-Girofla* by the French composer Alexandre Charles Lecocq is first performed, in Paris, France.
- The operetta *Die Fledermaus/The Bat* by the Austrian composer Johann Strauss is first performed, in Vienna, Austria. It is first performed in the United States the same year (in New York, New York), and in Britain in 1876 (in London, England).

Thought and Scholarship

- St. Louis historian John Fiske publishes *Outlines of Cosmic Philosophy*.
- The English philosopher Henry Sidgwick publishes *Methods of Ethics*.
- The U.S. historian Francis Parkman publishes *The Old Regime in Canada*.
- U.S. Presbyterian theologian Charles Hodge publishes *What Is Darwinism?*, a critique of Darwin's theory of evolution.
- U.S. writer John William Draper publishes *History of the Conflict Between Religion and Science*, an account of the debate gripping U.S. colleges and universities.
- The U.S. political thinker John Quincy Adams publishes his *Memoirs*.

SOCIETY

Education

- Hertford College is founded at Oxford University, England.
- Macalester College is founded in St. Paul, Minnesota.
- Ohio Methodists Lewis Miller and John H. Vincent establish the Chautauqua Society, which begins as a summer school for Sunday school teachers in Chautauqua, New York.

Everyday Life

- The city of Philadelphia, Pennsylvania, opens the nation's first public zoo.
- The first jeans with rivets are produced by Levi Strauss of San Francisco, California.
- U.S. confectioner Robert Green develops the ice-cream soda.

Media and Communication

- U.S. arms manufacturer Philo Remington begins manufacturing the typewriter designed by Christopher Latham Sholes.

NOVEMBER

7   In the an edition of *Harper's Weekly*, U.S. cartoonist Thomas Nast introduces the elephant as a symbol of the Republican Party.

Religion

- A group of women temperance advocates led by Annie Wittenmyer establishes the Woman's Christian Temperance Union in Cleveland, Ohio.
- The English statesman William Ewart Gladstone publishes the pamphlet *The Vatican Decrees*, an attack on papal infallibility.

MARCH

22   Educator Lewis May founds the first Young Men's Hebrew Association, in New York, New York.

Sports

- Lawn tennis is introduced to the United States by Mary Ewing Outerbridge of Staten Island, New York, at the Staten Island Cricket and Baseball Club. Around the same time U.S. physician James Dwight lays a court at Nahant, near Boston, Massachusetts.
- U.S. athlete Edward Payson Weston becomes the first person to walk 805 km/500 mi in six days. He finishes his walk in Newark, New Jersey.

MAY

14–15   The first football games under Harvard rules, a modified version of rugby and a precursor of American football, are played by Harvard University against McGill University in Montreal, Canada.

BIRTHS & DEATHS

JANUARY

16   Robert Service, British-born Canadian writer of popular verse who wrote "The Shooting of Dan McGrew," born in Preston, Lancashire, England (–1958).
25   W(illiam) Somerset Maugham, English novelist and playwright, born in Paris, France (–1965).
29   John D. Rockefeller, Jr., U.S. philanthropist who was instrumental in founding the United Nations in New York, New York, born in Cleveland, Ohio (–1960).

FEBRUARY

1   Hugo von Hofmannsthal, Austrian poet and dramatist, born in Vienna, Austria (–1929).
3   Gertrude Stein, U.S. avant-garde writer and eccentric, born in Allegheny, Pennsylvania (–1946).
9   Jules Michelet, French nationalist historian, dies in Hyères, France (75).
15   Ernest Shackleton, Irish explorer who tried to reach the South Pole, born in Kilkee, Ireland (–1922).
17   Adolphe Quetelet, Belgian mathematician who was one of the first to apply statistics to social phenomena, dies in Brussels, Belgium (77).

MARCH

8   Millard Fillmore, thirteenth president of the United States 1850–53, a Whig, dies in Buffalo, New York (74).
24   Harry Houdini (adopted name of Erich Weiss), Hungarian-born U.S. conjurer and escapologist, born in Budapest, Hungary (–1936).

24   Luigi Einaudi, first president of the Republic of Italy 1948–55, born in Carù, Italy (–1961).
26   Robert Frost, U.S. poet known for his use of colloquial language, born in San Francisco, California (–1963).

APRIL

25   Guglielmo Marconi, Italian physicist and inventor of radio, born in Bologna, Italy (–1937).

MAY

3   Vagn Walfrid Ekman, Swedish oceanographer noted for his studies of ocean currents, born in Stockholm, Sweden (–1954).
22   Daniel F. Malan, South African politician who instituted apartheid, born near Riebeck West, Cape Colony (–1959).
29   G(ilbert) K(eith) Chesterton, English author and literary critic, born in London, England (–1936).

JUNE

21   Anders Jonas Ångström, Swedish physicist who founded spectroscopy, dies in Uppsala, Sweden (59).

AUGUST

10   Herbert Hoover, thirty-first president of the United States 1929–33, a Republican, born in West Branch, Iowa (–1964).
31   Edward Lee Thorndike, U.S. psychologist and animal behaviorist who developed the theory of connectionism which states that behavioral responses are due to neural connections resulting from trial and error, born in Williamsburg, Massachusetts (–1949).

SEPTEMBER

13   Arnold Schoenberg, Austrian composer who developed a new "atonal" method of musical composition, born in Vienna, Austria (–1951).
21   Gustav Holst, English composer, author of the suite *The Planets* (1914–16), born in Cheltenham, Gloucestershire, England (–1934).

OCTOBER

12   François-Pierre-Guillaume Guizot, French politician and historian, dies in Val-Richer, France (87).
20   Charles Ives, U.S. composer, born in Danbury, Connecticut (–1954).

NOVEMBER

27   Chaim Weizmann, first president of Israel 1949–52, born in Motol, Poland, then part of the Russian Empire (–1952).
29   António Egas Moniz, Portuguese neurologist who introduced the lobotomy as a means of treating certain psychoses, born in Avança, Portugal (–1955).
30   Lucy Maude Montgomery, Canadian romantic novelist best known for *Anne of Green Gables*, born in Clifton, Prince Edward Island, Canada (–1942).
30   Winston Churchill, British prime minister 1940–45 and 1951–55, who led Britain through World War II, born at Blenheim Palace, Oxfordshire, England (–1965).

DECEMBER

17   W(illiam) L(yon) Mackenzie King, Prime Minister of Canada 1921–26, 1926–30, and 1935–48, a Liberal, born in Berlin, Ontario, Canada (–1950).

1875

POLITICS, GOVERNMENT, AND ECONOMICS

Business and Economics

- Henry John Heinz, his brother John, and cousin Frederick form their company in the United States. Heinz ketchup is one of the first products launched.
- U.S. tobacco merchant Richard Joshua Reynolds establishes R. J. Reynolds Tobacco in Winston, North Carolina.
- The total state expenditure in Great Britain is £73 million.

NOVEMBER

25 Britain buys 176,602 shares in the Suez Canal linking the Mediterranean with the Red Sea from Khedive Ismail of Egypt, the canal being a vital part of the route to India.

DECEMBER

12 The British financial expert Stephen Cave is sent to Egypt to inquire into its finances following a worsening of Egypt's debt crisis.

Human Rights

- U.S. social reformers Henry Bergh and Elbridge T. Gerry establish the Society for the Prevention of Cruelty to Children in the United States.

MARCH

1 The U.S. Congress passes the Civil-Rights Act of 1875, guaranteeing black Americans equal access to public facilities. The legislation also prohibits banning black Americans from jury duty.

Politics and Government

- A treaty of friendship is signed between Japan and Korea, after tension between the two.
- President Marie-Edmé-Patrice-Maurice MacMahon, duc de Magenta, arbitrates in the dispute over Delagoa Bay on the coast of southeast Africa (modern Mozambique), recognizing Portuguese claims against Britain.
- Russia has a standing army of 3,360,000 soldiers; Germany, 2,800,000; France, 412,000; Britain, 113,649.
- War breaks out between Egypt and Abyssinia (now Ethiopia) because of Egypt's eastward expansion.

JANUARY

9 King Alfonso XII of Spain lands at Barcelona, northeast Spain, but the Second Carlist War over the succession continues.

14 In an attempt to curb inflation, the U.S. Congress passes the Specie Resumption Act. The legislation authorizes the redemption of green backs for specie (coins), effective from January 1, 1879.

30 A Republican constitution in France is passed by one vote, establishing a democratically elected Chamber of Deputies, a Senate, and a president appointed for seven years.

30 The United States and Hawaii sign the Hawaiian Reciprocity Treaty, which stipulates that Hawaii will not allow itself to be annexed by another nation.

FEBRUARY

2 In the face of deteriorating relations with France, the German chancellor Otto von Bismarck endeavors to preserve Germany's entente with Russia.

25 Zaitian, nephew of the former coregent Cixi, becomes Guangxu emperor of China.

MARCH

3 In an attempt to promote the settlement of California, the U.S. Congress extends the Homestead Act of 1862. The new legislation makes available individual lots of 640 acres and relaxes absentee ownership restrictions.

3 Kálmán Tisza, the leader of the Left, forms a ministry in Hungary on the breakup of the party of Ferencz Deák, the architect of the dual monarchy of Austria-Hungary.

APRIL

4 Louis Decazes, the French foreign minister, appeals to Britain and Russia for support against Germany following pressure over France's military buildup.

8 An article ghosted by the German chancellor Otto von Bismarck entitled "Is War in Sight?" is printed in the *Berlin Post* and starts a war-scare with France.

14 The Japanese law courts are reformed, continuing the process of administrative modernization undertaken by Emperor Matsuhito.

MAY

5 Religious orders are abolished in Prussia by this year's May Laws against the Catholic Church in Germany.

10 In the so-called Whiskey Ring scandal, the U.S. Justice Department indicts approximately 240 whiskey distillers and Treasury Department officials for attempting to defraud the U.S. government of liquor taxes.

10 Czar Alexander II of Russia and his foreign minister, Prince Alexander Gorchakov, visit Berlin, Germany, to try to quell talk of war with France.

JULY

7 Risings occur in the Ottoman provinces of Bosnia and Herzegovina against Ottoman rule.

16   The law on the relation of the Public Powers delineates the powers of the French Chamber of Deputies and Senate and completes the French constitution of 1875.

SEPTEMBER

29   The British prime minister Benjamin Disraeli overrules the British Admiralty's ruling requiring the restitution of fugitive slaves picked up within U.S. territorial waters.

OCTOBER

12   Provincial governments are abolished in New Zealand and the government is centralized.

NOVEMBER

13   Egyptian forces are heavily defeated by the Abyssinians at Gundet, Abyssinia (modern Ethiopia), in the war between the two countries provoked by Egypt's eastward expansion.

DECEMBER

4   The notorious political operator William Marcy "Boss" Tweed escapes from prison in New York, New York, and heads for Cuba.

12   The Austrian foreign minister Gyula Andrássy, on behalf of the Eastern powers, calls for reform to improve the position of Christians in the Ottoman provinces of Bosnia and Herzegovina.

12   The sultan of the Ottoman Empire, Abdul Aziz, promises reforms throughout the Ottoman Empire to meet the demands of the rebels in the Ottoman provinces of Bosnia and Herzegovina.

SCIENCE, TECHNOLOGY, AND MEDICINE

Agriculture

- Inland lakes in the United States are stocked with Atlantic salmon by the U.S. Fish Commission; they soon become an important food.

JULY

20   The first experimental agricultural station is established at Wesleyan University, Connecticut.

Ecology

MAY

16   Colombia and Venezuela are struck by an earthquake that takes 16,000 lives.

SEPTEMBER

10   A group of U.S. conservationists establishes the American Forestry Association in Chicago, Illinois.

Health and Medicine

c. 1875   The Japanese navy eradicates beriberi among its sailors by providing them with extra meat, fish, and vegetables.

- Approximately 25,000 Fijians, over one-quarter of the population, die during an epidemic of measles.
- Dental cement, containing zinc oxyphosphate, becomes widely available; it is the forerunner of modern dental cements.
- German physiologist Leonard Landois demonstrates the danger of transfusions using animal blood by showing that red blood cells from one species clump together or burst when mixed with serum from another species.
- U.S. dentist George Green patents the electric dental drill.

Science

- French chemist Paul-Emile Lecoq de Boisbaudran discovers the metal gallium (atomic no. 31). Its existence had been predicted by Russian chemist Dmitry Ivanovich Mendeleyev on the basis of his periodic table, and its discovery results in acceptance of the table.
- French physiologist Paul Bert discovers that animals become ill at high altitudes because of the low oxygen content of the air. He creates the first life-support system when he sends two balloonists up with an oxygen supply in a bag made from cow's intestines. They fail to use it soon enough and one dies.
- German botanist Ferdinand Julius Cohn describes the production of endospores by the bacteria *Bacillus subtilis*. The discovery leads to the final rejection of the doctrine of spontaneous generation and becomes important in developing sterilization techniques.
- German embryologist Oskar Hertwig discovers that fertilization occurs with the fusion of the nuclei of the sperm and ovum.
- Scottish neurologist David Ferrier locates and maps the motor and sensory regions of the brain in primates.
- Tiny cuts in bones used by Neolithic cultures are identified by the British anthropologist E. R. Jones as tallies for counting game.

MAY

20   The International Bureau of Weights and Measures is established in France by a treaty signed in Paris. Located at Sèvres, its purpose is to unify systems of measurement, and to establish standards by providing a prototype meter and kilogram as the basis for all scientific and other measures.

Technology

- German-born British electrical engineer Charles William Siemens lays the first direct-link telegraph cable between Britain and the United States; previous ones have gone through either Ireland or Canada.

Transportation

- Austrian engineer Siegfried Marcus builds one of the first automobiles powered by gasoline. It is the oldest existing automobile.
- Irish-born U.S. engineer John Holland builds a submarine using water for ballast and with horizontal rudders to control diving.

ARTS AND IDEAS

Architecture

- The Opéra (the Opera House), designed by the French architect Charles Garnier, is completed in Paris, France. It is one of the outstanding examples of the ornate and flamboyant Beaux Arts style.
- The Watts Sherman House, designed by the U.S. architect Henry Hobson Richardson, is completed in Newport, Rhode Island.

Arts

- c. 1875 The French artist Gustave Moreau paints *Jupiter and Semele*.
- *Hermes*, a statue sculpted by the Ancient Greek artist Praxiteles, is unearthed at Olympia in Greece.
- The French artist Claude Monet paints *Boating at Argenteuil*.
- The French artist Edgar Degas paints *Ballet Rehearsal* and *Place de la Concorde*.
- The French artist Gustave Caillebotte paints *The Floor Strippers*.
- The German artist Adolf von Menzel paints *The Forge*.
- The German-born English artist Hubert Herkomer paints *The Last Muster: Sunday at the Royal Hospital, Chelsea*.
- The U.S. artist John Rogers sculpts *Checkers at the Farm*.

Literature and Language

- The Russian writer Leo Tolstoy publishes the first part of his novel *Anna Karenina*. The second part appears in 1876.

Music

- Bohemian composer Antonín Leopold Dvořák completes his Symphony No. 5 (once classified as No. 3). He revises it in 1887.
- Russian composer Peter Illyich Tchaikovsky completes his Piano Concerto No. 1 (Opus 23) and his Symphony No. 3, the *Polish*.
- The opera *Carmen* by the French composer Georges Bizet is first performed, in Paris, France. It is based on a story by the French writer Prosper Mérimée, published in 1840. It is first performed in both Britain and the United States in 1878 (in London, England, and New York, New York).
- The opera *Die Königin von Saba/Queen of Sheba* by the Hungarian composer Károly Goldmark is first performed, in Vienna, Austria.
- The operetta *Trial by Jury* by the English writer William Schwenk Gilbert and the English composer Arthur Seymour Sullivan is first performed, in London, England.

Theater and Dance

- The play *En fallit/The Bankrupt* by the Norwegian writer Bjørnstjerne Martinius Bjørnson is first performed, in Christiania (now Oslo), Norway.

Thought and Scholarship

- The French historian and critic Hippolyte Adolphe Taine publishes the first volume of *Les Origines de la France contemporaine/The Origins of Contemporary France*. The last volume appears in 1894.
- The German-born English orientalist Friedrich Max Müller publishes the first volume of his 51-volume *The Sacred Books of the East*. The last volume appears in 1903.

NOVEMBER

17 The Russian spiritualist Helena Blavatsky founds the Theosophical Society of America in New York, New York.

SOCIETY

Education

- Brigham Young University is founded by The Church of Jesus Christ of Latter-day Saints at Provo, Utah.
- Wellesley College opens in Wellesley, Massachusetts.

Everyday Life

- German chemist Ferdinand Tiemann patents synthetic vanilla flavoring, the first artificial flavor.
- The first canned baked beans are produced, for fishermen in Portland, Maine.
- The Swiss food company Nestlé develops the first milk chocolate.

Religion

- U.S. founder of the Christian Science movement Mary Baker Eddy publishes *Science and Health with Key to the Scriptures*, the first text of the Christian Science movement.

MARCH

15 The Catholic archbishop John McCloskey is invested as the first U.S. cardinal, in New York, New York.

Sports

- Snooker is invented by British colonel Neville Bowes Chamberlain at the Ooty Club, Ootacamund, Nilgiri, southern India.

MAY

17 Aristides, ridden by U.S. jockey Oliver Lewis, wins the inaugural Kentucky Derby horse race at Churchill Downs, Louisville, Kentucky.

17   The first ski races in Europe are held at Iverslöken, Norway.

August

24–25   The English swimmer Matthew Webb, a captain in the British Merchant Navy, becomes the first person to swim the English Channel. He takes 21 hours and 45 minutes to cross from Dover, England, to Calais, France.

BIRTHS & DEATHS

January

3   Pierre-Athanase Larousse, French encyclopedist, dies in Paris, France (57).

14   Albert Schweitzer, German theologian, philosopher, and doctor, born in Kaysensberg, Upper Alsace, Germany (–1965).

20   Jean-François Millet, French painter, dies in Barbizon, France (60).

22   D(avid Lewelyn) W(ark) Griffith, U.S. pioneer of filmmaking, born in Flodysfork, Kentucky (–1948).

23   Charles Kingsley, English clergyman and author, dies in Eversley, Hampshire, England (55).

February

22   (Jean-Baptiste-) Camille Corot, French landscape painter, dies in Paris, France (78).

22   Charles Lyell, Scottish geologist who developed uniformitarian geology which laid the foundation for evolutionary biology, dies in London, England (77).

March

7   Maurice Ravel, French composer, among whose well-loved pieces is the *Boléro*, born in Ciboure, France (–1937).

April

2   Walter Percy Chrysler, U.S. automobile manufacturer, born in Wamego, Kansas (–1940).

June

3   Georges (Alexandre-César-Léopold) Bizet, French composer, dies in Paris, France (36).

6   Thomas Mann, German novelist, born in Lübeck, Germany (–1955).

9   Henry Dale, British physiologist who isolated acetylcholine and described its role in the transmission of nerve impulses, born in London, England (–1968).

July

21   Andrew Johnson, seventeenth president of the United States 1865–69, a Democrat, dies near Carter Station, Tennessee (66). He is buried in Greenville, Tennessee.

23   Isaac Merrit Singer, U.S. inventor who developed and brought the sewing machine into popular use, dies in Torquay, Devon, England (63).

26   Carl Jung, Swiss psychologist who founded analytic psychology, born in Kesswil, Switzerland (–1961).

30   George Edward Pickett, Confederate general during the American Civil War, dies in Norfolk, Virginia (50).

August

4   Hans Christian Andersen, Danish storyteller, dies in Copenhagen, Denmark (70).

13   Samuel Coleridge-Taylor, English composer, born in London, England (–1912).

16   Charles Grandison Finney, U.S. lawyer and evangelical revivalist, dies in Oberlin, Ohio (82).

September

1   Edgar Rice Burroughs, U.S. author who created Tarzan, born in Chicago, Illinois (–1950).

3   Ferdinand Porsche, Austrian automotive engineer who designed the Volkswagen automobile, born in Maffersdorf, Austria (–1951).

16   J. C. Penny, U.S. merchant who established one of the largest department store chains in the United States, born in Hamilton, Missouri (–1971).

November

19   Mikhail Ivanovich Kalinin, head of state of the Soviet Union 1919–46, born in Verkhnyaya Troitsa, Tver Province, Russia (–1946).

December

4   Rainer Maria Rilke, Austro-German poet, born in Prague, Bohemia, in the Austro-Hungarian empire (–1926).

12   Gerd von Rundstedt, German field marshal during World War II, born in Aschersleben, near Magdeburg, Prussia (–1953).

1876

POLITICS, GOVERNMENT, AND ECONOMICS

Business and Economics

- The Chicago wholesaler Gustavus Swift establishes the nation's first meatpacking plant, shipping dressed beef rather than live cattle to eastern markets.
- The pharmaceutical company Eli Lilly is founded in the United States.

JANUARY

1   The Reichsbank, the central state bank of the new German Empire, is opened in Berlin, Prussia.

MARCH

3   The British financial expert Stephen Cave's highly critical report on Egyptian finances is published.

APRIL

8   Khedive Ismail of Egypt suspends payment of European debts in response to Egypt's financial crisis.

MAY

2   Khedive Ismail of Egypt allows the establishment of a Commission of Public Debts made up of French, Italian, Austro-Hungarian, and British representatives to deal with Egypt's debt crisis.

JULY

25 In an effort to relieve struggling debtors in his and other midwestern states, Missouri congressman Richard P. Bland introduces legislation providing for the unlimited coinage of silver.

Politics and Government

- A coup d'état in Bolivia leads to Hilarión Daza's presidency.
- In the U.S. Congressional elections, the Republicans retain a reduced majority in the Senate (39–36) while the Democrats maintain control of the House (153–140).
- The Russian anarchist Mikhail Alexandrovich Bakunin organizes "Land and Liberty," a secret society which becomes the spearhead of the revolutionary Russian Populist Movement.
- The U.S. Congress repeals the Southern Homestead Act of 1866, which set aside nearly 50 million acres of southern land for settlement by former slaves.

JANUARY

1   The cortes (national assembly) adopts a new constitution in Spain providing for a two-chamber legislature, elected on limited suffrage.
31 Sultan Abdul Aziz of the Ottoman Empire agrees to adopt the reform program of the Austrian foreign minister Gyula Andrássy for the Ottoman provinces of Bosnia and Herzegovina, but this is rejected by the insurgents who now demand that a third of the land be given to Christians.

FEBRUARY

26 Japan recognizes Korea as a state independent of China in a treaty that opens Korea to Japanese trade.
28 The Second Carlist War in Spain ends with the flight to France of the pretender Don Carlos following the defeat of his forces by the king's troops.

MARCH

2   The U.S. House adopts an impeachment resolution against Secretary of War William W. Belknap, who had been accused of various improprieties.
5–7 The Egyptians are defeated at Gura, Abyssinia (now Eritrea), by the Abyssinians, with whom they are at war because of Egypt's eastward expansion.
8   The rule of the National Assembly in France ends with the meeting of a new Senate (Conservative) and Chamber of Deputies (overwhelmingly Republican).
9–16 Ottoman troops massacre Bulgarians following a revolt against Ottoman rule.

MAY

10 The Ottoman Liberal leader Midhat Pasha forms a ministry in Constantinople.
13 A Berlin Memorandum from Germany, Russia, and Austria-Hungary to the Ottoman Empire calls for an armistice, the granting of reforms to the rebels against its rule in Bosnia, Herzegovina, and Bulgaria, and the supervision of Ottoman reforms by the three European powers.
30 Sultan Abdul Aziz of the Ottoman Empire is deposed and succeeded by his nephew who is proclaimed as Murad V.

JUNE

16 The Republicans nominate former Ohio governor Rutherford B. Hayes for president and New York congressman William A. Wheeler for vice president.
25 At the Battle of Little Bighorn, Sioux and Cheyenne warriors commanded by legendary chief Sitting Bull rout a force of U.S. soldiers led by General George A. Custer, killing Custer and over 200 of his soldiers.
29 The Democrats nominate New York governor Samuel A. Tilden for president and former Indiana governor Thomas A. Hendricks for vice president.

30 Serbia, under the nationalist leader Jovan Ristič, declares war on the Ottoman Empire.

JULY

2 Montenegro declares war on the Ottoman Empire in support of the revolt against Ottoman rule in Bosnia and Herzegovina.

AUGUST

1 Colorado becomes the 38th state in the Union.

31 Sultan Murad V of the Ottoman Empire is deposed because of his insanity and is succeeded by Abdul Hamid II.

SEPTEMBER

1 The Serbs, having declared war on the Ottoman Empire, are defeated at Alexinatz, Serbia, by Ottoman forces.

OCTOBER

31 The Ottoman Empire agrees to an eight-week armistice in its battle with Serbian rebels as a result of a Russian ultimatum.

NOVEMBER

7 With 20 electoral votes in dispute, the year's U.S. presidential election between Republican Rutherford B. Hayes and Democrat Samuel J. Tilden remains in the balance. The year will end with the result undecided.

11 Russia prepares for war against the Ottoman Empire in support of the rebellions in the Balkans against Ottoman domination.

23 Having been apprehended by Spanish authorities, the escaped fugitive William Marcy "Boss" Tweed is returned to the United States and imprisoned in New York, New York.

DECEMBER

5 In an unprecedented development, President Ulysses S. Grant apologizes to Congress for the corruption that plagued his administration.

12 New Hampshire congressman Henry W. Blair proposes a constitutional amendment prohibiting the production and distribution of liquor.

23 An Ottoman constitution is proclaimed by the reformist grand vizier (chief minister) Midhat Pasha, guaranteeing parliamentary government, freedom of worship, and a free press throughout the empire.

SCIENCE, TECHNOLOGY, AND MEDICINE

Agriculture

- British scientist Henry Wickham collects 70,000 seeds from the rubber plant *Hevea brasiliensis* in the Amazon jungle, and has them planted in Kew Gardens, England. The saplings are later transported to Ceylon (Sri Lanka), India, and Malaya where they form the beginning of the rubber industry.
- German physician Robert Koch discovers that anthrax spores can remain viable in the soil for years, thus explaining the reoccurrence of anthrax in long-disused fields.

December 1876–78 Drought in India results in famine that kills 5 million people.

December 1876–79 Famine in northern China results in the deaths of an estimated 9–13 million people.

Computing

- Scottish physicist William Thomson, develops the first analog computer, called the "Harmonic Analyzer." He uses it to solve differential equations to predict tides.

Ecology

- A rich deposit of nickel ore is discovered in the Pacific island of New Caledonia. Production begins in 1877 and it is the world's major source of nickel until 1905.
- Over 7,800 sq km/3,000 sq mi are flooded near Chittagong, India (now Bangladesh), when the storm surge of a cyclone obstructs the ebb tide in the Meghna River estuary. About 100,000 people die and a further 100,000 die subsequently from disease.

JUNE

15 An earthquake and a 30-m/100-ft-high tsunami kill more than 28,000 people in Japan.

Health and Medicine

- An outbreak of cholera in India leads to 3 million deaths.
- Swiss surgeon Emil Kocher is the first to remove the thyroid gland to treat goiter.

Science

- German cytologist Eduard Adolf Strasburger publishes *Über Zellbildung und Zellteilung/On Cell Formation and Cell Division*, in which he describes the process of mitosis.
- German electrical engineer Werner von Siemens develops a selenium cell in which electrical resistance decreases when it is illuminated—the first solar cell.
- U.S. physicist Henry Rowland discovers that a moving electric charge and an electric current have the same magnetic action.
- U.S. physicist Josiah Willard Gibbs publishes "On the Equilibrium of Heterogeneous Substances," which lays the theoretical foundation of physical chemistry.

JANUARY

1 The International System of Weights and Measures comes into effect in France.

Technology

- Automation of soldering makes the production of tin cans far more efficient in the United States.
- German engineer Karl von Linde develops the first really efficient refrigerator, replacing the potentially explosive methyl ether with ammonia. It opens the way for refrigerated railroad cars and ships.

- Russian electrical engineer Pavel Nikolayevich Yablochkov invents the "Yablochkov candle," an arc lamp widely used for street lighting in Paris, France, and other European cities before incandescent lamps.
- Swedish chemist Alfred Nobel patents gelatinous dynamite.
- U.S. inventor Julius Le Moyne develops the crematorium furnace. Corpses take about one hour to be reduced to ashes.

MARCH

7   Scottish-born U.S. inventor Alexander Graham Bell patents a device for transmitting human speech over electric wires. It consists of an identical microphone and receiver each made of a solenoid placed next to an iron membrane; vibration in the microphone's membrane induces a current in the solenoid that travels down the wire and causes the membrane in the receiver to vibrate.

Transportation

- German engineer Nikolaus Otto patents the four-stroke internal combustion engine, the prototype of modern engines. Its development marks the beginning of the end of the age of steam. More than 30,000 are built in the following decade.
- The 7.5-km/4.7-mi-long Hoosac Tunnel on the Boston and Maine Railroad, in Massachusetts, is completed: the world's longest railroad tunnel to date. The first pneumatic drills were used to build it.
- The Intercolonial railroad opens linking Ontario, New Brunswick, and Nova Scotia, Canada.
- U.S. engineer Charles Sharer Smith completes the Harrodsburg bridge across the Kentucky River; it is the first cantilever bridge in the United States.

ARTS AND IDEAS

Architecture

- The Museum of Fine Arts in Boston, Massachusetts, designed by the U.S. architects John Sturgis and Charles Brigham, is completed. It is the first purpose-built public art museum in the United States.
- Work begins on the Church of Sacré Coeur in Montmartre, Paris, France, designed by the French architect Paul Abadie.

Arts

- The English artist Hamo Thornycroft sculpts *Warrior Beasino: A Wounded Youth*.
- The English artist John Everett Millais paints *The North-West Passage*.
- The French artist Alfred Sisley paints *Floods at Port-Marly*.
- The French artist Auguste Rodin sculpts *The Age of Bronze*.
- The French artist Edgar Degas paints *The Glass of Absinth*.

- The French artist Gustave Moreau paints *Salomé Dancing Before Herod*.
- The French artist Gustave Caillebotte paints *Le Pont de l'Europe/The Bridge of Europe*.
- The French artist Pierre-Auguste Renoir paints *The Swing*.

Literature and Language

- The English writer and mathematician Lewis Carroll publishes his poem "The Hunting of the Snark."
- The English writer George Eliot publishes her novel *Daniel Deronda*.
- The English writer, designer, and social reformer William Morris publishes his long poem *Sigurd the Volsung*, based on Nordic myths.
- The French writer Stéphane Mallarmé publishes his poem *L'Après-midi d'un faune/The Afternoon of a Faun*.
- The Spanish writer Benito Pérez-Galdós publishes his novel *Doña Perfecta*. This is one of the finest novels in his 46-novel series *Episodios nacionales/National Episodes* (1873–1912), a vast picture of all aspects of 19th-century Spanish life.
- The U.S. writer Henry James publishes his novel *Roderick Hudson*.
- The U.S. writer Mark Twain publishes his novel *The Adventures of Tom Sawyer*.

Music

- Austrian composer Josef Anton Bruckner completes his Symphony No. 5.
- Bohemian composer Bedřich Smetana completes his String Quartet No. 1, *Z mého života/From My Life*. His opera *Hubička/The Kiss* is first performed, in Prague, Bohemia.
- French composer César Franck completes his symphonic poem *Les Eolides/The Breezes*.
- French composer Gabriel Fauré completes his Sonata for Piano and Violin No. 1.
- German composer Johannes Brahms completes his Symphony No. 1.
- Hungarian composer Franz Liszt completes his piano transcription of Camille St.-Saëns's *Danse macabre/Macabre Dance* (1874).
- Russian composer Alexander Porfiryevich Borodin completes his Symphony No. 2.
- The opera *La Gioconda* by the Italian composer Amilcare Ponchielli is first performed, in Milan, Italy. It is best remembered for its ballet sequence *Dance of the Hours*.
- The opera *Vakula the Smith* by the Russian composer Peter Illyich Tchaikovsky is first performed, in St. Petersburg, Russia. In the same year, he completes his symphonic fantasy *Francesca da Rimini* (Opus 32) and his String Quartet No. 3 (Opus 30).
- The operas *Siegfried* and *Götterdämmerung/The Twilight of the Gods* by the German composer Richard Wagner are first performed, in Bayreuth, Germany. They form the third part of his *Der Ring des Nibelungen/The Ring of the Nibelung* cycle of operas, which is now performed in its entirety.

- U.S. evangelist Ira David Sankey and U.S. poet Horatius Bonar write the hymn "What a Friend We Have in Jesus."
- U.S. songwriter Henry Clay Work writes the song "Grandfather's Clock."
- U.S. songwriter Thomas P. Westendorf writes the song "I'll Take You Home Again, Kathleen."

Theater and Dance

- The ballet *Sylvia, ou La Nymphe de Diane/Sylvia, or the Nymph of Diana* by the French composer Léo Delibes is first performed, in Paris, France. The choreography is by the French choreographer Louis Mérante.
- The Bayreuth Festspielhaus in the Germany opens for the first complete performance of Richard Wagner's *Der Ring des Nibelungen/The Ring of the Nibelung* cycle of operas.
- The verse play *Peer Gynt* by the Norwegian dramatist Henrik Ibsen is first performed, in Christiania (now Oslo), Norway. It was published in 1867.

Thought and Scholarship

- Columbia University librarian Melvil Dewey pioneers the Dewey Decimal System to facilitate classification of library books.
- Scottish philosopher Alexander Bain founds the journal *Mind* in Britain, the first psychology journal.
- The English philosopher Francis Herbert Bradley publishes *Ethical Studies*.
- The Italian professor of psychiatry Cesare Lembroso, of the University of Turin, publishes *The Criminal*, a work which founds the study of criminal anthropology.
- The New York, polymath Felix Adler founds the New York Society for Ethical Culture.

OCTOBER

6   A group of public and university librarians establishes the American Library Association to promote the enjoyment of reading.

SOCIETY

Education

- Harvard University students launch *The Harvard Lampoon*, the first undergraduate humor magazine at a U.S. college, in Cambridge, Massachusetts.
- Johns Hopkins University is founded in Baltimore, Maryland.
- Texas A&M University is founded at College Station, Texas.
- The University of Colorado is founded at Boulder, Colorado.
- The University of Montreal is founded in Montreal, Canada.
- The University of Oregon is founded in Eugene, Oregon.
- The U.S. Coast Guard Academy is founded at New London, Connecticut.

NOVEMBER

1   U.S. chef and culinary educator Juliet Corson opens the nation's first culinary institute, the New York Cooking School, in New York, New York.

Everyday Life

- Central Park, now fully constructed, opens to visitors in New York, New York.

BIRTHS & DEATHS

JANUARY

5   Konrad Adenauer, first chancellor of the Federal Republic of Germany (West Germany) 1949–63, born in Cologne, Germany (–1967).

12   Jack London (pseudonym of John Griffith Chaney), U.S. novelist and short-story writer, born in San Francisco, California (–1916).

FEBRUARY

16   George Macaulay Trevelyan, English historian, born in Welcombe, Warwickshire, England (–1964).

21   Constantin Brancusi, Romanian artist who pioneered abstract sculpture, born in Hobita, Romania (–1957).

MARCH

2   Pope Pius XII, Italian pope 1939–58, born in Rome, Italy (–1958).

JUNE

8   George Sand (pseudonym of Lucie Dudevant), French romantic novelist, dies in Nohant, France (71).

11   Alfred Louis Kroeber, U.S. anthropologist, born in Hoboken, New Jersey (–1960).

25   George A(rmstrong) Custer, U.S. cavalry officer and Civil War general, is killed at the Battle of Little Bighorn, Montana (36).

JULY

1   Mikhail Alexandrovich Bakunin, Russian revolutionary, dies in Bern, Switzerland (62).

17   Maxim Maximovich Litvinov, Soviet diplomat, born in Białystok, Poland (–1951).

AUGUST

2   "Wild Bill" (James Butler) Hickok, U.S. marksman, army scout, and gambler, is shot dead by a drunken stranger during a poker game in Deadwood, Dakota Territory (39).

7   Mata Hari, Dutch dancer and spy, born in Leeuwarden, the Netherlands (–1917).

SEPTEMBER

13   Sherwood Anderson, U.S. novelist and short-story writer, born in Camden, Ohio (–1941).

NOVEMBER

28   Karl Ernst von Baer, Estonian embryologist who established the science of comparative embryology, dies in Dorpat, Estonia (84).

DECEMBER

25   Muhammad Ali Jinnah, Indian/Pakistani Muslim politician, founder and first premier of Pakistan 1947–48, born in Karachi, India (now Pakistan) (–1948).

29   Pablo Casals, Spanish cellist, conductor, and composer, born in Vendrell, Spain (–1973).

- Fairmount Park in Philadelphia, Pennsylvania, opens—it is the largest public park in any U.S. city (1,538 hectares/3,845 acres).
- The clothing retailer John Wanamaker opens his Grand Depot department store in Philadelphia, Pennsylvania.
- U.S. brewer E. Anheuser and Co. launches Budweiser beer.
- The U.S. Justice Department opens the first federal reformatory for delinquent boys.

MAY

10 The Centennial Exposition, held in celebration of the 100th anniversary of the Declaration of Independence, opens in Philadelphia, Pennsylvania. It is an international trade fair and the first of its kind in the United States. Over 8,000 machines are exhibited in the Machinery Hall, all powered by a 2,500-horsepower steam engine built by the Corliss Steam Engine Co. There are 10 million visitors.

JULY

7   The First International (International Working Men's Association) is dissolved at the Philadelphia Congress, Pennsylvania.

SEPTEMBER

19 Melville R. Bissell of Grand Rapids, Michigan, patents the first practical carpet-sweeper, in response to his own allergy to dust; he will go on to form the Bissell Carpet Sweeper Co.

Media and Communication

- The *Corriere della sera* is launched in Milan, the first national newspaper in Italy.

MARCH

10 Scottish-born U.S. inventor Alexander Graham Bell transmits the first complete sentence by voice over wire using his newly invented telephone in the United States: "Mr. Watson, come here. I want you."

Sports

- At the Massosoit Convention in Springfield, Massachusetts, delegates from Harvard, Rutgers, Columbia, Princeton, and Yale universities agree to adopt the rugby-based Harvard rules of football, regarded as the first American football rules.
- Sportsmen introduce polo to the United States; the first match is played at Dickel's Riding Academy in New York, New York.
- The Glaciarium, the first artificially refrigerated ice rink, opens in Chelsea, London, England.

FEBRUARY

2   The National League of Professional Baseball Clubs, the first major league, is established in New York, New York, by representatives of eight teams brought together by the Chicago White Stockings president William A. Hulbert.

APRIL

22 Boston defeats Philadelphia 6–5 in the first official National League baseball game, before 3,000 spectators in Philadelphia.

JUNE

5   England competes against Ireland in Dublin, Ireland, in the first ever international athletics meeting.

AUGUST

- The first recorded lawn tennis tournament in the United States is staged at Nahant, near Boston, Massachusetts. James Dwight defeats Richard Sears in the final.

SEPTEMBER

7   Joe Goss of England wins the bareknuckle heavyweight boxing championship, beating Tom Allen of the United States in a 27-round bout held in Covington, Kentucky.

◆

1877

POLITICS, GOVERNMENT, AND ECONOMICS

Business and Economics

- The Bell Telephone Company is founded in the United States.

JULY

17 Violence erupts in Martinsburg, West Virginia, when federal troops arrive to end a strike by employees of the Baltimore & Ohio Railroad.

20 Nine striking employees of the Baltimore & Ohio Railroad are killed in Baltimore, Maryland, when police fire into a crowd of protesters.

21 Industrial violence spreads west toward Pittsburgh, Pennsylvania, from Baltimore, as the railroad strike begins to sweep the nation.

26 The railroad strike reaches Chicago, Illinois, accompanied by more violence as U.S. president Rutherford B. Hayes again dispatches federal troops to quell the civil disorder.

Colonization

JANUARY

1   Queen Victoria of Britain is proclaimed empress of
    India.

APRIL

12 The British colonial administrator Theophilus Shepstone
    annexes the southern African Republic of Transvaal for
    Britain on grounds of bankruptcy and danger from
    Basutos and Zulus, though this annexation violates the
    Sand River Convention of 1852.

Human Rights

JUNE

15 Henry O. Flipper becomes the first black American to
    graduate from the U.S. Military Academy at West Point.

Politics and Government

• Anti-Chinese riots erupt in California where U.S.
  workers protest against foreign competition.
• The U.S. president Rutherford B. Hayes appoints John
  M. Harlan to the U.S. Supreme Court.
• The U.S. Supreme Court upholds state regulation of
  railroads in *Munn v. Illinois*.

JANUARY

2   Florida voters elect Democrat George F. Drew governor,
    thus ending Reconstruction in the state.
15 By the Budapest Convention between Russia and
    Austria-Hungary, Austria-Hungary undertakes to
    remain neutral in the event of a Russo-Ottoman war,
    and is to occupy the Ottoman provinces of Bosnia and
    Herzegovina if it sees fit. Thereafter Serbia, Montenegro,
    and Herzegovina are to form a neutral zone.
20 The Constantinople Conference fails to produce an
    accord between Russia and the Ottoman Empire in the
    Balkans and breaks up.
29 The U.S. Congress appoints a commission to decide the
    fate of 20 disputed electoral votes in the presidential
    election. The commission comprises 15 members (5
    senators, 5 congressmen, and 5 Supreme Court justices).
    Eight members are Republican, 7 are Democrat; the
    committee will vote along strict party lines.

FEBRUARY

5   Midhat Pasha, leader of the Ottoman Liberals, is
    dismissed from his office of grand vizier (chief minister).
28 A peace treaty is signed between the Ottoman Empire
    and Serbia ending the Serbian revolt against Ottoman
    rule, without significant concessions.

MARCH

2   On the basis of its committee's recommendation, the
    U.S. Congress awards all 20 disputed electoral votes in
    the previous December's presidential election to
    Republican Rutherford B. Hayes. The decision furnishes
    Hayes with a 185–184 majority over Democrat Samuel
    J. Tilden.
4   Rutherford B. Hayes is inaugurated as 19th president of
    the United States.

18 By an additional Russo-Austrian convention it is agreed
    that no large state is to be established in the Balkans
    from freed Ottoman territories.
19 The first Ottoman parliament meets, in Istanbul,
    convened under the provisions of the 1876 constitution.
31 The Welsh colonial administrator Henry Frere is
    appointed British high commissioner in southern Africa
    with instructions to work toward federation.

APRIL

• In exchange for Democratic acquiescence in the decision
  conferring the presidential election to Republican
  Rutherford B. Hayes, the Hayes administration
  withdraws federal troops from South Carolina and
  Louisiana, thereby leaving black Americans to the mercy
  of their former white oppressors.
24 Russia declares war on the Ottoman Empire and invades
    Romania in support of the Balkan revolts against
    Ottoman rule.

MAY

2   The dictator Porfirio Díaz becomes president of Mexico
    after overthrowing the government of President
    Sebastián Ierdo de Tejada the previous year.
5   Romania enters the war against the Ottoman Empire in
    support of the Balkan revolutions.
6   Britain sends a note to Russia warning it against an
    attempted blockade of the Red Sea port of Suez or
    occupation of Egypt during its war with the Ottoman
    Empire in support of the Balkan rebellions.
16 In the crisis of *Seize Mai* in France, President Marie-
    Edmé-Patrice-Maurice MacMahon, duc de Magenta,
    annoyed at Prime Minister Jules Simon's failure to stand
    up to the anticlerical Left, dismisses him and appoints
    Albert, duc de Broglie, to form a monarchist ministry.

JUNE

June–October   Nez Percé chief Joseph leads his followers
    into battle against U.S. troops over disputed land. The
    Nez Percé resistance ends after four months upon the
    U.S. capture of Chief Joseph.
14 Americans celebrate their first flag day, one hundred
    years after the Continental Congress adopted the symbol
    of the stars and stripes.

JULY

• A rebellion of the Japanese Satsuma samurai clan
  against modernization breaks out in Japan (the Satsuma
  Rebellion).
21 The British Cabinet decides to declare war on Russia if
    it occupies the Ottoman capital, Constantinople
    (Istanbul).

AUGUST

8   The first war between Britain and the native inhabitants
    of southern Africa breaks out following simmering
    tensions over British administration.

SEPTEMBER

9   The antidemocratic and anti-Western Satsuma Rebellion
    in Japan ends in defeat for the samurai at Kumamoto.

OCTOBER

10 Britain signs a treaty of commerce with Madagascar,
    which agrees to liberate slaves.
15 Russian forces defeat the Ottoman army at Aladja
    Dagh, Anatolia (modern Turkey), in the Russo-Ottoman
    War over the Balkans.

NOVEMBER

18   Russian troops storm the fortified Ottoman city of Kars in eastern Anatolia during the Russo-Ottoman War.

19   The French monarchist ministry of Prime Minister Albert, duc de Broglie, is forced to resign after a vote of no confidence from the Republican Chamber of Deputies and is succeeded by that of Gaetan de Grimaudet de Rochebouët, which also fails to win the confidence of the Chamber of Deputies.

23   The United States and Canada settle a dispute over fishing rights off the northeast coast of North America. As compensation for concessions, Canada receives $5.5 million from the United States.

DECEMBER

10   The Ottoman-held city of Plevna in Bulgaria falls to Russian forces.

12   The Ottoman Empire appeals to the powers of Europe to mediate in its war with Russia, but the German chancellor Otto von Bismarck declines and the British cabinet is divided over its response.

13   The Republican Armand Dufaure forms a ministry in France following the fall of the two previous unsupported monarchist ministries.

14   Serbia, siding with Russia, declares war on the Ottoman Empire.

26   The U.S. Workingmen's Party changes its name to the Socialist Labor Party at its annual convention in Newark, New Jersey.

SCIENCE, TECHNOLOGY, AND MEDICINE

Agriculture

- British entomologist Eleanor Anne Ormerod begins to publish the *Annual Report of Observations of Injurious Insects*. Used by agriculturalists worldwide, 170,000 of the pamphlets are printed yearly.
- Famine in Bengal kills nearly 4 million people.

Ecology

- Cotopaxi volcano in Ecuador erupts; over 1,000 people are killed by mudflows.

Health and Medicine

- British physician Patrick Manson shows how insects can be the carriers of infectious diseases, and demonstrates that the embryo of the *Filaria* worm, which causes elephantiasis, is transmitted by mosquitoes.
- British surgeon James Paget describes the bone inflammation disease known as *Osteitis deformans*, or Paget's disease.

Photography (1777–1888)

1777
- Swedish chemist Karl Wilhelm Scheele discovers that silver nitrate, when exposed to light, results in a blackening effect, an important discovery for the development of photography.

1790
- English chemist Thomas Wedgwood makes photograms— shadowlike photographic images—by placing objects on leather sensitized with silver nitrate.

1816
April   French photography pioneer Joseph-Nicéphore Niepce records a view from his workroom window on paper sensitized with silver chloride, but he is only partially able to fix the image.

1826
- Using a camera obscura and an eight-hour exposure, Niepce takes a crude photograph of his barnyard from a window on his estate. It is the world's first photograph. He uses light-sensitive bitumen of Judea (a type of asphalt) to fix the image on a pewter plate.

1835
- English pioneer of photography William Henry Fox Talbot creates *Picture of a Latticed Window*, the oldest existing photographic negative.

1837
- The French pioneer of photography Louis-Jacques-Mandé Daguerre takes *Still Life in Studio*, one of the earliest daguerreotypes, a photographic technique he invented.

1839
- English astronomer and chemist John Herschel, independently of Fox Talbot, invents the process of photography on sensitized paper. He is the first to apply the terms "positive" and "negative" to photographic images and uses sodium hyposulfite instead of sodium chloride.

1840
- Talbot improves his earlier photographic process and produces the calotype, a negative-positive photographic system.

1842
- The first photograph to be printed in a newspaper appears in the English newspaper *The Times*.

1848
- French scientists Alexandre Becquerel and Abel Niépce de Saint-Victor produce the first color photographs using coatings of silver chloride. They are unable to be fix the images.

1851
- Talbot takes the first high-speed flash photograph. He uses a spark produced from the discharge of a Leyden jar battery for the flash.

1851–60
- Photographic exposure times become short enough to capture movement.

- German urologist Max Nitze invents the cytoscope, a tubelike instrument with a light at the end that is passed through the urethra to view the inside of the bladder.

OCTOBER

26 English surgeon Joseph Lister performs the first operation to repair a fractured kneecap. Conducted under antiseptic conditions, its success convinces other surgeons of the value of antisepsis.

Science

- English physicist John William Strutt, Baron Rayleigh, publishes the first volume of his book *The Theory of Sound*, which discusses vibrations and resonances in solids and gases. The second volume appears in 1878.
- English scientists A. Downes and V. P. Blunt discover that ultraviolet rays can kill some microorganisms.
- French bacteriologist Louis Pasteur discovers that certain bacteria die when cultured with another type of bacteria, suggesting that the latter gives off a toxic substance—an antibiotic.
- German botanist Ferdinand Julius Cohn demonstrates that bacterial endospores are resistant to heat, which helps to dispel the idea of spontaneous generation.
- German botanist Wilhelm Friedrich Philipp Pfeffer devises a semipermeable membrane and publishes *Osmotische Untersuchungen: Studien zur Zellmechanik/ Osmotic Research: Studies on Cell Mechanics*, in which

he describes how osmotic pressure depends on the size of the molecules.
- German physician Robert Koch demonstrates new techniques of staining and fixing bacteria with heat for microscopic examination.
- Russian biologist Ilya Ilyich Metchnikov discovers the process of phagocytosis whereby certain ameba-like cells engulf other cells or foreign bodies such as dust or bacteria.
- The Como Bluff paleontological site is discovered in Wyoming. It contains a large number and variety of dinosaur remains, including the first specimens of *Stegosaurus*, *Brontosaurus* (now known as *Apatosaurus*), and *Allosaurus*.
- U.S. anthropologist Lewis Henry Morgan publishes *Ancient Society, or Researches in the Lines of Human Progress from Savagery through Barbarism to Civilization*, which is an evolutionary account of the development of civilization. Karl Marx and Friedrich Engels are heavily influenced by it in *Origin of the Family, Private Property, and the State*.

AUGUST

8 U.S. astronomer Asaph Hall discovers Deimos and Phobos, the two moons of Mars.

DECEMBER

2 French physicist Louis-Paul Cailletet liquifies oxygen; he later liquefies hydrogen, nitrogen, and air.

1861
- Scottish physicist James Clerk Maxwell demonstrates that color photographs can be produced by photographing through three primary-color filters and then combining the images.

1870
- Talbot reduces photographic exposure time to one-hundredth of a second, making moving pictures feasible.

1871
- English doctor Richard Leach Maddox and English chemist Joseph Wilson Swan replace the collodion wet-emulsion photographic plate with a dry, silver-bromide sensitized, gelatin-emulsion plate. The gelatin emulsions go on sale in 1873 and the plates in 1876. They revolutionize photography.

1877
- British-born U.S. photographer Eadweard Muybridge develops a camera with a shutter speed of 1/1000 of a second. He uses 12 of them to take still photographs of a horse galloping down a racetrack, demonstrating that at one point in the horse's gallop all four hooves leave the ground. The horse broke strings stretched across the track which tripped each shutter in turn, exposing a different phase of its stride.

1878
- U.S. photographer Frederik Eugene Ives develops the first halftone photographic printing process.

1879
- Joseph Wilson Swan patents bromide paper, which is used in modern photography.
- U.S. manufacturer George Eastman invents a machine that applies photographic emulsion to a gelatin plate, which allows him to mass-produce photographic dry-plates.

1884
- Eastman and U.S. inventor William H. Walker invent roll film. Negative images are still captured on paper and are then reproduced on glass.

1885
- Eastman patents a machine for manufacturing coated photographic paper in long continuous rolls. It spurs on the development of cameras that are easy to use.

1887
- U.S. clergyman Hannibal Goodwin develops celluloid photographic film. He sells the patent to Eastman.

1888

June   Eastman introduces the hand-held "Kodak" box camera. The first commercial roll film camera, it is simple to use and contains a 100-exposure roll of paper film. The entire camera is returned to his factory for the film to be developed and printed, and the camera reloaded. Costing $25, it revolutionizes photography by making it possible for large numbers of amateur photographers to take acceptable snapshots.

Technology

- British-born U.S. electrical engineer Elihu Thomson introduces resistance welding, whereby the heat for joining sheets of steel is generated by electrical resistance.
- British-born U.S. photographer Eadweard Muybridge develops a camera with a shutter speed of 1/1000 of a second. He uses 12 of them to take still photographs of a horse galloping down a racetrack, demonstrating that at one point in the horse's gallop all four hooves leave the ground. The horse broke strings stretched across the track which tripped each shutter in turn, exposing a different phase of its stride.
- U.S. inventor Thomas Alva Edison invents the carbon transmitter for the telephone, increasing its audibility.

DECEMBER

6   U.S. inventor Thomas Alva Edison patents the phonograph. Recording involves the transmission of sound vibrations through a large horn and a diaphragm to a stylus, which inscribes a groove on a rotating wax cylinder. Reproduction of the sound is achieved by reversing the process. The first reproduction of a human voice occurs on the November 29 when Edison utters the words "Mary had a little lamb."

14 German inventor Ernst Wermer patents the electric speaker.

Transportation

- British engineer John Isaac Thornycroft patents the first air-cushion machine, or hovercraft, although he does not build it.
- French gardener Joseph Monier produces reinforced concrete beams—used to manufacture railroad sleepers.
- Frozen meat is shipped from Argentina to France on the *Paraguay*, the first refrigerator ship.
- German aeronautical engineer Otto Lilienthal begins to build successful gliders with arched wings like a bird and which he steers by moving his legs. The Wright brothers draw heavily on his experiements.
- Italian inventor Enrico Forlanini constructs a steam-driven helicopter with two propellers, in which he reaches a height of 15 m/45 ft in a one-minute flight.

ARTS AND IDEAS

Architecture

- The Society for the Protection of Ancient Buildings from Injudicious Restoration is founded in London, England.
- The Trinity Church in Boston, Massachusetts, designed by the U.S. architect Henry Hobson Richardson, is completed. The interior is decorated by the U.S. artist John La Farge.

Arts

- The French artist Camille Pissarro paints *Red Roofs*.
- The French artist Claude Monet paints *Gare St Lazare*.

- The French artist Edouard Manet paints *Nana*.
- The French artist Gustave Caillebotte paints *Rue de Paris in the Rain*.
- The French artist Paul Cézanne paints *Madame Cézanne in a Red Armchair*.
- The U.S. artist Winslow Homer paints *The Cotton-Pickers*.

Literature and Language

- The English writer Anna Sewell publishes her novel *Black Beauty: The Autobiography of a Horse*, which becomes a classic of children's literature.
- The French writer Emile Zola publishes his novel *L'Assommoir/The Drunkard*, one of the *Les Rougon–Macquart* series.
- The French writer Gustave Flaubert publishes *Trois Contes/Three Tales*, which contains the story "Un Coeur simple"/"A Simple Heart."
- The literary review the *Nineteenth Century* is issued in London, England, edited by J. Knowles.
- The U.S. photographer William Henry Jackson publishes *Portraits of Native Americans*, a major photographic survey of Native Americans.
- The U.S. writer Henry James publishes his novel *The American*.
- The U.S. writer Sarah Orne Jewett publishes her short story collection *Deephaven*.

Music

- Bohemian composer Antonín Leopold Dvořák completes his oratorio *Stabat Mater*.
- German composer Johannes Brahms completes his Symphony No. 2.
- Hungarian composer Franz Liszt completes the last of his three volumes of piano works, *Année de pèlerinage: Italie/Years of Pilgrimage: Italy*.
- The opera *Samson et Delila/Samson and Delilah* by the French composer Camille St.-Saëns is first performed, in Weimar, Germany.

Theater and Dance

- The ballet *Lebedinoe ozero/Swan Lake* by the Russian composer Peter Illyich Tchaikovsky is first performed, in Moscow, Russia. The choreography is by the Austrian choreographer Wenzel Reisinger. A revised version is performed in St. Petersburg, Russia, in 1895.

SOCIETY

Education

- Compulsory education is introduced in Italy for children aged from six to nine years.
- The University of Manitoba is founded in Winnipeg, Ontario.

Everyday Life

- Labor and trades union membership has declined from 300,000 in 1869 to 50,000, in the United States.
- The Grands Magasins du Louvre in Paris, France, is the first store to be completely lit using electricity.
- The Red Crescent society is founded in the Ottoman Empire, a humanitarian organization active in Islamic nations, formed on the same principles as the Red Cross.

APRIL

4 U.S. manufacturer Charles Williams, Jr., who will manufacture Alexander Graham Bell's telephones, has the first telephones for private use installed in his home and office in the United States.

JULY

- Social reformers Annie Besant and Charles Bradlaugh are put on trial in Britain for reissuing *The Fruits of Philosophy: a Private Companion of Young Married People*, a guide to contraception.

AUGUST

1 Juliet Corson, who runs the New York Cooking School, in New York, New York, publishes a pamphlet entitled "Fifteen-Cent Dinners for Working-Men's Families."

OCTOBER

- A coalition of animal protection agencies forms the American Humane Society at Cleveland, Ohio.

Media and Communication

APRIL

3 Alexander Graham Bell makes the first long-distance telephone call, from New York, New York, to his assistant Thomas Watson in Boston, Massachusetts.

Sports

- The Victorian Football Association (for Australian Rules football) is formed in Melbourne, Australia.

BIRTHS & DEATHS

JANUARY

4 Cornelius Vanderbilt, U.S. shipping and railroad magnate, dies in New York, New York (82).

4 Marsden Hartley, U.S. modernist painter, born in Lewiston, Maine (–1943).

22 Hjalmar Schacht, German financial advisor who ended Germany's runaway inflation in the early 1920s, born in Tinglev, Germany (–1970).

FEBRUARY

7 Godfrey Harold Hardy, English mathematician whose work with prime number theory has applications in genetics, born in Cranleigh, Surrey, England (–1947).

17 André Maginot, French statesman who organized the construction of a defensive line along France's eastern frontiers between the two world wars, born in Paris, France (–1932).

APRIL

12 U.S. statesman Henry Clay, known as "the great pacificator," born in Hanover County, Virginia (–1852).

MAY

26 Isadora Duncan, U.S. interpretative dancer, born in San Francisco, California (–1927).

JUNE

21 Nathaniel B. Palmer, U.S. sea captain and Antarctic explorer, dies in San Francisco, California (77).

JULY

2 Hermann Hesse, German writer whose spiritual novels made him a cult figure, born in Calw, Württemberg, Germany (–1962).

AUGUST

28 Charles Stewart Rolls, English motorist and aviator, joint founder of the Rolls-Royce company, born in London, England (–1910).

29 Brigham Young, U.S. religious leader of The Church of Jesus Christ of Latter-day Saints who led converts to colonize the U.S. West and established a base at Salt Lake City, dies in Salt Lake City, Utah (76).

SEPTEMBER

1 Francis William Aston, English physicist who developed the mass spectrograph, born in Harborne, Birmingham, England (–1945).

2 Frederick Soddy, English chemist who developed the theory of isotopes, born in Eastbourne, Sussex, England (–1956).

3 Adolphe Thiers, French statesman, journalist, and historian, first president of the Third Republic 1871–73, dies in St.-Germain-en-Laye, near Paris, France (80).

5 Crazy Horse (Ta- Sunko-Whitko), Oglala Sioux chief who, with Chief Sitting Bull, defeated the U.S. general George Custer and his troops at the Battle of the Little Bighorn in 1876, is killed at Fort Robinson, Nebraska, while trying to escape from his U.S. captors (35).

11 James Jeans, English physicist and writer who believed that matter is continuously being created in the universe, born in London, England (–1946).

17 William Henry Fox Talbot, English chemist, archeologist, and pioneer of photography, dies in Melbury Abbas, Dorset, England (77).

24 Saigo Takamori, Japanese leader who led the rebellion that overthrew the Tokugawa shogunate and then later rebelled against the new Imperial government, is beheaded by one of his lieutenants in Kagoshima, Japan, after being mortally wounded (49).

OCTOBER

10 William Morris (Lord Nuffield), British industrialist and philanthropist who manufactured Morris automobiles, born in Worcestershire, England (–1963).

29 Nathan Bedford Forrest, Confederate cavalry general during the American Civil War, dies in Memphis, Tennessee (56).

NOVEMBER

9 Muhammad Iqbal, Indian poet and philosopher who urged the establishment of a separate Muslim state (later realized as Pakistan), born in Sailkot, Punjab, India (–1938).

DECEMBER

31 Gustave Courbet, French realist painter of everyday events, dies in La Tour-de-Peilz, Switzerland (58).

MARCH

15–19 Australia defeats England by 45 runs in the first ever Test cricket match, played in Melbourne, Australia. Approximately 20,000 spectators attend the match over the four days of play.

JULY

9–19 The first All England Lawn Tennis Championships are played at Wimbledon, London. A crowd of 200 people watches Spencer Gore defeat William Marshall in the final of the Gentlemen's Singles, the only event at the meeting.

SEPTEMBER

30 The New York Athletic Club holds the first amateur championship swimming races in the United States, at the Mott Haven Boat House on the Harlem River, New York, New York.

◆

1878

POLITICS, GOVERNMENT, AND ECONOMICS

Business and Economics

- U.S. electrical engineer and inventor Thomas Alva Edison founds the Edison Speaking Phonograph Company to produce his recording machine, the phonograph, commercially. However, the product's low reproduction quality means that it is not successful.

MAY

18 Colombia grants a French company a nine-year concession to build the Panama Canal.

Human Rights

- The German nationalist historian Heinrich von Treitschke complains of the growth of Jewish influence he alleges in Germany.

Politics and Government

- An Irredentist agitation begins in Italy to obtain Trieste and other Italian-speaking areas currently outside the kingdom of Italy.
- In the U.S. Congressional elections, the Democrats regain control of the House (149–130) and Senate (42–33) for the first time since 1858.

JANUARY

8 Russian forces defeat the Ottoman army at the Battle of Senova in eastern Anatolia during the Russo-Ottoman War.

9 Humbert I succeeds as king of Italy on the death of Victor Emmanuel II.

9 The Turks capitulate at Shipka Pass in the Balkans and appeal to Russia for an armistice in the war over the Balkans.

10 California senator Aaron A. Sargent introduces a women's suffrage amendment. Sargent's colleagues defeat the bill by a vote of 34–16.

14 The U.S. Supreme Court nullifies state laws requiring railroads to provide equal facilities for blacks and whites.

17 The United States and Samoa sign a treaty providing the United States with exclusive access to the coaling station at the Samoan port of Pago Pago.

20 Russian troops take the Ottoman-held port of Adrianople (now Edirne) in the Russo-Ottoman War over the Balkans.

23 The British cabinet sends a fleet to Constantinople (Istanbul) at the Ottoman sultan Abdul Hamid II's request for assistance in the Russo-Ottoman War over the Balkans.

28 Risings occur in the Ottoman province of Thessaly (now northern Greece) against Ottoman rule.

31 The Ottoman Empire signs an armistice ending its war with Russia over the Balkans.

FEBRUARY

2 Greece declares war on the Ottoman Empire in support of a revolt against Ottoman rule in Thessaly.

7 Cardinal Joachim Pecci is elected as Pope Leo XIII.

8 Britain decides to send another fleet to Constantinople (Istanbul) to support the Ottoman Empire against Russia, but Sultan Abdul Hamid II, under Russian pressure, refuses it permission to enter the Bosporus.

MARCH

3 By the preliminary Treaty of San Stefano ending the Russo-Ottoman War over the Balkans, Montenegro is to be enlarged with the port of Antivari; Romania, Montenegro, and Serbia are to be independent; reforms are to be undertaken in Bosnia and Herzegovina; Bulgaria is to be enlarged with a seaboard on the Aegean and most of Macedonia; and Russia is to receive the fortified cities of Ardahan, Kars, and Batum in

eastern Anatolia, while the Ottoman Empire is to pay Russia a huge indemnity.

25 The Russian diplomat Nikolay Pavlovich, Count Ignatyev, fails to reconcile Austria-Hungary to the Treaty of San Stefano of March 3 agreed between Russia and the Ottoman Empire.

27 Fearing further Russian aggression against the Ottoman Empire, the British cabinet calls out the army reserve and drafts Indian troops to Malta.

APRIL

8 Austria-Hungary evades the suggestions of the British foreign secretary Robert Cecil, Lord Salisbury, for common action against Russia in support of the Ottoman Empire.

MAY

8 Peter Andreyevich, Count Shuvalov, the Russian ambassador in London, England, returns to St. Petersburg to try to agree a division of Bulgaria that is acceptable to Britain.

30 A secret Anglo-Russian agreement is made to reduce the proposed size of Bulgaria specified in the Treaty of San Stefano.

JUNE

2 A radical, Karl Nobiling, shoots and seriously wounds Emperor Wilhelm I of Germany.

4 A secret Anglo-Ottoman agreement is made to check the Russian advance in Asia Minor, by which Britain promises to defend the Ottoman Empire against further attack and Britain is allowed to occupy Cyprus.

6 An Anglo-Austrian agreement is made to limit the size of Bulgaria, to be created following the Russian defeat of the Ottoman Empire in their war over the Balkans.

11 The U.S. Congress establishes a new government of the District of Columbia. The government consists of two residents and one U.S. Army officer, all of whom are appointed by the president.

13–July 13 The Berlin Congress meets, attended by the Austro-Hungarian foreign minister Gyula Andrássy; the German chancellor Otto von Bismarck; the Russian ambassador to London, Peter Andreyevich, Count Shuvalov; the French foreign minister William Waddington; the Italian foreign minister Count Luigi Corti; the British prime minister Benjamin Disraeli; and the British foreign minister Robert Cecil, Lord Salisbury, to discuss the fate of Ottoman possessions in the Balkans.

JULY

13 By the Treaty of Berlin, Bulgaria is split into (a) autonomous Bulgaria, north of the Balkans, (b) Eastern Rumelia with a special organization under the Ottoman Empire, and (c) Macedonia, where reforms are to be undertaken; Austria-Hungary is given a mandate to occupy Bosnia and Herzegovina; Romania is awarded the region of Dobrudja but has to hand over South Bessarabia to Russia; Montenegro is given the port of Antivari; Montenegro, Romania, and Serbia become independent states; Russia receives the towns of Batum, Kars, and Ardaham; and the British occupation of Cyprus is confirmed. Italian and Greek demands are shelved, while promises for reforms in Macedonia and Asia Minor lead to agitation.

30 In the German Reichstag (legislative assembly) elections the Conservatives gain seats at the expense of the National Liberals following the failure of the latter to take action against radical elements.

OCTOBER

11 Germany and Austria-Hungary annul the clause in the 1866 Peace of Prague over the plebiscite for North Schleswig, confirming German power there.

17 The Canadian politician and former prime minister John Macdonald becomes premier of Canada when the Conservatives win the general election on a protectionist platform.

18 An anti-Socialist law in Germany prohibits public meetings, publications, and collections, thus driving socialism underground.

21 The Irish National Land League is founded to agitate for Irish rights, with the Irish nationalist politician Charles Stuart Parnell as its president.

DECEMBER

11 Henry Frere, the British high commissioner to southern Africa, delivers an ultimatum to the Zulus demanding that they submit to British protection.

12 Franco-British dual control in Egypt is suspended on Khedive Ismail's introduction of ministerial government.

SCIENCE, TECHNOLOGY, AND MEDICINE

Agriculture

- U.S. entrepreneur Albert Durant introduces the first milking machine.

Ecology

- Daily weather maps begin to be published in the United States.

Exploration

- Welsh-born U.S. explorer Henry Stanley publishes his account of his travels in Africa, *Through the Dark Continent*.

December 1878–79 Swedish explorer and scientist Nils Adolf Eric Nordenskjöld leads an expedition in which the survey ship *Vega* travels successfully from Norway to the Pacific via the Northeast Passage across the north coast of Russia.

December 1878–82 Pundit Kishen Singh of the British India Survey undertakes a double crossing of Tibet from India to the Gobi Desert. On his return to India, his calculation of his position is out by only 16 km/10 mi.

Health and Medicine

- About 4,500 people die in New Orleans, Louisiana, and another 5,150 in Memphis, Tennessee, from a yellow fever epidemic; 14,000 die altogether.

- Dutch doctor Aletta Jacobs opens the first contraceptive clinic in the world, in Amsterdam, the Netherlands.

Science

- English physiologist Michael Foster begins publishing the *Journal of Physiology*.
- French chemists Jacques Soret and Marc Delafontaine discover the rare-earth metal holmium (atomic no. 67); it is discovered independently the following year by Swedish chemist Per Teodor Cleve, who names it after his hometown of Stockholm.
- French physiologist Paul Bert publishes *La Pression barométrique, recherches de physiologie expérimentale/ Barometric Pressure: Researches in Experimental Physiology*, in which he shows that high barometric pressure forces nitrogen to dissolve in the blood forming bubbles that block the capillaries if decompression occurs too quickly.
- Swiss chemist Jean-Charles-Gallinard de Marignac discovers the rare earth metal ytterbium (atomic no. 70), which he names after the Swedish town of Ytterby.
- The complete skeletons of several dozen *Iguanodon* are discovered in a coal mine in Belgium. They provide the first evidence that some dinosaurs traveled in herds.

December 1878–86 German engineer Karl Humann, under the auspices of the Berlin Museum, excavates the ancient Greek city of Pergamum, which contains some of the best examples of Hellenistic sculpture.

Technology

- Bohemian photographer Karl Klic develops the photoengraving method of photogravure. He exposes a positive transparency through a screen onto carbon tissue that is then used to etch the image, now composed of dots, onto a metal plate for printing.
- British metallurgists Sidney Thomas and Percy Gilchrist perfect the "basic" process for steel production by lining the Bessemer furnace with dolomite, which removes phosphorous oxides that otherwise result in the production of brittle steel.
- British engineer James Wimshurst invents an electrostatic generator. It uses two counterrotating plates and is capable of producing very high voltages. Electrostatic generators are later used to accelerate charged particles in nuclear bombardment experiments.
- French scientist Augustin Mouchot develops a solar generator that produces enough energy to power a steam engine.
- German-born British inventor Charles William Siemens invents the electric arc furnace, the first to use electricity to make steel.
- Swiss army officer Major Rubin invents the jacketed bullet. It consists of a lead nucleus encased in a hardened-metal jacket of cupronickel.
- The Remington Model 2 typewriter is introduced in the United States. It is the first typewriter to have a shift key to write both upper and lower case letters; earlier typewriters had only capitals.
- U.S. astronomer and physicist Samuel Pierpont Langley invents the bolometer, a type of radiometer used to measure temperature differences of one hundred-

thousandth of a degree. He uses it to study the infrared spectrum of the sun and to measure the intensity of solar radiation at particular wavelengths.

- U.S. inventor Charles Francis Brush develops a variable-voltage, constant-current generator; the voltage is determined by the load.
- U.S. inventor Thomas Alva Edison patents a new type of telephone receiver called the "loud speaker."
- British-born U.S. inventor David Hughes patents the carbon microphone. It is an essential element in the telephone.
- U.S. photographer Frederik Eugene Ives develops the first halftone photographic printing process.

NOVEMBER

30 English chemist and physicist William Crookes describes an early form of the cathode-ray tube, now known as Crooke's tube, to the Royal Society. It is a forerunner of the television tube.

DECEMBER

18 English physicist Joseph Swan demonstrates his electric "glow lamp," in Newcastle, England. It is the first practical carbon-filament incandescent light bulb.

Transportation

- A ship's log which can be read without removing it from the water is invented by English navigator Thomas Walker.
- U.S. entrepreneur Augustus Pope begins to manufacture bicycles in the United States.

ARTS AND IDEAS

Architecture

- The Dresden Opera House in Germany, designed by the German architect Gottfried Semper, is completed.
- The Memorial Hall at Harvard University, Cambridge, Massachusetts, designed by the U.S. architects William Robert Ware and Henry van Brunt, is completed.
- The Nott Memorial Library (later the Alumni Hall) of Union College, Schenectady, New York, designed by the U.S. architect Edward Potter, is completed.

Arts

- The Egyptian obelisk, Cleopatra's Needle, from the ancient city of Heliopolis, is moved from Alexandria, Egypt, to London, England.
- The French artist Auguste Rodin sculpts *Walking Man*.
- The French artist Pierre Puvis de Chavannes completes his fresco *The Life of St. Geneviève*, painted for the Panthéon in Paris, France.
- The U.S. artist Albert Bierstadt paints *The Sierra Nevada*.

Film

- British-born U.S. photographer Eadweard Muybridge develops the zoopraxiscope, a type of magic lantern used to project moving photographs, particularly of animals in locomotion. It is an early forerunner of modern motion pictures.

Literature and Language

- In a major concession by the Belgian government, Flemish becomes the official language in Flanders.
- The English poet Algernon Charles Swinburne publishes *Poems and Ballads*.
- The English writer Thomas Hardy publishes his novel *The Return of the Native*.
- The French writer Sully Prudhomme publishes his poem "La Justice"/"Justice."
- The German writer Theodor Fontane publishes his novel *Vor dem Sturm/Before the Storm*.
- The U.S. writer Henry James publishes his story "Daisy Miller" and his novel *The Europeans*.

Music

- Bohemian composer Antonín Dvořák completes his *Slavonic Rhapsodies* and the first series of *Slavonic Dances*.

- German composer Johannes Brahms completes his Violin Concerto No. 1 (Opus 77).
- Russian composer Peter Illyich Tchaikovsky completes his Symphony No. 4, his Violin Concerto, and his choral work *Liturgy of St John Chrysostom*.
- The comic opera *HMS Pinafore, or the Lass Who Loved a Sailor*, by the English writer William Schwenk Gilbert and the English composer Arthur Seymour Sullivan, is first performed at the Opera Comique in London, England.
- The opera *Tajemstvì/The Secret* by the Bohemian composer Bedřich Smetana is first performed, in Prague, Bohemia.

Theater and Dance

- The play *Samfundets støtter/The Pillars of Society*, by the Norwegian dramatist Henrik Johan Ibsen, is first performed, in Christiania (now Oslo), in Norway. It was published in 1877.

BIRTHS & DEATHS

JANUARY
6   Carl Sandburg, U.S. poet, historian, and novelist, born in Galesburg, Illinois (–1967).
29 Barney Oldfield, U.S. automobile racing driver who set several world speed records in the early 1900s, born near Wauseon, Ohio (–1946).

FEBRUARY
5   André-Gustave Citroën, French engineer who established one of the largest automobile-manufacturing firms in Europe, born in Paris, France (–1935).
7   Pope Pius IX, Italian pope 1846–78, dies in Rome, Italy (85).
8   Martin Buber, German Jewish religious philosopher, born in Vienna, Austria (–1965).
10 Claude Bernard, French physiologist who discovered the role of the pancreas and liver in digestion, and the regulation of blood supply by vasomotor nerves, dies in Paris, France (64).
14 Julius Arthur Nieuwland, Belgian-born U.S. chemist who developed neoprene, the first synthetic rubber, born in Hansbeke, Belgium (–1936).

MARCH
16 Reza Shah Pahlavi, Shah of Persia 1925–41, born in Alasht, Persia (–1944).

21 Jack Johnson, U.S. boxer and the first black person to win the world heavyweight boxing championship (1908–15), born in Galveston, Texas (–1946).

APRIL
25 Anna Sewell, British author who wrote *Black Beauty*, dies in Old Catton, Norfolk, England (58).
28 Frank Gotch, U.S. professional wrestler who won 154 of his 160 matches, born in Humboldt, Iowa (–1917).

MAY
10 Gustav Stresemann, Chancellor of Germany 1923, and foreign minister 1923 and 1924–29, born in Berlin, Germany (–1929).
28 Lord John Russell, Earl Russell, British prime minister 1846–52 and 1865–66, a Liberal, dies in Pembroke Lodge, Richmond Park, Surrey, England (85).

JUNE
5   Francisco "Pancho" Villa, Mexican revolutionary who fought against the regimes of Porfirio Díaz and Victoriano Huerto, born in Hacienda de Rio Grande, Mexico (–1923).

JULY
3   George M. Cohan, U.S. actor, playwright, composer, director, and producer, born in Providence, Rhode Island (–1942).

AUGUST
19 Manuel Quezon, Filipino independence leader and first president of the Philippine Commonwealth 1935–44, born in Baler, Philippines (–1944).
28 George Hoyt Whipple, U.S. pathologist whose research into the liver led to a successful treatment for anemia, born in Ashland, New Hampshire (–1976).

SEPTEMBER
13 Dorothea Lambert Chambers, English tennis player who dominated women's tennis prior to World War I, born in Ealing, Middlesex, England (–1960).

OCTOBER
8   Alfred James Munnings, English painter who excelled in racing and hunting scenes, born in Suffolk, England (–1959).
15 Paul Reynaud, French premier in 1940, who opposed compromise with Hitler, born in Barcelonette, France (–1966).

NOVEMBER
27 William Orpen, Irish painter and official World War I artist, born in Stillorgan, County Dublin, Ireland (–1931).

DECEMBER
25 Louis Chevrolet, Swiss-born U.S. automobile designer, born in Chaux de Fonds, Switzerland (–1941).

Thought and Scholarship

- The Canadian-born English naturalist Georges John Romanes publishes his theological work *A Candid Examination of Theism*.
- The German philosopher Friedrich Nietzsche publishes *Menschliches, Allzumenschliches/Human, All Too Human*.

SOCIETY

Education

- German immigrant Maximilian Berlitz opens his first language school in Providence, Rhode Island.
- Lady Margaret Hall is founded at Oxford University, England.
- Massachusetts secondary school teachers attend the nation's first formal summer school on Martha's Vineyard.
- The University of Western Ontario is founded in London, Canada.

Everyday Life

- Swedish scientist Carl de Laval invents the centrifugal cream separator. It eliminates the need to leave milk in large pans to separate and leads to an expansion of the butter industry in Denmark, the Netherlands, and the United States.
- The British sugar manufacturer Henry Tate introduces sugar cubes.

JANUARY
1 The Knights of Labor elect Terence Vincent Powderly Grand Master Workman at their annual convention in the United States. Powderly will catapult the industrial union into national prominence.

Media and Communication

- The *Philadelphia Times* begins publishing a Sunday edition and becomes the first daily in the United States to launch a successful Sunday paper.

JANUARY
28 The first commercial telephone exchange opens in New Haven, Connecticut; it has 21 subscribers. The following month the first telephone directory is published by the New Haven Telephone Co. with 50 subscribers listed.

Religion

- The English evangelist leader William Booth begins his "Christian Mission" in the East End in London, England. This forms the basis of the Salvation Army.

Sports

- The first hard tennis court, an asphalt surface, is laid at St. Kilda, Melbourne, Australia. It is also Australia's first tennis court.
- The United States's first bicycle club, the Boston Bicycle Club, organizes the first recorded bicycle race in the United States, at Beacon Park, Boston, Massachusetts. The winner is C. A. Parker of Harvard University, who covers the 4.8-km/3-mi course in 12 minutes 27 seconds.

JULY
5 By winning the Visitor's Challenge Cup, Columbia University becomes the first U.S. victor at the Henley Regatta, England.

1879

POLITICS, GOVERNMENT, AND ECONOMICS

Business and Economics

- The Scott Paper Company begins operations in Philadelphia, Pennsylvania.
- U.S. attorney Samuel C. V. Dodd creates the blueprint for the Standard Oil Trust, enabling Standard Oil to attain a virtual monopoly of the oil industry.

AUGUST

17 The French Panama Canal Company is formed under French diplomat Ferdinand de Lesseps in order to construct a link between the Pacific Ocean and the Atlantic Ocean.

Human Rights

- The Afrikaner Bond is founded in southern Africa to work for the official recognition of the Dutch language.

OCTOBER

21 The Irish National Land League is founded in Dublin, Ireland, by Charles Stewart Parnell to agitate for fairer rents and to enable tenants to buy their own land.

Politics and Government

- The radical and terrorist Will of the People Society is founded in Russia.

JANUARY

1   The United States resumes specie payment (coins) for the first time since the outbreak of the Civil War in 1861.
5   The Republicans gain seats in the French senatorial elections.
12 Frederic Thesiger, Lord Chelmsford, invades Zululand and begins the war between the British and the Zulus.
22 Zulu warriors massacre British troops at Isandhlwana, Zululand.
24 Germany signs a commercial treaty with Samoa.
30 Following Republican gains in the senatorial elections, President Marie-Edmé-Patrice-Maurice MacMahon, duc de Magenta, resigns and François-Paul-Jules Grévy, a moderate Republican, is elected president of France.

FEBRUARY

4   William Henry Waddington becomes French prime minister of a government comprising center left and radical left deputies.

14 Chile begins a war with Peru and Bolivia over the control of nitrate-producing regions.
15 The U.S. Congress grants female attorneys the privilege to argue cases before the U.S. Supreme Court.
18 The pro-Western Nubar ministry in Egypt falls following an army demonstration engineered by Ismail, Khedive of Egypt.
22 A constitution including a national assembly is granted in Bulgaria, and is given Russian protection by the Treaty of Berlin.

APRIL

29 Alexander of Battenberg, the nephew of Czar Alexander II of Russia, is elected Prince Alexander I of Bulgaria, ruling until 1886.

MAY

7   Californian voters ratify a new constitution prohibiting the hiring of Chinese laborers.
11 U.S. president Rutherford B. Hayes vetoes legislation restricting Chinese immigration. The Burlingame Treaty of 1868 previously had established unlimited immigration between China and the United States.
26 Following the cessation of hostilities between Britain and Afghanistan by the Treaty of Gandamak, British forces occupy the Khyber Pass, paying the amir of Afghanistan an annual subsidy.

JUNE

6   A law is made restricting the influence of Jesuits in France, as Republicans attempt to undermine clerical influence in the country.
25 Ismail, Khedive of Egypt, is deposed by the Ottoman sultan following protests from the European powers at the sacking of Egypt's European financial advisors. Ismail is succeeded by his son Tewfik Pasha.

JULY

4   The Zulu chief Cetewayo is defeated by Lord Chelmsford's British force in the decisive battle of the Zulu war at Ulundi, Zululand.
12 Protectionist laws for industry and agriculture, introduced in Germany in response to foreign competition, split the National Liberal Party.

AUGUST

4   Alsace-Lorraine, seized from France as a result of the war of 1870–71 between France and Germany, is declared an integral part of the German Reich under the rule of a governor-general.
8   Count Eduard Taaffe forms a government in Austria-Hungary and ends German predominance in Austria-Hungary, using Bohemian and Polish support to uphold the position of the Austrian emperor Franz Josef I.
28 British troops capture the Zulu chief Cetewayo in Ulundi, Zululand, during the Zulu War.

SEPTEMBER

1   The British sign a peace treaty with the Zulu chiefs with whom they are at war.

3   Afghan troops massacre the British legation at Kabul, reigniting the Anglo-Afghan war ended by the Treaty of Gandamak on May 26.

4   Following the deposition of Khedive Ismail on June 25 by the Ottoman sultan, Anglo-French dual control of Egypt is reestablished after having been suspended in December 1878.

15 The Treaty of Livadiya between Russia and China gives Russia key areas in the Ili Valley, China.

OCTOBER

•   The British invade Afghanistan following the attack on the British legation in Kabul, Afghanistan.

•   The Russian diplomat P. A. Saburov fails in his mission in Berlin, Germany, to arrange a renewal of a Russo-German alliance.

7   An Austro-German dual alliance is agreed for a period of five years (subsequently renewed until 1918).

19 The Afghan amir Yakub abdicates and surrenders to the British forces with whom he has been at war.

NOVEMBER

1   Chile invades Peru and Bolivia.

24–December 9 In the Midlothian Campaign the veteran Liberal statesman William Ewart Gladstone denounces the British Conservative government for imperialism and the mishandling of domestic affairs.

27 The French chamber returns to Paris from Versailles, its seat since the war of 1870.

DECEMBER

28 Charles Freycinet forms a ministry in France with the support of Léon Gambetta's Republican Union, which has forced out Henry Waddington's government.

SCIENCE, TECHNOLOGY, AND MEDICINE

Agriculture

•   The Irish harvest fails.

Ecology

MARCH

3   The U.S. Congress creates the U.S. Geological Survey as a branch of the Department of the Interior, to measure the discharge of rivers.

•   The last of the Southern bison herd are killed at Buffalo Springs, Texas.

Health and Medicine

•   French bacteriologist Louis Pasteur discovers that chickens infected with weakened cholera bacteria are immune to the normal form of the disease. It leads to the development of vaccines.

•   German physician Albert Neisser discovers the bacterium *Neisseria gonorrhea*, which is responsible for the venereal disease gonorrhea.

Science

•   Austrian physicist Josef Stefan discovers the fourth-power law of blackbody radiation, which states that the energy radiating from a blackbody is proportional to the fourth power of its temperature.

•   British-born U.S. electrical engineer Elihu Thomson shows how induction coils can be used to increase current and step down voltage—the basic principle of the transformer developed a few years later.

•   Swedish chemist Lars Fredrik Nilson discovers the rare-earth element scandium (atomic no. 24). Its existence had been predicted by Dmitry Ivanovich Mendeleyev on the basis of his periodic table.

•   Swedish chemist Per Teodor Cleve discovers the rare-earth metal thulium (atomic no. 69); he names it after the old name for Scandinavia.

•   U.S. chemist Ira Remsen and his German student Constantin Fahlberg discover the artificial sweetener saccharin at Johns Hopkins University in Baltimore, Maryland; it is 500 times sweeter than sugar.

Technology

•   English inventor Henry Fleuss develops the first self-contained oxygen-rebreather, used for diving.

•   English physicist and chemist Joseph Wilson Swan patents bromide paper, which is used in modern photography.

•   French engineer François Hennebique is the first to use reinforced concrete to build floor slabs.

•   Scottish engineer Dugald Clark invents the two-stroke internal combustion engine.

•   The first extrusion machine, in which materials are extruded through a nozzle in a continuous string, is patented. Employing an Archimedes screw it is used in the rubber industry.

•   U.S. inventor Charles Francis Brush develops an electric arc lamp, 12 of which are used to light a public square in Cleveland, Ohio—the first public installation of arc lamps in the United States.

•   U.S. inventor Thomas Alva Edison invents the incandescent light.

•   U.S. manufacturer George Eastman invents a machine that applies photographic emulsion to a gelatin plate, which allows him to mass-produce photographic dry-plates.

OCTOBER

21 U.S. inventor Thomas Alva Edison demonstrates his carbon-filament incandescent lamp light. He lights his Menlo Park power station with 30 lamps that burn for two days; later filaments burn for several hundred hours. Each light can be turned on or off separately in the first demonstration of parallel circuit.

NOVEMBER

4   U.S. bar owner James Jacob Ritty of Dayton, Ohio, patents the cash register, developed to prevent theft in his bar, which he calls "Ritty's Incorruptible Cashier."

DECEMBER

3   U.S. inventor Thomas Alva Edison and his assistant Francis Upton demonstrate an improved carbon-filament electric lamp, based in part on the research of the English physicist Joseph Wilson Swan.

Transportation

- German electrical engineer Werner von Siemens demonstrates an electric streetcar at the Berlin Exhibition in Germany. The first electrically powered locomotive, it runs on a track 500 m/1,640 ft long.
- The Australian liner *Orient* enters service. The first ship to have electric lighting, it is also the second largest ship afloat (135 m/445 ft long) after the *Great Eastern*.
- The first funicular railroad is installed on the slopes of Mt. Vesuvius, Italy.
- U.S. industrialist George Mortimer Pullman builds the first railroad Pullman dining-car.

MAY

8   U.S. inventor George Baldwin Selden files the first patent for an automobile, although he does not build one.

DECEMBER

28   The Tay River Bridge, Scotland, built in 1877, collapses as a train is crossing it; 300 passengers are killed.

ARTS AND IDEAS

Architecture

- The Provident and Life Trust Company Building in Philadelphia, Pennsylvania, designed by the U.S. architect Frank Furness, is completed. It is later destroyed.
- The Votivkirche, a church in Vienna, Austria, designed by the Austrian architect Heinrich von Ferstel, is completed.

Arts

c. 1879   The French artist Pierre-Auguste Renoir paints *The Skiff*.
- Maria, the 12-year-old daughter of Spanish nobleman Marcelino de Sautuola, discovers prehistoric paintings of bison and other animals in Altamira Cave, Spain. They are initially dismissed as forgeries.
- The English artist John Everett Millais paints *Cherry Ripe*.
- The French artist Edgar Degas paints *Miss Lala at the Fernando Circus*.
- The French artist Jules Bastien-Lepage paints his *Portrait of Sarah Bernhardt* and *Joan of Arc*.
- The French artist Pierre-Auguste Renoir paints his *Portrait of Mme Charpentier and Her Children*.
- The U.S. artist John Singer Sargent paints *The Luxembourg Gardens at Twilight*.

Literature and Language

- German priest Johann Martin Schleyer devises Volapük, an artificial language based on a simplified form of German.
- The English philologist Walter William Skeat publishes the first volume of his *Etymological English Dictionary*. The final volume appears in 1882.
- The English writer George Meredith publishes his novel *The Egoist*.
- The Russian writer Fyodor Mikhailovich Dostoyevsky publishes the first part of his novel *Bratia Karamazovy/ The Brothers Karamazov*. The second part appears in 1880.
- The Scottish writer Robert Louis Stevenson publishes *Travels with a Donkey in the Cévennes*.
- The Spanish writer Juan Valera y Alcalá Galiano publishes his novel *Doña Luz*.
- The Swedish writer Johan August Strindberg publishes his novel *Röda rummet/The Red Room*.
- The U.S. writer William Dean Howells publishes his novel *The Lady of the Aroostook*.

Music

- Bohemian composer Bedřich Smetana completes his cycle of symphonic poems *Má Vlast/My Country*.
- French composer César Franck completes his oratorio *Les Béatitudes/The Beatitudes*.
- German composer Johannes Brahms completes his Violin Sonata No. 1 (Opus 78).
- The comic opera *The Pirates of Penzance, or The Slave of Duty*, by the English writer William Schwenk Gilbert and the English composer Arthur Seymour Sullivan, is first performed, in Paignton, Devon, England.
- The first volume of the first edition of the *Dictionary of Music and Musicians*, edited by George Grove, is published. The last volume of this four-volume edition appears in 1889.
- The opera *Eugene Onegin* by the Russian composer Peter Illyich Tchaikovsky is first performed, in Moscow, Russia. It is based on a long poem written in 1833 by the Russian poet Alexander Pushkin.

Theater and Dance

- The play *En dukkehjem/A Doll's House* by the Norwegian dramatist Henrik Johan Ibsen is first performed, in Christiania (now Oslo), Norway.

Thought and Scholarship

- German psychologist Wilhelm Max Wundt founds the first experimental psychology laboratory at Leipzig, Germany.
- The English social scientist Herbert Spencer publishes the first volume of his *Principles of Ethics*. The final volume appears in 1893.
- The Scottish statesman and philosopher Arthur James Balfour publishes *Defence of Philosophic Doubt*.
- The German historian Heinrich von Treitschke publishes the first volume of his *Deutsche Geschichte im*

XIX Jahrhundert/History of Germany in the XIXth Century. The final volume appears in 1895.

- The U.S. economist Henry George publishes the first part of his *Progress and Poverty*, proposing a land tax to alleviate debt and poverty. The second part also appears in 1879.

SOCIETY

Education

- Somerville College and St. Anne's College are founded at Oxford University, England.

JULY

1 State primary education in Belgium is secularized as the government bans religious instruction in school hours in the ongoing struggle between clericals and Liberals.

Everyday Life

- English-U.S. chemist Robert A. Chesebrough produces Vaseline (petroleum jelly).
- Store clerk Frank Winfield Woolworth opens a "five-and-ten" store in the United States, which will become the basis of his retail empire.
- The tenants of the British landowner Charles Cunningham Boycott in Ireland refuse to harvest his crops in protest against absentee landlordism, the origin of the term "boycott" to describe a politically motivated withdrawal of custom.

Media and Communication

AUGUST

- The first telephone exchange for general rather than business subscribers opens in London, England.

NOVEMBER

25 The daily newspaper *Asahi Shimbun* begins publication in Japan.

BIRTHS & DEATHS

JANUARY

1 E(dward) M(organ) Forster, English novelist best known for *Howards End* (1910) and *A Passage to India* (1924), born in London, England (–1970).

1 William Fox, Hungarian-born U.S. motion-picture magnate who founded Twentieth-Century Fox studios, born in Tulchva, Hungary (–1952).

FEBRUARY

11 Honoré Daumier, French caricaturist and painter known for his satirization of French politicians and society, dies in Valmondois, France (70).

MARCH

8 Otto Hahn, German chemist who, with Fritz Strassmann, discovered nuclear fission, born in Frankfurt am Main, Germany (–1968).

14 Albert Einstein, German-born U.S. physicist who developed the theory of relativity, born in Ulm, Württemberg, Germany (–1955).

27 Edward Steichen, U.S. pioneer photographer known for his portraits of celebrities in the 1930s and 1940s, born in Luxembourg (–1973).

APRIL

16 St. Bernadette of Lourdes, French peasant girl and nun whose visions of the Virgin Mary led to the establishment of the shrine at Lourdes, dies in Nevers, France (35).

MAY

19 Nancy Witcher Langhorne, Lady Astor, British politician and the first woman to sit in the House of Commons, born in Danville, Virginia (–1964).

24 William Lloyd Garrison, U.S. newspaper editor and leader of the abolitionist (antislavery) movement, dies in New York, New York (73).

JUNE

1 Knud Johan Victor Rasmussen, Danish explorer and ethnologist who studied the Inuit tribes across the Arctic, born in Jakobshavn, Greenland (–1933).

JULY

9 Ottorino Respighi, Italian composer, born in Bologna, Italy (–1936).

AUGUST

8 Emiliano Zapata, Mexican revolutionary who led a guerrilla force during the Mexican Revolution, born in Anenecuilo, Mexico (–1919).

27 Rowland Hill, British administrator who introduced the penny postage stamp, dies in Hampstead, near London, England (83).

OCTOBER

8 Chen Duxiu, Chinese revolutionary who founded the Chinese Communist Party, born in Huaining County, Anhui Province, China (–1942).

29 Franz von Papen, German statesman who was instrumental in dissolving the Weimar Republic and bringing Hitler to power, born in Werl, Germany (–1969).

31 Joseph Hooker, Union general in the American Civil War, dies in Garden City, Long Island, New York (64).

NOVEMBER

4 Will Rogers, U.S. actor and humorist, born near Oologah, Indian Territory (later Oklahoma) (–1935).

5 James Clerk Maxwell, Scottish physicist who formulated the theory of electromagnetism, dies in Cambridge, England (48).

7 Leon Trotsky (adopted name of Lev Davidovitch Bronstein), communist theorist and activist, a leader in Russia's October Revolution of 1917, born in Ianovka, Ukraine, Russian Empire (–1940).

DECEMBER

18 Paul Klee, Swiss Abstract artist, born in Münchenbuchsee, near Bern, Switzerland (–1940).

21 Joseph Stalin (adopted name, Russian for steel, of Josef Vissarionovich Dzhugashvili), secretary-general of the Communist Party of the Soviet Union 1922–53, and premier 1941–53, born in Gori, Georgia, Russian Empire (–1953).

29 Billy Mitchell, U.S. Army officer who recommended establishing a separate U.S. air force, born in Nice, France (–1936).

Religion

- The U.S. religious leader Mary Baker Eddy becomes pastor of the First Church of Christ, Scientist in Boston, Massachusetts.

Sports

- Colonel Albert A. Pope begins publishing *Bicycling World* in the United States, which includes news and technical information. A year later it becomes the official journal of the League of American Wheelmen.

1880

POLITICS, GOVERNMENT, AND ECONOMICS

Business and Economics

- Cecil Rhodes forms the De Beers Mining Corporation to exploit the mineral wealth of southern Africa.
- Entrepreneur William H. Forbes leads a team of Boston investors in creating the American Bell Telephone Company in the United States.
- Thomas Alva Edison founds the Edison Electrical Illuminating Company in the United States to provide electricity to the financial district of New York, New York. Edison's company is backed by J. P. Morgan and other investors.

JULY

17 Egyptian finances are reorganized by its Anglo-French advisors, and money is set aside to begin paying off its European debts.

Colonization

JUNE

29 France annexes the Pacific island of Tahiti.

Politics and Government

- Captain Charles Cunningham Boycott, a land agent in County Mayo, Ireland, is "boycotted" for refusing to accept rents at the reduced levels fixed by tenants, and starts a war of attrition between farmers and landlords.
- The first federal confederation assembly meets in Sydney, New South Wales, under Henry Parkes.
- U.S. president Rutherford B. Hayes appoints Georgia jurist William B. Woods to the U.S. Supreme Court.

FEBRUARY

17 A bomb in the Winter Palace in Moscow, Russia, kills ten people but fails to kill Czar Alexander II, its intended target.

MARCH

1 The U.S. Supreme Court declares it illegal for states to exclude black Americans from jury duty.

29–30 Decrees in France make it compulsory for religious associations to obtain the approval of the state, and provide for the dispersal of the Jesuits.

APRIL

28 William Ewart Gladstone forms a Liberal ministry in Britain in which he is also chancellor of the Exchequer, with Lord Granville as foreign secretary, William Harcourt as home secretary, and Joseph Chamberlain as president of the Board of Trade.

MAY

5 Acute rivalry begins between France and Italy in Tunis, Tunisia.

5 The authoritarian liberal Mikhail Tariyelovich, Count Loris-Melikov, becomes Russian minister of the interior, with wide powers for dealing with the revolutionary Nihilists.

26 Chilean forces are victorious over the Peru–Bolivia coalition at the Battle of Tacna.

JUNE

6 France, alarmed at Henry Morton Stanley's advance along the Congo for King Leopold II of Belgium, sends the explorer Pierre de Brazza to treat with chiefs on the north side of the river.

6 The Clericals defeat their ideological rivals, the Liberals, in the Belgian elections and begin a long era of power which extends until 1914.

8 The Republicans nominate Ohio congressman James A. Garfield for president and former New York customs commissioner Chester A. Arthur for vice president.

23 The British secularist member of Parliament Charles Bradlaugh is excluded from the House of Commons for refusing to swear the oath of allegiance.

24 The Democrats nominate Pennsylvania war hero Winfield Hancock for president and Indiana politician William H. English for vice president.

25 The parliament of Cape Colony rejects a British program for a South African federation.

29 The papal nuncio is expelled from Belgium during a crisis over educational policy.

JULY

- A new penal code based on the French system is introduced in Japan as the country continues to introduce Western style reforms.

3 Moroccan independence is universally recognized in the Convention of Madrid.

11 A French law grants an amnesty to the Marquis de Rochefort and other Communards for their antigovernment insurrection of 1871.

AUGUST

2 The Relief of Distress Act for Ireland extends the power of local government boards to provide assistance for unemployed and very poor agricultural laborers.

SEPTEMBER

25 Jules Ferry becomes the French prime minister on the fall of Charles Freycinet's ministry over calls for tougher anticlerical legislation.

OCTOBER

13 The Transvaal declares itself independent from Britain in opposition to Britain's annexation of the Boer Transvaal Republic in 1877.

NOVEMBER

2 The Irish Land League is prosecuted for conspiracy.

2 The Republican candidate James A. Garfield is elected as president of the United States. In the Congressional elections, Republicans and Democrats share the seats in the Senate (37–37), but the Republicans regain control of the House (147–135).

17 The United States and China sign the Chinese Exclusion Treaty, granting the United States the right to regulate Chinese immigration.

26 The Ottoman Empire yields to diplomatic pressure and permits Montenegro to occupy Dulcigno, a district of the Ottoman province of Albania in place of the territory assigned by the Berlin Congress of 1878.

DECEMBER

30 The Transvaal Boers, in revolt from British rule, declare a republic under their leader Paul Kruger.

SCIENCE, TECHNOLOGY, AND MEDICINE

Agriculture

APRIL

- Midwestern farmers in the United States form the National Farmers' Alliance, predecessor to the People's (Populist) Party. The organization aims to protect producers from exorbitant storage and distribution rates.

Ecology

- Prospectors strike gold in Juneau, Alaska, precipitating settlement there.

Exploration

- British explorer, mountaineer, and artist Edward Whymper visits the Andes in Ecuador, and climbs many of its peaks, including the 6,000-m/20,000-ft Mt. Chimborazo and the volcanic Mt. Cotopaxi.

Health and Medicine

- Austrian physician Josef Breuer relieves the symptoms of a patient being treated for hysteria by getting her to recall past experiences while under hypnosis. One of the forebears of psychoanalysis, he argues that unconscious processes produce neurotic symptoms that can be cured when the processes are made conscious. His work had a large influence on Sigmund Freud.
- German bacteriologist Karl Joseph Eberth discovers the *Salmonella typhii* bacteria responsible for typhoid.
- The parathyroid gland, which secretes parathormone that regulates calcium levels in the blood, is first described by Swedish physiologist Ivar Sandström.
- U.S. dentist Norman Kingsley publishes procedures for treating irregularly positioned teeth, thus founding orthodontics.

Math

- French mathematician Jules-Henri Poincaré publishes important results on automorphic functions, a subject of great importance in modern algebra.

Science

- French chemist Paul-Emile Lecoq de Boisbaudran discovers the rare-earth metal samarium (atomic no. 62).
- French physicists Pierre and Paul-Jacques Curie discover that electricity is produced when pressure is placed on certain crystals including quartz—the "piezoelectric" effect.
- German chemist Adolf von Baeyer synthesizes indigo.
- German cytologist Eduard Adolf Strasburger announces that new cell nuclei arise from the division of old nuclei.
- Scottish chemist James Ballantyne Hannay makes the first artificial diamonds by subjecting paraffin, oil, and lithium to high pressure, in a sealed steel cylinder.
- Swiss chemist Jean-Charles-Gallinard de Marignac discovers the rare-earth element gadolinium (atomic no. 64).
- U.S. astronomer Henry Draper photographs the Orion Nebula, the first photograph of a nebula.

Technology

c. 1880 Typewriters with letters mounted on wheels appear; pressing a key brings the correct letter into position.

c. 1880   U.S. inventor W. E. Sawyer and French scientist Maurice Leblanc suggest scanning images line by line. It creates the possibility of transmitting images along a single wire and is a basic principle of television.
- British geologist John Milne invents the modern seismograph for measuring the strength of earthquakes.
- German engineer Paul von Mauser improves the design of his rifle by adding a five-round tubular magazine; it becomes regular issue in the Prussian army in 1884 and is subsequently adopted or copied by armies throughout the world.
- U.S. bank clerk George Eastman of Rochester, New York, begins producing photographic plates for commercial sale.

JUNE
3   Scottish-born U.S. inventor Alexander Graham Bell patents the photophone which transmits sound on a beam of light.

Transportation

- Irish veterinarian John Boyd Dunlop develops the pneumatic bicycle tire.
- Railroad mileage in operation stands at 140,481 km/ 87,801 mi in the United States, 28,696 km/17,935 mi in Britain, 26,288 km/16,430 mi in France, and 19,520 km/12,200 mi in Russia.
- The French diplomat Ferdinand de Lesseps begins excavation of the Panama Canal. Disease, corruption, and poor planning put an end to it in 1889.
- The Suez Canal linking the Mediterranean and the Red Sea is used by 4,344,000 tons of shipping, 70% of which is British.
- The Tangent & Coventry Tricycle Co. (later the Rudge company) launches the Bicyclette in Britain, designed by H. J. Lawson. It is the first commercially made safety bicycle (a bicycle with wheels of equal size).

MAY
- The steamship USS *Columbia* has 115 of Thomas Alva Edison's incandescent lights installed—the first commercial installation of electric incandescent lights.

ARTS AND IDEAS

Arts

c. 1880   The French artist Aimé-Jules Dalou sculpts *Woman Taking off Her Stockings.*
c. 1880   The U.S. artist Albert Pinkham Ryder paints *Mending the Harness.*
- The French artist Auguste Rodin sculpts *St. Jean Baptiste/St. John the Baptist.* He also begins work on his monumental *Gates of Hell,* meant to be a doorway to the Museum of Decorative Art in Paris, France. Still unfinished at his death in 1917, the motifs for the project turned into some of his best-known works, such as *The Thinker.*

- The French artist Edgar Degas sculpts *The Little 14-year-old Dancer.*
- The German artist Adolph von Hildebrand sculpts *The Water Carrier.*
- The Swiss artist Arnold Böcklin paints *Isle of the Dead.*
- The U.S. artist Eastman Johnson paints *In the Fields.*

Literature and Language

- The Danish writer Jens Peter Jacobsen publishes his novel *Niels Lyhne.*
- The English poet James Thomson publishes his poetry collection *The City of Dreadful Night.*
- The English statesman and writer Benjamin Disraeli, Earl of Beaconsfield, publishes *Endymion,* his last novel.
- The English writer Joseph Henry Shorthouse publishes his novel *John Inglesant.*
- The French writer Emile Zola publishes his novel *Nana,* one of the *Les Rougon–Macquart* series, and *Le Roman expérimental/The Experimental Novel,* setting out his theories on the novel.
- The French writer Guy de Maupassant publishes his short story "Boule de Suif"/"Ball of Fat."
- The U.S. writer and historian Henry Brooks Adams publishes his novel *Democracy: An American Novel.*
- The U.S. writer Lewis Wallace publishes his historical novel *Ben-Hur.*

Music

- Austrian composer Gustav Mahler completes his cantata *Das klagende Lied/The Song of Sorrow.*
- Bohemian composer Antonín Dvořák completes his Symphony No. 6 (once classified as No. 1) and his *Gipsy Songs* (Opus 55), one of which is the well-known "Songs My Mother Taught Me."
- French composer Gabriel Fauré completes his song setting *Nell, le voyageur/Nell, the Traveler* of a poem by the French writer Charles-Marie-René Leconte de Lisle.
- German composer Johannes Brahms completes his Piano Concerto No. 2 (Opus 83) and his orchestral work *Akademische Fest-Ouvertüre/Academic Festival Overture.*
- German composer Max Bruch completes his *Scottish Fantasia* for violin and orchestra.
- German composer Richard Strauss completes his Symphony No. 1.
- Hungarian composer Franz Liszt completes his piano transcription of Peter Illyich Tchaikovsky's *Eugene Onegin: Polonaise.*
- Italian composer Giuseppe Verdi completes his *Ave Maria* for soprano and strings.
- Russian composer Alexander Porfiryevich Borodin completes his tone poem *In the Steppes of Central Asia.*
- Russian composer Peter Illyich Tchaikovsky completes his Piano Concerto No. 2, his *Serenade for Strings* (Opus 48), and his orchestral work *Capriccio italien/ Italian Caprice* (Opus 45).

Thought and Scholarship

- *Economic Studies* by the English social scientist and literary critic Walter Bagehot is published posthumously.

SOCIETY

Education

- The University of Southern California is founded in Los Angeles, California.

Everyday Life

- British baker Samuel Thomas introduces the English muffin to the United States.
- Electric street lights are installed in New York, New York.
- Greenwich Mean Time is established as the legal time in the British Isles.
- Salmon, meat, and fruit are all available in cans.
- Schweppes launches Schweppes Tonic Water in Britain.
- Soft canvas shoes, known in Britain as "plimsolls," catch on with the increasing popularity of lawn tennis as a sport.
- The Empire Cheese Co. launches Philadelphia cream cheese in the United States.
- The Lambert Pharmaceutical Co. launches the antiseptic mouthwash Listerine in the United States.
- The U.S. Census lists the nation's population at 50,155,783, a significant increase on the approximate figure of 39,905,000 in 1870.

Media and Communication

- Fifty thousand private telephones are in use in the United States.
- There are 80 German language daily newspapers, 466 German language weeklies, and 95 other German language periodicals in the United States.
- The *New York Daily Graphic* is the first newspaper to print a photographic illustration, a screened halftone of a shanty town.

Religion

- A U.S. branch of the British Salvation Army is set up in Pennsylvania.

Sports

- George Ligowsky of Cincinnati, Ohio, develops the first workable mechanical clay pigeon trap.
- Table tennis, called "Gossima," is invented by James Gibb, an English engineer and founder member of the Amateur Athletic Association. It does not sell well until it is renamed "Ping Pong."
- The Amateur Boxing Association (ABA) is founded in Britain.
- The Society of American Wheelmen, the first national cycling organization in the United States, is founded.
- The world's first ice hockey club is formed at McGill University, Montreal, Canada.

APRIL

24 The Amateur Athletic Association (AAA), the world's first national governing body for athletics, is founded at a meeting in Oxford, England.

BIRTHS & DEATHS

c. 1880 Ibn Saud, Arabian tribal and Muslim leader who founded the modern state of Saudi Arabia in 1932 and began to exploit its oil resources, born in Riyadh, Arabia (–1953).

JANUARY

17 Mack Sennett, Canadian film director and producer who created the Keystone Kops, born in Richmond, Quebec, Canada (–1960).

26 Douglas MacArthur, U.S. general who commanded the Allied forces in the Pacific during World War II, born in Little Rock, Arkansas (–1964).

29 W. C. Fields (adopted name of William Claude Dukenfield), U.S. comic actor and screenwriter, born in Philadelphia, Pennsylvania (–1946).

MARCH

29 Oswald Spengler, German philosopher, born in Blankenburg, Germany (–1936).

APRIL

15 Max Wertheimer, Bohemian psychologist who cofounded gestalt psychology, born in Prague, Bohemia (–1943).

MAY

6 Ernst Ludwig Kirchner, German expressionist painter, born in Aschaffenberg, Bavaria, Germany (–1938).

8 Gustave Flaubert, French realist novelist best known for *Madame Bovary* (1857), dies in Croisset, France (58).

JUNE

11 Jeanette Rankin, U.S. feminist, the first woman member of Congress 1917–19, born near Missoula, Montana (–1973).

27 Helen Keller, U.S. educator and writer who was deaf and blind, born in Tuscumbia, Alabama (–1968).

AUGUST

2 Arthur Dove, U.S. painter, an early exponent of abstract expressionism, born in Canandaigua, New York (–1946).

31 Wilhelmina, Queen of the Netherlands 1890–1948, born in The Hague, the Netherlands (–1962).

SEPTEMBER

12 H(enry) L(ouis) Mencken, U.S. humorist and critic, born in Baltimore, Maryland (–1956).

OCTOBER

5 Jacques Offenbach, French composer who created the *opérette*, or comic opera, dies in Paris, France (61).

DECEMBER

2 George Eliot (pseudonym of Mary Anne Evans), English novelist, dies in London, England (61).

28 Richard Henry Tawney, English economic historian and social critic, born in Calcutta, India (–1962).

31 George C. Marshall, U.S. general and Army chief of staff during World War II, and then secretary of state 1947–49, and secretary of defense 1950–51, born in Uniontown, Pennsylvania (–1959).

1881

POLITICS, GOVERNMENT, AND ECONOMICS

Business and Economics

- At the Midvale Steel Company in the United States, U.S. engineer Frederick Winslow Taylor begins investigating how manufacturing operations are organized; his work leads to modern production planning.

JANUARY

24   The U.S. Supreme Court upholds the federal income tax of 1862 in *Springer v. United States*.

SEPTEMBER

4   U.S. electrical engineer Thomas Alva Edison supplies electricity to the first customers of the Edison Electrical Illuminating Company in New York, New York.

DECEMBER

12   The Canadian Pacific Railroad Company is founded to develop the transport infrastructure of Canada.

Colonization

APRIL

5   The South African Republic of Transvaal achieves independence by the Treaty of Pretoria with Britain.

MAY

12   Tunisia becomes a French Protectorate.

Human Rights

- There is a moderate extension of the Italian franchise.

Politics and Government

- Flogging is abolished in both the Royal Navy and the British Army.
- Freedom of the press is granted in France, reversing the authoritarian legislation used by the Moral Order governments under President Marie-Edmé-Patrice-Maurice MacMahon, duc de Magenta.
- Political parties are founded in Japan following an imperial decree that an assembly will be convened in 1890.
- U.S. president James A. Garfield appoints Ohio senator Stanley Matthews and Massachusetts jurist Horace Gray to the U.S. Supreme Court.

JANUARY

25   The trial of Irish leader Charles Stewart Parnell ends in deadlock.

28   In the pursuance of their revolt against British rule, the Transvaal Boers repulse a British force under the command of General Sir George Colley at Laing's Nek, Natal.

31–February 2   Irish members of Parliament obstruct the passage of the repressive Coercion Bill for Ireland. The House of Commons sits for 41 hours continuously until, on February 2, the Speaker Sir Henry Brand takes a division (vote) on the first reading of the bill.

FEBRUARY

1   Nationalist army officers stage a rising in Egypt against Ottoman rule.

24   Under the Treaty of St. Petersburg, China pays an indemnity to Russia for the return of the Ili Valley, China, ceded in 1879.

27   Boer irregular forces defeat a British force led by General Sir George Colley at Majuba Hill, Natal, during the First Anglo-Boer War.

MARCH

2   The Habeas Corpus Act is suspended in Ireland following disturbances over land rents.

2   The Protection of Persons and Property Act gives Irish authorities the power to detain suspects at will.

4   James A. Garfield is inaugurated as 20th president of the United States.

12   France occupies Tunis, Tunisia, following raids into Algiers, Algeria, by Krumir tribes.

13   Czar Alexander II of Russia calls an assembly of Russian nobles and is assassinated by terrorists the same day. Alexander III succeeds.

APRIL

5   Britain and the Boers sign the Treaty of Pretoria, ending the First Anglo-Boer War and recognizing the independence of the South African Republic of Transvaal.

19   On the death of Benjamin Disraeli, Lord Beaconsfield, Robert Cecil, Lord Salisbury, becomes leader of the Conservatives in the British House of Lords and Sir Stafford Northcote becomes leader in the Commons.

30   The French navy seizes Bizerte, Tunisia, while French troops invade Tunisia, from Algeria.

MAY

12   By the Treaty of Bardo, Tunis, Tunisia, accepts its new status as a French protectorate.

JUNE

June 1881–July 1883   Risings against the French are put down in the hinterlands of Tunis and Algeria.

6   An immigration act is introduced in New Zealand to restrict Japanese immigration.

18 The Three Emperors' League, a secret alliance between Germany, Austria-Hungary, and Russia is signed for a three-year term.

28 A secret Austro-Serbian convention puts Serbia under Austro-Hungarian protection.

JULY

2 A disgruntled campaign worker, Charles J. Guiteau, shoots U.S. president James A. Garfield, who dies on September 19.

3 Britain persuades the Ottoman Empire to sign a convention with Greece, granting Greece possession of Thessaly and part of Epirus, as was promised at the Berlin Congress of 1878.

13 The constitution of Bulgaria is revised, including the formation of a new ministry of Russian officers.

AUGUST

16 British prime minister William Ewart Gladstone's Irish Land Act fixes tenures and establishes a land court to deal with excessive rents.

SEPTEMBER

9 A nationalist rising takes place in Egypt under the war minister Arabi Pasha.

20 One day after the death of President James A. Garfield, Chester A. Arthur is sworn in as 21st president of the United States.

OCTOBER

13 Charles Stewart Parnell, leader of the Irish National Land League and member of Parliament, is imprisoned for inciting Irish farmers to intimidate tenants taking advantage of Gladstone's Irish Land Act rather than holding out for better terms.

18 Charles Stewart Parnell's "No Rent Manifesto" calls for tenants to pay no more rent until the government agrees to reforms.

20 The Irish National Land League is proclaimed an unlawful and criminal association.

NOVEMBER

14 Charles J. Guiteau goes on trial for assassinating U.S. president James A. Garfield.

14 The Radical Léon Gambetta forms a ministry in France when Prime Minister Jules Ferry resigns over attacks on his Tunisian policy.

SCIENCE, TECHNOLOGY, AND MEDICINE

Ecology

- A typhoon in China kills over 300,000 people.
- Nearly 300,000 people die when a typhoon hits Haiphong, Vietnam.

Health and Medicine

- Austrian surgeon Theodor Christian Albert Billroth initiates modern abdominal surgery by removing the cancerous lower part of a patient's stomach.

- Cuban physician Carlos Juan Finlay discovers that the mosquito *Aëdes aegypti* is the carrier of yellow fever. His results are published in 1886 but his experiments are ignored until 1900.
- U.S. Army physician George Miller Sternberg discovers the bacillus responsible for pneumonia.
- U.S. surgeon William Stewart Halsted discovers that blood can be returned to a patient's body after it has been aerated.
- The modern device for eliminating saliva from a patient's mouth during dental work is introduced.

Math

- English mathematician John Venn introduces the idea of using pictures of circles to represents sets, subsequently known as Venn diagrams.
- U.S. scientist Josiah Willard Gibbs develops the theory of vectors in three dimensions.

Science

- At Dier el-Bahri, Egypt, French Egyptologist Gaston Camille Charles Maspero discovers a royal tomb containing 40 mummies, including those of Egyptian pharaohs Amenhotep I, Ramses II, Seti I, and Thutmose III.
- Dutch physicist Johannes van der Waals develops a version of the gas law, now known as the van der Waals equation, which takes into account the size and attraction of atoms and molecules.
- English anthropologist Edward Burnett Tylor publishes *Anthropology*, the first textbook on the subject.
- French physicist Marcel Deprez shows that increasing the voltage allows electricity to be carried over longer distances.
- German botanist Wilhelm Friedrich Philipp Pfeffer publishes *Pflanzenphysiologie: Ein Hanbuch des Stoffwechsels und Kraftwechsels in der Pflanz/The Physiology of Plants: A Treatise Upon the Metabolism and Sources of Energy in Plants*, which becomes the basic handbook on plant physiology.
- German chemist Emil Hermann Fischer demonstrates the association of caffeine, theobromine, uric acid, xanthine, and other nitrous compounds with purine.
- German-born U.S. physicist Albert Michelson develops an interferometer to measure distances between stars. He later uses it to measure the speed of the earth through the "ether."
- U.S. astronomer Edward Emerson Barnard is the first to discover a comet using photography.

MAY

5 French microbiologist Louis Pasteur vaccinates sheep against anthrax. It is the first infectious disease to be treated effectively with an antibacterial vaccine, and his success lays the foundations of immunology.

JUNE

24 English astronomer William Huggins and U.S. astronomer Henry Draper take the first photograph of the spectrum of a comet.

Technology

- British engineer Henry Simon and German engineer Albert Hussner independently develop a method of producing high quality coke and recovering coal gas, oil, and tar at the same time.
- British engineers William Edward Ayrton and John Perry invent a dynamometer for measuring electrical force.
- British inventor Percival Everitt patents the first practical vending machine, which supplies goods when a coin is inserted into it.
- French engineer Fernand Forest introduces the first air-cooled internal combustion engine.
- French engineers Abel Pifre and Augustin Mouchout demonstrate the use of solar energy. Using a 2.2-m/7-ft parabolic mirror, they focus the sun's energy on a small boiler, which produces sufficient steam to drive a steam engine, which they then use to run a small printing press.
- Hungarian inventor David Gestetner develops a duplicating machine which uses wax stencils.
- The British Parliament passes the Electric Light Act, which permits local authorities to take over privately owned electric power stations after 21 years. The act discourages the development of such power stations.
- The first all-wire telephone circuit is established between Boston, Massachusetts, and Providence, Rhode Island. By using two wires it eliminates the "cross-talk" that occurs when the conducting circuit consists of a wire in one direction and the ground in the other.
- The first experiment in wired broadcasting takes place, in Paris, France. Sound picked up by microphones placed on a concert stage is transmitted to receivers in a nearby room and broadcast to the listening audience.
- U.S. engineer Henry W. Seeley patents the first electric iron.
- U.S. inventor Alexander Graham Bell develops an induction balance metal detector. He uses it to locate the bullets fired into President Garfield when he is assassinated.
- U.S. inventor Thomas Alva Edison installs incandescent lamps in a factory in New York, New York. They are installed in over 150 other factories during the next two years.
- U.S. photographer Friedrich Eugene Ives produces the first color photograph with a fixed image.

JANUARY
12 The world's first public power station begins operating in London, England, at the Holburn Viaduct; it lights 30 homes.

OCTOBER
11 U.S. inventor David Henderson Houston patents a camera that takes roll film.

Transportation

- Russian explosives manufacturer Nikolay Ivanovich Kibalchich conceives the design for a multistage rocket airplane.
- Refrigerated railroad cars are used to transport meat from Chicago, Illinois, and Kansas City, Missouri, to eastern cities.

- Steam-powered cable cars begin to replace horsecars in cities.
- The British liner *Servia* enters service; it is the first steel-hulled ocean liner.
- The first solid-rubber tires appear on hansom cabs in London, England.

ARTS AND IDEAS

Architecture

- The Natural History Museum in London, England, designed by the English architect Alfred Waterhouse, is completed. It opens to the public on April 4.
- The Vanderbilt House in New York, New York, designed by the U.S. architect Richard Morris Hunt, is completed.
- Workmen complete the $3-million home of William K. Vanderbilt at the corner of Fifth Avenue and 52nd Street in New York, New York. Like other industrialists, Vanderbilt has it built as a grandiose display of his wealth.

Arts

- The French artist Auguste Rodin sculpts *The Thinker*, a motif derived from his *Gates of Hell* project.
- The French artist Claude Monet paints *Sunshine and Snow*.
- The French artist Edouard Manet paints *Bar at the Folies-Bergères*.
- The French artist Pierre Puvis de Chavannes paints *The Poor Fisherman*.
- The French artist Pierre-Auguste Renoir paints *Boating Party Luncheon*.
- The German artist Max Liebermann paints *An Asylum for Old Men*.
- The U.S. architect Frank Furness publishes *The Nature and Function of Art*.

Literature and Language

- Swiss author Johanna Spyri writes the children's classic *Heidi*.
- The Brazilian writer Joaquim Machado De Assis publishes his novel *Memorias postumas/Epitaph for a Small Winner*.
- The English artist and poet Dante Gabriel Rossetti publishes *Ballads and Sonnets*.
- The English writer Christina Georgina Rossetti publishes her poetry collection *A Pageant and Other Poems*.
- The English writer Mark Rutherford publishes his novel *The Autobiography of Mark Rutherford, Dissenting Minister*.
- The French writer Anatole France publishes his novel *Le Crime de Sylvestre Bonnard/The Crime of Sylvestre Bonnard*.

- The French writer Guy de Maupassant publishes his short story collection *La Maison Tellier/The Tellier House*.
- The French writer Paul Verlaine publishes his poetry collection *Sagesse/Wisdom*.
- The Irish writer Oscar Wilde publishes *Poems*.
- The Italian writer Giovanni Verga publishes his novel *I Malavoglia/The House by the Medlar Tree*.
- The Scottish writer Robert Louis Stevenson publishes his collection of essays *Virginibus Puerisque/On Girls and Boys*.
- The Spanish writer Benito Pérez-Galdós publishes his novel *La desheredada/The Disinherited*, another installment in his 46-novel series *Episodios nacionales/National Episodes*.
- The unfinished novel *Bouvard et Pécuchet/Bouvard and Pécuchet*, by the French writer Gustave Flaubert, is published posthumously.
- The U.S. novelist Henry James publishes his novels *Washington Square* and *Portrait of a Lady*.

Music

- Austrian composer Josef Anton Bruckner completes his Symphony No. 6.
- French composer Charles-François Gounod completes his oratorio *La Rédemption/The Redemption*. He began work on it in 1868.
- German composer Max Bruch completes his *Kol Nidrei* for cello and orchestra.
- Hungarian composer Franz Liszt completes his orchestral work *Mephistowaltzer/Mephisto Waltz* No. 2 and the transcription for piano of *Mephistowaltzer/Mephisto Waltz* Nos. 1 and 2.
- Joel Chandler Harris publishes *Uncle Remus: His Songs and Sayings*, an anthology of traditional Southern black American slave stories and songs.
- The German composer Johannes Brahms completes his *Tragische-ouvertüre/Tragic Overture* (Opus 81).
- The opera *Les Contes d'Hoffmann/The Tales of Hoffmann*, by the German-born French composer Jacques Offenbach, is first performed, in Paris, France.
- The opera *The Maid of Orleans* by the Russian composer Peter Illyich Tchaikovsky is first performed, in St. Petersburg, Russia. It is based on a play about Joan of Arc by the German dramatist Friedrich Johann Christoph von Schiller.
- U.S. composer Edward MacDowell completes his *First Modern Suite* for piano.

Theater and Dance

- English impresario Richard D'Oyly Carte builds the Savoy Theatre, the first public building in England to be lit by electricity.
- The play *Mäster Olof/Master Olaf*, by the Swedish writer Johan August Strindberg, is first performed, in Stockholm, Sweden.

DECEMBER

8 The Ring Theater in Vienna, Austria, catches fire, killing 850 people.

Thought and Scholarship

- Massachusetts legal scholar Oliver Wendell Holmes, Jr., publishes *Common Law*, arguing that law must evolve along with society.
- Massachusetts reformer Helen Hunt Jackson publishes *Century of Dishonor*, an account of the white man's oppression of the Native Americans.
- U.S. sociologist William Graham Sumner publishes "Sociology," delineating a *laissez-faire* philosophy at odds with his peers' interventionist bias.

SOCIETY

Education

- The University of Connecticut is founded at Storrs, Connecticut.
- U.S. financier-manufacturer Joseph Wharton endows the nation's first business school with a $100,000 gift to the University of Pennsylvania.

JULY

4 The Tuskegee Institute, a vocational institute for black Americans, opens in Tuskegee, Alabama. Its first president is the noted black American educator Booker T. Washington.

Everyday Life

- Population in the United States stands at 53 million; in Germany, 45.2 million; in France, 37.6 million; in Italy, 28.4 million; in Britain, 29.7 million; and in Ireland, 5.1 million.
- Populations of the chief European and North American cities stand at 3.3 million in London, England; 2.2 million in Paris, France; 1.2 million in New York, New York; 1.1 million in Berlin, Germany; 1 million in Vienna, Austria; 0.8 million in Tokyo, Japan; 0.6 million in St. Petersburg, Russia; and 0.1 million in Brussels, Belgium.
- The Barnum & Bailey Circus is created when P. T. Barnum's "Greatest Show on Earth" merges with John Anthony Bailey's Circus.
- U.S. judge James Logan creates the loganberry, a cross between a raspberry and a blackberry.

MAY

21 Clara Barton, a nurse during the Civil War, founds a U.S. branch of the Red Cross, in Washington, D.C.

JULY

July 1881–90 Emigration to the United States is 807,357 from Britain and 655,482 from Ireland.

Sports

- The first ski school is started by Mikkel and Torjus Hemmesvedt at Christiania (now Oslo), Norway.

AUGUST

- The first official U.S. lawn tennis championships are held at Newport, Rhode Island, by the recently formed U.S. National Lawn Tennis Association. Richard Sears of the United States wins the meeting's only event, the men's singles.

OCTOBER

15 William C. Harris of Philadelphia, Pennsylvania, begins publishing the United States's first fishing journal, *American Angler*.

NOVEMBER

2 The American Association of Base Ball Clubs, a rival professional league to the National League, is founded at Cincinnati, Ohio. It is dubbed the "Beer Ball League," partly because unlike the National League it permits the sale of alcohol at games.

BIRTHS & DEATHS

- (Mustafa) Kemal Atatürk, Turkish soldier, statesman, and reformer, founder and first president of the Republic of Turkey 1923–38, born in Greece (–1938).

JANUARY

1 Auguste Blanqui, French socialist revolutionary, dies in Paris, France (75).

17 Alfred Reginald Radcliffe-Brown, British structural-functionalist anthropologist, born in Birmingham, England (–1955).

FEBRUARY

4 Fernand Léger, French painter who developed "machine art," born in Argentan, France (–1955).

4 Thomas Carlyle, Scottish historian and essayist, dies in London, England (86).

9 Fyodor Mikhailovich Dostoyevsky, Russian novelist best known for *Crime and Punishment* (1866) and *The Brothers Karamazov* (1879–80), dies in St. Petersburg, Russia (59).

12 Anna Pavlova, Russian ballerina, born in St. Petersburg, Russia (–1931).

MARCH

11 Theodore von Kármán, Austrian-born U.S. engineer who pioneered the use of mathematics in aeronautics and astronautics, born in Budapest, Hungary (–1963).

13 Alexander II, Czar of Russia 1855–81 who was responsible for emancipating the Russian serfs, is assassinated in St. Petersburg, Russia (62).

25 Béla Bartók, Hungarian composer, born in Nagyszentmiklós, Hungary (–1945).

28 Modest Petrovich Mussorgsky, Russian composer, dies in St. Petersburg, Russia (42).

APRIL

3 Alcide de Gasperi, Prime Minister of Italy 1945–53 who signed the peace treaty with the Allies after World War II, born in Pieve Tesino, Italy (–1954).

19 Benjamin Disraeli, Earl of Beaconsfield, British prime minister 1868 and 1874–80, a Conservative, dies in London, England (76).

MAY

1 Pierre Teilhard de Chardin, French Jesuit priest, philosopher, and paleontologist, born in Sarcenat, France (–1955).

4 Alexander Kerensky, Russian revolutionary and head of the Russian provisional government July–October 1917, born in Simbirsk, Russia (–1970).

20 Władysław Sikorski, Polish soldier and statesman, leader of Poland's government-in-exile during World War II, born in Tuszów Narodowy, Poland (–1943).

JUNE

17 James Starkey, British inventor who developed the first true bicycle, dies in Coventry, Warwickshire, England (51).

21 Ferdinand Keller, Swiss archeologist who excavated prehistoric Alpine lake dwellings on Lake Zürich, dies in Zürich, Switzerland (80).

23 Matthias Schleiden, German botanist who, with Theodor Schwann, established cell theory, dies in Frankfurt am Main, Germany (77).

JULY

13 John Clifford Pemberton, Confederate general in the American Civil War who unsuccessfully defended Vicksburg, Mississippi, dies in Penllyn, Pennsylvania (66).

AUGUST

6 Alexander Fleming, Scottish bacteriologist who discovered penicillin, born in Lochfield, Ayr, Scotland (–1955).

12 Cecil B. de Mille, U.S. motion-picture director and producer known for his spectacular films, born in Ashfield, Massachusetts (–1959).

SEPTEMBER

19 James A. Garfield, twentieth president of the United States in 1881, a Republican, dies in Elberon, New Jersey, after being shot nearly three months earlier (49).

OCTOBER

22 Clinton Joseph Davisson, U.S. physicist who showed that electrons possess both wave and particle-like characteristics, born in Bloomington, Illinois (–1958).

25 Pablo Picasso, Spanish painter and sculptor who, with Georges Braque, founded cubism, born in Málaga, Spain (–1973).

NOVEMBER

22 Enver Pasha, Ottoman general who was largely responsible for the Ottoman Empire entering World War I on the side of Germany, born in Constantinople, Anatolia (modern Turkey) (–1922).

25 John III, Roman Catholic pope 1958–63 who convened the Second Vatican Council, born in Sotto il Monte, Italy (–1963).

DECEMBER

17 Lewis Henry Morgan, U.S. anthropologist whose study of kinship among the Iroquois helped establish anthropology in the United States, dies in Rochester, New York (63).

24 Juan Ramón Jiménez, Spanish poet, born in Moguer, Spain (–1958).

1882

POLITICS, GOVERNMENT, AND ECONOMICS

Business and Economics

- Cotton duties are abolished in India.
- During the year there are 2,590 agrarian outrages in Ireland and 10,457 families are evicted in the struggle over tenant farmers' rights.
- The Bank of Japan is founded.
- The English economist William Stanley Jevons publishes *The State in Relation to Labour*.
- The U.S. oil company now known as the Mobil Corporation is incorporated as the Standard Oil Co. of New York (Socony).

MAY

2 The Kilmainham Treaty is agreed by the Irish nationalist leader Charles Stewart Parnell (imprisoned in Kilmainham jail) and the British government, allowing for the arrears owed by Irish tenants to be paid by the government on condition that Parnell seeks to end disorder in Ireland. Lord Cowper, Lord Lieutenant of Ireland, and his chief secretary resign in protest.

22 The United States and Korea sign a commercial treaty.

AUGUST

3 The U.S. Congress passes immigration legislation imposing a 50-cent head tax on immigrants and barring convicts, the mentally impaired, and individuals unable to care for themselves.

Colonization

- The American Colonial Society is founded in the United States.

DECEMBER

12 Italy takes over Assab Bay in the Red Sea and establishes the colony of Eritrea.

Human Rights

December 1882–92 Around 1,400 black Americans are lynched in the United States.

Politics and Government

- The Married Women's Property Act in Britain gives married women the right of separate ownership of property of all kinds.
- The Republican Party is founded in Portugal.
- U.S. president Chester A. Arthur appoints Massachusetts jurist Horace Gray to the U.S. Supreme Court.

JANUARY

8 The French prime minister Léon Gambetta sends a note to Egypt from France and Britain, supporting the khedive against the nationalists.

22 Electoral reform in Italy lowers the tax requirements and age limit of electors.

27 The government of Léon Gambetta falls in France and Charles Freycinet forms a new ministry.

FEBRUARY

2 A Pan-Slavic speech in Paris, France, by the Russian general Mikhail Dmitriyevich Skobelev raises fears of Russian expansionism.

27 Khedive Tewfik of Egypt is forced to appoint a nationalist ministry following revolts against his rule.

MARCH

6 Prince Milan Obrenovič proclaims himself king of Serbia, with Austro-Hungarian support.

16 The U.S. Senate ratifies the Geneva Convention of 1864, establishing guidelines for the care of soldiers wounded in war.

22 The U.S. Congress passes the Edmunds Act, prohibiting polygamy in U.S. territories. The legislation is aimed at polygamous practices of The Church of Jesus Christ of Latter-day Saints.

31 The U.S. Congress establishes a pension for the widows of former U.S. presidents.

APRIL

4 The Prussian legation is restored at the Vatican following a severance of relations during the campaign against Catholics by the German government.

MAY

6 Fenians murder the new Irish chief secretary, Lord Frederick Cavendish, and V. H. Burke, the Irish undersecretary, in Phoenix Park, Dublin, Ireland.

6 The U.S. Congress adopts the Exclusion Act, prohibiting Chinese immigration for ten years.

20 Italy joins the Austro-German alliance for a period of five years, thereby forming the Triple Alliance (which is subsequently renewed until 1915). This assures Italy of support in the event of attack by France, commits Italy to support Germany in the event of a French attack on

Germany, and guarantees Italian neutrality in the event of war between Austria-Hungary and Russia.

JUNE

6   The Hague Convention fixes a three-mile limit for territorial waters.

12   Antiforeign riots occur in Alexandria, Egypt, led by the nationalist war minister Arabi Pasha.

28   An Anglo-French agreement is made over the boundaries of Sierra Leone and French Guinea.

JULY

7   The repressive Prevention of Crimes Bill for Ireland suspends trial by jury and grants police wide powers of search and arrest as a means to combat the disturbances in the country.

11   Britain's Royal Navy bombards Alexandria, Egypt, in response to anti-Western activities.

15   John Bright resigns from the British government in protest at the bombardment of Alexandria, Egypt.

30   Charles J. Guiteau is executed for the murder of U.S. president James A. Garfield on September 19, 1881.

AUGUST

2   The U.S. Congress overrides President Chester A. Arthur's veto to pass an $18-million public works program.

17   An Irish family named Joyce is murdered at Maamtrasna by the Invincibles, a secret Irish terrorist society.

SEPTEMBER

13   The British general Sir Garnet Wolseley defeats the Egyptians at Tel-el-Kebir, Lower Egypt, and proceeds to occupy Egypt and the Sudan.

15   A British force occupies Cairo, Egypt, in response to anti-Western demonstrations. The nationalist leader Arabi Pasha surrenders and is subsequently banished to Ceylon (Sri Lanka).

NOVEMBER

7   In the U.S. Congressional elections, the Democrats retain a majority in the House (197–118) but surrender control of the Senate (38–36) to the Republicans.

9   Anglo-French dual control of Egypt is reestablished following its suspension during Arabi Pasha's period of influence.

SCIENCE, TECHNOLOGY, AND MEDICINE

Agriculture

- Crop failure in Japan leads to starvation and mass emigration.

Ecology

- U.S. meteorologist Elias Loomis publishes the first precipitation map, which shows mean annual precipitation throughout the world, using isohyets connecting places having equal rainfall.

MARCH

1–30 Floods along the Mississippi River in the United States leave about 85,000 people homeless.

JUNE

5   A storm and tidal wave at Bombay, India, kill over 100,000 people.

Health and Medicine

- Dutch physician Aletta Jacobs begins the first systematic work on contraception.
- German cytologist Eduard Adolf Strasburger coins the words "cytoplasm" for the body of the cell, and "nucleoplasm" to describe the nucleus.
- British physiologist Sydney Ringer discovers that immersion in a saline solution containing calcium and potassium keeps an excised frog's heart beating longer. The solution, now known as Ringer's solution, is widely used to prolong the survival of excised tissue.

MARCH

24   German physician Robert Koch announces the discovery of *Mycobacterium tuberculosis*, the bacillus responsible for tuberculosis. This is the first time a microorganism has been definitively associated with a human disease.

Math

- Ferdinand Lindemann proves π is a transcendental number.
- German mathematician Carl Louis Ferdinand von Lindemann proves that it is impossible to construct a square with the same area as a given circle using a ruler and compass. This had been a classic mathematical problem dating back to ancient Greece.

Science

- English astronomer Ralph Copeland observes the transit of Venus, in Jamaica.
- English philosopher Henry Sidgwick founds and becomes the first president of the Society for Psychical Research.
- French physicist Jacques-Arsène d'Arsonval invents the d'Arsonval galvanometer to measure weak electric currents. Using the torque created when an electric current passes through a coil located between the poles of a magnet, it is still the most commonly used galvanometer.
- German anatomist Walther Flemming publishes *Zellsubstanz, Kern und Zelltheilung/Cell Substance, Nucleus and Cell Division* in which he describes how animal cell nuclei are derived from the division of preexisting nuclei—a process now known as mitosis.
- German bacteriologists Friedrich August Johannes Löffler and Wilhelm Schütz identify *Pfeifferella (Malleomyces) mallei* as the causative organism of glanders, a contagious disease of horses.
- German chemist Emil Hermann Fischer shows that proteins are polymers, or large molecules, comprised of amino acids.
- German electrical engineer Oskar von Miller transmits electrical energy over a 57-km/35-mi wire.

- German-born U.S. physicist Albert Michelson determines the speed of light to be 299,853 kps/186,329 mps.
- Scottish physicist Balfour Stewart postulates the existence of an electrically conducting layer of the outer atmosphere (now known as the ionosphere) to account for the daily variation in the earth's magnetic field.

Technology

- A hydraulic system is installed in London, England, to deliver water under high pressure to drive machinery in factories.
- English gunsmith George Kynoch develops a brass cartridge-case.
- French physiologist Etienne Marey invents a photographic "gun," which can take a sequence of pictures using a revolving photographic plate.
- Henry Seeley of New York, New York, patents an electric flatiron.
- German engineer Gottlieb Daimler builds a gasoline engine.

SEPTEMBER

4   U.S. inventor Thomas Alva Edison opens the Pearl Street electric generating station in New York, New York. The first in the United States, it employs three 125-horsepower steam generators to supply direct current (DC) to 225 houses.

30 The world's first hydroelectric generating plant opens at Appleton, Wisconsin. It consists of two direct current generators powered by a 107-cm/42-in waterwheel. It produces 2.5 kW of power.

Transportation

- China's first railroad is built between T'ang-shan and Feng-nan. Used for carrying coal, it is 11 km/7 mi long. It is extended to 128 km/80 mi to Tianjin in 1888.

ARTS AND IDEAS

Architecture

- The 15-km/9.3-mi long St. Gotthard railroad tunnel opens. Connecting Italy and Switzerland, it is one of the longest railroad tunnels in the world.
- The idea of a Channel Tunnel is first discussed in Britain, but military authorities disapprove.

Arts

c. 1882 The U.S. artist Albert Pinkham Ryder paints *Toilers of the Sea*.
- The French artist Auguste Rodin sculpts *The Crouching Woman*, a motif derived from his *Gates of Hell* project.
- The German artist Wilhelm Leibl paints *Three Women in Church*.
- The U.S. artist John Singer Sargent paints *The Daughters of Edward Darley Boit*.

- The U.S. artist Ralph Albert Blakelock paints *Moonlight*.

Film

- French physiologist Etienne-Jules Marey invents a rifle-shaped camera that records 12 successive photographs a second. In order to study the flight of birds, he mounts images on a rotating glass plate to simulate motion, and then projects them. They are the first motion pictures taken with a single camera.

Literature and Language

- The book *Dieu et l'Etat/God and the State* by the Russian anarchist Mikhail Alexandrovich Bakunin is published posthumously.
- The Danish writer Jens Peter Jacobsen publishes his collection of short stories *Morgens og andre Noveller/Morgens and Other Stories*.
- The English writer and social reformer Walter Besant publishes *All Sorts and Conditions of Men*, a novel describing slums in London, England.
- The first volume of the British *Dictionary of National Biography*, edited by the English critic and biographer Leslie Stephen, is published. The last volume of this edition appears in 1900.
- The French writer Guy de Maupassant publishes his short-story collection *Mademoiselle Fifi*.
- The Italian writer Carlo Collodi (Italian journalist and author Carlo Lorenzini) publishes his children's novel *Le avventure di Pinocchio: Storia di un burattino/The Adventures of Pinocchio: The Story of a Puppet*.
- The Italian writer Gabriele D'Annunzio publishes his poetry collection *Canto novo/New Poem*.
- The U.S. poet Walt Whitman publishes *Specimen Days and Collect*, a collection of prose works including diaries and notebooks.
- The U.S. writer Mark Twain publishes his novel *The Prince and the Pauper*.

Music

- Bohemian composer Antonín Dvořák completes his choral work *Vpřírodě/Amid Nature*.
- French composer César Franck completes his symphonic poem *Le Chasseur maudit/The Accursed Hunter*.
- German composer Johannes Brahms completes his Piano Trio No. 2 (Opus 87).
- Russian composer Peter Illyich Tchaikovsky completes his choral work *Russian Vespers*.
- The Berlin Philharmonic Orchestra is founded in Germany.
- The comic opera *Iolanthe, or The Peer and the Peri*, by the English writer William Schwenk Gilbert and the English composer Arthur Seymour Sullivan, is first performed, at the Savoy Theatre in London, England.
- The opera *Parsifal* by the German composer Richard Wagner is first performed, in Bayreuth, Germany. Wagner did not want the opera performed anywhere but at Bayreuth, but illegal performances are given, one of the first being in the United States in 1903, in New York, New York.

BIRTHS & DEATHS

- Alexander Gardner, U.S. photographer of the American Civil War and of Native North Americans, dies in Washington, D.C. (c. 60).

JANUARY

6　Sam Rayburn, U.S. Democratic Party leader and speaker of the House of Representatives 1937–54, born in Roane County, Tennessee (–1961).

11　Theodor Schwann, German histologist who founded modern cell theory, dies in Cologne, Germany (71).

13　Wiremu Kingi (also known as William King or Te Rangitake), Maori chief who led the resistance to European colonization of New Zealand's North Island, dies in Kaingaru, New Zealand (c. 89).

18　A(lan) A(lexander) Milne, English author who created Winnie-the-Pooh, born in London, England (–1956).

25　Virginia Woolf, English author and critic, born in London, England (–1941).

26　Léon Gambetta, French politician who organized the defense of France during the Franco-Prussian War 1870–71, dies in Ville-d'Avray, near Paris, France (43).

30　Franklin Delano Roosevelt, U.S. statesman, thirty-second president of the United States 1933–45 (reelected three times), a Democrat, born in Hyde Park, New York (–1945).

FEBRUARY

- Johnny Torrio, U.S. gangster who, with other crime bosses, formed a national crime syndicate c. 1934, born in Orsara, Italy (–1957).

2　James Joyce, Irish novelist and poet, born in Dublin, Ireland (–1941).

15　John Barrymore, U.S. actor in the early "talkies," born in Philadelphia, Pennsylvania (–1942).

MARCH

18　(Gian) Francesco Malipiero, Italian composer who combined modern techniques with the stylistic quality of early music, born in Venice, Italy (–1973).

24　Henry Wadsworth Longfellow, U.S. poet, dies in Cambridge, Massachusetts (75).

26　Thomas Hill Green, English philosopher, dies in Oxford, England (45).

APRIL

3　Jesse James, U.S. bank and train robber, is shot in the back of the head near Centerville, Missouri, by one of his gang members to claim a $10,000 reward (34).

9　Dante Gabriel Rossetti, English Pre-Raphaelite painter and poet, dies in Birchington-on-Sea, Kent, England (54).

18　Leopold Stokowski, U.S. composer who promoted contemporary music and was involved in new music technology in the 1930s, born in London, England (–1977).

19　Charles Robert Darwin, English naturalist who developed the theory of evolution through natural selection, dies in Downe, Kent, England (73).

21　Percy Williams Bridgman, U.S. physicist who was the first to experiment on materials subjected to extremely high pressures, winner of the Nobel Prize for Physics in 1946, born in Cambridge, Massachusetts (–1961).

27　Ralph Waldo Emerson, U.S. writer and leading proponent of New England Transcendentalism, dies in Concorde, Massachusetts (78).

MAY

9　Henry Kaiser, U.S. industrialist, born in Sprout Brook, New York (–1967).

13　Georges Braque, French painter who helped develop cubism, born in Argenteuil, France (–1963).

JUNE

2　Giuseppe Garibaldi, Italian soldier whose conquest of Sicily and Naples helped unify Italy, dies in Caprera, Italy (74).

17　Igor Stravinsky, Russian composer, born in Oranienbaum, near St. Petersburg, Russia (–1971).

21　Rockwell Kent, U.S. painter of nature and adventure scenes, writer, illustrator, and social critic, born in Tarrytown Heights, New York (–1971).

JULY

27　Geoffrey de Havilland, English aircraft designer who made some of the first jet airplanes, born in Haslemere, Surrey, England (–1965).

AUGUST

2　Jack L. Warner, U.S. film producer who, with his three brothers, established Warner Brothers, which pioneered talking pictures, born in London, Ontario, Canada (–1978).

27　Samuel Goldwyn, U.S. pioneer Hollywood filmmaker and producer, one of the founders of Metro-Goldwyn-Mayer (MGM), born in Warsaw, Poland (–1974).

SEPTEMBER

22　Wilhelm Keitel, German field marshal who was head of the German armed forces high command during World War II, born

in Helmscherode, Germany (–1946).

23　Friedrich Wöhler, U.S. chemist who first synthesized urea and developed a method for making metallic aluminum, dies in Eschersheim, near Frankfurt am Main (82).

30　Hans Geiger, German physicist who invented the Geiger counter to measure radioactivity, born in Neustadt-an-der-Haardt, Germany (–1945).

OCTOBER

5　Robert Goddard, U.S. astronautics pioneer who developed modern rockets used for launching spacecraft, born in Worcester, Massachusetts (–1945).

13　Joseph-Arthur Gobineau, French ethnologist whose theories of race influenced European racial policies, dies in Turin, Italy (64).

14　Eamon de Valéra, Irish politician and revolutionary, president 1959–73 who took Ireland out of the British Commonwealth, born in New York, New York (–1975).

24　Sybil Thorndike, English stage actress of great versatility, born in Gainsborough, Lincolnshire, England (–1976).

30　William F. Halsey, U.S. naval commander during World War II, born in Elizabeth, New Jersey (–1959).

NOVEMBER

11　Gustavus VI (or Gustaf VI), King of Sweden 1950–73, born in Stockholm, Sweden (–1973).

18　Jacques Maritain, French Roman Catholic philosopher, born in Paris, France (–1973).

DECEMBER

6　(Jean-Joseph-Charles-) Louis Blanc, French socialist who developed the idea of worker-controlled "social workshops," dies in Cannes, France (71).

6　Anthony Trollope, English novelist, dies in London, England (67).

11　Max Born, German physicist who shared the Nobel Prize for Physics in 1954 for his statistical description of the behavior of subatomic particles, born in Breslau, Germany (now Wrocław, Poland) (–1970).

28　Arthur Stanley Eddington, English astronomer, mathematician, and physicist who was the first to provide concrete evidence of Einstein's theory of relativity, born in Kendal, Westmorland (now Cumbria), England (–1944).

- The opera *Snegurochka/The Snow Maiden* by the Russian composer Nikolay Andreyevich Rimsky-Korsakov is first performed, in St. Petersburg, Russia.
- U.S. composer Edward MacDowell completes his Piano Concerto No. 1.

Theater and Dance

- The melodrama *The Silver King* by the English dramatists Henry Arthur Jones and Henry Herman is first performed, in London, England.
- The melodrama *Féodora* by the French dramatist Victorien Sardou is first performed, in Paris, France. It was written for the actress Sarah Bernhardt.
- The play *Gengangere/Ghosts* by the Norwegian dramatist Henrik Johan Ibsen is first performed, in Christiania (now Oslo), Norway.
- The play *Les Corbeaux/The Vultures* by the French dramatist Henry-François Becque is first performed, in Paris, France.
- William Cody begins his "Buffalo Bill's Wild West" show, an extravaganza that attempts to capture life on the frontier; it tours across the United States and Europe in subsequent years.

Thought and Scholarship

- The German philosopher Friedrich Nietzsche publishes *Die fröhliche Wissenschaft/The Gay Science*.
- The Scottish economist William Cunningham publishes *Growth of English Industry and Commerce*, which remains the standard work until the 1930s.
- The Italian historian Pasquale Villari publishes his biography *Niccolò Machiavelli*.
- The Irish writer Oscar Wilde delivers his "Lectures on the Decorative Arts" in Canada and the United States, explaining the principles of the aesthetic movement.

September 1882–83 U.S. psychologist Granville Stanley Hall writes about children's lies and children's minds, pioneering child psychology.

SOCIETY

Education

- Regent Street Polytechnic opens in London, England.
- Selwyn College is founded at Cambridge University, England.
- The Bohemian National University is opened in Prague, Bohemia, and becomes a center for Bohemian nationalism.

MARCH

29 A law is passed by the French Republican government to make primary education in France free, compulsory, and nonsectarian.

APRIL

28 New York industrialist John Fox Slater endows the $1-million John F. Slater Fund to promote education among emancipated slaves.

Everyday Life

- The first electrically lit Christmas tree is switched on in New York, New York, in the home of Thomas Alva Edison's associate Edward H. Johnson.
- The Spiegel, May, Stern Company in the United States begins to offer its goods by mail via its catalog.

Media and Communication

- The *Berliner Tageblatt* newspaper is launched in Germany.

Religion

FEBRUARY

2 A priest, Michael Joseph McGiveny, of New Haven, Connecticut, founds the Catholic fraternal organization Knights of Columbus.

Sports

c. 1882 The Irish game of handball is introduced to the United States in New York by Irish immigrants.

- The first judo *kodokan* (training hall) is established at Shitaya, Japan, by Jigoro Kano.
- The first U.S. country club, the Myopia Hunt Club, is founded in Winchester, Massachusetts.

1883

POLITICS, GOVERNMENT, AND ECONOMICS

Business and Economics

- U.S. petroleum production stands at 23,450,000 barrels.

MAY

1 Chancellor Otto von Bismarck introduces a state sickness insurance program in Germany to lessen the appeal of socialism to the working classes.

Colonization

- Britain declines the request by the British colony of Queensland to annex New Guinea.
- French troops begin the conquest of the Upper Niger.

AUGUST

25 France proclaims a protectorate in Annam and Tonkin, in Southeast Asia.

SEPTEMBER

9 The Boer republic of Stellaland is founded in Bechuanaland (later Botswana).

Politics and Government

JANUARY

16 The U.S. Congress passes the Pendleton Act, establishing the Civil Service Commission. The legislation aims to replace the spoils system with a merit system.

30 Armand Fallières forms a ministry in France which lasts just three weeks, one of several short-lived governments in a period of political turbulence.

FEBRUARY

21 The Left Republican Jules Ferry forms his second ministry in France which lasts until 1885.

MARCH

3 The U.S. Congress authorizes production of new Navy vessels made of steel, and reduces postage from three cents to two cents per half ounce.

15 Irish-American terrorists attempt to blow up *The Times* office and the local government board in London, England.

20 Eleven countries sign the International Convention for the Protection of Industrial Property, in Paris, France, which establishes international rights in patents, designs,

trademarks, and so on. It comes into effect on July 7, 1884.

APRIL

16 The Transvaal leader Paul Kruger becomes president of the South African Republic.

24 Germany begins settlements in southwest Africa and Angra Pequeña, prompting Britain to state that any claims to sovereignty in the territory between the Cape Colony and Angola will be regarded as an infringement of its rights.

MAY

1 The Organic Law in Egypt, based on the report by Lord Dufferin of February 6, establishes a legislative council and a general assembly, though authority remains vested in the British agent.

JUNE

June–December 1885 The French wage a war with Madagascar when the Hova government rejects the island's status as a French protectorate, created in 1882.

8 France gains effective control of Tunisia under the Convention of Marsa agreed with the bey of Tunis.

AUGUST

18 The Corrupt and Illegal Practices Act limits the spending of both individual candidates and political parties in a British general election in an attempt to prevent corruption. The limit for a party is set at £800,000.

24 Henri, comte de Chambord, Legitimist (Bourbon) pretender to the French throne, dies without an heir.

SEPTEMBER

11 Sir Evelyn Baring, Lord Cromer, arrives in Egypt in the role of British consul general and agent, because Britain is still unwilling to make Egypt a full protectorate.

30 Alexander of Bulgaria restores the constitution of 1879, dismissing the Russian ministers appointed during his spell of autocratic rule from 1881, and thereby alienating Russia.

OCTOBER

15 The U.S. Supreme Court dismembers the Civil Rights Act of 1875, declaring that the federal government may not regulate private discrimination.

20 By the peace of Ancón, hostilities between Peru and Chile are concluded. Peru cedes territory to Chile, which is to occupy the disputed provinces of Tacna and Arica for ten years, at the end of which a plebiscite is to be held.

30 A secret Austro-Romanian alliance, which will last until 1914, is agreed following Romanian fears of Russia.

NOVEMBER

5 The Sudanese followers of the dervish Mahdi (prophet) Mohammed Ahmed of Dongola defeat an Egyptian force under the British general William Hicks at El

Obeid, in Anglo-Egyptian Sudan, and the British decide to evacuate the country.

11 The Nationalist Radical party revolts against the Serbian government when it is excluded from power despite electoral victory.

SCIENCE, TECHNOLOGY, AND MEDICINE

Ecology

- Austrian meteorologist Julius von Hann publishes *Handbook of Climatology*, which is a compilation of meterological knowledge and world climate.
- One of the world's largest deposits of nickel and copper is discovered at Sudbury, Ontario, Canada, during the construction of the Canadian Pacific Railroad.

AUGUST

27 Krakatoa volcano, Indonesia, explodes in one of the most catastrophic volcanic eruptions in history. The explosion is heard nearly 4,830 km/3,000 mi away. Over 36,000 people in Sumatra and Java are drowned by an ensuing tsunami 35 m/115 ft high, and dust, which is thrown 80 km/50 mi into the air, drifts around the world, causing spectacular sunsets for over a year.

Health and Medicine

- Antipyrine, a powder used to reduce fever and pain, is introduced. It is the first analgesic to be synthesized.
- Russian physician Openchowski freezes parts of the cerebral cortex of dogs using a probe frozen by the evaporation of ether. He discovers that adjacent tissues are little damaged. His experiments are the forerunner of cryosurgery.
- German bacteriologist Robert Koch discovers preventive inoculation against anthrax.
- German bacteriologists Edwin Klebs and Friedrich August Johannes Löffler discover *Corynebacterium diptheriae*, the diphtheria bacillus.
- German physician Robert Koch discovers the cholera bacillus.
- The world's first national compulsory health insurance program is introduced in Germany.

Science

- British metallurgist Robert Abbott Hadfield patents manganese steel, the first special alloy of steel, and one that is exceptionally hard.
- English anthropologist and eugenicist Francis Galton suggests that humans can be improved by selective breeding in his *Enquiries into Human Faculty*. He introduces the term "eugenics."
- French anthropologist Alphonse Bertillon publishes *Ethnographie moderne des races sauvages/Modern Ethnography of the Savage Races.*

- German chemist Johann Friedrich Wilhelm Adolph von Baeyer formulates the structure of the dye indigo; manufacture begins in the 1890s.
- German physiologist Paul Ehrlich publishes "The Requirement of the Organism for Oxygen," in which he shows that different tissues consume oxygen at different rates and that the rate of consumption can be used to measure biological activity.
- Irish physicist George Francis FitzGerald suggests that electromagnetic waves (radio waves) can be created by oscillating an electric current. A later demonstration of such waves by the German physicist Heinrich Hertz leads to the development of wireless telegraphy.
- Italian physiologist Camillo Golgi discovers a network of small fibers, cavities, and granules in nerve cells. Now known as the Golgi apparatus, it may be involved in membrane construction, transport of substances across the cell membrane, and in protein and lipid storage.
- Scottish physicist William Thomson gives a discourse to the Royal Institution on the size of atoms.
- Scottish-born U.S. inventor Alexander Graham Bell founds the journal *Science* with his father-in-law G. G. Hubbard.
- U.S. inventor Thomas Alva Edison observes the flow of current between a hot electrode and a cold electrode in one of his vacuum bulbs. Known as the "Edison effect," it results from the thermionic emission of electrons from the hot electrode, and is the principle behind the working of the electron tube, which is to form the basis of the electronics industry.

August 1883–88 Austrian geologist Eduard Suess publishes *Das Antlitz der Erde/Face of the Earth*, in which he postulates the existence of an ancient supercontinent in the southern hemisphere called Gondwanaland, and discusses how various processes are responsible for the present features of the earth's surface.

Technology

- English physicist and chemist Joseph Wilson Swan patents a method of creating nitrocellulose (cellulose nitrate) fiber by squeezing it though small holes. It becomes a basic process in the artificial textile industry.

Transportation

- Belgian-born U.S. inventor Charles Joseph Van Depoele obtains a patent for an electric railroad.
- French inventor Léon Paul Charles Malandin runs a four-wheeled vehicle powered by a four-stroke two-cylinder internal combustion engine which burns gasoline.
- The Calais–Nice–Rome railroad line between France and Italy is completed.
- The Oslo–Bergen railroad is completed in Norway.
- The Southern Pacific Railroad is completed, linking New Orleans, Louisiana, and San Francisco, California.
- The Sydney–Melbourne railroad opens in Australia.
- To end the confusion caused by scores of different local times in the United States, U.S. railroads divide the country into four time zones: Eastern, Central, Rocky Mountain and Pacific.

MAY

24 The Brooklyn Bridge over the East River between Brooklyn and Manhattan, New York, New York, opens. Designed by German-born U.S. engineer Augustus Roebling, and completed by his son Washington Roebling, the suspension bridge is the first to use steel cable wire and is the longest in the world, with a span of 486 m/1,595 ft.

SEPTEMBER

8 The Northern Pacific Railroad, joining St. Paul, Minnesota, and Seattle, Oregon, is completed, providing a northern route to the western United States. Construction began in 1873.

OCTOBER

4 The luxury train the Orient Express leaves on its first trip. Europe's first transcontinental express train, it runs 2,740 km/1,700 mi from Paris, France, to Varna, Bulgaria, where passengers disembark to be ferried to Constantinople (Istanbul), Turkey.

8 French engineers Albert and Gaston Tissandier are the first to successfully power an airship with an electric motor.

DECEMBER

14 The Portuguese government grants a concession to a U.S. promoter for a railroad from Delagoa Bay, Mozambique, to the Transvaal.

ARTS AND IDEAS

Architecture

- U.S. architect William Lebaron Jenney completes construction of the ten-story Home Insurance Building in Chicago, Illinois. The world's first true skyscraper, it consists of a steel-girder framework on which the outer covering of masonry hangs. It sparks a boom in the construction of skyscrapers in Chicago.
- The Historical Museum in Moscow, Russia, designed by the Russian architect (of English descent) Vladimir Ossipovich Sherwood, is completed.
- The Palace of Justice in Brussels, Belgium, designed by the Belgian architect Joseph Poelaert, is completed.
- The Parliament House in Vienna, Austria, designed by the Danish architect Theophil von Hansen, is completed.

Arts

- The Belgian artist James Ensor paints *Portrait of the Artist in a Flowery Hat*.
- The French artist Claude Monet paints *The Cliffs at Etretat*.
- The French artist Paul Cézanne paints *Paysage rocheux/ Rocky Landscape*.
- The Russian artist Ilya Yefimovich Repin paints *The Procession in the Region of Kursk* and *The Return of the Exile*.
- The U.S. artist Winslow Homer paints *Inside the Bar, Tynemouth*.

Literature and Language

- British explorer and translator Richard Burton translates the Indian classic the *Kama Sutra*.
- The Belgian writer Emile Verhaeren (writing in French) publishes his poetry collection *Les Flamandes/The Flemish*.
- The Boer writer Olive Schreiner publishes her novel *The Story of an African Farm*.
- The first part of *Fragments d'un journal intime/ Fragments of an Intimate Journal*, by the Swiss writer and philosopher Henri Frédéric Amiel, is published posthumously. The second part appears in 1884.
- The French historian Ernest Renan publishes *Souvenirs d'enfance et de jeunesse/Memories of Childhood and Youth*.
- The French writer Auguste, comte Villiers de L'Isle-Adam, publishes his short stories *Contes cruels/Cruel Tales*.
- The French writer Guy de Maupassant publishes his novel *Une Vie/A Life*.
- The German writer Detlev, Baron von Liliencron, publishes his poetry collection *Adjutantenritte und andere Gedichte/Rides of the Adjutant and Other Poems*.
- The Irish writer George Augustus Moore publishes his novel *A Modern Lover*.
- The Scottish writer Robert Louis Stevenson publishes his adventure novel *Treasure Island*. It first appeared as a serial in the magazine *Young Folks* from 1881 to 1882 under the title *The Sea Cook, or Treasure Island*.
- The U.S. writer Mark Twain publishes his autobiographical *Life on the Mississippi*.
- U.S. English teachers establish the Modern Language Association to promote the study of literature and linguistics.

Music

- Austrian composer Josef Anton Bruckner completes his Symphony No. 7.
- Bohemian composer Bedřich Smetana completes his String Quartet No. 2.
- French composer Alexis Emmanuel Chabrier completes his orchestral rhapsody *España/Spain*.
- German composer Johannes Brahms completes his Symphony No. 3.
- The opera *Lakmé* by the French composer Léo Delibes is first performed, in Paris, France.
- U.S. composer Edward MacDowell completes his *Second Modern Suite* for piano.

Theater and Dance

- The Metropolitan Opera (the "Met") is founded in New York, New York.
- The play *En folkefiende/An Enemy of the People* by the Norwegian dramatist Henrik Johan Ibsen is first performed, in Christiania (now Oslo), Norway.

Thought and Scholarship

- The English jurist and historian Henry James Sumner Maine publishes *Early Law and Custom*.
- The German philosopher Friedrich Nietzsche publishes the first part of his *Also sprach Zarathustra/Thus Spake Zarathustra*. The final part appears in 1885. It is in this work that he develops his concept of the *übermensch* (superman).
- U.S. sociologist Lester Frank Ward publishes *Dynamic Sociology*, arguing that mankind's judicious use of science can affect the course of evolution.
- U.S. sociologist William Graham Sumner publishes *What Social Classes Owe Each Other*, in which he argues that in fact they owe one another nothing; anything more will ensure the survival of the least fit.
- The British philosopher Francis Herbert Bradley publishes *The Principles of Logic*.
- The English historian John Robert Seeley publishes *The Expansion of England*.
- The French writer and critic Paul-Charles-Joseph Bourget publishes *Essais de psychologie contemporaine/ Essays in Contemporary Psychology*.

SOCIETY

Education

- Jacksonville State University is founded in Jacksonville, Florida.
- The Royal College of Music is founded under George Grove in London, England.
- The University of Texas is founded in Austin, Texas.

Everyday Life

- George S. Parker invents the *Game of Banking* in the United States, a popular board game of the day.
- German electrical engineer Oskar von Miller organizes the Munich Electrical Exposition, the first in Germany.
- James and William Horlick manufacture Horlicks Malted Milk in the United States, a powder to add nutrition to milk and help sleeping.

OCTOBER

4 The Boys' Brigade, an association for young Christian men, is founded by William Smith in Glasgow, Scotland.

NOVEMBER

18 To facilitate railroad timetables, the United States and Canada standardize time.

BIRTHS & DEATHS

JANUARY

3 Clement Attlee, Earl Attlee, British prime minister 1945–51, a member of the Labour Party, born in London, England (–1967).

FEBRUARY

13 (Wilhelm) Richard Wagner, German dramatic composer and theorist who wrote the operatic sequence *Der Ring des Nibelungen/The Ring of the Nibelung*, dies in Venice, Italy (69).

23 Karl Jaspers, German Existentialist philosopher, born in Oldenburg, Germany (–1969).

MARCH

2 Leonard Colebrook, English physician who introduced the first sulfonamide drug (Prontosil) into Britain, born in Guildford, Surrey, England (–1967).

14 Karl Marx, Prussian political theorist, economist, and sociologist whose ideas formed the basis of communism, dies in London, England (65).

APRIL

1 Lon Chaney, U.S. actor known for his grotesque characterizations, born in Colorado Springs, Colorado (–1930).

19 Getúlio Vargas, President of Brazil 1930–45 whose economic and social policies helped modernize the country, born in São Borja, Brazil (–1954).

30 Edouard Manet, French realist painter and important 19th-century artist, dies in Paris, France (51).

MAY

18 Walter Gropius, German architect, born in Berlin, Germany (–1969).

23 Douglas Fairbanks, U.S. star of early films, born in Denver, Colorado (–1939).

JUNE

5 John Maynard Keynes, English economist concerned with the causes and solutions of long-term unemployment, born in Cambridge, England (–1946).

28 Pierre Laval, French politician, leader of the collaboration Vichy government during World War II, born in Châteldon, France (–1945).

JULY

3 Franz Kafka, Bohemian-born German writer, born in Prague, Bohemia (–1924).

19 Benito Mussolini, "Il Duce," Italian prime minister 1922–43, first of Europe's fascist dictators, born in Predappio, Italy (–1945).

AUGUST

19 Coco (Gabrielle) Chanel, French couturier whose classic designs have been widely copied, born in Saumur, France (–1971).

SEPTEMBER

4 Ivan Sergeyevich Turgenev, Russian novelist, poet, and playwright, dies in Bougival, near Paris, France (65).

14 Margaret Sanger, U.S. birth control advocate who opened the first birth control clinic in the United States, born in Corning, New York (–1966).

NOVEMBER

8 Arnold Bax, English composer, born in London, England (–1953).

8 Charles Demuth, U.S. painter, born in Lancaster, Pennsylvania (–1935).

19 Charles William Siemens, German-born British engineer whose telegraph company made the first direct telegraph link between the United States and Britain, dies in London, England (–1883).

23 José Clemente Orozco, Mexican painter of murals, born in Cuidad Guzmán, Mexico (–1949).

DECEMBER

3 Anton Webern, Austrian composer, born in Vienna, Austria (–1945).

Media and Communication

- *La Tribune* newspaper is launched in France.
- The humorous magazine *Life* is launched in the United States.

Religion

- U.S. theologian Charles Augustus Briggs publishes *Biblical Study*.

Sports

- The first international toboggan competition is staged on a 3.2-km/2-mi course between Davos and Klosters in Switzerland.
- The inaugural West of the Pecos Rodeo, described as a "Cowboy Tournament," is held at Pecos, Texas. It is one of the first organized rodeo events with cash prizes and paying spectators.

JUNE

16 The New York Giants baseball team holds a ladies' day on which all women are admitted to the ballpark for free.

1884

POLITICS, GOVERNMENT, AND ECONOMICS

Business and Economics

JANUARY

1 Poll tax, a relic of serfdom, is abolished in Russia.

Colonization

- The Imperial Federation League is founded in Canada to work for closer association within the British Empire.

APRIL

April–August Germany occupies South West Africa, Togoland, and Cameroon.

JUNE

6 By the Treaty of Hué the emperor of Annam (now part of Vietnam) recognizes the proclamation of Annam as a French protectorate.

DECEMBER

16 Britain follows the lead of the United States and Germany in recognizing the International Association of the Congo, organized by the Belgian Comité d'Etudes du Haut-Congo in 1882 for the purposes of exploiting the region.

Human Rights

- U.S. female suffrage advocates establish the National Equal Rights Party.

Politics and Government

- The Norwegian constitution is reformed.
- A Royal Commission is appointed to investigate the housing of the working classes in Britain, with the Radical member of Parliament Charles Dilke as chairman.

JANUARY

31 The Russians take Merv, Afghanistan, from Sher Ali, the amir of Afghanistan.

FEBRUARY

4 Sudanese forces under Osman Digna, lieutenant of the dervish Mahdi (prophet) Mohammed Ahmed of Dongola, defeat an Anglo-Egyptian force at El Teb, in Anglo-Egyptian Sudan.

18 The British general Charles George Gordon reaches Khartoum, capital of Anglo-Egyptian Sudan, but the dervish Mahdi Mohammed Ahmed of Dongola rejects his offer of negotiations over control of the country.

26 Britain recognizes Portugal's right to territory at the mouth of the Congo River in order to frustrate Belgian designs on the area.

27 The London Convention establishes the Transvaal as an independent state, although Britain still claims suzerainty.

MARCH

17 Germany, Austria, and Russia renew the Three Emperors' Alliance of June 1881.

APRIL

4 By the Treaty of Valparaíso, Bolivia cedes the disputed province of Atacama to Chile following a period of war between the two.

MAY

29 The U.S. Congress creates the Bureau of Animal Industry within the Department of Agriculture.

JUNE

6 A group of independent Republicans in the United States, known as Mugwumps, leave the Republican convention upon the nomination of James G. Blaine as presidential candidate. Reconvening on June 16, they pledge their votes to the Democrats, on condition that the Democrats nominate a reform-minded candidate.

6 The Republicans nominate Massachusetts congressman James G. Blaine for president and Illinois general John A. Logan for vice president.

26 Britain is forced to retract its support (given on February 26) to Portuguese claims to territory at the mouth of the Congo River after protests from France and Germany.

27 The U.S. Congress creates the Bureau of Labor within the Department of the Interior.

28–August 2 An international conference on Egyptian finance is held in London, England, at which German chancellor Otto von Bismarck and French prime minister Jules Ferry oppose Britain's attempts to use Egyptian revenues for paying the costs of the Anglo-Egyptian military campaign in the Sudan against the dervish Mahdi Mohammed Ahmed of Dongola.

JULY

11 The Democrats nominate New York governor Grover Cleveland for president and former Indiana governor Thomas A. Hendricks for vice president.

27 Divorce, abolished in 1816, is reestablished in France.

AUGUST

5 Members of former dynasties are excluded from the presidency of France and life senatorships are abolished.

OCTOBER

13 The Sudanese followers of the dervish Mahdi Mohammed Ahmed of Dongola capture the city of Omdurman, near Khartoum in Anglo-Egyptian Sudan, from Anglo-Egyptian forces.

NOVEMBER

11 Britain annexes land stretching from St. Lucia Bay to Natal to prevent the Boers in Zululand from gaining access to the east coast of Africa.

15 The 14-nation Berlin Conference on African Affairs, organized by German chancellor Otto von Bismarck and French prime minister Jules Ferry, provides for free trade on the Congo River and the abolition of slavery and the slave trade.

DECEMBER

1 The Redistribution of Seats Bill is passed in the British Parliament, giving more seats to counties in return for Conservative support for parliamentary reform.

SCIENCE, TECHNOLOGY, AND MEDICINE

Ecology

- German meteorologist Vladimir Peter Köppen introduces a classification of the world's climate zones based on the number of months whose temperatures remain above or below certain means.
- British zoologist Edwin Ray Lankester founds the Marine Biological Association.

Women's Suffrage (1776–1884)

1776

March 31 "Remember the Ladies," Abigail Adams, wife of American Continental Congressman and future president John Adams, admonishes her husband in a letter. "If particular care and attention is not paid to the Ladies we are determined to foment a Rebellion and will not hold ourselves bound by any Laws in which we have no voice, or Representation."

1777

- New York adopts a constitution denying women, even those with property, the right to vote.

1792

- The English writer and feminist Mary Wollstonecraft publishes her *Vindication of the Rights of Woman*.

1848

July 19 U.S. women's rights advocates Lucretia Mott and Elizabeth Cady Stanton convoke the Seneca Falls Convention where, along with a host of others, they issue the "Declaration of Sentiments," demanding full citizenship rights.

1853

February 1 Paulina Wright Davis and Caroline H. Dall publish *Una*, the first women's suffrage magazine, in Washington, D.C.

1868

- U.S. suffragist Susan B. Anthony introduces the suffrage newspaper *The Revolution*.
- Women's rights advocates Julia Ward Howe and Carolina Severance establish the New England Woman's Club to promote the civil rights of women.

1869

May Elizabeth Cady Stanton and Susan B. Anthony establish the National Woman Suffrage Association.

December The Wyoming Territory becomes the first U.S. state or territory to grant suffrage to women.

1872

November 5 Susan B. Anthony and several others are arrested for casting ballots in the presidential election.

1878

January 10 California senator Aaron A. Sargent introduces a women's suffrage amendment. Sargent's colleagues defeat the bill by a vote of 34–16.

1884

- U.S. female suffrage advocates establish the National Equal Rights Party.

Health and Medicine

- Austrian surgeon Carl Koller is the first to use cocaine as a local anesthetic, which he uses during eye operations to block nerve impulses. He uses it on a suggestion from Sigmund Freud. U.S. surgeon William Stewart Halsted experiments with it on himself the following year and becomes addicted.
- German physician Arthur Nikolaier discovers the tetanus bacillus, *Clostridium tetani*.

NOVEMBER

25 German-born British surgeon Rickman John Godlee performs the first operation to remove a brain tumor.

Science

- English physicist Oliver Lodge discovers electrical precipitation.
- French scientist Paul-Marie Eugène Vieille adds stabilizers to nitrocellulose (cellulose nitrate) to make smokeless powder. Stable and reliable, it quickly replaces black gunpowder.

MAY

- Swedish chemist Svante Arrhenius suggests that electrolytes (solutions or molten compounds that conduct electricity) disassociate into ions (atoms or groups of atoms that carry an electrical charge).

Technology

- British engineer Charles Parsons constructs the first practical high-speed steam turbine for generating electricity. The blades, on a series of rotors, are arranged so that the steam expands in stages, enabling the maximum extraction of energy. It is capable of 10 hp at 18,000 rpm. It leads to the development of the modern steam turbine.
- German chemists Friedrich Otto Schott and Carl Zeiss develop the heat- and shock-resistant Jena glass. It finds wide application in the manufacture of thermometers, eye-glasses, scientific instruments, and in industry.
- French chemist Hilaire Bernigaud, comte de Chardonnet, patents a process for making artificial silk, or rayon. The fiber is produced by extruding a cellulose nitrate solution through glass capillaries.
- German inventor Paul Gottlieb Nipkow patents a mechanical scanning device consisting of a rotating disc with a spiral of holes. All television systems later use the disc, or a modified version of it, to scan images, until electronic scanning is invented.
- German-born U.S. inventor Ottmar Mergenthaler patents the first Linotype typesetting machine. Characters are cast as metal type in complete lines rather than as individual letters as in a monotype machine.
- New York, New York, bans the installation of overhead electric cables, thereby stimulating the development of underground cables.
- U.S. insurance agent Lewis Edson Waterman develops the fountain pen with controlled ink flow.
- U.S. inventor Charles Sumner Tainter invents the Dictaphone.

- U.S. inventor Hiram Stevens Maxim develops the first automatic machine gun. Consisting of a single barrel and a belt feed, it harnesses the recoil to work the bolt, expel the used cartridge, and reload. Water-cooled, it can fire 600 shots per minute. The British army adopts it in 1889, followed by other armies and navies later.
- U.S. inventor Lewis Edson Waterman makes the first practical fountain pen. Ink is fed to the nib by capillary action.
- U.S. manufacturer George Eastman and U.S. inventor William H. Walker invent roll film. Negative images are still captured on paper and are then reproduced on glass.

Transportation

- H. J. Lawson patents the first ladies' bicycle with no crossbar, in Britain.
- Streetcars supplied with electricity from overhead wires appear in Germany.

AUGUST

9 French army engineers Charles Renard and Arthur Krebs fly their dirigible *La France* on an 8-km/5 mi-circular flight. It is the first dirigible capable of being steered in any direction and of returning to its point of departure.

ARTS AND IDEAS

Architecture

- The Spanish architect Antoni Gaudí begins work on the Sagrada Familia Church in Barcelona, Spain, an extravagant and idiosyncratic building that is still unfinished at his death in 1926.
- The Washington Monument, Washington, D.C., is completed. At 169 m/555 ft high it is the world's tallest structure.

AUGUST

5 Construction begins on the Statue of Liberty on Bedloe's Island in New York harbor, New York.

Arts

- "Les Vingt"/"The Twenty," an exhibiting society, is founded by the Belgian artist James Ensor in Brussels. It is supported by artists such as the French painters Georges Seurat, Paul Gauguin, Paul Cézanne, and by the Dutch painter Vincent van Gogh. The society ceases to exhibit in 1894.
- The English artist Edward Burne-Jones paints *King Cophetua and the Beggar Maid*.
- The French artist Edgar Degas paints *Laundresses*.
- The French artist Georges Seurat paints *Bathers at Asnières*.
- The French artist Gustave Moreau paints *Chimeras*.
- The French artist Pierre-Auguste Renoir paints *Umbrellas*.

- The U.S. artist John Singer Sargent paints *Madame X (Madame Gautreau)*.
- The U.S. artist William Merritt Chase paints *Sunlight and Shadow*.
- The U.S. artist Winslow Homer paints *The Life Line*.

Literature and Language

- The first volume of the *Oxford English Dictionary*, edited by the English lexicographer James Murray, is published. The last volume of this first edition appears in 1928.
- The French writer Charles-Marie-René Leconte de Lisle publishes his poetry collection *Poèmes tragiques/Tragic Poems*.
- The French writer Joris Karl Huysmans publishes his novel *A Rebours/Against the Grain*.
- The French writer Paul Verlaine publishes his poetry collection *Jadis et naguère/Yesteryear and Yesterday*. He also publishes *Les Poètes maudits/The Accursed Poets*, studies of six poets including Rimbaud and Mallarmé.
- The Greek-born French writer Jean Moréas publishes his poetry collection *Les Syrtes*.
- The Russian writer Anton Chekhov publishes *Skazki Melpomeny/Tales of Melpomene*, his first collection of short stories.
- The Russian writer Leo Tolstoy publishes *Ispoved/A Confession*, an account of the development of his religious beliefs.
- The Swedish writer Johan August Strindberg publishes his short story collection *Giftas/Marriage*.
- The Swiss writer Conrad Ferdinand Meyer publishes his novella *Die Hochzeit des Mönchs/The Monk's Wedding*.
- The U.S. writer and historian Henry Brooks Adams publishes his novel *Esther*.
- The U.S. writer Henry James publishes his essay "The Art of Fiction" in *Longman's Magazine*.
- The U.S. writer Joel Chandler Harris publishes *Mingo and Other Sketches in Black and White*, a collection of tales.
- The U.S. writer Mark Twain publishes his novel *The Adventures of Huckleberry Finn*.

Music

- Austrian composer Josef Anton Bruckner completes his *Te Deum* for chorus and orchestra.
- Bohemian composer Antonín Dvořák completes his choral work *Svatebni kosile/The Specter's Bride*.
- British composers James Molloy and C. Clifton Bingham write the song "Love's Old Sweet Song."
- German composer Richard Strauss completes his Symphony No. 2.
- The Austrian composer Gustav Mahler completes his song cycle *Lieder eines fahrenden Gesellen/Songs of a Wayfarer*, which he revises in 1896.
- The comic opera *Princess Ida, or Castle Adamant*, by the English writer William Schwenk Gilbert and the English composer Arthur Seymour Sullivan, is first performed in London, England.
- The opera *Canterbury Pilgrims* by the Irish composer Charles Villiers Stanford is first performed, in London, England. It is based on the *Canterbury Tales* by the 14th-century English poet Geoffrey Chaucer.

- The opera *Manon* by the French composer Jules Massenet is first performed, in Paris, France. It is based on the novel *Manon Lescaut* by the French writer Antoine-François Prévost d'Exiles, published in 1731.
- The opera *Mazeppa* by the Russian composer Pyotr Ilyich Tchaikovsky is first performed, in Moscow, Russia.
- U.S. composer Edward MacDowell completes his *Forest Idyls* for piano.
- U.S. composer I. Canning writes the song "Rock-a-bye Baby."

Thought and Scholarship

- The American Historical Association is founded, indicating the growing importance of historical writing in the post-Civil War era.
- U.S. history teachers found the American Historical Association in Saratoga Springs, New York.
- The English social scientist Herbert Spencer publishes *The Man versus the State*.
- The Fabian Society, an association of intellectual British socialists, is founded.

SOCIETY

Education

- Temple University is founded in Philadelphia, Pennsylvania.
- The University of North Dakota is founded at Grand Forks, North Dakota.

OCTOBER

6 The U.S. Naval War College, intended to provide naval officers with postgraduate training in science, law, and warfare, opens in Newport, Rhode Island.

Everyday Life

- Quaker Oats, the first commercially available breakfast cereal, is launched in the United States in prefilled packages.
- The Young Women's Christian Association (YWCA) in Boston, Massachusetts, opens its first building, which includes a gymnasium.
- U.S. entrepreneur John Mayenberg patents evaporated milk in the United States.
- Washington, D.C., plays host to an international conference resulting in the adoption of worldwide standard time, based on a prime meridian running through the British Royal Observatory at Greenwich, England.

MARCH

21 Labor unions in France are legalized.

Media and Communication

- *Le Matin* newspaper is launched in France.
- The newspaper *Svenska Dagbladet* is launched in Stockholm, Sweden.

Sports

- In a precursor to baseball's World Series, the Providence Grays of the National League defeats the New York Metropolitan Club of the American Association 2–1.
- Moses Fleetwood Walker becomes the first black American major league baseball player when he makes his American Association league debut for the Toledo Blue Stockings.

- Scotland wins the first soccer British International Championship, the world's oldest international soccer championship.
- The Cresta toboggan run is built at St. Moritz, Switzerland.

JULY

5–19　At the Wimbledon tennis championships in London, England, the British player Maud Watson wins the first ever women's singles event, and James and William Renshaw, also from Britain, win the first ever men's doubles.

30　The U.S. boxer Jack Dempsey beats fellow countryman George Fulljames in New York, New York, to win the world middleweight boxing championship. This is the first world title to be fought with padded gloves and conducted under the Queensberry rules.

BIRTHS & DEATHS

- Damon Runyon, U.S. short-story writer and journalist who wrote *Guys and Dolls*, born in Manhattan, Kansas (–1946).

JANUARY

19　Ivan Maysky, Russian diplomat, negotiator at the Yalta and Potsdam conferences, born (–1975).

26　Edward Sapir, German-born U.S. linguist and anthropologist, born in Lauenburg, Pomerania, Germany (–1939).

MARCH

24　François Mignet, French historian and archivist, dies in Paris, France (87).

31　Sean O'Casey, Irish playwright whose plays depict the reality of Dublin's slums, born in Dublin, Ireland (–1964).

APRIL

4　Yamamoto Isoroku, Japanese naval officer who planned and carried out the attack on Pearl Harbor in 1941, born in Nagaoka, Japan (–1943).

7　Bronislaw Malinowski, Polish-born British anthropologist who founded the study of social anthropology in Britain, born in Krakow, Poland (–1942).

MAY

8　Harry S. Truman, thirty-third president of the United States 1945–53, a Democrat, born in Lamar, Missouri (–1972).

13　Cyrus Hall McCormick, U.S. industrialist who invented the first practical reaper, dies in Chicago, Illinois (75).

28　Eduard Beneš, Bohemian statesman and president 1935–38, 1941–45 in exile, and 1946–48, one of the founders of the state of Czechoslovakia, born in Kozlany, Bohemia (–1948).

JUNE

13　Etienne Gilson, French Christian philosopher and international scholar of medieval thought, born in Paris, France (–1978).

18　Edouard Daladier, French premier in 1933, 1934, and 1938–40, who signed the Munich Agreement of 1938 allowing Hitler to occupy Czechoslovakia unopposed, born in Carpentras, France (–1970).

JULY

6　Gregor Mendel, Austrian monk and botanist who laid the mathematical foundations of genetics, dies in Brünn, Austro-Hungarian Empire (61).

12　Amedeo Modigliani, Italian painter and sculptor, born in Livorno, Italy (–1920).

SEPTEMBER

24　Ismet Inönü, Turkish statesman, president of Turkey 1939–46 and in three coalition governments 1961–65, born in Smyrna, Ottoman Empire (now Izmir, Turkey) (–1973).

OCTOBER

11　Eleanor Roosevelt, United Nations diplomat and wife of U.S. president Franklin Delano Roosevelt, born in New York, New York (–1962).

NOVEMBER

8　Hermann Rorschach, Swiss psychiatrist who developed the inkblot test that bears his name, born in Zürich, Switzerland (–1922).

DECEMBER

30　Hideki Tojo, Prime Minister of Japan during most of World War II 1941–44, born in Tokyo, Japan (–1948).

1885

POLITICS, GOVERNMENT, AND ECONOMICS

Business and Economics

- The American Bell Telephone Company charters American Telephone and Telegraph Company (AT&T) to build and operate a long-distance telephone service in the United States.
- The U.S. games manufacturer Parker Brothers is founded in Salem, Massachusetts, by George Swinerton Parker.
- Steel production stands at 2.4 million tons in Britain, 1.2 million tons in Germany, and 0.5 million tons in France.
- U.S. economists found the American Economic Association at Saratoga Springs, New York.

FEBRUARY
12 The German East Africa Company is chartered to exploit eastern Africa.

Colonization

- Britain proclaims a protectorate in Southern New Guinea, following German annexation of the north part of the island.

JANUARY
9 Spain proclaims a protectorate in Spanish Guinea.

FEBRUARY
5 The Congo State is established as a personal possession of King Leopold II of Belgium.
6 Italy occupies Massawa, Eritrea, in a continuation of its imperial expansion in East Africa.
25 Germany annexes Tanganyika and Zanzibar, forming German East Africa and continuing its expansion into East Africa.

MARCH
3 Britain proclaims a protectorate in North Bechuanaland, ending the Boer Stellaland Republic.

APRIL
26 Britain occupies Port Hamilton, Korea, remaining in possession until February 1887.

MAY
17 Germany annexes Northern New Guinea and the Bismarck Archipelago.

JUNE
5 The British proclaim a protectorate in the Niger River region of West Africa.

DECEMBER
17 France acquires control of Madagascar's foreign relations.

Politics and Government

- The Belgian Labor Party is founded with demands for universal suffrage.

JANUARY
22 Germany and the newly independent South African Republic sign a treaty of friendship.
26 The Sudanese followers of the dervish Mahdi (prophet) Mohammed Ahmed of Dongola capture the city of Khartoum, capital of Anglo-Egyptian Sudan, massacring the inhabitants and the occupying Anglo-Egyptian forces, and killing the Anglo-Egyptian commander, British general Charles Gordon.
28 A British relief force under Sir Garnet Wolseley arrives at Khartoum, Sudan, and the Sudan is evacuated.

FEBRUARY
25 The U.S. Congress passes legislation prohibiting western ranchers from erecting fences on public lands.
26 The U.S. Congress passes the Contract Labor Law (Foran Act), outlawing foreign contract labor.

MARCH
4 Grover Cleveland is inaugurated 22nd president of the United States.
30 The Russian occupation of Penjdeh, Afghanistan, provokes a crisis in Anglo-Russian relations.
31 Jules Ferry's ministry falls in France following a defeat at Langson, near Hanoi, in Tonkin, in the French war with China over piracy and political domination of Southeast Asia.

APRIL
18 China and Japan agree to withdraw troops from Korea under the Convention of Tientsin, following tension over Korea's status as a Chinese vassal.

JUNE
9 British prime minister William Ewart Gladstone resigns when his government, already weakened by the fall of Khartoum and the Irish Question, is defeated in a budget to tax beers and spirits.
9 The Treaty of Tientsin between France and China recognizes the French protectorate of Annam, in Southeast Asia.
21 The dervish Mahdi (prophet) Mohammed Ahmed of Dongola dies, probably of typhoid, in Omdurman, Sudan, and is succeeded by his son Abdullah.

25 Robert Cecil, Lord Salisbury, forms a Conservative ministry in Britain, with himself taking the position of foreign secretary as well as prime minister, Michael Hicks Beach as chancellor of the Exchequer, and Richard Cross as home secretary.

JULY

30 The dervishes take Kassala in the Sudan, extending their control to all Sudan except its Red Sea forts.

AUGUST

14 Lord Ashbourne's Act authorizes loans to enable Irish tenants to buy holdings on easy terms.

14 The first secretary of state for Scotland, the Duke of Richmond, is appointed.

SEPTEMBER

10 Britain makes a compromise settlement with Russia over the Afghanistan frontier.

18 A coup puts the Ottoman province of Eastern Rumelia under Bulgarian rule.

NOVEMBER

11 The boundary between Liberia and the British protectorate of Sierra Leone is defined.

13 Serbia invades Bulgaria following the union of Bulgaria and former Ottoman province of Eastern Rumelia, to force compensation for the territorial gains of its neighbor.

16 Canadian rebel Louis Riel is hanged after leading a second rebellion against the federal government.

17 The Serbs are defeated at Slivnitza, Bulgaria, by Bulgarian forces, but Austrian intervention saves Serbia from invasion.

21 The Irish nationalist leader Charles Stewart Parnell calls on the Irish in Britain to vote Conservative, believing them to be more sympathetic to Home Rule.

27 The Bulgarians take Pirot, Serbia, but are nevertheless forced to withdraw from Serbia in the war between the two.

28 British troops occupy Mandalay, Burma.

DECEMBER

19 Papal arbitration finds for Spain in the German–Spanish dispute over the Pacific Caroline Islands.

19 The conservative Republican François-Paul-Jules Grévy is reelected president of France.

SCIENCE, TECHNOLOGY, AND MEDICINE

Agriculture

- German bacteriologist Friedrich August Johannes Löffler discovers the microorganisms responsible for swine erysipelas and swine plague.
- French horticulturist Pierre-Marie-Alexis Millardet develops Bordeaux Mixture, a blend of copper sulfate and hydrated lime. The first successful fungicide, it rapidly achieves worldwide usage.

Ecology

- Banff National Park is established in Canada, the country's first national park.

Exploration

- Ney Elias crosses the Pamirs plateau in central Asia, from east to west.

Health and Medicine

- Polish surgeon Johannes von Mikulicz-Radecki is the first to suture a perforated gastric ulcer.
- U.S. surgeon William West Grant performs the first successful appendectomy in the United States, at Davenport, Iowa.
- Scottish physician Thomas Lauder Brunton publishes *A Textbook of Pharmacology, Therapeutics, and Materia Medica*, the first thorough treatise on pharmacology.

JULY

6 French chemist and microbiologist Louis Pasteur develops a vaccine against rabies and uses it to save the life of a young boy, Joseph Meister, who has been bitten by a rabid dog.

Science

- Austrian chemist Carl Auer Freiherr von Welsbach discovers the rare-earth elements neodymium (atomic no. 60) and praseodymium (atomic no. 59).
- English anthropologist and eugenicist Francis Galton proves the permanence and individuality of fingerprints, and devises an identification system based on them.
- Italian physicist Galileo Ferraris develops a rotating magnetic field by placing electromagnets at right angles to one another and supplying them with alternating current 90° out of phase. The principle is used in self-starting electric motors and polyphase motors.
- U.S. physicist Henry Augustus Rowland invents the concave diffraction grating, in which 20,000 lines to the inch are engraved on spherical concave mirrored surfaces. The grating revolutionizes spectrometry by dispersing light and permitting spectral lines to be focused.

July 1885–90 British astronomer David Gill photographs over 450,000 stars of 11th magnitude or brighter in the southern hemisphere, in southern Africa. The plates are cataloged by Dutch astronomer Jacobus Cornelius Kapteyn to produce the Cape Photographic Durchmusterung star catalog in 1900.

Technology

- Austrian physicist Ernst Mach uses the light from sparks to take high-speed photographs of bullets in flight.
- French chemist Eugène Turpin invents the first bursting charge artillery shell which explodes on impact.
- French inventor Etienne Lenoir develops the electrical spark plug.

- The development of permanent ink gives a huge boost to typewriter sales.
- The first refuse incinerator in the United States begins operating at Governors Island, New York, New York.
- The U.S. firm Singer demonstrates the first electric sewing machine, at the Philadelphia Electric Exhibition.
- U.S. inventor Tolbert Lanston invents the Monotype typesetting machine. Type is cast in individual letters, using a 120-key keyboard.
- U.S. manufacturer George Eastman patents a machine for manufacturing coated photographic paper in long continuous rolls. It spurs on the development of cameras that are easy to use.

MAY

- Serbian-born U.S. inventor Nikola Tesla sells his polyphase system of alternating current (AC) dynamos, transformers, and motors to U.S. industrialist George Westinghouse, who begins a power struggle to establish alternating current (AC) technology over U.S. inventor Thomas Alva Edison's direct current (DC) systems.

Transportation

- British inventor John Starley builds the "Rover" safety bicycle, the forerunner of modern bicycles. In the same year, French engineer G. Juzan designs the "bicyclette moderne," a bicycle with equal-sized wheels and a chain-driven rear wheel.
- German mechanical engineers Gottlieb Daimler and Wilhelm Maybach develop a successful lightweight high-speed internal combustion gasoline engine, and fit it to a bicycle to create the prototype of the present-day motorcycle.

JANUARY

26 German mechanical engineer Karl Friedrich Benz patents a three-wheeled vehicle powered by a two-cycle, single-cylinder internal combustion engine, pioneering the development of the automobile. His vehicle achieves a speed of 14.4 kph/9 mph.

NOVEMBER

7 The Canadian Pacific Railroad is completed. Begun in 1867, it is Canada's first transcontinental railroad, and one of the longest in the world.
28 The Cape Railway reaches Kimberley, Cape Colony, in southern Africa.

ARTS AND IDEAS

Architecture

- The Casa Vincens, near Barcelona in Spain, designed by the Spanish architect Antonio Gaudí, is completed.
- The Home Insurance Building in Chicago, Illinois, designed by the U.S. architect William Le Baron Jenney, is completed (later demolished). This is one of the first successful attempts to use an iron framework to support a building, and is considered the first true skyscraper.
- The Reliance Building in Chicago, Illinois, designed by the U.S. architect Daniel Hudson Burnham, is completed.

- The Rijksmuseum (national art gallery) in Amsterdam, the Netherlands, designed by the Dutch architect Petrus Josephus Hubertus Cuyper, is completed.

Arts

c. 1885 The French artist Auguste Rodin sculpts *Old Woman and Winter (The Old Courtesan)* and *Meditation*.
c. 1885 The U.S. artist Albert Pinkham Ryder paints *Jonah*.
- The Dutch artist Vincent van Gogh paints *The Potato Eaters*.
- The French artist Auguste Rodin sculpts *The Burghers of Calais*.
- The French artist Edgar Degas paints *Woman Drying Her Feet*.
- The French artist Gustave Moreau paints *The Unicorns*.
- The U.S. artist Mary Cassatt paints *Lady at the Teatable*.
- The U.S. artist William Michael Harnett paints *After the Hunt*.
- The French historian and critic Hippolyte-Adolphe Taine publishes *La Philosophie de l'art/The Philosophy of Art*.
- The U.S. artist James Abbot McNeill Whistler publishes *The Ten O'Clock Lectures*, which contains the fullest expression of his views on art.

Literature and Language

- Former American Civil War general and president Ulysses S. Grant publishes his *Personal Memoirs*; it becomes a best seller.
- The English explorer and translator Richard Burton publishes the first volume of *The Arabian Nights*, translations of a collection of Arabic tales. The final volume appears in 1888.
- The English writer and critic Walter Horatio Pater publishes his novel *Marius the Epicurean*.
- The English writer George Meredith publishes his novel *Diana of the Crossways*.
- The English writer (Henry) Rider Haggard publishes his adventure novel *King Solomon's Mines*.
- The French writer Emile Zola publishes his novel *Germinal*, one of the *Les Rougon–Macquart* series.
- The French writer Guy de Maupassant publishes his novel *Bel-Ami/Fair Friend*.
- The French writer Jules Laforgue publishes his poetry collection *L'Imitation de Notre-Dame la Lune/The Imitation of Our Lady the Moon*.
- The French writer Paul-Charles-Joseph Bourget publishes his novel *Cruelle Enigme/Cruel Enigma*.
- The U.S. writer William Dean Howells publishes his novel *The Rise of Silas Lapham*.

Music

- Bohemian composer Antonín Dvořák completes his Symphony No. 7 (once classified as No. 2).
- French composer César Franck completes his orchestral work *Symphonic Variations*.
- German composer Johannes Brahms completes his Symphony No. 4.

- Hungarian composer Franz Liszt completes his piano works *Mephistowaltzer/Mephisto Waltz* No. 3 and No. 4 and the last of his *19 Hungarian Rhapsodies*. The first was completed in 1846.
- Russian composer Peter Illyich Tchaikovsky completes his symphonic fantasy *The Manfred Symphony*.
- The American Opera Company is formed in New York, New York.
- The comic opera *The Mikado, or The Town of Titipu* by the English writer William Schwenk Gilbert and the English composer Arthur Seymour Sullivan is first performed, at the Savoy Theatre in London, England.
- U.S. composer Edward MacDowell completes his Piano Concerto No. 2.

Theater and Dance

- The play *La Parisienne/The Parisienne*, by the French dramatist Henry-François Becque, is first performed in Paris, France.
- The play *Vildanden/The Wild Duck*, and the verse play *Brand*, by the Norwegian dramatist Henrik Johan Ibsen,

are first performed in Christiania (now Oslo), Norway. *Brand* was written in 1886.

Thought and Scholarship

- The French historian Albert Sorel publishes the first volume of his eight-volume *L'Europe et la révolution/Europe and the French Revolution*. The last volume appears in 1904.
- The second volume of *Das Kapital/Capital* by the German political philosopher Karl Marx is published posthumously.
- The U.S. philosopher Josiah Royce publishes *Religious Aspects of Philosophy*.
- The English philosopher Bernard Bosanquet publishes *Knowledge and Reality*.
- The English theologian James Martineau publishes *Types of Ethical Theory*.
- U.S. historian John Fiske publishes *The Idea of God as Affected by Modern Knowledge*.

BIRTHS & DEATHS

JANUARY
21 Duncan Grant, Scottish innovative postimpressionist painter and designer, born in Rothiemurchus, Inverness, Scotland (–1978).
26 Charles George Gordon ("Chinese Gordon"), British general who suppressed rebellions in China, is killed defending Khartoum, Sudan (51).

FEBRUARY
7 Sinclair Lewis, U.S. novelist and social critic, born in Sauk Center, Minnesota (–1951).
9 Alban Berg, Austrian composer, born in Vienna, Austria (–1935).
24 Chester W. Nimitz, U.S. commander in chief of the Pacific Fleet and all land and sea forces in the area during World War II, born in Fredericksburg, Texas (–1966).

MARCH
6 Ring Lardner, U.S. short-story writer, satirist, and sportswriter, born in Niles, Michigan (–1933).
9 Tamara Karsavina, Anglo-Russian ballerina who partnered Nijinsky in Michel Fokine's avant-garde ballets, born in St. Petersburg, Russia (–1978).
11 Malcolm Campbell, English car and motorboat speed-record holder, born in Chislehurst, Kent, England (–1948).

APRIL
13 György S. von Lukács, Hungarian Marxist philosopher, author, and literary critic, born in Budapest, Hungary (–1971).

MAY
2 Victor Hugo, French romantic novelist, dies in Paris, France (83).
13 Friedrich Henle, German pathologist who pioneered histology, dies in Göttingen, Germany (75).
14 Otto Klemperer, German conductor and composer, born in Breslau, Germany (–1973).
20 Faisal I, King of Iraq 1921–33 and promoter of pan-Arab nationalism, born in Mecca, Saudi Arabia (–1933).

JULY
4 Louis B. Mayer, U.S. film executive, head of Metro-Goldwyn-Mayer (MGM) 1924–48, born in Minsk, Russia (–1957).
8 Ernest Bloch, German Marxist philosopher who developed the "philosophy of hope," born in Ludwigshafen, Germany (–1977).
23 Ulysses S. Grant, U.S. general who commanded the Union army during the last two years of the American Civil War and president 1863–1877, dies in Mt. McGregor, New York (63).

AUGUST
26 Jules Romains, French novelist, dramatist, and poet, a founder of the literary movement *Unanimisme*, born in St.-Julien-Chapteuil, France (–1972).

SEPTEMBER
11 D(avid) H(erbert) Lawrence, English poet and novelist, author of the controversial *Lady Chatterley's*

Lover, born in Eastwood, Nottinghamshire, England (–1930).

OCTOBER
7 Niels Bohr, Danish physicist who developed the science of quantum mechanics, born in Copenhagen, Denmark (–1962).
11 François Mauriac, French novelist and playwright, born in Bordeaux, France (–1970).
30 Ezra Pound, U.S. poet and literary critic, born in Hailey, Idaho (–1972).

NOVEMBER
11 George S. Patton, U.S. general during World War II, born in San Gabriel, California (–1945).
16 Louis Riel, Canadian Métis leader who led an uprising against the Canadian government, dies in Assiniboia, Canada (41).
20 Albert Kesselring, German field marshal and commander in chief (south) of the German armed forces 1941–44, born in Marktstedt, Bavaria, Germany (–1960).
25 U.S. vice president Thomas A. Hendricks dies (66), and is buried in Indianapolis, Indiana.

DECEMBER
8 William Henry Vanderbilt, U.S. railroad magnate and philanthropist, dies in New York, New York (64).

SOCIETY

Education

- Arizona State University is founded in Tempe, Arizona.
- Bryn Mawr College (for women) is founded in Bryn Mawr, Pennsylvania.
- Stanford University (officially the Leland Stanford Junior University) is founded in Stanford, California.
- The Georgia Institute of Technology is founded in Atlanta, Georgia.
- The University of Arizona is founded in Tucson, Arizona.

Everyday Life

- Allen Dodworth publishes *Dancing and Its Relation to Education and Social Life*, a manual about ballroom dancing.
- British soap manufacturer William Lever launches Sunlight soap.
- Pope Leo XIII excommunicates the Knights of Labor, the U.S. labor organization, but later withdraws his censure.
- William Jacob launches his brand of cream crackers, in Ireland.

JANUARY
24 The New Orleans Exposition (World's Fair) opens to visitors.

MARCH
3 The U.S. Post Office introduces special delivery service.

Media and Communication

- The magazine *Good Housekeeping* begins publication in Springfield, Massachusetts.

Sports

- The British golfer Allan MacFie wins the first British Amateur Championship, at Hoylake, England.
- The English jockey Fred Archer rides a record 246 winners in a season, a total which is not exceeded until 1933 when Gordon Richards rides 259 winners.
- The first black U.S. baseball team, the Cuban Giants, is formed, at Long Island, New York. They tour the country playing against white teams.
- The U.S. runner Laurence "Lon" Myers runs 805 m/ 880 yds in 1 minute 55.4 seconds, his seventh world record at this distance since 1880 at a track meeting in the United States.

1886

POLITICS, GOVERNMENT, AND ECONOMICS

Business and Economics

MAY
1 The Japanese foreign minister calls a conference in Tokyo, Japan, but fails to abolish extraterritorial concessions.

JULY
10 The British Royal Niger Company is chartered, giving official recognition to the conglomerate of merchants exploiting the region.

Colonization

JANUARY
1 Britain annexes Upper Burma, though guerrilla warfare continues.
13 Lagos becomes a British colony, separate from Nigeria.

Human Rights

NOVEMBER
20 The "Plan of Campaign" drawn up by the Irish nationalists William O'Brien and John Dillon calls on Irish tenants to organize themselves in their efforts to secure better conditions.

Politics and Government

- The first Indian National Congress meets, but lacks Muslim support.
- The U.S. Supreme Court, in *Wabash, St Louis, and Pacific Railway Company v. Illinois*, restricts the authority of the states to regulate railroads.

JANUARY

7   Charles Freycinet forms a broadly based Radical ministry in France in opposition to the Conservatives, who have made electoral gains.

7   General Georges Boulanger, who voices the French desire for revenge on Germany for the Franco-Prussian War, becomes war minister in Charles Freycinet's cabinet.

19 The death of Vice President Thomas A. Hendricks in November 1885 prompts the U.S. Congress to pass the Presidential Succession Act. It stipulates that in the event of the death, resignation, or incapacitation of the president or vice president, the office will be filled by cabinet officers in the order in which the cabinet offices were created.

FEBRUARY

12 The Radical British member of Parliament Charles Dilke appears as co-respondent in a sensational divorce suit.

MARCH

3   The Peace of Bucharest ends the war between Serbia and Bulgaria on the basis of the status quo.

APRIL

5   Abdul Hamid II, the Ottoman sultan, appoints Alexander of Bulgaria governor of Eastern Rumelia in a compromise that keeps the area under Ottoman sovereignty but places it under Bulgarian rule.

8   The British prime minister William Ewart Gladstone introduces a Home Rule Bill for Ireland.

26 The major powers send an ultimatum to Greece demanding that it stop supporting the revolution in Eastern Rumelia and halt its plans for war with the Ottoman Empire.

27 The French explorer Pierre de Brazza is appointed commissioner general of the French Congo.

MAY

May–June The European powers blockade Greece, forcing the status quo to be maintained in the disputed former Ottoman province of Eastern Rumelia.

4   Seven police officers are killed and 60 wounded by a bomb thrown in Haymarket Square, Chicago, Illinois, during a demonstration against the police killing of a striking worker outside the McCormick Harvesting Machine Co. on May 3. Several supposedly anarchist labor leaders are arrested and the incident sets off a wave of antilabor union hysteria in the United States.

10 In *Yick Wo v. Hopkins*, the U.S. Congress rules that aliens are persons in the eyes of the U.S. Constitution and are therefore protected by U.S. law.

JUNE

8   British prime minister William Ewart Gladstone's Liberal government is defeated on the second reading of the Irish Home Rule Bill, with 93 Liberals, including John Bright, Joseph Chamberlain, and the Marquess of Hartington voting with the opposition.

19–June 26, 1893 Eight anarchists go on trial in Chicago, Illinois, for allegedly conspiring in the bombing of Haymarket Square in May. All are found guilty on August 20; four are hung on November 11; one commits suicide in prison and the last three are pardoned on June 26, 1893 by Illinois governor John Peter Altgeld.

23 The Bonaparte and Orléans families are banished from France.

JULY

14 An Anglo-German agreement defines the frontiers of the Gold Coast and Togoland.

24 An Anglo-Chinese agreement recognizes Britain's position in Burma, its influence having been achieved by force.

26 British prime minister Robert Cecil, Lord Salisbury, forms a Conservative government following the party's electoral victory.

AUGUST

20–21 A military coup is effected in Sofia, Bulgaria, by discontented pro-Russian army officers.

SEPTEMBER

4   King Alexander of Bulgaria abdicates following the coup and Stefan Nikolov Stambulov becomes regent.

OCTOBER

11–16 The first congress of the French Federation of Labor Unions meets in Lyon, France.

NOVEMBER

1   An Anglo-German agreement delimits Britain's and Germany's respective spheres of influence in East Africa.

2   In the U.S. Congressional elections, the Republicans retain a narrow majority in the Senate (39–37), while the Democrats retain control of the House (169–152).

10 Prince Waldemar of Denmark is elected king of Bulgaria, but refuses to serve because he lacks the support of Czar Alexander III of Russia.

DECEMBER

12 A conflict begins in the German Reichstag (legislative assembly) over the army bill, with the Liberals attempting to secure greater control over government spending.

15 René Goblet forms a ministry in France following the fall of Charles Freycinet.

23 The British chancellor of the Exchequer Lord Randolph Churchill resigns because of faltering support in the cabinet over his budget calling for economies in the army and navy.

30 A German–Portuguese agreement is made over the boundaries between Angola and German southwestern African territories.

SCIENCE, TECHNOLOGY, AND MEDICINE

Agriculture

December 1886–96 Blizzards and overgrazing in the west of the United States reduce livestock populations by 60%.

Ecology

•   Gold is discovered at Witwatersrand reef, Transvaal, sparking a gold rush.

Health and Medicine

- German psychiatrist Richard Krafft–Ebing publishes *Psychopathia Sexualis*, the first study of abnormal sexual practices in humans.
- German surgeon Ernst Gustav Benjamin von Bergmann introduces steam sterilization of surgical instruments and dressings, in Berlin, Germany.
- U.S. pharmaceutical company Johnson and Johnson produces the first individually wrapped ready-to-use sterile surgical dressings.
- The synthetic drugs pyramidon (aminopyrine) and antifebrin are discovered.
- Acetanilide is used to relieve fever. Later it is discovered to relieve pain as well and is used as an alternative to aspirin.

Science

- Austrian chemist Carl Auer Freiherr von Welsbach invents the gas mantle, which greatly increases the light given out by gas lanterns.
- French chemist Eugène-Anatole Demarçay discovers the rare-earth metal europium (atomic no. 63), named for Europe.
- French chemist Henri Moissan isolates the highly reactive halogen element fluorine (atomic no. 9).
- French chemist Paul-Emile Lecoq de Boisbaudran discovers the rare-earth element dysprosium (atomic no. 66) and obtains an almost pure sample of the rare-earth element gadolinium (atomic no. 64).
- German biologist August Friedrich Leopold Weismann states that reproductive cells, or "germ plasm" cells, remain unchanged from generation to generation and that they contain some hereditary substance, which is now known as chromosomes, DNA, and genes.
- German chemist Clemens Alexander Winkler discovers germanium (atomic no. 32). It is the third element to be discovered which had been predicted by Dmitri Mendeleyev on the basis of his periodic table.
- Swedish chemist Svante August Arrhenius introduces the idea that acids are substances that disassociate in water to yield hydrogen ions (H+) and that bases are substances that disassociate to yield hydroxide ions (OH–), thus explaining the properties of acids and bases through their ability to yield ions.
- U.S. astronomer and physicist Samuel Pierpont Langley begins the first systematic aerodynamic research. He measures lift and drag on models of wings and other objects, which he attaches to a counterweighted beam, mounted on a pivot, that may be rotated at a speed of up to 112 kph/70 mph.
- U.S. chemist Charles Martin Hall and French chemist Paul-Louis-Toussaint Héroult, working independently, each develop a method for the production of aluminum by the electrolysis of aluminum oxide. The process reduces the price of the metal dramatically and brings it into widespread use.

Technology

- English inventor Thomas Crapper invents the modern flush toilet, with a water reserve tank placed a good

height above the bowl, a chain and lever system to discharge the water and expel and dilute the material in the bowl, and a U-bend in the pipe leading to the sewer system so that the water in the bowl is always clean.
- The French army is equipped with the Lebel rifle, which uses smokeless powder.
- U.S. inventors Charles Sumner Tainter and Chichester A. Bell improve Edison's tinfoil phonograph cylinder and rigid stylus by patenting a wax-coated cardboard cylinder and flexible stylus.
- U.S. inventors Chichester Bell and Charles Tainter patent the Graphophone in the United States, the first recording machine able to successfully reproduce music.

July

3   The *New York Tribune* is the first newspaper to put into operation the linotype machine, an automatic typesetting machine invented by Ottmar Mergenthaler in 1884.

Transportation

- Daniel Albone begins manufacturing the first tandem safety bicycle (a bicycle with wheels of equal size) in Britain.
- The British submarine *Nautilus* is launched. The first electric-powered submarine, it uses two electric 50-horsepower motors powered by a 100-cell storage battery to achieve a speed of 6 knots. The need for frequent battery recharges limits its range to 130 km/ 80 mi.
- The first oil tanker, the 90-m/300-ft-long German ship *Gluckhauf*, is launched. Oil is carried in tanks located along the hull. Previously, oil was transported in barrels on regular merchant ships. By 1900, 99% of oil carried by sea will be carried in such ships.
- The 7.2-km/4.5-mi Severn Tunnel opens in Britain.
- The Glasgow subway opens in Scotland, the second in the world after the London system in England.

ARTS AND IDEAS

Architecture

- Construction of the Niagara Falls hydroelectric installations begins in New York state.

October

28   The Statue of Liberty is dedicated on Liberty Island (Bedloe's Island) in New York Harbor, New York, by U.S. president Grover Cleveland. Designed by the French artist Frédéric-Auguste Bartholdi, on a frame built by Gustave Eiffel, it was presented to the United States by the French government to celebrate the 100th anniversary of U.S. independence. Made of copper, it is 46 m/152 ft high. Its full name is *Liberty Enlightening the World*.

Arts

- The Australian artist Tom Roberts paints *Bourke Street, Melbourne, 1885–86*.

- The eighth and last impressionist art exhibition is held in Paris, France.
- The English artist John Everett Millais paints *Bubbles*.
- The French artist Claude Monet paints *Lady with a Parasol*.
- The French artist Georges Seurat paints *Sunday on the Island of Grande Jatte*.
- The French artist Henri Rousseau paints *Carnival Evening*.
- The Norwegian artist Edvard Munch paints *The Sick Child*.
- The U.S. artist John Singer Sargent paints *Carnation, Lily, Lily, Rose*.
- The New English Art Club is founded by the U.S. artist James Abbot McNeill Whistler and the English artists Philip Wilson Steer and Walter Richard Sickert in London, England.

Literature and Language

- British explorer and translator Richard Burton translates the Arabian classic *The Perfumed Garden*.
- The collection of prose poems *Les Illuminations/ Illuminations*, by the French poet Arthur Rimbaud, is published by his friend and fellow poet Paul Verlaine. Rimbaud was thought to be dead, but was in fact living in Africa. The poems were written between 1872 and 1874 when he was aged 17–19.
- The English photographer Peter Henry Emerson publishes *Life and Landscape of the Norfolk Broads*.
- The English writer George Robert Gissing publishes his novel *Demos*.
- The English-born U.S. writer Frances Hodgson Burnett publishes her children's novel *Little Lord Fauntleroy*.
- The French writer and critic Melchior Vogüé publishes *Le Roman russe/The Russian Novel*, an influential critical study of contemporary Russian fiction.
- The French writer Pierre Loti publishes his novel *Pêcheur d'Islande/An Iceland Fisherman*.
- The Russian writer Leo Tolstoy publishes his novella *Smeat Ivana Ilyicha/The Death of Ivan Ilyich*.
- The Scottish writer Robert Louis Stevenson publishes his novels *The Strange Case of Dr Jekyll and Mr Hyde* and *Kidnapped*.
- The Swedish writer Johan August Strindberg publishes the first part of his autobiographical novel *Tjänstekvinnans son/The Son of a Servant*. The final part appears in 1887.
- The U.S. writer Henry James publishes his novels *The Bostonians* and *The Princess Casamassima*.
- The U.S. writer Sarah Orne Jewett publishes her short story "A White Heron."
- The U.S. writer William Dean Howells publishes his novel *Indian Summer*.

Music

- Bohemian composer Antonín Dvořák completes his second series of *Slavonic Dances* and his oratorio *St. Ludmila*.
- French composer Camille St.-Saëns completes his orchestral work *Carnaval des animaux/Carnival of the Animals*, though he forbids a performance of the work during his lifetime.

- German composer Johannes Brahms completes his Violin Sonatas No. 2 (Opus 100), his Piano Trio No. 3 (Opus 101), and his Cello Sonata No. 2 (Opus 99).
- German composer Richard Strauss completes his symphonic fantasy *Aus Italien*.

Theater and Dance

- The Russian writer Leo Tolstoy completes his play *Vlast tmy/The Power of Darkness*. It is first performed in Moscow, Russia, in 1895.

Thought and Scholarship

- The English jurist Albert Venn Dicey publishes *The Law of the Constitution*.
- The German philosopher Friedrich Nietzsche publishes *Jenseits von Gut und Böse/Beyond Good and Evil*.
- The Scottish-born U.S. industrialist and philanthropist Andrew Carnegie publishes *Triumphant Democracy*.
- The first English translation of the first volume of *Das Kapital*, by the German political philosopher Karl Marx, is published as *Capital*. The German edition appeared in 1867.
- The German theologian Adolph von Harnack publishes the first volume of his *Lehrbuch der Dogmengeschichte/ History of Dogma*. The last volume appears in 1890.

NOVEMBER

11 The British School of Archaeology opens in Athens, Greece.

SOCIETY

Everyday Life

- The first "Avon ladies," door-to-door saleswomen for the Avon Calling cosmetics company, start working in the United States.
- The food store Fauchon opens in Paris, France.
- U.S. hotelier Joel Cheek develops Maxwell House coffee, named for the establishment in Nashville, Tennessee, in which it is first served.
- U.S. physician Stanton Cott establishes The Neighborhood Guild in New York, New York, the nation's first settlement house.

MAY

4 The Knights of Labor, the first important national labor organization in the United States, riot in Chicago, Illinois.

8 John S. Pemberton invents the soft drink Coca-Cola in the United States: it goes on sale in Atlanta, Georgia, as "the intellectual beverage and temperance drink," and is claimed to be a cure for headaches and dyspepsia.

OCTOBER

- The tuxedo gets its name when tobacco heir Griswold Lorilland wears a short black dinner jacket with satin lapels in place of the traditional tails to the Tuxedo Club in New York, New York.

8   New York cigar maker Samuel Gompers establishes the American Federation of Labor (AFL), an alliance of national craft unions, at Columbus, Ohio.

Media and Communication

- The periodical *Cosmopolitan* is first published in Rochester, New York.

Religion

- U.S. Congregational minister Josiah Strong publishes *Our Country*, one of the core texts of the social gospel movement.

Sports

- Great Britain defeats the United States in the inaugural Westchester Cup polo match (originally called the International Cup) at Newport, Rhode Island; it is the first-ever polo international.
- John Collinson compiles the rules of bridge in Britain, after seeing the game played during a trip to Constantinople in the Ottoman Empire.
- Lexington becomes the champion U.S. race horse for the 16th time. He is sold to stud for a U.S. record price of $15,000 and becomes the greatest U.S. sire of the 19th century. Around 40% of his foals are winners, earning over $1 million in the United States and Canada.
- Ormonde, ridden by the English jockey Fred Archer, wins the Two Thousand Guineas, Epsom Derby, and St. Leger to become the fourth horse to capture the English Triple Crown.

BIRTHS & DEATHS

FEBRUARY
9   Winfield Scott Hancock, Union general during the American Civil War and Democratic presidential candidate in 1880, dies in Governor's Island, New York, New York (61).
27   Hugo Lafayette Black, U.S. associate justice of the Supreme Court 1931–71 who championed the Bill of Rights, born in Clay County, Alabama (–1971).

MARCH
1   Oskar Kokoschka, Austrian expressionist painter, writer, poet, and dramatist, born in Pöchlarn, Austria (–1980).
8   Edward Calvin Kendall, U.S. chemist who isolated cortisone and other hormones, born in South Norwalk, Connecticut (–1972).
27   Ludwig Mies van der Rohe, German-born U.S. architect who worked in the International Style, born in Aachen, Germany (–1969).
30   Stanisław Leśniewski, Polish mathematician and logician, born in Serpukhov, Russia (–1939).

APRIL
5   Frederick Lindemann Cherwell, Viscount Cherwell, English physicist who evolved a mathematical theory of aircraft spin, born in Baden-Baden, Germany (–1957).
27   Henry Hobson Richardson, U.S. architect who revived the Romanesque style in the United States, dies in Brookline, Massachusetts (47).

MAY
10   Karl Barth, Swiss theologian, born in Basel, Switzerland (–1968).

15   Emily Dickinson, U.S. poet, dies in Amherst, Massachusetts (55).
23   Leopold von Ranke, German historian, dies in Berlin, Germany (91).
26   Al Jolson (adopted name of Asa Yoelson), U.S. popular singer and comedian, star of *The Jazz Singer* (1927), the first feature film with synchronized speech and music, born in Srednike, Russia (–1950).
28   Jim Thorpe, U.S. professional football and baseball player, Olympic gold medallist in the pentathlon and decathlon, born near Prague, Indian Territory (later Oklahoma) (–1953).

JULY
23   Arthur Whitten Brown, British aviator who, with John W. Alcock, was the first person to fly nonstop across the Atlantic (1919), born in Glasgow, Scotland (–1948).
23   Salvador de Madariaga, Spanish author, historian, and diplomat involved in the League of Nations, born in La Coruña, Spain (–1978).
31   Franz (Ferencz) Liszt, Hungarian pianist and composer, dies in Bayreuth, Germany (74).

AUGUST
16   Ramakrishna, Hindu religious leader, dies in Calcutta, India (50).
20   Paul Tillyich, German-born U.S. theologian and philosopher, born in Starzeddel, Brandenburg, Germany (–1965).

SEPTEMBER
13   Robert Robinson, English chemist whose research into plant biology and alkaloids was important in the development of antimalarial drugs,

born near Chesterfield, Derbyshire, England (–1975).

OCTOBER
16   David Ben-Gurion, Zionist statesman and first prime minister of the newly formed state of Israel 1948–53 and 1955–63, born in Płońsk, Poland (–1973).

NOVEMBER
18   Chester A. Arthur, twenty-first president of the United States dies and is buried at Albany, New York. (56)
20   Karl von Frisch, German zoologist who discovered how bees communicate, born in Vienna, Austria (–1982).

DECEMBER
1   Rex Stout, U.S. mystery writer who created the character Nero Wolfe, born in Noblesville, Indiana (–1975).
9   Clarence Birdseye, U.S. businessman who invented a process for freezing packaged foods, born in New York, New York (–1956).
18   Ty Cobb (nicknamed "the Georgia Peach"), U.S. baseball player whose lifetime batting average (.367) remains unequaled, born in Narrows, Georgia (–1961).
18   Zhu De, Chinese military leader and founder of the Chinese communist army, born in I-lung, Szechwan Province, China (–1976).
25   Franz Rosenzweig, German-Jewish Existentialist theologian, born in Kassel, Germany (–1929).
26   John A. Logan, U.S. congressman and Union general during the Civil War, dies in Washington, D.C. (60).

- The first official world chess championships take place in London, England. Wilhelm Steinitz of Austria defeats J. H. Zukertort of Prussia.
- Yale University is the national college football champion, with an unprecedented 13–0 season record.

JULY

13 The British tennis player William Renshaw wins the men's singles at the Wimbledon championships for the sixth successive year, a feat that has never been equaled.

AUGUST

23 The English runner Walter George wins a professional 1.6-km/1-mi race against the Scottish runner William Cummings in a world record time of 4 minutes 12.75 seconds. His time will not be bettered by an amateur runner until 1915.

NOVEMBER

8 The English jockey Fred Archer, not long after becoming champion jockey for the thirteenth successive year, commits suicide at the age of 29.

1887

POLITICS, GOVERNMENT, AND ECONOMICS

Business and Economics

MAY

26 The British East Africa Company is chartered to coordinate trade and development in the region.

Colonization

- France organizes Cochin China, Cambodia, Annam, and Tonkin as the *Union Indo-Chinoise* (French Indochina).

JANUARY

20 New Zealand annexes the Kermadec Islands in the Pacific Ocean.

APRIL

4 The first colonial conference opens in London, England, allowing representatives from the British territories and dominions to meet.

JUNE

21 Britain annexes Zululand, blocking the attempt by Transvaal to gain a direct link with the coast.

OCTOBER

1 The frontier territory of Baluchistan, in which Britain has had influence, is united with the British possession of India.

NOVEMBER

16 An Anglo-French condominium is placed over the New Hebrides islands in the Pacific.

DECEMBER

1 Portugal secures the cession of the important port and commercial center Macao from China.

Politics and Government

- The Central American states, under the leadership of Guatemala, sign a treaty of amity and consider a draft federal constitution.
- The U.S. Congress passes the Edmunds–Tucker Act, stripping The Church of Jesus Christ of Latter-day Saints of its corporate charter. The legislation is precipitated by outcry at the Latter-day Saints endorsement of polygamy.

JANUARY

11 Chancellor Otto von Bismarck advocates a larger German army.
14 George Joachim Goschen is appointed chancellor of the Exchequer in Britain, in succession to Lord Randolph Churchill, and William Henry Smith is appointed leader of the House of Commons.
20 The U.S. Navy leases Pearl Harbor on the Hawaiian island of Oahu.

FEBRUARY

3 The U.S. Congress passes the Electoral Count Act, designed to prevent the sort of confusion that marred the 1876 presidential election. Individual states will now be responsible for determining their own electoral vote counts.
4 U.S. president Grover Cleveland signs the Interstate Commerce Act, establishing the Interstate Commerce Commission and prohibiting railroad pools.
8 The U.S. Congress passes the Dawes Severalty Act, designed to reform U.S. treatment of Native Americans. Rather than assigning vast tracts of land to whole groups, the new legislation disperses acreage to individual families to farm or ranch in the hope that

private proprietorship will render Natives more "American."

12 An Anglo-Italian agreement is signed for the purpose of maintaining the status quo in the Mediterranean region.

20 The Triple Alliance between Germany, Austria-Hungary, and Italy is renewed for a further three years.

MARCH

2 U.S. president Grover Cleveland signs the Hatch Act, providing for the creation of agricultural colleges in states with land-grant colleges.

20 A drastic Irish Crimes Act is introduced in the British Parliament, its passage being aided by articles in *The Times* on "Parnellism and Crime."

24 Austria-Hungary becomes a signatory to the Anglo-Italian agreement on maintaining the status quo in the Mediterranean region.

APRIL

20 Tension grows between France and Germany following the conviction in a German court of Schnaebele, a French frontier official, for espionage.

MAY

4 Spain supports the Anglo-Italian agreement of February 12 for maintaining the status quo in the Mediterranean region.

16 René Goblet's cabinet falls in France over demands for a more aggressive policy toward Germany following its treatment of the border official Schnaebele.

18 Maurice Rouvier forms a ministry in France from which Georges Boulanger is excluded, as increasing numbers of Republicans fear his potential power.

22 The British joint commissioner in Egypt, Sir Henry Drummond Wolff, signs a convention with Egypt by which Britain agrees to evacuate Egypt after three years, with the right to return if there are further disorders. The agreement is nullified by French opposition.

JUNE

17 A Liberal ministry under Jan Heemskerk reforms suffrage in the Netherlands, widening the franchise.

18 A secret German–Russian Reinsurance Treaty is signed to replace the expiring Three Emperors' Alliance (including Austria-Hungary), which Russia refuses to renew.

21 Queen Victoria's golden jubilee celebrates her fifty years as queen of the United Kingdom.

JULY

7 Bulgaria elects Prince Ferdinand of Saxe-Coburg as king, a candidate put forward by Russia.

31 Francesco Crispi, a member of Garibaldi's "Thousand," forms a ministry in Italy following the death of Agostino Depretis.

OCTOBER

• The popularity of the radical nationalist French general Georges Boulanger increases with revelations of scandals connected with President François-Paul-Jules Grévy's family.

NOVEMBER

13 "Bloody Sunday" occurs with over 100 casualties in Trafalgar Square, London, England, at a socialist meeting attended by Irish agitators. Many arrests are made.

DECEMBER

2 François-Paul-Jules Grévy resigns the presidency of France following financial scandals connected with his son-in-law Daniel Wilson, who trafficked in medals of the Legion of Honor. Marie-François-Sadi Carnot is elected president.

12 Britain, Austria-Hungary, and Italy sign a treaty for the maintenance of the status quo in the Near East, apprehensive at Russian attempts at expansion in the area.

SCIENCE, TECHNOLOGY, AND MEDICINE

Ecology

• Throughout the spring, China's Yellow River floods, inundating 129,500 sq km/50,000 sq mi of land. Between 1 and 1.5 million people die from famine.

JANUARY

6–13 Kansas, Montana, North Dakota, South Dakota, and Wyoming are ravaged by a blizzard that kills millions of cattle, and in some areas wipes out 80% of the herd.

Exploration

DECEMBER

13 Welsh-born U.S. explorer Henry Stanley explores Lake Albert Edward Nyanza, in Africa.

Health and Medicine

• German ophthalmologist A. E. Fick invents the contact lens.

• Phenacetin (acetophenetidin), an analgesic drug, is discovered; it replaces acetanilide.

Science

• British astronomer Joseph Norman Lockyer publishes *The Chemistry of the Sun*, which describes his spectroscopic analysis of sunlight.

• British physicist Oliver Heaviside shows that the distortion of the electrical signal on long-distance telephone lines can be reduced by increasing the inductance of the circuit. It makes long-distance telephone service practical.

• English naturalist H. G. Seeley classifies dinosaurs into two groups, those with birdlike pelvises, the *Ornithischia*, and those with reptile-like pelvises, the *Saurischia*.

• German chemist Emil Hermann Fischer synthesizes fructose and determines its molecular structure.

• German chemist Robert Wilhelm Bunsen invents the vapor calorimeter for measuring heat.

- German physicist Heinrich Hertz produces radio waves at his laboratory at Karlsruhe, Germany, and demonstrates that they are reflected in a manner similar to light waves. The existence of such waves had earlier been predicted by James Clerk Maxwell. Hertz's experiments now support Maxwell's theory that light is also electromagnetic in nature.
- German physicist Heinrich Hertz discovers the photoelectric effect, in which a material gives off charged particles when it absorbs radiant energy, when he observes that ultraviolet light affects the voltage at which sparking between two metal plates takes place. Later work on this phenomenon leads to the conclusion that light is composed of particles called photons.
- The Paris Observatory in France enlists 18 observatories around the world to make a photographic map of 10 million stars, and to catalog all stars of 12th magnitude or brighter. The map, known as the *Carte du ciel*, is still incomplete, but the catalog is completed in 1958.
- U.S. physicist Albert Michelson and U.S. chemist Edward Williams Morley fail in an attempt to measure the velocity of the earth through the "ether" by measuring the speed of light in two directions. Their failure discredits the idea of the ether and leads to the conclusion that the speed of light is a universal constant, a fundamental premise of Einstein's theory of relativity.

Technology

- French engineer Léon Bolle invents a "machine à calculer," the first calculator to multiply figures directly rather than making multiple additions.
- German-born U.S. inventor Emil Berliner patents his phonograph, a machine that plays discs or records. He also patents the records and develops a method of making them. Easier to manufacture than cylinders, they also minimize distortions caused by gravity since the stylus moves across the record rather than up and down as on the cylinders.
- Scottish chemists John S. MacArthur, Robert W. Forrest, and William Forrest invent the cyanide process for extracting gold and silver from their ores.
- Swedish scientist Carl Gustaf Patrik de Laval develops an impulse steam turbine; it achieves 42,000 rpm.
- The first leaf-type shutters appear on cameras.
- The German firm of Siemens and Haskle introduces the first electric elevator, at the industrial exhibition at Mannheim, Germany.
- U.S. clergyman Hannibal Goodwin develops celluloid photographic film. He sells the patent to U.S. manufacturer George Eastman.
- U.S. inventors Dorr Eugene Felt and Robert Tarrant introduce the "Comptometer," the first multiple-column key-operated calculating machine.

JANUARY
- The Tokyo Electric Light Company begins generating electricity for household use, in Japan.

Transportation

MARCH
4   German mechanical engineer Gottlieb Daimler fits his engine to a four-wheeled carriage to produce a four-wheeled automobile. During the same year he fits his internal combustion engine to a boat, creating the first motor boat.

ARTS AND IDEAS

Architecture

- The Marshall Field Wholesale Store in Chicago, Illinois, designed by the U.S. architect Henry Hobson Richardson, is completed.

Arts

- The Dutch artist Vincent van Gogh paints his *Portrait of Père Tanguy*.
- The French artist Edgar Degas paints *Evening: Women on the Terrace of a Café*.
- The French artist Emile Bernard paints *The Bridge at Asnières*.
- The French artist Paul Cézanne paints *Mont Ste.-Victoire with a Great Pine*, one of several pictures by him of this mountain.
- The French artist Pierre-Auguste Renoir paints *The Bathers*.
- The Russian artist Ilya Yefimovich Repin paints his *Portrait of Tolstoy*.

Literature and Language

- Polish philologist Luwik Lejzer Zamenhof devises Esperanto: based on phonetic spelling and a very simple grammar, it becomes the most widely accepted of the artificial languages. He invents it as a way of combatting nationalism.
- Joel Chandler Harris of Georgia, United States, who writes for the daily newspaper *The Atlanta Constitution*, publishes *Free Joe and Other Sketches*; it includes the Uncle Remus stories that purport to capture black folk life under slavery and during the Reconstruction.
- The English writer (Henry) Rider Haggard publishes his adventure novel *She*.
- The English writer Mark Rutherford publishes his novel *The Revolution in Tanner's Lane*.
- The English writer Thomas Hardy publishes his novel *The Woodlanders*.
- The German writer Hermann Sudermann publishes his novel *Frau Sorge/Dame Care*.
- The Scottish writer Arthur Conan Doyle publishes *A Study in Scarlet*, the first Sherlock Holmes novel.

Music

- Austrian composer Josef Anton Bruckner completes his Symphony No. 8. He revises it in 1890.

- English composer John Stainer completes his oratorio *The Crucifixion*.
- French composer Gabriel Fauré completes his song setting *Clair de lune/Moonlight* of a poem by the French writer Paul Verlaine.
- German composer Johannes Brahms completes his Concerto for Violin and Cello (Opus 102) and his *Zigeunerlieder/Gypsy Songs* (Opus 103).
- Russian composer Alexander Porfiryevich Borodin dies, leaving his opera *Prince Igor* unfinished. Completed by others, it is first performed in 1890.
- The comic opera *Ruddigore, or The Witch's Curse*, by the English writer William Schwenk Gilbert and the English composer Arthur Seymour Sullivan, is first performed at the Savoy Theatre in London, England.
- The opera *Otello* by the Italian composer Giuseppe Verdi is first performed, in Milan, Italy. It is based on Shakespeare's tragedy *Othello, the Moor of Venice*.

- The opera *The Sorceress* by the Russian composer Peter Illyich Tchaikovsky is first performed, in St. Petersburg, Russia.

Theater and Dance

- The French actor and director André Antoine founds the Théâtre Libre in Paris, France, for production of contemporary plays, particularly those experimenting with Naturalism. He produces plays by the French dramatist Henry-François Becque, and introduces the works of Strindberg, Ibsen, and Hauptmann to French theater.
- The play *Fadren/The Father*, by the Swedish writer Johan August Strindberg, is first performed, in Copenhagen, Denmark.
- The play *Ivanov* by the Russian writer Anton Chekhov is first performed, in Moscow, Russia.
- The play *La Tosca* by the French dramatist Victorien Sardou is first performed, in Paris, France.

BIRTHS & DEATHS

JANUARY

5 Bernard Leach, British potter who influenced ceramic design, born in Hong Kong (–1979).

28 Artur Rubinstein, Polish-born U.S. virtuoso pianist, born in Lódź, Poland (–1982).

FEBRUARY

27 Alexander Borodin, Russian composer, dies in St. Petersburg, Russia (53).

MARCH

7 Helen Parkhurst, U.S. educator and author who established a system of continuous assessed work for children instead of examinations, born in Durrand, Wisconsin (–1973).

8 James Buchanan Eads, U.S. engineer who built the first major bridge over the Mississippi River in 1874 at St. Louis, Missouri, dies in Nassau, Bahamas (66).

MAY

25 George (Francis) Abbott, U.S. playwright, theater director, and producer, born in Forestville, New York (–1995).

JUNE

5 Ruth Benedict, U.S. anthropologist who developed the culture and personality school, born in New York, New York (–1948).

20 Kurt Schwitters, German dada artist and poet, born in Hanover, Germany (–1948).

22 Julian Sorell Huxley, English biologist, philosopher, and author influential in the development of embryology, born in London, England (–1975).

JULY

7 Marc Chagall, Russian painter, born in Vitebsk, Russia (–1985).

14 Alfred Krupp, German industrialist who manufactured armaments, dies in Essen, Germany (75).

18 Vidkun Quisling, Norwegian army officer who collaborated with the Germans during World War I and whose name has become synonymous with "traitor," born in Fyresdal, Norway (–1945).

28 Marcel Duchamp, French artist whose *Nude Descending a Staircase, No 2* (1912) caused a sensation, born in Blainville, France (–1968).

AUGUST

12 Erwin Schrödinger, Austrian physicist who developed the wave theory of matter, born in Vienna, Austria (–1961).

SEPTEMBER

28 Avery Brundage, U.S. sports administrator and controversial president of the International Olympic Committee 1952–72, born in Detroit, Michigan (–1975).

OCTOBER

6 Le Corbusier (assumed name of Charles-Edouard Jeanneret), Swiss architect and city planner whose designs combined expressionism and Functionalism, born in Chaux-de-Fonds, Switzerland (–1965).

6 Martín Luiz Guzmán, Mexican novelist during the Mexican revolution, born in Chihuahua, Mexico (–1976).

17 Gustav Robert Kirchoff, German physicist who, with Robert Wilhelm von Bunsen, helped establish spectrum analysis, dies in Berlin, Germany (63).

31 Jiang Jie Shi (Chiang Kai-shek), Chinese statesman, leader of the Nationalist government 1928–49, and then of the Chinese Nationalist government in exile on Taiwan, born in Zhejiang Province, China (–1975).

NOVEMBER

8 Doc (John Henry) Holliday, U.S. gambler, dentist, and gunslinger, dies in Glenwood Springs, Colorado (35).

15 Georgia O'Keeffe, U.S. artist who painted semiabstract forms of color and light and many large flower paintings, born near Sun Prairie, Wisconsin (–1986).

15 Marianne Moore, U.S. poet, critic, and translator, born in St. Louis, Missouri (–1972).

17 Bernard L. Montgomery ("Monty"), British field marshal and commander during World War II, born in London, England (–1976).

23 Boris Karloff, English actor known for his horror films, born in London, England (–1969).

DECEMBER

6 Hisamitsu Shimazu, Japanese feudal lord who was one of the leaders in the rebellion against the Tokugawa shogunate, dies in Kagoshima, Japan (70).

25 Conrad Hilton, U.S. entrepreneur and founder of the Hilton Hotel Corporation, born in San Antonio, New Mexico (–1979).

- The play *Rosmersholm* by the Norwegian dramatist Henrik Ibsen is first performed, in Christiania (now Oslo), Norway. It was published in 1886.
- The Swedish writer Johan August Strindberg completes his play *Komraterna/Comrades*, which is first performed in 1905.

Thought and Scholarship

- The German philosopher Friedrich Nietzsche publishes *Zur Genealogie der Moral/The Genealogy of Morals*.
- The Scottish writer Andrew Lang publishes *Myth, Ritual and Religion*.

SOCIETY

Education

- Clark University is founded in Worcester, Massachusetts.
- Pomona College opens in Claremont, California.
- Troy State University is founded in Troy, Alabama.

Everyday Life

c. 1887 The British tobacco company W. D. & H. O. Wills introduces cigarette cards, initially images printed on the cardboard used to stiffen the packaging.

MAY
26 Racetrack betting becomes legal for the first time in New York state.

SEPTEMBER
5 New York state observes labor day for the first time.

Media and Communication

- Telephone subscribers reach the following levels: United States, 150,000; Great Britain, 26,000; Germany, 22,000; Canada, 12,000; Sweden, 12,000; France, 9,000.

Religion

MARCH
3 Protestant zealots in Iowa create the American Protective Association, a secret society designed to curb the allegedly pernicious influence of U.S. Catholics.

Sports

- At the U.S. lawn tennis championships, Ellen Hansell of the United States wins the inaugural women's singles event. Fellow U.S. player Richard Sears wins the men's singles for the eighth successive year.
- Commercials from Limerick defeats Young from Louth in the inaugural All-Ireland Gaelic Football Championship in Dublin, Ireland.
- George Hancock of the Farragut Boat Club, Chicago, Illinois, invents softball as an indoor version of baseball. The game later becomes known as "mush-ball" or "kitten-ball"; it is not called "softball" until the 1920s.
- The first women's cricket club, the White Heather Club, is formed in Yorkshire, England. It remains in existence until the 1950s.
- The first women's hockey club, the Molesey Ladies Hockey Club, is founded in England.
- The Foxburg Golf Club, in Foxburg, Pennsylvania, regarded by many authorities as the first golf club in the United States, is founded.

JANUARY
21 The American Athletic Union is founded to preserve amateurism in sport.

MARCH
- The American Trotting Association is founded in Detroit, Michigan.

APRIL
20 The first motor race, organized by the French cycling magazine *La Vélocipède*, is held in Paris. The winner (and only entrant) is Georges Bouton on a four-seater steam quadricycle.

JULY
6 The British tennis player Lottie Dod, aged 15 years and 8 months, wins the women's singles at the Wimbledon championships, London, England.

SEPTEMBER
19 The Lillie Bridge Stadium in London, England, is burned to the ground by angry crowds after two professional runners fail to appear for a race over 110 m/120 yds for a prize of £200. Large amounts of money had been laid on the race by two rival gangs who both wanted their runner to lose in order to achieve a betting coup.

1888

POLITICS, GOVERNMENT, AND ECONOMICS

Business and Economics

- George Parker founds the Parker Pen Co. in Janesville, Wisconsin. It will become the largest producer of fountain pens in the world.
- Protective tariffs are introduced in New Zealand and Sweden in response to the commercial and agricultural depression.
- The British colonial entrepreneur Cecil Rhodes amalgamates the Kimberley diamond companies in Cape Colony.

OCTOBER

14 Hamburg and Bremen join the German customs union.

Colonization

FEBRUARY

11 King Lobengula of Matabele accepts the creation of a British protectorate over his kingdom.

MARCH

17 Britain proclaims a protectorate in Sarawak, Malaysia, which has been ruled by a British rajah since 1841.

MAY

12 The British proclaim a protectorate in North Borneo and Brunei.

DECEMBER

11 The French colony of Gabon is united with the French Congo.

Politics and Government

- Five female prostitutes are murdered in the Whitechapel area of London, England, by an unidentified assailant known popularly as "Jack the Ripper."
- U.S. president Grover Cleveland appoints interior secretary Lucius Q. C. Lamar to the U.S. Supreme Court and names Illinois jurist Melville W. Fuller chief justice.

JANUARY

28 A military agreement between Germany and Italy provides for the use of Italian troops against France in the event of a Franco-German war.

FEBRUARY

3 Chancellor Otto von Bismarck publishes the German–Austrian alliance of 1879 as a warning to Russia, following Russian opposition to the accession of Ferdinand of Coburg as ruler of Bulgaria.

11 Franco-Italian relations become tense, as Italy fears the French fleet will attack Spezia, Italy.

MARCH

9 Frederick III succeeds as emperor of Germany following the death of Wilhelm I.

27 General Georges Boulanger retires from the French army, thereby becoming eligible for election to the French chamber.

APRIL

15 Following election to the French chamber, General Georges Boulanger begins a campaign for the revision of the constitution with the intention of making himself dictator. Charles Floquet forms a cabinet which stands until February 1889.

MAY

13 Serfdom is abolished in Brazil by Dom Pedro II following a protracted campaign.

JUNE

4 New York governor David B. Bill signs legislation replacing hanging with electrocution as the state's chosen method of execution.

5 The Democrats renominate Grover Cleveland for president and nominate former Ohio senator Allen G. Thurman for vice president.

15 Wilhelm II becomes emperor of Germany on the death of his father, Frederick III.

25 The Republicans nominate Indiana senator Benjamin Harrison for president and New York banker Levi P. Morton for vice president.

SEPTEMBER

9 Coastal Arabs rise against German rule in East Africa.

OCTOBER

6 The Ottoman Empire grants a concession to Germany to build a railroad to Ankara, Anatolia, in the first stage of the Baghdad Railroad.

29 Under the terms of the Suez Canal Convention, signed at Constantinople, Anatolia, the canal is open to all nations in war as in peace.

30 France provides Russia with a loan following the refusal of Germany to do so, beginning a Franco-Russian *entente*.

30 King Lobengula grants the British entrepreneur Cecil Rhodes mining rights in Matabeleland.

NOVEMBER

6 The Republican candidate Benjamin Harrison is elected as president of the United States after winning the

electoral vote, even though his opponent wins the greater share of the popular vote. In the Congressional elections, the Republicans attain narrow majorities in both the House (166–159) and Senate (39–37).

DECEMBER

12 Italy supports Menelek of Shoa, Ethiopia, in his revolt against Yohannes IV of Ethiopia.

SCIENCE, TECHNOLOGY, AND MEDICINE

Ecology

MARCH

11–14 A blizzard hits the states of New England, leaving 4.6-m/15-ft-high snowdrifts; more than 800 people die.

Exploration

- Charles Montagu Doughty publishes *Travels in Arabia Deserta*.
- Norwegian explorer Fridtjof Nansen crosses Greenland.

Health and Medicine

- Compulsory national health insurance is introduced in Austria.
- German surgeon Ernst Gustav Benjamin von Bergmann publishes *Die Chirurgische Behandlung der Hirnkrankheiten/The Surgical Treatment of Brain Disorders*, one of the first works on cranial surgery.

Math

- German mathematician Richard Dedekind publishes *Was sind und was sollen die Zahlen?/The Nature and Meaning of Numbers*. He gives a rigorous foundation for arithmetic, later known as the Peano axioms.

Science

- Argentine criminal investigator Juan Vucetich publishes *Dactiloscopia, Comparada/Comparative Fingerprinting*, which outlines a system of classifying fingerprints for personal identification.
- British astronomer Joseph Norman Lockyer describes the evolution of a star from birth to extinction.
- Danish astronomer Ludvig Emil Dreyer publishes the *New General Catalogue of Nebulae and Clusters of Stars*, which lists over 8,000 nebulae. This number is increased to 13,000 by 1895; stellar objects are known by their catalog designations, such as NGC1898.
- Dutch geneticist Hugo Marie de Vries uses the term "mutation" to describe varieties that arise spontaneously in cultivated primroses.

- German cytologist Eduard Adolf Strasburger determines that germ cell nuclei of flowering plants undergo meiosis.
- Swedish chemist Alfred Bernhard Nobel develops balistite, the first nitroglycerin smokeless blasting powder.
- Swedish geologist Alfred Elis Törnebohm presents the theory that mountain ranges are the result of overthrusting, in which the upper surface of a fault plane moves over the rocks of the lower surface.
- The Marine Biological Laboratory is established at Woods Hole, Massachusetts, as an independent research and educational organization.
- The National Geographic Society is founded in Washington, D.C., and begins publication of the *National Geographic* magazine. By the 1990s it is the largest scientific and educational organization in the world, with over 11 million members.
- The Pasteur Institute is founded in Paris, France, with the aim of conducting research into the prevention and treatment of rabies.
- The word "chromosome" is first used.
- U.S. physicist Henry Augustus Rowland publishes *Photographic Map of the Normal Solar Spectrum*, an 11-m/35-ft-long spectrogram of the sun, which serves as a standard reference for astronomers.

Technology

- German chemist George W. Kahlbaum makes the first plastic bottles.
- French physiologist Etienne-Jules Marey invents the chambre chronophotographique, the forerunner of the cinematograph.
- Hungarian inventor David Gestetner introduces the first typewriter stencil, in London, England.
- Serbian-born U.S. inventor Nikola Tesla invents the first alternating current (AC) electric motor, which serves as the model for most modern electric motors. He sells the patent to George Westinghouse, who manufactures the motors in competition with Edison's direct current (DC) electric generators.
- Belgian-born U.S. inventor Charles Joseph Van Depoele patents a carbon commutator brush for electric motors, which produces less sparking than that caused by metal brushes.
- The first coal-loading machine, the Stanley Header, is tested in Colorado.
- U.S. inventor Theophilus Van Kannel installs the first revolving door, in the lobby of an office building in Philadelphia, Pennsylvania.

JUNE

- U.S. manufacturer George Eastman introduces the hand-held "Kodak" box camera. The first commercial roll-film camera, it is simple to use and contains a 100-exposure roll of paper film. The entire camera is returned to Eastman's factory for the film to be developed and printed, and the camera reloaded. Costing $25, it revolutionizes photography by making it possible for large numbers of amateur photographers to take acceptable snapshots.

Transportation

- French engineer Gustave Zédé launches *Gymnote*, an electric-powered submarine.
- The first refrigerated railroad truck is used.

FEBRUARY

2 U.S. engineer Frank Julian Sprague begins the first successful electric trolley car service, at Richmond, Virginia. Running on a 19-km/12-mi-track, the cars are lit with incandescent bulbs and travel at 24 kph/15 mph. Within 10 years there are 40,000 of them in the United States.

OCTOBER

31 Scottish veterinary surgeon John Boyd Dunlop patents the pneumatic bicycle tire.

ARTS AND IDEAS

Architecture

OCTOBER

9 The Washington Monument, 202.2 m/555 ft high and built at a cost of $1.2 million, opens to the public in Washington, D.C.

Arts

- *c.* 1888 The English artist Walter Richard Sickert paints *The Red Shop*.
- The Belgian artist James Ensor paints *The Entry of Christ into Brussels*.
- The Dutch artist Vincent van Gogh paints *Sunflowers* and *The Night Café*.
- The French artist Henri de Toulouse-Lautrec paints *At the Circus Fernando*.
- The French artist Paul Gauguin paints *Vision After the Sermon* and *The Awakening of Spring*.
- The French artist Paul Sérusier paints *'The Talisman': Landscape in the Bois d'Amour in Brittany*.
- The U.S. artist Albert Bierstadt paints *The Last of the Buffalo*.
- The German art historian Heinrich Wölfflin publishes *Renaissance und Barock/Renaissance and Baroque*.

Literature and Language

- British explorer and translator Richard Burton publishes the final volume of his translation of the Arabian classic *The Arabian Nights*. The first volume appeared in 1885.
- Irish inventor John Robert Gregg publishes *Light-line Phonography*, which presents a phonetic shorthand alphabet based on the cursive motion of the hand. In 1893 he takes it to the United States where it becomes the main shorthand system.
- The English writer and critic Arthur Quiller-Couch publishes his novel *Astonishing History of Troy Town*.
- The English writer Rudyard Kipling publishes his collection of short stories *Plain Tales from the Hills*.

- The English-born Australian writer Rolf Boldrewood publishes his novel *Robbery under Arms*, a romantic novel set in the Australian outback.
- The French writer and politician Maurice Barrès publishes his novel *Sous l'Oeil des barbares/Under the Eyes of the Barbarians*, the first volume of his trilogy *Le Culte du moi/The Cult of Self*.
- The French writer Emile Zola publishes his novel *La Terre/Earth*, one of the *Les Rougon–Macquart* series.
- The French writer Guy de Maupassant publishes his novel *Pierre et Jean/Pierre and Jean*.
- The French writer Sully Prudhomme publishes his poem "Le Bonheure"/"Happiness."
- The Russian writer Anton Chekhov publishes his story "Step"/"The Steppe."
- The U.S. writer Edward Bellamy publishes his utopian novel *Looking Backwards, 2000–1887*.
- The U.S. writer Henry James publishes his short novel *The Aspern Papers*.

Music

- Austrian composer Gustav Mahler completes his Symphony No. 1. A much revised version appears in 1898.
- Austrian composer Hugo Wolf completes his song cycle *Mörike-Lieder*, inspired by the work of the German poet Eduard Mörike.
- Belgian woodcarver Pierre Degeyter and French transport worker Eugène Pettier write "L'Internationale," which will become the communist anthem.
- English composer Charles Hubert Parry completes his oratorio *Judith*.
- French composer César Franck completes his Symphony in D minor.
- French composer Claude Debussy completes his cantata *La Damoiselle élue/The Blessed Damozel*.
- French composer Erik Satie completes his three piano pieces *Gymnopédies*. The first and third are orchestrated by the French composer Debussy in 1896.
- German composer Richard Strauss completes his tone poem *Don Juan*.
- Russian composer Nikolay Andreyevich Rimsky-Korsakov completes his symphonic suite *Scheherazade*.
- Russian composer Peter Illyich Tchaikovsky completes his Symphony No. 5 and his overture *Hamlet*.
- The comic opera *The Yeoman of the Guard, or The Merryman and His Maid* by the English writer William Schwenk Gilbert and the English composer Arthur Seymour Sullivan is first performed, in London, England.
- U.S. composer Edward MacDowell completes his *Romance* for cello and orchestra.

Theater and Dance

- The comedy *Sweet Lavender* by the English dramatist Arthur Wing Pinero is first performed, in London, England.

Thought and Scholarship

- Scottish-U.S. theologian James McCosh publishes *The Religious Aspect of Evolution*, an account of evolution as evidence of God's creation.
- The Canadian-born English naturalist George John Romanes publishes *Mental Evolution in Man*.
- The English jurist and statesman James Bryce publishes *The American Commonwealth*.
- The English philosopher Bernard Bosanquet publishes *Logic, or the Morphology of Thought*.
- The English theologian James Martineau publishes *A Study of Religion*.
- The U.S. statesman Theodore Roosevelt publishes *Essays on Practical Politics*.
- The German philosopher Friedrich Nietzsche publishes *Der Antichrist/The Anti-Christ*, and *Ecce Homo/Behold the Man*.

SOCIETY

Education

- The University of Rhode Island is founded in Kingston, Rhode Island.

Everyday Life

- The deodorant Mum is launched in the United States.
- The first vending machines in the United States appear on platforms of the elevated railroad of New York, New York; they dispense chewing gum.

BIRTHS & DEATHS

JANUARY
24 Ernst Heinrich Heinkel, German aircraft designer who built the first rocket-powered aircraft, born in Grunbach, Germany (–1958).

29 Edward Lear, English landscape painter and writer of nonsense verse, dies in San Remo, Italy (75).

30 Asa Gray, U.S. botanist who classified much of the flora of the United States, dies in Cambridge, Massachusetts (77).

FEBRUARY
11 William Kelly, U.S. steelmaker who invented the pneumatic method of making steel, dies in Louisville, Kentucky (76).

25 John Foster Dulles, U.S. secretary of state 1953–59 who was responsible for many of the Cold War policies with respect to the USSR, born in Washington, D.C. (–1959).

27 Lotte Lehman, German-born U.S. soprano particularly associated with the songs of Robert Schumann, born in Perleberg, Germany (–1976).

MARCH
6 Louisa May Alcott, U.S. author of children's books, best known for *Little Women* (1869), dies in Boston, Massachusetts (65).

19 Josef Albers, German-born U.S. painter, poet, teacher, and theoretician of art, born in Bottrop, Germany (–1976).

APRIL
15 Matthew Arnold, English poet and social critic, dies in Liverpool, England (65).

MAY
11 Irving Berlin, U.S. composer, born in Temum, Russia (–1989).

JULY
10 Giorgio de Chirico, Greek-born Italian painter, one of the founders of the school of Metaphysical Painting, born in Vólos, Greece (–1978).

22 Selman Abraham Waksman, Ukranian-born U.S. microbiologist who discovered the antibiotic streptomycin, born in Priluka, Ukraine, in the Russian Empire (–1973).

23 Raymond Chandler, U.S. author, creator of the private detective Philip Marlowe, born in Chicago, Illinois (–1959).

AUGUST
5 Philip H. Sheridan, Union general in the American Civil War, dies in Nonquitt, Massachusetts (57).

13 John Logie Baird, Scottish engineer who was the first to televise moving pictures, born in Helensburgh, Dunbarton, Scotland (–1946).

15 T(homas) E(dward) Lawrence ("Lawrence of Arabia"), British scholar, military strategist, and author, born in Tremadoc, Caernarvonshire, Wales (–1935).

24 Rudolf Clausius, German physicist who formulated the second law of thermodynamics, dies in Bonn, Germany (66).

SEPTEMBER
5 Sarvepalli Radhakrishnan, Indian scholar, philosopher, and prime minister of India 1962–67, born in Tiruttani, India (–1975).

12 Maurice Chevalier, French actor and singer, born in Paris, France (–1972).

26 T(homas) S(tearns) Eliot, U.S.-born British modernist poet and playwright who had a strong influence on 20th-century poetry, born in St. Louis, Missouri (–1965).

OCTOBER
6 Li Dazhao, Chinese scholar and cofounder of the Chinese Communist Party, born in Hopeh Province, China (–1927).

14 Katherine Mansfield (born Beauchamp, pseudonym of Kathleen Murry), New Zealand-born English short-story writer, born in Wellington, New Zealand (–1923).

16 Eugene O'Neill, U.S. dramatist, born in New York, New York (–1953).

25 Richard E. Byrd, U.S. pilot and polar explorer, born in Winchester, Virginia (–1957).

NOVEMBER
9 Jean Monnet, French political economist and diplomat who rebuilt France's economy after World War II, born in Cognac, France (–1979).

10 Andrey Nikolayevich Tupolev, Russian aircraft designer who helped develop the world's first supersonic passenger airliner, born in Pustomazovo, Russia (–1972).

10 George Charles Bingham, Lord Lucan, British cavalry commander who mistakenly ordered the Charge of the Light Brigade (October 25, 1854) during the Crimean War, dies in London, England (87).

APRIL

4   The first aeronautical exhibition is held in Vienna, Austria.

SEPTEMBER

19 The first beauty contest takes place in Spa, Belgium, with the first selection being made from 350 photographs.

Media and Communication

- The *Collier's Weekly* newspaper is launched in Britain.
- The *Financial Times* newspaper is launched in Britain.

OCTOBER

- The magazine *National Geographic* is launched in the United States.

Sports

JUNE

9   The U.S. jockey Jimmy McLaughlin wins the Belmont Stakes for the third successive year, a feat he previously achieved in 1882–84.

NOVEMBER

14 Scottish golfer John Reid founds the St. Andrews Golf Club, Yonkers, New York.

1889

POLITICS, GOVERNMENT, AND ECONOMICS

Business and Economics

OCTOBER

29 The British South Africa Company, headed by Cecil Rhodes, is granted a royal charter giving extensive powers for expanding its territory at the expense of Transvaal.

Colonization

JANUARY

10 France proclaims a protectorate over the Ivory Coast.

MAY

2   By the Treaty of Ucciali with Menelek of Ethiopia, Italy proclaims a protectorate over Ethiopia.

JUNE

14 The United States, Britain, and Germany sign a treaty establishing Samoa as a joint protectorate.

Human Rights

- Manhood suffrage, the right of adult male citizens to vote, is granted in New Zealand.

JUNE

6   The Brussels Conference agrees on the abolition of the slave trade and the suppression of traffic in arms and liquor to the extra-European world.

Politics and Government

- New Jersey amends its corporation laws, encouraging the development of holding companies.
- The London County Council is formed in England, and Archibald Primrose, Lord Rosebery, is elected its first chairman on February 12.
- U.S. president Benjamin Harrison appoints Kansas jurist David J. Brewer to the U.S. Supreme Court.

JANUARY

19 Georgia becomes the first state to make Confederate general Robert E. Lee's birthday a holiday in the United States.

27 A demonstration is held in Paris, France, urging General Georges Boulanger to stage a coup, but he fails to seize his opportunity.

30 Crown Prince Archduke Rudolf of Austria-Hungary, only son of Emperor Franz Josef and Hapsburg heir, commits suicide at Mayerling, near Vienna.

FEBRUARY

- Pierre Tirard forms a ministry in France, relying on the Left Republicans and the Republican Union for support.
11 A constitution is granted in Japan with a two-chamber diet, but the emperor retains extensive powers.
11 The U.S. Congress makes the Department of Agriculture a Cabinet office.

MARCH

4   Benjamin Harrison is inaugurated as 23rd president of the United States.

6   King Milan of Serbia abdicates in favor of his son with Jovan Ristič acting as regent.

APRIL

1   General Georges Boulanger, fearing trial for treason, flees from France. In the subsequent elections the Republicans triumph.

22 At 12 noon, the U.S. government opens nearly 2 million acres of Oklahoma land to settlement, inaugurating a furious land rush.

MAY

5 Germany establishes provisions for a state old-age pension.

JULY

- A crisis in Italian–Vatican relations is precipitated by the Italian prime minister Francesco Crispi's treatment of the church.

17 A French law is passed to forbid multiple candidates in elections in order to prevent a mass vote in favor of General Georges Boulanger.

OCTOBER

2 An International Conference of American States convenes in Washington, D.C., to promote comity and trade.

10 Antonio Blanco, President of Venezuela since 1870, is deprived of office while absent in Europe.

NOVEMBER

2 North and South Dakota become the 39th and 40th states to join the U.S. Union.

8 Montana becomes the 41st state to join the Union.

11 Washington becomes the 42nd state to join the Union.

11 With Italian support, Menelek triumphs in the disputed succession which follows the death of Yohannes IV on March 12, and becomes king of Ethiopia.

15 Brazil is proclaimed a republic on the abdication of Dom Pedro II following a coup.

DECEMBER

6 A Calvinist–Catholic coalition is formed in the Netherlands following the fall of the anticlerical Liberals.

SCIENCE, TECHNOLOGY, AND MEDICINE

Ecology

- A swarm of locusts covering an estimated 5,180 sq km/ 2,000 sq mi crosses the Red Sea.
- U.S. geologist Clarence Edward Dutton discovers a method of determining the epicentre of earthquakes and accurately measuring the speed of seismic waves.

MAY

31 Johnstown, Pennsylvania, is hit by a flash flood when the South Fork Dam collapses and sends a wall of water down the Conemaugh River Valley; over 2,200 people are killed.

Health and Medicine

- French bacteriologist Emile Roux and Swiss bacteriologist Alexandre Yersin show that diphtheria bacteria produce a toxin which is the active agent in the disease.

- German physiologists Oskar Minkowski and Joseph von Mering remove the pancreas from a dog, which then develops diabetic symptoms. It leads them to conclude that the pancreas secretes an antidiabetic substance, which is now known as insulin.

May 1889–90 A pandemic of influenza, called the Russian flu, spreads round the world. Beginning in Russia, it spreads to the rest of Europe, China, and North America by 1890. It kills nearly 250,000 people in Europe and about 500,000 people worldwide.

Science

- Canadian-born U.S. chemist Herbert Henry Dow patents an electrolytic method of removing bromine (which is used in the pharmaceutical and photographic industries) from brine.
- English anthropologist and eugenicist Francis Galton publishes *Natural Inheritance*, in which he develops the application of advanced statistical techniques in relation to the study of human beings.
- English chemist Frederick Augustus Abel and Scottish chemist James Dewar invent the smokeless explosive cordite.
- German aeronautical engineer Otto Lilienthal writes *Der Vogelflug als Grundlage der Fliegekumst/Bird Flight as a Basis of Aviation*, a basic work on aeronautics in which he shows that the curved wings of birds are advantageous for flight.
- Italian astronomer Giovanni Schiaparelli determines that both Mercury and Venus rotate on their axes and circle the sun at the same rate so that one side of each planet always faces the sun.
- Swedish chemist Svante August Arrhenius theorizes that molecules require a given amount of energy, which he calls activation energy, before they can react with other substances.
- U.S. astronomer Edward Emerson Barnard takes the first photograph of the Milky Way.

Technology

- French engineer Léon François Edoux installs the world's first elevators with transparent walls, in the Eiffel Tower, Paris, France. Nearly 160 m/525 ft high, they are also higher and faster than previous elevators.
- Swedish workman F. W. Lindqvist invents a wickless stove, in Sweden, and sells the production rights to B. A. Hjorth, who markets it under the name Primus stove.
- The U.S. firm Otis installs the world's first commercial electric passenger elevators, in the Demarest building, New York, New York.
- U.S. engineer Lester Allen Pelton patents an impulse turbine that uses the maximum amount of energy from flowing water; it contains bucket-shaped blades that divide the flow of water.
- U.S. inventor Angus Campbell develops an automatic cotton-picking machine, although it is not produced commercially until 1927.
- U.S. manufacturer George Eastman produces celluloid roll film, which replaces paper roll film.

- U.S. manufacturer Isaac Merritt Singer produces the first electric sewing machine. It is not fully successful as a marketable machine until mains electricity is widely available in the 1920s.
- The first commercial recordings, for the Edison wax cylinder, are made by Frank Goede, playing piccolo and flute music, in the United States. There is no means of duplicating them.

Transportation

- Most maritime nations adopt the International Regulations for Preventing Collisions at Sea, which specify which lights must be shown, how ships must navigate with respect to one another, and so on.
- The "safety" bicycle, which has equal-sized wheels, is introduced into the United States.
- The first European electric trolley enters service in Northfleet, Kent, England.

NOVEMBER

14 U.S. reporter Elizabeth Cochrane ("Nellie Bly") sails from New York, New York, to travel around the world in an attempt to break the record of the Jules Verne fictional character Phileas Fogg.

ARTS AND IDEAS

Architecture

- The Auditorium Building in Chicago, Illinois, designed by the U.S. architects Dankman Adler and Louis Sullivan, is completed.
- The Eiffel Tower, designed by the French engineer Gustave Eiffel and started in 1887, is completed in Paris, France, for the World Fair. It is 300 m/984 ft high—making it the highest building in the world—and is made of 12,000 prefabricated wrought iron parts. It opens on May 6 and quickly becomes the most famous landmark in the city.
- The Palau Güell in Barcelona, Spain, designed by the Spanish architect Antonio Gaudí, is completed.
- U.S. architect William Holabird completes the Tacoma building in Chicago, Illinois. It is the first building to have a framework entirely made of steel rather than having just steel supports, as in William Le Baron Jenney's Home Insurance Building.

Arts

- The Belgian artist James Ensor paints *Two Skeletons Warming Themselves by a Stove*.
- The Dutch artist Vincent van Gogh paints *Cornfield, Cypress Tree*, *Self-Portrait with Bandaged Ear*, and *Olive Trees*.
- The French artist Henri Rousseau paints *Bois de Boulogne*.
- The French artist Paul Gauguin paints *Harvest in Brittany*, *The Yellow Christ*, and *The Schuffenecker Family*.

- The German artist Max Klinger completes his series of engravings *On Death*.
- The U.S. artist Frederic Remington paints *A Dash for the Timber*.
- The U.S. artist John Singer Sargent paints *Paul Hellau Sketching With His Wife*.
- The U.S. artist Ralph Albert Blakelock paints *Moonlight, Indian Encampment*.
- The English photographer Peter Henry Emerson publishes *Naturalistic Photography for Students of the Art*, a book that has a major impact on the development of photography.

Film

- German photographer Ottmar Anshütz develops the first coin-operated "What-the-Butler-Saw" machine in Vienna, Austria. A precursor to motion pictures, it consists of a series of photographs turned by a handle which creates the illusion of movement.
- British inventor William Friese-Greene develops a camera that takes ten photographs per second, on a roll of perforated film moving behind a shutter. The first true motion-picture camera, he uses it to film scenes at Hyde Park Corner, London, England.
- U.S. inventor William Kennedy Laurie Dickson makes the world's first motion picture on celluloid. Entitled *Fred Ott's Sneeze*, it is a close-up of an Edison factory worker sneezing. It is also the world's first copyrighted motion picture.

Literature and Language

- The Belgian writer Maurice Maeterlinck publishes his poetry collection *Serres chaudes/Hot House Blooms*.
- The English writer Jerome K. Jerome publishes his comic novel *Three Men in a Boat*.
- The French writer André Gide publishes his autobiographical first novel *Les Cahiers d'André Walter/The Notebooks of André Walter*.
- The French writer and politician Maurice Barrès publishes his novel *Un Homme libre/A Free Man*, the second volume of his trilogy *Le Culte du moi/The Cult of Self*.
- The Irish poet W. B. Yeats publishes his first collection of poems, *The Wanderings of Oisin and Other Poems*.
- The Norwegian writer Bjørnstjerne Martinius Bjørnson publishes his novel *På Guds veje/In God's Way*.
- The Scottish writer J. M. Barrie publishes his collection of stories *A Window in Thrums*.
- The Scottish writer Robert Louis Stevenson publishes his novel *The Master of Ballantrae*.
- The U.S. writer Mark Twain publishes his novel *A Connecticut Yankee in King Arthur's Court*.
- The U.S. writer Walt Whitman publishes his poetry collection *November Boughs*, with the preface "A Backward Glance o'er Travl'd Roads," in which he explains his aims in writing.

Music

- Bohemian composer Antonín Dvořák completes his Symphony No. 8 (once classified as No. 4).
- French composer Claude Debussy completes his work for piano duet *Petite Suite/Little Suite*.
- The comic opera *The Gondoliers, or The King of Barataria* by the English writer William Schwenk Gilbert and the English composer Arthur Seymour Sullivan is first performed, at the Savoy Theatre in London, England.
- U.S. composer John Philip Sousa completes his march *Washington Post*.

Theater and Dance

- The play *Fröken Julie/Miss Julie* by the Swedish writer Johan August Strindberg is first performed, in Copenhagen, Denmark. It was published in 1888.
- The play *Fruen fra Haven/The Lady from the Sea* by the Norwegian dramatist Henrik Johan Ibsen is first performed, in Christiania (now Oslo), Norway.
- The play *Vor Sonnenaufgang/Before Dawn* by the German dramatist Gerhardt Hauptmann is first performed, in Berlin, Germany. Its stark realism makes Hauptmann famous overnight.

Thought and Scholarship

- The Australian philosopher Samuel Alexander publishes *Moral Order and Progress*.

BIRTHS & DEATHS

FEBRUARY

13 Grant Wood, U.S. painter of stylized landscapes of the rural Midwest, born in Mapleton, Iowa (–1942).

17 H(aroldson) L(afayette) Hunt, U.S. oil billionaire, born in Ramsey, Illinois (–1974).

22 R(obin) G(eorge) Collingwood, English philosopher who related history to philosophy, born in Cartnel Fell, Lancashire, England (–1943).

MARCH

8 John Ericsson, Swedish-born U.S. naval engineer who invented the screw propeller, dies in New York, New York (85).

20 Albrecht Ritschl, German Lutheran theologian, dies in Göttingen, Germany (66).

APRIL

14 Arnold Toynbee, English historian whose 12-volume *A Study of History* provoked much debate, born in London, England (–1975).

15 Thomas Hart Benton, U.S. painter and muralist, born in Neosho, Missouri (–1975).

16 Charlie Chaplin, British-born U.S. actor and director of the silent film era, who gained fame playing a pathetic but humorous character, born in London, England (–1977).

20 Adolf Hitler, German fascist leader of the National Socialist (Nazi) Party, dictator of Germany 1933–45, born in Braunau, Germany (–1945).

26 Ludwig Wittgenstein, Austrian-born British philosopher, one of the most influential in the 20th century, born in Vienna, Austria (–1951).

28 Antonio Salazar, Prime Minister of Portugal 1932–68, born in Vimiero, Portugal (–1970).

MAY

25 Igor Sikorsky, Russian-born U.S. aircraft designer who developed the helicopter, born in Kiev, Russia (–1972).

JUNE

1 C. K. Ogden, British writer and linguist, born in Fleetwood, Lancashire, England (–1957).

23 Anna Akhmatova, Russian poet, born in Bolshoy Fontan, near Odessa, Russia (–1966).

JULY

5 Jean Cocteau, French writer, actor, and painter, born in Maisons-Lafitte, near Paris, France (–1963).

17 Erle Stanley Gardner, U.S. lawyer and author who created the private detective Perry Mason, born in Malden, Massachusetts (–1970).

30 Vladimir Zworykin, Russian-born U.S. electronic engineer who pioneered the development of television, born in Murmon, Russia (–1982).

AUGUST

5 Conrad Aiken, U.S. novelist, short-story writer, poet, and critic, born in Savannah, Georgia (–1973).

SEPTEMBER

23 Walter Lippmann, U.S. political columnist and author, born in New York, New York (–1974).

26 Martin Heidegger, German Existentialist philosopher, born in Messkirch, Schwarzwald, Germany (–1976).

29 Louis Faidherbe, French colonial administrator who was instrumental in establishing France's colonial empire in Africa, dies in Paris, France (71).

OCTOBER

11 James Prescott Joule, English physicist who demonstrated that the various forms of energy can be transformed one into another, dies in Sale, Cheshire, England (70).

25 Abel Gance, French film director, born in Paris, France (–1981).

NOVEMBER

12 DeWitt Wallace, U.S. publisher who started *Reader's Digest* magazine, born in St. Paul, Minnesota (–1981).

14 Jawaharlal Nehru, first prime minister of independent India 1947–64, born in Allahabad, India (–1964).

16 George S. Kaufman, U.S. playwright and stage director, born in Pittsburgh, Pennsylvania (–1961).

20 Edwin Powell Hubble, U.S. astronomer who provided the first proof that the universe is expanding, born in Marshfield, Missouri (–1953).

30 Edgar Adrian, English physiologist who won the Nobel Prize for Physiology or Medicine in 1932 for his discoveries concerning nerve impulses, born in London, England (–1977).

DECEMBER

6 Jefferson Davis, President of the Confederate States of America 1861–65, dies in New Orleans, Louisiana (81).

7 Gabriel Marcel, French Existentialist philosopher, born in Paris, France (–1973).

12 Robert Browning, English poet, dies in Venice, Italy (77).

21 Sewall Wright, U.S. geneticist, one of the founders of population genetics, born in Melrose, Massachusetts (–1988).

- The English scientist and philosopher Thomas Henry Huxley publishes *Agnosticism*.
- The Irish writer George Bernard Shaw publishes *Fabian Essays*, a collection of his political essays.
- The French philosopher Henri Bergson publishes *Essai sur les données immédiates et la conscience/Essay on the Immediate Data of Consciousness*.
- The U.S. statesman Theodore Roosevelt publishes the first volume of his study of American history *The Winning of the West*. The last volume appears in 1896.
- The U.S. writer and historian Henry Brooks Adams publishes the first volume of his nine-volume *History of the United States during the Administrations of Thomas Jefferson and James Madison*. The last volume appears in 1891.
- U.S. industrialist Andrew Carnegie publishes "Wealth" (also known as "The Gospel of Wealth"), arguing that the rich must serve as guardians of the public trust.
- U.S. writer Robert Ingersoll publishes "Why I Am an Agnostic," a rationalist critique of religious belief.

DECEMBER

14 U.S. social scientists establish the American Academy of Political and Social Science in Philadelphia, Pennsylvania.

SOCIETY

Education

- Barnard College (for women) is founded in New York, New York.
- Chicago entrepreneur John Crerar bequeaths $2.5 million to endow the John Crerar Library for scientific research.
- The British Parliament passes the Welsh Intermediate Education Act and establishes secondary education in Wales.
- The Catholic University in Washington, D.C., is founded.
- The University of Idaho is founded in Moscow, Idaho.
- The University of New Mexico is founded in Albuquerque.

Everyday Life

- Fire destroys much of Seattle, Washington.
- Foster's beer is launched in Collingwood, Victoria, Australia.
- The British are the largest consumers per capita of sugar in the world.
- The French corset-maker Hermine Cadolle creates the first bra, which frees women from the restrictions of corsets.
- U.S. reformers Jane Addams and Ellen Gates Starr establish Hull House, a settlement house dedicated to settlement work among the immigrant poor, in Chicago, Illinois.

December 1889–90 The Smithsonian Institute establishes the National Zoological Park in Washington, D.C.

JUNE

10 Diverse societies of Confederate war veterans unite to form the United Confederate Veterans in the United States.

AUGUST

6 The Savoy opens in London, England, the first hotel with private bathrooms.

Media and Communication

- U.S. inventor William Gray installs the first coin-operated telephone, in Hartford, Connecticut.

JULY

8 The *Wall Street Journal* is launched in the United States.

Sports

- The U.S. football player Walter Camp chooses the first All-American football team in *Collier's Weekly*.

JULY

8 In the last major bareknuckle championship prize fight, the U.S. boxer J. L. Sullivan defeats fellow countryman Jake Kilrain over 75 rounds at Richburg, Mississippi.

AUGUST

29 The first professional lawn tennis competition is held at Newport, Rhode Island.

1890

POLITICS, GOVERNMENT, AND ECONOMICS

Business and Economics

- It is estimated that 1% of the U.S. population holds more than half of the nation's wealth.
- James Buchanan Duke incorporates the American Tobacco Company in the United States.
- The industrial union Knights of Labor initiates a strike against operators of the New York Central Railroad.
- The U.S. Congress passes the McKinley Tariff Act, raising tariffs to record heights.
- U.S. politician Henry George leads delegates to the Single Tax National League meeting in New York, New York, in adopting a single tax platform.

MARCH
15–28   An international Congress for the Protection of the Workers is held in Berlin, Germany.

JULY
29   Industrial courts are established in Germany to adjudicate in wage disputes.

OCTOBER
10   Liberals in Canada press for the negotiation of a reciprocity agreement with the United States when, on the basis of the McKinley Tariff Act, the United States implements increased tariffs on imports from nations not having such agreements.
28   The German East Africa Company cedes its territorial rights to Germany.

NOVEMBER
- Barings, the English merchant bank, collapses following overspeculation in South America.

Colonization

- Bechuanaland is placed under a British governor.

MAY
24   Italy reorganizes the Red Sea territories as the colony of Eritrea.
24   By the Mackinnon Treaty between King Leopold II of Belgium and the British East Africa Company, the latter recognizes Leopold's rights on the west bank of the Upper Nile in return for territory near Lake Tanganyika.

JULY
1   Under an Anglo-German convention, Britain exchanges the North Sea island of Heligoland for Zanzibar and Pemba in East Africa.

SEPTEMBER
12   The British South Africa Company founds the city of Salisbury in Mashonaland.

NOVEMBER
14   An Anglo-Portuguese agreement on the Zambezi and Congo rivers grants Britain the control of the Lower Zambezi and the right to colonize central territory up to the Congo.

DECEMBER
18   Sir Frederick Lugard occupies Uganda for the British East Africa Company.

Human Rights

MARCH
27   Universal suffrage is restored in Spain following a respite from political disturbances since 1886.

Politics and Government

- The beginnings of the Armenian nationalist revolutionary movement are formed.
- U.S. president Benjamin Harrison appoints Michigan jurist Henry B. Brown to the U.S. Supreme Court.

FEBRUARY
4   The U.S. Senate ratifies the Samoan treaty, which establishes a joint U.S.-British-German protectorate over Samoa.
10   The U.S. government opens 11 million acres of South Dakota land, formerly under the possession of the Sioux, to settlement.

MARCH
20   The German chancellor Otto von Bismarck is dismissed by the new emperor Wilhelm II and Leo, Count von Caprivi, becomes chancellor.

APRIL
4   The Conservatives are defeated in the New Zealand elections by the Labor and Liberal parties.
14   Delegates to the International Conference of American States establish the Pan-American Union.

MAY
- The first May Day labor celebrations are held in Germany.
2   The U.S. Congress creates the Oklahoma Territory.

JUNE

18   Germany allows the lapse of former chancellor Otto von Bismarck's Reinsurance Treaty with Russia of June 1887, despite Russian attempts to open negotiations for a renewal.

27   The U.S. Congress passes the Dependent Pension Act, a pension for veterans of the U.S. Army. By 1890 there are 970,000 veterans receiving pensions at a cost of $135 million.

JULY

2   U.S. president Benjamin Harrison signs the Sherman Antitrust Act, designed to encourage competition by prohibiting unlawful monopolies.

3   Idaho becomes the 43rd state to join the Union.

7   The first Japanese general election is held for the country's newly created national assembly.

14   The U.S. Congress passes the Sherman Silver Purchase Act, authorizing the Treasury Department to buy 4.5 million ounces of silver per month and issue notes against it.

17   The British colonial entrepreneur Cecil Rhodes becomes premier of Cape Colony.

AUGUST

5   An Anglo-French convention defines spheres of influence in Nigeria, the British protectorate in Zanzibar and Pemba, and the French protectorate in Madagascar.

17   In a meeting at Narva, Russia, Czar Alexander III of Russia fails to persuade Emperor Wilhelm II of Germany to form an *entente*.

OCTOBER

1   The German antisocialist law of 1878 proscribing the Social Democratic Party (SPD) expires and is not renewed.

1   The U.S. Congress creates the Weather Bureau within the Department of Agriculture.

22   The British Parliament grants responsible government to the colony of Western Australia.

NOVEMBER

1   Mississippi adopts a new state constitution with literacy laws designed to disenfranchise black Americans.

4   In U.S. Congressional elections, Republicans retain their majority in the Senate (47-39), but surrender to the Democrats control of the House (235-88).

12   The Catholic prelate cardinal Charles Lavigerie's "Algiers Toast" calls on all Frenchmen to rally to the constitution, in an attempt to reconcile the Roman Catholic Church with the republic.

17   The Irish nationalist member of Parliament Captain William Henry O'Shea is granted a decree nisi against his wife Katherine, citing party leader Charles Stewart Parnell as corespondent.

23   On the death of William III and the accession of Queen Wilhelmina, the Grand Duchy of Luxembourg is separated from the Netherlands.

29   The first Japanese diet is opened following elections.

DECEMBER

10   U.S. Army troops capture Sioux chief Sitting Bull, who resists the white settlement of South Dakota. Sitting Bull is then shot dead by his captors when his Sioux followers attempt to liberate him.

12   Charles Stewart Parnell resigns as member of Parliament following the scandal of his citation as corespondent in

a divorce suit and is succeeded as leader of the Irish Nationalists by Justin McCarthy.

29   Some 500 U.S. Army troops massacre 300 Sioux—men, women, and children—at the so-called "Battle" of Wounded Knee, South Dakota. The massacre effectively ends Native American resistance to U.S. settlement in North America.

SCIENCE, TECHNOLOGY, AND MEDICINE

Ecology

•   The first offshore oil wells are drilled near Santa Barbara, California.

•   The U.S. Congress creates Rock Creek Park, a 2,213-acre oasis in Washington, D.C., Sequoia National Park from 386,863 acres of central California wilderness, and Yosemite National Park from 761,320 acres of wilderness in California's Tuolumne River Valley. The Sequoia and Yosemite parks are created to preserve stands of the *Sequoia giganteo* trees, the largest trees in the world.

Health and Medicine

•   French physician A. Pinard establishes the antenatal clinic Maternité Baudelocque, in Paris, France; it is the world's first public health clinic.

•   German bacteriologist Emil von Behring, along with Japanese bacteriologist Shibasaburo Kitazato, develop tetanus and diphtheria antitoxins, in Berlin, Germany. They inject minute amounts of the toxins into animals, which then produce the antitoxin.

•   The world's first infant welfare clinics are established in Barcelona, Spain.

•   U.S. surgeon William Stewart Halsted improves antiseptic surgical procedures by pioneering the use of thin rubber gloves.

•   U.S. dentist C. H. Land invents the porcelain crown for teeth.

•   U.S. dentist Willoughby Dayton Miller correctly identifies the microorganism involved in tooth decay.

Science

•   French electrical engineer Edouard Branly invents the coherer, a device for detecting radio waves. It consists of a tube containing iron filings which "cohere," or coalesce, in the presence of a radio frequency and permit the passage of an electric current.

•   Swedish chemist Per Teodor Cleve develops a method of dating glacial deposits by classifying the diatom (unicellular alga) fossils in the deposits.

•   German organic chemist Theodor Curtius obtains azoimide (compound of hydrogen and nitrogen) from organic sources.

- The first version of the Henry Draper Star Catalog is published. Produced by astronomers at Harvard College Observatory, it lists the position, magnitude, and type of over 10,000 stars, and begins the alphabetical system of naming stars according to temperature. Subsequent editions increase the listing to 400,000 stars.

Technology

- British-born U.S. electrical engineer Elihu Thomson creates the high-frequency generator.
- The first British electrical power station opens, in Deptford (now in Greater London).
- The first electric ovens to be manufactured in the United States are introduced by the Carpenter Electric Heating Manufacturing Company, St. Paul, Minnesota.
- The first hydroelectric plant to produce alternating current (AC), as opposed to direct current (DC), is built on the Willamette River, Oregon.
- The leakproof pipeline coupling is invented, a breakthrough in gas transportation technology.
- U.S. inventor and statistician Herman Hollerith uses punched cards to automate counting the U.S. census. The holes, which represent numerical data, are sorted and tabulated by an electric machine, the forerunner of modern computers. In 1896 Hollerith forms the Tabulating Machine Company, which later changes its name to International Business Machines (IBM).
- U.S. scientists Harold P. Brown and E. A. Kenneally invent the electric chair as a modern and humane method of execution. New York state prisoner William Kemmer is the first person to be executed with it.

Transportation

- English civil engineer Benjamin Baker completes the Firth railroad bridge over the Firth of Forth in Scotland. One of the first cantilever bridges, and having the world's longest span (two each 521 m/1,710 ft), it costs £3 million to build, and uses 54,000 tons of steel.
- Railroad mileage at this time is as follows: United States, 268,409 km/167,756 mi; Great Britain, 27,811 km/17,382 mi.
- The City and South London Railway's "tube" railroad line opens. The world's first electric underground railroad, the 4.8-km/3-mi line runs beneath the River Thames. Fares cost two pence.
- U.S. inventor John William Lambert builds the first automobile in the United States to be powered by an internal combustion engine: a single-cylinder, three-wheeled vehicle which he tests in 1891 at Ohio City, Ohio, achieving a speed of 24 kph/15 mph.

JANUARY

25 *New York World* reporter Elizabeth Cochrane ("Nellie Bly") completes her trip around the world in 72 days, 6 hours, 11 minutes, and 14 seconds to beat the achievement of Phileas Fogg, the fictional hero of Jules Verne's novel *Around the World in Eighty Days*.

OCTOBER

9 French engineer Clément Ader's bat-winged, steam-driven monoplane *Eole* flies 50 m/160 ft to become the first full-sized aircraft to leave the ground under its own power.

ARTS AND IDEAS

Architecture

- New Scotland Yard in London, England, designed by the English architect Richard Norman Shaw, is completed.

Arts

c. 1890 The French artist Paul Cézanne paints *Woman with a Coffee Pot*.
- The Dutch artist Vincent van Gogh paints his *Portrait of Dr Gachet*, *Field with a Stormy Sky*, and *Starry Night*.
- The English artist Frederic Leighton paints *The Bath of Psyche*.
- The French artist Aimé-Jules Dalou sculpts *The Triumph of the Republic*.
- The French artist Henri de Toulouse-Lautrec paints *Dance at the Moulin Rouge*.
- The French artist Odilon Redon completes his album of lithographs *Les Fleurs du mal/Flowers of Evil*, inspired by the poem of the same title by the French poet Charles Baudelaire.
- The Russian artist Mikhail Alexandrovich Vrubel paints *Demon Sitting Down*.
- The U.S. artist Albert Pinkham Ryder paints *Moonlight Marine*.
- The U.S. artist Childe Hassam paints *Washington Arch, Spring*.
- The U.S. artist Thomas Eakins takes the photograph *Walt Whitmann, Seated in a Chair*.
October 1890–91 The French artist Claude Monet paints his *Poplars* series.

Literature and Language

- *Poems*, a selection of the poems of the U.S. writer Emily Dickinson, who died in 1886, is published posthumously. Although she wrote over 1,000 poems, only six were published in her lifetime, all without her permission.
- The French writer Anatole France publishes his novel *Thaïs*, based on the opera by the French composer Jules Massenet.
- The French writer Auguste, comte de Villiers de L'Isle-Adam, publishes his long prose poem *Axël*.
- The French writer Emile Zola publishes his novel *La Bête humaine/The Human Beast*.
- The Indian writer Rabindranath Tagore publishes his Bengali poetry collection *Manasi/Mind's Creation*.
- The Norwegian writer Knut Hamsun publishes his novel *Sult/Hunger*.
- The Russian writer Leo Tolstoy publishes his story *Kreitserova sonata/The Kreutzer Sonata*.
- The Scottish writer Arthur Conan Doyle publishes *The Sign of Four*, the second Sherlock Holmes novel.
- The U.S. artist James Abbot McNeill Whistler publishes *The Gentle Art of Making Enemies*, his memoirs.
- The U.S. writer Henry James publishes his novel *The Tragic Muse*.

- The U.S. writer John Greenleaf Whittier publishes his poetry collection *At Sundown*.
- The U.S. writer Sarah Orne Jewett publishes *Tales of New England*.
- The U.S. writer William Dean Howells publishes his novel *A Hazard of New Fortunes*.

Music

- French composer Claude Debussy completes his piano work *Suite Bergamasque*.
- French composer Gabriel Fauré completes his *Requiem* for chorus and orchestra.
- German composer Richard Strauss completes his symphonic poem *Tod und Verklärung/Death and Transfiguration*.
- The opera *Cavalleria rusticana* by the Italian composer Pietro Mascagni is first performed, in Rome, Italy. It is based on a story by the Italian writer Giovanni Verga.
- The opera *Pikovaya dama/The Queen of Spades* by the Russian composer Peter Illyich Tchaikovsky is first performed, in St. Petersburg, Russia. It is based on a short story written in 1834 by the Russian poet Alexander Pushkin.
- The opera *Prince Igor* by the Russian composer Alexander Porfiryevich Borodin (and completed by Rimsky-Korsakov and Glazunov after his death in 1887) is first performed, in St. Petersburg, Russia.

Theater and Dance

- A new version of the ballet *Spyashchaya krasavitsa/The Sleeping Beauty* by the Russian composer Peter Illyich Tchaikovsky is first performed, in St. Petersburg, Russia. The choreography is by the French choreographer Marius Petipa.
- The play *Creditörer/Creditors* by the Swedish writer Johan August Strindberg is first performed, in Copenhagen, Denmark.
- The play *Das Friedensfest/The Reconciliation* by the German dramatist Gerhardt Hauptmann is first performed, in Berlin, Germany.

Thought and Scholarship

- Danish-American Jacob Riis publishes *How the Other Half Lives*, an indictment of tenement housing in New York, New York.
- The English economist Alfred Marshall publishes his classic *Principles of Economics*.
- The English evangelist leader William Booth publishes *In Darkest England and the Way Out*.
- The French police officer Alphonse Bertillon publishes *Photographie judiciare/Forensic Photography*, in which he sets out a system (widely adopted) for identifying criminals based on detailed measurements of body and facial features.
- The Scottish anthropologist and folklorist James George Frazer publishes the first volume of his 12-volume *The Golden Bough: A Study in Comparative Religion*, which details the cults, legends, myths, and rites of the world's peoples. The final volume appears in 1915.

- The U.S. historian Alfred Thayer Mahan publishes the first volume of *The Influence of Sea Power on History, 1660–1812*. The final volume appears in 1892.
- U.S. psychologist William James publishes *Principles of Psychology*, in which he pioneers the functional approach to physiological psychology.
- William Thomas Stead founds and edits the journal *Review of Reviews* in London, England.

SOCIETY

Education

- Classes begin at the University of Chicago, Illinois.
- Oklahoma State University is founded in Stillwater, Oklahoma.
- The University of Oklahoma is founded in Norman, Oklahoma.
- Washington State University is founded in Pullman, Washington.

Everyday Life

c. 1890 It is becoming acceptable for women to smoke in private, but not in public, in the United States and Europe.
- North Carolina pharmacist Lunsford Richardson invents what will become Vicks VapoRub, a decongestant for cold and cough sufferers, and calls it Richardson's Croup and Pneumonia Salve.
- The National Carbon Co. launches Ever Ready batteries in the United States, the first dry-cell battery to be made commercially.
- The U.S. Census lists the nation's population at 62,947,714, an increase from the 1880 figure of 50,155,783.
- U.S. coal miners establish the United Mine Workers of America, a union within the American Federation of Labor.

JUNE
6 The Swiss federal government introduces a state sponsored program of social insurance.

OCTOBER
11 The patriotic organization Daughters of the American Revolution is founded in Washington, D.C.
- The English writer, designer, and social reformer William Morris founds Kelmscott Press at Hammersmith in London, England.

Religion

OCTOBER
6 The Church of Jesus Christ of Latter-day Saints renounces polygamy.

BIRTHS & DEATHS

- Ho Chi Minh (original name Nguyen That Thanh), founder of the Indochina Communist Party in 1930 and president of North Vietnam 1945–69, born in Hoang Tru, Vietnam (–1969).

JANUARY

9   Karel Čapek, Bohemian novelist and playwright whose works explore philosophical ideas and who introduced the term "Robot," born in Malé Svatonovice, Hungary (–1938).

10   Johann Joseph Ignaz von Döllinger, German historian and theologian who was excommunicated for refusing to accept the Vatican Council's doctrine of the pope's infallibility, dies in Munich, Germany (91).

FEBRUARY

10   Boris Pasternak, Russian poet and novelist who wrote *Dr Zhivago*, born in Moscow, Russia (–1960).

17   Christopher Latham Sholes, U.S. inventor of the typewriter, dies in Milwaukee, Wisconsin (71).

MARCH

9   Vyacheslav Mikhaylovich Molotov, Russian diplomat who negotiated at the international conferences following World War II, born in Kukaida, Vyatka (–1986).

12   Vaslav Nijinsky, Russian-born ballet dancer and choreographer, born in Kiev, Russia (–1950).

20   Beniamino Gigli, Italian operatic tenor, born in Recanati, near Ancona, Italy (–1957).

21   (William) Lawrence Bragg, Australian-born British physicist and X-ray crystallographer who shared the Nobel Prize for Physics with his father William Bragg in 1915, born in Adelaide, Australia (–1971).

28   Paul Whiteman, U.S. bandleader known as the "King of Jazz," born in Denver, Colorado (–1967).

APRIL

6   Anthony Fokker, Dutch aircraft manufacturer who made the first machine gun able to shoot through the blades of an airplane's propeller, born in Kediri, Java, Netherlands East Indies (–1939).

11   Joseph Merrick, the "Elephant Man," severely deformed professional "freak," dies in London, England (27).

16   Donald Forsha Jones, U.S. geneticist who produced the first high-yield hybrid corn, born in Hutchinson, Kansas (–1963).

MAY

10   Alfred Jodl, German general who was head of Germany's armed forces operations staff and helped plan most of the country's military operations during World War II, born in Würzburg, Germany (–1946).

15   Katherine Anne Porter, U.S. Pulitzer prizewinning writer and teacher whose 1962 novel *Ship of Fools* was filmed in 1965, born in Indian Creek, Texas (–1980).

JUNE

16   Stan Laurel, U.S. comedian who, with Oliver Hardy, formed the first successful motion-picture comedian team, born in Ulverston, Lancashire, England (–1965).

JULY

6   Edwin Chadwick, English physician and social reformer, dies in East Sheen, Surrey, England (90).

13   John C(harles) Frémont, U.S. explorer who opened up California for development, dies in New York, New York (77).

16   Gottfried Keller, Swiss writer, dies in Zürich, Switzerland (71).

29   Vincent van Gogh, Dutch painter whose work inspired the expressionists, dies in Auvers-sur-Oise, near Paris, France (37).

AUGUST

5   Naum Gabo, Russian-born U.S. pioneering sculptor in Constructivist art, born in Bryansk, Russia (–1977).

11   John Henry Newman, English clergyman who led the Oxford Movement in the Church of England and later became a Roman Catholic cardinal, dies in Birmingham, England (89).

17   Harry L. Hopkins, U.S. administrator and President Franklin D. Roosevelt's personal advisor during World War II, born in Sioux City, Iowa (–1946).

27   Man Ray, U.S. dada and surrealist photographer, painter, and filmmaker, born in Philadelphia, Pennsylvania (–1976).

SEPTEMBER

9   Harland ("Colonel") Sanders, U.S. businessman, founder of the Kentucky Fried Chicken fast-food restaurants, born near Henryville, Indiana (–1980).

10   Mortimer Wheeler, British archeologist, author, and broadcaster who believed in popularizing archeology, born in Glasgow, Scotland (–1976).

15   Agatha Christie (born Miller), English author of detective novels and creator of Hercule Poirot and Miss Marple, born in Torquay, Devon, England (–1976).

15   Frank Martin, Swiss composer, pianist, harpsichordist, and teacher, born in Geneva, Switzerland (–1974).

OCTOBER

2   Groucho (real name Julius) Marx, U.S. comedian of stage, film, radio, and television along with two of his brothers, Harpo and Chico, born in New York, New York (–1977).

8   Edward (Eddie) Rickenbacker, U.S. flying ace of World War I, later an airline executive, born in Columbus, Ohio (–1973).

14   Dwight David Eisenhower, thirty-fourth president of the United States 1953–61, a Republican, born in Denison, Texas (–1969).

20   Richard (Francis) Burton, English explorer and translator who with John Speke discovered Lake Tanganyika in East Africa, dies in Trieste, Austria-Hungary (70).

NOVEMBER

8   César (-Auguste) Franck, Belgian-born French composer, dies in Paris, France (67).

10   (Jean-Nicolas-) Arthur Rimbaud, French Symbolist poet, dies in Marseille, France (37).

22   Charles de Gaulle, French general and president of France 1958–69, born in Lille, France (–1970).

DECEMBER

5   Fritz Lang, Austrian-born U.S. film director who made *Metropolis*, born in Vienna, Austria (–1976).

11   Mark Tobey, U.S. abstract painter who often used white on a dark background, born in Centerville, Wisconsin (–1976).

15   Sitting Bull, Sioux chief who was responsible for the alliance of Sioux people resulting in the utter defeat of George A(rmstrong) Custer and all the men under his command at the Battle of the Little Bighorn, is killed on the Grand River, South Dakota (c. 59).

18   Edwin Howard Armstrong, U.S. inventor who developed the heterodyne circuit and frequency modulation (FM) for radio, born in New York, New York (–1954).

21   Hermann Joseph Muller, U.S. geneticist who demonstrated that X-rays speed up the mutation rate, born in New York, New York (–1967).

26   Heinrich Schliemann, German archeologist who excavated Troy, Mycenae, and Tiryns, dies in Naples, Italy (68).

Sports

October 1891–1900 The pneumatic-tyred safety bicycle revolutionizes cycling both as means of leisure and sport.

OCTOBER

11 At the U.S. Amateur Athletic Union championships on Anastolan Island, Washington, D.C., U.S. runner John Owen becomes the first person to beat 10 seconds for the 90 m/100 yds in a major race.

1891

POLITICS, GOVERNMENT, AND ECONOMICS

Business and Economics

- American Express introduces American Express Traveler's Checks in the United States.
- Félix Méline introduces strict protection against foreign imports in France in response to the economic depression.
- Swiss industrialist Karl Elsener designs the Swiss Army knife and goes on to found the Victorinox Cutlery Co. in Switzerland.

APRIL

15 The Katanga Company is formed under the direction of King Leopold II of Belgium to exploit copper deposits in central Africa.

JUNE

10 Leander Starr Jameson becomes administrator of the territories of the British South Africa Company.

Colonization

APRIL

4 The Pan-German League is founded, a popular association dedicated to agitating for German expansionism.
11 A further Anglo-Portuguese convention is agreed on territories north and south of the Zambezi River. Portugal assigns Barotseland to Britain and Nyasaland is subsequently proclaimed a British protectorate.

Human Rights

- The states of Alabama, Arkansas, Georgia, and Tennessee adopt legislation designed to disenfranchise black Americans.

Politics and Government

- The International Copyright Act is passed in the United States, giving foreign authors protection against pirate editions.
- The Wahehe war begins in German East Africa between the indigenous inhabitants and their colonial rulers.

JANUARY

6 The Chilean congress declares the dictator José Manuel Balmaceda deposed.
31 Antonio Rudini, Marquis de Starabba, forms a right-wing coalition in Italy on the deposition by parliament of ex-revolutionary Francesco Crispi.

FEBRUARY

9 Emperor Menelek of Ethiopia denounces Italian claims to a protectorate in Ethiopia.
24 A federal constitution is introduced in Brazil.

MARCH

March–July A Sydney convention led by Henry Parkes draws up a federal constitution for Australia, but the program is dropped as a result of the opposition of New South Wales.
3 Congress creates the U.S. Circuit Court of Appeals to relieve the Supreme Court of some of its appellate burden.
14 A mob in New Orleans, Louisiana, lynches 11 Sicilian immigrants indicted for murder of the city's Irish police chief. The incident sparks international condemnation.
24 Britain and Italy make an agreement over Ethiopia defining the frontiers of their respective Red Sea colonies. The issues are defined further in the convention of April 15.

MAY

6 The Triple Alliance of Germany, Austria-Hungary, and Italy is renewed for 12 years.
19 U.S. farmers launch the People's (Populist) Party in Cincinnati, Ohio. The Party aims to protect farmers from unscrupulous creditors, railroad owners, and grain storage operators.

JUNE

1 A state law introduces the thorough inspection of factories in Germany.

16 John Abbot becomes premier of Canada following the death of Sir John Macdonald, premier since 1878 and the force behind making Canada a dominion.

20 Britain and the Netherlands define their boundaries in Borneo.

JULY

4   Kaiser Wilhelm II of Germany visits London, England, hoping Britain might join the Triple Alliance of Germany, Austria-Hungary, and Italy as a counterweight to the Franco-Russian alliance.

23 Relations between France and Russia are strengthened when a French squadron visits Kronstadt, Russia, and a French loan is floated to finance the Trans-Siberian Railroad.

AUGUST

27 A Franco-Russian *entente* is made as a result of friendlier relations following the break between Germany and Russia.

SEPTEMBER

19 The dictator José Balmaceda is driven from office in Chile following civil war with the congress.

22 The U.S. government opens nearly 1 million acres of Oklahoma land—formerly under the possession of the Sac, Fox, and Potawatomi peoples—to U.S. settlement.

30 The French nationalist General Georges Boulanger commits suicide while in exile in Brussels, Belgium.

OCTOBER

10 The British Liberal party adopts the "Newcastle Programme", which advocates Irish Home Rule, disestablishment of the Welsh church, reform of the House of Lords, triennial parliaments, abolition of the plural franchise, and a local veto on sales of liquor.

16 U.S.-Chilean relations deteriorate after sailors from the warship USS *Baltimore* are assaulted in Valparaíso, Chile.

NOVEMBER

23 The autocratic president of Brazil, Deodoroda Fonseca, is driven from office by a naval revolt and is succeeded by Florians Peixoto, who also governs dictatorially.

SCIENCE, TECHNOLOGY, AND MEDICINE

Ecology

- U.S. botanist Nathaniel Lord Britton establishes the New York Botanical Garden in the Bronx, New York, New York; it is the leading botanical research center in the United States.

MARCH

3   U.S. Congress passes the Forest Reserves Act, which establishes the first national forests in order to preserve their water, timber, wildlife, and other resources. Over 13 million acres are set aside over the next 2–3 years.

OCTOBER

28 An earthquake hits Mino-Owari, Japan, killing 7,300 people.

Health and Medicine

- Compulsory national health insurance is introduced in Hungary.
- German medical scientist Paul Ehrlich treats malaria with methylene blue. Its use marks the beginning of chemotherapy.
- Serbian-born U.S. inventor Nikola Tesla discovers that the application of high frequency alternating current (AC) to bodily tissues results in heat. He suggests this phenomena may have a medical application. It leads to the development of the physical therapy method now known as diathermy.
- The Public Health Act is introduced in Britain.
- U.S. surgeon Daniel Hale Williams establishes Provident Hospital in Chicago, Illinois. It is the first interracial hospital in the United States and provides training for black interns and nurses.

Science

- German electrical engineer Oskar von Miller develops a cable that can transmit alternating current (AC) at 25,000 volts over long distances.
- In an attempt to produce artificial diamonds, U.S. inventor Edward Goodrich Acheson discovers Carborundum (silicon carbide), the hardest synthetic material known until 1929. It is used as an industrial abrasive.
- Irish physicist Johnstone Stoney introduces the term "electron."
- Serbian-born U.S. inventor Nikola Tesla invents the Tesla coil, which produces a high-frequency high-voltage current.
- The "blink" comparator is invented. It permits the discovery of objects in the solar system by comparison of two photographs, taken a few hours apart, of the same region of the sky. Stars remain fixed, while planets and asteroids move or "blink."
- U.S. chemist Herman Frasch patents the Frasch process for the recovery of sulfur from underground deposits. Superheated water is pumped into the deposits, melting the sulfur and bringing it to the surface. The process allows the exploitation of deposits which would otherwise be prohibitively expensive. The liquid sulfur is more than 99% pure. It is first used successfully in Texas and Louisiana in 1894.

Technology

- British inventor Thomas Rudolphus Dallmeyer patents the first telephoto lens.
- French physicist Louis Ducos du Hauron patents the anaglyph, a device for taking three-dimensional photographs; images are viewed with different colored filters in order to give the three-dimensional impression.
- The world's first long-distance high-voltage line for transmitting electricity is established between Lauffen and Frankfurt am Main, Germany. Over 8,000 volts are carried over a distance of 177 km/120 mi.

Transportation

- French inventors René Panhard and Emile Levassar create an automobile to a design which becomes the basis for modern automobiles, by putting the engine at the front (which improves traction for the front wheels) and by replacing the typical leather drive-belt with a transmission, gear shift, and clutch. It is the first vehicle to be designed as an automobile rather than a modified "horseless" carriage.
- German aeronautical engineer Otto Lilienthal builds the first glider capable of carrying a person; he takes off by running downhill into the wind.

October 1891–1900   Electric streetcars replace horse-drawn streetcars in Europe and the United States.

October 1891–1904   The Trans-Siberian Railroad is built. Construction begins simultaneously from Moscow and Vladivostok and covers a distance of 9,311 km/ 5,786 mi, making it the longest railroad in the world.

ARTS AND IDEAS

Architecture

- The Monadnock Building in Chicago, Illinois, designed by the U.S. architects Daniel Hudson Burnham and John Wellborn Root, is completed.
- The Wainwright Building in St. Louis, Missouri, designed by the U.S. architect Louis Sullivan, is completed. Combining recent technological developments in building—particularly the use of a steel framework—the Wainwright Building is one of the first masterpieces in the development of the skyscraper.

Arts

- The French artist Auguste Rodin sculpts *Large Head of Iris*.
- The French artist Claude Monet paints his *Haystacks* series.
- The French artist Georges Seurat paints *Circus*.
- The French artist Henri de Toulouse-Lautrec draws the poster *Moulin Rouge: La Goulue/Moulin Rouge: The Glutton*.
- The French artist Jean-Edouard Vuillard paints *Woman in a Check Dress Darning a Stocking*.
- The French artist Paul Gauguin paints *Two Tahitian Women on a Beach*.
- The French artist Pierre Bonnard paints *Woman with a Dog*.
- The German-born English artist Hubert Herkomer paints *On Strike*.
- The Irish-born U.S. artist Augustus St.-Gaudens sculpts the Adams Memorial in Rock Creek Cemetery, Washington, D.C.

- The Italian artist Giovanni Segantini paints *Ploughing of the Engadine*.
- The U.S. artist Albert Pinkham Ryder paints *Siegried and the Rhine Maidens*.
- The U.S. artist John La Farge paints *Maua, Our Boatman*.

Film

- U.S. electrical engineer Thomas Edison, with his assistant William Dickson, develops the Kinetoscope, a predecessor of the motion-picture projector. It consists of a strip of film, viewed through a peephole in a box while being wound from one reel to another, producing the illusion of persons and objects in motion. Edison sees it as a toy and fails to consider projection of the images.

Literature and Language

- The English writer George Gissing publishes his novel *New Grub Street*.
- The English writer Rudyard Kipling publishes his novel *The Light that Failed*.
- The English writer Thomas Hardy publishes his novel *Tess of the D'Urbervilles*.
- The French writer and politician Maurice Barrès publishes his novel *Le Jardin de Bérénice/The Garden of Bernice*, the last volume of his trilogy *Le Culte du moi/ The Cult of Self*.
- The French writer Joris Karl Huysmans publishes his novel *Là-bas/Down There*.
- The Irish writer Oscar Wilde publishes his novel *The Picture of Dorian Gray* and *Lord Arthur Savile's Crime and Other Stories*.
- The Scottish writer Arthur Conan Doyle publishes the first of his Sherlock Holmes stories in *Strand Magazine*.
- The Scottish writer J. M. Barrie publishes his novel *The Little Minister*.
- The U.S. writer Ambrose Bierce publishes his short story collection *Tales of Soldiers and Civilians* (later called *In the Midst of Life*).
- The U.S. writer and editor Harriet Monroe publishes her poetry collection *Valeria and Other Poems*.
- The U.S. writer Hamlin Garland publishes his collection of prose sketches *Main-Traveled Roads*.
- The U.S. writer Herman Melville completes his short novel *Billy Budd*, which is not published until 1924. It provides the basis of the opera *Billy Budd*, which is written in 1951 by the English composer Benjamin Britten.
- The U.S. writer Mary Wilkins Freeman publishes her short story collection *A New England Nun and Other Stories*.
- The U.S. writer Walt Whitman publishes *Good-Bye, My Fancy*, his last collection of poems and prose.

Music

- Austrian composer Hugo Wolf completes his orchestral work *Italienische Serenade/Italian Serenade* and

the first volume of his song cycle *Italienisches Liederbuch/Italian Songbook*.
- Lottie Collins sings "Ta-ra-ra-boom-de-ay" in *Dick Whittington* at the Grand Theatre in Islington, London, England.
- Russian composer Sergey Rachmaninov completes his Piano Concerto No. 1, which he revises in 1917.

Theater and Dance

- The Carnegie Music Hall opens in New York, New York.
- The Dutch-born English theater manager Jack Thomas Grein founds the Independent Theatre Society, in London, England. His aim is to introduce plays by Henrik Johan Ibsen and other European dramatists to the English stage.
- The German dramatist Frank Wedekind publishes his tragedy *Frühlings Erwachen/Spring's Awakening*, its sexual explicitness causing a scandal. It is first performed in 1905.
- The play *Hedda Gabler* by the Norwegian dramatist Henrik Ibsen is first performed, in Christiania (now Oslo), Norway. One of Ibsen's finest plays, and one of the classic works of modern theater, it was published in 1890.
- The play *Thermidor* by the French dramatist Victorien Sardou is first performed, in Paris, France.

BIRTHS & DEATHS

JANUARY
23 Antonio Gramsci, Italian politician and intellectual who helped found the Italian Communist Party in 1921, born in Ales, Sardinia (–1937).
26 Frank Costello, U.S. gangster, born in Cosenza, Italy (–1973).
26 Nikolaus August Otto, German engineer who developed the four-stroke internal combustion engine, dies in Cologne, Germany (58).
27 Ilya Grigoryevich Ehrenburg, Russian writer, born in Kiev, Russia (–1967).

FEBRUARY
13 David Dixon Porter, Union naval officer during the American Civil War, dies in Washington, D.C. (77).
14 William Tecumseh Sherman, Union general during the American Civil War, dies in New York, New York (71).
27 David Sarnoff, U.S. radio broadcaster who promoted the sale of radios and formed the National Broadcasting Company (NBC), born in Minsk, Russia (–1971).

MARCH
19 Earl Warren, U.S. chief justice 1953–69 and chairman of the committee that investigates Kennedy's assassination, born in Los Angeles, California (–1974).
21 Joseph E. Johnston, Confederate general, dies in Washington, D.C. (84).

APRIL
2 Max Ernst, German painter and sculptor, one of the founders of surrealism, born in Brühl, Germany (–1976).
7 David Low, New Zealand-born British journalist and cartoonist, born in Dunedin, New Zealand (–1963).

7 P(hineas) T(aylor) Barnum, U.S. showman and promoter who popularized the three-ring circus, dies in Bridgeport, Connecticut (80).
11 Sergey Sergeyevich Prokofiev, Russian composer, born in Sontsovka, Ukraine, Russia (–1953).

MAY
11 Henry Morgenthau, U.S. secretary of the treasury 1934–45, born in New York, New York (–1967).
18 Rudolf Carnap, U.S. philosopher of logical positivism, born in Ronsdorf, Germany (–1970).

JUNE
6 John A. Macdonald, first prime minister of Canada 1867–73 and 1878–91, a Liberal-Conservative, dies in Ottawa, Ontario, Canada (76).
20 John Aloysius Costello, Prime Minister of Eire (the Republic of Ireland) 1948–51 and 1954–57, born in Dublin, Ireland (–1976).
21 Pier Luigi Nervi, Italian engineer and architect, born in Sondrio, Italy (–1979).

AUGUST
2 Arthur (Edward Drummond) Bliss, English composer, born in London, England (–1975).
12 James Russell Lowell, U.S. poet, critic, and diplomat, dies in Cambridge, Massachusetts (72).
22 Jacques Lipchitz, Russian-born French sculptor whose style was based on cubism, and who was one of the originators of nonrepresentational sculpture, born in Druskininkai, Russia (–1973).

SEPTEMBER
28 Herman Melville, U.S. novelist, short-story writer, and poet who wrote *Moby Dick*, dies in New York, New York (72).

OCTOBER
6 Charles Stewart Parnell, Irish nationalist who led the movement for Irish home rule, dies in Brighton, Sussex, England (45).
12 Fumimaro Konoe, Prime Minister of Japan 1937–39 and 1940–41, born in Tokyo, Japan (–1945).
20 James Chadwick, English physicist who discovered the neutron in 1932, born in Manchester, England (–1974).
26 Helmuth, Count von Moltke, chief of the Prussian and German general staff 1857–88 whose victories over Denmark, Austrias and France led the way to German unification, dies in Berlin, Germany (90).
29 Fanny Bryce, U.S. comedienne, born in New York, New York (–1951).

NOVEMBER
14 Frederick Grant Banting, Canadian physician who discovered insulin, born in Alliston, Canada (–1941).
15 Erwin Rommel, German field marshal who commanded the Afrika Korps during World War II, born in Heidenheim an der Brentz, Württemberg, Germany (–1944).
15 W. Averell Harriman, U.S. diplomat, a negotiator in the Nuclear Test-Ban Treaty of 1963, born in New York, New York (–1986).

DECEMBER
26 Henry Miller, U.S. novelist, born in New York, New York (–1980).
30 Antoine Pinay, French finance minister and premier of France in 1952 who brought inflation in France under control after World War II and introduced a new franc by devaluating the old one, born in St.-Symphorien-sur-Coise, France (–1994).

Thought and Scholarship

- *History of the Oxford Movement* by the English churchman and historian Richard William Church is published posthumously.
- University of California naturalist Joseph Le Conte publishes *Evolution and Its Relation to Religious Thought.*

SOCIETY

Education

- Rice University is founded in Houston, Texas.
- The California Institute of Technology is founded in Pasadena, California.

Everyday Life

- Dr. John S. Pemberton sells the rights to the soft drink Coca-Cola to Atlanta pharmacist Asa Briggs Candler.
- The U.S. Carpenter Electric Manufacturing Co. produces the first electric kettle.
- U.S. inventor Whitcomb L. Judson patents the zipper under the name of "Clasp Locker or Unlocker." It is initially designed for use on shoes and boots, and is not called the "zipper" until 1926.

Media and Communication

- A telephone link is established between London, England, and Paris, France.
- The newspaper *Il mattino* is launched in Italy.

Religion

- The religious leader John Clifford founds the Union of General and Particular Baptists in England.

MAY

15 Pope Leo XIII issues the papal encyclical "Rerum novarum"/"Of News Things," a study of the condition of working classes that earns him the name of "the working man's pope."

Sports

- The Canadian educator James Naismith, an instructor at the YMCA Training School in Springfield, Massachusetts, invents the game of basketball, attaching two peach baskets to the tops of ladders at opposite ends of a gymnasium floor.
- U.S. jockey Isaac Murphy becomes the first rider to win the Kentucky Derby in two successive years and the first to win it three times, having first won the race in 1884.
- Weightlifters from Britain, Belgium, Germany, and Italy compete in London, England, in what is promoted as the first world weightlifting championships.

JULY

4 The U.S. athlete Luther Cary becomes the first person to run the 100 meters in under 11 seconds, at a meeting in Paris, France.

1892

POLITICS, GOVERNMENT, AND ECONOMICS

Business and Economics

- Edison General and Thomson-Houston merge to form the General Electric Company in the United States.
- The U.S. economist Irving Fisher publishes *Mathematical Investigations in the Theory of Value and Prices.*

1892–97 The U.S. economy experiences a depression.

JUNE

30 Iron and steel workers begin a strike in the United States.

JULY

6 Violence erupts during a labor strike at a Carnegie Steel plant in Homestead, Pennsylvania. By the time the state militia restores order on July 12, thirteen people have been killed and scores more injured.

NOVEMBER

10 The Panama Canal financial scandal breaks in France and the canal's builder Ferdinand de Lesseps and his associates are committed for trial for corruption and mismanagement.

Human Rights

NOVEMBER

22 A Belgian force in the Upper Congo suppresses a rising of Arab slaveholders protesting at European disruption of their trade.

Politics and Government

- France fights a second war against the king of Dahomey in West Africa following opposition to the imposition of a French protectorate. The revolt is put down by General Alfred A. Dodds.
- U.S. president Benjamin Harrison appoints Pennsylvania jurist George Shiras, Jr., to the U.S. Supreme Court.

November 1892–94 Anarchist outrages occur across France.

JANUARY

7 At the age of 18, Abbas succeeds Tewfik as khedive of Egypt, ruling until 1914 and demonstrating hostility toward British influence.

FEBRUARY

1 Germany signs commercial treaties with Austria-Hungary, Italy, Switzerland, and Belgium.

MARCH

3 A Prussian bill for the religious education of children by the clergy is withdrawn after acrimonious debate.

26 A state labor department is formed in Germany.

APRIL

12 The U.S. government pays $25,000 indemnity to families of the 11 Sicilians lynched in New Orleans, Louisiana, in March 1891.

MAY

5 Giovanni Giolitti replaces Antonio Rudini, Marquis di Starabba, as premier of Italy.

5 The U.S. Congress passes the Geary Chinese Exclusion Act, extending the Exclusion Act of 1882.

JUNE

6 The pro-Western Prince Hirobumi Ito becomes premier of Japan.

11 Republicans renominate Benjamin Harrison for president and nominate New York editor Whitelaw Reid for vice president.

23 Democrats nominate former president Grover Cleveland for president and Illinois politician Adlai Ewing Stevenson for vice president.

AUGUST

11 Following electoral defeat in the British general election, the Conservative prime minister Lord Salisbury resigns and William Ewart Gladstone forms a Liberal ministry, with Lord Rosebery as foreign secretary, William Harcourt as chancellor of the Exchequer, and Herbert Asquith as home secretary.

17 A Franco-Russian military convention is agreed, developing the *entente* between the two powers.

SEPTEMBER

9 The reformer Sergey Witte becomes Russian finance minister.

OCTOBER

15 An Anglo-German convention recognizes a German protectorate in the Cameroons.

15 The U.S. Congress opens 1.8 million acres of land in Montana, formerly the Crow Native American reservation, to U.S. settlement.

NOVEMBER

8 Democratic candidate Grover Cleveland is elected president of the United States. In the Congressional elections, the Democrats attain majorities in both the House (218–127) and Senate (44–38).

DECEMBER

5 John Thompson becomes premier of Canada on the resignation of John Abbot.

12 A Pan-Slavic conference opens in Kraków, Poland, to work for the closer union of Slavic peoples.

SCIENCE, TECHNOLOGY, AND MEDICINE

Agriculture

- Russia is hit by a serious famine.
- Canadian botanist Charles Saunders develops Marquis wheat by crossing Red Fife wheat with an early ripening Indian variety. Made available to farmers in 1900, it dominates spring wheat in the United States and Canada for 50 years.

Ecology

- U.S. naturalist John Muir founds the Sierra Club to preserve scenic resources in the United States.
- Adirondack Park is established in the state of New York. The country's largest forest reserve, it covers 2.4 million acres.

December 1892–94 Over 1 million people die from drought-induced famine in China.

APRIL

19 An earthquake strikes in California, causing widespread devastation.

Health and Medicine

- A cholera epidemic strikes Hamburg, Germany, but its neighboring city of Altona, which has a water filtration system, escapes. It provides dramatic evidence of the value of treating water.
- Canadian physician William Osler publishes *The Principles and Practice of Medicine*, the most comprehensive and popular textbook on medicine of the time.

Math

- German mathematician Georg Cantor demonstrates that there are different kinds of infinity.

Science

- Dutch geneticist Hugo Marie de Vries, through a program of plant breeding, establishes the same laws of heredity discovered by Gregor Mendel in 1865.
- English anthropologist and eugenicist Francis Galton publishes *Fingerprints*, in which he describes the use of fingerprints for identification.
- French chemist Ferdinand-Frédéric Henri Moissan invents the first electric-arc furnace. He uses it to vaporize and fuse different elements and create new materials.
- French physicist Jacques-Arsène d'Arsonval demonstrates that humans can conduct alternating current (AC) strong enough to light an electric lamp.
- German embryologist and anatomist Oscar Hertwig establishes the science of cytology by suggesting that the processes that go on inside the cell are reflections of organismic processes.
- German-born U.S. electrical engineer Charles Proteus Steinmetz discovers the law of hysteresis, which, by explaining why all electrical devices lose power when magnetic action is converted to heat, allows engineers to improve the efficiency of electric motors, generators, and transformers through design, rather than trial and error.
- Presaging an aspect of Einstein's theory of relativity, Irish physicist George Francis FitzGerald suggests that a body contracts when in motion and that this contraction affects scientific instruments.
- Russian microbiologist Dimitry Iosifovich Ivanovsky publishes "On Two Diseases of Tobacco" in which he announces that mosaic disease in tobacco is caused by microorganisms too small to be seen through a microscope. Now known as viruses, his discovery pioneers the science of virology.
- Russian scientist Konstantin Eduardovich Tsiolkovsky pioneers the study of aerodynamics by building a series of wind tunnels to measure air resistance on moving vehicles.
- Scottish chemist William Ramsay discovers argon (atomic no. 18), the first inert gas.
- U.S. astronomer Edward Emerson Barnard discovers Jupiter's fifth moon, Amalthea.
- U.S. geologist Clarence Edward Dutton publishes the paper "On Some of the Greater Problems of Physical Geology," in which he advances the idea of isostasy, whereby lighter material in the earth's crust rises to form continents and mountains, while heavier material sinks, to form basins and oceans.

Technology

- British chemists Charles Cross, Edward Bevan, and Clayton Beadle dissolve cellulose to create viscose rayon. In 1905, the British textile company Courtaulds buy the rights and begin commercial production.
- British physicist and chemist James Dewar invents the double-walled vacuum flask for storing liquefied gases.
- French engineer François Hennebique improves reinforced concrete by laying the reinforcing rods at right angles to one another. He builds an apartment complex in France using the reinforced concrete for walls, floors, columns, and beams.

- German engineer Rudolf Diesel patents the diesel engine, a new type of internal combustion engine which runs on a fuel cheaper than gasoline and which, because ignition of the fuel is achieved by compression rather than electric spark, is simpler in construction.
- German mechanical engineer Gottlieb Daimler improves the carburetor by mixing vaporized fuel with air to create an explosive gas.
- German inventor Hermann Ganswindt proposes using steel cartridges loaded with explosives to achieve escape velocity and leave the earth. He is the first to link rockets and space flight.
- U.S. inventor William Seward Burroughs patents and manufactures the "arithmometer," the first adding machine that prints out each entry as well as the total.
- U.S. undertaker Almon B. Strowger patents the first automatic telephone exchange where the caller determines who the receiver will be without the aid of an operator. Strowger develops it because he believes the operator is diverting his calls to her husband, who is also an undertaker.

MARCH
15 U.S. inventor Jess W. Reno patents "The Reno Inclined Elevator," the world's first escalator.

Transportation

- French inventors René Panhard and Emile Levassar build the first automobile equipped with pneumatic tires.
- Iowa blacksmith John Froehlich builds the first gasoline-powered tractor.
- The first elevated railroad in Chicago, Illinois, enters service; it forms the first section of the railroad that eventually circles the city and which becomes known as the "Loop."

SEPTEMBER
9 On completion of the Kimberley–Johannesburg leg of the South African Cape Railway, the first trains arrive at Johannesburg from Cape Town.

ARTS AND IDEAS

Architecture

- The Masonic Temple in Chicago, Illinois, designed by the U.S. architects Daniel Hudson Burnham and John Wellborn Root, is completed.

Arts

- c. 1892 The Norwegian artist Edvard Munch paints *Evening in Karl-Johann Street in Oslo* and *The Kiss*.
- The Belgian artist James Ensor paints *The Ray Fish*.
- The French artist Henri de Toulouse-Lautrec draws the poster *Aristide Bruant at the Ambassadeurs*, *La Goulue Entering the Moulin Rouge*, and *At the Moulin Rouge*.

- The French artist Paul Cézanne paints *The Cardplayers*.
- The French artist Paul Gauguin paints *The Spirit of the Dead Watching*.
- The French artist Pierre Puvis de Chavannes completes his fresco cycle in the Hôtel de Ville in Paris, France.
- The U.S. artist Mary Cassatt paints *The Bath*.
- The international photography society, the Linked Ring Brotherhood, is formed in London, England. Outstanding members include Frederick Evans and Alfred Stieglitz. The group is disbanded in 1910.
- The U.S. photographer Alfred Stieglitz photographs *The Terminal (New York)*.
- The Danish-born U.S. photographer Jacob Riis publishes *How The Other Half Lives*, photographs of the poor of New York, New York.

Literature and Language

- English writer George Grossmith writes the Victorian classic *Diary of a Nobody*, the life of Charles Pooter, clerk.
- The English writer Israel Zangwill publishes his novel *The Children of the Ghetto*.
- The English writer Marie Corelli publishes her novel *Lillith*. Her melodramas make her one of the most widely read novelists of her day.
- The English writer Rudyard Kipling publishes his verse collection *Barrack Room Ballads*, which includes "Gunga Din."
- The Irish writer W. B. Yeats publishes his poetry collection *The Countess Kathleen and Other Legends and Lyrics*, which include the verse play *The Countess Kathleen*.
- The Italian writer Italo Svevo publishes his novel *Una vita/A Life*.
- The Russian writer Anton Chekhov publishes his story "*Palata No. 6*/Ward 6."
- The Russian writer Maxim Gorky publishes "*Makar Chudra*," his first published short story.
- The Scottish writer Arthur Conan Doyle publishes his story collection *The Adventures of Sherlock Holmes*.
- U.S. writer Charlotte Perkins Gilman publishes "The Yellow Wallpaper," a story about the male medical establishment's confinement of women.

Music

- Bohemian composer Antonín Dvořák becomes director of New York National Conservatory.
- Danish composer Carl Nielsen completes his Symphony No. 1.
- English composer Charles Hubert Parry completes his oratorio *Job*.
- English songwriter Harry Dacre writes the song "Daisy Bell (A Bicycle Built for Two)."
- The opera *I pagliacci/The Clowns* by the Italian composer Ruggiero Leoncavallo is first performed, in Milan, Italy.
- The opera *Yolanta* by the Russian composer Pyotr Ilyich Tchaikovsky is first performed, in St. Petersburg, Russia.
- U.S. composer John Philip Sousa and his band are popular in the United States.

Theater and Dance

- A new version of the ballet *Shchelkunchik/Nutcracker* by the Russian composer Peter Illyich Tchaikovsky is first performed, in St. Petersburg, Russia. The choreography is by the Russian choreographer Lev Ivanovich Ivanov.
- The comedy *Lady Windermere's Fan* by the Irish writer Oscar Wilde is first performed, at the St. James Theatre in London, England.
- The play *Charley's Aunt*, by the English dramatist Brandon Thomas, is first performed, in London, England.
- The play *Widower's Houses* by the Irish writer George Bernard Shaw is first performed, in London, England.

Thought and Scholarship

- The U.S. philosopher William James publishes *The Will to Believe and Other Essays in Popular Philosophy*.
- The Canadian-born English naturalist George John Romanes publishes *Darwin and After Darwinism*.
- The English statesman William Ewart Gladstone delivers the first Romanes Lecture at Oxford University, England.

SOCIETY

Everyday Life

- A new immigrant receiving station is opened in the United States, on Ellis Island, in New York Bay, New York.
- British physicist Sir James Dewar invents the thermos flask.
- Membership in British labor unions stands at 1,576,000.
- The age of marriage for Italian girls is raised to 12.
- The Pioneer Club for Ladies is founded in London, England.
- U.S. salesman William Wrigley starts selling chewing gum, previously given away free with other sales, as his main line.

Media and Communication

- The world's first automatic telephone exchange begins operation at La Porte, Indiana.
- Stefan George founds the *Blätter fur die Kunst* newspaper in Germany.

Religion

- The English theologian Charles Gore founds the Anglican Community of the Resurrection in Oxford, England.

Sports

- The introduction of the bicycle-wheeled sulky improves speeds in harness racing.

BIRTHS & DEATHS

JANUARY

3   J(ohn) R(onald) R(euel) Tolkien, English novelist, known for his *Lord of the Rings* trilogy, born in Bloemfontein, South Africa (–1973).

10   Dumas Malone, U.S. historian, author of *Jefferson and his Time*, born in Coldwater, Mississippi (–1986).

14   Hal Roach, early Hollywood film director who directed the Laurel and Hardy films, born in Elmira, New York (–1992).

14   Martin Niemöller, German anti-Nazi theologian and clergyman, born in Lippstadt, Germany (–1984).

18   Oliver Hardy, U.S. comedian who, with his partner Stan Laurel, formed the first successful motion-picture comedy team, born in Harlem, Georgia (–1957).

31   Charles Spurgeon, English Baptist preacher and founder of churches and of Spurgeon's Bible College, dies (57).

MARCH

10   Arthur Honegger, Swiss composer, born in Le Havre, France (–1955).

26   Walt Whitman, U.S. journalist, essayist, and poet, dies in Camden, New Jersey (72).

29   William Bowman, English surgeon who discovered that the kidneys produce urine through the filtration of blood, dies in Dorking, Surrey, England (75).

APRIL

6   Donald Douglas, U.S. aircraft designer who founded the Douglas Aircraft Company, born in Brooklyn, New York (–1981).

6   Lowell Thomas, U.S. explorer, journalist, and radio commentator, born in Woodington, Ohio (–1981).

8   Richard Joseph Neutra, Austrian-born U.S. architect who introduced the International style into U.S. architecture, born in Vienna, Austria (–1970).

13   Arthur "Bomber" Harris, British Air Chief Marshal who originated "saturation bombing" by the Royal Air Force in World War II, born in Cheltenham, Gloucestershire, England (–1984).

13   Robert Watson-Watt, Scottish physicist who developed radar in England, born in Brechin, Forfarshire, Scotland (–1973).

14   Vere Gordon Childe, Australian historian and archeologist who developed the study of preliterate European cultures, born in Sydney, Australia (–1957).

18   Bolesław Bierut, Polish communist leader, born in Lublin, Poland (–1956).

MAY

2   Manfred, Baron von Richthofen (the "Red Baron"), German aviator and leading ace during World War I, born in Breslau, Germany (now Wrocław, Poland) (–1918).

3   George Thomson, English physicist who worked on the diffraction of electrons, born in Cambridge, England (–1975).

7   Archibald MacLeish, U.S. poet, professor, and assistant secretary of state 1944–45, born in Glencoe, Illinois (–1982).

25   Josip Broz Tito, Marshal of Yugoslavia 1943–53, President 1953–80, born in Kumrovec, near Zagreb, Croatia, Austria-Hungary (–1980).

JUNE

21   Reinhold Neibuhr, U.S. theologian who persuaded Christian pacifists to oppose Hitler, born in Wright City, Missouri (–1971).

26   Pearl Buck, U.S. writer who wrote novels about China, born in Hillsboro, West Virginia (–1973).

JULY

23   Haile Selassie, Ethiopian emperor 1930–74, who modernized the country but was deposed, born in Härer, Ethiopia (–1975).

AUGUST

•   (Charles) Dion O'Bannion, Chicago bootlegger and crime boss, born in Aurora, Illinois (–1924).

15   Louis-Victor, duc de Broglie, French physicist who discovered the wave nature of electrons, born in Dieppe, France (–1987).

17   Mae West, U.S. stage and film actress and sex symbol, born in Brooklyn, New York (–1980).

SEPTEMBER

4   Darius Milhaud, French composer, born in Aix-en-Provence, France (–1974).

6   Edward Victor Appleton, English physicist who received the Nobel Prize for Physics in 1947 for his discovery of the Appleton layer in the atmosphere which reflects radio waves, born in Bradford, Yorkshire (now West Yorkshire), England (–1965).

12   Alfred A. Knopf, U.S. publisher who founded a publishing house under his own name (which became a subsidiary of Random House in 1966), born in New York, New York (–1984).

23   John Pope, Union general during the American Civil War, dies in Sandusky, Ohio (70).

OCTOBER

2   (Joseph-) Ernest Renan, French philosopher, historian, and religious scholar, dies in Paris, France (69).

4   Engelbert Dollfuss, Austrian chancellor 1932–34 who abolished the Austrian republic and instituted a dictatorial regime, born in Texing, Austria (–1934).

6   Alfred, Lord Tennyson, English poet, dies in Aldworth, Surrey, England (83).

NOVEMBER

5   James Burdon Sanderson Haldane, English geneticist who pioneered population genetics, born in Oxford, England (–1964).

6   John William Alcock, English aviator who in 1919 made the first transatlantic flight, born in Manchester, England (–1919).

23   Erté (adopted name of Romain de Tirtoff), Russian-born fashion illustrator and designer particularly associated with the art deco movement of the 1920s and 1930s, born in St. Petersburg, Russia (–1990).

DECEMBER

4   Francisco Franco, Spanish leader of the right-wing nationalist forces in the Spanish Civil War 1936–39, then dictator for life, born in El Ferrol, Spain (–1975).

6   Werner von Siemens, German electrical engineer who developed the telegraph industry, dies in Charlottenburg, Berlin, Germany (75).

15   J(ohn) Paul Getty, U.S. oil billionaire, president of the Getty Oil Company and founder of the Getty Museum in Malibu, California, born in Minneapolis, Minnesota (–1976).

18   Richard Owen, British anatomist and paleontologist who described *archaeopteryx*, the first bird, dies in London, England (88).

21   Rebecca West, British novelist, critic, and journalist, who reported on the Nuremberg war-crime trials, born in London, England (–1983).

SEPTEMBER

7   The U.S. boxer James "Gentleman Jim" Corbett knocks out fellow U.S. boxer John L. Sullivan in the first round to win the first world heavyweight title fight to be fought under Queensberry rules, held in New Orleans, Louisiana.

NOVEMBER

11   William Walter "Pudge" Heffelfinger, a former Yale All-America player, becomes the first professional football player when he is paid $500 to play for the Allegheny Athletic Association against the Pittsburgh Athletic Club.

25   The French educational reformer and social philosopher Pierre Fredi, baron de Coubertin, calls for a revival of the Olympic Games in a speech at the Sorbonne (University of Paris), France.

1893

POLITICS, GOVERNMENT, AND ECONOMICS

Business and Economics

- A tariff war develops between France and Switzerland.
- Germany signs further commercial treaties with the Balkan states, thereby extending its economic influence in south-eastern Europe.
- U.S. crude petroleum production stands at 48,431,000 barrels.
- The U.S. economy continues to deteriorate as wary European investors begin to take their money elsewhere.
- U.S. watch retailer Richard Warren Sears joins merchant Alvah C. Roebuck to establish Sears, Roebuck & Company in Chicago, Illinois.

MAY

5–June 27   Panic grips Wall Street as stock prices dive in the United States. By the end of June, some 600 banks and 15,000 businesses have closed and 74 railroads have declared bankruptcy.

Colonization

- France proclaims a protectorate in Laos, continuing the expansion of its influence in Southeast Asia.

FEBRUARY

1   The United States recognizes the provisional government of Hawaii and declares Hawaii a U.S. protectorate.

MARCH

3   Gerald Portal hoists the British flag in Uganda, which is evacuated by the British East Africa Company.

10   The French colonies of French Guinea and the Ivory Coast are formally established.

APRIL

13   U.S. president Grover Cleveland's administration revokes Hawaii's status as a U.S. protectorate.

MAY

10   Britain grants Natal self-government following war over its declaration of independence.

NOVEMBER

11   A British force under Leander Starr Jameson crushes the Matabele revolt and occupies Bulawayo.

13   By the Pretoria Convention, Britain agrees to the annexation of Swaziland by the Transvaal.

17   Dahomey (later Benin) becomes a French protectorate.

Human Rights

- New Zealand becomes the first country to extend the franchise to women.
- Universal suffrage, for both women and men, is introduced in Belgium, with plural voting on the basis of wealth and education.

NOVEMBER

7   The state of Colorado in the United States adopts women's suffrage.

Politics and Government

- Germany suppresses the rebellion against its rule in German East Africa.
- The terrorist Internal Macedonian Revolutionary Organization is founded in Bulgaria to work for the independence of Macedonia.
- U.S. president Grover Cleveland appoints Tennessee jurist Howell E. Jackson to the U.S. Supreme Court.

JANUARY

- A Franco-Russian alliance is signed, formalizing the *entente* established between the two countries in August 1891.

1   Khedive Abbas of Egypt dismisses his pro-British ministers in a dispute over British financial reforms, but

the British agent in Egypt, Evelyn Baring, Lord Cromer, prevents a radical change in policy.

13 The Independent Labour Party is formed under Keir Hardie at a conference in Bradford, England.

17 Hawaiian revolutionaries depose Queen Liliuokalani, amid rumors of U.S. government complicity.

FEBRUARY

15 U.S. president Benjamin Harrison's administration submits a Hawaiian annexation treaty to the U.S. Senate, but on March 9 the newly inaugurated president Grover Cleveland retracts the treaty amid controversy over U.S. complicity in the Hawaiian revolution.

MARCH

1 The U.S. Congress passes the Diplomatic Appropriation Act, creating the rank of ambassador.

4 Grover Cleveland is inaugurated 24th president of the United States.

8 The trial of Ferdinand de Lesseps and his associates opens in France to investigate corruption in the construction of the Panama Canal.

APRIL

14 Alexander I of Serbia, now 18, declares himself of age and dissolves the regency council appointed to rule during his minority.

22 Paul Kruger is reelected president of Transvaal for the third time.

MAY

15 The U.S. Supreme Court rules the Chinese Exclusion Act of 1892 unconstitutional.

JUNE

6 A Franco-Russian commercial treaty is signed, continuing the development of good relations between the two countries since Germany allowed its alliance with Russia to lapse.

6 Alarmed at Belgian advances in the Congo, France sends an occupying force to forestall further annexations.

JULY

• The Matabele people rise against the rule of the British South Africa Company after they are prevented from raiding Mashonaland.

13 An army bill increases the size of the German army but reduces military service to two years.

15 Attempts by the French to gain greater control in Siam (modern Thailand) provoke a crisis in Franco-British relations.

17 U.S. president Grover Cleveland's administration releases a report acknowledging the complicity of the current U.S. minister to Hawaii, John L. Stevens, in the Hawaiian revolution.

31 France agrees to maintain Siam (modern Thailand) as a buffer state after British protests at French attempts to increase its influence in the area.

AUGUST

20–September 3 French elections result in an increased radical and socialist presence, and political instability.

SEPTEMBER

1 The second Irish Home Rule Bill is passed in the British House of Commons, proposing that 80 Irish representatives should sit at Westminster.

16 The U.S. government opens 6 million acres of land between Kansas and Oklahoma, formerly territory of the Cherokees, to U.S. settlement.

OCTOBER

13–29 In a gesture of comradeship the Russian fleet visits Toulon, France.

29 Count Eduard von Taaffe, premier of Austria-Hungary, resigns when the question of universal suffrage splits his coalition.

NOVEMBER

15 An Anglo-German agreement defines the Nigeria–Cameroon boundary, and leases Germany the territory east of Lake Chad to within 160 km/100 mi of the Nile.

DECEMBER

4 An Anglo-French agreement is made over Siam (modern Thailand), but British concessions to French ambitions dismay Germany.

9 The anarchist Auguste Vailland explodes a bomb in the Paris chamber of deputies, France.

10 Francesco Crispi forms a cabinet in Italy following the fall of Giovanni Giolitti's Liberal ministry as a result of bank scandals.

12 An Italian force defeats the extremist Muslim Mahdist forces when they attack the Italian colony of Eritrea.

SCIENCE, TECHNOLOGY, AND MEDICINE

Ecology

AUGUST

27 The southeastern coast of the United States between Charleston, South Carolina, and Savannah, Georgia, is hit by a tidal wave generated by a hurricane; over 1,000 people die.

Exploration

• Norwegian explorer Fridtjof Nansen leads an expedition to the North Pole.

August 1893–95 German archeologist Leo Hirsch, exploring southern Arabia, visits the fertile region of the Wadi Hadramaut—an area previously almost unknown to Europeans.

Health and Medicine

• British psychologist Robert Armstrong–Jones begins the modern treatment of mental diseases, at London County Council's Claybury Asylum.

• Canadian physician William Osler, U.S. surgeons William Stewart Halsted and Howard Atwood Kelly, and U.S. pathologist William Henry Welch establish Johns Hopkins Medical School in Baltimore, Maryland. Associated with Johns Hopkins Hospital, and created especially for teaching and research, it excels in clinical work and surgery, and sets an example that influences medical education in the United States.

August 1893–94   Millions of people die during a worldwide outbreak of cholera.

JULY

10   U.S. surgeon Daniel Hale Williams performs the first open-heart surgery, on a patient who has been wounded by a knife. The patient lives for another 20 years.

Science

- British physicist Oliver Heaviside theorizes that as the velocity of an electric charge increases so does its mass. It presages Einstein's special theory of relativity.
- French chemist Ferdinand-Frédéric Henri Moissan obtains pure chromium in his electric-arc furnace.
- German physicist Wilhelm Wien states that the maximum wavelength emitted by a hot body is inversely proportional to the absolute temperature of the body.
- German physiologist Adolf Magnus–Levy devises a test to measure the basal human metabolic rate.
- German-born U.S. electrical engineer Charles Proteus Steinmetz develops a mathematical method for making calculations about alternating current (AC) circuits. By allowing the performance and efficiency of electrical equipment to be predicted, it leads to the rapid development of devices using alternating current (AC).

Technology

- Australian inventor Lawrence Hargrave invents the box kite; its design influences subsequent airplane design.
- Belgian-born U.S. chemist Leo Hendrik Baekeland invents "Velox," the first commercially successful photographic paper that can be developed under artificial light.
- British physicist Oliver Heaviside suggests that coils be introduced at intervals along telephone lines to increase their length. The first "loaded" circuits are introduced in the United States in May 1900, doubling telephone line lengths.
- French inventor Léon Appert invents reinforced glass, which contains a wire mesh.
- German engineer Wilhelm Maybach invents a float-free carburetor for gasoline engines.
- Serbian-born U.S. inventor Nikola Tesla conducts the first public demonstration of his polyphase alternating current (AC) generating system, at the World's Columbian Exposition in Chicago, Illinois. He uses generators providing two voltages 90° out of phase with each other to supply electric power to motors and lamps. The same year he also demonstrates a remote-controlled model boat at Madison Square Garden, New York, New York.
- U.S. manufacturer Edward Drummond Libbey produces fabric woven from a mixture of fiberglass and silk, creating the first fiberglass.

APRIL

- U.S. industrialist Henry Ford tests his first gasoline-powered internal combustion engine.

Transportation

- Air brakes become mandatory on U.S. railroad trains.
- Automatic railroad signals are installed at Liverpool, England.
- Driving licenses are introduced in France. France also requires cars to display license plates, the first country to do so.
- German mechanical engineer Karl Friedrich Benz constructs his first four-wheeled automobile.
- Swedish scientist Carl Gustaf Patrik de Laval develops a reversible 15-horsepower steam turbine for ships.
- U.S. railroad magnate James J. Hill completes the Great Northern Railroad, connecting St. Paul, Minnesota, to Seattle, Washington.

AUGUST

6   The 6.5-km/4-mi Corinth ship canal is opened across the Isthmus of Corinth, connecting the Aegean and Ionian seas.

SEPTEMBER

22   At Springfield, Massachusetts, U.S. inventors Charles Edgar and James Frank Duryea demonstrate the first automobile built in the United States. It has a single-cylinder, water-cooled gasoline engine, electric ignition, rubber tires, and leather transmission.

ARTS AND IDEAS

Architecture

- The New Croton Aqueduct tunnel, New York, New York, is completed. Begun in 1885, it supplies the city of New York with water from the Croton Reservoir.

Arts

c. 1893   The French artist Jean-Edouard Vuillard paints *The Mother and Sister of the Artist*.

- The English artist Alfred Gilbert sculpts the Shaftesbury Memorial, better known as *Eros*, one of the first sculptures made of aluminum. It is later set up in Piccadilly Circus in central London, England.
- The first issue of the British art journal *The Studio* appears, with drawings by the English artist Aubrey Beardsley. The journal plays a major role in spreading the art nouveau style in architecture and interior decoration.
- The French artist Henri de Toulouse-Lautrec draws the poster *Jane Avril at the Jardin de Paris*.
- The French artist Paul Signac paints *The Port of St. Tropez*.
- The Irish writer George Augustus Moore publishes his critical work *Modern Painting*.
- The Italian artist Medardo Rosso sculpts *Conversation in the Garden*.
- The Norwegian artist Edvard Munch paints *The Scream*.
- The U.S. artist Winslow Homer paints *The Fox Hunt*.

- U.S. craftsman Louis Comfort Tiffany develops Favrile glass, and uses it to make lampshades and jewelry in New York, New York.

Literature and Language

- An edition of the 15th-century classic prose narrative *Morte d'Arthur/Death of Arthur* by Sir Thomas Malory is printed with illustrations by the English artist Aubrey Beardsley.
- The Cuban-born French poet José Maria de Heredia publishes his poetry collection *Les Trophées/Trophies*.
- The English writer Mark Rutherford publishes his novel *Catherine Furze*.
- The French writer Anatole France publishes his novel *La Rôtisserie de la Reine Pédauque/At the Sign of the Reine Pédauque*.
- The U.S. writer Ambrose Bierce publishes his collection of short stories *Can Such Things Be?*
- The U.S. writer Stephen Crane publishes his novel *Maggie: A Girl of the Streets*.

Music

- Bohemian composer Antonín Dvořák completes his Symphony No. 9 (once classified as No. 5); *Z nového světa/From the New World*; and his String Quartet in F major (Opus 96), the *American*.
- Finnish composer Jean Sibelius completes his *Impromptus* (Opus 5), Sonata in F (Opus 12), and *Karelia Suite*.
- French composer Gabriel Fauré completes his song cycle *La Bonne Chanson/The Good Song* of poems by the French writer Paul Verlaine.
- Russian composer Peter Illyich Tchaikovsky completes his Symphony No. 6, the *Pathétique/Pathetic*.
- The opera *Falstaff*, based on Shakespeare's comedy *The Merry Wives of Windsor* and composed by the Italian composer Giuseppe Verdi, is first performed, in Milan, Italy.
- The opera *Hänsel und Gretel/Hansel and Gretel*, by the German composer Engelbert Humperdinck, is first performed, in Weimar, Germany.
- The opera *Manon Lescaut* by the Italian composer Giacomo Puccini is first performed, in Turin, Italy. It is based on the novel *Manon Lescaut*, by the French writer Antoine-François Prévost d'Exiles, published in 1731.
- U.S. composer Edward MacDowell completes his Piano Sonata *Tragica*.
- U.S. composer Horatio Parker completes his oratorio *Hora Novissima*.
- U.S. composer John Philip Sousa completes his march *Liberty Bell*.

AUGUST

7   The musical *A Trip to Chinatown*, with music and lyrics by Percy Gaunt, is performed for the first time, at the Madison Square Theater, New York, New York.

Theater and Dance

- The comedy *A Woman of No Importance* by the Irish writer Oscar Wilde is first performed, at the Haymarket Theatre in London, England.

- The Empire Theater in New York, New York, opens with a performance of the new play *The Girl I Left Behind Me*, by the U.S. dramatist David Belasco.
- The farce *Boubouroche* by the French dramatist Georges Courteline is first performed, in Paris, France.
- The play *Bygmester Solness/The Master Builder* by the Norwegian dramatist Henrik Johan Ibsen is first performed, in Trondheim, Norway.
- The play *Die Weber/The Weavers* by the German dramatist Gerhardt Hauptmann is first performed, in Berlin, Germany.
- The play *Pelléas et Mélisande/Pelléas and Mélisande* by the Belgian writer Maurice Maeterlinck is first performed, in Paris, France. It was published in 1892. One of the finest examples of Symbolist drama, it is used as the basis for an opera of the same name by the French composer Claude Debussy, performed in 1902.
- The play *The Second Mrs Tanqueray* by the English dramatist Arthur Wing Pinero is first performed, in London, England.

Thought and Scholarship

- French sociologist Emile Durkheim publishes *The Division of Labour*, in which he suggests that material prosperity threatens society's equilibrium, and in which he first puts forth the idea that society is like an organism of interdependent parts.
- The British philosopher Francis Herbert Bradley publishes *Appearance and Reality*.

JULY

- U.S. historian Frederick Jackson Turner delivers his famous article "The Significance of the Frontier in American History," a seminal text in the discipline of American Studies, as a paper at the annual meeting of the American Historical Association.

SOCIETY

Education

- St. Hilda's College is founded at Oxford University, England.
- The American University is founded in Washington, D.C.

Everyday Life

- Shredded Wheat is produced by Henry D. Perky, founder of the Natural Food Co., in the United States.
- The Anti-Saloon League is founded in the United States to further the cause of Prohibition.
- The Coca-Cola trademark is registered.
- U.S. engineer Gale Ferris builds the world's first ferris wheel at a cost of $300,000, at the Chicago fair in Illinois. Over 76 m/250 ft in diameter, it has 36 passenger compartments, each of which seats 40 people.
- William Wrigley introduces Juicy Fruit and Spearmint to his chewing gum ranges. Wrigley's is the leading brand in the United States by 1910.

BIRTHS & DEATHS

JANUARY

12 Hermann Goering, German Nazi leader under Hitler, born in Rosenheim, Germany (–1946).

17 Rutherford B. Hayes, nineteenth president of the United States 1877–81, a Republican, dies in Fremont, Ohio (70).

18 Jorge Guillén, Spanish poet and critic, born in Valladolid, Spain (–1984).

31 Freya Madeline Stark, English traveler, mountaineer, and writer, born in Paris, France (–1993).

FEBRUARY

10 Jimmy Durante, U.S. comedian, born in New York, New York (–1980).

12 Omar N(elson) Bradley, U.S. army commander of the 12th Army Group in World War II, later the first chairman of the U.S. joint Chiefs of Staff, born in Clark, Missouri (–1981).

20 Bill Tilden, U.S. tennis player who dominated the sport during the early 1920s, born in Philadelphia, . Pennsylvania (–1953).

20 Pierre Gustave Toutant Beauregard, Confederate general during the American Civil War, dies in New Orleans, Louisiana (74).

21 Andrés Segovia, Spanish musician and concert guitarist, born in Linares, Spain (–1987).

MARCH

5 Hippolyte-Adolphe Taine, French critic and Positive historian, born in Vouziers, France (64).

18 Wilfred Owen, English poet noted for his war poems, born in Oswestry, Shropshire, England (–1918).

26 James B. Conant, U.S. scientist, president of Harvard University, and U.S. high commissioner for West Germany after World War II, born in Dorchester, Massachusetts (–1978).

28 Edmund Kirby-Smith, commander of all Confederate forces west of the Mississippi for two years during the American Civil War, dies in Sewanee, Tennessee (68).

APRIL

9 Mary Pickford, Canadian-born U.S. film actress of the silent era, known as "America's Sweetheart," born in Toronto, Ontario, Canada (–1979).

11 Dean Acheson, U.S. secretary of state 1949–53 and principal architect of U.S. foreign policy during the Cold War, born in Middletown, Connecticut (–1971).

20 Harold Lloyd, U.S. film comedian who first gained popularity in the silent era, born in Burchard, Nebraska (–1971).

20 Joan Miró, Catalan surrealist and abstract artist, born in Barcelona, Spain (–1983).

26 Anita Loos, U.S. writer and screenwriter best known for her fictitious diary *Gentlemen Prefer Blonds*, born in Sissons, California (–1981).

29 Harold Clayton Urey, U.S. chemist who discovered deuterium, the heavy form of hydrogen, born in Walkerton, Indiana (–1981).

30 Joachim von Ribbentop, German Nazi foreign minister who negotiated Germany's treaties prior to World War I, born in Wesel, Germany (–1946).

MAY

11 Martha Graham, U.S. choreographer of modern dance, born in Pittsburgh, Pennsylvania (–1991).

JUNE

7 Edwin Booth, U.S. actor of Shakespearean tragedy, dies in New York, New York (59).

9 Cole Porter, U.S. composer and lyricist, born in Peru, Indiana (–1964).

30 Walter Ulbricht, head of state of the German Democratic Republic 1960–73 who had the Berlin Wall erected, born in Leipzig, Germany (–1973).

JULY

6 Guy de Maupassant, French short-story writer in the Naturalist school, dies in Paris, France (42).

14 Johannes Gerhardus Strijdom, Prime Minister of South Africa 1954–58 who vigorously pursued a policy of apartheid, born in Willowmore, Cape Colony, southern Africa (–1958).

22 John Rae, Scottish physician and explorer of the Canadian Arctic, dies in London, England (79).

26 George Grosz, German artist, born in Berlin, Germany (–1959).

AUGUST

16 Jean-Martin Charcot, French physician and one of the founders of modern neurology, dies in Morvan, France (67).

22 Dorothy Parker, U.S. poet and writer of short stories, born in West End, New Jersey (–1967).

30 Huey Long, U.S. senator and governor of Louisiana known for his autocratic style, born near Winfield, Louisiana (–1935).

SEPTEMBER

16 Albert Szent-Gyorgyi, Hungarian biochemist who isolated vitamin C, born in Budapest, Hungary (–1986).

16 Alexander Korda, Hungarian-born British film director, born in Pusztaturpaszto, Hungary (–1956).

OCTOBER

14 Lilian Gish, U.S. silent film actress, born in Springfield, Ohio (–1993).

18 Charles-François Gounod, French operatic composer known best for *Faust* (1859), dies in St.-Cloud, France (75).

30 Charles Atlas, U.S. bodybuilder who marketed a mail-order bodybuilding course, born in Acri, Italy (–1972).

NOVEMBER

5 Raymond Loewy, French-born U.S. industrial designer, born in Paris, France (–1986).

6 Peter Illyich Tchaikovsky, leading 19th-century Russian composer who, among a great variety of works, composed the music for the ballets *Swan Lake*, *The Nutcracker*, and *Sleeping Beauty*, dies in St. Petersburg, Russia (53).

8 Francis Parkman, U.S. historian who wrote *England and France in North America*, dies in Jamaica Plain, Massachusetts (70).

13 Edward Adelbert Doisy, U.S. biochemist who discovered vitamin K, born in Hume, Illinois (–1987).

DECEMBER

12 Edward G. Robinson, U.S. film actor known for his gangster roles, born in Bucharest, Romania (–1973).

26 Mao Zedong, Chinese Marxist theorist who was chairman of the People's Republic of China 1949–59 and chairman of the Chinese Communist Party 1949–76, born in Shaoshan, Hunan Province, China (–1976).

MAY

1   The World's Columbian Exposition opens in Chicago, Illinois.

Media and Communication

- Wired broadcasting is developed in Budapest, Hungary. News, music, dramas, and stock market reports are broadcast over telephone lines to subscribers on a regular schedule. It also begins to be used in the United States and Europe, but is supplanted by radio early in the 20th century.

Sports

- Ice hockey is first played in the United States at Yale and Johns Hopkins universities.
- The French journalist and cyclist Henri Desgrange, the future founder of the Tour de France, sets a world one-hour record unpaced of 35.325 km/21.9 mi at the Buffalo Velodrome in Paris.
- The Stanley Cup is donated by Lord Stanley of Preston, Governor-General of Canada, and presented to the winners of a Canadian amateur ice hockey match. From 1894 to 1909 it is awarded to the winners of the Canadian amateur championship and from 1910 to the winners of the professional league play-offs (the National Hockey League from 1918).
- The U.S. cyclist Arthur Zimmermann wins both the 1-mi/1.6-km and 10-km/6.2-mi sprints at the first official world amateur track championships, in Chicago, Illinois.

MARCH

- The world's first competitive relay race is run at the University of Pennsylvania in Philadelphia.

JUNE

13   Lady Margaret Scott wins the inaugural British Ladies' Golf Championship, at Royal Lytham St. Anne's, Lancashire, England.

1894

POLITICS, GOVERNMENT, AND ECONOMICS

Business and Economics

- Agricultural laborers riot and working men's associations combine in opposition to repressive government measures in Sicily.

MARCH

25   U.S. social reformer Jacob S. Coxey departs Massilon, Ohio, for Washington, D.C., on a quixotic march designed to highlight the need for federal action to ease the widespread misery caused by the nation's economic depression. Coxey's army of 400 men arrive at the Capitol on April 30. They disband shortly thereafter.

APRIL

4   The British chancellor William Harcourt introduces death duties in the budget by which taxes are to be paid on land and investments received by the beneficiaries of testaments.

5   Eleven miners die in a riot during a labor strike at Connellsville, Pennsylvania.

20   Approximately 140,000 coal miners in Columbus, Ohio, strike for higher wages.

MAY

11   Workers at the Pullman Sleeping Car Company, outside Chicago, Illinois, strike against wage reductions.

JUNE

26   The American Railway Union initiates a nationwide railroad strike in sympathy for the striking workers of the Pullman Sleeping Car Company.

JULY

4   Violence erupts in and around Chicago, Illinois, between federal troops, striking workers, and local protestors. Before order is restored in mid-July, several people are killed and millions of dollars' worth of property is destroyed.

AUGUST

27   The Wilson–Gorman Tariff Act, introducing a 2% income tax, becomes law in the United States, passed by Congress without receiving the assent of U.S. president Grover Cleveland. It is the nation's first graduated income tax.

NOVEMBER

11   Banks in Newfoundland fail.

Colonization

- Revolts take place against foreign rule in the Netherlands East Indies.

JANUARY

1   The British colonial administrator Leander Starr
     Jameson completes the occupation of Matabeleland.

APRIL

11   Uganda is declared a British protectorate.

JUNE

22   The protectorate of Dahomey is proclaimed a French
     colony.

JULY

17   An Italian force takes Kassala, in the Sudan, from the
     dervishes.

23   Japanese troops seize the royal palace in Seoul, Korea,
     and take control of the country, which has traditionally
     been a Chinese fiefdom.

AUGUST

8   The U.S. administration of President Grover Cleveland
     recognizes the Republic of Hawaii.

SEPTEMBER

25   Britain annexes Pondoland in southern Africa, thereby
     connecting Cape Colony with Natal.

NOVEMBER

November–January 1896   French troops conquer
     Madagascar.

Politics and Government

• Parish councils are established in England and become
  the lowest tier of local administration.
• The Dutch Labor Party is founded.
• U.S. president Grover Cleveland appoints Louisiana
  senator Edward D. White to the U.S. Supreme Court.

November 1894–97   Christians are involved in risings
     against the Turks in Crete.

FEBRUARY

2   The British prime minister William Ewart Gladstone
     withdraws the Employers' Liability Bill after amendment
     by the House of Lords.

10   Germany signs a commercial treaty with Russia.

MARCH

15   A Franco-German agreement is made to establish the
     boundaries between the French Congo and the
     Cameroons.

17   The United States and China sign the Chinese Exclusion
     Treaty, by which China accedes to U.S. exclusion of
     Chinese laborers.

MAY

5   An Anglo-Italian agreement is made over territories in
     East Africa, and Italy is assigned Harar in Ethiopia.

12   Britain and Belgium sign an agreement which assigns
     territory on the left bank of the Upper Nile to King
     Leopold of Belgium.

JUNE

6   Germany thwarts attempts by Lord Rosebery to draw
     Britain closer to the Triple Alliance of Germany,
     Austria-Hungary, and Italy.

23–July 10   A colonial conference is held in Ottawa,
     Canada.

24   President Marie-François-Sadi Carnot of France is
     assassinated in Lyon, France, by an Italian anarchist and
     is succeeded by Jean Casimir-Périer.

28   The U.S. Congress proclaims Labor Day, the first
     Monday in September, a national holiday.

JULY

2   An Illinois federal court, invoking the Sherman Antitrust
     Act, enjoins the American Railway Union from
     interfering with delivery of the U.S. mail.

3   Despite an appeal for calm by Illinois governor John P.
     Altgeld, the U.S. president Grover Cleveland dispatches
     federal troops to Chicago, Illinois, to enforce the day-
     old injunction against the American Railway Union.

10   Eugene V. Debs, head of the American Railway Union,
     is arrested for violating the injunction of July 2.

11   Laws are introduced in Italy to suppress anarchist and
     socialist organizations.

27   The regent of Korea, under Japanese control, declares
     war on China.

AUGUST

1   Japan declares war on China over the right of influence
     in Korea.

8   The Glen Grey Act in Cape Colony introduces a new
     natives policy.

14   King Leopold II of Belgium abandons his claims to
     territory on the Upper Nile following protests from
     France.

18   As European immigrants continue to inundate U.S.
     shores, Congress creates the Bureau of Immigration.

18   The Carey Act in the United States grants lands in
     Colorado, Idaho, and six other states to encourage
     irrigation.

OCTOBER

15   Major Alfred Dreyfus, a Jewish French army officer, is
     arrested on a treason charge, accused of spying for
     Germany.

26   Prince Chlodwig von Hohenlohe succeeds Leo, Count
     von Caprivi, as German chancellor, the unpopularity of
     the February commercial treaty with Russia contributing
     to Caprivi's fall.

NOVEMBER

6   In the U.S. Congressional elections, the Republicans
     retain control of the House (244–105) and Senate (43–
     39).

21   Japanese forces are victorious over the Chinese at Port
     Arthur, China.

26   Nicolas II becomes czar of Russia following the death of
     Alexander III.

DECEMBER

14   Eugene V. Debs of the American Railway Union is
     convicted of violating a federal injunction during the
     Pullman strike in July. He is sentenced to six months in
     prison.

21   MacKenzie Bowell becomes Canadian premier following
     the death of John Thompson.

22   The Jewish French army officer Major Alfred Dreyfus is
     convicted of treason by a court martial, and is
     imprisoned on Devil's Island, French Guiana.

SCIENCE, TECHNOLOGY, AND MEDICINE

Ecology

- Gold is discovered in the Transvaal, southern Africa.

SEPTEMBER

1 In Hinckley, Minnesota, 480 people die as a result of a forest fire.

Health and Medicine

- U.S. physician Andrew Taylor Still founds the American School of Osteopathy at Kirksville, Illinois.

September 1894–1914 Between 80,000 and 100,000 people die from an outbreak of bubonic plague in Hong Kong and Canton, China. It spreads throughout the world, killing nearly 10 million people over the next 20 years. During the epidemic, Japanese bacteriologist Shibasaburo Kitasato and French bacteriologist Alexandre Yersin, simultaneously and independently, discover the bacillus *Pasteurella pestis* which is responsible.

Science

- British physicist James Dewar liquefies oxygen.
- British physicist John William Strutt (3rd Baron Rayleigh) and Scottish chemist William Ramsay isolate the inert gas argon (atomic no. 18).
- British physicist Oliver Joseph Lodge suggests that the sun is a source of radio waves.
- Dutch anatomist Marie Eugène Dubois announces the discovery, in Java, of the remains of the first specimen of *Homo erectus* ("upright man"), which he calls *Pithecanthropus erectus*, and which has a cranial capacity of 900 cc and is 0.5 to 1 million years old.
- French physiologist Etienne-Jules Marey adapts his motion-picture camera to the microscope.
- U.S. chemist Hamilton Young Castner develops an electrolytic process for making caustic soda.
- U.S. chemists Carl Kellner and Hamilton Young Castner develop, independently, a method for producing sodium hydroxide by the electrolysis of brine.

Technology

- At the annual meeting of the British Association for the Advancement of Science, British physicist Oliver Joseph Lodge gives the first demonstration of wireless telegraphy, transmitting signals over a distance of 60 m/180 ft; he fails to realize its practical implications.
- French chemists Auguste and Louis Lumière patent a prototype color film procedure.
- Hungarian inventor Eugene Porzolt invents a photographic method for composing type (photocomposition), in which characters are projected onto a sensitized plate. It is not commercially exploited until 50 years later.

- Hungarian-born U.S. physicist Michael Idvorsky Pupin improves multiplex telegraphy.
- Italian physicist Guglielmo Marconi begins experimenting with wireless telegraphy, sending signals over a distance of about 2.4 km/1.5 mi.
- Push button controls are introduced on electric elevators.
- U.S. metallurgist James Gayley improves the quality of steel by patenting a process to prevent water vapor, which absorbs heat, from entering a blast furnace with the air blast.

Transportation

- The 58-km/36-mi Manchester Ship Canal, which links Manchester and Eastham, Merseyside, is opened, providing large oceangoing vessels access to Manchester, England.
- U.S. engineer Simon Lake builds an experimental wooden-hulled submarine called *Argonaut, Jr.* It travels along the bottom of the sea on wheels turned by hand.
- U.S. entrepreneur Henry Meiggs builds the first railroad over the Andes, in Peru.
- U.S. inventor Elmer Ambrose Sperry begins to make the first electric automobiles built in the United States.
- Tower Bridge, across the River Thames in London, England, opens. One of the first double-leaf bascule type suspension bridges, it has a 61-m/200-ft center span that can be raised to allow ships to pass.

ARTS AND IDEAS

Architecture

- The Castel Bérenger, an apartment block in Paris, France, designed by the French architect Hector Guimard, is completed.

Arts

c. 1894 The U.S. artist George Innes paints *Autumn Landscape*.
- The Australian artist Tom Roberts paints *Mosman's Bay*.
- The French artist Claude Monet paints his *Rouen Cathedral* series.
- The French artist Henri de Toulouse-Lautrec paints *The Salon of the Moulin Rouge*.
- The French artist Henri Rousseau paints *War*.
- The French artist Paul Gauguin paints *The Day of the God*.
- The Norwegian artist Edvard Munch paints *Anguish*.
- The U.S. artist Henry Ossawa Tanner paints *The Thankful Poor*.
- The U.S. artist Mary Cassatt paints *The Boating Party*.
- The Lithuanian-born U.S. art historian Bernard Berenson publishes *The Venetian Painters of the Renaissance*.

Film

- *The Serpentine Dance*, directed by W. K. Laurie Dickson, is the first movie to be subjected to censorship in the United States, because the underwear of the actress Carmencita can be seen when she dances.
- U.S. inventor Thomas Edison's first Kinetoscope Parlor opens, in New York, New York. The Kinetescope soon become very popular.

Literature and Language

- The English novelist George Du Maurier publishes his popular novel *Trilby*.
- The English writer Anthony Hope publishes his novel *The Prisoner of Zenda*, which becomes a classic adventure novel.
- The English writer Hall Caine publishes his novel *The Manxman*.
- The English writer Rudyard Kipling publishes his collection of tales *The Jungle Book*.
- The English writer Stanley Weyman publishes his novel *Under the Red Robe*.
- The Irish writer George Augustus Moore publishes his novel *Esther Waters*.
- The Norwegian writer Knut Hamsun publishes his novel *Pan*.
- The Russian writer Anton Chekhov publishes his story "Chorny monakh"/"The Black Monk."
- The U.S. writer Kate Chopin publishes her short story collection *Bayou Folk*.
- The U.S. writer Mark Twain publishes his novels *The Tragedy of Pudd'nhead Wilson* and *Tom Sawyer Abroad*.

September 1894–97 The art and literature journal *The Yellow Book* is published in London, England, edited by the U.S. writer Henry Harland and with the English artist Aubrey Beardsley as art editor. Contributors include Max Beerbohm, W. B. Yeats, H. G. Wells, and Arnold Bennett.

Music

- Austrian composer Gustav Mahler completes his Symphony No. 2, the *Resurrection*.
- Austrian composer Josef Anton Bruckner completes the first three movements of his Symphony No. 9. The final one is completed in 1896.
- Bohemian composer Antonín Dvořák completes his piano work *Humoresques* (Opus 101).
- English composer Charles Hubert Parry completes his orchestral suite *Lady Radnor's Suite*.
- French composer Claude Debussy completes his tone-poem *Prélude à l'après-midi d'un faune/Prelude to "The Afternoon of a Faun,"* inspired by a poem by the French poet Stéhane Mallarmé. The Russian dancer Vaslav Nijinsky uses Debussy's music for a ballet of this name first performed in 1912.
- The opera *Thaïs*, by the French composer Jules Massenet, is first performed in Paris, France. It is based on a novel by the French writer Anatole France published in 1890.

- U.S. composer Charles Ives completes his choral work *The Circus Band*.

Theater and Dance

- The play *Arms and the Man* by the Irish writer George Bernard Shaw is first performed, at the Avenue Theatre in London, England.

Thought and Scholarship

- Chicago investigative journalist Henry Demarest Lloyd publishes *Wealth Against Commonwealth*, a critique of the United States's increasingly polarized society.
- The English economists and social historians Stanley and Beatrice Webb publish *History of Trade Unionism*.
- The English jurists Frederick Pollock and Frederic William Maitland publish *History of English Law*.
- The English social philosopher Benjamin Kidd publishes *Social Revolution*.

SOCIETY

Everyday Life

- Coca-Cola is bottled for the first time in the United States: however, most Coca-Cola is sold to drug stores as a syrup, to which carbonated water is added.
- French chef Auguste Escoffier creates the Pèche Melba dessert in honor of the Australian opera singer Nellie Melba, at the Savoy Hotel in London, England.
- U.S. chef Oscar Tschirky creates Eggs Benedict at the Waldorf-Astoria Hotel in New York, New York.
- U.S. confectioner Milton Hershey produces his first chocolate bar, the Hershey Milk Chocolate Bar.

AUGUST

3 The American Railway Union officially halts its strike against the Pullman Sleeping Car Company. With its leaders arrested, among them Eugene V. Debs, the union virtually disintegrates.

Sports

- Hugh Duffy of the Boston Nationals ends the baseball season with the highest average, .438, ever reached by a National League player.
- The New York Jockey Club is founded.

MAY

- Emanuel Lasker of Germany wins the world chess championship 12–7, defeating the Austrian player Wilhelm Steinitz who has held the title since 1886, in the United States.

JUNE

- At the Sorbonne (University of Paris), France, delegates from sports organizations around the world vote to reestablish the Olympic Games in Athens, Greece, in 1896. They also nominate an International Olympic Committee of 14 members.
- 14 At the Edison Laboratories, West Orange, New Jersey, the U.S. scientist Thomas Alva Edison makes the first

ever motion picture of a sporting event, a specially staged six-round boxing match between Mike Leonard and Jack Cushing.

JULY

- A trial run for automobiles from Paris to Rouen, France, is won by a Panhard at an average speed of 17.2 kph/10.7 mph.

BIRTHS & DEATHS

c. 1894   Jomo Kenyatta, Prime Minister of Kenya 1963–64 and then president 1964–78, born in Ichaweri, British East Africa (–1978).

JANUARY

1   Heinrich Hertz, German physicist, the first person to transmit and receive radio waves, dies in Bonn, Germany (36).

20   Walter Piston, U.S. neoclassical composer of symphonies and chamber music, born in Rockland, Maine (–1976).

FEBRUARY

3   Norman Rockwell, U.S. popular artist and illustrator of covers for the *Saturday Evening Post*, born in New York, New York (–1978).

6   Theodor Billroth, Austrian surgeon who founded modern abdominal surgery, dies in Abbazia, Austria (64).

8   King Vidor, U.S. film director who was a key Hollywood figure in the 1930s, born in Galveston, Texas (–1982).

10   Harold Macmillan, British politician, Conservative prime minister 1957–63, born in London, England (–1986).

14   Jack Benny, U.S. comedian, born in Chicago, Illinois (–1974).

MARCH

2   Jubal A. Early, Confederate general whose defeat in 1864 and 1865 led to the end of the American Civil War, dies in Lynchburg, Virginia (77).

20   Lajos Kossuth, Hungarian political reformer who led Hungary's fight to gain independence from Austria-Hungary, dies in Turin, Italy (92).

APRIL

10   Ben Nicholson, English abstract artist who painted geometric pictures, born in Denham, Buckinghamshire, England (–1982).

17   Nikita Sergeyevich Khrushchev, first secretary of the Communist Party of the Soviet Union 1953–64 and premier 1958–64, born in Kalinovka,

Ukraine, in the Russian Empire (–1971).

26   Rudolf Hess, German Nazi leader and deputy of Adolf Hitler, born in Alexandria, Egypt (–1987).

MAY

6   Alan Cobham, British pioneer long-distance aviator who developed in-flight refueling, born in London, England (–1973).

JUNE

6   Harry Greb, U.S. professional boxer who lost only 7 of 94 bouts between 1913 and 1926, born in Pittsburgh, Pennsylvania (–1926).

23   Alfred Charles Kinsey, U.S. zoologist who reported on the sexual behavior of over 18,500 men and women, born in Hoboken, New Jersey (–1956).

23   Edward VIII, King of Great Britain and Northern Ireland (January–December 1936) who abdicated to marry the U.S. divorcée Wallis Simpson, born in Richmond, Surrey, England (–1972).

JULY

2   André Kertész, Hungarian-born U.S. photographer and photojournalist, born in Budapest, Hungary (–1985).

5   Austen Henry Layard, English archeologist who excavated much of Mesopotamia, dies in London, England (77).

8   Peter Leonidovich Kapitsa, Soviet physicist who discovered superfluidity in helium, born in Kronshtadt, Russia (–1984).

9   Dorothy Thompson, U.S. feminist leader, broadcaster, and journalist, born in Lisbon, Portugal (–1961).

17   Georges Lemaître, Belgian astronomer who formulated the Big Bang theory of the origin of the universe, born in Charleroi, Belgium (–1966).

26   Aldous Huxley, English novelist best known for his science-fiction work *Brave New World* (1932), born in Godalming, Surrey, England (–1963).

SEPTEMBER

8   Hermann Helmholtz, German philosopher best known for articulating the law of conservation of energy, dies in Charlottenburg, Berlin, Germany (73).

15   Jean Renoir, French film director of both the silent and sound eras, son of the impressionist painter Pierre-Auguste Renoir, born in Paris, France (–1979).

OCTOBER

7   Oliver Wendell Holmes, U.S. physician and poet, dies in Cambridge, Massachusetts (85).

14   e e cummings, U.S. poet and painter, born in Cambridge, Massachusetts (–1962).

NOVEMBER

1   Alexander III, Emperor of Russia 1881–94 who instituted a policy of Russification, dies in Livadiya, Crimea, Russia (49).

26   Norbert Wiener, U.S. mathematician who pioneered the field of cybernetics, born in Columbia, Missouri (–1964).

DECEMBER

3   Robert Louis Stevenson, Scottish novelist who wrote *Kidnapped*, *Treasure Island*, and *The Strange Case of Dr Jekyll and Mr Hyde*, dies in Vailima, Samoa (44).

7   Ferdinand de Lesseps, French diplomat who built the Suez Canal, dies in La Chenaie, near Guilly, France (89).

8   Elzie Segar, U.S. cartoonist who created Popeye, born in Chester, Illinois (–1938).

8   James Thurber, U.S. writer and cartoonist, born in Columbus, Ohio (–1963).

17   Arthur Fiedler, U.S. conductor of the Boston Pops Orchestra for 50 years, born in Boston, Massachusetts (–1979).

20   Robert Menzies, Australian prime minister 1939–41 and 1949–66, born in Jeparit, Victoria, Australia (–1978).

28   Alfred Sherwood Romer, U.S. paleontologist, born in White Plains, New York (–1973).

DECEMBER

22   The United States Golf Association is founded, with the St. Andrews Golf Club of Yonkers, New York, the

Newport Golf Club in Rhode Island, the Country Club of Brookline, Massachusetts, and the Chicago Golf Club in Illinois as its founding members.

1895

POLITICS, GOVERNMENT, AND ECONOMICS

Business and Economics

- Small- and medium-sized U.S. manufacturers establish the National Association of Manufacturers to promote foreign trade.

JANUARY

1   The French labor union congress at Nantes, France, adopts the principle of a general strike.

FEBRUARY

8   To replenish diminishing gold reserves, the U.S. Treasury Department purchases $62 million of gold from financiers J. P. Morgan and August Belmont.

Colonization

- Risings occur against Spanish rule in Cuba, aimed at securing independence.

February 1895–99   The citizens of Mozambique rise against Portuguese rule.

JANUARY

1   The British Niger Company proclaims a protectorate over Busa, on the Middle Niger, and Nikki, near Dahomey.

MAY

2   Territory belonging to the British South Africa Company south of the Zambezi is organized to form Southern Rhodesia.

JUNE

11   Britain annexes Togoland in order to block the Transvaal's access to the sea.

JULY

1   The British government creates an East African protectorate on the dissolution of the British East Africa Company.

NOVEMBER

11   British Bechuanaland is annexed to Cape Colony.

Human Rights

MARCH

18   Two hundred black Americans depart from Savannah, Georgia, for Liberia in West Africa, established in 1822 as a colony for free blacks.

SEPTEMBER

18   Black American educator Booker T. Washington delivers his "Atlanta Exposition Address" at the Cotton States Exposition in Atlanta, Georgia, suggesting that black Americans would be willing to forsake their demand for immediate civil and political rights in return for genuine economic opportunity.

Politics and Government

- The U.S. Supreme Court, in *United States v. E C Knight Co*, rules that the Constitution grants Congress the authority to regulate commerce but not manufacturing.
- U.S. president Grover Cleveland appoints New York jurist Rufus W. Peckham to the U.S. Supreme Court.

JANUARY

13   French president Jean Casimir-Périer resigns at the decision of the French labor union congress to adopt the principle of the general strike.

17   Félix Faure and Alexandre Ribot form a government in France with the support of the Republican Union.

FEBRUARY

12   The Japanese navy achieves a resounding victory over Chinese forces at Weihaiwei during the Sino-Japanese war.

24   After the Cuban Revolution begins against Spain, the U.S. president Grover Cleveland exhorts Americans to refrain from aiding the Cuban revolutionaries.

MARCH

25   Italian troops advance into Abyssinia (Ethiopia) seeking to enlarge Italy's African empire.

28   The British undersecretary at the foreign office Sir Edward Grey announces that Britain would regard French occupation of the Upper Nile as an unfriendly act.

APRIL

17   China opens seven new ports and cedes Formosa, Port Arthur, and the Liaodong peninsula to Japan following defeat by Japan in war.

17 Under the Treaty of Shimonoseki, China and Japan recognize the independence of Korea following war over its status as a Chinese vassal state.

23 Russia, France, and Germany (with Britain abstaining at the last moment) protest against the cession of Chinese mainland territory to Japan under the treaty ending the Sino-Japanese war.

MAY

- The Irish writer Oscar Wilde is accused of sodomy after failing in a libel action against the Marquis of Queensberry. Found guilty, he is sentenced to two year's hard labor, which he serves in Reading Gaol.

8 Following international pressure, a revised treaty is constructed to conclude the Sino-Japanese war, and, in return for a huge indemnity Japan surrenders the Liaodong peninsula and Port Arthur to China.

15 The pro-German politician Agenor, Count Gołuchowski, becomes Austro-Hungarian foreign secretary.

JUNE

6 Raids are made into Macedonia from Bulgaria following the founding of the External Macedonian Revolutionary Organization in Sofia, Bulgaria.

28 Nicaragua, Honduras, and El Salvador form a union (ended in 1898 because of opposition by El Salvador).

JULY

8 The opening of the Delagoa Bay Railroad gives Transvaal in southern Africa an outlet to the Indian Ocean.

15 Former Bulgarian prime minister Stefan Nikolov Stambulov is murdered after he publicly opposes the marriage of Prince Alexander to Princess Marie-Louise of Parma.

20 The United States notifies Britain that a modification by force of the boundary between British Guiana and Venezuela would be a violation of the Monroe Doctrine. U.S.–British relations deteriorate.

AUGUST

1–8 Kaiser Wilhelm II of Germany holds conversations at Cowes, England, with the British prime minister Lord Salisbury who proposes the partition of Turkey, but the meeting is blighted by misunderstanding and profound mutual distrust.

SEPTEMBER

9 Casimir Badeni forms a ministry in Austria-Hungary and attempts to pacify the discontented Bohemians.

9 King Leopold II of Belgium agrees to cooperate with the French over the Upper Nile following tension over the area.

27 Irish nationals attending the Irish National Convention in Chicago, Illinois, raise the possibility of using force to achieve Irish independence from Britain.

OCTOBER

1 Muslim Turks massacre Christian Armenians in Constantinople, Turkey, leading to an international outcry.

8 The queen of Korea is assassinated with the connivance of Japan so that Japanese influence over Korea may be increased.

NOVEMBER

7 Russia plans to seize Constantinople, Turkey, in protest at the massacre of the Armenians but postpones action when its ally France is unwilling to risk a general war.

11 Léon Bourgeois, as prime minister, forms a Radical ministry in France following the defeat of Alexandre Ribot.

DECEMBER

7 Ethiopian forces defeat the invading Italians at Amba Alagi, Ethiopia.

17 The U.S. president Grover Cleveland asks the U.S. Congress to appoint a commission to obtain facts regarding the Venezuelan boundary question.

21 U.S. president Grover Cleveland urges the U.S. Congress to appoint a commission to arbitrate the border dispute between Venezuela and British Guiana.

29 Leander Starr Jameson stages the "Jameson raid" into independent Boer Transvaal from Bechuanaland in an attempt to incite an anti-Boer uprising among non-Boer whites.

SCIENCE, TECHNOLOGY, AND MEDICINE

Ecology

- U.S. meteorologist Jeanette Picard launches the first balloon to be used for atmospheric research.

AUGUST

26 The first large hydroelectric power station begins operating at Niagara Falls, New York. Fourneyron water turbines are used to turn three 5,000-horsepower Westinghouse electric generators, providing 3750 kW of alternating current to Buffalo, New York.

Exploration

- Russian scientist Konstantin Eduardovich Tsiolkovsky publishes *Gryozy o zemle i nebe/Dreams of Earth and Sky*. The first book about space travel, it discusses the possibility of space flight using liquid-fueled rockets, and the idea of designing spacecraft with a closed biological cycle to provide oxygen from plants for long flights.

Health and Medicine

- Austrian physicians Sigmund Freud and Josef Breuer publish *Studien über Hysterie/Studies in Hysteria*, which discusses their methods of treating hysteria.
- Belgian bacteriologist Jules Bordet discovers antibodies.
- The protozoa *Trypanosoma gambiense* is discovered to be the cause of African sleeping sickness.
- Belgian bacteriologist Emilie Pierre Marie Van Ermengem isolates the bacterium *Clostridium botulinum*, which is responsible for botulism.

Math

- Jules-Henri Poincaré publishes the first paper on topology, often referred to as "rubber sheet geometry."

Science

- *c.* 1895   Dutch microbiologist Martinus Wilhelm Beijerinck develops a method of creating pure cultures of microorganisms, which are invaluable for research purposes.
- German chemist Johann Wilhelm Goldschmidt develops the "Thermit" reaction for the reduction of metallic oxides to their molten metals.
- Scottish chemist William Ramsay discovers the inert gas helium (atomic no. 2) on earth. Its existence had been established in 1868 from the solar spectrum.
- U.S. physicist Wallace Clement Saline discovers that the acoustics of a building depend on its volume and the absorptivity of the materials used in its construction; he thus founds the science of architectural acoustics.

MARCH

- Russian physicist Aleksandr Stepanovich Popov constructs a lightning detector to register atmospheric electrical disturbances, and suggests that it can be used to detect radio waves.

NOVEMBER

8   German physicist Wilhelm Conrad Röntgen discovers X-rays. Named because of their unknown origin, they revolutionize medicine and usher in the age of modern physics.

Technology

- *c.* 1895   British inventor Frederick G. Creed constructs a machine that can transmit and receive typewritten messages over telephone cables, the forerunner of the teletypewriter.
- German engineer Carl von Linde invents a machine that liquefies air (at 40°K), separating it into its major components. He also develops the explosive known as "LOX," liquid oxygen explosive. It is widely used by Germany during World War I.
- John Howard Northrop invents an automatic loom.

MAY

27   British inventor Birt Acres patents a combination camera and projector. It has a device for forming a loop, essential to maintain constant tension on the film.

Transportation

- French bicycle tire manufacturer Edouard Michelin introduces his pneumatic car tires.
- French inventors André and Edouard Michelin enter the first automobile with tires containing inner tubes in the Paris–Bordeaux automobile race in France.
- More than 300 automobiles are in use in the United States.
- Pneumatic tires for bicycles are introduced commercially in the United States.

- The Automobile Club of France is founded, becoming the first such organization.
- The first electric elevated trains begin operating in Chicago, Illinois.
- The first electric locomotive in the United States enters service. It runs on 550 volt DC current.
- The German firm of Benz and Cie builds the first gasoline-powered bus. It carries eight passengers.
- The U.S. Baltimore and Ohio Railroad company electrifies part of its track in Baltimore to eliminate smoke and noise. It is the first main line railroad to be electrified.

JUNE

20   The 98-km/61-mi Kiel Canal, Germany, is opened, linking the North Sea with the Baltic Sea.

NOVEMBER

- U.S. inventor James Frank Duryea develops an improved version of his automobile, winning on Thanksgiving Day the 87.47-km/54.36-mi *Chicago Times – Herald* automobile race from Chicago to Evanston, Illinois, the first automobile race in the United States.

ARTS AND IDEAS

Architecture

- Biltmore, a country house in Ashville, North Carolina, designed by the U.S. architect Richard Morris Hunt, is completed.
- The Breakers, a country house in Newport, Rhode Island, designed by the U.S. architect Richard Morris Hunt, is completed. It is one of the most opulent mansions built in the United States toward the end of the 19th century.
- The Guaranty Building in Buffalo, New York, designed by the U.S. architects Dankman Adler and Louis Sullivan, is completed.
- The new Boston Public Library, designed by the U.S. architects Charles Follen McKim, William Rutherford Mead, and Stanford White, opens at Copley Square in Boston, Massachusetts.
- The Austrian architect Otto Wagner publishes his influential book *Moderne Architektur/Modern Architecture.*

Arts

- *c.* 1895   The English artist Walter Richard Sickert paints *The Gallery at the Old Bedford.*
- *c.* 1895   The U.S. artist John Henry Twachtman paints *Snowbound.*
- The French artist Henri de Toulouse-Lautrec paints *The Clown Cha-u-kao.*
- The French artist Odilon Redon paints *Meadow Flowers in a Vase.*
- The French artist Paul Cézanne paints *Boy in a Red Waistcoat.*
- The French artist Pierre Bonnard paints *The Cab Horse.*
- The Norwegian artist Edvard Munch paints *Self-Portrait in Hell.*

- The U.S. artist Frederic Remington sculpts *Bronco Buster*.
- The U.S. artist William Merritt Chase paints *A Friendly Call*.

Film

- Charles Pathé introduces Thomas Edison's Kinetoscope into France and works with Henry Joly to produce movies for it.
- Max and Emil Skladanowsky invent the Bioskop, a rudimentary motion picture animation system, in Germany.

FEBRUARY

13 French inventors Auguste and Louis Lumière patent the Cinématograph, a device for taking and projecting moving pictures. On December 28, 1895, in the basement of the Grande Café in Paris, France, they show the movie *La Sortie des ouvriers de l'usine Lumière/ Workers Leaving the Lumière Factory*, the first movie shown to a paying public. It sparks an entire new industry. It is also the first documentary motion picture, and projects at 16 frames per second. They make more than 40 movies during 1896 and record everyday French life.

Literature and Language

- Florence K. Upton's book *The Adventures of Two Dutch Dolls and a Golliwog* introduces the golliwog as a children's character.
- The English writer Hilaire Belloc publishes *Verses and Sonnets*.
- The English writer H. G. Wells publishes his fantasy novel *The Time Machine*.
- The French writer Joris Karl Huysmans publishes his novel *En Route*.
- The poem "Le Bateau ivre"/"The Drunken Boat," by the French poet Arthur Rimbaud, is published in a French literary journal by his friend Paul Verlaine. Rimbaud was thought to be dead, though he was in fact living in Africa. The poem was written in 1871 when Rimbaud was 16.
- The Polish-born English writer Joseph Conrad publishes *Almayer's Folly*, his first novel.
- The Russian writer Maxim Gorky publishes his short story "Chelkash."
- The Spanish writer Vicente Blasco Ibáñez publishes his novel *Flor de Mayo/Mayflower*.
- The U.S. writer Henry James publishes his autobiography *The Middle Years*.
- The U.S. writer Stephen Crane publishes his novel *The Red Badge of Courage*.

Music

- English conductor Henry Wood conducts the first of the Promenade Concerts (the "Proms") at the Queen's Hall in London, England.

- German composer Richard Strauss completes his symphonic poem *Till Eulenspiegel*.
- Russian composer Sergey Rachmaninov completes his Symphony No. 1.

Theater and Dance

- A new version of the ballet *Lebedinoe ozero/Swan Lake*, written in 1877 by the Russian composer Pyotr Ilyich Tchaikovsky, is first performed, in St. Petersburg, Russia. The choreography of this, the most familiar version, is by the French choreographer Marius Petipa and the Russian choreographer Lev Ivanovich Ivanov.
- The comedy *The Importance of Being Earnest* by the Irish writer Oscar Wilde is first performed, at the St. James Theatre in London, England.
- The play *Le Princesse lointaine/The Princess Faraway* by the French dramatist Edmond Rostand is first performed, in Paris, France, with the actress Sarah Bernhardt playing the lead role.

Thought and Scholarship

- French sociologist Emile Durkheim publishes *Les Règles de la méthode sociologique/The Rules of the Sociological Method*, in which he formulates the scientific methodology of sociology and establishes it as a discipline.
- Harvard law professor Oliver Wendell Holmes, Jr., delivers "The Soldier's Faith," a paean to the god of war, in the United States.
- The Bohemian statesman and philosopher Thomas Garrigue Masaryk publishes *The Czech Question*.
- The third volume of *Das Kapital/Capital* by the German political philosopher Karl Marx is published posthumously.
- The Astor, Lennox, and Tilden libraries merge to form the New York Public Library in New York, New York.
- The Scottish statesman and philosopher Arthur James Balfour publishes *The Foundations of Belief*.

SOCIETY

Education

AUGUST

30 Roman Catholic instruction becomes compulsory in Belgian state schools.

Sports

- The Penn Relays (running races) are held for the first time, at the University of Pennsylvania, in Philadelphia.
- The U.S. yachtsman Henry Haff becomes the first skipper to win two America's Cup contests when his yacht *Defender* defeats the British challenger *Valkyrie II* 3–0.

- U.S. golfer Charles Blair MacDonald wins the first U.S. Amateur Golf Championship, held at Newport, Rhode Island.

- Volleyball is invented by William G. Morgan, director of physical training at the Holyoke YMCA, Massachusetts. It is originally known as "mintonette."

BIRTHS & DEATHS

- Buckminster Fuller, U.S. architect and engineer who developed the geodesic dome, born in Milton, Massachusetts (–1983).
- César Sandino, Nicaraguan guerrilla leader who gave his name to the revolution group the Sandinistas, born in Niquinohomo (La Victoria) (–1934).
- Friedrich Engels, German socialist philosopher who, with Karl Marx, wrote *The Communist Manifesto* (1848) which laid the foundations of modern communism, dies in London, England (75).

JANUARY

1 J. Edgar Hoover, U.S. government official, director of the Federal Bureau of Investigation (FBI) 1924–72, born in Washington, D.C. (–1972).

21 Cristóbal Balenciaga, Spanish designer of elegant ball gowns and other classic clothing, born in Guetaria, Spain (–1972).

26 Arthur Cayley, English mathematician who was instrumental in founding the British school of pure mathematics, dies in Cambridge, England (73).

FEBRUARY

1 John Ford (adopted name of Sean O'Feeney), U.S. film director best known for his Westerns, born in Cape Elizabeth, Maine (–1973).

2 George Halas, U.S. founder, owner, and influential coach of the Chicago Bears in the National Football League, born in Chicago, Illinois (–1983).

6 (George Herman) "Babe" Ruth, U.S. professional baseball player, born in Baltimore, Maryland (–1948).

APRIL

4 Arthur Murray, U.S. dance teacher, born in New York, New York (–1991).

14 James Dana, U.S. geologist who developed geology in the United States, dies in New Haven, Connecticut (82).

MAY

6 Rudolph Valentino, Italian-born U.S. silent film star, known as the "Great Lover," born in Castellaneta, Italy (–1926).

8 Edmund Wilson, U.S. playwright, poet, essayist, critic, and influential editor, born in Red Bank, New Jersey (–1972).

21 Lázaro Cárdenas, President of Mexico 1934–40 who redistributed vast amounts of land to Mexican peasants, born in Jiquilpan, Mexico (–1970).

JUNE

11 Nikolay Alexandrovich Bulganin, Prime Minister of the Soviet Union 1955–58, born in Nizhny, Russia (–1975).

14 Louis Finkelstein, U.S. religious leader, born in Cincinnati, Ohio (–1991).

24 Jack Dempsey, U.S. world heavyweight boxing champion 1919–26, born in Manassa, Colorado (–1983).

29 Thomas Henry Huxley, English biologist known for his defense of Darwinian evolution, dies in Eastbourne, Sussex, England (70).

JULY

4 Irving Caesar, U.S. lyricist who wrote songs for Al Jolson, Shirley Temple, Frank Sinatra, Doris Day, and others, born in New York, New York (–1996).

10 Carl Orff, German composer also known for his innovations in musical education, born in Munich, Germany (–1982).

12 Kirsten Flagstad, Norwegian soprano, born in Hamar, Norway (–1962).

12 Oscar Hammerstein, U.S. lyricist and composer known for his work with Richard Rodgers, born in New York, New York (–1960).

SEPTEMBER

18 John Diefenbaker, Prime Minister of Canada 1957–63, a Progressive Conservative, born in Grey County, Ontario, Canada (–1979).

28 Louis Pasteur, French microbiologist who proved that microorganisms cause disease and fermentation and who developed the process of pasteurization, dies in St.-Cloud, near Paris, France (73).

OCTOBER

4 Buster Keaton, U.S. silent-film actor and director, born in Piqua, Kansas (–1966).

8 Juan Perón, President of Argentina 1946–55 and 1873–74, born in Buenos Aires, Argentina (–1974).

8 William Mahone, Confederate general during the American Civil War, railroad magnate, and politician, dies in Washington, D.C. (68).

19 Lewis Mumford, U.S. architectural critic and historian of urbanization, born in Flushing, New York (–1990).

NOVEMBER

4 Eugene Field, U.S. journalist and poet, dies in Chicago, Illinois (45).

10 John Knudson Northrop, U.S. aircraft designer who designed many commercial and military aircraft, born in Newark, New Jersey (–1981).

16 Paul Hindemith, German composer and musical theorist, born in Hanau, near Frankfurt am Main, Germany (–1963).

29 Busby Berkeley, U.S. choreographer and film director who used elaborate sets and teams of female dancers to create kaleidoscopic patterns when filmed from above, born in Los Angeles, California (–1976).

29 William V. S. Tubman, Liberian president 1943–71 who carried out many liberal reforms, born in Harper, Liberia (–1971).

DECEMBER

1 Georgy Konstantinovich Zhukov, Russian marshal, one of the USSR's most important military leaders in World War II, born in Kaluga Province, Russia (–1974)

3 Anna Freud, Austrian-born British psychoanalyst who founded child psychoanalysis, born in Vienna, Austria (–1982).

14 George VI, King of Great Britain and Northern Ireland 1936–52, born in Sandringham, Norfolk, England (–1952).

20 Susanne Langer, U.S. educator and philosopher of linguistic analysis and aesthetics, born in New York, New York (–1985).

MARCH

30 U.S.-born British cinematographic pioneer Birt Acres films the Oxford and Cambridge University Boat Race. This is the first sporting event to be filmed in Britain, and the first regular event in the sporting calendar to be filmed anywhere in the world.

MAY

29 The U.S.-born British cinematographic pioneer Birt Acres films the English horse-racing Derby at Epsom, Surrey.

JUNE

11–14 A 1,178-km/732-mi motor race from Paris to Bordeaux and back is organized in France by the Automobile Club de France and *Le Petit Journal*. This is the first long-distance motor race and the first to include gasoline-driven automobiles.

SEPTEMBER

3 Latrobe YMCA defeats Jeannette Athletic 12–0 in Latrobe, Pennsylvania, in the first-ever professional football game.

OCTOBER

4 English-born U.S. golfer Horace Rawlins receives $150 as the winner of the inaugural U.S. Open golf championship, which is played on a nine-hole course at Newport, Rhode Island.

NOVEMBER

2 The first organized automobile race in the United States is held in Chicago, Illinois, along a 84-km/52-mi course beside Lake Michigan.

9 The world's first women's track and field athletics meeting is held at Vassar College, New York.

◆

1896

POLITICS, GOVERNMENT, AND ECONOMICS

Colonization

MARCH

March–October The Matabele people rebel against British rule in Southern Rhodesia.

AUGUST

16 A British protectorate is proclaimed in Ashanti following military victory over the Ashanti people in the fourth Ashanti war.

18 France annexes Madagascar, whose external treaties with other states are annulled.

OCTOBER

26 The Italian Protectorate of Ethiopia is withdrawn.

Human Rights

MAY

18 The U.S. Supreme Court, in *Plessy v. Ferguson*, upholds the concept of separate railroad cars for black Americans, creating the basis for segregationist provision of separate-but-equal public facilities in the United States.

JUNE

29 The Liberal government in the Netherlands widens the franchise, but leaves the working class dissatisfied.

Politics and Government

• Queen Victoria becomes the longest-reigning British monarch.

• The "Red Flag Act" of 1865, which required a man on foot carrying a red flag to precede all carriages, is repealed.

• There is a revival of the Young Turk nationalist movement in Turkey in response to the controversy surrounding the Armenian massacres.

JANUARY

2 Leander Starr Jameson surrenders to Boer commandos at Doornkop, Transvaal, after his attempt to start an anti-Boer rising in Transvaal fails.

3 Kaiser Wilhelm II of Germany sends the "Kruger telegram" congratulating the Transvaal leader in southern Africa on suppressing the "Jameson raid," and provokes a crisis in Anglo-German relations.

4 Utah becomes the 45th state to join the Union, under a constitution granting women's suffrage.

6 Cecil Rhodes resigns the premiership of Cape Colony following the failure of the raid on Transvaal by his friend Leander Starr Jameson.

15 An Anglo-French agreement is made over Siam (modern Thailand).

18 Sir Francis Scott takes Coomassie, Ashanti, at the end of of Britain's fourth Ashanti war and imprisons the king, Prempeh.

FEBRUARY

2   A revolution inspired by the Greeks begins on the Ottoman island of Crete in the search for independence from Turkey.

2   Russia and Bulgaria are reconciled when Crown Prince Boris is converted to the Orthodox Christian faith.

19   Following the conversion of Crown Prince Boris to the Christian Orthodox Church, Ferdinand I of Bulgaria is finally recognized by Russia. Russian opposition to his candidature in the period 1887–88 had almost led to war.

28   The U.S. House of Representatives passes a resolution urging President Grover Cleveland to grant belligerent rights to the Cuban revolutionaries.

MARCH

1   The Ethiopians under King Menelek II defeat the attacking Italian force at Adowa, Ethiopia, forcing Italy to sue for peace.

3   New evidence is found in France which is favorable to Alfred Dreyfus, the Jewish army officer imprisoned for treason, but the evidence is suppressed.

5   Francesco Crispi's ministry falls in Italy following the failure of the Ethiopian war, and Antonio Rudini, Marquis di Starabba, forms a ministry with support from the Radicals under Felice Cavalotti.

12   In order to protect the Nile region from a French advance, Britain decides to undertake the reconquest of Anglo-Egyptian Sudan, evacuated in 1885 because of the hostility of the Sudanese followers of the dervish Mahdi (prophet) Mohammed Ahmed of Dongola.

17   Transvaal and the Orange Free State in southern Africa conclude an offensive and defensive alliance.

APRIL

4   Félix Méline, a progressive, forms a ministry in France.

MAY

1   The shah of Persia Nasir ud-Din is murdered and is succeeded by his son Muzaffar ud-Din.

JUNE

3   A treaty is signed in Moscow, Russia, by which China and Russia form a defensive alliance for 15 years and China grants Russia the right to operate a railroad in North Manchuria.

6   An expedition led by Major Jean Marchand leaves France and advances to Fashoda, Sudan.

9   A Russo-Japanese agreement recognizes Russia's position in Korea.

18   The Republicans nominate Ohio governor William McKinley for president and New Jersey lawyer Garret A. Hobart for vice president.

JULY

1   A treaty of federation is signed for Britain's Straits Settlements on the Malay peninsula.

3   The sultan of Turkey, Abdul Hamid II, agrees to introduce self-government in Crete as Greek support for the insurgents continues.

7   The Land Bill for Ireland extends the rights of tenants with regard to improvements they may have made on land they have rented.

11   Sir Wilfred Laurier forms a Liberal ministry in Canada following political scandals in the Conservative party.

11   The Democrats nominate former Nebraska congressman William Jennings Bryan for president and Maine businessman Arthur Sewall for vice president.

AUGUST

25   Ambassadors of the powers draw up a revised program for the semi-independence of Crete under a Christian governor, which is approved by Turkey.

26   Armenian revolutionaries attack the Ottoman Bank in Constantinople, Turkey, and provoke a three-day massacre of Armenians by Turks.

SEPTEMBER

12   The Cretan insurgents approve the move to place Crete under the rule of a Christian governor.

21   British general Horatio Kitchener takes Dongola as he advances through the Sudan.

24   Former British prime minister William Ewart Gladstone's last speech, in Liverpool, England, pleads for isolated action by Britain against Turkey following the Ottoman massacres of the Armenians.

30   A Franco-Italian convention is agreed regarding Tunis, Tunisia, by which Italy surrenders many of its claims.

30   Russia and China sign a convention over Manchuria.

OCTOBER

1   The U.S. Congress establishes free postal delivery to the nation's rural areas.

10   The British colonel Robert Stephenson Smyth Baden-Powell puts down the Matabele rising in Southern Rhodesia.

10   Czar Nicholas II of Russia visits Paris, France, and London, England

24   The former German chancellor Otto von Bismarck publishes the secret German–Russian Reinsurance Treaty of 1887, which was unknown to Austria.

26   By the Treaty of Addis Ababa the Italian protectorate of Ethiopia is withdrawn, following Italian military defeat by the Ethiopians.

NOVEMBER

3   Republican candidate William McKinley is elected president of the United States. In the Congressional elections, the Republicans retain majorities in the House (204–113) and Senate (47–34).

11   Russia plans to seize Constantinople, Turkey, if Britain intervenes in Crete.

26   The Aliens Immigration Act in Transvaal restricts the liberty of the press and public meetings (it is subsequently repealed in 1897 on British colonial secretary Joseph Chamberlain's protest that it violates the convention of 1884).

SCIENCE, TECHNOLOGY, AND MEDICINE

Agriculture

- U.S. agriculturalist George Washington Carver begins experimenting on peanuts and sweet potatoes, and eventually derives over 300 different products from peanuts and over 100 from sweet potatoes. His discoveries transform the economy of the U.S. South.

- The first significant organic chemical herbicide, Sinox, is developed in France.

Ecology

November 1896–97 Drought-induced famine in India results in 5 million deaths.

- Swedish chemist Svante August Arrhenius discovers a link between the amount of carbon dioxide in the atmosphere and global temperature.

JUNE

15 An earthquake and 30-m/98-ft tsunami kill 22–28,000 people in the Japanese city of Sanriku.

AUGUST

17 U.S. prospector George Washington Carmack discovers gold at Bonanza Creek, Yukon, Canada, which leads to the Klondike Gold Rush.

Health and Medicine

- Hungarian-born U.S. physicist Michael Idvorsky Pupin uses an X-ray photograph of a patient's broken arm as an aid to setting it. It is the first diagnostic use of X-rays in the United States.
- Polish surgeon Johannes von Mikulicz–Radecki introduces the gauze mask worn by surgeons during surgery.
- The Widal reaction test for typhoid fever is developed by French physician Georges Widal.
- The first dental X-rays are taken in the United States.

Math

- The prime number theorem is proved independently by mathematicians Jacques-Salomon Hadamard of France and Charles-Jean de la Vallée-Poussin of Belgium. This theorem gives an estimate of the number of primes there are up to a given number.

Science

c. 1896 U.S. psychologist John Dewey introduces the formal school of functionalism in psychology.

- British physicist Ernest Rutherford discovers that magnetic fields can be used to detect electromagnetic or radio waves.
- British-born U.S. electrical engineer Elihu Thomson deliberately exposes a finger to X-rays and subsequently provides the first description of the development of X-ray burns.
- German biochemist E. Baumann discovers iodine in the thyroid gland; it is absent in all other tissues.
- Hungarian-born U.S. physicist Michael Idvorsky Pupin discovers that atoms struck by X-rays emit secondary X-ray radiation.
- Scottish physicist Charles Thomson Rees Wilson develops the first cloud chamber. He builds it to duplicate the effects of clouds on mountain tops, but later realizes its potential in nuclear physics.

FEBRUARY

24 French physicist Antoine-Henri Becquerel reports to the Académie des Sciences his discovery that uranium is radioactive.

MARCH

- Russian physicist Aleksandr Stepanovich Popov demonstrates the transmission of radio waves, at the University of St. Petersburg, Russia.

Technology

- French magician Georges Méliès develops "stop-action" cinematography to perform seemingly miraculous tricks.
- French physicist Charles Edouard Guillaume discovers invar, an alloy of nickel and steel that does not expand or contract with changes in temperature. It finds widespread use in scientific instruments.
- U.S. inventor Charles Gordon Curtis patents a multistage impulse steam turbine which receives wide application in electric power plants and marine propulsion.
- U.S. inventor Edward Goodrich Acheson patents a method of making graphite from vaporizing silicon.
- U.S. inventor Elmer Ambrose Sperry develops the gyrocompass, which always points to true north. It is first installed on the U.S. battleship *Delaware*, in 1911, and later in torpedoes and airplanes.
- U.S. inventor F. W. Fellows develops a lathe that can produce almost any type of gear quickly.
- U.S. inventor John Moses Browning patents the automatic revolver. Containing seven cartridges, it uses the gases from the explosion to reload. Manufacture begins in 1900.

JUNE

- Italian physicist Guglielmo Marconi patents wireless telegraphy. In September, he gives public demonstrations, sending signals 6.4 km/4 mi over Salisbury Plain, England, and 14.5 km/9 mi over the Bristol channel.

DECEMBER

12 Guglielmo Marconi publically demonstrates his system for commercially viable radio communication in Britain and obtains a patent.

Transportation

- An electric submarine is constructed in France.
- British aeronautical engineer Percy Sinclair Pilcher builds a successful monoplane glider called the *Hawk*, which is controlled by moving the body from side to side under the wings.
- A 4-km/2.5-mi electric subway opens in Budapest, Hungary. It is the first subway on the European continent.
- French-born U.S. aeronautical engineer Octave Chanute builds stable gliders with rudders and segmented wings. He is the first to realize controlled glider flight.
- German engineer Gottlieb Daimler builds the first motor truck. It has a four horsepower engine and a belt drive with two forward and one reverse speeds.
- Scottish-born U.S. automobile manufacturer Alexander Winton begins to build gasoline-powered vehicles, and,

in 1898, begins to sell the first regularly produced U.S. automobile.
- The French firm of Panhard Levassar introduces the first four-cylinder automobile engine.
- The U.S. company Goodrich manufactures the first automobile tires in the United States.

JUNE
4   U.S. industrialist Henry Ford tests his "Quadricycle" automobile, in Detroit, Michigan. It consists of a buggy frame mounted on four bicycle wheels and is powered by a four-horsepower internal combustion engine.

ARTS AND IDEAS

Architecture

- The U.S. architect Louis Sullivan publishes his influential essay "The Tall Office Building Artistically Considered," setting out the aesthetic of the skyscraper. Sullivan's motto will dominate 20th-century U.S. architecture: "form follows function."

Arts

- The English artist Frederic Leighton paints *Clytie*.
- The French artist Henri de Toulouse-Lautrec paints *In Bed*.
- The French artist Paul Cézanne paints *The Great Pine* and *The Lake at Annecy*.
- The French artist Pierre Puvis de Chavannes completes his frescoes *The Inspiring Muses Acclaim Genius, Messenger of Light* in the Public Library in Boston, Massachusetts.
- The Irish-born U.S. artist Augustus St.-Gaudens sculpts the Robert Gould Shaw Memorial in Boston, Massachusetts.
- The U.S. artist Childe Hassam paints *Union Square in Spring*.

Film

- *Le Coucher de la Marie*, directed by Eugène Pirou, is released in France. The first pornographic movie, it stars Louise Willy.
- Charles and Emil Pathé found Pathé Frères, a cinematograph and motion-picture company.
- Early motion pictures demonstrate a tendency to focus on risqué subjects.
- The Biograph camera, a projector for animated pictures, is launched.
- The movie *The Widow's Kiss* features the first screen kiss, between actors May Irwin and John Rice.
- U.S. inventor Thomas Edison adapts the Vitascope, the first effective movie projector, created by U.S. inventor Thomas Armat, for use with his Kinetoscope film.

APRIL
23 The first public screening of a motion picture in the United States takes place at Koster and Bial's Music Hall in New York, New York.

Literature and Language

- Alfred Austin becomes poet laureate in Britain, a position he holds until 1913.
- The Australian writer Henry Lawson publishes *While the Billy Boils*, a collection of stories about life in the outback.
- The Belgian writer Emile Verhaeren (writing in French) publishes his poetry collection *Les Heures claires/The Sunlit Hours*.
- The English writer A. E. Housman publishes his poetry collection *A Shropshire Lad*.
- The English writer Thomas Hardy publishes his novel *Jude the Obscure*.
- The English writer, designer, and social reformer William Morris publishes an edition of Chaucer at his Kelmscott Press, with illustrations by the English artist Edward Burne-Jones.
- The Polish writer Henryk Sienkiewicz publishes his novel *Quo Vadis?*.
- The Russian writer Anton Chekhov publishes his story "Moya zhizn"/"My Life."
- The unfinished novel *Weir of Hermiston* by the Scottish writer Robert Louis Stevenson is published posthumously.
- The U.S. writer Sarah Orne Jewett publishes her collection of prose sketches *The Country of the Pointed Firs*.

April 1896–1908   The Swedish writer Johan August Strindberg writes his *Okulta dagboken/Occult Diary*. It is not published until 1963.

Music

- Austrian composer Gustav Mahler completes his Symphony No. 3.
- Bohemian composer Antonín Dvořák completes his symphonic poems *Polednice/The Noonday Witch* and *Holoubek/The Wood Dove*.
- Danish composer Carl Nielsen completes his choral work *Hymnus Amoris/Hymn of Love*.
- French composer Vincent d'Indy completes his *Deus Israël/The God of Israel*.
- German composer Johannes Brahms completes his song cycle *Vier ernste Gesänge/Four Serious Songs*, settings of texts from the Bible (Opus 121).
- German composer Richard Strauss completes his tone poem *Also sprach Zarathustra/Thus Spake Zarathustra*, based on a prose poem by the German philosopher Friedrich Nietzsche published in 1883.
- The comic opera *The Grand Duke, or The Statutory Duel* by the English writer William Schwenk Gilbert and the English composer Arthur Seymour Sullivan is first performed, in London, England.
- The opera *Der Corregidor/The Magistrate* by the Austrian composer Hugo Wolf is first performed, in Mannheim, Germany. He also completes the second, and final, volume of his song cycle "Italiensches Liederbuch"/"Italian Songbook."
- The opera *Ghisèle*, by the French composer César Franck, is first performed, in Monaco.

- The opera *La Bohème/The Bohemian Girl* by the Italian composer Giacomo Puccini is first performed, in Turin, Italy.
- U.S. songwriter Maude Nugent writes the song "Sweet Rosie O'Grady."
- U.S. songwriters James M. Black and Katherine E. Purvis write the song "When the Saints Go Marching In."
- The English composer Charles Hubert Parry publishes *The Evolution of the Art of Music*.

Theater and Dance

- The first version of the play *Chayka/The Seagull* by the Russian writer Anton Chekhov is performed, in St. Petersburg, Russia. A revised version is performed in Moscow in 1898.
- The play *Salomé* by the Irish writer Oscar Wilde is first performed, in Paris, France.
- The play *Ubu Roi/King Ubu* by the French writer Alfred Jarry is first performed, in Paris, France.

Thought and Scholarship

- Russian scientist Konstantin Eduardovich Tsiolkovsky publishes his essay "Exploration of Cosmic Space by Means of Reaction Devices," which deals with the theoretical problems of using rockets for space flight.

BIRTHS & DEATHS

JANUARY

8 Paul Verlaine, French lyric poet, leader of the Symbolists, dies in Paris, France (51).

14 John Dos Passos, U.S. novelist known for his trilogy *U.S.A.*, born in Chicago, Illinois (–1970).

15 Mathew Brady, U.S. photographer known for his photographs of the American Civil War, dies in New York, New York (72).

20 George Burns (originally Nathan Birnbaum), U.S. comedian, born in New York, New York (–1996).

23 Charlotte, Grand Duchess of Luxembourg 1919–64, who guarded Luxembourg's independence, born in Château de Berg, Luxembourg (–1985).

FEBRUARY

29 Morarji Ranchhodji Desai, independent India's first non-Congress Party prime minister 1977–79, as leader of the Janata party, born in Bhadeli, Gujarat, India (–1995).

APRIL

21 Henry de Montherlant, French novelist and playwright, born in Paris, France (–1972).

27 Roger Hornsby, U.S. baseball player, born in Winters, Texas (–1963).

28 Vicente Aleixandre, Spanish poet, born in Seville, Spain (–1984).

MAY

30 Howard Hawks, U.S. director of films starring the major actors of the time, born in Goshen, Indiana (–1977).

JUNE

7 Robert Sanderson Mulliken, U.S. chemist and physicist who worked on the electronic structure of molecules, born in Newburyport, Massachusetts (–1986).

JULY

1 Harriet Beecher Stowe, U.S. writer, author of *Uncle Tom's Cabin*, dies in Hartford, Connecticut (85).

13 German chemist Friedrich August Kekulé von Stradonitz, who laid the theoretical foundations of organic chemistry, dies in Bonn, Germany (66).

16 Edmond de Goncourt, French writer, dies in Champrosay, France (74).

16 Trygve Lie, Norwegian politician and first secretary-general of the United Nations 1946–52, born in Christiania (now Oslo), Norway (–1968).

19 A. J. Cronin, Scottish physician and novelist who combined realism, romance, and social criticism in his writing, born in Cardross, Dumbartonshire, Scotland (–1981).

AUGUST

9 Jean Piaget, Swiss psychologist who originated the field of developmental psychology, born in Neuchâtel, Switzerland (–1980).

9 Léonide Massine, Russian ballet dancer and innovative choreographer, born in Moscow, Russia (–1979).

10 Otto Lilienthal, German aeronautical pioneer who made more than 2,000 glider flights, dies in Berlin, Germany, after his glider crashes (47).

13 John Everett Millais, English painter who was a founding member of the Pre-Raphaelite Brotherhood, dies in London, England (67).

SEPTEMBER

10 Elsa Schiaparelli, Italian-born French dress designer who combined simplicity with flamboyant colors, born in Rome, Italy (–1973).

22 Henry Segrave, U.S.-born British car and boat racer who set three world land-speed records, born in Baltimore, Maryland (–1930).

24 F. Scott Fitzgerald, U.S. novelist and short-story writer, born in St. Paul, Minnesota (–1940).

27 Samuel James Ervin, Jr., U.S. Democratic senator and chairman of the Senate Select Committee on Presidential Campaign Activities (the Watergate Committee), born in Morganton, North Carolina (–1985).

OCTOBER

2 Bud (William A) Abbott, U.S. comedian, born in Asbury Park, New Jersey (–1974).

11 Josef Anton Bruckner, Austrian composer, dies in Vienna, Austria (72).

12 Eugenio Montale, Italian poet, author, translator, and editor, born in Genoa, Italy (–1981).

28 Howard Hanson, U.S. romantic composer, conductor, and teacher, born in Wahoo, Nebraska (–1981).

NOVEMBER

25 Virgil Thomson, U.S. composer, music critic, and conductor, born in Kansas City, Missouri (–1989).

DECEMBER

10 Alfred Nobel, Swedish chemist who invented dynamite and founded the Nobel prizes, dies in San Remo, Italy (63).

15 Carl Cori, U.S. biochemist whose research led to a greater understanding of diabetes, born in Prague, Bohemia (–1984).

28 Roger Sessions, U.S. composer and author of several books on music, born in Brooklyn, New York (–1985).

- The English essayist Goldsworthy Lowes Dickinson publishes his cultural and philosophical study *The Greek View of Life*.
- The French philosopher Henri Bergson publishes *Matière et mémoire/Matter and Memory*.
- The German psychologist Wilhelm Wundt publishes *Grundiss der Psychologie/Outlines of Psychology*.
- U.S. engineer Frederick Winslow Taylor publishes *The Adjustment of Wages to Efficiency*, which outlines the results of his time-and-motion studies of workers. His methods provide a quantitative method of organizing production and prove invaluable in the mass production of cars.

SOCIETY

Education

- Girton College is founded at Cambridge University, England.

Everyday Life

- Chop suey is invented in the United States, designed to appeal to both U.S. and Chinese tastes.
- Heinz uses the advertising slogan "57 varieties" for the first time.
- Italian immigrant Italo Marcioni creates the ice-cream cone in the United States.
- The Tootsie Roll, the first candy bar to be wrapped in paper, is launched in the United States.

Media and Communication

- Alfred Harmsworth founds the *Daily Mail* newspaper in Britain, which is advertised as "bright and breezy," and priced at one halfpenny.
- The first comic-strip in a newspaper appears in the *New York World*.

NOVEMBER

3   The world's first permanent wireless installation is set up at The Needles on the Isle of Wight, Hampshire, England, by the Marconi Wireless Telegraph Co. Ltd.

Sports

- Brian Gamlin of Bury, Lancashire, England, devises the numbering system currently in use for dartboards.

- Mathias Zdarsky, the Austrian pioneer of Alpine skiing, publishes his influential instructional book *Lilienfelder Schilauf-Technik*.
- The British Ladies' Football Club, the first ever women's soccer team, is founded by Lady Florence Dixie in Crouch End, London, England.
- The first amateur ice hockey league in the United States, the Amateur Hockey League, is formed in New York.
- The first figure skating world championships are held in St. Petersburg, Russia.
- The Kentucky Derby horse race is shortened from 2.4 km/1.5 mi to its present length of 2 km/1.25 mi.

FEBRUARY

8   In college sports, the Western (Big Ten) Conference is founded at a meeting of Midwestern universities.

APRIL

6–15   The first Olympic Games of the modern era are held in Athens, Greece, in the ancient Panathenaic stadium. Around 250 athletes (all men) from 14 nations assemble to compete in 44 track and field, swimming, cycling, fencing, Greco-Roman wrestling, gymnastics, shooting, tennis, and weightlifting events. The United States wins 11 gold medals (including 9 of the 12 track and field gold medals); Greece wins 10 gold medals; Germany, 7; France, 5; Great Britain, 3; Hungary, Austria, and Australia, 2 each. The marathon, using the ancient course covered by Pheidippides after the Battle of Marathon in 490 BC, is won by Spiridon Louis of Greece.

SEPTEMBER

7   The first automobile race on a track in the United States is held at Narragansett Park, Cranston, Rhode Island.

20   The first known motorcycle race is held in France. The winner, M. Chevalier, riding a Michelin-Dion tricycle, completes the 132-km/139-mi course from Paris to Nantes and back in 4 hours 10 minutes.

20   The first marathon to be run in the United States is put on by the New York Knickerbocker Athletic Club in New York, New York.

NOVEMBER

14   The Motor Car Club organizes the Emancipation Run from London to Brighton, England, to celebrate the repeal of the Red Flag Act. It is not intended to be a race but many of the drivers of the 33 vehicles taking part treat it as such. French motorist Léon Bollée on a Bollée tricycle arrives first, in a time of 3 hours 44 minutes and 35 seconds.

1897

POLITICS, GOVERNMENT, AND ECONOMICS

Business and Economics

- Foreigners invest $3.4 billion in the United States; U.S. interests invest $700 million overseas.

MARCH

28 Japan adopts the gold standard, linking its paper money directly to its gold reserves, the accepted Western base for a stable financial system.

JULY

2 Seventy-five thousand coal miners go on strike in Pennsylvania, Ohio, and West Virginia. Among their goals are an eight-hour day and the abolition of company stores.

24 Nelson Dingley's Tariff increases U.S. protection.

SEPTEMBER

10 Twenty striking miners are killed at Hazelton and Latimer, Pennsylvania, when local sheriffs fire into a group of protesters.

Colonization

JUNE

June–July The second Colonial Conference is held in London, England, presided over by the colonial secretary Joseph Chamberlain.

DECEMBER

1 Zululand is annexed to Natal.

25 Italy cedes Kassala, Sudan, to Egypt.

Human Rights

APRIL

6 The newly acceded sultan of Zanzibar Hammud bin Mohammed abolishes slavery in the British protectorate of Zanzibar.

Politics and Government

- The Austro-Hungarian Socialist Party splits into six nationalist groups corresponding with the major divisions within the empire.

- The Irish wit and playwright Oscar Wilde is released from Reading Gaol, after serving a two-year sentence for sodomy.

- The Workmen's Compensation Act in Britain makes employers liable to pay damages to any employee injured while working for them.

JANUARY

1 A federal convention with representatives from each Australian colony except Queensland meets in Hobart, Tasmania, to discuss a draft federal constitution.

FEBRUARY

2 The Cretan insurrection against Turkey is resumed, aiming at full independence following violence between Greeks and Turks.

6 Crete proclaims itself united with Greece.

10 Greece sends troops to assist the Cretans in their revolt against Turkey.

17 Britain rejects an Austro-Russian proposal for a blockade of Piraeus, a port of Athens, Greece, following direct Greek involvement in the Cretan revolt.

MARCH

2 U.S. president Grover Cleveland vetoes immigration legislation introducing a literacy test.

4 William McKinley is inaugurated 25th president of the United States.

18 The powers of Europe (Britain, France, Russia, Germany, and Austria-Hungary) blockade Crete when Greece refuses to withdraw troops from the island.

20 France, now enjoying greater influence in Addis Ababa, Ethiopia, following the Italian defeat at the hands of the Ethiopians, obtains a treaty with Ethiopia defining the Somali frontier.

APRIL

5 The Czech language is granted equality with the German language in Bohemia.

7 Turkey declares war on Greece in retaliation for its support for the revolt in Crete.

30 An Austro-Russian agreement is made to maintain the status quo in the Balkans during the crisis over the Cretan revolt.

MAY

8 Greece begs the powers of Europe (Britain, France, Russia, Germany, and Austria-Hungary) to intervene in support of the Cretan revolt.

12 Greek forces are defeated by the Turks in the Greco-Ottoman war, and the powers of Europe decide to intervene. They occupy Crete until appointing Prince George of Greece as governor in November 1898.

14 By a treaty with Ethiopia, Britain abandons certain claims in Somaliland, but Emperor Menelek refuses to surrender his claims to lands near the Nile.

19 An armistice is agreed in the Greco-Ottoman war.

JUNE

15 Alfred von Tirpitz is appointed German naval secretary.

20 Queen Victoria celebrates her diamond jubilee in Britain—60 years' reign.

JULY

7 A report of the parliamentary committee investigating the "Jameson raid" into Transvaal censures Cecil Rhodes, but acquits Joseph Chamberlain and the Colonial Office.

10 The French force advancing up the Sudan under General Jean Marchand occupies Fashoda, Sudan.

24 Britain denounces the treaties made by Canada with Belgium and Germany which would prevent Canadian preference.

AUGUST

7 An Egyptian force takes Abu Hamed in the Sudan.

8 The French expedition to the Sudan led by General Jean Marchand reaches the River Bahr al-Ghazal.

8 Alfred, Lord Milner, becomes British high commissioner in southern Africa.

8 The Franco-Russian alliance is reaffirmed and extended.

SEPTEMBER

9 Sudanese troops mutiny in Uganda; the mutiny is not suppressed until the next year.

OCTOBER

10 The king of Korea proclaims himself emperor and Russia and Japan intervene to preserve order, but leave the emperor independent.

20 Prince Bernhard von Bülow becomes German foreign secretary.

NOVEMBER

15 Mathieu Dreyfus discovers that the document which convicted his brother, Jewish army officer Major Alfred Dreyfus, of treason is composed in the handwriting of Major Count Walzin Esterházy.

28 Count Badeni is forced to resign in Austria-Hungary following German opposition to the language ordinance of April, and the Austro-Hungarian monarchy weathers the crisis with difficulty.

28 Germany occupies Jiaozhou, northern China, in retaliation for the murder of German missionaries, which provides Germany with a naval base in China.

DECEMBER

13 Russia occupies Port Arthur in Manchuria in response to Germany's seizure of Jiaozhou, China.

16 The Peace of Constantinople ends the war between Greece and Turkey.

SCIENCE, TECHNOLOGY, AND MEDICINE

Agriculture

- Severe famine takes hold in India.

Ecology

- A typhoon hits the Philippines and kills 10,000 people.
- Norwegian meteorologist Vilhelm Bjerknes develops mathematical theorems applicable to the motions of large-scale air masses, which are essential to weather forecasting.
- U.S. president Grover Cleveland sets aside 20 million acres of forest reserve.

Health and Medicine

- British bacteriologist Ronald Ross discovers the malaria parasite in the gastrointestinal tract of the *Anopheles* mosquito, and realizes that the insect is responsible for the transmission of the disease.
- Dutch physician Christian Eijkman, working in the Dutch East Indies (now Indonesia), shows that a beriberi-like disease is produced in chickens fed on a diet of polished rice. Although he believes it is caused by a toxin produced by microorganisms, his work eventually leads to the discovery of vitamins.
- English bacteriologist Almroth Edward Wright introduces a vaccine against typhoid. It is successfully tested on 3,000 troops sent to India.
- Plague breaks out in Poona, India.

Science

- Danish veterinarian Bernhard Lauritz Frederik Bang discovers the bacillus *Brucella abortus* (Bang's bacillus), which is responsible for contagious abortion in cattle, and brucellosis in human beings.
- English physicist John Joseph Thomson demonstrates the existence of the electron, the first known subatomic particle. It revolutionizes knowledge of atomic structure by indicating that the atom can be subdivided.
- French engineer and chemist Georges Claude discovers that acetylene can be safely transported if dissolved in acetone. It leads to an expansion of the acetylene industry.
- German chemist Eduard Buchner crushes yeast cells and shows that the fermentation of carbohydrates into carbon dioxide and oxygen can still occur in the press of juice. He thus reduces a life process to a nonliving system, demonstrating the importance of enzymes in a life process.
- German-born U.S. electrical engineer Charles Proteus Steinmetz publishes *Theory and Calculation of Alternating Current*, which outlines his method of making calculations concerning alternating current (AC) circuits.
- Russian physiologist Ivan Petrovich Pavlov publishes *Lectures on the Work of the Digestive Glands*, which discusses the gastrointestinal secretions involved in digestion and results in the idea of the conditioned reflex.
- Scottish physicist William Thomson, Lord Kelvin, experiments with cathode rays.
- U.S. astronomer Alvan Clark completes construction of the 101-cm/40-inch Yerkes optical refracting telescope in Wisconsin, the largest telescope in the world to date.

- U.S. physiologist John Jacob Abel isolates the endocrine hormone adrenaline.

Technology

- French-born U.S. metallurgist Guillame de Chalmot and U.S. salesman James T. Morehead produce the first high-carbon ferrochrome used to plate steel.
- German physicist Karl Ferdinand Braun improves the cathode-ray tube. By varying the voltage, he can control the narrow beam of electrons. His "Braun tube" is the forerunner of television tubes, radar screens, and oscilloscopes.
- Italian physicist Guglielmo Marconi uses wireless telegraphy to communicate with Italian warships, at a distance of 19 km/12 mi.
- U.S. engineer Thaddeus S. C. Lowe invents the "New Lowe Coke Oven," which improves the quality of coke used in the manufacture of steel.
- U.S. inventor Tolbert Lanston develops the Monotype typesetting machine, a machine that uses rolls of punched paper to direct the mechanism.
- German engineer Rudolf Diesel produces a 25-horsepower compression engine. Its high efficiency and simple design make it an immediate success.

Transportation

- c. 1897 The development of the electric streetcar makes the suburbs more accessible, leading to an expansion of the cities in the United States.
- English engineer Charles Parsons fits a steam turbine to the boat *Turbania*, which achieves a speed of 34.5 knots, making it the fastest boat of the time. It is the first time a steam turbine has been applied to propel a ship. Parsons demonstrates the boat to a crowd of thousands at Queen Victoria's Diamond Jubilee Review of the Fleet, by unexpectedly weaving in and out of the British fleet.
- Irish-born U.S. engineer John P. Holland launches the 16-m/53-ft submarine *Holland*. It has a crew of nine, and is propelled on the surface by a gasoline engine and underwater by an electric motor. It also has a torpedo tube on the bow.
- U.S. engineer Simon Lake launches the 11-m/36-ft submarine *Argonaut*. Equipped with wheels to travel on the ocean floor, and an airtight chamber that can be opened when the air pressure inside equals the water pressure outside, it is powered by a 30-horsepower gasoline engine.
- U.S. inventors Francis E. and Freelan O. Stanley begin to manufacture "Stanley Steamers," steam-driven automobiles.

September

1 The 2.4-km/1.5-mi Boston subway line opens, in Boston, Massachusetts; it employs trolley streetcars and is the first U.S. subway.

November

4 The Cape Railway reaches Bulawayo in Southern Rhodesia.

ARTS AND IDEAS

Arts

- The commercial Art Nouveau Gallery opens in Paris, France, with an exhibition of paintings by the Norwegian artist Edvard Munch. The gallery gives its name to the art nouveau or "new art" style.
- The French artist Camille Pissarro paints *Boulevard des Italiens*.
- The French artist Henri Rousseau paints *Sleeping Gypsy*.
- The French artist Henri Matisse paints *The Dinner Table*.
- The French artist Paul Gauguin paints *Where do we come from? What are we? Where are we going?*
- The Italian artist Giovanni Segantini paints *The Wicked Mothers*.
- The Tate Art Gallery, Millbank, in London, England, opens; with a donation of 65 paintings by Henry Tate, its emphasis is on modern British art (from the 19th century onward), though it will later acquire a fine collection of international modern art.
- The U.S. artist John Singer Sargent paints *Mr and Mrs Isaac Newton Phelps Stokes*.

Film

- British reporter Frederick Villiers films the first real-life battle scenes, when he covers the Battle of Volo in the Greco-Ottoman War.
- The United States passes legislation to protect U.S. movie manufacturers, imposing prohibitive taxes, which effectively prevents the French Cinématograph entering the country.

May

4 An explosion and resulting fire at a Cinématograph demonstration at the Charity Bazaar in Paris, France, kills 121 people and leads to a decrease in movie attendance.

Literature and Language

- The English writer Bram Stoker publishes his novel *Dracula*, a classic horror novel that launches the Dracula myth.
- The English writer H. G. Wells publishes his novel *The Invisible Man*.
- The English writer Rudyard Kipling publishes his novel *Captains Courageous*.
- The English writer Somerset Maugham publishes his novel *Liza of Lambeth*.
- The French writer Anatole France publishes his novel *L'Orme du mail/The Elm Tree on the Mall*.
- The French writer and politician Maurice Barrès publishes his novel *Le Déracinéa/The Uprooted*, the first volume of his trilogy *Le Roman de l'énergie nationale/The Novel of National Energy*.

- The French writer André Gide publishes *Les Nourritures terrestres/The Fruits of the Earth*, a hymn to the pleasures of life, in verse and prose.
- The German writer Stefan George publishes his poetry collection *Das Jahr der Seele/The Year of the Soul*.
- The Polish-born English writer Joseph Conrad publishes his novel *The Nigger of the 'Narcissus'*.
- The Russian writer Anton Chekhov publishes his story "Muzhiki"/"Peasants."
- The Swedish writer Johan August Strindberg publishes *Inferno*, a frank account of his recent mental crisis.
- The U.S. writer Edwin Arlington Robinson publishes his poetry collection *The Children of the Night*, which includes one of his best-known poems, "Richard Cory."
- The U.S. writer Henry James publishes his short novels *The Spoils of Poynton* and *What Maisie Knew*.

Music

- French composer Claude Debussy orchestrates two of the *Gymnopédies* of 1888 by the French composer Erik Satie.
- French composer Paul Dukas completes his symphonic poem *L'Apprenti sorcier/The Sorcerer's Apprentice*.
- Italian composer Giuseppe Verdi completes his *Stabat Mater* for choir and orchestra and his *Te Deum* for choir, soprano, and orchestra.
- The opera *Fervaal* by the French composer Vincent d'Indy is first performed, in Brussels, Belgium.
- U.S. bandleader John Philip Sousa writes the march "The Stars and Stripes Forever."
- U.S. composer Edward MacDowell completes his Orchestral Suite No. 2, the *Indian*.

BIRTHS & DEATHS

FEBRUARY

4 Ludwig Erhard, German statesman and economist responsible for Germany's postwar recovery, chancellor of the Federal Republic of Germany (West Germany) 1963–66, born in Fürth, Germany (–1977).

APRIL

3 Johannes Brahms, German composer, dies in Vienna, Austria (63).

17 Thornton Wilder, U.S. novelist and playwright, born in Madison, Wisconsin (–1975).

23 Lester B. Pearson, Canadian statesman and diplomat, prime minister of Canada 1963–68, born in Toronto, Ontario, Canada (–1972).

MAY

5 Kenneth Burke, U.S. philosopher and literary critic, born in Pittsburgh, Pennsylvania (–1993).

11 George P. Murdock, U.S. anthropologist who established the Human Relations Area Files, a cross-cultural database, born in Meriden, Connecticut (–1985).

18 Frank Capra, Italian-born U.S. film director who directed *It's a Wonderful Life* and *Mr Smith Goes to Washington*, born near Palermo, Sicily (–1991).

27 John Douglas Cockcroft, English physicist who shared the Nobel Prize for Physics in 1951 for his pioneering use of particle accelerators, born in Todmorden, Yorkshire (now West Yorkshire), England (–1967).

JUNE

12 Anthony Eden, Viscount Avon, British prime minister 1955–57, a Conservative, born in Windlestone, Durham, England (–1977).

13 Paavo Nurmi, Finnish track athlete who dominated long-distance running in the 1920s, born in Turku, Finland (–1973).

JULY

24 Amelia Earhart, U.S. aviator who in 1932 was the first woman to fly across the Atlantic alone, born in Atchison, Kansas (–1937).

AUGUST

8 Jacob Burckhardt, Swiss cultural historian, dies in Basel, Switzerland (79).

11 Enid Blyton, English author of children's stories, born in East Dulwich, London, England (–1968).

28 Charles Boyer, French actor, born in Figeac, France (–1978).

SEPTEMBER

5 A(rthur) C(harles) Nielsen, U.S. market-researcher who developed the Nielsen ratings for television programs, born in Chicago, Illinois (–1980).

12 Irène Joliot-Curie (born Irène Curie), French physicist who with her husband Jean-Frédéric Joliot-Curie created new radioactive elements artificially, born in Paris, France (–1956).

23 Paul Delvaux, Belgian surrealist renowned for his unearthly canvases portraying female nudes in settings of ruined, classical architecture, born in Antheit, Liège, Belgium (–1994).

25 William Faulkner, U.S. novelist, author of a series of novels known as the Yoknapatawpha cycle and winner of the Nobel Prize for Literature in 1949, born in New Albany, Mississippi (–1962).

26 Pope Paul VI (Giovanni Montini), pope 1963–78, born in Concesio, Italy (–1978).

30 St. Theresa, French Carmelite nun, canonized in 1925, dies in Lisieux, France (24).

OCTOBER

29 Joseph Goebbels, German Nazi leader, minister of propaganda under Hitler, born in Rehydt, Germany (–1945).

NOVEMBER

14 Paul Ricca ("The Waiter"), Chicago gangster, born in Naples, Italy (–1972).

24 Lucky Luciano (nickname of Charles Luciano), U.S. organized crime boss, born in Lercara Friddi, Sicily, Italy (–1962).

28 Uno Chiyo, Japanese novelist and kimono designer, born in Iwakuni, Japan (–1996).

DECEMBER

4 Robert Redfield, U.S. anthropologist who examined the relationship between folk and urban societies, born in Chicago, Illinois (–1958).

14 Kurt von Schuschnigg, Austrian chancellor 1934–38 who tried to prevent Austria's takeover by Nazi Germany in 1938, born in Riva del Garda, Trento, Austria-Hungary (–1977).

16 Alphonse Daudet, French novelist, dies in Paris, France (57).

Theater and Dance

- The play *Cyrano de Bergerac* by the French dramatist Edmond Rostand is first performed, in Paris, France.
- The play *The Devil's Disciple* by the Irish writer George Bernard Shaw is first performed, at the Fifth Avenue Theater in New York, New York.
- The play *John Gabriel Borkman* by the Norwegian dramatist Henrik Johan Ibsen is first performed, in Helsinki, Sweden (now Finland).

Thought and Scholarship

- French sociologist Emile Durkheim publishes *Le Suicide/Suicide*, in which he argues that the absence of social cohesion in modern society has produced a sense of rootlessness in people called "*anomie*," which is responsible for high suicide rates in European countries. He thus explains individual decisions by social forces.
- The English economists and social historians Stanley and Beatrice Webb publish *Industrial Democracy*.
- The English psychologist Havelock Ellis publishes the first volume of his *Studies in the Psychology of Sex*. One of the first objective studies of human sexuality, it causes an outcry and is initially banned as obscene. The final volume is published in 1928.
- U.S. philosopher William James publishes *The Will to Believe*, a meditation on belief, will, and the intellect.

SOCIETY

Education

- San Diego State University is founded in California.

Everyday Life

- Advertisement films start to be made in Britain, France, and the United States.
- British soap manufacturer William Lever launches Lifebuoy soap, which is advertised as being effective against body odor.
- Campbell's Soups are launched in the United States.
- Charles Bennet patents the jockstrap in the United States.
- The red light district of New Orleans, Louisiana, gets the name "Storyville," after the politician who demarcated the area.

FEBRUARY

17 U.S. educator and social activist Mrs. Theodore W. Birney helps establish the National Congress of Mothers.

Media and Communication

- Italian inventor Guglielmo Marconi founds the Wireless Telegraph and Signal Co. Ltd. in Britain, to manufacture radio equipment and maintain radio stations.

Religion

- A Zionist Conference is held in Basel, Switzerland, chaired by Theodor Herzl and Max Nordau.

Sports

- The Amateur Athletic Union organizes the first ever basketball tournament in the United States.

JANUARY

1 Atlanta University defeats Tuskegee Normal and Industrial Institute 10–0 in the first football game between black colleges.

MARCH

17 The British-born New Zealand fighter Bob Fitzsimmons wins the world professional heavyweight boxing title when he knocks out the defending champion, Jim Corbett of the United States, in 14 rounds at Carson City, Nevada. It is the first major fight to be filmed.

20 Yale defeats the University of Pennsylvania 32–10 in the first men's intercollegiate basketball game, at New Haven, Connecticut.

APRIL

19 The first Boston Marathon is held in Boston, Massachusetts, as part of the city's Patriot's Day celebrations. Fifteen runners enter the 38.6-km/24-mi race. John J. McDermott of New York, New York, wins in 2 hr 55 min 10 sec.

AUGUST

28 In harness racing, Star Pointer becomes the first horse to pace 1.6 km/1 mi in under two minutes, at Readville, Massachusetts.

NOVEMBER

29 The first race exclusively for two-wheeled motorcycles is held on an oval track at Sheen House, Richmond, Surrey, England. The winner, Charles Jarrott on a Fournier, completes the 1.6-km/1-mi course in 2 minutes 8 seconds.

1898

POLITICS, GOVERNMENT, AND ECONOMICS

Business and Economics

- The British parliamentary committee on old age-pensions, chaired by Lord Rothschild, is unable to accept any of the programs which are proposed. Old-age pensions are, however, introduced in New Zealand.

FEBRUARY

2 An international commission is appointed to control Greek finances when Greece defaults on its debts.

OCTOBER

12 Thirteen workers die when violence erupts during a United Mine Workers strike at Virden, Illinois.

NOVEMBER

27 Germany secures preliminary concessions from the Persian government for the proposed Baghdad Railroad.

Colonization

MARCH

27 China leases Port Arthur to Russia, and Weihaiwei and Kowloon to Britain.

APRIL

10 France obtains concessions in China.

AUGUST

12 The islands of Hawaii are annexed to the United States.

DECEMBER

10 Spain cedes Cuba, Puerto Rico, Guam and the Philippines to the United States at the end of the Spanish–American War.

Human Rights

- U.S. writer and feminist Charlotte Perkins Gilman publishes *Women and Economics*, arguing that women's subjugation to men has interrupted the course of natural selection, to the detriment of men and women alike.

JANUARY

13 French novelist Emile Zola publishes his "J'accuse!"/"I Accuse!," an open letter to the French president protesting that French army officer Alfred Dreyfus, accused of espionage, is the victim of an anti-Semitic plot.

Politics and Government

- The U.S. Supreme Court, in *Holden v. Hardy*, upholds the right of states to regulate labor conditions.
- U.S. president William McKinley appoints California jurist Joseph McKenna to the U.S. Supreme Court.

JANUARY

11 Major Count Walzin Esterházy is acquitted in his trial over the alleged forgery of the key document in the controversial espionage case surrounding French army officer Alfred Dreyfus.

25 British prime minister Lord Salisbury suggests a compromise on disputes over influence in China, but Russia declines to accept it.

FEBRUARY

9 Paul Kruger is reelected president of Transvaal, southern Africa, with a massive majority.

9 U.S. media magnate William Randolph Hearst publishes in the daily *New York Journal* an intercepted letter written by Spanish minister Enrique de Lome characterizing U.S. president William McKinley as weak. De Lome resigns.

15 The U.S. warship *Maine* explodes in Havana harbor, killing 269 U.S. Navy personnel. Despite a lack of evidence, Americans overwhelmingly blame Spain for the incident and begin to agitate for war.

23 Emile Zola is imprisoned for his article "J'accuse!/I Accuse!" published January 13, in which he espoused the cause of Alfred Dreyfus, Jewish French soldier, indicting the military authorities. Dreyfus was unjustly accused of delivering documents containing national and military security secrets to a foreign government, and transported to Devil's Island. He was of Jewish origin; Zola's pamphlet is also an attack on anti-Semitism.

MARCH

March–April Joseph Chamberlain, Secretary of the Colonies and leader of the Liberal Unionists, suggests an Anglo-German alliance but discussions come to nothing as a result of the German Navy Bill.

28 The first German Navy Bill is introduced by Alfred von Tirpitz and begins the expansion of the German navy and competition with Britain's naval power.

29 Bohemia is divided into Czech, German, and mixed districts.

APRIL

5 President William McKinley recalls U.S. consuls from Cuba.

8 The British general Horatio Kitchener is victorious at Atbara River in his advance up the Sudan.

11 President William McKinley asks Congress to authorize the use of U.S. force in Cuba.

19 The U.S. Congress adopts a resolution denying U.S. intent to annex Cuba, demanding that Spain should

Spanish–American War (1898)

FEBRUARY

15 The U.S. warship *Maine* explodes in Havana harbor, killing 269 U.S. Navy personnel. Despite a lack of evidence, Americans overwhelmingly blame Spain for the incident and begin to agitate for war.

APRIL

11 President William McKinley asks Congress to authorize the use of U.S. force in Cuba.

19 Congress adopts a resolution denying U.S. intent to annex Cuba, demanding that Spain should withdraw from Cuba, and authorizing President McKinley to use military force against Spain.

22 Congress passes the Volunteer Army Act, providing for the marshalling of the First Volunteer Cavalry, which becomes known as the Rough Riders.

22 President McKinley orders the blockade of Cuban ports.

22 The U.S. warship *Nashville* captures the Spanish ship *Buena Ventura*, in the first hostile action of the Spanish–American War.

23 President McKinley calls for 125,000 U.S. volunteers to fight against Spain.

24 The United States declares war on Spain, retroactive to April 21, and Spain declares war on the United States, formally beginning the Spanish–American War.

MAY

1 A U.S. force led by George Dewey destroys the Spanish fleet at Manila, the Philippines.

25 President McKinley calls for 75,000 more volunteers to fight against Spain.

JUNE

24 The United States defeats Spain in the Battle of Las Guasimas in Cuba.

JULY

1 U.S. troops seize El Caney and San Juan Heights in Cuba from Spain.

3 U.S. naval forces destroy the Spanish fleet in Cuba when it tries to depart from Santiago, Chile.

25 U.S. forces invade Puerto Rico.

26 Spain authorizes the French ambassador to the United States to seek terms of peace.

28 U.S. forces under the command of Major General Nelson D. Miles capture Ponce, Puerto Rico's second largest city.

AUGUST

12 The war between the United States and Spain ceases after Spain grants Cuban independence and cedes Puerto Rico and Guam to the United States. The fate of the Philippines remains to be negotiated.

DECEMBER

10 The United States and Spain sign the Treaty of Paris, in which Spain cedes Cuba, Puerto Rico, Guam, and also the Philippines (which is yet to be conquered) for $20 million, formally ending the Spanish–American War.

---

withdraw from Cuba, and authorizing President William McKinley to use military force against Spain.

22 The U.S. Congress passes the Volunteer Army Act, providing for the marshalling of the First Volunteer Cavalry, which becomes known as the Rough Riders.

22 The U.S. president William McKinley orders the blockade of Cuban ports.

22 The U.S. warship *Nashville* captures the Spanish ship *Buena Ventura*, in the first hostile action of the Spanish–American War.

23 President William McKinley calls for 125,000 U.S. volunteers to fight against Spain.

24 The United States declares war on Spain, retroactive to April 21, and Spain declares war on the United States, beginning the Spanish–American War.

MAY

1 A U.S. force led by George Dewey destroys the Spanish fleet at Manila, the Philippines.

3–8 Bread riots in Milan, Italy, are crushed with heavy loss of life.

13 The British colonial secretary Joseph Chamberlain criticizes Russia and bids for the friendship of the United States and Germany, which creates an unfavorable impression in Britain and overseas.

25 President William McKinley calls for 75,000 more U.S. volunteers to fight against Spain.

28 In a ruling bearing on the constitutionality of the Chinese Exclusion Act of 1892, the U.S. Supreme Court

rules that U.S. citizenship is race and color blind. Children born in the United States are to be deemed U.S. citizens and cannot lawfully be deported.

JUNE

1 The U.S. Congress passes the Erdman Arbitration Act, establishing a system of arbitration to settle labor disputes among interstate carriers. The legislation also forbids interstate carriers from discriminating against union members.

10 The U.S. Congress passes the War Revenue Act, authorizing the creation of $400 million in war bonds. The legislation also imposes taxes on, among other things, tobacco and liquor.

11–September 16 Emperor Guangxu initiates China's "100 days of Reform" under the guidance of Kang Youwei in response to the interest being shown in China by the Western powers.

14 An Anglo-French convention defines the boundaries of Nigeria and the Gold Coast.

15–17 The U.S. House of Representatives adopts a resolution approving the U.S. annexation of Hawaii. The Senate follows two days later.

24 The United States defeats Spain in the Battle of Las Guasimas in Cuba.

28 General Luigi Pelloux forms a ministry in Italy following the resignation of Antonio Rudini, Marquis de Starabba.

JULY

1　U.S. troops seize El Caney and San Juan Heights in Cuba from Spain.

3　U.S. naval forces destroy the Spanish fleet in Cuba when it tries to depart from Santiago, Chile.

25　U.S. forces invade Puerto Rico in the Spanish–American War.

26　Spain authorizes the French ambassador to the United States to seek terms of peace.

28　In the Spanish–American War, U.S. forces under the command of Major General Nelson D. Miles capture Ponce, Puerto Rico's second largest city.

30　Théophile Delcassé is appointed French foreign secretary and remains in the post until June 1905.

AUGUST

12　The war between the United States and Spain ceases after Spain grants Cuban independence and cedes Puerto Rico and Guam to the United States. The fate of the Philippines remains to be negotiated.

13　U.S. forces capture Manila in the Philippines.

24　Czar Nicholas II of Russia invites the European powers to cooperate in reducing armaments.

30　A secret Anglo-German agreement is made on the future of the African territories of Portugal should Portugal relinquish them as a consequence of its bankruptcy. Britain will obtain the area of Delagoa Bay, Mozambique, and Germany will receive other areas of Mozambique and of Angola.

30　The French officer Colonel Henry admits the forgery of a document in the Dreyfus case.

SEPTEMBER

2　General Horatio Kitchener defeats the dervishes at the Battle of Omdurman as his British force advances across the Sudan.

10　Empress Elizabeth of Austria-Hungary is murdered by an Italian anarchist in Geneva, Switzerland.

19　The British general Horatio Kitchener reaches Fashoda, the Sudan, on the left bank of the Nile.

21　Dowager Empress Zuxi of China seizes power and revokes the reforms of Emperor Guangxu.

OCTOBER

October–November　Kaiser Wilhelm II of Germany visits Palestine and Syria.

NOVEMBER

4　The French force occupying Fashoda, the Sudan, evacuates it under the threat of General Horatio Kitchener's British army.

8　In the U.S. Congressional elections, the Republicans retain majorities in the House (185–163) and Senate (53–26).

26　A Franco-Italian commercial treaty ends the tariff war which has existed between the two countries since 1886.

26　Following the Ottoman evacuation of Crete, Prince George of Greece is appointed high commissioner of the island.

DECEMBER

2　The United States, Britain, and Germany sign the Samoan Partition Treaty, dividing the Samoan Islands between the three signatories.

10　The United States and Spain sign the Treaty of Paris, in which Spain cedes Cuba, Puerto Rico, Guam, and also the Philippines (which is yet to be conquered) for $20 million, thus ending the Spanish–American War.

SCIENCE, TECHNOLOGY, AND MEDICINE

Ecology

- The 19,480-sq km/7,500-sq mi Kruger National Park is established (in part) in southern Africa.

Health and Medicine

- Canadian-born U.S. physician Daniel David Palmer founds the profession of chiropractic, by establishing the Palmer School of Chiropractic at Davenport, Iowa.
- German pharmaceutical company Farbenfabriken vormals Friedrich Bayer und Co. introduce a cough suppressant derived from opium, under the brand name "Heroin."
- Martinus Willem Beijerinck identifies the first virus; it is the cause of tobacco mosaic disease.
- Belgian bacteriologist Jules Bordet discovers hemolysis, the rupture of foreign red blood cells in blood serum. It soon leads to the discovery of blood groups.
- The U.S. meatpacking industry is reformed after more U.S. troops in the Spanish–American War die from eating contaminated meat than from war injuries.

December 1898–1907　An estimated 3 million people in China and India die from plague; at least 370,000 people die from cholera in India.

Science

- British chemists William Ramsay and Morris William Travers discover the noble gases neon (atomic no. 10), krypton (atomic no. 36), and xenon (atomic no. 54).
- British physicist and chemist James Dewar liquefies hydrogen.
- French chemists Pierre and Marie Curie discover the radioactive elements radium (atomic no. 88) and polonium (atomic no. 84). Radium is discovered in pitchblende and is the first element to be discovered radiochemically.
- German physicist Gerhard Carl Schmidt and French physicist Marie Curie demonstrate, independently, that thorium is radioactive; it stimulates interest in radioactivity.
- German physicist Wilhelm Wien discovers the proton. He also discovers that a magnetic field can deflect a beam of charged particles. His discovery lays the foundations of mass spectroscopy.
- The discovery of sesquisulfide of phosphorus makes the safety match possible.
- The word "photosynthesis" is introduced.

AUGUST

13　The asteroid Eros is discovered by German astronomer Gustav Witt.

Technology

- Austrian chemist Carl Auer Freiherr von Welsbach introduces the osmium filament in incandescent lights.

The first metallic filament, osmium is too rare for general use, but leads to the use of tungsten filaments in modern light bulbs.

- The first flashlight photograph is taken.
- U.S. inventor M. J. Owens invents an automatic bottle-making machine.

DECEMBER

1 Danish engineer Vlademar Poulsen patents the "telegraphone," a device for electromagnetically recording human speech on a steel wire. The world's first magnetic recording device, it finds little application.

Transportation

- Scottish-born U.S. automobile manufacturer Alexander Winton makes the first truck to be produced in the United States, a single-cylinder, six-horsepower delivery wagon.
- The French firm of Renault Frères produces the first automobile where the transmission is connected directly to the engine. It has three forward and one reverse gears, which are selected with a gear shift.
- The submarine *Argonaut* travels 1,280 km/800 mi from Norfolk, Virginia, to New York, New York. It is the first time a submarine has navigated extensively in the open ocean.

ARTS AND IDEAS

Architecture

- The Broadleys and Moor Crag houses at Gill Head, Windermere, in England, designed by the English architect Charles Voysey, are completed.
- The Secession Building in Vienna, Austria, designed by the Austrian architect Joseph Maria Olbricht, is completed.
- The Van Eetvelde House in Brussels, Belgium, designed by the Belgian architect Victor Horta, is completed.
- The Whitechapel Art Gallery in London, England, designed by the English architect Charles Harrison Townsend, is completed.

Arts

c. 1898 The French artist Jean-Edouard Vuillard paints *Portrait of Henri Toulouse-Lautrec.*
- The French artist Auguste Rodin sculpts *Monument to Balzac.*
- The French artist Odilon Redon paints *The Cyclops.*
- The French artist Paul Gauguin paints *The White Horse.*
- The U.S. photographer Frank Eugene takes *Nude – A Study.*

Film

- *The Campaign in Cuba*, a movie about the Spanish–American War, is released. Instead of Cuba, the footage has been shot in New Jersey.
- U.S. inventor Thomas Edison threatens legal moves in the United States against companies attempting to show foreign movies or developing rival projection systems.

Literature and Language

- The English philologist George Abraham Grierson publishes the first volume of his *Linguistic Survey of India*, which describes 179 Indian languages and 544 dialects. The last volume appears in 1928.
- The English writer H. G. Wells publishes his novel *The War of the Worlds.*
- The English writer John Galsworthy publishes his novel *Jocelyn* under the pseudonym John Sinjohn.
- The English writer Thomas Hardy publishes *Wessex Poems.*
- The French writer Joris Karl Huysmans publishes his novel *La Cathédrale/The Cathedral.*
- The Irish writer Oscar Wilde publishes his long poem "The Ballad of Reading Gaol," written while serving a prison sentence.
- The Italian writer Italo Svevo publishes his novel *Senilità/As a Man Grows Older.*
- The Norwegian writer Knut Hamsun publishes his novel *Victoria.*
- The Russian writer Anton Chekhov publishes his story "Dama s sobachkoi"/"Lady with a Dog."
- The U.S. writer Henry James publishes his story *The Turn of the Screw.*
- The U.S. writer Stephen Crane publishes *The Open Boat and Other Tales of Adventure*, which includes, along with the title story, "A Bride Comes to Yellow Sky."

Music

- English composer Samuel Coleridge-Taylor completes his cantata *Hiawatha's Wedding Feast*, based on the poem by the U.S. writer Henry Wadsworth Longfellow.
- English-U.S. songwriter James Thornton writes the song "When You Were Sweet Sixteen."
- French composer Claude Debussy completes his *Chansons de Bilitis/Songs of Bilitis*, inspired by the poems of French writer Pierre Louÿs.
- The opera *Fedora* by the Italian composer Umberto Giordano is first performed, in Milan, Italy.
- U.S. composer Charles Ives completes his Symphony No. 1.

Theater and Dance

- A revised version of the 1896 play *Chayka/The Seagull* by the Russian writer Anton Chekhov is performed in Moscow, Russia. Directed by Konstantin Sergeyevich Stanislavsky, this is the first production of the Moscow Art Theater.

APRIL

12   *The Belle of New York* is the first U.S. musical to be performed in the West End, London, England.

SOCIETY

Thought and Scholarship

- U.S. philosopher Josiah Royce publishes "The Problem of Job," a rationalist account of divine will and human suffering.

Everyday Life

- Cornflakes are introduced in the United States by John Harvey and William Keith Kellogg and manufactured by the Sanitas Nut Food Co., based in Battle Creek, Michigan.
- French jeweler Alfred Cartier opens a new store with his sons Louis, Jacques, and Pierre in Paris, France, which will be the foundation of a famous jewelry business.
- The Federation of American Zionists is organized, with Rabbi Stephen Wise as secretary.

BIRTHS & DEATHS

- Albert Lutuli, Zulu chief, president of the African National Congress 1952–60, and first African to be awarded the Nobel Peace Prize (1960), born in Zimbabwe (–1967).
- Liu Shaoqi, chairman of the People's Republic of China 1959–68, born in Ningxiang province, China (–1969).
- Trofim Denisovich Lysenko, Soviet biologist and agronomist who rejected conventional genetics, born in Karlovka, Ukraine, in the Russian Empire (–1976).
- Zhou Enlai, Prime Minister of China 1949–76, born in Huaian, Jiangsu Province, China (–1976).

JANUARY

14   Lewis Carroll (pen name of Charles Lutwidge Dodgson), English novelist who wrote *Alice's Adventures in Wonderland* (1865), dies in Guildford, Surrey, England (65).

23   Sergey Mikhaylovich Eisenstein, Russian film director, born in Riga, Latvia (–1948).

FEBRUARY

3   Alvar Aalto, Finnish architect, furniture designer, and city planner, born in Kuortane, Russia (–1976).

9   Steen Rasmussen, Danish architect and city planner, born (–1990).

10   Bertolt Brecht, German poet and playwright, born in Augsburg, Germany (–1956).

15   Masuji Ibuse, Japanese novelist and poet, author of *Kuroi ame/Black Rain*, born in Kamo, Japan (–1993).

MARCH

11   William Rosecrans, Union general during the American Civil War, dies in Redondo Junction, California (78).

15   Henry Bessemer, English engineer who invented the Bessemer converter for manufacturing steel

cheaply, dies in London, England (85).

APRIL

3   Henry R. Luce, U.S. magazine publisher who published *Time*, *Life*, and *Fortune* magazines, born in Shandong Province, China (–1967).

9   Paul Robeson, U.S. singer, film actor, and civil-rights activist, born in Princeton, New Jersey (–1976).

18   Gustave Moreau, French Symbolist painter, dies in Paris, France (72).

MAY

3   Golda Meir, Jewish politician, a founder and fourth prime minister 1969–74 of the state of Israel, born in Kiev, Ukraine, in the Russian Empire (–1978).

19   William Ewart Gladstone, Prime Minister of Britain 1868–74, 1880–85, 1886, and 1892–94, a Liberal, dies in Hawarden, Flintshire, Wales (88).

21   Armand Hammer, U.S. petroleum executive who maintained economic ties with the Soviet Union, born in New York, New York (–1990).

25   Gene Tunney, U.S. boxer, world heavyweight champion 1926–28, born in New York, New York (–1978).

31   Norman Vincent Peale, U.S. religious leader, born in Bowersville, Ohio (–1993).

JUNE

7   Imre Nagy, independent communist and premier of Hungary 1953–55 who tried to gain Hungary's independence from the Soviet Union, born in Kaposvár, Hungary, Austria-Hungary (–1958).

17   Edward Burne-Jones, English artist and designer, dies in Fulham, London, England (64).

17   M(aurits) C(ornelius) Escher, Dutch artist known for his optical effects, born in Leeuwarden, the Netherlands (–1971).

26   Willy Messerschmitt, German aircraft designer and engineer, born in Frankfurt am Main, Germany (–1978).

JULY

19   Herbert Marcuse, German-born U.S. political philosopher, born in Berlin, Germany (–1979).

22   Alexander Calder, U.S. sculptor who invented the mobile, born in Lawnton, Pennsylvania (–1976).

30   Henry Moore, British sculptor of abstract bronze and stone figures, born in Castleford, Yorkshire (now West Yorkshire), England (–1986).

30   Otto von Bismarck, founder and first chancellor of the German Empire 1871–90, dies in Hamburg, Germany (83).

SEPTEMBER

9   Stéphane Mallarmé, French Symbolist poet, dies in Valvins, near Fontainebleau, France (56).

24   Howard Florey, Australian pathologist who, with Ernst Boris Chain, purified penicillin for clinical use, born in Adelaide, Australia (–1968).

26   George Gershwin, U.S. composer and songwriter of Broadway musicals, born in Brooklyn, New York (–1937).

NOVEMBER

29   C(live) S(taples) Lewis, British academic and writer, born in Belfast, Ireland (–1963).

DECEMBER

6   Alfred Eisenstaedt, German-born U.S. photographer known for his war photographs, born in Dirschau, West Prussia (–1995).

- The Society of Harmonious Fists (Boxers), a Chinese antiforeign society resistant to westernization and Christianity, is founded.
- To prevent imitation, French luggage manufacturer Louis Vuitton begins to put his initials on his products.
- U.S. pharmacist Caleb Bradham produces a drink as a rival to Coca-Cola, calling it Pepsi Cola.

Sports

- The first table tennis sets, manufactured in England by John Jacques & Son Ltd., go on sale in London. The game was called Gossima, but it did not sell well until Jacques renamed it Ping Pong at the turn of the century.
- The National Basketball and the New England League, the first professional basketball leagues, are founded in the United States. Both leagues, however, are disbanded after two seasons.

JULY

16 The Irish athlete William Newburn is the first to exceed 7.3 m/24 ft in the long jump, at an athletics meeting in Dublin, Ireland.

1899

POLITICS, GOVERNMENT, AND ECONOMICS

Business and Economics

- Louis and Marcel Renault found the French automobile company Renault Frères.

FEBRUARY

2 China opposes Italy's demands for concessions at Chekiang.

APRIL

29 Labor violence erupts at Wardner, Idaho, after mine operators refuse to employ only people who are union members.

JULY

1 Giovanni Agnelli founds the Fabbrica Italiana Automobili di Torino (Italian Automobile Factory of Torino) or Fiat car company in Turin, Italy.

DECEMBER

23 Germany secures the Baghdad Railroad contract.

Colonization

JANUARY

9 The United States acquires Puerto Rico, Guam, and territory in the Philippines by its peace treaty with Spain. Cuba becomes independent.

FEBRUARY

12 Germany buys the Mariana, Caroline, and Pelew Islands from Spain.

AUGUST

9 Britain purchases the possessions of the British Niger Company (subsequently proclaimed a protectorate in January 1900).

Human Rights

FEBRUARY

15 Czar Nicholas II of Russia suppresses the liberties of his subjects in Finland.

Politics and Government

- Plans for a federal government of Australia are modified by a conference of premiers to meet the criticisms of New South Wales.
- Revisionist German Social Democrats abandon revolutionary Marxism for evolutionary change.
- The U.S. Justice Department establishes a system of juvenile courts.

JANUARY

1 Sir Henry Campbell-Bannerman succeeds William Harcourt as leader of the Liberals in the British House of Commons.

9 The U.S. Senate ratifies the peace treaty with Spain. The United States acquires Puerto Rico and Guam. Cuba becomes independent. The United States pays Spain $20 million for specified Spanish territory in the Philippines.

19 An Anglo-Egyptian convention on the Sudan fixes the extent of British interests in the Nile region and the French in the Congo.

FEBRUARY

4 Filipinos demand independence from the United States.

4 Philippine revolutionaries fire on the occupying U.S. forces at Manila.

18 Emile Loubet is elected president of France following the death of Félix Faure.

March

- The U.S. Congress appoints the Isthmian Canal Commission to draw up plans for a canal across the Isthmus of Panama.
- 4   Jacob G. Schurman's U.S. commission offers representative government to the Filipinos, but the revolt continues.
- 21   An Anglo-French convention on the hinterland of Tripoli, Libya, ends the Fashoda crisis, but Italy protests at the large concessions made to France in the Sahara.
- 24   In southern Africa, Johannesburg *Uitlanders* (white non-Boers) in the Transvaal send a petition to the British queen, Victoria, reciting their grievances against the Boers.
- 30   U.S. forces in the Philippines drive the Filipino revolutionary Emilio Aguinaldo off the island of Malolos to Tarlac.
- 31–June 5   At the Bloemfontein conference the British high commissioner in southern Africa, Alfred Milner, and Transvaal president Paul Kruger fail to reach an agreement on the widening of the Transvaal franchise to incorporate non-Boers.

April

- 28   A Filipino peace commission proposes armistice terms in the U.S.–Philippine War. The United States rejects the proposal, demanding unconditional surrender.

May

- 18–July 21   At the suggestion of Czar Nicholas II of Russia, 26 nations meet in the first peace conference at The Hague, the Netherlands, for the purpose of extending the Geneva Convention to naval warfare, explosive bullets, and poison gas, and authorizing the establishment of a permanent court of arbitration for international disputes.

June

- 3   A Cour de Cassation (Supreme Court of Appeal) annuls the first trial of French army officer Alfred Dreyfus for treason and orders a retrial.
- 22   René Waldeck-Rousseau, a moderate Republican, becomes French premier.

July

- 11   The Transvaal government decides that immigrants in Transvaal are to be enfranchised after a period of residence of seven years.
- 27   British colonial secretary Joseph Chamberlain proposes a joint British-Boer inquiry into the Transvaal franchise bills, but this is unacceptable to Transvaal president Paul Kruger.

August

- 9   The French foreign secretary Théophile Delcassé extends the Franco-Russian alliance while visiting St. Petersburg, Russia.

September

- 6   John Hay, U.S. secretary of state, sends the "open door" note to Britain, Germany, and Russia speaking against interference in China's treaty ports.
- 9   At a retrial at Rennes, France, a court martial condemns Alfred Dreyfus for treason though "with extenuating circumstances."
- 9   The fanatical "Mad Mullah" leads dervish raids on British and Italian Somaliland.
- 19   Alfred Dreyfus is pardoned by presidential decree.

October

- 3   The British Guiana–Venezuela boundary dispute is settled, largely in favor of Britain.
- 9   Transvaal president Paul Kruger sends an ultimatum to Britain to stop sending troops to southern Africa, or face war.
- 14   Under the secret Treaty of Windsor with Britain, Portugal undertakes to prevent the passage of munitions from Delagoa Bay to the Transvaal during the Anglo-Boer war.
- 17   The Boers are defeated by British forces at Glencoe, Natal.
- 17   The Bohemian language ordinances of April 1897, which gave parity of status to the Czech language with German, are repealed.
- 23   Cipriano Castro assumes power in Venezuela.
- 30   Boer general Piet Joubert wins the Battle of Nicholson's Nek, against a British force under Sir George White.

November

- 1   The town of Ladysmith, Natal, center of British operations in the Boer War, is besieged by Boer forces under General Piet Joubert.
- 14   Britain and Germany agree on the Togoland–Gold Coast frontier and the issue of Samoa, with Britain taking Tonga and the Savage Islands (confirmed on December 2).
- 19–25   Kaiser Wilhelm II of Germany and his foreign secretary Prince Bernhard von Bülow visit England to discuss a possible Anglo-German alliance.

December

- 10   A British force is defeated by Boer irregulars at Stromberg.
- 11   German foreign minister Prince Bernhard von Bülow rejects British advances for an alliance in a speech in the Reichstag (legislative assembly).
- 11   The British forces led by Lord Methuen are repulsed by General Piet Cronje at Magersfontein, Orange Free State, and on December 15 the "Black week" ends with Boer general Louis Botha repulsing the British forces under General Redvers Buller at Colenso, Natal.
- 12   Canadian and Australian volunteers land in southern Africa to assist Britain in the struggle against the Boers.
- 24   The Netherlands adopts proportional representation.

SCIENCE, TECHNOLOGY, AND MEDICINE

Agriculture

- The boll weevil *Antonomus grandis* enters the United States from Mexico, causing devastation to the U.S. cotton crop.

Ecology

- Mt. Rainier National Park is created in the state of Washington. The 95,264-ha/235,404-acre park encompasses an ancient volcano, which contains 41 glaciers on its summit.

December 1899–1900 Drought and ensuing famine in India kill 1.25 million people.

Health and Medicine

- German pharmaceutical company Farbenfabriken vormals Friedrich Bayer und Co. introduce aspirin; the drug is initially produced in powdered form, tablets appearing in 1915.
- U.S. Army Medical Corps physician Bailey Kelley Asford discovers that thymol and epsom salts eliminate hookworm.

Math

- French mathematician Jules-Henri Poincaré publishes *Les Méthodes nouvelles de la mécanique céleste/New Methods in Celestial Mechanics*, describing the interactions of objects in space due to gravity.
- German mathematician David Hilbert publishes *Grundlagen der Geometrie/Foundations of Geometry*, which provides a rigorous basis for geometry.

Science

- At Columbia University, New York, New York, German-born U.S. anthropologist Franz Boas founds the "historical particularism" school of anthropology, which emphasizes fieldwork, the history of individual cultures, and the rejection of cultural evolutionary theory.
- British physicist and chemist James Dewar solidifies hydrogen.
- British physicist Ernest Rutherford discovers alpha and beta rays, produced by the radioactivity of uranium.
- British zoologist Edwin Ray Lankester publishes "The Significance of the Increased Size of the Cerebrum in Recent as Compared with Extinct Animals," in which he argues that the ability to learn is inherited and plays a significant role in human evolution.
- Canadian-born U.S. astronomer Simon Newcomb helps establish the American Astronomical Society; he serves as its first president.
- English physicist John Joseph Thomson measures the charge of the electron.
- French chemist André-Louis Debierne discovers the radioactive element actinium (atomic no. 89) in pitchblende residues.
- German chemist Emil Fischer postulates the "lock and key" hypothesis to explain the specificity of enzyme action.
- The amino acid cystine is discovered to be a component of protein.
- U.S. astronomer William Henry Pickering discovers Phoebe, the ninth satellite of Saturn. He notes that it revolves around Saturn in a retrograde direction.

December 1899–1900 British archeologist Arthur John Evans excavates the palace of Knossos, Crete.

December 1899–1900 Serbian-born U.S. inventor Nikola Tesla discovers stationary terrestrial waves, demonstrating that the earth can act as a conductor of certain electromagnetic frequencies.

March

26 German archeologist Robert Koldewey begins an 18-year excavation of Babylon, Iraq. He discovers the Temple of Marduk, which he believes is the hanging gardens of Babylon, the Gate of Ishtar, and the Tower of Babylon.

Technology

- Danish engineer Valdemar Poulson makes the first magnetic recording of sound. He uses a machine called a "telegraphone" to record the sound on steel wire.
- French chemist Paul-Louis-Toussaint Héroult invents the first commercial electric furnace used for making steel.
- German physicist Karl Ferdinand Braun patents a sparkless antenna circuit. By inductively connecting the power from the transmitter to the antenna, he greatly increases the range of radio transmitters.
- U.S. engineers Frederick Winslow Taylor and Maunsel White develop a process of tempering steel such that its cutting edge is maintained even at the high temperatures produced by high cutting speeds. The high-speed steel improves the cutting capacities of blades 200–300%, and sparks a revolution in designing and cutting machine tools.
- U.S. inventor Charles Gordon Curtis patents the first U.S. gas turbine.

Transportation

- French inventor Camille Jenatzy's electric bullet-shaped automobile *La Jamais Contente* sets a world speed record of 108.46 kph/67.79 mph and is the first automobile to exceed 100 kph/60 mph.
- French naval engineer Maxime Laubeuf launches the *Narval*, the first double-hulled submarine. The space between the hulls is used for ballast.
- German mechanical engineer Karl Friedrich Benz constructs his first race automobile.
- The British ship *Oceanic* is launched. It is the largest ship in the world, measuring 215 m/704 ft.
- The Dortmund–Ems Canal, which links Germany's Ruhr industrial area with the North Sea, is completed.
- The first icebreaker, the *Ermak*, is built in Britain for the Russian government. It has 38-mm/1.5-in steel plating on its hull, and serves as the prototype for all other icebreakers.

December

24 Boston's last horse-drawn omnibus is replaced by a trolley.

ARTS AND IDEAS

Architecture

- The Faculty Club at the University of California, Berkeley, designed by the U.S. architect Bernard Ralph Maybeck, is completed.

- The Schlesinger and Mayer Department Store (later the Carson Pirie Scott Store) in Chicago, Illinois, designed by the U.S. architect Louis Sullivan, is completed.

Arts

c. 1899 The U.S. artist Thomas Eakins paints *Between Rounds*.
- The Belgian artist Henri Evenepoel paints *Sunday Promenade*.
- The English artist Hamo Thornycroft sculpts *Oliver Cromwell*, which is set up in Westminster, London, England.
- The French artist Claude Monet paints *Water Lilies*, the first of a long series that occupies him for the rest of his life (he dies in 1926).
- The French artist Jean-Edouard Vuillard paints *Landscape at l'Etang-la-Ville*.
- The French artist Paul Gauguin paints *Beasts and Flowers*.
- The U.S. artist John Singer Sargent paints *The Wyndham Sisters: Lady Elcho, Mrs Adeane, and Mrs Tennant*.
- The U.S. artist Robert Henri paints *Sidewalk Café*.
- The U.S. artist Winslow Homer paints *The Gulf Stream*.
- The German art historian Heinrich Wölfflin publishes *Das klassische Kunst: Eine Einführung in die italienische Renaissance/Classic Art: A Guide to the Italian Renaissance*.

Film

- *Monijigari/Viewing Scarlet Maple Leaves*, one of the first Japanese movies, is released in Japan, directed by Tsunekichi Shibata and starring Danjuro Ichikawa, a leading Kabuki actor.
- The French director Georges Méliès makes reconstructed newsreels about the Dreyfus affair: these are instrumental in starting public criticism of the handling of the trial in which the French army officer, Alfred Dreyfus was accused of espionage.

Literature and Language

- English novelist Ernest William Hornung publishes *The Amateur Cracksman*, the first in a series of adventures of the gentleman burglar Raffles.
- The English writer Edith Nesbit publishes her children's novel *The Story of the Treasure Seekers*.
- The English writer Rudyard Kipling publishes *Stalky and Co*, a collection of boy's stories.
- The German writer Stefan George publishes his poetry collection *Der Teppich des Lebens/The Carpet of Life*.
- The Italian writer Gabriele D'Annunzio publishes his poetry collection *Laudi del cielo del mare della terra e degli eroi/In Praise of Sky, Sea, Earth, and Heroes*.
- The Russian writer Leo Tolstoy publishes his novel *Voskreseniye/Resurrection*.
- The Russian writer Maxim Gorky publishes *Foma Gordeyev*, his first novel, and one of his best-known stories, "Dvadtsat shest i odna"/"Twenty-Six Men and A Girl."

- The U.S. statesman Theodore Roosevelt publishes *Rough Riders*, an account of his experiences in the Spanish–American War.
- The U.S. writer Frank Norris publishes his novel *McTeague*.
- The U.S. writer Henry James publishes his novel *The Awkward Age*.
- The U.S. writer Kate Chopin publishes her short novel *The Awakening*.
- The U.S. writer Mark Twain publishes his story "The Man That Corrupted Hadleyburg" in *Harper's Magazine*.
- The U.S. writer Stephen Crane publishes *The Monster and Other Stories*, which includes his story "The Blue Hotel."

Music

- Austrian composer Gustav Mahler completes his song cycle *Lieder aus Des Knabelns Wunderhorn/Songs of The Youth's Magic Horn*.
- English composer Edward Elgar completes his *Enigma Variations*.
- Finnish composer Jean Sibelius completes his Symphony No. 1, which is first performed in London, England, in 1903.
- French composer Camille St.-Saëns completes his String Quartet No. 1.
- French composer Maurice Ravel completes his piano work *Pavane pour une infante défunte/Pavane for a Dead Infanta*, which he orchestrates in 1910.
- Italian songwriters Eduardo de Capna and Giovanni Capurro write the song "O sole mio!/O, My Soul!."
- The opera *Čert a Káča/Kate and the Devil*, by the Bohemian composer Antonín Dvořák is first performed, in Prague, Bohemia.
- The opera *The Tsar's Bride* by the Russian composer Nikolay Rimsky-Korsakov is first performed, in Moscow, Russia.
- U.S. composer John Philip Sousa completes his march *Hands Across the Sea*.
- U.S. composer Scott Joplin writes the tune "Maple Leaf Rag," which increases the general popularity of ragtime music.

Theater and Dance

- The comedy *The Gay Lord Quex* by the English dramatist Arthur Wing Pinero is first performed, in London, England.
- The play *Dyadya Vanya/Uncle Vanya* by the Russian writer Anton Chekhov is first performed, in Moscow, Russia. It was published in 1897.

Thought and Scholarship

- Ernst Haeckel publishes *The Riddle of the Universe*.
- The *Prolegomena to Ethics* by the English philosopher Thomas Hill Green is published posthumously.
- The English philosopher James Ward publishes *Naturalism and Agnosticism*.

BIRTHS & DEATHS

JANUARY

2 Solomon Bandaranaike, Prime Minister of Ceylon (Sri Lanka) 1956–59, born in Colombo, Ceylon (–1959).

7 Francis Poulenc, French composer, born in Paris, France (–1963).

17 Al Capone, U.S. gangster, born in Brooklyn, New York, New York (–1947).

25 Paul Spaak, Belgian statesman who played a major role in the formation of the European Economic Community, NATO, and Benelux, born in Schaerbeek, near Brussels, Belgium (–1972).

30 Max Theiler, U.S. microbiologist who developed a vaccine for yellow fever, born in Pretoria, southern Africa (–1972).

FEBRUARY

15 Georges Auric, French composer of film scores and ballets, born in Lodève, France (–1983).

18 Arthur Bryant, British historian and biographer, born in Dersingham, Norfolk, England (–1985).

23 Erich Kästner, German novelist, poet, satirist, and author of children's books, born in Dresden, Germany (–1974).

25 Paul Julius, Baron von Reuter, German-born British reporter who established Reuter's news agency, dies in Paris, France (82).

27 Charles Best, U.S. physiologist who, with Frederick Grant Banting, discovered insulin, born in West Pembroke, Maine (–1978).

MARCH

11 Frederik IX, King of Denmark 1947–72, born in Sorgenfri Castle, near Copenhagen, Denmark (–1972).

17 Gloria Swanson, U.S. silent film star and glamor girl of the 1920s, born in Chicago, Illinois (–1983).

APRIL

22 Vladimir Nabokov, Russian-born U.S. author and critic, best known for his novel *Lolita*, born in St. Petersburg, Russia (–1977).

23 Ngaio Marsh, New Zealand author of mystery novels, born in Christchurch, New Zealand (–1982).

29 Duke Ellington, U.S. jazz composer, pianist, and big band leader, born in Washington, D.C. (–1974).

MAY

4 Fritz von Opel, German automobile manufacturer who built the first rocket-propelled automobile, born in Rüsselsheim, Germany (–1971).

8 Friedrich A. von Hayek, Austrian-born British economist who was opposed to Keynesian economics and the intervention of government in the economy, born in Vienna, Austria (–1992).

10 Fred Astaire (real name Frederick Austerlitz), U.S. dancer and actor, born in Omaha, Nebraska (–1987).

24 Suzanne Lenglen, French tennis player who dominated women's singles tennis between 1919 and 1926, born in Compiègne, France (–1938).

JUNE

3 Johann Strauss, Austrian composer of Viennese waltzes and operettas, dies in Vienna, Austria (74).

7 Elizabeth Bowen, Irish novelist and short-story writer, born in Dublin, Ireland (–1973).

11 Yasunari Kawabata, Japanese novelist, born in Osaka, Japan (–1972).

12 Fritz Albert Lipmann, German-born U.S. biochemist who discovered coenzyme A, born in Königsberg, Germany (–1986).

13 Carlos Chávez, Mexican composer and conductor who combined elements of folk songs with modern techniques, born in Mexico City, Mexico (–1978).

JULY

1 Charles Laughton, English-born U.S. actor, born in Scarborough, Yorkshire (now North Yorkshire), England (–1962).

7 George Cukor, U.S. film and theater director who won an Academy Award for the direction of *My Fair Lady* in 1964, born in New York, New York (–1983).

11 E(lwyn) B(rooks) White, U.S. essayist for the *New Yorker* magazine and author of the children's classic *Charlotte's Web*, born in Mt. Vernon, New York (–1985).

17 James Cagney, U.S. actor, born in New York, New York (–1986).

18 Horatio Alger, U.S. writer and biographer, dies in Natick, Massachusetts (65).

21 Ernest Hemingway, U.S. novelist who wrote *A Farewell to Arms* (1929) and *For Whom the Bell Tolls* (1941), born in Oak Park, Illinois (–1961).

AUGUST

9 P(amela) L(yndon) Travers, English author, creator of Mary Poppins, born in Maryborough, Australia (–1996).

13 Alfred Hitchcock, U.S. film director known for his films of suspense, born in London, England (–1980).

16 Robert Wilhelm von Bunsen, German chemist who discovered that each element emits light of a characteristic wavelength and who invented the Bunsen burner, dies in Heidelberg, Germany (88).

24 Jorge Luis Borges, Argentine poet, short-story writer, and essayist who established the modernist Ultraist movement in South America, born in Buenos Aires, Argentina (–1986).

SEPTEMBER

14 Hal B. Wallis, U.S. producer of almost 200 films, born in Chicago, Illinois (–1986).

NOVEMBER

22 Hoagy Carmichael, U.S. pianist and composer, born in Bloomington, Indiana (–1981).

22 Wiley Post, U.S. aviator who made the first solo flight round the world, born near Grand Saline, Texas (–1935).

DECEMBER

3 Ikeda Hayato, Prime Minister of Japan 1960–64 whose fiscal policies were responsible for Japan's rapid economic growth, born in Hiroshima Prefecture, Japan (–1965).

16 Noël Coward, English playwright, composer, and actor, born in Teddington, Middlesex, England (–1973).

25 Humphrey Bogart, U.S. actor, born in New York, New York (–1957).

30 James Paget, English surgeon and physiologist who was a founder of the modern study of pathology, dies in London, England (85).

- The English-born German historian Houston Stewert Chamberlain publishes *Grundlagen das Neunzehnten Jahrhunderts/The Foundations of the 19th Century*, in Vienna, Austria. It is translated into English in 1910.
- The Russian anarchist Peter Alexeyevich Kropotkin publishes his political tract *Fields, Factories and Workshops*, written in English and published in England.
- U.S. economist Thorstein Veblen publishes *The Theory of the Leisure Class*, decrying the "conspicuous consumption" of the moneyed class.

SOCIETY

Education

- San Francisco State University is founded in California.

Everyday Life

- Elbridge Amos Stuart markets Carnation evaporated milk in the United States, developed as a safe means of storing a sterilized milk product.
- Montgomery Ward's catalog has 1,036 pages, up from 32 pages in 1874.
- Oxo meat stock cubes are developed at Fray Bentos in Uruguay.
- The German company AEG produces the first hand-held electric hair-dryers.
- The Indian polo player Sir Pratap Singh of Jodhpur introduces jodhpurs into Britain.

Media and Communication

- Italian physicist Guglielmo Marconi establishes the first radio connection between England and France.
- An average copy of *Harper's*, which initially shunned advertisements, carries 135 pages of ads and 163 pages of editorial copy.

SEPTEMBER

- Guglielmo Marconi stimulates worldwide interest in radio by installing radios on two U.S. ships to report up-to-the-minute details of the America's Cup yacht race to New York newspapers.

Sports

- Six-day nonstop team cycling events are introduced in the United States as an alternative to the more dangerous individual endurance rides.
- The Milan Cricket and Football Club (now A. C. Milan) is founded in Italy.

JUNE

9   The U.S. fighter James Jeffries wins the world heavyweight boxing title when he knocks out the defending champion, the British-born New Zealander Bob Fitzsimmons, in the eleventh round at Coney Island, New York.

OCTOBER

16–20   In the America's Cup, the U.S. yacht *Columbia* defeats the British challenger *Shamrock*, owned by the British businessman Thomas Lipton, by three races to nil. Lipton makes further attempts, all unsuccessful, to win the trophy in 1901, 1903, 1920, and 1930.

1900

POLITICS, GOVERNMENT, AND ECONOMICS

Business and Economics

- Eldridge Johnson's Consolidated Talking Machine Company of Camden, New Jersey, markets the first phonograph records, in the United States, under the trademark "His Master's Voice"—a dog listening to a phonograph, taken from the painting by Francis Barraud.

JANUARY

1   A "National Union" is formed in Valladolid, Spain, to campaign for the modernization of taxation and government.

FEBRUARY

2   A coal famine hits Europe following heavy demand from industry. Prices rise and Russian import duty is suspended.

27   The Independent Labour Party, the Fabian Society, the Social Democratic Federation, and labor unions found the Labour Representation Committee in London, England, to work for the independent representation of labor in Parliament. Ramsay MacDonald is appointed secretary.

MARCH

14 The U.S. Congress passes the Currency Act, transferring all U.S. currency to the gold standard.

APRIL

2 Demonstrators protest about new taxes in cities throughout Spain including Madrid, Barcelona, and Seville.

JULY

7 Following an excellent vintage in both quantity and quality of wine, the French government reduces retail duties to enable wine growers to sell their stocks.

Colonization

JANUARY

1 The British government assumes direct control of land belonging to the Royal Niger Company, adding it to Britain's Niger Coast Protectorate to form southern Nigeria. Sir Frederick Lugard is appointed high commissioner.

APRIL

30 Hawaii is organized as a territory of the United States.

MAY

19 The Tonga Islands are made a British protectorate.

24 Field Marshal Frederick, Lord Roberts, announces the British annexation of the Orange Free State. It becomes the Orange River Colony.

JULY

9 Queen Victoria of Great Britain gives the royal assent to the Australian Federation Bill, which provides for the establishment of an autonomous Commonwealth of Australia from January 1, 1901.

SEPTEMBER

3 The British commander in the Second Anglo-Boer War, Field Marshal Frederick, Lord Roberts, formally proclaims the annexation of the Transvaal in southern Africa by Great Britain.

Politics and Government

JANUARY

10 Emperor Franz Josef of Austria appoints a ministry of bureaucrats under Ernst von Körber to resolve the conflict between German and Czech parties over the status of the Czech language.

10 Following four months of Boer advances in the Second Anglo-Boer War, Field Marshal Frederick, Lord Roberts ("Bobs"), lands in southern Africa as the new commander in chief of the British army, with Horatio, Lord Kitchener, as chief of staff.

25 In the Battle of Spion Kop, a Boer army forces the British troops under General Sir Redvers Buller to retreat with heavy losses.

FEBRUARY

6 U.S. president William McKinley appoints a commission, with Judge William Taft as president, to extend U.S. civil power in the Philippines. This begins in September with appropriations for the construction of roads and harbors.

15 A British army under General Sir John French relieves Kimberley, Northern Cape Province, which has been under siege by a Boer force since October 15, 1899.

22 A bitter parliamentary conflict begins in Italy, following a declaration by the Court of Cassation that the constitutional decrees of June 1899, which empower the government to ban political associations, are invalid.

27 The Boer commander Piet Cronje and his army surrender to General John French at Paardeberg, Orange Free State, southern Africa, having been besieged there since their defeat of February 18.

28 General Sir Redvers Buller relieves the town of Ladysmith in Natal, which has been besieged by a Boer force since October 30, 1899.

28 The Russian foreign minister Mikhail Nikolayevich, Count Muravyov, suggests that France and Germany put joint pressure on Britain to end the Second Anglo-Boer War, but Germany rejects this on March 3, while France takes advantage of Britain's plight to advance its interests in Morocco.

MARCH

• The Ashanti people rise against British colonial rule in West Africa.

5 President Paul Kruger of the Transvaal and President Martinus Steyn of the Orange Free State offer peace proposals to the British government, with a view to ending the Second Anglo-Boer War.

9 The Socialist Party of the United States nominates Indiana labor organizer Eugene V. Debs for president and California politician Job Harriman for vice president.

10 Britain and Uganda sign a treaty to regulate the Ugandan government, which will be advised by a British commissioner.

13 Field Marshal Frederick, Lord Roberts, captures Bloemfontein, capital of the Orange Free State.

APRIL

22 French troops defeat and kill the slave trader and raider Rabah Zobeir at the Battle of Lakhta in the Chad region of central Africa.

30 The U.S. Congress creates the Hawaii Territory.

MAY

1 The Foraker Act establishes civil government in Puerto Rico.

17–18 British forces under General Sir Redvers Buller relieve the town of Mafeking, southern Africa, following a seven-month siege by a Boer force.

24 Field Marshal Frederick, Lord Roberts, announces the British annexation of the Orange Free State following its defeat in the Second Anglo-Boer War.

31 British troops under Field Marshal Frederick, Lord Roberts, and General Sir Redvers Buller occupy Johannesburg and the Rand in the Transvaal.

JUNE

5 British troops in southern Africa capture Pretoria, capital of the Transvaal.

8 Czech members of the Austrian Reichsrat (parliament) disrupt it for seven hours with cymbals and trumpets, demanding that Czech be recognized as an official language in Bohemia.

10 A U.S.–British force under Admiral Henry Seymour lands at Tientsin, China, to combat the anti-European

Boxer movement. French, Russian, and Japanese forces join them later.

12 Germany attempts to rival Britain's naval mastery and passes a second Navy Bill, which provides for the creation of a fleet of 38 battleships over a period of 20 years.

13 The Boxer Rising by supporters of the Society of Harmonious Fists begins in China, in opposition to the growth of European influence there.

18 General Luigi Pelloux resigns as prime minister of Italy, following the success of the Left in the Italian elections.

20 The German ambassador Baron Klemens von Kettler is assassinated in Beijing, China, beginning the overt siege of foreign legations in the city by Chinese Boxer rebels.

21 The National Republican Convention in Philadelphia, Pennsylvania, renominates William McKinley for U.S. president and nominates Theodore Roosevelt for vice president.

21 U.S. Army general Arthur MacArthur grants amnesty to the Philippine revolutionaries.

JULY

5 The Democratic Party nominates former Congressman William Jennings Bryan of Nebraska for president and Illinois politician Adlai Ewing Stevenson for vice president.

23 An international expedition, including troops from the United States and Great Britain, is sent to China to combat the Boxer Rebellion, and is successful in taking Tientsin. The U.S. secretary of state John Hay restates U.S. "open door" policy in China, namely its commitment to equal trade opportunities for foreign traders.

29 An anarchist assassinates King Humbert I of Italy at Monza near Milan, Italy. Victor Emmanuel III succeeds to the throne.

AUGUST

14 The British armies commanded by Field Marshal Frederick, Lord Roberts, and General Sir Redvers Buller unite at Vlakfontein, southern Africa.

14 The international military force combating the Boxers in China relieves the besieged foreign legations in Beijing, China.

27 A Boer army under the command of Louis Botha is defeated by a British force at Bergendal.

SEPTEMBER

3 In southern Africa, Field Marshal Frederick, Lord Roberts, formally proclaims the annexation of the Transvaal by Britain.

4 Russian troops begin an invasion of the Chinese province of Manchuria.

9 The sultan of Turkey, Abdul Hamid II, announces the construction of the Hejaz railroad from Damascus to the holy places in Arabia. The railroad is to be built by popular subscription as a Pan-Islamic project, work continuing until 1908.

11 President Paul Kruger of Transvaal crosses from Transvaal into Portuguese Southeast Africa following defeat in the Second Anglo-Boer War, and subsequently leaves for Europe.

18 Hennepin County, Minnesota, hosts the nation's first direct presidential primary.

30 Arthur Griffith founds Cumann na nGaedhael ("The League of Gaels") in Ireland to promote the use of Gaelic. The organization adopts the slogan *Sinn Féin* ("We Ourselves").

OCTOBER

16 Britain and Germany sign the Yangzi Agreement to restrain foreign aggression in China, and to maintain the "open door" of trading opportunities.

16 In the "khaki" election in Great Britain, the Conservatives, successful in the Second Anglo-Boer War, remain in power with a majority of 134. The Conservatives and Unionists take 334 seats, the Liberal Unionists 68, the Liberals 184, the Irish Nationalists 82, and Labour 2. Prime Minister Lord Salisbury reconstructs his government, appointing Lord Lansdowne as foreign secretary.

17 Bernhard von Bülow succeeds the aged Prince Chlodwig von Hohenlohe as the German chancellor.

24 President Paul Kruger of the Transvaal, seeking assistance in Europe against the British, is denied an audience by Kaiser Wilhelm II of Germany.

31 A rising begins in Catalonia, Spain, in support of the pretender to the throne, Don Carlos, and in support of local autonomy.

NOVEMBER

• British forces put down a rising of the Ashanti people in West Africa.

5 The Spanish constitution is suspended following political unrest.

5–February 21, 1901 The Cuban constitutional convention sits in Havana, Cuba.

6 In the U.S. presidential elections, the Republican candidate William McKinley is reelected as president of the United States. In the Congressional elections, the Republicans retain majorities in the House (197–151) and Senate (55–31).

9 Russia, having completed the occupation of Manchuria with 100,000 troops, forces China to accept a secret convention recognizing the dominance of Russia in the region.

11 Following British conquests, the Boer forces under General Christiaan De Wet resort to guerrilla tactics, raiding communications and British outposts. Horatio, Lord Kitchener, orders that women and children related to Boer combatants be interred in concentration camps, and extends the "scorched earth" policy started by Field Marshal Frederick, Lord Roberts, destroying Boer farms.

DECEMBER

14 France and Italy make a secret agreement with a view to maintaining both French influence in Morocco and Italian interests in Tripoli, Libya.

SCIENCE, TECHNOLOGY, AND MEDICINE

Ecology

• German meteorologist Vladimir Peter Köppen develops a mathematical system for classifying climatic types, based on temperature and rainfall. It serves as the basis for subsequent classification systems.

- French meteorologist Léon-Philippe Teisserenc de Bort discovers that the earth's atmosphere consists of two main layers: the troposphere, where the temperature continually changes and is responsible for the weather, and the stratosphere, where the temperature is invariant.
- Less than 30 bison remain in the United States. Action by cattlemen and conservationists to protect them on government reserves, however, saves them from extinction.

SEPTEMBER

8   Galveston, Texas, is hit by a hurricane that kills over 6,000 people and causes $20 million in damages. It is the worst recorded natural disaster in U.S. history. In 1901, in order to speed its reconstruction, the running of the city is put in the hands of five commissioners. This structure is retained in a charter of 1903, inaugurating the "city manager" form of municipal government.

Health and Medicine

- Bubonic plague strikes Honolulu's Chinatown, in Hawaii. The fire department burns many of the buildings to control the rats, but the fire gets out of control and destroys a large part of the city.
- The American Society of Orthodontists is formed.
- U.S. army pathologist Walter Reed establishes that yellow fever is caused by the bite of an *Aëdes aegypti* mosquito infected with the yellow fever parasite, as discovered by Cuban physician Carlos Juan Finlay in 1881. His discovery leads to the creation of a vaccine and makes possible the completion of the Panama Canal.
- Austrian immunologist Karl Landsteiner discovers the ABO blood group.

Math

- German mathematician David Hilbert poses 23 problems at the International Congress of Mathematics as a challenge for the 20th century. Most of these problems are now solved.

Science

- British chemist and physicist William Crookes isolates uranium.
- Dutch geneticist Hugo Marie de Vries, German botanist Carl Erich Correns, and Austrian botanist Erich Tschermak von Seysenegg, simultaneously and independently, rediscover the Austrian monk Gregor Mendel's 1865 work on heredity.
- French physicist Antoine-Henri Becquerel demonstrates that the beta particle is the same thing as the electron.
- French physiologist Paul Ulrich Villard discovers gamma rays.
- German chemist Friedrich E. Dorn discovers the radioactive noble gas radon (atomic no. 86), which is generated by the radioactive decay of radium.

- German physicist Max Planck suggests that black bodies (perfect absorbers) radiate energy in packets or quanta, rather than continuously. He thus begins the science of quantum physics, which revolutionizes the understanding of atomic and subatomic processes.
- German physicists Johann Phillip Elster and Hans F. Geitel invent the first practical photoelectric cell.
- Lord Rayleigh publishes the second volume of his *Scientific Papers*.
- Swedish chemist Per Teodor Cleve publishes *The Seasonal Distribution of Atlantic Plankton Organisms*, which serves as a basic text on oceanography.
- The British archeologist Arthur Evans discovers an unknown Bronze Age civilization at Knossos on the Greek island of Crete. He names it "Minoan" after the legendary king of Crete, Minos.
- The Kral Collection of microorganisms is established in Prague, Czechoslovakia; it is the first collection of pure cultures of microorganisms used for research purposes.
- U.S. chemist Charles Skeel Palmer develops a new way of breaking down the heavy hydrocarbons ("cracking") of petroleum to obtain gasoline and other products.

JUNE

- The Galton–Henry fingerprint classification system is published. Scotland Yard in London, England, adopts it in 1901 in place of the Bertillon anthropometric system; other law enforcement agencies change over soon after.

Technology

- Canadian-born U.S. scientist Reginald Aubrey Fessenden discovers the principle of amplitude modulation (AM) of radio waves.
- Italian physicist Guglielmo Marconi files patents for improvements to his wireless telegraphy system, which allow several stations to transmit signals on different wavelengths without interference.
- Serbian-born U.S. inventor Nikola Tesla suggests that radio waves may be used to detect moving objects—the first time the idea of radar has been proposed.
- Swedish metallurgist Johann August Brinell develops the Brinell hardness test, which determines the hardness of a metal by pressing a steel ball against it with known force. The hardness of the metal is inversely proportional to the size of the dent made.

Transportation

- 40% of the 13,824 automobiles in the United States are steam-powered, 38% electric, and 22% gasoline-powered.
- 99% of oil transported by sea is carried by oil tanker.
- Italian engineer Enrico Forlanini builds the world's first hydrofoil.
- Railroad mileage at this time is as follows: United States, 311,094 km/194,433 mi; UK, 30,063 km/18,789 mi.
- The Chicago Sanitary and Ship Canal is opened in Chicago, Illinois. Intended to stop sewage entering Lake Michigan by reversing the flow of the Chicago River, the canal links the Chicago River with the Des Plains River at Lockport, Illinois, and ultimately with the Gulf of Mexico. Begun in 1885, excavation has involved the largest earth-moving project in the United States to date.

The Telephone (1861–1900)

1861

- German physicist Johann Reis transmits musical tones over 100 m/300 ft using a device he calls a telephone.

1874

- U.S. inventor Elisha Gray constructs a telephone receiver but does not have a transmitter.

1876

March 7   Scottish-born U.S. inventor Alexander Graham Bell patents a device for transmitting human speech over electric wires. It consists of an identical microphone and receiver each made of a solenoid placed next to an iron membrane; vibration in the microphone's membrane induces a current in the solenoid that travels down the wire and causes the membrane in the receiver to vibrate.

March 10   Bell, addressing his assistant, transmits the first complete sentence by voice over wire using his newly invented telephone: "Mr. Watson, come here. I want you."

1877

- The Bell Telephone Company is founded.
- U.S. inventor Thomas Edison invents the carbon transmitter for the telephone, increasing its audibility.

April 3   Bell makes the first long-distance telephone call, from New York, New York, to his assistant in Boston, Massachusetts.

April 4   U.S. manufacturer Charles Williams, Jr., who will manufacture Bell's telephones, has the first telephones for private use installed in his home and office in the United States.

1878

January 28   The first commercial telephone exchange opens in New Haven, Connecticut; it has 21 subscribers. The following month the first telephone directory is published by the New Haven Telephone Co. with 50 subscribers listed.

1879

August   The first telephone exchange for general rather than business subscribers opens in London, England.

1880

- Entrepreneur William H. Forbes leads a team of Boston investors in creating the American Bell Telephone Company in the United States.
- Fifty thousand private telephones are in use in the United States.

1885

- The American Bell Telephone Company charters American Telephone and Telegraph Company (AT&T) to build and operate a long-distance telephone service in the United States.

1889

- U.S. inventor William Gray installs the first coin-operated telephone, in Hartford, Connecticut.

1892

- U.S. undertaker Almon B. Strowger patents the first automatic telephone exchange where the caller determines who the receiver will be without the aid of an operator. Strowger develops it because he believes the operator is diverting his calls to her husband, who is also an undertaker.

1900

- There are now over 1,300,000 telephones in use in the United States.

- The Elbe–Lübeck Canal is constructed in Germany, providing a shortcut from the imperial naval base at Kiel, Germany, to the North Sea.
- The first stage of the Trans-Siberian Railroad opens, between Moscow and Irkutsk, Russia.
- The French firm of Renault Frères introduces the first glass-enclosed automobile.
- The nation's railroad companies employ more than 1 million workers and there are 320,192 km/198,964 mi of railroad track in the United States.
- There are now 8,000 automobiles on the roads in the United States.
- U.S. automobile manufacturer Herbert H. Franklin introduces the first automobile with an air-cooled engine.

June 1900–01   The French navy constructs four Sirène class submarines.

June 1900–10   Electric trolleys replace steam-powered cable cars in the United States and Europe.

APRIL

30   The U.S. engine driver John Luther "Casey" Jones dies on the footplate on his train, trying to stop it before it hits another engine, at Vaughan, Mississippi. Although this is only one of many accidents this year, it is immortalized in a popular song.

JULY

2   German inventor Ferdinand Graf von Zeppelin's lighter-than-air ship LZ-3D1 makes its first flight, at Lake Constance, Germany. It has an aluminum sheeting hull.

19   The 10-km/6.25-mi Paris Métro opens in France.

ARTS AND IDEAS

Architecture

- The Hôtel Solvay and the Maison du Peuple in Brussels, Belgium, designed by the Belgian architect Victor Horta, are completed.

Arts

- The French artist Henri Matisse paints *Male Model*.
- The French artist Henri de Toulouse-Lautrec paints *La Modiste/The Milliner*.
- The French artist Paul Cézanne paints *Still Life With Onions* and *Apples and Oranges*.
- The French artist Paul Gauguin paints *Nude Woman*.

- The Norwegian artist Edvard Munch paints *Golgotha*.
- The Spanish artist Pablo Picasso arrives in Paris, France, and paints *Moulin de la Galette/Windmill of Galette*, his first French painting.
- The U.S. artist Childe Hassam paints *Late Afternoon, Winter, New York*.
- The U.S. artist Frederic Remington paints *The Fight for the Waterhole*.
- The U.S. artist Robert Henri paints *East River Embankment*.
- The U.S. artist Thomas Eakins paints *Addie (Miss Mary Adeline Williams)*.
- The U.S. photographer Gertrude Käsebier photographs *Blessed Art Thou Amongst Women*.
- The English photographer Frank Evans photographs *On Sussex Downs*.
- The art dealer Ambroise Vollard holds the first exhibition of works by the Spanish artist Pablo Picasso, in Paris, France.
- The Wallace Collection—a collection of French art and furniture—opens in Manchester Square, London, England.

Film

- The movie *Hamlet's Duel* is released in France, starring Sarah Bernhardt.
- The Lumière Brothers' Cinématograph is the highlight at the Paris International Exhibition. Primitive color and sound film systems are also demonstrated.

NOVEMBER

16 The Edison Company in the United States registers for a U.S. patent for its moving animated cartoon entitled *The Enchanted Drawing*.

Literature and Language

- The *Oxford Book of English Verse* is published, edited by Arthur Quiller-Couch.
- The English writer H. G. Wells publishes his novel *Love and Mr Lewisham*.
- The French literary critic Emile Faguet publishes his *Histoire de la littérature française/History of French Literature*.

- The French poet and essayist Charles Péguy launches the bimonthly literary review *Les Cahiers de la quinzaine*. Published until 1914, it plays a major role in French intellectual life, introducing new writers and defending the army officer Alfred Dreyfus, who in 1894 was wrongly sent to prison for treason.
- The French writer Colette and her husband Henri Gauthier-Villars, writing under the pseudonym of Willy, publish their novel *Claudine à l'école/Claudine at School*. It is the first of their "Claudine" novels.
- The Polish-born English writer Joseph Conrad publishes his novel *Lord Jim*.
- The Russian writer Anton Chekhov publishes his story "V ovrage"/"In the Ravine."
- The U.S. statesman Theodore Roosevelt publishes *The Strenuous Life*, an expression of his philosophy of life.
- The U.S. writer Ellen Glasgow publishes her novel *The Voice of the People*.
- The U.S. writer Jack London publishes his story collection *The Son of Wolf*.
- The U.S. writer Theodore Dreiser publishes his novel *Sister Carrie*.
- The U.S. author Frank L. Baum writes the children's classic *The Wizard of Oz*.

Music

- Austrian composer Gustav Mahler completes his Symphony No. 4.
- English composer Edward Elgar completes his oratorio *The Dream of Gerontius*, based on a dramatic monologue by the English churchman Cardinal Newman.
- Finnish composer Jean Sibelius completes his revision of the orchestral work *Finlandia*.
- The opera *Louise* by the French composer Gustave Charpentier is first performed, in Paris, France.
- The opera *Tosca* by the Italian composer Giacomo Puccini is first performed, in Rome, Italy.
- The opera *Zazà* by the Italian composer Ruggiero Leoncavallo is first performed, in Milan, Italy.
- U.S. composer Edward MacDowell completes his Piano Sonata *Norse*.
- U.S. composers Harry Von Tilzer and Arthur J. Lamb write the song "A Bird in a Gilded Cage."

BIRTHS & DEATHS

c. 1900 Ruhollah Khomeini (Ruholla Hendi), Persian Shiite Muslim, organizer of the 1979 revolution after which he became political and religious leader of Iran for life, born in Khomeyn, Persia (–1989).

- Margaret Mitchell, U.S. novelist and author of *Gone with the Wind*, born in Atlanta, Georgia (–1949).

JANUARY

20 John Ruskin, English writer and artist who led the Gothic Revival movement, dies in Coniston, Lancashire, England (81).

25 Theodosius Dobzhansky, Russian-U.S. geneticist who combined evolutionary theory with genetics, born in Nemirov, Ukraine, in the Russian Empire (–1975).

27 Hyman G. Rickover, U.S. naval officer who developed the *Nautilus*, the world's first atomic-powered submarine, born in Markov, Russia (–1986).

FEBRUARY

4 Jacques Prévert, French poet and screenwriter, born in Neuilly-sur-Seine, France (–1977).

5 Adlai Ewing Stevenson, U.S. politician and diplomat, and Democratic presidential candidate in 1952 and 1956, who helped found the United Nations, born in Los Angeles, California (– 1965).

22 Luis Buñuel, Spanish surrealist filmmaker and director, born in Calanda, Spain (–1983).

22 Sean O'Faolain (born John Whelan), Irish novelist, short-story writer, critic, and biographer, born in Cork, Ireland (–1991).

March

2   Kurt Weill, German composer of popular satirical opera, born in Dessau, Germany (–1950).

6   Gottlieb Daimler, German mechanical engineer who built one of the first successful automobiles powered by an internal combustion engine, dies in Cannstatt, Germany (65).

9   Howard Hathaway Aiken, U.S. mathematician who invented the Harvard Mark 1 computer, the forerunner of modern computers, born in Hoboken, New Jersey (–1972).

13 George Seferis, Greek poet, essayist, and diplomat, born in Smyrna, Anatolia, Turkey (–1971).

19 Jean-Frédéric Joliot (after 1926 Joliot-Curie), French physicist who with his wife Irène Joliot-Curie created new radioactive elements artificially, born in Paris, France (–1958).

23 Erich Fromm, German-born U.S. psychoanalyst and philosopher, born in Frankfurt am Main, Germany (–1980).

29 Charles Sutherland Elton, English ecologist who defined the concept of food chains, born in Liverpool, England (–1991).

April

5   Spencer Tracey, U.S. actor, born in Milwaukee, Wisconsin (–1967).

25 Wolfgang Pauli, Austrian-born U.S. physicist, who discovered the principle that no two electrons in the same atom can have the same energy, born in Vienna, Austria (–1958).

26 Charles Francis Richter, U.S. seismologist who developed the Richter scale of earthquake magnitude, born near Hamilton, Ohio (–1985).

27 Walter Lantz, U.S. animator who created Woody Woodpecker, born in New Rochelle, New York (–1994).

28 Jan Hendrik Oort, Dutch astronomer who discovered that the Milky Way galaxy rotates and determined the sun's position in the galaxy, born in Franeker, the Netherlands (–1992).

30 Casey Jones, U.S. railroad engineer and folk hero, dies in a train crash near Vaughn, Mississippi (36).

May

4   Augustus Henry Lane-Fox Pitt-Rivers, English archeologist who stressed complete excavation of sites and stratigraphic analysis, dies in Rushmore, Wiltshire, England (73).

June

5   Dennis Gabor, Hungarian-born British electrical engineer, the inventor of holography, born in Budapest, Hungary (–1979).

5   Stephen Crane, U.S. novelist known for his book *The Red Badge of Courage* (1895), dies in Badenweiler, Germany (28).

11 Lawrence Edmund Spivak, U.S. journalist who founded the radio program *Meet the Press*, born in Brooklyn, New York (–1994).

25 Louis (Earl) Mountbatten, British statesman, naval commander, and last viceroy of India, born in Frogmore House, Windsor, England (–1979).

July

4   Louis Armstrong, U.S. jazz trumpeter, composer, and band leader, born in New Orleans, Louisiana (–1971).

10 Evelyn Laye, English theater actress and singer, born in London, England (–1996).

August

4   (Jean-Joseph-) Etienne Lenoir, Belgian inventor who built the first commercially successful internal combustion engine and the first automobile to be equipped with one, dies in La Varenne-St.-Hilaire, France (78).

7   Wilhelm Liebnecht, German socialist who cofounded the German Social Democratic Party, dies in Berlin, Germany (74).

12 Wilhelm Steinitz, Austrian chess master, world champion 1866–94, dies in Wards Island, New York (64).

19 Gilbert Ryle, English philosopher, a leading figure in the "Oxford Philosophy" movement, born in Brighton, Sussex, England (–1976).

25 Friedrich Nietzsche, German philosopher and critic, especially of Christianity, dies in Weimar, Thuringian States (55).

25 Hans Krebs, German-born British biochemist who discovered the chemical process whereby food is metabolized, born in Hildesheim, Germany (–1981).

September

3   Urho Kaleva Kekkonen, Finnish president 1956–81 who was determined to retain Finland's independence from the USSR, born in Pielavesi, Finland (–1986).

20 Willem Visser't Hooft, Dutch clergyman, secretary of the World Council of Churches 1938–66, born in Haarlem, the Netherlands (–1985).

23 Louise Nevelson, U.S. sculptor whose works are large, abstract, often monochromatic pieces, born in Kiev, Russia (–1988).

October

3   Thomas Clayton Wolfe, U.S. writer, born in Asheville, North Carolina (–1938).

7   Heinrich Himmler, German Nazi leader, head of the SS, and organizer of the Nazi death camps, born in Munich, Germany (–1945).

8   Geoffrey (Alan) Jellico, English landscape architect born in London, England (–1996).

8   Serge Chermayeff (originally Sergei Ivanovitch Issakovitch), Russian-born English architect, born in the Caucasus Mountains, Russia (–1996).

10 Helen Hayes, U.S. film and theater actress, born in Washington, D.C. (–1993).

22 Edward R. Stettinius, U.S. secretary of state and industrialist who helped establish the United Nations, born in Chicago, Illinois (–1949).

28 Max Müller, German Orientalist and philologist, dies in Oxford, England (76).

November

14 Aaron Copland, U.S. composer, born in Brooklyn, New York (–1990).

20 Chester Gould, U.S. cartoonist, the creator of Dick Tracy, born in Pawnee, Oklahoma (–1985).

22 Arthur Seymour Sullivan, British composer of operettas with William Schwenk Gilbert, dies in London, England (58).

30 Oscar Wilde, Irish poet and dramatist, dies in Paris, France (44).

December

9   Joseph Needham, English biochemist and historian of Chinese science, born in London, England (–1995).

16 Victor Saudon Pritchett, English short-story writer and novelist, born in Ipswich, England (–1997).

Theater and Dance

- The "Cakewalk" dance becomes a craze. It was first introduced in minstrel shows by the performers Harrigan and Hart in 1877 with the song "Walkin' for Dat Cake."
- The play *Danton* by the French writer Romain Rolland is first performed, in Paris, France.

Thought and Scholarship

- The Austrian psychiatrist Sigmund Freud publishes *Die Traumdeutung/The Interpretation of Dreams*.
- The Belgian historian Henri Pirenne publishes the first volume of his seven-volume *Histoire de Belgique/ History of Belgium*. The final volume appears in 1932.
- The multivolume British *Dictionary of National Biography* is completed, edited by Leslie Stephens and Sidney Lee. The first volume was published in 1882.
- The English historian Albert Frederick Pollard publishes *England under Protector Somerset*.
- The English historian Charles Harding Firth publishes *Oliver Cromwell and the Rule of the Puritans in England*.
- The English philosopher Bertrand Russell publishes *A Critical Exposition of the Philosophy of Leibniz*.
- The first volume of the *Victoria History of the Counties of England* is published, an encyclopedic account of every county and place in England. Volumes are still appearing.
- The French philosopher Henri Bergson publishes *Le Rire/On Laughter*.
- The Irish scholar John Bagnell Bury publishes his *History of Greece*.

SOCIETY

Everyday Life

- Automobile clubs begin in Germany, Austria, and Switzerland.
- British art teacher William Harbutt launches Plasticine, a substitute for modeling clay.
- French tire manufacturers André and Edouard Michelin launch the *Guide Michelin*, the first systematic guidebook to restaurants, hotels, and garages in Europe.
- The Norwegian Johann Vaaler patents paper clips in Germany.
- The clothes company Brooks Brothers introduces shirts with button-down collars in the United States.
- The Eastman Company, based in Rochester, New York, manufactures and markets 35 different kinds of cameras, including the Brownie Box Camera, selling for just $1.
- The U.S. Census lists the nation's population at 75,994,575, up from the figure of 62,947,714 recorded in 1890.
- The world population stands at 1.6 billion.
- There are more than 1,700 free libraries in the United States.

April

14–November 13 The Paris International Exhibition is held, having been opened by President Emile Loubet of France.

November

10 The first U.S. National Automobile Show opens at Madison Square Gardens, New York, New York, with 31 exhibitors.

Media and Communication

- There are 18,487 newspapers published in the United States, including 2,190 dailies.
- The Associated Press news agency moves from Chicago, Illinois, to New York, New York: Illinois law did not permit exclusive membership in the wire service and New York law allowed Associated Press to avoid pending antimonopoly prosecution.
- There are now over 1,300,000 telephones in use in the United States.
- Cyril Arthur Pearson publishes the *Express* in Britain; one of the paper's innovations is to have news on the front page.

Sports

c. 1900 The forerunner of the equestrian three-day event, the Championnat de Cheval d'Armes, comprising long-distance riding, steeplechasing, dressage, and show jumping, is introduced by the French army as a test for cavalry officers. The format is adopted by cavalry regiments in other countries, and from it the three-day event evolves.

- The Prince of Wales becomes the first racehorse owner to win the English Triple Crown (2,000 Guineas, Derby, and St. Leger) and the Grand National in the same year.
- The YMCA employs 244 physical training directors at its facilities across the United States.

January

29 Bancroft Byron "Ban" Johnson founds the American League of Professional Baseball Clubs in Chicago, Illinois, as a rival to the National Baseball League.

May

20–October 28 The second Olympic Games are held in Paris, France, in connection with the Paris International Exhibition, with events spread out over 23 weeks. 1,330 athletes from 22 nations compete in 80 events. France wins 26 gold medals; the United States, 18; Great Britain, 16; Belgium and Switzerland, 6 each; Germany, 3; and Australia, 2. Alvin Kraenzlein of the United States wins the 60 meters, 110-meter hurdles, 400-meter hurdles, and the long jump. Charlotte Cooper of Britain wins the women's tennis singles and doubles, the first women's events to be included in the Olympics.

June

14 The inaugural Gordon Bennett Cup motor race, the first international championship race, is held in France. The winner is M. F. Charron of France, driving a Panhard at an average speed of 62 kph/38.5 mph.

August

8–10 The U.S. public official Dwight Filley Davis presents an international challenge cup for lawn tennis, the Davis Cup. The United States wins the trophy, beating Britain 3–0 at Brookline, Massachusetts.

INDEX

TITLES INDEX